# Psychology

Fifth edition

**Saundra K. Ciccarelli**
*Gulf Coast State College*

**J. Noland White**
*Georgia College & State University*

 Pearson

330 Hudson Street, NY NY 10013

*Portfolio Manager:* Erin Mitchell
*Content Producer:* Pamela Weldin
*Content Developer:* Julie Swasey, Jennifer Stevenson
*Portfolio Manager Assistant:* Stephany Harrington
*Product Marketer:* Margaret Waples
*Content Producer Manager:* Amber Mackey
*Content Development Manager:* Sharon Geary
*Associate Director of Design:* Blair Brown

*Design Lead:* Kathryn Foot
*Technical Manager:* Caroline Fenton
*Digital Producer:* Lindsay Verge
*Full-Service Project Manager:* Melissa Sacco, Lumina Datamatics, Inc.
*Compositor:* Lumina Datamatics, Inc.
*Printer/Binder:* LSC Communications
*Cover Printer:* Phoenix Color
*Cover Design:* Pentagram

Credits and acknowledgments borrowed from other sources and reproduced, with permission, in this textbook appear on the appropriate page of appearance.

**Library of Congress Cataloging-in-Publication Data**

Names: Ciccarelli, Saundra K., author. | White, J. Noland, author.
Title: Psychology / Saundra K. Ciccarelli, Gulf Coast State College, J.
 Noland White, Georgia College & State University.
Description: Fifth edition. | Boston : Pearson, [2017] | Includes bibliographical references and index.
Identifiers: LCCN 2016022788 | ISBN 9780134477961 (alk. paper) | ISBN 0134477960 (alk. paper)
Subjects: LCSH: Psychology.
Classification: LCC BF121 .C52 2017 | DDC 150—dc23
LC record available at https://lccn.loc.gov/2016022788

6   18

Student Edition
ISBN-10: 0-13-447796-0
ISBN-13: 978-0-13-447796-1
Books a là Carte
ISBN-10: 0-13-457171-1
ISBN-13: 978-0-13-457171-3

# Brief Contents

# Contents

# Learner-Centered Approach

## Curiosity and Dialogue

Our goal is to awaken students' curiosity and energize their desire to learn by having them read and engage with the material. In the last edition, we extended that experience with the new REVEL format. Fully digital and highly engaging, REVEL offers an immersive learning experience designed for the way today's students read, think, and learn. Enlivening course content with media interactives and assessments, REVEL empowers educators to increase engagement with the course and to better connect with students. See **pearsonhighered.com/revel**.

The fifth edition builds upon the REVEL experience. This edition was written with digital learning materials clearly in mind. With the dynamic learning aids of previous editions as a foundation, the digital materials are interactive, allowing students to experience figures, graphs, and tables in an active learning process. Instead of simply looking and reading, the student is *doing* things with the digital materials. This format will truly help students engage in the learning process and will also help instructors make classroom presentations more vivid and attention grabbing.

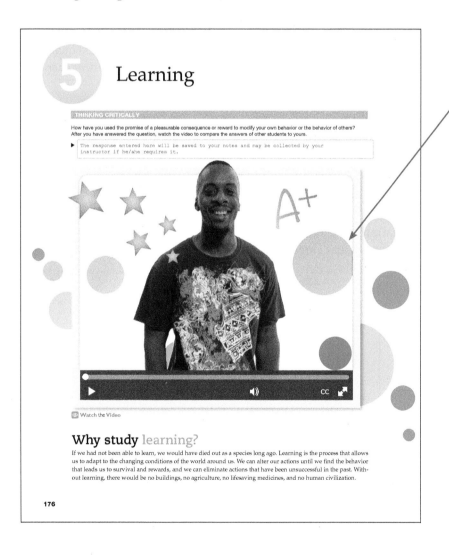

**Chapter-Opening Journal Prompts and Student Voice Videos**
Chapters open with videos in which psychology students share personal stories about how the chapter theme directly applies to their lives. For the fifth edition, we've added the ability for students to answer these questions for themselves before watching the video responses.

Watch the Video *Experiments: Experimental Group versus Control Group*

**New Introduction to Psychology Video Series**
More than twenty new videos have been filmed for this edition. These videos cover a variety of key topics in introductory psychology, from careers in psychology to experiments to diagnosing and classifying disorders.

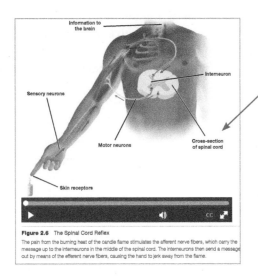

**Figure 2.6** The Spinal Cord Reflex
The pain from the burning heat of the candle flame stimulates the afferent nerve fibers, which carry the message up to the interneurons in the middle of the spinal cord. The interneurons then send a message out by means of the efferent nerve fibers, causing the hand to jerk away from the flame.

**New Biological Artwork and Animations**
A new art program designed for REVEL takes into account all of the visual media that students now interact with; the artwork is designed in a contemporary aesthetic that matches the graphical quality users see in other digital experiences such as video games.

## Emphasis on APA Learning Goals
We have used the APA goals and assessment recommendations as guidelines for structuring our content. For the fifth edition, we have placed even greater emphasis on these goals.

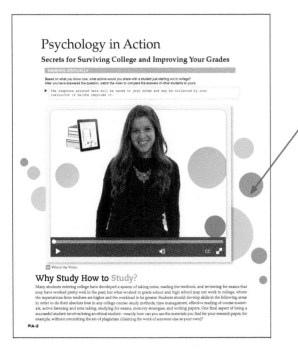

Psychology in Action
Secrets for Surviving College and Improving Your Grades

**Why Study How to Study?**
Many students entering college have developed a system of taking notes, reading the textbook, and reviewing for exams that may have worked pretty well in the past; but what worked in grade school and high school may not work in college, where the expectations from teachers are higher and the workload is far greater. Students should develop skills in the following areas in order to do their absolute best in any college course: study methods, time management, effective reading of course materials, active listening and note taking, studying for exams, memory strategies, and writing papers. One final aspect of being a successful student involves being an ethical student—exactly how can you use the materials you find for your research paper, for example, without committing the sin of plagiarism (claiming the work of someone else as your own)?

PIA-2

**Updated Psychology in Action Chapter**
This chapter has been restructured around eight modules, which address many of the APA learning goals for the undergraduate psychology major. Each module is accompanied by a study tip video: study skills, managing time, reading textbooks, getting the most out of lectures, studying for exams, writing papers, improving your memory, and your ethical responsibility.

## APA Goal 2: Scientific Inquiry and Critical Thinking

### Perceptual Influences on Metacognition

*Addresses APA Learning Objective 2.3 Engage in innovative and integrative thinking and problem-solving.*

As you can see, pun intended, what we perceive as being real does not always match the actual visual stimulus we are presented with. Perceptual information can also influence how we think about a given object. For example, many of us assume that things that are larger weigh more than things that are smaller. The color of an object can also have an influence (De Camp, 1917). Darker objects are often appraised to be heavier than comparable objects that are lighter in color (Walker et al., 2010). Both of these are examples of stimulus influences on perceptual expectations. But what about stimulus influences on expectations for a cognitive task, like assessing how well we will be able to remember something?

*Metacognition* is thinking about thinking. It includes being aware of our own thought processes, such as evaluating how well we actually understand something or how well we will remember something. For example, the font size of a given word appears to have an effect. In one study, words that were printed in a larger font were rated as being more memorable than words appearing in a smaller font (Rhodes & Castel, 2008). In other words, when evaluated as part of a sequential list, Psychology might be rated as being more memorable than macroeconomics. At least it was for one of your authors during college. Despite the initial ratings on memorability, when tested later, word font size did not yield significant effects on recall (Rhodes & Castel, 2008).

Research also suggests that students often report using study strategies, such as focusing primarily on **bold** or *italicized* terms in a textbook (Gurung, 2003, 2004), or over-reliance on strategies such as highlighting. These are methods that have less of an overall positive impact on retention of material, especially when compared to more robust study and memory strategies. Ⓛ Ⓘ Ⓝ Ⓚ to PIA 6 and Learning Objectives 6.5, 6.6.

---

**THINKING CRITICALLY**

Do you think that humans are as controlled by their biology as other animals? Why or why not?

▶ | The response entered here will be saved to your notes and may be collected by your instructor if he/she requires it.

Submit

---

Shared Writing: Ethical and Social Responsibility: The Biological Perspective

Dr. Z is conducting research on ADHD and is requiring members of his psychology class to participate. As part of the study, students are learning to control their brain activity by using feedback during an EEG. In doing so, half of the class is learning to enhance brain activity associated with improved attention. The other half is learning to increase brain activity associated with the inattentive symptoms of ADHD. He asks both groups to complete tests of attention and he shares the individual results students in class, calling them by name and displaying their individual results. He did not gain approval from his university's institutional review board to conduct this study, claiming it simply a pilot investigation. Refer back to the APA Ethical Guidelines discussed in Chapter One. What guidelines and standards are being violated?

*A minimum number of characters is required to post and earn points. After posting, your response can be viewed by your class and instructor, and you can participate in the class discussion.*

---

**New Chapter Feature on APA Goal 2: Scientific Reasoning and Critical Thinking**
Each chapter of the text now includes a special feature that reinforces scientific inquiry and critical thinking skills. Students are introduced to a psychological topic and then encouraged to practice their skills using a hands-on interactive example.

**Critical Thinking Journal Prompts**
Journal Prompts allow students to write short critical thinking–based journal entries about the chapter content. By reinforcing critical thinking, the prompts offer another way to expose students to the skills covered in APA Goal 2: Scientific Reasoning and Critical Thinking.

**New Shared Writing Prompts Focused on APA Goal 3: Ethical and Social Responsibility in a Diverse World**
Shared Writing prompts in each chapter foster collaboration and critical thinking skills by providing students the opportunity to write a brief response to a chapter-specific question and engage in peer-to-peer feedback on a discussion board. In this edition, Shared Writing Prompts focus on topics related to APA Goal 3: Ethical and Social Responsibility in a Diverse World.

## Embedded Interactive Content

Interactive content has been fully incorporated into all aspects of the text, allowing students a more direct way to access and engage with the material.

**Figure 5.12** Bandura's Bobo Doll Experiment
In Albert Bandura's famous Bobo doll experiment, the doll was used to demonstrate the impact of observing an adult model performing aggressive behavior on the later aggressive behavior of children. The children in these photos are imitating the adult model's behavior even though they believe they are alone and are not being watched.

Watch **Videos** of topics as they are explained.

**Interactive Figures and Tables** walk students through some of the more complex processes in psychology and offer students the ability to evaluate their knowledge of key topics.

**Figure 5.3**  Extinction and Spontaneous Recovery
This graph shows the acquisition, extinction, spontaneous recovery, and reacquisition of a conditioned salivary response. Typically, the measure of conditioning is the number of drops of saliva elicited by the CS on each trial. Note that on the day following extinction, the first presentation of the CS elicits quite a large response. This response is due to spontaneous recovery.

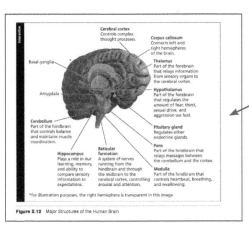

**Figure 2.12**  Major Structures of the Human Brain

**Interactive versions of brain-based figures** allow students to rotate the brain 360 degrees and isolate regions.

Simulate **experiments** and answer **surveys** right from the narrative.

**Survey**  DO YOU FLY OR FIGHT?

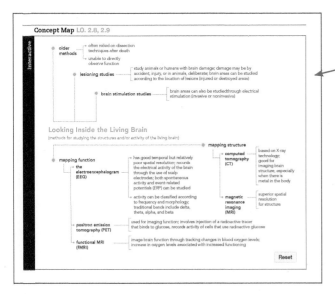

Reinforce connections across topics with **Interactive Concept Maps**.

Take **Practice Quizzes** as you read.

**Practice Quiz**   How much do you remember?

**THINKING CRITICALLY**

Some people think that taking human growth hormone (HGH) supplements will help reverse the effects of aging. If this were true, what would you expect to see in the news media or medical journals? How would you expect HGH supplements to be marketed as a result?

▸ The response entered here will be saved to your notes and may be collected by your instructor if he/she requires it.

Submit

**Writing Prompts** allow students to write about the chapter content and receive auto-feedback.

# Teaching and Learning Package

**INTEGRATION AND FEEDBACK**

It is increasingly true today that as valuable as a good textbook is, it is still only one element of a comprehensive learning package. The teaching and learning package that accompanies *Psychology*, 5e, is the most comprehensive and integrated on the market. We have made every effort to provide high-quality instructor resources that will save you preparation time and will enhance the time you spend in the classroom.

**MYPSYCHLAB**  MyPsychLab is an online homework, tutorial, and assessment program that truly engages students in learning. It helps students better prepare for class, quizzes, and exams—resulting in better performance in the course—and provides educators with a dynamic set of tools for gauging individual and class progress. MyPsychLab comes from Pearson, your partner in providing the best digital learning experience.

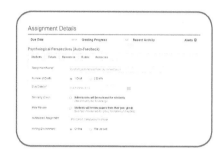

**LEARNING CATALYTICS**  Learning Catalytics is a "bring your own device" student engagement, assessment, and classroom intelligence system. It allows instructors to engage students in class with real-time diagnostics. Students can use any modern, web-enabled device (smartphone, tablet, or laptop) to access it.

**WRITING SPACE**  Better writers make great learners—who perform better in their courses. To help you develop and assess concept mastery and critical thinking through writing, we created the Writing Space in MyPsychLab. It's a single place to create, track, and grade writing assignments, provide writing resources, and exchange meaningful, personalized feedback with students, quickly and easily, including autoscoring for practice writing prompts. Plus, Writing Space has integrated access to Turnitin, the global leader in plagiarism prevention.

**PEARSON WRITER**  Good writing is an important skill that opens doors for you, whether at school or in the workplace. Pearson Writer offers writing support for anyone—regardless of skill level, subject, or discipline. It's affordable, built for mobile devices, and easy to use, so rather than spending time learning new software, you can just focus on your ideas. Pearson Writer takes care of the labor-intensive details of writing—gathering and citing sources, proofreading for grammar and usage, and staying organized—so you can concentrate on what matters to you. Your grades will improve, your thoughts will be clearer, and you will become a better writer.

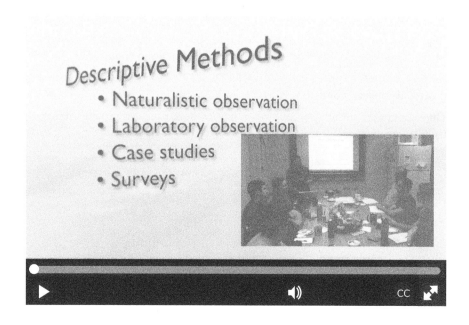

# Presentation and Teaching Resources

The Instructor's Resource Center (**www.pearsonhighered.com/irc**) provides information on the following supplements and downloadable files:

**Interactive PowerPoint Slides (ISBN 0-13-462372-X)** bring the Ciccarelli/White design into the classroom, drawing students into the lecture and providing appealing interactive activities, visuals, and videos. The slides are built around the text's learning objectives and offer many direct links to interactive exercises, simulations, and activities.

**Standard Lecture PowerPoint Slides (ISBN 0-13-462366-5)** These ADA PowerPoint slides provide an active format for presenting concepts from each chapter and feature relevant figures and tables from the text.

**Art PowerPoint Slides (ISBN 0-13-466664-X)** These slides contain only the photos, figures, and line art from the textbook.

**Instructor's Resource Manual (ISBN 0-13-462365-7)**, prepared by Alan Swinkels, St. Edward's University, offers detailed chapter lecture outlines, chapter summaries, learning objectives, activities, exercises, assignments, handouts, and demonstrations for in-class use, as well as useful guidelines for integrating the many Pearson media resources into your classroom and syllabus.

**Test Item File (ISBN 0-13-462364-9)** prepared by Jason Spiegelman, Community College of Baltimore County, contains more than 3,200 questions categorized by learning objective and question type (factual, conceptual, or applied). Rationales for each correct answer and the key distracter in the multiple-choice questions help instructors evaluate questions and provide more feedback to students.

**Pearson MyTest (ISBN: 0-13-462371-1)**, a powerful assessment generation program, helps instructors easily create and print quizzes and exams. Questions and tests can be authored online, allowing instructors ultimate flexibility! For more information, go to **www.PearsonMyTest.com**.

## APA Assessment Bank

Available within MyPsychLab, a unique bank of assessment items allows instructors to assess student progress against the American Psychological Association's Learning Goals and Outcomes.

## Accessing All Resources

For a list of all student resources available with Ciccarelli/White, *Psychology*, 5e, go to www.mypearsonstore.com and enter the text ISBN 0-13-447796-0, and check out the "Everything That Goes With It" section under the photo of the book cover.

For access to all instructor resources for Ciccarelli/White, *Psychology*, 5e, simply go to **http://pearsonhighered.com/irc**.

For technical support for any of your Pearson products, you and your students can contact **http://247.pearsoned.com**.

# Learning Outcomes and Assessment

## LEARNING OBJECTIVES

Based on APA recommendations, each chapter is structured around detailed learning objectives. All of the instructor and student resources are also organized around these objectives, making the text and resources a fully integrated system of study. The flexibility of these resources allows instructors to choose which learning objectives are important in their courses as well as which content they want their students to focus on.

---

### ⌄ Learning Objectives

**5.1**   Define the term *learning*.

**5.2**   Identify the key elements of classical conditioning as demonstrated in Pavlov's classic experiment.

**5.3**   Apply classical conditioning to examples of phobias, taste aversions, and drug dependency.

**5.4**   Identify the contributions of Thorndike and Skinner to the concept of operant conditioning.

**5.5**   Differentiate between primary and secondary reinforcers and positive and negative reinforcement.

**5.6**   Identify the four schedules of reinforcement.

**5.7**   Identify the effect that punishment has on behavior.

**5.8**   Explain the concepts of discriminant stimuli, extinction, generalization, and spontaneous recovery as they relate to operant conditioning.

**5.9**   Describe how operant conditioning is used to change animal and human behavior.

**5.10**   Explain the concept of latent learning.

**5.11**   Explain how Köhler's studies demonstrated that animals can learn by insight.

**5.12**   Summarize Seligman's studies on learned helplessness.

**5.13**   Describe the process of observational learning.

**5.14**   List the four elements of observational learning.

**5.15**   Describe an example of conditioning in the real world.

---

## GOALS AND STANDARDS

In recent years, many psychology departments have been focusing on core competencies and how methods of assessment can better enhance students' learning. In response, the American Psychological Association (APA) established recommended goals for the undergraduate psychology major beginning in 2008 with a set of 10 goals, and revised again in 2013 with a new set of 5 goals. Specific learning outcomes were established for each of the goals, and suggestions were made on how best to tie assessment practices to these goals. In writing this text, we have used the APA goals and assessment recommendations as guidelines for structuring content and integrating the teaching and homework materials. For details on the APA learning goals and assessment guidelines, please see **www.apa.org/**.

| APA LEARNING OBJECTIVES | CICCARELLI/WHITE TEXT LEARNING OBJECTIVES |

## 1 Knowledge Base in Psychology

Students should demonstrate fundamental knowledge and comprehension of the major concepts, theoretical perspectives, historical trends, and empirical findings to discuss how psychological principles apply to behavioral phenomena. Foundation students should demonstrate breadth in their knowledge and applications of psychological ideas to simple problems; baccalaureate students should show depth in their knowledge and application of psychological concepts and frameworks to problems of greater complexity.

**1.1** Describe key concepts, principles, and overarching themes in psychology.

**1.2** Develop a working knowledge of psychology's content domains.

**1.3** Describe applications of psychology.

**Intro: PIA.1**

**Ch 1:** 1.1–1.5, 1.10 and Applying Psychology to Everyday Life: Thinking Critically About Critical Thinking

**Ch 2:** 2.1–2.13 and Applying Psychology to Everyday Life: Paying Attention to Attention-Deficit/Hyperactivity Disorder

**Ch 3:** 3.1–3.11, 3.13–3.14 and Applying Psychology to Everyday Life: Beyond "Smoke and Mirrors"—The Psychological Science and Neuroscience of Magic

**Ch 4:** 4.1–4.10 and Applying Psychology to Everyday Life: Thinking Critically About Ghosts, Aliens, and Other Things that Go Bump in the Night

**Ch 5:** 5.1–5.8, 5.9–5.14 and Applying Psychology to Everyday Life: Can You Really Toilet Train Your Cat?

**Ch 6:** 6.1–6.13 and Applying Psychology to Everyday Life: Health and Memory

**Ch 7:** 7.1–7.4, 7.6–7.10 and Applying Psychology to Everyday Life: Mental and Physical Exercises Combine for Better Cognitive Health

**Ch 8:** 8.2–8.5, 8.7–8.11 and Applying Psychology to Everyday Life: Cross-Cultural Views on Death

**Ch 9:** 9.1–9.10 and Applying Psychology to Everyday Life: When Motivation is Not Enough

**Ch 10:** 10.1–10.9 and Applying Psychology to Everyday Life: The AIDS Epidemic in Russia

**Ch 11:** 11.1–11.10 and Applying Psychology to Everyday Life: Coping with Stress Through Mindfulness Meditation

**Ch 12:** 12.1–12.15 and Applying Psychology to Everyday Life: Peeking Inside the Social Brain

**Ch 13:** 13.1–13.15 and Applying Psychology to Everyday Life: Biological Bases of Personality

**Ch 14:** 14.1–14.15 and Applying Psychology to Everyday Life: Taking the Worry Out of Exams

**Ch 15:** 15.1–15.11 and Applying Psychology to Everyday Life: Virtual Reality Therapies

Major concepts are reinforced with learning tools: Writing Space, Experiment Simulations, MyPsychLab Video Series, Operation ARA, Visual Brain, and instructor's teaching and assessment package.

## 2 Scientific Inquiry and Critical Thinking

The skills in this domain involve the development of scientific reasoning and problem solving, including effective research methods. Foundation students should learn basic skills and concepts in interpreting behavior, studying research, and applying research design principles to drawing conclusions about behavior; baccalaureate students should focus on theory use as well as designing and executing research plans.

**2.1** Use scientific reasoning to interpret psychological phenomena.

**2.2** Demonstrate psychology information literacy.

**2.3** Engage in innovative and integrative thinking and problem solving.

**2.4** Interpret, design, and conduct basic psychological research.

**2.5** Incorporate sociocultural factors in scientific inquiry.

**Ch 1:** 1.6–1.12; APA Goal 2: Scientific Inquiry and Critical Thinking: A Sample Experiment; Applying Psychology to Everyday Life: Thinking Critically About Critical Thinking

**Ch 2:** 2.4, 2.8, 2.14; APA Goal 2: Scientific Reasoning and Critical Thinking: Phineas Gage and Neuroplasticity; Classic Studies in Psychology: Through the Looking Glass—Spatial Neglect

**Ch 3:** Applying Psychology to Everyday Life: Beyond "Smoke and Mirrors"—The Psychological Science and Neuroscience of Magic; APA Goal 2: Scientific Inquiry and Critical Thinking: Perceptual Influences on Metacognition

**Ch 4:** 4.10; Applying Psychology to Everyday Life: Thinking Critically About Ghosts, Aliens, and Other Things That Go Bump in the Night; APA Goal 2: Weight Gain and Sleep

**Ch 5:** 5.2–5.14 and Classic Studies in Psychology: Biological Constraints of Operant Conditioning; APA Goal 2: Scientific Inquiry and Critical Thinking: Spare the Rod, Spoil the Child?

**Ch 6:** Classic Studies in Psychology: Sperling's Iconic Memory Test; Classic Studies in Psychology: Elizabeth Loftus and Eyewitnesses; APA Goal 2: Scientific Inquiry and Critical Thinking: Effects of Supplements on Memory; Applying Psychology to Everyday Life: Health and Memory

**Ch 7:** 7.2–7.5; APA Goal 2: Scientific Inquiry and Critical Thinking: A Cognitive Advantage for Bilingual Individuals? Classic Studies in Psychology: Terman's Termites; Applying Psychology to Everyday Life: Mental and Physical Exercises for Better Cognitive Health

**Ch 8:** 8.1, 8.7, 8.10; Classic Studies in Psychology: The Visual Cliff; Classic Studies in Psychology: Harlow and Contact Comfort; APA Goal 2: Scientific Reasoning and Critical Thinking: The Facts About Immunizations

**Ch 9:** Classic Studies in Psychology: The Angry/Happy Man; APA Goal 2: Scientific Inquiry and Critical Thinking: Cultural Differences in the Use of Praise as a Motivator

**Ch 10:** 10.7; Classic Studies in Psychology: Masters and Johnson's Observational Study of the Human Sexual Response; APA Goal 2: Scientific Reasoning and Critical Thinking

**Ch 12:** 12.16; Classic Studies in Psychology: Brown Eyes, Blue Eyes; APA Goal 2: Scientific Inquiry and Critical Thinking: Cults and the Failure of Critical Thinking

**Ch 13:** 13.9 and Classic Studies in Psychology: Geert Hofstede's Four Dimensions of Cultural Personality; APA Goal 2: Scientific Inquiry and Critical Thinking: Personality, Family, and Culture

**Ch 14:** APA Goal 2: Scientific Inquiry and Critical Thinking: Learning More: Psychological Disorders

**Ch 15:** APA Goal 2: Scientific Inquiry and Critical Thinking: Does It Work? Psychological Treatment

**Appendix A: Statistics in Psychology**

Scientific methods are reinforced with learning tools: Writing Space, Experiment Simulations, MyPsychLab Video Series, Operation

## 3 Ethical and Social Responsibility

The skills in this domain involve the development of ethically and socially responsible behaviors for professional and personal settings. Foundation students should become familiar with the formal regulations that govern professional ethics in psychology and begin to embrace the values that will contribute to positive outcomes in work settings and in society. Baccalaureate students should have more direct opportunities to demonstrate adherence to professional values that will help them optimize their contributions.

**3.1** Apply ethical standards to psychological science and practice.

**3.2** Build and enhance interpersonal relationships.

**3.3** Adopt values that build community at local, national, and global levels.

**Ch 1:** 1.10; Shared Writing: The Science of Psychology
**Ch 2:** Shared Writing: The Biological Perspective
**Ch 3:** Shared Writing: Sensation and Perception
**Ch 4:** Shared Writing: Consciousness
**Ch 5:** 5.3; Shared Writing: Learning
**Ch 6:** Shared Writing: Memory
**Ch 7:** 7.9, 7.10; Classic Studies in Psychology: Terman's "Termites"; Shared Writing: Cognition: Thinking, Intelligence, and Language
**Ch 8:** 8.4, 8.11; Shared Writing: Development Across the Life Span
**Ch 9:** 9.3, 9.5, 9.10; Classic Studies in Psychology: The Angry/Happy Man; Shared Writing: Motivation and Emotion
**Ch 10:** 10.5; Applying Psychology to Everyday Life: The AIDS Epidemic in Russia; Shared Writing: Sexuality and Gender
**Ch 11:** 11.6, 11.9; Shared Writing: Stress and Health
**Ch 12:** 12.4; Scientific Inquiry and Critical Thinking: Cults and the Failure of Critical Thinking; Classic Studies in Psychology: Brown Eyes, Blue Eyes; Applying Psychology in Everyday Life: Peeking Inside the Social Brain
**Ch 13:** 13.12; Shared Writing: Theories of Personality
**Ch 14:** Shared Writing: Psychological Disorders
**Ch 15:** Shared Writing: Psychological Therapies

Ethics and values are reinforced with learning tools: Writing Space, Experiment Simulations, MyPsychLab Video Series, Operation ARA, Visual Brain, and instructor's teaching and assessment package.

## 4 Communication

Students should demonstrate competence in written, oral, and interpersonal communication skills. Foundation students should be able to write a cogent scientific argument, present information using a scientific approach, engage in discussion of psychological concepts, explain the ideas of others, and express their own ideas with clarity. Baccalaureate students should produce a research study or other psychological project, explain scientific results, and present information to a professional audience. They should also develop flexible interpersonal approaches that optimize information exchange and relationship development.

**4.1** Demonstrate effective writing in multiple formats.

**4.2** Exhibit effective presentation skills in multiple formats.

**4.3** Interact effectively with others.

**Intro:** PIA.6
**Ch 7:** 7.11
**Ch 8:** 8.8 and Applying Psychology to Everyday Life: Cross-Cultural Views on Death
**Ch 9:** 9.3
**Ch 10:** 10.5
**Ch 12:** 12.2–12.3, 12.8–12.9, 12.12 and Psychology in the News: Facing Facebook—The Social Nature of Online Networking; Applying Psychology to Everyday Life: Peeking Inside the Social Brain

Communication skills are reinforced with learning tools: Writing Space, Experiment Simulations, MyPsychLab Video Series, Operation ARA, Visual Brain, and instructor's teaching and assessment package.

## 5 Professional Development

The skills in this domain refer to abilities that sharpen student readiness for post-baccalaureate employment, graduate school, or professional school. The emphasis in the domain involves application of psychology-specific content and skills, effective self-reflection, project management skills, teamwork skills, and career preparation. These skills can be developed and refined both in traditional academic settings and extracurricular involvement. In addition, career professionals can be enlisted to support occupational planning and pursuit.

**5.1** Apply psychological content and skills to professional work.

**5.2** Exhibit self-efficacy and self-regulation.

**5.3** Refine project management skills.

**5.4** Enhance teamwork capacity.

**5.5** Develop meaningful professional direction for life after graduation.

**Intro: PIA.1-PIA.7**
**Ch 1:** 1.4, 1.12
**Ch 7:** Applying Psychology to Everyday Life: Mental and Physical Exercises for Better Cognitive Health
**Ch 9:** 9.1, 9.3–9.4, 9.10 and Applying Psychology to Everyday Life: When Motivation Is Not Enough
**Ch 10:** 10.5
**Ch 11:** 11.7–11.10
**Ch 12:** 12.1–12.3, 12.8–12.9

**Appendix B: Applied Psychology and Psychology Careers**

Professional development opportunities are reinforced with learning tools: Writing Space, Experiment Simulations, MyPsychLab Video Series, Operation ARA, Visual Brain, and instructor's teaching and assessment package.

# Acknowledgments

I have to thank my husband, Joe Ciccarelli, for his love and support while I spent many long hours writing and editing this textbook. My children, Al and Liz, also put up with my odd working hours and frequent trips and deserve my thanks as well.

There are so many people to thank for their support! Erin Mitchell and Dickson Musslewhite, of the editorial team supported and advised me—thank you all so much. Special thanks to Maggie Waples, Debi Doyle, and Kate Stewart for a fantastic marketing campaign.

The design is the collaborative work of Lumina, Blair Brown, and Kathryn Foot. New videos were the efforts of Kim Norbuta, Rebecca Green, and a variety of new contributors appearing on camera. New bio art and animations made possible by our phenomenal content producer Pamela Weldin. Thanks also to Ben Ferini and Liz Kincaid for their permissions work and Tom Scalzo, Caroline Fenton, and Diane Lombardo for their work on REVEL and MyPsychLab. A big, heartfelt thank you to Diana Murphy, supplement manager, and my supplement authors Jason Spiegelman, Alan Swinkels, and Editors, Inc. You are fantastic!

We are grateful to all of the instructors and students who have contributed to the development of this text and package over the last five editions. We thank the hundreds of folks who have reviewed content, participated in focus groups, evaluated learning tools, appeared in videos, and offered their feedback and assistance in numerous other ways. We thank you.

Special thanks to Julie Swasey, our development editor, who fits us like a glove and made the whole process of editing this edition so much easier. We love you, Julie! We know you are moving on to a new position and wish you all the best, and we'll miss you. Thanks also to Jennifer Stevenson, who took over Julie's chores at the "back end" of the editing process and did a great job!

And, of course, I can't forget Noland White, my coauthor, pal, and Grand High Expert. His expertise in neuropsychology and clinical psychology is a valuable resource, and his revisions of half of the chapters and all of the chapter maps have once again made this edition a real standout. Thank you from the bottom of my heart, buddy! And give my foster "grands" a hug from Nana Sandy.

Sandy Ciccarelli
Gulf Coast State College
Panama City, Florida
**sandy243@comcast.net**

I would like to personally thank:

My wife and best friend, Leah, and our wonderful children, Sierra, Alexis, and Landon, thank you for your love and patience through the long hours and many absences. I would not be able to do any of this without you;

My lead author and collaborator, Sandy Ciccarelli, for making all of this possible—and for your friendship, support, assistance, advice, and continuing to be the most amazing mentor and writing partner I could ever hope to work with!

My students, for your inspiration, encouragement, and for all of the things you continue to teach me;

The student and faculty users and reviewers of this text, for your support and ever-helpful comments and suggestions;

My friends and colleagues in the Department of Psychological Science at Georgia College, for your encouragement, frequent discussions, and feedback, with special thanks to Lee Gillis, John Lindsay, and Greg Jarvie for your input and support along the way. And to Walt Isaac, Kristina Dandy, and Diana Young, thank you for your contributions and willingness to be "on call" reviewers!

Julie Swasey and Erin Mitchell, for your guidance, creativity, collaboration, and for being so awesome!

Jen Stevenson, for tagging in and doing such an amazing job!

Pamela Weldin, Caroline Fenton, Melissa Sacco, Maggie Waples, Debi Doyle, Kate Stewart, Dickson Musslewhite, Stephany Harrington, and all of the other Pearson and associated staff, for your contributions and for continuing to make this such a great experience!

Noland White
Georgia College & State University
Milledgeville, Georgia
noland.white@gcsu.edu

# About the Authors

**SAUNDRA K. CICCARELLI** is a professor emeritus of psychology at Gulf Coast State College in Panama City, Florida. She received her Ph.D. in developmental psychology from George Peabody College of Vanderbilt University, Nashville, Tennessee. She is a member of the American Psychological Association and the Association for Psychological Science. Originally interested in a career as a researcher in the development of language and intelligence in developmentally delayed children and adolescents, Dr. Ciccarelli had publications in the *American Journal of Mental Deficiency* while still at Peabody. However, she discovered a love of teaching early on in her career. This led her to the position at Gulf Coast State College, where she taught Introductory Psychology and Human Development for more than 30 years. Her students loved her enthusiasm for the field of psychology and the many anecdotes and examples she used to bring psychology to life for them. Before writing this text, Dr. Ciccarelli authored numerous ancillary materials for several introductory psychology and human development texts.

**J. NOLAND WHITE** is a professor of psychology at Georgia College & State University (Georgia College), Georgia's Public Liberal Arts University, located in Milledgeville. He received his A.A. in psychology from Macon State College and both his B.S. and M.S. in psychology from Georgia College. After receiving his Ph.D. in counseling psychology from the University of Tennessee, he joined the faculty of Georgia College in 2001. He teaches Introductory Psychology, Psychology of Adjustment, Behavioral Neuroscience, Advanced Behavioral Neuroscience, Counseling and Clinical Psychology, Senior Seminar, and a section of Advanced Research Methods focusing on psychophysiology. He has an active lab and, with his students, is investigating the psychophysiological characteristics and neuropsychological performance of adults with and without ADHD. Outside of the lab, Dr. White is engaged in collaborative research examining the effectiveness of incorporating various technologies in and out of the college classroom to facilitate student learning. He also serves as a mentor for other faculty wanting to expand their use of technology with their classes. In April 2008, he was a recipient of the Georgia College Excellence in Teaching Award. Dr. White is also a licensed psychologist and has worked with adolescents and adults in a variety of clinical and community settings.

# Psychology

Fifth edition

# Psychology in Action

## Secrets for Surviving College and Improving Your Grades

Based on what you know now, what advice would you share with a student just starting out in college?
After you have answered the question, watch the video to compare the answers of other students to yours.

▶ The response entered here will be saved to your notes and may be collected by your instructor if he/she requires it.

👁 **Watch** the **Video**

## Why Study How to Study?

Many students entering college have developed a system of taking notes, reading the textbook, and reviewing for exams that may have worked pretty well in the past; but what worked in grade school and high school may not work in college, where the expectations from teachers are higher and the workload is far greater. Students should develop skills in the following areas in order to do their absolute best in any college course: study methods, time management, effective reading of course materials, active listening and note taking, studying for exams, memory strategies, and writing papers. One final aspect of being a successful student involves being an ethical student—exactly how can you use the materials you find for your research paper, for example, without committing the sin of plagiarism (claiming the work of someone else as your own)?

This introduction presents various techniques and information aimed at maximizing knowledge and skills in each of these eight areas. In addition, brief videos are available on each of these topics. These topics address aspects of the American Psychological Association's (APA) undergraduate learning goals. APA Goal 2 (Scientific Inquiry and Critical Thinking) is addressed in Chapter One and is the basis of a feature in every chapter.

## Learning Objectives

**PIA.1** Identify four methods of studying.

**PIA.2** Describe some strategies for time management.

**PIA.3** Describe how to read a textbook so that you get the most out of your reading efforts.

**PIA.4** Identify the best methods for taking notes and listening in class.

**PIA.5** Describe how to approach studying for exams.

**PIA.6** Explain how using mnemonics can help you improve your memory for facts and concepts.

**PIA.7** Describe the key steps in writing papers for college.

**PIA.8** Identify some of the key ethical considerations that you'll face as a student.

Some students find it helpful to hear the content in addition to reading it. This is especially true when learning a new language. This woman is listening to an audio recording from her textbook as she follows along and looks at the figures and photos.

◉ **Watch** the **Video** *Study Methods*

# Study Skills

### PIA.1 Identify four methods of studying.

 💬 I want to make better grades, but sometimes it seems that no matter how hard I study, the test questions turn out to be hard and confusing and I end up not doing very well. Is there some trick to getting good grades?

Many students would probably say that their grades are not what they want them to be. They may make the effort, but they still don't seem to be able to achieve the higher grades that they wish they could earn. A big part of the problem is that despite many different educational experiences, students are rarely taught how to study.

We learn many different kinds of things during our lives, and using only one method of learning probably isn't going to work for everyone. Students may have preferences for a particular study method or may find it useful to use a combination of different methods. *Verbal study methods* involve the use of words, expressed either through writing or speaking. For instance, after you read about a topic, you might put it into your own words, or you might write out longer, more detailed versions of the notes you took in class. *Visual learning methods* involve the use of pictures or images. Students using these methods may look at or create charts, diagrams, and figures to master the content. There are also those who prefer to learn by hearing the information (*auditory learning methods*). Listening to a recording of a lecture is a good example. Finally, there are people who use the motion of their own bodies to help them remember key information (*action learning methods*). For instance, you might construct a three-dimensional model to gain a better understanding of a topic.

**THINKING CRITICALLY**

Describe some other ways in which the various study methods can be put to use.

▶ | The response entered here will be saved to your notes and may be collected by your instructor if he/she requires it.

[ Submit ]

Table PIA.1 lists just some of the ways in which you can study. All of the methods listed in this table are good for students who wish to improve both their understanding of a subject and their grades on tests.

**Table PIA.1** Multiple Study Methods

| VERBAL METHODS (involve speaking or writing) | VISUAL METHODS (involve pictures, images) | AUDITORY METHODS (involve listening) | ACTION METHODS (involve physical activity) |
|---|---|---|---|
| Use flash cards to identify main points or key terms. | Make flash cards with pictures or diagrams to aid recall of key concepts or use the flashcards in REVEL. | Join or form a study group or find a study partner so that you can discuss concepts and ideas. | Sit near the front of the classroom. If online, give yourself room to walk around while studying. |
| Write out or recite key information in whole sentences or phrases in your own words. | Make charts and diagrams and sum up information in tables. | While studying, speak out loud or into a digital recorder that you can play back later or to the audio recordings in REVEL. | Take notes by making pictures or charts to help you remember key terms and ideas. |
| When looking at diagrams, write out a description. | | Make speeches. | Read out loud or use the audio feature in REVEL while walking around. |
| Use "sticky" notes to remind yourself of key terms and information, and put them in the notebook text or e-text or on a mirror that you use frequently. | Use different colors of highlighter for different sections of information in text, e-text, or notes. | Record the lectures (with permission). Take notes on the lecture sparingly, using the recording to fill in parts that you might have missed. | Study with a friend.
While exercising, listen to recordings of important information, either your own or those in REVEL. |
| | Visualize charts, diagrams, and figures. | Read notes or text material into a digital recorder or get study materials recorded and play back while exercising or doing chores. | Write out key concepts on a large board or poster. |
| Practice spelling words or repeating facts to be remembered. | Trace letters and words to remember key facts. | When learning something new, state or explain the information in your own words out loud or to a study partner. | Make your own flash cards, using different colors and diagrams, and lay them out in order on a large surface. |
| Rewrite things from memory. | Use the interactive figures and tables available in REVEL. | Use musical rhythms as memory aids, or put information to a rhyme or a tune. | Make a three-dimensional model.
Spend extra time in the lab.
Go to off-campus areas such as a museum or historical site to gain information. |
| | Redraw things from memory. | | |

### Concept Map L.O. PIA.1

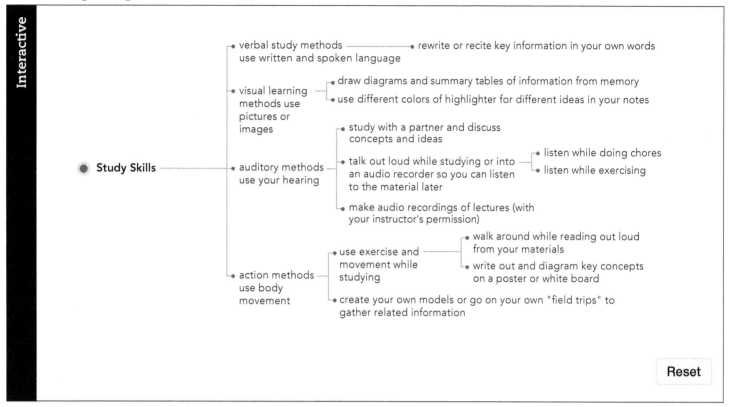

## Practice Quiz   How much do you remember?

*Pick the best answer.*

1. In an episode of a popular television program, a detective reconstructs a crime scene by using various foods from his dinner table. He uses ears of corn to represent the cars, mashed potatoes to form the sides of the road, and so on. What method of learning best fits the method this character seems to be using to think about the events of the crime?
   **a.** verbal
   **b.** visual
   **c.** auditory
   **d.** action

2. Gilbert has been advised by a learning expert to study using techniques like using flash cards, writing out important points in his own words and then reciting them, using sticky notes to emphasize important points, and creating descriptions of figures and images. Gilbert's tutor is recommending the use of _____ study methods.
   **a.** auditory
   **b.** action
   **c.** visual
   **d.** verbal

## Managing Time

**PIA.2  Describe some strategies for time management.**

One of the biggest failings of college students (and many others) is managing the time for all the tasks involved. Procrastination, the tendency to put off tasks until some later time that often does not arrive, is the enemy of time management. There are some strategies to defeating procrastination (The College Board, 2011):

- Make a map of your long-term goals. If you are starting here, what are the paths you need to take to get to your ultimate goal?

- Use a calendar to keep track of class times, time devoted to studying, time for writing papers, work times, social engagements, everything! Use the calendar app on your phone, tablet, or computer—or all three.

- Before you go to bed, plan your next day, starting with when you get up and prioritizing your tasks for that day. Mark tasks off as you do them.

- Go to bed. Getting enough sleep is a necessary step in managing your tasks. Eating right and walking or stretching between tasks is a good idea, too.

- If you have big tasks, break them down into smaller, more manageable pieces. For example, if you have to write a paper, divide the task into smaller ones, such as making an outline or writing the introductory paragraph. How do you eat an elephant? One bite at a time.

- Do small tasks, like taking a practice quiz or writing the first paragraph of a paper, in those bits of time you might otherwise dismiss: riding the bus to school or work, waiting in a doctor's office, and so on.

- Build in some play time—all work and no play pretty much ensures that you will fail at keeping your schedule. Use play time as a reward for getting tasks done.

- If your schedule falls apart, don't panic—just start again the next day. Even the best time managers have days when things don't go as planned.

Another problem that often interferes with time management is the enduring myth that we can effectively multitask. In today's world of technological interconnectedness, people tend to believe that they can learn to do more than one task at a time. The fact, however, is that the human mind is not meant to multitask, and trying to do so not only can lead to car wrecks and other disasters but also may result in changes in how individuals process different types of information, and not for the better. One study challenged college students to perform experiments that involved task switching, selective attention, and working memory (Ophir et al., 2009). The expectation was that students who were experienced at multitasking would outperform those who were not, but the results were just the opposite: the "chronic multitaskers" failed miserably at all three tasks. The results seemed to indicate that frequent multitaskers use their brains less effectively, even when focusing on a single task. Yet another study found that the grade point averages of students who multitasked while studying were negatively affected (Junco & Cotton, 2012).

Researchers also have found that people who think they are good at multitasking are actually not (Sanbonmatsu et al., 2013), while still another study indicates that video gamers, who often feel that their success at gaming is training them to be good multitaskers in other areas of life such as texting or talking while driving, are just as unsuccessful at multitasking as nongamers (Donohue et al., 2012). In short, it's better to focus on one task and only one task for a short period of time before moving on to another than to try to do two things at once.

👁 **Watch** the **Video** *Managing Time*

## Concept Map L.O. PIA.2

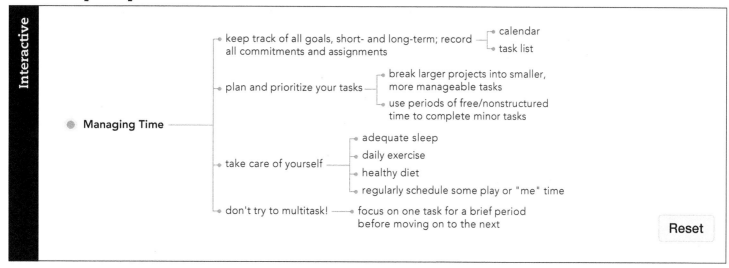

**Managing Time**

- keep track of all goals, short- and long-term; record all commitments and assignments
  - calendar
  - task list
- plan and prioritize your tasks
  - break larger projects into smaller, more manageable tasks
  - use periods of free/nonstructured time to complete minor tasks
- take care of yourself
  - adequate sleep
  - daily exercise
  - healthy diet
  - regularly schedule some play or "me" time
- don't try to multitask! — focus on one task for a brief period before moving on to the next

Reset

# Practice Quiz    How much do you remember?

*Pick the best answer.*

**1.** Which of the following is *not* a question that students should ask themselves in order to maximize their studying effectiveness?
   **a.** How can I most effectively highlight while I am reading my textbook?
   **b.** How should I improve my memory for facts and concepts?
   **c.** How can I best manage my time and avoid procrastination?
   **d.** How can I write good term papers?

**2.** Which of the following is a suggestion to help you with time management skills?
   **a.** When you have a big project to complete, try to complete it all at once rather than breaking it down into smaller pieces so that you don't put it off until later.

   **b.** Try to focus only on short-term goals, since looking at long-term goals can be defeating and upsetting.
   **c.** Build in some play time, using it as a reward for getting tasks done.
   **d.** If your schedule falls apart, make sure to panic immediately!

**3.** What does the research show in regard to multitasking?
   **a.** Chronic multitaskers have developed strategies that allow them to use their brains more effectively.
   **b.** Chronic multitasking may be related to less effective ways of processing different types of information.
   **c.** Multitasking is effective, but only if you limit the number of tasks to 5 or fewer.
   **d.** Video gamers are better at multitasking in all areas of life.

# Reading the Text: Textbooks Are Not Meatloaf

**PIA.3** **Describe how to read a textbook so that you get the most out of your reading efforts.**

No matter what the study method, students must read the textbook or other assigned course materials to be successful in the course. (While that might seem obvious to some, many students today seem to think that just taking notes on lectures or slide presentations will be enough.) This section deals with how to read textbooks—whether in print or online—for understanding rather than just to "get through" the material.

Students make two common mistakes in regard to reading a textbook. The first mistake is simple: Many students don't bother to read the textbook *before* watching the lecture that will cover that material. Trying to get anything out of a lecture without having read the material first is like trying to find a new, unfamiliar place without using a GPS or any kind of directions. It's easy to get lost. This is especially true because of the assumption that most instructors make when planning their lectures: They take for granted that the students have already read the assignment. The instructors then use the lecture to go into detail about the information the students supposedly got from the reading. If the students have not done the reading, the instructor's lecture isn't going to make a whole lot of sense.

The second mistake that most students make when reading textbook material is to try to read it the same way they would read a novel: They start at the beginning and read continuously. With a novel, it's easy to do this because the plot is usually interesting and people want to know what happens next, so they keep reading. It isn't necessary to remember every little detail—all they need to remember are the main plot points. One could say that a novel is like meatloaf—some meaty parts with lots of filler. Meatloaf can be eaten quickly, without even chewing for very long.

With a textbook, the material may be interesting but not in the same way that a novel is interesting. A textbook is a big, thick steak—all meat, no filler. Just as a steak has to be chewed to be enjoyed and to be useful to the body, textbook material has to be "chewed" with the mind. You have to read slowly, paying attention to every morsel of meaning.

So how do you do that? Probably one of the best-known reading methods is called SQ3R, first used by F. P. Robinson in a 1946 book called *Effective Study*. The letters S-Q-R-R-R stand for:

**SURVEY** Look at the chapter you've been assigned to read. Read the outline, learning objectives, or other opening materials. Then scan the chapter and read the headings of sections, and look at tables and figures. Quickly read through the chapter summary if one is provided.

It might sound like it takes too much time to do this, but you should just be skimming at this point—a couple of minutes is all it should take. Why do this at all? Surveying the chapter, or "previewing" it, as some experts call it, helps you form a framework in your head around which you can organize the information in the chapter when you read it in detail. Organization is one of the main ways to improve your memory for information. Ⓛ Ⓘ Ⓝ Ⓚ to Learning Objective 6.5.

**QUESTION** After previewing the chapter, read the heading for the first section. *Just* the first section! Try to think of a question based on this heading that the section should answer as you read. For example, in Chapter One there's a section titled "Pavlov, Watson, and the Dawn of Behaviorism." You could ask yourself, "What did Pavlov and Watson do for psychology?" or "What is behaviorism?" In this text, we've presented a list of learning objectives for the key concepts in the chapter that can be used with the SQ3R method. There are also student questions highlighted throughout the chapters that can serve the same purpose. Now when you read the section, you aren't *just* reading—you're reading to *find an answer*. That makes the material much easier to remember later on.

**READ** Now read the section, looking for the answers to your questions. As you read, take notes by making an outline of the main points and terms in the section. This is another area where some students make a big mistake. They assume that highlighting words and phrases is as good as writing notes. One of the author's former students conducted research on the difference between highlighting and note taking, and her findings were clear: Students who wrote their own notes during the reading of a text or while listening to a lecture scored significantly higher on their exam grades than students who merely highlighted the text (Boyd & Peeler, 2004). Highlighting requires no real mental effort (no "chewing," in other words), but writing the words down yourself requires you to read the words in depth and to understand them. When we study memory, you'll learn more about the value of processing information in depth. Ⓛ Ⓘ Ⓝ Ⓚ to Learning Objective 6.2.

**RECITE** It may sound silly, but reciting out loud what you can remember from the section you've just read is another good way to process the information more deeply and completely. How many times have you thought you understood something, only to

Before reading any chapter in a text, survey the chapter by reading the outline and the section headings.

As you read, take notes. Write down key terms and try to summarize the main points of each paragraph and section in the chapter. These notes will be useful when you later review the chapter material.

find that when you tried to explain it to someone, you didn't understand it at all? Recitation forces you to put the information in your own words—just as writing it in notes does. Writing it down accesses your visual memory; saying it out loud gives you an auditory memory for the same information. If you have ever learned something well by teaching it to someone else, you already know the value of recitation. If you feel self-conscious about talking to yourself, talk into a digital recorder—and it's a great way to review later.

Now repeat the Question, Read, and Recite instructions for each section, taking a few minutes' break after every two or three sections. Why take a break? There's a process that has to take place in your brain when you are trying to form a permanent memory for information, and that process takes a little time. When you take a break every 10 to 20 minutes, you are giving your brain the time to accomplish this process. A break will help you avoid a common problem in reading texts—finding yourself reading the same sentence over and over again because your brain is too overloaded from trying to remember what you just read.

**RECALL/REVIEW** Finally, you've finished reading the entire chapter. If you've used the guidelines listed previously, you'll only have to read the chapter as thoroughly this one time instead of having to read it over and over throughout the semester and just before exams. Once you've read the chapter, take a few minutes to try to remember as much of what you learned while reading it as you can. A good way to do this is to take any practice quizzes that might be available. For this text, we offer both practice quizzes within the print text and online quizzes and study materials in the e-text. If there are no quizzes, read the chapter summary in detail, making sure that you understand everything in it. If there's anything that's confusing, go back to that section in the chapter and read again until you understand it.

Some educators and researchers now add a fourth R: *Reflect*. To reflect means to try to think critically about what you have read by trying to tie the concepts into what you already know, thinking about how you can use the information in your own life, and deciding which of the topics you've covered interests you enough to look for more information on that topic (Richardson & Morgan, 1997). For example, if you have learned about the genetic basis for depression, you might better understand why that disorder seems to run in your best friend's family. ⓁⒾⓃⓀ to Learning Objective 14.9.

Reading textbooks in this way means that, when it comes time for the final exam, all you will have to do is carefully review your notes to be ready for the exam—you won't have to read the entire textbook all over again. What a time saver! Recent research suggests that the most important steps in this method are the three Rs: read, recite, and review. In two experiments with college students, researchers found that when compared with other study methods such as rereading and note-taking study strategies, the 3R strategy produced superior recall of the material (McDaniel et al., 2009).

After reading a chapter section, take time to reflect on what the information means and how it might relate to real-world situations.

◉ **Watch** the **Video** *Reading the Text*

---

## Concept Map L.O. PIA.3

Interactive

Reading the Text
- reading for learning is not the same as reading for pleasure
- break up your reading sessions so you have time to process and understand the information
- using a system of reading, reciting, and reviewing is very effective
  - SQ3R
  - SQ4R
  - 3R

Reset

# Practice Quiz    How much do you remember?

*Pick the best answer.*

**1.** What does the S in SQ3R stand for?
   **a.** survey          **c.** synthesize
   **b.** study           **d.** stand

**2.** As you read the text material, you should
   **a.** use a highlighter so that you don't waste time writing notes.
   **b.** avoid taking notes while reading so that you can concentrate on the material.
   **c.** make an outline of the main points and key terms.
   **d.** read the entire chapter all at once.

**3.** Candice has surveyed the material, developed questions to consider, and begun reading the material to find the answers to her questions. What should she do next?
   **a.** Recite out loud what she can remember from the section she just read.
   **b.** Reread the material a second time.
   **c.** Review the material from the chapter that she has read.
   **d.** Retain the material by committing it to memory.

---

# Getting the Most Out of Lectures

**PIA.4  Identify the best methods for taking notes and listening in class.**

As mentioned earlier, mastering course content means you have to attend the lectures. Even if lectures are online, you have to read or watch them. But just attending or reading or watching is not enough; you have to process the information just as you have to process the text material. To get the most out of lectures, you need to take notes on the content, and taking notes involves quite a bit more than just writing down the words the instructor says or printing out the PowerPoint slides.

One very important fact you must remember: PowerPoint slides are not meant to be notes at all; they are merely talking points that help the instructor follow a particular sequence in lecturing. Typically, the instructor will have more to say about each point on the slide, and that is the information students should be listening to and writing down. In Table PIA.1, the suggestion to use highlighters of different colors is not meant to replace taking notes but instead to supplement the notes you do take.

How should you take notes? As stated earlier, you should try to take notes while reading the chapter (*before* attending the lecture) by writing down the main points and the vocabulary terms *in your own words* as much as possible. This forces you to think about what you are reading. The more you think about it, the more likely it is that the concepts will become a part of your permanent memory. Ⓛ Ⓘ Ⓝ Ⓚ to Learning Objective 6.5.

Taking notes while listening to the lecture is a slightly different procedure. First, you should have your notes from your earlier reading in front of you, and it helps to leave plenty of space between lines to add notes from the lecture. A major mistake made by many students is to come to the lecture without having read the material first. This is an EXTREMELY BAD IDEA. If you come to the lecture totally unprepared, you will have no idea what is important enough to write down and what is just the instructor's asides and commentary. Reading the material first gives you a good idea of exactly what is important in the lecture and reduces the amount of notes you must take.

### THINKING CRITICALLY

What are some reasons why not relying on the instructor's PowerPoints might be beneficial in committing information to memory?

▶ | The response entered here will be saved to your notes and may be collected by your instructor if he/she requires it.

Submit

Here are two things that instructors love to see: attentive looks and note taking during the lecture. And for the student who learns better just listening, a small digital recorder (used with permission) can help for later review of the lecture. How should these students have prepared before coming to this class?

There is an art to really listening to someone, too, often called *active listening*. Active listeners make eye contact with the speaker and sit facing the speaker in a place where they can easily hear and see the speaker. Active listeners focus on what is being said rather than how the speaker looks or sounds (not always an easy task) and ask questions when they do not understand something or need a clarification. Asking questions during a lecture is a good way to stay engaged in actively processing the speaker's message.

Ask your instructor if you can bring a digital recorder to class to record the lecture. You will then be able to listen during the class and use the recording to take notes from later. Some students may prefer to jot down diagrams, charts, and other visual aids along with their written notes. When you have good notes taken while reading the text and from the lectures, you will also have ready-made study aids for preparing to take exams. The next section deals with the best ways to study for exams.

👁 **Watch** the **Video** *Lecture Notes*

---

**Concept Map** L.O. PIA.4

**Interactive**

● **Getting the Most Out of Lectures** —— ┬→ read your textbook and take notes before class so you can focus on the lecture—in the lecture only take notes on the most important ideas

├→ take notes and write information in your own words; create diagrams or charts

└→ engage in active listening; focus on what is being discussed and ask questions for clarification

Reset

---

# Practice Quiz    How much do you remember?

*Pick the best answer.*

**1.** To maximize success, which method of note-taking should Juan use?
  **a.** He should take notes in his own words as much as possible.
  **b.** He should write down every word from the PowerPoint slides used in class.
  **c.** He should highlight the text rather than writing his own notes.
  **d.** He should make sure that his notes contain the exact words used by his instructor.

**2.** Avery maintains eye contact when listening to her instructors. She also places herself so that she can see and hear the instructors. Additionally, she works to listen to the content of the lecture instead of focusing on how they look or what they are wearing. Avery would be described as a(n)
  **a.** accomplished student.
  **b.** active listener.
  **c.** passive listener.
  **d.** social listener.

---

# Studying for Exams: Cramming Is Not an Option

**PIA.5  Describe how to approach studying for exams.**

Inevitably, the time will come when your instructor wants some hard evidence that you have truly learned at least some of the material to which you have been exposed. There is a right way to study for a test, believe it or not. Here are some good things to remember when preparing for an exam, whether it's a quiz, a unit test, a midterm, or a final (Carter et al., 2005; Reynolds, 2002):

  • **Timing is everything.** One of the worst things that students can do is to wait until the last minute to study for an exam. Remember the analogy about "chewing" the steak? (Just as a steak has to be chewed to be enjoyed and to be useful to the body,

Could this be you? The scattered materials, the frantic phone call to a friend or professor, and the tense and worried facial expression are all hallmarks of that hallowed yet useless student tradition, cramming. Don't let this happen to you.

textbook material has to be "chewed" with the mind.) The same concept applies to preparing for an exam: You have to give yourself enough time. If you've read your text material and taken good notes as discussed in the previous sections, you'll be able to save a lot of time in studying for the exam, but you still need to give yourself ample time to go over all of those notes. The time management tips given earlier in this chapter will help you prioritize your studying.

- **Find out as much as you can about the type of test and the material it will cover.** The type of test can affect the way in which you want to study the material. An objective test, for example, such as multiple-choice or true/false, is usually fairly close to the text material, so you'll want to be very familiar with the wording of concepts and definitions in the text, although this is not a suggestion to memorize a lot of material.

These kinds of tests can include one of three types of questions:

- **Factual:** Questions that ask you to remember a specific fact from the text material. For example, "Who built the first psychological laboratory?" requires that you recognize a person's name. (The answer is Wilhelm Wundt.)

- **Applied:** Questions that ask you to use, or apply, information presented in the text. For example, consider the following question:

> Ever since she was scared by a dog as a young child, Angelica has been afraid of all dogs. The fact that she is afraid not only of the original dog but of all types of dogs is an example of
>
> **a.** stimulus generalization.
> **b.** stimulus discrimination.
> **c.** spontaneous recovery.
> **d.** shaping.
>
> This question requires you to take a concept (in this case, generalization) and apply it to a real-world example.

- **Conceptual:** Questions that demand that you think about the ideas or concepts presented in the text and demonstrate that you understand them by answering questions like the following: "Freud is to _____ as Watson is to _____." (The answers could vary, but a good set would be "the unconscious" and "observable behavior.")

Notice that although memorizing facts might help on the first type of question, it isn't going to help at all on the last two. Memorization doesn't always help on factual questions either, because the questions are sometimes worded quite differently from the text. It is far better to understand the information rather than be able to "spit it back" without understanding it. "Spitting it back" is memorization; understanding it is true learning. **LINK** to Learning Objective 6.5. There are different levels of analysis for information you are trying to learn, and the higher the level of analysis, the more likely you are to remember (Anderson et al., 2001; Bloom, 1956). *Factual questions* are the lowest level of analysis: knowledge. *Applied questions* are a higher level and are often preferred by instructors for that reason—it's hard to successfully apply information if you don't really understand it. *Conceptual questions* are a kind of analysis, a level higher than either of the other two. Not only do you have to understand the concept, you have to understand it well enough to compare and contrast it with other concepts. They might be harder questions to answer, but in the long run, you will get more "bang for your buck" in terms of true learning.

Subjective tests, such as essay tests and short-answer exams, require not only that you are able to recall and understand the information from the course but also that you are able to organize it in your own words. To study for a subjective test means that you need to be familiar with the material *and* that you need to be able to write it down. Make outlines of your notes. Rewrite both reading and lecture notes and make flash cards, charts, and drawings. Practice putting the flash cards in order. Talk out loud or study with someone else and discuss the possible questions that could be on an essay test. You might find that only a few of these methods work best for you, but the more ways in which you try to study, the better you will be able to retrieve the information when you need it. It may sound like a big investment of your time, but most students vastly underestimate how long it takes to study—and fail to recognize that many of these techniques are doable when first reading the textbook assignment and preparing for the classroom lecture. DON'T CRAM!

You might also look at old tests (if the instructor has made them available) to see what kinds of questions are usually asked. If this is not possible, make sure that you pay close attention to the kinds of questions asked on the first exam so that you will know how to prepare for future tests. Write out your own test questions as if you were the instructor. Not only does this force you to think about the material the way it will appear on the test, it also provides a great review tool. Other helpful advice:

- **Use SQ3R.** You can use the same method that you used to read the text material to go over your notes. Skim through your notes, try to think of possible test questions, recite the main ideas and definitions of terms, either out loud, into a digital recorder, or to a friend or study group. Review by summarizing sections of material or by making an outline or flash cards that you can use in studying important concepts.

- **Use the concept maps if provided.** When surveying the chapter, make sure you look over any concept maps. (In this text, they are provided at the end of each major section of the chapters, just before the practice quizzes). **Concept maps** are a visual organization of the key concepts, terms, and definitions that are found in each section and are an excellent way to "see" how various concepts are linked together (Carnot et al., 2001; Novak, 1995; Wu et al., 2004). They are also a great way to review the chapter once you have finished reading it, just to check for understanding—if the concept maps don't make sense, then you've missed something and need to go back over the relevant section. You can also make your own concept maps as you take notes on the chapter. A good resource for the background behind concept maps and how to use them is at cmap.ihmc.us/Publications/ResearchPapers/TheoryCmaps/TheoryUnderlyingConceptMaps.htm

- **Take advantage of all the publisher's test and review materials.** Practice does help, and most textbooks come with a study guide or a Web site. Those materials should have practice quizzes available—take them. We offer practice quizzes in both the print and REVEL versions of this text. The REVEL e-text also offers a variety of opportunities for students to quiz themselves on the information in tables, figures, and graphs. The more types of quiz questions you try to answer, the more successful you will be at interpreting the questions on the actual exam. You'll also get a very good idea of the areas that you need to go back and review again. And remember, retrieval practice, or actually testing your recall through tests or quizzes, is a great way to improve long-term learning (Karpicke, 2012; Karpicke & Blunt, 2011), even when just thinking about the information or rehearsing it in your mind (Smith et al., 2013)! Retrieval practice works better than simply restudying. The key is testing your retrieval of information, not your recognition of information. Also, a good resource of study helps created by Joe Landsberger is the Web site Study Guides and Strategies, available at www.studygs.net.

- **Make use of the resources.** If you find that you are having difficulty with certain concepts, go to the instructor well in advance of the exam for help. (This is another good reason to manage your study time so that you aren't trying to do everything in a few hours the night before the exam.) There are help centers on most college and university campuses with people who can help you learn to study, organize your notes, or tutor you in the subject area.

Many students studying for exams ignore one of the most valuable resources to which they have access: the instructor. Most instructors are happy to answer questions or schedule time for students who are having difficulty understanding the material.

**concept map**

an organized visual representation of knowledge consisting of concepts and their relationships to other concepts.

Holding your eyes open is not going to help you study when you are this tired. Sleep has been shown to improve memory and performance on tests, so get a good night's sleep before every exam.

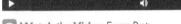

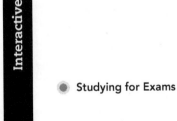

Watch the Video *Exam Prep*

• **Don't forget your physical needs.** Studies have shown that not getting enough sleep is bad for memory and learning processes (Stickgold et al., 2001; Vecsey et al., 2009). Try to stop studying an hour or so before going to bed at a reasonable time to give your body time to relax and unwind. Get a full night's sleep if possible. Do not take sleep-inducing medications or drink alcohol, as these substances prevent normal stages of sleep, including the stage that seems to be the most useful for memory and learning (Davis et al., 2003). Do eat breakfast; hunger is harmful to memory and mental performance. A breakfast heavy on protein and light on carbohydrates is the best for concentration and recall (Benton & Parker, 1998; Dani et al., 2005; Pollitt & Matthews, 1998; Stubbs et al., 1996).

• **Use your test time wisely.** When taking the test, don't allow yourself to get stuck on one question that you can't seem to answer. If an answer isn't clear, skip that question and go on to others. After finishing all of the questions that you can answer easily, go back to the ones you have skipped and try to answer them again. This accomplishes several things: You get to experience success in answering the questions that you can answer, which makes you feel more confident and relaxed; other questions on the test might act as memory cues for the exact information you need for one of those questions you skipped; and once you are more relaxed, you may find that the answers to those seemingly impossible questions are now clear because anxiety is no longer blocking them. This is a way of reducing stress by dealing directly with the problem, one of many ways of dealing effectively with stress. **(L I N K)** to Learning Objective 11.7.

**THINKING CRITICALLY**

Many elementary and secondary school programs now offer breakfast to their students. What foods would benefit these children the most and why?

▶ | The response entered here will be saved to your notes and may be collected by your instructor if he/she requires it.

Submit

## Concept Map  L.O. PIA.5

Interactive

Studying for Exams
- spacing out studying sessions (distributed practice) is more effective than cramming (massed practice); start early!
- knowing what kind of test questions to expect can help guide study efforts
- retrieval practice, testing your recall through tests or quizzes, works much better than simply rereading, restudying, or relying on recognition methods
- use effective time management strategies, both when studying and while taking exams
- don't forget to take care of yourself by getting enough sleep, proper nutrition, and exercise

Reset

# Practice Quiz    How much do you remember?

*Pick the best answer.*

1. Which category is the following question an example of? *True or False: Psychology is the study of behavior and mental processes.*
   a. factual question
   b. conceptual question
   c. applied question
   d. critical question

2. Which questions are the highest level of analysis and often considered the hardest to answer on a test?
   a. factual            c. conceptual
   b. applied            d. true/false

3. Tom is studying for his first psychology exam. What should he do to ensure he remembers all that he has studied?
   a. Wait to study until just before the scheduled exam, so that the information will be fresh in his mind.
   b. Study all night long before the exam—he can sleep after the test.
   c. Memorize as much of the information as possible.
   d. Begin studying many days in advance to give his brain time to commit the material to memory and repeatedly test his retrieval of information.

4. What is the value of retrieval practice?
   a. It helps increase long-term learning.
   b. It allows students more opportunities to study.
   c. It assists only in preparing for essay-based exams.
   d. No research exists to prove that retrieval practice is effective.

5. Simply spitting information back out on a test is likely more indicative of _____, while truly understanding information is more indicative of actual _____.
   a. memorization; learning
   b. learning; memorization
   c. behavior; action
   d. a process; a gift

# Improving Your Memory

**PIA.6**  **Explain how using mnemonics can help you improve your memory for facts and concepts.**

Everyone needs a little memory help now and then. Even memory experts use strategies to help them perform their unusual feats of remembering. These strategies may be unique to that individual, but there are many memory "tricks" that are quite simple and available for anyone to learn and use. A memory trick or strategy to help people remember is called a **mnemonic**, from the Greek word for memory. Take a look at **Figure PIA.1** to see examples of a few of the more popular mnemonics, some of which may sound familiar:

- **Linking.** Make a list in which items to be remembered are linked in some way. If trying to remember a list of the planets in the solar system, for example, a person

**mnemonic**

a strategy or trick for aiding memory.

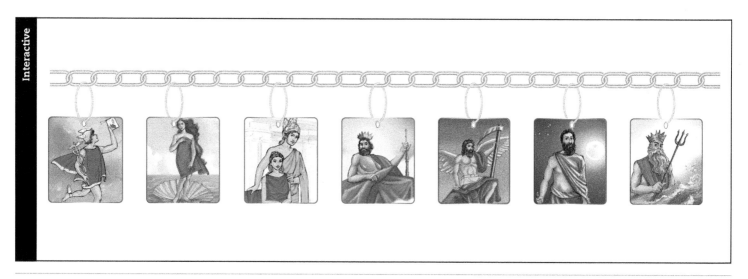

**Figure PIA.1**  Popular Mnemonics

could string the names of the planets together like this: *Mercury* was the messenger god, who carried lots of love notes to *Venus*, the beautiful goddess who sprang from the *Earth's* sea. She was married to *Mars*, her brother, which didn't please her father *Jupiter* or his father *Saturn*, and his uncle *Uranus* complained to the sea god, *Neptune*. That sounds like a lot, but once linked in this way, the names of the planets are easy to recall in proper order.

- **The peg-word method.** In this method, it is necessary to first memorize a series of "peg" words, numbered words that can be used as keys for remembering items associated with them. A typical series of peg words is:

| | |
|---|---|
| One is a bun. | Six is bricks. |
| Two is a shoe. | Seven is heaven. |
| Three is a tree. | Eight is a gate. |
| Four is a door. | Nine is a line. |
| Five is a hive. | Ten is a hen. |

- To use this method, each item to be remembered is associated with a peg word and made into an image. For instance, if you are trying to remember the parts of the nervous system, you might picture the brain stuck inside a bun, the spinal cord growing out of a shoe or with shoes hanging off of it, and the peripheral nerves as the branches of a tree.

- **The method of loci (LOW-kee or LOW-si).** In this method, the person pictures a very familiar room or series of rooms in a house or other building. Each point of the information is then made into an image and "placed" mentally in the room at certain locations. For example, if the first point was about military spending, the image might be a soldier standing in the doorway of the house throwing money out into the street. Each point would have its place, and all the person would need to do to retrieve the memories would be to take a "mental walk" around the house.

R O Y G B I V

- **Verbal/rhythmic organization.** How do you spell relief? If, when spelling a word with an *ie* or an *ei* in it, you resort to the old rhyme "I before E except after C, or when sounded as A as in neighbor or weigh," you have made use of a verbal/rhythmic organization mnemonic. "Thirty days hath September, April, June, and November …" is another example of this technique. Setting information into a rhyme aids memory because it uses verbal cues, rhyming words, and the rhythm of the poem itself to aid retrieval. Sometimes this method is accomplished through making a sentence by using the first letters of each word to be remembered and making them into new words that form a sentence. The colors of the rainbow are ROY G. BIV (red, orange, yellow, green, blue, indigo, and violet). The notes on the musical staff are "Every Good Boy Does Fine." There are countless examples of this technique.

Watch the Video *Improve Memory*

- **Put it to music (a version of the rhythmic method).** Some people have had success with making up little songs, using familiar tunes, to remember specific information. The best example of this? The alphabet song.

## Concept Map L.O. PIA.6

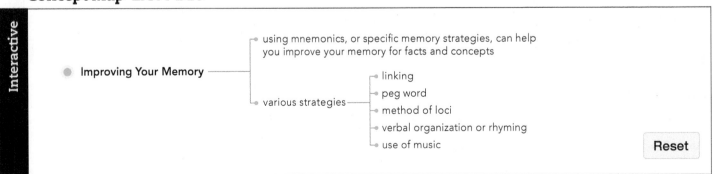

# Practice Quiz    How much do you remember?

*Pick the best answer.*

1. Which of the following is NOT one of the mnemonic techniques described in this chapter?
   **a.** method of loci
   **b.** rote memorization
   **c.** linking
   **d.** peg-word

2. "My very excellent mother just served us nine pizzas" is a mnemonic for remembering the order of the planets in our solar system (including poor, downgraded Pluto, of course). What kind of mnemonic is this?
   **a.** method of loci          **c.** peg-word
   **b.** linking                       **d.** verbal/rhythmic organization

# Writing Papers

**PIA.7  Describe the key steps in writing papers for college.**

Several steps are involved in writing a paper, whether it be a short paper or a long one. You should begin all of these steps well in advance of the due date for the paper (not the night before):

1. **Choose a topic.** The first step is to choose a topic for your paper. In some cases, the instructor may have a list of acceptable subjects, which makes your job easier. If that is not the case, don't be afraid to go to your instructor during office hours and talk about some possible topics. Try to choose a topic that interests you, one that you would like to learn more about. The most common mistake students make is to choose subject matter that is too broad. For example, the topic "autism" could fill a book. A narrower focus might discuss a single form of autism in detail. Again, your instructor can help you narrow down your topic choices.

2. **Do the research.** Find as many sources as you can that have information about your topic. Don't limit yourself to textbooks. Go to your school library and ask the librarian to point you in the direction of some good scientific journals that would have useful information on the subject. Be very careful about using the Internet to do research: Not everything on the Internet is correct or written by true experts—avoid other students' papers and "encyclopedia" Web sites that can be written and updated by darn near anyone.

3. **Take notes.** While reading about your topic, take careful notes to remember key points and write down the reference that will go along with the reading. References for psychology papers are usually going to be in APA (American Psychological Association) style, which can be found at www.apastyle.org.

   Taking good notes helps you avoid using the materials you find in their exact or nearly exact form, a form of cheating we'll discuss more in a later module of this chapter.

4. **Decide on the thesis.** The thesis is the central message of your paper—the message you want to communicate to your audience—which may be your instructor, your classmates, or both, depending on the nature of the assignment. Some papers are persuasive, which means the author is trying to convince the reader of a particular point of view, such as "Autism is not caused by immunizations." Some papers are informative, providing information about a topic to an audience that may have no prior knowledge, such as "Several forms of autism have been identified."

5. **Write an outline.** Using your notes from all your readings, create an outline of your paper—a kind of "road map" of how the paper will go. Start with an introduction (e.g., a brief definition and discussion of what autism is). Then decide what the body of the paper should be. If your paper is about a specific type of autism, for example, your outline might include sections about the possible causes of that type. The last section of your outline should be some kind of conclusion. For example, you might have

In earlier times, people actually had to write or type their first, second, and sometimes third drafts on real paper. The advent of computers with word-processing programs that allow simple editing and revision has no doubt saved a lot of trees from the paper mill. This also means there is no good excuse for failing to write a first draft and proofreading one's work.

recommendations about how parents of a child with autism can best help that child develop as fully as possible.

6. **Write a first draft.** Write your paper using the outline and your notes as guides. If using APA style, place citations with all of your statements and assertions. Failure to use citations (which point to the particular reference work from which your information came) is also a common mistake that many students make.

It is very important that you avoid plagiarism, as discussed in Step 3. When you use a source, you are supposed to explain the information that you are using in your own words *and* cite the source, as in the following example:

*In one study comparing both identical and fraternal twins, researchers found that stressful life events of the kind listed in the SRRS were excellent predictors of the onset of episodes of major depression (Kendler & Prescott, 1999).*

Your paper's reference section would have the following citation: Kendler, K. S., & Prescott, C. A. (1999). A population-based twin study of lifetime major depression in men and women. *Archives of General Psychiatry*, 56(1), 39–44. [Author's note: The number in front of the parentheses is the volume of the journal, the one inside is the issue number, and the last numbers are the page numbers of that article.]

7. **Let it sit.** Take a few days (if you have been good about starting the paper on time) to let the paper sit without reading it. Then go back over and mark places that don't sound right and need more explanation, a citation, or any other changes. This is much easier to do after a few days away from the paper; the need to reword will be more obvious.

8. **Write the revised draft.** Some people do more than one draft, while others do only a first draft and a final. In any case, revise the draft carefully, making sure to check your citations—and your spelling!

👁 **Watch** the **Video** *Paper Writing*

## Concept Map L.O. PIA.7

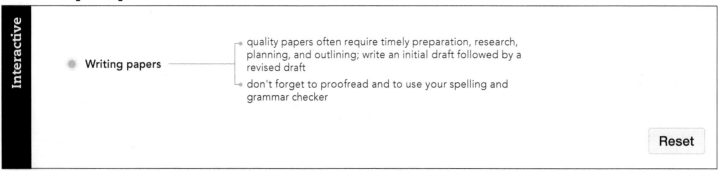

Interactive

**Writing papers** —
- quality papers often require timely preparation, research, planning, and outlining; write an initial draft followed by a revised draft
- don't forget to proofread and to use your spelling and grammar checker

Reset

# Practice Quiz    How much do you remember?

*Pick the best answer.*

1. Tamika has developed and researched a topic for her paper. What should she do next?
   a. Begin writing a rough draft of her paper.
   b. Begin writing as if her first draft will be her final draft.
   c. Develop an outline as a road map to help her stay on track when writing her paper.
   d. Let everything sit for a couple of days before beginning her rough draft.

2. Which of the following would be a more manageable topic for a term paper?
   a. mental illness
   b. learning
   c. causes of schizophrenia
   d. human development

3. Once you have written the first draft, what should you do?
   a. Submit it to the instructor, as your first draft is usually the best effort.
   b. Let it sit a few days before going back over it to make corrections.
   c. Immediately write the second or final draft before the material gets too stale for you to remember why you wrote it the way you did.
   d. Write the outline of the paper, which is easier to do once the paper is already.

# Your Ethical Responsibility as a Student

**PIA.8** **Identify some of the key ethical considerations that you'll face as a student.**

Many students have been tempted to take short-cuts in their educational process. Sometimes the short-cut takes the form of **plagiarism**, the copying of someone else's ideas or exact words (or a close imitation of the words) and presenting them as your own. When you cite someone else's work in your paper, you have to give them credit for that work. If you don't, you have committed plagiarism, whether you meant to do so or not, and this is theft. With all the tools instructors have at their beck and call these days, they are likely to uncover any plagiarism. In taking credit for someone else's work, you hurt yourself and your reputation in a number of ways. You don't actually learn anything (because if you don't put it in your own words, you haven't really understood it), which means you aren't giving yourself the chance to develop the skills and knowledge you will need in your future career. You also put your integrity and honesty as a person under close scrutiny. Plagiarism shows disrespect for your peers as well—they did their own work and expected you to do the same (Pennsylvania State University, 2014).

How can you avoid plagiarizing? First, remember that if you want to use the actual words from your source, you should put them inside quotation marks and then include the reference or citation, including page numbers. If you want to use the ideas but don't want to plagiarize, try taking brief notes on the source material (preferably from more than one source) and then use your notes—not the actual source—to write the ideas in your own words. There are some free online tools that can be used to check for plagiarism by both instructors and students, such as Plagiarism Checker at http://smallseotools.com/plagiarism-checker/ or Grammarly's Grammar and Plagiarism Checker at https://www.grammarly.com/plagiarism-checker.

There are also some good online resources for learning about what plagiarism is and how to avoid it. One is OWL, the Purdue Online Writing Lab at https://owl.english.purdue.edu/owl/resource/589/1/. Another is Indiana University's Writing Tutorial Services (WTS) at http://www.indiana.edu/~wts/pamphlets/plagiarism.shtml. Finally, Accredited Schools Online has a site called Understanding & Preventing Plagiarism: Strategies & Resources for Students and Teachers at http://www.accreditedschoolsonline.org/resources/preventing-plagiarism/. These and the plagiarism checker sites in the previous paragraph are just a few of many resources available online.

Another ethical responsibility that you have as a student is to not cheat. Most colleges and universities have honor codes about academic integrity, and cheating of any kind can have some fairly severe consequences. Cheating can also involve copying answers from someone else's test as you look over their shoulder, stealing tests to get the answers before the exam, or even having someone else take your test for you, among others. Sadly, cheating in school is still very common. A survey of more than 23,000 American high school students (both private and public as well as charter school students) conducted by the Josephson Institute Center for Youth Ethics (2012) found that in 2012, a little more than half of the students admitted to cheating on an exam at least once, and a little more than a fourth of the students said they had cheated more than once. Cheating at the college or university level also happens more often that it should, and even the most prestigious universities are not immune: In 2012 Harvard University investigated more than 125 undergraduates for plagiarism and other forms of cheating (Galante & Zeveloff, 2012).

Cheating involves many of the same concerns as plagiarism; you don't learn, and your instructors and peers will not respect you. In the long run, both plagiarism and cheating hurt you far more than any temporary relief you might get from these actions.

👁 **Watch** the **Video** *Ethics*

**plagiarism**
the copying of someone else's exact words (or a close imitation of the words) and presenting them as your own.

## Concept Map L.O. PIA.8

- Your Ethical Responsibility as a Student
  - maintain academic integrity for yourself and others; take responsibility for your learning and education; do not take shortcuts
  - do your own work and make sure you understand what constitutes academic dishonesty; do not plagiarize someone else's work and do not cheat

Reset

# Practice Quiz   How much do you remember?

*Pick the best answer.*

1. Michael is writing a paper for psychology. One of his sources is a text in which the following statement appears:

   When a deeply depressed mood comes on fairly suddenly and either seems to be too severe for the circumstances or exists without any external cause for sadness, it is called major depressive disorder.

   Which of the following would NOT be an acceptable way for Michael to use this material in his paper?
   a. Put the entire sentence in quotation marks and cite the author and textbook information where he found the quote.
   b. Summarize the ideas in the sentence in his own words.
   c. Use only part of the information, but make sure he uses his own language.
   d. All of the above are acceptable.

2. In the Josephson Center survey, how many students reported cheating at least once?
   a. About one fourth.
   b. A little more than half.
   c. A little more than three fourths.
   d. The survey found no reported incidences of cheating.

# Psychology in Action Summary

## Study Skills

### PIA.1 Identify four methods of studying.

- Research has shown that using multiple learning methods to study is a useful and effective strategy.
- Four common learning methods are verbal, visual, auditory, and action methods.

## Managing Time

### PIA.2 Describe some strategies for time management.

- Making or using a calendar of prioritized tasks, breaking tasks down into smaller ones, and avoiding multitasking are some ways to improve time management.

## Reading the Text: Textbooks Are Not Meatloaf

### PIA.3 Describe how to read a textbook so that you get the most out of your reading efforts.

- Textbooks must be read in a different way from novels or popular books.
- The SQ3R method is an excellent way to approach reading a textbook: survey, question, read, recite, review.

## Getting the Most Out of Lectures

### PIA.4 Identify the best methods for taking notes and listening in class.

- Notes should be in your own words and written or typed, not highlighted in the text or on handouts.
- When taking notes from a lecture, you should be prepared by having the notes from your reading in front of you; some people may benefit from recording the lecture and taking notes afterward.

## Studying for Exams: Cramming Is Not an Option

### PIA.5 Describe how to approach studying for exams.

- Don't wait until the last minute to study.
- Find out about the types of questions on the exam.
- Use concept maps, the SQ3R method, and publishers' practice-test materials.
- Engage in retrieval practice; test your recall, not just recognition, of content often.
- Get plenty of sleep and eat breakfast, preferably something with protein.

## Improving Your Memory

**PIA.6 Explain how using mnemonics can help you improve your memory for facts and concepts.**

• There are memory strategies called mnemonics, including methods that use imagery, rhymes, linking, and even music to improve memory.

## Writing Papers

**PIA.7 Describe the key steps in writing papers for college.**

• Key steps in writing a research paper are to choose a topic, read about the topic, take notes on your reading, decide upon the central message of your paper, write an outline, complete a first draft, and allow the paper to sit for a few days before going back and writing the final draft.

## Your Ethical Responsibility as a Student

**PIA.8 Identify some of the key ethical considerations that you'll face as a student.**

• Students need to realize that plagiarism and cheating in school are harmful to the students and disrespectful to others.

# Test Yourself

*Pick the best answer.*

1. Cody learns best whenever he can see things laid out before him. He uses flash cards and concept maps and often tries to redraw charts and figures from memory. What learning method does Cody seem to prefer?
   a. verbal
   b. visual
   c. auditory
   d. action

2. Which of the following is NOT one of the strategies for defeating procrastination?
   a. Make a map of long-term goals.
   b. Use a calendar.
   c. Stay up all night to finish your task.
   d. Break big tasks down into smaller, more manageable pieces.

3. What learning aid gives the student the ability to more effectively read and remember material?
   a. chapter summaries
   b. content maps
   c. SQ3R
   d. practice quizzes

4. Which of the following is NOT a mistake often made by students when taking notes?
   a. Taking notes while reading the chapter before going to the lecture.
   b. Highlighting material in the textbook as the instructor lectures.
   c. Make sure you have not read the chapter before the lecture so that the material will be fresher and more memorable.
   d. Use the PowerPoint slides as your notes.

5. What type of question requires that you understand the material so well that you are able to compare and contrast it to other material?
   a. factual
   b. applied
   c. conceptual
   d. true/false

6. Your mom wants you to eat some breakfast before going off to your first psychology exam. What will you tell her?
   a. No thanks. A big meal will probably put me to sleep.
   b. Sounds good. Can I have some cereal and toast?
   c. All I want is some coffee. Caffeine will help me do my best!
   d. Thank you. Just some ham and eggs and maybe a small slice of bread.

7. Tabitha is stuck on a question while taking her psychology exam. What should she do?
   a. Stay on that question until she can figure out what the answer is.
   b. Go on to the other questions. Maybe she can find a clue to the one she skipped.
   c. Take a guess as to the correct answer. She probably will get it correct anyway.
   d. Review the questions she already has answered to find a clue there.

8. Which mnemonic involves first memorizing a series of numbered words?
   a. linking
   b. peg-word
   c. method of loci
   d. verbal/rhythmic organization

9. What is one of the most common mistakes students make when choosing a topic for a research paper?
   a. The topic is too broad.
   b. The topic is too narrow.
   c. The topic is unclear.
   d. The topic has no research to support it.

10. Keela has finished a draft of her research paper almost 2 weeks before the date it is due. What should she do now?
    a. Let it sit for a few days before reviewing it.
    b. Complete the final draft immediately while the material is still fresh in her head.
    c. Hand in her rough draft as if it were the final draft. Most students tend to make their paper worse when they revise it.
    d. Keela needs to start again, since papers finished early tend not to be well written.

# The Science of Psychology

How would you define psychology? What do you hope to learn about psychology, yourself, and others after taking this course? After you have answered the question, watch the video to compare the answers of other students to yours.

▶ The response entered here will be saved to your notes and may be collected by your instructor if he/she requires it.

👁 Watch the Video

## Why study psychology?

Psychology not only helps you understand why people (and animals) do the things they do, but it also helps you better understand yourself and your reactions to others. Psychology can help you comprehend how your brain and body are connected, how to improve your learning abilities and memory, and how to deal with the stresses of life, both ordinary and extraordinary. In studying psychology, an understanding of the methods psychologists use is crucial because research can be flawed, and knowing how research should be done can bring those flaws to light. And finally, psychology and its research methods promote critical thinking, which can be used to evaluate not just research but also claims of all kinds, including those of advertisers and politicians.

# Learning Objectives

**1.1** Describe the contributions of some of the early pioneers in psychology.

**1.2** Summarize the basic ideas and the important people behind the early approaches known as Gestalt, psychoanalysis, and behaviorism.

**1.3** Summarize the basic ideas behind the seven modern perspectives in psychology.

**1.4** Differentiate between the various types of professionals within the field of psychology.

**1.5** Recall the five steps of the scientific approach.

**1.6** Compare and contrast some of the methods used to describe behavior.

**1.7** Explain how researchers use the correlational technique to study relationships between two or more variables.

**1.8** Identify the steps involved in designing an experiment.

**1.9** Recall two common sources of problems in an experiment and some ways to control for these effects.

**1.10** Identify some of the common ethical guidelines for doing research with people.

**1.11** Explain why psychologists sometimes use animals in their research.

**1.12** Recall the basic criteria for critical thinking that people can use in their everyday lives.

# The History of Psychology

Some people believe psychology is just the study of people and what motivates their behavior. Psychologists do study people, but they study animals as well. And to better understand what motivates behavior, psychologists study not only what people and animals do but also what happens in their bodies and in their brains as they do it. The study of psychology is not important only to psychologists: psychology is a *hub science* and findings from psychological research are cited and used in many other fields as diverse as cancer research, health, and even climate change (Cacioppo, 2013; McDonald et al., 2015; Roberto & Kawachi, 2014; Rothman et al., 2015; van der Linden et al., 2015). Before examining the field of psychology, participate in the survey *What Do You Know About Psychology?* to understand more about your own preconceived notions of people and human behavior.

**Survey** WHAT DO YOU KNOW ABOUT PSYCHOLOGY?

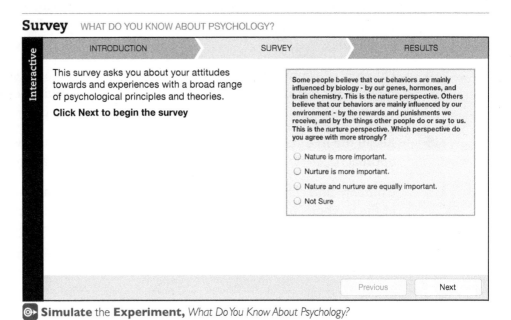

Simulate the Experiment, *What Do You Know About Psychology?*

**Psychology** is the scientific study of behavior and mental processes. *Behavior* includes all of our outward or overt actions and reactions, such as talking, facial expressions, and movement. The term *mental processes* refers to all the internal, covert (hidden) activity of our minds, such as thinking, feeling, and remembering. Why "scientific"? To study behavior and mental processes in both animals and humans, researchers must observe them. Whenever a human being observes anyone or anything, there's always a possibility that the observer will see only what he or she *expects* to see. Psychologists don't want to let these possible biases* cause them to make faulty observations. They want to be precise and to measure as carefully as they can—so they use a systematic** approach to study psychology scientifically.

 How long has psychology been around?

Psychology is a relatively new field in the realm of the sciences, only about 138 years old. It's not that no one thought about why people and animals do the things they do before then; on the contrary, there were philosophers,*** medical doctors, and physiologists**** who thought about little else—particularly with regard to people. See **Figure 1.1** for a timeline of the history

---

**psychology**

scientific study of behavior and mental processes.

*biases: personal judgments based on beliefs rather than facts.
**systematic: according to a fixed, ordered plan.
***philosophers: people who seek wisdom and knowledge through thinking and discussion.
****physiologists: scientists who study the physical workings of the body and its systems.

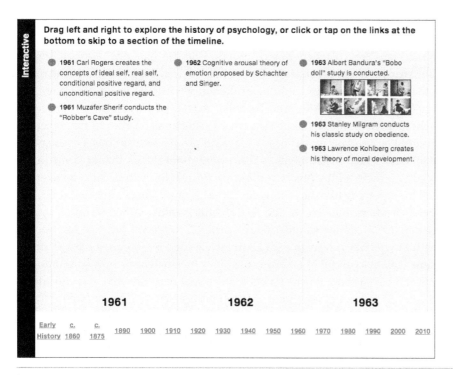

**Figure 1.1** Timeline of the History of Psychology

of psychology. Philosophers such as Plato, Aristotle, and Descartes tried to understand or explain the human mind and its connection to the physical body (Durrant, 1993; Everson, 1995; Kenny, 1968, 1994). Medical doctors and physiologists wondered about the physical connection between the body and the brain. For example, physician and physicist Gustav Fechner is often credited with performing some of the first scientific experiments that would form a basis for experimentation in psychology with his studies of perception (Fechner, 1860), and physician Hermann von Helmholtz (von Helmholtz, 1852, 1863) performed groundbreaking experiments in visual and auditory perception. Ⓛ Ⓘ Ⓝ Ⓚ to Learning Objectives 3.2, 3.6, and 3.8.

### IN THE BEGINNING: WUNDT, TITCHENER, AND JAMES

**1.1** Describe the contributions of some of the early pioneers in psychology.

It really all started to come together in a laboratory in Leipzig, Germany, in 1879. It was here that Wilhelm Wundt (VILL-helm Voont, 1832–1920), a physiologist, attempted to apply scientific principles to the study of the human mind. In his laboratory, students from around the world were taught to study the structure of the human mind. Wundt believed that consciousness, the state of being aware of external events, could be broken down into thoughts, experiences, emotions, and other basic elements. In order to inspect these nonphysical elements, students had to learn to think objectively about their own thoughts—after all, they could hardly read someone else's mind. Wundt called this process **objective introspection**, the process of objectively examining and measuring one's own thoughts and mental activities (Rieber & Robinson, 2001). For example, Wundt might place an object, such as a rock, in a student's hand and have the student tell him everything that he was feeling as a result of having the rock in his hand—all the sensations stimulated by the rock. (Objectivity* was—and is—important because scientists need to remain unbiased. Observations need to be clear and precise but unaffected by the individual observer's beliefs and values.)

This was really the first attempt by anyone to bring objectivity and measurement to the concept of psychology. This attention to objectivity, together with the establishment of the first true experimental laboratory in psychology, is why Wundt is known as the father of psychology.

---

*objectivity: expressing or dealing with facts or conditions as they really are without allowing the influence of personal feelings, prejudices, or interpretations.

**objective introspection**
the process of examining and measuring one's own thoughts and mental activities.

Structuralists would be interested in all of the memories and sensations this woman is experiencing as she smells the strawberries.

**TITCHENER AND STRUCTURALISM IN AMERICA**    One of Wundt's students was Edward Titchener (1867–1927), an Englishman who eventually took Wundt's ideas to Cornell University in Ithaca, New York. Titchener expanded on Wundt's original ideas, calling his new viewpoint **structuralism** because the focus of study was the structure of the mind. He believed that every experience could be broken down into its individual emotions and sensations (Brennan, 2002). Although Titchener agreed with Wundt that consciousness could be broken down into its basic elements, Titchener also believed that objective introspection could be used on thoughts as well as on physical sensations. For example, Titchener might have asked his students to introspect about things that are blue rather than actually giving them a blue object and asking for reactions to it. Such an exercise might have led to something like the following: "What is blue? There are blue things, like the sky or a bird's feathers. Blue is cool and restful, blue is calm …" and so on.

In 1894, one of Titchener's students at Cornell University became famous for becoming the first woman to receive a Ph.D. in psychology (Goodman, 1980; Guthrie, 2004). Her name was Margaret F. Washburn, and she was Titchener's only graduate student for that year. In 1908 she published a book on animal behavior that was considered an important work in that era of psychology, *The Animal Mind* (Washburn, 1908).

Structuralism was a dominant force in the early days of psychology, but it eventually died out in the early 1900s, as the structuralists were busily fighting among themselves over just which key elements of experience were the most important. A competing view arose not long after Wundt's laboratory was established, shortly before structuralism came to America.

**WILLIAM JAMES AND FUNCTIONALISM**    Harvard University was the first school in America to offer classes in psychology in the late 1870s. These classes were taught by one of Harvard's most illustrious instructors, William James (1842–1910). James began teaching anatomy and physiology, but as his interest in psychology developed, he began teaching it almost exclusively (Brennan, 2002). His comprehensive textbook on the subject, *Principles of Psychology*, is so brilliantly written that copies are still in print (James, 1890, 2015).

Unlike Wundt and Titchener, James was more interested in the importance of consciousness to everyday life than just its analysis. He believed that the scientific study of consciousness itself was not yet possible. Conscious ideas are constantly flowing in an ever-changing stream, and once you start thinking about what you were just thinking about, what you were thinking about is no longer what you *were* thinking about—it's what you *are* thinking about—and … excuse me, I'm a little dizzy. I think you get the picture, anyway.

Instead, James focused on how the mind allows people to *function* in the real world—how people work, play, and adapt to their surroundings, a viewpoint he called **functionalism.** (He was heavily influenced by Charles Darwin's ideas about *natural selection*, in which physical traits that help an animal adapt to its environment and survive are passed on to its offspring.) If physical traits could aid in survival, why couldn't behavioral traits do the same? Animals and people whose behavior helped them to survive would pass those traits on to their offspring, perhaps by teaching or even by some mechanism of heredity.* (Remember that this was early in the days of trying to understand how heredity worked.) For example, a behavior such as avoiding the eyes of others in an elevator can be seen as a way of protecting one's personal space—a kind of territorial protection that may have its roots in the primitive need to protect one's home and source of food and water from intruders (Manusov & Patterson, 2006) or as a way of avoiding what might seem like a challenge to another person (Brown et al., 2005; Jehn et al., 1999).

It is interesting to note that one of James's early students was Mary Whiton Calkins, who completed every course and requirement for earning a Ph.D. but was denied that degree by Harvard University because she was a woman. She was allowed to take those classes as

**structuralism**

early perspective in psychology associated with Wilhelm Wundt and Edward Titchener, in which the focus of study is the structure or basic elements of the mind.

**functionalism**

early perspective in psychology associated with William James, in which the focus of study is how the mind allows people to adapt, live, work, and play.

---

*heredity: the transmission of traits and characteristics from parent to offspring through the actions of genes.

a guest only. Calkins eventually established a psychological laboratory at Wellesley College. Her work was some of the earliest research in the area of human memory and the psychology of the self. In 1905, she became the first female president of the American Psychological Association (Furumoto, 1979, 1991; Zedler, 1995). Unlike Washburn, Calkins never earned the elusive Ph.D. degree despite a successful career as a professor and researcher (Guthrie, 2004).

Women were not the only minority to make contributions in the early days of psychology. In 1920, for example, Francis Cecil Sumner became the first African American to earn a Ph.D. in psychology at Clark University. He eventually became the chair of the psychology department at Howard University and is assumed by many to be the father of African American psychology (Guthrie, 2004). Kenneth and Mamie Clark worked to show the negative effects of school segregation on African American children (Lal, 2002). In the 1940s, Hispanic psychologist George (Jorge) Sanchez conducted research in the area of intelligence testing, focusing on the cultural biases in such tests (Tevis, 1994). Other names of noted minorities include Dr. Charles Henry Thompson, the first African American to receive a doctorate in educational psychology in 1925, Dr. Albert Sidney Beckham, senior assistant psychologist at the National Committee for Mental Hygiene at the Illinois Institute for Juvenile Research in the early 1930s; Dr. Robert Prentiss Daniel, who became president of Shaw University in North Carolina and finally the president of Virginia State College; Dr. Inez Beverly Prosser (1897–1934), who was the first African American woman to earn a Ph.D. in educational psychology; Dr. Howard Hale Long, who became dean of administration at Wilberforce State College in Ohio; and Dr. Ruth Howard, who was the first African American woman to earn a Ph.D. in psychology (not educational psychology) in 1934 from the University of Minnesota (Guthrie, 2004).

Since those early days, psychology has seen an increase in the contributions of all minorities, although the percentages are still small when compared to the population at large. The American Psychological Association's Office of Ethnic Minority Affairs features notable psychologists as part of their *Ethnicity and Health in America Series*. Their Web site provides brief biographies of ethnic minority psychologists and work or research highlights particularly related to chronic health conditions for several ethnic groups: African American, Asian American, Hispanic Latino, and Native American. For more information, visit http://www.apa.org/pi/oema/resources/ethnicity-health/psychologists/.

  Is functionalism still an important point of view in psychology?

In the new field of psychology, functionalism offered an alternative viewpoint to the structuralists. But like so many of psychology's early ideas, it is no longer a major perspective. Instead, one can find elements of functionalism in the modern fields of *educational psychology* (studying the application of psychological concepts to education) and *industrial/organizational psychology* (studying the application of psychological concepts to businesses, organizations, and industry), as well as other areas in psychology. (L)(I)(N)(K) to Learning Objective B.6. Functionalism also played a part in the development of one of the more modern perspectives, evolutionary psychology, discussed later in this chapter.

**THREE INFLUENTIAL APPROACHES: GESTALT, PSYCHOANALYSIS, AND BEHAVIORISM**

**1.2** **Summarize the basic ideas and the important people behind the early approaches known as Gestalt, psychoanalysis, and behaviorism.**

While the structuralists and functionalists argued with each other and among themselves, other psychologists were looking at psychology in several other ways.

**GESTALT PSYCHOLOGY: THE WHOLE IS GREATER THAN THE SUM OF ITS PARTS**  Max Wertheimer (VERT-hi-mer), like James, objected to the structuralist point of view, but for different reasons. Wertheimer believed that psychological events such as

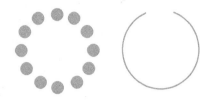

**Figure 1.2**  A Gestalt Perception

The eye tends to "fill in" the blanks here and sees both of these figures as circles rather than as a series of dots or a broken line.

perceiving* and sensing** could not be broken down into any smaller elements and still be properly understood. For example, you can take a smartphone apart, but then you no longer have a smartphone—you have a pile of unconnected bits and pieces. Or, just as a melody is made up of individual notes that can only be understood if the notes are in the correct relationship to one another, so perception can only be understood as a whole, entire event. Hence the familiar slogan, "The whole is greater than the sum of its parts." Wertheimer and others believed that people naturally seek out patterns ("wholes") in the sensory information available to them.

Wertheimer and others devoted their efforts to studying sensation and perception in this new perspective, **Gestalt psychology**. *Gestalt* (Gesh-TALT) is a German word meaning "an organized whole" or "configuration," which fit well with the focus on studying whole patterns rather than small pieces of them. See **Figure 1.2** for an example of Gestalt perceptual patterns. Today, Gestalt ideas are part of the study of *cognitive psychology*, a field focusing not only on perception but also on learning, memory, thought processes, and problem solving; the basic Gestalt principles of perception are still taught within this newer field (Ash, 1998; Kohler, 1925, 1992; Wertheimer, 1982). Ⓛ Ⓘ Ⓝ Ⓚ to Learning Objective 3.14. The Gestalt approach has also been influential in psychological therapy, becoming the basis for a therapeutic technique called *Gestalt therapy*. Ⓛ Ⓘ Ⓝ Ⓚ to Learning Objective 15.3.

**SIGMUND FREUD'S THEORY OF PSYCHOANALYSIS**    It should be clear by now that psychology didn't start in one place and at one particular time. People of several different viewpoints were trying to promote their own perspective on the study of the human mind and behavior in different places all over the world. Up to now, this chapter has focused on the physiologists who became interested in psychology, with a focus on understanding consciousness but little else. The medical profession took a whole different approach to psychology.

    💬 What about Freud? Everybody talks about him when they talk about psychology. Are his ideas still in use?

Sigmund Freud had become a noted physician in Austria while the structuralists were arguing, the functionalists were specializing, and the Gestaltists were looking at the big picture. Freud was a neurologist, a medical doctor who specializes in disorders of the nervous system; he and his colleagues had long sought a way to understand the patients who were coming to them for help.

Freud's patients suffered from nervous disorders for which he and other doctors could find no physical cause. Therefore, it was thought, the cause must be in the mind, and that is where Freud began to explore. He proposed that there is an *unconscious* (unaware) mind into which we push, or *repress*, all of our threatening urges and desires. He believed that these repressed urges, in trying to surface, created the nervous disorders in his patients (Freud et al., 1990). Ⓛ Ⓘ Ⓝ Ⓚ to Learning Objective 13.2.

Freud stressed the importance of early childhood experiences, believing that personality was formed in the first 6 years of life; if there were significant problems, those problems must have begun in the early years.

Some of his well-known followers were Alfred Adler, Carl Jung, Karen Horney, and his own daughter, Anna Freud. Anna Freud began what became known as the ego movement in psychology, which produced one of the best-known psychologists in the study of personality development, Erik Erikson. Ⓛ Ⓘ Ⓝ Ⓚ to Learning Objective 8.8.

Freud's ideas are still influential today, although in a somewhat modified form. He had a number of followers in addition to those already named, many of whom became famous by altering Freud's theory to fit their own viewpoints, but his basic ideas are still discussed and debated. Ⓛ Ⓘ Ⓝ Ⓚ to Learning Objective 13.3.

**Gestalt psychology**

early perspective in psychology focusing on perception and sensation, particularly the perception of patterns and whole figures.

*perceiving: becoming aware of something through the senses.
**sensing: seeing, hearing, feeling, tasting, or smelling something.

While some might think that Sigmund Freud was the first person to deal with people suffering from various mental disorders, the truth is that mental illness has a fairly long (and not very pretty) history. For more on the history of mental illness, see the Ⓛ Ⓘ Ⓝ Ⓚ to Learning Objective 14.1.

Freudian **psychoanalysis**, the theory and therapy based on Freud's ideas, has been the basis of much modern *psychotherapy* (a process in which a trained psychological professional helps a person gain insight into and change his or her behavior), but another major and competing viewpoint has actually been more influential in the field of psychology as a whole.

**PAVLOV, WATSON, AND THE DAWN OF BEHAVIORISM**    Ivan Pavlov, like Freud, was not a psychologist. He was a Russian physiologist who showed that a *reflex* (an involuntary reaction) could be caused to occur in response to a formerly unrelated stimulus. While working with dogs, Pavlov observed that the salivation reflex (which is normally produced by actually having food in one's mouth) could be caused to occur in response to a totally new stimulus, in this case, the sound of a ticking metronome. At the onset of his experiment, Pavlov would turn on the metronome and give the dogs food, and they would salivate. After several repetitions, the dogs would salivate to the sound of the metronome *before* the food was presented—a learned (or "conditioned") reflexive response (Klein & Mowrer, 1989). This process was called *conditioning*. Ⓛ Ⓘ Ⓝ Ⓚ to Learning Objective 5.2.

By the early 1900s, psychologist John B. Watson had tired of the arguing among the structuralists; he challenged the functionalist viewpoint, as well as psychoanalysis, with his own "science of behavior," or **behaviorism** (Watson, 1924). Watson wanted to bring psychology back to a focus on scientific inquiry, and he felt that the only way to do that was to ignore the whole consciousness issue and focus only on *observable behavior*—something that could be directly seen and measured. He had read of Pavlov's work and thought that conditioning could form the basis of his new perspective of behaviorism.

Watson was certainly aware of Freud's work and his views on unconscious repression. Freud believed that all behavior stems from unconscious motivation, whereas Watson believed that all behavior is learned. Freud had stated that a *phobia*, an irrational fear, is really a symptom of an underlying, repressed conflict and cannot be "cured" without years of psychoanalysis to uncover and understand the repressed material.

Watson believed that phobias are learned through the process of conditioning and set out to prove it. Along with his colleague Rosalie Rayner, he took a baby, known as "Little Albert," and taught him to fear a white rat by making a loud, scary noise every time the infant saw the rat until finally just seeing the rat caused the infant to cry and become fearful (Watson & Rayner, 1920). Even though "Little Albert" was not afraid of the rat at the start, the experiment worked very well—in fact, he later appeared to be afraid of other fuzzy things including a rabbit, a dog, and a sealskin coat. Ⓛ Ⓘ Ⓝ Ⓚ to Learning Objective 5.3.

💬 This sounds really bizarre—what does scaring a baby have to do with the science of psychology?

Watson wanted to prove that all behavior was a result of a stimulus–response relationship such as that described by Pavlov. Because Freud and his ideas about unconscious motivation were becoming a dominant force, Watson felt the need to show the world that a much simpler explanation could be found. Although scaring a baby sounds a little cruel, he felt that the advancement of the science of behavior was worth the baby's relatively brief discomfort.

A graduate student of Watson's named Mary Cover Jones later decided to repeat Watson and Rayner's study but added training that would "cancel out" the phobic reaction of the baby to the white rat. She duplicated the "Little Albert" study with another

American psychologist John Watson is known as the father of behaviorism. Behaviorism focuses only on observable behavior.

Mary Cover Jones, one of the early pioneers of behavior therapy, earned her master's degree under the supervision of John Watson. Her long and distinguished career also included the publication in 1952 of the first educational television course in child development (Rutherford, 2000).

**psychoanalysis**

an insight therapy based on the theory of Freud, emphasizing the revealing of unconscious conflicts; Freud's term for both the theory of personality and the therapy based on it.

**behaviorism**

the science of behavior that focuses on observable behavior only.

child, "Little Peter," successfully conditioning Peter to be afraid of a white rabbit (Jones, 1924). She then began a process of *counterconditioning*, in which Peter was exposed to the white rabbit from a distance while eating a food that he really liked. The pleasure of the food outweighed the fear of the faraway rabbit. Day by day, the situation was repeated with the rabbit being brought closer each time, until Peter was no longer afraid of the rabbit. Jones went on to become one of the early pioneers of behavior therapy. Behaviorism is still a major perspective in psychology today. It has also influenced the development of other perspectives, such as *cognitive psychology*.

## Concept Map LO. 1.1, 1.2

**Interactive**

• it has methods for studying phenomena

# What Is Psychology?
(it is the scientific study of behavior and mental processes)

A relatively new science that formally began in 1879 when Wilhelm Wundt ("father of psychology") established the first psychological laboratory in Leipzig, Germany

• studied nonphysical structure (i.e., thought, experiences, emotions, etc.) of the human mind
• used objective introspection to study processes that were the result of physical sensations
• first attempt to bring objectivity and measurement to psychology

was a student of Wundt's

**Structuralism**
founded by Edward Titchener

• expanded Wundt's original ideas; believed every experience could be broken down into individual emotions and sensations
• applied introspection method to thoughts as well as physical sensations

**Functionalism**
founded by William James

• influenced by Darwin's ideas about natural selection—focused on how the mind allows people to function in the real world
• interested in how behavioral traits could aid in survival
• influenced development of evolutionary psychology
• has elements in educational psychology and industrial/organizational psychology

# The History of Psychology
(has roots in several disciplines, including philosophy, medicine, and physiology, and has developed through several perspectives)

**Gestalt psychology**
founded by Max Wertheimer

did not believe that psychological events could be broken down into smaller elements; could only be understood as a whole, entire event; has influenced field of cognitive psychology and a form of psychological therapy, Gestalt therapy

**Psychoanalysis**
ideas put forth by Sigmund Freud

stressed importance of early life experiences, the role of the unconscious, and development through stages

**Behaviorism**
associated with work of John B. Watson, who was greatly influenced by Ivan Pavlov's work in conditioning/learning

wanted to bring focus back on scientific inquiry and believed only way to do so was to focus on observable behavior and ignore "consciousness" issue; early work examined phobias

Reset

# Practice Quiz    How much do you remember?

*Pick the best answer.*

1. In the definition of psychology, *mental processes* means
   a. internal, covert processes.
   b. unconscious processes.
   c. outward or overt actions and reactions.
   d. only human behavior.

2. Which early psychologist was the first to try to bring objectivity and measurement to the concept of psychology?
   a. Wilhelm Wundt
   b. William James
   c. John Watson
   d. Sigmund Freud

3. Which of the following early psychologists would have been most likely to agree with the statement, "The study of the mind should focus on how it functions in everyday life"?
   a. Wilhelm Wundt
   b. William James
   c. John Watson
   d. Sigmund Freud

4. Who was the first woman to complete the coursework for a doctorate at Harvard University?
   a. Mary Whiton Calkins
   b. Mary Cover Jones
   c. Margaret Washburn
   d. Ruth Howard

5. Which early perspective tried to return to a focus on scientific inquiry by ignoring the study of consciousness?
   a. behaviorism
   b. functionalism
   c. psychoanalysis
   d. Gestalt

---

# The Field of Psychology Today

Even in the twenty-first century, there isn't one single perspective that is used to explain all human behavior and mental processes. There are actually seven modern perspectives.

## MODERN PERSPECTIVES

### 1.3 Summarize the basic ideas behind the seven modern perspectives in psychology.

Two of psychology's modern perspectives are updated versions of psychoanalysis and behaviorism, while the others focus on people's goals, thought processes, social and cultural factors, biology, and genetics. Watch the video *Diverse Perspectives* to get a quick overview of the perspectives before we continue.

Watch the Video *Diverse Perspectives*

**PSYCHODYNAMIC PERSPECTIVE** Freud's theory is still used by many professionals in therapy situations. It is far less common today than it was a few decades ago, however, and even those who use his techniques modify them for contemporary use. In the more modern **psychodynamic perspective**, the focus may still include the unconscious mind and its influence over conscious behavior and on early childhood experiences, but with less of an emphasis on sex and sexual motivations and more emphasis on the development of a sense of self, social and interpersonal relationships, and the discovery of other motivations behind a person's behavior. ⓁⒾⓃⓀ to Learning Objective 13.3. Some modern psychodynamic practitioners have even begun to recommend that the link between neurobiology (the study of the brain and nervous system) and psychodynamic concepts should be more fully explored (Glucksman, 2006).

**BEHAVIORAL PERSPECTIVE** Like modern psychodynamic perspectives, behaviorism is still also very influential. When its primary supporter, John B. Watson, moved on to greener pastures in the world of advertising, B. F. Skinner became the new leader of the field.

Skinner not only continued research in classical conditioning, but he also developed a theory called *operant conditioning* to explain how voluntary behavior is learned (Skinner, 1938). In this theory, *behavioral* responses that are followed by pleasurable consequences are strengthened, or *reinforced*. For example, a child who cries and is rewarded by getting his mother's attention will cry again in the future. Skinner's work is discussed later in more depth. ⓁⒾⓃⓀ to Learning Objective 5.4. In addition to the psychodynamic and behavioral perspectives, there are five newer perspectives that have developed within the last 60 years.

**HUMANISTIC PERSPECTIVE** Often called the "third force" in psychology, humanism was really a reaction to both psychoanalytic theory and behaviorism. If you were a psychologist in the early to mid-1900s, you were either a psychoanalyst or a behaviorist—there weren't any other major viewpoints to rival those two.

In contrast to the psychoanalytic focus on sexual development and behaviorism's focus on external forces in guiding personality development, some professionals began to develop a perspective that would allow them to focus on people's ability to direct their own lives. Humanists held the view that people have *free will*, the freedom to choose their own destiny, and strive for *self-actualization*, the achievement of one's full potential. Two of the earliest and most famous founders of this view were Abraham Maslow (1908–1970) and Carl Rogers (1902–1987). Today, humanism exists as a form of psychotherapy aimed at self-understanding and self-improvement. ⓁⒾⓃⓀ to Learning Objective 15.3.

**COGNITIVE PERSPECTIVE** Cognitive psychology, which focuses on how people think, remember, store, and use information, became a major force in the field in the 1960s. It wasn't a new idea, as the Gestalt psychologists had themselves supported the study of mental processes of learning. The development of computers (which just happened to make pretty good models of human thinking) and discoveries in biological psychology all stimulated an interest in studying the processes of thought. The **cognitive perspective** with its focus on memory, intelligence, perception, thought processes, problem solving, language, and learning has become a major force in psychology. ⓁⒾⓃⓀ to Chapter Seven: Cognition.

Within the cognitive perspective, the relatively new field of **cognitive neuroscience** includes the study of the physical workings of the brain and nervous system when engaged in memory, thinking, and other cognitive processes. Cognitive neuroscientists use tools for imaging the structure and activity of the living brain, such as magnetic resonance imaging (MRI), functional magnetic resonance imaging (fMRI), and positron emission tomography (PET). ⓁⒾⓃⓀ to Learning Objective 2.9. The continually developing field of brain imaging is important in the study of cognitive processes.

Behaviorist B. F. Skinner puts a rat through its paces. What challenges might arise from applying information gained from studies with animals to human behavior?

**psychodynamic perspective**

modern version of psychoanalysis that is more focused on the development of a sense of self and the discovery of motivations behind a person's behavior other than sexual motivations.

**cognitive perspective**

modern perspective in psychology that focuses on memory, intelligence, perception, problem solving, and learning.

**cognitive neuroscience**

study of the physical changes in the brain and nervous system during thinking.

**SOCIOCULTURAL PERSPECTIVE**    Another modern perspective in psychology is the **sociocultural perspective**, which actually combines two areas of study: *social psychology*, which is the study of groups, social roles, and rules of social actions and relationships, and *cultural psychology*, which is the study of cultural norms,* values, and expectations. These two areas are related in that they are both about the effect that people have on one another, either individually or in a larger group such as a culture (Peplau & Taylor, 1997). (L)(I)(N)K  to Chapter Twelve: Social Psychology. Think about it: don't you behave differently around your family members than you do around your friends? Would you act differently in another country than you do in your native land? Russian psychologist Lev Vygotsky (1978) also used sociocultural concepts in forming his sociocultural theory of children's cognitive development. (L)(I)(N)K  to Learning Objective 8.7.

The sociocultural perspective is important because it reminds people that the way they and others behave (or even think) is influenced not only by whether they are alone, with friends, in a crowd, or part of a group but also by the social norms, fads, class differences, and ethnic identity concerns of the particular culture in which they live. *Cross-cultural research* also fits within this perspective. In cross-cultural research, the contrasts and comparisons of a behavior or issue are studied in at least two or more cultures. This type of research can help illustrate the different influences of environment (culture and training) when compared to the influence of heredity (genetics, or the influence of genes on behavior).

For example, in a classic study covered in Chapter Twelve: Social Psychology, researchers Dr. John Darley and Dr. Bibb Latané (1968) found that the presence of other people actually *lessened* the chances that a person in trouble would receive help. The phenomenon is called the "bystander effect," and it is believed to be the result of *diffusion of responsibility*, which is the tendency to feel that someone else is responsible for taking action when others are present. But would this effect appear in other cultures? There have been incidents in India that meet the criteria for the bystander effect: in 2002, a man under the influence of alcohol sexually assaulted a mentally challenged girl while the two were traveling on a train while five other passengers did nothing to stop the attack, and in 2012 a 20-year-old woman was molested outside a bar in Guwahati for thirty minutes in view of many witnesses who did nothing (Tatke, 2012). India is a country that is culturally quite different from the United States, and individuals in India are typically expected to act for the greater good of others, yet the bystander effect apparently exists even there (Hofstede, 1980; Hofstede et al., 2002). Questions about how human behavior differs or is similar in different social or cultural settings are exactly what the sociocultural perspective asks and attempts to answer, using cross-cultural research.

**BIOPSYCHOLOGICAL PERSPECTIVE**    *Biopsychology*, or the study of the biological bases of behavior and mental processes, isn't really as new a perspective as one might think. Also known as physiological psychology, biological psychology, psychobiology, and behavioral neuroscience, biopsychology is part of the larger field of *neuroscience*: the study of the physical structure, function, and development of the nervous system. Also, the previously discussed field of cognitive neuroscience often overlaps with biopsychology.

In the **biopsychological perspective**, human and animal behavior is seen as a direct result of events in the body. Hormones, heredity, brain chemicals, tumors, and diseases are some of the biological causes of behavior and mental events. (L)(I)(N)K  to Chapter Two: The Biological Perspective. Some of the topics researched by biopsychologists include sleep, emotions, aggression, sexual behavior, and learning and memory—as well as disorders. While disorders may have multiple causes (family issues, stress, or trauma, for example), research in biopsychology points clearly to biological factors as one of those causes.

---

*norms: standards or expected behavior.

**sociocultural perspective**
perspective that focuses on the relationship between social behavior and culture, in which thinking and behavior is seen as the product of learning and shaping within the context of one's family, social group, and culture.

**biopsychological perspective**
perspective that attributes human and animal behavior to biological events occurring in the body, such as genetic influences, hormones, and the activity of the nervous system.

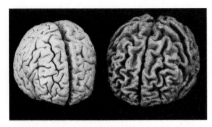

Compare the two preserved brains above. A "normal" brain is on the left while the one on the right is from someone diagnosed with Alzheimer's disease. Note the narrowed gyri (bulges) and widened sulci (grooves) in the brain on the right. This is due to progressive brain cell loss associated with Alzheimer's disease. In the case of dementia and other progressive diseases, one focus of the biological perspective is examining how thinking and behavior changes over time as the brain changes. You may also notice the brains are not identical in size. This is due to slight differences between individuals, and how individual specimens respond to the preservation and plastination processes.

For example, research suggests that human sexual orientation may be related to the developing baby's exposure in the womb to testosterone, especially in females (Breedlove, 2010; Grimbos et al., 2010), as well as the birth order of male children (Puts et al., 2006). The birth order study suggests that the more older brothers a male child has, the more likely he is to have a homosexual orientation (Puts et al., 2006). LINK to Learning Objective 10.8. The biopsychological perspective plays an even greater role in helping us understand psychological phenomena in other areas. There is clear evidence that genetics play a role in the development of *schizophrenia*, a mental disorder involving delusions (false beliefs), hallucinations (false sensory impressions), and extremely distorted thinking, with recent research pointing to greater risk for those who inherit variants of a gene that plays a role in removing extra connections between neurons in the brain (Flint & Munafò, 2014; Schizophrenia Working Group of the Psychiatric Genomics, 2014; Sekar, et al., 2016). LINK to Learning Objectives 2.1 and 14.4. In still another example, the progressive brain changes associated with Alzheimer's disease may begin more than 20 years prior to the onset of the clinical symptoms of dementia (Bateman et al., 2012). To date, no cure exists, and treatments only temporarily assist with some cognitive and behavioral symptoms. Early identification and tracking of cognitive performance in individuals at risk for Alzheimer's disease is one vital component of researchers' efforts to identify potential interventions and treatments for this devastating disease (Amariglio et al., 2015).

**EVOLUTIONARY PERSPECTIVE**   The **evolutionary perspective** focuses on the biological bases for universal mental characteristics that all humans share. It seeks to explain general mental strategies and traits, such as why we lie, how attractiveness influences mate selection, why fear of snakes is so common, or why people universally like music and dancing. This approach may also overlap with biopsychology and the sociocultural perspective.

In this perspective, the mind is seen as a set of information-processing machines, designed by the same process of natural selection that Darwin (1859) first theorized, allowing human beings to solve the problems faced in the early days of human evolution—the problems of the early hunters and gatherers. For example, *evolutionary psychologists* (psychologists who study the evolutionary origins of human behavior) would view the human behavior of not eating substances that have a bitter taste (such as poisonous plants) as an adaptive* behavior that evolved as early humans came into contact with such bitter plants. Those who ate the bitter plants would die, while those who spit them out survived to pass on their "I-don't-like-this-taste" genes to their offspring, who would pass on the genes to *their* offspring, and so on, until after a long period of time, there is an entire population of humans that naturally avoids bitter-tasting substances.

💬 That explains why people don't like bitter stuff, like the white part of an orange peel, but that's really a physical thing. How would the evolutionary perspective help us understand something psychological like relationships?

Relationships between men and women are one of the many areas in which evolutionary psychologists conduct research. For example, in one study, researchers surveyed young adults about their relationships with the opposite sex, asking the participants

**evolutionary perspective**
perspective that focuses on the biological bases of universal mental characteristics that all humans share.

*adaptive: having the quality of adjusting to the circumstances or need; in the sense used here, a behavior that aids in survival.

how likely they would be to forgive either a sexual infidelity or an emotional one (Shackelford et al., 2002). Evolutionary theory would predict that men would find it more difficult to forgive a woman who had sex with someone else than a woman who was only emotionally involved with someone, because the man wants to be sure that the children the woman bears are his (Geary, 2000, 2012). Why put all that effort into providing for children who could be another man's offspring? Women, on the other hand, should find it harder to forgive an emotional infidelity, as they are always sure that their children are their own, but (in evolutionary terms, mind you) they need the emotional loyalty of the men to provide for those children (Buss et al., 1992; Daly et al., 1982; Edlund et al., 2006). The results support the prediction: Men find it harder to forgive a partner's sexual straying and are more likely to break up with the woman than if the infidelity is purely emotional; for women, the opposite results were found. Other research concerning mating has found that women seem to use a man's kissing ability to determine his worthiness as a potential mate (Hughes et al., 2007; Walter, 2008), and men seem to prefer women with more curve in their spines, possibly because it makes them more capable of bearing the weight of pregnancy (Lewis et al., 2015).

You may have realized as you read through the various perspectives that no one perspective has all the answers. Some perspectives are more scientific (e.g., behavioral and cognitive), while others are based more in thinking about human behavior (e.g., psychodynamic and humanistic). Some, like sociocultural, biopsychological, and evolutionary perspectives, are related to each other. Psychologists will often take an *eclectic* perspective—one that uses the "bits and pieces" of several perspectives that seem to best fit a particular situation.

Psychologists with an evolutionary perspective would be interested in how this couple selected each other as partners.

Do you believe that violence is a part of human nature? Is violent behavior something that can someday be removed from human behavior or, at the very least, be controlled? Think about this question from each of the perspectives discussed in this chapter.

▶ | The response entered here will be saved to your notes and may be collected by your instructor if he/she requires it.

Submit

## PSYCHOLOGICAL PROFESSIONALS AND AREAS OF SPECIALIZATION

**1.4** **Differentiate between the various types of professionals within the field of psychology.**

Psychology is a large field, and the many professionals working within it have different training, different focuses, and may have different goals from the typical psychologist.

A **psychologist** has no medical training but has a doctorate degree. Psychologists undergo intense academic training, learning about many different areas of psychology before choosing a specialization. Because the focus of their careers can vary so widely, psychologists work in many different vocational* settings. **Figure 1.3a** on the next page shows the types of settings in which psychologists work. It is important to realize that not all psychologists are trained to do counseling, nor are all psychologists actually counselors. Psychologists who are in the counseling specialization must be licensed to practice in their states.

In contrast, a **psychiatrist** has a medical degree and is a physician who specializes in the diagnosis and treatment (including the prescription of medications) of psychological

**psychologist**

a professional with an academic degree and specialized training in one or more areas of psychology.

**psychiatrist**

a physician who specializes in the diagnosis and treatment of psychological disorders.

---

*vocational: having to do with a job or career.

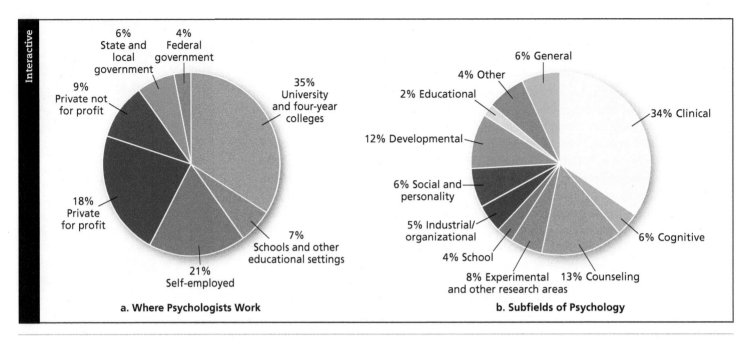

**Interactive**

a. Where Psychologists Work

- 6% State and local government
- 4% Federal government
- 9% Private not for profit
- 18% Private for profit
- 21% Self-employed
- 7% Schools and other educational settings
- 35% University and four-year colleges

b. Subfields of Psychology

- 6% General
- 4% Other
- 2% Educational
- 12% Developmental
- 6% Social and personality
- 5% Industrial/organizational
- 4% School
- 8% Experimental and other research areas
- 34% Clinical
- 6% Cognitive
- 13% Counseling

**Figure 1.3** Work Settings and Subfields of Psychology

(a) There are many different work settings for psychologists. Although not obvious from the chart, many psychologists work in more than one setting. For example, a clinical psychologist may work in a hospital setting and teach at a university or college (Michalski et al., 2011). (b) This pie chart shows the specialty areas of psychologists who recently received their doctorates (American Psychological Association, 2014).

disorders. A **psychiatric social worker** is trained in the area of social work and usually possesses a master's degree in that discipline. These professionals focus more on the environmental conditions that can have an impact on mental disorders, such as poverty, overcrowding, stress, and drug abuse. There are also *licensed professional counselors* and *licensed marriage and family therapists* who may have a master's or doctoral degree in a variety of areas and provide counseling services relative to their area of training. **L I N K** to Learning Objective B.3.

💬 You said not all psychologists do counseling. But I thought that was all that psychologists do—what else is there?

Although many psychologists do participate in delivering therapy to people who need help, there is a nearly equal number of psychologists who do other tasks: researching, teaching, designing equipment and workplaces, and developing educational methods, for example. Also, not every psychologist is interested in the same area of human—or animal—behavior, and most psychologists work in several different areas of interest, as shown in **Figure 1.3b**.

Those psychologists who do research have two types of research to consider: basic research versus applied research. **Basic research** is research for the sake of gaining scientific knowledge. For example, a researcher might want to know how many "things" a person can hold in memory at any one time. The other form of research is **applied research**, which is research aimed at answering real-world, practical problems. An applied researcher might take the information from the basic researcher's memory study and use it to develop a new study method for students. Some of the subfields in Figure 1.3b tend to do more basic research, such as experimental and cognitive psychologists, while others may focus more on applied research, such as educational, school, and industrial/organizational psychologists.

**psychiatric social worker**

a social worker with some training in therapy methods who focuses on the environmental conditions that can have an impact on mental disorders, such as poverty, overcrowding, stress, and drug abuse.

**basic research**

research focused on adding information to the scientific knowledge base.

**applied research**

research focused on finding practical solutions to real-world problems.

There are many other areas of specialization: Psychology can be used in fields such as health; sports performance; legal issues; business concerns; and even in the design of equipment, tools, and furniture. For a more detailed look at some of the areas in which psychological principles can be applied and a listing of careers that can benefit from a degree in psychology, watch the video *Careers in Psychology* and see Ⓛ Ⓘ Ⓝ Ⓚ to Appendix B: Applied Psychology.

Psychiatric social workers help many kinds and ages of people. The woman on the right might be going through a divorce, dealing with the loss of a spouse, or even recovering from drug abuse.

👁 **Watch** the **Video** *Careers in Psychology*

## Concept Map LO. 1.3, 1.4

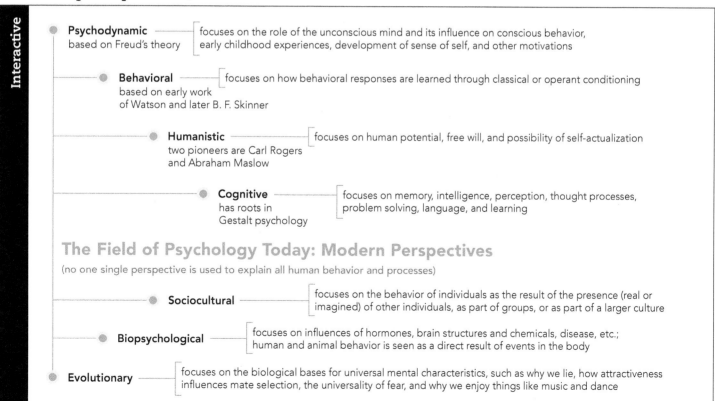

**Interactive**

**Psychodynamic** based on Freud's theory — focuses on the role of the unconscious mind and its influence on conscious behavior, early childhood experiences, development of sense of self, and other motivations

**Behavioral** based on early work of Watson and later B. F. Skinner — focuses on how behavioral responses are learned through classical or operant conditioning

**Humanistic** two pioneers are Carl Rogers and Abraham Maslow — focuses on human potential, free will, and possibility of self-actualization

**Cognitive** has roots in Gestalt psychology — focuses on memory, intelligence, perception, thought processes, problem solving, language, and learning

### The Field of Psychology Today: Modern Perspectives
(no one single perspective is used to explain all human behavior and processes)

**Sociocultural** — focuses on the behavior of individuals as the result of the presence (real or imagined) of other individuals, as part of groups, or as part of a larger culture

**Biopsychological** — focuses on influences of hormones, brain structures and chemicals, disease, etc.; human and animal behavior is seen as a direct result of events in the body

**Evolutionary** — focuses on the biological bases for universal mental characteristics, such as why we lie, how attractiveness influences mate selection, the universality of fear, and why we enjoy things like music and dance

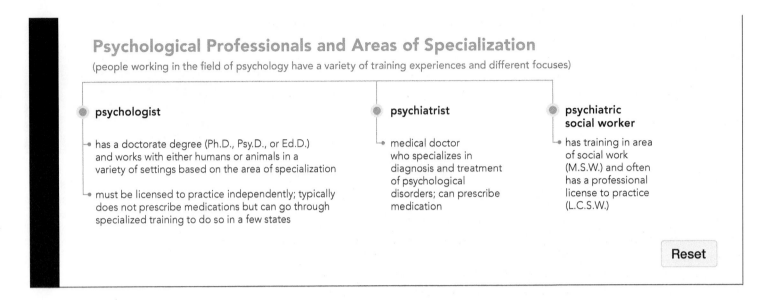

## Psychological Professionals and Areas of Specialization

(people working in the field of psychology have a variety of training experiences and different focuses)

**psychologist**

- has a doctorate degree (Ph.D., Psy.D., or Ed.D.) and works with either humans or animals in a variety of settings based on the area of specialization

- must be licensed to practice independently; typically does not prescribe medications but can go through specialized training to do so in a few states

**psychiatrist**

- medical doctor who specializes in diagnosis and treatment of psychological disorders; can prescribe medication

**psychiatric social worker**

- has training in area of social work (M.S.W.) and often has a professional license to practice (L.C.S.W.)

Reset

# Practice Quiz    How much do you remember?

*Pick the best answer.*

1. Which of the following perspectives focuses on the biological bases of universal mental characteristics?
   a. humanistic
   b. behavioral
   c. psychodynamic
   d. evolutionary

2. Which perspective offers the best explanation for schizophrenia?
   a. psychodynamic
   b. behavioral
   c. biopsychological
   d. humanistic

3. Wesley has learned that if he cries with his mother in public, she will often get him a new toy or a piece of candy so as to quiet him. Which of the following perspectives explains Wesley's behavior?
   a. psychodynamic
   b. cognitive
   c. behavioral
   d. biopsychological

4. Which perspective would a researcher be taking if she were studying a client's early childhood experiences and his resulting development of self?
   a. psychodynamic
   b. cognitive
   c. behavioral
   d. evolutionary

5. Which of the following professionals in psychology has a doctoral degree but it is not in medicine?
   a. psychiatrist
   b. psychiatric nurse
   c. psychiatric social worker
   d. psychologist

6. If Dr. Swasey is like most psychologists, where does she probably work?
   a. university/college
   b. self-employed
   c. federal government
   d. state or local government

# Scientific Research

Have you ever played the "airport game"? You sit at the airport (bus terminal, mall, or any other place where people come and go) and try to guess what people do for a living based only on their appearance. Although it's a fun game, the guesses are rarely correct. People's guesses also sometimes reveal the biases that they may have about certain physical appearances: men with long hair are musicians, people wearing suits are executives, and so on. Psychology is about trying to determine facts and reduce uncertainty and bias.

### THE SCIENTIFIC APPROACH

**1.5** **Recall the five steps of the scientific approach.**

**scientific approach**

system of gathering data so that bias and error in measurement are reduced.

In psychology, researchers want to see only what is really there, not what their biases might lead them to see. This can be achieved using the **scientific approach**, an approach to research intending to reduce the likelihood of bias and error in the measurement of data.

**PSYCHOLOGY'S GOALS**  Every science has the common goal of learning how things work. The goals specifically aimed at uncovering the mysteries of human and animal behavior are description, explanation, prediction, and control. The scientific approach is a way to accomplish these goals of psychology.

- **DESCRIPTION: WHAT IS HAPPENING?** The first step in understanding anything is to describe it. *Description* involves observing a behavior and noting everything about it: what is happening, where it happens, to whom it happens, and under what circumstances it seems to happen.

For example, a psychologist might wonder why so many computer scientists seem to be male. She makes further observations and notes that many "nontechies" stereotypically perceive the life and environment of a computer scientist as someone who lives and breathes at the computer and surrounds himself with computer games, junk food, and science-fiction gadgets—characteristics that add up to a very masculine ambiance.

That's what *seems* to be happening. The psychologist's observations are a starting place for the next goal: Why do females seem to avoid going into this environment?

- **EXPLANATION: WHY IS IT HAPPENING?** Based on her observations, the psychologist might try to come up with a tentative explanation, such as "women feel they do not belong in such stereotypically masculine surroundings." In other words, she is trying to understand or find an *explanation* for the lower proportion of women in this field. Finding explanations for behavior is a very important step in the process of forming theories of behavior. A *theory** is a general explanation of a set of observations or facts. The goal of description provides the observations, and the goal of explanation helps build the theory.

The preceding example comes from a real experiment conducted by psychologist Sapna Cheryan and colleagues (Cheryan et al., 2009). Professor Cheryan (who teaches psychology at the University of Washington in Seattle) set up four experiments with more than 250 female and male student participants who were not studying computer science. In the first experiment, students came into a small classroom that had one of two sets of objects: either Star Trek® posters, video-game boxes, and Coke™ cans, or nature posters, art, a dictionary, and coffee mugs (among other things). Told to ignore the objects because they were sharing the room with another class, the students spent several minutes in the classroom. While still sitting in the classroom, they were asked to fill out a questionnaire asking about their attitude toward computer science. While the attitudes of male students were not different between the two environments, women exposed to the stereotypically masculine setup were less interested in computer science than those who were exposed to the nonstereotypical environment. The three other similar experiments yielded the same results. Later studies found that when women were exposed to role models who dressed and acted according to the computer science stereotyped image, those women showed decreased interest in computer science as a career as well as decreased expectation of success in that field (Cheryan et al., 2011; Cheryan et al., 2013). In two similar follow-up studies with high school students, the researchers found that providing adolescent girls with an educational environment that did not fit current computer science stereotypes seemed to increase their interest in computer science courses (Master et al., 2015).

- **PREDICTION: WHEN WILL IT HAPPEN AGAIN?** Determining what will happen in the future is a *prediction*. In the original Cheryan et al. study, the prediction is clear: If we want more women to go into computer science, we must do something to change either the environment or the perception of the environment typically associated with this field. This is the purpose of the last of the four goals of psychology: changing or modifying behavior.

Is this an environment that you would want to work in? Some researchers have wondered if your answer might be influenced by your gender.

*theory: a general explanation of a set of observations or facts.

• **CONTROL: HOW CAN IT BE CHANGED?** The focus of control, or the modification of some behavior, is to change a behavior from an undesirable one (such as women avoiding a certain academic major) to a desirable one (such as more equality in career choices). Professor Cheryan suggests that changing the image of computer science may help increase the number of women choosing to go into this field.

Not all psychological investigations will try to meet all four of these goals. In some cases, the main focus might be on description and prediction, as it would be for a personality theorist who wants to know what people are like (description) and what they might do in certain situations (prediction). Some psychologists are interested in both description and explanation, as is the case with experimental psychologists who design research to find explanations for observed (described) behavior. Therapists may be more interested in controlling or influencing behavior and mental processes, although the other three goals would be important in achieving this objective.

**STEPS IN THE SCIENTIFIC APPROACH**   The first step in any investigation is to have a question to investigate, right? So the first step in the scientific approach is this:

1. **Perceiving the Question:** You notice something interesting happening in your surroundings for which you would like to have an explanation. An example might be that you've noticed that your children seem to get a little more aggressive with each other after watching a particularly violent children's cartoon program on Saturday morning. You wonder if the violence in the cartoon could be creating the aggressive behavior in your children. This step is derived from the goal of *description*: What is happening here?

    Once you have a question, you want an answer. The next logical step is to form a tentative* answer or explanation for the behavior you have seen. This tentative explanation is known as a **hypothesis**.

2. **Forming a Hypothesis:** Based on your initial observations of what's going on in your surroundings, you form an educated guess about the explanation for your observations, putting it into the form of a statement that can be tested in some way. Testing hypotheses is the heart of any scientific investigation and is the primary way in which support for theories is generated. In fact, a good theory should lead to the formation of hypotheses (predictions based on the theory). It might be helpful to think of an "if–then" statement: If the world is round, then a person should be able to sail in a straight line around the world and come back to where he or she started. "If the world is round" is the theory part of this statement, a theory based on many observations and facts gathered by observers, like observing that when a ship sails toward the horizon, it seems to "disappear" from the bottom up, indicating a curvature of the surface of the water. The "then" part of the statement is the hypothesis, a specific, *testable* prediction based on the theory. While it would be nice if all of our assumptions about what we observe are always correct, that isn't what happens and isn't necessarily what we want to happen—the scientific approach means you have to seek out information even though it might not agree with what you believed you would find. As odd as it might seem, hypotheses must be *falsifiable*: there must be a way not just to prove a hypothesis is true but also to prove a hypothesis is false. This is what being "testable" means: You have to be able to see if your hypothesis is true or false. In the example, the "then" part of the statement is testable because, as Christopher Columbus attempted to do, you actually can sail in a straight (more or less) line and see if your prediction comes true. Going back to the previous example, you might say, "If exposure to violence leads to increased aggression in children, then children who watch violent cartoons will become more aggressive." The last part of that statement is the hypothesis to be tested. (Forming a hypothesis based on observations is related to the goals of *description* and *explanation*.)

The scientific approach can be used to determine if children who watch violence on television are more likely to be aggressive than those who do not.

**hypothesis**

tentative explanation of a phenomenon based on observations.

---

*tentative: something that is not fully worked out or completed as yet.

The Science of Psychology

How do researchers go about testing the hypothesis? People have a tendency to notice only things that agree with their view of the world, a kind of selective perception called *confirmation bias.* Ⓛ Ⓘ Ⓝ Ⓚ to Learning Objective 7.4. For example, if a person is convinced that all men with long hair smoke cigarettes, that person will tend to notice only those long-haired men who are smoking and ignore all the long-haired men who don't smoke. As mentioned in the previous paragraph, the scientific approach is designed to overcome the tendency to look at only the information that confirms people's biases by forcing them to actively seek out information that might *contradict* their biases (or hypotheses). So when you test your hypothesis, you are trying to determine if the factor you suspect has an effect and that the results weren't due to luck or chance. That's why psychologists keep doing research over and over—to get more evidence that hypotheses are "supported" or "not supported." When you have a body of hypotheses that have been supported, you can build your theory around those observations.

3. **Testing the Hypothesis:** The approach you use to test your hypothesis will depend on exactly what kind of answer you think you might get. You could make more detailed observations or do a survey in which you ask questions of a large number of people, or you might design an experiment in which you would deliberately change one thing to see if it causes changes in the behavior you are observing. In the example, the best approach would probably be an experiment in which you select a group of children, show half of them a cartoon with violence and half of them a cartoon with no violence, and then find some way of measuring aggressive behavior in the two groups.

   What do you do with the results of your testing? Of course, testing the hypothesis is all about the goal of getting an *explanation* for behavior, which leads to the next step.

4. **Drawing Conclusions:** Once you know the results of your hypothesis testing, you will find that either your hypothesis was supported—which means that your experiment worked, and that your measurements supported your initial observations—or that they weren't supported, which means that you need to go back to square one and think of another possible explanation for what you have observed. (Could it be that Saturday mornings make children a little more aggressive? Or Saturday breakfasts?)

   The results of any form of hypothesis testing won't be just the raw numbers or measurements. Any data that come from your testing procedure will be analyzed with some kind of statistical method that helps to organize and refine the data. Ⓛ Ⓘ Ⓝ Ⓚ to Appendix A: Statistics. Drawing conclusions can be related to the goal of *prediction*: If your hypothesis is supported, you can make educated guesses about future, similar scenarios.

5. **Report Your Results:** You have come to some conclusion about your investigation's success or failure, and you want to let other researchers know what you have found.

  Why tell anyone what happened if it failed?

   Just because one experiment or study did not find support for the hypothesis does not necessarily mean that the hypothesis is incorrect. Your study could have been poorly designed, or there might have been factors out of your control that interfered with the study. But other researchers are asking the same kinds of questions that you might have asked. They need to know what has already been found out about the answers to those questions so that they can continue investigating and adding more knowledge about the answers to those questions. Even if your own investigation didn't go as planned, your report will tell other researchers what *not* to do in the future. So the final step in any scientific investigation is reporting the results.

At this point, you would want to write up exactly what you did, why you did it, how you did it, and what you found. If others can **replicate** your research (meaning, do exactly the same study over again and get the same results), it gives much more support to your findings. This allows others to predict behavior based on your findings and to use the results of those findings to modify or *control* behavior, the last goal in psychology. Replication of a study's results is not always an easy task, and some evidence suggests editors of peer-reviewed journals have tended to publish positive research results overall and not embrace direct replications of "old" knowledge (Nosek et al., 2012). Even when direct replication studies have been published, some results have not been as strong or did not reach the same level of statistical significance as the originals (Open Science Collaboration, 2015). While these and related concerns have been referred to as a *replicability crisis* in psychology, the field is responding to the challenge. There are focused and continued efforts of researchers to test and retest "what we think we know," providing additional evidence for many areas and suggesting we still have much work to do in other areas of psychology (Open Science Collaboration, 2015).

This might be a good place to make a distinction between questions that can be scientifically or empirically studied and those that cannot. For example, "What is the meaning of life?" is not a question that can be studied using the scientific or empirical approach. Empirical questions are those that can be tested through direct observation or experience. For example, "Has life ever existed on Mars?" is a question that scientists are trying to answer through measurements, experimentation, soil samples, and other methods. Eventually they will be able to say with some degree of confidence that life could have existed or could not have existed. That is an empirical question, because it can be supported or disproved by gathering real evidence. The meaning of life, however, is a question of belief for each person. One does not need proof to *believe*, but scientists need proof (in the form of objectively gathered evidence) to *know*. Questions that involve beliefs and values are best left to philosophy and religion.

In psychology, researchers try to find the answers to empirical questions. They can use a variety of research methods depending on the scientific question to be answered, as seen in the video *Research Methods*.

**replicate**

in research, repeating a study or experiment to see if the same results will be obtained in an effort to demonstrate reliability of results.

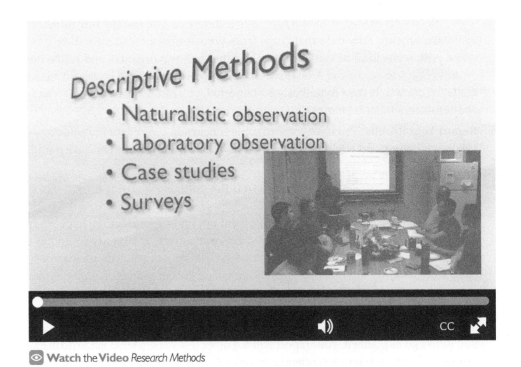

👁 **Watch** the **Video** *Research Methods*

## DESCRIPTIVE METHODS

### 1.6 Compare and contrast some of the methods used to describe behavior.

There are a number of different ways to investigate the answers to research questions, and which one researchers use depends on the kind of question they want to answer. If they only want to gather information about what has happened or what is happening, they would select a method that gives them a detailed description.

**NATURALISTIC OBSERVATION**    Sometimes all a researcher needs to know is what is happening to a group of animals or people. The best way to look at the behavior of animals or people is to watch them behave in their normal environment. That's why animal researchers go to where the animals live and watch them eat, play, mate, and sleep in their own natural surroundings. With people, researchers might want to observe them in their workplaces, in their homes, or on playgrounds. For example, if someone wanted to know how adolescents behave with members of the opposite sex in a social setting, that researcher might go to the mall on a weekend night.

What is the advantage of naturalistic observation? It allows researchers to get a realistic picture of how behavior occurs because they are actually watching that behavior in its natural setting. In a more controlled arranged environment, like a laboratory, they might get behavior that is contrived or artificial rather than genuine. Of course, precautions must be taken. An observer should have a checklist of well-defined and specific behavior to record, perhaps using their phone, tablet computer, or a special handheld computer to log each piece of data. In many cases, animals or people who know they are being watched will not behave normally—a process called the **observer effect**—so often the observer must remain hidden from view. When researching humans, remaining hidden is often a difficult thing to do. In the earlier example of the mall setting with the teenagers, a researcher might find that pretending to read a book is a good disguise, especially if one wears glasses to hide the movement of the eyes. Using such a scenario, researchers would be able to observe what goes on between the teens without them knowing that they were being watched. In other cases, researchers might use one-way mirrors, or they might actually become participants in a group, a technique called **participant observation**.

Are there disadvantages to this method? Unfortunately, yes. One of the disadvantages of naturalistic observation is the possibility of **observer bias**. That happens when the person doing the observing has a particular opinion about what he or she expects to see. If that is the case, sometimes that person recognizes only those actions that support the preconceived expectation and ignores actions that coincide with it. For example, if you think girls initiate flirting, you might not see the boys who initiate flirting. One way to avoid observer bias is to use *blind observers*: people who do not know what the research question is and, therefore, have no preconceived notions about what they "should" see. It's also a good idea to have more than one observer so that the various observations can be compared.

Another disadvantage is that each naturalistic setting is unique and unlike any other. Observations that are made at one time in one setting may not hold true for another time, even if the setting is similar, because the conditions are not going to be identical time after time—researchers don't have that kind of control over the natural world. For example, famed gorilla researcher Diane Fossey had to battle poachers who set traps for the animals in the area of her observations (Mowat, 1988). The presence and activities of the poachers affected the normal behavior of the gorillas she was trying to observe.

**LABORATORY OBSERVATION**    Sometimes observing behavior in animals or people is just not practical in a natural setting. For example, a researcher might want to observe the reactions of infants to a mirror image of themselves and to record the reactions with a camera mounted behind a one-way mirror. That kind of equipment might be difficult to set up in a natural setting. In a laboratory observation, the researcher would bring

This researcher is studying the behavior of a group of meerkats. Is this naturalistic observation? Why or why not?

The researcher in the foreground is watching the children through a one-way mirror to get a description of their behavior. Observations such as these are just one of many ways that psychologists have of investigating behavior. Why is it important for the researcher to be behind a one-way mirror?

**observer effect**

tendency of people or animals to behave differently from normal when they know they are being observed.

**participant observation**

a naturalistic observation in which the observer becomes a participant in the group being observed.

**observer bias**

tendency of observers to see what they expect to see.

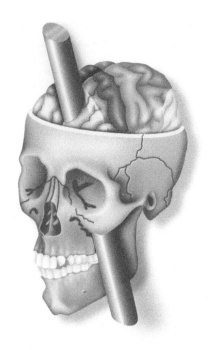

Phineas Gage survived a steel tamping rod going through his head after some explosive powder went off unexpectedly. The steel tamping rod entered above the left side of his mouth, passed through his left frontal lobe, and exited through the top of his skull.

the infant to the equipment, controlling the number of infants and their ages, as well as everything else that goes on in the laboratory.

As mentioned previously, laboratory settings have the disadvantage of being an artificial situation that might result in artificial behavior—both animals and people often react differently in the laboratory than they would in the real world. The main advantage of this method is the degree of control that it gives to the observer.

Both naturalistic and laboratory observations can lead to the formation of hypotheses that can later be tested.

**CASE STUDIES** Another descriptive technique is called the **case study**, in which one individual is studied in great detail. In a case study, researchers try to learn everything they can about that individual. For example, Sigmund Freud based his entire theory of psychoanalysis on case studies of his patients in which he gathered information about their childhoods and relationships with others from the very beginning of their lives to the present. Ⓛ Ⓘ Ⓝ Ⓚ to Learning Objective 13.2.

The advantage of the case study is the tremendous amount of detail it provides. It may also be the only way to get certain kinds of information. For example, one famous case study was the story of Phineas Gage, who, in an accident, had a large metal rod driven through his head and survived but experienced major personality and behavioral changes during the time immediately following the accident (Damasio et al., 1994; Ratiu et al., 2004; Van Horn et al., 2012). Researchers couldn't study that with naturalistic observation, and an experiment is out of the question. Imagine anyone responding to an ad in the newspaper that read:

> *Wanted: 50 people willing to suffer nonfatal brain damage for scientific study of the brain. Will pay all medical expenses.*

You certainly wouldn't get many volunteers. Case studies are good ways to study things that are rare.

The disadvantage of the case study is that researchers can't really apply the results to other similar people. In other words, they can't assume that if another person had the same kind of experiences growing up, he or she would turn out just like the person in their case study. People are unique and have too many complicating factors in their lives to be that predictable. So what researchers find in one case won't necessarily apply or generalize to others. Another weakness of this method is that case studies are a form of detailed observation and are vulnerable to bias on the part of the person conducting the case study, just as observer bias can occur in naturalistic or laboratory observation.

**SURVEYS** Sometimes what psychologists want to know about is pretty personal—like what people do in their sexual relationships, for example. (I'm pretty sure naturalistic observation of human sexual behavior could end in an arrest!) The only way to find out about very private (covert) behavior is to ask questions.

In the survey method, researchers will ask a series of questions about the topic they are studying. Surveys can be conducted in person in the form of interviews or on the telephone, the Internet, or with a questionnaire. The questions used in interviews or on the telephone can vary, but usually the questions in a survey are all the same for everyone answering the survey. In this way, researchers can ask lots of questions and survey literally hundreds of people. To gain a better understanding of what it is like to complete a survey, try your hand at the survey *Participating in a Research Survey* on the next page.

That is the big advantage of surveys, aside from their ability to get at private information. Researchers can get a tremendous amount of data on a very large group of people. Of course, there are disadvantages. For one, researchers have to be very careful about the group of people they survey. If they want to find out what college freshmen think about politics, for example, they can't really ask every single college freshman in the entire United States. But they can select a **representative sample** from that group. They

**case study**

study of one individual in great detail.

**representative sample**

randomly selected sample of subjects from a larger population of subjects.

**Survey**  PARTICIPATING IN A RESEARCH SURVEY

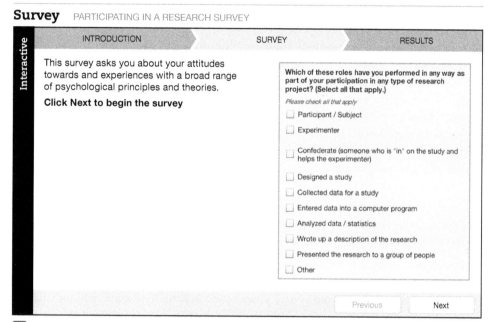

| INTRODUCTION | SURVEY | RESULTS |

This survey asks you about your attitudes towards and experiences with a broad range of psychological principles and theories.

**Click Next to begin the survey**

Which of these roles have you performed in any way as part of your participation in any type of research project? (Select all that apply.)

*Please check all that apply*

☐ Participant / Subject

☐ Experimenter

☐ Confederate (someone who is "in" on the study and helps the experimenter)

☐ Designed a study

☐ Collected data for a study

☐ Entered data into a computer program

☐ Analyzed data / statistics

☐ Wrote up a description of the research

☐ Presented the research to a group of people

☐ Other

Previous    Next

**Simulate** the **Experiment,** *Participating in a Research Survey*

could randomly* select a certain number of college freshmen from several different colleges across the United States, for example. Why randomly? Because the sample has to be *representative* of the **population**, which is the entire group in which the researcher is interested. If researchers selected only freshmen from Ivy League schools, for example, they would certainly get different opinions on politics than they might get from small community colleges. But if they take a lot of colleges and select their *participants* (people who are part of the study) randomly, they will be more certain of getting answers that a broad selection of college students would typically give.

Getting a representative sample is not always easy (Banerjee & Chaudhury, 2010). Many researchers (even more so in the past than now) use people for their samples who are readily available. Since many researchers work in educational settings, that means that they often use college students. College students aren't really good representatives of the general population even if you sampled many different kinds of schools as in the previous example—they are mostly white, well educated (and, in the early days of psychology, nearly all men). The general population is not all of those things, obviously. Sometimes the best way to get a truly representative sample is to pick names from a large phone book, starting by opening the book to a random page, closing one's eyes, and jabbing a finger at a name. Starting from that name and taking every tenth name from that point would be fairly random.

Another major disadvantage of the survey technique occurs because people aren't always going to give researchers accurate answers. The fact is, people tend to misremember things, distort the truth, and may lie outright—even if the survey is an anonymous** questionnaire. Remembering is not a very accurate process sometimes, especially when people think that they might not come off sounding very desirable or socially appropriate. Some people deliberately give the answer they think is more socially correct rather than their true opinion so that no one gets offended in a process called *courtesy bias*. Researchers must take their survey results with a big grain of salt***—they may not be as accurate as they would like them to be.

*"Next question: I believe that life is a constant striving for balance, requiring frequent tradeoffs between morality and necessity, within a cyclic pattern of joy and sadness, forging a trail of bittersweet memories until one slips, inevitably, into the jaws of death. Agree or disagree?"*

---

*randomly: in this sense, selected so that each member of the group has an equal chance of being chosen.

**anonymous: not named or identified.

***grain of salt: a phrase meaning to be skeptical; to doubt the truth or accuracy of something.

**population**

the entire group of people or animals in which the researcher is interested.

Both the wording of survey questions and the order in which they appear can affect the outcome. It is difficult to find a wording that will be understood in exactly the same way by all those who read the question. Questions can be worded in a way that the desired answer becomes obvious (often resulting in courtesy bias–type answers). For example, "Do you agree that the new procedures for registering for classes are too complicated?" is obviously looking for a confirmation, while "What is your opinion of the new procedures for registering for classes?" is much more open to differing responses. Even the order of questions in a survey matters: A question about how much should be spent on public safety might have a very different answer at the beginning of a survey than after a long list of questions about crimes and criminal activity.

### CORRELATIONS: FINDING RELATIONSHIPS

**1.7** **Explain how researchers use the correlational technique to study relationships between two or more variables.**

The methods discussed so far only provide descriptions of behavior. There are really only two methods that allow researchers to know more than just a description of what has happened: correlations and experiments. Correlation is actually a statistical technique, a particular way of organizing numerical information so that it is easier to look for patterns in the information. This method will be discussed here rather than in the statistics appendix found at the back of this text because correlation, like the experiment, is about finding relationships. In fact, the data from the descriptive methods just discussed are often analyzed using the correlational technique.

A **correlation** is a measure of the relationship between two or more variables. A *variable* is anything that can change or vary—scores on a test, temperature in a room, gender, and so on. For example, researchers might be curious to know whether cigarette smoking is connected to life expectancy—the number of years a person can be expected to live. Obviously, the scientists can't hang around people who smoke and wait to see when those people die. The only way (short of performing a very unethical and lengthy experiment) to find out if smoking behavior and life expectancy are related to each other is to use the medical records of people who have already died. (For privacy's sake, the personal information such as names and social security numbers would be removed, with only the facts such as age, gender, weight, and so on available to researchers.) Researchers would look for two facts from each record: the number of cigarettes the person smoked per day and the age of the person at death.

Now the researcher has two sets of numbers for each person in the study that go into a mathematical formula, Ⓛ Ⓘ Ⓝ Ⓚ to Learning Objective A.6, to produce a number called the **correlation coefficient**. The correlation coefficient represents two things: the direction of the relationship and its strength.

 Direction? How can a mathematical relationship have a direction?

Whenever researchers talk about two variables being related to each other, what they really mean is that knowing the value of one variable allows them to predict the value of the other variable. For example, if researchers found that smoking and life expectancy are indeed related, they should be able to predict how long someone might live if they know how many cigarettes a person smokes in a day. But which way does that prediction work? If a person smokes a lot of cigarettes, does that mean that he or she will live a longer life or a shorter one? Does life expectancy go up or down as smoking increases? That's what is meant by the *direction* of the relationship.

In terms of the correlation coefficient (represented by the small letter $r$), the number researchers get from the formula will either be a positive number or a negative number. If positive, the two variables increase in the same direction—as one goes up, the other

**correlation**

a measure of the relationship between two variables.

**correlation coefficient**

a number that represents the strength and direction of a relationship existing between two variables; number derived from the formula for measuring a correlation.

goes up; as one decreases, the other also decreases. If negative, the two variables have an inverse* relationship—as one increases, the other decreases. If researchers find that the more cigarettes a person smoked, the younger that person was when he or she died, it would mean that the correlation between the two variables is negative. (As smoking goes up, life expectancy goes down—an inverse relationship.)

The strength of the relationship between the variables will be determined by the actual number itself. That number will always range between +1.00 and −1.00.

The reason that it cannot be greater than +1.00 or less than −1.00 has to do with the formula and an imaginary line on a graph around which the data points gather, a graph called a scatterplot (see **Figure 1.4**). If the relationship is a strong one, the number will be closer to +1.00 or to −1.00. A correlation of +.89 for example, would be a very strong positive correlation. That might represent the relationship between scores on the SAT and an IQ test, for example. A correlation of −.89 would be equally strong but negative. That would be more like the correlation researchers would probably find between smoking cigarettes and the age at which a person dies.

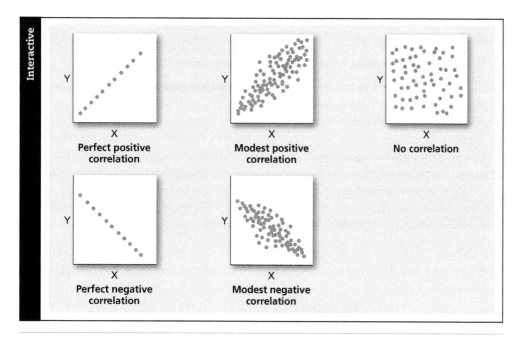

**Figure 1.4**   Five Scatterplots

These scatterplots show direction and strength of correlation. It should be noted that perfect correlations, whether positive or negative, rarely occur in the real world.

Notice that the closer the number is to zero, the weaker the relationship becomes. Researchers would probably find that the correlation coefficient for the relationship between people's weight and the number of freckles they have is pretty close to zero, for example.

 💬 Go back to the cigarette thing—if we found that the correlation between cigarette smoking and life expectancy was high, does that mean that smoking causes your life expectancy to be shortened?

Not exactly. The biggest error that people make concerning correlation is to assume that it means one variable is the cause of the other. Remember that *correlation does not prove causation*. Although adverse health effects from cigarette smoking account for

---

*inverse: opposite in order.

approximately 480,000 deaths each year in the United States alone, correlation by itself cannot be used to prove causation (U.S. Department of Health and Human Services, 2014). Just because two variables are related to each other, researchers cannot assume that one of them causes the other one to occur. They could both be related to some other variable that is the cause of both. For example, cigarette smoking and life expectancy could be linked only because people who smoke may be less likely to take care of their health by eating right and exercising, whereas people who don't smoke may tend to eat healthier foods and exercise more than smokers do.

To sum up, a correlation will tell researchers if there is a relationship between the variables, how strong the relationship is, and in what direction the relationship goes. If researchers know the value of one variable, they can predict the value of the other. If they know someone's IQ score, for example, they can predict approximately what score that person should get on the SAT—not the exact score, just a reasonable estimate. Also, even though correlation does not prove causation, it can provide a starting point for examining causal relationships with another type of study, the experiment.

## THE EXPERIMENT

### 1.8  Identify the steps involved in designing an experiment.

The only method that will allow researchers to determine the cause of a behavior is the **experiment**. In an experiment, researchers deliberately manipulate (change in some purposeful way) the variable they think is causing some behavior while holding all the other variables that might interfere with the experiment's results constant and unchanging. That way, if they get changes in behavior (an effect, in other words), they know that those changes must be due to the manipulated variable. For example, remember the discussion of the steps in the scientific approach. It talked about how to study the effects of watching violent cartoons on children's aggressive behavior. The most logical way to study that particular relationship is by an experiment.

**SELECTION**    First, researchers might start by selecting the children they want to use in the experiment. The best way to do that is through random selection of a sample of children from a "population" determined by the researchers—just as a sample would be selected for a survey. Ideally, researchers would decide on the age of child they wanted to study—say, children who are 3–4 years old. Then researchers would go to various day care centers and randomly select a certain number of children of that age. Of course, that wouldn't include the children who don't go to a day care center. Another way to get a sample in the age range might be to ask several pediatricians to send out letters to parents of children of that age and then randomly select the sample from those children whose parents responded positively.

**THE VARIABLES**    Another important step is to decide on the variable the researchers want to manipulate (which would be the one they think causes changes in behavior) and the variable they want to measure to see if there are any changes (this would be the effect on behavior of the manipulation). Often deciding on the variables in the experiment comes before selection of the participants or subjects.

In the example of aggression and children's cartoons, the variable that researchers think causes changes in aggressive behavior is the violence in the cartoons. Researchers would want to manipulate that in some way, and in order to do that they have to decide the meaning of the term *violent cartoon*. They would have to find or create a cartoon that contains violence. Then they would show that cartoon to the participants and try to measure their aggressive behavior afterward. In measuring the aggressive behavior, the researchers would have to describe exactly what they mean by "aggressive behavior" so that it can be measured. This description is called **operationalization** because it

The act of hitting each other could be part of an operationalization of aggressive behavior.

**experiment**

a deliberate manipulation of a variable to see if corresponding changes in behavior result, allowing the determination of cause-and-effect relationships.

**operationalization**

specific description of a variable of interest that allows it to be measured.

specifically names the operations (steps or procedures) that the experimenter must use to control or measure the variables in the experiment (Lilienfeld et al., 2015). An operationalization of aggressive behavior might be a checklist of very specific actions such as hitting, pushing, and so on that an observer can mark off as the children do the items on the list. If the observers were just told to look for "aggressive behavior," the researchers would probably get half a dozen or more different interpretations of what aggressive behavior is.

The name for the variable that is manipulated in any experiment is the **independent variable** because it is *independent* of anything the participants do. The participants in the study do not get to choose or vary the independent variable, and their behavior does not affect this variable at all. In the preceding example, the independent variable would be the presence or absence of violence in the cartoons.

The response of the participants to the manipulation of the independent variable *is* a dependent relationship, so the response of the participants that is measured is known as the **dependent variable**. Their behavior, if the hypothesis is correct, should *depend* on whether or not they were exposed to the independent variable, and in the example, the dependent variable would be the measure of aggressive behavior in the children. The dependent variable is always the thing (response of subjects or result of some action) that is measured to see just how the independent variable may have affected it.

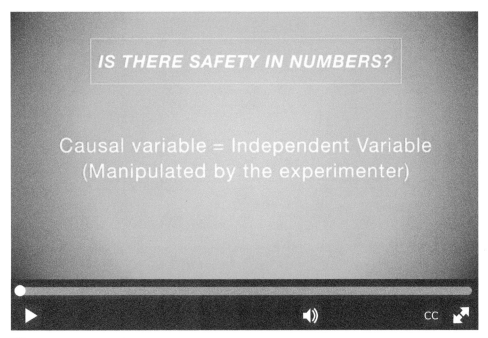

IS THERE SAFETY IN NUMBERS?

Causal variable = Independent Variable
(Manipulated by the experimenter)

 **Watch** the **Video** *Experiments: Independent versus Dependent Variables*

### THE GROUPS

💬 If researchers do all of this and find that the children's behavior is aggressive, can they say that the aggressive behavior was caused by the violence in the cartoon?

No, what has been described so far is not enough. The researchers may find that the children who watch the violent cartoon are aggressive, but how would they know if their aggressive behavior was caused by the cartoon or was just the natural aggression level of those particular children or the result of the particular time of day they were observed? Those sorts of *confounding variables* (variables that interfere with each other and their possible effects on some other variable of interest) are the kind researchers have to control for in some way. For example, if most children in this experiment just happened to be from a fairly aggressive family background, any effects the violent cartoon in the experiment might have

**independent variable**
variable in an experiment that is manipulated by the experimenter.

**dependent variable**
variable in an experiment that represents the measurable response or behavior of the subjects in the experiment.

had on the children's behavior could be confused (confounded) with the possible effects of the family background. The researchers wouldn't know if the children were being aggressive because they watched the cartoon or because they liked to play aggressively anyway.

The best way to control for confounding variables is to have two groups of participants: those who watch the violent cartoon and those who watch a nonviolent cartoon for the same length of time. Then the researchers would measure the aggressive behavior in both groups. If the aggressive behavior is significantly greater in the group that watched the violent cartoon (statistically speaking), then researchers can say that in this experiment, violent cartoon watching caused greater aggressive behavior.

The group that is exposed to the independent variable (the violent cartoon in the example) is called the **experimental group**, because it is the group that receives the experimental manipulation. The other group that gets either no treatment or some kind of treatment that should have no effect (like the group that watches the nonviolent cartoon in the example) is called the **control group** because it is used to *control* for the possibility that other factors might be causing the effect that is being examined. If researchers were to find that both the group that watched the violent cartoon and the group that watched the nonviolent cartoon were equally aggressive, they would have to assume that the violent content did not influence their behavior at all.

👁 **Watch** the **Video** *Experiments: Experimental Group versus Control Group*

**experimental group**

subjects in an experiment who are subjected to the independent variable.

**control group**

subjects in an experiment who are not subjected to the independent variable and who may receive a placebo treatment.

**random assignment**

process of assigning subjects to the experimental or control groups randomly, so that each subject has an equal chance of being in either group.

**THE IMPORTANCE OF RANDOMIZATION**   As mentioned previously, random selection is the best way to choose the participants for any study. Participants must then be assigned to either the experimental group or the control group. Not surprisingly, **random assignment** of participants to one or the other condition is the best way to ensure control over other interfering, or *extraneous*, variables. Random assignment means that each participant has an equal chance of being assigned to each condition. If researchers simply looked at the children and put all of the children from one day care center or one pediatrician's recommendations into the experimental group and the same for the control group, they would run the risk of biasing their research. Some day care centers may have more naturally aggressive children, for example, or some pediatricians may have a particular client base in which the children are very passive. So researchers want to take the entire participant group and assign each person randomly to one or the other of the groups in the study. Sometimes this is as simple as picking names out of a hat.

**1.9** **Recall two common sources of problems in an experiment and some ways to control for these effects.**

There are a few other problems that might arise in any experiment, even with the use of control groups and random assignment. These problems are especially likely when studying people instead of animals, because people are often influenced by their own thoughts or biases about what's going on in an experiment.

**THE PLACEBO EFFECT AND THE EXPERIMENTER EFFECT**  For example, say there is a new drug that is supposed to improve memory in people who are in the very early stages of *Alzheimer's disease* (a form of mental deterioration that occurs in some people as they grow old). Ⓛ Ⓘ Ⓝ Ⓚ to Learning Objective 6.13. Researchers would want to test the drug to see if it really is effective in helping improve memory, so they would get a sample of people who are in the early stages of the disease, divide them into two groups, give one group the drug, and then test for improvement. They would probably have to do a test of memory both before and after the administration of the drug to be able to measure improvement.

 💬 Let me see if I've got this straight. The group that gets the drug would be the experimental group, and the one that doesn't is the control group, right?

Right, and getting or not getting the drug is the independent variable, whereas the measure of memory improvement is the dependent variable. But there's still a problem with doing it this way. What if the researchers do find that the drug group had greater memory improvement than the group that received nothing? Can they really say that the drug itself caused the improvement? Or is it possible that the participants who received the drug *knew* that they were supposed to improve in memory and, therefore, made a major effort to do so? The improvement may have had more to do with participants' *belief* in the drug than the drug itself, a phenomenon* known as the **placebo effect**: The expectations and biases of the participants in a study can influence their behavior. In medical research, the control group is often given a harmless substitute for the real drug, such as a sugar pill or an injection of salt water, and this substitute (which has no medical effect) is called the *placebo*. If there is a placebo effect, the control group will show changes in the dependent variable even though the participants in that group received only a placebo.

Another way that expectations about the outcome of the experiment can influence the results, even when the participants are animals rather than people, is called the **experimenter effect**. It has to do with the expectations of the experimenter, not the participants. As discussed earlier in the section about naturalistic observations, sometimes observers are biased—they see what they expect to see. Observer bias can also happen in an experiment. When the researcher is measuring the dependent variable, it's possible that he or she could give the participants clues about how they are supposed to respond—through the use of body language, tone of voice, or even eye contact. Although not deliberate, it does happen. It could go something like this in the memory drug example mentioned earlier: You, the Alzheimer's patient, are in the experimenter's office to take your second memory test after trying the drug. The experimenter seems to pay a lot of attention to you and to every answer that you give in the test, so you get the feeling that you are supposed to have improved a lot. So you try harder, and

This elderly woman has Alzheimer's disease, which causes a severe loss of recent memory. If she were given a new drug in the very early stages of her disease, in the attempt to improve her memory, the researcher could not be certain that any improvement shown was caused by the drug rather than by the elderly woman's belief that the drug would work. The expectations of any person in an experimental study can affect the outcome of the study, a phenomenon known as the placebo effect.

**placebo effect**

the phenomenon in which the expectations of the participants in a study can influence their behavior.

**experimenter effect**

tendency of the experimenter's expectations for a study to unintentionally influence the results of the study.

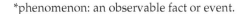

*phenomenon: an observable fact or event.

any improvement you show may be caused only by your own increased effort, not by the drug. That's an example of the experimenter effect in action: The behavior of the experimenter caused the participant to change his or her response pattern.

**SINGLE-BLIND AND DOUBLE-BLIND STUDIES**   There are ways to control these effects. The classic way to avoid the placebo effect is to give the control group an actual placebo—some kind of treatment that doesn't affect behavior at all. In the drug experiment, the placebo would have to be some kind of sugar pill or saline (salt) solution that looks like and is administered just like the actual drug. The participants in both the experimental and the control groups would not know whether they got the real drug or the placebo. That way, if their expectations have any effect at all on the outcome of the experiment, the experimenter will be able to tell by looking at the results for the control group and comparing them to the experimental group. Even if the control group improves a little, the drug group should improve significantly more if the drug is working. This is called a **single-blind study** because the participants are "blind" to the treatment they receive.

For a long time, that was the only type of experiment researchers carried out in psychology. But researchers found that when teachers were told that some students had a high potential for success and others a low potential, the students showed significant gains or decreases in their performance on standardized tests depending on which "potential" they were supposed to have (Rosenthal & Jacobson, 1968). Actually, the students had been selected randomly and were randomly assigned to one of the two groups, "high" or "low." Their performances on the tests were affected by the attitudes of the teachers concerning their potential. This study and similar ones after it highlighted the need for the experimenter to be "blind" as well as the participants in research. So in a **double-blind study**, neither the participants nor the person or persons measuring the dependent variable know who got what. That's why every element in a double-blind experiment gets coded in some way, so that only after all the measurements have been taken can anyone determine who was in the experimental group and who was in the control group.

**single-blind study**

study in which the subjects do not know if they are in the experimental or the control group.

**double-blind study**

study in which neither the experimenter nor the subjects know if the subjects are in the experimental or the control group.

## Concept Map LO. 1.5, 1.6, 1.7, 1.8 , 1.9

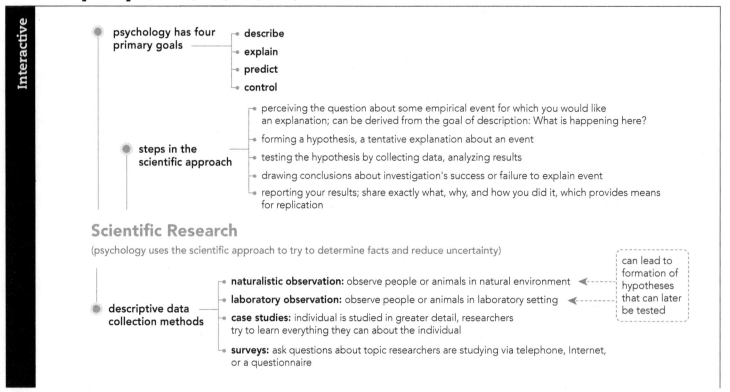

Interactive

- psychology has four primary goals
  - describe
  - explain
  - predict
  - control

- steps in the scientific approach
  - perceiving the question about some empirical event for which you would like an explanation; can be derived from the goal of description: What is happening here?
  - forming a hypothesis, a tentative explanation about an event
  - testing the hypothesis by collecting data, analyzing results
  - drawing conclusions about investigation's success or failure to explain event
  - reporting your results; share exactly what, why, and how you did it, which provides means for replication

### Scientific Research
(psychology uses the scientific approach to try to determine facts and reduce uncertainty)

- descriptive data collection methods
  - **naturalistic observation:** observe people or animals in natural environment
  - **laboratory observation:** observe people or animals in laboratory setting
  - **case studies:** individual is studied in greater detail, researchers try to learn everything they can about the individual
  - **surveys:** ask questions about topic researchers are studying via telephone, Internet, or a questionnaire

can lead to formation of hypotheses that can later be tested

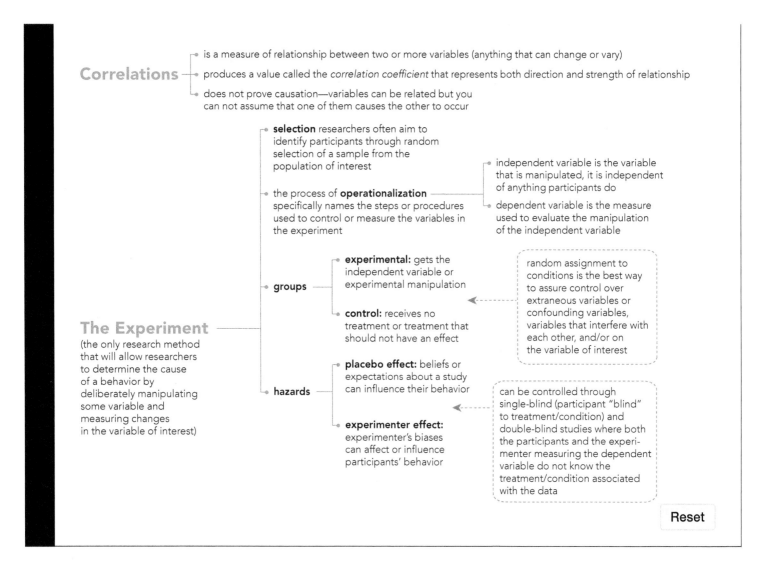

**Correlations**
- is a measure of relationship between two or more variables (anything that can change or vary)
- produces a value called the *correlation coefficient* that represents both direction and strength of relationship
- does not prove causation—variables can be related but you can not assume that one of them causes the other to occur

**The Experiment**
(the only research method that will allow researchers to determine the cause of a behavior by deliberately manipulating some variable and measuring changes in the variable of interest)

- **selection** researchers often aim to identify participants through random selection of a sample from the population of interest
- the process of **operationalization** specifically names the steps or procedures used to control or measure the variables in the experiment
  - independent variable is the variable that is manipulated, it is independent of anything participants do
  - dependent variable is the measure used to evaluate the manipulation of the independent variable

**groups**
- **experimental:** gets the independent variable or experimental manipulation
- **control:** receives no treatment or treatment that should not have an effect

random assignment to conditions is the best way to assure control over extraneous variables or confounding variables, variables that interfere with each other, and/or on the variable of interest

**hazards**
- **placebo effect:** beliefs or expectations about a study can influence their behavior
- **experimenter effect:** experimenter's biases can affect or influence participants' behavior

can be controlled through single-blind (participant "blind" to treatment/condition) and double-blind studies where both the participants and the experimenter measuring the dependent variable do not know the treatment/condition associated with the data

Reset

# Practice Quiz    How much do you remember?

*Pick the best answer.*

**1.** Dr. White noticed something odd happening to the behavior of his students as midterm exams neared. He decided to take notes about this behavior to find out exactly what was happening and the circumstances surrounding the behavior. His goal is clearly
**a.** description.
**b.** explanation.
**c.** prediction.
**d.** control.

**2.** Which of the following is an example of observer bias?
**a.** You ask your fellow students to be participants in a study of adult memory.
**b.** You ask people from your church to participate in a study of family values.
**c.** You develop an opinion of what you expect to see in an experiment.
**d.** You allow a student to quit an experiment simply because he or she is bored.

**3.** The main advantage of a survey is that
**a.** only a small number of subjects need to be accessed.
**b.** a large amount of data can be gathered.
**c.** the chance of experimenter error is removed.

**d.** subjects will not know if they are part of a control or experimental group.

**4.** Which of the following would indicate the weakest relationship and thus be close to complete randomness?
**a.** +1.04
**b.** −0.89
**c.** +0.01
**d.** −0.98

**5.** In an experiment to examine the effects of sleep deprivation on completion of a puzzle, one group is allowed to sleep 8 hours while another group is made to stay awake. In this experiment, the control group is
**a.** the group that gets to sleep.
**b.** the group that remains awake.
**c.** the puzzle.
**d.** the difference in time for each group to complete the puzzle.

**6.** In a _____ study, the participants do not know if they are part of the control group or the experimental group. Only the experimenter knows who is in each group.
**a.** placebo
**b.** single-blind
**c.** double-blind
**d.** triple-blind

# APA Goal 2: Scientific Inquiry and Critical Thinking

## A Sample Experiment

*Addresses APA LO 2.4: Interpret, design, and conduct basic psychological research.*

Many people have a somewhat negative stereotype of college athletes' academic abilities—believing that they are graded and promoted based on their athletic performance rather than their classroom performance. Evidence does exist for poorer performance on academic tests of athletes when compared to nonathletes in college (National Collegiate Athletic Association, 2002; Purdy et al., 1982; Upthegrove et al., 1999). But is this negative performance the result of poor academic ability, or could it be the effect of the negative stereotype itself? The following experiment (Jameson et al., 2007) was designed to examine the latter possibility.

In the experiment, 72 male college athletes from the sports teams of a university were given an intellectual test. Half of the athletes answered a brief questionnaire *before* taking the test, whereas the other half received the same questionnaire *after* taking the test. The questionnaire asked three questions, with the third question being, "Rate your likelihood of being accepted to the university without the aid of athletic recruiting." This item was designed to bring the negative stereotype of athletes ("dumb jocks") to the forefront of students' minds, *operationalizing* a "high threat" for that stereotype. The difference in threat level between the two groups before taking the intellectual test represents the *independent variable* in this experiment.

Those students who answered the "high threat" question *before* the intellectual test (the *experimental* group) scored significantly lower on that test (the measurement of the *dependent* variable) than those who answered the question *after* the test (the *control* group). The researchers also found a correlation between the students' exposure to the "high threat" stereotype condition and accuracy on the intellectual test: The more students believed that they got into college primarily because of their ability in sports (based on their rating of that third question), the worse they performed on the subsequent test. The researchers concluded that obvious negative stereotypes in higher education may be an important cause underlying the tendency of college athletes to underperform in academics.

**APA Goal 2**   A Sample Experiment                                              ❓

Interactive

**Match the term to the correct element of the experiment.**

Feeling of stereotype threat [        ]

Intellectual test scores [        ]

Group answering questionnaire before taking intellectual test
[        ]

Group answering questionnaire after taking intellectual test
[        ]

WORD BANK
- Experimental group
- Control group
- Independent variable
- Dependent variable

Start Over     Check Answers

# Ethics of Psychological Research

 💬 The study that Dr. Watson did with "Little Albert" and the white rat seems pretty cruel when you think about it. Do researchers today do that kind of study?

Actually, as the field and scope of psychology began to grow and more research with people and animals was being done, psychologists began to realize that some protections had to be put in place. No one wanted to be thought of as a "mad scientist," and if studies were permitted that could actually harm people or animals, the field of psychology might die out pretty quickly. (L)(I)(N)(K) to Learning Objectives 5.3 and 12.3.

## THE GUIDELINES FOR DOING RESEARCH WITH PEOPLE

**1.10** **Identify some of the common ethical guidelines for doing research with people.**

Scientists in other areas of research were also realizing that ethical treatment of the participants in studies had to be ensured in some way. Ethical treatment, of course, means that people who volunteer for a study will be able to expect that no physical or psychological harm should come to them. The video *The Ethics of Psychological Research with People* explains how researchers in the field of psychology draw the line between what is ethical and what is not and explains some of the safeguards in place today.

👁 **Watch** the **Video** *The Ethics of Psychological Research with People*

Universities and colleges (where most psychological research is carried out) usually have *institutional review boards*, groups of psychologists or other professionals who look over each proposed study and judge it according to its safety and consideration for the research participants. These review boards look at all aspects of the projected study, from the written materials that explain the research to the potential subjects to the equipment that may be used in the study itself.

There are quite a few ethical concerns when dealing with human subjects in an experiment or other type of study. Here is a list of some of the most common ethical guidelines:

1. **Rights and well-being of participants must be weighed against the study's value to science.** In other words, people come first, research second.

2. **Participants must be allowed to make an informed decision about participation.** This means that researchers have to explain the study to the people they want to include before they do anything to them or with them—even children—and it has to be in terms that the participants can understand. If researchers are using infants or children, their parents have to be informed and give their consent, a legal term known as *informed consent*. Even in single- or double-blind studies, it is necessary to tell the participants that they may be members of either the experimental or the control group—they just won't find out which group they were actually in until after the experiment is concluded.

3. **Deception must be justified.** In some cases, it is necessary to deceive the participants because the study wouldn't work any other way. For example, if you intend to give the participants a test of memory at the end but don't want them to know about the test beforehand, you would have to withhold that part of the experiment. The participants have to be told after the study exactly why the deception was important. This is called *debriefing*.

4. **Participants may withdraw from the study at any time.** The participants must be allowed to drop out for any reason. For example, sometimes people get bored with the study, decide they don't have the time, or don't like what they have to do. Children participating in studies often decide to stop "playing" (play is a common part of studies of children). Researchers have to release them, even if it means having to get more participants.

5. **Participants must be protected from risks or told explicitly of risks.** For example, if researchers are using any kind of electrical equipment, care must be taken to ensure that no participant will experience a physical shock from faulty electrical equipment.

6. **Investigators must debrief participants, telling the true nature of the study and expectations of results.** This is important in all types of studies but particularly in those involving a deception.

7. **Data must remain confidential.** Freud recognized the importance of confidentiality, referring to his patients in his books and articles with false names. Likewise, psychologists and other researchers today tend to report only group results rather than results for a single individual so that no one could possibly be recognized.

8. **If for any reason a study results in undesirable consequences for the participant, the researcher is responsible for detecting and removing or correcting these consequences.** Sometimes people react in unexpected ways to the manipulations in an experiment, despite the researcher's best efforts to prevent any negative impact on participants. If this happens, the researcher must find some way of helping the participant overcome that impact (American Psychological Association, 2002).

## THINKING CRITICALLY

You are testing a new drug to treat a serious, often fatal medical condition. Before your experiment is over, it becomes obvious that the drug is working so well that the people in the experimental group are going to recover completely. Should you stop the experiment to give the drug to the people in the control group?

▶ The response entered here will be saved to your notes and may be collected by your instructor if he/she requires it.

Submit

## ANIMAL RESEARCH

**1.11** **Explain why psychologists sometimes use animals in their research.**

Psychologists also study animals to find out about behavior, often drawing comparisons between what the animals do and what people might do under similar conditions.

  But why not just study people in the first place?

Some research questions are extremely important but difficult or impossible to answer by using human participants. Animals live shorter lives, so looking at long-term effects becomes much easier. Animals are also easier to control—the scientist can control diet, living arrangements, and even genetic relatedness. The white laboratory rat has become a recognized species different from ordinary rats, bred with its own kind for many decades until each white rat is essentially a little genetic "twin" of all the others. Animals also engage in much simpler behavior than humans do, making it easier to see the effects of manipulations. But the biggest reason that researchers use animals in some research is that animals can be used in ways that researchers could never use people. For example, it took a long time for scientists to prove that the tars and other harmful substances in tobacco cause cancer, because they had to do correlational studies with people and experiments only with animals. There's the catch—researchers can do many things to animals that they can't do to people. That might seem cruel at first, but when you think that without animal research there would be no vaccines for deadly diseases, no insulin treatments for diabetics, no transplants, and so on, then the value of the research and its benefits to humankind far outweigh the hazards to which the research animals are exposed. Still, some animal rights activists disagree with this point of view.

There are also ethical considerations when dealing with animals in research, just as there are with humans. With animals, though, the focus is on avoiding exposing them to any *unnecessary* pain or suffering. So if surgery is part of the study, it is done under anesthesia. If the research animal must die for the effects of some drug or other treatment to be examined in a necropsy (autopsy performed on an animal), the death must be accomplished humanely. Animals are used in only about 7 percent of all psychological studies (Committee on Animal Research and Ethics, 2004).

"He says he wants a lawyer."

## Concept Map LO. 1.10, 1.11

**Interactive**

**guidelines for research with humans**
- rights and well-being of participants must be weighed against the study's value to science
- participants must be allowed to make an informed decision about participating (informed consent)
- deception must be justified
- participants may withdraw from the study at any time
- participants must be protected from risks or told explicitly of risks
- investigator must debrief participants, telling the true nature of the study and expectations of results
- data must remain confidential

**Ethics of Psychological Research**
(psychological scientists have a primary goal of protecting the health and welfare of their animal or human participants)

**research with animals**
- any animal research is also covered by ethical considerations; primary focus is on avoiding any unnecessary pain or suffering
- why use animals?
  - some research questions are important but can be difficult or dangerous to answer with human participants
  - animals are easier to control
  - animals have shorter lives; easier to study long-term effects

Reset

# Practice Quiz  How much do you remember?

1. What is the first guideline for doing research with people?
   a. Participants have to give informed consent.
   b. Deception cannot be used in any studies with human beings.
   c. The rights and well-being of the participants must come first.
   d. Data must remain confidential.

2. What happens when the results of a study create an undesirable outcome for the participant?
   a. The participants signed permission forms and must take their chances.
   b. The researcher must find some way of helping the participant deal with the negative impact.
   c. The participant is institutionalized for further study.
   d. The researcher simply adds an addendum to the report of the study's results.

3. What is the biggest reason we use animals in research?
   a. Animals have simple behavior that makes it easy to see changes.
   b. Animals don't live as long as humans.
   c. We can do things to animals that we can't do to people.
   d. Animals are easier to control.

4. Which of the following is an ethical consideration when using animals in research?
   a. Avoiding exposing them to unnecessary pain.
   b. Animals cannot be killed during the course of an experiment.
   c. Animals must not experience any pain during an experiment.
   d. There are no ethical considerations when using animals in research.

## Applying Psychology to Everyday Life
### Thinking Critically About Critical Thinking

**1.12** **Recall the basic criteria for critical thinking that people can use in their everyday lives.**

💬 What good is all this focus on science and research going to do for me? I live in the real world, not a laboratory.

The real world is full of opportunities for scientific thinking. Think about all the commercials on television for miracle weight loss, hair restoration, or herbal remedies for arthritis, depression, and a whole host of physical and mental problems. Wouldn't it be nice to know how many of these claims people should believe? Wouldn't you like to know how to evaluate statements like these and possibly save yourself some time, effort, and money? That's exactly the kind of "real-world" problem that critical thinking can help sort out.

**Critical thinking** means making reasoned judgments (Beyer, 1995). The word *reasoned* means that people's judgments should be logical and well thought out. Critical thinking also includes the ability to ask and seek answers for critical questions at the right time (Browne & Keeley, 2009). (A relevant example of a critical question might be, "Is someone paying you to do this research, and is this a conflict of interest?" or "Do you have any good evidence for your assertions, or are you just giving your opinion?") Critical thinking can also help us avoid false beliefs that may lead to poor decisions or even prove dangerous to our mental and physical health.

While the word *critical* is often viewed as meaning "negative," that is not the use of this term here. Instead, it's more related to the word *criteria*,* as in thinking that meets certain high criteria or standards (Nosich, 2008). There are four basic criteria for critical thinking that people should remember when faced with statements about the world around them (Browne & Keeley, 2009; Gill, 1991; Shore, 1990):

1. **There are very few "truths" that do not need to be subjected to testing.**
   Although people may accept religious beliefs and personal values on faith, everything else in life needs to have supporting evidence. Questions that can be investigated

**critical thinking**

making reasoned judgments about claims

_____
* criteria: standards on which a judgment or decision may be based.

empirically should be examined using established scientific approaches. One shouldn't accept anything at face value but should always ask, "How do you know that? What is the evidence? Can you be more specific in your terms?" (These are more examples of those important questions to ask when thinking critically.) For example, many people still believe that astrology, the study of the supposed influence of the stars and planets on the birth of an infant, can be used to make predictions about that infant's personality and life events as he or she grows. But scientific investigations have shown us, time after time, that astrology is without any basis in truth or scientific fact (Dean & Kelly, 2000; Hines, 2003; Kelly, 1980; Wiseman, 2007).

2. **All evidence is not equal in quality.** One of the most important, often overlooked steps in critical thinking is evaluating how evidence is gathered before deciding that it provides good support for some idea. For example, there are poorly done experiments, incorrect assumptions based on correlations rather than experiments, studies that could not be replicated, and studies in which there was either no control group or no attempt made to control for placebo effects or experimenter effects. There are also studies that have been deliberately manipulated to produce the findings that the researcher (or whoever is paying the researcher) would prefer. For example, the results of a study on the effectiveness of a particular drug would be immediately suspect if the researcher is being paid by the company making the drug. As a critical thinker, you should be aware that the more wild the claim, the better the evidence should be: For example, I have not yet seen any evidence that convinces me of alien visitations or abductions!

3. **Just because someone is considered to be an authority or to have a lot of expertise does not make everything that person claims automatically true.** One should always ask to see the evidence rather than just take some expert's word for anything. How good is the evidence? Are there other alternative explanations? Is the alternative explanation simpler? If there are two explanations for some phenomenon and both account for the phenomenon equally well, the *simplest* explanation is *more often* the best one—a rule of thumb known as *the law of parsimony*. For example, let's look at crop circles, those geometric patterns of flattened crop stalks that have at times been discovered in farmers' fields. Two possible explanations for crop circles exist: Either they are made by aliens in spaceships—as is the

Many people believe that crop circles are created by alien visitors, despite clear evidence that crop circles are hoaxes created by ordinary people.

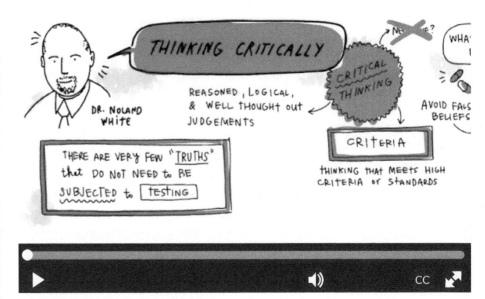

◉ **Watch** the **Video** *Critical Thinking*

claim by many alleged experts—or they are made by human beings as a hoax.* Which explanation is simpler? Obviously, the hoax rationalization is the simplest, and it turned out to be correct for the crop circles that appeared in England in the late 1970s and 1980s: David Bower and Doug Chorley, two British men, confessed to creating the crop circles as a prank, thought up in a barroom and meant to make fun of people who believe in alien visitations (Nickell, 1995; M. Ridley, 2002; Schnabel, 1994).

4. **Critical thinking requires an open mind.** Although it is good to be a little skeptical, people should not close their minds to things that are truly possible. At the same time, it's good for people to have open minds but not so open that they are gullible** and apt to believe anything. Critical thinking requires a delicate balance between skepticism and willingness to consider possibilities—even possibilities that contradict previous judgments or beliefs. For example, scientists have yet to find any convincing evidence that there was once life on Mars. That doesn't mean that scientists totally dismiss the idea, just that there is no convincing evidence *yet*. I don't believe that there are Martians on Mars, but if I were shown convincing evidence, I would have to be willing to change my thinking—as difficult as that might be.

Questions for Further Discussion

1. How might critical thinking be applied to the issue of global climate change?
2. Why do you think some people (even very smart people) sometimes avoid thinking critically about issues such as politics, the existence of ESP, or the supernatural?

---

*hoax: something intended to fool people, a trick or lie.
**gullible: easily fooled or cheated.

# Chapter Summary

## The History of Psychology

**1.1 Describe the contributions of some of the early pioneers in psychology.**

- Psychology is the scientific study of behavior and mental processes.
- In 1879, psychology began as a science of its own in Germany with the establishment of Wundt's psychology laboratory. He developed the technique of objective introspection.
- Titchener, a student of Wundt, brought psychology in the form of structuralism to America. Structuralism died out in the early twentieth century.
- William James proposed a countering point of view called functionalism, which stressed the way the mind allows us to adapt.
- Many of psychology's early pioneers were minorities such as Hispanic and African Americans who, despite prejudice and racism, made important contributions to the study of human and animal behavior.
- Functionalism influenced the modern fields of educational psychology, evolutionary psychology, and industrial/organizational psychology.

**1.2 Summarize the basic ideas and the important people behind the early approaches known as Gestalt, psychoanalysis, and behaviorism.**

- Wertheimer and others studied sensation and perception, calling the new perspective Gestalt (an organized whole) psychology.
- Freud proposed that the unconscious mind controls much of our conscious behavior in his theory of psychoanalysis.
- Watson proposed a science of behavior called behaviorism, which focused only on the study of observable stimuli and responses.
- Watson and Rayner demonstrated that a phobia could be learned by conditioning a baby to be afraid of a white rat.
- Mary Cover Jones, one of Watson's more famous students in behaviorism and child development, later demonstrated that a learned phobia could be counterconditioned.

## The Field of Psychology Today

**1.3 Summarize the basic ideas behind the seven modern perspectives in psychology.**

- Modern Freudians such as Anna Freud, Jung, and Adler changed the emphasis in Freud's original theory into a kind of neo-Freudianism.
- Skinner's operant conditioning of voluntary behavior became a major force in the twentieth century. He introduced the concept of reinforcement to behaviorism.

- Humanism, which focuses on free will and the human potential for growth, was developed by Maslow and Rogers, among others, as a reaction to the deterministic nature of behaviorism and psychoanalysis.
- Cognitive psychology is the study of learning, memory, language, and problem solving and includes the field of cognitive neuroscience.
- Biopsychology emerged as the study of the biological bases of behavior, such as hormones, heredity, chemicals in the nervous system, structural defects in the brain, and the effects of physical diseases.
- The principles of evolution and the knowledge we currently have about evolution are used in the evolutionary perspective to look at the way the mind works and why it works as it does. Behavior is seen as having an adaptive or survival value.

**1.4 Differentiate between the various types of professionals within the field of psychology.**

- Psychologists have academic doctoral degrees and can do counseling, teaching, and research and may specialize in any one of a large number of areas within psychology.
- There are many different areas of specialization in psychology, including clinical, counseling, developmental, social, and personality as areas of work or study.
- Psychiatrists are medical doctors who provide diagnosis and therapy for persons with mental disorders.
- Psychiatric social workers are social workers with special training in the influences of the environment on mental illness.
- Besides social workers, other psychology professions, such as licensed professional counselors and licensed marriage and family therapists, may only require a master's degree.

## Scientific Research

**1.5 Recall the five steps of the scientific approach.**

- The four goals of psychology are description, explanation, prediction, and control.
- The scientific approach is a way to determine facts and control the possibilities of error and bias when observing behavior. The five steps are perceiving the question, forming a hypothesis, testing the hypothesis, drawing conclusions, and reporting the results.

**1.6 Compare and contrast some of the methods used to describe behavior.**

- Naturalistic observations involve watching animals or people in their natural environments but have the disadvantage of lack of control.
- Laboratory observations involve watching animals or people in an artificial but controlled situation, such as a laboratory.

- Case studies are detailed investigations of one subject, whereas surveys involve asking standardized questions of large groups of people that represent a sample of the population of interest.

- Information gained from case studies cannot be applied to other cases. People responding to surveys may not always tell the truth or remember information correctly.

**1.7  Explain how researchers use the correlational technique to study relationships between two or more variables.**

- Correlation is a statistical technique that allows researchers to discover and predict relationships between variables of interest.

- Positive correlations exist when increases in one variable are matched by increases in the other variable, whereas negative correlations exist when increases in one variable are matched by decreases in the other variable.

- Correlations cannot be used to prove cause-and-effect relationships.

**1.8  Identify the steps involved in designing an experiment.**

- Experiments are tightly controlled manipulations of variables that allow researchers to determine cause-and-effect relationships.

- The independent variable in an experiment is the variable that is deliberately manipulated by the experimenter to see if related changes occur in the behavior or responses of the participants and is given to the experimental group.

- The dependent variable in an experiment is the measured behavior or responses of the participants.

- The control group receives either a placebo treatment or nothing.

- Random assignment of participants to experimental groups helps control for individual differences both within and between the groups that might otherwise interfere with the experiment's outcome.

**1.9  Recall two common sources of problems in an experiment and some ways to control for these effects.**

- Experiments in which the subjects do not know if they are in the experimental or control groups are single-blind studies, whereas experiments in which neither the experimenters nor the subjects know this information are called double-blind studies.

- An experiment studying the effect of negative stereotypes on test performance of athletes found that exposure to negative stereotypes prior to taking a test resulted in poorer performance by athletes than the performance of athletes whose exposure came after the test.

## Ethics of Psychological Research

**1.10  Identify some of the common ethical guidelines for doing research with people.**

- Ethical guidelines for doing research with human beings include the protection of rights and well-being of participants, informed consent, justification when deception is used, the right of participants to withdraw at any time, protection of participants from physical or psychological harm, confidentiality, and debriefing of participants at the end of the study. Researchers are also responsible for correcting any undesirable consequences that may result from the study.

**1.11  Explain why psychologists sometimes use animals in their research.**

- Animals in psychological research make useful models because they are easier to control than humans, they have simpler behavior, and they can be used in ways that are not permissible with humans.

## Applying Psychology to Everyday Life: Thinking Critically About Critical Thinking

**1.12  Recall the basic criteria for critical thinking that people can use in their everyday lives.**

- Critical thinking is the ability to make reasoned judgments. The four basic criteria of critical thinking are that there are few concepts that do not need to be tested, evidence can vary in quality, claims by experts and authorities do not automatically make something true, and keeping an open mind is important.

# Test Yourself

*Pick the best answer.*

1. In the definition of psychology, the term *behavior* means
   - **a.** internal, covert processes.
   - **b.** outward behavior.
   - **c.** overt actions and reactions.
   - **d.** only animal behavior.

2. Who is considered to be the father of African American psychology?
   - **a.** Charles Henry Thompson
   - **b.** Robert V. Guthrie
   - **c.** Francis Cecil Sumner
   - **d.** Howard Hale Long

3. Sigmund Freud's psychoanalysis focused on
   - **a.** observable behavior.
   - **b.** Gestalt perceptions.
   - **c.** introspection.
   - **d.** early childhood experiences.

4. Which psychologist dared to ignore the whole consciousness issue and return to a study of scientific inquiry by focusing on observable behavior?
   - **a.** Ivan Pavlov
   - **b.** John Watson
   - **c.** Sigmund Freud
   - **d.** William James

5. Which perspective is often referred to as the "third force" in psychology and focuses on a person's freedom of choice in determining their behavior?
   a. biopsychological perspective
   b. behaviorism
   c. cognitive psychology
   d. humanism

6. Which perspective best explains the bystander effect whereby individuals will be less likely to help someone in need because of the presence of others close by?
   a. psychoanalysis
   b. behaviorism
   c. cognitive psychology
   d. sociocultural

7. If Dr. Byers uses an eclectic approach in her clinical treatment of children, what is it that she is doing?
   a. She is relying primarily on one psychological perspective to treat all her patients.
   b. She is using medications with all her patients, especially those suffering from depression.
   c. She relies heavily on the Freudian psychodynamic perspective to help children who show abnormal behavior.
   d. She is using a combination of perspectives to treat different clients.

8. Dr. Colton identifies himself with the largest subfield of psychology. What kind of psychologist is he?
   a. counseling
   b. clinical
   c. school
   d. experimental

9. Micah has recently been diagnosed with a psychological disorder that is best addressed initially with medication. He would likely benefit the most by first seeing a _____.
   a. psychiatrist
   b. psychoanalyst
   c. psychiatric social worker
   d. psychologist

10. A psychologist is interested in finding out why married couples seemingly begin to look like each other after several years of marriage. This psychologist is most interested in the goal of
    a. description.
    b. explanation.
    c. prediction.
    d. control.

11. Which step in the scientific approach is derived from the goal of description?
    a. reporting your results
    b. perceiving a question
    c. drawing conclusions
    d. forming a hypothesis

12. Brianne wants to find an explanation for the behavior of her lab rats in her study. Which step in the scientific approach is she currently focusing on?
    a. testing a hypothesis
    b. perceiving the question
    c. drawing conclusions
    d. reporting her results

13. The famous study of Phineas Gage, who survived when a metal rod pierced his skull, is an example of a
    a. laboratory experiment.
    b. correlation.
    c. case study.
    d. survey.

14. A researcher finds that as her subjects increased the number of hours they spent exercising, the overall weight of her subjects decreased. This would be an example of a _____ correlation.
    a. positive
    b. negative
    c. zero
    d. causal

15. A researcher wants to study the effects of texting on driving. Students in Group A drive a car in a computer game and see how many virtual accidents they have. Students in Group B are asked to drive the same virtual car but they must respond to and send at least three texts. The number of virtual accidents is measured for each group. What is the independent variable?
    a. the virtual car
    b. texting
    c. the number of virtual accidents
    d. the group assignment

16. A researcher asks an assistant to conduct a study on her behalf. She specifically tells her assistant only to share the results anonymously and not include the names of the students along with their scores. Such an experiment would be considered a
    a. double-blind experiment.
    b. single-blind experiment.
    c. correlational study.
    d. laboratory observation.

17. Double-blind studies control for
    a. the placebo effect.
    b. the experimenter effect.
    c. the placebo effect and the experimenter effect.
    d. extrinsic motivation.

18. In the stereotypes-and-athletes study, who was the control group?
    a. those students who completed the survey prior to the intelligence test
    b. those students who completed the survey after the intelligence test
    c. those students who were not asked to complete the intelligence test
    d. those students who did not take part in the study at all

19. Dr. Calvin needs just one more participant to complete her experiment. Lisa, a student of Dr. Calvin, has almost completed the experiment when she announces she wants to quit because the experiment is boring. What options does Dr. Calvin have?
    a. Dr. Calvin can require that Lisa finish because students don't have the same rights to quit an experiment as the general public does.
    b. Dr. Calvin can require that Lisa finish because boredom is not an acceptable excuse for quitting.
    c. Dr. Calvin can make Lisa stay since she is a student of hers and she requires students to take part in her experiments.
    d. Dr. Calvin must let Lisa go and find another participant.

20. A famous golfer advertises a new golf bracelet that helps minimize fatigue while playing. If Bethany decides to order the bracelet because she believes that such a well-known personality should know if it works or not, she has made an error in which of the following?
    a. Few "truths" do not need to be tested.
    b. All evidence is not equal in quality.
    c. Authority or expertise does not make the claims of the authority or expert true.
    d. Critical thinking requires an open mind.

# The Biological Perspective

What do you see as the brain's role in our behavior? How much do you think your behavior is influenced by hormones and chemicals in the nervous system?

After you have answered the question, watch the video to compare the answers of other students to yours.

▶ The response entered here will be saved to your notes and may be collected by your instructor if he/she requires it.

👁 Watch the Video

# Why study the nervous system and the glands?

How could we possibly understand any of our behavior, thoughts, or actions without knowing something about the incredible organs that allow us to act, think, and react? If we can understand how the brain, the nerves, and the glands interact to control feelings, thoughts, and behavior, we can begin to truly understand the complex organism called a human being.

# Learning Objectives

**2.1** Identify the parts of a neuron and the function of each.

**2.2** Explain the action potential.

**2.3** Describe how neurons use neurotransmitters to communicate with each other and with the body.

**2.4** Describe how the brain and spinal cord interact and respond to external experiences.

**2.5** Differentiate the roles of the somatic and autonomic nervous systems.

**2.6** Explain why the pituitary gland is known as the "master gland."

**2.7** Recall the role of various endocrine glands.

**2.8** Describe how lesioning studies and brain stimulation are used to study the brain.

**2.9** Compare and contrast neuroimaging techniques for mapping the structure and function of the brain.

**2.10** Identify the different structures of the hindbrain and the function of each.

**2.11** Identify the structures of the brain that are involved in emotion, learning, memory, and motivation.

**2.12** Identify the parts of the cortex that process the different senses and those that control movement of the body.

**2.13** Name the parts of the cortex that are responsible for higher forms of thought, such as language.

**2.14** Explain how some brain functions differ between the left and right hemispheres.

**2.15** Identify some potential causes of attention-deficit/hyperactivity disorder.

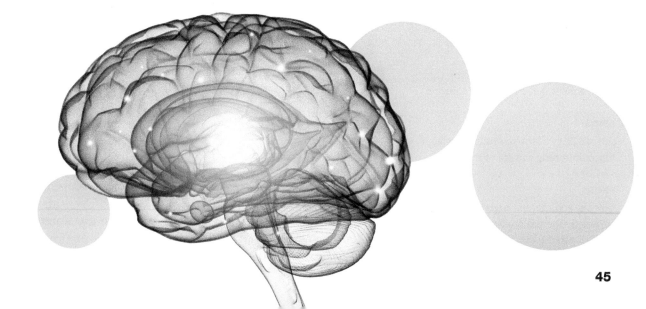

# Neurons and Nerves: Building the Network

This chapter will explore a complex system of cells, chemicals, and organs that work together to produce behavior, thoughts, and actions. The first part of this complex arrangement is the **nervous system**, a network of cells that carries information to and from all parts of the body. The field of **neuroscience** is a branch of the life sciences that deals with the structure and functioning of the brain and the neurons, nerves, and nervous tissue that form the nervous system. **Biological psychology, or behavioral neuroscience**, is the branch of neuroscience that focuses on the biological bases of psychological processes, behavior, and learning, and it is the primary area associated with the biological perspective in psychology.

## STRUCTURE OF THE NEURON: THE NERVOUS SYSTEM'S BUILDING BLOCK

### 2.1 Identify the parts of a neuron and the function of each.

In 1887, Santiago Ramón y Cajal, a doctor studying slides of brain tissue, first theorized that the nervous system was made up of individual cells (Ramón y Cajal, translation, 1995). Although the entire body is composed of cells, each type of cell has a special purpose and function and, therefore, a special structure. For example, skin cells are flat, but muscle cells are long and stretchy. Most cells have three things in common: a nucleus, a cell body, and a cell membrane holding it all together. The **neuron** is the specialized cell in the nervous system that receives and sends messages within that system. Neurons are one of the messengers of the body, and that means that they have a very special structure, which we will explore in the **Figure 2.1**.

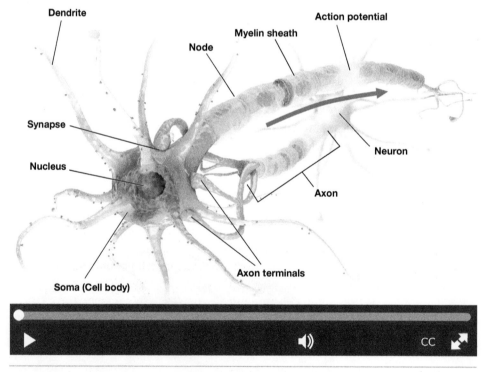

**Figure 2.1**   The Structure of the Neuron

The parts of the neuron that receive messages from other cells are called the **dendrites**. The name *dendrite* means "tree-like," or "branch," and this structure does indeed look like the branches of a tree. The dendrites are attached to the cell body, or **soma**, which is the part of the cell that contains the nucleus and keeps the entire cell alive and functioning. The word *soma* means "body." The **axon** (from the Greek for "axis") is a fiber attached to the soma, and its job is to carry messages out to other cells. The end of

**nervous system**

an extensive network of specialized cells that carries information to and from all parts of the body.

**neuroscience**

a branch of the life sciences that deals with the structure and function of neurons, nerves, and nervous tissue.

**biological psychology or behavioral neuroscience**

branch of neuroscience that focuses on the biological bases of psychological processes, behavior, and learning.

**neuron**

the basic cell that makes up the nervous system and that receives and sends messages within that system.

**dendrites**

branchlike structures of a neuron that receive messages from other neurons.

**soma**

the cell body of the neuron responsible for maintaining the life of the cell.

**axon**

tubelike structure of neuron that carries the neural message from the cell body to the axon terminals, for communication with other cells.

the axon branches out into several shorter fibers that have swellings or little knobs on the ends called **axon terminals** (may also be called *presynaptic terminals*, *terminal buttons*, or *synaptic knobs*), which are responsible for communicating with other nerve cells.

Neurons make up a large part of the brain, but they are not the only cells that affect our thinking, learning, memory, perception, and all of the other facets of life that make us who we are. The other primary cells are called glia, or **glial cells**, which serve a variety of functions. While historically viewed as support cells for neurons, the expanded roles of glia are still being discovered. And while they help maintain a state of *homeostasis*, or sense of balance in the nervous system, they are increasingly being better understood as partner cells, not just support cells (Kettenmann & Ransom, 2013; Verkhratsky et al., 2014). Some glia serve as a sort of structure on which the neurons develop and work and that hold the neurons in place. For example, during early brain development, radial glial cells (extending from inner to outer areas like the spokes of a wheel) help guide migrating neurons to form the outer layers of the brain. Other glia are involved in getting nutrients to the neurons, cleaning up the remains of neurons that have died, communicating with neurons and other glial cells, and insulating the axons of some neurons.

Glial cells affect both the functioning and structure of neurons, and specific types also have properties similar to stem cells, which allow them to develop into new neurons, both during prenatal development and in adult mammals (Bullock et al., 2005; Gotz et al., 2015; Kriegstein & Alvarez-Buylla, 2009). Glial cells are also being investigated for their possible role in a variety of neurodevelopmental diseases like *autism spectrum disorder*, degenerative disorders such as Alzheimer's disease, and psychiatric disorders including *major depressive disorder* and *schizophrenia* (Molofsky et al., 2012; Peng et al., 2015; Sahin & Sur, 2015; Verkhratsky et al., 2014; Yamamuro et al., 2015). Ⓛ Ⓘ Ⓝ Ⓚ to Learning Objectives 8.7, 14.9, and 14.14. Glial cells also play important roles in learning, behavior, and neuroplasticity by affecting synaptic connectivity and facilitating communication between neurons in specific neural networks (Hahn et al., 2015; Martín et al., 2015).

Two special types of glial cells, called *oligodendrocytes* and *Schwann cells*, generate a layer of fatty substances called **myelin**. Oligodendrocytes produce myelin for the neurons in the brain and spinal cord (the central nervous system); Schwann cells produce myelin for the neurons of the body (the peripheral nervous system). Myelin wraps around the shaft of the axons, forming an insulating and protective sheath. Bundles of myelin-coated axons travel together as "cables" in the central nervous system called *tracts*, and in the peripheral nervous system bundles of axons are called **nerves**. Myelin from Schwann cells has a unique feature that can serve as a tunnel through which damaged nerve fibers can reconnect and repair themselves. That's why a severed toe might actually regain some function and feeling if sewn back on in time. Unfortunately, myelin from oligodendrocytes covering axons in the brain and spinal cord does not have this feature, and these axons are more likely to be permanently damaged.

The myelin sheath is a very important part of the neuron. It not only insulates and protects the neuron, it also speeds up the neural message traveling down the axon. As shown in Figure 2.1, sections of myelin bump up next to each other on the axon, similar to the way sausages are linked together. The places where the myelin seems to bump are actually small spaces on the axon called nodes, which are not covered in myelin. Myelinated and unmyelinated sections of axons have slightly different electrical properties. There are also far more ion channels at each node. Both of these features affect the speed at which the electrical signal is conducted down the axon. When the electrical impulse that is the neural message travels down an axon coated with myelin, the electrical impulse is regenerated at each node and appears to "jump" or skip rapidly from node to node down the axon (Koester & Siegelbaum, 2013; Schwartz et al., 2013). That makes the message go much faster down the coated axon than it would down an uncoated axon of a neuron in the brain. In the disease called *multiple sclerosis* (MS), the myelin sheath is destroyed (possibly by the individual's own immune system), which leads to diminished

**axon terminals**

enlarged ends of axonal branches of the neuron, specialized for communication between cells.

**glial cells**

cells that provide support for the neurons to grow on and around, deliver nutrients to neurons, produce myelin to coat axons, clean up waste products and dead neurons, influence information processing, and, during prenatal development, influence the generation of new neurons.

**myelin**

fatty substances produced by certain glial cells that coat the axons of neurons to insulate, protect, and speed up the neural impulse.

**nerves**

bundles of axons coated in myelin that travel together through the body.

or complete loss of neural functioning in those damaged cells. Early symptoms of MS may include fatigue; changes in vision; balance problems; and numbness, tingling, or muscle weakness in the arms or legs. Just as we are learning more about the expanded roles of glial cells, our knowledge about the structure and function of myelin is also expanding far beyond myelin simply being an insulator of axons. Myelin thickness varies, and myelin distribution may vary along the length of an axon, likely affecting communication properties of those neurons and impacting larger neural networks (Fields, 2014; Tomassy et al., 2014).

**GENERATING THE MESSAGE WITHIN THE NEURON: THE NEURAL IMPULSE**
**2.2** Explain the action potential.

  Exactly how does this "electrical message" work inside the cell?

A neuron that's at rest—not currently firing a neural impulse or message—is actually electrically charged. Inside and outside of the cell is a semiliquid (jelly-like) solution in which there are charged particles, or *ions*. Although both positive and negative ions are located inside and outside of the cell, the relative charge of ions inside the cell is mostly negative, and the relative charge of ions outside the cell is mostly positive due to both **diffusion**, the process of ions moving from areas of high concentration to areas of low concentration, and *electrostatic pressure*, the relative balance of electrical charges when the ions are at rest. The cell membrane itself is *semipermeable*, meaning that some molecules may freely pass through the membrane while others cannot. Some molecules that are outside the cell enter through tiny protein openings, or *channels*, in the membrane, while molecules inside the cell can pass through the same channels to the outside of the cell. Many of these channels are gated—they open or close based on the electrical potential of the membrane—more about that in a minute. Inside the cell is a concentration of both smaller positively charged potassium ions and larger negatively charged protein ions. The negatively charged protein ions, however, are so big that they can't get out, which leaves the inside of the cell primarily negative when at rest. Outside the cell are lots of positively charged sodium ions and negatively charged chloride ions, but they are unable to enter the cell membrane when the cell is at rest because the ion channels that would allow them in are closed. But because the outside sodium ions are positive and the inside ions are negative, and because opposite electrical charges attract each other, the sodium ions will cluster around the membrane. This difference in charges creates an electrical potential.

Think of the ions inside the cell as a baseball game inside a stadium (the cell walls). The sodium ions outside the cell are all the fans in the area, and they want to get inside to see the game. When the cell is resting (the electrical potential is in a state called the **resting potential**, because the cell is at rest), the fans are stuck outside. The sodium ions cannot enter when the cell is at rest, because even though the cell membrane has all these channels, the *particular channels* for the big sodium ions aren't open yet. But when the cell receives a strong enough stimulation from another cell (at the dendrites or soma), the cell membrane opens up those particular channels, one after the other, all down its surface, allowing the sodium ions (the "fans") to rush into the cell. That causes the inside of the cell to become mostly positive and the outside of the cell to become mostly negative, because many of the positive sodium ions are now inside the cell—at the point where the first ion channel opened. This electrical charge reversal will start at the part of the axon closest to the soma, the *axon hillock*, and then proceed down the axon in a kind of chain reaction. (Picture a long hallway with many doors in which the first door opens, then the second, and so on all the way down the hall.) This electrical charge reversal is known as the **action potential** because the electrical potential is now in action rather than at rest.

**diffusion**

process of molecules moving from areas of high concentration to areas of low concentration.

**resting potential**

the state of the neuron when not firing a neural impulse.

**action potential**

the release of the neural impulse, consisting of a reversal of the electrical charge within the axon.

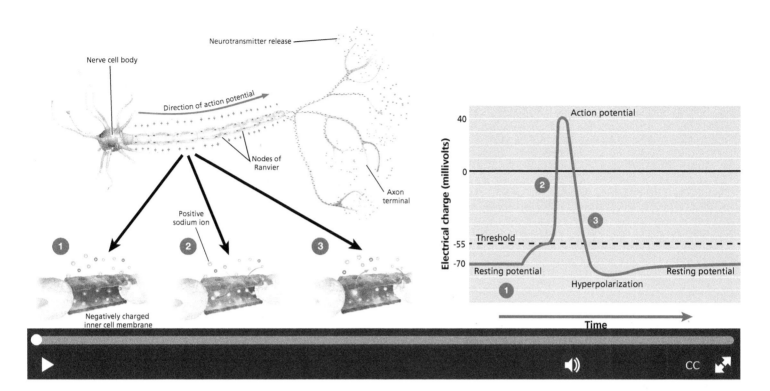

**Figure 2.2**  The Neural Impulse Action Potential

Voltage is graphed at a given axonal node over 2 to 3 milliseconds (thousandths of a second). From an initial resting state, enough stimulation is received that the threshold of excitation is reached and an action potential is triggered. The resulting rapid depolarization, repolarization, brief hyperpolarization, and return to resting potential coincide with movement of sodium and potassium ions across the cell membrane.

Each action potential sequence takes about one thousandth of a second, so the neural message travels very fast—from 2 miles per hour in the slowest, shortest neurons to 270 miles per hour in other neurons. (See **Figure 2.2**.)

Now the action potential is traveling down the axon. When it gets to the end of the axon, something else happens: the message will get transmitted to another cell (that step will be discussed momentarily). Meanwhile, what is happening to the parts of the cell that the action potential has already left behind? How does the cell get the "fans" back outside? Remember, the action potential means that the cell is now positive inside and negative outside at the point where the channel opened. Several things happen to return the cell to its resting state. First, the sodium ion channels close immediately after the action potential has passed, allowing no more "fans" (sodium ions) to enter. The cell membrane also literally pumps the positive sodium ions back outside the cell, kicking the "fans" out until the next action potential opens the ion channels again. This pumping process is a little slow, so another type of ion gets into the act. Small, positively charged potassium ions inside the neuron move rapidly out of the cell after the action potential passes, helping more quickly restore the inside of the cell to a negative charge. Now the cell becomes negative inside and positive outside, and the neuron is capable of "firing off" another message. Once the sodium pumps finish pumping out the sodium ions, the neuron can be said to have returned to its full resting potential, poised and ready to do it all again.

To sum all that up, when the cell is stimulated, the first ion channel opens and the electrical charge *at that ion channel* is reversed. Then the next channel opens and *that* charge is reversed, but in the meantime the *first* ion channel has been closed and the charge is returning to what it was when it was at rest. The action potential is the *sequence* of ion channels opening all down the length of the cell's axon.

💬 So if the stimulus that originally causes the neuron to fire is very strong, will the neuron fire more strongly than it would if the stimulus were weak?

Neurons actually have a threshold for firing, and all it takes is a stimulus that is just strong enough to get past that threshold to make the neuron fire. Here's a simple version of how this works: Each neuron is receiving many signals from other neurons. Some of these signals are meant to cause the neuron to fire, whereas others are meant to prevent the neuron from firing. The neuron constantly adds together the effects of the "fire" messages and subtracts the "don't fire" messages, and if the fire messages are great enough, the threshold is crossed and the neuron fires. When a neuron does fire, it fires in an **all-or-none** fashion. That is, neurons are either firing at full strength or not firing at all—there's no such thing as "partial" firing of a neuron. It would be like turning on a light switch—it's either on or it's off. Once the switch is turned to the on position, the light will come on. When it's turned to the off position, the light is off.

So, what's the difference between strong stimulation and weak stimulation? A strong message will cause the neuron to fire repeatedly (as if someone flicked the light switch on and off as quickly as possible), and it will also cause more neurons to fire (as if there were a lot of lights going on and off instead of just one).

### NEUROTRANSMISSION

**2.3** **Describe how neurons use neurotransmitters to communicate with each other and with the body.**

💬 Now that we know how the message travels within the axon of the cell, what is that "something else" that happens when the action potential reaches the end of the axon?

**all-or-none**

referring to the fact that a neuron either fires completely or does not fire at all.

**synaptic vesicles**

saclike structures found inside the synaptic knob containing chemicals.

**neurotransmitters**

chemical found in the synaptic vesicles that, when released, has an effect on the next cell.

Once a neural signal reaches the axon terminals of a neuron, several events take place to allow neurons to communicate with each other. These events are dependent upon key structures within a neuron and on the surface of adjacent neurons.

**SENDING THE MESSAGE TO OTHER CELLS: THE SYNAPSE** Look once again at the axon terminals in Figure 2.1. **Figure 2.3** shows an axon terminal enlarged to giant scale. Notice that the presynaptic terminal is not empty. It has a number of little saclike structures in it called **synaptic vesicles**. The word *vesicle* is Latin and means a "little blister" or "fluid-filled sac."

Inside the synaptic vesicles are chemicals suspended in fluid, which are molecules of substances called **neurotransmitters**. The name is simple enough—they are inside a neuron and they are going to transmit a message. (Neurons have traditionally been viewed as containing a single type of neurotransmitter, but it is now accepted that neurons

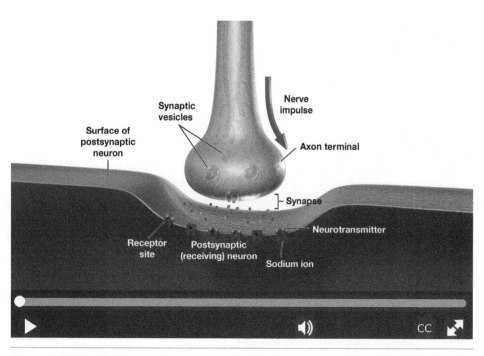

**Figure 2.3** The Synapse

The nerve impulse reaches the axon terminal, triggering the release of neurotransmitters from the synaptic vesicles. The molecules of neurotransmitter cross the synaptic gap to fit into the receptor sites that fit the shape of the molecule, opening the ion channel and allowing sodium ions to rush in.

may release more than one neurotransmitter. For simplicity and unless otherwise specified, our discussion throughout the text will assume a single, predominant neurotransmitter is being released.) Next to the axon terminal is the dendrite of another neuron (see **Figure 2.3**). Between them is a fluid-filled space called the **synapse** or the **synaptic gap**. Instead of an electrical charge, the vesicles at the end of the axon (also called the presynaptic membrane) contain the molecules of neurotransmitters, and the surface of the dendrite next to the axon (the postsynaptic membrane) contains ion channels that have **receptor sites**, proteins that allow only particular molecules of a certain shape to fit into it, just as only a particular key will fit into a keyhole. Synapses can also occur on the soma of the postsynaptic cell, as the surface membrane of the soma also has receptor sites.

How do the neurotransmitters get across the gap? Recall the action potential making its way down the axon after the neuron has been stimulated. When that action potential, or electrical charge, reaches the synaptic vesicles, the synaptic vesicles release their neurotransmitters into the synaptic gap. The molecules then float across the synapse, and many of them fit themselves into the receptor sites, opening the ion channels and allowing sodium to rush in, activating the next cell. It is this very activation that stimulates, or releases, the action potential in that cell. It is important to understand that the "next cell" may be a neuron, but it may also be a cell on a muscle or a gland. Muscles and glands have special cells with receptor sites on them, just like on the dendrite or soma of a neuron.

So far, we've been talking about the synapse as if neurotransmitters always cause the next cell to fire its action potential (or, in the case of a muscle or gland, to contract or start secreting its chemicals). But the neurons must have a way to be turned *off* as well as on. Otherwise, when a person burns a finger, the pain signals from those neurons would not stop until the burn was completely healed. Muscles are told to contract or relax, and glands are told to secrete or stop secreting their chemicals. The neurotransmitters found at various synapses around the nervous system can either turn cells on (called an *excitatory* effect) or turn cells off (called an *inhibitory* effect), depending on exactly what synapse is being affected. Although some people refer to neurotransmitters that turn cells on as *excitatory* neurotransmitters and the ones that turn cells off as *inhibitory* neurotransmitters, it's really more correct to refer to **excitatory synapses** and **inhibitory synapses**. In other words, it's not the neurotransmitter itself that is excitatory or inhibitory, but rather it is the effect of that neurotransmitter that is either excitatory or inhibitory at the receptor sites of a particular synapse.

**NEUROTRANSMITTERS: MESSENGERS OF THE NETWORK**  The first neurotransmitter to be identified was named *acetylcholine* (ACh). It is found at the synapses between neurons and muscle cells. Acetylcholine stimulates the skeletal muscles to contract but actually slows contractions in the heart muscle. If acetylcholine receptor sites on the muscle cells are blocked in some way, then the acetylcholine can't get to the site and the muscle will be incapable of contracting—paralyzed, in other words. This is exactly what happens when *curare*, a drug used by South American Indians on their blow darts, gets into the nervous system. Curare's molecules are just similar enough to fit into the receptor site without actually stimulating the cell, making curare an **antagonist** (a chemical substance that blocks or reduces the effects of a neurotransmitter) for ACh.

What would happen if the neurons released too much ACh? The bite of a black widow spider does just that. Its venom stimulates the release of excessive amounts of ACh and causes convulsions and possible death. Black widow spider venom is an **agonist** (a chemical substance that mimics or enhances the effects of a neurotransmitter) for ACh.

ACh also plays a key role in memory, arousal, and attention. For example, ACh is found in the hippocampus, an area of the brain that is responsible for forming new

---

**synapse (synaptic gap)**

microscopic fluid-filled space between the axon terminal of one cell and the dendrites or soma of the next cell.

**receptor sites**

three-dimensional proteins on the surface of the dendrites or certain cells of the muscles and glands, which are shaped to fit only certain neurotransmitters.

**excitatory synapse**

synapse at which a neurotransmitter causes the receiving cell to fire.

**inhibitory synapse**

synapse at which a neurotransmitter causes the receiving cell to stop firing.

**antagonists**

chemical substances that block or reduce a cell's response to the action of other chemicals or neurotransmitters

**agonists**

chemical substances that mimic or enhance the effects of a neurotransmitter on the receptor sites of the next cell, increasing or decreasing the activity of that cell.

The venom of the black widow spider causes a flood of acetylcholine to be released into the body's muscle system, causing convulsions.

memories, and low levels of ACh have been associated with Alzheimer's disease, the most common type of dementia. (L I N K) to Learning Objective 6.13. We will focus more on agonists and antagonists later in the chapter.

*Dopamine* (DA) is a neurotransmitter found in the brain, and like some of the other neurotransmitters, it can have different effects depending on the exact location of its activity. For example, if too little DA is released in a certain area of the brain, the result is Parkinson's disease—the disease that is currently being battled by actor Michael J. Fox, and that affected the late former boxing champ Muhammad Ali (Almasay, 2016; Ahlskog, 2003). If too much DA is released in other areas, the result is a cluster of symptoms that may be part of schizophrenia (Akil et al., 2003). (L I N K) to Learning Objective 14.13.

*Serotonin* (5-HT) is a neurotransmitter originating in the lower part of the brain that can have either an excitatory or inhibitory effect, depending on the particular synapses being affected. It is associated with sleep, mood, anxiety, and appetite. For example, low levels of 5-HT activity have been linked to depression. (L I N K) to Learning Objective 14.9.

Although ACh was the first neurotransmitter found to have an excitatory effect at the synapse, the nervous system's major excitatory neurotransmitter is *glutamate.* Like ACh, glutamate plays an important role in learning and memory and may also be involved in the development of the nervous system and in synaptic plasticity (the ability of the brain to change connections among its neurons). However, an excess of glutamate results in overactivation and neuronal damage and may be associated with the cell death that occurs after stroke or head injury or in degenerative diseases like Alzheimer's disease and Huntington disease (Julien et al., 2011; Siegelbaum et al., 2013).

Another neurotransmitter is *gamma-aminobutyric acid* or GABA. Whereas glutamate is the major neurotransmitter with an excitatory effect, GABA is the most common neurotransmitter producing inhibition in the brain. GABA can help calm anxiety, for example, by binding to the same receptor sites that are affected by tranquilizing drugs and alcohol. In fact, the effect of alcohol is to enhance the effect of GABA, which causes the general inhibition of the nervous system associated with getting drunk. This makes alcohol an agonist for GABA. (L I N K) to Learning Objective 4.13. **Table 2.1** below lists some neurotransmitters and their functions.

A group of substances known as *neuropeptides* can serve as neurotransmitters or hormones or influence the action of other neurotransmitters (Schwartz & Javitch, 2013).

| Table 2.1 | Some Neurotransmitters and Their Functions |
| --- | --- |
| **Neurotransmitters** | **Functions** |
| Acetylcholine (ACh) | Excitatory or inhibitory; involved in arousal, attention, memory, and controls muscle contractions |
| Norepinephrine (NE) | Mainly excitatory; involved in arousal and mood |
| Dopamine (DA) | Excitatory or inhibitory; involved in control of movement and sensations of pleasure |
| Serotonin (5-HT) | Excitatory or inhibitory; involved in sleep, mood, anxiety, and appetite |
| Gamma-aminobutyric acid (GABA) | Major inhibitory neurotransmitter; involved in sleep and inhibits movement |
| Glutamate | Major excitatory neurotransmitter; involved in learning, memory formation, nervous system development, and synaptic plasticity |
| Endorphins | Inhibitory neural regulators; involved in pain relief |

You may have heard of the set of neuropeptides called *endorphins*—pain-controlling chemicals in the body. When a person is hurt, a neurotransmitter that signals pain is released. When the brain gets this message, it triggers the release of endorphins. The endorphins bind to receptors that open the ion channels on the axon. This causes the cell to be unable to fire its pain signal, and the pain sensations eventually lessen. For example, you might bump your elbow and experience a lot of pain at first, but the pain will quickly subside to a much lower level. Athletes may injure themselves during an event and yet not feel the pain until after the competition is over, when the endorphin levels go down.

The name *endorphin* comes from the term *endogenous morphine*. (*Endogenous* means "native to the area"—in this case, native to the body.) Scientists studying the nervous system found receptor sites that fit morphine molecules perfectly and decided that there must be a natural substance in the body that has the same effect as morphine. Endorphins are one reason that heroin and the other drugs derived from opium are so addictive—when people take morphine or heroin, their bodies neglect to produce endorphins. When the drug wears off, they are left with no protection against pain at all, and *everything* hurts. This pain is one reason most people want more heroin, creating an addictive cycle of abuse. (L) (I) (N) K to Learning Objective 4.11.

💬 If the neurotransmitters are out there in the synaptic gap and in the receptor sites, what happens to them when they aren't needed anymore?

**CLEANING UP THE SYNAPSE: REUPTAKE AND ENZYMES** The neurotransmitters have to get out of the receptor sites before the next stimulation can occur. Some just drift away through the process of diffusion, but most will end up back in the presynaptic neuron to be repackaged into the synaptic vesicles in a process called **reuptake**. (Think of a little suction tube, sucking the chemicals back into the vesicles.) That way, the synapse is cleared for the next release of neurotransmitters. Some drugs, like cocaine, affect the nervous system by blocking the reuptake process, as shown in **Figure 2.4** .

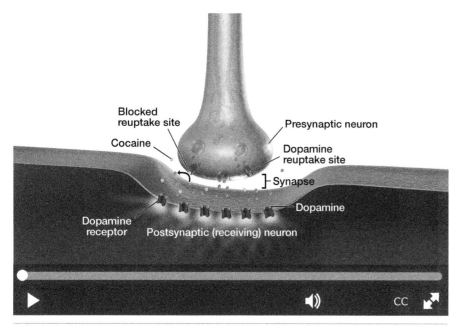

**Figure 2.4** Neurotransmitters: Reuptake

**reuptake**

process by which neurotransmitters are taken back into the synaptic vesicles.

There is one neurotransmitter that is not taken back into the vesicles, however. Because ACh is responsible for muscle activity, and muscle activity needs to happen rapidly and continue happening, it's not possible to wait around for the "sucking up" process to occur. Instead, an enzyme* specifically designed to break apart ACh clears the synaptic gap very quickly (a process called **enzymatic degradation**.) There are enzymes that break down other neurotransmitters as well.

🗨 I think I understand the synapse and neurotransmitters now, but how do I relate that to the real world?

Knowing how and why drugs affect us can help us understand why a doctor might prescribe a particular drug or why certain drugs are dangerous and should be avoided. Because the chemical molecules of various drugs, if similar enough in shape to the neurotransmitters, can fit into the receptor sites on the receiving neurons just like the neurotransmitters do, drugs can act as agonists or antagonists. Drugs acting as agonists, for example, can mimic or enhance the effects of neurotransmitters on the receptor sites of the next cell. This can result in an increase or decrease in the activity of the receiving cell, depending on what the effect of the original neurotransmitter (excitatory or inhibitory) was going to be. So if the original neurotransmitter was excitatory, the effect of the agonist will be to increase that excitation. If it was inhibitory, the effect of the agonist will be to increase that inhibition. Another deciding factor is the nervous system location of the neurons that use a specific neurotransmitter.

For example, some antianxiety medications, such as diazepam (Valium®), are classified as benzodiazepines (Ⓛ Ⓘ Ⓝ K to Learning Objective 15.10.) and are agonists for GABA, the primary inhibitory neurotransmitter in the brain. Areas of the brain that you will learn about later that play a role in controlling anxiety, agitation, and fear include the amygdala, orbitofrontal cortex, and the insula (LeDoux & Damasio, 2013; Zilles & Amunts, 2012). By increasing the inhibitory (calming) action of GABA, the benzodiazepines directly calm these specific brain areas (Julien et al., 2011; Preston et al., 2008).

Other drugs act as antagonists, blocking or reducing a cell's response to the action of other chemicals or neurotransmitters. Although an antagonist might sound like it has only an inhibitory effect, it is important to remember that if the neurotransmitter that the antagonist affects is inhibitory itself, the result will actually be an *increase* in the activity of the cell that would normally have been inhibited; the antagonist *blocks* the inhibitory effect.

Last, some drugs yield their agonistic or antagonistic effects by impacting the amount of neurotransmitter in the synapse. They do so by interfering with the regular reuptake or enzymatic degradation process. Remember that the neurotransmitter serotonin helps regulate and adjust people's moods, but in some people the normal process of adjustment is not working properly. Some of the drugs used to treat depression are called SSRIs (selective serotonin reuptake inhibitors). SSRIs block the reuptake of serotonin, leaving more serotonin available in the synapse to bind with receptor sites. Over several weeks, the individual's mood improves. Although the reason for this improvement is not as simple as once believed (i.e., low levels of serotonin = low levels of mood) or fully understood, SSRIs are effective for depression, anxiety, and obsessive-compulsive disorder (Hyman & Cohen, 2013; Julien et al., 2011; Stahl, 2013).

This section covered the neuron and how neurons communicate. The next section looks at the bigger picture—the nervous system itself.

**enzymatic degradation**
process by which the structure of a neurotransmitter is altered so it can no longer act on a receptor.

---

*enzyme: a complex protein that is manufactured by cells.

## Concept Map LO. 2.1, 2.2, 2.3

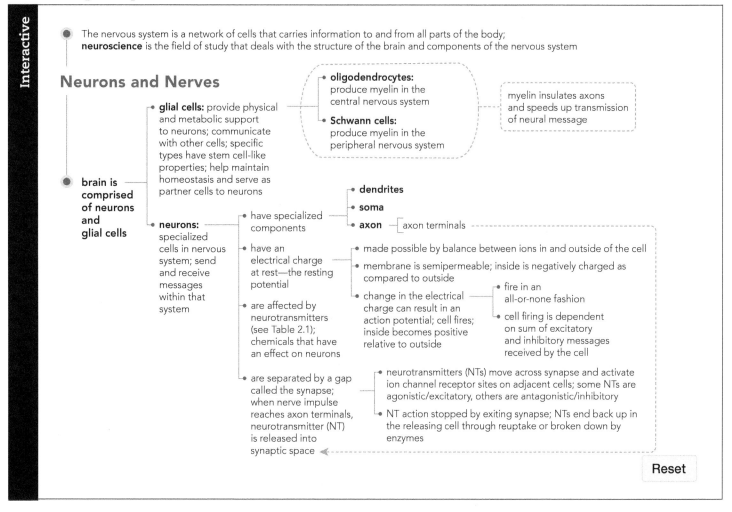

The nervous system is a network of cells that carries information to and from all parts of the body; **neuroscience** is the field of study that deals with the structure of the brain and components of the nervous system

**Neurons and Nerves**

**glial cells:** provide physical and metabolic support to neurons; communicate with other cells; specific types have stem cell-like properties; help maintain homeostasis and serve as partner cells to neurons

**oligodendrocytes:** produce myelin in the central nervous system

**Schwann cells:** produce myelin in the peripheral nervous system

myelin insulates axons and speeds up transmission of neural message

**brain is comprised of neurons and glial cells**

**neurons:** specialized cells in nervous system; send and receive messages within that system

have specialized components
- dendrites
- soma
- axon — axon terminals

have an electrical charge at rest—the resting potential
- made possible by balance between ions in and outside of the cell
- membrane is semipermeable; inside is negatively charged as compared to outside
- change in the electrical charge can result in an action potential; cell fires; inside becomes positive relative to outside
  - fire in an all-or-none fashion
  - cell firing is dependent on sum of excitatory and inhibitory messages received by the cell

are affected by neurotransmitters (see Table 2.1); chemicals that have an effect on neurons

are separated by a gap called the synapse; when nerve impulse reaches axon terminals, neurotransmitter (NT) is released into synaptic space
- neurotransmitters (NTs) move across synapse and activate ion channel receptor sites on adjacent cells; some NTs are agonistic/excitatory, others are antagonistic/inhibitory
- NT action stopped by exiting synapse; NTs end back up in the releasing cell through reuptake or broken down by enzymes

Reset

Interactive

## Practice Quiz    How much do you remember?

*Pick the best answer.*

1. Which part of the neuron carries messages to other cells?
   a. axon
   b. dendrite
   c. soma
   d. myelin

2. Which one of the following is NOT a function of glial cells?
   a. getting nutrients to the neurons
   b. generating action potentials
   c. cleaning up the remains of dead neurons
   d. generating myelin

3. When a neuron's resting potential is occurring, the neuron is _____ charged on the inside.
   a. positively
   b. negatively
   c. both positively and negatively
   d. neutrally

4. Neurotransmitters must pass from an axon terminal to the next dendrite by crossing a fluid-filled space called the
   a. synapse.
   b. reuptake inhibitor.
   c. neuron.
   d. glial cell.

5. The venom of a black widow spider acts as a(n) _____ by mimicking the effects of acetylcholine.
   a. agonist
   b. antagonist
   c. protagonist
   d. glial cell

6. Which of the following is associated with pain relief?
   a. acetylcholine
   b. glutamate
   c. serotonin
   d. endorphins

## An Overview of the Nervous System

Now that we have looked at the cells that make up the nervous system and ways in which they process and communicate information, take a look at **Figure 2.5**. This fig-ure shows the organization of the various parts of the nervous system and will help in

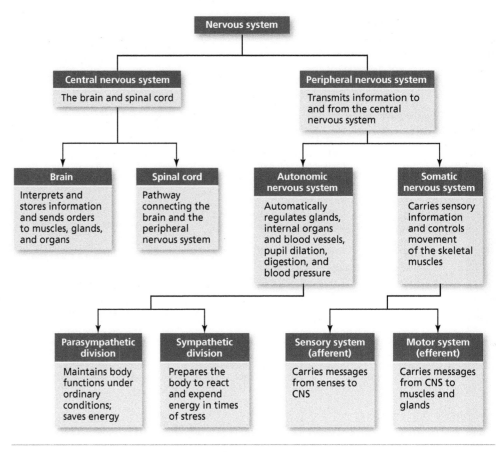

**Figure 2.5** An Overview of the Nervous System

understanding how all the different parts work together in controlling the way people and animals think, act, and feel.

THE CENTRAL NERVOUS SYSTEM: THE "CENTRAL PROCESSING UNIT"

**2.4** **Describe how the brain and spinal cord interact and respond to external experiences.**

The **central nervous system (CNS)** is composed of the brain and the spinal cord. Both the brain and the spinal cord are composed of neurons and glial cells that control the life-sustaining functions of the body as well as all thought, emotion, and behavior.

**THE BRAIN** The brain is the core of the nervous system, the part that makes sense of the information received from the senses, makes decisions, and sends commands out to the muscles and the rest of the body, if needed. Many different areas of the brain are involved in preparing us for an appropriate response to the information received, and the brain is responsible for cognition and thoughts, including learning, memory, and language. Later parts of this chapter will cover the brain in more detail, but for now, you should know the brain is organized into different regions, each with primary functions. While the neurons in each of the different areas work in much the same way, it is the groups of cells and the connections between them and other parts of the brain or components of the nervous system, and our experiences, that influence the various functions found in specific brain areas (Amaral & Strick, 2013; Heimer, 1995; Squire & Kandel, 2009).

**THE SPINAL CORD** The **spinal cord** is a long bundle of neurons that serves two vital functions for the nervous system. Look at the cross-section of the spinal cord in **Figure 2.6**. Notice that it seems to be divided into two areas, a lighter outer section and a darker inner section. If it were a real spinal cord, the outer section would appear to be white and the inner section

**central nervous system (CNS)**

part of the nervous system consisting of the brain and spinal cord.

**spinal cord**

a long bundle of neurons that carries messages between the body and the brain and is responsible for very fast, lifesaving reflexes.

would seem gray. That's because the outer section is composed mainly of myelinated axons and nerves, which appear white, whereas the inner section is mainly composed of cell bodies of neurons, which appear gray. The purpose of the outer section is to carry messages from the body up to the brain and from the brain down to the body. It is simply a message "pipeline."

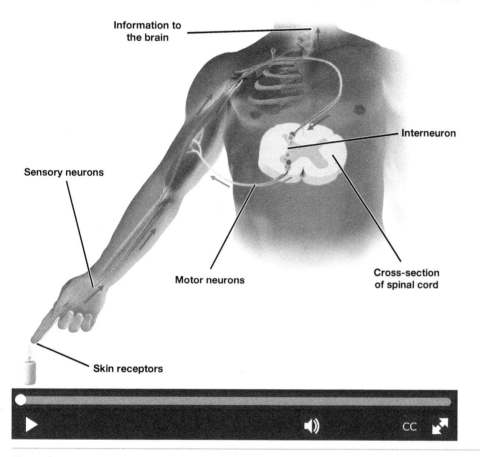

**Figure 2.6** The Spinal Cord Reflex

The pain from the burning heat of the candle flame stimulates the afferent nerve fibers, which carry the message up to the interneurons in the middle of the spinal cord. The interneurons then send a message out by means of the efferent nerve fibers, causing the hand to jerk away from the flame.

The inside section, which is made up of cell bodies separated by glial cells, is actually a primitive sort of "brain." This part of the spinal cord is responsible for certain reflexes—very fast, lifesaving reflexes. To understand how the spinal cord reflexes work, it is important to know there are three basic types of neurons: **afferent (sensory) neurons** that carry messages from the senses to the spinal cord, **efferent (motor) neurons** that carry messages from the spinal cord to the muscles and glands, and **interneurons** that connect the afferent neurons to the efferent neurons (and make up the inside of the spinal cord and much of the brain itself). (See Figure 2.6.) Touch a flame or a hot stove with your finger, for example, and an afferent neuron will send the pain message up to the spinal column, where it enters into the central area of the spinal cord. The interneuron in that central area will then receive the message and send out a response along an efferent neuron, causing your finger to pull back. This all happens very quickly. If the pain message had to go all the way up to the brain before a response could be made, the response time would be greatly increased and more damage would be done to your finger. So having this kind of **reflex arc** controlled by the spinal cord alone allows for very fast response times. (A good way to avoid mixing up the terms *afferent* and *efferent* is to remember "<u>a</u>fferent neurons <u>a</u>ccess the spinal cord, <u>e</u>fferent neurons <u>e</u>xit." The pain message does eventually get to the brain, where other motor responses may be triggered, like saying "Ouch!" and putting the finger in your mouth.

**afferent (sensory) neuron**

a neuron that carries information from the senses to the central nervous system.

**efferent (motor) neuron**

a neuron that carries messages from the central nervous system to the muscles of the body.

**interneuron**

a neuron found in the center of the spinal cord that receives information from the afferent neurons and sends commands to the muscles through the efferent neurons. Interneurons also make up the bulk of the neurons in the brain.

**reflex**

an involuntary response, one that is not under personal control or choice.

The look on this young woman's face clearly indicates that she has experienced pain in her shoulder. Pain is a warning signal that something is wrong. What might be some of the problems encountered by a person who could feel no pain at all?

**DAMAGE TO THE CENTRAL NERVOUS SYSTEM, NEUROPLASTICITY, AND NEUROGENESIS**

Damage to the central nervous system was once thought to be permanent. Neurons in the brain and spinal cord were not seen as capable of repairing themselves. When people recovered from a stroke, for example, it was assumed that it was primarily due to healthy brain cells taking over the functions of the damaged ones. Scientists have known for a while now that some forms of central nervous system damage can be repaired by the body's systems, and in recent years great strides have been made in repairing spinal cord damage. The brain actually exhibits a great deal of **neuroplasticity**, the ability to constantly change both the structure and function of many cells in the brain in response to trauma or experience (Neville & Bavelier, 2000; Rossini et al., 2007; Sanders et al., 2008). For example, dendrites grow and new synapses are formed in at least some areas of the brain as people learn new things throughout life (Sanes & Jessell, 2013a, 2013b). The video *Overview of Neuroplasticity* explains some aspects of neuroplasticity in more detail.

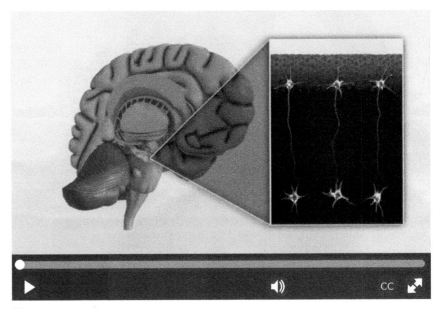

◉ **Watch** the **Video** *Overview of Neuroplasticity*

**neuroplasticity**

the ability within the brain to constantly change both the structure and function of many cells in response to experience or trauma.

**neurogenesis**

the formation of new neurons; occurs primarily during prenatal development but may also occur at lesser levels in some brain areas during adulthood.

**stem cells**

special cells found in all the tissues of the body that are capable of becoming other cell types when those cells need to be replaced due to damage or wear and tear.

The brain may also change through **neurogenesis**, the formation of new neurons, and an important process during the development of our nervous system. The greatest period of neurogenesis takes place prior to birth, during the prenatal period. And while not at the same level as during early development, the brains of most mammals continue to produce neurons well into adulthood, primarily in the *hippocampus* and *olfactory bulb*. Humans are an exception. We do not appear to have any new neurons produced in our olfactory bulbs as we grow older (Bergmann et al., 2012). However, we do continue to generate new neurons in the hippocampus throughout adulthood, with only a slight decline as we get older (Spalding et al., 2013). And most recently, researchers have found strong but preliminary evidence of human adult neurogenesis in the *striatum* (Ernst et al., 2014; Ernst & Frisen, 2015), an important area of the brain related to motor control, voluntary movement, and other functions.

Scientists are exploring ways to facilitate both neurogenesis and neuroplasticity. In efforts to repair spinal cord damage, they are examining the application of special proteins that are typically involved in the development and survival of new neurons and in the maintenance of existing neurons (Harvey et al., 2015). Researchers are also examining the effects of implanting Schwann cells from the peripheral nervous system to the central nervous system to aid in treating spinal cord injuries (Deng et al., 2013).

Researchers are constantly looking for new ways to repair the brain. One avenue of research has involved scientists investigating the possibility of transplanting **stem cells** to repair damaged or diseased brain tissue. Stem cells can become any cell in the body and may offer promise for addressing diseases such as Parkinson's and Alzheimer's or the repair of damaged spinal cords or brain tissue. If stem cells can be implanted into areas that have been damaged, the newly developed neurons may assume the roles that the original (now damaged) neurons can no longer perform. Besides transplantation, researchers are also examining the feasibility of activating stem cells through electrical stimulation (Huang et al., 2015).

Efforts to promote neurogenesis, neuroplasticity, or to aid in rehabilitation, have also examined a variety of other areas, including sleep, cognitive training, pharmacological intervention, and physical activity. Research with animals suggests sustained aerobic activity increases neurogenesis in the hippocampus, at least for some that are genetically inclined to benefit from aerobic exercise (Nokia et al., 2016). Physical exercise also appears to benefit neuroplasticity in humans (Mueller et al., 2015; Prakash et al., 2015). Sleep is another important factor. Brain wave activity changes have been recorded during sleep following specific learning experiences, and changes have been noted to coincide with symptoms observed in some psychological disorders (Tesler et al., 2016; Wilhelm et al., 2014).

While not a rehabilitative approach, ongoing research is investigating how neuroplasticity and functioning of the nervous system are influenced through **epigenetics**, or the interaction between genes and environmental factors that influence gene activity. Such factors include our physical environment, nutritional status, and life experiences. We cannot reverse time, but new life experiences can influence our brain, impact future behavior, and impact our resiliency and ability to cope with life's challenges (Caldji et al., 1998; Goossens et al., 2015; McEwen et al., 2015; Tammen et al., 2013).

## THE PERIPHERAL NERVOUS SYSTEM: NERVES ON THE EDGE

**2.5** **Differentiate the roles of the somatic and autonomic nervous systems.**

💬 Okay, that takes care of the central nervous system, except for the detail on the brain. How does the central nervous system communicate with the rest of the body?

The term *peripheral* refers to things that are not in the center or that are on the edges of the center. The **peripheral nervous system** or **PNS** (see **Figure 2.7** and also refer to Figure 2.5) is made up of all the nerves and neurons that are not contained in the brain and spinal cord. It is this system that allows the brain and spinal cord to communicate with the sensory systems of the eyes, ears, skin, and mouth and allows the brain and spinal cord to control the muscles and glands of the body. The PNS can be divided into two major systems: the **somatic nervous system**, which consists of nerves that control the voluntary muscles of the body, and the **autonomic nervous system (ANS)**, which consists of nerves that control the involuntary muscles, organs, and glands.

**THE SOMATIC NERVOUS SYSTEM** One of the parts of a neuron is the soma, or cell body (remember that the word *soma* means "body"). The somatic nervous system is made up of the **sensory pathway**, which comprises all the nerves carrying messages from the senses to the central nervous system (those nerves containing afferent neurons), and the **motor pathway**, which is all of the nerves carrying messages from the central nervous system to the voluntary, or skeletal,* muscles of the body—muscles that allow people to move their bodies (those nerves composed of efferent neurons). When people are walking, raising their hands in class, lifting a flower to smell, or directing their gaze toward the person they are talking to or to look at a pretty picture, they are using the somatic nervous system. (As seen in the discussion of spinal cord reflexes, although these muscles are called the "voluntary muscles," they can move involuntarily when a reflex response occurs.

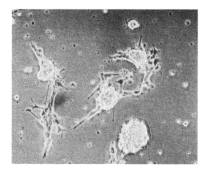
This electron micrograph shows a stem cell in the process of becoming a neuron.

**epigenetics**
the interaction between genes and environmental factors that influence gene activity; environmental factors include diet, life experiences, and physical surroundings.

**peripheral nervous system (PNS)**
all nerves and neurons that are not contained in the brain and spinal cord but that run through the body itself.

**somatic nervous system**
division of the PNS consisting of nerves that carry information from the senses to the CNS and from the CNS to the voluntary muscles of the body.

**autonomic nervous system (ANS)**
division of the PNS consisting of nerves that control all of the involuntary muscles, organs, and glands.

**sensory pathway**
nerves coming from the sensory organs to the CNS consisting of afferent neurons.

**motor pathway**
nerves coming from the CNS to the voluntary muscles, consisting of efferent neurons.

*skeletal: having to do with the bones of the body, or skeleton.

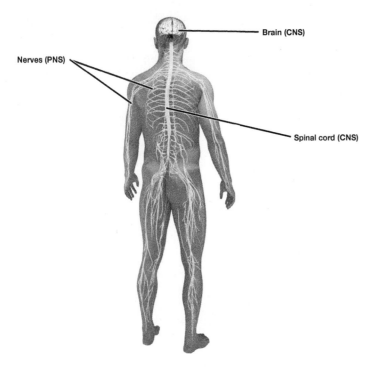

**Figure 2.7** The Peripheral Nervous System

They are called "voluntary" because they *can* be moved at will but are not limited to only that kind of movement.)

Involuntary* muscles, such as the heart, stomach, and intestines, together with glands such as the adrenal glands and the pancreas, are all controlled by clumps of neurons located on or near the spinal column. (The words *on or near* are used quite deliberately here. The neurons *inside* the spinal column are part of the central nervous system, not the peripheral nervous system.) These large groups of neurons near the spinal column make up the *autonomic nervous system.*

**THE AUTONOMIC NERVOUS SYSTEM** The word *autonomic* suggests that the functions of this system are more or less automatic, which is basically correct. Whereas the somatic division of the peripheral nervous system controls the senses and voluntary muscles, the autonomic division controls everything else in the body—organs, glands, and involuntary muscles. The autonomic nervous system is divided into two systems, the *sympathetic division* and the *parasympathetic division.* (See **Figure 2.8.**) (For a schematic representation of how all the various sections of the nervous system are organized, look back at Figure 2.5.)

**THE SYMPATHETIC DIVISION** The **sympathetic division** of the autonomic nervous system is primarily located on the middle of the spinal column—running from near the top of the rib-cage to the waist area. It may help to think of the name in these

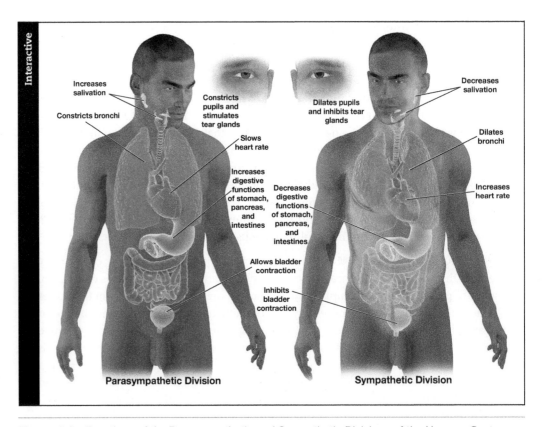

**Figure 2.8** Functions of the Parasympathetic and Sympathetic Divisions of the Nervous System

**sympathetic division**

part of the ANS that is responsible for reacting to stressful events and bodily arousal; "fight-or-flight system."

*involuntary: not under deliberate control.

terms: The *sympathetic* division is in *sympathy* with one's emotions. In fact, the sympathetic division is usually called the "fight-or-flight system" because it allows people and animals to deal with all kinds of stressful events. (L)(I)(N)(K) to Learning Objective 11.4. Emotions during these events might be anger (hence the term *fight*) or fear (that's the "flight" part, obviously) or even extreme joy or excitement. Yes, even joy can be stressful. The sympathetic division's job is to get the body ready to deal with the stress. Many of us have experienced a fight-or-flight moment at least once in our lives. Participate in the survey *Do You Fly or Fight?* to learn more about how your body responds.

**Survey**   DO YOU FLY OR FIGHT?

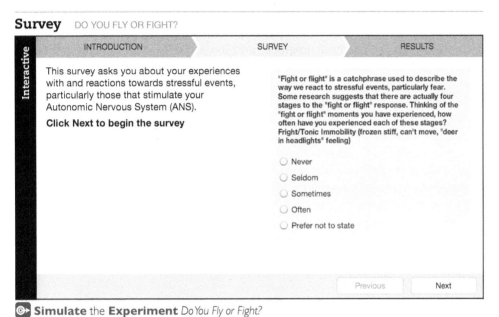

**Simulate** the **Experiment** *Do You Fly or Fight?*

What are the specific ways in which this division readies the body to react? (See Figure 2.8.) The pupils seem to get bigger, perhaps to let in more light and, therefore, more information. The heart starts pumping faster and harder, drawing blood away from nonessential organs such as the skin (so at first the person may turn pale) and sometimes even away from the brain itself (so the person might actually faint). Blood needs lots of oxygen before it goes to the muscles, so the lungs work overtime, too (the person may begin to breathe faster). One set of glands in particular receives special instructions. The adrenal glands will be stimulated to release certain stress-related chemicals (members of a class of chemicals released by glands called *hormones*) into the bloodstream. These stress hormones will travel to all parts of the body, but they will only affect certain target organs. Just as a neurotransmitter fits into a receptor site on a cell, the molecules of the stress hormones fit into receptor sites at the various target organs—notably, the heart, muscles, and lungs. This further stimulates these organs to work harder. But not every organ or system will be stimulated by the activation of the sympathetic division. Digestion of food and excretion* of waste are not necessary functions when dealing with stressful situations, so these systems tend to be shut down or inhibited. Saliva, which is part of digestion, dries right up (ever try whistling when you're scared?). Food that was in the stomach sits there like a lump. Usually, the urge to go to the bathroom will be suppressed, but if the person is really scared, the bladder or bowels may actually empty (this is why people who die under extreme stress, such as hanging or electrocution, will release their urine and waste). The sympathetic division is also going to demand that the body burn a tremendous amount of fuel, or blood sugar.

Now, all this bodily arousal is going on during a stressful situation. If the stress ends, the activity of the sympathetic division will be replaced by the activation of the parasympathetic division. If the stress goes on too long or is too intense, the person

*excretion: in this sense, the act of eliminating waste products from the body.

Speaking in public is something many people find to be particularly stressful. Which part of the speaker's autonomic nervous system is most likely to be working hard at this moment?

might actually collapse (as a deer might do when being chased by another animal). This collapse occurs because the parasympathetic division overresponds in its inhibition of the sympathetic activity. The heart slows, blood vessels open up, blood pressure in the brain drops, and fainting can be the result.

**THE PARASYMPATHETIC DIVISION** If the sympathetic division can be called the fight-or-flight system, the **parasympathetic division** might be called the "eat-drink-and-rest" system. The neurons of this division are located at the top and bottom of the spinal column, on either side of the sympathetic division neurons (*para* means "beyond" or "next to" and in this sense refers to the neurons located on either side of the sympathetic division neurons).

In looking at Figure 2.8, it might seem as if the parasympathetic division does pretty much the opposite of the sympathetic division, but it's a little more complex than that. The parasympathetic division's job is to return the body to normal functioning after a stressful situation ends. It slows the heart and breathing, constricts the pupils, and reactivates digestion and excretion. Signals to the adrenal glands stop because the parasympathetic division isn't connected to the adrenal glands. In a sense, the parasympathetic division allows the body to restore all the energy it burned—which is why people are often very hungry *after* the stress is all over.

The parasympathetic division does more than just react to the activity of the sympathetic division. It is the parasympathetic division that is responsible for most of the ordinary, day-to-day bodily functioning, such as regular heartbeat and normal breathing and digestion. People spend the greater part of their 24-hour day eating, sleeping, digesting, and excreting. So it is the parasympathetic division that is typically active. At any given moment, then, one or the other of these divisions, sympathetic or parasympathetic, will determine whether people are aroused or relaxed.

**parasympathetic division**

part of the ANS that restores the body to normal functioning after arousal and is responsible for the day-to-day functioning of the organs and glands; "eat-drink-and-rest system."

## Concept Map LO. 2.4, 2.5

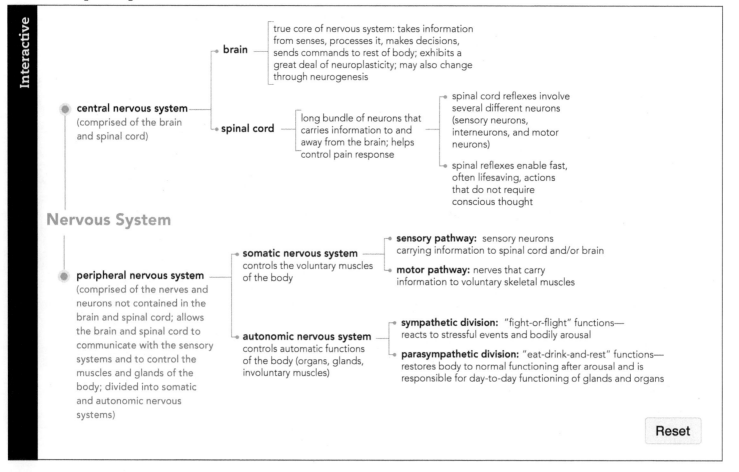

# Practice Quiz    How much do you remember?

*Pick the best answer.*

**1.** If you touch a hot stove, your spinal cord can prompt you to withdraw your hand without having to send the message all the way to the brain. This is due to what scientists call
   **a.** the reflex arc.
   **b.** neuroplasticity.
   **c.** the parasympathetic nervous system.
   **d.** the sympathetic nervous system.

**2.** What is the process whereby the structure and function of brain cells change in response to trauma, damage, or even learning?
   **a.** shallow lesioning      **c.** cell regeneration
   **b.** deep lesioning      **d.** neuroplasticity

**3.** The neurons of the sensory pathway contain
   **a.** efferent neurons.      **c.** both efferent and afferent neurons.
   **b.** afferent neurons.      **d.** voluntary muscle fibers.

**4.** Yvonne's ability to reach for and pick up her book is largely due to the functions of the _____ pathway of the _____ nervous system.
   **a.** sensory; somatic
   **b.** motor; somatic
   **c.** autonomic; peripheral
   **d.** parasympathetic; autonomic

**5.** Which of the following would be active if you have just had an automobile accident?
   **a.** sympathetic division
   **b.** parasympathetic division
   **c.** somatic division
   **d.** motor division

# Distant Connections:
# The Endocrine Glands

 How do the glands fit into all of this? Aren't there more glands than just the adrenal glands? How do they affect our behavior?

Earlier we addressed neurons and the neurotransmitters and how they release into the synapse to communicate with postsynaptic neurons. This type of chemical communication is fairly specific, primarily affecting neurons in the immediate vicinity of the originating neuron, and also very fast (almost immediate). Other structures also use chemical communication but do so at a different rate and act in a more far-reaching manner. For example, glands are organs in the body that secrete chemicals. Some glands, such as salivary glands and sweat glands, secrete their chemicals directly onto the body's tissues through tiny tubes, or ducts. This kind of gland affects the functioning of the body but doesn't really affect behavior. Other glands, called **endocrine glands**, have no ducts and secrete their chemicals directly into the bloodstream (see **Figure 2.9**). The chemicals secreted by this type of gland are called **hormones**. As mentioned earlier in the chapter when talking about the sympathetic division of the autonomic nervous system, these hormones flow into the bloodstream, which carries them to their target organs. The molecules of these hormones then fit into receptor sites on those organs to fulfill their function, affecting behavior as they do so. As compared to synaptic communication, endocrine communication is generally slower due to the time it takes hormones to travel to target organs, and the behaviors and responses they affect may not occur until hours, weeks, or years later.

The hormones affect behavior and emotions by stimulating muscles, organs, or other glands of the body. Some theories of emotion state that the surge in certain hormones actually triggers the emotional reaction (Izard, 1988; Zajonc, 1980, 1984). ⓁⒾⓃⓀ to Learning Objective 9.9. Some of the hormones produced by endocrine glands also influence the activity of the brain, producing excitatory or inhibitory effects (Schwartz & Javitch, 2013).

**endocrine glands**
glands that secrete chemicals called hormones directly into the bloodstream.

**hormones**
chemicals released into the bloodstream by endocrine glands.

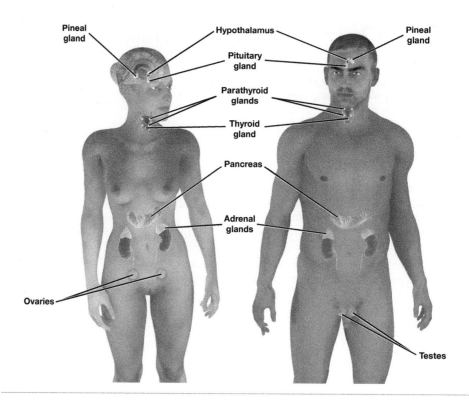

**Figure 2.9**  The Endocrine Glands

The endocrine glands secrete hormones directly into the bloodstream, which carries them to organs in the body, such as the heart, pancreas, and sex organs.

### THE PITUITARY: MASTER OF THE HORMONAL UNIVERSE

#### 2.6  Explain why the pituitary gland is known as the "master gland."

The **pituitary gland** is located under the brain, just below the hypothalamus. The hypothalamus controls the glandular system by influencing the pituitary. That is because the pituitary gland is the *master gland*, the one that controls or influences all of the other endocrine glands.

Part of the pituitary secretes several hormones that influence the activity of the other glands. One of these hormones is a *growth hormone* that controls and regulates the increase in size as children grow from infancy to adulthood. There are also hormones that stimulate the gonads (ovaries and testes) to release female or male sex hormones, which in turn influence the development and functioning of the reproductive organs, development of secondary sex characteristics in puberty, and reproductive behavior in general. **L I N K** to Learning Objective 10.1. Male and female sex hormones have also been implicated in cognitive changes as we grow older. One study has found a correlation between lower levels of the male sex hormone androgen and cognitive decline in older men (Hsu et al., 2015), and for females, hormonal therapy during a limited postmenopausal time window may lower the risk of mild cognitive impairment later in their lives (Scott et al., 2012). Another part of the pituitary controls things associated with pregnancy and levels of water in the body.

### THINKING CRITICALLY

Some people think that taking human growth hormone (HGH) supplements will help reverse the effects of aging. If this were true, what would you expect to see in the news media or medical journals? How would you expect HGH supplements to be marketed as a result?

▶  The response entered here will be saved to your notes and may be collected by your instructor if he/she requires it.

Submit

**pituitary gland**

gland located in the brain that secretes human growth hormone and influences all other hormone-secreting glands (also known as the master gland).

The hormone that controls aspects of pregnancy is called **oxytocin**, and it is involved in a variety of ways with both reproduction and parental behavior. It stimulates contractions of the uterus in childbirth. The word itself comes from the Greek word *oxys*, meaning "rapid," and *tokos*, meaning "childbirth," and injections of oxytocin are frequently used to induce or speed up labor and delivery. It is also responsible for the *milk letdown reflex*, which involves contraction of the mammary gland cells to release milk for the nursing infant. The hormone that controls levels of water in our body is called *vasopressin*, and it essentially acts as an antidiuretic, helping the body to conserve water.

You may have seen oxytocin covered in the news lately, as its role in human social behavior has been making headlines. Sometimes referred to in the media as the "love hormone" or the "trust hormone," it is prompting a great deal of research. While the role of oxytocin and vasopressin has been demonstrated in the formation of social bonds in nonhuman animals such as prairie voles, the exact role of these hormones in human social behavior is still under investigation (Ferguson et al., 2001; Lim & Young, 2006; Miller, 2013; Stoesz et al., 2013; Winslow et al., 1993).

From investigations of receptor genes to direct impact on social behaviors, both of these hormones are gathering a lot of attention (Donaldson & Young, 2008; Poulin et al., 2012; Scheele et al., 2012). One study has suggested men in monogamous relationships were more likely to keep a greater distance between themselves and an attractive female during their first meeting after receiving oxytocin (Scheele et al., 2012). The result suggested may help men in heterosexual monogamous relationships remain faithful to their partners.

There is additional evidence that oxytocin may have different effects for different individuals under different conditions. Men less socially proficient at recognizing social cues performed better on a task of empathic accuracy after receiving nasal administration of oxytocin, whereas more socially proficient males did not (Bartz et al., 2010). Especially in light of growing interest in the potential role of oxytocin as a treatment for a variety of psychiatric behaviors where social behavior is impacted (e.g., autism, social anxiety), researchers need to be aware of the different impacts oxytocin may have on different individuals in different situations (Bartz et al., 2011). Oxytocin's effects depend on what people believe about themselves in relation to other people and what they believe about achieving close social relationships (Bartz et al., 2015). Besides the prosocial affects most often studied, some researchers have suggested it may be tied more to increasing the importance of social stimuli. As such, administration of oxytocin has also been tied to increased aggressive responses (Ne'eman et al., 2016).

### OTHER ENDOCRINE GLANDS

**2.7** **Recall the role of various endocrine glands.**

As the master gland, the pituitary forms a very important part of a feedback system, one that includes the hypothalamus and the organs targeted by the various hormones. The balance of hormones in the entire endocrine system is maintained by feedback from each of these "players" to the others.

**THE PINEAL GLAND** The **pineal gland** is located in the brain, near the back, directly above the brain stem. It plays an important role in several biological rhythms. The pineal gland secretes a hormone called *melatonin*, which helps track day length (and seasons). In some animals, this influences seasonal behaviors such as breeding and molting. In humans, melatonin levels are more influential in regulating the sleep–wake cycle. LINK to Learning Objective 4.3.

**THE THYROID GLAND** The **thyroid gland** is located inside the neck and secretes hormones that regulate growth and metabolism. One of these, a hormone called *thyroxin*,

**oxytocin**
hormone released by the posterior pituitary gland that is involved in reproductive and parental behaviors.

**pineal gland**
endocrine gland located near the base of the cerebrum; secretes melatonin.

**thyroid gland**
endocrine gland found in the neck; regulates metabolism.

When the pancreas does not excrete enough insulin, the result is diabetes. A person with diabetes must keep a close watch on blood sugar levels. Some people test more than once a day while others are able to test only a few times a week. Devices such as the one in use here make it much easier—and far less painful—to test blood sugar levels than in years past.

**pancreas**

endocrine gland; controls the levels of sugar in the blood.

**gonads**

sex glands; secrete hormones that regulate sexual development and behavior as well as reproduction.

**ovaries**

the female gonads or sex glands.

**testes**

the male gonads or sex glands.

**adrenal glands**

endocrine glands located on top of each kidney that secrete over 30 different hormones to deal with stress, regulate salt intake, and provide a secondary source of sex hormones affecting the sexual changes that occur during adolescence.

regulates metabolism (how fast the body burns its available energy). As related to growth, the thyroid plays a crucial role in body and brain development.

**PANCREAS** The **pancreas** controls the level of blood sugar in the body by secreting *insulin* and *glucagon*. If the pancreas secretes too little insulin, it results in *diabetes*. If it secretes too much insulin, it results in *hypoglycemia*, or low blood sugar, which causes a person to feel hungry all the time and often become overweight as a result. Ⓛ Ⓘ Ⓝ Ⓚ to Learning Objective 9.6.

**THE GONADS** The **gonads** are the sex glands, including the **ovaries** in the female and the **testes** in the male. They secrete hormones that regulate sexual behavior and reproduction. They do not control all sexual behavior, though. In a very real sense, the brain itself is the master of the sexual system—human sexual behavior is not controlled totally by instincts and the actions of the glands as in some parts of the animal world, but it is also affected by psychological factors such as attractiveness. Ⓛ Ⓘ Ⓝ Ⓚ to Learning Objective 10.1.

**THE ADRENAL GLANDS** Everyone has two **adrenal glands**, one on top of each kidney. The origin of the name is simple enough; *renal* comes from a Latin word meaning "kidney" and *ad* is Latin for "to," so *adrenal* means "to or on the kidney." Each adrenal gland is actually divided into two sections, the *adrenal medulla* and the *adrenal cortex*. It is the adrenal medulla that releases epinephrine and norepinephrine when people are under stress and aids in sympathetic arousal.

The adrenal cortex produces more than 30 different hormones called *corticoids* (also called steroids) that regulate salt intake, help initiate* and control stress reactions, and also provide a source of sex hormones in addition to those provided by the gonads. One of the most important of these adrenal hormones is *cortisol*, released when the body experiences stress, both physical stress (such as illness, surgery, or extreme heat or cold) and psychological stress (such as an emotional upset). Cortisol is important in the release of glucose into the bloodstream during stress, providing energy for the brain itself, and the release of fatty acids from the fat cells that provide the muscles with energy.

———————————

*initiate: begin or start.

## Concept Map LO. 2.6, 2.7

**Interactive**

**glands** are organs in the body that secrete chemicals; some affect functioning of the body but not behavior; others have widespread influence on the body and behavior

### Distant Connections: The Endocrine Glands

**endocrine glands** secrete chemicals called *hormones* into bloodstream; affect behavior and emotions by influencing the activity of the brain and by controlling muscles and organs such as the heart, pancreas, and sex organs

- pituitary gland
- pineal gland
- thyroid gland
- pancreas
- gonads
- adrenal glands

Reset

# Practice Quiz   How much do you remember?

*Pick the best answer.*

**1.** Your friend Melissa has suffered from diabetes for her entire life. She regularly tests her blood to make sure her sugar levels are not too high or low. Which gland in her endocrine system is responsible for regulating her blood sugar?
  **a.** pancreas
  **b.** thyroid
  **c.** pituitary
  **d.** adrenal

**2.** Andrew has always been thin. In fact, he often seems to be able to eat whatever he wants without gaining weight. The doctor told his parents that Andrew's _____ gland is the cause of his fast metabolism.
  **a.** pituitary
  **b.** adrenal
  **c.** thyroid
  **d.** pancreas

**3.** Although oxytocin has been tied to a variety of prosocial behaviors such as "love" and "trust," some researchers believe that in humans, it may actually work to increase _____.
  **a.** heart rate and empathy
  **b.** the importance of some social stimuli
  **c.** negative pair bonding
  **d.** social loafing

**4.** Which gland(s) have the greatest influence over other components of the endocrine system?
  **a.** gonads
  **b.** pineal
  **c.** pituitary
  **d.** pancreas

# Looking Inside the Living Brain

Scientists can't be sure what brain tissue really looks like when it's inside the skull of a living person—nor can they be certain that it looks identical to that of a brain sitting on a dissecting table. How can scientists find out if the brain is intact, if parts are missing or damaged, or what the various parts of the brain do?

**METHODS FOR STUDYING SPECIFIC REGIONS OF THE BRAIN**

**2.8  Describe how lesioning studies and brain stimulation are used to study the brain.**

Researchers are able to learn about the brain through accidental damage or through intentional manipulation of brain tissue. When appropriate, such manipulation can be accomplished through lesioning or stimulation methods.

**LESIONING STUDIES**   One way to get some idea of the functions that various areas of the brain control is to study animals or people with damage in those areas. In animals, that may mean researchers will deliberately damage a part of the brain, after which they test the animal to see what has happened to its abilities. In such an experiment, once the test animal is anesthetized and given medication for pain, an electrode, which is a thin wire or probe insulated everywhere but at its tip, is surgically inserted into the brain. An electrical current strong enough to kill off the target neurons is sent through the tip of the wire. This procedure is called **lesioning**.

It should be obvious that researchers cannot destroy areas of brains in living human beings. One method they can use is to study and test people who already have brain damage. However, this is not an ideal way to study the brain. No two case studies of humans are likely to present damage in exactly the same area of the brain, nor would the cases involve exactly the same amount of damage.

**BRAIN STIMULATION**   In contrast to lesioning, a less harmful way to study the brain is to temporarily disrupt or enhance the normal functioning of specific brain areas through electrical stimulation and then study the resulting changes in behavior or cognition. The procedure of stimulating a specific area of the brain is much the same as in lesioning, but the much milder current in this research does no damage to the neurons. It does cause the neurons to react as if they had received a message. This is called *electrical stimulation of the brain*, or *ESB*. It has become an important technique in psychology, as its use in animals (and humans under very special circumstances such as testing before surgery to address seizure disorders) has informed us in many areas of investigation, including new directions for therapy.

**lesioning**
insertion of a thin, insulated electrode into the brain through which an electrical current is sent, destroying the brain cells at the tip of the wire.

**INVASIVE TECHNIQUES: STIMULATING FROM THE INSIDE** A specific type of ESB called *deep brain stimulation (DBS)* has been shown to be very helpful in some disorders in humans. In this procedure, neurosurgeons place electrodes in specific deep-brain areas and then route the electrode wires to a pacemaker-like device called an impulse generator that is surgically implanted under the collarbone. The impulse generator then sends impulses to the implanted electrodes, stimulating the specific brain areas of interest. DBS has been widely used as a treatment for Parkinson's disease and may play an important role in the treatment of seizure disorder, chronic pain, and possibly some psychiatric disorders (Fisher et al., 2010; Rabins et al., 2009; Weaver et al., 2009), among other areas. Also, using DBS for specific disorders allows researchers to learn about other effects DBS may have on the brain such as affecting an individual's mood or memory. It should be noted that invasive techniques such as DBS are typically only used after all other less intrusive treatments have been shown to be ineffective or whose side effects have been deemed undesirable. For example, DBS is being investigated for the treatment of anorexia nervosa in individuals for whom other treatments have not been effective (Lipsman et al., 2013).

One of the newest and fastest developing areas in brain stimulation is *optogenetics*, where neurons can be activated by light rather than electricity. While currently only used in animal models, it is being employed across a variety of areas to enhance our understanding of the brain, cognition, and behavior (Burguière et al., 2013; Miocinovic et al., 2013). Furthermore, the technique is not only being used to refine existing DBS methods, it is also being paired with other methods, such as *fMRI*, to further enhance our understanding of brain function in both normal and disordered behavior (Creed et al., 2015; Ferenczi et al., 2016).

**NONINVASIVE TECHNIQUES: STIMULATING FROM THE OUTSIDE** There are also noninvasive techniques for stimulating the brain that contribute to research and our knowledge of the brain in a variety of areas. In *transcranial magnetic stimulation* (TMS), magnetic pulses are applied to the cortex using special copper wire coils that are positioned over the head. The resulting magnetic fields stimulate neurons in the targeted area of the cortex. Longer-lasting stimulation results when the pulses are administered in a repetitive fashion, which is referred to as *repetitive TMS* (rTMS). Another procedure, called *transcranial direct current stimulation* (tDCS), uses scalp electrodes to pass very low-amplitude direct current to the brain to change the excitability of cortical neurons directly below the electrodes. Both rTMS and tDCS are being evaluated as research tools in studies of cognition such as memory retrieval and decision making (Boggio et al., 2010; Boggio et al., 2009) and as possible treatment options for a variety of psychological disorders including posttraumatic stress disorder (PTSD) and depression and physical disorders due to suffering a stroke (Boggio, Rocha, et al., 2009; Nitsche et al., 2009; Williams et al., 2010).

Bear in mind that stimulating the cortex may facilitate specific functions or behaviors but impair others. For example, if someone is counting from 1 to 20 and the brain is stimulated in the correct location of the motor cortex, the person's speech would be disrupted, but perhaps stimulating in other areas of the frontal lobe may assist the person in attending to the counting task. Furthermore, the brain has widespread connections, so stimulation in one area is likely to affect other areas. In one study, inhibitory stimulation of the left prefrontal cortex resulted in reduced blood oxygenation on both the left and right sides of the prefrontal cortex (Tupak et al., 2013).

**Note:** tDCS is NOT the same as electroconvulsive therapy, which uses much higher levels of current through the entire brain, resulting in a grand mal seizure and changes in the brain chemistry associated with depression. **Ⓛ Ⓘ Ⓝ Ⓚ** to Learning Objective 15.11.

### NEUROIMAGING TECHNIQUES

**2.9** **Compare and contrast neuroimaging techniques for mapping the structure and function of the brain.**

All of these methods of stimulation yield important information about the brain and behavior, but they do not allow us to see what is going on with the brain as a whole.

This person is participating in a study that involves repetitive transcranial magnetic stimulation (rTMS). This procedure uses magnetic pulses to stimulate specific areas of the cortex. rTMS is being used in both studies of cognition, as seen here, and in the exploration of new potential treatments for a variety of psychological disorders.

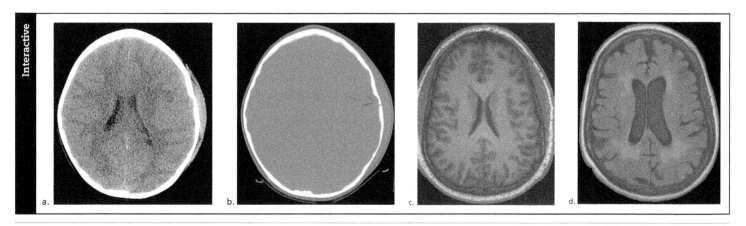

**Figure 2.10**  Mapping Brain Structure

Fig 2.10a: CT scan from a 5-year-old girl with a head injury and skull fracture, depicting the brain and swelling associated with the injury. Fig 2.10b: Same CT scan highlighting the skull fracture (indicated by the red arrow). Contrast the brain detail of Fig 2.10a with the MRI scan in Fig 2.10c (different, adult individual). Note the scans are in the horizontal plane, separating the brain into upper and lower portions. Fig 2.10d: Different type of MRI image from an older adult, with cortical cell loss (atrophy) and white matter changes. Notice the enlarged ventricles and widening of the grooves (sulci) in the outer cortex as compared to 2.10c. Figs 2.10a, b, c, and d images created with OsiriX software; CT and MRI data courtesy of N. White.

Instead, various neuroimaging techniques can do this, either by directly imaging the brain's structure (the different parts) or its function (how the parts work). These methods also vary in their degree of spatial resolution (ability to see fine detail) and temporal resolution (ability to time lock a recorded event).

**MAPPING STRUCTURE**   As hinted at earlier, aside from observing the person's behavior, scientists had to wait until a person died to fully investigate if there were changes or damage to the individual's brain. Fortunately, modern neuroimaging allows us to image the brain's structure while the person is still alive.

**COMPUTED TOMOGRAPHY (CT)**   Scientists have several ways to look inside the human brain without causing harm to the person. One way is to take a series of X-rays of the brain, aided by a computer. This is accomplished during a **CT scan (computed tomography** involves mapping "slices" of the brain by computer). CT scans can show stroke damage, tumors, injuries, and abnormal brain structure. (See **Figure 2.10a**.) A CT scan is also the structural imaging method of choice when there is metal in the body (e.g., a bullet or surgical clips) and useful for imaging possible skull fractures. (See **Figure 2.10b**.)

**MAGNETIC RESONANCE IMAGING (MRI)**   As useful as a CT scan can be for imaging the skull, it doesn't show very small details within the brain. The relatively newer technique of **magnetic resonance imaging, or MRI**, provides much more detail (see **Figure 2.10c** and **Figure 2.10d**), even allowing doctors to see the effects of very small strokes. The person getting an MRI scan is placed inside a machine that generates a powerful magnetic field to align hydrogen atoms in the brain tissues (these normally spin in a random fashion); then radio pulses are used to make the atoms spin at a particular frequency and direction. The time it takes for the atoms to return to their normal spin allows a computer to create a three-dimensional image of the brain and display "slices" of that image on a screen.

Using MRI as a basis, several techniques have been developed that allow us to study other aspects of the brain. *MRI spectroscopy* allows researchers to estimate the concentration of specific chemicals and neurotransmitters in the brain. Another fascinating technique is called *DTI*, or *diffusion tensor imaging*. The brain has two distinct color regions, *gray matter*, the outer areas consisting largely of neurons with unmyelinated axons, and *white matter*, the fiber tracts consisting of myelinated axons (the myelin is responsible for the lighter color). DTI uses MRI technology to provide a way to measure connectivity in the brain by imaging these white matter tracts. DTI has been used to investigate normal

**computed tomography (CT) scan**
brain-imaging method using computer-controlled X-rays of the brain.

**magnetic resonance imaging (MRI)**
brain-imaging method using radio waves and magnetic fields of the body to produce detailed images of the brain.

function, such as structural changes associated with different levels of memory performance, and various disorders and conditions including Alzheimer's disease, MS, and traumatic brain injury (Hayes et al., 2016; Ly et al., 2016; Muthuraman et al., 2016; Wang et al., 2016).

**MAPPING FUNCTION** In addition to imaging the different parts of the brain to understand what may or may not be present, examining the function of the brain is also important in understanding behavior and mental processes.

**THE ELECTROENCEPHALOGRAM (EEG)** As important as imaging brain structure is, it is sometimes important to know how different brain areas function. A fairly harmless way to study the activity of the living brain is to record the electrical activity of the cortex just below the skull using a device called an **electroencephalograph**. The first **electroencephalogram (EEG)** recording in humans was accomplished in 1924 by Hans Berger (Niedermeyer, 2005). Recording the EEG involves using small metal disks or sponge-like electrodes placed directly on the scalp and a special solution to help conduct the electrical signals from the cortex just below. These electrodes are connected to an amplifier and then to a computer to view the information. The resulting electrical output forms waves that indicate many things, such as stages of sleep, seizures, and even the presence of tumors. The EEG can also be used to help determine which areas of the brain are active during various mental tasks that involve memory and attention. EEG activity can be classified according to appearance and frequency, and different waves are associated with different brain activity. For example, *alpha waves* in the back of the brain are one indication of relaxed wakefulness (seen in bottom two lines in **Figure 2.11a**). EEG waveforms are covered in more detail in Chapter Four. (L)(I)(N)K to Learning Objective 4.5.

Another common EEG–based technique focuses on *event-related potentials*, or *ERPs*. In ERP studies, multiple presentations of a stimulus are measured during an EEG and then averaged to remove variations in the ongoing brain activity that is normally recorded during the EEG. The result is a measurement of the response of the brain related to the stimulus event itself, or an event-related potential. ERPs allow the study of different stages of cognitive processing. For example, the use of ERPs has allowed researchers to investigate differences in brain processing associated with the recognition of facial expression of emotion in individuals with and without schizophrenia (Lee et al., 2010). In other studies, ERPs are being studied as a possible method of lie detection (Hu et al., 2013; Labkovsky & Rosenfeld, 2014; Rosenfeld et al., 2008).

**electroencephalogram (EEG)**

a recording of the electrical activity of large groups of cortical neurons just below the skull, most often using scalp electrodes.

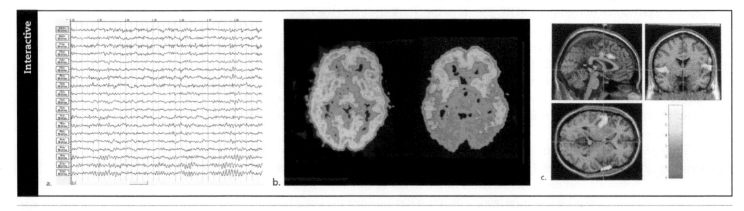

**Figure 2.11** Mapping Brain Function

Various methods for mapping brain function. An EEG record is shown in 2.11a, a PET scan image in 2.11b, and an image from an fMRI study in 2.11c. Data and figure for 2.11a courtesy of N. White.

**MAGNETOENCEPHALOGRAPHY (MEG)**  While the EEG alone does not allow for the direct identification of areas of brain activation, a closely related technique does. *Magneto-encephalography* (MEG) uses devices that are very sensitive to magnetic fields called superconducting quantum interference devices, which are contained in a helmet-like device that is placed over the individual's head. MEG has many applications and is being used to differentiate dementia disorders and to explore cognitive processes in autism (M. A. Williams & Sachdev, 2010).

**POSITRON EMISSION TOMOGRAPHY (PET)**  The functional neuroimaging methods discussed so far rely on the electrical activity of the brain. Other techniques make use of other indicators of brain activity, including energy consumption or changes in blood oxygen levels (if areas of the brain are active, they are likely using fuel and oxygen). In **positron emission tomography (PET)**, the person is injected with a radioactive glucose (a kind of sugar). The computer detects the activity of the brain cells by looking at which cells are using up the radioactive glucose and projecting the image of that activity onto a monitor. The computer uses colors to indicate different levels of brain activity. For example, lighter colors may indicate greater activity. (See **Figure 2.11b**.) With this method, researchers can actually have the person perform different tasks while the computer shows what his or her brain is doing during the task. A related technique is *single photon emission computed tomography (SPECT)*, which measures brain blood flow and takes advantage of more easily obtainable radioactive tracers than those used for PET (Bremmer, 2005).

**FUNCTIONAL MRI (FMRI)**  Although traditional MRI scans only show structure, **functional MRI (fMRI)**, in which the computer tracks changes in the oxygen levels of the blood (see **Figure 2.11c**), provides information on the brain's function as well. By superimposing information about where oxygen is being used in the brain over an image of the brain's structure, researchers can identify what areas of the brain are most active during specific tasks. By combining such images taken over a period of time, a sort of "movie" of the brain's functioning can be made (Lin et al., 2007). Functional MRIs can give more detail, tend to be clearer than PET scans, and are an incredibly useful tool for research into the workings of the brain. For example, fMRI has been used to demonstrate that older adults with a genetic risk for Alzheimer's disease show greater activation in brain areas associated with semantic knowledge and word retrieval when compared to older adults without that genetic risk. This finding may one day help clinicians and researchers identify individuals at risk for Alzheimer's much earlier in the disease process (Wierenga et al., 2010). There is also exciting research suggesting individuals can use fMRI to learn how to regulate their own brain processes. Individuals with schizophrenia were able to use real-time fMRI (rtfMRI) to learn how to control a portion of their brain that ass-ists in recognition of facial emotions, which is a common deficit in schizophrenia (Ruiz et al., 2013). Functional neuroimaging is also helping researchers understand how various types of treatment and therapy affect the brain in a variety of disorders (Ball et al., 2014; Fournier & Price, 2014; Miller et al., 2015).

## THINKING CRITICALLY

You may see a lot of brain imaging studies in the news or on the Internet. Thinking back to the research methods discussed in Chapter One (Learning Objectives 1.6 through 1.11), what kinds of questions should you ask about these studies before accepting the findings as valid?

▶  The response entered here will be saved to your notes and may be
   collected by your instructor if he/she requires it.

 Submit

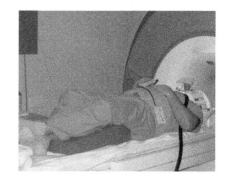

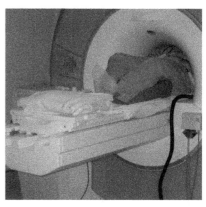

As part of an fMRI study on attention, one of your authors is fitted with headphones, an angled mirror, and a hand response pad. During the study, the headphones will allow him to hear audio instructions and stimuli, and the mirror will allow him to view task items projected on a rear screen placed outside of the scanner. The response pad is used to indicate answers for the various tasks.

**positron emission tomography (PET)**

brain-imaging method in which a radioactive sugar is injected into the subject and a computer compiles a color-coded image of the activity of the brain.

**functional magnetic resonance imaging (fMRI)**

MRI-based brain-imaging method that allows for functional examination of brain areas through changes in brain oxygenation.

## Concept Map LO. 2.8, 2.9

Interactive

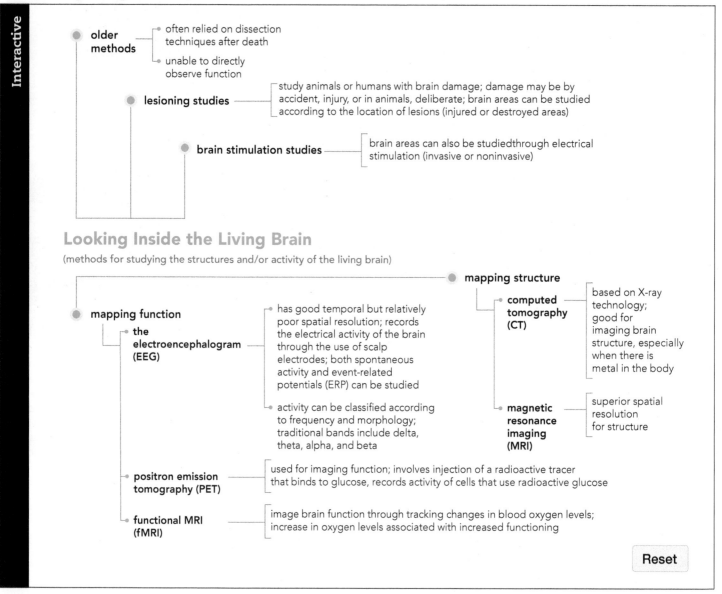

- **older methods**
  - often relied on dissection techniques after death
  - unable to directly observe function

- **lesioning studies** — study animals or humans with brain damage; damage may be by accident, injury, or in animals, deliberate; brain areas can be studied according to the location of lesions (injured or destroyed areas)

- **brain stimulation studies** — brain areas can also be studied through electrical stimulation (invasive or noninvasive)

### Looking Inside the Living Brain

(methods for studying the structures and/or activity of the living brain)

- **mapping structure**
  - **computed tomography (CT)** — based on X-ray technology; good for imaging brain structure, especially when there is metal in the body
  - **magnetic resonance imaging (MRI)** — superior spatial resolution for structure

- **mapping function**
  - **the electroencephalogram (EEG)**
    - has good temporal but relatively poor spatial resolution; records the electrical activity of the brain through the use of scalp electrodes; both spontaneous activity and event-related potentials (ERP) can be studied
    - activity can be classified according to frequency and morphology; traditional bands include delta, theta, alpha, and beta
  - **positron emission tomography (PET)** — used for imaging function; involves injection of a radioactive tracer that binds to glucose, records activity of cells that use radioactive glucose
  - **functional MRI (fMRI)** — image brain function through tracking changes in blood oxygen levels; increase in oxygen levels associated with increased functioning

Reset

# Practice Quiz    How much do you remember?

*Pick the best answer.*

1. Which of the following techniques involves passing a mild current through the brain to activate certain structures without damaging them?
   a. electroconvulsive tomography (ECT)
   b. magnetic resonance imaging (MRI)
   c. deep brain lesioning
   d. electrical stimulation of the brain (ESB)

2. Which of the following techniques analyzes blood oxygen levels to look at the functioning of the brain?
   a. EEG
   b. CT
   c. fMRI
   d. PET

3. Dr. Roll is conducting a research study. She wants to measure the physical connectivity in the research participants' brains by imaging their white matter. Which of the following methods will she use?
   a. diffusion tensor imaging (DTI)
   b. MRI spectroscopy
   c. functional magnetic resonance imaging (fMRI)
   d. computed tomography (CT)

4. If you were suffering from neurological problems and your neurologist wanted to have a study done of your brain and its electrical functioning, which of the following techniques would be most appropriate?
   a. PTI
   b. EEG
   c. PET
   d. DTI

# From the Bottom Up: The Structures of the Brain

 💬 Okay, now I understand a little more about how we look inside the brain. What exactly IS inside the brain?

Now it's time to look at the various structures of the brain, starting from the bottom and working up to the top. The video *Parts of the Brain* describes the major parts of the brain and their functions. This text won't be discussing every single part of the brain, only major areas of interest to psychologists as explorers of behavior. Many areas also have multiple roles, but a full understanding of the brain is not possible within one chapter of an introductory psychology text. Furthermore, while there may be brain and behavior differences according to sex or gender, despite what you may have read in the popular press, there is little evidence of people having a "female" versus a "male" brain (Joel et al., 2015). Human brains can simply not be categorized that way.

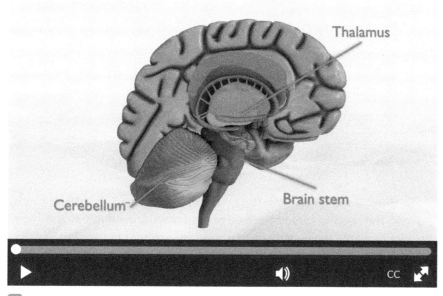

👁 **Watch** the **Video** *Parts of the Brain*

## THE HINDBRAIN

**2.10** **Identify the different structures of the hindbrain and the function of each.**

The brain can be divided into three main divisions early in our development that later subdivide into smaller divisions. The three primary divisions are the forebrain, the midbrain, and the hindbrain. The forebrain includes the cortex, the basal ganglia, and the limbic system. The midbrain is important for both sensory and motor functions. The hindbrain includes the medulla, pons, and cerebellum.

**MEDULLA**    The **medulla** is located at the top of the spinal column. In **Figure 2.12**, it is the first "swelling" at the top of the spinal cord, just at the very bottom of the brain. This is the part of the brain that a person would least want to have damaged, as it controls life-sustaining functions such as heartbeat, breathing, and swallowing. It is in the medulla that the sensory nerves coming from the left and right sides of the body cross over, so that sensory information from the left side of the body goes to the right side of the brain and vice versa.

**medulla**

the first large swelling at the top of the spinal cord, forming the lowest part of the brain, which is responsible for life-sustaining functions such as breathing, swallowing, and heart rate.

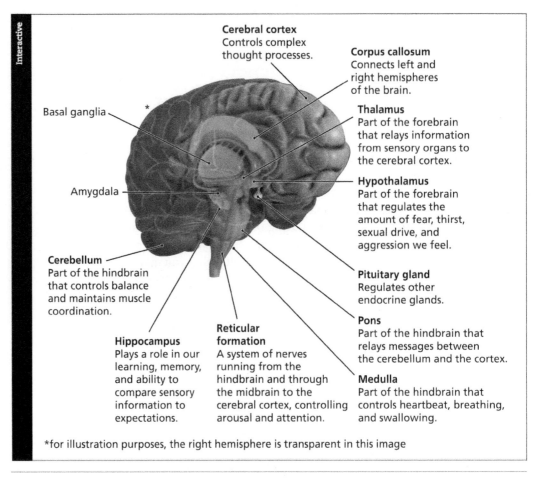

**Figure 2.12**  Major Structures of the Human Brain

**PONS**  The **pons** is the larger "swelling" just above the medulla. This term means "bridge," and the pons is indeed the bridge between the cerebellum and the upper sections of the brain. As in the medulla, there is a crossover of nerves, but in this case it is the motor nerves carrying messages from the brain to the body. This allows the pons to coordinate the movements of the left and right sides of the body. (It will be useful to remember these nerve crossovers when reading about the functions of the left and right sides of the brain in a later part of this chapter.) The pons also influences sleep, dreaming, and arousal. The role that the pons plays in sleep and dreams will be discussed in more detail in Chapter Four. **(L)(I)(N)K** to Learning Objective 4.7.

**THE RETICULAR FORMATION**  The **reticular formation (RF)** is a network of neurons running through the middle of the medulla and the pons and slightly beyond. These neurons are responsible for people's ability to generally attend to certain kinds of information in their surroundings. Basically, the RF allows people to ignore constant, unchanging information (such as the noise of an air conditioner) and become alert to changes in information (for example, if the air conditioner stopped, most people would notice immediately).

The reticular formation is also the part of the brain that helps keep people alert and aroused. One part of the RF is called the *reticular activating system* (RAS), and it stimulates the upper part of the brain, keeping people awake and alert. When a person is driving and someone suddenly pulls out in front of the vehicle, it is the RAS that brings that driver to full attention. It is also the system that lets a mother hear her baby cry in the night, even though she might sleep through other noises. The RAS has also been suggested by brain-scanning studies as a possible area involved in attention-deficit/hyperactivity

**pons**

the larger swelling above the medulla that relays information from the cortex to the cerebellum, and that plays a part in sleep, dreaming, left-right body coordination, and arousal.

**reticular formation (RF)**

an area of neurons running through the middle of the medulla and the pons and slightly beyond that is responsible for general attention, alertness, and arousal.

disorder, in which children or adults have difficulty maintaining attention to a single task (Durston, 2003).

Studies have shown that when the RF of rats is electrically stimulated while they are sleeping, they immediately awaken. If the RF is destroyed (by deep lesioning, for example), they fall into a sleeplike coma from which they never awaken (Moruzzi & Magoun, 1949; Steriade & McCarley, 1990). The RF is also implicated in comas in humans (Plum & Posner, 1985).

**CEREBELLUM** At the base of the skull, behind the pons and below the main part of the brain, is a structure that looks like a small brain. This is the **cerebellum** (meaning "little brain"). The cerebellum is the part of the lower brain that controls all involuntary, rapid, fine motor movement. People can sit upright because the cerebellum controls all the little muscles needed to keep them from falling out of their chair. It also coordinates voluntary movements that have to happen in rapid succession, such as walking, skating, dancing, playing a musical instrument, and even the movements of speech. Learned reflexes, skills, and habits are also stored here, which allows them to become more or less automatic. Because of the cerebellum, people don't have to consciously think about their posture, muscle tone, and balance.

🗨 So if your cerebellum is damaged, you might be very uncoordinated?

This gymnast must count on her cerebellum to help her balance and coordinate the many fine motor commands that allow her to balance on this narrow beam. What other kinds of professions depend heavily on the activity of the cerebellum?

Yes. In fact, this happens in a disease called *spinocerebellar degeneration*, where the first symptoms of cerebellum deterioration are tremors, an unsteady walk, slurred speech, dizziness, and muscle weakness. The person suffering from this disease will eventually be unable to walk, stand, or even get a spoon to his or her own mouth (Schöls et al., 1998). These symptoms are similar to what one might see in a person who is suffering from alcohol intoxication.

Just like we are starting to better understand the various roles of glial cells, researchers and scientists are still working to better understand other functions of the cerebellum. Research suggests the cerebellum is involved in much more than motor control and may be involved with a variety of higher functions, with parts of the cerebellum activated during sensorimotor tasks and other parts involved in cognitive or emotional tasks (Stoodley & Schmahmann, 2009). Research continues to investigate the role of the cerebellum in these and other tasks once believed to be the domain of other lobes of the brain, in a large part by examining the connections between the cerebellum and other functional areas and patterns of brain activation during specific tasks (Strick et al., 2009; Voogd & Ruigrok, 2012). Studies using fMRI have investigated such higher-level cognitive functions as language and working memory and the timing of perceptual tasks like visual attention (Kellermann et al., 2012; Stoodley et al., 2012). While much is still to be learned, evidence exists that the cerebellum is involved in both perceptual processes and disorders that are characterized by perceptual disturbances such as schizophrenia and autism spectrum disorder (Baumann et al., 2015).

### STRUCTURES UNDER THE CORTEX: THE LIMBIC SYSTEM

**2.11** Identify the structures of the brain that are involved in emotion, learning, memory, and motivation.

The forebrain includes the two cerebral hemispheres of the brain, including the cortex, which is discussed in detail later in this chapter, and a number of important structures located under the cortex in each hemisphere. These subcortical structures (the prefix *sub* means "under" or "below") play a part in our thinking and behavior. While there are subcortical structures that influence motor control and the learning of motor skills, the *basal ganglia*, and white matter fiber pathways that connect the cortex to other parts of the

**cerebellum**

part of the lower brain located behind the pons that controls and coordinates involuntary, rapid, fine motor movement, and may have some cognitive functions.

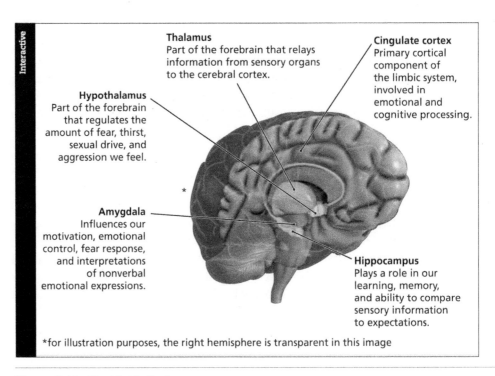

Interactive

**Thalamus**
Part of the forebrain that relays information from sensory organs to the cerebral cortex.

**Cingulate cortex**
Primary cortical component of the limbic system, involved in emotional and cognitive processing.

**Hypothalamus**
Part of the forebrain that regulates the amount of fear, thirst, sexual drive, and aggression we feel.

**Amygdala**
Influences our motivation, emotional control, fear response, and interpretations of nonverbal emotional expressions.

**Hippocampus**
Plays a role in our learning, memory, and ability to compare sensory information to expectations.

*for illustration purposes, the right hemisphere is transparent in this image

**Figure 2.13** The Limbic System

**limbic system**

a group of several brain structures located primarily under the cortex and involved in learning, emotion, memory, and motivation.

**thalamus**

part of the limbic system located in the center of the brain, this structure relays sensory information from the lower part of the brain to the proper areas of the cortex and processes some sensory information before sending it to its proper area.

**olfactory bulbs**

two bulb-like projections of the brain located just above the sinus cavity and just below the frontal lobes that receive information from the olfactory receptor cells.

**hypothalamus**

small structure in the brain located below the thalamus and directly above the pituitary gland, responsible for motivational behavior such as sleep, hunger, thirst, and sex.

**hippocampus**

curved structure located within each temporal lobe, responsible for the formation of long-term declarative memories.

brain and spinal cord, we will focus on the subcortical structures that have been collectively referred to as the *limbic system*. (See **Figure 2.13**.)

The **limbic system** (the word *limbic* means limbus or "margin," referring to a border around something, and these structures are found between the upper brain and brain stem) includes the thalamus, hypothalamus, hippocampus, amygdala, and the cingulate cortex. In general, the limbic system is involved in emotions, motivation, memory, and learning.

**THALAMUS**   The **thalamus** ("inner chamber") is in some ways similar to a triage* nurse. This somewhat round structure in the center of the brain acts as a kind of relay station for incoming sensory information. Like a nurse, the thalamus might perform some processing of that sensory information before sending it on to the part of the cortex that deals with that kind of sensation—hearing, sight, touch, or taste. Damage to the thalamus might result in the loss or partial loss of any or all of those sensations. Recent research has also suggested the thalamus may affect the functioning of task-specific regions of the cortex. For example, a study of children with dyslexia found abnormal connections between the thalamus and brain areas associated with reading behavior (Fan et al., 2014).

The sense of smell is unique in that signals from the neurons in the sinus cavity go directly into special parts of the brain called **olfactory bulbs**, just under the front part of the brain. Smell is the only sense that does not have to first pass through the thalamus.

**HYPOTHALAMUS**   A very small but extremely powerful part of the brain is located just below and in front of the thalamus (see **Figure 2.13**). The **hypothalamus** ("below the inner chamber") regulates body temperature, thirst, hunger, sleeping and waking, sexual activity, and emotions. It sits right above the pituitary gland. The hypothalamus controls the pituitary, so the ultimate regulation of hormones lies with the hypothalamus.

**HIPPOCAMPUS**   Like many structures in the brain, the **hippocampus** was named based on its appearance. Hippocampus is the Greek word for "seahorse," and it was

---

*triage: a process for sorting injured people into groups based on their need for, or likely benefit from, immediate medical treatment.

given to this brain structure because the first scientists who dissected the brain thought it looked like a seahorse. The hippocampus is located within the medial temporal lobe on each side of the brain (medial means "toward the middle"). Research has shown that the hippocampus is instrumental in forming long-term (permanent) declarative memories that are then stored elsewhere in the brain (Squire & Kandel, 2009). (L)(I)(N)K to Learning Objective 6.12. As mentioned earlier, ACh, the neurotransmitter involved in muscle control, is also involved in the memory function of the hippocampus. People who have Alzheimer's disease, for example, have much lower levels of ACh in that structure than is normal, and the drugs given to these people boost the levels of ACh.

**AMYGDALA**    The **amygdala** ("almond") is another area of the brain named for its shape and appearance. It is located near the hippocampus. The amygdala is involved in fear responses and memory of fear. Information from the senses goes to the amygdala before the upper part of the brain is even involved, so that people can respond to danger very quickly, sometimes before they are consciously aware of what is happening. In 1939 researchers found that monkeys with large amounts of their temporal lobes removed—including the amygdala—were completely unafraid of snakes and humans, both normally fear-provoking stimuli (Klüver & Bucy, 1939). This effect came to be known as the *Klüver-Bucy syndrome*. Rats that have damaged amygdala structures will also show no fear when placed next to a cat (Maren & Fanselow, 1996). Case studies of humans with damage to the amygdala also show a link to decreased fear response (Adolphs et al., 2005). Although the amygdala plays a vital role in forming emotional memories, it is still unclear if the memories are stored in the amygdala (Squire & Kandel, 2009). One study has suggested activity in the amygdala impacts hippocampal neuroplasticity by facilitating structural changes in the hippocampus, possibly underlying the influence of stress on fear memories (Giachero et al., 2015).

**CINGULATE CORTEX**    The *cingulate cortex* is the limbic structure that is actually found in the cortex. It is found right above the corpus callosum in the frontal and parietal lobes and plays an important role in both emotional and cognitive processing. The cingulate cortex can be divided into up to four regions that play different roles in processing emotional, cognitive, and autonomic information (Vogt & Palomero-Gallagher, 2012). It has been shown to be active during a variety of cognitive tasks such as selective attention, written word recognition, and working memory (Cabeza & Nyberg, 2000) and has been implicated in a variety of psychological and mental disorders including attention-deficit/hyperactivity disorder (Bush et al., 1999; Bush et al., 2008), schizophrenia, major depressive disorder, and bipolar disorder (Fornito et al., 2009; Maletic et al., 2007). The next section further explores the cortex and its functions.

### THE CORTEX

**2.12** Identify the parts of the cortex that process the different senses and those that control movement of the body.

As stated earlier, the **cortex** ("rind" or outer covering) is the outermost part of the brain, which is the part of the brain most people picture when they think of what the brain looks like. It is made up of tightly packed neurons and actually is only about one tenth of an inch thick on average (Fischl et al., 2001; MacDonald et al., 2000; Zilles, 1990). The cortex is very recognizable surface anatomy because it is full of wrinkles.

 Why is the cortex so wrinkled?

The wrinkling of the cortex allows a much larger area of cortical cells to exist in the small space inside the skull. If the cortex were to be taken out, ironed flat, and measured, it would be about 2 to 3 square feet. (The owner of the cortex would also be dead, but that's fairly obvious, right?) As the brain develops before birth, it forms a smooth outer

This young woman's thirst is regulated by her hypothalamus.

**amygdala**

brain structure located near the hippocampus, responsible for fear responses and memory of fear.

**cortex**

outermost covering of the brain consisting of densely packed neurons, responsible for higher thought processes and interpretation of sensory input.

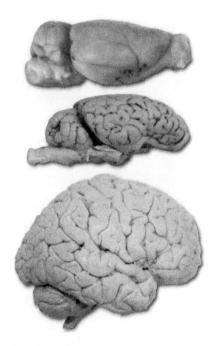

From top to bottom, a rat brain, sheep brain, and human brain (not to scale!). Note the differences in the amount of corticalization, or wrinkling, of the cortex between these three brains. Greater amounts of corticalization are associated with increases in size and complexity.

covering on all the other brain structures. This will be the cortex, which will get more and more wrinkled as the brain increases in size and complexity. This increase in wrinkling is called "corticalization."

**CEREBRAL HEMISPHERES**   The cortex is divided into two sections called the **cerebral hemispheres**, which are connected by a thick, tough band of neural fibers (axons) called the **corpus callosum** (literally meaning "hard body," as calluses on the feet are hard). (Refer to Figure 2.12.) The corpus callosum allows the left and right hemispheres to communicate with each other. Each hemisphere can be roughly divided into four sections or lobes by looking at the deeper wrinkles, or fissures, in its surface. The lobes are named for the skull bones that cover them (see **Figure 2.14**).

   Another organizational feature of the cortex is that for specific regions, each hemisphere is responsible for the opposite side of the body, either for control or for receiving information. For example, the motor cortex controls the muscles on the opposite side of the body. If we are writing with our right hand, the motor cortex in the left hemisphere is responsible for controlling those movements. This feature, referred to as *contralateral organization*, plays a role in information coming from many of the sense organs to the brain and in the motor commands originating in the brain going to the rest of the body.

   Information from our body can also be transmitted to both sides of the brain, or *bilaterally* (as in hearing and vision), or to only one side of the brain, or *ipsilaterally* (as in taste and olfaction). These aspects are also important in the study of *brain lateralization*, which we will come back to later in the chapter. Why do we have this arrangement for some functions and not for others? No one really knows, but at least for some information, it assists with identifying where information from the environment is coming from. For auditory information from the ears, having sensory information projected to both hemispheres allows us to localize sounds by comparing the slightly different information coming from each ear.

**OCCIPITAL LOBES**   At the base of the cortex, toward the back of the brain, is an area called the **occipital lobe**. This area processes visual information from the eyes in the *primary visual cortex*. The *visual association cortex*, also in this lobe and in parts of the

**cerebral hemispheres**

the two sections of the cortex on the left and right sides of the brain.

**corpus callosum**

thick band of neurons that connects the right and left cerebral hemispheres.

**occipital lobe**

section of the brain located at the rear and bottom of each cerebral hemisphere containing the primary visual centers of the brain.

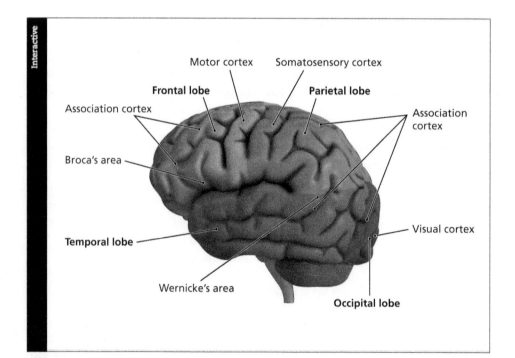

**Figure 2.14**   Lobes and Cortical Areas of the Brain

temporal and parietal lobes, helps identify and make sense of the visual information from the eyes. The famed neurologist Oliver Sacks once had a patient who had a tumor in his right occipital lobe area. He could still see objects and even describe them in physical terms, but he could not identify them by sight alone. When given a rose, the man began to describe it as a "red inflorescence" of some type with a green tubular projection. Only when he held it under his nose (stimulating the sense of smell) did he recognize it as a rose (Sacks, 1990). Each area of the cortex has these association areas that help people make sense of sensory information.

**PARIETAL LOBES**    The **parietal lobes** are at the top and back of the brain, just under the parietal bone in the skull. This area contains the **somatosensory cortex**, an area of neurons (see **Figure 2.15**) at the front of the parietal lobes on either side of the brain. This area processes information from the skin and internal body receptors for touch, temperature, and body position. The somatosensory cortex is laid out in a rather interesting way—the cells at the top of the brain receive information from the bottom of the body, and as one moves down the area, the signals come from higher and higher in the body. It's almost as if a little upside-down person were laid out along this area of cells.

**TEMPORAL LOBES**    The beginnings of the **temporal lobes** are found just behind the temples of the head. These lobes contain the *primary auditory cortex* and the *auditory association area*. Also found in the left temporal lobe is an area that in most people is particularly involved with language. We have already discussed some of the medial structures of the temporal lobe, the amygdala and hippocampus, that are involved in aspects of learning and memory. There are also parts of the temporal lobe that help us process visual information.

**FRONTAL LOBES**    These lobes are at the front of the brain, hence, the name **frontal lobes**. (It doesn't often get this easy in psychology; feel free to take a moment to appreciate it.) Here are found all the higher mental functions of the brain—planning, personality, memory storage, complex decision making, and (again in the left hemisphere in most people) areas devoted to language. The frontal lobe also helps in controlling emotions by means of its connection to the limbic system. The most forward part of the frontal lobes is called the prefrontal cortex. The middle area toward the center (medial prefrontal cortex) and bottom surface above the eyes (orbitofrontal prefrontal cortex—right above the orbits of the eye) have strong connections to the limbic system. Phineas Gage, who was mentioned in Chapter One, suffered damage to his left frontal lobe (Ratiu et al., 2004). He lacked emotional control for some time immediately after the accident because of the damage to his prefrontal and orbitofrontal cortex, and the connections with limbic system structures. Overall, he had connections damaged from the left frontal cortex to many other parts of the brain (Van Horn et al., 2012). People with damage to the frontal lobe may also experience problems with performing mental or motor tasks, such as getting stuck on one step in a process or on one wrong answer in a test and repeating it over and over again, or making the same movement over and over, a phenomenon called *perseveration* (Asp & Tranel, 2013; Luria, 1965).

The frontal lobes also contain the **motor cortex**, a band of neurons located at the back of each lobe. (See **Figure 2.15**.) These cells control the movements of the body's voluntary muscles by sending commands out to the somatic division of the peripheral nervous system. The motor cortex is laid out just like the somatosensory cortex, which is right next door in the parietal lobes.

This area of the brain has been the focus of a great deal of research, specifically as related to the role of a special type of neuron. These neurons are called **mirror neurons**, which fire when an animal performs an action—but they also fire when an animal observes that same action being performed by another. Previous brain-imaging studies in humans suggested that we, too, have mirror neurons in this area of the brain (Buccino et al., 2001;

This boxer must rely on his parietal lobes to sense where his body is in relation to the floor of the ring and the other boxer, his occipital lobes to see his target, and his frontal lobes to guide his hand and arm into the punch.

**parietal lobes**

sections of the brain located at the top and back of each cerebral hemisphere containing the centers for touch, temperature, and body position.

**somatosensory cortex**

area of cortex at the front of the parietal lobes responsible for processing information from the skin and internal body receptors for touch, temperature, and body position.

**temporal lobes**

areas of the cortex located along the side of the brain, starting just behind the temples, containing the neurons responsible for the sense of hearing and meaningful speech.

**frontal lobes**

areas of the brain located in the front and top, responsible for higher mental processes and decision making as well as the production of fluent speech.

**motor cortex**

rear section of the frontal lobe, responsible for sending motor commands to the muscles of the somatic nervous system.

**mirror neurons**

neurons that fire when an animal or person performs an action and also when an animal or person observes that same action being performed by another.

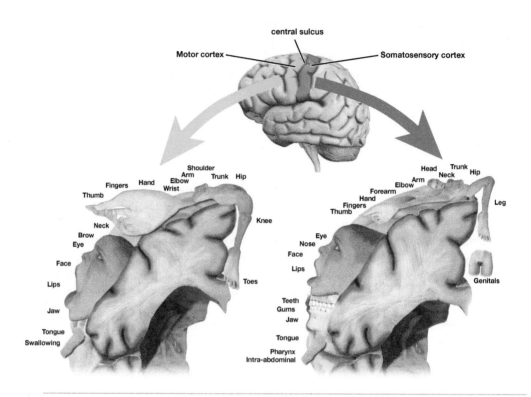

**Figure 2.15** The Motor and Somatosensory Cortex

The motor cortex in the frontal lobe controls the voluntary muscles of the body. Cells at the top of the motor cortex control muscles at the bottom of the body, whereas cells at the bottom of the motor cortex control muscles at the top of the body. Body parts are drawn larger or smaller according to the number of cortical cells devoted to that body part. For example, the hand has many small muscles and requires a larger area of cortical cells to control it. The somatosensory cortex, located in the parietal lobe just behind the motor cortex, is organized in much the same manner and receives information about the sense of touch and body position.

As this boy imitates the motions his father goes through while shaving, certain areas of his brain are more active than others, areas that control the motions of shaving. But even if the boy were only *watching* his father, those same neural areas would be active—the neurons in the boy's brain would *mirror* the actions of the father he is observing.

**association areas**

areas within each lobe of the cortex responsible for the coordination and interpretation of information, as well as higher mental processing.

Buccino et al., 2004; Iacoboni et al., 1999). However, single-cell and multicell recordings in humans have demonstrated that neurons with mirroring functions are found not only in motor regions but also in parts of the brain involved in vision and memory, suggesting such neurons provide much more information than previously thought about our own actions as compared to the actions of others (Mukamel et al., 2010). These findings may have particular relevance for better understanding or treating specific clinical conditions that are believed to involve a faulty mirror system in the brain, such as autism (Oberman & Ramachandran, 2007; Rizzolatti et al., 2009). (L I N K) to Learning Objective 8.7.

### THE ASSOCIATION AREAS OF THE CORTEX

**2.13** **Name the parts of the cortex that are responsible for higher forms of thought, such as language.**

You've mentioned association cortex a few times. Do the other lobes of the brain contain association cortex as well?

**Association areas** are made up of neurons in the cortex that are devoted to making connections between the sensory information coming into the brain and stored memories, images, and knowledge. In other words, association areas help people make sense of the incoming sensory input. Although association areas in the occipital and temporal lobes have already been mentioned, much of the brain's association cortex is in the frontal lobes. Furthermore, some special association areas are worth talking about in more detail.

**BROCA'S AREA**   In the left frontal lobe of most people is an area of the brain associated with the production of speech. (In a small portion of the population, this area is in the right frontal lobe.) More specifically, this area allows a person to speak smoothly and fluently. It is called *Broca's area* after nineteenth-century neurologist Paul Broca, who first provided widely accepted clinical evidence that deficits in fluent and articulate speech result from damage to this area (Finger, 1994). However, it appears that Broca's area is not responsible for the production of speech itself but rather for the interaction between frontal, temporal, and motor areas responsible for speech production (Flinker et al., 2015). Damage to Broca's area causes a person to be unable to get words out in a smooth, connected fashion. People with this condition may know exactly what they want to say and understand what they hear others say, but they cannot control the actual production of their own words. Speech is halting and words are often mispronounced, such as saying "cot" instead of "clock" or "non" instead of "nine." Some words may be left out entirely, such as "the" or "for." This is called **Broca's aphasia**. *Aphasia* refers to an inability to use or understand either written or spoken language (Goodglass et al., 2001). (Stuttering is a somewhat different problem in getting words *started* rather than mispronouncing them or leaving them out, but it may also be related to Broca's area.)

**WERNICKE'S AREA**   In the left temporal lobe (again, in most people) is an area called *Wernicke's area*, named after the physiologist and Broca's contemporary, Carl Wernicke, who first studied problems arising from damage in this location. This area of the brain appears to be involved in understanding the meaning of words (Goodglass et al., 2001). A person with **Wernicke's aphasia** would be able to speak fluently and pronounce words correctly, but the words would be the wrong ones entirely. For example, Elsie suffered a stroke to the temporal lobe, damaging this area of the brain. As the ER nurse inflated a blood pressure cuff, Elsie said, "Oh, that's so Saturday hard." Elsie *thought* she was making sense. She also had trouble understanding what the people around her were saying to her. In another instance, Ernest suffered a stroke at the age of 80 and also showed signs of Wernicke's aphasia. For example, he asked his wife to get him some milk out of the air conditioner. Right idea, wrong word. To hear audio examples of aphasia, (( Listen to the **Audio File** Broca's Aphasia, and (( Listen to the **Audio File** Wernicke's Aphasia.

**Broca's aphasia**

condition resulting from damage to Broca's area, causing the affected person to be unable to speak fluently, to mispronounce words, and to speak haltingly.

**Wernicke's aphasia**

condition resulting from damage to Wernicke's area, causing the affected person to be unable to understand or produce meaningful language.

As this woman applies make-up to the right side of her face, is she really "seeing" the left side? If she has spatial neglect, the answer is "no." While her eyes work just fine, her damaged right hemisphere refuses to notice the left side of her visual field.

# Classic Studies in Psychology
## Through the Looking Glass—Spatial Neglect

Dr. V. S. Ramachandran reported in his fascinating book, *Phantoms in the Brain* (Ramachandran & Blakeslee, 1998), the case of a woman with an odd set of symptoms. When Ellen's son came to visit her, he was shocked and puzzled by his formerly neat and fastidious* mother's appearance. The woman who had always taken pride in her looks, who always had her hair perfectly done and her nails perfectly manicured, looked messy and totally odd. Her hair was uncombed on the left side. Her green shawl was hanging neatly over her right shoulder but hanging onto the floor on the left. Her lipstick was neatly applied to the right side of her lips, and *only to the right side—the left side of her face was completely bare of makeup!* Yet her eyeliner, mascara, and blush were all neatly applied to the right side of her face.

What was wrong? The son called the doctor and was told that his mother's stroke had left her with a condition called **spatial neglect**, or unilateral neglect, in which a person with damage to the right parietal and occipital lobes of the cortex will ignore

*fastidious: having demanding standards, difficult to please.

everything in the left visual field. Damage to areas of the frontal and temporal lobes may also play a part along with the parietal damage. Spatial neglect can affect the left hemisphere, but this condition occurs less frequently and in a much milder form than right-hemisphere neglect (Corbetta et al., 2005; Heilman et al., 1993; Springer & Deutsch, 1998).

When the doctor examined this woman, he tried to get her to notice her left side by holding up a mirror (remember, she was not blind—she just would not notice anything on her left side unless her attention was specifically called to it). She responded correctly when asked what the mirror was and she was able to describe her appearance correctly, but when an assistant held a pen just within the woman's reach, reflected in the mirror on her left side, she tried to reach *through the mirror* to get the pen with her good right hand. When the doctor told her that he wanted her to grab the real object and not the image of it in the mirror, she told him that the pen was *behind* the mirror and even tried to reach around to get it.

Clearly, persons suffering from spatial neglect can no longer perceive the world in the same way as other people do. For these people, the left sides of objects, bodies, and spaces are somewhere "through the looking glass."

### Questions for Further Discussion

1. If a person with spatial neglect only eats the food on the right side of the plate, what could caregivers do to help that person get enough to eat?

2. What other odd things might a person with spatial neglect do that a person with normal functioning would not? What other things might a person with spatial neglect fail to do?

**THE CEREBRAL HEMISPHERES: ARE YOU IN YOUR RIGHT MIND?**

**2.14** **Explain how some brain functions differ between the left and right hemispheres.**

💬 I've heard that some people are right brained and some are left brained. Are the two sides of the brain really that different?

Most people tend to think of the two cerebral hemispheres as identical twins. Both sides have the same four lobes and are arranged in much the same way. But language seems to be confined to only the left hemisphere in about 90 percent of the population (Toga & Thompson, 2003). What other special tasks do the two halves of the **cerebrum** (the upper part of the brain consisting of the two hemispheres and the structures connecting them) engage in, and how do researchers know about such functions? Participate in the experiment simulation *Hemispheric Specialization* to test the language abilities of the two hemispheres 🔘 **Simulate** the **Experiment,** *Hemispheric Specialization.*

**SPLIT-BRAIN RESEARCH**    Roger Sperry was a pioneer in the field of hemisphere specialization. He won a Nobel Prize for his work in demonstrating that the left and right hemispheres of the brain specialize in different activities and functions (Sperry, 1968). In looking for a way to cure epilepsy (severe muscle spasms or seizures resulting from brain damage), Sperry cut through the corpus callosum, the thick band of neural fibers that joins the two hemispheres. In early research with animals, this technique worked and seemed to have no side effects. The first people to have this procedure done also experienced relief from their severe epileptic symptoms, but testing found that (in a sense) they now had two brains in one body.

The special testing involves sending messages to only one side of the brain, which is now possible because the connecting tissue, the corpus callosum, has been cut. Remember that each hemisphere is largely responsible for controlling, or receiving information from, the opposite side of the body. **Figure 2.16** shows what happens with a typical split-brain patient.

**spatial neglect**

condition produced most often by damage to the parietal lobe association areas of the right hemisphere, resulting in an inability to recognize objects or body parts in the left visual field.

**cerebrum**

the upper part of the brain consisting of the two hemispheres and the structures that connect them.

Interactive

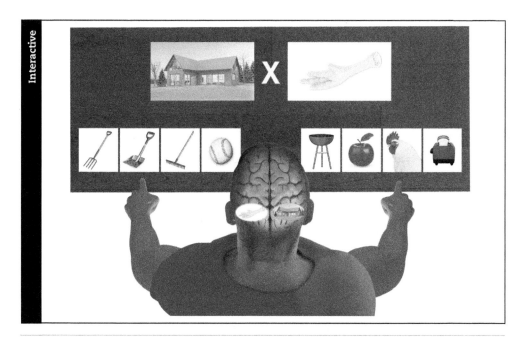

**Figure 2.16**   The Split-Brain Experiment

Building off methods developed by Roger Sperry, Michael Gazzaniga and Joseph LeDoux used this simultaneous concept test to further investigate functions of the left and right hemispheres of the brain

In a split-brain patient, if a picture of a ball is flashed to the right side of the screen, the image of the ball will be sent to the left occipital lobe. The person will be able to say that he or she sees a ball. If a picture of a hammer is flashed to the left side of the screen, the person will not be able to *verbally* identify the object or be able to state with any certainty that something was seen. But if the left *hand* (controlled by the right hemisphere) is used, the person can point to the hammer he or she "didn't see." The right occipital lobe clearly saw the hammer, but the person could not *verbalize* that fact (Sperry, 1968). By doing studies such as these, researchers have found that the left hemisphere specializes in language, speech, handwriting, calculation (math), sense of time and rhythm (which is mathematical in nature), and basically any kind of thought requiring analysis. The right hemisphere appears to specialize in more global (widespread) processing involving perception, visualization, spatial perception, recognition of patterns, faces, emotions, melodies, and expression of emotions. It also comprehends simple language but does not produce speech. (See **Table 2.2**.)

In general, the left hemisphere processes information in a sequence and is good at breaking things down into smaller parts, or performing analysis (Springer & Deutsch, 1998). The right hemisphere, by contrast, processes information all at once and simultaneously, a more global or holistic* style of processing. Remember the discussion in Chapter One of the early days of psychology, the structuralists, and the Gestalt psychologists? One could almost say that the left hemisphere of the brain is a structuralist who wants to break everything down into its smallest parts, and the right side of the brain is a Gestaltist, who wants to study only the whole.

💬 So there really are left-brained and right-brained people?

Actually, unless one is a split-brain patient, the two sides of the brain are always working together as an integrated whole. For example, the right side might recognize someone's face, while the left side struggles to recall the person's name. People aren't really left- or right-brained, they are "whole-brained." Michael Gazzaniga was one of Roger Sperry's students, his collaborator, and is a long-time researcher in the area of brain asymmetry and cognitive neuroscience. Gazzaniga's continuing work in brain lateralization has led to insights

*holistic: relating to or concerned with complete systems or wholes.

**Table 2.2** Specialization of the Two Hemispheres

| Left Hemisphere | Right Hemisphere |
|---|---|
| Controls the right hand | Controls the left hand |
| Spoken language | Nonverbal |
| Written language | Visual–spatial perception |
| Mathematical calculations | Music and artistic processing |
| Logical thought processes | Emotional thought and recognition |
| Analysis of detail | Processes the whole |
| Reading | Pattern recognition |
| | Facial recognition |

of the integrated mind, and he continues to work in related areas including human consciousness, perception, and neuroethics (Gazzaniga, 2006, 2009).

**HANDEDNESS**   The separate functions of the left and right sides of the brain are often confused with handedness, or the tendency to use one hand for most fine motor skills. Roughly 90% of individuals are right handed, and handedness appears to be influenced largely through genetics (Corballis, 2009; Ocklenburg et al., 2013). While most right-handed people also have their left hemisphere in control of their other fine motor skills, such as speech, a few right-handers actually have their language functions in the right hemisphere, in spite of the dominance of the left hemisphere for controlling the right hand. Among left-handed people, there are also many who, although right-brain dominant for motor control, still have their language functions on the left side of the brain. One study suggests approximately 4% of right-handed, 15% of ambidextrous, and 27% of left-handed people have language functions in the right hemisphere (Knecht et al., 2000).

## Concept Map LO. 2.10, 2.11, 2.12, 2.13, 2.14

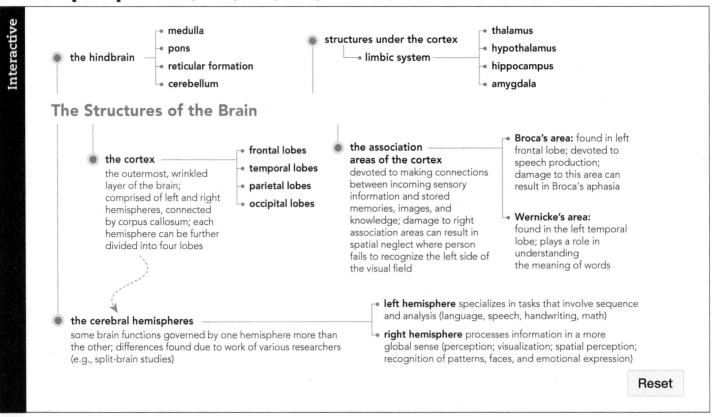

Interactive

The Structures of the Brain

- the hindbrain
  - medulla
  - pons
  - reticular formation
  - cerebellum

- structures under the cortex
  - limbic system
    - thalamus
    - hypothalamus
    - hippocampus
    - amygdala

- the cortex
  the outermost, wrinkled layer of the brain; comprised of left and right hemispheres, connected by corpus callosum; each hemisphere can be further divided into four lobes
  - frontal lobes
  - temporal lobes
  - parietal lobes
  - occipital lobes

- the association areas of the cortex
  devoted to making connections between incoming sensory information and stored memories, images, and knowledge; damage to right association areas can result in spatial neglect where person fails to recognize the left side of the visual field
  - **Broca's area:** found in left frontal lobe; devoted to speech production; damage to this area can result in Broca's aphasia
  - **Wernicke's area:** found in the left temporal lobe; plays a role in understanding the meaning of words

- the cerebral hemispheres
  some brain functions governed by one hemisphere more than the other; differences found due to work of various researchers (e.g., split-brain studies)
  - **left hemisphere** specializes in tasks that involve sequence and analysis (language, speech, handwriting, math)
  - **right hemisphere** processes information in a more global sense (perception; visualization; spatial perception; recognition of patterns, faces, and emotional expression)

Reset

# Practice Quiz   How much do you remember?

*Pick the best answer.*

**1.** Which brain structure allows us to pay attention to certain stimuli while ignoring others?
   **a.** medulla
   **b.** cerebellum
   **c.** reticular formation
   **d.** pons

**2.** Which brain structure relays incoming sensory information?
   **a.** thalamus
   **b.** hypothalamus
   **c.** reticular formation
   **d.** pons

**3.** If you were to develop a rare condition in which you were not able to remember to be afraid of certain situations, animals, or events, which part of the brain would most likely be damaged?
   **a.** cingulate cortex
   **b.** hypothalamus
   **c.** thalamus
   **d.** amygdala

**4.** What part of the brain can sometimes be referred to as the "rind" or outer covering?
   **a.** thalamus
   **b.** medulla
   **c.** corpus callosum
   **d.** cortex

**5.** In which of the following lobes of the cortex would you find the primary visual cortex?
   **a.** frontal
   **b.** temporal
   **c.** occipital
   **d.** parietal

**6.** You have a dream in which you wake up to find that people around you are using words that make no sense. What's more, your friends don't seem to understand you when you speak. At one point in your dream, your mom tells you that you almost forgot your tree limb today. When you give her a puzzled look, she holds up your lunchbox and repeats, "You know, your tree limb." Your predicament in your dream is most like which of the following disorders?
   **a.** Wernicke's aphasia
   **b.** Broca's aphasia
   **c.** apraxia
   **d.** spatial neglect

# APA Goal 2: Scientific Reasoning and Critical Thinking

## Phineas Gage and Neuroplasticity

*Addresses APA LO 2.2: Demonstrate psychology information literacy.*

Earlier in the chapter you read about neuroplasticity as well as the role of the frontal lobes in the case of Phineas Gage. There is little question about the significant changes that likely occurred in Phineas's behavior and personality immediately following the accident and trauma to his brain. However, based on what you know about the brain, his injury, and neuroplasticity and recovery, what questions might you have regarding his behavior and personality immediately before and after the injury and later in his life?

With regard to initial changes, it was reported that Gage went from being well balanced, energetic, and a smart business man to being fitful, irreverent, and impatient to the point that those who knew him said he was "no longer Gage" (Harlow, 1848). In turn, many reports in psychology (including many psychology textbooks!) have previously suggested Gage's behavior and personality were permanently altered (Griggs, 2015; Macmillan, 2000; Macmillan & Lena, 2010). It is also important to note that at the time of Gage's accident, not as much was known about specific aspects of brain function and injury, much less recovery from brain injury.

As you have read, the actual amount of brain damage was not as well understood until relatively recently. Recent investigations using reconstructions of his skull and other methods have identified the most likely areas of brain damage. These studies have revealed damage to the left frontal lobe, primarily the prefrontal and orbitofrontal areas, and the white matter connections between the left frontal lobe and other parts of the brain (Ratiu et al., 2004; Van Horn et al., 2012). Given these brain areas' involvement in goal-directed behavior, planning, personality, emotional control, and the connections to other brain areas, it is easy to imagine the profound changes initially reported in Gage's behavior.

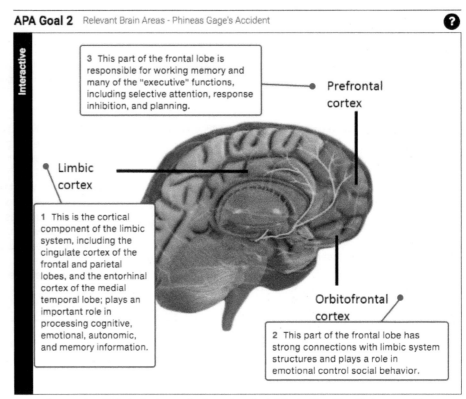

**APA Goal 2**   Relevant Brain Areas - Phineas Gage's Accident                              ❓

Interactive

3  This part of the frontal lobe is responsible for working memory and many of the "executive" functions, including selective attention, response inhibition, and planning.

Prefrontal cortex

Limbic cortex

1  This is the cortical component of the limbic system, including the cingulate cortex of the frontal and parietal lobes, and the entorhinal cortex of the medial temporal lobe; plays an important role in processing cognitive, emotional, autonomic, and memory information.

Orbitofrontal cortex

2  This part of the frontal lobe has strong connections with limbic system structures and plays a role in emotional control social behavior.

Phineas Gage experienced behavioral and personality changes immediately following his accident. Explore some of the brain areas that were either injured or affected by his injury.

But what about his behavior later in life? Although he has historically been portrayed as being permanently altered, there has been some evidence to suggest he experienced a fair amount of recovery. After a period of time in which he exhibited himself and the tamping iron at least twice, there has not been any confirmation that he was actually in a "freak show" and in contrast, he traveled throughout the New England area of the United States, found employment in a horse stable, and later traveled to Chile for work to drive a horse-drawn coach (Harlow, 1868; Macmillan & Lena, 2010). This was not a single horse-and-buggy setup, but rather a six-horse stagecoach that was loaded with passengers and luggage. Although some may consider the work menial, it certainly had to provide some challenges as he had to take care of the horses, tend to the needs of his passengers, and most likely learn something about local customs (Macmillan & Lena, 2010; Van Horn et al., 2012).

There has also been an image of Phineas discovered although the date is not known. What does the portrait below suggest with regard to Phineas's confidence, demeanor, etc.?

From this information and what you know in your study of psychology thus far, can you answer the following questions?

**THINKING CRITICALLY**

1. What type of questions should you ask yourself when referring to case studies? Do the questions differ based on the case studies being modern or historical?

2. What kind of supports and structure might have been provided to Phineas through his postaccident jobs that would have possibly helped him with his recovery?

3. How might the modern study of psychology help us better understand other historical case studies?

Submit

# Paying Attention to Attention-Deficit/ Hyperactivity Disorder

**2.15** **Identify some potential causes of attention-deficit/hyperactivity disorder.**

Attention-deficit/hyperactivity disorder (ADHD) is a developmental disorder involving behavioral and cognitive aspects of inattention, impulsivity, and hyperactivity. Despite what many people have been told over the years, it is not due to bad parenting, too much junk food, or certain types of food coloring, and while symptoms may change somewhat, people do not outgrow the disorder. ADHD is a biological disorder that is related to genetics, environmental influences, and variations in brain structure and function.

Previously referred to as attention deficit disorder (ADD), there are currently three diagnostic categories for this disorder in the *Diagnostic and Statistical Manual of Mental Disorders (DSM-5)*. These include ADHD predominantly hyperactive/impulsive presentation, ADHD predominantly inattentive presentation, and ADHD combined presentation (American Psychiatric Association, 2013). Although ADHD is most commonly diagnosed in children, the disorder tends to persist into adolescence and adulthood. Inattention and impulsivity are often reported in adults, whereas symptoms of hyperactivity tend to decline with age. The ADHD–related problems in adults can range from strained relations with family, friends, or a significant other to problems with substance abuse, traffic accidents, or job stability (Barkley et al., 2008). A longitudinal study found a group of males diagnosed with ADHD in childhood were more likely to have issues across a variety of domains when followed up with as adults. At a mean age of 41, the men with ADHD had significantly worse educational, occupational, economic, and social outcomes and more divorces than non–ADHD comparisons (Klein et al., 2012).

There are not only ongoing issues from the disorder itself but also with the medications used to treat it. In the United States there is a growing concern over the misuse of prescription drugs on college campuses, for example, by students without ADHD in the attempt to improve their attention or concentration when studying. And for some students, the most common source of the medication is a friend with a prescription (Garnier-Dykstra et al., 2012). Furthermore, an ongoing increase in the number of ADHD diagnoses and prescriptions for stimulant medications appears to coincide with the use of ADHD medications as "neuroenhancers" in otherwise healthy children and adolescents and has prompted the American Academy of Neurology to publish a position paper against such practices (Graf et al., 2013).

The brain areas involved in the behavioral and cognitive characteristics of ADHD are typically divided into those responsible for regulating attention and cognitive control and those responsible for alertness and motivation (Nigg, 2010). Cortical and subcortical brain areas involved and found to be smaller in neuroimaging studies of ADHD are the prefrontal cortex (primarily on the right side), basal ganglia (subcortical structures involved in response control), cerebellum, and corpus callosum (Giedd et al., 2015; Nigg, 2006).

Since ADHD involves a variety of behaviors and cognitive aspects, research has often looked for specific markers that may lead to the actual causes of the disorder. These markers may be biological, cognitive, or behavioral measures (Nigg, 2010). To assess individual markers, researchers may combine neuroimaging and electrophysiological studies of individuals with ADHD while at rest or while they perform specific cognitive tasks (like various tests of attention). Some studies use EEG or ERPs (Clarke et al., 2007; Loo et al., 2009; Missonnier et al., 2013; van der Stelt et al., 2010; White et al., 2005), whereas others use MRI, fMRI, or PET (Bush et al., 2008; Mostert et al., 2016; Volkow et al., 2007).

Some research suggests that some aspects of attention are actually normal in individuals with ADHD. The aspect of attention with which individuals with ADHD do have problems is vigilance (being able to "watch out" for something important). Another cognitive area that appears to be impaired is being able to effectively control one's own cognitive processes such as staying on task, maintaining effort, or engaging in self-control (Nigg, 2010).

These findings have prompted researchers to reexamine the causes of ADHD and have highlighted the likelihood of more than one cause and more than one brain route to ADHD. Research is looking at a variety of areas including environmental factors such as low-level lead exposure, genetic influences, the role of heredity and familial factors, and personality factors (Forster & Lavie, 2016; Nigg, 2010; Nigg et al., 2016). Furthermore, causes for the prevalence of ADHD continue to be examined, with variables ranging from the impact of sleep, circadian rhythms, and environmental light exposure (Arns et al., 2013) to the manner in which ADHD symptoms are characterized and diagnosed. While some of these areas of investigation are not completely new and have been examined before, the possibility of multiple causes and interactions between these causes has not been examined as closely as it is being examined in current ADHD research.

### Questions for Further Discussion

1. How might a psychology professional help parents or teachers understand the neuroimaging techniques and brain areas associated with ADHD?

2. If a college student has ADHD, what aspects of their school or personal lives might be impacted by problems with vigilance or cognitive control?

3. What kinds of problems may arise in individuals taking ADHD medications when they do not have the actual symptoms of the disorder?

# Chapter Summary

## Neurons and Nerves: Building the Network

### 2.1 Identify the parts of a neuron and the function of each.

- The nervous system is a complex network of cells that carries information to and from all parts of the body.

- The brain is made up of two types of cells, neurons and glial cells.

- Neurons have four primary components: dendrites that receive input, a soma or cell body, axons that carry the neural message to other cells, and axon terminals that are the site of neurotransmitter release.

- Glial cells separate, support, and insulate the axons of some neurons; they influence thinking, memory, and other forms of cognition.

- Myelin insulates and protects the axons of some neurons. Some axons bundle together in "cables" called nerves. Myelin also speeds up the neural message.

- A neuron contains charged particles called ions. When at rest, the neuron is negatively charged on the inside and positively charged on the outside. When stimulated, this reverses the charge by allowing positive sodium ions to enter the cell. This is the action potential.

- Neurons fire in an all-or-nothing manner. It is the speed and number of neurons firing that tell researchers the strength of the stimulus.

### 2.2 Explain the action potential.

- Synaptic vesicles in the end of the axon terminal release neurotransmitter chemicals into the synapse, or gap, between one cell and the next. The neurotransmitter molecules fit into receptor sites on the next cell, stimulating or inhibiting that cell's firing. Neurotransmitters may be either excitatory or inhibitory.

### 2.3 Describe how neurons use neurotransmitters to communicate with each other and with the body.

- The first known neurotransmitter was acetylcholine (ACh). It stimulates muscles, helps in memory formation, and plays a role in arousal and attention.

- GABA is the major inhibitory neurotransmitter; high amounts of GABA are released when drinking alcohol.

- Serotonin (5-HT) is associated with sleep, mood, and appetite.

- Dopamine (DA) is associated with Parkinson's disease and schizophrenia.
- Endorphins are neural regulators that control our pain response.
- Most neurotransmitters are taken back into the synaptic vesicles in a process called reuptake.
- ACh is cleared out of the synapse by enzymes that break up the molecules.

## An Overview of the Nervous System

**2.4 Describe how the brain and spinal cord interact and respond to external experiences.**

- The central nervous system consists of the brain and the spinal cord.
- The spinal cord serves two functions. The outer part of the cord transmits messages to and from the brain, whereas the inner part controls lifesaving reflexes such as the pain response.
- Spinal cord reflexes involve afferent neurons, interneurons, and efferent neurons, forming a simple reflex arc.
- Neuroplasticity refers to the brains ability to modify its structure and function as the result of experience or injury; researchers are examining ways to capitalize on this feature to assist individuals with brain injury or disease.

**2.5 Differentiate the roles of the somatic and autonomic nervous systems.**

- The peripheral nervous system is all the neurons and nerves that are not part of the brain and spinal cord and that extend throughout the body.
- There are two systems within the peripheral nervous system, the somatic nervous system and the autonomic nervous system.
- The somatic nervous system contains the sensory pathway, or neurons carrying messages to the central nervous system, and the motor pathway, or neurons carrying messages from the central nervous system to the voluntary muscles.
- The autonomic nervous system consists of the parasympathetic division and the sympathetic division. The sympathetic division is our fight-or-flight system, reacting to stress, whereas the parasympathetic division is our eat-drink-and-rest system that restores and maintains normal day-to-day functioning of the organs.

## Distant Connections: The Endocrine Glands

**2.6 Explain why the pituitary gland is known as the "master gland."**

- Endocrine glands secrete chemicals called hormones directly into the bloodstream, influencing the activity of the muscles and organs.
- The pituitary gland is found in the brain just below the hypothalamus. Among its many functions, it helps us conserve water and controls oxytocin, a hormone involved in the onset of labor and lactation. The pituitary also regulates growth hormone and influences the activity of the other glands.

**2.7 Recall the role of various endocrine glands.**

- The pineal gland is also located in the brain. It secretes melatonin, a hormone that regulates the sleep–wake cycle, in response to changes in light.
- The thyroid gland is located inside the neck. It controls metabolism (the burning of energy) by secreting thyroxin.
- The pancreas controls the level of sugar in the blood by secreting insulin and glucagons. Too much insulin produces hypoglycemia, whereas too little causes diabetes.
- The gonads are the ovaries in women and testes in men. They secrete hormones to regulate sexual growth, activity, and reproduction.
- The adrenal glands, one on top of each kidney, control the stress reaction through the adrenal medulla's secretion of epinephrine and norepinephrine. The adrenal cortex secretes more than 30 different corticoids (hormones), controlling salt intake, stress, and sexual development.

## Looking Inside the Living Brain

**2.8 Describe how lesioning studies and brain stimulation are used to study the brain.**

- We can study the brain by using lesioning techniques to destroy certain areas of the brain in laboratory animals or by electrically stimulating those areas (ESB).
- We can use case studies of human brain damage to learn about the brain's functions but cannot easily generalize from one case to another.
- rTMS and tDCS are noninvasive methods for stimulating the brain.

**2.9 Compare and contrast neuroimaging techniques for mapping the structure and function of the brain.**

- Different neuroimaging methods allow scientists to investigate the structure or the function of the living brain.
- The electroencephalograph allows researchers to look at the electroencephalogram (EEG), or electrical activity of the surface of the brain, through the use of electrodes placed on the scalp that are then amplified and viewed using a computer. ERPs allow researchers to look at the timing and progression of cognitive processes.
- CT scans are computer-aided X-rays of the brain and show the skull and brain structure.
- MRI scans use a magnetic field, radio pulses, and a computer to give researchers an even more detailed look at the structure of the brain.
- fMRI allows researchers to look at the activity of the brain over a time period.
- PET scans use a radioactive sugar injected into the bloodstream to track the activity of brain cells, which is enhanced and color-coded by a computer. SPECT allows for the imaging of brain blood flow.

## From the Bottom Up: The Structures of the Brain

**2.10 Identify the different structures of the hindbrain and the function of each.**

- The medulla is at the very bottom of the brain and at the top of the spinal column. It controls life-sustaining functions such as breathing and swallowing. The nerves from each side of the body also cross over in this structure to opposite sides.
- The pons is above the medulla and acts as a bridge between the cerebellum and the cerebrum. It influences sleep, dreaming, arousal, and coordination of movement on the left and right sides of the body.
- The reticular formation runs through the medulla and the pons and controls our general level of attention and arousal.
- The cerebellum is found at the base and back of the brain and coordinates fine, rapid motor movement, learned reflexes, posture, and muscle tone. It may also be involved in some cognitive and emotional functions.

**2.11 Identify the structures of the brain that are involved in emotion, learning, memory, and motivation.**

- The limbic system consists of the thalamus, hypothalamus, hippocampus, and amygdala.
- The thalamus is the relay station that sends sensory information to the proper areas of the cortex.
- The hypothalamus controls hunger, thirst, sexual behavior, sleeping and waking, and emotions. It also controls the pituitary gland.
- The hippocampus is the part of the brain responsible for the formation of long-term declarative memories.
- The amygdala controls our fear responses and memory of fearful stimuli.

**2.12 Identify the parts of the cortex that process the different senses and those that control movement of the body.**

- The cortex is the outer covering of the cerebrum and consists of a tightly packed layer of neurons about one tenth of an inch in thickness. Its wrinkles, or corticalization, allow for greater cortical area and are associated with greater brain complexity.
- The cortex is divided into two cerebral hemispheres connected by a thick band of neural fibers called the corpus callosum.
- The occipital lobes at the back and base of each hemisphere process vision and contain the primary visual cortex.
- The parietal lobes at the top and back of the cortex contain the somatosensory area, which processes our sense of touch, temperature, and body position.

- The temporal lobes contain the primary auditory area and are also involved in understanding language.
- The frontal lobes contain the motor cortex, which controls the voluntary muscles, and are also where all the higher mental functions occur, such as planning, language, and complex decision making.

**2.13 Name the parts of the cortex that are responsible for higher forms of thought, such as language.**

- Association areas of the cortex are found in all the lobes but particularly in the frontal lobes. These areas help people make sense of the information they receive from primary sensory areas and the lower areas of the brain.
- A region called Broca's area in the left frontal lobe is critical in the production of fluent, understandable speech. If damaged, the person has Broca's aphasia, in which words will be halting and pronounced incorrectly.
- An area called Wernicke's area in the left temporal lobe is important for the understanding of language. If damaged, the person has Wernicke's aphasia, in which speech is fluent but nonsensical. The wrong words are used.

**2.14 Explain how some brain functions differ between the left and right hemispheres.**

- Studies with split-brain patients, in which the corpus callosum has been severed to correct epilepsy, reveal that the left side of the brain seems to control language, writing, logical thought, analysis, and mathematical abilities. The left side also processes information sequentially.
- The right side of the brain processes information globally and controls emotional expression, spatial perception, recognition of faces, patterns, melodies, and emotions. Information presented only to the left hemisphere can be verbalized, but information only sent to the right cannot.

## Applying Psychology to Everyday Life: Paying Attention to Attention-Deficit/Hyperactivity Disorder

**2.15 Identify some potential causes of attention-deficit/hyperactivity disorder.**

- ADHD is often diagnosed in children but may persist into adulthood. Multiple causes are possible, including genetic and environmental factors and several differences in brain structure and function.

# Test Yourself

*Pick the best answer.*

1. In the structure of the neuron, the _____ receives messages from other cells.
   a. axon
   b. dendrite
   c. soma
   d. myelin

2. Oligodendrocytes and Schwann cells generate a fatty substance known as
   a. glial.
   b. soma.
   c. myelin.
   d. neurilemma.

3. Which of the following insulates and protects a neuron's axon, as well as helps speed along electrical impulses?
   a. synaptic knobs
   b. receptor sites
   c. myelin sheath
   d. neuromodulators

4. When a neuron is in the resting potential state, the neuron is negatively charged on the _____ and positively charged on the _____.
   a. inside; outside
   b. outside; inside
   c. top; bottom
   d. bottom; top

5. Which neurotransmitter stimulates muscle cells to contract but slows contractions in the heart?
   a. acetylcholine
   b. GABA
   c. serotonin
   d. endorphin

6. Heroin mimics the actions of endorphins, inhibiting pain signals and creating a "high" feeling. Heroin is an example of a(n):
   a. protagonist.
   b. antagonist.
   c. agonist.
   d. glial cell.

7. Involuntary muscles are controlled by the _____ nervous system.
   a. somatic
   b. autonomic
   c. sympathetic
   d. parasympathetic

8. As you take notes, your heart beats at a normal rate. Your breathing is normal and your stomach slowly digests your earlier meal. What division of the peripheral nervous system is currently in action?
   a. sympathetic
   b. parasympathetic
   c. autonomic
   d. somatic

9. Robert has had difficulty sleeping for the past 6 months, and his body seemingly no longer differentiates between night and day. His doctor believes the problem lies with Robert's endocrine system. What gland will Robert's physician focus on?
   a. pituitary
   b. adrenal
   c. thyroid
   d. pineal

10. Which gland(s) is/are known to influence all other glands within the endocrine system?
    a. pineal gland
    b. pituitary gland
    c. thyroid gland
    d. adrenal glands

11. Danielle is a subject in a study on memory and problem solving. The researcher is applying magnetic pulses to her brain through copper wire coils positioned directly above her scalp. Danielle study would best be described as a(n)
    a. invasive stimulation technique.
    b. noninvasive stimulation technique.
    c. EEG technique.
    d. PET technique.

12. Which technique of studying the brain involves injecting the patient with radioactive glucose?
    a. EEG
    b. CT
    c. MRI
    d. PET

13. Maria often sleeps soundly and rarely awakens to any outside noise. However, the cries of Maria's baby can awaken her immediately. What part of the brain is responsible for this reaction?
    a. medulla
    b. pons
    c. reticular formation
    d. cerebellum

14. Nicole and Camille are synchronized swimmers for their college swim team. They often work long hours to ensure the movements in their routine are perfectly timed. What part of their brains must Camille and Nicole rely most upon?
    a. medulla
    b. pons
    c. reticular formation
    d. cerebellum

15. Your psychology professor refers to this as the great relay station of the brain. What part is he or she referring to?
    a. thalamus
    b. hypothalamus
    c. hippocampus
    d. amygdala

16. Which part of the brain is involved in the creation of memories and is often linked to Alzheimer's disease?
    a. hippocampus
    b. thalamus
    c. hypothalamus
    d. amygdala

17. Madison suffered a severe blow to the back of her head when she was thrown to the mat during a judo match. Subsequently, her occipital lobe has been injured. Which of her senses has the highest chance of being affected?
    a. hearing
    b. touch
    c. taste and smell
    d. vision

18. Jaime's grandfather recently suffered a stroke and has had difficulty with language production ever since. Most likely, he has experienced damage to the _____ area of his brain.
    a. right rear
    b. left frontal
    c. left rear
    d. right frontal

19. Felicia is recovering from a brain injury. She is able to speak fluently but often uses incorrect words in a sentence. In one instance at a friend's birthday party, she said, "I would like something to drink. Can I have some battery?" Felicia's problem is known as
    a. spatial neglect.
    b. visual agnosia.
    c. Broca's aphasia.
    d. Wernicke's aphasia.

20 Although the brain works largely as a whole, which of the following is *not* a correct pairing of hemisphere and function?
    a. left; control of right-handed motor functions
    b. right; control of right-handed motor functions
    c. right; recognition of faces
    d. left; reading

# 3 Sensation and Perception

Which of your sensory abilities do you rely on most during a typical day? Are certain senses more important than others depending on the social context or setting?

After you have answered the question, watch the video to compare the answers of other students to yours.

▶ The response entered here will be saved to your notes and may be collected by your instructor if he/she requires it.

👁 Watch the Video

## Why study sensation and perception?

Without sensations to tell us what is outside our own mental world, we would live entirely in our own minds, separate from one another and unable to find food or any other basics that sustain life. Sensations are the mind's window to the world that exists around us. Without perception, we would be unable to understand what all those sensations mean—perception is the process of interpreting the sensations we experience so that we can act upon them.

# Learning Objectives

**3.1** Describe how we get information from the outside world into our brains.

**3.2** Describe the difference and absolute thresholds.

**3.3** Explain why some sensory information is ignored.

**3.4** Describe how light travels through the various parts of the eye.

**3.5** Explain how light information reaches the visual cortex.

**3.6** Compare and contrast two major theories of color vision, and explain how color-deficient vision occurs.

**3.7** Explain the nature of sound, and describe how it travels through the various parts of the ear.

**3.8** Summarize three theories of how the brain processes information about pitch.

**3.9** Identify types of hearing impairment and treatment options for each.

**3.10** Explain how the sense of taste works.

**3.11** Explain how the sense of smell works.

**3.12** Describe how we experience the sensations of touch, pressure, temperature, and pain.

**3.13** Describe the systems that tell us about balance and position and movement of our bodies.

**3.14** Describe how perceptual constancies and the Gestalt principles account for common perceptual experiences.

**3.15** Explain how we perceive depth using both monocular and binocular cues.

**3.16** Identify some common visual illusions and the factors that influence our perception of them.

**3.17** Describe how the neuroscientific study of magic can help to explain visual and cognitive illusions.

# The ABCs of Sensation

Information about the world has to have a way to get into the brain, where it can be used to determine actions and responses. The way into the brain is through the sensory organs and the process of sensation.

### TRANSDUCTION

**3.1** **Describe how we get information from the outside world into our brains.**

**Sensation** occurs when special receptors in the sense organs—the eyes, ears, nose, skin, and taste buds—are activated, allowing various forms of outside stimuli to become neural signals in the brain. This process of converting outside stimuli, such as light, into neural activity is called **transduction**.

The *sensory receptors* are specialized forms of neurons, the cells that make up the nervous system. Instead of receiving neurotransmitters from other cells, these receptor cells are stimulated by different kinds of energy—for example, the receptors in the eyes are stimulated by light, whereas the receptors in the ears are activated by vibrations. Touch receptors are stimulated by pressure or temperature, and the receptors for taste and smell are triggered by chemical substances. Each receptor type transduces the physical information into electrical information in different ways, which then either depolarizes or hyperpolarizes the cell, causing it to fire more or to fire less based on the timing and intensity of information it is detecting from the environment (Gardner & Johnson, 2013).

In some people, the sensory information gets processed in unusual, but fascinating ways. Taria Camerino is a pastry chef who experiences music, colors, shapes, and emotions as taste; Jamie Smith is a sommelier, or wine steward, who experiences smells as colors and shapes; and James Wannerton is an information technology consultant who experiences sounds, words, and colors as tastes and textures (Carlsen, 2013, March 18). All three of these individuals have a condition known as **synesthesia**, which literally means "joined sensation." Studies suggest at least 4 to 5 percent of the population may experience some form of synesthesia (Hubbard & Ramachandran, 2005; Simner, 2013; Simner et al., 2006). While the causes of synesthesia are still being investigated, it appears that in some forms, signals that come from the sensory organs, such as the eyes or the ears, either go to places in the brain where they weren't originally meant to be or they are processed differently. Overall, there is increased communication between sensory regions that results in synesthetes experiencing the world differently than others.

### SENSORY THRESHOLDS

**3.2** **Describe the difference and absolute thresholds.**

Ernst Weber (1795–1878) did studies trying to determine the smallest difference between two weights that could be detected. His research led to the formulation known as Weber's law of **just noticeable differences (jnd,** or the **difference threshold**). A jnd is the smallest difference between two stimuli that is detectable 50 percent of the time, and Weber's law simply means that whatever the difference between stimuli might be, it is always a *constant*. If to notice a difference the amount of sugar a person would need to add to a cup of coffee that is already sweetened with 5 teaspoons is 1 teaspoon, then the percentage of change needed to detect a just noticeable difference is one fifth, or 20 percent. So if the coffee has 10 teaspoons of sugar in it, the person would have to add another 20 percent, or 2 teaspoons, to be able to taste the difference half of the time. Most people would not typically drink a cup of coffee with 10 teaspoons of sugar in it, let alone 12 teaspoons, but you get the point.

**sensation**

the process that occurs when special receptors in the sense organs are activated, allowing various forms of outside stimuli to become neural signals in the brain.

**transduction**

the process of converting outside stimuli, such as light, into neural activity.

**synesthesia**

disorder in which the signals from the various sensory organs are processed in the wrong cortical areas, resulting in the sense information being interpreted as more than one sensation.

**just noticeable difference (jnd or the difference threshold)**

the smallest difference between two stimuli that is detectable 50 percent of the time.

In some parts of the United States, "coffee regular" refers to coffee with two creams and two sugars. How much more sugar would you need to add to taste a difference?

| Table 3.1 | Examples of Absolute Thresholds |
|---|---|
| **Sense** | **Threshold** |
| Sight | A candle flame at 30 miles on a clear, dark night |
| Hearing | The tick of a watch 20 feet away in a quiet room |
| Smell | One drop of perfume diffused throughout a three-room apartment |
| Taste | 1 teaspoon of sugar in 2 gallons of water |
| Touch | A bee's wing falling on the cheek from 1 centimeter above |

To see a visual example of this, participate in the experiment *Weber's Law* and discover the amount of change needed to detect a just noticeable difference between two circles of light. ◉▶ **Simulate** the **Experiment,** *Weber's Law*

Gustav Fechner (1801–1887) expanded on Weber's work by studying something he called the **absolute threshold** (Fechner, 1860). An absolute threshold is the lowest level of stimulation that a person can consciously detect 50 percent of the time the stimulation is present. (Remember, the jnd is detecting a difference *between two* stimuli.) For example, assuming a very quiet room and normal hearing, how far away can someone sit and you might still hear the tick of their analog watch on half of the trials? For some examples of absolute thresholds for various senses, see **Table 3.1**.

💬 I've heard about people being influenced by stuff in movies and on television, things that are just below the level of conscious awareness. Is that true?

Stimuli that are below the level of conscious awareness are called *subliminal stimuli*. (The word *limin* means "threshold," so *sublimin* means "below the threshold.") These stimuli are just strong enough to activate the sensory receptors but not strong enough for people to be consciously aware of them. Many people believe that these stimuli act upon the unconscious mind, influencing behavior in a process called *subliminal perception*.

At one time, many people believed that a market researcher named James Vicary had demonstrated the power of subliminal perception in advertising. In 1957, Vicary claimed that over a 6-week period, 45,699 patrons at a movie theater in Fort Lee, New Jersey, were shown two advertising messages, *Eat Popcorn* and *Drink Coca-Cola*, while they watched the film *Picnic*. According to Vicary, these messages were flashed for 3 milliseconds once every 5 seconds. Vicary claimed that over the 6-week period the sales of popcorn rose 57.7 percent and the sales of Coca-Cola rose 18.1 percent. It was 5 years before Vicary finally admitted that he had never conducted a real study (Merikle, 2000; Pratkanis, 1992). Furthermore, many researchers have gathered scientific evidence that subliminal perception does not work in advertising (Bargh et al., 1996; Broyles, 2006; Moore, 1988; Pratkanis & Greenwald, 1988; Trappey, 1996; Vokey & Read, 1985).

This is not to say that subliminal perception does not exist—there is a growing body of evidence that we process some stimuli without conscious awareness, especially stimuli that are fearful or threatening (LeDoux & Phelps, 2008; Öhman, 2008). In this effort, researchers have used *event-related potentials* (ERPs) and functional magnetic resonance imaging (fMRI) to verify the existence of subliminal perception and associated learning in the laboratory (Babiloni et al., 2010; Bernat et al., 2001; Fazel-Rezai & Peters, 2005; Sabatini et al., 2009). ⓛⓘⓝⓚ to Learning Objective 2.9. The stimuli used in these studies are detectable by our sensory systems but below

**absolute threshold**
the lowest level of stimulation that a person can consciously detect 50 percent of the time the stimulation is present.

the level of full conscious perception. Participants are not aware or conscious that they have been exposed to the stimuli due to masking or manipulation of attention. Furthermore, the stimuli typically influence automatic reactions (such as an increase in facial tension) rather than direct voluntary behaviors (such as going to buy something suggested by advertising).

Another useful way of analyzing what stimuli we respond to is based on signal detection theory. **Signal detection theory** is used to compare our judgments, or the decisions we make, under uncertain conditions. The ability to detect any physical stimulus is based on how strong it is and how mentally and physically prepared the individual is. It was originally developed to help address issues associated with research participants guessing during experiments and is a way to measure accuracy (Green & Swets, 1966; Macmillan & Creelman, 1991).

For example, a stimulus can be either present or absent. In turn, an individual can either detect a stimulus when present, a "hit," or say it is not there, a "miss." He or she can also falsely report a stimulus as present when it actually isn't, a "false alarm," or correctly state it isn't there, a "correct rejection."

**HABITUATION AND SENSORY ADAPTATION**

### 3.3 Explain why some sensory information is ignored.

Some of the lower centers of the brain filter sensory stimulation and "ignore" or prevent conscious attention to stimuli that do not change. The brain is primarily interested in changes in information. That's why people don't really "hear" the noise of the air conditioner unless it suddenly cuts off, or the noise made in some classrooms, unless it gets very quiet or someone else directs their attention toward it. Although they actually are *hearing* it, they aren't paying attention to it. This is called **habituation**, and it is the way the brain deals with unchanging information from the environment. (L)(I)(N)(K) to Learning Objective 2.10.

> Sometimes I can smell the odor of the garbage can in the kitchen when I first come home, but after a while the smell seems to go away—is this also habituation?

Although different from habituation, **sensory adaptation** is another process by which constant, unchanging information from the sensory receptors is effectively ignored. In habituation, the sensory receptors are still responding to stimulation, but the lower centers of the brain are not sending the signals from those receptors to the cortex. The process of sensory adaptation differs because the receptor cells *themselves* become less responsive to an unchanging stimulus—garbage odors included—and the receptors no longer send signals to the brain.

For example, when you eat, the food that you put in your mouth tastes strong at first, but as you keep eating the same thing, the taste does fade somewhat, doesn't it? Generally speaking, all of our senses are subject to sensory adaptation.

You might think, then, that if you stare at something long enough, it would also disappear, but the eyes are a little different. Even though the sensory receptors in the back of the eyes adapt to and become less responsive to a constant visual stimulus, under ordinary circumstances, the eyes are never entirely still. There's a constant movement of the eyes, tiny little vibrations called "microsaccades" or "saccadic movements," that people don't consciously notice. These movements keep the eyes from adapting to what they see. (That's a good thing, because otherwise many students would no doubt go blind from staring off into space.)

This young woman does not feel the piercings on her ear and nose because sensory adaptation allows her to ignore a constant, unchanging stimulation from the metal rings. What else is she wearing that would cause sensory adaptation?

**signal detection theory**

provides a method for assessing the accuracy of judgments or decisions under uncertain conditions; used in perception research and other areas. An individual's correct "hits" and rejections are compared against their "misses" and "false alarms."

**habituation**

tendency of the brain to stop attending to constant, unchanging information.

**sensory adaptation**

tendency of sensory receptor cells to become less responsive to a stimulus that is unchanging.

## Concept Map L.O. 3.1, 3.2, 3.3

Interactive

### The ABCs of Sensation

**sensation**
process by which information
from the outside world
enters the brain

- related to the activation of receptors in the various sense organs and transduction of that information into neural signals
- related to changes in physical stimuli

- detected by sensory receptors
- influenced by both absolute and difference thresholds; responses can also be examined through signal detection theory
- sometimes "ignored" through sensory adaptation or cognitive habituation

Reset

## Practice Quiz    How much do you remember?

*Pick the best answer.*

1. _____ involves the detection of physical stimuli from our environment and is made possible by the activation of specific receptor cells.
   a. Perception
   b. Sublimation
   c. Adaptation
   d. Sensation

2. The lowest level of stimulation that a person can consciously detect 50 percent of the time the stimulation is present is called
   a. absolute threshold.
   b. just noticeable difference.
   c. sensation.
   d. sensory adaptation.

3. After being in class for a while, _____ is a likely explanation for not hearing the sound of the lights buzzing above you until someone says something about it.
   a. accommodation
   b. adaptation
   c. sublimation
   d. habituation

4. You are drinking a strong cup of coffee that is particularly bitter. After a while, the coffee doesn't taste as strong as it did when you first tasted it. What has happened?
   a. sensory adaptation
   b. subliminal perception
   c. habituation
   d. perceptual defense

# The Science of Seeing

💬 I've heard that light is waves, but I've also heard that light is made of particles—which is it?

Light is a complicated phenomenon. Although scientists have long argued over the nature of light, they finally have agreed that light has the properties of both waves and particles. The following section gives a brief history of how scientists have tried to "shed light" on the mystery of light.

### LIGHT AND THE EYE

**3.4  Describe how light travels through the various parts of the eye.**

It was Albert Einstein who first proposed that light is actually tiny "packets" of waves. These "wave packets" are called *photons* and have specific wavelengths associated with them (Lehnert, 2007; van der Merwe & Garuccio, 1994).

When people experience the physical properties of light, they are not really aware of its dual, wavelike and particle-like, nature. With regard to its psychological properties, there are three aspects to our perception of light: *brightness*, *color*, and *saturation*.

*Brightness* is determined by the amplitude of the wave—how high or how low the wave actually is. The higher the wave, the brighter the light appears to be. Low waves are dimmer. *Color*, or hue, is largely determined by the length of the wave. Short wavelengths (measured in nanometers) are found at the blue end of the *visible spectrum* (the portion of the whole spectrum of light that is visible to the human eye; see **Figure 3.1**), whereas longer wavelengths are found at the red end.

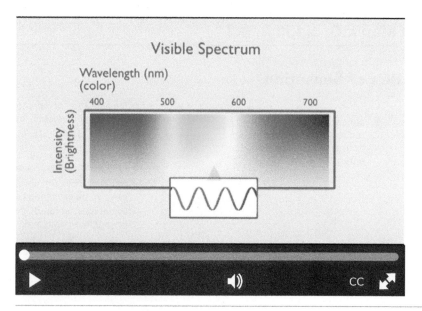

**Figure 3.1** The Visible Spectrum

*Saturation* refers to the purity of the color people perceive: A highly saturated red, for example, would contain only red wavelengths, whereas a less-saturated red might contain a mixture of wavelengths. For example, when a child is using the red paint from a set of poster paints, the paint on the paper will look like a pure red, but if the child mixes in some white paint, the paint will look pink. The hue is still red, but it will be less of a saturated red because of the presence of white wavelengths. Mixing in black or gray would also lessen the saturation. (Note that when combining different colors, light works differently than pigments or paint. We will look at this distinction when we examine perception of color.)

**THE STRUCTURE OF THE EYE**    The best way to talk about how the eye processes light is to talk about what happens to an image being viewed as the photons of light from that image travel through the eye. Refer to **Figure 3.2** to follow the path of the image.

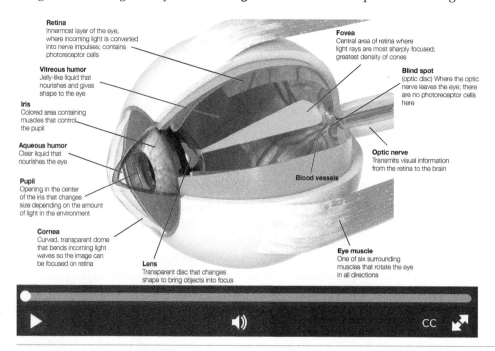

**Figure 3.2** Structure of the Eye

Light enters the eye through the cornea and pupil. The iris controls the size of the pupil. From the pupil, light passes through the lens to the retina, where it is transformed into nerve impulses. The nerve impulses travel to the brain along the optic nerve.

**FROM FRONT TO BACK: THE PARTS OF THE EYE**  Light enters the eye directly from a source (such as the sun) or indirectly by reflecting off of an object. To see clearly, a single point of light from a source or reflected from an object must travel through the structures of the eye and end up on the retina as a single point. Light bends as it passes through substances of different densities, through a process known as refraction. For example, have you ever looked at a drinking straw in a glass of water through the side of the glass? It appears that the straw bends, or is broken, at the surface of the water. That optical illusion is due to the refraction of light. The structures of the eye play a vital role in both collecting and focusing of light so we can see clearly.

The surface of the eye is covered in a clear membrane called the *cornea*. The cornea not only protects the eye but also is the structure that focuses most of the light coming into the eye. The cornea has a fixed curvature, like a camera that has no option to adjust the focus. However, this curvature can be changed somewhat through vision-improving techniques that change the shape of the cornea. For example, ophthalmologists, physicians who specialize in medical and surgical treatment of eye problems, can use both *photoreactive keratectomy (PRK)* and *laser-assisted in situ keratomileusis (LASIK)* procedures to remove small portions of the cornea, changing its curvature and thus the focus in the eye.

The next visual layer is a clear, watery fluid called the *aqueous humor*. This fluid is continually replenished and supplies nourishment to the eye. The light from the visual image then enters the interior of the eye through a hole, called the *pupil*, in a round muscle called the *iris* (the colored part of the eye). The iris can change the size of the pupil, letting more or less light into the eye. That also helps focus the image; people try to do the same thing by squinting.

Behind the iris, suspended by muscles, is another clear structure called the *lens*. The flexible lens finishes the focusing process begun by the cornea. In a process called **visual accommodation**, the lens changes its shape from thick to thin, enabling it to focus on objects that are close or far away. The variation in thickness allows the lens to project a sharp image on the retina. People lose this ability as the lens hardens through aging (a disorder called *presbyopia*). Although people try to compensate* for their inability to focus on things that are close to them, eventually they usually need bifocals because their arms just aren't long enough anymore. In nearsightedness, or *myopia*, visual accommodation may occur, but the shape of the eye causes the focal point to fall short of the retina. In farsightedness, or *hyperopia*, the focus point is beyond the retina (see **Figure 3.3**). Glasses, contacts, or corrective surgery like LASIK or PRK can correct these issues.

Once past the lens, light passes through a large, open space filled with a clear, jelly-like fluid called the *vitreous humor*. This fluid, like the aqueous humor, also nourishes the eye and gives it shape.

This photo illustrates an optical illusion caused by the refraction of light. The straw is not really broken, although it appears that way.

**visual accommodation**

the change in the thickness of the lens as the eye focuses on objects that are far away or close.

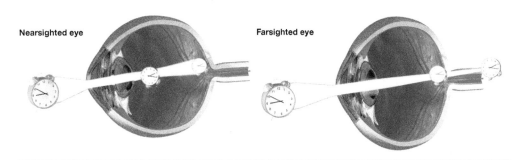

Nearsighted eye          Farsighted eye

**Figure 3.3**  Nearsightedness and Farsightedness

---

*compensate: to correct for an error or defect.

**RETINA, RODS, AND CONES** The final stop for light within the eye is the *retina*, a light-sensitive area at the back of the eye containing three layers: ganglion cells, bipolar cells, and the **rods** and **cones**, special receptor cells (*photoreceptors*) that respond to the various wavelengths of light. The video *Rods and Cones* provides an overview.

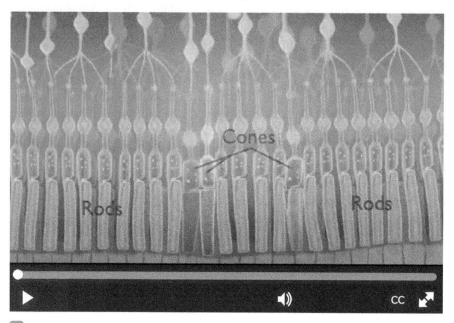

👁 **Watch** the **Video** *Rods and Cones*

While the retina is responsible for absorbing and processing light information, the rods and the cones are the business end of the retina—the part that actually receives the photons of light and turns them into neural signals for the brain, sending them first to the *bipolar cells* (a type of interneuron; called bipolar or "two-ended" because they have a single dendrite at one end and a single axon on the other; ⓁⒾⓃⓀ to Learning Objective 2.1) and then to the retinal *ganglion cells* whose axons form the optic nerve.

The rods and cones are responsible for different aspects of vision. There are 6 million cones in each eye; of these, 50,000 have a private line to the optic nerve (one bipolar cell for each cone). This means that the cones are the receptors for visual acuity, or ability to see fine detail. Cones are located all over the retina but are more concentrated at its very center where there are no rods (the area called the *fovea*). Cones also need a lot more light to function than the rods do, so cones work best in bright light, which is also when people see things most clearly. Cones are also sensitive to different wavelengths of light, so they are responsible for color vision.

The rods (about 100 million of them in each eye) are found all over the retina except the *fovea* but are concentrated in the periphery. Rods are sensitive to changes in brightness but not to a variety of wavelengths, so they see only in black and white and shades of gray. They can be very sensitive because many rods are connected to a single bipolar cell, so that if even only one rod is stimulated by a photon of light, the brain perceives the whole area of those rods as stimulated. But because the brain doesn't know exactly what part of the area (which rod) is actually sending the message, the visual acuity (sharpness) is quite low. That's why things seen in low levels of light, such as twilight or a dimly lit room, are fuzzy and grayish. Because rods are located on the periphery of the retina, they are also responsible for peripheral vision.

The eyes don't adapt to constant stimuli under normal circumstances because of saccadic movements. But if people stare with one eye at one spot long enough, small

**rods**

visual sensory receptors found at the back of the retina, responsible for non-color sensitivity to low levels of light.

**cones**

visual sensory receptors found at the back of the retina, responsible for color vision and sharpness of vision.

**Figure 3.4** The Blind Spot

Hold the book in front of you. Close your right eye and stare at the picture of the dog with your left eye. Slowly bring the book closer to your face. The picture of the cat will disappear at some point because the light from the picture of the cat is falling on your blind spot. If you cannot seem to find your blind spot, trying moving the book more slowly.

objects that slowly cross their visual field may at one point disappear briefly because there is a "hole" in the retina—the place where all the axons of those ganglion cells leave the retina to become the optic nerve, the *optic disk*. There are no rods or cones here, so this is referred to as the **blind spot**. You can demonstrate the blind spot for yourself by following the directions in **Figure 3.4**.

### THE VISUAL PATHWAY

**3.5** **Explain how light information reaches the visual cortex.**

You may want to first look at **Figure 3.5** for a moment before reading this section. Light entering the eyes can be separated into the left and right visual fields. Light from the right visual field falls on the left side of each eye's retina; light from the left visual field falls on the right side of each retina. Light travels in a straight line through the cornea and lens, resulting in the image projected on the retina actually being upside down and reversed from left to right as compared to the visual fields. Thank goodness our brains can compensate for this!

The areas of the retina can be divided into halves, with the halves toward the temples of the head referred to as the temporal retinas and the halves toward the center, or nose, called the nasal retinas. Look at Figure 3.5 again. Notice that the information from the left visual field (falling on the right side of each retina) goes to the right visual cortex, while the information from the right visual field (falling on the left side of each retina) goes to the left visual cortex. This is because the axons from the temporal halves of each retina project to the visual cortex on the same side of the brain, while the axons from the nasal halves cross over to the visual cortex on the opposite side of the brain. The optic chiasm is the point of crossover.

Because rods work well in low levels of light, they are also the cells that allow the eyes to adapt to low light. **Dark adaptation** occurs as the eye recovers its ability to see when going from a brightly lit state to a dark state. (The light-sensitive pigments that allow us to see are able to regenerate or "recharge" in the dark.) The brighter the light was, the longer it takes the rods to adapt to the new lower levels of light (Bartlett, 1965). This is why the bright headlights of an oncoming car can leave a person less able to see for a while after that car has passed. Fortunately, this is usually a temporary condition because the bright light was on so briefly and the rods readapt to the dark night relatively quickly. Full dark adaptation, which occurs when going from more constant light to darkness, such as turning out one's bedroom lights, takes about 30 minutes. As people get older this process takes longer, causing many older persons to be less able to see at night and in darkened rooms (Klaver et al., 1998). This age-related change can cause *night blindness*, in which a person has difficulty seeing well enough to drive at night or get around in a darkened

**blind spot**

area in the retina where the axons of the three layers of retinal cells exit the eye to form the optic nerve; insensitive to light.

**dark adaptation**

the recovery of the eye's sensitivity to visual stimuli in darkness after exposure to bright lights.

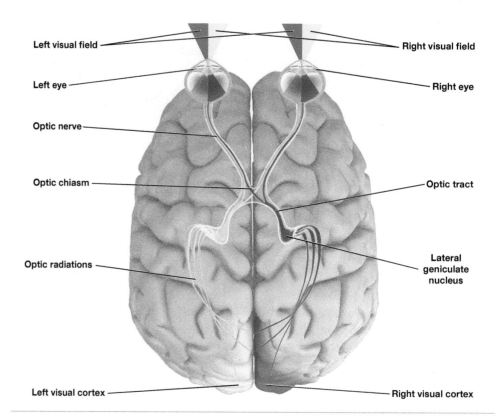

**Figure 3.5**    Crossing of the Optic Nerve

Light falling on the left side of each eye's retina (from the right visual field, shown in yellow) will stimulate a neural message that will travel along the optic nerve to the thalamus and then on to the visual cortex in the occipital lobe of the left hemisphere. Notice that the message from the temporal half of the left retina goes to the left occipital lobe, while the message from the nasal half of the right retina crosses over to the left hemisphere (the optic chiasm is the point of crossover). The optic nerve tissue from both eyes joins together to form the left optic tract before going on to the lateral geniculate nucleus of the thalamus, the optic radiations, and then the left occipital lobe. For the left visual field (shown in blue), the messages from both right sides of the retinas will travel along the right optic tract to the right visual cortex in the same manner.

While this deer may seem to see relatively well at night, the oncoming headlights of a car will briefly blind it. It may only take a few seconds for light adaption to occur, but until it does, the deer is unable to fully see, so it does not move.

**light adaptation**

the recovery of the eye's sensitivity to visual stimuli in light after exposure to darkness.

**trichromatic theory**

theory of color vision that proposes three types of cones: red, blue, and green; "three colors" theory.

room or house. Some research indicates that taking supplements such as vitamin A can reverse or relieve this symptom in some cases (Jacobson et al., 1995). When going from a darkened room to one that is brightly lit, the opposite process occurs. The cones have to adapt to the increased level of light, and they accomplish this **light adaptation** much more quickly than the rods adapt to darkness—it takes a few seconds at most (Hood, 1998).

## PERCEPTION OF COLOR

**3.6** **Compare and contrast two major theories of color vision, and explain how color-deficient vision occurs.**

💬 Earlier you said the cones are used in color vision. There are so many colors in the world—are there cones that detect each color? Or do all cones detect all colors?

Although experts in the visual system have been studying color and its nature for many years, at this point in time there is an ongoing theoretical discussion about the role the cones play in the sensation of color.

**TRICHROMATIC THEORY**    Two theories about how people see colors were originally proposed in the 1800s. The first is called the **trichromatic ("three colors") theory**. First proposed by Thomas Young in 1802 and later modified by Hermann von Helmholtz in 1852, this theory proposed three types of cones: red cones, blue cones, and green cones, one for each of the three primary colors of light.

Most people probably think that the primary colors are red, yellow, and blue, but these are the primary colors when talking about *painting*—not when talking about *light*. Paints *reflect* light, and the way reflected light mixes is different from the way direct light mixes. For example, if an artist were to blend red, yellow, and blue paints together, the result would be a mess—a black mess. The mixing of paint (reflected light) is subtractive, removing more light as you mix in more colors. As all of the colors are mixed, more light waves are absorbed and we see black. But if the artist were to blend a red, green, and blue light together by focusing lights of those three colors on one common spot, the result would be white, not black (see **Figure 3.6**). The mixing of direct light is additive, resulting in lighter colors, more light, and when mixing red, blue, and green, we see white, the reflection of the entire visual spectrum.

In the trichromatic theory, different shades of colors correspond to different amounts of light received by each of these three types of cones. These cones then fire their message to the brain's vision centers. It is the combination of cones and the rate at which they are firing that determine the color that will be seen. For example, if the red and green cones are firing in response to a stimulus at fast enough rates, the color the person sees is yellow. If the red and blue cones are firing fast enough, the result is magenta. If the blue and green cones are firing fast enough, a kind of cyan color (blue-green) appears.

Paul K. Brown and George Wald (1964) identified three types of cones in the retina, each sensitive to a range of wavelengths, measured in nanometers (nm), and a peak sensitivity that roughly corresponds to three different colors (although hues/colors can vary depending on brightness and saturation). The peak wavelength of light the cones seem to be most sensitive to turns out to be just a little different from Young and von Helmholtz's original three corresponding colors: Short-wavelength cones detect what we see as blue-violet (about 420 nm), medium-wavelength cones detect what we see as green (about 530 nm), and long-wavelength cones detect what we see as green-yellow (about 560 nm). Interestingly, none of the cones identified by Brown and Wald have a peak sensitivity to light where most of us see red (around 630 nm). Keep in mind, though, each cone responds to light across a range of wavelengths, not just its wavelength of peak sensitivity. Depending on the intensity of the light, both the medium and long wavelength cones respond to light that appears red, as shown in **Figure 3.7**.

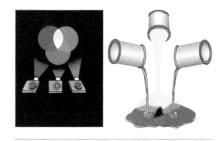

**Figure 3.6** Mixing Light

The mixing of direct light is different than the mixing of reflected light. The mixing of red, blue, and green light is additive, resulting in white light. The mixing of multiple colors of paint (reflected light) is subtractive, resulting in a dark gray or black color.

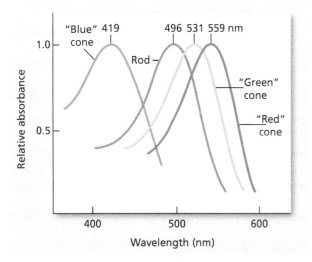

**Figure 3.7** Absorbance of Light from Rods and Three Types of Cones

**OPPONENT-PROCESS THEORY**   The trichromatic theory would, at first glance, seem to be more than adequate to explain how people perceive color. But there's an interesting phenomenon that this theory cannot explain. If a person stares at a picture of the American flag for a little while—say, a minute—and then looks away to a blank white wall or sheet of paper, that person will see an afterimage of the flag. **Afterimages** occur when a visual sensation persists for a brief time even after the original stimulus is removed. The person would also notice rather quickly that the colors of the flag in the afterimage are all wrong—green for red, black for white, and yellow for blue. If you follow the directions for **Figure 3.8**, in which the flag is yellow, green, and black, you should see a flag with the usual red, white, and blue.

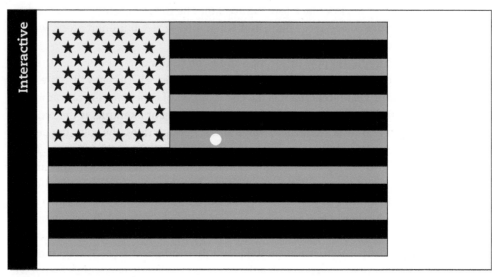

**Figure 3.8**   Color Afterimage

 💬 Hey, now the afterimage of the flag has normal colors! Why does this happen?

The phenomenon of the color afterimage is explained by the second theory of color perception, called the **opponent-process theory** (De Valois & De Valois, 1993; Hurvich & Jameson, 1957), based on an idea first suggested by Edwald Hering in 1874 (Finger, 1994). In opponent-process theory, there are four primary colors: red, green, blue, and yellow. The colors are arranged in pairs, with each member of the pair as opponents. Red is paired with its opponent green, and blue is paired with its opponent yellow. If one member of a pair is strongly stimulated, the other member is inhibited and cannot be working—so there are no reddish-greens or bluish-yellows.

So how can this kind of pairing cause a color afterimage? From the level of the bipolar and ganglion cells in the retina, all the way through the thalamus, and on to the visual cortical areas in the brain, some neurons (or groups of neurons) are stimulated by light from one part of the visual spectrum and inhibited by light from a different part of the spectrum. For example, let's say we have a red-green ganglion cell in the retina whose baseline activity is rather weak when we expose it to white light. However, the cell's activity is increased by red light, so we experience the color red. If we stimulate the cell with red light for a long enough period of time, the cell becomes fatigued. If we then swap out the red light with white light, the fatigued cell responds even less than the original baseline. Now we experience the color green, because green is associated with a decrease in the responsiveness of this cell.

So which theory is the right one? Both theories play a part in color vision. Trichromatic theory can explain what is happening with the raw stimuli, the actual detection of various wavelengths of light. Opponent-process theory can explain afterimages and

**afterimages**

images that occur when a visual sensation persists for a brief time even after the original stimulus is removed.

**opponent-process theory**

theory of color vision that proposes visual neurons (or groups of neurons) are stimulated by light of one color and inhibited by light of another color.

other aspects of visual perception that occur after the initial detection of light from our environment. In addition to the retinal bipolar and ganglion cells, opponent-process cells are contained inside the thalamus in an area called the lateral geniculate nucleus (LGN). The LGN is part of the pathway that visual information takes to the occipital lobe. It is when the cones in the retina send signals through the retinal bipolar and ganglion cells that we see the red versus green pairings and blue versus yellow pairings. Together with the retinal cells, the cells in the LGN appear to be the ones responsible for opponent-processing of color vision and the afterimage effect.

> 💬 So which theory accounts for color blindness? I've heard that there are two kinds of color blindness, when you can't tell red from green and when you can't tell blue from yellow.

**COLOR BLINDNESS**    From the mention of red-green and yellow-blue color blindness, one might think that the opponent-process theory explains this problem. But in reality, "color blindness" is caused by defective cones in the retina of the eye and, as a more general term, *color-deficient vision* is more accurate, as most people with "color blindness" have two types of cones working and can see many colors.

There are really three kinds of color-deficient vision. In a very rare type, *monochrome color blindness*, people either have no cones or have cones that are not working at all. Essentially, if they have cones, they only have one type and, therefore, everything looks the same to the brain—shades of gray. The other types of color-deficient vision, or *dichromatic vision*, are caused by the same kind of problem—having one cone that does not work properly. So instead of experiencing the world with normal vision based on combinations of three cones or colors, trichromatic vision, individuals with dichromatic vision experience the world with essentially combinations of two cones or colors. Red-green color deficiency is due to the lack of functioning red or green cones. In both of these, the individual confuses reds and greens, seeing the world primarily in blues, yellows, and shades of gray. In one real-world example, a November 2015 professional American football game had one team in all green uniforms and the other in all red uniforms. The combination caused problems for some viewers, who were unable to tell the teams apart! A lack of functioning blue cones is much less common and causes blue-yellow color deficiency. These individuals see the world primarily in reds, greens, and shades of gray. To get an idea of what a test for color-deficient vision is like, look at **Figure 3.9.**

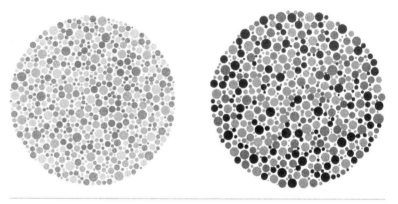

**Figure 3.9**    The Ishihara Color Test

In the circle on the left, the number 8 is visible only to those with normal color vision. In the circle on the right, people with normal vision will see the number 96, while those with red-green color blindness will see nothing but a circle of dots.

 💬 Why are most of the people with color-deficient vision men?

Color-deficient vision involving one set of cones is inherited in a pattern known as *sex-linked inheritance.* The gene for color-deficient vision is *recessive.* To inherit a recessive trait, you normally need two of the genes, one from each parent. Ⓛⓘⓝⓚ to Learning Objective 8.3. But the gene for color-deficient vision is attached to a particular chromosome (a package of genes) that helps determine the sex of a person. Men have one X chromosome and one smaller Y chromosome (named for their shapes), whereas women have two X chromosomes. The smaller Y has fewer genes than the larger X, and one of the genes missing is the one that would suppress the gene for color-deficient vision. For a woman to have color-deficient vision, she must inherit two recessive genes, one from each parent, but a man only needs to inherit *one* recessive gene—the one passed on to him on his mother's X chromosome. His odds are greater; therefore, more males than females have color-deficient vision.

## Concept Map L.O. 3.4, 3.5, 3.6

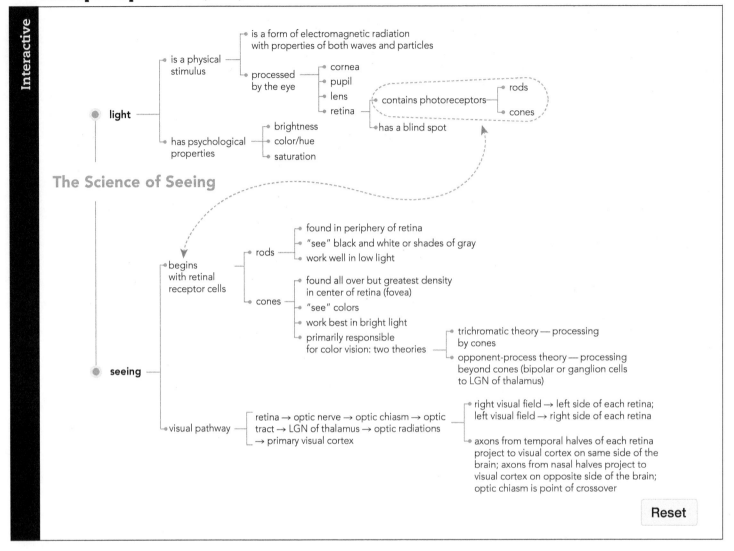

The Science of Seeing

- **light**
  - is a physical stimulus
    - is a form of electromagnetic radiation with properties of both waves and particles
    - processed by the eye
      - cornea
      - pupil
      - lens
      - retina
        - contains photoreceptors
          - rods
          - cones
        - has a blind spot
  - has psychological properties
    - brightness
    - color/hue
    - saturation

- **seeing**
  - begins with retinal receptor cells
    - rods
      - found in periphery of retina
      - "see" black and white or shades of gray
      - work well in low light
    - cones
      - found all over but greatest density in center of retina (fovea)
      - "see" colors
      - work best in bright light
      - primarily responsible for color vision: two theories
        - trichromatic theory — processing by cones
        - opponent-process theory — processing beyond cones (bipolar or ganglion cells to LGN of thalamus)
  - visual pathway
    - retina → optic nerve → optic chiasm → optic tract → LGN of thalamus → optic radiations → primary visual cortex
      - right visual field → left side of each retina; left visual field → right side of each retina
      - axons from temporal halves of each retina project to visual cortex on same side of the brain; axons from nasal halves project to visual cortex on opposite side of the brain; optic chiasm is point of crossover

Reset

# Practice Quiz    How much do you remember?

*Pick the best answer.*

1. Which of the following is largely determined by the length of a light wave?
   a. color
   b. brightness
   c. saturation
   d. duration

2. Aside from the lens, damage to the _____ can affect the eye's ability to focus light.
   a. iris
   b. cornea
   c. pupil
   d. retina

3. In farsightedness, also known as _____, the focal point is _____ the retina.
   a. presbyopia; above
   b. myopia; below
   c. hyperopia; beyond
   d. presbyopia; in front of

4. Colleen stares at a fixed spot in her bedroom using only one eye. After a while, what might happen to her vision?
   a. Any small object that crosses her visual field very slowly may at one point disappear.
   b. Any object that she focuses on will begin to rotate, first clockwise, then counterclockwise.
   c. Objects will become more focused the longer she looks at them.
   d. Objects will become more distorted the longer she looks at them.

5. What are the three primary colors as proposed by the trichromatic theory?
   a. red, yellow, blue
   b. red, green, blue
   c. white, black, brown
   d. white, black, red

6. Which of the following best explains afterimages?
   a. trichromatic theory
   b. opponent-process theory
   c. color-deficient vision
   d. monochrome color blindness

# The Hearing Sense: Can You Hear Me Now?

💬 If light works like waves, then do sound waves have similar properties?

The properties of sound are indeed similar to those of light, as both senses rely on waves. But the similarity ends there, as the physical properties of sound are different from those of light.

## SOUND WAVES AND THE EAR

**3.7 Explain the nature of sound, and describe how it travels through the various parts of the ear.**

Sound waves do not come in little packets the way light comes in photons. Sound waves are simply the vibrations of the molecules of air that surround us. Sound waves do have the same properties of light waves though—wavelength, amplitude, and purity. Wavelengths are interpreted by the brain as frequency or *pitch* (high, medium, or low). Amplitude is interpreted as *volume*, how soft or loud a sound is. (See **Figure 3.10**.) Finally, what

*"And only you can hear this whistle?"*

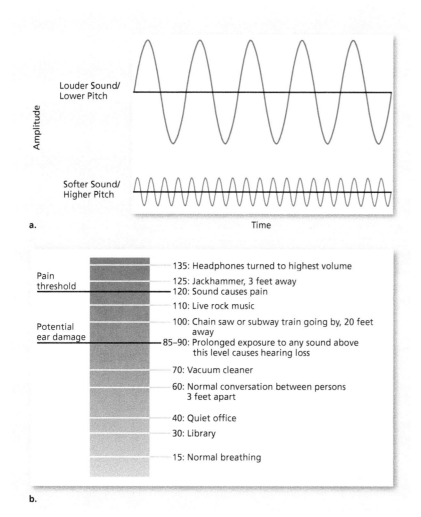

**Figure 3.10** Sound Waves and Decibels

(a) Two sound waves. The higher the wave, the louder the sound; the lower the wave, the softer the sound. If the waves are close together in time (high frequency), the pitch will be perceived as a high pitch. Waves that are farther apart (low frequency) will be perceived as having a lower pitch. (b) Decibels of various stimuli. A *decibel* is a unit of measure for loudness. Psychologists study the effects that noise has on stress, learning, performance, aggression, and psychological and physical well-being.

would correspond to saturation or purity in light is called *timbre* in sound, a richness in the tone of the sound. And just as people rarely see pure colors in the world around us, they also seldom hear pure sounds. The everyday noises that surround people do not allow them to hear many pure tones.

Just as a person's vision is limited by the visible spectrum of light, a person is also limited in the range of frequencies he or she can hear. Frequency is measured in cycles (waves) per second, or **hertz (Hz)**. Human limits are between 20 and 20,000 Hz, with the most sensitivity from about 2,000 to 4,000 Hz, very important for conversational speech. (In comparison, dogs can hear between 50 and 60,000 Hz, and dolphins can hear up to 200,000 Hz.) To hear the higher and lower frequencies of a piece of music on their iPod® or iPhone®, for example, a person would need to increase the amplitude or volume—which explains why some people like to "crank it up."

**THE STRUCTURE OF THE EAR: FOLLOW THE VIBES**   The ear is a series of structures, each of which plays a part in the sense of hearing, as shown in **Figure 3.11**.

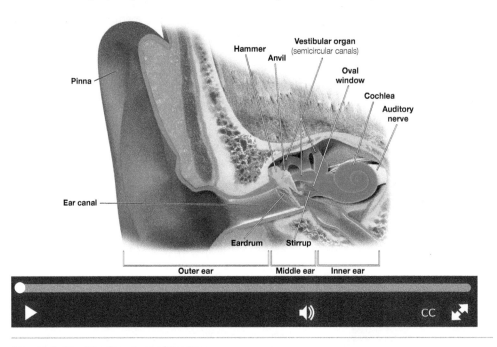

**Figure 3.11**   The Structure of the Ear

**THE OUTER EAR**   The **pinna** is the visible, external part of the ear that serves as a kind of concentrator, funneling* the sound waves from the outside into the structure of the ear. The pinna is also the entrance to the **auditory canal** (or ear canal), the short tunnel that runs down to the *tympanic membrane*, or eardrum. When sound waves hit the eardrum, they cause three tiny bones in the middle ear to vibrate.

**THE MIDDLE EAR: HAMMER, ANVIL, AND STIRRUP**   The three tiny bones in the middle ear are known as the hammer (*malleus*), anvil (*incus*), and stirrup (*stapes*), each name stemming from the shape of the respective bone. Collectively they are referred to as the *ossicles* and they are the smallest bones in the human body. The vibration of these three bones amplifies the vibrations from the eardrum. The stirrup, the last bone in the chain, causes a membrane covering the opening of the inner ear to vibrate.

**THE INNER EAR**   This membrane is called the *oval window*, and its vibrations set off another chain reaction within the inner ear. The inner ear is a snail-shaped structure called the **cochlea**, which is filled with fluid. When the oval window vibrates, it causes

**hertz (Hz)**

cycles or waves per second, a measurement of frequency.

**pinna**

the visible part of the ear.

**auditory canal**

short tunnel that runs from the pinna to the eardrum.

**cochlea**

snail-shaped structure of the inner ear that is filled with fluid.

---

*funneling: moving to a focal point.

the fluid in the cochlea to vibrate. This fluid surrounds a membrane running through the middle of the cochlea called the *basilar membrane*.

The *basilar membrane* is the resting place of the *organ of Corti*, which contains the receptor cells for the sense of hearing. When the basilar membrane vibrates, it vibrates the organ of Corti, causing it to brush against a membrane above it. On the organ of Corti are special cells called *hair cells*, which are the receptors for sound. When these auditory receptors or hair cells are bent up against the other membrane, it causes them to send a neural message through the **auditory nerve** (which contains the axons of all the receptor neurons) and into the brain, where after passing through the thalamus, the auditory cortex will interpret the sounds (the transformation of the vibrations of sound into neural messages is transduction). The louder the sound in the outside world, the stronger the vibrations that stimulate more of those hair cells—which the brain interprets as loudness.

> 💬 I think I have it straight—but all of that just explains how soft and loud sounds get to the brain from the outside. How do we hear different kinds of sounds, like high pitches and low pitches?

### PERCEIVING PITCH

**3.8** **Summarize three theories of how the brain processes information about pitch.**

**Pitch** refers to how high or low a sound is. For example, the bass beats in the music pounding through the wall of your apartment from the neighbors next door are low pitch, whereas the scream of a 2-year-old child is a very high pitch. *Very* high. There are three primary theories about how the brain receives information about pitch.

**PLACE THEORY**   The oldest of the three theories, **place theory**, is based on an idea proposed in 1863 by Hermann von Helmholtz and elaborated on and modified by Georg von Békésy, beginning with experiments first published in 1928 (Békésy, 1960). In this theory, the pitch a person hears depends on where the hair cells that are stimulated are located on the organ of Corti. For example, if the person is hearing a high-pitched sound, all of the hair cells near the oval window will be stimulated, but if the sound is low pitched, all of the hair cells that are stimulated will be located farther away on the organ of Corti.

**FREQUENCY THEORY**   **Frequency theory**, developed by Ernest Rutherford in 1886, states that pitch is related to how fast the basilar membrane vibrates. The faster this membrane vibrates, the higher the pitch; the slower it vibrates, the lower the pitch. (In this theory, all of the auditory neurons would be firing at the same time.)

So which of these first two theories is right? It turns out that both are right—up to a point. For place theory to be correct, the basilar membrane has to vibrate unevenly—which it does when the frequency of the sound is *above* 1,000 Hz. For the frequency theory to be correct, the neurons associated with the hair cells would have to fire as fast as the basilar membrane vibrates. This only works up to 1,000 Hz, because neurons don't appear to fire at exactly the same time and rate when frequencies are faster than 1,000 times per second. Not to mention the maximum firing rate for neurons is approximately 1,000 times per second due to the refractory period.

**VOLLEY PRINCIPLE**   The frequency theory works for low pitches, and place theory works for moderate to high pitches. Is there another explanation? Yes, and it is a third theory, developed by Ernest Wever and Charles Bray, called the **volley principle** (Wever, 1949; Wever & Bray, 1930), which appears to account for pitches from about 400 Hz up to about 4,000 Hz. In this explanation, groups of auditory neurons take turns firing in a process called *volleying*. If a person hears a tone of about 3,000 Hz, it means that three groups of neurons have taken turns sending the message to the brain—the first group for the first 1,000 Hz, the second group for the next 1,000 Hz, and so on.

**auditory nerve**
bundle of axons from the hair cells in the inner ear.

**pitch**
psychological experience of sound that corresponds to the frequency of the sound waves; higher frequencies are perceived as higher pitches.

**place theory**
theory of pitch that states that different pitches are experienced by the stimulation of hair cells in different locations on the organ of Corti.

**frequency theory**
theory of pitch that states that pitch is related to the speed of vibrations in the basilar membrane.

**volley principle**
theory of pitch that states that frequencies from about 400 Hz to 4000 Hz cause the hair cells (auditory neurons) to fire in a volley pattern, or take turns in firing.

**3.9** Identify types of hearing impairment and treatment options for each.

*Hearing impairment* is the term used to refer to difficulties in hearing. A person can be partially hearing impaired or totally hearing impaired, and the treatment for hearing loss will vary according to the reason for the impairment.

**CONDUCTION HEARING IMPAIRMENT** *Conduction hearing impairment*, or conductive hearing loss, refers to problems with the mechanics of the outer or middle ear and means that sound vibrations cannot be passed from the eardrum to the cochlea. The cause might be a damaged eardrum or damage to the bones of the middle ear (usually from an infection). In this kind of impairment, the causes can often be treated, for example, hearing aids may be of some use in restoring hearing.

**NERVE HEARING IMPAIRMENT** In *nerve hearing impairment*, or sensorineural hearing loss, the problem lies either in the inner ear or in the auditory pathways and cortical areas of the brain. This is the most common type of permanent hearing loss. Normal aging causes loss of hair cells in the cochlea, and exposure to loud noises can damage hair cells. *Tinnitus* is a fancy word for an extremely annoying ringing in one's ears, and it can also be caused by infections or loud noises—including loud music in headphones. Prolonged exposure to loud noises further leads to permanent damage and hearing loss, so you might want to turn down that stereo or personal music player!

Because the damage is to the nerves or the brain, nerve hearing impairment cannot typically be helped with ordinary hearing aids, which are basically sound amplifiers, or the hearing aids are not enough. A technique for restoring some hearing to those with irreversible nerve hearing impairment makes use of an electronic device called a *cochlear implant*. This device sends signals from a microphone worn behind the ear to a sound processor worn on the belt or in a pocket, which then translates those signals into electrical stimuli that are sent to a series of electrodes implanted directly into the cochlea, allowing transduction to take place and stimulating the auditory nerve. (See **Figure 3.12**.) The brain then processes the electrode information as sound.

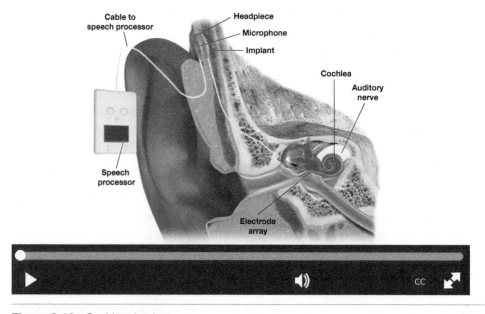

**Figure 3.12** Cochlear Implant

In a cochlear implant, a microphone implanted just behind the ear picks up sound from the surrounding environment. A speech processor, attached to the implant and worn outside the body, selects and arranges the sound picked up by the microphone. The implant itself is a transmitter and receiver, converting the signals from the speech processor into electrical impulses that are collected by the electrode array in the cochlea and then sent to the brain.

How might someone who has had total hearing loss from birth react to being able to hear?

▶ The response entered here will be saved to your notes and may be collected by your instructor if he/she requires it.

Submit

---

## Concept Map L.O. 3.7, 3.8, 3.9

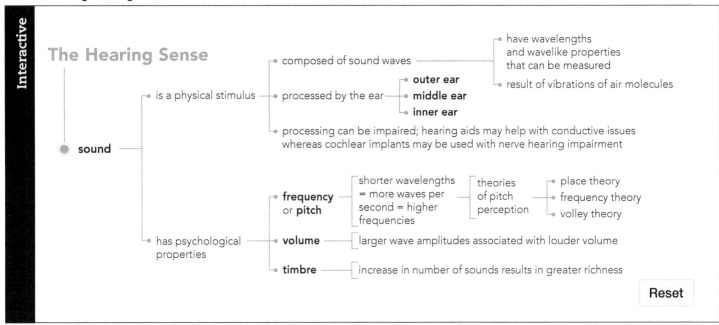

**Interactive**

**The Hearing Sense**

sound
- is a physical stimulus
  - composed of sound waves
    - have wavelengths and wavelike properties that can be measured
    - result of vibrations of air molecules
  - processed by the ear
    - **outer ear**
    - **middle ear**
    - **inner ear**
  - processing can be impaired; hearing aids may help with conductive issues whereas cochlear implants may be used with nerve hearing impairment
- has psychological properties
  - **frequency or pitch** — shorter wavelengths = more waves per second = higher frequencies
    - theories of pitch perception
      - place theory
      - frequency theory
      - volley theory
  - **volume** — larger wave amplitudes associated with louder volume
  - **timbre** — increase in number of sounds results in greater richness

Reset

---

# Practice Quiz    How much do you remember?

*Pick the best answer.*

1. The part of the ear that can be seen is also called the
   a. pinna.
   b. oval window.
   c. organ of Corti.
   d. cochlea.

2. The oval window is found in what part of the ear?
   a. outer ear
   b. middle ear
   c. inner ear
   d. The oval window is not a structure of the ear.

3. Which theory cannot adequately account for pitches above 1,000 Hz?
   a. place
   b. frequency
   c. volley
   d. adaptive

4. Yoshi has suffered minor damage to the bones in his left middle ear. What treatment, if any, might help restore his hearing?
   a. a hearing aid
   b. a cochlear implant
   c. Both a hearing aid and a cochlear implant will be needed.
   d. Such damage is permanent and cannot be remedied.

5. Which is considered the most common type of permanent hearing loss?
   a. psychological hearing loss
   b. conductive hearing loss
   c. frequency-based hearing loss
   d. sensorineural hearing loss

---

# Chemical Senses: It Tastes Good and Smells Even Better

The sense of taste (taste in food, not taste in clothing or friends) and the sense of smell are very closely related. As Dr. Alan Hirsch, a researcher on smell and taste, explains in the video *Smell and Taste*, about 90 percent of what we deem taste is really smell. Have you ever noticed that when your nose is all stopped up, your sense of taste is affected, too? That's because the sense of taste is really a combination of taste and smell. Without the input from the nose, there are actually only four, or possibly five, kinds of taste sensors in the mouth.

👁 **Watch** the **Video** *Smell and Taste*

### GUSTATION: HOW WE TASTE THE WORLD

**3.10** **Explain how the sense of taste works.**

Our food preferences, or aversions, start to form very early in life, very early! Taste is one of our earliest developed senses. Research suggests developing babies are exposed to substances the mother inhales or digests, and these impart flavor to the amniotic fluid, which the baby also ingests. Along with exposure to different flavors early in life after we are born, these experiences may affect food choices and nutritional status, that is, picking certain foods over others, for a long time to come (Beauchamp & Mennella, 2011; Mennella & Trabulsi, 2012).

**TASTE BUDS**  *Taste buds* are the common name for the taste receptor cells, special kinds of neurons found in the mouth that are responsible for the sense of taste, or **gustation**. Most taste buds are located on the tongue, but there are a few on the roof of the mouth, the cheeks, under the tongue, and in the throat as well. How sensitive people are to various tastes depends on how many taste buds they have; some people have only around 500, whereas others have 20 times that number. The latter are called "supertasters" and need far less seasoning in their food than those with fewer taste buds (Bartoshuk, 1993).

 💬 So taste buds are those little bumps I can see when I look closely at my tongue?

No, those "bumps" are called *papillae*, and the taste buds line the walls of these papillae. (See **Figure 3.13**.)

Each taste bud has about 20 receptors that are very similar to the receptor sites on receiving neurons at the synapse. Ⓛ Ⓘ Ⓝ Ⓚ to Learning Objective 2.3. In fact, the receptors on taste buds work exactly like receptor sites on neurons—they receive molecules of various substances that fit into the receptor like a key into a lock. Taste is often called a chemical sense because it works with the molecules of foods people eat in the same way the neural receptors work with neurotransmitters. When the molecules (dissolved in saliva) fit into the receptors, a signal is fired to the brain, which then interprets the taste sensation.

**gustation**

the sensation of a taste.

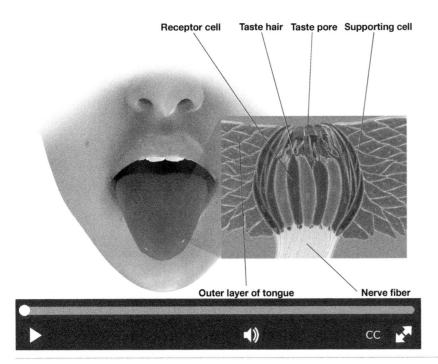

Receptor cell    Taste hair   Taste pore  Supporting cell

Outer layer of tongue          Nerve fiber

**Figure 3.13** The Tongue and Taste Buds.

Taste buds are located inside the papillae of the tongue and are composed of small cells that send signals to the brain when stimulated by molecules of food.

> 💬 What happens to the taste buds when I burn my tongue? Do they repair themselves? I know when I have burned my tongue, I can't taste much for a while, but the taste comes back.

In general, the taste receptors get such a workout that they have to be replaced every 10 to 14 days (McLaughlin & Margolskee, 1994). And when the tongue is burned, the damaged cells no longer work. As time goes on, those cells get replaced and the taste sense comes back.

**THE FIVE BASIC TASTES**    In 1916 a German psychologist named Hans Henning proposed that there are four primary tastes: sweet, sour, salty, and bitter. Lindemann (1996) supported the idea that there is a fifth kind of taste receptor that detects a pleasant "brothy" taste associated with foods like chicken soup, tuna, kelp, cheese, and soy products, among others. Lindemann proposed that this fifth taste be called *umami*, a Japanese word first coined in 1908 by Dr. Kikunae Ikeda of Tokyo Imperial University to describe the taste. Dr. Ikeda had succeeded in isolating the substance in kelp that generated the sensation of umami—glutamate (Beyreuther et al., 2007). Ⓛ Ⓘ Ⓝ Ⓚ to Learning Objective 2.3. Glutamate exists not only in the foods listed earlier but is also present in human breast milk and is the reason that the seasoning MSG—monosodium *glutamate*—adds a pleasant flavor to foods. Although not yet widely accepted, researchers have recently suggested there may be yet another basic taste. The proposed name for this potential sixth taste is *oleogustus*, the taste of fatty acids in the food we eat (Running et al., 2015).

Although researchers used to believe that certain tastes were located on certain places on the tongue, it is now known that all of the taste sensations are processed all over the tongue (Bartoshuk, 1993). The taste information is sent to the gustatory cortex, found in the front part of the *insula* and the *frontal operculum*. (See **Figure 3.14**.) These areas are involved in the conscious perception of taste, whereas the texture, or "mouth-feel," of foods is processed in the somatosensory cortex of the parietal lobe (Buck & Bargmann, 2013; Pritchard, 2012; Shepherd, 2012). The five taste sensations work together, along with the sense of smell and the texture, temperature, and "heat" of foods, to produce thousands

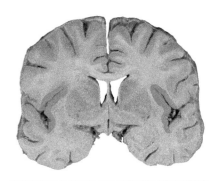

**Figure 3.14** The Gustatory Cortex

The gustatory cortex is found in the anterior insula and frontal operculum. The insula is an area of cortex covered by folds of overlying cortex, and each fold is an operculum. In the coronal section of a human brain above, the gustatory cortex is found in the regions colored a light red.

of taste sensations, which are further affected by our culture, personal expectations, and past learning experiences. For example, boiled peanuts are not an uncommon snack in parts of the southern United States, but the idea of a warm, soft and mushy, slightly salty peanut may not be appealing in other parts of the country. The cortical taste areas also project to parts of the limbic system, which helps explain why tastes can be used for both positive and negative reinforcement (Pritchard, 2012). Ⓛ Ⓘ Ⓝ Ⓚ to Learning Objective 5.5.

Just as individuals and groups can vary on their food preferences, they can also vary on level of perceived sweetness. For example, obese individuals have been found to experience less sweetness than individuals who are not obese; foods that are both sweet and high in fat tend to be especially attractive to individuals who are obese (Bartoshuk et al., 2006). Such differences (as well as genetic variations like the supertasters) complicate direct comparison of food preferences. One possible solution is to have individuals rate taste in terms of an unrelated "standard" sensory experience of known intensity, such as the brightness of a light or loudness of a sound or preference in terms of all pleasurable experiences, and not just taste (Bartoshuk et al., 2005; Snyder & Bartoshuk, 2009).

Turning our attention back to how things taste for us as individuals, have you ever noticed that when you have a cold, food tastes very bland? Everything becomes bland or muted because you can taste only sweet, salty, bitter, sour, and umami—and because your nose is stuffed up with a cold, you don't get all the enhanced variations of those tastes that come from the sense of smell.

### THE SENSE OF SCENTS: OLFACTION

### 3.11 Explain how the sense of smell works.

Like the sense of taste, the sense of smell is a chemical sense. The ability to smell odors is called **olfaction**, or the **olfactory sense**.

The outer part of the nose serves the same purpose for odors that the pinna and ear canal serve for sounds: Both are merely ways to collect the sensory information and get it to the part of the body that will translate it into neural signals.

The part of the olfactory system that transduces odors—turns odors into signals the brain can understand—is located at the top of the nasal passages. This area of olfactory receptor cells is only about an inch square in each cavity yet contains about 10 million olfactory receptors. (See **Figure 3.15**.)

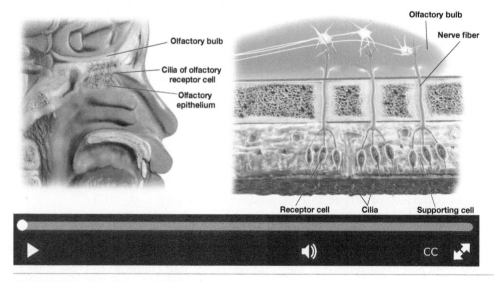

**Figure 3.15** The Olfactory Receptors

(a) A cross-section of the nose and mouth. This drawing shows the nerve fibers inside the nasal cavity that carry information about smell directly to the olfactory bulb just under the frontal lobe of the brain (shown in green). (b) A diagram of the cells in the nose that process smell. The olfactory bulb is on top. Notice the cilia, tiny hairlike cells that project into the nasal cavity. These are the receptors for the sense of smell.

**olfaction (olfactory sense)**
the sensation of smell.

**OLFACTORY RECEPTOR CELLS**   The *olfactory receptor cells* each have about a half dozen to a dozen little "hairs," called *cilia*, that project into the cavity. Like taste buds, there are receptor sites on these hair cells that send signals to the brain when stimulated by the molecules of substances that are in the air moving past them.

 💬 Wait a minute—you mean that when I can smell something like a skunk, there are little particles of skunk odor IN my nose?

Yes. When a person is sniffing something, the sniffing serves to move molecules of whatever the person is trying to smell into the nose and into the nasal cavities. That's okay when it's the smell of baking bread, apple pie, flowers, and the like, but when it's skunk, rotten eggs, dead animals—well, try not to think about it too much.

Olfactory receptors are like taste buds in another way, too. Olfactory receptors also have to be replaced as they naturally die off, about every 5–8 weeks. Unlike the taste buds, there are many more than 5 types of olfactory receptors—in fact, there are at least 1,000 of them.

Signals from the olfactory receptors in the nasal cavity do not follow the same path as the signals from all the other senses. Vision, hearing, taste, and touch all pass through the thalamus and then on to the area of the cortex that processes that particular sensory information. But the sense of smell has its own special place in the brain—the olfactory bulbs.

**THE OLFACTORY BULBS**   The **olfactory bulbs** are located right on top of the sinus cavity on each side of the brain directly beneath the frontal lobes. (Refer to Figure 3.15.) The olfactory receptors send their neural signals directly up to these bulbs, bypassing the thalamus, the relay center for all other sensory information. The olfactory information is then sent from the olfactory bulbs to higher cortical areas, including the primary olfactory cortex (the *piriform cortex*), the orbitofrontal cortex, and the amygdala (remember from Chapter Two that the orbitofrontal cortex and amygdala play important roles in emotion). Ⓛ Ⓘ Ⓝ Ⓚ to Learning Objectives 2.11 and 2.12.

**olfactory bulbs**

two bulb-like projections of the brain located just above the sinus cavity and just below the frontal lobes that receive information from the olfactory receptor cells.

### Concept Map L.O. 3.10, 3.11

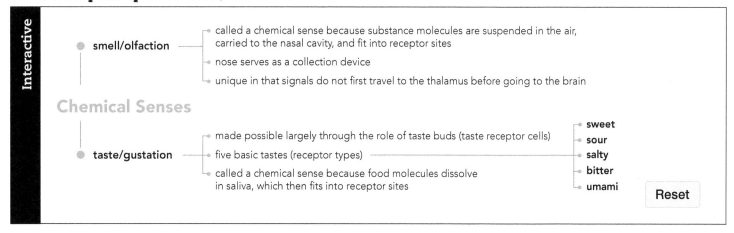

## Practice Quiz   How much do you remember?

*Pick the best answer.*

**1.** Taste is often called a _____ sense because it works with the molecules of foods that people eat.
   **a.** physical
   **b.** psychological
   **c.** chemical
   **d.** electrical

**2.** Research has found that taste information is sent to the
   **a.** pons and medulla.
   **b.** suprachiasmatic nucleus.
   **c.** cerebellum and parietal lobe.
   **d.** insula and frontal operculum.

**3.** How often are olfactory receptors replaced by new olfactory receptors?
   **a.** every 12–24 hours
   **b.** every 2–3 days
   **c.** every 30 days
   **d.** every 5–8 weeks

**4.** Olfactory receptors project directly to the _____ and are unique in that signals do not first connect to the thalamus.
   **a.** occipital lobe
   **b.** olfactory bulbs
   **c.** hypothalamus
   **d.** gustatory cortex

The sense of touch allows individuals that are blind to "read" a Braille book with their fingers. The fingertips are extremely sensitive to fine differences in texture, allowing readers to distinguish between small dots representing the different letters of the alphabet.

**somesthetic senses**

the body senses consisting of the skin senses, the kinesthetic and proprioceptive senses, and the vestibular sense.

# The Other Senses: What the Body Knows

So far, this chapter has covered vision, hearing, taste, and smell. That leaves touch. What is thought of as the sense of touch is really several sensations, originating in several different places in—and on—the body. It's really more accurate to refer to these as the body senses, or **somesthetic senses**. The first part of that word, *soma*, means "body," as mentioned in Chapter Two. The second part, *esthetic*, means "feeling," hence the name. We will discuss four somesthetic sense systems.

## SOMESTHETIC SENSES

**3.12** **Describe how we experience the sensations of touch, pressure, temperature, and pain.**

Here's a good trivia question: What organ of the body is about 20 square feet in size? The answer is the skin. Skin is an organ. Its purposes include more than simply keeping bodily fluids in and germs out; skin also receives and transmits information from the outside world to the central nervous system (specifically, to the somatosensory cortex). ⓛ ⓘ ⓝ ⓚ to Learning Objective 2.12. Information about light touch, deeper pressure, hot, cold, and even pain is collected by special receptors in the skin's layers.

**TYPES OF SENSORY RECEPTORS IN THE SKIN** There are about half a dozen different receptors in the layers of the skin. (See **Figure 3.16**.) Some of them will respond to only one kind of sensation. For example, the *Pacinian corpuscles* are just beneath the skin and respond to changes in pressure. There are nerve endings that wrap around the ends of the hair follicles, a fact people may be well aware of when they tweeze their eyebrows or when someone pulls their hair. These nerve endings are sensitive to both pain and touch. There are *free nerve endings* just beneath the uppermost layer of the skin that respond to changes in temperature and to pressure—and to pain.

 How exactly does pain work? Why is it that sometimes I feel pain deep inside? Are there pain receptors there, too?

Yes, there are pain nerve fibers in the internal organs as well as receptors for pressure. How else would people have a stomachache or intestinal* pain—or get that full feeling of pressure when they've eaten too much or their bladder is full?

There are actually different types of pain. There are receptors that detect pain (and pressure) in the organs, a type of pain called *visceral pain*. Pain sensations in the skin, muscles, tendons, and joints are carried on large nerve fibers and are called *somatic pain*. Somatic pain is the body's warning system that something is being or is about to be damaged and tends to be sharp and fast. Another type of somatic pain is carried on small nerve fibers and is slower and more of a general ache. This somatic pain acts as a kind of reminder system, keeping people from further injury by reminding them that the body has already been damaged. For example, if you hit your thumb with a hammer, the immediate pain

**Figure 3.16** Cross-Section of the Skin and Its Receptors

The skin is composed of several types of cells that process pain, pressure, and temperature. Some of these cells are wrapped around the ends of the hairs on the skin and are sensitive to touch on the hair itself, whereas others are located near the surface and still others just under the top layer of tissue.

Labels in figure: Hair; Skin surface; Pain-sensitive and touch-sensitive free nerve endings; Pressure-sensitive nerves; Skin layers; Meissner's corpuscle; Sweat gland; Subcutaneous fat; Blood vessels; Pacinian corpuscle; Ruffini ending

*intestinal: having to do with the tubes in the body that digest food and process waste material.

sensation is of the first kind—sharp, fast, and bright. But later the bruised tissue simply aches, letting you know to take it easy on that thumb.

**PAIN: GATE-CONTROL THEORY**    One explanation for how the sensation of pain works is called *gate-control theory*, first proposed by Ronald Melzack and Patrick Wall (1965) and later refined and expanded (Melzack & Wall, 1996). In this theory, the pain signals must pass through a "gate" located in the spinal cord. The activity of the gate can be closed by nonpain signals coming into the spinal cord from the body and by signals coming from the brain. The gate is not a physical structure but instead represents the relative balance in neural activity of cells in the spinal cord that receive information from the body and then send information to the brain. Additional research has revealed that the activity of relay centers in the brain can also be influenced, and the exact locations and mechanisms are still being investigated. The video *Gate-Control Theory* provides a simulation of how pain signals travel along the spinal cord.

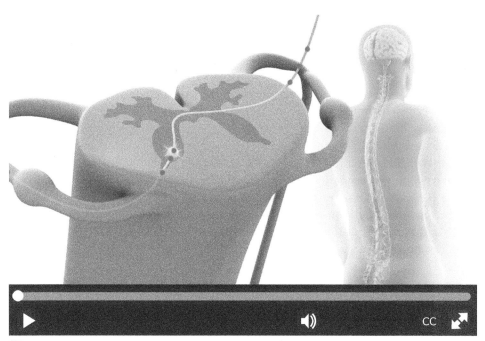

👁 **Watch** the **Video** *Gate-Control Theory of Pain*

Stimulation of the pain receptor cells releases a neuromodulator called *substance P* (for "pain," naturally). Substance P released into the spinal cord activates other neurons that send their messages through spinal gates (opened by the pain signal). From the spinal cord, the message goes to the brain, activating cells in the thalamus, somatosensory cortex, areas of the frontal lobes, and the limbic system. The brain then interprets the pain information and sends signals that either open the spinal gates farther, causing a greater experience of pain, or close them, dampening the pain. Of course, this decision by the brain is influenced by the psychological aspects of the pain-causing stimulus. Anxiety, fear, and helplessness intensify pain, whereas laughter, distraction, and a sense of control can diminish it. (This is why people might bruise themselves and not know it if they were concentrating on something else.) Pain can also be affected by competing signals from other skin senses, which is why rubbing a sore spot can reduce the feeling of pain.

Those same psychological aspects can also influence the release of the *endorphins*, the body's natural version of morphine. Ⓛ Ⓘ Ⓝ Ⓚ to Learning Objective 2.3. Endorphins can inhibit the transmission of pain signals in the brain, and in the spinal cord they can inhibit the release of substance P.

💬 I've always heard that women are able to stand more pain than men. Is that true?

On the contrary, research has shown that women apparently feel pain more intensely than do men, and they also report pain more often than men do (Chesterton et al., 2003; Faucett et al., 1994; Norrbrink et al., 2003). Men have been shown to cope better with many kinds of pain, possibly because men are often found to have a stronger belief than women that they can (or should) control their pain by their own efforts (Jackson et al., 2002).

**PAIN DISORDERS**   People may not like pain, but its function as a warning system is vitally important. There are people who are born without the ability to feel pain, rare conditions called *congenital analgesia* and *congenital insensitivity to pain with anhidrosis (CIPA)*. Children with these disorders cannot feel pain when they cut or scrape themselves, leading to an increased risk of infection when the cut goes untreated (Mogil, 1999). They fear nothing—which can be a horrifying trial for the parents and teachers of such a child. These disorders affect the neural pathways that carry pain, heat, and cold sensations. (Those with CIPA have an additional disruption in the body's heat–cold sensing perspiration system [anhidrosis], so that the person is unable to cool off the body by sweating.)

A condition called *phantom limb pain* occurs when a person who has had an arm or leg removed sometimes "feels" pain in the missing limb (Nikolajsen & Jensen, 2001; Woodhouse, 2005). As many as 50–80 percent of people who have had amputations experience various sensations: burning, shooting pains, or pins-and-needles sensations where the amputated limb used to be. Once believed to be a psychological problem, some now believe that it is caused by the traumatic injury to the nerves during amputation (Ephraim et al., 2005). Other research suggests it may be due to maladaptive neuroplasticity, or reorganization of some parts of the somatosensory cortex (Flor et al., 1995; Karl et al., 2001; Raffin et al., 2016), and yet others suggest this may not be the cause for the pain, at least not in all individuals (Makin et al., 2015).

**THINKING CRITICALLY**

What kinds of changes in your life would you have to make if you suddenly could not feel pain?

▶ The response entered here will be saved to your notes and may be collected by your instructor if he/she requires it.

Submit

**BODY MOVEMENT AND POSITION**

**3.13 Describe the systems that tell us about balance and position and movement of our bodies.**

Besides the systems already covered, there are other senses that tell us about our body. *Kinesthesia* and *proprioception*, awareness of body movement and position, are based on somesthetic information. Information affecting our balance comes from the vestibular system, which informs us about head and whole-body movement and position.

**KINESTHETIC AND PROPRIOCEPTIVE SENSES**   Special receptors located in the muscles, tendons, and joints provide information about body movement and the movement and location of the arms, legs, and so forth in relation to one another. Some of these receptors increase awareness of the body's own movements, or **kinesthesia**, from the Greek words *kinein* ("to move") and *aesthesis* ("sensation"). Changes in the skin stretching as body parts move also provide kinesthetic information.

Congenital insensitivity to pain with anhidrosis (CIPA) is a rare genetic disorder that makes 5-year-old Ashlyn unable to feel pain. She must be examined carefully for scrapes and cuts after recess at school because she cannot feel when she hurts herself, putting her at risk for infection. What are some of the problems that Ashlyn and her parents may face as she grows older?

**kinesthesia**

the awareness of body movement

These special receptors also provide proprioceptive information, letting us know where our body parts are and their position in space. This awareness is called **proprioception**. When you close your eyes and raise your hand above your head, you know where your hand is because these receptors, called proprioceptors, tell you about joint movement or the muscles stretching or contracting.

If you have ever gotten sick from traveling in a moving vehicle, it has not been because of these proprioceptors. The culprits are actually special structures in the ear that tell us about the position of the body in relation to the ground and movement of the head that make up the **vestibular sense**—the sense of balance.

**THE VESTIBULAR SENSE**   The name of this particular sense comes from a Latin word that means "entrance" or "chamber." The structures for this sense are located in the innermost chamber of the ear. There are two kinds of vestibular organs, the otolith organs and the semicircular canals.

The *otolith organs* are tiny sacs found just above the cochlea. These sacs contain a gelatin-like fluid within which tiny crystals are suspended (much like pieces of fruit in a bowl of Jell-O®). The head moves and the crystals cause the fluid to vibrate, setting off some tiny hairlike receptors on the inner surface of the sac, telling the person that he or she is moving forward, backward, sideways, or up and down. (It's pretty much the way the cochlea works but with movement being the stimulus instead of sound vibrations.)

The *semicircular canals* are three somewhat circular tubes that are also filled with fluid that will stimulate hairlike receptors when rotated. Having three tubes allows one to be located in each of the three planes of motion. Remember learning in geometry class about the *x*-, *y*-, and *z*-axes? Those are the three planes through which the body can rotate, and when it does, it sets off the receptors in these canals. When you spin around and then stop, the fluid in the horizontal canal is still rotating and will make you feel dizzy because your body is telling you that you are still moving, but your eyes are telling you that you have stopped. The horizontal canals are also critical in helping us navigate our environments, as they provide important information about which direction we are facing (Valerio & Taube, 2016).

This disagreement between what the eyes say and what the body says is pretty much what causes *motion sickness*, the tendency to get nauseated when in a moving vehicle, especially one with an irregular movement. Normally, the vestibular sense coordinates with the other senses. But for some people, the information from the eyes may conflict a little too much with the vestibular organs, and dizziness, nausea, and disorientation are the result. This explanation of motion sickness is known as **sensory conflict theory** (Oman, 1990; Reason & Brand, 1975). The dizziness is the most likely cause of the nausea. Many poisons make a person dizzy, and the most evolutionarily adaptive thing to do is to expel the poison. Even without any poison in a case of motion sickness, the nausea occurs anyway (Treisman, 1977).

One way some people overcome motion sickness is to focus on a distant point or object. This provides visual information to the person about how he or she is moving, bringing the sensory input into agreement with the visual input. This is also how ballerinas and ice skaters manage not to get sick when turning rapidly and repeatedly—they focus their eyes at least once on some fixed object every so many turns.

Astronauts, who travel in low-gravity conditions, can get a related condition called space motion sickness (SMS). This affects about 60 percent of those who travel in space, typically for about the first week of space travel. After that time of adjustment, the astronauts are able to adapt and the symptoms diminish. Repeated exposure to some environment that causes motion sickness—whether it is space, a car, a train, or some other vehicle—is actually one of the best ways to overcome the symptoms (Hu & Stern, 1999).

**vestibular sense**
the awareness of the balance, position, and movement of the head and body through space in relation to gravity's pull

**proprioception**
awareness of where the body and body parts are located in relation to each other in space, and to the ground.

**sensory conflict theory**
an explanation of motion sickness in which the information from the eyes conflicts with the information from the vestibular senses, resulting in dizziness, nausea, and other physical discomfort.

## Concept Map L.O. 3.12, 3.13

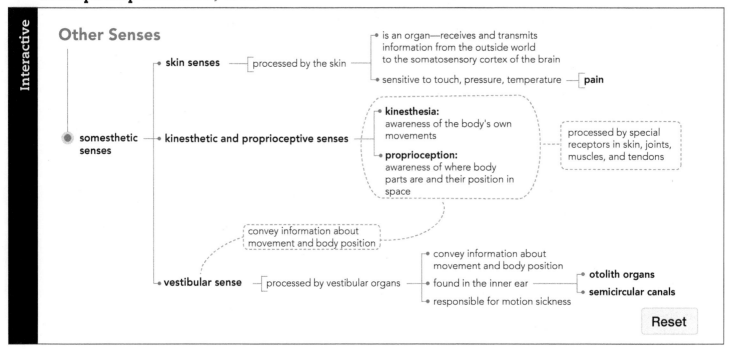

## Practice Quiz    How much do you remember?

*Pick the best answer.*

**1.** _____ are tactile receptors that are located just beneath the skin and respond to changes in pressure.
  **a.** Oligodendrocytes    **c.** Tactile interneurons
  **b.** Free nerve endings   **d.** Pacinian corpuscles

**2.** In gate-control theory, substance P
  **a.** opens the spinal gates for pain.
  **b.** closes the spinal gates for pain.
  **c.** is unrelated to pain.
  **d.** is similar in function to endorphins.

**3.** When you close your eyes and raise your hand above your head, you know where your hand is due to information from
  **a.** your otolith organs.    **c.** your proprioceptors.
  **b.** the horizontal canals.   **d.** the semicircular canals.

**4.** Motion sickness often results from conflicting signals sent from the _____ and from the _____.
  **a.** eyes; vestibular organs    **c.** conscious; unconscious
  **b.** brain; internal organs     **d.** extremities; brain

# The ABCs of Perception

**Perception** is the method by which the brain takes all the sensations a person experiences at any given moment and allows them to be interpreted in some meaningful fashion. Perception has some individuality to it. For example, two people might be looking at a cloud, and while one thinks it's shaped like a horse, the other thinks it's more like a cow. They both *see* the same cloud, but they *perceive* that cloud differently.

### HOW WE ORGANIZE OUR PERCEPTIONS

**3.14 Describe how perceptual constancies and the Gestalt principles account for common perceptual experiences.**

As individual as perception might be, some similarities exist in how people perceive the world around them. As such, there are some circumstances during which stimuli are seemingly automatically perceived in almost the same way by various individuals.

**THE CONSTANCIES: SIZE, SHAPE, AND BRIGHTNESS**    One form of perceptual constancy* is **size constancy**, the tendency to interpret an object as always being the same

**perception**

the method by which the sensations experienced at any given moment are interpreted and organized in some meaningful fashion.

**size constancy**

the tendency to interpret an object as always being the same actual size, regardless of its distance.

_____

* constancy: something that remains the same; the property of remaining stable and unchanging.

size, regardless of its distance from the viewer (or the size of the image it casts on the retina). So if an object that is normally perceived to be about 6 feet tall appears very small on the retina, it will be interpreted as being very far away.

Another perceptual constancy is the tendency to interpret the shape of an object as constant, even when it changes on the retina. This **shape constancy** is why a person still perceives a coin as a circle even if it is held at an angle that makes it appear to be an oval on the retina. Dinner plates on a table are also seen as round, even though from the angle of viewing they are oval. (See **Figure 3.17**.)

A third form of perceptual constancy is **brightness constancy**, the tendency to perceive the apparent brightness of an object as the same even when the light conditions change. If a person is wearing black pants and a white shirt, for example, in broad daylight the shirt will appear to be much brighter than the pants. But if the sun is covered by thick clouds, even though the pants and shirt have less light to reflect than previously, the shirt will still appear to be just as much brighter than the pants as before—because the different amount of light reflected from each piece of clothing is still the same difference as before (Zeki, 2001).

**THE GESTALT PRINCIPLES** Remember the discussion of the Gestalt theorists in Chapter One? Their original focus on human perception can still be seen in certain basic principles today, including the Gestalt tendency to group objects and perceive whole shapes.

**FIGURE–GROUND RELATIONSHIPS** Take a look at the drawing of the cube in **Figure 3.18**. Which face of the cube is in the front? Look again—do the planes and corners of the cube seem to shift as you look at it?

This is called the "Necker cube." It has been around officially since 1832, when Louis Albert Necker, a Swiss scientist who was studying the structure of crystals, first drew it in his published papers. The problem with this cube is that there are conflicting sets of depth cues, so the viewer is never really sure which plane or edge is in the back and which is in the front—the visual presentation of the cube seems to keep reversing its planes and edges.

A similar illusion can be seen in **Figure 3.19**. In this picture, the viewer can switch perception back and forth from two faces looking at each other to the outline of a goblet in the middle. Which is the figure in front and which is the background?

**Figure–ground** relationships refer to the tendency to perceive objects or figures as existing on a background. People seem to have a preference for picking out figures from

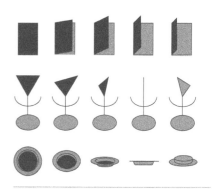

**Figure 3.17** Shape Constancy

Three examples of shape constancy are shown here. The opening door is actually many different shapes, yet we still see it as basically a rectangular door. We do the same thing with a triangle and a circle—and, although when we look at them from different angles they cast differently shaped images on our retina, we experience them as a triangle and a circle because of shape constancy.

### shape constancy

the tendency to interpret the shape of an object as being constant, even when its shape changes on the retina.

### brightness constancy

the tendency to perceive the apparent brightness of an object as the same even when the light conditions change.

### figure–ground

the tendency to perceive objects, or figures, as existing on a background.

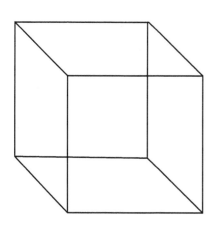

**Figure 3.18** The Necker Cube

This is an example of a reversible figure. It can also be described as an ambiguous figure, since it is not clear which pattern should predominate.

**Figure 3.19** Figure–Ground Illusion

What do you see when you look at this picture? Is it a wine goblet? Or two faces looking at each other? This is an example in which the figure and the ground seem to "switch" each time you look at the picture.

**Figure 3.20**  Gestalt Principles of Grouping

The Gestalt principles of grouping are shown here. These are the human tendency to organize isolated stimuli into groups on the basis of five characteristics: proximity, similarity, closure, continuity, and common region.

*Proximity:* The dots on the left can be seen as horizontal or vertical rows—neither organization dominates. But just by changing the proximity of certain dots, as in the other two examples, we experience the dots as vertical columns (middle) or horizontal rows (right).

*Similarity:* The similarity of color here makes you perceive these dots as forming black squares and color squares rather than two rows of black and colored dots.

*Closure:* Even though the lines are broken, we still see these figures as a circle and a square—an example of how we tend to "close" or "fill in" missing parts from what we know of the whole.

*Continuity:* Because of continuity, we are much more likely to see the figure on the left as being made up of two lines, A to B and C to D, than we are to see it as a figure made up of lines A to D and C to B or A to C and B to D.

*Common Region:* Similarity would suggest that people see two groups, stars and circles. But the colored backgrounds define a visible common region, and the tendency is to perceive three different groups.

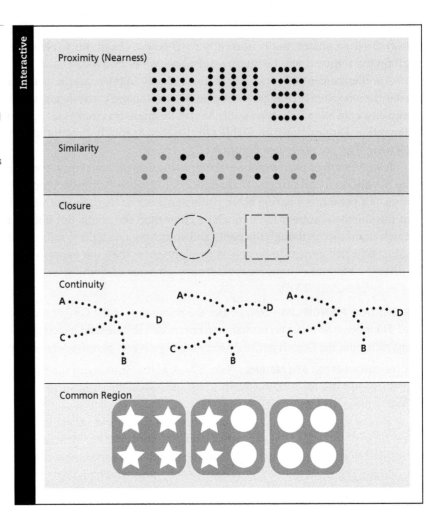

**reversible figures**

visual illusions in which the figure and ground can be reversed.

**proximity**

a Gestalt principle of perception, the tendency to perceive objects that are close to each other as part of the same grouping; physical or geographical nearness.

**similarity**

a Gestalt principle of perception, the tendency to perceive things that look similar to each other as being part of the same group.

**closure**

a Gestalt principle of perception, the tendency to complete figures that are incomplete.

**continuity**

a Gestalt principle of perception, the tendency to perceive things as simply as possible with a continuous pattern rather than with a complex, broken-up pattern.

backgrounds even as early as birth. The illusions in Figures 3.18 and 3.19 are **reversible figures**, in which the figure and the ground seem to switch back and forth.

**PROXIMITY**   Another very simple rule of perception is the tendency to perceive objects that are close to one another as part of the same grouping, a principle called **proximity**, or "nearness." (See **Figure 3.20**.)

**SIMILARITY**   **Similarity** refers to the tendency to perceive things that look similar as being part of the same group. When members of a sports team wear uniforms that are all the same color, it allows people viewing the game to perceive them as one group even when they are scattered around the field or court.

**CLOSURE**   **Closure** is the tendency to complete figures that are incomplete. A talented artist can give the impression of an entire face with just a few cleverly placed strokes of the pen or brush—the viewers fill in the details.

**CONTINUITY**   The principle of **continuity** is easier to see than it is to explain in words. It refers to the tendency to perceive things as simply as possible with a continuous pattern rather than with a complex, broken-up pattern. Look at Figure 3.20 for an example of continuity. Isn't it much easier to see the figure on the left as two wavy lines crossing each other than as the little sections in the diagrams to the right?

**CONTIGUITY** **Contiguity** isn't shown in Figure 3.20 because it involves not just nearness in space but nearness in time also. Basically, contiguity is the tendency to perceive two things that happen close together in time as being related. Usually the first occurring event is seen as causing the second event. Ventriloquists* make vocalizations without appearing to move their own mouths but move their dummy's mouth instead. The tendency to believe that the dummy is doing the talking is due largely to contiguity.

There is one other principle of perceptual grouping that was not one of the original principles. It was added to the list (and can be seen at the bottom of Figure 3.20) by Stephen Palmer (Palmer, 1992). In *common region*, the tendency is to perceive objects that are in a common area or region as being in a group. In Figure 3.20, people could perceive the stars as one group and the circles as another on the basis of similarity. But the colored backgrounds so visibly define common regions that people instead perceive three groups—one of which has both stars and circles in it.

### DEPTH PERCEPTION

**3.15** **Explain how we perceive depth using both monocular and binocular cues.**

The capability to see the world in three dimensions is called **depth perception**. It's a handy ability, because without it you would have a hard time judging how far away objects are. How early in life do humans develop depth perception? It seems to develop very early in infancy, if it is not actually present at birth. People who have had sight restored have almost no ability to perceive depth if they were blind from birth. Depth perception, like the constancies, seems to be present in infants at a very young age. Ⓛ Ⓘ Ⓝ Ⓚ to Learning Objective 8.6.

Various cues exist for perceiving depth in the world. Some require the use of only one eye (**monocular cues**) and some are a result of the slightly different visual patterns that exist when the visual fields of both eyes are used (**binocular cues**).

**MONOCULAR CUES** Monocular cues are often referred to as **pictorial depth cues** because artists can use these cues to give the illusion of depth to paintings and drawings. Examples of these cues are discussed next and can be seen in **Figure 3.21**.

1. **Linear perspective:** When looking down a long interstate highway, the two sides of the highway appear to merge together in the distance. This tendency for lines that are actually parallel to *seem* to converge** on each other is called **linear perspective**. It works in pictures because people assume that in the picture, as in real life, the converging lines indicate that the "ends" of the lines are a great distance away from where the people are as they view them.

2. **Relative size:** The principle of size constancy is at work in **relative size**, when objects that people expect to be of a certain size appear to be small and are, therefore, assumed to be much farther away. Movie makers use this principle to make their small models seem gigantic but off in the distance.

3. **Overlap:** If one object seems to be blocking another object, people assume that the blocked object is behind the first one and, therefore, farther away. This cue is also known as **interposition**.

4. **Aerial (atmospheric) perspective:** The farther away an object is, the hazier the object will appear to be due to tiny particles of dust, dirt, and other pollutants in the air, a perceptual cue called **aerial (atmospheric) perspective**. This is why

---

*ventriloquist: an entertainer who, through the use of misdirection and skill, makes other objects, such as a dummy, appear to talk.

**converge: come together.

**contiguity**
a Gestalt principle of perception, the tendency to perceive two things that happen close together in time as being related.

**depth perception**
the ability to perceive the world in three dimensions

**monocular cues (pictorial depth cues)**
cues for perceiving depth based on one eye only.

**binocular cues**
cues for perceiving depth based on both eyes.

**linear perspective**
monocular depth perception cue, the tendency for parallel lines to appear to converge on each other.

**relative size**
monocular depth perception cue, perception that occurs when objects that a person expects to be of a certain size appear to be small and are, therefore, assumed to be much farther away.

**interposition**
monocular depth perception cue, the assumption that an object that appears to be blocking part of another object is in front of the second object and closer to the viewer.

**aerial (atmospheric) perspective**
monocular depth perception cue, the haziness that surrounds objects that are farther away from the viewer, causing the distance to be perceived as greater.

Interactive

a.

c.

b.

d.

**Figure 3.21** Examples of Pictorial Depth Cues

(a) Both the lines of the trees and the sides of the road appear to come together or converge in the distance. This is an example of *linear perspective*. (b) Notice how the larger pebbles in the foreground seem to give way to smaller and smaller pebbles near the middle of the picture. *Texture gradient* causes the viewer to assume that as the texture of the pebbles gets finer, the pebbles are getting farther away. (c) In *aerial* or *atmospheric perspective*, the farther away something is the hazier it appears because of fine particles in the air between the viewer and the object. Notice that the shed and grassy area in the foreground are in sharp focus while the mountain ranges are hazy and indistinct. (d) The depth cue of *relative size* appears in this photograph. Notice that the flowers in the distance appear much smaller than those in the foreground. Relative size causes smaller objects to be perceived as farther away from the viewer.

distant mountains often look fuzzy, and buildings far in the distance are blurrier than those that are close.

**texture gradient**

monocular depth perception cue, the tendency for textured surfaces to appear to become smaller and finer as distance from the viewer increases.

5. **Texture gradient:** If there are any large expanses of pebbles, rocks, or patterned roads (such as a cobblestone street) nearby, go take a look at them one day. The pebbles or bricks that are close to you are very distinctly textured, but as you look farther off into the distance, their texture becomes smaller and finer. **Texture gradient** is another trick used by artists to give the illusion of depth in a painting.

**motion parallax**

monocular depth perception cue, the perception of motion of objects in which close objects appear to move more quickly than objects that are farther away.

6. **Motion parallax:** The next time you're in a car, notice how the objects outside the car window seem to zip by very fast when they are close to the car, and objects in the distance, such as mountains, seem to move more slowly. This discrepancy in motion of near and far objects is called **motion parallax**.

**accommodation**

as a monocular cue of depth perception, the brain's use of information about the changing thickness of the lens of the eye in response to looking at objects that are close or far away.

7. **Accommodation:** A monocular cue that is not one of the pictorial cues, **accommodation** makes use of something that happens inside the eye. The lens of the human eye is flexible and held in place by a series of muscles. The discussion of the eye earlier in this chapter mentioned the process of visual accommodation as the tendency of the lens to change its shape, or thickness, in response to objects near or far away. The brain can use this information about accommodation as a cue for distance. Accommodation is also called a "muscular cue."

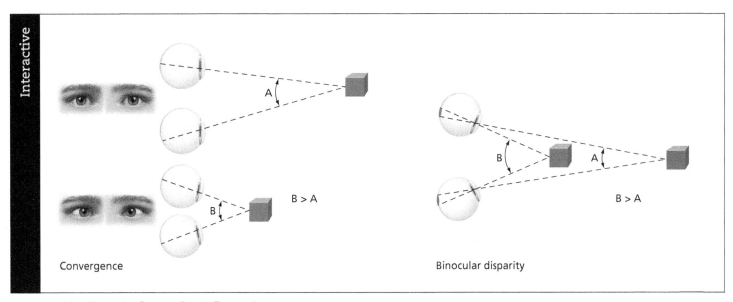

**Figure 3.22** Binocular Cues to Depth Perception

(Left) Convergence is a depth cue that involves the muscles of the eyes. When objects are far away, the eye muscles are more relaxed; when objects are close, the eye muscles move together, or converge. (Right) Binocular disparity. Because your eyes are separated by several centimeters, each eye sees a slightly different image of the object in front of you. In A, the object is far enough away that the difference is small. In B, while the object is closer, there is a greater difference between what each eye sees. The brain interprets this difference as the distance of the object.

**BINOCULAR CUES**    As the name suggests, these cues require the use of two eyes.

1. **Convergence:** Another muscular cue, **convergence**, refers to the rotation of the two eyes in their sockets to focus on a single object. If the object is close, the convergence is pretty great (almost as great as crossing the eyes). If the object is far, the convergence is much less. Hold your finger up in front of your nose, and then move it away and back again. That feeling you get in the muscles of your eyes is convergence. (See **Figure 3.22**, left.)

2. **Binocular disparity: Binocular disparity** is a scientific way of saying that because the eyes are a few inches apart, they don't see exactly the same image. The brain interprets the images on the retina to determine distance from the eyes. If the two images are very different, the object must be pretty close. If they are almost identical, the object is far enough away to make the retinal disparity very small. You can demonstrate this cue for yourself by holding an object in front of your nose. Close one eye, note where the object is, and then open that eye and close the other. There should be quite a difference in views. But if you do the same thing with an object that is across the room, the image doesn't seem to "jump" or move nearly as much, if at all. (See **Figure 3.22**, right.)

In spite of all the cues for perception that exist, even the most sophisticated perceiver can still fail to perceive the world as it actually is, as the next section demonstrates.

**PERCEPTUAL ILLUSIONS**

3.16 **Identify some common visual illusions and the factors that influence our perception of them.**

💬 You've mentioned the word *illusion* several times. Exactly what are illusions, and why is it so easy to be fooled by them?

An *illusion* is a perception that does not correspond to reality: People *think* they see something when the reality is quite different. Another way of thinking of illusions is as visual

**convergence**
binocular depth perception cue, the rotation of the two eyes in their sockets to focus on a single object, resulting in greater convergence for closer objects and lesser convergence if objects are distant.

**binocular disparity**
binocular depth perception cue, the difference in images between the two eyes, which is greater for objects that are close and smaller for distant objects.

**Figure 3.23** The Hermann Grid

Look at this matrix of squares. Do you notice anything interesting at the white intersections? What happens if you focus your vision directly on one of the intersections?

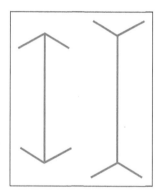

The Müller-Lyer optical illusion features two lines, with one appearing to be longer than the other. In reality, both lines are equal in length.

**Müller-Lyer illusion**

illusion of line length that is distorted by inward-turning or outward-turning corners on the ends of the lines, causing lines of equal length to appear to be different.

stimuli that "fool" the eye. (Illusions are not hallucinations: An illusion is a distorted perception of something that is really there, but a hallucination originates in the brain, not in reality.)

Research involving illusions can be very useful for both psychologists and neuroscientists. These studies often provide valuable information about how the sensory receptors and sense organs work and how humans interpret sensory input.

Sometimes illusions are based on early sensory processes, subsequent processing, or higher-level assumptions made by the brain's visual system (Eagleman, 2001; Macknik et al., 2008).

We've already discussed one visual illusion, color afterimages, which is due to opponent-processes in the retina or LGN of the thalamus after light information has been detected by the rods and cones. Another postdetection but still rather early process has been offered for yet another illusion.

**THE HERMANN GRID**  Look at the matrix of squares in **Figure 3.23**. Notice anything interesting as you look at different parts of the figure, particularly at the intersections of the white lines? You probably see gray blobs or diamonds that fade away or disappear completely when you try to look directly at them. This is the Hermann grid.

One explanation for this illusion is attributed to the responses of neurons in the primary visual cortex that respond best to bars of light of a specific orientation (Schiller & Carvey, 2005). Such neurons are called "simple cells" and were first discovered by David Hubel and Torsten Wiesel (Hubel & Wiesel, 1959). They also discovered other cells including "complex cells," which respond to orientation and movement, and "end-stopped cells," which respond best to corners, curvature, or sudden edges. Collectively these cells have been referred to as *feature detectors* because they respond to specific features of a stimulus. Hubel and Wiesel were later awarded the Nobel Prize for extensive work in the visual system. Other research into the Hermann grid illusion has documented that straight edges are necessary for this illusion to occur, as the illusion disappears when the edges of the grid lines are slightly curved, and further suggests that the illusion may be due to a unique function of how our visual system processes information (Geier et al., 2008).

**MÜLLER-LYER ILLUSION**  One of the most famous visual illusions, the **Müller-Lyer illusion**, is shown in the image to the left. The distortion happens when the viewer tries to determine if the two lines are exactly the same length. They are identical, but one line looks longer than the other. (It's always the line with the angles on the end facing outward.) You can try to determine the length of the lines yourself in the experiment, *Müller-Lyer Illusion* **Simulate** the **Experiment**, *Müller-Lyer Illusion*.

Why is this illusion so powerful? The explanation is that most people live in a world with lots of buildings. Buildings have corners. When a person is outside a building, the corner of the building is close to that person, while the walls seem to be moving away (like the line with the angles facing inward). When the person is inside a building, the corner of the room seems to move away from the viewer while the walls are coming closer (like the line with the angles facing outward). In their minds, people "pull" the inward-facing angles toward them like the outside corners of a building, and they make the outward-facing angles "stretch" away from them like the inside corners of the room (Enns & Coren, 1995; Gregory, 1990).

Marshall Segall and colleagues (Segall et al., 1966) found that people in Western cultures, having carpentered buildings with lots of straight lines and corners (Segall and colleagues refer to this as a "carpentered world"), are far more susceptible to this illusion than people from non-Western cultures (having round huts with few corners—an "uncarpentered world"). Richard Gregory (1990) found that Zulus, for example, rarely see this illusion. They live in round huts arranged in circles, use curved tools and toys, and experience few straight lines and corners in their world.

**THE MOON ILLUSION**  Another common illusion is the *moon illusion*, in which the moon on the horizon* appears to be much larger than the moon in the sky (Plug & Ross, 1994). One explanation for this is that the moon high in the sky is all alone, with no cues for depth surrounding it. But on the horizon, the moon appears behind trees and houses, cues for depth that make the horizon seem very far away. The moon is seen as being behind these objects and, therefore, farther away from the viewer. Because people know that objects that are farther away from them yet still appear large are very large indeed, they "magnify" the moon in their minds—a misapplication of the principle of size constancy. This explanation of the moon illusion is called the *apparent distance hypothesis*. This explanation goes back to the second century A.D., first written about by the Greek–Egyptian astronomer Ptolemy and later further developed by an eleventh-century Arab astronomer, Al-Hazan (Ross & Ross, 1976).

**ILLUSIONS OF MOTION**  Sometimes people perceive an object as moving when it is actually still. One example of this takes place as part of a famous experiment in conformity called the *autokinetic effect*. In this effect, a small, stationary light in a darkened room will appear to move or drift because there are no surrounding cues to indicate that the light is *not* moving. Another is the *stroboscopic motion* seen in motion pictures, in which a rapid series of still pictures will seem to be in motion. Many a student has discovered that drawing little figures on the edges of a notebook and then flipping the pages quickly will also produce this same illusion of movement.

Another movement illusion related to stroboscopic motion is the *phi phenomenon*, in which lights turned on in sequence appear to move. For example, if a light is turned on in a darkened room and then turned off, and then another light a short distance away is flashed on and off, it will appear to be one light moving across that distance. This principle is used to suggest motion in many theater marquee signs, flashing arrows indicating direction that have a series of lights going on and off in a sequence, and even in strings of decorative lighting, such as the "chasing" lights seen on houses at holiday times.

What about seeing motion in static images? There are several examples, both classic and modern, of illusory movement or apparent motion being perceived in a static image. The debate about the causes for such illusions, whether they begin in the eyes or the brain, has been going on for at least 200 years (Troncoso et al., 2008).

Look at **Figure 3.24**. What do you see?

There have been a variety of explanations for this type of motion illusion, ranging from factors that depend on the image's luminance and/or the color arrangement to possibly slight differences in the time it takes the brain to process this information. When fMRI and equipment used to track eye movements were used to investigate participants' perception of a similar illusion, researchers found that there was an increase in brain

The moon illusion. When this moon is high in the night sky, it will still be the same size to the eye as it is now. Nevertheless, it is perceived to be much larger when on the horizon. In the sky, there are no objects for comparison, but on the horizon, objects such as this tree are seen as being in front of a very large moon.

---

*horizon: the place where the earth apparently meets the sky.

**Figure 3.24** Perceived Motion

Notice anything as you move your eyes over this image? The image is not moving; seeing the circles move is due at least in part to movements of your eyes.

**Figure 3.25** "Reinterpretation of Enigma"

As in **Figure 3.24**, the motion you see in this static image is because of movements of your eyes, this time due more to tiny movements called *microsaccades*. Created by and courtesy of Jorge Otero-Millan, Martinez-Conde Laboratory, Barrow Neurological Institute.

**perceptual set (perceptual expectancy)**

the tendency to perceive things a certain way because previous experiences or expectations influence those perceptions.

activity in a visual area sensitive to motion. However, this activity was greatest when accompanied by guided eye movements, suggesting eye movements play a significant role in the perception of the illusion (Kuriki et al., 2008).

Eye movements have also been found to be a primary cause for the illusory motion seen in images based on a 1981 painting by Isia Levant, *Enigma*. Look at the center of **Figure 3.25**; notice anything within the green rings? Many people will see the rings start to "sparkle" or the rings rotating. Why does this occur? By using special eye-tracking equipment that allowed them to record even the smallest of eye movements, researchers found that tiny eye movements called *microsaccades*, discussed earlier in the chapter, are directly linked to the perception of motion in *Enigma* and are at least one possible cause of the illusion (Troncoso et al., 2008).

These two studies highlight some of the advances researchers have made in examining questions related to visual perception. For more information about the study of visual illusions as used in magic and the study of such illusions from a neuroscientific perspective see the Applying Psychology section at the end of the chapter.

**OTHER FACTORS THAT INFLUENCE PERCEPTION**  Human perception of the world is obviously influenced by things such as culture and misinterpretations of cues. Following are other factors that cause people to alter their perceptions.

People often misunderstand what is said to them because they were expecting to hear something else. People's tendency to perceive things a certain way because their previous experiences or expectations influence them is called **perceptual set** or **perceptual expectancy**. Although expectancies can be useful in interpreting certain stimuli, they can also lead people down the wrong path. What you see depends upon what you expect to see. Participate in the experiment *Ambiguous Figures* to see how perceptual set influences how you identify various ambiguous figures. ◉► **Simulate** the **Experiment**, *Ambiguous Figures*

The way in which people *interpret* what they perceive can also influence their perception. For example, people can try to understand what they perceive by using information they already have (as is the case of perceptual expectancy). But if there is no existing information that relates to the new information, they can look at each feature of what they perceive and try to put it all together into one whole.

Anyone who has ever worked on a jigsaw puzzle knows that it's a lot easier to put it together if there is a picture of the finished puzzle to refer to as a guide. It also helps to have worked the puzzle before—people who have done that already know what it's going to look like when it's finished. In the field of perception, this is known as **top-down processing**—the use of existing knowledge to organize individual features into a unified whole. This is also a form of perceptual expectancy.

If the puzzle is one the person has never worked before or if that person has lost the top of the box with the picture on it, he or she would have to start with a small section, put it together, and keep building up the sections until the recognizable picture appears. This analysis of smaller features and building up to a complete perception is called **bottom-up processing** (Cave & Kim, 1999). In this case, there is no expectancy to help organize the perception, making bottom-up processing more difficult in some respects. Fortunately, the two types of processing are often used together in perceiving the surrounding world.

Would people of different cultures perceive objects differently because of different expectancies? Some research suggests that this is true. For example, take a look at **Figure 3.26**. This figure is often called the "devil's trident." Europeans and North Americans insist on making this figure three dimensional, so they have trouble looking at it—the figure is impossible if it is perceived in three dimensions. But people in less technologically oriented cultures have little difficulty with seeing or even reproducing this figure, because they see it as a two-dimensional drawing, quite literally a collection of lines and circles rather than a solid object (Deregowski, 1969). By contrast, if you give Europeans and North Americans the task of reproducing a drawing of an upside-down face, their drawings tend to be more accurate because the upside-down face has become a "collection of lines and circles." That is, they draw what they actually see in terms of light and shadow rather than what they "think" is there three dimensionally.

The Ames Room illusion. This illusion is influenced by our past experiences and expectancies. The viewer perceives the room as a rectangle, but in reality, it is actually a trapezoid with angled walls and floor.

**Figure 3.26** The Devil's Trident

At first glance, this seems to be an ordinary three-pronged figure. But a closer look reveals that the three prongs cannot be real as drawn. Follow the lines of the top prong to see what goes wrong.

**top-down processing**

the use of preexisting knowledge to organize individual features into a unified whole.

**bottom-up processing**

the analysis of the smaller features to build up to a complete perception.

**Concept Map** L.O. 3.14, 3.15, 3.16

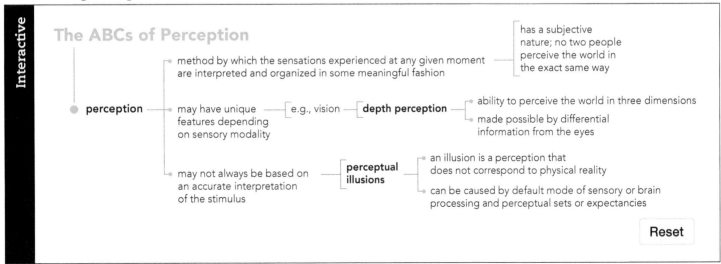

The ABCs of Perception

perception
- method by which the sensations experienced at any given moment are interpreted and organized in some meaningful fashion
  - has a subjective nature; no two people perceive the world in the exact same way
- may have unique features depending on sensory modality
  - e.g., vision — depth perception
    - ability to perceive the world in three dimensions
    - made possible by differential information from the eyes
- may not always be based on an accurate interpretation of the stimulus
  - perceptual illusions
    - an illusion is a perception that does not correspond to physical reality
    - can be caused by default mode of sensory or brain processing and perceptual sets or expectancies

Reset

Interactive

# Practice Quiz    How much do you remember?

*Pick the best answer.*

1. When opening a door, the actual image on your retina changes drastically, but you still perceive the door as a rectangle. This is an example of
   - **a.** size constancy.
   - **b.** shape constancy.
   - **c.** color constancy.
   - **d.** brightness constancy.

2. Hunters who wear camouflage so that they can blend in with their surroundings are relying on which principle of perception?
   - **a.** shape constancy
   - **b.** expectancy
   - **c.** figure–ground relationships
   - **d.** depth perception

3. What monocular depth cue can best explain why railroad tracks appear to come together in the distance?
   - **a.** convergence
   - **b.** linear perspective
   - **c.** overlap
   - **d.** texture gradient

4. The Müller-Lyer illusion occurs more frequently in
   - **a.** children than adults.
   - **b.** men than women.
   - **c.** people living in a Western culture.
   - **d.** individuals living in poverty.

5. Jason's uncle claimed to have seen a black panther in the trees beside the highway, although no one else saw it. Knowing that his uncle has been looking for a black panther for years, Jason attributes his uncle's "sighting" to
   - **a.** perceptual set.
   - **b.** perceptual defense.
   - **c.** bottom-up processing.
   - **d.** cognitive convergence.

6. The first time Megan had to install a ceiling fan in her new home, it took a long time. But later when she helped install a ceiling fan in her best friend's home, she completed the job very quickly. Her improved speed and skill can partially be attributed to
   - **a.** bottom-up processing.
   - **b.** top-down processing.
   - **c.** perceptual expectancy.
   - **d.** perceptual set.

# APA Goal 2: Scientific Inquiry and Critical Thinking

## Perceptual Influences on Metacognition

*Addresses APA Learning Objective 2.3 Engage in innovative and integrative thinking and problem-solving.*

As you can see, pun intended, what we perceive as being real does not always match the actual visual stimulus we are presented with. Perceptual information can also influence how we think about a given object. For example, many of us assume that things that are larger weigh more than things that are smaller. The color of an object can also have an influence (De Camp, 1917). Darker objects are often appraised to be heavier than comparable objects that are lighter in color (Walker et al., 2010). Both of these are examples of stimulus influences on perceptual expectations. But what about stimulus influences on expectations for a cognitive task, like assessing how well we will be able to remember something?

*Metacognition* is thinking about thinking. It includes being aware of our own thought processes, such as evaluating how well we actually understand something or how well we will remember something. For example, the font size of a given word appears to have an effect. In one study, words that were printed in a larger font were rated as being more memorable than words appearing in a smaller font (Rhodes & Castel, 2008). In other words, when evaluated as part of a sequential list, Psychology might be rated as being more memorable than macroeconomics. At least it was for one of your authors during college. Despite the initial ratings on memorability, when tested later, word font size did not yield significant effects on recall (Rhodes & Castel, 2008).

Research also suggests that students often report using study strategies, such as focusing primarily on **bold** or *italicized* terms in a textbook (Gurung, 2003, 2004), or over-reliance on strategies such as highlighting. These are methods that have less of an overall positive impact on retention of material, especially when compared to more robust study and memory strategies. (L)(I)(N)K to PIA.6 and Learning Objectives 6.5, 6.6.

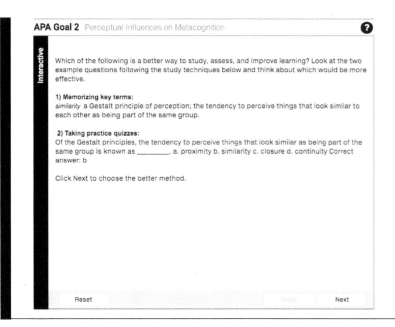

Which of the following is a better way to study, assess, and improve learning? Look at the two example questions following the study techniques below and think about which would be more effective.

**1) Memorizing key terms:**
*similarity* a Gestalt principle of perception; the tendency to perceive things that look similar to each other as being part of the same group.

**2) Taking practice quizzes:**
Of the Gestalt principles, the tendency to perceive things that look similar as being part of the same group is known as _____. a. proximity b. similarity c. closure d. continuity Correct answer: b

Click Next to choose the better method.

Reset    Back    Next

## Applying Psychology to Everyday Life

# Beyond "Smoke and Mirrors"—The Psychological Science and Neuroscience of Magic

**3.17** Describe how the neuroscientific study of magic can help to explain visual and cognitive illusions.

Many people enjoy watching magic acts in person or on television. Perhaps you have been amazed by a Mindfreak® performed by Criss Angel or the performance and edgy antics of Penn & Teller. If you are one of those people, you likely witnessed a performance that included many various illusions. And like many of us, you probably wondered at some point in the performance, "How did they do that?" Did you think the tricks were due to some type of special device (such as a fake thumb tip for hiding a scarf), or perhaps they were accomplished with "smoke and mirrors," or maybe the magician distracted the audience with one movement while actually doing something else to pull off the illusion? Magicians use many techniques to take advantage of, or manipulate, our actual level of awareness of what is happening right in front of us or perhaps to manipulate our attention.

Though magic is not a new topic of interest in psychology, there has been renewed interest in recent years, especially in the neuroscientific study of magic. This view suggests that researchers can work alongside magicians so we may be able to gain a better understanding of various cognitive and perceptual processes by not only examining the sensory or physical mechanics behind magic tricks, or even the psychological explanations, but to look further by examining what is happening in the brain (Macknik & Martinez-Conde, 2009).

Dr. Stephen L. Macknik and Dr. Susanna Martinez-Conde of the Barrow Neurological Institute are two neuroscientists who have teamed up with professional magicians to study their techniques and tricks in the effort to better understand the brain mechanisms underlying the illusions and how that information can be used by researchers in the laboratory.

Penn & Teller have performed together for more than 30 years and have joined neuroscientists in the effort to gain insights into the brain mechanisms behind magical illusions.

They have identified several types of illusions that can be used alone or in combination with others to serve as a basis for various magic tricks; two of these are visual illusions and cognitive illusions (Macknik et al., 2008).

As discussed earlier in the chapter, visual illusions occur when our individual perception does not match a physical stimulus. These illusions are caused by organizational or processing biases in the brain. Furthermore, our brain activity from the perception does not directly match the brain activity associated with the physical stimulus (Macknik et al., 2008). One example Dr. Macknik and Dr. Martinez-Conde point out is similar to a trick you may have performed yourself in grade school. Did you ever take a pencil or pen, grasp it in the middle, and then shake or wiggle it up and down? If you did it correctly, the pen or pencil would appear to bend or be made of rubber. Magicians use this illusion when they "bend" solid objects, such as spoons. So what is the brain explanation? We have special neurons in the visual cortex that are sensitive to both motion and edges called *end-stopped neurons*. These neurons respond differently if an object is bouncing or moving up and down quickly, causing us to perceive a solid spoon or pencil as if it is bending.

Another effect or trick that is based on the functioning of our visual system is when a magician makes an object disappear, such as a ball vanishing into the air or perhaps the outfit of an assistant changing suddenly. By showing the audience the target object, such as the ball or outfit, and then removing it very quickly from the visual field, the *persistence of vision* effect will make it appear that the object is still there. This is due to a response in vision neurons called the after-discharge, which will create an afterimage that lasts for up to 100 milliseconds after a stimulus is removed (Macknik et al., 2008). Again, you may have performed a similar trick if you have ever taken a lit sparkler or flashlight and twirled it around quickly to make a trail of light in the dark.

## Questions for Further Discussion

1. The examples highlighted in this discussion are based on visual illusions; can you think of a magic trick or performance that may have been based on an illusion in a different sensory modality?

2. Of the neuroimaging methods covered in Chapter Two, which methods might be best for examining the brain activity of someone who is watching a magic performance? Why?

# Chapter Summary

## The ABCs of Sensation

### 3.1 Describe how we get information from the outside world into our brains.

- Sensation is the activation of receptors located in the eyes, ears, skin, nasal cavities, and tongue.
- Sensory receptors are specialized forms of neurons that are activated by different stimuli such as light and sound.

### 3.2 Describe the difference and absolute thresholds.

- A just noticeable difference is the point at which a stimulus is detectable half the time it is present.

- Weber's law of just noticeable differences states that the just noticeable difference between two stimuli is always a constant.
- Absolute thresholds are the smallest amount of energy needed for conscious detection of a stimulus at least half the time it is present.

### 3.3 Explain why some sensory information is ignored.

- Subliminal stimuli are stimuli presented just below the level of conscious awareness, and subliminal perception has been demonstrated in the laboratory. It has not been shown to be effective in advertising.
- Habituation occurs when the brain ignores a constant stimulus.

- Sensory adaptation occurs when the sensory receptors stop responding to a constant stimulus.

## The Science of Seeing

**3.4 Describe how light travels through the various parts of the eye.**

- Brightness corresponds to the amplitude of light waves, whereas color corresponds to the length of the light waves.
- Saturation is the psychological interpretation of wavelengths that are all the same (highly saturated) or varying (less saturated).
- Light enters the eye and is focused through the cornea, passes through the aqueous humor, and then through the hole in the iris muscle called the pupil.
- The lens also focuses the light on the retina, where it passes through ganglion and bipolar cells to stimulate the rods and cones.

**3.5 Explain how light information reaches the visual cortex.**

- Visual pathway = retina -> optic nerve -> optic chiasm -> optic tract -> LGN of thalamus -> optic radiations -> primary visual cortex.
- Light from right visual field projects to left side of each retina; light from left visual field projects to right side of each retina.
- Axons from temporal halves of each retina project to visual cortex on same side of the brain; axons from nasal halves of each retina project to visual cortex on opposite side of the brain; optic chiasm is point of crossover.

**3.6 Compare and contrast two major theories of color vision, and explain how color-deficient vision occurs.**

- Rods detect changes in brightness but do not see color and function best in low levels of light. They are found everywhere in the retina except the center, or fovea.
- Cones are sensitive to colors and work best in bright light. They are responsible for the sharpness of visual information and are found in the fovea.
- The trichromatic theory of color perception assumes three types of cones: red, green, and blue. All colors would be perceived as various combinations of these three.
- The opponent-process theory of color perception assumes four primary colors of red, green, blue, and yellow. Colors are arranged in pairs, and when one member of a pair is activated, the other is not.
- Color blindness is a total lack of color perception, whereas color-deficient vision refers to color perception that is limited primarily to yellows and blues or reds and greens only.

## The Hearing Sense: Can You Hear Me Now?

**3.7 Explain the nature of sound, and describe how it travels through the various parts of the ear.**

- Sound has three aspects: pitch (frequency), loudness, and timbre (purity).

- Sound enters the ear through the visible outer structure, or pinna, and travels to the eardrum and then to the small bones of the middle ear.
- The bone called the stirrup rests on the oval window, causing the cochlea and basilar membrane to vibrate with sound.
- The organ of Corti on the basilar membrane contains the auditory receptors, which send signals to the brain about sound qualities as they vibrate.

**3.8 Summarize three theories of how the brain processes information about pitch.**

- Place theory states that the locations of the hair cells on the organ of Corti correspond to different pitches of sound. This can explain pitch above 1,000 Hz.
- Frequency theory states that the speed with which the basilar membrane vibrates corresponds to different pitches of sound. This can explain pitch below 1,000 Hz.
- The volley principle states that neurons take turns firing for sounds above 400 Hz and below 4,000 Hz.

**3.9 Identify types of hearing impairment and treatment options for each.**

- Conduction hearing impairment is caused by damage to the outer or middle ear structures, whereas nerve hearing impairment is caused by damage to the inner ear or auditory pathways in the brain.
- Hearing aids may be used for those with conductive hearing impairment, while cochlear implants may restore some hearing to those with nerve hearing impairment.

## Chemical Senses: It Tastes Good and Smells Even Better

**3.10 Explain how the sense of taste works.**

- Gustation is the sense of taste. Taste buds in the tongue receive molecules of substances, which fit into receptor sites.
- Gustation is a chemical sense that involves detection of chemicals dissolved in saliva.
- The five basic types of taste are sweet, sour, salty, bitter, and umami (brothy).

**3.11 Explain how the sense of smell works.**

- Olfaction is the sense of smell. The olfactory receptors in the upper part of the nasal passages receive molecules of substances and create neural signals that then go to the olfactory bulbs under the frontal lobes.
- Olfaction is a chemical sense that involves detection of chemicals suspended in the air.

## The Other Senses: What the Body Knows

**3.12 Describe how we experience the sensations of touch, pressure, temperature, and pain.**

- The skin senses are one part of our somesthetic senses.
- Pacinian corpuscles respond to pressure, certain nerve endings around hair follicles respond to pain and pressure, and free nerve endings respond to pain, pressure, and temperature.

- The gate-control theory of pain states that when receptors sensitive to pain are stimulated, a neurotransmitter called substance P is released into the spinal cord, activating other pain receptors by opening "gates" in the spinal column and sending the message to the brain.

### 3.13 Describe the systems that tell us about balance and position and movement of our bodies.

- The kinesthetic sense allows the brain to know about movement of the body.
- Proprioception, or information about where the body and its parts are in relation to each other and the ground, comes from the activity of special receptors responsive to movement of the joints and limbs.
- The vestibular sense also contributes to the body's sense of spatial orientation and movement through the activity of the otolith organs (up-and-down movement) and the semicircular canals (movement through arcs).
- Motion sickness is explained by sensory conflict theory, in which information from the eyes conflicts with information from the vestibular sense, causing nausea.

## The ABCs of Perception

### 3.14 Describe how perceptual constancies and the Gestalt principles account for common perceptual experiences.

- Perception is the interpretation and organization of sensations.
- Size constancy is the tendency to perceive objects as always being the same size, no matter how close or far away they are.
- Shape constancy is the tendency to perceive objects as remaining the same shape even when the shape of the object changes on the retina of the eye.
- Brightness constancy is the tendency to perceive objects as a certain level of brightness, even when the light changes.
- The Gestalt psychologists developed several principles of perception that involve interpreting patterns in visual stimuli. The principles are figure–ground relationships, closure, similarity, continuity, contiguity, and common region.

### 3.15 Explain how we perceive depth using both monocular and binocular cues.

- Depth perception is the ability to see in three dimensions.
- Monocular cues for depth perception include linear perspective, relative size, overlap, aerial (atmospheric) perspective, texture gradient, motion parallax, and accommodation.
- Binocular cues for depth perception include convergence and binocular overlap.

### 3.16 Identify some common visual illusions and the factors that influence our perception of them.

- Illusions are perceptions that do not correspond to reality or are distortions of visual stimuli.
- Perceptual set or expectancy refers to the tendency to perceive objects and situations in a particular way because of prior experiences.
- Top-down processing involves the use of existing knowledge to organize individual features into a unified whole.
- Bottom-up processing involves the analysis of smaller features, building up to a complete perception.

## Applying Psychology to Everyday Life: Beyond "Smoke and Mirrors"—The Psychological Science and Neuroscience of Magic

### 3.17 Describe how the neuroscientific study of magic can help to explain visual and cognitive illusions.

- Magicians take advantage of some well-known properties of our visual system to accomplish a variety of magic tricks.
- By collaborating with magicians, psychologists and neuroscientists can learn more about magic and the brain processes responsible for our perception of magic tricks.

# Test Yourself

*Pick the best answer.*

1. In making a large pot of chili for a family reunion, you find that you have to add 1 onion to your pot of chili that already has 5 onions mixed in it to notice a difference. According to Weber's Law, how many onions would you have to add to notice a difference if you are making twice as much chili with 10 onions?
   a. 1
   b. 2
   c. 4
   d. 5

2. A study purportedly conducted by James Vicary teaches us what about the power of subliminal perception and its effect on advertising?
   a. Subliminal advertising can profoundly affect a consumer's decision-making process.
   b. Subliminal advertising affects a consumer's decision-making process but only when it involves comfort foods such as popcorn and soda.
   c. Subliminal advertising is effective on those who believe in the power of the unconscious.
   d. Subliminal advertising was never supported, since Vicary ultimately admitted that he never truly conducted such a study.

**3.** You detect the strong smell of cedar when you enter a furniture store. However, after a short while in the store, you no longer can detect the smell. This process is known as
   **a.** sensory adaptation.
   **b.** habituation.
   **c.** perceptual constancy.
   **d.** accommodation.

**4.** Which of the following terms refers to the amplitude of a light wave such as how high or low the wave is?
   **a.** color
   **b.** brightness
   **c.** pitch
   **d.** hue

**5.** When an ophthalmologist surgically corrects a patient's vision through LASIK or PRK, the doctor is making adjustments to the patient's
   **a.** cornea.
   **b.** lens.
   **c.** retina.
   **d.** iris.

**6.** What part of the eye hardens as we age, thus causing many to suffer from presbyopia?
   **a.** rods
   **b.** cones
   **c.** lens
   **d.** vitreous humor

**7.** A deer's inability to quickly respond to the headlights of an approaching car is due to what sensory phenomenon?
   **a.** dark adaptation
   **b.** light adaptation
   **c.** afterimage
   **d.** opponent-process theory

**8.** The hammer, the anvil, and the stirrup are part of the
   **a.** outer ear.
   **b.** middle ear.
   **c.** inner ear.
   **d.** cochlea.

**9.** John has played his music loudly for years. Now, in his 20s, he finds he has a continuous ringing in both of his ears. What would John probably be diagnosed with?
   **a.** Tinnitus, which is a nerve-based disorder that has no permanent cure.
   **b.** Conduction-based hearing impairment; however, hearing aids may be able to help.
   **c.** Damage to the pinna, which can be corrected with surgery.
   **d.** Regardless of the disorder, John will ultimately require a cochlear implant.

**10.** Studies show that taste preference can typically begin
   **a.** before a baby is born.
   **b.** in the first 3 to 6 months after birth.
   **c.** by age 1.
   **d.** during preschool.

**11.** Jude is suffering from a severe cold. His nose has been stopped up for several days. What effect, if any, might his cold have on his sense of taste?
   **a.** His sense of taste will be increased since he isn't receiving additional sensory input from his smell.
   **b.** His sense of taste will be dulled since taste and smell often work together.
   **c.** His sense of taste will get better but not until 48 hours after he loses his sense of smell.
   **d.** His sense of taste will be no better or worse since the senses of taste and smell are completely separate.

**12.** If a child suffers from congenital analgesia, why must he or she be careful when outside playing?
   **a.** The child often cannot hear sounds unless he or she is within 3 feet of the source.
   **b.** The child cannot feel pain and can suffer injuries without even knowing it.
   **c.** The child lacks the ability to react to a dangerous situation.
   **d.** The child's sense of smell does not work properly.

**13.** If Tabitha closes her eyes when she rides in her parents' car, she can still tell that the car is moving. This is due to the movement of tiny crystals in the
   **a.** outer ear.
   **b.** cochlea.
   **c.** otolith organs.
   **d.** middle ear.

**14.** A child may sometimes play by quickly turning around in a circle. When the child stops, he or she often feels like his or her head is still spinning. What is responsible for this sensation?
   **a.** fluid still rotating in the semicircular canals
   **b.** proprioceptors
   **c.** compression of the otolith organs
   **d.** disruption of the otolith crystals

**15.** Little Karla is with her mother at the docks waiting for her daddy to return from his naval deployment. While the boat is still a way out, her mother says, "There is daddy's boat." Karla is confused. She cannot understand how her dad can be on a boat that is so small that she can hold up her thumb and cover the entire boat. It's safe to assume that Karla does not yet understand
   **a.** size constancy.
   **b.** shape constancy.
   **c.** brightness constancy.
   **d.** color constancy.

**16.**  XX  XX  XX      XXXXX
        XX  XX  XX      XXXXX
        XX  XX  XX      XXXXX

In viewing the items above, seeing three columns of Xs on the left versus three rows of Xs on the right can be explained by the Gestalt principle of _____.
   **a.** closure
   **b.** similarity
   **c.** proximity
   **d.** contiguity

**17.** From experience, you know that commercial jets typically fly around 500 miles per hour at a height of 30,000 feet. However, as you watch one fly high overhead, it seems to slowly pass by. What monocular depth cue best explains this?
   **a.** motion parallax
   **b.** linear perspective
   **c.** overlap
   **d.** texture gradient

**18.** The Müller-Lyer illusion is influenced greatly by one's
   **a.** age.
   **b.** gender.
   **c.** level of intellect.
   **d.** culture.

**19.** Allison opened her new jigsaw puzzle but soon realized that she had the same puzzle when she was a child. With her past experience to rely upon, Allison will probably use _____ to help her reassemble the puzzle.
   **a.** bottom-up processing
   **b.** top-down processing
   **c.** perceptual expectancy
   **d.** perceptual set

**20.** Kip enjoys playing with sparklers on the 4th of July. He always loves watching a friend run with a sparkler and the momentary trail of light that seems to be left behind. Which aspect of our visual system best explains this trail of light?
   **a.** lateral inhibition
   **b.** microsaccades of the eyes
   **c.** persistence of vision
   **d.** achromatopsia

# 4 Consciousness

What are some ways in which you multitask throughout the day? How does multitasking impact your awareness or affect the quality of your work, if at all?
After you have answered the question, watch the video to compare the answers of other students to yours.

▶ The response entered here will be saved to your notes and may be collected by your instructor if he/she requires it.

👁 Watch the Video

# Why study consciousness?

In a very real sense, to understand consciousness is to understand what it means to be who we are. Waking, sleeping, dreaming, daydreaming, and other forms of conscious awareness make up the better part of the human experience. Lack of sleep may increase the likelihood of diabetes, interfere with the onset of puberty changes, decrease memory for learning, and increase weight gain. Drug use can affect consciousness as well, and not always to our benefit. Clearly, an understanding of the workings of the conscious mind is important to both our mental and our physical well-being.

# Learning Objectives

**4.1** Define what it means to be conscious.

**4.2** Differentiate between the different levels of consciousness.

**4.3** Describe the biological process of the sleep–wake cycle.

**4.4** Explain why we sleep.

**4.5** Identify the different stages of sleep.

**4.6** Differentiate among the various sleep disorders.

**4.7** Compare and contrast two explanations of why people dream.

**4.8** Identify commonalities and differences in the content of people's dreams.

**4.9** Explain how hypnosis affects consciousness.

**4.10** Compare and contrast two views of why hypnosis works.

**4.11** Distinguish between physical dependence and psychological dependence upon drugs.

**4.12** Identify the effects and dangers of using stimulants.

**4.13** Identify the effects and dangers of using depressants.

**4.14** Identify the effects and dangers of using hallucinogens.

**4.15** Describe how the workings of our consciousness can explain "supernatural" visitations.

# What Is Consciousness?

💬 What exactly is meant by the term *consciousness*? I've heard it a lot, but I'm not sure that I know everything it means.

*Consciousness* is one of those terms that most people think they understand until someone asks them to define it. Various sorts of scientists, psychologists, neuroscientists, philosophers, and even computer scientists (who have been trying to develop an artificial intelligence for some time now) have tried to define consciousness, and so there are several definitions—one for nearly every field in which consciousness is studied.

### DEFINITION OF CONSCIOUSNESS

### 4.1 Define what it means to be conscious.

Philosopher Daniel Dennett, in his 1991 book *Consciousness Explained*, asserts that (contrary to the opinion of William James in his 1894 text) there is no single stream of consciousness but rather multiple "channels," each of which is handling its own tasks (Dennett, 1991). All of these channels operate in parallel, a kind of chaos of consciousness. People must somehow organize all this conscious experience, and that organization is influenced by their particular social groups and culture.

Do animals experience consciousness in the same way as people? That is a question too complex to answer fully here, but many researchers of animal behavior, language, and cognition have some reason to propose that there is a kind of consciousness in at least some animals, although its organization would naturally not be the same as human consciousness (Block, 2005; Browne, 2004; Hurley & Nudds, 2006; Koch & Mormann, 2010). Chapter Seven in this text includes a discussion of animal language that touches on some of these issues. (L)(I)(N)(K) to Learning Objective 7.14.

 💬 So where does that leave us in the search for a working definition of consciousness?

For our purposes, a more useful definition of consciousness might be the following: **Consciousness** is your awareness of everything that is going on around you and inside your own head at any given moment, which you use to organize your behavior (Farthing, 1992), including your thoughts, sensations, and feelings. In a cognitive neuroscience view, consciousness is generated by a set of action potentials in the communication among neurons just sufficient to produce a specific perception, memory, or experience in our awareness (Crick & Koch, 1990, 2003; Koch & Mormann, 2010). In other words, your eyes see a dog, the neurons along the optic pathway to the occipital lobe's visual cortex are activated, and the visual association cortex is activated to identify the external stimulus as a "dog." Bam!—consciousness! (L)(I)(N)(K) to Learning Objective 2.12.

### ALTERED STATES OF CONSCIOUSNESS

### 4.2 Differentiate between the different levels of consciousness.

Much of people's time awake is spent in a state called **waking consciousness** in which their thoughts, feelings, and sensations are clear and organized, and they feel alert. But there are many times in daily activities and in life when people experience states of consciousness that differ from this organized waking state. These variations are called "altered states of consciousness."

**consciousness**

a person's awareness of everything that is going on around him or her at any given time.

**waking consciousness**

state in which thoughts, feelings, and sensations are clear, organized, and the person feels alert.

An **altered state of consciousness** occurs when there is a shift in the quality or pattern of your mental activity. Thoughts may become fuzzy and disorganized, and you may feel less alert, or your thoughts may take bizarre turns, as they so often do in dreams. Sometimes being in an altered state may mean being in a state of *increased* alertness, as when under the influence of a stimulant. You may also divide your conscious awareness, as when you drive to work or school and then wonder how you got there—one level of conscious awareness was driving, while the other was thinking about the day ahead, perhaps. This altered state of divided consciousness can be a dangerous thing, as many people who try to drive and talk on a cell phone at the same time have discovered. People are often unaware that there are two kinds of thought processes, *controlled processes* and *automatic processes* (Bargh et al., 2012; Huang & Bargh, 2014). Controlled processes are those that require our conscious attention to a fairly high degree, such as driving, carrying on a conversation, or taking notes in your psychology class (you are taking notes, right?). Automatic processes require far less of a conscious level of attention—we are aware of these actions at a low level of conscious awareness, and examples would be brushing one's hair or well-practiced actions such as walking or riding a bicycle. Driving a car along a familiar path can become fairly automatic, hence the experience of driving somewhere and not knowing how you got there—driving is really a control process, not an automatic one, but we often forget to pay attention to this fact. Controlled processes such as driving or carrying on a conversation should only be done one at a time, while you can do an automatic process and a controlled process at the same time without too much trouble. Talking on a cell phone while brushing your hair is okay, for example, but talking on a cell phone while driving your car is not. Studies have shown that driving while talking on a cell phone, even a hands-free phone, puts a person at the same degree of risk as driving under the influence of alcohol (Alm & Nilsson, 1995; Briem & Hedman, 1995; Strayer & Drews, 2007; Strayer & Johnston, 2001; Strayer et al., 2006, 2014). Texting while driving is more than risky—it can be murderous (Centers for Disease Control, 2015d; Eastern Virginia Medical School, 2009; Wang et al., 2012). Ⓛ Ⓘ Ⓝ Ⓚ to Learning Objective PIA.2. Participate in the survey *What Altered States Have You Experienced?* to discover more about your own encounters with various states of consciousness.

The driver of this car has several competing demands on his attention: working his cell phone, listening to the passenger read to him, and driving his car. If he manages to get himself and his passenger safely to their destination—and by multitasking while driving he is certainly endangering both of their lives, and others as well—it's possible that he won't even remember the trip; he may be driving in an altered state of consciousness.

**Survey**   WHAT ALTERED STATES HAVE YOU EXPERIENCED?

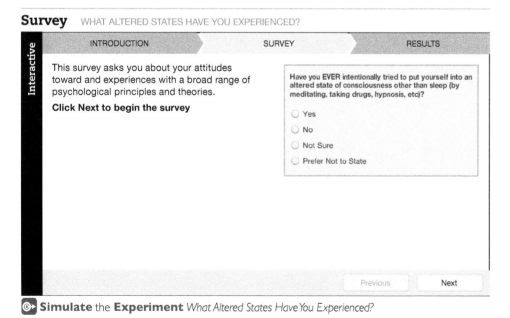

Interactive

| INTRODUCTION | SURVEY | RESULTS |

This survey asks you about your attitudes toward and experiences with a broad range of psychological principles and theories.

**Click Next to begin the survey**

Have you EVER intentionally tried to put yourself into an altered state of consciousness other than sleep (by meditating, taking drugs, hypnosis, etc)?

○ Yes
○ No
○ Not Sure
○ Prefer Not to State

Previous    Next

◉► **Simulate** the **Experiment** *What Altered States Have You Experienced?*

There are many forms of altered states of consciousness. For example, daydreaming, being hypnotized, or achieving a meditative state are usually considered to be altered states. Ⓛ Ⓘ Ⓝ Ⓚ to Learning Objective 11.10. Being under the influence of certain drugs

**altered state of consciousness**
state in which there is a shift in the quality or pattern of mental activity as compared to waking consciousness.

such as caffeine, tobacco, or alcohol is definitely an example of altered states. Over several decades, there has been a definite rise in the use of stimulants that would ordinarily be prescribed for children and adolescents with attention-deficit/hyperactivity disorder but are also used by college students and older adults who feel that the drugs give them an "edge" (Partnership for Drug-Free Kids, 2014; Szalavitz, 2009; Zuvekas & Vitlielo, 2012). But the most common altered state people experience is the one they spend about a third of their lives in on a nightly basis—sleep.

## Concept Map L.O. 4.1, 4.2

Interactive

### What Is Consciousness?

- people's awareness of everything that is going on around them at any given moment (thoughts, sensations, and feelings); much of the day is spent in waking consciousness where these are clear and organized

- altered states of consciousness occur when there is a shift in the quality or pattern of mental activity as compared to waking consciousness; alertness, thought content, and focus can vary greatly

Reset

## Practice Quiz    How much do you remember?

*Pick the best answer.*

1. A change in the quality or pattern of mental activity, such as increased alertness or divided consciousness, is called a(n)
   a. waking consciousness.
   b. altered state of consciousness.
   c. transient state of consciousness.
   d. hallucination.

2. Consciousness can be defined as a set of action potentials occurring among neurons in which of the following views?
   a. behavioral
   b. sociocultural
   c. cognitive neuroscience
   d. evolutionary

3. Which of the following is an example of an automatic process?
   a. Driving a car.          c. Doing math problems.
   b. Talking on a cell phone.   d. Brushing your teeth.

4. Which of the following statements is false?
   a. It is safe to drive and talk on a cell phone as long as it is hands free.
   b. Brushing your hair while talking on the phone is easy to do.
   c. Texting while driving is more dangerous than talking on a cell phone while driving.
   d. Driving while talking on a cell phone is as risky as driving while under the influence of alcohol.

# Sleep

Have you ever wondered why people have to sleep? They could get so much more work done if they didn't have to sleep, and they would have more time to play and do creative things.

### THE BIOLOGY OF SLEEP

#### 4.3 Describe the biological process of the sleep–wake cycle.

Sleep was once referred to as "the gentle tyrant" (Webb, 1992). People can try to stay awake, and sometimes they may go for a while without sleep, but eventually they *must* sleep. One reason for this fact is that sleep is one of the human body's *biological rhythms*, natural cycles of activity that the body must go through. Some biological rhythms are monthly, like the cycle of a woman's menstruation, whereas others are far shorter—the beat of the heart is a biological rhythm. But many biological rhythms take place on a daily basis, like the rise and fall of blood pressure and body temperature or the production of certain body chemicals (Moore-Ede et al., 1982). The most obvious of these is the sleep–wake cycle (Baehr et al., 2000).

**THE RHYTHMS OF LIFE: CIRCADIAN RHYTHMS**    The sleep–wake cycle is a **circadian rhythm**. The term actually comes from two Latin words, *circa* ("about") and *diem* ("day"). So a circadian rhythm is a cycle that takes "about a day" to complete.

For most people, this means that they will experience several hours of sleep at least once during every 24-hour period. The sleep–wake cycle is ultimately controlled by the brain, specifically by an area within the *hypothalamus*, the tiny section of the brain that influences the glandular system. Ⓛ Ⓘ Ⓝ Ⓚ to Learning Objective 2.11.

💬 There was a big fuss over something called melatonin a few years ago—isn't melatonin supposed to make people sleep?

**THE ROLE OF THE HYPOTHALAMUS: THE MIGHTY MITE**    A lot of people were buying supplements of *melatonin* (a hormone normally secreted by the pineal gland) several years ago, hoping to sleep better and perhaps even slow the effects of aging (Folkard et al., 1993; Herxheimer & Petrie, 2001; Young, 1996). The release of melatonin is influenced by a structure deep within the tiny hypothalamus in an area called the *suprachiasmatic* (SOO-prah-ki-AS-ma-tik) *nucleus*, the internal clock that tells people when to wake up and when to fall asleep (Gandhi et al., 2015; Quintero et al., 2003; Yamaguchi et al., 2003; Zisapel, 2001). The suprachiasmatic nucleus, or SCN, is sensitive to changes in light. As daylight fades, the SCN tells the pineal gland (located in the base of the brain) to secrete melatonin (Bondarenko, 2004; Delagrange & Guardiola-Lemaitre, 1997). As melatonin accumulates, a person will feel sleepy. As the light coming into the eyes increases (as it does in the morning), the SCN tells the pineal gland to stop secreting melatonin, allowing the body to awaken. That's a lot of control for such a small part of the brain.

Melatonin supplements are often used to treat a condition called *jet lag*, in which the body's circadian rhythm has been disrupted by traveling to another time zone. There is some evidence that melatonin may be linked to a healthier metabolism (Cardinali et al., 2013; Gandhi et al., 2015). It may help people who suffer from sleep problems due to shift work. Shift-work sleep problems, often attributed to the custom of having workers change shifts against their natural circadian rhythms (e.g., from a day shift to a night shift, and then back again to an evening shift), have been linked to increased accident rates, increased absence from work due to illness, and lowered productivity rates (Folkard & Tucker, 2003; Folkard et al., 1993; Folkard et al., 2005). In addition to melatonin supplements, it has been found that gradually changing the shifts that workers take according to the natural cycle of the day (e.g., from day shift to evening shift to night shift, rather than from day shift directly to night shift) has significantly reduced the problems (Czeisler et al., 1982; Folkard et al., 2006).

Melatonin is not the whole story, of course. Several neurotransmitters are associated with arousal and sleep regulation, including serotonin. It was once theorized that serotonin promoted sleepiness. However, it is not that simple. Serotonin-producing neurons are most active during wakefulness, less active during deep sleep, and relatively inactive during the type of sleep in which dreams typically occur (Elmenhorst et al., 2012; Hornung, 2012; Siegel, 2011). Furthermore, effects differ based on which serotonin-producing cells are firing and which brain structures are receiving those messages. Last, some serotonin receptors are excitatory and others are inhibitory. For example, some

Sleep, according to Webb (1992), is the "gentle tyrant." As this picture shows, when the urge to sleep comes upon a person, it can be very difficult to resist—no matter where that person is at the time. Can you think of a time or place when you fell asleep without meaning to do so? Why do you think it happened?

**circadian rhythm**

a cycle of bodily rhythm that occurs over a 24-hour period.

receptors facilitate some stages of sleep, while others inhibit other stages (Siegel, 2011; Zhang et al., 2015).

Body temperature plays a part in inducing sleep, too. The suprachiasmatic nucleus, as part of the hypothalamus, controls body temperature. The higher the body temperature, the more alert people are; the lower the temperature, the sleepier they are. When people are asleep at night, their body temperature is at its lowest level. Be careful: The research on the effects of serotonin and body temperature on sleep is correlational, so we cannot assume causation, and there are many different factors involved in sleep. Ⓛ Ⓘ Ⓝ Ⓚ to Learning Objective 1.7.

In studies in which volunteers spend several days without access to information about day or night, their sleep–wake cycles lengthened (Czeisler, 1995; Czeisler et al., 1980). The daily activities of their bodies—such as sleeping, waking, waste production, blood pressure rise and fall, and so on—took place over a period of 25 hours rather than 24 hours. Our circadian rhythms are synchronized to a 24-hour day consistent with the day-night cycle due to the suprachiasmatic nucleus, which receives direct input from some retinal ganglion cells responding to light (McCormick & Westbrook, 2013).

In the same studies, body temperature dropped consistently even in the absence of light (Czeisler et al., 1980). As body temperature dropped, sleep began, giving further support to the importance of body temperature in the regulation of sleep.

### WHY WE SLEEP

### 4.4 Explain why we sleep.

How much sleep is enough sleep? The answer varies from person to person because of each person's age and possibly inherited sleep needs (Feroah et al., 2004), but most young adults need about 7–9 hours of sleep each 24-hour period in order to function well (see **Figure 4.1**). Some people are short sleepers, needing only 4 or 5 hours, whereas others are long sleepers and require more than 9 hours of sleep (McCann & Stewin, 1988). As we age, we seem to sleep less during each night until the average length of sleep approaches only 6 hours. As sleep researcher Dr. Jerry Siegel describes in the video *How Much Sleep Do We Need?*, the amount of sleep that we get can have an impact on our health.

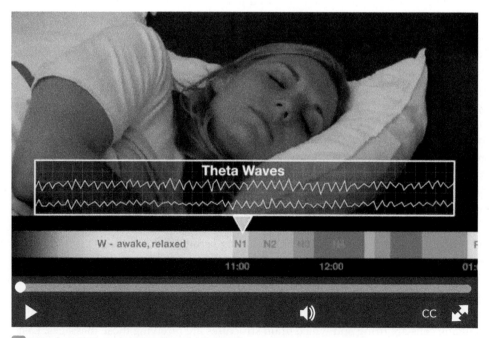

👁 **Watch** the **Video** *How Much Sleep Do We Need?*

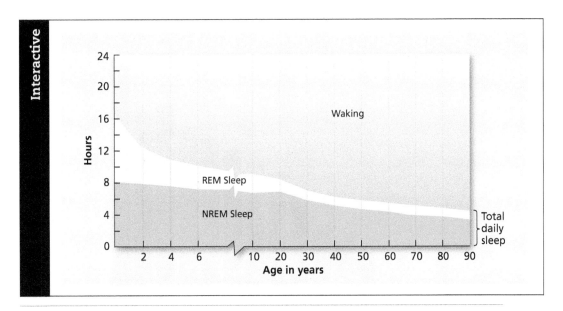

**Figure 4.1** Sleep Patterns of Infants and Adults

Infants need far more sleep than older children and adults. Both REM sleep and NREM sleep decrease dramatically in the first 10 years of life, with the greatest decrease in REM sleep. Nearly 50 percent of an infant's sleep is REM, compared to only about 20 percent for a normal, healthy adult (Roffwarg, 1966).

Although people can do without sleep for a while, they cannot do without it altogether. In one experiment, rats were placed on moving treadmills over water. They couldn't sleep normally because they would then fall into the water and be awakened, but they did drift repeatedly into **microsleeps**, or brief sidesteps into sleep lasting only seconds (Goleman, 1982; Konowal et al., 1999). People can have microsleeps, too, and if this happens while they are driving a car or a truck, it's obviously bad news (Åkerstedt et al., 2013; Dinges, 1995; Lyznicki et al., 1998; Thomas et al., 1998). Microsleep periods are no doubt responsible for a lot of car accidents that occur when drivers have had very little sleep.

💬 Okay, so we obviously need to sleep. But what does it do for us? Why do we have to sleep at all?

**THEORIES OF SLEEP** While it's clear that sleep is essential to life, theories about *why*—the purpose of sleep—differ.

**THE ADAPTIVE THEORY OF SLEEP** Sleep is a product of evolution (Webb, 1992) according to the **adaptive theory** of sleep. It proposes that animals and humans evolved different sleep patterns to avoid being present during their predators' normal hunting times, which typically would be at night. For example, if a human or a prey animal (one a predator will eat) is out and about at night, they are more at risk of being eaten. However, if during active hunting hours the prey is in a safe place sleeping and conserving energy, it is more likely to remain unharmed. If this theory is true, then one would expect prey animals to sleep mostly at night and for shorter periods of time than predator animals; you would also expect that predators could sleep in the daytime—virtually as much as they want. This seems to be the case for predators like lions that have very few natural predators themselves. Lions will sleep nearly 15 hours a day, whereas animals such as gazelles that are lions' prey sleep a mere 4 hours a day, usually in short naps. Nocturnal animals

**microsleeps**

brief sidesteps into sleep lasting only a few seconds.

**adaptive theory**

theory of sleep proposing that animals and humans evolved sleep patterns to avoid predators by sleeping when predators are most active.

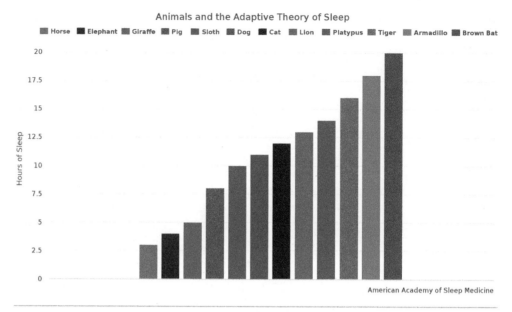

**Figure 4.2** Animals and the Adaptive Theory of Sleep

such as the opossum can afford to sleep during the day and be active at night (when their food sources are available), because they are protected from predators by sleeping high up in trees (see **Figure 4.2**).

**THE RESTORATIVE THEORY OF SLEEP**   The other major theory of why organisms sleep is called **restorative theory**, which states that sleep is necessary to the physical health of the body. During sleep, chemicals that were used up during the day's activities are replenished, other chemicals that were secreted in excess and could become toxic if left in the system are removed, and cellular damage is repaired (Adam, 1980; Moldofsky, 1995; Xie et al., 2013). As discussed earlier, brain plasticity is enhanced by sleep, and there is evidence that most bodily growth and repair occur during the deepest stages of sleep, when enzymes responsible for these functions are secreted in higher amounts (Saper et al., 2001).

Sleep is also important for forming memories. Studies have shown that the physical changes in the brain that occur when we form memories are strengthened during sleep, and particularly so for children (Racsmány et al., 2010; Wilhelm et al., 2013). Ⓛ Ⓘ Ⓝ K to Learning Objective 6.14. This memory effect is no doubt due, at least in part, to the finding that sleep enhances the synaptic connections among neurons, thus increasing the plasticity of the brain—the brain's ability to adapt to experiences (Aton et al., 2009; Bushey et al., 2011; Cirelli et al., 2012; Frank & Benington, 2006). Sleep may also reduce the activity of neurons associated with forgetting, leading to memory retention (Berry et al., 2015), and people who learn tasks right before they go to sleep are able to both recall and perform those tasks better than if they had not slept after learning (Kurdziel et al., 2013; Stickgold & Ellenbogen, 2008). Ⓛ Ⓘ Ⓝ K to Learning Objective 2.4.

Which of these theories is correct? The answer is that both are probably needed to understand why sleep occurs the way it does. Adaptive theory explains why people sleep *when* they do, and restorative theory (including the important function of memory formation) explains why people *need* to sleep.

**SLEEP DEPRIVATION**   While we've already discussed the importance of being able to sleep and the dangers of microsleeps, just how much sleep loss can occur before serious problems start to happen? What will losing out on just one night's sleep do to a

**restorative theory**

theory of sleep proposing that sleep is necessary to the physical health of the body and serves to replenish chemicals and repair cellular damage.

person? For most people, a missed night of sleep will result in concentration problems and the inability to do simple tasks that normally would take no thought at all, such as loading a DVD into a player. More complex tasks, such as math problems, suffer less than these simple tasks because people *know* they must concentrate on a complex task (Chee & Choo, 2004; Lim et al., 2007).

Even so, **sleep deprivation**, or loss of sleep, is a serious problem, which many people have without realizing it. Students, for example, may stay up all night to study for an important test the next day. In doing so, they will lose more information than they gain, as a good night's sleep is important for memory and the ability to think well (Gillen-O'Neel et al., 2012). ⓁⒾⓃⓀ to Learning Objective PIA.5. Even a few nights of poor sleep have serious consequences for mental and physical functioning (Jackson et al., 2013; Van Dongen et al., 2003). Some typical symptoms of sleep deprivation include trembling hands, inattention, staring off into space, droopy eyelids, and general discomfort (Naitoh et al., 1989), as well as emotional symptoms such as irritability and even depression. ⓁⒾⓃⓀ to Learning Objective 14.9. Add to that list an increased risk of insulin resistance, which can lead to diabetes (Matthews et al., 2012), and even possible delays in the onset of puberty (Shaw et al., 2012). And if you are a Twitter user, beware—a study found that users suffering from sleep deprivation tend to create more negative tweets, a sign of increased risk for psychological issues (McIver et al., 2015). As you will see in the feature titled "Weight Gain and Sleep" later on in this chapter, one common cause of sleep deprivation is a disturbance of the sleep–wake cycle, something that is a common problem among college students.

In one study, researchers found that air-traffic controllers, such as the man pictured here, were significantly more impaired in performance after working an 8-hour midnight shift as compared to a day or evening shift of equal length (Heslegrave & Rhodes, 1997).

## THE STAGES OF SLEEP

**4.5** **Identify the different stages of sleep.**

 So are there different kinds of sleep? Do you go from being awake to being asleep and dreaming—is it instant?

There are actually two kinds of sleep: **rapid eye movement sleep (R; REM)** and **non-rapid eye movement sleep (N; NREM)**. REM sleep is a relatively psychologically active type of sleep when most of a person's dreaming takes place, whereas NREM sleep spans from lighter stages to a much deeper, more restful kind of sleep. In REM sleep, the voluntary muscles are inhibited, meaning that the person in REM sleep moves very little, whereas in NREM sleep the person's body is free to move around (including kicking one's bed partner!). There are also several different stages of sleep that people go through each night in which REM sleep and NREM sleep occur. A machine called an electro-encephalograph allows scientists to record the brain-wave activity as a person passes through the various stages of sleep and to determine what type of sleep the person has entered (Aserinsky & Kleitman, 1953).

A person who is wide awake and mentally active will show a brain-wave pattern on the electroencephalogram (EEG) called **beta waves**. Beta waves are very small and very fast. As the person relaxes and gets drowsy, slightly larger and slower **alpha waves** appear. The alpha waves are eventually replaced by even slower and larger **theta waves**. In the deepest stages of sleep, the largest and slowest waves appear, called **delta waves**.

Before moving on to the topic of the stages of sleep, it is worth mentioning that the terminology we now use for the various types and stages of sleep has changed in recent years, replacing older terminology that dated back to the 1960s (Carskadon & Dement, 2011; Iber et al., 2007; Rechtschaffen & Kales, 1968). If you find yourself reading older sleep research and see terms like REM (now R), NREM (now N), or four stages of NREM sleep instead of the three stages we will examine shortly, it is due to this change in the guidelines set forth by the American Academy of Sleep Medicine (Iber et al., 2007).

**sleep deprivation**
any significant loss of sleep, resulting in problems in concentration and irritability.

**rapid eye movement sleep (R, REM)**
stage of sleep in which the eyes move rapidly under the eyelids and the person is typically experiencing a dream.

**non-REM (N, NREM) sleep**
any of the stages of sleep that do not include REM.

**beta waves**
smaller and faster brain waves, typically indicating mental activity.

**alpha waves**
brain waves that indicate a state of relaxation or light sleep.

**theta waves**
brain waves indicating the early stages of sleep.

**delta waves**
long, slow brain waves that indicate the deepest stage of sleep.

**N1: LIGHT SLEEP**    As theta wave activity increases and alpha wave activity fades away, people are said to be entering stage N1 sleep, or light sleep. Several rather interesting things can happen in this stage of sleep. If people are awakened at this point, they will probably not believe that they were actually asleep. They may also experience vivid visual events called *hypnogogic images* or *hallucinations* (Kompanje, 2008; Mavromatis, 1987; Mavromatis & Richardson, 1984; Vitorovic & Biller, 2013). (The Greek word *hypnos* means "sleep.") Many researchers now believe that people's experiences of ghostly visits, alien abductions, and near-death experiences may be most easily explained by these hallucinations (Kompanje, 2008; Moody & Perry, 1993). For more about hypnogogic experiences and the role they may play in "hauntings," see the Applying Psychology section at the end of this chapter.

A much more common occurrence is called the *hypnic jerk* (Cuellar et al., 2015; Mahowald & Schenck, 1996; Oswald, 1959). Have you ever been drifting off to sleep when your knees, legs, or sometimes your whole body gives a big "jerk"? Although experts have no solid proof of why this occurs, many believe that it has something to do with the possibility that our ancestors slept in trees: The relaxation of the muscles as one drifts into sleep causes a "falling" sensation, at which point the body jerks awake to prevent the "fall" from the hypothetical tree (Coolidge, 2006; Sagan, 1977).

**N2: SLEEP SPINDLES**    As people drift further into sleep, the body temperature continues to drop. Heart rate slows, breathing becomes more shallow and irregular, and the EEG will show the first signs of *sleep spindles*, brief bursts of activity lasting only a second or two. Theta waves still predominate in this stage, but if people are awakened during this stage, they will be aware of having been asleep.

**N3: DELTA WAVES ROLL IN**    In the third stage of sleep, the slowest and largest waves make their appearance. These waves are called delta waves. These waves increase during this stage from about 20 percent to more than 50 percent of total brain activity. Now the person is in the deepest stage of sleep, often referred to as slow-wave sleep (SWS) or simply deep sleep (Carskadon & Dement, 2011).

It is during this stage that growth hormones (often abbreviated as GH) are released from the pituitary gland and reach their peak. The body is at its lowest level of functioning. Eventually, the delta waves become the dominant brain activity for this stage of sleep. See **Figure 4.3**, which shows progression, including brain activity, through the sleep stages throughout one night.

People in deep sleep are very hard to awaken. If something does wake them, they may be very confused and disoriented at first. It is not unusual for people to wake up in this kind of disoriented state only to hear the crack of thunder and realize that a storm has come up. Children are even harder to wake up when in this state than are adults. Deep sleep is the time when body growth occurs. This may explain why children in periods of rapid growth need to sleep more and also helps explain why children who are experiencing disrupted sleep (as is the case in situations of domestic violence) suffer delays in growth (Gilmour & Skuse, 1999; Saper et al., 2001; Swanson, 1994).

The fact that children do sleep so deeply may explain why certain sleep disorders are more common in childhood. Indeed, many sleep disorders are more common in boys than in girls because boys sleep more deeply than do girls due to high levels of the male hormone testosterone (Miyatake et al., 1980; Thiedke, 2001).

**R: RAPID EYE MOVEMENT**    After spending some time in N3, the sleeping person will go back up through N2 and then into a stage in which body temperature increases to near-waking levels, the eyes move rapidly under the eyelids, the heart beats much faster, and brain waves resemble beta waves—the kind of brain activity that usually signals wakefulness. The person is still asleep but in the stage known as rapid eye movement sleep (R) and sometimes referred to as paradoxical sleep.

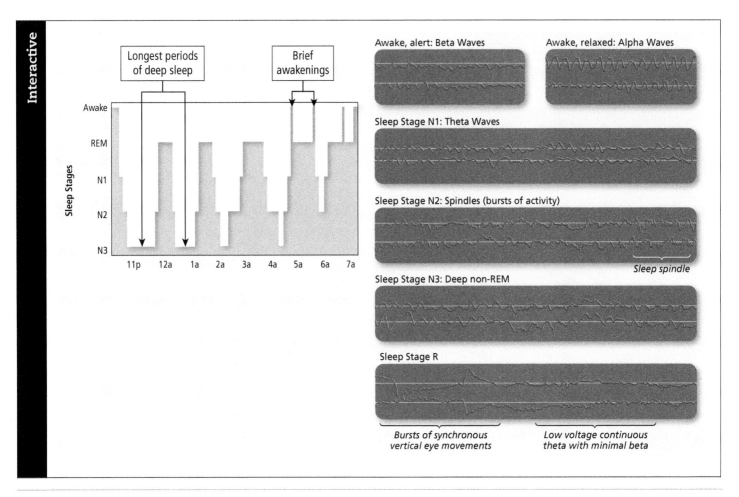

**Figure 4.3**  Brain Activity During Sleep

The EEG reflects brain activity during both waking and sleep. This activity varies according to level of alertness while awake (top two segments) and the stage of sleep. Stage N3 of sleep is characterized by the presence of delta activity, which is much slower and accounts for the larger, slower waves on these graphs. R sleep has activity that resembles alert wakefulness but has relatively no muscle activity except rapid eye movement. The graph shows the typical progression through the night of Stages N1–N3 and R. The R sleep periods occur about every 90 minutes throughout the night (based on Dement, 1974). EEG data and images in this figure are courtesy of Dr. Leslie Sherlin.

**REM SLEEP: PERCHANCE TO DREAM?**   When a person in stage R is awakened, he or she almost always reports being in a dream state (Shafton, 1995). REM sleep is, therefore, associated with dreaming, and 90 percent of dreams actually take place in REM sleep. People do have dreams in the other non-REM sleep stages, but REM sleep dreams tend to be more vivid, more detailed, longer, and more bizarre than the dreams of NREM sleep. NREM sleep dreams tend to be more like thoughts about daily occurrences and far shorter than REM sleep dreams (Foulkes & Schmidt, 1983; Takeuchi et al., 2003). Fortunately, the body is unable to act upon these dreams under normal conditions because the voluntary muscles are paralyzed during REM sleep, a condition known as **sleep paralysis**. (This is why you sometimes have a dream in which you are trying to run or move and can't—you are partially aware of sleep paralysis.)

**WHAT IS THE PURPOSE OF REM SLEEP?**   Why two kinds of sleep? And why would REM sleep ever be considered restful when the body is almost awake and the brain is so active? REM sleep seems to serve a different purpose than does NREM, or deep sleep. After a very physically demanding day, people tend to spend more time in NREM deep sleep than is usual. But an emotionally stressful day leads to increased time in REM sleep

**sleep paralysis**

the inability of the voluntary muscles to move during REM sleep.

While this infant is sleeping, an increased amount of REM sleep (occurring about half of the time she is asleep) allows her brain to make new neural connections.

Nightmares of being chased by a monster or a similar frightening creature are common, especially in childhood.

**REM rebound**

increased amounts of REM sleep after being deprived of REM sleep on earlier nights.

**nightmares**

bad dreams occurring during REM sleep.

**REM behavior disorder (RBD)**

a rare disorder in which the mechanism that blocks the movement of the voluntary muscles fails, allowing the person to thrash around and even get up and act out nightmares.

(Horne & Staff, 1983). Perhaps the dreams people have in REM sleep are a way of dealing with the stresses and tensions of the day, whereas physical activity would demand more time for recovery of the body in NREM sleep. Also, if deprived of REM sleep (as would occur with the use of sleeping pills or other depressant drugs), a person will experience greatly increased amounts of REM sleep the next night, a phenomenon called **REM rebound** (Lo Bue et al., 2014; Vogel, 1975, 1993).

An early study of REM sleep deprivation (Dement, 1960) seemed to suggest that people deprived of REM sleep would become paranoid, seemingly mentally ill from lack of this one stage of sleep. This is called the *REM myth* because later studies failed to reliably produce the same results (Dement et al., 1969).

Other early research attempted to link REM sleep with the physical changes that occur during storing a memory for what one has recently learned, but the evidence today suggests that no one particular stage of sleep is the "one" in which this memory process occurs; rather, the evidence is mounting for sleep in general as necessary to the formation of memory (Ellenbogen et al., 2006; Kurdziel et al., 2013; Maquet et al., 2003; Seehagen et al., 2015; Siegel, 2001; Stickgold et al., 2001; Walker, 2005).

REM sleep in early infancy differs from adult REM sleep in several ways: Babies spend nearly 50 percent of their sleep in REM sleep as compared to adults' 20 percent, the brain-wave patterns on EEG recordings are not exactly the same in infant REM sleep when compared to adult REM sleep recordings, and infants can and do move around quite a bit during REM sleep (Carskadon & Dement, 2005; Davis et al., 2004; Sheldon, 2002; Tucker et al., 2006). These differences can be explained: When infants are engaged in REM sleep, they are not dreaming but rather forming new connections between neurons (Carskadon & Dement, 2005; Davis et al., 2004; Seehagen et al., 2015; Sheldon, 2002). The infant brain is highly plastic, and much of brain growth and development takes place during REM sleep. (L I N) K to Learning Objective 2.3. As the infant's brain nears its adult size by age 5 or 6, the proportion of REM sleep has also decreased to a more adult-like ratio of REM sleep to NREM sleep. For infants, to sleep is perchance to grow synapses.

**SLEEP DISORDERS**

**4.6** **Differentiate among the various sleep disorders.**

What happens when sleep goes wrong? Nightmares, sleepwalking, and being unable to sleep well are all examples of sleep disorders.

💬 What would happen if we could act out our dreams? Would it be like sleepwalking?

**NIGHTMARES AND REM SLEEP BEHAVIOR DISORDER**  Being able to act out one's dreams, especially nightmares, is a far more dangerous proposition than sleepwalking. **Nightmares** are bad dreams, and some nightmares can be utterly terrifying. Children tend to have more nightmares than adults do because they spend more of their sleep in the REM sleep state, as discussed earlier. As they age, they have fewer nightmares because they have less opportunity to have them. But some people still suffer from nightmares as adults.

Some people have a rare disorder in which the brain mechanisms that normally inhibit the voluntary muscles fail, allowing the person to thrash around and even get up and act out nightmares. This disorder is called **REM behavior disorder (RBD)**, which is a fairly serious condition (Nihei et al., 2012; Shafton, 1995). Usually seen in men over age 60, it can happen in younger men and in women. Researchers have found support for the possibility that the breakdown of neural functioning in RBD may be a warning sign for future degeneration of neurons, leading to brain diseases such as Alzheimer's and

Parkinson's disorders (Peever et al., 2014). This has positive implications for early detection and treatment of these disorders.

**NIGHT TERRORS** Often seen as a rare disorder, **night terrors** have been found to occur in up to 56 percent of children between the ages of 1½ to 13 years old, with greatest prevalence around 1½ years of age (34.4%) and rapidly decreasing as the child grows older (13.4% at 5 years; 5.3% at 13 years; Petit et al., 2015). A night terror is essentially a state of panic experienced while sound asleep. People may sit up, scream, run around the room, or flail at some unseen attacker. It is also not uncommon for people to feel unable to breathe while they are in this state. Considering that people suffering a night-terror episode are in a deep stage of sleep and breathing shallowly, one can understand why breathing would seem difficult when they are suddenly active. Most people do not remember what happened during a night-terror episode, although a few people can remember vividly the images and terror they experienced.

💬 But that sounds like the description of a nightmare—what's the difference?

Some very real differences exist between night terrors and nightmares. Nightmares are usually vividly remembered immediately upon waking. A person who has had a nightmare, unlike a person experiencing a night terror, will actually be able to awaken and immediately talk about the bad dream. Perhaps the most telling difference is that nightmares occur during REM sleep rather than deep NREM, slow wave sleep, which is the domain of night terrors, which means that people don't move around in a nightmare as they do in a night-terror experience.

**SLEEPWALKING** Real **sleepwalking,** or **somnambulism**, occurs in approximately 29 percent of children overall between the ages of 2½ to 13 years and is most likely between the ages of 10 and 13 years, at about 13 percent (Petit, et al., 2015). Sleepwalking is at least partially due to heredity, with greatest risk for children of parents who are or were sleepwalkers (Kales et al., 1980; Petit et al., 2015). The prevalence for children without parents having a history of sleepwalking is 22.5 percent, increasing to 47.4 percent where one parent did, and reaches 61.5 percent for children where both parents were sleepwalkers. In other words, children with one or both parents having a history of sleepwalking are three to seven times more likely to be sleepwalkers themselves (Petit, et al., 2015). A person who is sleepwalking may do nothing more than sit up in bed. But other episodes may involve walking around the house, looking in the refrigerator or even eating, and getting into the car. Most people typically do not remember the episode the next day. One student said that her brother walked in his sleep, and one morning his family found him sound asleep behind the wheel of the family car in the garage. Fortunately, he had not been able to find the keys in his sleep.

Many people with this disorder grow out of their sleepwalking by the time they become adolescents. Many parents have found that preventing sleep loss makes sleepwalking a rare occurrence. This is most likely due to the deeper stage N3 sleep becoming even deeper during sleep loss, which would make fully waking even more difficult (Pilon et al., 2008; Zadra et al., 2008, 2013). The only real precaution that the families of people who sleepwalk should take is to clear their floors of obstacles and to put not-easy-to-reach locks on the doors. And although it is typically not dangerous to wake sleepwalkers, they may strike out before awakening.

There have been incidents in which people who claimed to be in a state of sleepwalking (or more likely RBD) have committed acts of violence, even murder (Mahowald et al., 2005; Martin, 2004; Morris, 2009). In some cases the sleepwalking defense led to the acquittal of the accused person.

"Wait! Don't! It can be dangerous to wake them."

**night terrors**

relatively rare disorder in which the person experiences extreme fear and screams or runs around during deep sleep without waking fully.

**sleepwalking (somnambulism)**

occurring during deep sleep, an episode of moving around or walking around in one's sleep.

Do you think that sleepwalking is an adequate defense for someone who has harmed or killed another person? Should a person who has done harm while sleepwalking be forced by the courts to take preventive actions, such as installing special locks on bedroom doors? How might this affect the person's safety, such as in a fire?

> The response entered here will be saved to your notes and may be collected by your instructor if he/she requires it.

Submit

**INSOMNIA**  Most people think that **insomnia** is the inability to sleep. Although that is the literal meaning of the term, in reality insomnia is the inability to get to sleep, stay asleep, or get a good quality of sleep (Kryger et al., 1999; Mayo Clinic Staff, 2014). There are many causes of insomnia, both psychological and physiological. Some of the psychological causes are worrying, trying too hard to sleep, or having anxiety. Some of the physiological causes are too much caffeine, indigestion, or aches and pain.

There are several steps people can take to help them sleep. Obvious ones are consuming no caffeinated drinks or foods that cause indigestion before bedtime, taking medication for pain, and dealing with anxieties in the daytime rather than facing them at night. That last bit of advice is easy to say but not always easy to do. Here are some other helpful hints (Kupfer & Reynolds, 1997; Mayo Clinic Staff, 2014; National Sleep Foundation, 2009):

1. **Go to bed only when you are sleepy.** If you lie in bed for 20 minutes and are still awake, get up and do something like reading or other light activity (avoid watching TV or being in front of a computer screen) until you feel sleepy, and then go back to bed.

2. **Don't do anything in your bed but sleep.** Your bed should be a cue for sleeping, not for studying or watching television. Using the bed as a cue for sleeping is a kind of learning called *classical conditioning*, or the pairing of cues and automatic responses. **LINK** to Learning Objective 5.2. Studies have shown that the light emitted by television screens and particularly e-readers can be very disruptive to the natural sleep cycle (Chang et al., 2015).

3. **Don't try too hard to get to sleep, and especially do not look at the clock and calculate how much sleep you aren't getting.** That just increases the tension and makes it harder to sleep.

4. **Keep to a regular schedule.** Go to bed at the same time and get up at the same time, even on days that you don't have to go to work or class.

5. **Don't take sleeping pills or drink alcohol or other types of drugs that slow down the nervous system (see the category Depressants later in this chapter).** These drugs force you into deep sleep and do not allow you to get any REM sleep or lighter stages of sleep. When you try to sleep without these drugs the next night, you will experience REM rebound, which will cause you to feel tired and sleepy the next day. REM rebound is one way to experience the form of insomnia in which a person sleeps but sleeps poorly.

6. **Exercise.** Exercise is not only good for your health, it's good for your quality of sleep, too. Exercise is particularly useful for combatting *hypersomnia*, or excessive sleepiness in the daytime—one cause of insomnia (Rethorst et al., 2015).

If none of these things seems to be working, there are sleep clinics and sleep experts who can help people with insomnia. The American Academy of Sleep Medicine has an excellent Web site at www.aasmnet.org that provides links to locate sleep clinics in any area. One treatment that seems to have more success than any kind of sleep medication is the use of cognitive-behavior therapy, a type of therapy in which both rational thinking and controlled behavior are stressed (Bastien et al., 2004; Ellis & Barclay, 2014; Irwin et al., 2006; Morin et al., 2006). **LINK** to Learning Objective 15.5.

**insomnia**
the inability to get to sleep, stay asleep, or get a good quality of sleep.

**SLEEP APNEA**   Gerald was a snorer. Actually, that's an understatement. Gerald could give a jet engine some serious competition. Snoring is fairly common, occurring when the breathing passages (nose and throat) get blocked. Most people snore only when they have a cold or some other occasional problem, but some people snore every night and quite loudly, like Gerald. It is this type of snoring that is often associated with a condition called **sleep apnea**, in which the person stops breathing for 10 seconds or more. When breathing stops, there will be a sudden silence, followed shortly by a gasping sound as the person struggles to get air into the lungs. Many people do not wake up while this is happening, but they do not get a good, restful night's sleep because of the apnea.

Apnea is a serious problem. According to the National Institutes of Health (2011), from 5 to 25 percent of adults in the United States suffer from apnea (it is difficult to be precise, as many people are unaware that they have apnea). Apnea can cause heart problems as well as poor sleep quality and depression (Edwards et al., 2015; Flemons, 2002; National Institute of Neurological Disorders and Stroke, 2015). If a person suspects the presence of apnea, a visit to a physician is the first step in identifying the disorder and deciding on a treatment. While some people can benefit from wearing a nasal opening device, losing weight (obesity is often a primary cause of apnea), or using a nasal spray to shrink the nasal tissues, others must sleep with a device that delivers a continuous stream of air under mild pressure, called a *continuous positive airway pressure (CPAP) device*. Still others undergo a simple surgery in which the *uvula* (the little flap that hangs down at the back of the throat) and some of the soft tissues surrounding it are removed.

Some very young infants also experience a kind of apnea due to immaturity of the brain stem. These infants are typically placed on monitors that sound an alarm when breathing stops, allowing caregivers to help the infant begin breathing again. Although sleep apnea in infants is often associated with sudden infant death syndrome, or SIDS, it is not necessarily caused by it: Many infants who die of SIDS were never diagnosed with sleep apnea (Blackmon et al., 2003).

**NARCOLEPSY**   A disorder affecting 1 in every 2,000 persons, **narcolepsy** is a kind of "sleep seizure." In narcolepsy, the person may slip suddenly into REM sleep during the day (especially when the person experiences strong emotions). Another symptom is excessive daytime sleepiness that results in the person falling asleep throughout the day at inappropriate times and in inappropriate places (Overeem et al., 2001). These sleep attacks may occur many times and without warning, making the operation of a car or other machinery very dangerous for the person with narcolepsy. The sudden REM attacks are especially dangerous because of the symptom of *cataplexy*, or a sudden loss of muscle tone. This sleep paralysis may cause injuries if the person is standing when the attack occurs. The same hypnogogic images that may accompany stage N1 sleep may also occur in the person with narcolepsy. There may be new hope for sufferers of narcolepsy: Researchers have been developing a new drug to treat narcolepsy, and while still in the stages of animal testing, it looks very promising (Nagahara et al., 2015). **Table 4.1** has a more detailed list of known sleep disorders.

| **Table 4.1**   Sleep Disorders | |
| --- | --- |
| **Name of Disorder** | **Primary Symptoms** |
| Somnambulism | Sitting, walking, or performing complex behavior while asleep |
| Night terrors | Extreme fear, agitation, screaming while asleep |
| Restless leg syndrome | Uncomfortable sensations in legs causing movement and loss of sleep |
| Nocturnal leg cramps | Painful cramps in calf or foot muscles |
| Hypersomnia | Excessive daytime sleepiness |
| Circadian rhythm disorders | Disturbances of the sleep–wake cycle such as jet lag and shift work |
| Enuresis | Urinating while asleep in bed |

**sleep apnea**

disorder in which the person stops breathing for 10 seconds or more.

**narcolepsy**

sleep disorder in which a person falls immediately into REM sleep during the day without warning.

## Concept Map L.O. 4.3, 4.4, 4.5, 4.6

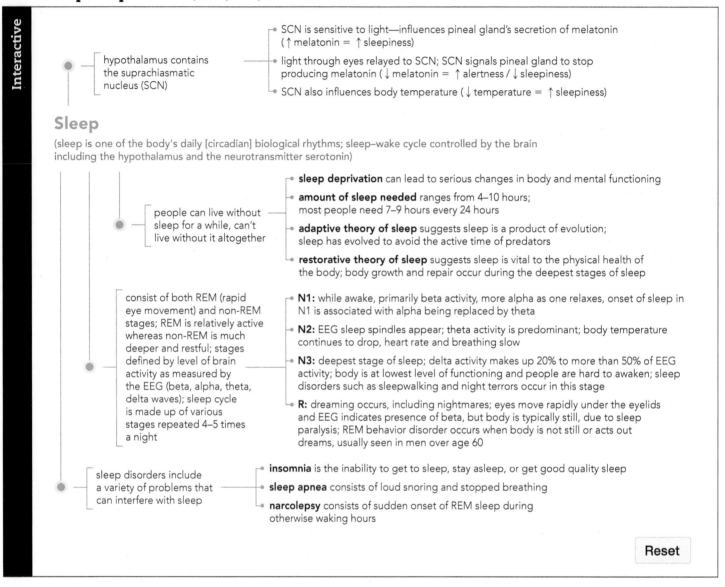

Interactive

**Sleep**

(sleep is one of the body's daily [circadian] biological rhythms; sleep–wake cycle controlled by the brain including the hypothalamus and the neurotransmitter serotonin)

hypothalamus contains the suprachiasmatic nucleus (SCN)
- SCN is sensitive to light—influences pineal gland's secretion of melatonin (↑ melatonin = ↑ sleepiness)
- light through eyes relayed to SCN; SCN signals pineal gland to stop producing melatonin (↓ melatonin = ↑ alertness / ↓ sleepiness)
- SCN also influences body temperature (↓ temperature = ↑ sleepiness)

people can live without sleep for a while, can't live without it altogether
- **sleep deprivation** can lead to serious changes in body and mental functioning
- **amount of sleep needed** ranges from 4–10 hours; most people need 7–9 hours every 24 hours
- **adaptive theory of sleep** suggests sleep is a product of evolution; sleep has evolved to avoid the active time of predators
- **restorative theory of sleep** suggests sleep is vital to the physical health of the body; body growth and repair occur during the deepest stages of sleep

consist of both REM (rapid eye movement) and non-REM stages; REM is relatively active whereas non-REM is much deeper and restful; stages defined by level of brain activity as measured by the EEG (beta, alpha, theta, delta waves); sleep cycle is made up of various stages repeated 4–5 times a night
- **N1:** while awake, primarily beta activity, more alpha as one relaxes, onset of sleep in N1 is associated with alpha being replaced by theta
- **N2:** EEG sleep spindles appear; theta activity is predominant; body temperature continues to drop, heart rate and breathing slow
- **N3:** deepest stage of sleep; delta activity makes up 20% to more than 50% of EEG activity; body is at lowest level of functioning and people are hard to awaken; sleep disorders such as sleepwalking and night terrors occur in this stage
- **R:** dreaming occurs, including nightmares; eyes move rapidly under the eyelids and EEG indicates presence of beta, but body is typically still, due to sleep paralysis; REM behavior disorder occurs when body is not still or acts out dreams, usually seen in men over age 60

sleep disorders include a variety of problems that can interfere with sleep
- **insomnia** is the inability to get to sleep, stay asleep, or get good quality sleep
- **sleep apnea** consists of loud snoring and stopped breathing
- **narcolepsy** consists of sudden onset of REM sleep during otherwise waking hours

Reset

# Practice Quiz How much do you remember?

*Pick the best answer.*

**1.** The sleep–wake cycle typically follows a 24-hour cycle and is regulated by the _____.
a. cerebellum
b. frontal lobe
c. pituitary gland
d. suprachiasmatic nucleus

**2.** The pineal gland receives instructions from the _____ to release _____.
a. thalamus; dopamine
b. occipital lobe; serotonin
c. suprachiasmatic nucleus; melatonin
d. spinal cord; acetylcholine

**3.** Which of the following is involved in determining when we sleep?
a. body position
b. digestion
c. body temperature
d. GABA

**4.** Which theory states that sleep is a product of evolution?
a. restorative theory
b. reactive theory
c. adaptive theory
d. REM theory

**5.** Which of the following is a characteristic of stage N3, or slow-wave sleep?
a. paralysis of voluntary muscles
b. increased heart rate
c. deepest level of sleep
d. increased body temperature

**6.** Sleepwalking occurs in stage _____ sleep, whereas nightmares occur in stage _____ sleep.
a. N1; N2
b. R; N3
c. N2; N1
d. N3; R

# APA Goal 2: Scientific Inquiry and Critical Thinking

## Weight Gain and Sleep

*Addresses APA Learning Objective 2.1: Use scientific reasoning to interpret psychological phenomena.*

Many people have heard that it's common for young people going off to college or university for the first time to gain weight. There's even a name for it, the "freshman 15." Some of the reasons people have given for this weight gain, citing "commonsense" reasoning, include being away from home (and parental supervision) for the first time, more partying than studying, and mass consumption of junk food, among others. But common sense, as we've seen, doesn't always give an accurate picture of what is really happening. For accuracy, we need to determine what science says about the freshman 15.

First we need to ask, do first-year college students really put on weight their first year of school? The answer seems to be yes, but not quite as much as rumor has it. The actual freshman weight gain tends to be about 3.5 to 6 pounds (Holm-Denoma et al., 2008; Roane et al., 2015). Score one for science, not so much for common sense.

Now that we know there is a weight gain, what could be the cause or causes of that gain? We do know that college students probably don't get the amount of sleep recommended by experts, which is a little over 9 hours a night (Dahl & Lewin, 2002; Hirshkowitz et al., 2015). Sleep deprivation can make you eat more, and there's evidence that when teens and young adults are sleep deprived, they tend to go for sweet foods that are high in calories and low in nutrition (Simon et al., 2015).

But is it the fewer hours of sleep or the timing of the amount of sleep freshman do get? Students often get to bed much later when away at school than when at home, and one study has shown that for every hour bedtime was pushed back, there was a gain of about two points in body mass index or BMI, an indicator of how much body fat a person has (Asarnow et al., 2015).

A more recent study suggests that in addition to all of these factors, the weight gain experienced by many freshman college students may also be a result of irregular sleep patterns: Not only do students get less sleep and go to bed later, but they also go to sleep at different times due to different class schedules and social activities. While a person who is working has a schedule of getting up at a certain time and going to bed by a certain time on a regular basis, students may get to bed at midnight and get up at 7 A.M. one night but go to bed at 2 A.M. the following night and get up at 9 A.M. Even though both nights are 7 hours of sleep, the shift in the schedule is what may cause more sleep deprivation symptoms, according to a study conducted by researchers at Brown University in Providence, Rhode Island (Roane et al., 2015). When your sleep–wake cycle is shifted daily by 2 to nearly 3 hours, it's like having daily jet lag—just like shift workers and frequent flyers.

So the "freshman fifteen" is real, but more like the "freshman five," and the causative factors are not as simple as common sense might tell us. The sleep deprivation symptoms brought on by not only less sleep but also frequent variability in sleep cycles lead to fatigue (which leads to less exercise) and eating more sweets for quick energy boosts, eventually leading to weight gain. In the Brown study, this weight gain amounted to about 6 pounds in only 9 weeks!

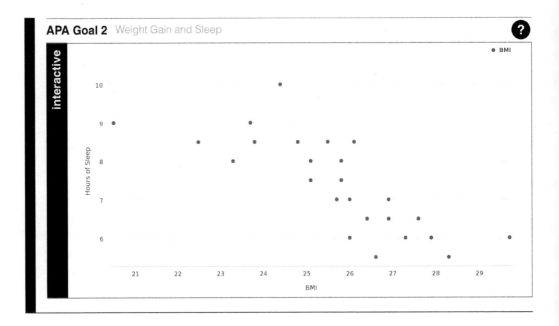

**APA Goal 2** Weight Gain and Sleep

# Dreams

"To sleep, perchance to dream" is a well-known and often-quoted line from Act II of *Hamlet* by William Shakespeare (Shakespeare & Hubler, 1987). But how important is dreaming? What is the purpose of dreaming?

## WHY DO WE DREAM?

**4.7** Compare and contrast two explanations of why people dream.

Dreams have long been a source of curiosity. People of ancient times tried to find meaning in dreams. Some viewed dreams as prophecy, some as messages from the spirits. But the real inquiry into the process of dreaming began with the publication of Freud's *The Interpretation of Dreams* (1900).

**FREUD'S INVTERPRETATION: DREAMS AS WISH FULFILLMENT** Sigmund Freud (1856–1939) believed that the problems of his patients stemmed from conflicts and events that had been buried in their unconscious minds since childhood. These early traumas were seen as the cause of behavior problems in adulthood, in which his patients suffered from symptoms such as a type of paralysis that had no physical basis or repetitive, ritualistic* hand washing. One of the ways Freud devised to get at these early memories was to examine the dreams of his patients, believing that conflicts, events, and desires of the past would be represented in symbolic** form in the dreams. Freud believed dreams to be a kind of wish fulfillment for his patients. **LINK** to Learning Objective 13.1.

The *manifest content* of a dream is the actual content of the dream itself. For example, if Chad has a dream in which he is trying to climb out of a bathtub, the manifest content of the dream is exactly that—he's trying to climb out of a bathtub.

But, of course, Freud would no doubt find more meaning in Chad's dream than is at first evident. He believed that the true meaning of a dream was hidden, or *latent*, and only expressed in symbols. In the dream, the water in the tub might symbolize the waters of birth, and the tub itself might be his mother's womb. Using a Freudian interpretation, Chad may be dreaming about being born.

© The New Yorker Collection 1973 Dana Fradon from cartoonbank.com. All Rights Reserved.

---

*ritualistic: referring to an action done in a particular manner each time it is repeated, according to some specific pattern.
**symbolic: having the quality of representing something other than itself.

🗨 Seems like quite a stretch. Wouldn't there be lots of other possible interpretations?

Yes, and today many professionals are no longer as fond of Freud's dream analysis as they once were. But there are still some people who insist that dreams have symbolic meaning. For example, dreaming about being naked in a public place is very common, and most dream analyzers interpret that to mean feeling open and exposed, an expression of childhood innocence, or even a desire for sex. Exactly how the dream is interpreted depends on the other features of the dream and what is happening in the person's waking life.

The development of techniques for looking at the structure and activity of the brain (see Ⓛ Ⓘ Ⓝ Ⓚ to Learning Objective 2.9) has led to an explanation of why people dream that is more concrete than that of Freud.

**THE ACTIVATION-SYNTHESIS HYPOTHESIS** Using brain-imaging techniques such as a PET scan (see Chapter Two), researchers have found evidence that dreams are products of activity in the pons (Hobson, 1988; Hobson & McCarley, 1977; Hobson et al., 2000; Weber et al., 2015). This lower area inhibits the neurotransmitters that would allow movement of the voluntary muscles while sending random signals to the areas of the cortex that interpret vision, hearing, and so on (see **Figure 4.4**).

When signals from the pons bombard* the cortex during waking consciousness, the association areas of the cortex interpret those signals as seeing, hearing, and so on. Because those signals come from the real world, this process results in an experience of reality. But when people are asleep, the signals from the brain stem are random and not necessarily attached to actual external stimuli, yet the brain must somehow interpret these random signals. It *synthesizes* (puts together) an explanation of the cortex's activation from memories and other stored information.

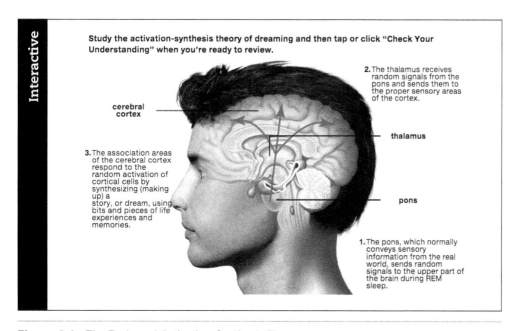

**Interactive**

Study the activation-synthesis theory of dreaming and then tap or click "Check Your Understanding" when you're ready to review.

2. The thalamus receives random signals from the pons and sends them to the proper sensory areas of the cortex.

cerebral cortex

thalamus

3. The association areas of the cerebral cortex respond to the random activation of cortical cells by synthesizing (making up) a story, or dream, using bits and pieces of life experiences and memories.

pons

1. The pons, which normally conveys sensory information from the real world, sends random signals to the upper part of the brain during REM sleep.

**Figure 4.4** The Brain and Activation-Synthesis Theory

According to the activation-synthesis theory of dreaming, the pons in the brainstem sends random signals to the upper part of the brain during REM sleep. These random signals pass through the thalamus, which sends the signals to the proper sensory areas of the cortex. Once in the cortex, the association areas of the cortex respond to the random activation of these cortical cells by synthesizing (making up) a story, or dream, using bits and pieces of life experiences and memories.

---

*bombard: to attack or press.

In this theory, called the **activation-synthesis hypothesis**, a dream is merely another kind of thinking that occurs when people sleep. It is less realistic because it comes not from the outside world of reality but from within people's memories and experiences of the past. The frontal lobes, which people normally use in daytime thinking, are more or less shut down during dreaming, which may also account for the unrealistic and often bizarre nature of dreams (Macquet & Franck, 1996).

💬 My dreams can be really weird, but sometimes they seem pretty ordinary or even seem to mean something. Can dreams be more meaningful?

**THE ACTIVATION-INFORMATION-MODE (AIM) MODEL**    There are dream experts who suggest that dreams may have more meaning than Hobson and McCarley originally theorized. A survey questioning subjects about their dream content, for example, concluded that much of the content of dreams is meaningful, consistent over time, and fits in with past or present emotional concerns rather than being bizarre, meaningless, and random (Domhoff, 1996, 2005).

Hobson and colleagues have reworked the activation-synthesis hypothesis to reflect concerns about dream meaning, calling it the **activation-information-mode model,** or **AIM** (Hobson et al., 2000). In this newer version, information that is accessed during waking hours can have an influence on the synthesis of dreams. In other words, when the brain is "making up" a dream to explain its own activation, it uses meaningful bits and pieces of the person's experiences from the previous day or the last few days rather than just random items from memory.

#### WHAT DO PEOPLE DREAM ABOUT?

**4.8** **Identify commonalities and differences in the content of people's dreams.**

Calvin Hall believed that dreams are just another type of cognitive process, or thinking, that occurred during sleep in his *cognitive theory of dreaming* (Hall, 1953). He collected more than 10,000 dreams and concluded that most dreams reflect the events that occur in everyday life (Hall, 1966). Although most people dream in color, people who grew up in the era of black-and-white television sometimes have dreams in black and white. There are gender differences, although whether those differences are caused by hormonal/genetic influences, sociocultural influences, or a combination of influences remains to be seen. In his book *Finding Meaning in Dreams*, Dr. William Domhoff (1996) concluded that across many cultures, men more often dream of other males whereas women tend to dream about males and females equally. Men across various cultures also tend to have more physical aggression in their dreams than do women, and women are more often the victims of such aggression in their own dreams. Domhoff also concluded that where there are differences in the content of dreams across cultures, the differences make sense in light of the culture's "personality." For example, American culture is considered fairly aggressive when compared to the culture of the Netherlands, and the aggressive content of the dreams in both cultures reflects this difference: There were lower levels of aggression in the dreams of those from the Netherlands when compared to the Americans' dream content.

Girls and women tend to dream about people they know, personal appearance concerns, and issues related to family and home. Boys and men tend to have more male characters in their dreams, which are also typically in outdoor or unfamiliar settings and may involve weapons, tools, cars, and roads. Men also report more sexual dreams, usually with unknown and attractive partners (Domhoff, 1996; Domhoff & Schneider, 2008; Foulkes, 1982; Horikawa et al., 2013; Van de Castle, 1994).

In dreams people run, jump, talk, and do all of the actions that they do in normal daily life. Nearly 50 percent of the dreams recorded by Hall (1966) had sexual content, although later research has found lower percentages (Van de Castle, 1994). Then there

**activation-synthesis hypothesis**

premise that states that dreams are created by the higher centers of the cortex to explain the activation by the brain stem of cortical cells during REM sleep periods.

**activation-information-mode model,** or **AIM**

revised version of the activation synthesis explanation of dreams in which information that is accessed during waking hours can have an influence on the synthesis of dreams.

are dreams of flying, falling, and of trying to do something and failing—all of which are very common dreams, even in other cultures (Domhoff, 1996). So is that often-recounted dream of being naked in public! Take the survey *Are Dreams Meaningful?* to discover more about your own experiences and attitudes toward dreams.

**Survey**   ARE DREAMS MEANINGFUL?

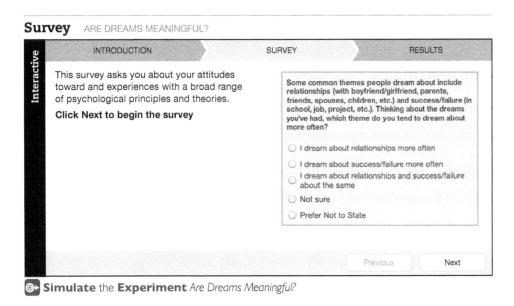

○ **Simulate** the **Experiment** *Are Dreams Meaningful?*

**Concept Map** L.O. 4.7, 4.8

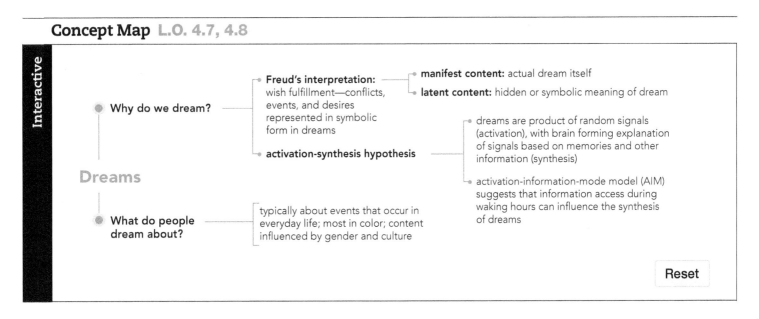

# Practice Quiz    How much do you remember?

*Pick the best answer.*

1. In Freud's theory, the actual content of a dream is called
   a. manifest content.
   b. latent content.
   c. symbolic content.
   d. hidden content.

2. Michael finds that most of his dreams are little more than random images that seemingly have been put into a strange storyline. Which theory of dreams best explains this?
   a. Freudian dream theory
   b. dreams for survival theory
   c. activation-synthesis hypothesis
   d. Hall's dreams as reflections of everyday life

3. According to Calvin Hall, around what are most dreams centered?
   a. everyday life
   b. unfulfilled fantasies
   c. frightening events
   d. past childhood

4. Studies show that most people tend to
   a. dream in black and white.
   b. dream in color.
   c. only have nightmares.
   d. not dream at all.

# Hypnosis

Contrary to what you may have seen in the movies or on television, people who are hypnotized are not in a trance (Lynn et al., 2015). **Hypnosis** is simply a state of consciousness in which a person is especially susceptible to suggestion. Although a lot of misunderstandings exist about hypnosis, it can be a useful tool when properly managed.

## HOW HYPNOSIS WORKS

**4.9** **Explain how hypnosis affects consciousness.**

There are four key steps in inducing hypnosis (Druckman & Bjork, 1994):

1. The hypnotist tells the person to focus on what is being said.
2. The person is told to relax and feel tired.
3. The hypnotist tells the person to "let go" and accept suggestions easily.
4. The person is told to use vivid imagination.

The real key to hypnosis seems to be a heightened state of suggestibility.* People can be hypnotized when active and alert, but only if they are willing to be hypnotized. Only 80 percent of all people can be hypnotized, and only 40 percent are good hypnotic subjects. The ability to be hypnotized may lie in the way the brain functions. Using brain-scanning techniques, researchers found that two areas in the brains of highly hypnotizable people, areas associated with decision making and attention, seem to be more active and connected when compared to people who cannot be hypnotized (Hoeft et al., 2012).

A test of *hypnotic susceptibility*, or the degree to which a person is a good hypnotic subject, often makes use of a series of ordered suggestions. The more suggestions in the ordered list the person responds to, the more susceptible** that person is. (See **Table 4.2** for examples of the types of items on a typical hypnotic susceptibility scale.)

💬 Is it true that people can be hypnotized into doing things that they would never do under normal conditions?

Although the popular view is that the hypnotized person is acting involuntarily, the fact is that the hypnotist may only be a guide into a more relaxed state, while the subject actually hypnotizes himself or herself (Kirsch & Lynn, 1995). People cannot be hypnotized against their will. The tendency to act as though their behavior is automatic and out of their control is called the *basic suggestion effect* (Kihlstrom, 1985); it gives people an excuse to do things they might not otherwise do because the burden of responsibility for their actions falls on the hypnotist.

**Table 4.2** Examples of Items That Would Appear on a Hypnotic Susceptibility Scale

| | |
|---|---|
| 1. Movement of the body back and forth | 5. Responding to posthypnotic suggestion |
| 2. Closing eyes and unable to open them | 6. Loss of memory for events during the session |
| 3. Fingers locked together | 7. Unable to state one's own name |
| 4. One arm locked into position | 8. Seeing or hearing nonexistent stimuli |

**SOURCE:** Based on Hilgard, E, Hypnotic Susceptibility, 1965.

**hypnosis**

state of consciousness in which the person is especially susceptible to suggestion.

*suggestibility: being readily influenced.
**susceptible: easily affected emotionally.

As the video *Hypnosis in Therapy and Recovered Memories* explains, hypnosis is also a controversial tool when used in therapy to help people "recover" what are thought to be repressed memories. Ⓛ Ⓘ Ⓝ Ⓚ to Learning Objective 6.9.

👁 **Watch** the **Video** *Hypnosis In Therapy and Recovered Memories*

In general, hypnosis is a handy way to help people relax and/or to control pain. These subjective experiences are very much under people's mental influence, and hypnosis is not the only way to achieve them. The same kind of effects (such as hallucinations, reduction of pain, and memory loss) can be achieved without any hypnotic suggestion (Lynn et al., 2015). Actual physical behavior is harder to change, and that is why hypnosis is not as effective at changing eating habits or helping people stop smoking (Druckman & Bjork, 1994). Hypnosis is sometimes used in psychological therapy to help people cope with anxiety or deal with cravings for food or drugs. For a concise look at what hypnosis can and cannot do, see **Table 4.3**.

**THEORIES OF HYPNOSIS**

**4.10** **Compare and contrast two views of why hypnosis works.**

There are two views of why hypnosis works. One emphasizes the role of **dissociation**, or a splitting of conscious awareness, whereas the other involves a kind of social role-playing.

| Table 4.3    Facts About Hypnosis | |
|---|---|
| **Hypnosis Can:** | **Hypnosis Cannot:** |
| Create amnesia for whatever happens during the hypnotic session, at least for a brief time (Bowers & Woody, 1996). | Give people superhuman strength. (People may use their full strength under hypnosis, but it is no more than they had before hypnosis.) |
| Relieve pain by allowing a person to remove conscious attention from the pain (Holroyd, 1996). | Reliably enhance memory. (There's an increased risk of false-memory retrieval because of the suggestive state hypnosis creates.) |
| Alter sensory perceptions. (Smell, hearing, vision, time sense, and the ability to see visual illusions can all be affected by hypnosis.) | Regress people back to childhood. (Although people may *act* like children, they do and say things children would not.) |
| Help people relax in situations that normally would cause them stress, such as flying on an airplane (Muhlberger et al., 2001). | Regress people to some "past life." There is no scientific evidence for past-life regression (Lilienfeld et al., 2004). |

**dissociation**

divided state of conscious awareness.

Stage hypnotists often make use of people's willingness to believe that something ordinary is extraordinary. This woman was hypnotized and suspended between two chairs after the person supporting her middle stepped away. The hypnotist led the audience to believe that she could not do this unless hypnotized, but in reality anyone can do this while fully conscious.

**HYPNOSIS AS DISSOCIATION: THE HIDDEN OBSERVER**  Ernest Hilgard (1991; Hilgard & Hilgard, 1994) believed that hypnosis worked only on the immediate conscious mind of a person, while a part of that person's mind (a "hidden observer") remained aware of all that was going on. It's the same kind of dissociation that takes place when people drive somewhere familiar and then wonder how they got there. One part of the mind, the conscious part, is thinking about dinner or a date or something else, while the other part is doing the actual driving. When people arrive at their destination, they don't really remember the actual trip. In the same way, Hilgard believes that there is a hidden part of the mind that is very much aware of the hypnotic subject's activities and sensations, even though the "hypnotized" part of the mind is blissfully unaware of these same things.

In one study (Miller & Bowers, 1993), subjects were hypnotized and told to put their arms in ice water, although they were instructed to feel no pain. There had to be pain—most people can't even get an ice cube out of the freezer without *some* pain—but subjects reported no pain at all. The subjects who were successful at denying the pain also reported that they imagined being at the beach or in some other place that allowed them to dissociate* from the pain.

**HYPNOSIS AS SOCIAL ROLE-PLAYING: THE SOCIAL-COGNITIVE EXPLANATION**  The other theory of why hypnosis works began with an experiment in which participants who were *not* hypnotized were instructed to behave as if they were (Sarbin & Coe, 1972). These participants had no trouble copying many actions previously thought to require a hypnotic state, such as being rigidly suspended between two chairs. The researchers also found that participants who were not familiar with hypnosis and had no idea what the "role" of a hypnotic subject was supposed to be could not be hypnotized.

Add to those findings the later findings that expectancies of the hypnotized person play a big part in how the person responds and what the person does under hypnosis (Kirsch, 2000). The **social-cognitive theory of hypnosis** assumes that people who are hypnotized are not in an altered state but are merely playing the role expected of them in the situation. They might believe that they are hypnotized, but in fact it is all a very good performance, so good that even the "participants" are unaware that they are role-playing. Social roles are very powerful influences on behavior, as anyone who has ever worn a uniform can understand—the uniform stands for a particular role that becomes very easy to play (Zimbardo, 1970; Zimbardo et al., 2000). (L)(I)(N)(K) to Learning Objective 12.14.

**social-cognitive theory of hypnosis** theory that assumes that people who are hypnotized are not in an altered state but are merely playing the role expected of them in the situation.

## Concept Map L.O. 4.9, 4.10

**Interactive**

**Hypnosis**
(state of consciousness during which person is more susceptible to suggestion)

- can be assessed by scale of hypnotic susceptibility
- induction typically involves relaxed focus and "permission to let go"; person being hypnotized is in control and cannot be hypnotized against his or her will
- can be used in therapy—helps people deal with pain, anxiety, or cravings (e.g., food, drug)
- theories
  - **dissociation:** one part of the mind is aware of actions/activities taking place, while the "hypnotized" part is not
  - **social-cognitive theory** suggests that people assume roles based on expectations for a given situation

Reset

*dissociate: break a connection with something.

# Practice Quiz   How much do you remember?

*Pick the best answer.*

1. The primary key to hypnosis is finding someone who
   a. accepts suggestions easily.
   b. has a vivid imagination.
   c. is already very tired.
   d. is easily distracted.

2. Some researchers have suggested that hypnosis may work due to an individual's personal expectations about what being hypnotized is supposed to be like and the individual's ability to play a particular role in the given social situation. Which theory of hypnosis best accounts for these possible explanations for an individual's behavior while hypnotized?
   a. dissociative theory
   b. expectancy theory
   c. social-cognitive theory
   d. biological theory

3. Your friend tells you she is seeing a therapist who wishes to use hypnosis as part of her therapy. However, your friend is concerned that she might be hypnotized without knowing it. What might you tell her?
   a. Be careful. Hypnotists are in control of you while hypnotized.
   b. Not to worry. Hypnotists can only control their patient's behavior about 40 percent of the time.
   c. That you actually hypnotize yourself and you cannot be hypnotized against your will.
   d. Don't worry. Hypnosis is just an illusion and doesn't really work.

4. Which theory of hypnosis includes the idea of a "hidden observer"?
   a. social cognitive
   b. biological
   c. expectancy
   d. dissociative

# The Influence of Psychoactive Drugs

Whereas some people seek altered states of consciousness in sleep, daydreaming, meditation, or even hypnosis, others try to take a shortcut. They use **psychoactive drugs**, chemical substances that alter thinking, perception, memory, or some combination of those abilities. Many of the drugs discussed in the following sections are very useful and were originally developed to help people. Some put people to sleep so that surgeries and procedures that would otherwise be impossible can be performed, whereas others help people deal with the pain of injuries or disease. Still others may be used in helping to control various conditions such as sleep disorders or attention deficits in children and adults.

## DEPENDENCE

### 4.11 Distinguish between physical dependence and psychological dependence upon drugs.

The usefulness of these drugs must not blind us to the dangers of misusing or abusing them. When taken for pleasure, to get "high," or to dull psychological pain or when taken without the supervision of a qualified medical professional, these drugs can pose serious risks to one's health and may even cause death. One danger of such drugs is their potential to create either a physical or psychological dependence, both of which can lead to a lifelong pattern of abuse as well as the risk of taking increasingly larger doses, leading to one of the clearest dangers of dependence: a drug overdose. Drug overdoses do not happen only with illegal drugs; even certain additives in so-called natural supplements can have a deadly effect. One survey found that more than 23,000 emergency room visits per year could be attributed to the use and abuse of dietary supplements (Geller et al., 2015).

**PHYSICAL DEPENDENCE**  Drugs that people can become physically dependent on cause the user's body to crave the drug (Abadinsky, 1989; Fleming & Barry, 1992; Pratt, 1991). After using the drug for some period of time, the body becomes unable to function normally without the drug and the person is said to be dependent or addicted, a condition commonly called **physical dependence**.

One sign of physical dependence is the development of a **drug tolerance** (Pratt, 1991). As the person continues to use the drug, larger and larger doses of the drug are needed to achieve the same initial effects of the drug.

Another sign of a physical dependence is that the user experiences symptoms of **withdrawal** when deprived of the drug. Depending on the drug, these symptoms can range from headaches, nausea, and irritability to severe pain, cramping, shaking, and

**psychoactive drugs**
chemical substances that alter thinking, perception, and memory.

**physical dependence**
condition occurring when a person's body becomes unable to function normally without a particular drug.

**drug tolerance**
the decrease of the response to a drug over repeated uses, leading to the need for higher doses of drug to achieve the same effect.

**withdrawal**
physical symptoms that can include nausea, pain, tremors, crankiness, and high blood pressure, resulting from a lack of an addictive drug in the body systems.

dangerously elevated blood pressure. These physical sensations occur because the body is trying to adjust to the absence of the drug. Many users will take more of the drug to alleviate the symptoms of withdrawal, which makes the entire situation worse. This is actually an example of *negative reinforcement*, the tendency to continue a behavior that leads to the removal of or escape from unpleasant circumstances or sensations. Negative reinforcement is a very powerful motivating factor, and scores of drug-dependent users exist as living proof of that power. ⓁⓘⓃⓚ to Learning Objective 5.3.

This learned behavioral effect has led to nondrug treatments that make use of behavioral therapies such as *contingency-management therapy* (an operant conditioning strategy), in which patients earn vouchers for negative drug tests (Tusel et al., 1994). The vouchers can be exchanged for healthier, more desirable items like food. These behavioral therapies can include residential and outpatient approaches. ⓁⓘⓃⓚ to Learning Objective 15.4. *Cognitive-behavioral interventions* work to change the way people think about the stresses in their lives and react to those stressors, working toward more effective coping without resorting to drugs.

The brain itself plays an important part in dependency. Drugs that can lead to dependence cause the release of dopamine in a part of the brain called the mesolimbic pathway, a neural track that begins in the midbrain area (just above the pons, an area called the *ventral tegmental area* or *VTA*) and connects to limbic system structures, including the amygdala, the hippocampus, and the *nucleus accumbens*, and continues to the middle of the prefrontal cortex (Hnasko et al., 2010; Salgado & Kaplitt, 2015; Schmitt & Reith, 2010). ⓁⓘⓃⓚ to Learning Objective 2.11. When a drug enters the body, it goes quickly to this area, known as the brain's "reward pathway," causing a release of dopamine and intense pleasure (see **Figure 4.5**). The brain tries to adapt to this large amount of dopamine by decreasing the number of synaptic receptors for dopamine. The next time the user takes the drug, he or she needs more of it to get the same pleasure response because of the reduced number of receptors—drug tolerance has developed (Koob & Le Moal, 2005; Laviolette et al., 2008; Salamone & Correa, 2012). This system of structures in the reward pathway is the

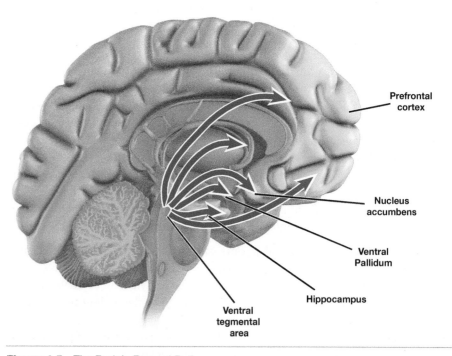

**Figure 4.5** The Brain's Reward Pathway

A pleasure center has been discovered in the mesotelencephalic dopamine pathway. The cells in this pathway communicate via the neurotransmitter dopamine. The pathway between the ventral tegmental area and the nucleus accumbens is most likely the site for the rewarding effects of natural rewards (e.g. eating, drinking, sex) and drug effects (e.g. euphoria, pleasure).

most important pathway of neurons in the brain tied to all forms of addiction and may be involved in the depression that occurs in some mood disorders (Glangetas et al., 2015; Mahr et al., 2013; Russo & Nestler, 2013). (L)(I)(N)(K) to Learning Objective 14.9.

💬 But not all drugs produce physical dependence, right? For example, some people say that you can't get physically dependent on marijuana. If that's true, why is it so hard for some people to quit smoking pot?

**PSYCHOLOGICAL DEPENDENCE**  Not all drugs cause physical dependence; some cause **psychological dependence**, or the belief that the drug is needed to continue a feeling of emotional or psychological well-being, which is a very powerful factor in continued drug use. The body may not need or crave the drug, and people may not experience the symptoms of physical withdrawal or tolerance, but they will continue to use the drug because they *think* they need it. In this case, it is the rewarding properties of using the drug that cause a dependency to develop. This is an example of *positive reinforcement*, or the tendency of a behavior to strengthen when followed by pleasurable consequences. (L)(I)(N)(K) to Learning Objective 5.5. Negative reinforcement is also at work here, as taking the drug will lower levels of anxiety.

Although not all drugs produce physical dependence, *any* drug can become a focus of psychological dependence. Indeed, because there is no withdrawal to go through or to recover from, psychological dependencies can last forever. Some people who gave up smoking marijuana decades ago still say that the craving returns every now and then (Roffman et al., 1988).

The effect of a particular drug depends on the category to which it belongs and the particular neurotransmitter the drug affects. (L)(I)(N)(K) to Learning Objective 2.3. In this current chapter we will describe several of the major drug categories, including **stimulants** (drugs that increase the functioning of the nervous system), **depressants** (drugs that decrease the functioning of the nervous system), and **hallucinogenics** (drugs that alter perceptions and may cause hallucinations).

One of the dangers of psychoactive drugs is that they may lead to physical or psychological dependence.

### STIMULANTS: UP, UP, AND AWAY

**4.12 Identify the effects and dangers of using stimulants.**

Stimulants are a class of drugs that cause either the sympathetic division or the central nervous system (or both) to increase levels of functioning, at least temporarily. In simple terms, stimulants "speed up" the nervous system—the heart may beat faster or the brain may work faster, for example. Many of these drugs are called "uppers" for this reason.

**AMPHETAMINES**  Amphetamines are stimulants that are synthesized (made) in laboratories rather than being found in nature. Among the amphetamines are drugs like Benzedrine, Methedrine, and Dexedrine. A related compound, *methamphetamine*, is sometimes used to treat attention-deficit/hyperactivity disorder or narcolepsy. "Crystal meth" is a crystalline form that can be smoked and is used by "recreational" drug users, people who do not need drugs but instead use them to gain some form of pleasure.

Like other stimulants, amphetamines cause the sympathetic nervous system to go into overdrive. (L)(I)(N)(K) to Learning Objective 2.5. Some truck drivers use amphetamines to stay awake while driving long hours. Stimulants won't give people any extra energy, but they will cause people to burn up whatever energy reserves they do have. They also depress the appetite, which is another function of the sympathetic division. Many doctors used to prescribe these drugs as diet pills. Today they are only used on a short-term basis and under strict medical supervision, often in the treatment of attention-deficit hyperactivity disorder (Safer, 2015). Diet pills sold over the counter usually contain another relatively mild stimulant, caffeine.

**psychological dependence**
the feeling that a drug is needed to continue a feeling of emotional or psychological well-being.

**stimulants**
drugs that increase the functioning of the nervous system.

**depressants**
drugs that decrease the functioning of the nervous system.

**hallucinogenics**
drugs including hallucinogens and marijuana that produce hallucinations or increased feelings of relaxation and intoxication.

**amphetamines**
stimulants that are synthesized (made) in laboratories rather than being found in nature.

When the energy reserves are exhausted, or the drug wears off, a "crash" is inevitable and the tendency is to take more pills to get back "up." The person taking these pills finds that it takes more and more pills to get the same stimulant effect (drug tolerance). Nausea, vomiting, high blood pressure, and strokes are possible, as is a state called "amphetamine psychosis." This condition causes addicts to become delusional (losing contact with what is real) and paranoid. They think people are out to "get" them. Violence is a likely outcome, against both the self and others (Dickinson, 2015; Kratofil et al., 1996; Paparelli et al., 2011).

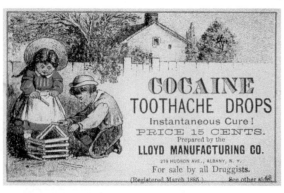

Far from being illegal, cocaine was once used in many health drinks and medications, such as this toothache medicine used in the late 1800s.

**COCAINE** Unlike amphetamines, **cocaine** is a natural drug found in coca plant leaves. It produces feelings of euphoria (a feeling of great happiness), energy, power, and pleasure. It also deadens pain and suppresses the appetite. It was used rather liberally by both doctors and dentists (who used it in numbing the mouth prior to extracting a tooth, for example) near the end of the nineteenth century and the beginning of the twentieth century, until the deadly effects of its addictive qualities became known. Many patent medicines contained minute traces of cocaine, including the now famous Coca-Cola™ (this popular soft drink was originally marketed as a nerve tonic). The good news is that even in 1902, there wasn't enough cocaine in a bottle of cola to affect even a fly, and by 1929, all traces of cocaine were removed (Allen, 1994).

Cocaine is a highly dangerous drug, not just for its addictive properties. Some people have convulsions and may even die when using cocaine for the first time (Lacayo, 1995). It can have devastating effects on the children born to mothers who use cocaine and has been associated with increased risk of learning disabilities, delayed language development, and an inability to cope adequately with stress, among other symptoms (Cone-Wesson, 2005; Eiden et al., 2009; Kable et al., 2008; Morrow et al., 2006). Laboratory animals have been known to press a lever to give themselves cocaine rather than eating or drinking, even to the point of starvation and death (Chahua et al., 2015; Glangetas et al., 2015; Iwamoto & Martin, 1988; Ward et al., 1996).

Although cocaine users do not go through the same kind of physical withdrawal symptoms that users of heroin, alcohol, and other physically addictive drugs go through, users will experience a severe mood swing into depression (the "crash"), followed by extreme tiredness, nervousness, an inability to feel pleasure, and paranoia. The brain is the part of the body that develops the craving for cocaine because of chemical changes caused by the drug (Glanetas et al., 2015; Hurley, 1989; Schmitt & Reith, 2010). Ⓛ Ⓘ Ⓝ ᴋ to Learning Objective 2.3.

As addictive as cocaine is, there is one other stimulant that is usually described as even more addictive. Most experts in addiction seem to agree that although crack cocaine (a less pure, cheaper version found on the streets) produces addiction in nearly three fourths of the people who use it, nicotine produces addiction in 99 percent of the people who use it (Benowitz, 1988; Centers for Disease Control and Prevention [CDC], 2002, 2004; Franklin, 1990; Henningfield et al., 1991; Hilts, 1998; Jamal et al., 2015); Perrine, 1997).

 💬 Hasn't nicotine just been the victim of a lot of bad press? After all, it's legal, unlike cocaine and heroin.

**NICOTINE** Every year, nearly 480,000 people in the United States die from illnesses related to smoking, costing more than $300 billion in health care and productivity losses annually. That's more people than those who die from accidents in motor vehicles, alcohol, cocaine, heroin and other drug abuse, AIDS, suicide, and homicide *combined* (Jamal et al., 2015; U.S. Department of Health and Human Services, 2010). Remember, cocaine, heroin, morphine, and many other currently controlled substances

**cocaine**

a natural drug derived from the leaves of the coca plant.

or illegal drugs once used to be legal. One has to wonder what would have been the fate of these drugs if as many people had been making money off of them at that time as do those who farm, manufacture, and distribute tobacco products today.

**Nicotine** is a relatively mild but nevertheless toxic stimulant, producing a slight "rush" or sense of arousal as it raises blood pressure and accelerates the heart, as well as providing a rush of sugar into the bloodstream by stimulating the release of adrenalin in addition to raising dopamine levels in the brain's reward pathway (Kovacs et al., 2010; Rezvani & Levin, 2001). As is the case with many stimulants, it also has a relaxing effect on most people and seems to reduce stress (Pormerleau & Pormerleau, 1994).

Although fewer Americans are smoking (down to about 17% from more than 40% in the 1960s), men are more likely to smoke than women, an incidence of about 19% for men and 15% for women (CDC, 2015b). The heaviest smokers (20%) are those adults aged 25–44 years. This is alarming news when one considers the toxic nature of nicotine: In the 1920s and 1930s it was used as an insecticide and is considered to be highly toxic and fast acting (Gosselin et al., 1984; Mayer, 2014). Although the amount of nicotine in a cigarette is low, first-time smokers often experience nausea as a result of the toxic effects after just a few puffs.

Why is it so difficult to quit using tobacco products? Aside from the powerfully addictive nature of nicotine, the physical withdrawal symptoms can be as bad as those resulting from alcohol, cocaine, or heroin abuse (Epping-Jordan et al., 1998). People don't think about nicotine as being as bad as cocaine or heroin because nicotine is legal and easily obtainable, but in terms of its addictive power, it is *more powerful* than heroin or alcohol (CDC, 2010; Henningfield et al., 1990; Jamal et al., 2015). Using smokeless tobacco (e-cigarettes or "vaping") may actually be more harmful, as one study found higher levels of exposure to nicotine and toxins in those users than in users of regular tobacco products (Rostron et al., 2015).

**THINKING CRITICALLY**

What might happen if the use of nicotine products became illegal?

▶   The response entered here will be saved to your notes and may be collected by your instructor if he/she requires it.

Submit

**CAFFEINE**  Although many people will never use amphetamines or take cocaine, and others will never smoke or will quit successfully, there is one stimulant that almost everyone uses, with many using it every day. This, of course, is **caffeine**, the stimulant found in coffee, tea, most sodas, energy drinks, chocolate, and even many over-the-counter drugs.

Caffeine is another natural substance, like cocaine and nicotine, and is found in coffee beans, tea leaves, cocoa nuts, and at least 60 other types of plants (Braun, 1996). It is a mild stimulant, helps maintain alertness, and can increase the effectiveness of some pain relievers such as aspirin. Caffeine is often added to pain relievers for that reason and is the key ingredient in medications meant to keep people awake.

Contrary to popular belief, coffee does not help induce sobriety. All one would get is a wide-awake drunk. Coffee is fairly acidic, too, and acids are not what the stomach of a person with a hangover needs. (And since the subject has come up, drinking more alcohol or "hair of the dog that bit you" just increases the problem later on—the best cure for a hangover is lots of water to put back all the fluids that alcohol takes out of the body, and sleep.)

Research suggests that, in modest amounts of perhaps two cups a day, coffee may actually be good for you. Studies have found that coffee consumption is associated with lowered risk of Type 2 diabetes and a lower risk of death overall (Ding et al., 2014, 2015).

**nicotine**
the active ingredient in tobacco.

**caffeine**
a mild stimulant found in coffee, tea, and several other plant-based substances.

That isn't a cloud of smoke coming from this woman's mouth. She's using an e-cig, or electronic cigarette. There are many different brands of this battery-operated device currently on the market. Each e-cig can deliver nicotine (with flavorings and other chemicals) in the form of a vapor rather than smoke. Often promoted as safer than a regular cigarette, the health risks of using such devices is not yet determined.

While most people probably get their caffeine dose in the form of coffee or caffeinated sodas, many people are turning to highly-caffeinated energy drinks such as the one pictured here. What problems might arise from using such heavily sweetened beverages?

Actor Cory Allan Michael Monteith was known for his role as Finn Hudson on the Fox television series *Glee*. On July 13, 2013, after a long battle with addiction, he died from a toxic drug interaction of heroin and alcohol.

### barbiturates

depressant drugs that have a sedative effect.

### benzodiazepines

drugs that lower anxiety and reduce stress.

### alcohol

the chemical resulting from fermentation or distillation of various kinds of vegetable matter.

Although many young adults see drinking as a rite of passage into adulthood, few may understand the dangers of "binge" drinking, or drinking four to five drinks within a limited amount of time. Inhibitions are lowered and poor decisions may be made, such as driving while intoxicated. Binge drinking, a popular activity on some college campuses, can also lead to alcoholism.

**DOWN IN THE VALLEY: DEPRESSANTS**

## 4.13 Identify the effects and dangers of using depressants.

Another class of psychoactive drugs is *depressants*, drugs that slow the central nervous system.

**MAJOR AND MINOR TRANQUILIZERS** Commonly known as the *major tranquilizers* (drugs that have a strong depressant effect) or sleeping pills, **barbiturates** are drugs that have a sedative (sleep-inducing) effect. Overdoses can lead to death as breathing and heart action are stopped.

The *minor tranquilizers* (drugs having a relatively mild depressant effect) include the **benzodiazepines**. These drugs are used to lower anxiety and reduce stress. Some of the most common are Valium, Xanax, Halcion, Ativan, and Librium.

Both major and minor tranquilizers can be addictive, and large doses can be dangerous, as can an interaction with alcohol or other drugs (Breslow et al., 2015; Olin, 1993).

Rohypnol is a benzodiazepine tranquilizer that has become famous as the "date rape" drug. Unsuspecting victims drink something that has been doctored with this drug, which causes them to be unaware of their actions, although still able to respond to directions or commands. Rape or some other form of sexual assault can then be carried out without fear that the victim will remember it or be able to report it (Armstrong, 1997; Gable, 2004).

**ALCOHOL** The most commonly used and abused depressant is **alcohol**, the chemical resulting from fermentation or distillation of various kinds of vegetable matter. Anywhere from 10 to 20 million people in the United States suffer from alcoholism. In 2014, nearly 25 percent of people aged 18 or older reported that they had participated in binge drinking within the past month (National Institute on Alcohol Abuse and Alcoholism [NIAAA], 2016). Aside from the obvious health risks to the liver, brain, and heart, alcohol is associated with loss of work time, loss of a job, and loss of economic stability.

Many people are alcoholics but deny the fact. They believe that getting drunk, especially in college, is a ritual of adulthood. Many college students and even older adults engage in binge drinking (drinking four or five drinks within a limited amount of time, such as at "happy hour"). Binge drinking quickly leads to being drunk, and drunkenness is a major sign of alcoholism. Some other danger signs are feeling guilty about drinking, drinking in the morning, drinking to recover from drinking, drinking alone, being sensitive about how much one drinks when others mention it, drinking so much that one does and says things one later regrets, drinking enough to have blackouts or memory loss, drinking too fast, lying about drinking, and drinking enough to pass out.

The dangers of abusing alcohol cannot be stressed enough. According to the Centers for Disease Control and Prevention (CDC, 2011, 2015a), the number of alcohol-related deaths in the period from 2006 to 2010 was around 88,000 deaths. This figure does *not* include deaths due to accidents and homicides that may be related to abuse of alcohol—only those deaths that are caused by the body's inability to handle the alcohol. The National Institute on Alcohol Abuse and Alcoholism (NIAAA, 2016) has statistics showing that nearly 88,000 people *per year* die from alcohol-related causes, a figure that probably *does* include those accidents and homicides, making alcohol the fourth leading cause of death in the United States.

Pregnant women should not drink at all, as alcohol can damage the growing embryo, causing a condition of mental retardation and physical deformity known as fetal alcohol syndrome (Truong et al., 2012; Williams & Smith, 2015). (L)(I)(N)(K) to Learning Objective 8.5. Increased risk of loss of bone density (known as osteoporosis) and heart disease has also been linked to alcoholism (Abbott et al., 1994). These are just a few of the many health problems that alcohol can cause.

If you are concerned about your own drinking or are worried about a friend or loved one, there is a free and very simple online assessment at this site on the Internet: www.alcoholscreening.org.

> 💬 I have friends who insist that alcohol is a stimulant because they feel more uninhibited when they drink, so why is it considered a depressant?

Alcohol is often confused with stimulants. Many people think this is because alcohol makes a person feel "up" and euphoric (happy). Actually, alcohol is a depressant that gives the illusion of stimulation, because the very first thing alcohol depresses is a person's natural inhibitions, or the "don'ts" of behavior. Inhibitions are all the social rules people have learned that allow them to get along with others and function in society. Inhibitions also keep people from taking off all their clothes and dancing on the table at a crowded bar—inhibitions are a good thing.

Many people are unaware of exactly what constitutes a "drink." **Table 4.4** explains this and shows the effects of various numbers of drinks on behavior. Alcohol indirectly stimulates the release of a neurotransmitter called GABA, the brain's major depressant (Brick, 2003; Santhakumar et al., 2007). GABA slows down or stops neural activity. As more GABA is released, the brain's functioning actually becomes more and more inhibited, depressed, or slowed down. The areas of the brain that are first affected by alcohol are unfortunately the areas that control social inhibitions, so alcohol (due to its simulation of GABA) has the effect of depressing the inhibitions. As the effects continue, motor skills, reaction time, and speech are all affected.

Some people might be surprised that only one drink can have a fairly strong effect. People who are not usually drinkers will feel the effects of alcohol much more quickly than those who have built up a tolerance. Women also feel the effects sooner, as their

| **Table 4.4**   Blood Alcohol Level and Behavior Associated With Amounts of Alcohol |

A drink is a drink. Each contains half an ounce of alcohol.
So a drink is...
• 1 can of beer (12 oz.; 4–5% alcohol)
• 1 glass of wine (4 oz.; 12% alcohol)
• 1 shot of most liquors (1 oz.; 40–50% alcohol)
At times "a drink" is really the equivalent of more than just one drink, like when you order a drink with more than one shot of alcohol in it, or you do a shot followed by a beer.

| Average Number of Drinks | Blood Alcohol Level | Behavior |
| --- | --- | --- |
| 1–2 drinks | 0.05% | Feeling of well-being, uninhibited, poor judgment, coordination, and alertness Impaired driving |
| 3–5 drinks | 0.10% | Slow reaction time Muscle control, vision, and speech impaired Crash risk greatly increased |
| 6–7 drinks | 0.15% | Major increases in reaction time |
| 8–10 drinks | 0.20% | Loss of balance, fine motor skills, legally blind and unable to drive for up to 10 hours |
| 10–14 drinks | 0.20% and 0.25% | Staggering and severe motor disturbances |
| 10–14 drinks | 0.30% | Not aware of surroundings |
| 10–14 drinks | 0.35% | Surgical anesthesia Lethal dosage for a small percentage of people |
| 14–20 drinks | 0.40% | Lethal dosage for about 50% of people Severe circulatory/respiratory depression Alcohol poisoning/overdose |

**SOURCE:** Adapted from the *Moderate Drinking Skills Study Guide* (2004). Eau-Claire, WI: University of Wisconsin.

bodies process alcohol differently than men's bodies do. (Women are typically smaller, too, so alcohol has a quicker impact on women.)

**OPIATES: I FEEL YOUR PAIN** **Opiates** are a type of depressant that suppress the sensation of pain by binding to and stimulating the nervous system's natural receptor sites for endorphins (called *opioid receptors*), the neurotransmitters that naturally deaden pain sensations (Levesque, 2014; Olin, 1993). Because they also slow down the action of the nervous system, drug interactions with alcohol and other depressants are possible—and deadly. All opiates are a derivative of a particular plant-based substance—opium.

**OPIUM** **Opium**, made from the opium poppy, has pain-relieving and euphoria-inducing properties that have been known for at least 2,000 years. Highly addictive, it mimics the effects of endorphins, the nervous system's natural painkillers. The nervous system slows or stops its production of endorphins. When the drug wears off, there is no protection against any kind of pain, causing the severe symptoms of withdrawal associated with these drugs. It was not until 1803 that opium was developed for use as a medication by a German physician. The new form—morphine—was hailed as "God's own medicine" (Hodgson, 2001).

**MORPHINE** **Morphine** was created by dissolving opium in an acid and then neutralizing the acid with ammonia. Morphine was thought to be a wonder drug, although its addictive qualities soon became a major concern to physicians and their patients. Morphine is still used today to control severe pain, but in carefully controlled doses and for very short periods of time.

**HEROIN** Ironically, **heroin** was first hailed as the new wonder drug—a derivative of morphine that did not have many of the disagreeable side effects of morphine. The theory was that heroin was a purer form of the drug and that the impurities in morphine were the substances creating the harmful side effects. It did not take long, however, for doctors and others to realize that heroin was even more powerfully addictive than morphine or opium. Although usage as a medicine ceased, it is still used by many people.

The United States has seen an increase in the use of heroin among both men and women in various age groups and levels of income (CDC, 2015c). People are not only using heroin but are combining it with other drugs, particularly cocaine and prescription painkillers containing opiates, which has of course led to an increase in overdose deaths. The rate of heroin-related overdose deaths quadrupled in only an 11-year period, from 2002–2013 (CDC, 2015c).

Drugs such as *methadone, buprenorphine,* and *naltrexone* may be used to control withdrawal symptoms and help treat opiate addictions (Kahan & Sutton, 1998; Kakko et al., 2003; Ward et al., 1999). Eventually, as the addicted person is weaned from these drugs, the natural endorphin system starts to function more normally.

### HALLUCINOGENS: HIGHER AND HIGHER

**4.14** **Identify the effects and dangers of using hallucinogens.**

**Hallucinogens** actually cause the brain to alter its interpretation of sensations (Olin, 1993) and can produce sensory distortions very similar to *synesthesia* (Ⓛ Ⓘ Ⓝ Ⓚ to Chapter Three: Sensation and Perception), in which sensations cross over each other—colors have sound, sounds have smells, and so on. False sensory perceptions, called *hallucinations*, are often experienced, especially with the more powerful hallucinogens. There are two basic types of hallucinogens—those that are created in a laboratory and those that are from natural sources.

**MANUFACTURED HIGHS** There are several drugs that were developed in the laboratory instead of being found in nature. Perhaps because these drugs are manufactured, they are often more potent than drugs found in the natural world.

**opiates**

a class of opium-related drugs that suppress the sensation of pain by binding to and stimulating the nervous system's natural receptor sites for endorphins.

**opium**

substance derived from the opium poppy from which all narcotic drugs are derived.

**morphine**

narcotic drug derived from opium, used to treat severe pain.

**heroin**

narcotic drug derived from opium that is extremely addictive.

**hallucinogens**

drugs that cause false sensory messages, altering the perception of reality.

**LSD**   LSD, or **lysergic acid diethylamide**, is synthesized from a grain fungus called *ergot*. Ergot fungus commonly grows on rye grain but can be found on other grains as well. First manufactured in 1938, LSD is one of the most potent, or powerful, hallucinogens (Johnston et al., 2007; Lee & Shlain, 1986). It takes only a very tiny drop of LSD to achieve a "high."

People who take LSD usually do so to get that high feeling. Some people feel that LSD helps them expand their consciousness or awareness of the world around them. Colors seem more intense, sounds more beautiful, and so on. But the experience is not always a pleasant one, just as dreams are not always filled with positive emotions. "Bad trips" are quite common, and there is no way to control what kind of "trip" the brain is going to decide to take.

One of the greater dangers in using LSD is the effect it has on a person's ability to perceive reality. Real dangers and hazards in the world may go unnoticed by a person "lost" in an LSD fantasy, and people under the influence of this drug may make poor decisions, such as trying to drive while high. A person who has taken LSD can have flashbacks—spontaneous hallucinations—even years after taking the drug, and chronic uses of the drug can develop *hallucinogen persisting perception disorder (HPPD)*, an irreversible condition in which hallucinations and altered perceptions of reality can occur repeatedly, accompanied by depression and physical discomfort (Brodrick & Mitchell, 2016; Lerner et al., 2002).

**PCP**   Another synthesized drug was found to be so dangerous that it remains useful only in veterinary medicine as a tranquilizer. The drug is **PCP** (which stands for *phenyl cyclohexyl piperidine*, a name which is often contracted as *phencyclidine*) and can have many different effects. Depending on the dosage, it can be a hallucinogen, stimulant, depressant, or an analgesic (painkilling) drug. As with LSD, users of PCP can experience hallucinations, distorted sensations, and very unpleasant effects. PCP can also lead to acts of violence against others or suicide (Brecher, 1988; Cami et al., 2000; Johnston et al., 2007; Morris & Wallach, 2014). Users may even physically injure themselves unintentionally because PCP causes them to feel no warning signal of pain.

**MDMA**   The last synthetic drug we will address here is technically an amphetamine, but it is capable of producing hallucinations as well. In fact, both **MDMA** (a "designer drug" known on the streets as *Ecstasy, molly,* or simply *X*) and PCP are now classified as **stimulatory hallucinogenics**, drugs that produce a mixture of psychomotor stimulant and hallucinogenic effects (National Institute on Drug Abuse, 2016; Shuglin, 1986). Although many users of MDMA believe that it is relatively harmless, the fact is that it—like many other substances—can be deadly when misused. MDMA causes the release of large amounts of serotonin and also blocks the reuptake of this neurotransmitter (Hall & Henry, 2006; Liechti & Vollenweider, 2001; Montgomery & Fisk, 2008; United Nations Office on Drugs and Crime [UNODC], 2014). The user feels euphoric, energized, and may feel increased emotional warmth toward others. But there is some evidence that MDMA may damage the serotonin receptors, which could lead to depression. Other negative effects include severe dehydration and raised body temperature, which can lead to excessive intake of liquids—with possible fatal results (Laws & Kokkalis, 2007; Leccese et al., 2000; Meyer, 2013; UNODC, 2014). It should also be noted that since MDMA is illegal, illicit drug manufacturers try to stay ahead of the legal system by manufacturing novel psychoactive substances (NPS) such as "ivory wave" or "bath salts" that are similar in effect to MDMA but just different enough to skirt the law, at least for a while (Baumeister et al., 2015; Bright, 2013; European Monitoring Centre for Drugs and Drug Addiction [EMCDDA], 2015).

**NONMANUFACTURED HIGH: MARIJUANA**   One of the best known and most commonly abused of the hallucinogenic drugs, **marijuana** (also called "pot" or "weed") comes

**LSD (lysergic acid diethylamide)**
powerful synthetic hallucinogen.

**PCP**
synthesized drug now used as an animal tranquilizer that can cause stimulant, depressant, narcotic, or hallucinogenic effects.

**MDMA: (Ecstasy or X)**
designer drug that can have both stimulant and hallucinatory effects.

**stimulatory hallucinogenics**
drugs that produce a mixture of psychomotor stimulant and hallucinogenic effects.

**marijuana**
mild hallucinogen (also known as "pot" or "weed") derived from the leaves and flowers of a particular type of hemp plant.

from the leaves and flowers of the hemp plant called *Cannabis sativa*. (*Hashish* is the concentrated substance made by scraping the resin from these leaves, and both marijuana and hashish contain *cannabinoids*.) The most psychoactive cannabinoid, and the active ingredient in marijuana, is *tetrahydrocannabinol* (THC). Marijuana is best known for its ability to produce a feeling of well-being, mild intoxication, and mild sensory distortions or hallucinations.

The effects of marijuana are relatively mild compared to those of the other hallucinogens. In fact, an inexperienced user who doesn't know what to expect upon smoking that first marijuana cigarette may feel nothing at all. Most people do report a feeling of mild euphoria and relaxation, along with an altered time sense and mild visual distortions. Higher doses can lead to hallucinations, delusions, and the all-too-common paranoia. Most studies of marijuana's effects have concluded that while marijuana can create a powerful psychological dependency, it does not produce physical dependency or physical withdrawal symptoms (Gordon et al., 2013). However, after alcohol and nicotine, cannabis dependence is the most common form of drug dependence in the United States, Canada, and Australia (Hall & Degenhardt, 2009). Even at mild doses, it is not safe to operate heavy machinery or drive a car while under the influence of marijuana because it negatively affects reaction time and perception of surroundings; the drug reduces a person's ability to make the split-second decisions that driving a car or other equipment requires. Information processing in general, attention, and memory are all likely to be impaired in a person who has used marijuana.

Marijuana is most commonly smoked like tobacco, but some people have been known to eat it baked into brownies or other foods. This is a kind of double duty for the doctored food, as marijuana stimulates the appetite.

Although no one has ever been known to die from an overdose of marijuana, smoking it is not a healthy habit. Research linking marijuana smoking and lung cancer is not definitive due to the fact that many studies have not been able to control for confounding variables, such as cigarette smoking, alcohol use, or other risk factors (Berthiller et al., 2008; Hall & Degenhardt, 2009). **Ⓛ Ⓘ Ⓝ Ⓚ** to Learning Objective 1.9. Aside from those previously mentioned, probable adverse effects from chronic nonmedical marijuana use also include increased risk of motor vehicle crashes, chronic bronchitis or other lung problems, and cardiovascular disease. In adolescents who are regular users, psychosocial development, educational attainment, and mental health can be negatively impacted (Borgelt et al., 2013; Gordon et al., 2013; Hall & Degenhardt, 2009; Hirvonen et al., 2011; Madras, 2014). With regard to the possible mental health problems, there especially appears to be an increased risk for psychotic symptoms and disorders later in life for adolescents who are regular and heavier users (Hall & Degenhardt, 2009; Hirvonen et al., 2011; Madras, 2014; Moore et al., 2007).

There are some legitimate medical uses for marijuana, and 25 states and the District of Columbia have legalized medical marijuana since 1996 (Hasin et al., 2015). Aside from uses in treating the nausea resulting from chemotherapy for both cancer and autoimmune deficiency disease (AIDS), medical marijuana has either proven useful or is showing great promise in treating chronic pain, depression, and posttraumatic stress disorder, for example (Greer et al., 2014; Haj-Dahmane & Shen, 2014; Ware et al., 2015). Despite fears that availability of medical marijuana would lead to an increase of marijuana use among adolescents, studies over the past 24 years have found no evidence of such increases (Hasin et al., 2015; Johnson et al., 2015).

**Table 4.5** summarizes the various types of drugs, their common names, and their effects on human behavior.

This is a medical marijuana dispensary in Ypsilanti, Michigan. How might having marijuana available in such legal stores change the illegal drug business?

## Table 4.5  How Drugs Affect Consciousness

| Drug Classification | Common Name | Main Effect | Adverse Effects |
|---|---|---|---|
| **Stimulants** | | Stimulation, excitement | |
| Amphetamines | Methamphetamine, speed, Ritalin, Dexedrine | | Risk of addiction, stroke, fatal heart problems, psychosis |
| Cocaine | Cocaine, crack | | Risk of addiction, stroke, fatal heart problems, psychosis |
| Nicotine | Tobacco | | Addiction, cancer |
| Caffeine | Coffee, tea, energy drinks | | Addiction, high blood pressure |
| **Depressants** | | Relaxation | |
| Barbiturates (major tranquilizers) | Nembutal, Seconal | | Addiction, brain damage, death |
| Benzodiazepines (minor tranquilizers) | Valium, Xanax, Halcion, Ativan, Rohypnol | | Lower risk of overdose and addiction when taken alone |
| Alcohol | Beer, wine, spirits | | Alcoholism, health problems, depression, increased risk of accidents, death |
| Opiates | Opium, Morphine, heroin | Euphoria | Addiction, death |
| **Hallucinogens** | LSD, PCP, MDMA (Ecstasy), marijuana | Distorted consciousness, altered perception | Possible permanent memory problems, bad "trips," suicide, overdose, and death |

## Concept Map  L.O. 4.11, 4.12, 4.13, 4.14

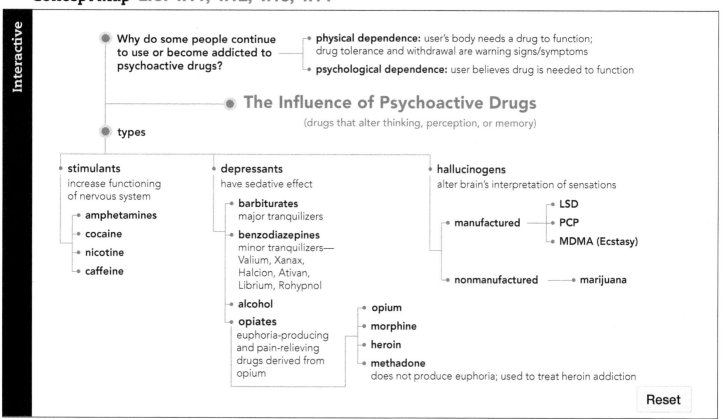

## Practice Quiz   How much do you remember?

*Pick the best answer.*

**1.** As consequences to stopping drug use, headaches, nausea, shaking, and elevated blood pressure are all signs of
**a.** withdrawal.
**b.** overdose.
**c.** psychological dependency.
**d.** amphetamine toxicity.

**2.** What drug's physical withdrawal symptoms include severe mood swings (crash), paranoia, extreme fatigue, and an inability to feel pleasure?
**a.** heroin
**b.** caffeine
**c.** alcohol
**d.** cocaine

**3.** Which of the following statements about nicotine is true?
   **a.** In terms of addictive power, nicotine is more powerful than heroin or alcohol.
   **b.** Nicotine can slow the heart and therefore create a sense of relaxation.
   **c.** Overall, the number of Americans smoking is on the increase.
   **d.** Overall, the number of women and teenagers smoking is on the decrease.

**4.** _____ is a tranquilizer that is also known as the "date rape" drug.
   **a.** Halcion
   **b.** Librium
   **c.** Rohypnol
   **d.** Xanax

**5.** Typically, opiates have the ability to
   **a.** cause intense hallucinations.
   **b.** suppress the sensation of pain.
   **c.** stimulate the user.
   **d.** cause deep levels of depression.

**6.** Most studies of marijuana's effects have found that
   **a.** it creates a powerful psychological dependency.
   **b.** it creates a strong physical dependency.
   **c.** it produces intense withdrawal symptoms.
   **d.** it is easy to overdose on the substance.

## Applying Psychology to Everyday Life
## Thinking Critically About Ghosts, Aliens, and Other Things That Go Bump in the Night

**4.15** Describe how the workings of our consciousness can explain "supernatural" visitations.

Down through the ages, people have been visited by ghosts, spirits, and other sorts of mystical or mysterious visitors—or so they have believed. In more modern times, ghostly visitations have often given way to aliens, who may perform some sort of medical examination or who may abduct the person, only to return them to their beds. And it is to their beds that they are usually returned, and such visitations typically are experienced when the person is in bed. Is there a simpler explanation for these experiences?

As mentioned earlier in this chapter, a type of hallucination can occur just as a person is entering stage N1 sleep, called a *hypnogogic hallucination* (Lana-Peixoto, 2014; Ohayon et al., 1996; Siegel & West, 1975). If you remember that people in N1, when awakened, will deny having been asleep, a simple explanation for so-called supernatural visitations does present itself. Hypnogogic hallucinations are not dreamlike in nature. Instead, they feel very real to the person experiencing them (who does not think he or she is asleep, remember). Most common are the auditory hallucinations, in which a person might hear a voice calling out the person's name, not all that unusual and probably not remembered most of the time.

Imagine for a moment, though, that your hypnogogic hallucination is that of some person whom you know to be dead or ill, or a strange and frightening image, perhaps with equally strange and frightening sound effects. That you will remember, especially since you are likely to wake up right after *and be completely convinced that you were awake at the time of the hallucination*. Combine this experience with the natural tendency many people have to want to believe that there is life after death or that there are other sentient life forms visiting our planet, and *voilà!*—a ghost/spirit/alien has appeared.

Sometimes people have a similar experience in the middle of the night. They awaken to find that they are paralyzed and that something—ghost, demon, alien—is standing over them and perhaps doing strange things to their helpless bodies. When a hallucination happens just as a person is in the between-state of being in REM sleep (in which the voluntary muscles are paralyzed) and not yet fully awake, it is called a *hypnopompic hallucination* and is once again a much simpler explanation of visits by aliens or spirits during the night than any supernatural explanation. Such visitations are not as rare as you might think, but once again, it is only the spectacular, frightening, or unusual ones that will be remembered (Cheyne, 2003; Greeley, 1987; Mantoan et al., 2013; Ohayon et al., 1996).

Individuals sometimes awaken with the very real feeling that they have been visited by aliens or a ghost, demon, or even an angel. The more logical explanation is that they have been startled awake from either a hypnogogic or hypnopompic hallucination experienced at some point as they were sleeping.

1. Have you ever had one of these experiences? Can you now understand how that experience might have been one that you would remember?

2. Talk to friends or family about their similar experiences, looking for the simpler explanation.

# Chapter Summary

## What Is Consciousness?

### 4.1 Define what it means to be conscious.

• Consciousness is a person's awareness of everything that is going on at any given moment. Most waking hours are spent in waking consciousness.

### 4.2 Differentiate between the different levels of consciousness.

• Altered states of consciousness are shifts in the quality or pattern of mental activity.

• Controlled processes are those tasks that require a higher degree of conscious attention, while automatic processes can be done at a far lower level of conscious awareness.

## Sleep

### 4.3 Describe the biological process of the sleep–wake cycle.

• Sleep is a circadian rhythm, lasting 24 hours, and is a product of the activity of the hypothalamus, the hormone melatonin, the neurotransmitter serotonin, and body temperature.

### 4.4 Explain why we sleep.

• Adaptive theory states that sleep evolved as a way to conserve energy and keep animals safe from predators that hunt at night.

• Restorative theory states that sleep provides the body with an opportunity to restore chemicals that have been depleted during the day as well as the growth and repair of cell tissue.

• The average amount of sleep needed by most adults is about 7 to 9 hours within each 24-hour period.

### 4.5 Identify the different stages of sleep.

• N1 sleep is light sleep.

• N2 sleep is indicated by the presence of sleep spindles, bursts of activity on the EEG.

• N3 is highlighted by the first appearance of delta waves, the slowest and largest waves, and the body is at its lowest level of functioning.

• R sleep occurs four or five times a night, replacing N1 after a full cycle through N1–N3 and then ascending back to lighter stages of sleep. It is accompanied by paralysis of the voluntary muscles but rapid movement of the eyes.

### 4.6 Differentiate among the various sleep disorders.

• Sleepwalking and sleeptalking occur in N3, during slow-wave sleep.

• Voluntary muscles are paralyzed during REM sleep.

• Night terrors are attacks of extreme fear that the victim has while sound asleep.

• Nightmares are bad or unpleasant dreams that occur during REM sleep.

• REM behavior disorder is a rare condition in which sleep paralysis fails and the person moves violently while dreaming, often acting out the elements of the dream.

• Insomnia is an inability to get to sleep, stay asleep, or get enough sleep.

• Sleep apnea occurs when a person stops breathing for 10 seconds or more.

• Narcolepsy is a genetic disorder in which the person suddenly and without warning collapses into REM sleep.

## Dreams

### 4.7 Compare and contrast two explanations of why people dream.

• Manifest content of a dream is the actual dream and its events. Latent content of a dream is the symbolic content, according to Freud.

• Without outside sensory information to explain the activation of the brain cells in the cortex by the pons area, the association areas of the cortex synthesize a story, or dream, to explain that activation in the activation-synthesis hypothesis.

• A revision of activation-synthesis theory, the activation-information-mode model (AIM), states that information experienced during waking hours can influence the synthesis of dreams.

### 4.8 Identify commonalities and differences in the content of people's dreams.

• Calvin Hall believed that dreams are just another type of cognitive process that occurred during sleep, called the cognitive theory of dreaming

• Common dream content includes normal activities that people do while awake along with more fanciful actions such as flying or being naked in public.

## Hypnosis

### 4.9 Explain how hypnosis affects consciousness.

• Hypnosis is a state of consciousness in which a person is especially susceptible to suggestion.

• The hypnotist will tell the person to relax and feel tired, to focus on what is being said, to let go of inhibitions and accept suggestions, and to use vivid imagination.

- Hypnosis cannot give increased strength, reliably enhance memory, or regress people to an earlier age or an earlier life, but it can produce amnesia, reduce pain, and alter sensory impressions.

**4.10 Compare and contrast two views of why hypnosis works.**

- Hilgard believed that a person under hypnosis is in a state of dissociation, in which one part of consciousness is hypnotized and susceptible to suggestion, while another part is aware of everything that occurs.
- Other theorists believe that the hypnotized subject is merely playing a social role—that of the hypnotized person. This is called the social-cognitive theory of hypnosis.

## The Influence of Psychoactive Drugs

**4.11 Distinguish between physical dependence and psychological dependence upon drugs.**

- Drugs that are physically addictive cause the user's body to crave the drug. When deprived of the drug, the user will go through physical withdrawal.
- Drug tolerance occurs as the user's body becomes conditioned to the level of the drug. After a time, the user must take more and more of the drug to get the same effect.
- In psychological dependence, the user believes that he or she needs the drug to function well and maintain a sense of well-being. Any drug can produce psychological dependence.

**4.12 Identify the effects and dangers of using stimulants.**

- Stimulants are drugs that increase the activity of the nervous system, particularly the sympathetic division and the central nervous system.
- Amphetamines are synthetic drugs such as Benzedrine or Dexedrine. They help people stay awake and reduce appetite but are highly physically addictive.
- Cocaine is highly addictive and can cause convulsions and death in some first-time users.
- Nicotine is a mild stimulant and is very physically addictive.
- Caffeine is the most commonly used stimulant, found in coffee, tea, chocolate, and many sodas.

**4.13 Identify the effects and dangers of using depressants.**

- Barbiturates, also known as major tranquilizers, have a sedative effect and are used as sleeping pills.

- The minor tranquilizers are benzodiazepines such as Valium or Xanax.
- Alcohol is the most commonly used and abused depressant.
- Alcohol can interact with other depressants.
- Excessive use of alcohol can lead to alcoholism, health problems, loss of control, and death.
- Opiates are pain-relieving drugs of the depressant class that are derived from the opium poppy.
- Opium is the earliest form of this drug and is highly addictive because it directly stimulates receptor sites for endorphins. This causes natural production of endorphins to decrease.
- Morphine is a more refined version of opium but is highly addictive.
- Heroin was believed to be a purer form of morphine and, therefore, less addictive but in fact is even more powerfully addictive.
- Methadone has the ability to control the symptoms of heroin or morphine withdrawal without the euphoria, or "high," of heroin or morphine.

**4.14 Identify the effects and dangers of using hallucinogens.**

- Hallucinogens are stimulants that alter the brain's interpretation of sensations, creating hallucinations. Three synthetically created hallucinogens are LSD, PCP, and MDMA.
- Marijuana is a mild hallucinogen, producing a mild euphoria and feelings of relaxation in its users. Larger doses can lead to hallucinations and paranoia. It contains substances that may be carcinogenic and impairs learning and memory.
- Many states in the U.S. have now legalized marijuana use for medical purposes, such as treatment of the nausea and other side effects of chemotherapy.

## Applying Psychology to Everyday Life: Thinking Critically About Ghosts, Aliens, and Other Things That Go Bump in the Night

**4.15 Describe how the workings of our consciousness can explain "supernatural" visitations.**

- Vivid, realistic hallucinations that occur in N1 sleep are called hypnogogic hallucinations and are often misinterpreted as ghosts or other supernatural visitations.
- Similar hallucinations that occur when awakening from REM sleep are called hypnopompic hallucinations.

# Test Yourself

*Pick the best answer.*

1. Jane is aware that she is sitting in her psychology class and it is almost lunchtime. She is also aware of how tired she is after staying up late to watch a movie. Thus, if Jane is aware of what is going on around her and what is going on within her, then it is safe to say that she is in a(n)
   a. state of waking consciousness.
   b. altered state of consciousness.
   c. unconscious state.
   d. preconscious state.

2. What part of the brain is influential in determining when to sleep?
   a. hippocampus        c. thalamus
   b. hypothalamus       d. frontal lobe

3. As the sun begins to set, Winston finds himself becoming more and more sleepy. What structure is sensitive to light and influences when to go to sleep and when to awaken?
   a. corpus callosum     c. thalamus
   b. occipital lobe      d. suprachiasmatic nucleus

**4** Carlos is pulling an all-nighter in preparation for his big psychology test tomorrow. According to the research, what is the result on Carlos's memory when he deprives himself of sleep the night prior to his exam?

   **a.** Carlos will retain information from staying up all night, but only if his test is early in the morning.

   **b.** The ability to retain information can be influenced by the presence of sunlight. Thus, if the sun is shining, Carlos will remember more than if it is a cloudy day.

   **c.** Carlos will actually remember less if he deprives himself of sleep the night before.

   **d.** Carlos's memory will not be affected in any way assuming he only stays awake for one all-night study session.

**5.** Your uncle Karl, who recently retired, has mentioned how he doesn't sleep as well as he did when he was younger. For many years, he regularly slept about 7 to 8 hours, but now that he is in his 60s he tends to get only 5 to 6 hours of sleep per night. What would you tell him?

   **a.** Getting less sleep seems to be a common consequence of aging.

   **b.** Getting less sleep as we age is not normal, since studies show we need more sleep as we age.

   **c.** Getting less sleep is dangerous as we age. People should seek medical intervention to help them sleep.

   **d.** Getting less sleep is associated with mental health problems in our later years. Uncle Karl should consider seeing a psychologist.

**6.** You find yourself driving very late at night. As you are driving, you realize that you actually were falling off to sleep for a couple of seconds. Such a phenomenon is known as

   **a.** microsleep.          **c.** circadian rhythms.

   **b.** daydreaming.          **d.** hypnic jerk.

**7.** Studies have found that certain chemicals that help repair damaged cells only function while we sleep. What theory best explains this?

   **a.** circadian rhythm of sleep     **c.** restorative theory of sleep

   **b.** adaptive theory of sleep      **d.** sleep deprivation theory

**8.** In which stage of sleep do sleep spindles occur?

   **a.** N1          **c.** N3

   **b.** N2          **d.** R

**9.** Josef has had a very demanding day. Though his work is not physically challenging, it tends to mentally drain him. Which type of sleep will Josef probably require more of?

   **a.** N1          **c.** N3

   **b.** N2          **d.** R

**10.** Your doctor has told you that your youngest son suffers from somnambulism. What is another name for somnambulism?

   **a.** insomnia          **c.** sleep apnea

   **b.** sleepwalking          **d.** narcolepsy

**11.** Gerald has difficulty falling off to sleep. Harley can fall off to sleep easily but often wakes up early. Dale typically sleeps for 10 hours. All three are tired and not rested upon rising. Who seems to be experiencing insomnia?

   **a.** Gerald          **c.** Dale

   **b.** Harley          **d.** All three suffer from insomnia.

**12.** Very young infants who suffer from sleep apnea may be more at risk for SIDS, or sudden infant death syndrome. Why might these infants have difficulty breathing?

   **a.** Many of these infants are obese and therefore their airways are obstructed.

   **b.** The brain stem is not yet fully mature.

   **c.** The tissue lining in the nasal passageway may be obstructing their airflow.

   **d.** No medical explanation has been determined.

**13.** Bill suddenly and without warning slips into REM sleep during the day. He often falls to the ground and is difficult to awaken. Bill may have a condition called

   **a.** sleep apnea.          **c.** narcolepsy.

   **b.** insomnia.          **d.** epilepsy.

**14.** Calvin had a dream about his dog Snoopy in which he constantly looked for him but couldn't find him. In reality, Calvin's dog had died after being hit by a car. According to Sigmund Freud, his dream in which he was searching for his dog is an example of _____, while the inner meaning that he misses his dog terribly is an example of _____.

   **a.** wish fulfillment; manifest content

   **b.** latent content; wish fulfillment

   **c.** latent content; manifest content

   **d.** manifest content; latent content

**15.** When Tawny is asked to write down her dreams as a class assignment, she is bothered by the fact that her dreams often seem to jump randomly from scene to scene with little meaning. What theory best explains her dreams?

   **a.** activation-synthesis     **c.** sociocultural theory

   **b.** dreams-for-survival     **d.** Freudian

**16.** Anthony's therapist is using hypnosis to help him recall the night he was supposedly abducted by aliens. Danny's therapist is using hypnosis to help him prepare for the pain of dental surgery because Danny is allergic to the dentist's painkillers. Patrick's therapist is using hypnosis to help him quit drinking and smoking. Which client has the highest chance for success?

   **a.** Anthony

   **b.** Danny

   **c.** Patrick

   **d.** All three can benefit from hypnosis because each technique is proven effective.

**17.** Bobby agreed to be hypnotized during a comedy routine. While hypnotized, he stood on his chair and crowed like a rooster. Later, when his friends asked why he did this, Bobby replied that he didn't know, it must have been because he was hypnotized. What theory best explains his behavior?

   **a.** the hidden observer theory of hypnosis

   **b.** the social-cognitive explanation of hypnosis

   **c.** the biological theory of hypnosis

   **d.** the behavioral theory of hypnosis

**18.** Jackie has found that when she tries to quit drinking, she gets headaches, has night sweats, and shakes uncontrollably. Such a reaction is an example of

   **a.** psychological dependence.     **c.** withdrawal.

   **b.** overdose.          **d.** learned behavior.

**19.** What is the most commonly used and abused depressant?

   **a.** alcohol          **c.** tranquilizers

   **b.** Prozac          **d.** caffeine

**20.** Which drug, depending on the dosage, can be a hallucinogen, stimulant, depressant, or painkiller?

   **a.** marijuana

   **b.** opium

   **c.** PCP

   **d.** caffeine

# 5 Learning

**THINKING CRITICALLY**

How have you used the promise of a pleasurable consequence or reward to modify your own behavior or the behavior of others? After you have answered the question, watch the video to compare the answers of other students to yours.

▶ The response entered here will be saved to your notes and may be collected by your instructor if he/she requires it.

👁 Watch the Video

# Why study learning?

If we had not been able to learn, we would have died out as a species long ago. Learning is the process that allows us to adapt to the changing conditions of the world around us. We can alter our actions until we find the behavior that leads us to survival and rewards, and we can eliminate actions that have been unsuccessful in the past. Without learning, there would be no buildings, no agriculture, no lifesaving medicines, and no human civilization.

# Learning Objectives

**5.1** Define the term *learning*.

**5.2** Identify the key elements of classical conditioning as demonstrated in Pavlov's classic experiment.

**5.3** Apply classical conditioning to examples of phobias, taste aversions, and drug dependency.

**5.4** Identify the contributions of Thorndike and Skinner to the concept of operant conditioning.

**5.5** Differentiate between primary and secondary reinforcers and positive and negative reinforcement.

**5.6** Identify the four schedules of reinforcement.

**5.7** Identify the effect that punishment has on behavior.

**5.8** Explain the concepts of discriminant stimuli, extinction, generalization, and spontaneous recovery as they relate to operant conditioning.

**5.9** Describe how operant conditioning is used to change animal and human behavior.

**5.10** Explain the concept of latent learning.

**5.11** Explain how Köhler's studies demonstrated that animals can learn by insight.

**5.12** Summarize Seligman's studies on learned helplessness.

**5.13** Describe the process of observational learning.

**5.14** List the four elements of observational learning.

**5.15** Describe an example of conditioning in the real world.

# Definition of Learning

## 5.1 Define the term *learning*.

The term *learning* is one of those concepts whose meaning is crystal clear until one has to put it in actual words. "Learning is when you learn something." "Learning is learning how to do something." A more useful definition is as follows: **Learning** is any relatively permanent change in behavior brought about by experience or practice.

> 💬 What does "relatively permanent" mean? And how does experience change what we do?

The "relatively permanent" part of the definition refers to the fact that when people learn anything, some part of their brain is physically changed to record what they've learned (Farmer et al., 2013; Loftus & Loftus, 1980). This is actually a process of memory, for without the ability to remember what happens, people cannot learn anything. Although there is no conclusive proof as yet, research suggests that once people learn something, it may be present somewhere in memory in physical form (Barsalou, 1992; Smolen et al., 2006). They may be unable to "get" to it, but it's there. ⓁⒾⓃⓀ to Learning Objective 6.5.

As for the inclusion of experience or practice in the definition of learning, think about the last time you did something that caused you a lot of pain. Did you do it again? Probably not. You didn't want to experience that pain again, so you changed your behavior to avoid the painful consequence.\* This is how children learn not to touch hot stoves. In contrast, if a person does something resulting in a very pleasurable experience, that person is more likely to do that same thing again. This is another change in behavior and is explained by the law of effect, a topic we will discuss later in the chapter.

Not all change is accomplished through learning. Changes like an increase in height or the size of the brain are another kind of change, controlled by a genetic blueprint. This kind of change is called *maturation* and is due to biology, not experience. For example, practice alone will not allow a child to walk. Children learn to walk because their nervous systems, muscle strength, and sense of balance have reached the point where walking is physically possible for them—all factors controlled by maturation. Once that maturational readiness has been reached, then practice and experience play their important part.

# It Makes Your Mouth Water: Classical Conditioning

In the early 1900s, research scientists were unhappy with psychology's focus on mental activity. ⓁⒾⓃⓀ to Learning Objective 1.2. Many were looking for a way to bring some kind of objectivity and scientific research to the field. It was a Russian *physiologist* (a person who studies the workings of the body) named Ivan Pavlov (1849–1936) who pioneered the empirical study of the basic principles of a particular kind of learning (Pavlov, 1906, 1926).

### PAVLOV AND THE SALIVATING DOGS

## 5.2 Identify the key elements of classical conditioning as demonstrated in Pavlov's classic experiment.

Studying the digestive system in his dogs, Pavlov had built a device that would accurately measure the amount of saliva produced by the dogs when they were fed a measured amount of food. Normally, when food is placed in the mouth of any animal, the

**learning**

any relatively permanent change in behavior brought about by experience or practice.

---

\*consequence: an end result of some action.

salivary glands automatically start releasing saliva to help with chewing and digestion. This is a normal **reflex**—an unlearned, involuntary response that is not under personal control or choice—one of many that occur in both animals and humans. The food causes a particular reaction, the salivation. A *stimulus* can be defined as any object, event, or experience that causes a *response*, the reaction of an organism. In the case of Pavlov's dogs, the food is the stimulus and salivation is the response.

Pavlov soon discovered that his dogs began salivating when they weren't supposed to be salivating. Some dogs would start salivating when they saw the lab assistant bringing their food, others when they heard the clatter of the food bowl from the kitchen, and still others when it was the time of day they were usually fed. Switching his focus, Pavlov spent the rest of his career studying what eventually he termed **classical conditioning**, learning to elicit* an involuntary, reflex-like response to a stimulus other than the original, natural stimulus that normally produces the response.

**ELEMENTS OF CLASSICAL CONDITIONING**    Pavlov eventually identified several key elements that must be present and experienced in a particular way for conditioning to take place.

**UNCONDITIONED STIMULUS**    The original, naturally occurring stimulus is called the **unconditioned stimulus (UCS)**. The term *unconditioned* means "unlearned." This is the stimulus that ordinarily leads to the involuntary response. In the case of Pavlov's dogs, the food is the unconditioned stimulus.

**UNCONDITIONED RESPONSE**    The automatic and involuntary response to the unconditioned stimulus is called the **unconditioned response (UCR)** for much the same reason. It is unlearned and occurs because of genetic "wiring" in the nervous system. For example, in Pavlov's experiment, the salivation to the food is the UCR (unconditioned response).

**CONDITIONED STIMULUS**    Pavlov determined that almost any kind of stimulus could become associated with the unconditioned stimulus (UCS) if it is paired with the UCS often enough. In his original study, the sight of the food dish itself became a stimulus for salivation *before* the food was given to the dogs. Every time they got food (to which they automatically salivated), they saw the dish. At this point, the dish was a **neutral stimulus (NS)** because it had no effect on salivation. After being paired with the food so many times, the dish came to produce a salivation response, although a somewhat weaker one, as did the food itself. When a previously neutral stimulus, through repeated pairing with the unconditioned stimulus, begins to cause the same kind of involuntary response, learning has occurred. The previously neutral stimulus can now be called a **conditioned stimulus (CS)**. (*Conditioned* means "learned," and, as mentioned earlier, *unconditioned* means "unlearned.")

**CONDITIONED RESPONSE**    The response that is given to the CS (conditioned stimulus) is not usually quite as strong as the original unconditioned response (UCR), but it is essentially the same response. However, because it comes as a learned response to the conditioned stimulus (CS), it is called the **conditioned response (CR)**.

**PUTTING IT ALL TOGETHER: PAVLOV'S CANINE CLASSIC, OR TICK TOCK TICK TOCK**
Pavlov did a classic experiment in which he paired the ticking sound of a metronome (a simple device that produces a rhythmic ticking sound) with the presentation of food to see if the dogs would eventually salivate at the sound of the metronome (Pavlov, 1927). Since the metronome's ticking did not normally produce salivation, it was a neutral stimulus (NS) before any conditioning took place. The repeated pairing of an NS and the UCS (unconditioned stimulus) is usually called *acquisition*, because the organism is in the process of acquiring learning. **Figure 5.1** explains how each element of the conditioning relationship worked in Pavlov's experiment.

---

*elicit: to draw forth.

Dr. Ivan Pavlov and students working in his laboratory. Pavlov, a Russian physiologist, was the first to study and write about the basic principles of classical conditioning.

**reflex**

an involuntary response, one that is not under personal control or choice.

**classical conditioning**

learning to make an involuntary response to a stimulus other than the original, natural stimulus that normally produces the response.

**unconditioned stimulus (UCS)**

in classical conditioning, a naturally occurring stimulus that leads to an involuntary and unlearned response.

**unconditioned response (UCR)**

in classical conditioning, an involuntary and unlearned response to a naturally occurring or unconditioned stimulus.

**neutral stimulus (NS)**

in classical conditioning, a stimulus that has no effect on the desired response prior to conditioning.

**conditioned stimulus (CS)**

in classical conditioning, a previously neutral stimulus that becomes able to produce a conditioned response, after pairing with an unconditioned stimulus.

**conditioned response (CR)**

in classical conditioning, a learned response to a conditioned stimulus.

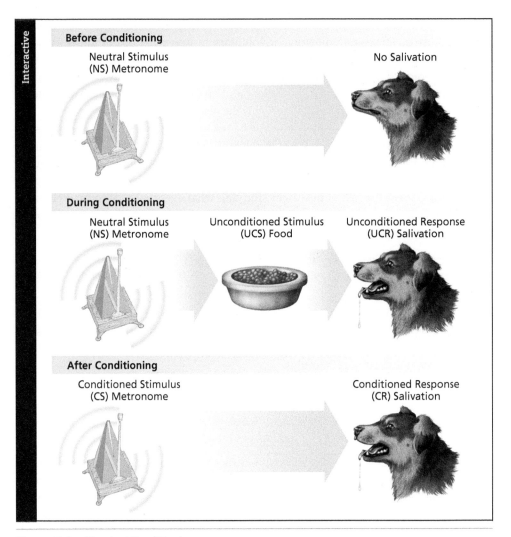

**Figure 5.1**  Classical Conditioning

Before conditioning takes place, the sound of the metronome does not cause salivation and is a neutral stimulus, or NS. During conditioning, the sound of the metronome occurs just before the presentation of the food, the UCS. The food causes salivation, the UCR. When conditioning has occurred after several pairings of the metronome with the food, the metronome will begin to elicit a salivation response from the dog without any food. This is learning, and the sound of the metronome is now a CS and the salivation to the metronome is the CR.

Notice that the responses, CR (conditioned response) and UCR (unconditioned response), are very similar—salivation. However, they differ not only in strength but also in the stimulus to which they are the response. An *unconditioned* stimulus (UCS) is always followed by an *unconditioned* response (UCR), and a *conditioned* stimulus (CS) is always followed by a *conditioned* response (CR).

Is this rocket science? No, not really. Classical conditioning is actually one of the simplest forms of learning. It's so simple that it happens to people all the time without them even being aware of it. Does your mouth water when you merely *see* an advertisement for your favorite food on television? Do you feel anxious every time you hear the high-pitched whine of the dentist's drill? These are both examples of classical conditioning. Over the course of many visits to the dentist, for example, the body comes to associate that sound (CS) with the anxiety or fear (UCR) the person has felt while receiving a painful dental treatment (UCS), and so the sound produces a feeling of anxiety (CR) whether that person is in the chair or just in the outer waiting area.

Pavlov and his fellow researchers did many experiments with the dogs. In addition to the metronome, whistles, tuning forks, various visual stimuli, and bells were used

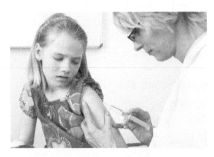

If you find yourself cringing at the mere sight of a hypodermic needle, your cringing is a CR to the CS of the needle. The pain of the shot would be the original UCS.

(Thomas, 1994). Although classical conditioning happens quite easily, Pavlov and his other researchers formulated a few basic principles about the process (although we will see that there are a few exceptions to some of these principles):

1. The CS must come *before* the UCS. If Pavlov sounded the metronome just after he gave the dogs the food, they did not become conditioned (Rescorla, 1988).

2. The CS and UCS must come very close together in time—ideally, no more than 5 seconds apart. When Pavlov tried to stretch the time between the potential CS and the UCS to several minutes, no association or link between the two was made. Too much could happen in the longer interval of time to interfere with conditioning (Pavlov, 1926; Ward et al., 2012; Wasserman & Miller, 1997). Studies have found that the interstimulus interval (ISI, or the time between the CS and UCS) can vary depending on the nature of the conditioning task and even the organism being conditioned. In these studies, shorter ISIs (less than 500 milliseconds) have been found to be ideal for conditioning (Polewan et al., 2006).

3. The neutral stimulus must be paired with the UCS several times, often many times, before conditioning can take place (Pavlov, 1926).

4. The CS is usually some stimulus that is distinctive* or stands out from other competing stimuli. The metronome, for example, was a sound that was not normally present in the laboratory and, therefore, distinct (Pavlov, 1927; Rescorla, 1988).

 💬 That seems simple enough. But I wonder—would Pavlov's dogs salivate to other ticking sounds?

**STIMULUS GENERALIZATION AND DISCRIMINATION**   Pavlov did find that similar sounds would produce a similar conditioned response from his dogs. He and other researchers found that the strength of the response to similar sounds was not as strong as it was to the original one, but the more similar the other sound was to the original sound (be it a metronome or any other kind of sound), the more similar the strength of the response was (Siegel, 1969; see **Figure 5.2**). The tendency to respond to a stimulus that is similar to the original conditioned stimulus is called **stimulus generalization**. For example, a person who reacts with anxiety to the sound of a dentist's drill might react with some slight anxiety to a similar-sounding machine, such as an electric coffee grinder.

Of course, Pavlov did not give the dogs any food after the similar ticking sound. They only got food following the correct CS. It didn't take long for the dogs to stop responding (generalizing) to the "fake" ticking sounds altogether. Because only the real CS was followed with food, they learned to tell the difference, or to *discriminate*, between the fake ticking and the CS ticking, a process called **stimulus discrimination**. Stimulus discrimination occurs when an organism learns to respond to different stimuli in different ways. For example, although the sound of the coffee grinder might produce a little anxiety in the dental-drill-hating person, after a few uses that sound will no longer produce anxiety because it isn't associated with dental pain.

**EXTINCTION AND SPONTANEOUS RECOVERY**   What would have happened if Pavlov had stopped giving the dogs food after the real CS? Pavlov did try just that, and the dogs gradually stopped salivating to the sound of the ticking. When the metronome's ticking (CS or conditioned stimulus) was repeatedly presented in the absence of the UCS (unconditioned stimulus or food, in this case), the salivation (CR or conditioned response) "died out" in a process called **extinction**.

---

*distinctive: separate, having a different quality from something else.

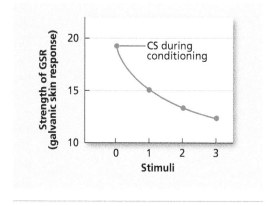

**Figure 5.2**   Strength of the Generalized Response

An example of stimulus generalization. The UCS was an electric shock and the UCR was the galvanic skin response (GSR), a measure associated with anxiety. The subjects had been conditioned originally to a CS tone (0) of a given frequency. When tested with the original tone, and with tones 1, 2, and 3 of differing frequencies, a clear generalization effect appeared. The closer the frequency of the test tone to the frequency of tone 0, the greater was the magnitude of the galvanic skin response to the tone (Hovland, 1937).

**stimulus generalization**

the tendency to respond to a stimulus that is only similar to the original conditioned stimulus with the conditioned response.

**stimulus discrimination**

the tendency to stop making a generalized response to a stimulus that is similar to the original conditioned stimulus because the similar stimulus is never paired with the unconditioned stimulus.

**extinction**

the disappearance or weakening of a learned response following the removal or absence of the unconditioned stimulus (in classical conditioning) or the removal of a reinforcer (in operant conditioning).

Why does the removal of an unconditioned stimulus lead to extinction of the conditioned response? One theory is that the presentation of the CS alone leads to new learning. During extinction, the CS–UCS association that was learned is weakened, as the CS no longer predicts the UCS. In the case of Pavlov's dogs, through extinction they learned to not salivate to the metronome's ticking, as it no longer predicted that food was on its way.

Look back at Figure 5.1. Once conditioning is acquired, the conditioned stimulus (CS) and conditioned response (CR) will always come *before* the original unconditioned stimulus (UCS). The UCS, which comes after the CS and CR link, now serves as a strengthener, or reinforcer, of the CS–CR association. Remove that reinforcer, and the CR it strengthens will weaken and disappear—at least for a while.

The term *extinction* is a little unfortunate in that it seems to mean that the original conditioned response is totally gone, dead, never coming back, just like the dinosaurs. Remember the definition of learning is any relatively *permanent* change in behavior. The fact is that once people learn something, it's almost impossible to "unlearn" it. People can learn new things that replace it or lose their way to it in memory, but it's still there. In the case of classical conditioning, this is easily demonstrated.

After extinguishing the conditioned salivation response in his dogs, Pavlov waited a few weeks, putting the conditioned stimulus (i.e., the metronome) away. There were no more training sessions, and the dogs were not exposed to the metronome's ticking in that time at all. But when Pavlov took the metronome back out and set it ticking, the dogs all began to salivate, although it was a fairly weak response and didn't last very long. This brief recovery of the conditioned response proves that the CR is "still in there" somewhere (remember, learning is *relatively permanent*). It is just suppressed or inhibited by the lack of an association with the unconditioned stimulus of food (which is no longer reinforcing or strengthening the CR). As time passes, this inhibition weakens, especially if the original conditioned stimulus has not been present for a while. In **spontaneous recovery** the conditioned response can briefly reappear when the original CS returns, although the response is usually weak and short lived. See **Figure 5.3** for a graph showing both extinction and spontaneous recovery.

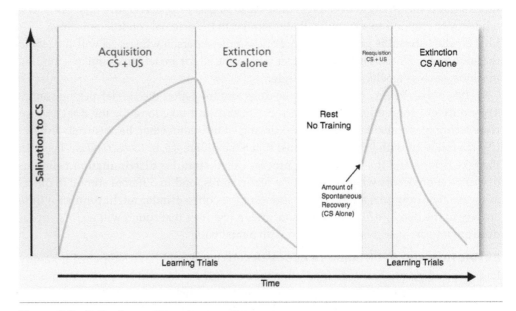

**Figure 5.3** Extinction and Spontaneous Recovery

This graph shows the acquisition, extinction, spontaneous recovery, and reacquisition of a conditioned salivary response. Typically, the measure of conditioning is the number of drops of saliva elicited by the CS on each trial. Note that on the day following extinction, the first presentation of the CS elicits quite a large response. This response is due to spontaneous recovery.

**spontaneous recovery**

the reappearance of a learned response after extinction has occurred.

**HIGHER-ORDER CONDITIONING**   Another concept in classical conditioning is **higher-order conditioning** (see **Figure 5.4**). This occurs when a strong conditioned stimulus is paired with a neutral stimulus. The strong CS can actually play the part of a UCS, and the previously neutral stimulus becomes a *second* conditioned stimulus.

For example, let's revisit the point when Pavlov has conditioned his dogs to salivate at the sound of the metronome. What would happen if just before Pavlov turned on the metronome, he snapped his fingers? The sequence would now be "snap-ticking-salivation," or "NS–CS–CR" ("neutral stimulus/conditioned stimulus/conditioned response"). If this happens enough times, the finger snap will eventually also produce a salivation response. The finger snap becomes associated with the ticking through the same process that the ticking became associated with the food originally and is now another conditioned stimulus. Of course, the food (UCS) would have to be presented every now and then to maintain the original conditioned response to the metronome's ticking. Without the UCS, the higher-order conditioning would be difficult to maintain and would gradually fade away.

**WHY DOES CLASSICAL CONDITIONING WORK?**   Pavlov believed that the conditioned stimulus, through its association close in time with the unconditioned stimulus, came to activate the same place in the animal's brain that was originally activated by the unconditioned stimulus. He called this process *stimulus substitution*. But if a mere association in time is all that is needed, why would conditioning *fail to happen* when the CS is presented immediately *after* the UCS?

Robert Rescorla (1988) found that the CS has to provide some kind of information about the coming of the UCS in order to achieve conditioning. In other words, the CS must predict that the UCS is coming. In one study, Rescorla exposed one group of rats to a tone, and just after the tone's onset and while the tone was still able to be heard, an electric shock was administered for some of the tone presentations. Soon the rats became agitated* and

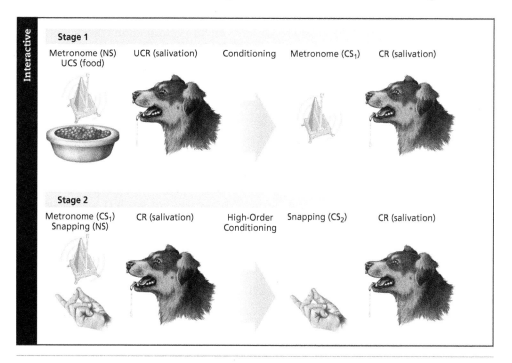

**Figure 5.4** Higher-Order Conditioning

In Stage 1, a strong salivation response is conditioned to occur to the sound of the metronome (CS$_1$). In Stage 2, finger snapping (NS) is repeatedly paired with the ticking of the metronome (CS$_1$) until the dog begins to salivate to the finger snapping alone (now CS$_2$). This is called "higher-order conditioning," because one CS is used to create another, "higher" CS.

*agitated: excited, upset.

**higher-order conditioning**
occurs when a strong conditioned stimulus is paired with a neutral stimulus, causing the neutral stimulus to become a second conditioned stimulus.

reacted in fear by shivering and squealing at the onset of the tone, a kind of conditioned emotional response. But with a second group of rats, Rescorla again sounded a tone but administered the electric shock only *after* the tone *stopped*, not while the tone was being heard. That group of rats responded with fear to the *stopping* of the tone (Rescorla, 1968).

The tone for the second group of rats provided a different kind of information than the tone in the first instance. For the first group, the tone means the shock is coming, whereas for the second group, the tone means there is no shock while the tone is on. It was the particular *expectancy* created by pairing the tone or absence of tone with the shock that determined the particular response of the rats. Because this explanation involves the mental activity of consciously expecting something to occur, it is an example of an explanation for classical conditioning called the **cognitive perspective**.

### CLASSICAL CONDITIONING APPLIED TO HUMAN BEHAVIOR

**5.3** Apply classical conditioning to examples of phobias, taste aversions, and drug dependency.

Later scientists took Pavlov's concepts and expanded them to explain not only animal behavior but also human behavior. One of the earliest of these studies showed that even an emotional response could be conditioned.

**PHOBIAS** In the first chapter of this text, John B. Watson's classic experiment with "Little Albert" and the white rat was discussed. This study was a demonstration of the classical conditioning of a phobia—an irrational fear response (Watson & Rayner, 1920).

Watson paired the presentation of the white rat to the baby with a loud, scary noise. Although the baby was not initially afraid of the rat, he was naturally afraid of the loud noise and started to cry. After only seven pairings of the noise with the rat, every time the baby saw the rat, he started to cry. In conditioning terms, the loud noise was the UCS, the fear of the noise the UCR, the white rat became the CS, and the fear of the rat (the phobia) was the CR (see **Figure 5.5**). (It should be pointed out that Watson didn't really "torture" the baby—Albert's fright was temporary. Still, no ethics committee today would approve an experiment in which an infant experiences psychological distress like this.)

Little Albert remains a topic of interest for many researchers and students of psychology alike. Researchers have suggested his true identity was Douglas Merritte, the son of a wet nurse at the hospital where the study took place (Beck & Irons, 2011; Beck et al., 2009). And, if in fact Little Albert was really Douglas Merritte, additional research has revealed that Douglas was neurologically impaired at the time he was tested by Watson and Rayner (due to hydrocephalus, brain infections, and serious allergic reactions) and sadly, later died at six years of age (Fridlund et al., 2012). And while Watson and Rayner's original study still prompts curiosity and controversy, so do the recent investigations, as not everyone believes that Little Albert's identity has been found (Harris, 2011; Powell, 2010; Reese, 2010).

The learning of phobias is a very good example of a certain type of classical conditioning, the **conditioned emotional response (CER)**. Conditioned emotional responses are some of the easiest forms of classical conditioning to accomplish, and our lives are full of them. It's easy to think of fears people might have that are conditioned or learned: a child's fear of the doctor's office, a puppy's fear of a rolled-up newspaper, or the fear of dogs that is often shown by a person who has been attacked by a dog in the past. But other emotions can be conditioned, too.

It is even possible to become classically conditioned by simply watching someone else respond to a stimulus in a process called **vicarious conditioning** (Bandura & Rosenthal, 1966; Hygge & Öhman, 1976; Jones & Menzies, 1995). For example, one of the authors (we're not saying who, but her name rhymes with "candy") grew up watching her mother react very badly to any stray dog. The mother had been bitten and had to get rabies shots, so her fear was understandable. Her daughter had never been bitten or attacked yet developed an irrational and strong fear of all dogs as a result of watching her mother's reaction.

**Figure 5.5** Conditioning of "Little Albert"

After "Little Albert" had been conditioned to fear a white rat, he also demonstrated fear of a rabbit, a dog, and a sealskin coat (although it remains uncertain if stimulus generalization actually occurred, as this fear was of a single rabbit, a single dog, etc.). Can you think of any emotional reactions you experience that might be classically conditioned emotional responses?

**cognitive perspective**

modern perspective in psychology that focuses on memory, intelligence, perception, problem solving, and learning.

**conditioned emotional response (CER)**

emotional response that has become classically conditioned to occur to learned stimuli, such as a fear of dogs or the emotional reaction that occurs when seeing an attractive person.

**vicarious conditioning**

classical conditioning of an involuntary response or emotion by watching the reaction of another person.

The next time you watch television, watch the commercials closely. Advertisers often use certain objects or certain types of people in their ads to generate a specific emotional response in viewers, hoping that the emotional response will become associated with their product. Sexy models, cute little babies, and adorable puppies are some of the examples of stimuli the advertising world uses to tug at our heartstrings, so to speak. But advertisers also use vicarious classical conditioning, often showing people reacting emotionally in the ad (either positively or negatively) to a product. They hope that the viewer will become conditioned to experience that same emotion when seeing the same product on store shelves.

The good news is that the same learning principles that can contribute to phobias and anxiety disorders can also be used to treat them, as we'll see in the video *Using Classical Conditioning to Treat Disorders.*

👁 **Watch** the **Video** *Using Classical Conditioning to Treat Disorders*

**CONDITIONED TASTE AVERSIONS**    Some kinds of associations in classical conditioning seem to be easier to make than others. For example, are there any foods that you just can't eat anymore because of a bad experience with them? Believe it or not, your reaction to that food is a kind of classical conditioning.

Many experiments have shown that laboratory rats will develop a **conditioned taste aversion** for any liquid or food they swallow up to 6 hours before becoming nauseated. Researchers (Garcia et al., 1989; Garcia & Koelling, 1966) found that rats that were given a sweetened liquid and then injected with a drug or exposed to radiation* that caused nausea would not touch the liquid again. In a similar manner, alcoholics who are given a drug to make them violently nauseated when they drink alcohol may learn to avoid drinking any alcoholic beverage. The chemotherapy drugs that cancer patients receive also can create severe nausea, which causes those people to develop a taste aversion for any food they have eaten before going in for the chemotherapy treatment (Berteretche et al., 2004).

> 💬 But I thought that it took several pairings of these stimuli to bring about conditioning. How can classical conditioning happen so fast?

**conditioned taste aversion**
development of a nausea or aversive response to a particular taste because that taste was followed by a nausea reaction, occurring after only one association.

It's interesting to note that birds, which find their food by sight, will avoid any object or insect that simply *looks* like the one that made them sick. There is a certain species of moth with coloring that mimics the monarch butterfly. That particular

*radiation: beams of electromagnetic energy.

Conditioned taste aversions in nature. This moth is not poisonous to birds, but the monarch butterfly whose coloring the moth imitates is quite poisonous. Birds find their food by vision and will not eat anything that resembles the monarch.

butterfly is poisonous to birds, but the moth isn't. The moth's mimicry causes birds to avoid eating it, even though it is quite edible. Researchers have found that some associations between certain stimuli and responses are far easier to form than others and that this is true in both animals and people. This is called **biological preparedness**. While mammals are biologically prepared to associate taste with illness, birds are biologically prepared to associate visual characteristics with illness (Shapiro et al., 1980).

As for phobias, fear is a natural emotional response that has ties to survival—we need to remember what the fear-inducing stimuli are so we can safely avoid them in the future. Nausea and fear are both examples of involuntary reactions that help organisms survive to reproduce and pass on their genetic material, so the innate tendency to make quick and strong associations between stimuli and these reactions has evolutionary importance.

Biological preparedness for fear of objects that are dangerous makes sense for survival, but when objects are not typically dangerous, it turns out to be very difficult to condition a fear of those objects. In one study, monkeys easily learned to be afraid of a toy snake or crocodile by watching videos of other monkeys reacting fearfully to these stimuli (a good example of vicarious classical conditioning). But the monkeys never learned to fear flowers or a toy rabbit by the same means (Cook & Mineka, 1989). Snakes and crocodiles are predators; flowers and rabbits are not.

**DRUG DEPENDENCY** The "high" of drug use, whether it comes from an opiate derivative, a stimulant, or a depressant such as alcohol, often takes place in certain surroundings, with certain other people, and perhaps even using certain objects, such as the tiny spoons used by cocaine addicts. These people, settings, and objects can become conditioned stimuli that are associated with the drug high and can produce a conditioned "high" response. The presence of these cues can make it even harder to resist using the drug because the body and mind have become classically conditioned to associate drug use with the cues.

**biological preparedness**

referring to the tendency of animals to learn certain associations, such as taste and nausea, with only one or few pairings due to the survival value of the learning.

## Concept Map L.O. 5.1, 5.2, 5.3

**Interactive**

### Definition of Learning

(any relatively permanent change in behavior brought about by experience or practice)

- "relatively permanent" aspect of learning refers to learning being associated with physical changes in the brain
- although physical changes may be present we may not always be able to "get" to the information

- **discovered by Ivan Pavlov** — focused on observable, measurable behavior
  worked with salivating dogs

- **several key elements must be present and experienced**
  - **unconditioned stimulus (UCS):** original, naturally occurring stimulus that ordinarily leads to an involuntary response
  - **unconditioned response (UCR):** involuntary response to the unconditioned stimulus
  - **conditioned stimulus (CS):** previously neutral stimulus that begins to cause the same kind of involuntary response when paired repeatedly with the UCS
  - **conditioned response (CR):** response that is given to the CS

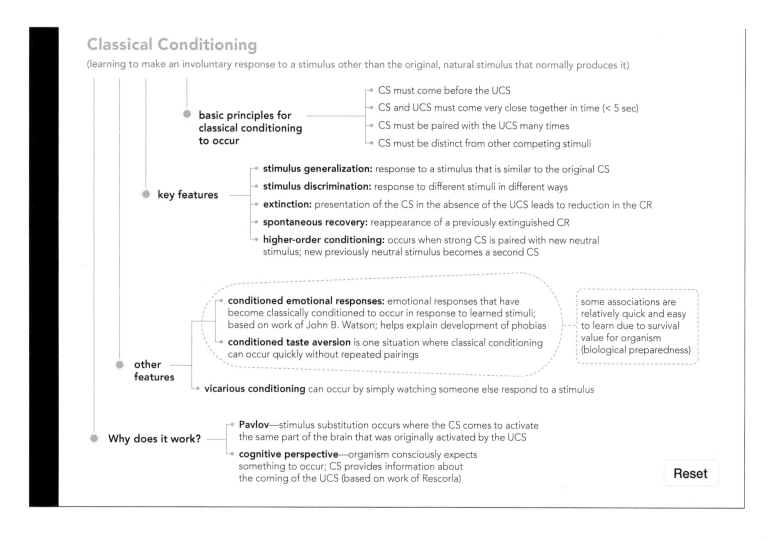

## Classical Conditioning

(learning to make an involuntary response to a stimulus other than the original, natural stimulus that normally produces it)

**basic principles for classical conditioning to occur**
- CS must come before the UCS
- CS and UCS must come very close together in time (< 5 sec)
- CS must be paired with the UCS many times
- CS must be distinct from other competing stimuli

**key features**
- **stimulus generalization:** response to a stimulus that is similar to the original CS
- **stimulus discrimination:** response to different stimuli in different ways
- **extinction:** presentation of the CS in the absence of the UCS leads to reduction in the CR
- **spontaneous recovery:** reappearance of a previously extinguished CR
- **higher-order conditioning:** occurs when strong CS is paired with new neutral stimulus; new previously neutral stimulus becomes a second CS

**other features**
- **conditioned emotional responses:** emotional responses that have become classically conditioned to occur in response to learned stimuli; based on work of John B. Watson; helps explain development of phobias
- **conditioned taste aversion** is one situation where classical conditioning can occur quickly without repeated pairings
- some associations are relatively quick and easy to learn due to survival value for organism (biological preparedness)
- **vicarious conditioning** can occur by simply watching someone else respond to a stimulus

**Why does it work?**
- **Pavlov**—stimulus substitution occurs where the CS comes to activate the same part of the brain that was originally activated by the UCS
- **cognitive perspective**—organism consciously expects something to occur; CS provides information about the coming of the UCS (based on work of Rescorla)

Reset

# Practice Quiz    How much do you remember?

*Pick the best answer.*

**1.** Michael noticed that whenever he moved his dog's food dish, his dog would come into the kitchen and act hungry and excited. He reasoned that because he feeds the dog using that dish, the sound of the dish had become a(n)
- **a.** unconditioned stimulus.
- **b.** conditioned stimulus.
- **c.** unconditioned response.
- **d.** conditioned response.

**2.** Ever since she was scared by a dog as a young child, Angelica has been afraid of all dogs. The fact that she is afraid of not only the original dog but all types of dogs is an example of
- **a.** extinction.
- **b.** spontaneous recovery.
- **c.** stimulus discrimination.
- **d.** stimulus generalization.

**3.** In Watson's experiment with "Little Albert," the conditioned stimulus was
- **a.** the white rat.
- **b.** the loud noise.
- **c.** the fear of the rat.
- **d.** the fear of the noise.

**4.** Which of the following would be an example of vicarious classical conditioning?
- **a.** As a young child, Tony frequently observed his older sisters jump around and scream whenever any of them saw a spider, as they were very afraid of them. Subsequently, Tony experiences feelings of fear when he sees a spider.

- **b.** Tommy is told about a new product by a close friend and decides to buy it for himself.
- **c.** A cat responds to the sound of a bell because it sounds similar to a bell it hears on the television.
- **d.** Tonja watches her grandfather check the air pressure in her bike tire and then use a hand pump to add air to the tire. She is later able to check the air pressure and pump up the tire herself.

**5.** Cindy had cheesy tacos at a local Mexican restaurant. Later she became terribly ill and suffered bouts of nausea and vomiting. What might we predict based on conditioned taste aversion research?
- **a.** Cindy will probably develop a strong liking for cheesy tacos.
- **b.** Cindy will probably be able to eat cheesy tacos with no nausea at all.
- **c.** Cindy will probably get nauseated the next time she tries to eat cheesy tacos.
- **d.** Cindy will probably continue to eat cheesy tacos except when she feels nauseous.

**6.** Rescorla found that the CS must _____ the UCS for conditioning to take place.
- **a.** replace
- **b.** come after
- **c.** come at the same time as
- **d.** predict

# What's In It for Me?
# Operant Conditioning

🗨 So far, all learning seems to involve involuntary behavior, but I know that I am more than just automatic responses. People do things on purpose, so is that kind of behavior also learned?

There are two kinds of behavior that all organisms are capable of doing: involuntary and voluntary. If Inez blinks her eyes because a gnat flies close to them, that's a reflex and totally involuntary. But if she then swats at the gnat to frighten it, that's a voluntary choice. She *had* to blink, but she *chose* to swat.

Classical conditioning is the kind of learning that occurs with automatic, involuntary behavior. In this section we'll describe the kind of learning that applies to voluntary behavior, which is both different from and similar to classical conditioning.

## THE CONTRIBUTIONS OF THORNDIKE AND SKINNER

**5.4 Identify the contributions of Thorndike and Skinner to the concept of operant conditioning.**

While classical conditioning involves the learning of involuntary, automatic responses, operant conditioning is about how organisms learn voluntary responses. **Operant conditioning** is based on the research of Edward L. Thorndike and B. F. Skinner.

**FRUSTRATING CATS: THORNDIKE'S PUZZLE BOX AND THE LAW OF EFFECT**   Thorndike (1874–1949) was one of the first researchers to explore and attempt to outline the laws of learning voluntary responses, although the field was not yet called operant conditioning. Thorndike placed a hungry cat inside a "puzzle box" from which the only escape was to press a lever located on the floor of the box. Thorndike placed a dish of food *outside* the box, so the hungry cat is highly motivated to get out. Thorndike observed that the cat would move around the box, pushing and rubbing up against the walls in an effort to escape. Eventually, the cat would accidentally push the lever, opening the door. Upon escaping, the cat was fed from a dish placed just outside the box. The lever is the stimulus, the pushing of the lever is the response, and the consequence is both escape (good) and food (even better).

The cat did not learn to push the lever and escape right away. After a number of trials (and many errors) in a box like this one, the cat took less and less time to push the lever that would open the door (see **Figure 5.6**). It's important not to assume that the cat had "figured out" the connection between the lever and freedom—Thorndike kept moving the lever to a different position, and the cat had to learn the whole process over again. The cat would simply continue to rub and push in the same general area that led to food and freedom the last time, each time getting out and fed a little more quickly.

Based on this research, Thorndike developed the **law of effect**: If an action is followed by a pleasurable consequence, it will tend to be repeated. If an action is followed by an unpleasant consequence, it will tend not to be repeated (Thorndike, 1911). This is the basic principle behind learning voluntary behavior. In the case of the cat in the box, pushing the lever

**operant conditioning**

the learning of voluntary behavior through the effects of pleasant and unpleasant consequences to responses.

**law of effect**

law stating that if an action is followed by a pleasurable consequence, it will tend to be repeated, and if followed by an unpleasant consequence, it will tend not to be repeated.

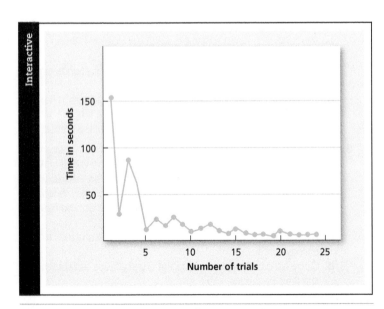

**Figure 5.6**   Graph of the Time to Learn in Thorndike's Experiment

This is one of the earliest "learning curves" in the history of the experimental study of conditioning. The time required by one of Thorndike's cats to escape from the puzzle box gradually decreased with trials but with obvious reversals.

was followed by a pleasurable consequence (getting out and getting fed), so pushing the lever became a repeated response.

**B. F. SKINNER: THE BEHAVIORIST'S BEHAVIORIST**   B. F. Skinner (1904–1990) was the behaviorist who assumed leadership of the field after John Watson. He was even more determined than Watson that psychologists should study only measurable, observable behavior. In addition to his knowledge of Pavlovian classical conditioning, Skinner found in the work of Thorndike a way to explain all behavior as the product of learning. He even gave the learning of voluntary behavior a special name: *operant conditioning* (Skinner, 1938). Voluntary behavior is what people and animals do to *operate* in the world. When people perform a voluntary action, it is to get something they want or to avoid something they don't want, right? So voluntary behavior, for Skinner, is **operant** behavior, and the learning of such behavior is operant conditioning.

The heart of operant conditioning is the effect of consequences on behavior. Thinking back to the section on classical conditioning, learning an involuntary behavior really depends on what comes *before* the response—the unconditioned stimulus and what will become the conditioned stimulus. These two stimuli are the *antecedent* stimuli (antecedent means something that comes before another thing). But in operant conditioning, learning depends on what happens *after* the response—the consequence. In a way, operant conditioning could be summed up as this: "If I do this, what's in it for me?"

**THE CONCEPT OF REINFORCEMENT**

**5.5**  **Differentiate between primary and secondary reinforcers and positive and negative reinforcement.**

"What's in it for me?" represents the concept of **reinforcement**, one of Skinner's major contributions to behaviorism. The word itself means "to strengthen," and Skinner defined reinforcement as anything that, when following a response, causes that response to be more likely to happen again. Typically, this means that reinforcement is a consequence that is in some way pleasurable to the organism, which relates back to Thorndike's law of effect. The "pleasurable consequence" is what's "in it" for the organism. (Keep in mind that a pleasurable consequence might be something like getting food when hungry or a paycheck when you need money, but it might also mean *avoiding* a tiresome chore, like doing the dishes or taking out the garbage. I'll do almost anything to get out of doing the dishes, myself!)

Going back to Thorndike's puzzle-box research, what was in it for the cat? We can see that the escape from the box and the food that the cat received after getting out are both *reinforcement* of the lever-pushing response. Every time the cat got out of the box, it got reinforced for doing so. In Skinner's view, this reinforcement is the reason that the cat learned anything at all. In operant conditioning, reinforcement is the key to learning.

Skinner had his own research device called a "Skinner box" or "operant conditioning chamber" (see **Figure 5.7**). His early research often involved placing a rat in one of these chambers and training it to push down on a bar to get food.

**PRIMARY AND SECONDARY REINFORCERS**   The events or items that can be used to reinforce behavior are not all alike. Let's say that a friend of yours asks you to help her move some books from the trunk of her car to her apartment on the second floor. She offers you a choice of $25 or a candy bar. Unless you've suffered recent brain damage, you'll most likely choose the money, right? With $25, you could buy more than one candy bar. (At today's prices, you might even be able to afford three.)

Now pretend that your friend offers the same deal to a 3-year-old child who lives downstairs for carrying up some of the paperback books: $25 or a candy bar. Which reward will the child more likely choose? Most children at that age have no real idea of the value of money, so the child will probably choose the candy bar. The money and the candy bar represent two basic kinds of **reinforcers**, items or events that when following

**Figure 5.7**   A Typical Skinner Box
This rat is learning to press the bar in the wall of the cage in order to get food (delivered a few pellets at a time in the food trough on lower left). In some cases, the light on the top left might be turned on to indicate that pressing the bar will lead to food or to warn of an impending shock delivered by the grate on the floor of the cage.

**operant**
any behavior that is voluntary and not elicited by specific stimuli.

**reinforcement**
any event or stimulus, that when following a response, increases the probability that the response will occur again.

**reinforcers**
any events or objects that, when following a response, increase the likelihood of that response occurring again.

a response will strengthen it. The reinforcing properties of money must be learned, but candy gives immediate reward in the form of taste and satisfying hunger.

A reinforcer such as a candy bar that fulfills a basic need like hunger is called a **primary reinforcer**. Examples would be any kind of food (hunger drive), liquid (thirst drive), or touch (pleasure drive). Infants, toddlers, preschool-age children, and animals can be easily reinforced by using primary reinforcers. (It's not a good idea, however, to start thinking of reinforcers as rewards—freedom from pain is also a basic need, so pain itself can be a primary reinforcer when it is *removed*. Removal of a painful stimulus fills a basic need just as eating food when hungry fills the hunger need.)

A **secondary reinforcer** such as money, however, gets its reinforcing properties from being associated with primary reinforcers in the past. A child who is given money to spend soon realizes that the ugly green paper can be traded for candy and treats—primary reinforcers—and so money becomes reinforcing in and of itself. If a person praises a puppy while petting him (touch, a primary reinforcer), the praise alone will eventually make the puppy squirm with delight.

 That sounds very familiar. Isn't this related to classical conditioning?

Secondary reinforcers do indeed get their reinforcing power from the process of classical conditioning. After all, the pleasure people feel when they eat, drink, or get a back rub is an automatic response, and any automatic response can be classically conditioned to occur to a new stimulus. In the case of money, the candy is a UCS for pleasure (the UCR), and the money is present just before the candy is obtained. The money becomes a CS for pleasure, and people certainly do feel pleasure when they have a lot of that green stuff, don't they?

In the case of the puppy, the petting is the UCS, the pleasure at being touched and petted is the UCR. The praise, or more specifically the tone of voice, becomes the CS for pleasure. Although classical and operant conditioning often "work together," as in the creation of secondary reinforcers, they are two different processes. **Table 5.1** presents a brief look at how the two types of conditioning differ from each other.

**THE NEURAL BASES OF LEARNING** As new ways of looking at the brain and the workings of neurons advance, researchers are investigating the neural bases of both classical and operant conditioning (Gallistel & Matzel, 2013). One important area involved in learning consists of neurons in the anterior cingulate cortex (ACC), located in the frontal lobe above the front of the corpus callosum (Apps et al., 2015). The ACC also connects to

**primary reinforcer**

any reinforcer that is naturally reinforcing by meeting a basic biological need, such as hunger, thirst, or touch.

**secondary reinforcer**

any reinforcer that becomes reinforcing after being paired with a primary reinforcer, such as praise, tokens, or gold stars.

**Table 5.1** Comparing Two Kinds of Conditioning

| Operant Conditioning | Classical Conditioning |
|---|---|
| End result is an increase in the rate of an already-occurring response. | End result is the creation of a new response to a stimulus that did not normally produce that response. |
| Responses are voluntary, emitted by the organism. | Responses are involuntary and automatic, elicited by a stimulus. |
| Consequences are important in forming an association. | Antecedent stimuli are important in forming an association. |
| Reinforcement should be immediate. | CS must occur immediately before the UCS. |
| An expectancy develops for reinforcement to follow a correct response. | An expectancy develops for UCS to follow CS. |

the nucleus accumbens. Remember our discussion of drug dependence and the reward pathway in Chapter Four? (L)(I)(N)(K) to Learning Objective 4.11. The nucleus accumbens was a part of that pathway, and both of these areas of the brain are involved in the release of dopamine (Gale et al., 2016; Morita et al., 2013; Yavuz et al., 2015).

Given the role it plays in amplifying some input signals and decreasing the intensity of others in the nucleus accumbens (Floresco, 2015), it makes sense that dopamine would be involved in the process of reinforcement. Think about what happens when you hear the particular sound from your cell phone when you have an incoming message, for example. We like getting messages, so much so that we will often ignore the live person we are with to look at the message. Have you ever been accused of being "addicted" to your phone? If you think about it, that little sound—be it chime, ding, or whatever you have chosen—has become a kind of conditioned stimulus. We find reading the messages themselves pleasurable, so the message could be seen as a kind of unconditioned stimulus for pleasure, and the sound becomes a CS for the CR of pleasure. But what is happening in the brain when you hear that sound followed by rewarding activities is excitatory activity in several areas, accompanied by increased dopamine activity, to signal that the behavior was beneficial and to do it again. Just as dopamine and the reward pathway are involved in drug dependency, they also seem to be heavily involved in our "learned" addictions, too.

**POSITIVE AND NEGATIVE REINFORCEMENT**    Reinforcers can also differ in the way they are used. Most people have no trouble at all understanding that following a response with some kind of pleasurable consequence (like a reward) will lead to an increase in the likelihood of that response being repeated. This is called **positive reinforcement**, the reinforcement of a response by the *addition* or experience of a pleasurable consequence, such as a reward or a pat on the back.

But many people have trouble understanding that the opposite is also true: Following a response with *the removal or escape* from something *unpleasant* will also increase the likelihood of that response being repeated—a process called **negative reinforcement**. Remember the idea that pain can be a primary reinforcer if it is removed? If a person's behavior gets pain to stop, the person is much more likely to do that same thing again—which is part of the reason people can get addicted to painkilling medication. Watch the video *Negative Reinforcement* for another example.

👁 **Watch** the **Video** *Negative Reinforcement*

**positive reinforcement**

the reinforcement of a response by the addition or experiencing of a pleasurable stimulus.

**negative reinforcement**

the reinforcement of a response by the removal, escape from, or avoidance of an unpleasant stimulus.

Let's consider a few examples of each of these types of reinforcement. Getting money for working is an example of *positive reinforcement* because the person *gets* money (an added, pleasurable consequence) for the behavior of working. That one everyone understands. But what about avoiding a penalty by turning one's income tax return in on time? That is an example of *negative reinforcement* because the behavior (submitting the return before the deadline) results in *avoiding* an *unpleasant* stimulus (a penalty). The likelihood that the person will behave that way again (turn it in on time in the future) is therefore *increased*—just as positive reinforcement will increase a behavior's likelihood. It is very important to remember that BOTH positive AND negative reinforcement *increase* the likelihood of the behavior they follow—they *both* have the effect of strengthening, or reinforcing, the behavior. Examples are the best way to figure out the difference between these two types of reinforcement, so try to figure out which of the following examples would be positive reinforcement and which would be negative reinforcement:

1. Pedro's father nags him to wash his car. Pedro hates being nagged, so he washes the car so his father will stop nagging.
2. Napoleon learns that talking in a funny voice gets him lots of attention from his classmates, so now he talks that way more often.
3. Allen is a server at a restaurant and always tries to smile and be pleasant because that seems to lead to bigger tips.
4. An Li turns her report in to her teacher on the day it is due because papers get marked down a letter grade for every day they are late.

Here are the answers:

1. Pedro is being negatively reinforced for washing his car because the nagging (unpleasant stimulus) stops when he does so.
2. Napoleon is getting positive reinforcement in the form of his classmates' attention.
3. Allen's smiling and pleasantness are positively reinforced by the customers' tips.
4. An Li is avoiding an unpleasant stimulus (the marked-down grade) by turning in her paper on time, which is an example of negative reinforcement.

**THINKING CRITICALLY**

What type of reinforcement worked best for you when you were in grade school? Positive or negative? Did this change in high school?

▶ | The response entered here will be saved to your notes and may be collected by your instructor if he/she requires it.

Submit

## SCHEDULES OF REINFORCEMENT: WHY THE ONE-ARMED BANDIT IS SO SEDUCTIVE

### 5.6 Identify the four schedules of reinforcement.

The timing of reinforcement can make a tremendous difference in the speed at which learning occurs and the strength of the learned response. However, Skinner (1956) found that reinforcing every response was not necessarily the best schedule of reinforcement for long-lasting learning, as we'll see in the video *Schedules of Reinforcement*.

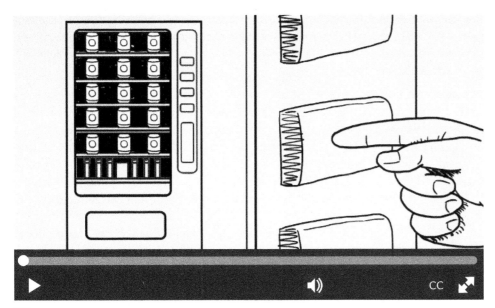

Watch the **Video** *Schedules of Reinforcement*

**THE PARTIAL REINFORCEMENT EFFECT**   Consider the following scenario: Alicia's mother agrees to give her a quarter every night she remembers to put her dirty clothes in the clothes hamper. Bianca's mother agrees to give her a dollar at the end of the week, but only if she has put her clothes in the hamper every night. Alicia learns to put her clothes in the hamper more quickly than does Bianca because responses that are reinforced each time they occur are more easily and quickly learned. After a time, the mothers stop giving the girls the money. Which child is more likely to stop putting her clothes in the hamper?

The answer might surprise you. It is more likely that Alicia, who has expected to get a reinforcer (the quarter) after *every single response*, will stop putting her clothes in the hamper. As soon as the reinforcers stop for her, the behavior is no longer reinforced and is likely to extinguish. In contrast, Bianca has expected to get a reinforcer only after *seven correct responses*. When the reinforcers stop for her, she might continue to put the clothes in the hamper for several more days or even another whole week, hoping that the reinforcer will eventually come anyway. Bianca may have learned more slowly than Alicia, but once she learned the connection between putting her clothes in the hamper and getting that dollar, she is less likely to stop doing it—even when her mother fails to give the dollar as expected.

Bianca's behavior illustrates the **partial reinforcement effect** (Skinner, 1956): A response that is reinforced after some, but not all, correct responses will be more resistant to extinction than a response that receives **continuous reinforcement** (a reinforcer for each and every correct response). Although it may be easier to teach a new behavior using continuous reinforcement, partially reinforced behavior is not only more difficult to suppress but also more like real life. Imagine being paid for every hamburger you make or every report you turn in. In the real world, people tend to receive partial reinforcement rather than continuous reinforcement for their work.

Partial reinforcement can be accomplished according to different patterns or schedules. For example, it might be a certain interval of time that's important, such as an office safe that can only be opened at a certain time of day. It wouldn't matter how many times one tried to open the safe if the effort didn't come at the right *time*. On the other hand, it might be the number of responses that is important, as it would be if one had to sell a certain number of raffle tickets in order to get a prize. When the timing of the response is more important, it is called an *interval schedule*. When it is the number of responses that is important, the schedule is called a *ratio schedule* because a certain number of responses is required for each reinforcer (e.g., 50 raffle tickets for each prize). The other way in which schedules of reinforcement can

"Remember, every time he gives you a pellet, reinforce that behavior by pulling the lever."

**partial reinforcement effect**
the tendency for a response that is reinforced after some, but not all, correct responses to be very resistant to extinction.

**continuous reinforcement**
the reinforcement of each and every correct response.

differ is in whether the number of responses or interval of time is *fixed* (the same in each case) or *variable* (a different number or interval is required in each case). So it is possible to have a fixed interval schedule, a variable interval schedule, a fixed ratio schedule, and a variable ratio schedule (Skinner, 1961).

**FIXED INTERVAL SCHEDULE OF REINFORCEMENT** If you receive a paycheck once a week, you are familiar with what is called a **fixed interval schedule of reinforcement**, in which a reinforcer is received *after* a certain, fixed interval of time has passed. If Professor Conner were teaching a rat to press a lever to get food pellets, she might require it to push the lever *at least once* within a 2-minute time span to get a pellet. It wouldn't matter how many times the rat pushed the bar; the rat would only get a pellet at the end of the 2-minute interval if it had pressed the bar at least once. It is the *first* correct response that gets reinforced at the end of the interval.

As shown in **Figure 5.8**, a fixed interval schedule of reinforcement does not produce a fast rate of responding (notice that the line doesn't go "up" as fast as in the blue fixed ratio line). Since it only matters that at least *one* response is made *during* the specific interval of time, speed is not that important. Eventually, the rat will start pushing the lever only as the interval of time nears its end, causing the *scalloping* effect you see in the graph. The response rate goes up just before the reinforcer and then drops off immediately after, until it is almost time for the next food pellet. This is similar to the way in which factory workers speed up production just before payday and slow down just after payday (Critchfield et al., 2003).

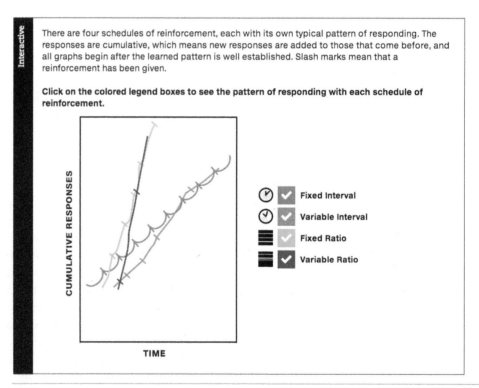

There are four schedules of reinforcement, each with its own typical pattern of responding. The responses are cumulative, which means new responses are added to those that come before, and all graphs begin after the learned pattern is well established. Slash marks mean that a reinforcement has been given.

**Click on the colored legend boxes to see the pattern of responding with each schedule of reinforcement.**

Fixed Interval
Variable Interval
Fixed Ratio
Variable Ratio

**Figure 5.8** Schedules of Reinforcement

These four graphs show the typical pattern of responding for both fixed and variable interval and ratio schedules of reinforcement. The responses are cumulative, which means new responses are added to those that come before, and all graphs begin after the learned pattern is well established. Slash marks mean that a reinforcement has been given. In both the fixed interval and fixed ratio graphs, there is a pause after each reinforcement as the learner briefly "rests." The "scalloped" shape of the fixed interval curve is a typical indicator of this pause, as is the stair-step shape of the fixed ratio curve. In the variable interval and ratio schedules, no such pause occurs, because the reinforcements are unpredictable. Notice that both fixed and variable interval schedules are slower (less steep) than the two ratio schedules because of the need to respond as quickly as possible in the ratio schedules.

**fixed interval schedule of reinforcement**

schedule of reinforcement in which the interval of time that must pass before reinforcement becomes possible is always the same.

Paychecks aren't the only kind of fixed schedule that people experience. When do you study the hardest? Isn't it right before a test? If you know when the test is to be given, that's like having a fixed interval of time that is predictable, and you can save your greatest studying efforts until closer to the exam. (Some students save *all* of their studying for the night before the exam, which is not the best strategy.) Another example of a fixed interval schedule would be the way that many people floss and brush their teeth most rigorously* for a few days before their next dental exam—especially those who have not been flossing until just before their appointment! In this case, they are probably hoping for negative reinforcement. The cleaner they get their teeth before the appointment, the less time they might have to spend in that chair.

 💬 So if a scheduled test is a fixed interval, then would a pop quiz be a variable interval schedule?

**VARIABLE INTERVAL SCHEDULE OF REINFORCEMENT**   Pop quizzes are unpredictable. Students don't know exactly what day they might be given a pop quiz, so the best strategy is to study a little every night just in case there is a quiz the next day. Pop quizzes are good examples of a **variable interval schedule of reinforcement**, where the interval of time after which the individual must respond in order to receive a reinforcer (in this case, a good grade on the quiz) changes from one time to the next. In a more basic example, a rat might receive a food pellet when it pushes a lever, every 5 minutes on average. Sometimes the interval might be 2 minutes, sometimes 10, but the rat must push the lever at least once *after* that interval to get the pellet. Because the rat can't predict how long the interval is going to be, it pushes the bar more or less continuously, producing the smooth graph in Figure 5.8. Once again, speed is not important, so the rate of responding is slow but steady.

Another example of a variable interval schedule might be the kind of fishing in which people put the pole in the water and wait—and wait—and—wait, until a fish takes the bait, if they are lucky. They only have to put the pole in once, but they might refrain from taking it out for fear that just when they do, the biggest fish in the world would swim by. Dialing a busy phone number is also this kind of schedule, as people don't know *when* the call will go through, so they keep dialing and dialing.

**FIXED RATIO SCHEDULE OF REINFORCEMENT**   In ratio schedules, it is the number of responses that counts. In a **fixed ratio schedule of reinforcement**, the number of responses required to receive each reinforcer will always be the same number.

Notice two things about the fixed ratio graph in Figure 5.8. The rate of responding is very fast, especially when compared to the fixed interval schedule, and there are little "breaks" in the response pattern immediately after a reinforcer is given. The rapid response rate occurs because the rat wants to get to the next reinforcer just as fast as possible, and the number of lever pushes counts. The pauses or breaks come right after a reinforcer, because the rat knows "about how many" lever pushes will be needed to get to the next reinforcer because it's always the same. Fixed schedules—both ratio and interval—are predictable, which allows rest breaks.

In human terms, anyone who does piecework, in which a certain number of items have to be completed before payment is given, is reinforced on a fixed ratio schedule. Some sandwich shops use a fixed ratio schedule of reinforcement with their customers by giving out punch cards that get punched one time for each sandwich purchased. When the card has 10 punches, for example, the customer might get a free sandwich.

**VARIABLE RATIO SCHEDULE OF REINFORCEMENT**

💬 The purple line in Figure 5.8 is also very fast, but it's so much smoother, like the variable interval graph. Why are they similar?

―――――――――
*rigorously: strictly, consistently.

When people go fishing, they never know how long they may have to dangle the bait in the water before snagging a fish. This is an example of a variable interval schedule of reinforcement and explains why some people, such as this father and son, are reluctant to pack up and go home.

**variable interval schedule of reinforcement**

schedule of reinforcement in which the interval of time that must pass before reinforcement becomes possible is different for each trial or event.

**fixed ratio schedule of reinforcement**

schedule of reinforcement in which the number of responses required for reinforcement is always the same.

Slot machines provide reinforcement in the form of money on a variable ratio schedule, making the use of these machines very addictive for many people. People don't want to stop for fear the next pull of the lever will be that "magic" one that produces a jackpot.

A **variable ratio schedule of reinforcement** is one in which the number of responses changes from one trial to the next. In the rat example, the rat might be expected to push the bar an *average* of 20 times to get reinforcement. That means that sometimes the rat would push the lever only 10 times before a reinforcer comes, but at other times it might take 30 lever pushes or more.

Figure 5.8 shows a purple line that is just as rapid a response rate as the fixed ratio schedule because the *number* of responses still matters. But the graph is much smoother because the rat is taking no rest breaks. It can't afford to do so because it *doesn't know* how many times it may have to push that lever to get the next food pellet. It pushes as fast as it can and eats while pushing. It is the *unpredictability* of the variable schedule that makes the responses more or less continuous—just as in a variable interval schedule.

In human terms, people who shove money into the one-armed bandit, or slot machine, are being reinforced on a variable ratio schedule of reinforcement (they hope). They put their coins in (response), but they don't know how many times they will have to do this before reinforcement (the jackpot) comes. People who do this tend to sit there until they either win or run out of money. They don't dare stop because the "next one" might hit that jackpot. Buying lottery tickets is much the same thing, as is any kind of gambling. People don't know how many tickets they will have to buy, and they're afraid that if they don't buy the next one, that will be the ticket that would have won, so they keep buying and buying.

Regardless of the schedule of reinforcement one uses, two additional factors contribute to making reinforcement of a behavior as effective as possible. The first factor is *timing*: In general, a reinforcer should be given as immediately as possible *after* the desired behavior. Delaying reinforcement tends not to work well, especially when dealing with animals and small children. (For older children and adults who can think about future reinforcements, such as saving up one's money to buy a highly desired item, some delayed reinforcement can work—for them, just saving the money is reinforcing as they think about their future purchase.) The second factor in effective reinforcement is to reinforce *only* the desired behavior. This should be obvious, but we all slip up at times; for example, many parents make the mistake of giving a child who has not done some chore the promised treat anyway, which completely undermines the child's learning of that chore or task. And who hasn't given a treat to a pet that has not really done the trick?

### THE ROLE OF PUNISHMENT IN OPERANT CONDITIONING

**5.7** **Identify the effect that punishment has on behavior.**

💬 So I think I get reinforcement now, but what about punishment? How does punishment fit into the big picture?

Let's go back to the discussion of positive and negative reinforcement. These strategies are important for *increasing* the likelihood that the targeted behavior will occur again. But what about behavior that we do not want to recur?

**DEFINING PUNISHMENT** People experience two kinds of things as consequences in the world: things they like (food, money, candy, sex, praise, and so on) and things they don't like (spankings, being yelled at, and experiencing any kind of pain, to name a few). In addition, people experience these two kinds of consequences in one of two ways: Either people experience them directly (such as getting money for working or getting yelled at for misbehaving) or they don't experience them, such as losing an allowance for misbehaving or avoiding a scolding by lying about misbehavior. These four consequences are named and described in **Table 5.2**.

**variable ratio schedule of reinforcement**

schedule of reinforcement in which the number of responses required for reinforcement is different for each trial or event.

**Table 5.2** Four Ways to Modify Behavior

| | Reinforcement | Punishment |
|---|---|---|
| Positive (Adding) | Something valued or desirable | Something unpleasant |
| | *Positive Reinforcement* | *Punishment by Application* |
| | Example: getting a gold star for good behavior in school | Example: getting a spanking for disobeying |
| Negative (Removing/Avoiding) | Something unpleasant | Something valued or desirable |
| | *Negative Reinforcement* | *Punishment by Removal* |
| | Example: fastening a seat belt to stop the alarm from sounding | Example: losing a privilege such as going out with friends |

As you can see from this table, **punishment** is actually the opposite of reinforcement. It is any event or stimulus that, when following a response, causes that response to be *less* likely to happen again. People often confuse negative reinforcement with punishment because "negative" sounds like it ought to be something bad, like a kind of punishment. But reinforcement (no matter whether it is positive or negative) *strengthens* a response, while punishment *weakens* a response.

Just as there are two ways in which reinforcement can happen, there are also two ways in which punishment can happen.

**Punishment by application** occurs when something unpleasant (such as a spanking, scolding, or other unpleasant stimulus) is added to the situation or *applied*. This is the kind of punishment that most people think of when they hear the word *punishment*. This is also the kind of punishment that many child development specialists strongly recommend parents avoid using with their children because it can easily escalate into abuse (Dubowitz & Bennett, 2007; Durrant & Ensom, 2012; Straus, 2000; Trocmé et al., 2001). A spanking might be *physically* harmless if it is only two or three swats with a hand, but if done in anger or with a belt or other instrument, it becomes abuse, both physical and emotional.

**Punishment by removal**, on the other hand, is the kind of punishment most often confused with negative reinforcement. In this type of punishment, behavior is punished by the removal of something pleasurable or desired after the behavior occurs. "Grounding" a teenager is removing the freedom to do what the teenager wants to do and is an example of this kind of punishment. Other examples would be placing a child in time-out (removing the attention of the others in the room), fining someone for disobeying the law (removing money), and punishing aggressive behavior by taking away television privileges. This type of punishment is typically far more acceptable to child development specialists because it involves no physical aggression and avoids many of the problems caused by more aggressive punishments.

The confusion over the difference between negative reinforcement and punishment by removal makes it worth examining the difference just a bit more. Negative reinforcement occurs when a response is followed by the *removal* of an *unpleasant* stimulus. If something unpleasant has just gone away as a consequence of that response, wouldn't that response tend to happen again and again? If the response increases, the consequence has to be a kind of *reinforcement*. The problem is that the name sounds like it should be some kind of punishment because of the word *negative*, and that's exactly the problem that many people experience when they are trying to understand negative reinforcement. Many people get negative reinforcement mixed up with punishment by removal, in which a *pleasant* thing is removed (like having your driver's license taken away because you caused a bad accident). Because something is removed (taken away) in both cases, it's easy to think that they will both have the effect of punishment, or weakening a response. The difference between them lies in *what* is taken away: In the case of negative reinforcement, it is an *unpleasant* thing; in the case of punishment by removal, it is a *pleasant* or desirable thing. Many textbooks refer to punishment by

This young girl's father is applying punishment by removal by forcing her to cut up her credit card.

**punishment**

any event or object that, when following a response, makes that response less likely to happen again.

**punishment by application**

the punishment of a response by the addition or experiencing of an unpleasant stimulus.

**punishment by removal**

the punishment of a response by the removal of a pleasurable stimulus.

**Table 5.3**  Negative Reinforcement Versus Punishment by Removal

| Example of Negative Reinforcement | Example of Punishment by Removal |
|---|---|
| Stopping at a red light to avoid getting in an accident. | Losing the privilege of driving because you got into too many accidents. |
| Fastening your seat belt to get the annoying warning signal to stop. | Having to spend some of your money to pay a ticket for failure to wear a seat belt. |
| Obeying a parent before the parent reaches the count of "three" to avoid getting a scolding. | Being "grounded" (losing your freedom) because of disobedience. |

application as positive punishment and punishment by removal as negative punishment. While technically these terms are correct, they just add to the confusion, and as a result, your authors have chosen to stay with the more descriptive terms. For a head-to-head comparison of negative reinforcement and this particular type of punishment by removal, see **Table 5.3**.

**PROBLEMS WITH PUNISHMENT**   Although punishment can be effective in reducing or weakening a behavior, it has several drawbacks. The job of punishment is much harder than that of reinforcement. In using reinforcement, all one has to do is strengthen a response that is already there. But punishment is used to weaken a response, and getting rid of a response that is already well established is not that easy. (Ask any parent or pet owner.) Many times punishment only serves to temporarily suppress or inhibit a behavior until enough time has passed. For example, punishing a child's bad behavior doesn't always eliminate the behavior completely. As time goes on, the punishment is forgotten and the "bad" behavior may occur again in a kind of spontaneous recovery of the old (and probably pleasurable for the child) behavior.

Look back at Table 5.2 under the "Punishment" column. Punishment by application can be quite severe, and severe punishment does do one thing well: It stops the behavior immediately (Bucher & Lovaas, 1967; Carr & Lovaas, 1983). It may not stop it permanently, but it does stop it. In a situation in which a child might be doing something dangerous or self-injurious, this kind of punishment is sometimes more acceptable (Duker & Seys, 1996). For example, if a child starts to run into a busy street, the parent might scream at the child to stop and then administer several rather severe swats to the child's rear. If this is NOT typical behavior on the part of the parent, the child will most likely never run into the street again.

Other than situations of immediately stopping dangerous behavior, severe punishment has too many drawbacks to be really useful (Berlin et al., 2009; Boutwell et al., 2011). It should also be discouraged because of its potential for leading to abuse (Dubowitz & Bennett, 2007; Hecker et al., 2014; Gershoff, 2000, 2010; Lee et al., 2013; McMillan et al., 1999; Trocmé et al., 2001):

- Severe punishment may cause the child (or animal) to avoid the punisher instead of the behavior being punished, so the child (or animal) learns the wrong response.
- Severe punishment may encourage lying to avoid the punishment (a kind of negative reinforcement)—again, not the response that is desired.
- Severe punishment creates fear and anxiety, emotional responses that do not promote learning (Baumrind, 1997; Gershoff, 2002, 2010). If the point is to teach something, this kind of consequence isn't going to help.
- Hitting provides a successful model for aggression (Gershoff, 2000, 2010; Milner, 1992; Österman et al., 2014; Taylor et al., 2010).

That last point is worth a bit more discussion. In using an aggressive type of punishment, such as spanking, the adult is actually modeling (presenting a behavior to be imitated by the child). After all, the adult is using aggression to get what the adult wants from the child. Children sometimes become more likely to use aggression to get what they want when they receive this kind of punishment (Bryan & Freed, 1982; Larzelere, 1986), and the adult has lost an opportunity to model a more appropriate way to deal with parent–child disagreements. Since aggressive punishment does tend to stop the undesirable behavior, at least for a while, the parent who is punishing actually experiences a kind of negative reinforcement: "When I spank, the unpleasant behavior goes away." This may increase the tendency to use aggressive punishment over other forms of discipline and could even lead to child abuse (Dubowitz & Bennett, 2007). There is some evidence that physical punishment that would not be considered abusive (i.e., pushing, shoving, grabbing, hitting) is associated with an increased risk of mental illness for the child in later life (Afifi et al., 2012; Ma et al., 2012). Finally, some children are so desperate for attention from their parents that they will actually misbehave on purpose. The punishment is a form of attention, and these children will take whatever attention they can get, even negative attention.

Punishment by removal is less objectionable to many parents and educators and is the only kind of punishment that is permitted in many public schools. But this kind of punishment also has its drawbacks—it teaches the child what *not* to do but not what the child should do. Both punishment by removal and punishment by application are usually only temporary in their effect on behavior. After some time has passed, the behavior will most likely return as the memory of the punishment gets weaker, allowing spontaneous recovery.

🗨 If punishment doesn't work very well, what can a parent do to keep a child from behaving badly?

The way to make punishment more effective involves remembering a few simple rules:

1. **Punishment should immediately follow the behavior it is meant to punish.** If the punishment comes long after the behavior, it will not be associated with that behavior. (This is also true of reinforcement.)

2. **Punishment should be consistent.** This actually means two things. First, if the parent says that a certain punishment will follow a certain behavior, then the parent must make sure to follow through and do what he or she promised to do. Second, punishment for a particular behavior should stay at the same intensity or increase slightly but never decrease. For example, if a child is scolded for jumping on the bed the first time, the second time this behavior happens the child should also be punished by scolding or by a stronger penalty, such as removal of a favorite toy. But if the first misbehavior is punished by spanking and the second by only a scolding, the child learns to "gamble" with the possible punishment.

3. **Punishment of the wrong behavior should be paired, whenever possible, with reinforcement of the right behavior.** Instead of yelling at a 2-year-old for eating with her fingers, the parent should pull her hand gently out of her plate while saying something such as, "No, we do not eat with our fingers. We eat with our fork," and then placing the fork in the child's hand and praising her for using it. "See, you are doing such a good job with your fork. I'm so proud of you." Pairing punishment (the mild correction of pulling her hand away while saying "No, we do not eat with our fingers") with reinforcement allows parents (and others) to use a much milder punishment and still be effective. It also teaches the desired behavior rather than just suppressing the undesired one.

A few examples of these methods are explained in the video *Alternatives to Using Punishment.*

👁 **Watch** the **Video** *Alternatives to Using Punishment*

## OTHER ASPECTS OF OPERANT CONDITIONING

**5.8** **Explain the concepts of discriminant stimuli, extinction, generalization, and spontaneous recovery as they relate to operant conditioning.**

We've discussed the role of the antecedent stimulus in classical conditioning, as well as the concepts of extinction, generalization, and spontaneous recovery. These concepts are also important in operant conditioning, but in slightly different ways.

**STIMULUS CONTROL: SLOW DOWN, IT'S THE COPS**   You see a police car in your rear-view mirror and automatically slow down, even if you weren't speeding. The traffic light turns red, so you stop. When you want to get into a store, you head for the door and push or pull on the handle. All of these things—slowing down, stopping, using the door handle—are learned. But how do you know what learned response to make and when? The police car, the stoplight, and the door handle are all cues, or stimuli, which tell you what behavior will get you what you want.

A **discriminative stimulus** is any stimulus that provides an organism with a cue for making a certain response in order to obtain reinforcement—specific cues would lead to specific responses, and discriminating between the cues leads to success. For example, a police car is a discriminative stimulus for slowing down and a red stoplight is a cue for stopping because both of these actions are usually followed by negative reinforcement—people don't get a ticket or don't get hit by another vehicle. A doorknob is a cue for where to grab the door in order to successfully open it. In fact, if a door has a knob, people always turn it, but if it has a handle, people usually pull it, right? The two kinds of opening devices each bring forth a different response from people, and their reward is opening the door.

**EXTINCTION, GENERALIZATION, AND SPONTANEOUS RECOVERY IN OPERANT CONDITIONING**   *Extinction* in classical conditioning involves the removal of the UCS, the unconditioned stimulus that eventually acts as a reinforcer of the CS–CR bond. It should come as no surprise, then, that extinction in operant conditioning involves the removal of the reinforcement. Have you ever seen a child throw a temper tantrum in the checkout line because the little one wanted some candy or toy? Many exasperated*

One way to deal with a child's temper tantrum is to ignore it. The lack of reinforcement for the tantrum behavior will eventually result in extinction.

**discriminative stimulus**

any stimulus, such as a stop sign or a doorknob, that provides the organism with a cue for making a certain response in order to obtain reinforcement.

*exasperated: irritated or annoyed.

parents will cave in and give the child the treat, positively reinforcing the tantrum. The parent is also being negatively reinforced for giving in, because the obnoxious* behavior stops. The only way to get the tantrum behavior to stop is to remove the reinforcement, which means no candy, no treat, and if possible, no attention from the parent. (Not only is this hard enough to do while enduring the tantrum, but also the tantrum behavior may actually get worse before it extinguishes!)

Just as in classical conditioning, operantly conditioned responses also can be generalized to stimuli that are only *similar* to the original stimulus. For example, what parent has not experienced that wonderful moment when Baby, who is just learning to label objects and people, says "Dada" in response to the presence of her father and is reinforced by his delight and attention to her. But in the beginning, Baby may cause Dad to cringe when she generalizes her "Dada" response to any man. As other men fail to reinforce her for this response, she'll learn to discriminate among them and her father and only call her father "Dada." In this way, the man who is actually her father becomes a discriminative stimulus just like the stoplight or the doorknob mentioned earlier.

*Spontaneous recovery* (in classical conditioning, the recurrence of a conditioned response after extinction) will also happen with operant responses. Anyone who has ever trained animals to do several different tricks will say that when first learning a new trick, most animals will try to get reinforcers by performing their *old* tricks.

### APPLICATIONS OF OPERANT CONDITIONING: SHAPING AND BEHAVIOR MODIFICATION

**5.9** **Describe how operant conditioning is used to change animal and human behavior.**

Operant conditioning is more than just the reinforcement of simple responses. It can be used to modify the behavior of both animals and humans.

 How do the circus trainers get their animals to do all those complicated tricks?

**SHAPING**   When you see an animal in a circus or in a show at a zoo perform tricks, you are seeing the result of applying the rules of conditioning—both classical and operant—to animals. But the more complex tricks are a process in operant conditioning called **shaping**, in which small steps toward some ultimate goal are reinforced until the goal itself is reached.

For example, if Jody wanted to train his dog to jump through a hoop, he would have to start with some behavior that the dog is already capable of doing on its own. Then he would gradually "mold" that starting behavior into the jump—something the dog is capable of doing but not likely to do on its own. Jody would have to start with the hoop on the ground in front of Rover's face and then call the dog through the hoop, using the treat as bait. After Rover steps through the hoop (as the shortest way to the treat), Jody should give Rover the treat (positive reinforcement). Then he could raise the hoop just a little, reward him for walking through it again, raise the hoop, reward him … until Rover is jumping through the hoop to get the treat. The goal is achieved by reinforcing each *successive approximation* (small steps one after the other that get closer and closer to the goal). This process is shaping (Skinner, 1974). Through pairing of a sound such as a whistle or clicker with the primary reinforcer of food, animal trainers can use the sound as a secondary reinforcer and avoid having an overfed learner. Watch the video *Shaping* to see this process in action.

**shaping**
the reinforcement of simple steps in behavior through successive approximations that lead to a desired, more complex behavior.

---

*obnoxious: highly offensive or undesirable.

Shaping

👁 **Watch** the **Video** *Shaping*

While animals can learn many types of behavior through the use of operant conditioning, it seems that not every animal can be taught *anything*—see the following section on biological constraints for more on this topic.

## Classic Studies in Psychology

# Biological Constraints on Operant Conditioning

Raccoons are fairly intelligent animals and are sometimes used in learning experiments. In a typical experiment, a behaviorist would use shaping and reinforcement to teach a raccoon a trick. The goal might be to get the raccoon to pick up several coins and drop them into a metal container, for which the raccoon would be rewarded with food. The behaviorist starts by reinforcing the raccoon for picking up a single coin. Then the metal container is introduced and the raccoon is now required to drop the coin into the slot on the container in order to get reinforcement.

It is at this point that operant conditioning seems to fail. Instead of dropping the coin in the slot, the raccoon puts the coin in and out of the slot and rubs it against the inside of the container, then holds it firmly for a few seconds before finally letting it go. When the requirement is upped to two coins, the raccoon spends several minutes rubbing them against each other and dipping them into the container without actually dropping them in. In spite of the fact that this dipping and rubbing behavior is not reinforced, it gets worse and worse until conditioning becomes impossible.

Keller and Marian Breland, in their attempt to train a raccoon, found that this problem was not limited to the raccoon (Breland & Breland, 1961). They ran into a similar difficulty with a pig that was being trained to pick up a total of five large wooden coins and put them into a "piggy bank." Although at first successful, the pig became slower and slower at the task over a period of weeks, dropping the coin, rooting (pushing) it around with its nose, picking it up, dropping it again, and rooting some more. This behavior became so persistent that the pig actually did not get enough to eat for the day.

The Brelands concluded that the raccoon and the pig were reverting* to behavior that was instinctual for them. Instinctual behavior is genetically determined and not under the

*reverting: to go back in action, thought, speech, and so on.

influence of learning. Apparently, even though the animals were at first able to learn the tricks, as the coins became more and more associated with food, the animals began to drift back into the instinctual patterns of behavior that they used with real food. Raccoons rub their food between their paws and dip it in and out of water. Pigs root and throw their food around before eating it. The Brelands called this tendency to revert to genetically controlled patterns **instinctive drift**.

In their 1961 paper describing these and other examples of instinctive drift, the Brelands (both trained by Skinner himself) determined that, contrary to Skinner's original ideas:

1. The animal does NOT come to the laboratory a *tabula rasa*, or "blank slate," and cannot be taught just *any* behavior.
2. Differences between species of animals matter in determining what behavior can or cannot be conditioned.
3. Not all responses are equally able to be conditioned to any stimulus.

As became quickly obvious in their studies with these animals, each animal comes into the world (and the laboratory) with certain genetically determined instinctive patterns of behavior already in place. These instincts differ from species to species, with the result that there are some responses that simply cannot be trained into an animal regardless of conditioning.

### Questions for Further Discussion

1. What other kinds of limitations do animals have in learning?
2. What kinds of behavior might people do that would be resistant to conditioning?
3. How can these research findings about animal behavior be generalized to human behavior?

Raccoons commonly dunk their food in and out of water before eating. This "washing" behavior is controlled by instinct and difficult to change even using operant techniques.

**BEHAVIOR MODIFICATION**  Operant conditioning principles such as reinforcement and the process of shaping have been used for many years to change undesirable behavior and create desirable responses in animals and humans—particularly in schoolchildren. The term **behavior modification** refers to the application of operant conditioning (and sometimes classical conditioning) to bring about such changes. The video *How to Make Healthier Choices* describes a sample behavior modification plan for someone who wants to watch less television and exercise more.

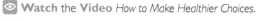
Watch the Video *How to Make Healthier Choices.*

**instinctive drift**
tendency for an animal's behavior to revert to genetically controlled patterns.

**behavior modification**
the use of learning techniques to modify or change undesirable behavior and increase desirable behavior.

As another example, if a teacher wants to use behavior modification to help a child learn to be more attentive during the teacher's lectures, the teacher may do the following:

1. Select a target behavior, such as making eye contact with the teacher.

2. Choose a reinforcer. This may be a gold star applied to the child's chart on the wall, for example.

3. Put the plan in action. Every time the child makes eye contact, the teacher gives the child a gold star. Inappropriate behavior (such as looking out the window) is not reinforced with gold stars.

4. At the end of the day, the teacher gives the child a special treat or reward for having a certain number of gold stars. This special reward is decided on ahead of time and discussed with the child.

The gold stars in this example can be considered *tokens*, secondary reinforcers that can be traded in for other kinds of reinforcers. The use of tokens to modify behavior is called a **token economy**. (L I N K) to Learning Objective 15.4. In the example, the child is collecting gold stars to "buy" the special treat at the end of the day. When one thinks about it, the system of money is very much a token economy. People are rewarded for working with money, which they then trade for food, shelter, and so on. Credit card companies encourage the use of their card by offering reward points that can be exchanged for desirable goods and services, and airlines offer frequent flyer miles. Many fast-food restaurants offer punch cards or stamps that are exchanged for free food when filled up. The points, miles, and punches on the cards are all forms of tokens.

Another tool that behaviorists can use to modify behavior is the process of *time-out*. Time-out is a form of mild punishment by removal in which a misbehaving animal, child, or adult is placed in a special area away from the attention of others. Essentially, the organism is being "removed" from any possibility of positive reinforcement in the form of attention. When used with children, a time-out should be limited to 1 minute for each year of age, with a maximum time-out of 10 minutes (longer than that and the child can forget why the time-out occurred).

**Applied behavior analysis (ABA)** is the modern term for a form of behavior modification that uses both analysis of current behavior and behavioral techniques to address a socially relevant issue. In ABA, skills are broken down to their simplest steps and then taught to the child through a system of reinforcement. Prompts (such as moving a child's face back to look at the teacher or the task) are given as needed when the child is learning a skill or refuses to cooperate. As the child begins to master a skill and receives reinforcement in the form of treats or praise, the prompts are gradually withdrawn until the child can do the skill independently. Applied behavior analysis is a growing field, with many colleges and universities offering degrees at both the undergraduate and graduate levels. A person graduating from one of these programs may act as a consultant* to schools or other institutions or may set up a private practice. Typical uses for ABA are treating children with disorders, training animals, and developing effective teaching methods for children and adults of all levels of mental abilities (Baer et al., 1968; Du et al., 2015; Klein & Kemper, 2016; Mohammadzaheri et al., 2015).

An example of how ABA can be used is found in the use of shaping to mold desirable, socially acceptable behavior in individuals with *autism*. Autism is a disorder in which the person has great difficulty in communicating with others, often refusing to look at another person. People who have autism may also fail to learn to speak at all, and they normally do not like to be touched. (L I N K) to Learning Objective 8.7. This specific application of ABA can be said to have begun with the work of Dr. O. Ivar Lovaas (1964) and his associates, although the basic general techniques are those first outlined by Skinner. Lovaas used small pieces of candy as reinforcers to teach social skills and language to children with autism. Other techniques for modifying responses have been developed so that even biological responses that are normally considered involuntary such as blood

**token economy**

the use of objects called tokens to reinforce behavior in which the tokens can be accumulated and exchanged for desired items or privileges.

**applied behavior analysis (ABA)**

modern term for a form of functional analysis and behavior modification that uses a variety of behavioral techniques to mold a desired behavior or response.

---

*consultant: someone who offers expert advice or services.

pressure, muscle tension, and hyperactivity can be brought under conscious control. For nearly 60 years, scientists have known how to use feedback from a person's biological information (such as heart rate) to create a state of relaxation (Margolin & Kubic, 1944). **Biofeedback** is the traditional term used to describe this kind of biological feedback of information, and through its use many problems can be relieved or controlled.

A relatively newer biofeedback technique called **neurofeedback** involves trying to change brain activity. (L I N K) to Learning Objective 2.4. Although this technique uses the latest in technology, the basic principles behind it are much older. Traditionally, this technique was based on recording the electrical activity of the brain, or EEG. To record the EEG, a person would have to be connected to a stand-alone *electroencephalograph*, a machine that amplifies and records the brain's electrical activity. Modern biofeedback and neurofeedback amplifiers are often connected to a computer that records and analyzes the physiological activity of the brain. Neurofeedback can be integrated with video game–like programs that individuals can use to learn how to produce brain waves or specific types of brain activity associated with specific cognitive or behavioral states (e.g., increased attention, staying focused, relaxed awareness). Individuals learn to make these changes through the principles of operant conditioning (Sherlin et al., 2011). Neurofeedback using the EEG continues to be investigated in specific disorders such as attention-deficit/hyperactivity disorder (ADHD) and in new areas such as the control of chronic pain (Arns et al., 2009; Jensen et al., 2013) and the treatment of epilepsy (Koberda, 2015; Micoulaud-Franchi et al., 2014; Strehl et al., 2014). Other recent neurofeedback studies have incorporated MRI or fMRI to examine the effects of EEG-based neurofeedback on the brain (Ghaziri et al., 2013; Ros et al., 2013). And in some studies, fMRI is being used as a neurofeedback method in and of itself (Ruiz et al., 2013; Scharnowski et al., 2012; Stoeckel et al., 2014; Sulzer et al., 2013).

**biofeedback**

using feedback about biological conditions to bring involuntary responses, such as blood pressure and relaxation, under voluntary control.

**neurofeedback**

form of biofeedback using brain-scanning devices to provide feedback about brain activity in an effort to modify behavior.

## Concept Map L.O. 5.4, 5.5, 5.6, 5.7, 5.8, 5.9

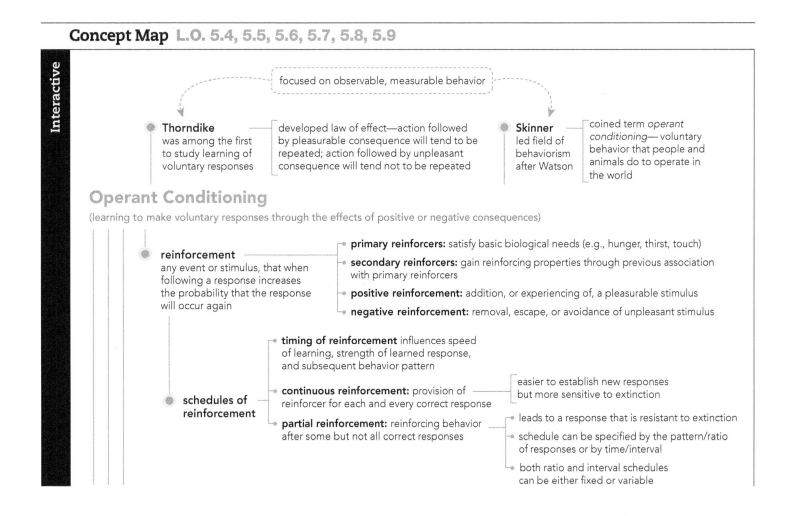

Interactive

focused on observable, measurable behavior

**Thorndike** was among the first to study learning of voluntary responses — developed law of effect—action followed by pleasurable consequence will tend to be repeated; action followed by unpleasant consequence will tend not to be repeated

**Skinner** led field of behaviorism after Watson — coined term *operant conditioning*— voluntary behavior that people and animals do to operate in the world

### Operant Conditioning
(learning to make voluntary responses through the effects of positive or negative consequences)

**reinforcement** any event or stimulus, that when following a response increases the probability that the response will occur again
- **primary reinforcers:** satisfy basic biological needs (e.g., hunger, thirst, touch)
- **secondary reinforcers:** gain reinforcing properties through previous association with primary reinforcers
- **positive reinforcement:** addition, or experiencing of, a pleasurable stimulus
- **negative reinforcement:** removal, escape, or avoidance of unpleasant stimulus

**schedules of reinforcement**
- **timing of reinforcement** influences speed of learning, strength of learned response, and subsequent behavior pattern
- **continuous reinforcement:** provision of reinforcer for each and every correct response — easier to establish new responses but more sensitive to extinction
- **partial reinforcement:** reinforcing behavior after some but not all correct responses —
  - leads to a response that is resistant to extinction
  - schedule can be specified by the pattern/ratio of responses or by time/interval
  - both ratio and interval schedules can be either fixed or variable

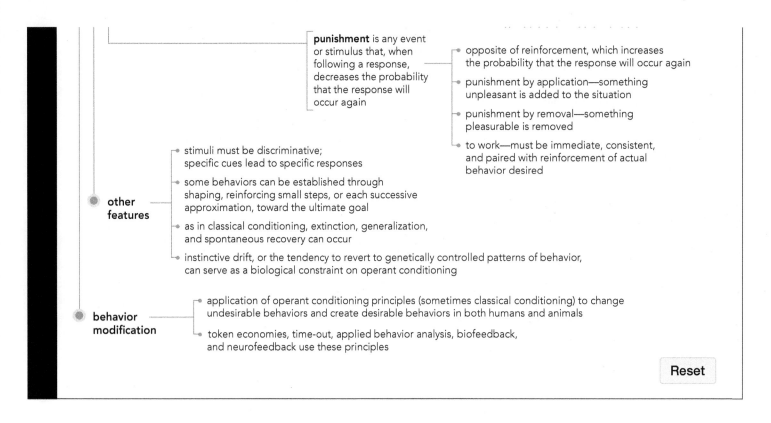

**punishment** is any event or stimulus that, when following a response, decreases the probability that the response will occur again
- opposite of reinforcement, which increases the probability that the response will occur again
- punishment by application—something unpleasant is added to the situation
- punishment by removal—something pleasurable is removed
- to work—must be immediate, consistent, and paired with reinforcement of actual behavior desired

**other features**
- stimuli must be discriminative; specific cues lead to specific responses
- some behaviors can be established through shaping, reinforcing small steps, or each successive approximation, toward the ultimate goal
- as in classical conditioning, extinction, generalization, and spontaneous recovery can occur
- instinctive drift, or the tendency to revert to genetically controlled patterns of behavior, can serve as a biological constraint on operant conditioning

**behavior modification**
- application of operant conditioning principles (sometimes classical conditioning) to change undesirable behaviors and create desirable behaviors in both humans and animals
- token economies, time-out, applied behavior analysis, biofeedback, and neurofeedback use these principles

Reset

# Practice Quiz   How much do you remember?

*Pick the best answer.*

**1.** To a dog, _____ is an example of a primary reinforcer, whereas _____ is an example of a secondary reinforcer.
   **a.** a paycheck; money
   **b.** dog food; a Frisbee
   **c.** dog food; dog treats
   **d.** a gold star; candy

**2.** Edgar cannot sleep because he is terribly worried about his research paper. So Edgar decides to get out of bed and continue working on the paper. Although he stays up to nearly 3 A.M., he is relieved that it is done and easily falls off to sleep. In the future, Edgar will be more likely to finish his work before going to bed so that he can avoid the worry and sleeplessness. Such behavior is an example of
   **a.** positive reinforcement.
   **b.** negative reinforcement.
   **c.** punishment.
   **d.** classical conditioning.

**3.** Joe owned a small repair shop. Each day, he would check the mail to see if any of his customers mailed in a payment for the work he had done for them. Some days, he would receive a check or two. At other times, he would have to wait days before getting another payment. What schedule of reinforcement is evident here?
   **a.** fixed interval
   **b.** fixed ratio
   **c.** variable interval
   **d.** variable ratio

**4.** Little Jimmie's mother was upset to find that Jimmie had not picked up his building blocks after repeated requests to do so. The next morning, Jimmie found all his blocks had been picked up and put into a bag on top of the refrigerator. Jimmie's mother told him that he couldn't play with his blocks for the next 2 days. Which type of discipline did she use?
   **a.** negative reinforcement
   **b.** punishment by application
   **c.** punishment by removal
   **d.** positive reinforcement

**5.** Tabitha signed up for a new credit card that offers reward miles for every purchase. Tabitha plans to make as many purchases as she can so that she can accumulate enough miles to go on a trip over spring break. Such an approach is an example of
   **a.** a token economy.
   **b.** shaping.
   **c.** a schedule of reinforcement.
   **d.** a form of negative reinforcement.

**6.** Which of the following is the best example of applied behavior analysis?
   **a.** Tiffany works with children by asking them what they want to accomplish and then helping them attain that goal through different forms of classical conditioning.
   **b.** Bethany has children watch her repeatedly so as to understand how a task is to be done. Once they have finished the observation, then they are asked to imitate the behavior.
   **c.** Agatha observes a child to see what purpose a disruptive classroom behavior serves and identifies a new replacement behavior. She then implements a training program for the new behavior, reinforcing often at the simplest levels and gradually removing reinforcers as the child demonstrates the behavior independently.
   **d.** Camille wants children to learn a new behavior and uses punishment as the basis for the behavior change.

# APA Goal 2: Scientific Inquiry and Critical Thinking

## Spare the Rod, Spoil the Child?

*Addresses APA Learning Objectives 2.1: Use scientific reasoning to interpret psychological phenomena; 2.2: Demonstrate psychology information literacy; and 2.5: Incorporate sociocultural factors in scientific inquiry.*

To spank or not to spank has been a controversial issue for many years now. In the past, across many cultures, spanking a child for misbehavior was an accepted form of discipline, but with the rise in both awareness and incidence of child abuse, critical thinking demands asking the next question: Does it work, or does it do more harm than good?

Finland was the second country in the world (after Sweden) to enact a law that banned any kind of physical punishment of children, including by their own parents. This law was put into effect in 1983. The results of a survey conducted nearly 30 years later on a sample of 4, 609 males and females between the ages of 15 and 80 years of age showed a significant decrease in reports of physical discipline (e.g., being beaten with an object or slapped) among those participants who were born after the law went into effect. There were also far fewer murdered children. Those participants who had been exposed to more physical punishment than average were found to be more likely to abuse alcohol and suffer from mental health issues such as depression and were also more likely to be divorced or to have attempted suicide (Österman et al., 2014). In other countries where a ban against corporal punishment has been enacted, there has also been a decrease in child abuse (Zolotor & Puzia, 2010). In this case it definitely seems that physical punishment such as spanking actually does more harm.

In the last 40 years in the United States, spanking has decreased as a means of disciplining children but is still used by the parents of about 80 percent of preschool-aged children. While in addition to Finland and Sweden 24 other countries have officially banned corporal punishment in about the same time period, spanking is still common across many cultures (Runyan et al., 2010; Zolotor & Puzia, 2010; Zolotor et al., 2011). Regardless of country of origin, research has found that spanking and other forms of harsh physical discipline are more common in places where income is low and parents are less educated (Runyan et al., 2010).

### APA Goal 2: Spare the Road and Spoil the Child? Countries that Have Banned Corporal Punishment

| Country | Year Corporal Punishment Banned | Country | Year Corporal Punishment Banned | Country | Year Corporal Punishment Banned |
|---|---|---|---|---|---|
| San Marino | 2014 | Republic of Moldova | 2008 | Iceland | 2003 |
| Brazil | 2014 | Liechtenstein | 2008 | Turkmenistan | 2002 |
| Argentina | 2014 | Costa Rica | 2008 | Bulgaria | 2000 |
| Malta | 2014 | Togo | 2007 | Germany | 2000 |
| Bolivia | 2014 | Uruguay | 2007 | Israel | 2000 |
| Honduras | 2013 | Netherlands | 2007 | Croatia | 1999 |
| TFYR Macedonia | 2013 | Spain | 2007 | Latvia | 1998 |
| Cabo Verde | 2013 | Portugal | 2007 | Denmark | 1997 |
| South Sudan | 2011 | Venezuela | 2007 | Cyprus | 1994 |
| Albania | 2010 | New Zealand | 2007 | Austria | 1989 |
| Tunisia | 2010 | Greece | 2006 | Norway | 1987 |
| Republic of Congo | 2010 | Hungary | 2005 | Finland | 1983 |
| Poland | 2010 | Romania | 2004 | Sweden | 1979 |
| Kenya | 2010 | Ukraine | 2004 | | |
| Luxembourg | 2008 | | | | |

**SOURCE:** The Global Initiative to End All Corporal Punishment of Children, 2016

# Cognitive Learning Theory

In the early days of behaviorism, the focus of Watson, Skinner, and many of their followers was on observable, measurable behavior. Anything that might be occurring inside a person's or animal's head during learning was considered to be of no interest to the behaviorist because it could not be seen or directly measured. Other psychologists, however, were still interested in the mind's influence over behavior. Gestalt psychologists, for instance, were studying the way that the human mind tried to force a pattern onto stimuli in the world around the person. **L I N K** to Learning Objective 1.2. This continued interest in the mind was followed, in the 1950s and 1960s, by the comparison of the human mind to the workings of those fascinating "thinking machines," computers. Soon after, interest in *cognition*, the mental events that take place inside a person's mind while behaving, began to dominate experimental psychology. Many behavioral psychologists could no longer ignore the thoughts, feelings, and expectations that clearly existed in the mind and that seemed to influence observable behavior, and eventually began to develop a cognitive learning theory to supplement the more traditional theories of learning (Kendler, 1985). Three important figures often cited as key theorists in the early days of the development of cognitive learning theory were the Gestalt psychologists Edward Tolman and Wolfgang Köhler and modern psychologist Martin Seligman.

### TOLMAN'S MAZE-RUNNING RATS: LATENT LEARNING

#### 5.10  Explain the concept of latent learning.

One of Gestalt psychologist Edward Tolman's best-known experiments in learning involved teaching three groups of rats the same maze, one at a time (Tolman & Honzik, 1930). In the first group, each rat was placed in the maze and reinforced with food for making its way out the other side. The rat was then placed back in the maze, reinforced upon completing the maze again, and so on until the rat could successfully solve the maze with no errors (see **Figure 5.9**).

"Bathroom? Sure, it's just down that hall to the left, jog right, left, another left, straight past two more lefts, then right, and it's at the end of the third corridor on your right."

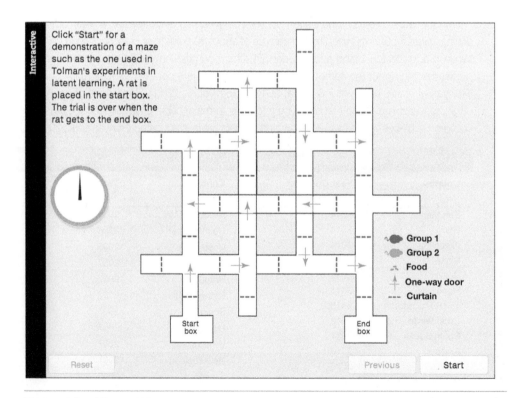

**Figure 5.9**  A Typical Maze

This is an example of a maze such as the one used in Tolman's experiments in latent learning. A rat is placed in the start box. The trial is over when the rat gets to the end box.

The second group of rats was treated exactly like the first, except that they never received any reinforcement upon exiting the maze. They were simply put back in again and again, until the 10th day of the experiment. On that day, the rats in the second group began to receive reinforcement for getting out of the maze. The third group of rats, serving as a control group, was also not reinforced and was not given reinforcement for the entire duration of the experiment.

A strict Skinnerian behaviorist would predict that only the first group of rats would learn the maze successfully because learning depends on reinforcing consequences. At first, this seemed to be the case. The first group of rats did indeed solve the maze after a certain number of trials, whereas the second and third groups seemed to wander aimlessly around the maze until accidentally finding their way out.

On the 10th day, however, something happened that would be difficult to explain using only Skinner's basic principles. The second group of rats, upon receiving the reinforcement for the first time, *should* have then taken as long as the first group to solve the maze. Instead, they began to solve the maze almost immediately (see **Figure 5.10**).

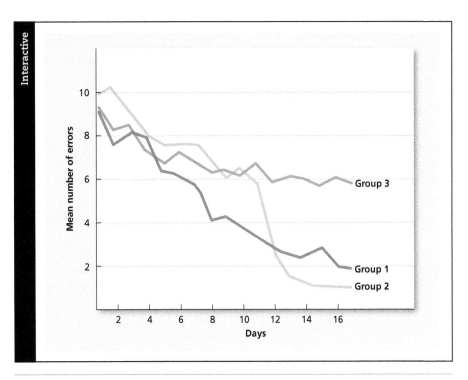

**Figure 5.10** Learning Curves for Three Groups of Rats

In the results of the classic study of latent learning, Group 1 was rewarded on each day, while Group 2 was rewarded for the first time on Day 10. Group 3 was never rewarded. Note the immediate change in the behavior of Group 2 on Day 12 (Tolman & Honzik, 1930).

Tolman concluded that the rats in the second group, while wandering around in the first 9 days of the experiment, had indeed learned where all the blind alleys, wrong turns, and correct paths were and stored this knowledge away as a kind of "mental map," or *cognitive map* of the physical layout of the maze. The rats in the second group had learned and stored that learning away mentally but had not *demonstrated* this learning because there was no reason to do so. The cognitive map had remained hidden, or latent, until the rats had a reason to demonstrate their knowledge by getting to the food. Tolman called this **latent learning**. The idea that learning could happen without reinforcement and then later affect behavior was not something traditional operant conditioning could explain. To see a real-life example of latent learning, participate in the experiment *Learning* ⊙ **Simulate** the **Experiment,** *Latent Learning.*

### KÖHLER'S SMART CHIMP: INSIGHT LEARNING

5.11 **Explain how Köhler's studies demonstrated that animals can learn by insight.**

Another exploration of the cognitive elements of learning came about almost by accident. Wolfgang Köhler (1887–1967) was a Gestalt psychologist who became marooned* on an island in the Canaries (a series of islands off the coast of North Africa) when World War I broke out. Stuck at the primate research lab that had first drawn him to the island, he turned to studies of animal learning.

In one of his more famous studies (Köhler, 1925), he set up a problem for one of the chimpanzees. Sultan the chimp was faced with the problem of how to get to a banana that was placed just out of his reach outside his cage. Sultan solved this problem relatively easily, first trying to reach through the bars with his arm, then using a stick that was lying

**latent learning**

learning that remains hidden until its application becomes useful.

---

* marooned: in this sense, being placed on an island from which escape is impossible.

in the cage to rake the banana into the cage. As chimpanzees are natural tool users, this behavior is not surprising and is still nothing more than simple trial-and-error learning.

But then the problem was made more difficult. The banana was placed just out of reach of Sultan's extended arm with the stick in his hand. At this point there were two sticks lying around in the cage, which could be fitted together to make a single pole that would be long enough to reach the banana. Sultan tried first one stick, then the other (simple trial and error). After about an hour of trying, Sultan seemed to have a sudden flash of inspiration. He pushed one stick out of the cage as far as it would go toward the banana and then pushed the other stick behind the first one. Of course, when he tried to draw the sticks back, only the one in his hand came. He jumped up and down and was very excited, and when Köhler gave him the second stick, he sat on the floor of the cage and looked at them carefully. He then fitted one stick into the other and retrieved his banana. Köhler called Sultan's rapid "perception of relationships" **insight** and determined that insight could not be gained through trial-and-error learning alone (Köhler, 1925). Although Thorndike and other early learning theorists believed that animals could not demonstrate insight, Köhler's work seems to demonstrate that insight requires a sudden "coming together" of all the elements of a problem in a kind of "aha" moment that is not predicted by traditional animal learning studies. (L I N K) to Learning Objective 7.3. More recent research has also found support for the concept of animal insight (Heinrich, 2000; Heyes, 1998; Zentall, 2000), but there is still controversy over how to interpret the results of those studies (Wynne, 1999).

**SELIGMAN'S DEPRESSED DOGS: LEARNED HELPLESSNESS**

**5.12** Summarize Seligman's studies on learned helplessness.

Martin Seligman is now famous for founding the field of *positive psychology*, a new way of looking at the entire concept of mental health and therapy that focuses on the adaptive, creative, and psychologically more fulfilling aspects of human experience rather than on mental disorders. But in the mid- to late 1960s, learning theorist Seligman (1975) and his colleagues were doing classical conditioning experiments on dogs. They accidentally discovered an unexpected phenomenon, which Seligman called **learned helplessness**, the tendency to fail to act to escape from a situation because of a history of repeated failures. Their original intention was to study escape and avoidance learning. Seligman and colleagues presented a tone followed by a harmless but painful electric shock to one group of dogs (Overmier & Seligman, 1967; Seligman & Maier, 1967). The dogs in this group were harnessed so that they could not escape the shock. The researchers assumed that the dogs would learn to fear the sound of the tone and later try to escape from the tone before being shocked.

These dogs, along with another group of dogs that had not been conditioned to fear the tone, were placed in a special box containing a low fence that divided the box into two compartments. The dogs, which were now unharnessed, could easily see over the fence and jump over if they wished—which is precisely what the dogs that had not been conditioned did as soon as the shock occurred (see **Figure 5.11**). Imagine the researchers' surprise when, instead of jumping over the fence when the tone sounded, the previously conditioned dogs just sat there. In fact, these dogs showed distress but didn't try to jump over the fence *even when the shock itself began.*

Why would the conditioned dogs refuse to move when shocked? The dogs that had been harnessed while being conditioned had apparently learned in the original tone/shock situation that there was nothing they could do to escape the shock. So when placed in a situation in which escape was possible, the dogs still did nothing because they had learned to be "helpless." They believed they could not escape, so they did not try.

Another of Köhler's chimpanzees, Grande, has just solved the problem of how to get to the banana by stacking boxes. Does this meet the criteria for insight, or was it simple trial-and-error learning?

**insight**

the sudden perception of relationships among various parts of a problem, allowing the solution to the problem to come quickly.

**learned helplessness**

the tendency to fail to act to escape from a situation because of a history of repeated failures in the past.

**Figure 5.11** Seligman's Apparatus

In Seligman's studies of learned helplessness, dogs were placed in a two-sided box. Dogs that had no prior experience with being unable to escape a shock would quickly jump over the hurdle in the center of the box to land on the "safe" side. Dogs that had previously learned that escape was impossible would stay on the side of the box in which the shock occurred, not even trying to go over the hurdle.

More recently, Seligman's colleague and coresearcher in those early studies, Steven F. Maier, has revisited the phenomenon of learned helplessness from a neuroscientific approach, and this work has provided some new insights. Maier and others have investigated the brain mechanisms underlying this phenomenon, focusing on an area of the brain stem that releases serotonin and can play a role in activating the amygdala (which plays an important role in fear and anxiety) but also participates in decreasing activity in brain areas responsible for the "fight-or-flight" response. This combination of increased fear/anxiety with non-escape or freezing is the very behavior associated with learned helplessness. This part of the brain stem (the dorsal raphe nucleus) is a much older part of the brain and not able to determine what type of stressors are controllable. Their research suggests that a higher-level area, a part of the frontal lobe called the *ventromedial prefrontal cortex* (vmPFC), is able to help determine what is controllable. In turn, the vmPFC inhibits the brain stem area and calms the amygdala's response, allowing an animal to effectively respond to a stressor and exhibit control (Amat et al., 2005; Maier et al., 2006; Maier & Watkins, 2005). In other words, it is possible that the dogs in the early studies, rather than learning to be helpless, were *not* learning how to relax and take control of the situation. Maier and colleagues suggest that both training and input from the vmPFC are necessary for animals to learn how to take control (Maier et al., 2006).

> 💬 I know some people who seem to act just like those dogs—they live in a horrible situation but won't leave. Is this the same thing?

Seligman extended the concept of learned helplessness to explain some behaviors characteristic of *depression*. Depressed people seem to lack normal emotions and become somewhat apathetic, often staying in unpleasant work environments or bad marriages or relationships rather than trying to escape or better their situation. Seligman proposed that this depressive behavior is a form of learned helplessness. Depressed people may have learned in the past that they seem to have no control over what happens to them (Alloy & Clements, 1998). A sense of powerlessness and hopelessness is common to depressed people, and certainly this would seem to apply to Seligman's dogs as well. Maier's recent work also has implications here, especially the focus on the components necessary for learning how to relax and exhibit control: input from the vmPFC and training (repeated exposures to stressors). This combination provides a mechanism not only for understanding resilience* but also for possibly helping people foster resilience and avoid anxiety or mood disorders such as posttraumatic stress disorder (PTSD) or depression (Maier et al., 2006). ⓛⓘⓝⓚ to Learning Objectives 14.6 and 14.9. Maier and colleagues are continuing to study the brain foundations of learned helplessness and examining how factors related to control and controllability impact not only immediate events but future stressful events as well (Amat et al., 2010; Rozeske et al., 2011; Varela et al., 2012).

Think about how learned helplessness might apply to other situations. Perceived control or learned helplessness can play an important role in coping with chronic or acute health conditions, either for the person with the disorder or for the family member making medical decisions for a loved one (Camacho et al., 2013; Sullivan et al., 2012). What about college? There are many students who feel that they are bad at math because they have had problems with it in the past. Is it possible that this belief could make them not try as hard or study as much as they should? Is this kind of thinking also an example of learned helplessness, or is it possible that these students have simply not had enough experiences of success or control?

Cognitive learning is also an important part of a fairly well-known form of learning, often simplified as "monkey see, monkey do." Let's take a look at learning through watching the actions of others.

---

*resilience: the ability to recover quickly from change and/or stress.

## Concept Map L.O. 5.10, 5.11, 5.12

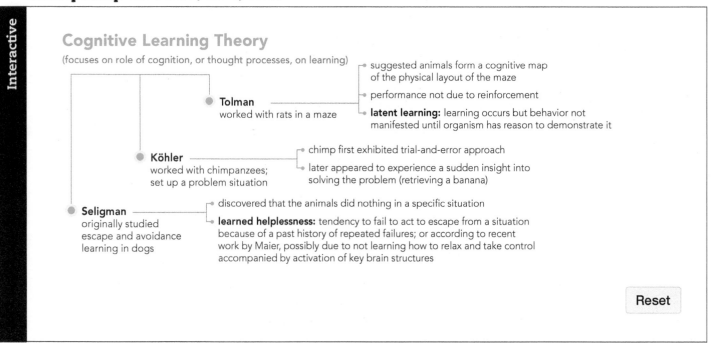

# Practice Quiz   How much do you remember?

*Pick the best answer.*

**1.** In Tolman's maze study, the fact that the group of rats receiving reinforcement only after day 10 of the study solved the maze far more quickly than did the rats who had been reinforced from the first day can be interpreted to mean that these particular rats
**a.** were much smarter than the other rats.
**b.** had already learned the maze in the first 9 days.
**c.** had the opportunity to cheat by watching the other rats.
**d.** were very hungry and, therefore, learned much more quickly.

**2.** Lisa's parents have decided to take a 3-week trip to Europe. Consequently, Lisa's mother will not be able to make her famous pies for the upcoming bake sale. When her mother encourages Lisa to bake the pies herself, Lisa panics at first, but then she finds that she knows how to put the recipe together. Her ability to prepare the recipe is an example of
**a.** latent learning.       **c.** insight learning.
**b.** learned helplessness.  **d.** discovery learning.

**3.** Which theory is commonly referred to as the "aha!" phenomenon?
**a.** Tolman's latent learning theory
**b.** Köhler's insight theory
**c.** Seligman's learned helplessness theory
**d.** Bandura's observational learning

**4.** Research by Steven Maier suggests that learned helplessness may be due to a higher-level region of the brain known as the _____, which helps subjects determine what is controllable.
**a.** amygdala
**b.** hippocampus
**c.** dorsal raphe nucleus
**d.** ventromedial prefrontal cortex (vmPFC)

# Observational Learning

**Observational learning** is the learning of new behavior through watching the actions of a model (someone else who is doing that behavior). Sometimes that behavior is desirable, and sometimes it is not, as the next section describes.

## BANDURA AND THE BOBO DOLL

### 5.13  Describe the process of observational learning.

Albert Bandura's classic study in observational learning involved having a preschool child in a room in which the experimenter and a model interacted with toys in the room in front of the child (Bandura et al., 1961). In one condition, the model interacted with the toys in a nonaggressive manner, completely ignoring the presence of a "Bobo" doll (a punch-bag doll in the shape of a clown). In another condition, the model became very aggressive with the doll, kicking it and yelling at it, throwing it in the air and hitting it with a hammer.

When each child was left alone in the room and had the opportunity to play with the toys, a camera filming through a one-way mirror caught the children who were exposed to the aggressive model beating up on the Bobo doll, in exact imitation of the model (see **Figure 5.12**). The children who saw the model ignore the doll did not act aggressively toward the toy. Obviously, the aggressive children had learned their aggressive actions from merely watching the model—with no reinforcement necessary. The fact that learning can take place without actual performance (a kind of latent learning) is called **learning/performance distinction**.

💬 Ah, but would that child have imitated the model if the model had been punished? Wouldn't the consequences of the model's behavior make a difference?

In later studies, Bandura showed a film of a model beating up the Bobo doll. In one condition, the children saw the model rewarded afterward. In another, the model was punished. When placed in the room with toys, the children in the first group beat up the doll, but the children in the second group did not. But when Bandura told the children in the second group that he would give them a reward if they could show him

**observational learning**
learning new behavior by watching a model perform that behavior.

**learning/performance distinction**
referring to the observation that learning can take place without actual performance of the learned behavior.

**Figure 5.12**  Bandura's Bobo Doll Experiment

In Albert Bandura's famous Bobo doll experiment, the doll was used to demonstrate the impact of observing an adult model performing aggressive behavior on the later aggressive behavior of children.

what the model in the film did, each child duplicated the model's actions. Both groups had learned from watching the model, but only the children watching the successful (rewarded) model imitated the aggression with no prompting (Bandura, 1965). Apparently, consequences do matter in motivating a child (or an adult) to imitate a particular model. The tendency for some movies and television programs to make "heroes" out of violent, aggressive "bad guys" is particularly disturbing in light of these findings. In fact, Bandura began this research to investigate possible links between children's exposure to violence on television and aggressive behavior toward others.

In one nationwide study of youth in the United States, it was found that young people ages 8 to 18 spend on average almost 7.5 hours per day involved in media consumption (television, computers, video games, music, cell phones, print, and movies), 7 days a week. Furthermore, given the prevalence of media multitasking (using more than one media device at a time), they are packing in approximately 10 hours and 45 minutes of media during those 7.5 hours (Rideout et al., 2010)! While not all media consumption is of violent media, it is quite easy to imagine that some of that media is of a violent nature.

Hundreds of studies stretching over nearly three decades and involving hundreds of thousands of participants strongly indicate that a link exists between viewing violent media and an increased level of aggression in children and young adults (Anderson et al., 2015; Bushman & Huesmann, 2001; Huesmann & Eron, 1986). Ⓛⓘⓝⓚ to Learning Objective 1.7. While some of these studies involved correlations, and correlations do not prove that viewing violence on various media is the *cause* of increased violence, one cannot help but be concerned, especially given the continuing rise of media consumption in young people, coupled with the multiple ways young people interact with media. Although still a topic of debate for some (Boxer et al., 2015; Ferguson, 2015; Gentile, 2015; Rothstein & Bushman, 2015), there appears to be a strong body of evidence that exposure to media violence does have immediate and long-term effects, increasing the likelihood of aggressive verbal and physical behavior and aggressive thoughts and emotions—and the effects appear to impact children, adolescents, and adults (Anderson et al., 2003, 2015).

Prosocial behavior, which is behavior aimed at helping others, has also been shown to be influenced by media consumption. Studies have shown that when children watch media that models helping behavior, aggressive behavior decreases and prosocial behavior increases (Anderson et al., 2015; Prot et al., 2014). (L) (I) (N) K to Learning Objectives 12.15, 12.16.

**THINKING CRITICALLY**

Do you think that watching violence on television increases violence and aggression in viewers? Why or why not?

▶ | The response entered here will be saved to your notes and may be collected by your instructor if he/she requires it. |

Submit

### THE FOUR ELEMENTS OF OBSERVATIONAL LEARNING

**5.14** List the four elements of observational learning.

Bandura (1986) concluded, from his studies and others, that observational learning required the presence of four elements.

**ATTENTION**   To learn anything through observation, the learner must first pay *attention* to the model. For example, a person at a fancy dinner party who wants to know which utensil to use has to watch the person who seems to know what is correct. Certain characteristics of models can make attention more likely. For example, people pay more attention to those they perceive as similar to them and to those they perceive as attractive.

**MEMORY**   The learner must also be able to retain the *memory* of what was done, such as remembering the steps in preparing a dish that was first seen on a cooking show.

**IMITATION**   The learner must be capable of reproducing, or *imitating*, the actions of the model. A 2-year-old might be able to watch someone tie shoelaces and might even remember most of the steps, but the 2-year-old's chubby little fingers will not have the dexterity* necessary for actually tying the laces. A person with extremely weak ankles might be able to watch and remember how some ballet move was accomplished but will not be able to reproduce it. The mirror neurons discussed in Chapter Two may be willing, but the flesh is weak. (L) (I) (N) K to Learning Objective 2.12.

**DESIRE**   Finally, the learner must have the desire or *motivation* to perform the action. That person at the fancy dinner, for example, might not care which fork or which knife is the "proper" one to use. Also, if a person expects a reward because one has been given in the past or has been promised a future reward (like the children in the second group of Bandura's study) or has witnessed a model getting a reward (like the children in the first group), that person will be much more likely to imitate the observed behavior. Successful models are powerful figures for imitation, but rarely would we be motivated to imitate someone who fails or is punished.

(An easy way to remember the four elements of modeling is to remember the letters AMID, which stand for the first letters of each of the four elements. This is a good example of using a strategy to improve memory. (L) (I) (N) K to Learning Objective PIA.6.)

---

*dexterity: skill and ease in using the hands.

## Concept Map  L.O. 5.13, 5.14

Interactive

### Observational Learning

(the learning of a new behavior through the observation of a model; typically associated with classic work of Bandura and "Bobo doll" study) ——————— **key elements for learner** ———

- pay attention to the model
- able to remember what was done
- capable of reproducing, or imitating, the actions of the model
- have the desire or motivation to perform the action

**children observing** ——————— an adult model's aggressive or nonaggressive behaviors tended to later act in the same manner they saw modeled; no reinforcement was necessary

later research suggested that potential consequences can influence motivation to imitate a particular model

Reset

# Practice Quiz    How much do you remember?

*Pick the best answer.*

**1.** Bandura's studies found that learning can take place without actual performance. What is this referred to as?
   **a.** learning/performance distinction
   **b.** insight-based learning
   **c.** ARID
   **d.** cognitive learning

**2.** Which of the following statements is false?
   **a.** There is a strong link between viewing violent media and an increase in aggressive behavior among young people.
   **b.** Prosocial behavior can be positively influenced by the viewing/playing of prosocial media.
   **c.** Young people spend more than 7 hours a day viewing various forms of media.
   **d.** Adults are not negatively affected by viewing or playing violent media.

**3.** What is the correct sequence of the four elements of observational learning?
   **a.** Attention, Imitation, Desire, Memory
   **b.** Attention, Memory, Imitation, Desire
   **c.** Desire, Attention, Memory, Imitation
   **d.** Memory, Attention, Desire, Imitation

**4.** Leticia wanted to help her father prepare breakfast. She had watched him crack eggs into a bowl many times, paying careful attention to how he did it. But when she went to crack her own eggs, they smashed into many pieces. Which of the following elements of observational learning was Leticia's problem?
   **a.** attention
   **b.** memory
   **c.** imitation
   **d.** desire

## Applying Psychology to Everyday Life
# Can You Really Toilet Train Your Cat?

**5.15  Describe an example of conditioning in the real world.**

(This article has been excerpted with permission of the author and cat trainer extraordinaire Karawynn Long. Karawynn Long is a published writer and Web designer who lives in Seattle with her family. Sadly, since this article was written, her cat, Misha, has passed away. Ms. Long can be reached at her Web site, **www.karawynn.name/mishacat/toilet.html**. The italicized words in brackets are the textbook author's "editorial" comments.)

There have been more books and articles about toilet-training cats than you'd think. In the summer of 1989, when Misha was a small kitten with big ears and enough meow for five cats, I searched out and read a half-dozen of them. And then tried it myself, and discovered there were a couple of things they all failed to mention … here's what worked for me and Misha.

The central idea is that the transition from litter box to toilet should be accomplished in a series of stages. [*This is shaping.*] You make a small change and then give your cat time to adjust before you make another small change. If at any time Felix gives the whole thing up and goes on the rug instead, you're pushing him too far too fast; back up a stage or two and try again, more slowly.

The very most important thing to remember is: Lid Up, Seat Down. Post a note on the back of the door or the lid of the toilet if you think you (or your housemates or guests) might forget. And if you are accustomed to closing the bathroom door when it's empty, you'll have to break that habit too. [*In operant conditioning, this is part of "preparing the training arena."*]

Begin by moving the cat's current litter box from wherever it is to one side of the toilet. Make sure he knows where it is and uses it. Rest (this means doing nothing for a period of between a day and a week, depending on how flappable your cat is). Next put something—a stack of newspapers, a phone book, a cardboard box—under the litter box to raise it, say, about an inch. (Magazines are too slick; you don't want the litter box sliding around and making your cat feel insecure. Tape the litter box down if you need to.) Rest. Get another box or phone book and raise it a little higher. Rest. Continue this process until the bottom of the litter box is level with the top of the toilet seat. (For Misha I raised it about two inches per day.) [*Notice that this is the step-by-step process typically used in shaping.*]

At the beginning of this process, your cat could just step into the litter box; later he began jumping up into it, until at some point he probably started jumping up onto the toilet seat first and stepping into the box from there. Lift the seat on your toilet and measure the inside diameter of the top of the bowl at its widest point. Venture forth and buy a metal mixing bowl of that diameter. Do not (I discovered this the hard way) substitute a plastic bowl. A plastic bowl will not support the cat's weight and will bend, dropping into the toilet bowl and spilling litter everywhere, not to mention startling the cat.

Now you move the litter box over so that it's sitting directly over the toilet seat. (If your cat has shown reluctance over previous changes, you might want to split this into two stages, moving it halfway onto the seat and then fully over.) Take away the stack of phone books or whatever you used. Rest. [*Again, notice that everything has to be done in small steps. This is the heart of the shaping process—requiring too large a step will stop the process.*]

Here's the cool part. Take away the litter box entirely. (Ta da!) Nestle the metal mixing bowl inside the toilet bowl and lower the seat. Fill the bowl with about two inches of litter (all of this is much easier if you have the tiny granules of litter that can be scooped out and flushed).

Naturally, any humans using the toilet at this point will want to remove the metal bowl prior to their own use and replace it afterward. The next week or two the whole process is likely to be something of an annoyance; if you begin to think it's not worth it, just remember that you will never have to clean a litter box again.

Watch your cat using the bathroom in the metal bowl. Count the number of feet he gets up on the toilet seat (as opposed to down in the bowl of litter). The higher the number, the luckier you are and the easier your job is going to be …

… because next you have to teach him proper squatting posture. Catch him beginning to use the toilet as much of the time as possible and show him where his feet are supposed to go. Just lift them right out of the bowl and place them on the seat (front legs in the middle, hind legs on the outside). If he starts out with three or, heaven forbid, all four feet in the bowl, just get the front two feet out first. Praise him all over the place every time he completes the activity in this position. [*The praise is the positive reinforcement and should be done with each successful step.*]

(Misha is very doglike in that he craves approval and praise. If your cat is indifferent to this sort of thing, you can also reward him with small food treats and wean him from them later when the toilet behavior has "set." Just keep the treats as small and infrequent as

This cat is being trained to use the toilet employing the learning techniques discussed in this section.

Part of the training may include learning to press the flush handle.

possible—half a Pounce™ or similar treat per occasion should be plenty.) [*If treats are too frequent, it will make it difficult to phase out the reinforcer after the behavior is well learned*.]

When he is regularly using the toilet with his front feet out (and some cats naturally start from this position), begin lifting a hind foot out and placing it on the seat outside the front paws. Your cat will probably find this awkward at first and try to replace the foot in the litter. Be persistent. Move that foot four times in a row if you have to, until it stays there. Praise and/or treat.

Repeat with the other hind foot, until your cat learns to balance in that squat. Once he's getting all four feet regularly on the seat, it's all easy from here.

Which is fortunate, because the last bit is also the most unpleasant. I suggest that you postpone this stage until you have at least a weekend, and preferably several days, when you (or another responsible party) will be at home most of the time. I skipped through this part in about two days; I only hope that your cat allows you to move along that fast.

Begin reducing the litter in the bowl. Go as fast as he'll feel comfortable with, because as the litter decreases, the odor increases. You'll want to be home at this point so that you can praise him and dump out the contents of the bowl immediately after he's finished, to minimize both the smell and the possibility that your cat, in a confused attempt to minimize the smell on his own, tries to cover it up with litter that no longer exists and ends up tracking unpleasantness into the rest of the house.

By the time you're down to a token teaspoonful of litter in the bottom of the bowl, your next-door neighbors will probably be aware of the precise instant your cat has used the toilet. This is as bad as it gets. The next time you rinse out the metal bowl, put a little bit of water in the bottom. Increase the water level each time, just as you decreased the litter level. Remember—if at any point Felix looks nervous enough about the change to give the whole thing up and take his business to the corner behind the door, back up a step or two and try the thing again more slowly. [*Shaping takes a lot of patience, depending on the behavior being shaped and the learning ability of the animal—or person*.]

Once the water in the mixing bowl is a couple of inches deep and your cat is comfortable with the whole thing, you get to perform the last bit of magic. Take the mixing bowl away, leaving the bare toilet. (Lid Up, Seat Down.)

### Questions for Further Discussion

1. Why would this technique probably not work with a dog?
2. Are there any safety concerns with teaching a cat in this way?
3. Are there any other difficulties that might arise when doing this training?

# Chapter Summary

### Definition of Learning

**5.1** Define the term *learning*.

- Learning is any relatively permanent change in behavior brought about by experience or practice and is different from maturation, which is genetically controlled.

### It Makes Your Mouth Water: Classical Conditioning

**5.2** Identify the key elements of classical conditioning as demonstrated in Pavlov's classic experiment.

- Pavlov accidentally discovered the phenomenon in which one stimulus can, through pairing with another stimulus, come to produce a similar response. He called this "classical conditioning."

- The unconditioned stimulus (UCS) is the stimulus that is naturally occurring and produces the innate, or involuntary, unconditioned response (UCR). Both are called "unconditioned" because they are not learned.

- The conditioned stimulus (CS) begins as a neutral stimulus, but when paired with the unconditioned stimulus, it eventually begins to elicit an involuntary, and automatic behavior on its own. The response to the conditioned stimulus is called the "conditioned response" (CR), and both stimulus and response are learned.

- Pavlov paired a sound with the presentation of food to dogs and discovered several principles for classical conditioning: The neutral stimulus (NS) and UCS must be paired several times, and the CS must precede the UCS by only a few seconds.

- Other important aspects of classical conditioning include stimulus generalization, stimulus discrimination, extinction, spontaneous recovery, and higher-order conditioning.

## 5.3 Apply classical conditioning to examples of phobias, taste aversions, and drug dependency.

- Watson was able to demonstrate that an emotional disorder called a phobia could be learned through classical conditioning by exposing a baby to a white rat and a loud noise, producing conditioned fear of the rat in the baby.
- Conditioned taste aversions occur when an organism becomes nauseated some time after eating a certain food, which then becomes aversive to the organism.
- Some kinds of conditioned responses are more easily learned than others because of biological preparedness.
- Pavlov believed that the NS became a substitute for the UCS through association in time.
- The cognitive perspective asserts that the CS has to provide some kind of information or expectancy about the coming of the UCS in order for conditioning to occur.

## What's In It for Me? Operant Conditioning

## 5.4 Identify the contributions of Thorndike and Skinner to the concept of operant conditioning.

- Thorndike developed the law of effect: A response followed by a pleasurable consequence will be repeated, but a response followed by an unpleasant consequence will not be repeated.
- B. F. Skinner named the learning of voluntary responses "operant conditioning" because voluntary responses are what we use to operate in the world around us.

## 5.5 Differentiate between primary and secondary reinforcers and positive and negative reinforcement.

- Skinner developed the concept of reinforcement, the process of strengthening a response by following it with a pleasurable, rewarding consequence.
- A primary reinforcer is something such as food or water that satisfies a basic, natural drive, whereas a secondary reinforcer is something that becomes reinforcing only after being paired with a primary reinforcer.
- In positive reinforcement, a response is followed by the presentation of a pleasurable stimulus, whereas in negative reinforcement, a response is followed by the removal or avoidance of an unpleasant stimulus.
- Shaping is the reinforcement of successive approximations to some final goal, allowing behavior to be molded from simple behavior already present in the organism.
- Extinction, generalization and discrimination, and spontaneous recovery also occur in operant conditioning.

## 5.6 Identify the four schedules of reinforcement.

- Continuous reinforcement occurs when each and every correct response is followed by a reinforcer.

- Partial reinforcement, in which only some correct responses are followed by reinforcement, is much more resistant to extinction. This is called the partial reinforcement effect.
- In a fixed interval schedule of reinforcement, at least one correct response must be made within a set interval of time to obtain reinforcement.
- In a variable interval schedule of reinforcement, reinforcement follows the first correct response made after an interval of time that changes for each reinforcement opportunity.
- In a fixed ratio schedule of reinforcement, a certain number of responses is required before reinforcement is given.
- In a variable ratio schedule of reinforcement, a varying number of responses is required to obtain reinforcement.

## 5.7 Identify the effect that punishment has on behavior.

- Punishment is any event or stimulus that, when following a response, makes that response less likely to happen again.
- In punishment by application, a response is followed by the application or experiencing of an unpleasant stimulus, such as a spanking.
- In punishment by removal, a response is followed by the removal of some pleasurable stimulus, such as taking away a child's toy for misbehavior.
- A person who uses aggressive punishment, such as spanking, can act as a model for aggressive behavior. This will increase aggressive behavior in the one being punished, which is an undesirable response.
- Punishment of both kinds normally has only a temporary effect on behavior.
- Punishment can be made more effective by making it immediate and consistent and by pairing punishment of the undesirable behavior with reinforcement of the desirable one.

## 5.8 Explain the concepts of discriminant stimuli, extinction, generalization, and spontaneous recovery as they relate to operant conditioning.

- Discriminative stimuli are cues, such as a flashing light on a police car or a sign on a door that says "Open," which provide information about what response to make in order to obtain reinforcement.
- Shaping, extinction, generalization and discrimination, and spontaneous recovery are other concepts in operant conditioning.
- Instinctive drift is the tendency for an animal that is being trained by operant conditioning to revert to instinctive patterns of behavior rather than maintaining the trained behavior.

## 5.9 Describe how operant conditioning is used to change animal and human behavior.

- Operant conditioning can be used in many settings on both animals and people to change, or modify, behavior. This use is termed *behavior modification* and includes the use of reinforcement and shaping to alter behavior.
- Token economies are a type of behavior modification in which secondary reinforcers, or tokens, are used.

- Applied behavior analysis (ABA) is the modern version of behavior modification and makes use of functional analysis and behavioral techniques to change human behavior.
- Neurofeedback is a modified version of biofeedback in which a person learns to modify the activity of his or her brain.

## Cognitive Learning Theory

**5.10  Explain the concept of latent learning.**

- Cognitive learning theory states that learning requires cognition, or the influence of an organism's thought processes.
- Tolman found that rats that were allowed to wander in a maze but were not reinforced still showed evidence of having learned the maze once reinforcement became possible. He termed this hidden learning *latent learning*, a form of cognitive learning.

**5.11  Explain how Köhler's studies demonstrated that animals can learn by insight.**

- Köhler found evidence of insight, the sudden perception of the relationships among elements of a problem, in chimpanzees.

**5.12  Summarize Seligman's studies on learned helplessness.**

- Seligman found that dogs that had been placed in an inescapable situation failed to try to escape when it became possible to do so, remaining in the painful situation as if helpless to leave.

Seligman called this phenomenon "learned helplessness" and found parallels between learned helplessness and depression.

## Observational Learning

**5.13  Describe the process of observational learning.**

- Observational learning is acquired by watching others perform, or model, certain actions.
- Bandura's famous Bobo doll experiment demonstrated that young children will imitate the aggressive actions of a model even when there is no reinforcement for doing so.

**5.14  List the four elements of observational learning.**

- Bandura determined that four elements needed to be present for observational learning to occur: attention, memory, imitation, and desire.

## Applying Psychology to Everyday Life: Can You Really Toilet Train Your Cat?

**5.15  Describe an example of conditioning in the real world.**

- Writer Karawynn Long used shaping, reinforcement, and classical conditioning to train her cat to use the toilet in her bathroom instead of a litter box.

# Test Yourself

*Pick the best answer.*

1. Sheila almost got hit by a car at a street corner because she was too busy texting on her phone. From that day on, Sheila looks before she reaches the street corner. Her change in behavior is a result of
   a. learning.
   b. memory.
   c. motivation.
   d. both sensation and perception.

2. At home, you rattle the chain on your dog's leash every time you prepare to take him for a walk. After several episodes like this, you find that your dog comes running to the front door even when you pick up the leash to put it back in the closet. In this example, what is the conditioned stimulus?
   a. going for a walk
   b. the sound of the leash
   c. the front door
   d. the dog runs to the door

3. A child has been classically conditioned to fear a white rat. If the child does not show fear when shown a black rat, this is called
   a. stimulus generalization.
   b. stimulus discrimination.
   c. spontaneous recovery.
   d. extinction.

4. During the cold winter, you have stopped taking your dog for walks. What's more, your dog has gotten used to the fact that when you accidentally rattle his leash, he isn't going for a walk, and subsequently he doesn't come running to the front door. What has occurred?
   a. stimulus generalization
   b. stimulus discrimination
   c. spontaneous recovery
   d. extinction

5. Rhonda had tartar sauce with her fish one night. The next morning she was nauseated and sick for much of the day. The next time she was offered the chance to go out for fish, she felt queasy and declined. Her queasiness at the thought of fish with tartar sauce was probably due to
   a. higher-order conditioning.
   b. a conditioned taste aversion.
   c. stimulus substitution.
   d. stimulus generalization.

6. Caitlin works in the psychology department's rat lab. In her studies, she found that many of her lab rats would develop a conditioned taste aversion to certain foods after as little as one trial. Caitlin's psychology professor refers to this as a classic example of
   a. biological preparedness.
   b. psychological preparedness.
   c. instinctive drift.
   d. stimulus substitution.

7. Blake finds that if he washes his car prior to going out on the town, more of his friends want to ride along with him. What theory would best explain his willingness to always wash and clean his car before going out?
   a. Thorndike's law of effect
   b. Skinner's theory of operant conditioning
   c. Pavlov's theory of classical conditioning

8. In classical conditioning, behavior typically is _____, whereas with operant conditioning, behavior is _____.
   a. rewarded; punished
   b. biological; internal
   c. voluntary; involuntary
   d. involuntary; voluntary

9. Where do secondary reinforcers get their power from?
   a. Classical conditioning
   b. Law of effect
   c. Observational theory
   d. Insight theory

10. Positive reinforcement results in _____ in the target behavior and negative reinforcement results in _____ in the target behavior.
    a. an increase; a decrease
    b. an increase; an increase
    c. a decrease; a decrease
    d. a decrease; an increase

11. Belinda has a terrible headache. If she takes some aspirin so as to make her headache go away, this would be an example of
    a. positive reinforcement.
    b. negative reinforcement.
    c. punishment.
    d. generalization.

12. Ben gets paid every 2 weeks. In one 2-week period, he works a total of 20 hours. During another 2-week period, he worked a total of 50 hours. Regardless of the total number of hours he works each week, he is paid every 2 weeks. What schedule of reinforcement is being used?
    a. fixed ratio
    b. variable ratio
    c. fixed interval
    d. variable interval

13. Denise is grounded for coming home after curfew. Additionally, her parents have taken away her cell phone for a month. Losing her cell phone privileges is an example of
    a. negative reinforcement.
    b. punishment by application.
    c. punishment by removal.
    d. learned helplessness.

14. What is the relationship between negative reinforcement and punishment?
    a. Both tend to strengthen a response.
    b. Both tend to weaken a response.
    c. Negative reinforcement strengthens a response, while punishment weakens a response.
    d. Negative reinforcement weakens a response, while punishment strengthens a response.

15 Which of the following is an example of the use of extinction with operant conditioning?
    a. A mother ignores her child's temper tantrum so that the behavior ultimately goes away.
    b. A mother gives in to her child's demands for candy by buying the child some chocolate so as to quiet him or her.
    c. A mother spanks a child when he or she starts throwing a tantrum.
    d. A mother gives a child chocolate prior to him or her asking for it so as to keep a tantrum from occurring in the first place.

16. Studies by Keller and Marian Breland found that many animals exhibit instinctive drift. What does this mean?
    a. The animals studied could not learn any skills even with the use of reinforcement.
    b. The animals studied would learn skills through reinforcement but eventually revert to their genetically controlled patterns of behavior.
    c. The animals studied would learn skills through reinforcement, and they remained that way no matter how much reinforcement they were given.
    d. The animals studied could only learn skills similar to those found in the wild.

17. Jose was lying in bed when he suddenly realized how he might deal with a fast-approaching deadline at work. When his coworkers asked how he came up with his idea, he said, "It just came to me out of nowhere." Psychologists would refer to this as
    a. latent learning.
    b. learned helplessness.
    c. insight learning.
    d. observational learning.

18. Jody failed repeatedly in college algebra. Finally, she gave up and was seriously considering dropping out of college. One day, her best friend offered to personally help her if she signed up for college algebra again, but she refused. What concept might explain her reluctance?
    a. latent learning
    b. learned helplessness
    c. insight learning
    d. observational learning

19. What does AMID stand for?
    a. Attention, Memory, Intention, Detention
    b. Attention, Memory, Imitation, Desire
    c. Ask, Memory, Imitate, Develop
    d. Association, Memory, Imitation, Desires

20. Darla has noticed how some of her friends have lost weight and gotten trim by exercising 1 to 2 hours each day. However, she has no plans to imitate their behavior. What component of Bandura's model of observational learning will explain why Darla has not started a similar weight-loss program?
    a. Darla's unconscious does not believe she can achieve the goal.
    b. Darla is not motivated, nor does she have the desire to begin the program.
    c. Darla's self-esteem must first be addressed.
    d. Darla's unwillingness may be a sign of mental disorder.

# 6 Memory

How is your memory of events? Do you find that you remember events from your past differently than others who were also present at that time?
After you have answered the question, watch the video to compare the answers of other students to yours.

▶ The response entered here will be saved to your notes and may be collected by your instructor if he/she requires it.

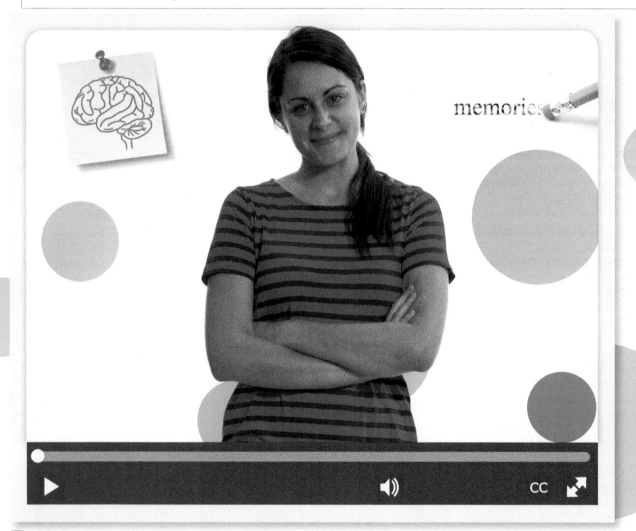

👁 Watch the Video

## Why study memory?

Without memory, how would we be able to learn anything? The ability to learn is the key to our very survival, and we cannot learn unless we can remember what happened the last time a particular situation arose. Why study forgetting? If we can learn about the ways in which we forget information, we can apply that learning so that unintended forgetting occurs less frequently.

# Learning Objectives

**6.1** Identify the three processes of memory.

**6.2** Explain how the different models of memory work.

**6.3** Describe the process of sensory memory.

**6.4** Describe short-term memory, and differentiate it from working memory.

**6.5** Explain the process of long-term memory, including nondeclarative and declarative forms.

**6.6** Identify the effects of cues on memory retrieval.

**6.7** Differentiate the retrieval processes of recall and recognition.

**6.8** Describe how some memories are automatically encoded into long-term memory.

**6.9** Explain how the constructive processing view of memory retrieval accounts for forgetting and inaccuracies in memory.

**6.10** Describe the "curve of forgetting."

**6.11** Identify some common reasons people forget things.

**6.12** Explain the biological bases of memory in the brain.

**6.13** Identify the biological causes of amnesia.

**6.14** Explain how sleep, exercise, and diet affect memory.

# What Is Memory?

Is memory a place or a process? The answer to that question is not simple. In reading through this chapter, it will become clear that memory is a process but that it also has a "place" in the brain as well. Perhaps the best definition of **memory** is an active system that receives information from the senses, puts that information into a usable form, organizes it as it stores it away, and then retrieves the information from storage (adapted from Baddeley, 1996, 2003).

## THREE PROCESSES OF MEMORY

**6.1** **Identify the three processes of memory.**

Although there are several different models of how memory works, all of them involve the same three processes: getting the information into the memory system, storing it there, and getting it back out.

**PUTTING IT IN: ENCODING**   The first process in the memory system is to get sensory information (sight, sound, etc.) into a form that the brain can use. This is called **encoding**. Encoding is the set of mental operations that people perform on sensory information to convert that information into a form that is usable in the brain's storage systems. For example, when people hear a sound, their ears turn the vibrations in the air into neural messages from the auditory nerve (*transduction*), which make it possible for the brain to interpret that sound. **L I N K** to Learning Objective 3.1.

 💬 It sounds like memory encoding works just like the senses—is there a difference?

Encoding is not limited to turning sensory information into signals for the brain. Encoding is accomplished differently in each of three different storage systems of memory. In one system, encoding may involve rehearsing information over and over to keep it in memory, whereas in another system, encoding involves elaborating on the meaning of the information—but let's elaborate on that later.

**KEEPING IT IN: STORAGE**   The next step in memory is to hold on to the information for some period of time in a process called **storage**. The period of time will actually be of different lengths, depending on the system of memory being used. For example, in one system of memory, people hold on to information just long enough to work with it, about 20 seconds or so. In another system of memory, people hold on to information more or less permanently.

**GETTING IT OUT: RETRIEVAL**   The biggest problem many people have is **retrieval**, that is, getting the information they know they have out of storage. Have you ever handed in an essay test and *then* remembered several other things you could have said? Retrieval problems are discussed thoroughly in a later section of this chapter.

## MODELS OF MEMORY

**6.2** **Explain how the different models of memory work.**

Exactly how does memory work? When the storage process occurs, where does that information go and why? Memory experts have proposed several different ways of looking at memory. The model that many researchers once felt was the most comprehensive* and has perhaps been the most influential over the last several decades is the **information-processing model**. This approach focuses on the way information

---

*comprehensive: all-inclusive, covering everything.

## memory

an active system that receives information from the senses, puts that information into a usable form, and organizes it as it stores it away, and then retrieves the information from storage.

## encoding

the set of mental operations that people perform on sensory information to convert that information into a form that is usable in the brain's storage systems.

## storage

holding on to information for some period of time.

## retrieval

getting information that is in storage into a form that can be used.

## information-processing model

model of memory that assumes the processing of information for memory storage is similar to the way a computer processes memory in a series of three stages.

is handled, or processed, through three different systems of memory. The processes of encoding, storage, and retrieval are seen as part of this model.

While it is common to refer to the three systems of the information-processing model as *stages* of memory, that term seems to imply a sequence of events. While many aspects of memory formation may follow a series of steps or stages, there are those who see memory as a simultaneous* process, with the creation and storage of memories taking place across a series of mental networks "stretched" across the brain (McClelland & Rumelhart, 1988; Plaut & McClelland, 2010; Rumelhart et al., 1986). This simultaneous processing allows people to retrieve many different aspects of a memory all at once, facilitating much faster reactions and decisions. This model of memory, derived from work in the development of artificial intelligence (AI), is called the **parallel distributed processing (PDP) model**. In the AI world, PDP is related to *connectionism*, the use of artificial neural networks to explain the mental abilities of humans (Bechtel & Abrahamsen, 2002; Clark, 1991; Marcus, 2001; Schapiro & McClelland, 2009).

The information-processing model assumes that the length of time that a memory will be remembered depends on the stage of memory in which it is stored. Other researchers have proposed that a memory's duration.** depends on the depth (i.e., the effort made to understand the meaning) to which the information is processed or encoded (Cermak & Craik, 1979; Craik & Lockhart, 1972). If the word *BALL* is flashed on a screen, for example, and people are asked to report whether the word was in capital letters or lowercase, the word itself does not have to be processed very much at all—only its visual characteristics need enter into conscious attention. But if those people were to be asked to use that word in a sentence, they would have to think about what a ball is and how it can be used. They would have to process its meaning, which requires more mental effort than processing just its "looks." This model of memory is called the **levels-of-processing model**. Numerous experiments have shown that thinking about the meaning of something is a deeper level of processing and results in longer retention of the word (Cermak & Craik, 1979; Craik & Tulving, 1975; Paul et al., 2005; Watson et al., 1999).

👁 **Watch** the **Video** *Depth of Processing*

---

*simultaneous: all at the same time.
**duration: how long something lasts.

**parallel distributed processing (PDP) model**

a model of memory in which memory processes are proposed to take place at the same time over a large network of neural connections.

**levels-of-processing model**

model of memory that assumes information that is more "deeply processed," or processed according to its meaning rather than just the sound or physical characteristics of the word or words, will be remembered more efficiently and for a longer period of time.

 So which model is right?

"Which model is right?" is not the correct question. The correct question is, *Which model explains the findings of researchers about how memory works?* The answer to that question is that all of these models can be used to explain some, if not all, research findings. Each of these views of the workings of memory can be seen as speaking to different aspects of memory. For example, the information-processing model provides a "big picture" view of how the various memory systems relate to each other—how the "memory machine" works. The PDP model is less about the mechanics of memory and more about the connections and timing of memory processes. The depth to which information is processed can be seen to address the strength of those parallel connections within each of the three memory systems, with strength and duration of the memory increasing as the level of processing deepens.

While the information-processing model is no longer the primary way current memory researchers view the processes of memory, it is historically important and provides a handy way to talk about how memory seems to work. We're going to explore a lot of memory concepts in this chapter and will look at many of these concepts in the framework of this older model just because it's a little easier to talk about these concepts in these terms—terms many of you have probably heard in daily use. If you should decide to specialize in the study of memory, you'll no doubt have a better grasp of the latest memory theories because you understand the historical view from which they arose. Many of those more current ideas will also be covered in later sections of this chapter as well.

## Concept Map L.O. 6.1, 6.2

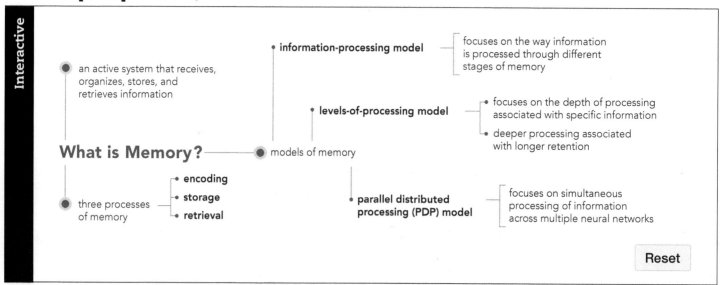

# Practice Quiz How much do you remember?

*Pick the best answer.*

**1.** Human memory consists of multiple systems that have the ability to store information for periods of time that range from _____ to _____.

    **a.** seconds; hours     **c.** minutes; decades

    **b.** seconds; our lifetime     **d.** hours; our lifetime

**2.** Ruth has just finished her research paper and handed it in. As she walks out of the classroom, she realizes that there were a few more things she should have included in the paper. Ruth's problem is in the memory process of

    **a.** encoding.     **c.** retrieval.

    **b.** storage.     **d.** retention.

**3.** Which model of memory suggests that memory processes occur throughout a neural network simultaneously?
   **a.** levels-of-processing model
   **b.** parallel distributed processing model
   **c.** information-processing model
   **d.** three-stage model

**4.** Research has demonstrated you can enhance your memory for a specific word if you think about its meaning, how it can be used, and by giving a personal example of its use. This is best accounted for by which model of memory?
   **a.** levels-of-processing model
   **b.** parallel distributed processing model
   **c.** information-processing model
   **d.** three-stage model

# The Information-Processing Model: Three Memory Systems

The link between cognitive psychology and information-processing theory was discussed briefly in Chapter One. Information-processing theory, which looks at how memory and other thought processes work, bases its model for human thought on the way that a computer functions (Massaro & Cowan, 1993). Data are encoded in a manner that the computer can understand and use. The computer stores that information on a disc, hard drive, or—these days—a memory stick, and then the data are retrieved out of storage as needed. It was also information-processing theorists who first proposed that there are three types of memory systems (see **Figure 6.1**), sensory memory, short-term memory, and long-term memory (Atkinson & Shiffrin, 1968).

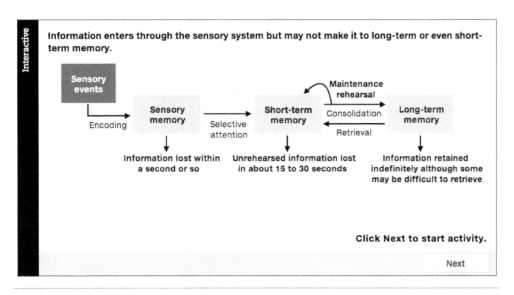

**Figure 6.1** Three-Stage Process of Memory

Information enters through the sensory system, briefly registering in sensory memory. Selective attention filters the information into short-term memory, where it is held while attention (rehearsal) continues. If the information receives enough rehearsal (maintenance or elaborative), it will enter and be stored in long-term memory.

**SENSORY MEMORY: WHY DO PEOPLE DO DOUBLE TAKES?**

**6.3** Describe the process of sensory memory.

**Sensory memory** is the first system in the process of memory, the point at which information enters the nervous system through the sensory systems—eyes, ears, and so on. Think of it as a door that is open for a brief time. Looking through the door, one can see many people and objects, but only some of them will actually make it through the door itself. Sensory memory is a kind of door onto the world.

**sensory memory**

the very first stage of memory, where raw information from the senses is held for a very brief period of time.

Information is encoded into sensory memory as neural messages in the nervous system. As long as those neural messages are traveling through the system, it can be said that people have a "memory" for that information that can be accessed if needed. For example, imagine that Elaina is driving down the street, looking at the people and cars on either side of her vehicle. All of a sudden she thinks, "What? Was that man wearing any pants?" and she looks back to check. How did she know to look back? Her eyes had already moved past the possibly pantless person, but some part of her brain must have just processed what she saw (most likely it was the reticular formation, which notices new and important information). This is called a "double take" and can only be explained by the presence, however brief, of a memory for what she saw. (L)(I)(N)(K) to Learning Objective 2.10.

There are two kinds of sensory memory that have been studied extensively. They are the iconic (visual) and echoic (auditory) sensory systems.

**ICONIC SENSORY MEMORY**   The example of seeing the possibly pantless person is an example of how the visual sensory system works. The visual sensory system is often called **iconic memory**, and it only lasts for a fraction of a second. *Icon* is the Greek word for "image." Iconic memory was studied in several classic experiments by George Sperling (1960), as shown in the *Classic Studies in Psychology* feature.

---

# Classic Studies in Psychology
## Sperling's Iconic Memory Test

George Sperling had found in his early studies that if he presented a grid of letters using a machine that allowed very fast presentation, his subjects could only remember about four or five of the letters, no matter how many had been presented.

Sperling became convinced that this method was an inaccurate measure of the capacity of iconic memory because the human tendency to read from top to bottom took long enough that the letters on the bottom of the grid may have faded from memory by the time the person had "read" the letters at the top. He developed a technique called the *partial report method,* in which he showed a grid of letters similar to those in **Figure 6.2** but immediately sounded a high, medium, or low tone just after the grid was shown. Subjects were told to report the top row of letters if they heard the high tone, the middle row for the medium tone, or the lowest row for the low tone. As they didn't hear the tone until after the grid went away, they couldn't look at just one row in advance.

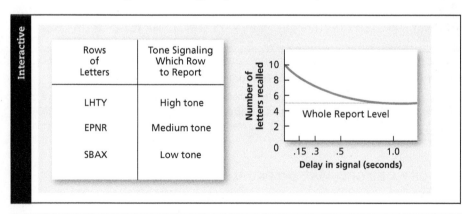

**Figure 6.2**   Iconic Memory Test

Sample grid of letters for Sperling's test of iconic memory. To determine if the entire grid existed in iconic memory, Sperling sounded a tone associated with each row after the grid's presentation. Participants were able to recall the letters in the row for which they heard the tone. The graph shows the decrease in the number of letters recalled as the delay in presenting the tone increased.

**iconic memory**

visual sensory memory, lasting only a fraction of a second.

Using this technique, Sperling found that subjects could accurately report any of the three rows. This meant that the entire grid was in iconic memory and available to the subjects. The capacity of iconic memory is everything that can be seen at one time.

Sperling also found that if he delayed the tone for a brief period of time, after about a second, subjects could no longer recall letters from the grid any better than they had during the whole report procedure. The iconic information had completely faded out of sensory memory in that brief time.

### Questions for Further Discussion

1. How might the results of the partial report method be different for people from cultures in which text is read from right to left or top to bottom?
2. Would the results be different if more detailed pictures were used instead of letters?

In real life, information that has just entered iconic memory will be pushed out very quickly by new information, a process called *masking* (Cowan, 1988). Research suggests that after only a quarter of a second, old information is replaced by new information.

Although it is rare, some people do have what is properly called **eidetic imagery**, or the ability to access a visual sensory memory over a long period of time. Although the popular term *photographic memory* is often used to mean this rare ability, some people claiming to have photographic memory actually mean that they have an extremely good memory. Having a very good memory and having eidetic imagery ability are two very different things. People with eidetic imagery ability might be able to look quickly at a page in a book, then by focusing on a blank wall or piece of paper, "read" the words from the image that still lingers in their sensory memory. Although it might sound like a great ability to have while in college, it actually provides little advantage when taking tests, because it's just like having an open-book test. If a student can't *understand* what's written on the pages, having the book open is useless. It is unknown why some people have this ability, but it is more common in children and tends to diminish by adolescence or young adulthood (Haber, 1979; Leask et al., 1969; Stromeyer & Psotka, 1971).

  If iconic memory lasts such a brief time, what use is it to us?

Iconic memory actually serves a very important function in the visual system. Chapter Three discussed the way the eyes make tiny little movements called *microsaccades* that keep vision from adapting to a constant visual stimulus, so that what is stared at steadily doesn't slowly disappear. Iconic memory helps the visual system view surroundings as continuous and stable in spite of these saccadic movements. It also allows enough time for the brain stem to decide if the information is important enough to be brought into consciousness—like the possibly pantless person.

**ECHOIC SENSORY MEMORY** Another type of sensory system is **echoic memory**, or the brief memory of something a person has heard. A good example of echoic memory is the "What?" phenomenon. You might be reading or concentrating on the television, and your parent, roommate, or friend walks up and says something to you. You sit there for a second or two and then say "What? Oh—yes, I'm ready to eat now," or whatever comment is appropriate. You didn't really process the statement from the other person as he or she said it. You heard it, but your brain didn't interpret it immediately. Instead, it took several seconds for you to realize that (1) something was said, (2) it may have been important, and (3) you'd better try to remember what it was. If you realize all this within about 4 seconds (the duration of echoic memory), you will more than likely be able to "hear" an echo of the statement in your head, a kind of "instant replay."

Pablo Picasso was one of the most creative artists of his time. Here he is seen drawing an abstract of a woman in the air with a flashlight, using multiple exposures of the camera. What does his ability to "hold" the light image in his head long enough to complete the abstract tell us about his visual memory?

**eidetic imagery**
the ability to access a visual memory for 30 seconds or more.

**echoic memory**
auditory sensory memory, lasting only 2–4 seconds.

Once these piano strings have been attached to the tuning pins, the piano can be tuned. Tuning a piano requires the use of echoic sensory memory. What other occupations might find a good echoic memory to be an asset?

Echoic memory's capacity is limited to what can be heard at any one moment and is smaller than the capacity of iconic memory, although it lasts longer—about 2–4 seconds (Schweickert, 1993).

Echoic memory is very useful when a person wants to have meaningful conversations with others. It allows the person to remember what someone said just long enough to recognize the meaning of a phrase. As with iconic memory, it also allows people to hold on to incoming auditory information long enough for the lower brain centers to determine whether processing by higher brain centers is needed. It is echoic memory that allows a musician to tune a musical instrument, for example. The memory of the tuning fork's tone lingers in echoic memory long enough for the person doing the tuning to match that tone on the instrument.

💬 What happens if the lower brain centers send the information on to the higher centers?

### SHORT-TERM MEMORY

**6.4** **Describe short-term memory, and differentiate it from working memory.**

If an incoming sensory message is important enough to enter consciousness, that message will move from sensory memory to the next process of memory, called **short-term memory (STM)**. Unlike sensory memory, short-term memories may be held for up to 30 seconds and possibly longer through *maintenance rehearsal*.

**SELECTIVE ATTENTION: HOW INFORMATION ENTERS**   **Selective attention** is the ability to focus on only one stimulus from among all sensory input (Broadbent, 1958). It is through selective attention that information enters our STM system. In Dr. Donald E. Broadbent's original filter theory, a kind of "bottleneck" occurs between the processes of sensory memory and short-term memory. Only a stimulus that is "important" enough (determined by a kind of "pre-analysis" accomplished by the attention centers in the brain stem) will make it past the bottleneck to be consciously analyzed for meaning in STM. When a person is thinking actively about information, that information is said to be conscious and is also in STM. 🅛🅘🅝🅚 to Learning Objective 4.1.

It is somewhat difficult to use Broadbent's selective-attention filter to explain the "cocktail-party effect" that has been long established in studies of perception and attention (Bronkhorst, 2000; Cherry, 1953; Handel, 1989). If you've ever been at a party where there's a lot of noise and several conversations going on in the background but you are still able to notice when someone says your name, you have experienced this effect. In this kind of a situation, the areas of the brain that are involved in selective attention had to be working—even though you were not consciously aware of it. Then, when that important bit of information (your name) "appeared," those areas somehow filtered the information into your conscious awareness—in spite of the fact that you were not paying conscious attention to the other background noise (Hopfinger et al., 2000; Mesgarani & Chang, 2012; Stuss et al., 2002).

Dr. Anne M. Treisman (Treisman, 2006; Triesman & Gelade, 1980) proposed that selective attention operates in a two-stage filtering process: In the first stage, incoming stimuli in sensory memory are filtered on the basis of simple physical characteristics, similar to Broadbent's original idea. Instead of moving to STM or being lost, however, there is only a lessening (*attenuation*) of the "signal strength" of unselected sensory stimuli in comparison to the selected stimuli. In the second stage, only the stimuli that meet a certain threshold of importance are processed. Since the attenuated stimuli are still present at this second stage, something as subjectively important as one's own name may be able to be "plucked" out of the attenuated incoming stimuli. Even when deeply asleep, when the selective attention filter is not working at its peak level, it still functions:

**short-term memory (STM)**

the memory system in which information is held for brief periods of time while being used.

**selective attention**

the ability to focus on only one stimulus from among all sensory input.

A sleeping mother will awake to her infant's cries while sleeping through louder, less important sounds such as a passing train (LaBerge, 1980).

What happens when information does pass through the selective attention filter and into short-term memory? Short-term memory tends to be encoded primarily in auditory (sound) form. That simply means that people tend to "talk" inside their own heads. Although some images are certainly stored in STM in a kind of visual "sketchpad" (Baddeley, 1986), auditory storage accounts for much of short-term encoding. Even a dancer planning out moves in her head will not only visualize the moves but also be very likely to verbally describe the moves in her head as she plans. An artist planning a painting certainly has visual information in STM but may also keep up an internal dialogue that is primarily auditory. Research in which participants were asked to recall numbers and letters showed that errors were nearly always made with numbers or letters that *sounded like* the target but not with those that *looked like* the target word or number (Acheson et al., 2010; Conrad & Hull, 1964).

Each person at this gathering is involved in a conversation with others, with dozens of such conversations going on at the same time all around. Yet if a person in another conversation says the name of one of the people in the crowd, that person in the crowd will be able to selectively attend to his or her name. This is known as the "cocktail-party effect."

**WORKING MEMORY**   Some memory theorists use the term *working memory* as another way of referring to short-term memory—they see no difference between the two concepts. Others feel that the two systems are quite different. In this discussion, we will use short-term memory to refer to simple storage and working memory as relating to storage and manipulation of information (Baddeley, 2012). Short-term memory has traditionally been thought of as a thing or a place into which information is put. As mentioned earlier, current memory researchers prefer to think of memory in terms of a more continuous system, where information flows from one form of representation to another, rather than a series of "boxes." **Working memory** is therefore thought of as an active system that processes the information present within short-term memory. Working memory is thought to consist of three interrelated systems: a central executive (a kind of "CEO" or "Big Boss") that controls and coordinates the other two systems, the visuospatial "sketchpad" of sorts that was mentioned earlier, and a kind of auditory action "recorder" or phonological loop (Baddeley, 1986, 2012; Baddeley & Hitch, 1974; Baddeley & Larsen, 2007; Engle & Kane, 2004). The central executive acts as interpreter for both the visual and auditory information, and the visual and auditory information are themselves contained in short-term memory. For example, when a person is reading a book, the sketchpad will contain images of the people and events of the particular passage being read, while the recorder "plays" the dialogue in the person's head. The central executive helps interpret the information from both systems and pulls it all together. In a sense, then, short-term memory can be seen as being a part of the working memory system (Acheson et al., 2010; Bayliss et al., 2005; Colom et al., 2006; Kail & Hall, 2001).

Another way to think about short-term memory is as a desk where you do your work. You might pull some files out of storage (permanent memory), or someone might hand you some files (sensory input). While the files are on your desk, you can see them, read them, and work with them (working memory). The "files" are now conscious material and will stay that way as long as they are on the desk. Less important files may get "thrown out" (forgotten as you fail to pay attention to them), while more important files might get stored away (permanent memory), where they are not conscious until they are once again retrieved—brought out of the desk.

**CAPACITY: THE MAGICAL NUMBER SEVEN, OR FIVE, OR FOUR**   George Miller (1956) wanted to know how much information humans can hold in short-term memory at any one time (or how many "files" will fit on the "desk"). He reviewed several memory studies, including some using a memory test called the *digit-span test*, in which a series of numbers is read to subjects in the study who are then asked to recall the numbers in order. Each series gets longer and longer, until the subjects cannot recall any of the numbers in order.

**working memory**
an active system that processes the information in short-term memory.

What you will discover is that most everyone you test will get past the first two sequences of numbers, but some people will make errors on the six-digit span, about half of the people you test will slip up on the seven-digit span, and very few will be able to get past the nine-digit span without errors. This led Miller to conclude that the capacity of STM is about seven items or pieces of information, plus or minus two items, or from five to nine bits of information. Miller called this the magical number seven, plus or minus two. Since Miller's review of those early studies and subsequent conclusion about the capacity of STM being about seven items, research methods have improved, as has our knowledge and understanding of memory processes. Current research suggests younger adults can hold three to five items of information at a time if a strategy of some type is not being used. When the information is in the form of longer, similar-sounding, or unfamiliar words, however, that capacity reduces until it is only about four items (Cowan, 2001; Cowan et al., 2005; Palva et al., 2010).

There is a way to "fool" STM into holding more information than is usual. (Think of it as "stacking" related files on the desk.) If the bits of information are combined into meaningful units, or chunks, more information can be held in STM. If someone were to recode the last sequence of numbers as "654-789-3217," for example, instead of 10 separate bits of information, there would only be three "chunks" that read like a phone number. This process of recoding or reorganizing the information is called *chunking*. Chances are that anyone who can easily remember more than eight or nine digits in the digit-span test is probably recoding the numbers into chunks. To see how well you do at remembering numbers, participate in the *Digit Span* experiment ⊙ **Simulate** the **Experiment,** *Digit Span*.

**WHY DO YOU THINK THEY CALL IT "SHORT TERM"?** How long is the "short" of short-term memory? Research has shown that short-term memory lasts from about 12 to 30 seconds without rehearsal (Atkinson & Shiffrin, 1968; J. Brown, 1958; Peterson & Peterson, 1959). After that, the memory seems to rapidly "decay" or disappear. In fact, the findings of one study with mice suggest that in order to form new memories, old memories must be "erased" by the formation of newly formed neurons (Kitamura et al., 2009). The hippocampus only has so much storage room, and while many of the memories formed there will be transferred to more permanent storage in other areas of the brain, some memories, without rehearsal, will decay as new neurons (and newer memories) are added to the already existing neural circuits.

💬 What do you mean by rehearsal? How long can short-term memories last if rehearsal is a factor?

Most people realize that saying something they want to remember over and over again in their heads can help them remember it longer. We sometimes do this with names we want to remember, or a phone number we want to remember long enough to enter into our phone's contacts. This is a process called **maintenance rehearsal**. With maintenance rehearsal, a person is simply continuing to pay attention to the information to be held in memory, and since attention is how that information got into STM in the first place, it works quite well (Atkinson & Shiffrin, 1968; Rundus, 1971). With this type of rehearsal, information will stay in short-term memory until rehearsal stops. When rehearsal stops, the memory rapidly decays and is forgotten. If anything interferes with maintenance rehearsal, memories are also likely to be lost. For example, if someone is trying to count items by reciting each number out loud while counting, and someone else asks that person the time and interferes with the counting process, the person who is counting will probably forget what the last number was and have to start all over again. Short-term memory helps people keep track of things like counting.

Interference in STM can also happen if the amount of information to be held in STM exceeds its capacity. Information already in STM may be "pushed out" to make room for newer information. This is why it might be possible to remember the first few

This restaurant server is taking the woman's order without writing it down. Which memory system is he using? Do you think that his capacity for items in this system may be greater than someone who does not try to remember items like this often?

**maintenance rehearsal**

practice of saying some information to be remembered over and over in one's head in order to maintain it in short-term memory.

names of people you meet at a party, but as more names are added, they displace the older names. A better way to remember a person's name is to associate the name with something about the person's appearance, a process that may help move the name from STM into more permanent storage. This more permanent storage is the process of long-term memory, which is the topic of the next section.

Working memory is an important area of research and has implications for understanding not only intelligence but also learning and attention disorders such as attention-deficit/hyperactivity disorder, and various dementia-related memory problems (Alloway et al., 2009; Kensinger et al., 2003; Martinussen et al., 2005). Researchers have trained mice to improve their working memory and found that the mice become more intelligent with improved working memory (e.g., Light et al., 2010). Other researchers have found that working memory is helpful in solving mathematical problems but may actually hurt the ability to solve creative problems (Wiley & Jarosz, 2012). Creative problem solving seems to benefit from a less focused approach than the focused attention taking place in working memory.

### LONG-TERM MEMORY

**6.5** **Explain the process of long-term memory, including nondeclarative and declarative forms.**

The third stage of memory is **long-term memory (LTM)**, the system into which all the information is placed to be kept more or less permanently. In terms of capacity, LTM seems to be unlimited for all practical purposes (Bahrick, 1984; Barnyard & Grayson, 1996). In fact, researchers now think the capacity of the human brain may be as much as 10 times greater than previously estimated (Bartol et al., 2015). Think about it: Would there ever really come a time when you could not fit one more piece of information into your head? When you could learn nothing more? If humans lived much longer lives, there might be a finite end to the capacity of LTM stores. But in practical terms, there is always room for more information (in spite of what some students may believe).

**DURATION** As for duration, the name *long term* says it all. There is a relatively permanent physical change in the brain itself when a memory is formed. That means that many of the memories people have stored away for a long, long time—even since childhood—may still be there. That does not mean that people can always retrieve those memories. The memories may be *available* but not *accessible*, meaning that they are still there, but for various reasons (discussed later under the topic of forgetting) people cannot "get to" them. It's like knowing that there is a certain item on the back of the top shelf of the kitchen cabinet but having no ladder or step stool to reach it. The item is there (available), but you can't get to it (not accessible).

"Long term" also does not mean that *all* memories are stored forever; our personal memories are too numerous to be permanently retained, for example. Nor do we store every single thing that has ever happened to us. We only store long-lasting memories of events and concepts that are meaningful and important to us.

> 💬 I once memorized a poem by repeating it over and over— that's maintenance rehearsal, right? Since I still remember most of the poem, it must be in long-term memory. Is maintenance rehearsal a good way to get information into long-term memory?

Information that is rehearsed long enough may actually find its way into long-term memory. After all, it's how most people learned their Social Security number and the letters of the alphabet (although people cheated a little on the latter by putting the alphabet to music, which makes it easier to retrieve). Most people tend to learn poems and the multiplication tables by maintenance rehearsal, otherwise known as rote learning.

These students are rehearsing for a concert. They will use maintenance rehearsal (repeating the musical passages over and over) until they can play their parts perfectly. The movements of their fingers upon their instruments will be stored in long-term memory. How is this kind of long-term memory different from something like the memorized lines of one's part in a play?

**long-term memory (LTM)**

the system of memory into which all the information is placed to be kept more or less permanently.

*Rote* is like "rotating" the information in one's head, saying it over and over again. But maintenance rehearsal is not the most efficient way of putting information into long-term storage, because to get the information back out, one has to remember it almost exactly as it went in. Try this: What is the 15th letter of the alphabet? Did you have to recite or sing through the alphabet song to get to that letter?

Although many long-term memories are encoded as images (think of the *Mona Lisa*), sounds, smells, or tastes (Cowan, 1988), in general, LTM is encoded in meaningful form, a kind of mental storehouse of the meanings of words, concepts, and all the events that people want to keep in mind. Even the images, sounds, smells, and tastes involved in these events have some sort of meaning attached to them that gives them enough importance to be stored long term. If STM can be thought of as a working "surface" or desk, then LTM can be thought of as a huge series of filing cabinets behind the desk, in which files are stored in an organized fashion, according to meaning. Files have to be placed in the cabinets in a certain organized fashion to be useful—how could anyone ever remember any kind of information quickly if the files were not in some order? The best way to encode information into LTM in an organized fashion is to make it meaningful through *elaborative rehearsal.*

**ELABORATIVE REHEARSAL**    **Elaborative rehearsal** is a way of increasing the number of *retrieval cues* (stimuli that aid in remembering) for information by connecting new information with something that is already well known (Craik & Lockhart, 1972; Postman, 1975). For example, the French word *maison* means "house." A person could try to memorize that (using maintenance rehearsal) by saying over and over, "*Maison* means house, *maison* means house." But it would be much easier and more efficient if that person simply thought, "*Maison* sounds like masons, and masons build houses." That makes the meaning of the word tie in with something the person already knows (masons, who lay stone or bricks to build houses) and helps in remembering the French term. In older versions of this concept, elaborative rehearsal was seen as a way of transferring information from STM to LTM, but that makes the two forms of memory sound like boxes. The "memory stores as boxes" idea is one of the main criticisms of the information-processing model because it makes it seem as though there is nothing in between STM and LTM. This is not the case; research has shown that information can exist anywhere along the continuum of actively paying attention to an experience and permanent storage of that experience (Raaijmakers, 1993; Raaijmakers & Shiffrin, 2003).

As discussed in the beginning of this chapter, Craik and Lockhart (1972) theorized that information that is more "deeply processed," or processed according to its meaning rather than just the sound or physical characteristics of the word or words, will be remembered more efficiently and for a longer period of time. As the levels-of-processing approach predicts, elaborative rehearsal is a deeper kind of processing than maintenance rehearsal and so leads to better long-term storage (Craik & Tulving, 1975).

💬 I can remember a lot of stuff from my childhood. Some of it is stuff I learned in school and some of it is more personal, like the first day of school. Are these two different kinds of long-term memories?

**TYPES OF LONG-TERM INFORMATION**    Long-term memories include general facts and knowledge, personal facts, and even skills that can be performed. Memory for skills is a type of *nondeclarative memory*, or *implicit memory*, because the skills have to be demonstrated and not reported. Memory for facts is called *declarative memory*, or *explicit memory*, because facts are things that are known and can be declared (stated outright). These two types of long-term memory are quite different, as the following sections will explain.

**NONDECLARATIVE (IMPLICIT) LTM**    Memories for things that people know how to do, like tying shoes and riding a bicycle, are a kind of LTM called **nondeclarative (implicit) memory**. The fact that people have the knowledge of how to tie their shoes, for example, is *implied* by

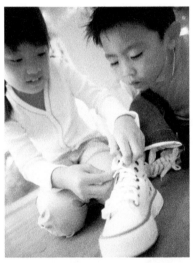

Nondeclarative knowledge, such as tying one's shoes, often must be learned by doing, as it is difficult to put into words. Once this child learns how to tie shoes, the knowledge will always be there to retrieve.

**elaborative rehearsal**

a method of transferring information from STM into LTM by making that information meaningful in some way.

**nondeclarative (implicit) memory**

type of long-term memory including memory for skills, procedures, habits, and conditioned responses. These memories are not conscious but are implied to exist because they affect conscious behavior.

the fact that they can actually tie them. Nondeclarative memories also include emotional associations, habits, and simple conditioned reflexes that may or may not be in conscious awareness, which are often very strong memories (Schacter & Wagner, 2013; Squire & Kandel, 2009). Ⓛ Ⓘ Ⓝ Ⓚ to Learning Objective 5.2, 5.3, 5.5. Referring to Chapter Two, the amygdala is the most probable location for emotional associations, such as fear, and the cerebellum in the hind-brain is responsible for storage of memories of conditioned responses, skills, and habits (Dębiec et al., 2010; Kandel & Siegelbaum, 2013; Squire et al., 1993).

Evidence that separate areas of the brain control nondeclarative memory comes from studies of people with damage to the hippocampal area of the brain. This damage causes them to have **anterograde amnesia**, in which new long-term declarative memories cannot be formed. (This disorder is fairly accurately represented by the character of Lenny in the 2000 motion picture *Memento*.) One of the more famous anterograde amnesia patients, H.M., is discussed in detail later in this chapter.

In one study of nondeclarative memory (Cohen et al., 1985), patients with this disorder were taught how to solve a particular puzzle called the Tower of Hanoi (see **Figure 6.3**). Although the patients were able to learn the sequence of moves necessary to solve the puzzle, when brought back into the testing room at a later time, they could not remember ever having seen the puzzle before—or, for that matter, the examiner. Yet they were able to solve the puzzle even while claiming that they had never seen it before. Their nondeclarative memories for how to solve the puzzle were evidently formed and stored in a part of the brain separate from the part controlling the memories they could no longer form. Even people with Alzheimer's disease, who also suffer from anterograde amnesia, do not forget how to walk, talk, fasten clothing, or even tie shoes (although they do lose motor ability because the brain eventually fails to send the proper signals). These are all implicit, nondeclarative memories. In fact, it would be rare to find someone who has lost nondeclarative memory. Literally, these are the kind of memories people "never forget."

Nondeclarative memories are not easily retrieved into conscious awareness. Have you ever tried to tell someone how to tie shoes without using your hands to show them? The subjects in the Tower of Hanoi study also provide a good example of implicit memory, as they could solve the puzzle but had no conscious knowledge of how to do so. Such knowledge is in people's memories because they use this information, but they are often not consciously aware of this knowledge (Roediger, 1990). A memory from one's early childhood of being frightened by a dog, for example, may not be a conscious memory in later childhood but may still be the cause of that older child's fear of dogs. Conscious memories for events in childhood, on the other hand, are usually considered to be a different kind of long-term memory called declarative memory.

**DECLARATIVE (EXPLICIT) LTM**  Nondeclarative memory is about the things that people can *do*, but **declarative (explicit) memory** is about all the things that people can *know*—the facts and information that make up knowledge. People know things such as the names of the planets in the solar system, that adding 2 and 2 makes 4, and that a noun is the name of a person, place, or thing. These are general facts, but people also know about the things that have happened to them personally. For example, I know what I ate for breakfast this morning and what I saw on the way to work, but I don't know what you had for breakfast or what you might have seen. There are two types of declarative long-term memories, *semantic* and *episodic* (Nyberg & Tulving, 1996).

One type of declarative memory is general knowledge that anyone has the ability to know. Most of this information is what is learned in school or by reading. This kind of LTM is called **semantic memory**. The word *semantic* refers to meaning, so this kind of knowledge is the awareness of the meanings of words, concepts, and terms as well as names of objects, math skills, and so on. This is also the type of knowledge that is used on game shows such as *Jeopardy*. Semantic memories, like nondeclarative memories, are relatively permanent. But it is possible to "lose the way" to this kind of memory, as discussed later in the section on forgetting.

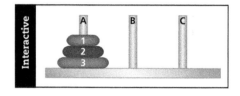

**Figure 6.3**  Tower of Hanoi

The Tower of Hanoi is a puzzle that is solved in a series of steps by moving one disk at a time. The goal is to move all of the disks from peg A to peg C; the rules are that a larger disk cannot be moved on top of a smaller one and a disk cannot be moved if there are other disks on top of it. Amnesic patients were able to learn the procedure for solving the puzzle but could not remember that they knew how to solve it.

**anterograde amnesia**

loss of memory from the point of injury or trauma forward, or the inability to form new long-term memories.

**declarative (explicit) memory**

type of long-term memory containing information that is conscious and known.

**semantic memory**

type of declarative memory containing general knowledge, such as knowledge of language and information learned in formal education.

The other kind of factual memory is the personal knowledge that each person has of his or her daily life and personal history, a kind of autobiographical* memory (LePort et al., 2012). Memories of what has happened to people each day, certain birthdays, anniversaries that were particularly special, childhood events, and so on are called **episodic memory**, because they represent episodes from their lives. Unlike nondeclarative and semantic long-term memories, episodic memories tend to be updated and revised more or less constantly. You can probably remember what you had for breakfast today, but what you had for breakfast 2 years ago on this date is most likely a mystery. Episodic memories that are especially *meaningful,* such as the memory of the first day of school or your first date, are more likely to be kept in LTM (although these memories may not be as exact as people sometimes assume they are). The updating process is a kind of survival mechanism, because although semantic and nondeclarative memories are useful and necessary on an ongoing basis, no one really needs to remember every little detail of every day. As becomes obvious later, the ability to forget some kinds of information is very necessary.

Episodic and semantic memories are explicit memories because they are easily made conscious and brought from long-term storage into short-term memory. The knowledge of semantic memories such as word meanings, science concepts, and so on can be brought out of the "filing cabinet" and placed on the "desk" where that knowledge becomes *explicit*, or obvious. The same is often true of personal, episodic memories.

 But sometimes I can't remember all the names of the planets or what I had for breakfast yesterday. Doesn't that make these memories implicit instead of explicit?

The difference between implicit memories, such as how to balance on a bicycle, and explicit memories, such as naming all the planets, is that it is impossible or extremely difficult to bring implicit memories into consciousness. Explicit memories can be forgotten but always have the potential to be made conscious. When someone reminds you of what you had for breakfast the day before, for example, you will remember that you had that knowledge all along—it was just temporarily "mislaid." For a look at the connections among all these types of LTM, see **Figure 6.4.**

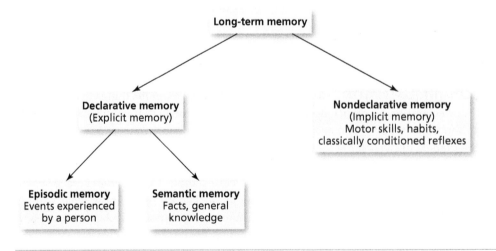

**Figure 6.4**  Types of Long-Term Memories

Long-term memory can be divided into declarative memories, which are factual and typically conscious (explicit) memories, and nondeclarative memories, which are skills, habits, and conditioned responses that are typically unconscious (implicit). Declarative memories are further divided into episodic memories (personal experiences) and semantic memories (general knowledge).

**episodic memory**

type of declarative memory containing personal information not readily available to others, such as daily activities and events.

*autobiographical: the story of a person's life as told by that person.

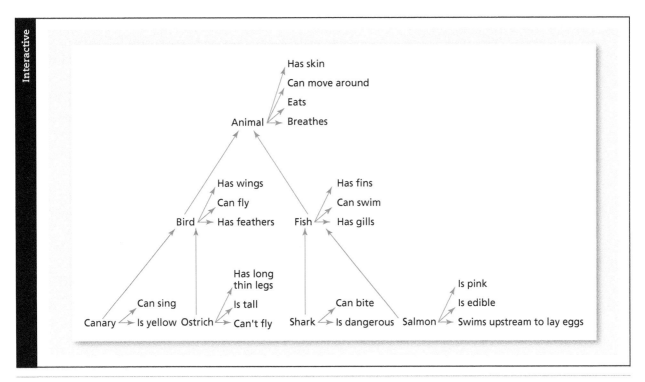

**Figure 6.5** An Example of a Semantic Network

In the semantic network model of memory, concepts that are related in meaning are thought to be stored physically near each other in the brain. In this example, canary and ostrich are stored near the concept node for "bird," whereas shark and salmon are stored near "fish." But the fact that a canary is yellow is stored directly with that concept.

**LONG-TERM MEMORY ORGANIZATION**   As stated before, LTM has to be fairly well organized for retrieval to be so quick. Can you remember the name of your first-grade teacher? If you can, how long did it take you to pull that name out of LTM and pull it into STM? It probably took hardly any time at all.

Research suggests that long-term memory is organized in terms of related meanings and concepts (Collins & Loftus, 1975; Collins & Quillian, 1969). In their original study, Allan Collins and M. Ross Quillian (1969) had subjects respond "true" or "false" as quickly as possible to sentences such as "a canary is a bird" and "a canary is an animal." Looking at **Figure 6.5**, it is apparent that information exists in a kind of network, with nodes (focal points) of related information linked to each other in a kind of hierarchy.* To verify the statement "a canary is a bird" requires moving to only one node, but "a canary is an animal" would require moving through two nodes and should take longer. This was exactly the result of the 1969 study, leading the researchers to develop the **semantic network model**, which assumes that information is stored in the brain in a connected fashion with concepts that are related to each other stored physically closer to each other than concepts that are not highly related (Collins & Quillian, 1969).

The PDP model (Rumelhart et al., 1986) discussed earlier in this chapter can be used to explain how rapidly the different points on the networks can be accessed. Although the access of nodes within a particular category (for example, *birds*) may take place in a serial fashion, explaining the different response times in the Collins and Quillian (1969) study, access across the entire network may take place in a parallel fashion, allowing several different concepts to be targeted at the same time (for example, one might be able to think about *birds, cats,* and *trees* simultaneously).

Perhaps the best way to think of how information is organized in LTM is to think about the Internet. A person might go to one Web site and from that site link to many other

**semantic network model**

model of memory organization that assumes information is stored in the brain in a connected fashion, with concepts that are related stored physically closer to each other than concepts that are not highly related.

*hierarchy: a ranked and ordered list or series.

related sites. Each related site has its own specific information but is also linked to many other related sites, and a person can have more than one site open at the same time. This may be very similar to the way in which the mind organizes the information stored in LTM.

---

**THINKING CRITICALLY**

In thinking about a typical day, how do you use each type of memory: nondeclarative, episodic, and semantic?

▶ | The response entered here will be saved to your notes and may be collected by your instructor if he/she requires it. |

Submit

---

## Concept Map  L.O. 6.3, 6.4, 6.5

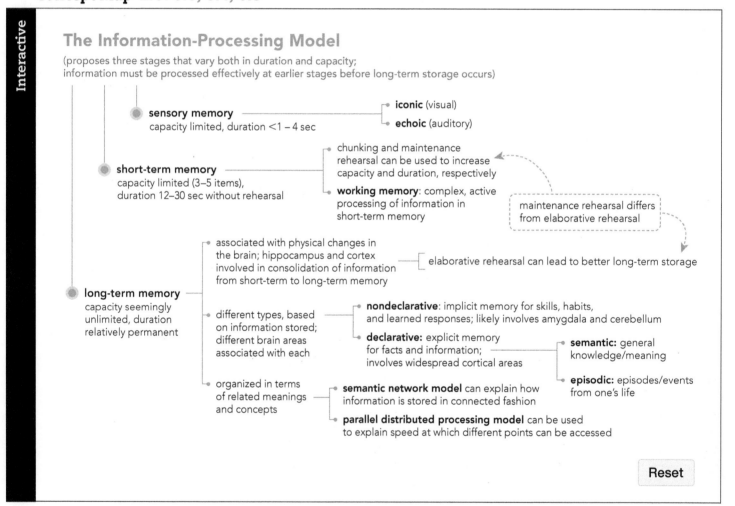

**Interactive**

### The Information-Processing Model

(proposes three stages that vary both in duration and capacity; information must be processed effectively at earlier stages before long-term storage occurs)

**sensory memory**
capacity limited, duration <1 – 4 sec
  - **iconic** (visual)
  - **echoic** (auditory)

**short-term memory**
capacity limited (3–5 items), duration 12–30 sec without rehearsal
  - chunking and maintenance rehearsal can be used to increase capacity and duration, respectively
  - **working memory**: complex, active processing of information in short-term memory

maintenance rehearsal differs from elaborative rehearsal

**long-term memory**
capacity seemingly unlimited, duration relatively permanent
  - associated with physical changes in the brain; hippocampus and cortex involved in consolidation of information from short-term to long-term memory
    - elaborative rehearsal can lead to better long-term storage
  - different types, based on information stored; different brain areas associated with each
    - **nondeclarative**: implicit memory for skills, habits, and learned responses; likely involves amygdala and cerebellum
    - **declarative**: explicit memory for facts and information; involves widespread cortical areas
      - **semantic**: general knowledge/meaning
      - **episodic**: episodes/events from one's life
  - organized in terms of related meanings and concepts
    - **semantic network model** can explain how information is stored in connected fashion
    - **parallel distributed processing model** can be used to explain speed at which different points can be accessed

Reset

---

# Practice Quiz    How much do you remember?

*Pick the best answer.*

**1.** _____ memories are said to linger in the mind for a few seconds, allowing people the chance to keep up with the flow of conversations and remember what was just said.
   **a.** Iconic
   **b.** Echoic
   **c.** Short-term
   **d.** Long-term

**2.** Information enters into short-term memory through a process known as _____.
   **a.** recency effect
   **b.** primacy effect
   **c.** selective attention
   **d.** repetition

**3.** Of the following, which is the most similar to the concept of long-term memory?
   **a.** a computer hard drive    **c.** a computer mouse
   **b.** a computer monitor    **d.** a computer keyboard

**4.** Amber meets a cute guy named Carson at a party. She wants to make sure she remembers his name, so she reminds herself that he has the same name as the capital of Nevada (Carson City). This transferring of information from short-term memory to long-term memory is an example of what type of rehearsal?
   **a.** repetitive    **c.** elaborative
   **b.** imagery    **d.** maintenance

**5.** Brenda has been able to tie her shoes since she was 4 but now finds it difficult to explain to her baby brother how to tie his shoes, but she can easily demonstrate it for him. Brenda's memory for shoe tying is best characterized as a _____ memory.
   **a.** declarative (explicit)    **c.** episodic
   **b.** semantic    **d.** nondeclarative (implicit)

**6.** When you take your final exam in your psychology class, what type of memory will you most certainly need to access to answer each question?
   **a.** nondeclarative    **c.** episodic
   **b.** semantic    **d.** working

# Getting It Out: Retrieval of Long-Term Memories

💬 My problem isn't so much getting information into my head; it's finding it later that's tough.

Oddly enough, most people's problems with getting information stored in LTM back out again have to do with *how* they put that information *into* LTM. Take the survey *What Do You Remember?* to learn more about what factors influence your own memories of events.

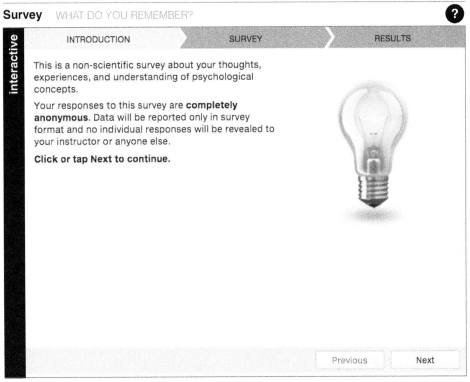

**Survey**  WHAT DO YOU REMEMBER?  ❓

| INTRODUCTION | SURVEY | RESULTS |
|---|---|---|

This is a non-scientific survey about your thoughts, experiences, and understanding of psychological concepts.

Your responses to this survey are **completely anonymous**. Data will be reported only in survey format and no individual responses will be revealed to your instructor or anyone else.

**Click or tap Next to continue.**

Previous    Next

⊙→ **Simulate** the **Experiment** *What Do You Remember?*

## RETRIEVAL CUES

**6.6  Identify the effects of cues on memory retrieval.**

Remember the previous discussion about maintenance rehearsal versus elaborative rehearsal? One of the main reasons that maintenance rehearsal is not a very good way

The results of the Godden and Baddeley (1975) study indicated the retrieval of words learned while underwater was higher when the retrieval also took place underwater. Similarly, words learned while out of water (on land) were retrieved at a higher rate out of the water.

When this bride and groom dance together later on in their marriage, they will be able to recall this moment at their wedding and the happiness they felt at that time. State-dependent learning makes it easier for people to recall information stored while in a particular emotional state (such as the happiness of this couple) if the recall occurs in a similar emotional state.

**encoding specificity**

the tendency for memory of information to be improved if related information (such as surroundings or physiological state) that is available when the memory is first formed is also available when the memory is being retrieved.

to get information into LTM is that saying something over and over gives only one kind of retrieval cue, the sound of the word or phrase. When people try to remember a piece of information by thinking of what it means and how it fits in with what they already know, they are giving themselves multiple cues for meaning in addition to sound. The more retrieval cues stored with a piece of information, the easier the retrieval of that information will be (Karpicke, 2012; Pyc et al., 2014; Roediger, 2000; Roediger & Guynn, 1996), which is the primary reason elaborative rehearsal enhances the formation of a memory. Ⓛ Ⓘ Ⓝ Ⓚ to Learning Objective PIA.6. Furthermore, we are not always aware of what cues are being associated. Remember from the discussion of nondeclarative memory, *priming* can occur where experience with information or concepts can improve later performance. And in many situations, we are not aware the improvement has taken place.

Although most people would assume that cues for retrieval would have to be directly related to the concepts being studied, the fact is that almost anything in one's surroundings is capable of becoming a cue. If you usually watch a particular television show while eating peanuts, for example, the next time you eat peanuts you might find yourself thinking of the show you were watching. This connection between surroundings and remembered information is called *encoding specificity*.

**ENCODING SPECIFICITY: CONTEXT EFFECTS ON MEMORY RETRIEVAL**   Have you ever had to take a test in a different classroom than the one in which you learned the material being tested? Do you think that your performance on that test was hurt by being in a different physical context? Researchers have found strong evidence for the concept of **encoding specificity**, the tendency for memory of any kind of information to be improved if retrieval conditions are similar to the conditions under which the information was encoded (Tulving & Thomson, 1973). These conditions, or cues, can be internal or external. *Context-dependent learning* may refer to the physical surroundings a person is in when they are learning specific information. For example, encoding specificity would predict that the best place to take one's chemistry test is in the same room in which you learned the material. Also, it's very common to walk into a room and know that there was something you wanted, but in order to remember it, you have to go back to the room you started in to use your surroundings as a cue for remembering.

In one study, researchers had students who were learning to scuba dive in a pool also learn lists of words while they were either out of the pool or in the pool under the water (Godden & Baddeley, 1975). Subjects were then asked to remember the two lists in each of the two conditions. Words that were learned while out of the pool were remembered significantly better when the subjects were out of the pool, and words that were learned underwater were more easily retrieved if the subjects were underwater while trying to remember.

**ENCODING SPECIFICITY: STATE-DEPENDENT LEARNING**   Physical surroundings at the time of encoding a memory are not the only kinds of cues that can help in retrieval. In another form of encoding specificity called *state-dependent learning*, memories formed during a particular physiological or psychological state will be easier to remember while in a similar state. For example, when you are fighting with someone, it's much easier to remember all of the bad things that person has done than to remember the good times. In one study (Eich & Metcalfe, 1989), researchers had subjects try to remember words that they had read while listening to music. Subjects read one list of words while listening to sad music (influencing their mood to be sad) and another list of words while listening to happy music. When it came time to recall the lists, the researchers again manipulated the mood of the subjects. The words that were read while subjects were in a happy mood were remembered better if the manipulated mood was also happy but far less well if the mood was sad. The reverse was also true.

## RECALL AND RECOGNITION

**6.7** **Differentiate the retrieval processes of recall and recognition.**

  Why do multiple-choice tests seem so much easier than essay tests?

There are two kinds of retrieval of memories, *recall* and *recognition*. It is the difference between these two retrieval methods that makes some kinds of exams seem harder than others. In **recall**, memories are retrieved with few or no external cues, such as filling in the blanks on an application form. **Recognition**, on the other hand, involves looking at or hearing information and matching it to what is already in memory. A word-search puzzle, in which the words are already written down in the grid and simply need to be circled, is an example of recognition. The following section takes a closer look at these two important processes.

**RECALL: HMM ... LET ME THINK** When someone is asked a question such as "Where were you born?" the question acts as the cue for retrieval of the answer. This is an example of recall, as are essay, short-answer, and fill-in-the-blank tests that are used to measure a person's memory for information (Borges et al., 1977; Gillund & Shiffrin, 1984; Raaijmakers & Shiffrin, 1992).

Whenever people find themselves struggling for an answer, recall has failed (at least temporarily). Sometimes the answer seems so very close to the surface of conscious thought that it feels like it's "on the tip of the tongue." (If people could just get their tongues out there far enough, they could read it.) This is sometimes called the *tip of the tongue (TOT)* phenomenon (Brown & McNeill, 1966; Burke et al., 1991). Although people may be able to say how long the word is or name letters that start or even end the word, they cannot retrieve the sound or actual spelling of the word to allow it to be pulled into the auditory "recorder" of STM so that it can be fully retrieved. This particular memory problem gets more common as we get older, although it should not be taken as a sign of oncoming dementia unless the increase is sudden (Osshera et al., 2012).

How can a person overcome TOT? The best solution is the one "everyone" seems to know: Forget about it. When you "forget about it," the brain apparently continues to work on retrieval. Sometime later (perhaps when you run across a similar-sounding word in your surroundings), the word or name will just "pop out." This can make for interesting conversations, because when that particular word does "pop out," it usually has little to do with the current conversation.

Another interesting feature of recall is that it is often subject to a kind of "prejudice" of memory retrieval, in which information at the beginning and the end of a list, such as a poem or song, tends to be remembered more easily and accurately. This is called the **serial position effect** (Murdock, 1962).

A good demonstration of this phenomenon involves instructing people to listen to and try to remember words that are read to them that are spaced about 4 or 5 seconds apart. People typically use maintenance rehearsal by repeating each word in their heads. They are then asked to write as many of the words down as they can remember. If the frequency of recall for each word in the list is graphed, it will nearly always look like the graph in **Figure 6.6** on the next page. To try this demonstration for yourself, participate in the *Serial Position Effect* experiment ▶ **Simulate** the **Experiment,** *Serial Position Effect.*

Words at the very beginning of the list tend to be remembered better than those in the middle of the list. This effect is called the **primacy effect** and is due to the fact that the first few words, when the listener has nothing already in STM to interfere with their rehearsal, will receive far more rehearsal time than the words in the middle, which are constantly being replaced by the next word on the list (Craik, 1970; Murdock, 1962).

At the end of the graph there is another increase in recall. This is the **recency effect**; it is usually attributed to the fact that the last word or two was *just heard* and is still in short-term memory for easy retrieval, with no new words entering to push the most

**recall**

type of memory retrieval in which the information to be retrieved must be "pulled" from memory with very few external cues.

**recognition**

the ability to match a piece of information or a stimulus to a stored image or fact.

**serial position effect**

tendency of information at the beginning and end of a body of information to be remembered more accurately than information in the middle of the body of information.

**primacy effect**

tendency to remember information at the beginning of a body of information better than the information that follows.

**recency effect**

tendency to remember information at the end of a body of information better than the information that precedes it.

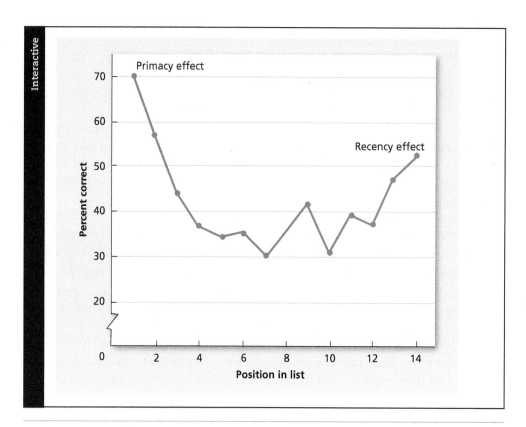

**Figure 6.6** Serial Position Effect

In the serial position effect, information at the beginning of a list will be recalled at a higher rate than information in the middle of the list (primacy effect), because the beginning information receives more rehearsal and may enter LTM. Information at the end of a list is also retrieved at a higher rate (recency effect), because the end of the list is still in STM, with no information coming after it to interfere with retrieval.

These people are waiting to audition for a play. The person who auditioned first and the one who auditioned last have the greatest chance of being remembered when the time comes for the director to choose. The serial position effect will cause the impression made by the actors who come in the "middle" to be less memorable.

recent word or words out of memory (Bjork & Whitten, 1974; Murdock, 1962). The serial position effect works with many different kinds of information. In fact, business schools often teach their students that they should try not to be "in the middle" for job interviews. Going first or last in the interview process is much more likely to make a person's interview more memorable.

Can knowledge of the serial position effect be of help to students trying to remember the information they need for their classes? Yes—students can take advantage of the recency effect by skimming back over their notes just before an exam. Knowing that the middle of a list of information is more likely to be forgotten means that students should pay more attention to that middle, and breaking the study sessions up into smaller segments helps reduce the amount of "middle to muddle." (Students can also use *mnemonic strategies* to help offset this memory problem, as well as others. Ⓛ Ⓘ Ⓝ Ⓚ to Learning Objective PIA.6.) Watch the video *Methods for Remembering* for additional mnemonic strategies.

Speaking of students and classes, practicing retrieval is obviously very important to the process of learning. In education, this is often called the *testing effect*, the fact that long-term memory is increased when students practice retrieving the information to be learned (Karpicke & Blunt, 2011; Karpicke, 2012; Pyc et al., 2014; Roediger & Karpicke, 2006). Retrieval practice is essentially what testing is all about, so even though you might want to groan over yet another test your instructor hands out, be grateful—it's all in the best interests of memory!

**RECOGNITION: HEY, DON'T I KNOW YOU FROM SOMEWHERE?** The other form of memory retrieval is *recognition*, the ability to match a piece of information or a stimulus to a

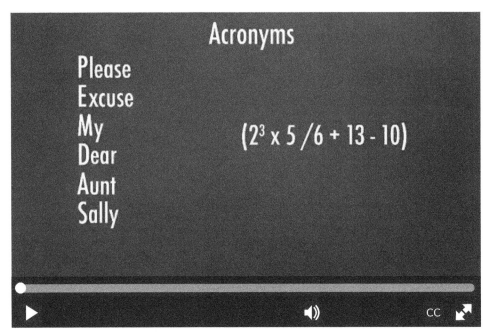

Acronyms

Please
Excuse
My
Dear
Aunt
Sally

$(2^3 \times 5 / 6 + 13 - 10)$

👁 **Watch** the **Video** *Methods for Remembering*

stored image or fact (Borges et al., 1977; Gillund & Shiffrin, 1984; Raaijmakers & Shiffrin, 1992). Recognition is usually much easier than recall because the cue is the actual object, word, sound, and so on that one is simply trying to detect as familiar and known. Examples of tests that use recognition are multiple-choice, matching, and true–false tests. The answer is right there and simply has to be matched to the information already in memory.

Recognition tends to be very accurate for images, especially human faces. In one study, more than 2,500 photographs were shown to participants at the rate of one every 10 seconds. Participants were then shown pairs of photographs in which one member of each pair was one of the previously seen photographs. Accuracy for identifying the previous photos was between 85 and 95 percent (Standing et al., 1970).

Recognition isn't foolproof, however. Sometimes, there is just enough similarity between a stimulus that is not already in memory and one that is in memory so that a *false positive* occurs (Muter, 1978). A false positive occurs when a person thinks that he or she has recognized (or even recalled) something or someone but in fact does not have that something or someone in memory.

False positives can become disastrous in certain situations. In one case, in a series of armed robberies in Delaware, word had leaked out that the suspect sought by police might be a priest. When police put Father Bernard Pagano in a lineup for witnesses to identify, he was the only one in the lineup wearing a priest's collar. Seven eyewitnesses identified him as the man who had robbed them. Fortunately for Father Pagano, the real robber confessed to the crimes halfway through Pagano's trial (Loftus, 1987). Eyewitness recognition can be especially prone to false positives, although most people seem to think that "seeing is believing." For more about the problems with eyewitnesses, see the following Classic Studies in Psychology.

ED? TED? FRED? NED? TIM? JIM?

WILL? BILL? HARRY? LARRY? BARRY?

*"Hey, good buddy! How you doin'?"*

*"Can't kick, big fella. What's shakin'?"*

# Classic Studies in Psychology
## Elizabeth Loftus and Eyewitnesses

Elizabeth Loftus is a distinguished professor of social ecology, a professor of law, and a professor of cognitive science at the University of California in Irvine. For more than 30 years, Dr. Loftus has been one of the world's leading researchers in the area of memory. Her focus has been on the accuracy of recall of memories—or rather, the inaccuracies of memory retrieval. She has been an expert witness or consultant in hundreds of trials, including that of Ted Bundy, the serial killer who eventually was executed in Florida (Neimark, 1996).

Loftus and many others have demonstrated time and again that memory is not an unchanging, stable process but rather is a constantly changing one. People continually update and revise their memories of events without being aware that they are doing so, and they incorporate information gained after the actual event, whether correct or incorrect.

Here is a summary of one of Loftus's classic studies concerning the ways in which eyewitness testimony can be influenced by information given after the event in question (Loftus, 1975).

In this experiment, Loftus showed subjects a 3-minute video clip taken from the movie. In this clip, eight demonstrators run into a classroom and eventually leave after interrupting the professor's lecture in a noisy confrontation. At the end of the video, two questionnaires were distributed containing one key question and 90 "filler" questions. The key question for half of the subjects was, "Was the leader of the four demonstrators who entered the classroom a male?" The other half were asked, "Was the leader of the twelve demonstrators who entered the classroom a male?" One week later, a new set of questions was given to all subjects in which the key question was, "How many demonstrators did you see entering the classroom?" Subjects who were previously asked the question incorrectly giving the number as "four" stated an average recall of 6.4 people, whereas those who were asked the question incorrectly giving the number as "twelve" recalled an average of 8.9 people. Loftus concluded that subjects were trying to compromise the memory of what they had actually seen—eight demonstrators—with later information. This study, along with the Father Pagano story and many others, clearly demonstrates the heart of Loftus's research: What people see and hear about an event after the fact can easily affect the accuracy of their memories of that event.

### Questions for Further Discussion

1. How might police officers taking statements about a crime avoid getting inaccurate information from eyewitnesses?

2. The Innocence Project (**www.innocenceproject.org**) helps prisoners prove their innocence through DNA testing. More than 300 people in the United States have been freed by this testing, and the average time they served in prison before release is 13 years. Is eyewitness testimony enough, or should DNA evidence be required for sending someone to prison?

Dr. Elizabeth Loftus is an internationally known expert on the accuracy of eyewitness testimony. She is often called on to testify in court cases.

## AUTOMATIC ENCODING: FLASHBULB MEMORIES

**6.8 Describe how some memories are automatically encoded into long-term memory.**

Although some long-term memories need extensive maintenance rehearsal or effortful encoding in the form of elaborative rehearsal to enter from STM into LTM, many other kinds of long-term memories seem to enter permanent storage with little or no effort at all, in a kind of **automatic encoding** (Kvavilashvili et al., 2009; Mandler, 1967; Schneider et al., 1984). People unconsciously notice and seem able to remember a lot of things, such as the passage of time, knowledge of physical space, and frequency of events. For example, a person might make no effort to remember how many times cars have passed down the street but when asked can give an answer of "often," "more than usual," or "hardly any."

A special kind of automatic encoding takes place when an unexpected event or episode in a person's life has strong emotional associations, such as fear, horror, or joy. Memories of highly emotional events can often seem vivid and detailed, as if the person's mind took a "flash picture" of the moment in time. These kinds of memories are called **flashbulb memories** (Hirst & Phelps, 2016; Kraha & Boals, 2014; Neisser, 1982; Neisser & Harsch, 1992; Winningham et al., 2000).

Many people share certain flashbulb memories. People of the "baby boomer" generation remember exactly where they were when the news came that President John F. Kennedy had been shot or the moment that Neil Armstrong first stepped on the surface of the moon. Younger generations may remember the horrific events of September 11, 2001, and the disastrous Hurricane Katrina. But personal flashbulb memories also exist. These memories tend to be major positive or negative emotional events, such as the first date, graduation, an embarrassing event, or a particularly memorable birthday party.

Why do flashbulb memories seem so vivid and exact? The answer lies in the emotions felt at the time of the event. Emotional reactions stimulate the release of hormones that have been shown to enhance the formation of long-term memories (Dolcos et al., 2005; McEwen, 2000; McGaugh, 2004; Sharot et al., 2004). But is this kind of memory really all that accurate? Although some researchers have found evidence for a high degree of accuracy in flashbulb memories of *major events*, such as the reelection of President Barack Obama in November 2012 or the tragic death of actor and comedian Robin Williams in 2014, others have found that while flashbulb memories are often convincingly real, they are just as subject to decay and alterations over time as other kinds of memories (Neisser & Harsch, 1992). In fact, memory of highly stressful events such as experiencing a crime has been shown to be less accurate than other memories (Loftus, 1975). Apparently, no memories are completely accurate after the passage of time. The next section will discuss some of the reasons for faulty memories.

Robin Williams died on August 11, 2014. His suicide shocked a multitude of fans and admirers. Events like this are so emotional for many people that the memories for the event are stored automatically, as if the mind had taken a "flash" picture of that moment in time. Such "flashbulb" memories seem to be very accurate but are actually no more accurate than any other memory.

### THE RECONSTRUCTIVE NATURE OF LONG-TERM MEMORY RETRIEVAL: HOW RELIABLE ARE MEMORIES?

**6.9** **Explain how the constructive processing view of memory retrieval accounts for forgetting and inaccuracies in memory.**

> 💬 I think my memory is pretty good, but my brother and I often have arguments about things that happened when we were kids. Why don't we have the same exact memories? We were both there!

People tend to assume that their memories are accurate when, in fact, memories are revised, edited, and altered on an almost continuous basis. The reason for the changes that occur in memory has to do with the way in which memories are formed as well as how they are retrieved.

**CONSTRUCTIVE PROCESSING OF MEMORIES** Many people have the idea that when they recall a memory, they are recalling it as if it were an "instant replay." As new memories are created in LTM, old memories can get "lost," but they are more likely to be changed or altered in some way (Baddeley, 1988). In reality, memories (including those very vivid flashbulb memories) are never quite accurate, and the more time that passes, the more inaccuracies creep in. The early twentieth-century memory schema

**automatic encoding**

tendency of certain kinds of information to enter longterm memory with little or no effortful encoding.

**flashbulb memories**

type of automatic encoding that occurs because an unexpected event has strong emotional associations for the person remembering it.

These men may engage in "Monday morning quarterbacking" as they apply hindsight to their memories of this game. Their memories of the game may be altered by information they get afterward from the television, newspapers, or their friends.

theorist Sir Frederic Bartlett (1932) saw the process of memory as more similar to creating a story than reading one already written. He viewed memory as a problem-solving activity in which the person tries to retrieve the particulars of some past event (the problem) by using current knowledge and inferring from evidence to create the memory (the solution; Kihlstrom, 2002).

Elizabeth Loftus, along with other researchers (Hyman, 1993; Hyman & Loftus, 1998, 2002), has provided ample evidence for the **constructive processing** view of memory retrieval. In this view, memories are literally "built," or reconstructed, from the information stored away during encoding. Each time a memory is retrieved, it may be altered or revised in some way to include new information or to exclude details that may be left out of the new reconstruction.

An example of how memories are reconstructed occurs when people, upon learning the details of a particular event, revise their memories to reflect their feeling that they "knew it all along." They will discard any incorrect information they actually had and replace it with more accurate information gained after the fact. This tendency of people to falsely believe that they would have accurately predicted an outcome without having been told about it in advance is called **hindsight bias** (Bahrick et al., 1996; Hoffrage et al., 2000). People who have ever done some "Monday morning quarterbacking" by saying that they knew all along who would win the game have fallen victim to hindsight bias.

## THINKING CRITICALLY

Think about the last time you argued with a family member about something that happened when you were younger. How might hindsight bias have played a part in your differing memories of the event?

▶ | The response entered here will be saved to your notes and may be collected by your instructor if he/she requires it. |

Submit

**MEMORY RETRIEVAL PROBLEMS**   Some people may say that they have "total recall." What they usually mean is that they feel that their memories are more accurate than those of other people. As should be obvious by now, true total recall is not a very likely ability for anyone to have. Here are some reasons people have trouble recalling information accurately.

**THE MISINFORMATION EFFECT**   Police investigators sometimes try to keep eyewitnesses to crimes or accidents from talking with each other. The reason is that if one person tells the other about something she has seen, the other person may later "remember" that same detail, even though he did not actually see it at the time. Such false memories are created by a person being exposed to information after the event. That misleading information can become part of the actual memory, affecting its accuracy (Loftus et al., 1978). This is called the **misinformation effect**. Loftus, in addition to her studies concerning eyewitness testimony, has also done several similar studies that demonstrate the misinformation effect. In one study, subjects viewed a slide presentation of a traffic accident. The actual slide presentation contained a stop sign, but in a written summary of the presentation, the sign was referred to as a yield sign. Subjects who were given this misleading information after viewing the slides were far less accurate in their memories for the kind of sign present than were subjects given no such information. One of the interesting points made by this study is that information that comes not only after the original event but also in an entirely different format (i.e., written instead of visual) can cause memories of the event to be incorrectly reconstructed.

**FALSE MEMORY SYNDROME**   If memory gets edited and changed when individuals are in a state of waking consciousness, alert and making an effort to retrieve information, how much more might memory be changed when individuals are being influenced by others or in an altered state of consciousness, such as hypnosis? *False-memory syndrome* refers to the creation of inaccurate or false memories through the suggestion of others, often while

**constructive processing**

referring to the retrieval of memories in which those memories are altered, revised, or influenced by newer information.

**hindsight bias**

the tendency to falsely believe, through revision of older memories to include newer information, that one could have correctly predicted the outcome of an event.

**misinformation effect**

the tendency of misleading information presented after an event to alter the memories of the event itself.

the person is under hypnosis (Frenda et al., 2014; Hochman, 1994; Laney & Loftus, 2013; Roediger & McDermott, 1995).

For example, research has shown that, although hypnosis may make it easier to recall some real memories, it also makes it easier to create false memories. Hypnosis also has been found to increase the confidence people have in their memories, regardless of whether those memories are real or false (Bowman, 1996). False memories have been accidentally created by therapists' suggestions during hypnotic therapy sessions. **LINK** to Learning Objective 4.9. For more information on false-memory syndrome, visit the Web site at **www.fmsfonline.org**.

Research suggests that false memories are created in the brain in much the same way as real memories are formed, especially when visual images are involved (Gonsalves et al., 2004). Researchers, using fMRI scans, looked at brain activity of individuals who were looking at real visual images and then were asked to imagine looking at visual images. They found that these same individuals were often unable to later distinguish between the images they had really seen and the imagined images when asked to remember which images were real or imagined. This might explain why asking people if they saw a particular person at a crime scene (causing them to imagine the image of that person) might affect the memories those people have of the crime when questioned sometime later—the person they were asked to think about may be falsely remembered as having been present. Other evidence suggests that false memories have much in common with the confabulations (stories that are made up but not intended to deceive) of people with dementia-related memory problems and that both forms of false memories involve a lower-than-normal level of activity in the part of the frontal lobe associated with doubt and skepticism (Mendez & Fras, 2011). Clearly, memories obtained through hypnosis should not be considered accurate without solid evidence from other sources.

 But I've heard about people who under hypnosis remember being abused as children. Aren't those memories sometimes real?

The fact that some people recover false memories under certain conditions does not mean that child molestation does not really happen; nor does it mean that a person who was molested might not push that unwanted memory away from conscious thought. Molestation is a sad fact, with one conservative estimate stating that nearly 20 percent of all females and 7 percent of all males have experienced molestation during childhood (Abel & Osborn, 1992). There are also many therapists and psychological professionals who are quite skilled at helping clients remember events of the past without suggesting possible false memories, and they find that clients do remember information and events that were true and able to be verified but were previously unavailable to the client (Dalenberg, 1996). False-memory syndrome is not only harmful to the persons directly involved but also makes it much more difficult for genuine victims of molestation to be believed when they do recover their memories of the painful traumas of childhood.

So can we trust any of our memories at all? There is evidence to suggest that false memories cannot be created for just any kind of memory content. The *memories* must at least be plausible, according to the research of cognitive psychologist and memory expert Kathy Pezdek, who with her colleagues has done several studies demonstrating the resistance of children to the creation of implausible false memories (Hyman et al., 1998; Pezdek et al., 1997; Pezdek & Hodge, 1999).

In the 1999 study, Pezdek and Hodge asked children to read five different summaries of childhood events. Two of these events were false, but only one of the two false events was plausible (e.g., getting lost). Although the children all were told that all of the events happened to them as small children, the results indicated that the plausible false events were significantly more likely to be "remembered" as false memories than were the implausible

As this young woman observes the activity outside the window, she is storing some of the things she sees in memory while ignoring others. If she were to witness a crime, how would investigators know if her memories of the events were accurate? Would hypnotizing her to help her remember be effective? Why or why not?

false events (e.g., getting a rectal enema). A second experiment (Pezdek & Hodge, 1999) found similar results: Children were significantly less likely to form a false memory for an implausible false event than for a plausible false event.

The idea that only plausible events can become false memories runs contrary to the earlier work of Loftus and colleagues and to research concerning some very implausible false memories that have been successfully implanted, such as a memory for satanic rituals and alien abductions (Mack, 1994). Loftus and colleagues (Mazzoni et al., 2001) conducted several experiments in which they found that implausible events could be made more plausible by having the experimenters provide false feedback to the participants, who read articles telling of the implausible events as if they had actually happened to other people. The false feedback involved telling the participants that their responses to a questionnaire about fears were typical of people who had been through one of the false events (much as a well-meaning therapist might suggest to a client that certain anxieties and feelings are typical of someone who has been abused). These manipulations were so successful that participants not only developed false memories for the events but also even contradicted their own earlier statements in which they denied having these experiences in childhood. The researchers concluded that there are two steps that must occur before people will be likely to interpret their thoughts and fantasies about false events as true memories:

1. The event must be made to seem as plausible as possible.
2. Individuals are given information that helps them believe that the event could have happened to them personally.

The personality of the individual reporting such a memory also matters, it seems. In one study, people who claimed to have been abducted by aliens (an implausible event) were compared to a control group with no such memories on a measure of false-memory recall and false recognition. Those who reported recovered memories of alien abduction were far more likely to recall or recognize items that were false than were the controls (Clancy et al., 2002). Other variables that predicted a higher false recall and recognition response were susceptibility to hypnosis, symptoms of depression, and the tendency to exhibit odd behavior and unusual beliefs (such as past-life regression or the healing ability of crystals).

## Concept Map L.O. 6.6, 6.7, 6.8, 6.9

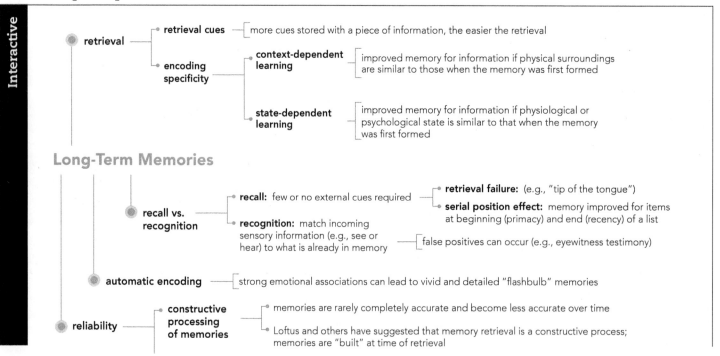

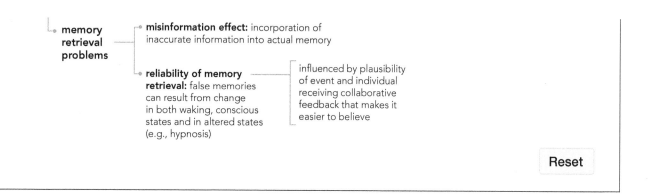

&#8627; **memory retrieval problems**

—&#8226; **misinformation effect:** incorporation of inaccurate information into actual memory

&#8627; **reliability of memory retrieval:** false memories can result from change in both waking, conscious states and in altered states (e.g., hypnosis)

influenced by plausibility of event and individual receiving collaborative feedback that makes it easier to believe

Reset

# Practice Quiz    How much do you remember?

*Pick the best answer.*

1. What concept suggests that the best place to study for your psychology final to ensure good retrieval of concepts is your psychology classroom?
   a. serial position effect
   b. encoding specificity
   c. tip-of-the-tongue phenomenon
   d. automatic encoding

2. Jaclynn had written a grocery list but accidentally left it at home. Trying to remember the list, Jaclynn remembers what was at the beginning of the list and what was at the end but not those things in the middle. This is an example of
   a. encoding specificity.
   b. the serial position effect.
   c. the tip-of-the-tongue effect.
   d. flashbulb memory.

3. Multiple-choice test questions typically rely on _____, while essay questions rely on _____.
   a. rehearsal; recall
   b. relearning; rehearsing
   c. recall; recognition
   d. recognition; recall

4. Felisha can recall with great detail the day of her wedding and all that occurred. What might psychologists say about these particular flashbulb memories?
   a. The memories were likely enhanced in part by the hormones released during emotional moments.
   b. The memories should last up to 15 to 20 years.
   c. The memories are unusually accurate.
   d. The memories are stored as nondeclarative memories.

5. In Loftus's 1978 study, subjects viewed a slide presentation of an accident. Later, some of the subjects were asked a question about a yield sign when the actual slides contained pictures of a stop sign. When presented with this inaccurate information, how did these subjects typically respond?
   a. Most corrected Loftus and recalled seeing a stop sign.
   b. Many began seeing both a stop sign and a yield sign.
   c. Many subjects' overall accuracy dropped when confronted with conflicting information.
   d. Subjects were confused, but only briefly, at which point their accuracy of recalling the event returned.

6. A key component for any person to believe that a false event is in fact true is to make sure that the false information is
   a. as plausible as possible.
   b. introduced as soon after the event as possible.
   c. introduced by a source perceived as trustworthy.
   d. introduced no sooner than 24 hours after the event but no later than 15 days.

# APA Goal 2: Scientific Inquiry and Critical Thinking

## Effects of Supplements on Memory

*Addresses APA Learning Objectives 2.1: Use scientific reasoning to interpret psychological phenomena, and 2.3: Engage in innovative and integrative thinking and problem solving.*

More and more people are turning to various supplements that promise to improve memory, ward off or even alleviate Alzheimer's, and prevent other forms of cognitive decline. But what does science say about the claims of these various supplements? Are they really helpful? Could they be harmful? Here's a look at some of the more popular supplements and the research examining their claims.

### Gingko Biloba

The gingko biloba supplement is an extract from the leaf of the gingko biloba tree. The Chinese have used this supplement for thousands of years to improve various aspects of health, and you might think that anything that people have used for that long must work, right? But think about other reasons that people might continue to use a dietary supplement that have little or nothing to do with actual health results. It's a cultural habit and tradition, for example. People may take the supplement and think they feel better or think better because of the placebo effect. **(L I N K)** to Learning Objective 1.9. The only way to really know if gingko biloba actually has any positive effect on memory is to look at the scientific research.

So what does the research say? There are numerous studies over the past decade that strongly indicate the failure of gingko biloba supplements in improving memory in healthy people or in preventing dementia-related memory problems such as those found in Alzheimer's disease (Birks & Evans, 2009; Cooper et al., 2013; Laws et al., 2012; Mancuso et al., 2012; Snitz et al., 2009). A large review of current research did find that the extract may slow the decline in cognitive abilities, including memory, for people who already have symptoms of dementia (Tan et al., 2015). The conclusion: Don't bother with this supplement unless you actually have dementia, and even then your doctor should be monitoring you for possible side effects. This supplement can change your insulin levels, make bleeding harder to stop, increase bruising, blur vision, cause any number of gastric distress symptoms, affect your sense of taste, cause fluid retention—the list goes on.

### Coconut Oil and Fish Oil

Another popular type of supplement is coconut oil, an extract from the meat of coconuts that is high in saturated fat. While there are many health claims for this supplement, the one we will examine is the claim that consuming coconut oil can treat and even cure Alzheimer's disease. This claim is based on the idea that people with Alzheimer's disease have neurons in their brains that cannot use glucose (blood sugar) properly, leading to "starving" brain cells. Coconut oil is supposed to provide an alternative energy source for these cells, but at the present time the scientific evidence has yielded mixed results (Connor et al., 2012; Naqvi, et al., 2013). There is a clinical trial going on now in the United States, but the results will not be available until 2017.

So is it safe to take coconut oil? It is a saturated fat, and high cholesterol levels may occur with the accompanying increased risk of stroke, heart disease, and—ironically—dementia.

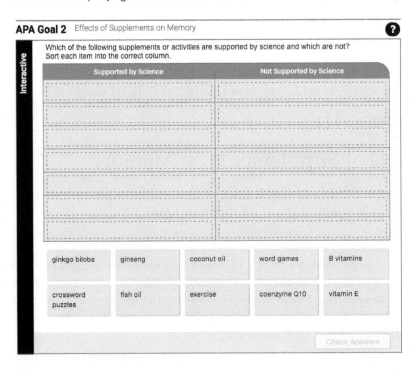

**APA Goal 2** Effects of Supplements on Memory ❓

Which of the following supplements or activities are supported by science and which are not? Sort each item into the correct column.

| Supported by Science | Not Supported by Science |
| --- | --- |
| | |
| | |
| | |
| | |
| | |
| | |

ginkgo biloba    ginseng    coconut oil    word games    B vitamins

crossword puzzles    fish oil    exercise    coenzyme Q10    vitamin E

Check Answers

If you do not have Alzheimer's or another dementia, taking coconut oil may not do much of anything except adversely affect your blood work on your next trip to the doctor.

Fish oil supplements have a slightly better track record for helping slow the rates of cognitive decline in people with Alzheimer's disease but may do very little for healthy people (Connor et al., 2012; Daiello et al., 2014). The safest advice to improve your memory and possibly prevent or postpone any symptoms of dementia may simply be to remain mentally active (Naqvi et al., 2013). Work crossword puzzles, read, and keep those neurons firing!

# What Were We Talking About? Forgetting

 Why do we forget things? And why do we forget some things but not others?

Most of us, at some point in our busy lives, have trouble remembering things, especially events from the distant past. What if you could remember nearly every day of your life? This rare ability is possessed by Brad Williams, who is known as the "Human Google." Brad is one of a small group of individuals with a syndrome called *hyperthymesia* (hī-pər-thī-mē-sē-uh). A person with hyperthymesia not only has an astonishing and rare ability to recall specific events from his or her personal past but also spends an unusually large amount of time thinking about that personal past. Brad can recall almost any news event or personal event he himself has experienced, particularly specific dates—and even the weather on those dates.

You may think that being able to remember everything like Brad Williams would be wonderful. But it's important to consider that people with hyperthymesia not only have the ability to remember nearly everything but also have the inability to *forget*. The ability to forget may be nearly as vital to human thought processes as the ability to remember. William James, one of the founders of the field of psychology, said, "If we remembered everything, we should on most occasions be as ill off as if we remembered nothing" (James, 1890, 2002). *Adaptive forgetting* is the idea that being able to suppress information that we no longer need makes it easier to remember what we do need (Kuhl et al., 2007; MacLeod, 1998; Nairne, 2015; Wimber et al., 2015.) Learn more about Brad Williams and hyperthymesia in the video *Reasons for Forgetting*.

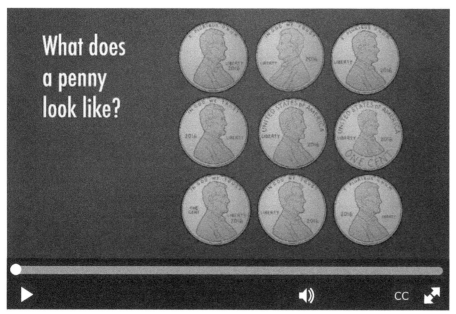

👁 **Watch** the **Video** *Reasons for Forgetting*

A similar problem was experienced in the case of A. R. Luria's (1968) famous *mnemonist*, Mr. S. (A mnemonist is a memory expert or someone with exceptional memory ability.) Mr. S. was a performing mnemonist, astonishing his audiences with lists of numbers that he memorized in minutes. But Mr. S. found that he *was unable to forget* the lists. He also could not easily separate important memories from trivial ones, and each time he looked at an object or read a word, images stimulated by that object or word would flood his mind. He eventually invented a way to "forget" things—by writing them on a piece of paper and then burning the paper (Luria, 1968).

The ability to forget seems necessary to one's sanity if the experience of Mr. S. is any indicator. But how fast do people forget things? Are there some things that are harder or easier to forget?

### EBBINGHAUS AND THE FORGETTING CURVE

**6.10** Describe the "curve of forgetting."

Hermann Ebbinghaus (1913) was one of the first researchers to study forgetting. Because he did not want any verbal associations to aid him in remembering, he created several lists of "nonsense syllables," pronounceable but meaningless (such as GEX and WOL). He memorized a list, waited a specific amount of time, and then tried to retrieve the list, graphing his results each time. The result has become a familiar graph: the **curve of forgetting**. This graph clearly shows that forgetting happens quickly within the first hour after learning the lists and then tapers off gradually. (See **Figure 6.7**.) In other words, forgetting is greatest just after learning. This curve can be applied to other types of information as well. Although meaningful material is forgotten much more slowly and much less completely, the pattern obtained when testing for forgetting is similar (Conway et al., 1992).

In his early studies, Ebbinghaus (1885) found that it is also important not to try to "cram" information you want to remember into your brain. Research has found that spacing out one's study sessions, or **distributed practice**, will produce far better retrieval of information studied in this way than does *massed practice*, or the attempt to study a body of material all at once. For example, studying your psychology material for 3 hours may make you feel that you've done some really hard work, and you have. Unfortunately, you won't remember as much of what you studied as you would if you had

**curve of forgetting**

a graph showing a distinct pattern in which forgetting is very fast within the first hour after learning a list and then tapers off gradually.

**distributed practice**

spacing the study of material to be remembered by including breaks between study periods.

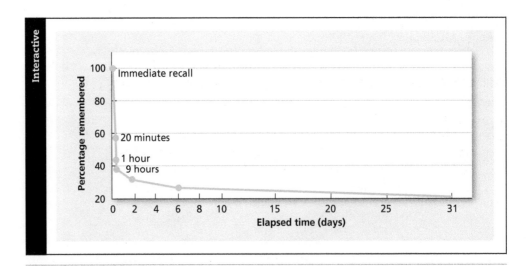

**Figure 6.7** Curve of Forgetting

Ebbinghaus found that his recall of words from his memorized word lists was greatest immediately after learning the list but rapidly decreased within the first hour. After the first hour, forgetting leveled off.

shorter study times of 30 minutes to an hour followed by short breaks (Cepeda et al., 2006; Dempster & Farris, 1990; Donovan & Radosevich, 1999; Simon & Bjork, 2001). Ⓛⓘⓝⓚ to Learning Objective PIA.5.

REASONS WE FORGET

**6.11** **Identify some common reasons people forget things.**

There are several reasons people forget things. We'll examine three theories here.

**ENCODING FAILURE**    One of the simplest is that some things never get encoded in the first place. Your friend, for example, may have said something to you as he walked out the door, and you may have heard him, but if you weren't paying attention to what he said, it would not get past sensory memory. This isn't forgetting so much as it is **encoding failure**, the failure to process information into memory. Researchers (Nickerson & Adams, 1979) developed a test of long-term memory using images of a common object for many people, a penny. Look at **Figure 6.8**. Which view of a stop sign is the correct one? People see stop signs nearly every day, but how many people actually look at them that closely so the information is encoded into long-term memory?

The fact that this man can remember the things shown in the pictures even after many years makes it unlikely that the memory trace decay theory can explain all forgetting in long-term memory.

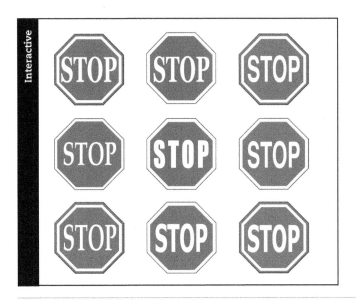

Interactive

**Figure 6.8**  Stop!
Many people look at stop signs multiple times a day. Which of these stop signs is closest to an actual stop sign? The answer can be found on the next page.

**MEMORY TRACE DECAY THEORY**    One of the older theories of forgetting involves the concept of a **memory trace**. A memory trace is some physical change in the brain, perhaps in a neuron or in the activity between neurons, which occurs when a memory is formed (Brown, 1958; Peterson & Peterson, 1959). Over time, if these traces are not used, they may **decay**, fading into nothing. It would be similar to what happens when a number of people walk across a particular patch of grass, causing a path to appear in which the grass is trampled down and perhaps turning brown. But if people stop using the path, the grass grows back and the path disappears.

Forgetting in sensory memory and short-term memory seems easy to explain as decay: Information that is not brought to attention in sensory memory or continuously rehearsed in STM will fade away. But is decay a good explanation for forgetting from long-term memory? When referring to LTM, decay theory is usually called **disuse**, and the phrase "use it or lose it" takes on great meaning (Bjork & Bjork, 1992). Although the fading of information from LTM through disuse sounds logical, there are many

**encoding failure**
failure to process information into memory.

**memory trace**
physical change in the brain that occurs when a memory is formed.

**decay**
loss of memory due to the passage of time, during which the memory trace is not used.

**disuse**
another name for decay, assuming that memories that are not used will eventually decay and disappear.

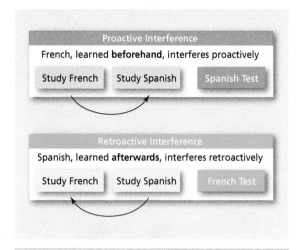

**Figure 6.9**  Proactive and Retroactive Interference
If a student were to study for a French exam and then a Spanish exam, interference could occur in two directions. When taking the Spanish exam, the French information studied first may proactively interfere with the learning of the new Spanish information. But when taking the French exam, the more recently studied Spanish information may retroactively interfere with the retrieval of the French information.

The answer to **Figure 6.8** is the middle right image.

**proactive interference**

memory problem that occurs when older information prevents or interferes with the learning or retrieval of newer information.

**retroactive interference**

memory problem that occurs when newer information prevents or interferes with the retrieval of older information.

times when people can recall memories they had assumed were long forgotten. There must be other factors involved in the forgetting of long-term memories.

**INTERFERENCE THEORY**   A possible explanation of LTM forgetting is that although most long-term memories may be stored more or less permanently in the brain, those memories may not always be accessible to attempted retrieval because other information interferes (Anderson & Neely, 1995). (And even memories that are accessible are subject to constructive processing, which can lead to inaccurate recall.) An analogy might be this: The can of paint that Phillip wants may very well be on some shelf in his storeroom, but there's so much other junk in its way that he can't see it and can't get to it. In the case of LTM, interference can come from two different "directions."

**PROACTIVE INTERFERENCE**   Have you ever switched from driving a car with the gearshift on the steering wheel to one with the gearshift on the floor of the car? If the answer is yes, you probably found that you had some trouble when you first got into the new car. You may have grabbed at the wheel instead of reaching to the gearshift on the floor. The reason you reached for the gearshift in the "old" place is called **proactive interference**: the tendency for older or previously learned material to interfere with the learning (and subsequent retrieval) of new material. (See **Figure 6.9**.)

Another example of proactive interference often occurs when someone gets a new cell phone number. People in this situation often find themselves remembering their old cell phone number or some of its digits instead of the new cell phone number when they are trying to give the new number to friends.

**RETROACTIVE INTERFERENCE**   When newer information interferes with the retrieval of older information, this is called **retroactive interference**. (See Figure 6.9.) What happens when you change back from the car with the gearshift on the floor to the older car with the gearshift on the wheel? You'll probably reach down to the floor at least once or twice because the newer skill retroactively interferes with remembering the old way of doing it.

How might interference work in each of the following cases?

1. Moving from the United States to England, where people drive on the left instead of the right side of the road.
2. Trying to use the controls on your old Blu-ray® player after having used the new one for a year.
3. Moving from one type of cell phone system to another, such as going from an iPhone® to an Android® system.

The different ways that forgetting occurs are summarized in **Table 6.1**.

| Table 6.1    Reasons for Forgetting | |
|---|---|
| **Reason** | **Description** |
| Encoding Failure | The information is not attended to and fails to be encoded. |
| Decay or Disuse | Information that is not accessed decays from the storage system over time. |
| Proactive Interference | Older information already in memory interferes with the learning of newer information. |
| Retroactive Interference | Newer information interferes with the retrieval of older information. |

## Concept Map  L.O. 6.10, 6.11

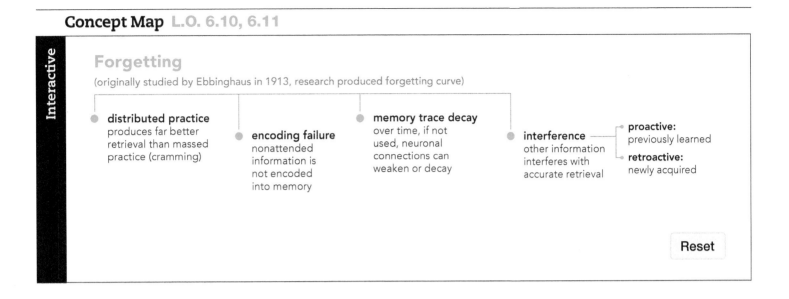

*Interactive*

**Forgetting**
(originally studied by Ebbinghaus in 1913, research produced forgetting curve)

- **distributed practice** produces far better retrieval than massed practice (cramming)
- **encoding failure** nonattended information is not encoded into memory
- **memory trace decay** over time, if not used, neuronal connections can weaken or decay
- **interference** other information interferes with accurate retrieval
  - **proactive:** previously learned
  - **retroactive:** newly acquired

Reset

# Practice Quiz   How much do you remember?

*Pick the best answer.*

**1.** Raven has just finished learning a list of nonsense words given to her by her psychology instructor as part of a class activity. She had 100 percent recall at the end of class. According to Ebbinghaus's curve of forgetting, how quickly will Raven likely forget about 40 percent of the information she has just learned?
 **a.** within the first 20 minutes after leaving the class
 **b.** within the first day after leaving the class
 **c.** nearly a week after the class
 **d.** nearly a month after the class

**2.** Collin is asked to repeat what his mother just told him. He says he "forgot," but in reality Collin wasn't paying attention to his mother at all. This is an example of the _____ explanation of forgetting.
 **a.** interference
 **b.** memory trace
 **c.** encoding failure
 **d.** repression

**3.** Shantel spent a year living abroad in Spain. During that time, her ability to read and speak Spanish grew tremendously. However, now, 2 years later, Shantel feels she can no longer travel there because she can barely remember a thing. Her problem is most likely due to
 **a.** encoding failure.
 **b.** retroactive interference.
 **c.** proactive interference.
 **d.** decay theory.

**4.** Noland bought a fancy new smart phone. It was a different brand of phone than his old phone, so he spent quite a few frustrating hours learning to use the new one. The problem was that he kept trying to tap icons on the new phone in the places they had been on his old phone. Noland's problem was most likely due to
 **a.** encoding failure.
 **b.** retroactive interference.
 **c.** proactive interference.
 **d.** decay theory.

# Neuroscience of Memory

Researchers have evidence that specific areas of the brain may be the places in which memories are physically formed and that these areas are different for different types of memory.

**THE BIOLOGICAL BASES OF MEMORY**

**6.12** **Explain the biological bases of memory in the brain.**

Nondeclarative memories seem to be stored in the cerebellum (Boyd & Winstein, 2004; Daum & Schugens, 1996). Research involving PET scanning techniques strongly suggests that short-term memories are stored in the prefrontal cortex (the very front of the frontal lobe) and the temporal lobe (Goldman-Rakic, 1998; Rao et al., 1997). Memories related to fear seem to be stored in the amygdala (Dębiec et al., 2010).

As for semantic and episodic long-term memories, evidence suggests that these memories are also stored in the frontal and temporal lobes but not in exactly the same places, nor in the same location as short-term memories (Binder et al., 2009; Weis et al., 2004).

💬 All that explains is the "where" of memory. Did scientists ever find out the "what" or the exact physical change that happens in the brain when memories are stored?

Several studies have offered evidence that memory is not simply one physical change but many: changes in the number of receptor sites, changes in the sensitivity of the synapse through repeated stimulation (called *long-term potentiation*), and changes in the dendrites and specifically in the proteins within the neurons (Alkon, 1989; Kandel & Schwartz, 1982; Squire & Kandel, 1999). The changes underlying synaptic plasticity and memory storage have been attributed to six molecular mechanisms (*cAMP, PKA, CRE, CREB-1* and *CREB-2, CPEB*) that signify information changing from short-term memory to long-term memory, and apply to both explicit and implicit memory (Kandel, 2012). In addition to multiple changes occurring, changes in synaptic function have to occur across collections of neurons as part of a larger circuit (Kandel, 2012). Collectively, the synaptic alterations, changes in neuronal structure, protein synthesis, and other changes that take place as a memory is forming are called **consolidation** (Deger et al., 2012; Fioriti et al., 2015; Griggs et al., 2013; Hill et al., 2015; Krüttner et al., 2012). Consolidation may take only a few minutes for some memories, such as learning a new friend's name, but may take years for others, such as learning a new language (Dudai, 2004).

In the discussion of the *hippocampus* (a part of the limbic system) in Chapter Two, it was identified as the part of the brain that is responsible for the formation of new long-term declarative memories. One of the clearest pieces of evidence of this function comes from the study of a man known as H.M. (Milner et al., 1968).

H.M. was 16 when he began to suffer from severe epileptic seizures. Eleven years later, H.M.'s hippocampi and adjacent medial temporal lobe structures were removed in an experimental operation that the surgeon hoped would stop his seizures. The last thing H.M. could remember was being rolled to the operating room, and from then on his ability to form new declarative memories was profoundly impaired. The hippocampus was not the source of his problem (his seizures were reduced but not eliminated), but it was apparently the source of his ability to consolidate and store any new factual information he encountered, because without either hippocampus, he was completely unable to remember new events or facts. Consolidation had become impossible. He had a magazine that he carried around, reading and rereading the stories, because each time he did so the stories were completely new to him. As with most amnesic patients of this type (although H.M.'s case was quite severe), his nondeclarative memory was still intact*. It was only new declarative memory—both semantic and episodic—that was lost. H.M., who can now be revealed as Henry Gustav Molaison, died in December 2008 at the age of 82. His experience and his brain will continue to educate students and neuroscientists, as he agreed many years ago that his brain would be donated for further scientific study upon his death. It has now been cut into 2,401 slices, each about the width of a human hair, in preparation for further study. You can read more about H.M.'s contributions to science at Suzanne Corkin's Web site at **http://web.mit.edu/bnl/publications.htm**. To learn about the H.M. postmortem project being conducted go to **http://thebrainobservatory.org** (Carey, 2009).

There is some evidence that memories of the same event may involve different areas of the hippocampus (Collin et al., 2015). The different areas seem to correspond to different degrees of memory detail for the event, such as remembering reading a specific text message from your partner before going to class (a fine detail) or recalling going out to eat after class (a broader event).

Another area of the brain involved in the formation of long-term memories is the *posterior cingulate,* an area of the cortex located near the rear of the corpus callosum.

**consolidation**

the changes that take place in the structure and functioning of neurons when a memory is formed.

---

*intact: whole or complete.

L I N K to Learning Objective 2.12. This is one of the areas of the brain that shows damage in people with Alzheimer's disease. It is involved in consolidation, as researchers have found evidence that the posterior cingulate is not only activated when engaging in active rehearsal to first remember specific information, but it is also active when retrieving that memory (Bird et al., 2015). Furthermore, improved memory appears to be related to how similar brain activity during retrieval is to the activity in this same area during active rehearsal. It is possible that active rehearsal and activity in the posterior cingulate strengthens memory by helping link both episodic and semantic information (Binder et al., 2009; Bird et al., 2015).

### WHEN MEMORY FAILS: ORGANIC AMNESIA

#### 6.13  Identify the biological causes of amnesia.

From movies and TV, many people are familiar with the concept of repression, a type of psychologically motivated forgetting in which a person supposedly cannot remember a traumatic event. L I N K to Learning Objective 14.7. But what about an inability to remember brought about by some physical cause? There are two forms of severe loss of memory disorders caused by problems in the functioning of the memory areas of the brain. These problems can result from concussions, brain injuries brought about by trauma, alcoholism (Korsakoff's syndrome), or disorders of the aging brain.

**RETROGRADE AMNESIA**   If the hippocampus is that important to the formation of declarative memories, what would happen if it got temporarily "disconnected"? People who are in accidents in which they received a head injury often are unable to recall the accident itself. Sometimes they cannot remember the last several hours or even days before the accident. This type of amnesia (literally, "without memory") is called **retrograde amnesia**, which is loss of memory from the point of injury backward (Hodges, 1994). What apparently happens in this kind of memory loss is that the consolidation process, which was busy making the physical changes to allow new memories to be stored, gets disrupted and loses everything that was not already nearly "finished."

Think about this: You are working on your computer, trying to finish a history paper that is due tomorrow. Your computer saves the document every 10 minutes, but you are working so furiously that you've written a lot in the last 10 minutes. Then the power goes out—horrors! When the power comes back on, you find that while all the files you had already saved are still intact, your history paper is missing that last 10 minutes' worth of work. This is similar to what happens when someone's consolidation process is disrupted. All memories that were in the process of being stored—but are not yet permanent—are lost.

One of the therapies for severe depression is *ECT*, or *electroconvulsive therapy*, in use for this purpose for many decades. L I N K to Learning Objective 15.11. One of the common side effects of this therapy is the loss of memory, specifically retrograde amnesia (Meeter et al., 2011; Sackeim et al., 2007; Squire & Alvarez, 1995; Squire et al., 1975). While the effects of the induced seizure seem to significantly ease the depression, the shock also seems to disrupt the memory consolidation process for memories formed prior to the treatment. While some researchers in the past found that the memory loss can go back as far as three years for certain kinds of information (Squire et al., 1975), later research suggests that the loss may not be a permanent one (Meeter et al., 2011).

**ANTEROGRADE AMNESIA**   Concussions can also cause a more temporary version of the kind of amnesia experienced by H.M. This kind of amnesia is called *anterograde amnesia*, or the loss of memories from the point of injury or illness forward (Squire & Slater, 1978). People with this kind of amnesia, like H.M., have difficulty remembering anything new. This is also the kind of amnesia most often seen in people with *senile dementia*, a mental disorder in which severe forgetfulness, mental confusion, and mood swings are the primary symptoms. (Dementia patients also may suffer from retrograde amnesia in addition to anterograde amnesia.) If retrograde amnesia is like losing a document in the computer because of a power loss, anterograde amnesia is like discovering that your hard drive has become

**retrograde amnesia**
loss of memory from the point of some injury or trauma backwards, or loss of memory for the past.

**Figure 6.10** (a) Sometimes a blow to the head, such as might be sustained in an accident like this one, can lead to the loss of memories from the time of the injury backwards—a loss of recent memory which may be only a few minutes to several hours or days, or in some cases, even years of the past. This is called retrograde amnesia, because "retro" means "relating to the recent past. (b) Anterograde amnesia involves the loss of the ability to form new memories. Memories of the distant past may still be intact, but newer memories such as the name of the person you just met or whether you took your medication or not seem unable to "stick." That's why a person with this type of amnesia (common in dementia) might not remember a conversation that just took place or a visit from the day before.

defective—you can read data that are already on the hard drive, but you can't store any new information. As long as you are looking at the data in your open computer window (i.e., attending to it), you can access it, but as soon as you close that window (stop thinking about it), the information is lost, because it was never transferred to the hard drive (long-term memory). This makes for some very repetitive conversations, such as being told the same story or being asked the same question numerous times in the space of a 20-minute conversation. See **Figure 6.10** for a comparison of retrograde and anterograde amnesia.

**ALZHEIMER'S DISEASE** Nearly 5.3 million Americans have Alzheimer's disease (Alzheimer's Association, 2015). It is the most common type of dementia found in adults and the elderly, accounting for nearly 60 to 80 percent of all cases of dementia. It is estimated that 1 out of 9 people over the age of 65 has Alzheimer's disease. It has also become the sixth-leading cause of death in the United states and the fifth-leading cause of death in people 65 years and older, with only heart disease and cancer responsible for more deaths (Alzheimer's Association, 2015; Antuono et al., 2001; National Center for Health Statistics, 2015).

With Alzheimer's disease, the primary memory problem, at least in the beginning, is anterograde amnesia. Memory loss may be rather mild at first but becomes more severe over time, causing the person to become more and more forgetful about everyday tasks. Eventually more dangerous forgetting occurs, such as taking extra doses of medication or leaving something cooking on the stove unattended. As Alzheimer's disease progresses, memories of the past seem to begin "erasing" as retrograde amnesia also takes hold. It is a costly disease to care for, and caregivers often face severe emotional and financial burdens in caring for a loved one who is slowly becoming a stranger.

What causes Alzheimer's disease is not completely understood. While it is normal for the brain to begin to form beta-amyloid protein deposits (plaques) and for strands of the protein tau to become twisted ("tangles"), people who suffer from Alzheimer's disease are found to have far more of these physical signs of an aging brain (Chen et al., 2012; Lim et al., 2012). One of the neurotransmitters involved in the formation of memories in the hippocampus is acetylcholine, and the neurons that produce this chemical break down in the early stages of the disease (Martyn et al., 2012). While one early-onset form of Alzheimer's appears to be heavily genetically influenced and involves several different genetic variations, this seems to be the case for fewer than 5 percent of the total cases of the disease (Alzheimer's Association, 2010; Bertram & Tanzi, 2005; Haass et al., 1995). The sad truth is that there is not one cause but many, and even those who do NOT have Alzheimer's disease are not safe from other forms of dementia, such as dementia caused by strokes, dehydration, medications, and so on (Karantzoulis, & Galvin, 2011).

Treatments can slow but not halt or reverse the course of the disease. Five drugs are currently approved for treatment, but as yet only slow down the symptoms for an average of 6 to 12 months. What is known is that the risk factors for Alzheimer's (and many other forms of dementia) are something that can be managed: high cholesterol, high blood pressure, smoking, obesity, Type II diabetes, and lack of exercise all contribute (Alzheimer's Association, 2010; Baumgart et al., 2015). Keeping the brain mentally active is also a way to help prolong good cognitive health. One study's findings indicate that continued everyday learning stimulates brain-derived neurotrophic factors (BDNF), a key protein involved in the formation of memories (L. Y. Chen et al., 2010). A more recent study suggests that a drug intended for use in treating diabetes, AC253, may be able to restore memory to Alzheimer's-affected brain cells (Kimura et al., 2012), while another new drug, ORM-12741, also shows promise (Rouru et al., 2013).

We also know that Alzheimer's is *not* caused by eating food from aluminum pots and pans, using the artificial sweetener aspartame, having silver dental fillings, or getting a flu shot—all myths you may have seen on the Internet or social media. None of these are true (Alz.org®: Alzheimer's Association, 2015).

People with dementia or traumatic brain injuries may end up with both types of amnesia. In a study of a recent case of anterograde amnesia, a musician suffering brain damage from a bad case of encephalitis (brain inflammation) no longer remembers his past life, friends, or relatives (retrograde amnesia) and can no longer learn new information (anterograde amnesia). Yet he can still play his cello, read music, and can not only play pieces from before his brain injury but can also learn new pieces (Finke et al., 2012). These are nondeclarative skills, and this type of memory is typically unaffected by amnesia, suggesting that a different area of the brain is involved.

💬 I've tried to remember things from when I was a baby, but I don't seem to be able to recall much. Is this some kind of amnesia, too?

**INFANTILE AMNESIA** What is the earliest memory you have? Chances are you cannot remember much that happened to you before age 3. When a person does claim to "remember" some event from infancy, a little investigation usually reveals that the "memory" is really based on what family members have told the person about that event and is not a genuine memory at all. This type of "manufactured" memory often has the quality of watching yourself in the memory as if it were a movie and you were an actor. In a genuine memory, you would remember the event through your own eyes—as if you were the camera.

Why can't people remember events from the first 2 or 3 years of life? One explanation of **infantile amnesia** involves the type of memory that exists in the first few years of life, when a child is still considered an infant. Early memories tend to be implicit, and, as stated earlier in this chapter, implicit memories are difficult to bring to consciousness. Explicit memory, which is the more verbal and conscious form of memory, does not really develop until after about age 2, when the hippocampus is more fully developed and language skills blossom (Carver & Bauer, 2001).

Katherine Nelson (1993) also gives credit to the social relationships that small children have with others. As children are able to talk about shared memories with adults, they begin to develop their **autobiographical memory**, or the memory for events and facts related to one's personal life story.

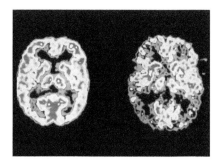

To track the cell death that occurs in Alzheimer's disease, researchers used MRI technology to scan both patients with Alzheimer's disease and normal elderly subjects. Using supercomputers, the UCLA team created color-coded maps that revealed the degenerative sequence of the disease through novel brain-mapping methods. The wave of gray matter loss was strongly related to the progressive decline in cognitive functioning that is a key feature of the disease. Other researchers have used PET scans, as in the image above, to illustrate differences in brain activity between individuals with and without Alzheimer's disease.

**infantile amnesia**

the inability to retrieve memories from much before age 3.

**autobiographical memory**

the memory for events and facts related to one's personal life story.

## Concept Map L.O. 6.12, 6.13

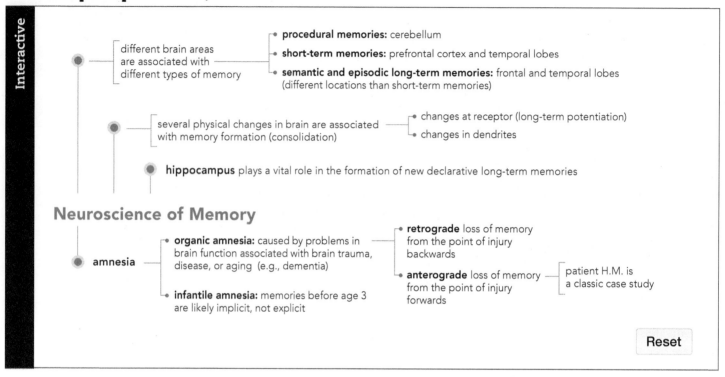

### Neuroscience of Memory

Interactive

- different brain areas are associated with different types of memory
  - **procedural memories:** cerebellum
  - **short-term memories:** prefrontal cortex and temporal lobes
  - **semantic and episodic long-term memories:** frontal and temporal lobes (different locations than short-term memories)
- several physical changes in brain are associated with memory formation (consolidation)
  - changes at receptor (long-term potentiation)
  - changes in dendrites
- **hippocampus** plays a vital role in the formation of new declarative long-term memories
- amnesia
  - **organic amnesia:** caused by problems in brain function associated with brain trauma, disease, or aging (e.g., dementia)
    - **retrograde** loss of memory from the point of injury backwards
    - **anterograde** loss of memory from the point of injury forwards — patient H.M. is a classic case study
  - **infantile amnesia:** memories before age 3 are likely implicit, not explicit

Reset

# Practice Quiz   How much do you remember?

1. Chantal is very afraid of clowns, no doubt because she was frightened by one when she was very young. Chantal's memories of that fearful encounter are likely to be associated with the
   a. cerebellum.
   b. prefrontal cortex.
   c. posterior cingulate cortex.
   d. amygdala.

2. Henry Gustav Molaison (H.M.) suffered from profound anterograde amnesia after his _____ were surgically removed in an attempt to control his seizures.
   a. hippocampi
   b. amygdalae
   c. frontal lobes
   d. thalami

3. What type of amnesia do you have when you cannot remember things that happened before a traumatic accident?
   a. retrograde amnesia
   b. anterograde amnesia
   c. psychogenic amnesia
   d. infantile amnesia

4. Which neurotransmitter is no longer readily produced in Alzheimer's patients?
   a. dopamine
   b. endorphins
   c. GABA
   d. acetylcholine

## Applying Psychology to Everyday Life
# Health and Memory

### 6.14 Explain how sleep, exercise, and diet affect memory.

Several recent studies highlight three important factors in improving or maintaining your memory's health: getting enough sleep, moderate exercise, and a diet high in DHA.

Sleep: As discussed in the chapter on consciousness, sleep is an important part of how the brain functions, particularly in forming memories. Recent studies have found that:

1. Memories that are rehearsed during sleep as well as during waking are more likely to be consolidated and therefore remembered better later on (Oudiette et al., 2013). This isn't really news for memories that already have high value, such as memories

associated with making more money. But researchers found that by pairing lower-value memories with a characteristic sound and then playing that sound back to the sleeping participants, those low-value items were better recalled—even better than when those same sound cues were played during waking periods. Sleep is necessary to rehearse and consolidate the things we want to remember from our waking day.

2. Can you learn while asleep? That has long been a hope of many a college student who has played a recording of lectures while sleeping, but it has never worked. It turns out that the mistake was not in trying to learn while asleep but trying to learn *something new* while asleep. Participants in one study learned how to play two previously unfamiliar tunes. They were then allowed to take a 90-minute nap, during which researchers (using information from an EEG) presented one of the tunes they had practiced during slow-wave sleep, a stage of sleep associated with memory consolidation. Sure enough, the tune presented during sleep was remembered significantly better than the one that was not presented (Antony et al., 2012).

3. Sleep deprivation severely interferes with the functioning of the hippocampus, the part of the brain that is vital for forming new memories (Basner et al., 2013; Poe et al., 2010). Ⓛ Ⓘ Ⓝ Ⓚ to Learning Objective 2.11. People who live a lifestyle that is typically sleep deprived—such as college students, doctors, nurses, and so on—are doing their memories no favors.

4. Sleep also helps prevent forgetting. We already know that interference causes forgetting, and it should come as no surprise that sleep reduces the amount of interference. But researchers have also found that sleep may protect new memories by inhibiting the workings of the neurotransmitter dopamine, a chemical in certain areas of the brain that is involved in forgetting (Berry et al., 2015). Remember to sleep, because we sleep to remember!

Exercise: It turns out that even brief exercise can be good for your memory (Petersen, 2015). Researchers had people 50 to 85 years old look at pleasant images, such as photos of animals and nature scenes (Segal et al., 2012). Some of these participants also had memory deficits. Immediately after viewing the pictures, half of the participants rode a stationary exercise bicycle for 6 minutes. One hour later all, participants were given a surprise recall test on the previously viewed pictures. Regardless of memory impairment, the participants who exercised showed substantially improved memory when compared to those who did not exercise. The possible explanation for this improved memory may lie in the extra norepinephrine released during exercise. Norepinephrine, a neurotransmitter found in the brain, plays a strong role in the formation of memories.

Diet: How many times have you heard that fish is brain food? Well, it turns out that it probably is brain food, at least when it comes to improving memory. Fish, particularly salmon, bluefin or albacore tuna, and swordfish, have high levels of an omega-3 fatty acid called DHA (docosahexaenoic acid). In a recent study, researchers fed a high-DHA diet to lab animals and found that, when compared to lab animals not fed the special diet, there was a 30 percent increase in DHA levels in the hippocampus of the brain (Connor et al., 2012). DHA appears to help memory cells communicate with each other better, resulting in improved memory function. Other foods high in DHA include ground flax seeds, walnuts, grass-fed beef, and soybeans, and of course there are numerous fish oil supplements on the market.

Questions for Further Discussion

1. Why do you think learning something new while asleep does not work?
2. What might be the dangers in using supplements to get DHA in your diet?

# Chapter Summary

## What Is Memory?

### 6.1 Identify the three processes of memory.

- Memory can be defined as an active system that receives information from the senses, organizes and alters it as it stores it away, and then retrieves the information from storage.
- The three processes are encoding, storage, and retrieval.

### 6.2 Explain how the different models of memory work.

- In the levels-of-processing model of memory, information that gets more deeply processed is more likely to be remembered.
- In the parallel distributed processing model of memory, information is simultaneously stored across an interconnected neural network that stretches across the brain.

## The Information-Processing Model: Three Memory Systems

### 6.3 Describe the process of sensory memory.

- Iconic memory is the visual sensory memory, in which an afterimage or icon will be held in neural form for about one fourth to one half second.
- Echoic memory is the auditory form of sensory memory and takes the form of an echo that lasts for up to 4 seconds.

### 6.4 Describe short-term memory and differentiate it from working memory.

- Short-term memory is where information is held while it is conscious and being used. It holds about three to five items of information and lasts about 30 seconds without rehearsal.
- STM can be lost through failure to rehearse, decay, interference by similar information, and the intrusion of new information into the STM system, which pushes older information out.

### 6.5 Explain the process of long-term memory, including nondeclarative and declarative forms.

- Long-term memory is the system in which memories that are to be kept more or less permanently are stored and is unlimited in capacity and relatively permanent in duration.
- Information that is more deeply processed, or processed according to meaning, will be retained and retrieved more efficiently.
- Nondeclarative, or implicit, memories are memories for skills, habits, and conditioned responses. Declarative, or explicit, memories are memories for general facts and personal experiences and include both semantic memories and episodic memories.
- Implicit memories are difficult to bring into conscious awareness, whereas explicit memories are those that a person is aware of possessing.
- LTM is organized in the form of semantic networks, or nodes of related information spreading out from a central piece of knowledge.

## Getting It Out: Retrieval of Long-Term Memories

### 6.6 Identify the effects of cues on memory retrieval.

- Retrieval cues are words, meanings, sounds, and other stimuli that are encoded at the same time as a new memory.
- Encoding specificity occurs when context-dependent information becomes encoded as retrieval cues for specific memories.
- State-dependent learning occurs when physiological or psychological states become encoded as retrieval cues for memories formed while in those states.

### 6.7 Differentiate the retrieval processes of recall and recognition.

- Recall is a type of memory retrieval in which the information to be retrieved must be "pulled" out of memory with few or no cues, whereas recognition involves matching information with stored images or facts.
- The serial position effect, or primacy or recency effect, occurs when the first items and the last items in a list of information are recalled more efficiently than items in the middle of the list.
- Loftus and others have found that people constantly update and revise their memories of events. Part of this revision may include adding information acquired later to a previous memory. That later information may also be in error, further contaminating the earlier memory.

### 6.8 Describe how some memories are automatically encoded into long-term memory.

- Automatic encoding of some kinds of information requires very little effort to place information in long-term memory.
- Memory for particularly emotional or traumatic events can lead to the formation of flashbulb memories, memories that seem as vivid and detailed as if the person were looking at a snapshot of the event but that are no more accurate than any other memories.

## The Reconstructive Nature of Long-Term Memory Retrieval: How Reliable Are Memories?

### 6.9 Explain how the constructive processing view of memory retrieval accounts for forgetting and inaccuracies in memory.

- Memories are reconstructed from the various bits and pieces of information that have been stored away in different places at the time of encoding in a process called constructive processing.
- Hindsight bias occurs when people falsely believe that they knew the outcome of some event because they have included knowledge of the event's true outcome in their memories of the event itself.
- The misinformation effect refers to the tendency of people who are asked misleading questions or given misleading information to incorporate that information into their memories for a particular event.

- Rather than improving memory retrieval, hypnosis makes the creation of false memories more likely.
- False-memory syndrome is the creation of false or inaccurate memories through suggestion, especially while hypnotized.
- Pezdek and colleagues assert that false memories are more likely to be formed for plausible false events than for implausible ones.

## What Were We Talking About? Forgetting

### 6.10 Describe the "curve of forgetting."

- Ebbinghaus found that information is mostly lost within 1 hour after learning and then gradually fades away. This is known as the curve of forgetting.

### 6.11 Identify some common reasons people forget things.

- Some "forgetting" is actually a failure to encode information.
- Memory trace decay theory assumes the presence of a physical memory trace that decays with disuse over time.
- Forgetting in LTM is most likely due to proactive or retroactive interference.

## Neuroscience of Memory

### 6.12 Explain the biological bases of memory in the brain.

- Evidence suggests that nondeclarative memories are stored in the cerebellum, whereas short-term memories are stored in the prefrontal and temporal lobes of the cortex.
- Semantic and episodic memories may be stored in the frontal and temporal lobes as well but in different locations than short-term memory, whereas memory for fear of objects is most likely stored in the amygdala.
- Consolidation consists of the physical changes in neurons that take place during the formation of a memory.
- The hippocampus appears to be responsible for the formation of new long-term declarative memories. If it is removed, the ability to store anything new is completely lost.

### 6.13 Identify the biological causes of amnesia.

- In retrograde amnesia, memory for the past (prior to the injury) is lost, which can be a loss of only minutes or a loss of several years.
- ECT, or electroconvulsive therapy, can disrupt consolidation and cause retrograde amnesia.
- In anterograde amnesia, memory for anything new becomes impossible, although old memories may still be retrievable.
- The primary memory difficulty in Alzheimer's disease is anterograde amnesia, although retrograde amnesia can also occur as the disease progresses.
- Alzheimer's disease has multiple causes, many of which are not yet identified.
- There are various drugs in use or in development for use, with the hopes of slowing, or possibly in the future halting, the progression of Alzheimer's disease.
- Most people cannot remember events that occurred before age 2 or 3. This is called infantile amnesia and is most likely due to the implicit nature of infant memory.

## Applying Psychology to Everyday Life: Health and Memory

### 6.14 Explain how sleep, exercise, and diet affect memory.

- Good nutrition, physical exercise, and adequate sleep contribute to memory functions.
- Research results suggest diets high in omega-3s, and especially DHA, may help hippocampal cells communicate better, whereas norepinephrine release during physical exercise appears to strengthen memories. Sleep is a critical component, both in the consolidation of memories and normal functioning of the hippocampus.

# Test Yourself

1. The steps to memory can best be described as follows:
   a. finding it, using it, storing it, using it again
   b. putting it in, keeping it in, getting it out
   c. sensing it, perceiving it, remembering it, forgetting it
   d. a series of passive data files

2. According to Sperling, what is the capacity of iconic memory?
   a. Everything that can be seen at one time.
   b. Everything that can be heard in 1 minute.
   c. Everything that can be sensed in 1 second.
   d. Everything that can be perceived in a lifetime.

3. Which type of memory system best explains the "What?" phenomenon?
   a. iconic sensory system
   b. echoic sensory system
   c. short-term memory system
   d. tactile sensory system

4. For information to travel from either the iconic or echoic sensory system to short-term memory, it must first be _____ and then encoded primarily into _____ form.
   a. unconsciously chosen; auditory
   b. selectively attended to; visual
   c. biologically chosen; visual
   d. selectively attended to; auditory

5. You are introduced to someone at a party. While talking with the person, you realize that you have already forgotten the person's name. What amount of time does it typically take before such information is lost from short-term memory?
   a. approximately ¼ of a second
   b. usually no more than 4 seconds
   c. typically between 12 and 30 seconds
   d. Short-term memories typically last a lifetime.

6. Early studies of the capacity of short-term memory suggested that most people could remember approximately _____ bits of information.
   a. two
   b. three
   c. seven
   d. ten

7. Mary has just met an attractive man named Austin at a party. She wants to make sure she remembers his name. What should she do?
   a. Mary should repeat the name continuously so as to commit it to long-term memory.
   b. Mary should chunk it by remembering the first three letters as a set and then remembering the remaining letters as a set.
   c. Mary should make it more meaningful. For example, she might remind herself that Austin has the same name as the capital of Texas.
   d. Mary should create a song to help her remember his name.

8. _____ memory includes what people can do or demonstrate, whereas _____ memory is about what people know and can report.
   a. Nondeclarative; declarative
   b. Declarative; nondeclarative
   c. Semantic; nondeclarative
   d. Episodic; semantic

9. The semantic network model of memory suggests that the _____ nodes you must pass through to access information, the longer it will take for you to recall information.
   a. fewer
   b. more
   c. bigger the
   d. more complex the

10. Phineas walks out of his office and into the conference room. However, after he leaves his office, he forgets what he was coming into the conference room for. According to the encoding specificity hypothesis, what should Phineas do to regain his lost memory?
    a. Phineas should return to his office to help him remember what he had forgotten.
    b. Phineas should ask someone else, "What did I come in here for?"
    c. Phineas should remain in the conference room and simply relax so that his memory should return.
    d. Phineas should consider seeing a doctor, since such memory loss can be a sign of mental illness.

11. Which of the following is an example of a test using recognition?
    a. short answer
    b. essay
    c. fill in the blanks
    d. true–false

12. When creating a presentation, many public-speaking instructors will tell you to develop a strong opening or attention getter to your presentation as well as a good summary and finish. What aspect of memory best explains these suggestions?
    a. parallel distributed processing model of memory
    b. chunking
    c. elaborative rehearsal theory
    d. serial position effect

13. Your mother tells you to dress for success at your interview because it's all about "first impressions." In other words, she is telling you that people often remember what they see first. This belief is in line with what element of memory?
    a. the primacy effect
    b. the tip-of-the-tongue phenomenon
    c. the recency effect
    d. the power of false positives

14. Research by Elizabeth Loftus shows that eyewitness recognition is very prone to what psychologists call
    a. automatic encoding.
    b. a false positive.
    c. a flashbulb memory.
    d. a recency effect.

15. The tendency of certain elements to enter long-term memory with little or no effort to encode and organize them is what defines
    a. encoding specificity.
    b. automatic encoding.
    c. flashbulb memories.
    d. eidetic imagery.

16. The ability to remember where you were and what you were doing when the United States was attacked on September 11, 2001, is an example of
    a. eyewitness testimony.
    b. encoding specificity hypothesis.
    c. false-memory syndrome.
    d. flashbulb memory.

17. In Hermann Ebbinghaus's classic study on memory and the forgetting curve, how long after learning the lists does most forgetting happen?
    a. Forgetting started immediately.
    b. 1 hour
    c. 5 hours
    d. 9 hours

18. You are surprised by the fact that you cannot remember if Abraham Lincoln's head faces the left or the right on a penny. This is all the more surprising given the fact that you work with money at your job on nearly a daily basis. What would best explain such an inability to recall this information?
    a. encoding failure
    b. decay theory
    c. interference theory
    d. distributed practice effect

19. Henry Gustav Molaison, infamously known as H.M., was unable to form new declarative memories. He suffered from what psychologists call
    a. psychogenic amnesia.
    b. retrograde amnesia.
    c. retroactive amnesia.
    d. anterograde amnesia.

20. Your English instructor has given you an assignment to write down your most favorite memory from when you were 12 months old. What might you tell him?
    a. Memories from this time are exceptionally vivid because of the exciting nature of childhood.
    b. Students will not be able to recall such memories if they had yet to develop the ability to talk by age 1.
    c. Students' memories are detailed but often inaccurate.
    d. Students will probably not be able to recall events from such an early age.

# Cognition: Thinking, Intelligence, and Language

Do you tend to rely more on instinctual or deliberate thought processes? How do your thought processes and decision-making strategies vary depending on the situation?

After you have answered the question, watch the video to compare the answers of other students to yours.

▶ | The response entered here will be saved to your notes and may be collected by your instructor if he/she requires it.

👁 **Watch** the Video

# **Why study** the nature of thought?

To fully understand how we do any of the things we do (such as learning, remembering, and behaving), we need to understand how we think. How do we organize our thoughts? How do we communicate those thoughts to others? What do we mean by intelligence? Why are some people able to learn so much faster than others?

# Learning Objectives

**7.1** Explain how mental images are involved in the process of thinking.

**7.2** Describe how concepts and prototypes influence our thinking.

**7.3** Identify some methods that people use to solve problems and make decisions.

**7.4** Identify three common barriers to successful problem solving.

**7.5** Recall some characteristics of creative, divergent thinking.

**7.6** Compare and contrast different theories on the nature of intelligence.

**7.7** Compare and contrast some methods of measuring intelligence.

**7.8** Identify ways to evaluate the quality of a test.

**7.9** Define intellectual disability, giftedness, and emotional intelligence.

**7.10** Evaluate the influence of heredity and environment on the development of intelligence.

**7.11** Identify the different elements and structure of language.

**7.12** Explain how language develops.

**7.13** Evaluate whether or not language influences how people think.

**7.14** Summarize the research on the ability of animals to communicate and use language.

**7.15** Identify some methods for improving your cognitive health.

# How People Think

What does it mean to think? People are thinking all the time and talking about thinking as well: "What do you think?" "Let me think about that." "I don't think so." So, what does it mean to think? **Thinking, or cognition** (from a Latin word meaning "to know"), can be defined as mental activity that goes on in the brain when a person is processing information—organizing it, understanding it, and communicating it to others. Thinking includes memory, but it is much more. When people think, they are not only aware of the information in the brain but also are making decisions about it, comparing it to other information, and using it to solve problems. Also, how often do you simply respond without knowing how or why you do the things you do, say, or think? How much of your conscious experience involves effortful, mindful attention and decision making?

These two types of thinking, sometimes referred to as System 1 and System 2, characterize much of how we think and process information (Kahneman, 2011; Stanovich & West, 2000). System 1, which involves making quick decisions and using cognitive shortcuts, is guided by our innate abilities and personal experiences. System 2, which is relatively slow, analytical, and rule based, is dependent more on our formal educational experiences. Overall, our thinking has to be governed by the interplay between the two.

Thinking also includes more than just a kind of verbal "stream of consciousness." When people think, they often have images as well as words in their minds.

## MENTAL IMAGERY

**7.1** **Explain how mental images are involved in the process of thinking.**

As stated in Chapter Six, short-term memories are encoded in the form of sounds and also as visual images, forming a mental picture of the world. Thus, **mental images** (representations that stand in for objects or events and have a picture-like quality) are one of several tools used in the thought process.

Here's an interesting demonstration of the use of mental images. Get several people together and ask them to tell you *as fast as they can* how many windows are in the place where they live. Usually you'll find that the first people to shout out an answer have fewer windows in their houses than the ones who take longer to respond. You'll also notice that most of them look up, as if looking at some image that only they can see. If asked, they'll say that to determine the number of windows, they pictured where they live and simply counted windows as they "walked through" the image they created in their mind.

💬 So more windows means more time to count them in your head? I guess mentally "walking" through a bigger house in your head would take longer than "walking" through a smaller one.

That's what researchers think, too. They have found that it does take longer to view a mental image that is larger or covers more distance than a smaller, more compact one (Kosslyn et al., 2001; Ochsner & Kosslyn, 1994). In one study (Kosslyn et al., 1978), participants were asked to look at a map of an imaginary island (see **Figure 7.1**). On this map were several landmarks, such as a hut, a lake, and a grassy area. After viewing the map and memorizing it, participants were asked to imagine a specific place on the island, such as the hut, and then to "look" for another place, like the lake. When they mentally "reached" the second place, they pushed a button that recorded reaction time. The greater the physical distance on the map between the two locations, the longer it took participants to scan the image for the second location. The participants were apparently looking at their mental image and scanning it just as if it were a real, physical map.

People are even able to mentally rotate, or turn, images (Shepherd & Metzler, 1971). Kosslyn (1983) asked participants questions such as the following: "Do frogs have lips and a stubby tail?" He found that most participants reported visualizing a frog, starting

**thinking (cognition)**
mental activity that goes on in the brain when a person is organizing and attempting to understand information and communicating information to others.

**mental images**
mental representations that stand for objects or events and have a picture-like quality.

with the face ("no lips"), then mentally rotating the image so it was facing away from them, and then "zooming in" to look for the stubby tail ("yes, there it is"). A very important aspect of the research on mental rotation is that we tend to engage *mental* images in our mind much like we engage or interact with *physical* objects. When we rotate an object in our minds (or in other ways interact with or manipulate mental images), it is not instantaneous—it takes time, just as it would if we were rotating a physical object with our hands. To see how well you are able to mentally rotate images, try the *Mental Rotation* experiment. ⊙ **Simulate** the **Experiment,** *Mental Rotation*

In the brain, creating a mental image is almost the opposite of seeing an actual image. With an actual image, the information goes from the eyes to the visual cortex of the occipital lobe and is processed, or interpreted, by other areas of the cortex that compare the new information to information already in memory. Ⓛ Ⓘ Ⓝ Ⓚ to Learning Objective 2.12. In creating a mental image, areas of the cortex associated with stored knowledge send information to the visual cortex, where the image is perceived in the "mind's eye" (Kosslyn et al., 1993; Sparing et al., 2002). PET scans show areas of the visual cortex being activated during the process of forming an image, providing evidence for the role of the visual cortex in mental imagery (Kosslyn et al., 1993, 1999, 2001).

Through the use of functional magnetic resonance imagery (fMRI), researchers have been able to see the overlap that occurs in brain areas activated during visual mental imagery tasks as compared to actual tasks involving visual perception (Ganis et al., 2004). During both types of tasks, activity was present in the frontal cortex (cognitive control), temporal lobes (memory), parietal lobes (attention and spatial memory), and occipital lobes (visual processing). However, the amount of activity in these areas differed between the two types of tasks. For example, activity in the visual cortex was stronger during perception than in imagery, suggesting sensory input activates this area more strongly than memory input. And an important finding overall is that those areas activated during visual imagery were a subset of those activated during visual perception, with the greatest similarity in the frontal and parietal regions rather than the temporal and occipital regions. What does this mean? Simply that there is commonality between the processes of visual imagery and visual perception but it *is not* a complete overlap, and, as the authors point out, the greater overlap *was not* in the temporal and occipital regions (memory and vision functions) that might be assumed to be the most likely areas of overlap given the visual nature of the tasks (Ganis et al., 2004).

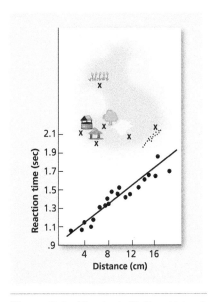

**Figure 7.1** Kosslyn's Fictional Island
In Kosslyn's 1978 study, participants were asked to push a button when they had imagined themselves moving from one place on the island to another. As the graph below the picture shows, participants took longer times to complete the task when the locations on the image were farther apart. *Source:* Kosslyn et al. (1978).

## CONCEPTS AND PROTOTYPES

### 7.2 Describe how concepts and prototypes influence our thinking.

  Images are not the only way we think, are they?

Mental images are only one form of mental representation. Another aspect of thought processes is the use of concepts. **Concepts** are ideas that represent a class or category of objects, events, or activities. People use concepts to think about objects or events without having to think about all the specific examples of the category. For example, a person can think about "fruit" without thinking about every kind of fruit there is in the world, which would take far more effort and time. This ability to think in terms of concepts allows us to communicate with each other: If I mention a bird to you, you know what I am referring to, even if we aren't actually thinking of the same *type* of bird.

Concepts not only contain the important features of the objects or events people want to think about, but also they allow the identification of new objects and events that may fit the concept. For example, dogs come in all shapes, sizes, colors, and lengths of fur. Yet most people have no trouble recognizing dogs as dogs, even though they may never before have seen that particular breed of dog. Friends of the author have a dog called a briard, which is a kind of sheepdog. In spite of the fact that this dog is easily the size of a small pony, the author had no trouble recognizing it as a dog, albeit a huge and extremely shaggy one.

**concepts**

ideas that represent a class or category of objects, events, or activities.

Concepts can have very strict definitions, such as the concept of a square as a shape with four equal sides. Concepts defined by specific rules or features are called *formal concepts* and are quite rigid. To be a square, for example, an object must be a two-dimensional figure with four equal sides and four angles adding up to 360 degrees. Mathematics is full of formal concepts. For example, in geometry there are triangles, squares, rectangles, polygons, and lines. In psychology, there are double-blind experiments, sleep stages, and conditioned stimuli, to name a few. Each of these concepts must fit very specific features to be considered true examples.

💬 But what about things that don't easily fit the rules or features? What if a thing has some, but not all, features of a concept?

People are surrounded by objects, events, and activities that are not as clearly defined as formal concepts. What is a vehicle? Cars and trucks leap immediately to mind, but what about a bobsled or a raft? Those last two objects aren't quite as easy to classify as vehicles immediately, but they fit some of the rules for "vehicle." These are examples of *natural concepts*, concepts people form not as a result of a strict set of rules but rather as the result of experiences with these concepts in the real world (Ahn, 1998; Barton & Komatsu, 1989; Rosch, 1973). Formal concepts are well defined, but natural concepts are "fuzzy" (Hampton, 1998). Natural concepts are important in helping people understand their surroundings in a less structured manner than school-taught formal concepts, and they form the basis for interpreting those surroundings and the events that may occur in everyday life.

When someone says "fruit," what's the first image that comes to mind? More than likely, it's a specific kind of fruit like an apple, pear, or orange. It's less likely that someone's first impulse will be to say "guava" or "papaya" or even "banana," unless that person comes from a tropical area. In the United States, apples are a good example of a **prototype**, a concept that closely matches the defining characteristics of the concept (Mervis & Rosch, 1981; Rosch, 1977). Fruit is sweet, grows on trees, has seeds, and is usually round—all very apple-like qualities. Coconuts are sweet and they also grow on trees, but many people in the Northern Hemisphere have never actually seen a coconut tree. They have more likely seen countless apple trees. So people who do have very different experiences with fruit, for instance, will have different prototypes, which are the most basic examples of concepts.

💬 What about people who live in a tropical area? Would their prototype for fruit be different? And would people's prototypes vary in other cultures?

More than likely, prototypes develop according to the exposure a person has to objects in that category. So someone who grew up in an area where there are many coconut trees might think of coconuts as more prototypical than apples, whereas someone growing up in the northwestern United States would more likely see apples as a prototypical fruit (Aitchison, 1992). Culture also matters in the formation of prototypes. Research on concept prototypes across various cultures found greater differences and variations in prototypes between cultures that were dissimilar, such as Taiwan and America, than between cultures that are more similar, such as Hispanic Americans and non–Hispanic Americans living in Florida (Lin et al., 1990; Lin & Schwanenflugel, 1995; Schwanenflugel & Rey, 1986).

How do prototypes affect thinking? People tend to look at potential examples of a concept and compare them to the prototype to see how well they match—which is why it takes most people much longer to think about olives and tomatoes as fruit because they aren't sweet, one of the major characteristics of the prototype of fruit (Rosch & Mervis, 1975). As the video *The Mind Is What the Brain Does* explains, we use a combination of cognitive processes including concepts, prototypes, and mental images to identify objects in our daily lives.

A duck-billed platypus is classified as a mammal yet shares features with birds, such as webbed feet and a bill, and it also lays eggs. The platypus is an example of a "fuzzy" natural concept. Courtesy of Dave Watts, Nature Picture Library.

Both of these animals are dogs. They both have fur, four legs, a tail—but the similarities end there. With so many variations in the animals we call "dogs," what is the prototype for "dog"?

**prototype**

an example of a concept that closely matches the defining characteristics of the concept.

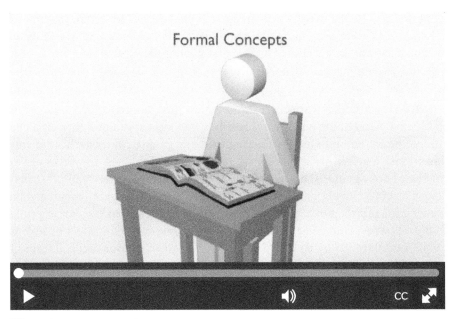

## Formal Concepts

 **Watch** the **Video** *The Mind Is What the Brain Does*

No matter what type, concepts are one of the ways people deal with all the information that bombards* their senses every day, allowing them to organize their perceptions of the world around them. This organization may take the form of *schemas*, mental generalizations about objects, places, events, and people (for example, one's schema for "library" would no doubt include books and bookshelves), or *scripts*, a kind of schema that involves a familiar sequence of activities (for example, "going to a movie" would include traveling there, getting the ticket, buying snacks, finding the right theater, etc.). Concepts not only help people think, but also they are an important tool in *problem solving*, a type of thinking that people engage in every day and in many different situations.

### PROBLEM-SOLVING AND DECISION-MAKING STRATEGIES

**7.3** Identify some methods that people use to solve problems and make decisions.

💬 Problem solving is certainly a big part of any college student's life. Is there any one "best" way to go about solving a problem?

Think about it as you read on and solve the following: Put a coin in a bottle and then cork the opening. How can you get the coin out of the bottle without pulling out the cork or breaking the bottle? (For the solution, see the section on Insight.)

As stated earlier, images and concepts are mental tools that can be used to solve problems and make decisions. For the preceding problem, you are probably trying to create an image of the bottle with a coin in it. **Problem solving** occurs when a goal must be reached by thinking and behaving in certain ways. Problems range from figuring out how to cut a recipe in half to understanding complex mathematical proofs to deciding what to major in at college. Problem solving is one aspect of **decision making**, or identifying, evaluating, and choosing among several alternatives. There are several different ways in which people can think in order to solve problems.

**TRIAL AND ERROR (MECHANICAL SOLUTIONS)**    One method is to use **trial and error**, also known as a **mechanical solution**. Trial and error refers to trying one solution after

*bombards: attacks again and again.

This child may try one piece after another until finding the piece that fits. This is an example of trial-and-error learning.

**problem solving**

process of cognition that occurs when a goal must be reached by thinking and behaving in certain ways.

**decision making**

process of cognition that involves identifying, evaluating, and choosing among several alternatives.

**trial and error (mechanical solution)**

problem-solving method in which one possible solution after another is tried until a successful one is found.

another until finding one that works. For example, if Shelana has forgotten the PIN for her online banking Web site, she can try one combination after another until she finds the one that works, if she has only a few such PINs that she normally uses. Mechanical solutions can also involve solving by *rote*, or a learned set of rules. This is how word problems were solved in grade school, for example. One type of rote solution is to use an algorithm.

**ALGORITHMS**  **Algorithms** are specific, step-by-step procedures for solving certain types of problems. Algorithms will always result in a correct solution if there is a correct solution to be found and you have enough time to find it. Mathematical formulas are algorithms. When librarians organize books on bookshelves, they also use an algorithm: Place books in alphabetical order within each category, for example. Many puzzles, like a Rubik's Cube®, have a set of steps that, if followed exactly, will always result in solving the puzzle. But algorithms aren't always practical to use. For example, if Shelana didn't have a clue what those four numbers might be, she *might* be able to figure out her forgotten PIN by trying *all possible combinations* of four digits, 0 through 9. She would eventually find the right four-digit combination—but it might take a very long while! Computers, however, can run searches like this one very quickly, so the systematic search algorithm is a useful part of some computer programs.

**HEURISTICS**  Unfortunately, humans aren't as fast as computers and need some other way to narrow down the possible solutions to only a few. One way to do this is to use a heuristic. A **heuristic**, or "rule of thumb," is a simple rule that is intended to apply to many situations. Whereas an algorithm is very specific and will always lead to a solution, a heuristic is an educated guess based on prior experiences that helps narrow down the possible solutions for a problem. For example, if a student is typing a paper in a word-processing program and wants to know how to format the page, he or she could try to read an entire manual on the word-processing program. That would take a while. Instead, the student could use an Internet search engine or type "format" into the help feature's search program. Doing either action greatly reduces the amount of information the student will have to look at to get an answer. Using the help feature or clicking on the appropriate toolbar word will also work for similar problems.

**REPRESENTATIVENESS HEURISTIC**  Will using a rule of thumb always work, like algorithms do? Using a heuristic is faster than using an algorithm in many cases, but unlike algorithms, heuristics will *not* always lead to the correct solution. What you gain in speed is sometimes lost in accuracy. For example, a **representativeness heuristic** is used for categorizing objects and simply assumes that any object (or person) that shares characteristics with the members of a particular category is also a member of that category. This is a handy tool when it comes to classifying plants but doesn't work as well when applied to people. The representativeness heuristic can cause errors due to ignoring base rates, the actual probability of a given event. Are all people with dark skin from Africa? Does everyone with red hair also have a bad temper? Are all blue-eyed blondes from Sweden? See the point? The representativeness heuristic can be used—or misused— to create and sustain stereotypes (Kahneman & Tversky, 1973; Kahneman et al., 1982).

**AVAILABILITY HEURISTIC**  Another heuristic that can have undesired outcomes is the **availability heuristic**, which is based on our estimation of the frequency or likelihood of an event based on how easy it is to recall relevant information from memory or how easy it is for us to think of related examples (Tversky & Kahneman, 1973). Imagine, for example, that after you have already read this entire textbook (it could happen!) you are asked to estimate how many words in the book start with the letter *K* and how many have the letter *K* as the third letter in the word. Which place do you think is more frequent, the first letter or as the third letter? Next, what do you think the ratio of the more frequent placement is to the less frequent placement? What is easier to think of, words that begin with the letter *K* or words that have *K* as the third letter? Tversky and Kahneman (1973) asked this same question of 152 participants for five consonants (*K, N, L, R, V*) that appear more frequently

Smartphones and other portable devices provide tools for easy navigation. How might the use or overuse of these tools affect our ability to navigate when we do not have access to them?

**algorithms**

very specific, step-by-step procedures for solving certain types of problems.

**heuristic**

an educated guess based on prior experiences that helps narrow down the possible solutions for a problem. Also known as a "rule of thumb."

**representativeness heuristic**

assumption that any object (or person) sharing characteristics with the members of a particular category is also a member of that category.

**availability heuristic**

estimating the frequency or likelihood of an event based on how easy it is to recall relevant information from memory or how easy it is for us to think of related examples.

in the third position as compared to the first in a typical text. Sixty-nine percent of the participants indicated that the first position was the more frequent placement and the median estimated ratio was 2:1 for the letter *K*—however, there are typically twice as many words with *K* as the third letter as compared to the first. Can you think of an example where you may have used the availability heuristic and it did not work in your favor?

**WORKING BACKWARD**    A useful heuristic that *does* work much of the time is to *work backward from the goal.* For example, if you want to know the shortest way to get to the new coffee shop in town, you already know the goal, which is finding the coffee shop. There are probably several ways to get there from your house, and some are shorter than others. Assuming you have the address of the store, for many the best way to determine the shortest route is to look up the location of the store on an Internet map, a GPS, or a smartphone and compare the different routes by the means of travel (walking versus driving). People actually used to do this with a physical map and compare the routes manually! Think about it: Does technology help or hinder some aspects of problem solving? What are, if any, the benefits to using technology for solving some problems as compared to actively engaging in problem solving as a mental challenge?

 💬 What if my problem is writing a term paper? Starting at the end isn't going to help me much!

**SUBGOALS**    Sometimes it's better to break a goal down into *subgoals* so that as each subgoal is achieved, the final solution is that much closer. Writing a term paper, for example, can seem overwhelming until it is broken down into steps: Choose a topic, research the topic, organize what has been gathered, write one section at a time, and so on. 🔗 L I N K to Learning Objective PIA.7. Other examples of heuristics include making diagrams to help organize the information concerning the problem or testing possible solutions to the problem one by one and eliminating those that do not work.

💬 Sometimes I have to find answers to problems one step at a time, but in other cases the answer seems to just "pop" into my head all of a sudden. Why do some answers come so easily to mind?

**INSIGHT**    When the solution to a problem seems to come suddenly to mind, it is called insight. Chapter Five contained a discussion of Köhler's (1925) work with Sultan the chimpanzee, which demonstrated that even some animals can solve problems by means of a sudden insight. 🔗 L I N K to Learning Objective 5.11. In humans, insight often takes the form of an "aha!" moment—the solution seems to come in a flash. A person may realize that this problem is similar to another one that he or she already knows how to solve or might see that an object can be used for a different purpose than its original one, like using a dime as a screwdriver.

Remember the problem of the bottle discussed earlier in this chapter? The task was to get the coin out of the bottle without removing the cork or breaking the bottle. The answer is simple: *Push the cork into the bottle and shake out the coin. Aha!*

Insight is not really a magical process, although it can seem like magic. What usually happens is that the mind simply reorganizes a problem, sometimes while the person is thinking about something else (Durso et al., 1994).

Here's a problem that can be solved with insight: Marsha and Marjorie were born on the same day of the same month of the same year to the same mother and the same father yet they are not twins. How is that possible? Think about it and then look for the answer in the section on Mental Sets.

In summary, thinking is a complex process involving the use of mental imagery and various types of concepts to organize the events of daily life. Problem solving is a

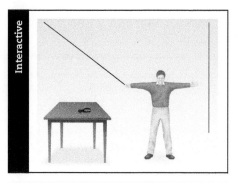

**Figure 7.2** The String Problem

How do you tie the two strings together if you cannot reach them both at the same time?

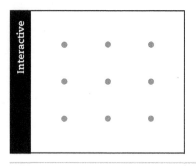

**Figure 7.3** The Dot Problem

Can you draw four straight lines so that they pass through all nine dots *without lifting your pencil from the page and without touching any dot more than once?*

**functional fixedness**

a block to problem solving that comes from thinking about objects in terms of only their typical functions.

**mental set**

the tendency for people to persist in using problem-solving patterns that have worked for them in the past.

**confirmation bias**

the tendency to search for evidence that fits one's beliefs while ignoring any evidence that does not fit those beliefs.

special type of thinking that involves the use of many tools, such as trial-and-error thinking, algorithms, and heuristics, to solve different types of problems.

## PROBLEMS WITH PROBLEM SOLVING AND DECISION MAKING

**7.4** **Identify three common barriers to successful problem solving.**

Using insight to solve a problem is not always foolproof. Sometimes a solution to a problem remains just "out of reach" because the elements of the problem are not arranged properly or because people get stuck in certain ways of thinking that act as barriers* to solving problems. Such ways of thinking occur more or less automatically, influencing attempts to solve problems without any conscious awareness of that influence. Here's a classic example:

Two strings are hanging from a ceiling but are too far apart to allow a person to hold one and walk to the other. (See **Figure 7.2**.) Nearby is a table with a pair of pliers on it. The goal is to tie the two pieces of string together. How? For the solution to this problem, read on.

People can become aware of automatic tendencies to try to solve problems in ways that are not going to lead to solutions and, in becoming aware, can abandon the "old" ways for more appropriate problem-solving methods. Three of the most common barriers to successful problem solving are functional fixedness, mental sets, and confirmation bias.

**FUNCTIONAL FIXEDNESS**   One problem-solving difficulty involves thinking about objects only in terms of their typical uses, which is a phenomenon called **functional fixedness** (literally, "fixed on the function"). Have you ever searched high and low for a screwdriver to fix something around the house? All the while there are several objects close at hand that could be used to tighten a screw: a butter knife, a key, or even a dime in your pocket. Because the tendency is to think of those objects in terms of cooking, unlocking, and spending, we sometimes ignore the less obvious possible uses. The string problem introduced before is an example of functional fixedness. The pair of pliers is often seen as useless until the person realizes it can be used as a weight. (See answer in the section on Creativity.)

**MENTAL SETS**   Functional fixedness is actually a kind of **mental set**, which is defined as the tendency for people to persist in using problem-solving patterns that have worked for them in the past. Solutions that have worked in the past tend to be the ones people try first, and people are often hesitant or even unable to think of other possibilities. Look at **Figure 7.3** and see if you can solve the dot problem.

People are taught from the earliest grades to stay within the lines, right? That tried-and-true method will not help in solving the dot problem. The solution involves drawing the lines beyond the actual dots, as seen in the solution in the section on Creativity.

Answer to insight problem: *Marsha and Marjorie are two of a set of triplets. Gotcha!*

**CONFIRMATION BIAS**   Another barrier to effective decision making or problem solving is **confirmation bias**, the tendency to search for evidence that fits one's beliefs while ignoring any evidence to the contrary. This is similar to a mental set, except that what is "set" is a belief rather than a method of solving problems. Believers in ESP tend to remember the few studies that seem to support their beliefs and psychic predictions that worked out while at the same time "forgetting" the cases in which studies found no proof or psychics made predictions that failed to come true. They remember only that which confirms their bias toward a belief in the existence of ESP.

Another example is that people who believe that they are good multitaskers and can safely drive a motor vehicle while talking or texting on their cell phones may tend to remember their own personal experiences, which may not include any vehicle accidents or "near-misses" (that they are aware of). Recent research on sensory processing in the brain has found that when faced with multiple sources of sensory information, we can actually become overloaded under high-demand situations and experience temporary

*barrier: something that blocks one's path; an obstacle preventing a solution.

blindness or deafness due to inattention. In one study, researchers found that when faced with a very demanding visual task, participants lost the ability to detect auditory information (Molloy et al., 2015).

While it might be tempting to think of one's self as a "supertasker," research suggests otherwise. When tested on driving simulators while having to perform successfully on two attention-demanding tasks, more than 97 percent of individuals are unable to do so without significant impacts on their performance. During the dual-task condition, only 2.5 percent of individuals were able to perform without problems (Watson & Strayer, 2010). Research also suggests the people that are most likely to talk on their cell phone while driving, as indicated by self-report, are actually the worst at multitasking when tested (Sanbonmatsu et al., 2013). It is estimated that at least 27 percent of all traffic crashes are caused by drivers using their cell phone and/or texting (National Safety Council, 2015).

The driver of this train was texting from his cell phone immediately before this crash that killed 25 people and injured more than 130 others.

## CREATIVITY

### 7.5 Recall some characteristics of creative, divergent thinking.

 💬 So far, we've only talked about logic and pretty straightforward thinking. How do people come up with totally new ideas, things no one has thought of before?

Not every problem can be answered by using information already at hand and the rules of logic in applying that information. Sometimes a problem requires coming up with entirely new ways of looking at the problem or unusual, inventive solutions. This kind of thinking is called **creativity**: solving problems by combining ideas or behavior in new ways (Csikszentmihalyi, 1996; pronounced chĭck-sĕnt-mē-HĪ-ē). Before we learn more, take the survey *What Is Creativity?* to examine your own beliefs about creativity.

**Survey**  WHAT IS CREATIVITY?

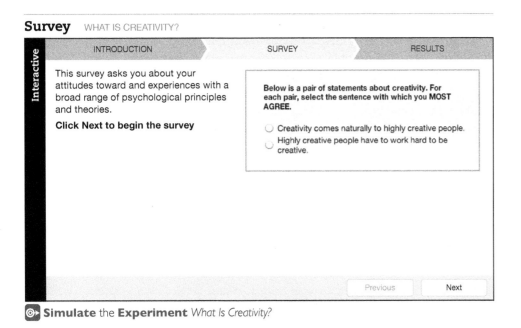

This survey asks you about your attitudes toward and experiences with a broad range of psychological principles and theories.

**Click Next to begin the survey**

Below is a pair of statements about creativity. For each pair, select the sentence with which you MOST AGREE.

○ Creativity comes naturally to highly creative people.
○ Highly creative people have to work hard to be creative.

Previous    Next

⊙ **Simulate** the **Experiment** *What Is Creativity?*

**creativity**
the process of solving problems by combining ideas or behavior in new ways.

**convergent thinking**
type of thinking in which a problem is seen as having only one answer, and all lines of thinking will eventually lead to that single answer, using previous knowledge and logic.

The logical method for problem solving that has been discussed so far is based on a type of thinking called **convergent thinking**. In convergent thinking, a problem is seen as having only one answer, and all lines of thinking will eventually lead to (converge on) that single answer by using previous knowledge and logic (Ciardiello, 1998). For example, the question "In what ways are a pencil and a pen alike?" can be answered

**Solution to the String Problem**

The solution to the string problem is to use the pliers as a pendulum to swing the second string closer to you.

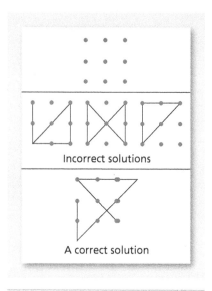

Incorrect solutions

A correct solution

**Solution to the Dot Problem**

When people try to solve this problem, a mental set causes them to think of the dots as representing a box, and they try to draw the line while staying in the box. The only way to connect all nine dots without lifting the pencil from the paper is to draw the lines so they extend out of the box of dots—literally "thinking outside the box."

**divergent thinking**

type of thinking in which a person starts from one point and comes up with many different ideas or possibilities based on that point.

by listing the features that the two items have in common: Both can be used to write, have similar shapes, and so on, in a simple comparison process. Convergent thinking works well for routine problem solving but may be of little use when a more creative solution is needed.

**Divergent thinking** is the reverse of convergent thinking. Here a person starts at one point and comes up with many different, or divergent, ideas or possibilities based on that point (Finke, 1995). For example, if someone were to ask the question, "What is a pencil used for?" the convergent answer would be "to write." But if the question is put this way: "How many different uses can you think of for a pencil?" the answers multiply: "writing, poking holes, a weight for the tail of a kite, a weapon." Divergent thinking has been attributed not only to creativity but also to intelligence (Guilford, 1967).

What are the characteristics of a creative, divergent thinker? Theorists in the field of creative thinking have found through examining the habits of highly creative people that the most productive periods of divergent thinking for those people tend to occur when they are doing some task or activity that is more or less automatic, such as walking or swimming (Csikszentmihalyi, 1996; Gardner, 1993a; Goleman, 1995). These automatic tasks take up some attention processes, leaving the remainder to devote to creative thinking. The fact that all of one's attention is not focused on the problem is actually a benefit, because divergent thinkers often make links and connections at a level of consciousness just below alert awareness, so that ideas can flow freely without being censored* by the higher mental processes (Goleman, 1995). In other words, having part of one's attention devoted to walking, for example, allows the rest of the mind to "sneak up on" more creative solutions and ideas.

Divergent thinkers will obviously be less prone to some of the barriers to problem solving, such as functional fixedness. For example, what would most people do if it suddenly started to rain while they are stuck in their office with no umbrella? How many people would think of using a see-through vinyl tote bag as a makeshift umbrella?

Creative, divergent thinking is often a neglected topic in the education of young people. Although some people are naturally more creative, it is possible to develop one's creative ability. The ability to be creative is important—coming up with topics for a research paper, for example, is something that many students have trouble doing. Cross-cultural research (Basadur et al., 2002; Colligan, 1983) has found that divergent thinking and problem-solving skills cannot be easily taught in the Japanese or Omaha Native American cultures, for example. In these cultures, creativity in many areas is not normally prized, and the preference is to hold to well-established cultural traditions, such as traditional dances that have not varied for centuries. See **Table 7.1** for some ways to become a more divergent thinker.

Many people have the idea that creative people are also a little different from other people. There are artists and musicians, for example, who actually encourage others

| **Table 7.1** | Stimulating Divergent Thinking |
|---|---|
| Brainstorming | Generate as many ideas as possible in a short period of time without judging each idea's merits until all ideas are recorded. |
| Keeping a Journal | Carry a journal to write down ideas as they occur or a recorder to capture those same ideas and thoughts. |
| Freewriting | Write down or record everything that comes to mind about a topic without revising or proofreading until all of the information is written or recorded in some way. Organize it later. |
| Mind or Subject Mapping | Start with a central idea and draw a "map" with lines from the center to other related ideas, forming a visual representation of the concepts and their connections. |

*censored: blocked from conscious awareness as unacceptable thoughts.

to see them as eccentric. But the fact is that creative people are actually pretty normal. According to Csikszentmihalyi (1997):

1. Creative people usually have a broad range of knowledge about a lot of subjects and are good at using mental imagery.
2. Creative people aren't afraid to be different—they are more open to new experiences than many people, and they tend to have more vivid dreams and daydreams than others do.
3. Creative people value their independence.
4. Creative people are often unconventional in their work, but not otherwise.

A DJ performing before an audience. What aspects of creativity apply to the work of a DJ?

## Concept Map L.O. 7.1, 7.2, 7.3, 7.4, 7.5

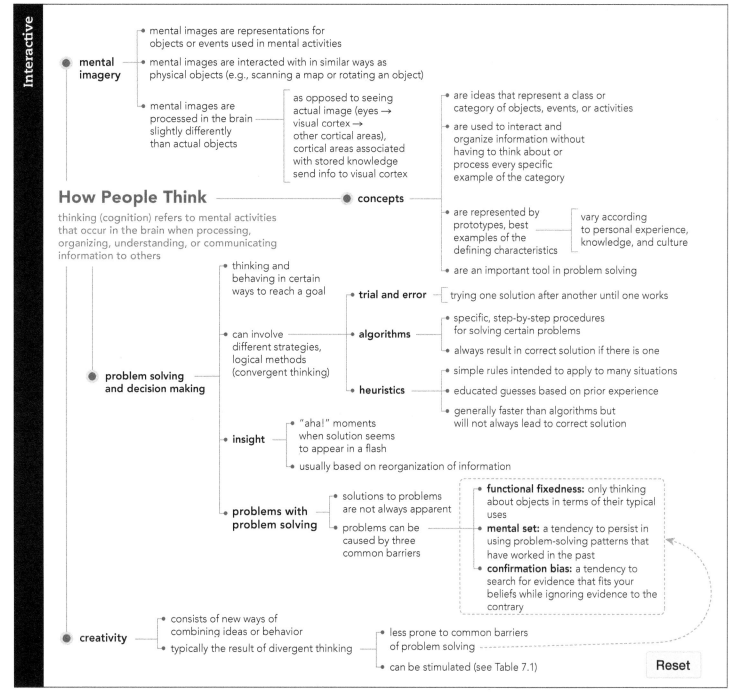

**Interactive**

**mental imagery**
- mental images are representations for objects or events used in mental activities
- mental images are interacted with in similar ways as physical objects (e.g., scanning a map or rotating an object)
- mental images are processed in the brain slightly differently than actual objects — as opposed to seeing actual image (eyes → visual cortex → other cortical areas), cortical areas associated with stored knowledge send info to visual cortex

## How People Think

thinking (cognition) refers to mental activities that occur in the brain when processing, organizing, understanding, or communicating information to others

**concepts**
- are ideas that represent a class or category of objects, events, or activities
- are used to interact and organize information without having to think about or process every specific example of the category
- are represented by prototypes, best examples of the defining characteristics — vary according to personal experience, knowledge, and culture
- are an important tool in problem solving

**problem solving and decision making**
- thinking and behaving in certain ways to reach a goal
- can involve different strategies, logical methods (convergent thinking)
  - **trial and error** — trying one solution after another until one works
  - **algorithms**
    - specific, step-by-step procedures for solving certain problems
    - always result in correct solution if there is one
  - **heuristics**
    - simple rules intended to apply to many situations
    - educated guesses based on prior experience
    - generally faster than algorithms but will not always lead to correct solution

**insight**
- "aha!" moments when solution seems to appear in a flash
- usually based on reorganization of information

**problems with problem solving**
- solutions to problems are not always apparent
- problems can be caused by three common barriers
  - **functional fixedness:** only thinking about objects in terms of their typical uses
  - **mental set:** a tendency to persist in using problem-solving patterns that have worked in the past
  - **confirmation bias:** a tendency to search for evidence that fits your beliefs while ignoring evidence to the contrary

**creativity**
- consists of new ways of combining ideas or behavior
- typically the result of divergent thinking
- less prone to common barriers of problem solving
- can be stimulated (see Table 7.1)

Reset

# Practice Quiz    How much do you remember?

*Pick the best answer.*

1. What is thinking?
   a. mental activity that involves processing, organizing, understanding, and communicating information
   b. spontaneous, nondirected, and unconscious mental activity
   c. simply and succinctly, it is only our ability to remember
   d. all mental activity except memory

2. People in the United States often think of a sports car when asked to envision a fun, fast form of travel. In this example, a sports car would be considered a
   a. prototype.              c. formal concept.
   b. natural concept.        d. mental image.

3. While taking a shower, Miguel suddenly realizes the solution to a problem at work. When later asked how he solved this problem, Miguel said, "The answer just seemed to pop into my head." Miguel's experience is an example of
   a. a mechanical solution.   c. an algorithm.
   b. a heuristic.             d. insight.

4. Alicia leaves her office building only to find it is raining. She returns to her office and gets a trash bag out of the supply cabinet. Using a pair of scissors, she cuts the bag so that she can put her head and arms through the bag without getting wet. In using the trash bag as a makeshift rain jacket, Alicia has overcome
   a. functional fixedness.    c. creativity bias.
   b. confirmation bias.       d. confirmation fixedness.

5. Randall believes that aliens are currently living deep under the ocean. When looking for information about this on the Internet, he ignores any sites that are skeptical of his belief and only visits sites that support his belief. This is an example of
   a. functional fixedness.    c. creativity bias.
   b. confirmation bias.       d. confirmation fixedness.

6. Which of the following is the best way to encourage divergent, creative thinking?
   a. Go for a walk or engage in some other automatic activity.
   b. Stare at a blank sheet of paper until a new, innovative solution comes to mind.
   c. Engage in many activities simultaneously.
   d. Force yourself to think of something new and creative.

---

# Intelligence

What does it mean to be "smart"? Is this the same as being intelligent? It is likely the answer depends on the immediate task or context. What exactly do we mean by the term *intelligence*?

## THEORIES OF INTELLIGENCE

### 7.6 Compare and contrast different theories on the nature of intelligence.

Is intelligence merely a score on some test, or is it practical knowledge of how to get along in the world? Is it making good grades or being a financial success or a social success? Ask a dozen people and you will probably get a dozen different answers. Psychologists have come up with a workable definition that combines many of the ideas just mentioned: They define **intelligence** as the ability to learn from one's experiences, acquire knowledge, and use resources effectively in adapting to new situations or solving problems (Sternberg & Kaufman, 1998; Wechsler, 1975). These are the characteristics that individuals need in order to survive in their culture.

Although we have defined intelligence in a general way, there are differing opinions of the specific knowledge and abilities that make up the concept of intelligence. We will discuss several theories that offer different explanations of the nature and number of intelligence-related abilities.

**SPEARMAN'S G FACTOR**    Charles Spearman (1904) saw intelligence as two different abilities. The ability to reason and solve problems was labeled **g factor** for *general intelligence*, whereas task-specific abilities in certain areas such as music, business, or art are labeled **s factor** for *specific intelligence*. A traditional IQ test would most likely measure g factor, but Spearman believed that superiority in one type of intelligence predicts superiority overall. Although his early research found some support for specific intelligences, other researchers (Guilford, 1967; Thurstone, 1938) felt that Spearman had oversimplified the concept of intelligence. Intelligence began to be viewed as composed of numerous factors. In fact, Guilford (1967) proposed that there were 120 types of intelligence.

**intelligence**
the ability to learn from one's experiences, acquire knowledge, and use resources effectively in adapting to new situations or solving problems.

**g factor**
the ability to reason and solve problems, or general intelligence.

**s factor**
the ability to excel in certain areas, or specific intelligence.

**GARDNER'S MULTIPLE INTELLIGENCES**   One of the later theorists to propose the existence of several kinds of intelligence is Howard Gardner (1993b, 1999a). Although many people use the terms *reason*, *logic*, and *knowledge* as if they are the same ability, Gardner believes that they are different aspects of intelligence, along with several other abilities. He originally listed seven different kinds of intelligence but later added an eighth type and then proposed a tentative ninth (Gardner, 1998, 1999b). The nine types of intelligence are described in the video *Theories of Intelligence: Gardner's Theory* and summarized in **Table 7.2**.

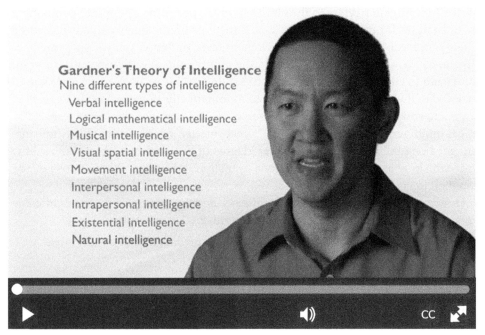

Gardner's Theory of Intelligence
Nine different types of intelligence
  Verbal intelligence
  Logical mathematical intelligence
  Musical intelligence
  Visual spatial intelligence
  Movement intelligence
  Interpersonal intelligence
  Intrapersonal intelligence
  Existential intelligence
  Natural intelligence

◉ **Watch** the **Video** *Theories of Intelligence: Gardner's Theory*

| **Table 7.2**  Gardner's Nine Intelligences | | |
|---|---|---|
| **Type of Intelligence** | **Description** | **Sample Occupation** |
| Verbal/linguistic | Ability to use language | Writers, speakers |
| Musical | Ability to compose and/or perform music | Musicians, even those who do not read musical notes but can perform and compose |
| Logical/ mathematical | Ability to think logically and to solve mathematical problems | Scientists, engineers |
| Visual/spatial | Ability to understand how objects are oriented in space | Pilots, astronauts, artists, navigators |
| Movement | Ability to control one's body motions | Dancers, athletes |
| Interpersonal | Sensitivity to others and understanding motivation of others | Psychologists, managers |
| Intrapersonal | Understanding of one's emotions and how they guide actions | Various people-oriented careers |
| Naturalist | Ability to recognize the patterns found in nature | Farmers, landscapers, biologists, botanists |
| Existentialist (a candidate intelligence) | Ability to see the "big picture" of the human world by asking questions about life, death, and the ultimate reality of human existence | Various careers, philosophical thinkers |

**SOURCE**: Gardner, 1998, 1999b.

The idea of multiple intelligences has great appeal, especially for educators. However, some argue that there are few scientific studies providing evidence for the concept of multiple intelligences (Waterhouse, 2006a, 2006b), while others claim that the evidence does exist (Gardner & Moran, 2006). Some critics propose that such intelligences are no more than different abilities and that those abilities are not necessarily the same thing as what is typically meant by *intelligence* (E. Hunt, 2001).

**STERNBERG'S TRIARCHIC THEORY**   Robert Sternberg (1988a, 1997b) has theorized that there are three kinds of intelligence. Called the **triarchic theory of intelligence** (*triarchic* means three), this theory includes *analytical, creative,* and *practical intelligence.* **Analytical intelligence** refers to the ability to break problems down into component parts, or analysis, for problem solving. This is the type of intelligence that is measured by intelligence tests and academic achievement tests, or "book smarts" as some people like to call it. **Creative intelligence** is the ability to deal with new and different concepts and to come up with new ways of solving problems (divergent thinking, in other words); it also refers to the ability to automatically process certain aspects of information, which frees up cognitive resources to deal with novelty (Sternberg, 2005). **Practical intelligence** is best described as "street smarts," or the ability to use information to get along in life. People with a high degree of practical intelligence know how to be tactful, how to manipulate situations to their advantage, and how to use inside information to increase their odds of success.

How might these three types of intelligence be illustrated? All three might come into play when planning and completing an experiment. For example:

- *Analytical:* Being able to run a statistical analysis on data from the experiment.
- *Creative:* Being able to design the experiment in the first place.
- *Practical:* Being able to get funding for the experiment from donors.

Practical intelligence has become a topic of much interest and research. Sternberg (1996, 1997a, 1997b) has found that practical intelligence predicts success in life but has a surprisingly low relationship to academic (analytical) intelligence. However, when practical intelligence is taken into account or used to supplement standardized tests, studies have found that college, high school, and elementary school programs benefit in a variety of areas due to the diverse range of individuals being included (Sternberg, 2015).

**CATTELL-HORN-CARROLL (CHC) THEORY**   Another influential theory of intelligence is actually based on the culmination of work from several theorists, Raymond Cattell, John Horn, and John Carroll (Flanagan & Dixon, 2013; McGrew, 2009; Schneider & McGrew, 2012). Interestingly, Cattell was a student of Charles Spearman and Horn was a student of Cattell (Schneider & McGrew, 2012). Raymond Cattell suggested intelligence was composed of *crystalized intelligence,* which represents acquired knowledge and skills, versus *fluid intelligence,* or problem solving and adaptability in unfamiliar situations. John Horn expanded on Cattell's work and added other abilities based on visual and auditory processing, memory, speed of processing, reaction time, quantitative skills, and reading-writing skills (Flanagan & Dixon, 2013). Based on an extensive factor analysis of data from more than 460 studies, John Carroll developed a three-tier hierarchical model of cognitive abilities that fit so well with the Cattell-Horn crystalized and fluid intelligence models that a new theory was suggested, the Cattell-Horn-Carroll (CHC) Theory of Intelligence (McGrew, 2009).

One component of the CHC framework is general intelligence, or *g.* It is also composed of 16 broad abilities including general brain-based factors comprising fluid reasoning, short-term memory, long-term storage and retrieval, processing speed, reaction and decision speed, and psychomotor speed (see **Figure 7.4**). Four abilities are based on Cattell's description of crystalized intelligence: comprehension-knowledge,

**triarchic theory of intelligence**

Sternberg's theory that there are three kinds of intelligence: analytical, creative, and practical.

**analytical intelligence**

the ability to break problems down into component parts, or analysis, for problem solving.

**creative intelligence**

the ability to deal with new and different concepts and to come up with new ways of solving problems.

**practical intelligence**

the ability to use information to get along in life and become successful.

domain-specific knowledge, reading and writing, and quantitative knowledge. Other abilities are tied to sensory systems and their respective primary and association areas of the cortex: visual processing, auditory processing, olfactory abilities, tactile abilities, kinesthetic abilities, and psychomotor abilities (Schneider & McGrew, 2012).

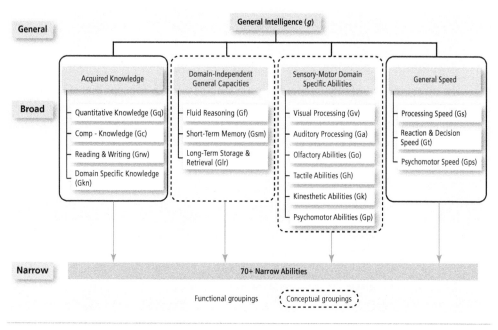

**Figure 7.4**   Cattell-Horn-Carroll (CHC) Theory of Intelligence. Based on and adapted from Schneider & McGrew (2012, 2013).

Of all of the theories of intelligence, it has been suggested that CHC theory is the most researched, empirically supported, and comprehensive (Flanagan & Dixon, 2013). In fact, many new assessments of intelligence and revisions of earlier assessments have been driven by CHC theory (Keith & Reynolds, 2010).

**NEUROSCIENCE THEORIES**    It is probably no surprise that the brain has been closely linked to intelligence. Not only have specific brain areas and brain functions been tied to differences in intellectual ability, but differing levels of specific cognitive abilities have also been a topic of study. With regard to brain area and function, some researchers have suggested that the frontal and parietal brain areas play the most important roles, and these areas are actually components of one of the leading neuroscience theories of intelligence, the *Parieto-Frontal Integration Theory*, or P-FIT (Jung & Haier, 2007). **Ⓛ Ⓘ Ⓝ Ⓚ** to Learning Objectives 2.11, 2.12. Researchers have expanded on P-FIT and suggested other areas such as the posterior cingulate cortex, insular cortex, and specific subcortical areas also play critical roles (Basten et al., 2015). For specific cognitive abilities, working memory has been tied to *fluid intelligence*, or the ability to adapt and deal with new problems or challenges the first time you encounter them, without having to depend on knowledge you already possess. Working memory in of itself is a contributing factor to a variety of higher cognitive functions. **Ⓛ Ⓘ Ⓝ Ⓚ** to Chap 6.4. When examined in relation to fluid intelligence, individual differences in working memory components such as capacity, attention control, and ability to retrieve items from long-term memory appear to be most influential, and that overall, the ability to reliably preserve relevant information for successful cognitive processing appears to be vital (Colom et al., 2015; Unsworth et al., 2014, 2015).

## 7.7 Compare and contrast some methods of measuring intelligence.

The history of intelligence testing spans the twentieth century and has at times been marked by controversies and misuse. A full history of how intelligence testing developed would take at least an entire chapter, so this section will discuss only some of the better-known forms of testing and how they came to be.

> 💬 It doesn't sound like intelligence would be easy to measure on a test—how do IQ tests work, anyway?

The measurement of intelligence by some kind of test is a concept that is less than a century old. It began when educators in France realized that some students needed more help with learning than others did. They thought that if a way could be found to identify these students more in need, they could be given a different kind of education than the more capable students.

**BINET'S MENTAL ABILITY TEST** In those early days, a French psychologist named Alfred Binet was asked by the French Ministry of Education to design a formal test of intelligence that would help identify children who were unable to learn as quickly or as well as others so that they could be given remedial education. Eventually, he and colleague Théodore Simon came up with a test that distinguished not only between fast and slow learners but also between children of different age groups as well (Binet & Simon, 1916). They noticed that the fast learners seemed to give answers to questions that older children might give, whereas the slow learners gave answers that were more typical of a younger child. Binet decided that the key element to be tested was a child's *mental age*, or the average age at which children could successfully answer a particular level of questions.

**STANFORD-BINET AND IQ** Lewis Terman (1916), a researcher at Stanford University, adopted German psychologist William Stern's method for comparing mental age and *chronological age* (number of years since birth) for use with the translated and revised Binet test. Stern's (1912) formula was to divide the mental age (MA) by the chronological age (CA) and multiply the result by 100 to get rid of any decimal points. The resulting score is called an **intelligence quotient, or IQ**. (A *quotient* is a number that results from dividing one number by another.)

$$IQ = MA/CA \times 100$$

For example, if a child who is 10 years old takes the test and scores a mental age of 15 (is able to answer the level of questions typical of a 15-year-old), the IQ would look like this:

$$IQ = 15/10 \times 100 = 150$$

The quotient has the advantage of allowing testers to compare the intelligence levels of people of different age groups. While this method works well for children, it produces IQ scores that start to become meaningless as the person's chronological age passes 16 years. (Once a person becomes an adult, the idea of questions that are geared for a particular age group loses its power. For example, what kind of differences would there be between questions designed for a 30-year-old versus a 40-year-old?) Most intelligence tests today, such as the *Stanford-Binet Intelligence Scales, Fifth Edition* (*SB5*; Roid, 2003) and the Wechsler tests (see the following section), use age-group comparison norms instead. The SB5 is often used by educators to make decisions about the placement of students into special educational programs, both for those with disabilities and for those with exceptionalities. Many children are given this test in the second grade, or age 7 or 8. The SB5 yields an overall estimate of intelligence, verbal and nonverbal domain scores, all composed of five primary areas of cognitive ability—fluid reasoning, knowledge, quantitative processing, visual–spatial processing, and working memory (Roid, 2003). Test

**intelligence quotient (IQ)**

a number representing a measure of intelligence, resulting from the division of one's mental age by one's chronological age and then multiplying that quotient by 100.

items vary by task and difficulty and are typically completed successfully at different ages. Test items include tasks such as inserting correct shapes into matching holes on a form board (Age 2), digit reversal or being able to repeat four digits backward (Age 9), and testing vocabulary by defining 20 words from a list (Average adult; Roid, 2003).

**THE WECHSLER TESTS** Although the original Stanford-Binet Test is now in its fifth edition and includes different questions for people of different age groups, it is not the only IQ test that is popular today. David Wechsler was the first to devise a series of tests designed for specific age groups. Originally dissatisfied with the fact that the Stanford-Binet test was designed for children but being administered to adults, he developed an IQ test specifically for adults. He later designed tests specifically for older school-age children and preschool children, as well as those in the early grades. The Wechsler Adult Intelligence Scale (WAIS-IV; Wechsler, 2008), Wechsler Intelligence Scale for Children (WISC-V; Wechsler, 2014), and the Wechsler Preschool and Primary Scale of Intelligence (WPPSI-IV; Wechsler, 2012) are the three current versions of this test, and in the United States these tests are now used more frequently than the Stanford-Binet. In earlier editions, another way these tests differed from the Stanford-Binet was by having both a verbal and performance (nonverbal) scale, as well as providing an overall score of intelligence (the original Stanford-Binet was composed predominantly of verbal items). While still using both verbal and nonverbal items, the Wechlser tests now provide an overall score of intelligence and index scores related to cognitive domains. **Table 7.3** has sample items for each of the four index scales from the WAIS-IV.

| Table 7.3 | Simulated Sample Items From the Wechsler Adult Intelligence Scale (WAIS-IV) |
|---|---|
| **Simulated Sample Test Items** | |
| **Verbal Comprehension Index** | |
| Similarities | In what way are a circle and a triangle alike? In what way are a saw and a hammer alike? |
| Vocabulary | What is a hippopotamus? What does "resemble" mean? |
| Information | What is steam made of? What is pepper? Who wrote *Tom Sawyer*? |
| **Perceptual Reasoning Index** | |
| Block Design | After looking at a pattern or design, try to arrange small cubes in the same pattern. |
| Matrix Reasoning | After looking at an incomplete matrix pattern or series, select an option that completes the matrix or series. |
| Visual Puzzles | Look at a completed puzzle and select three components from a set of options that would recreate the puzzle, all within a specified time limit. |
| **Working Memory Index** | |
| Digit Span | Recall lists of numbers, some lists forward and some lists in reverse order, and recall a mixed list of numbers in correct ascending order. |
| Arithmetic | Three women divided 18 golf balls equally among themselves. How many golf balls did each person receive? If two buttons cost $0.15, what will be the cost of a dozen buttons? |
| **Processing Speed Index** | |
| Symbol Search | Visually scan a group of symbols to identify specific target symbols, within a specified time limit. |
| Coding | Learn a different symbol for specific numbers and then fill in the blank under the number with the correct symbol. (This test is timed.) |

Simulated items and descriptions similar to those in the *Wechsler Adult Intelligence Scale—Fourth Edition (2008)*.

### 7.8 Identify ways to evaluate the quality of a test.

All tests are not equally good tests. Some tests may fail to actually test what they are designed for. Others may fail to give the same results on different occasions for the same person when that person has not changed. These tests would be considered invalid and unreliable, respectively.

**RELIABILITY AND VALIDITY** Reliability of a test refers to the test producing consistent results each time it is given to the same individual or group of people. For example, if Nicholas takes a personality test today and then again in a month or so, the results should be very similar if the personality test is reliable. Other tests might be easy to use and even reliable, but if they don't actually measure what they are supposed to measure, they are also useless. These tests are thought of as "invalid" (untrue) tests. **Validity** is the degree to which a test actually measures what it's supposed to measure. Another aspect of validity is the extent to which an obtained score accurately reflects the intended skill or outcome in real-life situations, or *ecological validity*, not just validity for the testing or assessment situation. For example, we hope that someone who passes his or her test for a driver's license will also be able to safely operate a motor vehicle when they are actually on the road. When evaluating a test, consider what a specific test score means and to what or to whom it is compared.

Take the hypothetical example of Professor Stumpwater, who—for reasons best known only to him—believes that intelligence is related to a person's golf scores. Let's say that he develops an adult intelligence test based on golf scores. What do we need to look at to determine if his test is a good one?

**STANDARDIZATION OF TESTS** First of all, we would want to look at how he tried to standardize his test. *Standardization* refers to the process of giving the test to a large group of people that represents the kind of people for whom the test is designed. One aspect of standardization is in the establishment of consistent and standard methods of test administration. All test subjects would take the test under the same conditions. In the professor's case, this would mean that he would have his sample members play the same number of rounds of golf on the same course under the same weather conditions, and so on. Another aspect addresses the comparison group whose scores will be used to compare individual test results. Standardization groups are chosen randomly from the population for whom the test is intended and, like all samples, must be representative of that population. Ⓛ Ⓘ Ⓝ Ⓚ to Learning Objectives A.1 and 1.8. If a test is designed for children, for example, then a large sample of randomly selected children would be given the test.

**NORMS** The scores from the standardization group would be called the *norms*, the standards against which all others who take the test would be compared. Most tests of intelligence follow a *normal curve*, or a distribution in which the scores are the most frequent around the *mean*, or average, and become less and less frequent the farther from the mean they occur (see **Figure 7.5**). Ⓛ Ⓘ Ⓝ Ⓚ to Learning Objectives A.2, A.3, and A.4.

On the Wechsler IQ test, the percentages under each section of the normal curve represent the percentage of scores falling within that section for each *standard deviation (SD)* from the mean on the test. The standard deviation is the average variation of scores from the mean. Ⓛ Ⓘ Ⓝ Ⓚ to Learning Objective A.4.

In the case of the professor's golf test, he might find that a certain golf score is the average, which he would interpret as average intelligence. People who scored extremely well on the golf test would be compared to the average, as well as people with unusually poor scores.

The normal curve allows IQ scores to be more accurately estimated than the old IQ scoring method formula devised by Stern. Test designers replaced the old ratio IQ of the earlier versions of IQ tests with **deviation IQ scores**, which are based on the normal curve

**reliability**

the tendency of a test to produce the same scores again and again each time it is given to the same people.

**validity**

the degree to which a test actually measures what it's supposed to measure.

**deviation IQ scores**

a type of intelligence measure that assumes that IQ is normally distributed around a mean of 100 with a standard deviation of about 15.

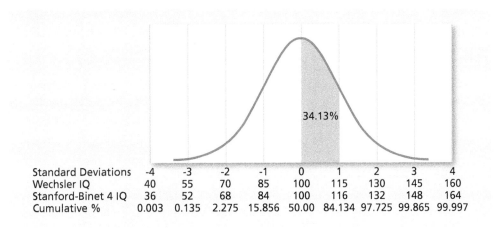

| Standard Deviations | -4 | -3 | -2 | -1 | 0 | 1 | 2 | 3 | 4 |
|---|---|---|---|---|---|---|---|---|---|
| Wechsler IQ | 40 | 55 | 70 | 85 | 100 | 115 | 130 | 145 | 160 |
| Stanford-Binet 4 IQ | 36 | 52 | 68 | 84 | 100 | 116 | 132 | 148 | 164 |
| Cumulative % | 0.003 | 0.135 | 2.275 | 15.856 | 50.00 | 84.134 | 97.725 | 99.865 | 99.997 |

**Figure 7.5** The Normal Curve

The percentages under each section of the normal curve represent the percentage of scores falling within that section for each *standard deviation (SD)* from the mean. Scores on intelligence tests are typically represented by the normal curve. The dotted vertical lines each represent one standard deviation from the mean, which is always set at 100. For example, an IQ of 115 on the Wechsler represents one standard deviation above the mean, and the area under the curve indicates that 34.13 percent of the population falls between 100 and 115 on this test. (L)(I)(N)(K) to Learning Objectives A.2, A.3, A.4, and 1.8. Note: The figure shows the mean and standard deviation for the Stanford-Binet Fourth Edition (Stanford-Binet 4). The Stanford-Binet Fifth Edition was published in 2003 and now has a mean of 100 and a standard deviation of 15 for composite scores.

distribution (Eysenck, 1994): IQ is assumed to be normally distributed with a mean IQ of 100 and a typical standard deviation of about 15 (the standard deviation can vary according to the particular test). An IQ of 130, for example, would be two standard deviations above the mean, whereas an IQ of 70 would be two standard deviations below the mean, and in each case the person's score is being compared to the population's average score.

With respect to validity and reliability, the professor's test fares poorly. If the results of the professor's test were compared with other established intelligence tests, there would probably be no relationship at all. Golf scores have nothing to do with intelligence, so the test is not a valid, or true, measure of intelligence.

On the other hand, his test might work well for some people and poorly for others on the question of reliability. Some people who are good and regular golfers tend to score about the same for each game that they play, so for them, the golf score IQ would be fairly reliable. But others, especially those who do not play golf or play infrequently, would have widely varying scores from game to game. For those people, the test would be very unreliable, and if a test is unreliable for some, it's not a good test.

A test can fail in validity but still be reliable. If for some reason Professor Stumpwater chose to use height as a measure of intelligence, an adult's score on Stumpwater's "test" would always be the same, as height does not change by very much after the late teens. But the opposite is not true. If a test is unreliable, how can it accurately measure what it is supposed to measure? For example, adult intelligence remains fairly constant. If a test meant to measure that intelligence gave different scores at different times, it's obviously not a valid measure of intelligence.

💬 Just because an IQ test gives the same score every time a person takes it doesn't mean that the score is actually measuring real intelligence, right?

That's right—think about the definition of intelligence for a moment: the ability to learn from one's experiences, acquire knowledge, and use resources effectively in adapting to new situations or solving problems. How can anyone define what "effective use of resources" might be? Does everyone have access to the same resources? Is everyone's "world" necessarily perceived as being the same? Intelligence tests are useful measuring devices but should not necessarily be assumed to be measures of all types of intelligent behavior, or even good measures for all groups of people, as the next section discusses.

**IQ TESTS AND CULTURAL BIAS** The problem with trying to measure intelligence with a test that is based on an understanding of the world and its resources is that not everyone comes from the same "world." People raised in a different culture, or even a different economic situation, from the one in which the designer of an IQ test is raised are not likely to perform well on such a test—not to mention the difficulties of taking a test that is written in an unfamiliar language or dialect. In the early days of immigration, people from non–English-speaking countries would score very poorly on intelligence tests, in some cases being denied entry to the United States on the basis of such tests (Allen, 2006).

How might these two women, apparently from different cultures, come to an agreement on what best defines intelligence?

It is very difficult to design an intelligence test that is completely free of *cultural bias*, a term referring to the tendency of IQ tests to reflect, in language, dialect, and content, the culture of the person or persons who designed the test. A person who comes from the same culture (or even socioeconomic background) as the test designer may have an unfair advantage over a person who is from a different cultural or socioeconomic background (Helms, 1992). If people raised in an Asian culture are given a test designed within a traditional Western culture, many items on the test might make no sense to them. For example, one kind of question might be: Which one of the five is least like the other four?

*DOG—CAR—CAT—BIRD—FISH*

The answer is supposed to be "car," which is the only one of the five that is not alive. But a Japanese child, living in a culture that relies on the sea for so much of its food and culture, might choose "fish," because none of the others are found in the ocean. That child's test score would be lower but not because the child is not intelligent.

In 1971, Adrian Dove designed an intelligence test to highlight the problem of cultural bias. Dove, an African-American sociologist, created the Dove Counterbalance General Intelligence Test in an attempt to demonstrate that a significant language/dialect barrier exists among children of different backgrounds. Questions on this test were derived from African-American culture in the southeastern United States during the 1960s and 1970s. Anyone not knowledgeable of this culture will probably score very poorly on this test, including African-American people from other geographical regions. The point is simply this: Tests are created by people from a particular culture and background. Questions and answers that test creators might think are common knowledge may relate to their own experiences and not to people of other cultures, backgrounds, or socioeconomic levels.

Attempts have been made to create intelligence tests that are as free of cultural influences as is humanly possible. Many test designers have come to the conclusion that it may be impossible to create a test that is completely free of cultural bias (Carpenter et al., 1990). Instead, they are striving to create tests that are at least *culturally fair*. These tests use questions that do not create a disadvantage for people whose culture differs from that of the majority. Many items on a "culture-fair" test require the use of nonverbal abilities, such as rotating objects, rather than items about verbal knowledge that might be culturally specific. One example is Raven's Progressive Matrices, a test of abstract reasoning. The test consists of a series of items containing abstract patterns, either in a $2 \times 2$ or $2 \times 3$ matrix, from which test takers have to identify a missing portion that best completes a pattern (see **Figure 7.6**). However, although once believed to be largely culture free, or at least fair, even this test is not immune to the influence of culture, as age, generational cohort, and education appear to impact performance (Brouwers et al., 2009; Fox & Mitchum, 2013).

**Figure 7.6**   Raven's Progressive Matrices Example

Facsimile of an item that may be found in Raven's Progressive Matrices.  Which of the bottom images completes the pattern?

**THINKING CRITICALLY**

What kind of questions would you include on an intelligence test to minimize cultural bias?

▶ | The response entered here will be saved to your notes and may be collected by your instructor if he/she requires it.

Submit

 💬 If intelligence tests are so flawed, why do people still use them?

**USEFULNESS OF IQ TESTS**   IQ tests are generally valid for predicting academic success and job performance (Sackett et al., 2008). This may be more true for those who score at the higher and lower ends of the normal curve. (For those who score in the average range of IQ, the predictive value is less clear.) The kinds of tests students are given in school are often similar to intelligence tests, and so people who do well on IQ tests typically do well on other kinds of academically oriented tests as well, such as the SAT, the American College Test (ACT), the Graduate Record Exam (GRE), and actual college examinations. These achievement tests are very similar to IQ tests but are administered to groups of people rather than to individuals. However, research suggests skills in self-regulation or levels of motivation may impact IQ measures and raises concerns about situations or circumstances in which IQ scores may not be unbiased predictors of academic or job success (Duckworth et al., 2011; Duckworth & Seligman, 2005; Nisbett et al., 2012).

Intelligence testing also plays an important role in neuropsychology, where specially trained psychologists use intelligence tests and other forms of cognitive and behavioral testing to assess neurobehavioral disorders in which cognition and behavior are impaired as the result of brain injury or brain malfunction (National Academy of Neuropsychology, 2001). As part of their profession, neuropsychologists use intelligence testing in diagnosis (e.g., head injury, learning disabilities, neuropsychological disorders), tracking progress of individuals with such disorders, and in monitoring possible recovery. ⓁⒾⓃⓀ to Learning Objective B.5.

Neuropsychologists often work with individuals who have traumatic brain injury (TBI). Many traumatic brain injuries can also be permanent, impacting the day-to-day functioning of both individuals and their loved ones for the rest of their lives. Depending on the area or areas of the brain injured and the severity of the trauma, some possible outcomes might include difficulty thinking, speech disturbances, memory problems, reduced attention span, headaches, sleep disturbances, frustration, mood swings, and personality changes. Not only do these outcomes negatively impact formal tests of intelligence, the deficits from such injuries may also affect thinking, problem solving, and cognition in general.

Mild TBI, or concussion, is an impairment of brain function for minutes to hours following a head injury. Concussions may include a loss of consciousness for up to 30 minutes, "seeing stars," headache, dizziness, and sometimes nausea or vomiting (Blumenfeld, 2010; Ruff et al., 2009). Amnesia for the events immediately before or after the accident is also a primary symptom and more likely to be anterograde in nature. Ⓛ Ⓘ Ⓝ Ⓚ to Learning Objective 6.5 and 6.13.

The effects of repeated concussions and the long-term effects of head injuries in general are of particular interest to neuropsychologists and other health professionals because the potential issues (memory problems, changes in personality, etc.) may not be evident until many years later. American football is one sport in which athletes may have extended playing careers. The possibility of an increased risk for depression, dementia, or other neurological risks for these athletes after they have quit playing has spawned ongoing research with professional football players (Guskiewicz et al., 2007; Hazrati et al., 2013; G. Miller, 2009). Former players who had three or more concussions were three times more likely to have significant memory problems and five times more likely to be diagnosed with mild cognitive impairment, often a precursor to Alzheimer's disease. *Chronic traumatic encephalopathy* (CTE) is a progressive brain disease linked to repetitive TBIs. In one recent study, of 66 brains examined from individuals that had participated in contact sports, 21 had brain changes and pathology consistent with CTE. Furthermore, of 198 brains from individuals that did not play contact sports, no CTE signs were detected, even in the brains of 33 individuals that suffered from a single TBI (Bieniek et al., 2015).

As part of the effort to protect players, modern football helmets are being designed so they better fit individual players, and engineered to further minimize both front and side impacts to the head.

### INDIVIDUAL DIFFERENCES IN INTELLIGENCE

## 7.9 Define intellectual disability, giftedness, and emotional intelligence.

Another use of IQ tests is to help identify people who differ from those of average intelligence by a great degree. Although one such group is composed of those who are sometimes called "geniuses" (who fall at the extreme high end of the normal curve for intelligence), the other group is made up of people who, for various reasons, are considered intellectually disabled and whose IQ scores fall well below the mean on the normal curve.

**INTELLECTUAL DISABILITY** Intellectual disability (intellectual developmental disorder), formerly *mental retardation* or *developmentally delayed*, is a neurodevelopmental disorder and is defined in several ways. First, the person exhibits deficits in mental abilities, which is typically associated with an IQ score approximately two standard deviations below the mean on the normal curve, such as below 70 on a test with a mean of 100 and standard deviation of 15. Second, the person's *adaptive behavior* (skills that allow people to live independently, such as being able to work at a job, communicate well with others, and grooming skills such as being able to get dressed, eat, and bathe with little or no help) is severely below a level appropriate for the person's age. Finally, these limitations must begin in the developmental period. Intellectual disability occurs in about 1 percent of the population (American Psychiatric Association, 2013).

**Intellectual disability (intellectual developmental disorder)**

condition in which a person's behavioral and cognitive skills exist at an earlier developmental stage than the skills of others who are the same chronological age; may also be referred to as developmentally delayed. This condition was formerly known as mental retardation.

💬 So how would a professional go about deciding whether or not a child has an intellectual disability? Is the IQ test the primary method?

**DIAGNOSIS**  Previous editions of the *Diagnostic and Statistical Manual of Mental Disorders (DSM)* relied heavily on IQ tests for determining the diagnosis of *mental retardation* and level of severity. Recognizing tests of IQ are less valid as one approaches the lower end of the IQ range, and the importance of adaptive living skills in multiple life areas, levels of severity are now based on the level of adaptive functioning and level of support the individual requires (American Psychiatric Association, 2013). Thus, a *Diagnostic and Statistical Manual of Mental Disorders, Fifth Edition (DSM-5)* (American Psychiatric Association, 2013) diagnosis of intellectual disability is based on deficits in intellectual functioning, determined by standardized tests of intelligence and clinical assessment, which impact adaptive functioning across three domains. The domains include: conceptual (memory, reasoning, language, reading, writing, math, and other academic skills), social (empathy, social judgment, interpersonal communication, and other skills that impact the ability to make and maintain friendships), and practical (self-management skills that affect personal care, job responsibilities, school, money management, and other areas; American Psychiatric Association, 2013). Symptoms must begin during the developmental period.

Intellectual disability can vary from mild to profound. According to the *DSM-5* (American Psychiatric Association, 2013), individuals with mild intellectual disability may not be recognized as having deficits in the conceptual domain until they reach school age, where learning difficulties become apparent; as adults, they are likely to be fairly concrete thinkers. In the social domain, they are at risk of being manipulated, as social judgment and interactions are immature as compared to same-age peers. In the practical domain, they are capable of living independently with proper supports in place but will likely require assistance with more complex life skills such as health care decisions, legal issues, or raising a family (American Psychiatric Association, 2013). This category makes up the vast majority of those with intellectual disabilities. Other classifications in order of severity are moderate, severe, and profound. Conceptually, individuals with profound intellectual disability have a very limited ability to learn beyond simple matching and sorting tasks and, socially, have very poor communication skills, although they may recognize and interact nonverbally with well-known family members and other caretakers. In the practical domain, they may be able to participate by watching or assisting but are likely totally dependent on others for all areas of their care (American Psychiatric Association, 2013). All of these skill deficits are likely compounded by multiple physical or sensory impairments.

**CAUSES**  What causes intellectual disability? Unhealthy living conditions can affect brain development. Examples of such conditions are lead poisoning from eating paint chips (Lanphear et al., 2000), exposure to PCBs (Darvill et al., 2000), prenatal exposure to mercury (Grandjean et al., 1997), as well as other toxicants (Eriksson et al., 2001; Eskenazi et al., 1999; Schroeder, 2000). Deficits may also be attributed to factors resulting in inadequate brain development or other health risks associated with poverty. Examples include malnutrition, health consequences as the result of not having adequate access to health care, or lack of mental stimulation through typical cultural and educational experiences.

Some of the biological causes of intellectual disability include Down syndrome ((L I N K) to Learning Objective 8.3), fetal alcohol syndrome, and fragile X syndrome. *Fetal alcohol syndrome* is a condition that results from exposing a developing embryo to alcohol, and intelligence levels can range from below average to levels associated with intellectual disability (Olson & Burgess, 1997). In *fragile X syndrome*, an individual (more frequently a male) has a defect in a gene on the X chromosome of the 23rd pair, leading to a deficiency in a protein needed for brain development. Depending on the severity of the damage to this gene, symptoms of fragile X syndrome can range from mild to severe or profound intellectual disability (Dykens et al., 1994; Valverde et al., 2007).

There are many other causes of intellectual disability (Murphy et al., 1998). Lack of oxygen at birth, damage to the fetus in the womb from diseases, infections, or drug use

This middle-aged man, named Jack, lives in a small town in Arkansas and serves as a deacon in the local church. He is loved and respected and leads what, for him, is a full and happy life. Jack also has Down syndrome, but he has managed to find his place in the world.

by the mother, and even diseases and accidents during childhood can lead to intellectual disability.

One thing should always be remembered: Intellectual disability affects a person's *intellectual* capabilities and adaptive behaviors. Individuals with an intellectual disability are just as responsive to love and affection as anyone else and need to be loved and to have friends just as all people do. Intelligence is only one characteristic; warmth, friend-liness, caring, and compassion also count for a great deal and should not be underrated.

**GIFTEDNESS**    At the other end of the intelligence scale* are those who fall on the upper end of the normal curve (see Figure 7.4), above an IQ of 130 (about 2 percent of the population). The term applied to these individuals is **gifted**, and if their IQ falls above 140 to 145 (less than half of 1 percent of the population), they are often referred to as highly advanced or *geniuses*.

> 💬 I've heard that geniuses are sometimes a little "nutty" and odd. Are geniuses, especially the really high-IQ ones, "not playing with a full deck," as the saying goes?

People have long held many false beliefs about people who are very, very intel-ligent. Such beliefs have included that gifted people are weird and socially awkward, physically weak, and more likely to suffer from mental illnesses. From these beliefs come the "mad scientist" of the cinema and the "evil geniuses" of literature.

These beliefs were shattered by a groundbreaking study that was initiated in 1921 by Lewis M. Terman, the same individual responsible for the development of the Stanford-Binet Test. Terman (1925) selected 1,528 children to participate in a longitudinal study. ⓁⒾⓃⓀ to Learning Objective 8.1. These children, 857 boys and 671 girls, had IQs (as measured by the Stanford-Binet) ranging from 130 to 200. The early findings of this major study (Terman & Oden, 1947) demonstrated that the gifted were socially well adjusted and often skilled lead-ers. They were also above average in height, weight, and physical attractiveness, putting an end to the myth of the weakling genius. Terman was able to demonstrate not only that his gifted children were *not* more susceptible to mental illness than the general population, but he was also able to show that they were actually more resistant to mental illnesses than those of average intelligence. Only those with the highest IQs (180 and above) were found to have some social and behavioral adjustment problems *as children* (Janos, 1987).

Terman's "Termites," as they came to be called, were also typically successful as adults. They earned more academic degrees and had higher occupational and financial success than their average peers (at least, the men in the study had occupational success—women at this time did not typically have careers outside the home). Researchers Zuo and Cramond (2001) examined some of Terman's gifted people to see if their identity formation as adolescents was related to later occupational success. ⓁⒾⓃⓀ to Learning Objective 8.11. They found that most of the more successful "Termites" had in fact suc-cessfully achieved a consistent sense of self, whereas those who were less successful had not done so. For more on Terman's famous study, see Classic Studies in Psychology.

A book by Joan Freeman called *Gifted Children Grown Up* (Freeman, 2001) describes the results of a similar longitudinal study of 210 gifted and nongifted children in Great Britain. One of the more interesting findings from this study is that gifted children who are "pushed" to achieve at younger and younger ages, sitting for exams long before their peers would do so, often grow up to be disappointed, somewhat unhappy adults. Freeman points to differing life conditions for the gifted as a major factor in their success, adjustment, and well-being: Some lived in poverty and some in wealth, for example.

Stanford University psychologist Lewis Terman is pictured at his desk in 1942. Terman spent a good portion of his career researching children with high IQ scores and was the first to use the term *gifted* to describe these children.

**gifted**

the 2 percent of the population falling on the upper end of the normal curve and typically possessing an IQ of 130 or above.

---

*scale: a graded series of tests or performances used in rating individual intelligence or achievement.

# Classic Studies in Psychology
## Terman's "Termites"

Terman's (1925) longitudinal study is still providing information today. Terman himself died in 1956, but several other researchers (including Robert Sears, one of the original Termites, who died in 1989) kept track of the remaining Termites over the years (Holahan & Sears, 1996).

As adults, the Termites were relatively successful, with a median income in the 1950s of $10,556, compared to the national median at that time of $5,800 a year. Most of them graduated from college, many earning advanced degrees. Their occupations included doctors, lawyers, business executives, university professors, scientists, and even one famous science fiction writer and an Oscar-winning director.

By 2000, only about 200 Termites were still living. Although the study was marred by several flaws, it still remains one of the most important and rich sources of data on an entire generation. Terman's study was actually the first truly longitudinal study (LINK to Learning Objective 8.1) ever to be accomplished, and scientists have gotten data about the effects of phenomena such as World War II and the influence of personality traits on how long one lives from the questionnaires filled out by the participants over the years.

Terman and Oden (1959) compared the 100 most successful men in the group to the 100 least successful by defining "successful" as holding jobs that related to or used their intellectual skills. The more successful men earned more money, had careers with more prestige, and were healthier and less likely to be divorced or alcoholics than the less successful men. The IQ scores were relatively equal between the two groups, so the differences in success in life had to be caused by some other factor or factors. Terman and Oden found that the successful adults were different from the others in three ways: They were more goal oriented, more persistent in pursuing those goals, and were more self-confident than the less successful Termites.

What were the flaws in this study? Terman acquired his participants by getting recommendations from teachers and principals, not through random selection, so that there was room for bias in the pool of participants from the start. It is quite possible that the teachers and principals were less likely, especially in 1921, to recommend students who were "troublemakers" or different from the majority. Consequently, Terman's original group consisted of almost entirely white, urban, and middle-class children, with the majority (857 out of 1,528) being male. There were only two African Americans, six Japanese Americans, and one Native American.

Another flaw is the way Terman interfered in the lives of his "children." In any good research study, the investigator should avoid becoming personally involved in the lives of the participants in the study to reduce the possibility of biasing the results. Terman seemed to find it nearly impossible to remain objective (Leslie, 2000). He became like a surrogate father to many of them.

Flawed as it may have been, Terman's groundbreaking study did accomplish his original goal of putting to rest the myths that existed about genius in the early part of the twentieth century. Gifted children and adults are no more prone to mental illnesses or odd behavior than any other group, and they also have their share of failures as well as successes. Genius is obviously not the only factor that influences success in life—personality and experiences are strong factors as well. For example, the homes of the children in the top 2 percent of Terman's group had an average of 450 books in their libraries, a sign that the parents of these children valued books and learning, and these parents were also more likely to be teachers, professionals, doctors, and lawyers. The experiences of these gifted children growing up would have been vastly different from those in homes with less emphasis on reading and lower occupational levels for the parents.

Yet another longitudinal study (Torrance, 1993) found that in both gifted students and gifted adults, there is more to success in life than intelligence and high academic achievement. In that study, liking one's work, having a sense of purpose in life, a high energy level, and persistence were also very important factors. If the picture of the genius as mentally unstable is a myth, so, too, is the belief that being gifted will always lead to success, as even Terman found in his original study.

**EMOTIONAL INTELLIGENCE** What about people who have a lot of "book smarts" but not much common sense? There are some people like that who never seem to get ahead in life in spite of having all that so-called intelligence. It is true that not everyone who is intellectually able is going to be a success in life (Mehrabian, 2000). Sometimes the people who are most successful are those who didn't do all that well in the regular academic setting.

One explanation for why some people who do poorly in school succeed in life and why some who do well in school don't do so well in the "real" world is that success relies on a certain degree of **emotional intelligence**, the accurate awareness of and ability to manage one's own emotions to facilitate thinking and attain specific goals, and the ability to understand what others feel (Mayer & Salovey, 1997; Mayer, Salovey, et al., 2008).

The concept of emotional intelligence was first introduced by Peter Salovey and John Mayer (1990) and later popularized by Dan Goleman (1995). And while Goleman originally suggested emotional intelligence was a more powerful influence on success in life than more traditional views of intelligence, his work and the work of others used the term in a variety of different ways than originally proposed, and claims by some were not backed by scientific evidence. For example, studies have been criticized for their lack of validity and, thus, their applicability (Antonakis, 2004). Furthermore, emotional intelligence is not the same as having high self-esteem or being optimistic. One who is emotionally intelligent possesses self-control of emotions such as anger, impulsiveness, and anxiety. Empathy, the ability to understand what others feel, is also a component, as are an awareness of one's own emotions, sensitivity, persistence even in the face of frustrations, and the ability to motivate oneself (Mayer & Salovey, 1997; Salovey & Mayer, 1990).

That all sounds very nice, but how can anything like this be measured?

Is there research to support this idea? In one study, researchers asked 321 participants to read passages written by nonparticipants and try to guess what the nonparticipants were feeling while they were writing (Mayer & Geher, 1996). The assumption was that people who were good at connecting thoughts to feelings would also have a high degree of empathy and emotional intelligence. The participants who more correctly judged the writers' emotional experiences (assessed by both how well each participant's emotional judgments agreed with a group consensus and the nonparticipant's actual report of feelings) also scored higher on the empathy measure and lower on

**emotional intelligence**

the awareness of and ability to manage one's own emotions to facilitate thinking and attain goals, as well as the ability to understand emotions in others.

the defensiveness measure. These same participants also had higher SAT scores (self-reported), leading Mayer and colleagues to conclude not only that emotional intelligence is a valid and measurable concept but also that general intelligence and emotional intelligence may be related: Those who are high in emotional intelligence are also smarter in the traditional sense (Mayer et al., 2000). Another review found individuals with higher emotional intelligence tended to have better social relationships for both children and adults, better family and intimate relationships, were perceived more positively by others, had better academic achievement, were more successful at work, and experienced greater psychological well-being (Mayer, Roberts, et al., 2008).

Another example of research supporting the role of emotional intelligence in real-world settings has been in the field of medicine. Studies have supported that medical school students with higher emotional intelligence tended to perform better in courses related to patient relationships, or "bedside manners" (Libbrecht et al., 2014). In this sample of students, success appeared to be related more to the individual's ability to regulate their own emotions, as compared to their ability to understand the emotions of others. There has also been reported evidence for emotional intelligence being related to physician competence and areas of improved physician–patient interactions, including enhanced communication and more empathic and compassionate patient care (Arora et al., 2010).

Emotional intelligence includes empathy, which is the ability to feel what others are feeling. This doctor is not only able to listen to her patient's problems but also is able to show by her facial expression, body language, and gestures that she understands how the patient feels.

### THE NATURE/NURTURE ISSUE REGARDING INTELLIGENCE

### 7.10 Evaluate the influence of heredity and environment on the development of intelligence.

Are people born with all of the "smarts" they will ever have, or do experience and learning count for something in the development of intellect? The influence of nature (heredity or genes) and nurture (environment) on personality traits has long been debated in the field of human development, and intelligence is one of the traits that has been examined closely. Ⓛ Ⓘ Ⓝ Ⓚ to Learning Objective 8.2.

**TWIN AND ADOPTION STUDIES** The problem with trying to separate the role of genes from that of environment is that controlled, perfect experiments are neither practical nor ethical. Instead, researchers find out what they can from *natural experiments*, circumstances existing in nature that can be examined to understand some phenomenon. *Twin studies* are an example of such circumstances.

Identical twins are those who originally came from one fertilized egg and, therefore, share the same genetic inheritance. Any differences between them on a certain trait, then, should be caused by environmental factors. Fraternal twins come from two different eggs, each fertilized by a different sperm, and share only the amount of genetic material that any two siblings would share. Ⓛ Ⓘ Ⓝ Ⓚ to Learning Objective 8.3. By comparing the IQs of these two types of twins reared together (similar environments) and reared apart (different environments), as well as persons of other degrees of relatedness, researchers can get a general, if not exact, idea of how much influence heredity has over the trait of intelligence (see **Figure 7.7**). As can be easily seen from the chart, the greater the degree of genetic relatedness, the stronger the correlation is between the IQ scores of those persons. The fact that genetically identical twins show a correlation of 0.86 means that the environment must play a part in determining some aspects of intelligence as measured by IQ tests. If heredity alone were responsible, the correlation between genetically identical twins should be 1.00. At this time, researchers have determined that the estimated **heritability** (proportion of change in IQ within a population that is caused by hereditary factors) for intelligence is about .50 or 50 percent (Plomin & DeFries, 1998; Plomin & Spinath, 2004). Furthermore, the impact of genetic factors increases with increasing age, but the set of genes or genetic factors remains the same. The effects of the same set of genes becomes larger with increasing age (Posthuma et al., 2009).

**heritability**

degree to which the changes in some trait within a population can be considered to be due to genetic influences; the extent individual genetic differences affect individual differences in observed behavior; in IQ, proportion of change in IQ within a population that is caused by hereditary factors.

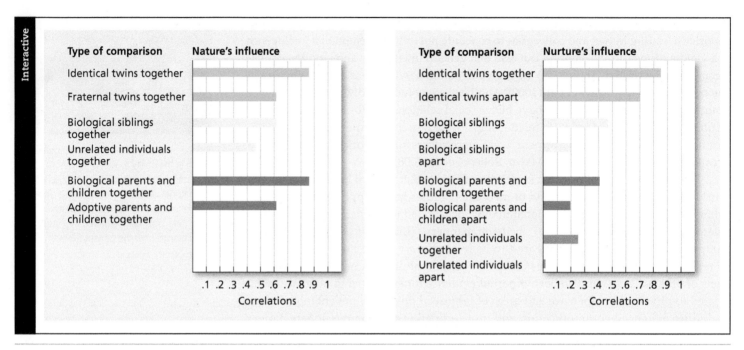

**Figure 7.7** Correlations Between IQ Scores of Persons With Various Relationships

In the graph on the left, the degree of genetic relatedness seems to determine the agreement (correlation) between IQ scores of the various comparisons. For example, identical twins, who share 100 percent of their genes, are more similar in IQ than fraternal twins, who share only about 50 percent of their genes, even when raised in the same environment. In the graph on the right, identical twins are still more similar to each other in IQ than are other types of comparisons, but being raised in the same environment increases the similarity considerably.

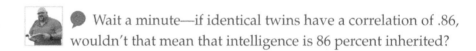 Wait a minute—if identical twins have a correlation of .86, wouldn't that mean that intelligence is 86 percent inherited?

Although the correlation between identical twins is higher than the estimated heritability of .50, that similarity is not entirely due to the twins' genetic similarity. Twins who are raised in the same household obviously share very similar environments as well. Even twins who are reared apart, as seen in adoption studies, are usually placed in homes that are similar in socioeconomic and ethnic background—more similar than one might think. So when twins who are genetically similar are raised in similar environments, their IQ scores are also going to be similar. However, similar environmental influences become less important over time (where genetic influences increase over time), accounting for only about 20 percent of the variance in intelligence by age 11 or 12 (Posthuma et al., 2009). In turn, environmental influences tend not to be a factor by adolescence, and with the increasing impact of genetic factors, it has been suggested that the heritability of intelligence might be as high as .91 or 91 percent by the age of 65 (Posthuma et al., 2009).

One of the things that people need to understand about heritability is that estimates of heritability apply only to changes in IQ within a *group* of people, *not to the individual people themselves*. Each individual is far too different in experiences, education, and other nongenetic factors to predict exactly how a particular set of genes will interact with those factors in that one person. Only differences among people *in general* can be investigated for the influence of genes (Dickens & Flynn, 2001). Genes always interact with environmental factors, and in some cases extreme environments can modify even very heritable traits, as would happen in the case of a severely malnourished child's growth pattern. Enrichment, on the other hand, could have improved outcomes. Even a family's socioeconomic status is influenced by genetics, and a child's socioeconomic status during infancy through adolescence is positively correlated with his or her intelligence development (Trzaskowski et al., 2014; von Stumm & Plomin, 2015). Some observations suggest IQ scores are steadily increasing over time, from generation to generation, in modernized countries, a phenomenon called the *Flynn effect* (Flynn, 2009).

How might you determine whether flute-playing ability is a highly heritable trait? If you want to improve your flute playing and someone tells you that musical ability is heritable, should you stop practicing?

▶ | The response entered here will be saved to your notes and may be collected by your instructor if he/she requires it.

Submit

**THE BELL CURVE AND MISINTERPRETATION OF STATISTICS**    One of the other factors that has been examined for possible heritable differences in performance on IQ tests is the concept of race. (The term *race* is used in most of these investigations as a way to group people with common skin colors or facial features, and one should always be mindful of how suspect that kind of classification is. Cultural background, educational experiences, and socioeconomic factors typically have far more to do with similarities in group performances than does the color of one's skin.) In 1994, Herrnstein and Murray published the controversial book *The Bell Curve*, in which they cite large numbers of statistical studies (never published in scientific journals prior to the book) that led them to make the claim that IQ is largely inherited. These authors go further by also implying that people from lower economic levels are poor because they are unintelligent.

In their book, Herrnstein and Murray made several statistical errors and ignored the effects of environment and culture. First, they assumed that IQ tests actually do measure intelligence. As discussed earlier, IQ tests are not free of cultural or socioeconomic bias. Furthermore, as the video *Intelligence Tests and Stereotypes* explains, just being aware of negative stereotypes can result in an individual scoring poorly on intelligence tests, a response called **stereotype threat** (Steele & Aronson, 1995). So all they really found was a correlation

👁 **Watch** the **Video** *Intelligence Tests and Stereotypes*

**stereotype threat**
condition in which being made aware of a negative performance stereotype interferes with the performance of someone that considers himself or herself part of that group.

Although *The Bell Curve* stated that Japanese Americans are genetically superior in intelligence, the book's authors overlook the influence of cultural values. Many Japanese American parents put much time and effort into helping their children with schoolwork.

between race and *IQ*, not race and *intelligence*. Second, they assumed that intelligence itself is very heavily influenced by genetics, with a heritability factor of about .80. The current estimate of the heritability of intelligence is about .50 (Plomin & DeFries, 1998; Plomin & Spinath, 2004).

Herrnstein and Murray also failed to understand that heritability only applies to differences that can be found *within* a group of people as opposed to those *between* groups of people or individuals (Gould, 1981). Heritability estimates can only be made truly from a group that was exposed to a similar environment.

One of their findings was that Japanese Americans are at the top of the IQ ladder, a finding that they attribute to racial and genetic characteristics. They seem to ignore the cultural influence of intense focus on education and achievement by Japanese-American parents (Neisser et al., 1996). Scientists (Beardsley, 1995; Kamin, 1995) have concluded that, despite the claims of *The Bell Curve*, there is no real scientific evidence for genetic differences in intelligence *between* different racial groups. A series of studies, using blood-group testing for racial grouping (different racial groups have different rates of certain blood groups, allowing a statistical estimation of ancestry), found no significant relationship between ethnicity and IQ (Neisser et al., 1996).

## Concept Map L.O. 7.6, 7.7, 7.8, 7.9, 7.10

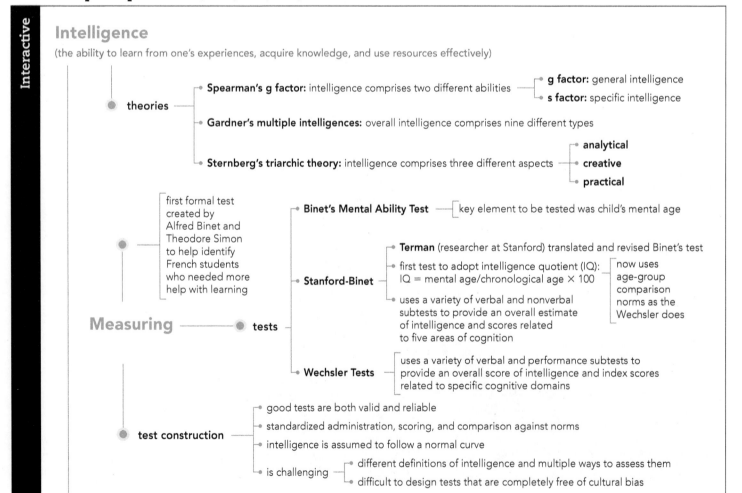

**Intelligence** (the ability to learn from one's experiences, acquire knowledge, and use resources effectively)

- theories
  - **Spearman's g factor:** intelligence comprises two different abilities
    - **g factor:** general intelligence
    - **s factor:** specific intelligence
  - **Gardner's multiple intelligences:** overall intelligence comprises nine different types
  - **Sternberg's triarchic theory:** intelligence comprises three different aspects
    - **analytical**
    - **creative**
    - **practical**

**Measuring**
- first formal test created by Alfred Binet and Theodore Simon to help identify French students who needed more help with learning
- tests
  - **Binet's Mental Ability Test** — key element to be tested was child's mental age
  - **Stanford-Binet**
    - **Terman** (researcher at Stanford) translated and revised Binet's test
    - first test to adopt intelligence quotient (IQ): IQ = mental age/chronological age × 100 — now uses age-group comparison norms as the Wechsler does
    - uses a variety of verbal and nonverbal subtests to provide an overall estimate of intelligence and scores related to five areas of cognition
  - **Wechsler Tests** — uses a variety of verbal and performance subtests to provide an overall score of intelligence and index scores related to specific cognitive domains
- test construction
  - good tests are both valid and reliable
  - standardized administration, scoring, and comparison against norms
  - intelligence is assumed to follow a normal curve
  - is challenging
    - different definitions of intelligence and multiple ways to assess them
    - difficult to design tests that are completely free of cultural bias

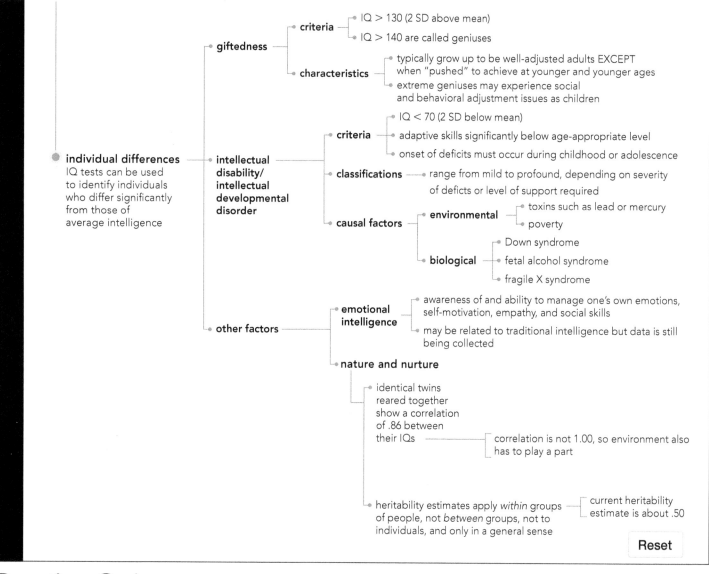

giftedness
- criteria
  - IQ > 130 (2 SD above mean)
  - IQ > 140 are called geniuses
- characteristics
  - typically grow up to be well-adjusted adults EXCEPT when "pushed" to achieve at younger and younger ages
  - extreme geniuses may experience social and behavioral adjustment issues as children

individual differences
IQ tests can be used to identify individuals who differ significantly from those of average intelligence

intellectual disability/ intellectual developmental disorder
- criteria
  - IQ < 70 (2 SD below mean)
  - adaptive skills significantly below age-appropriate level
  - onset of deficits must occur during childhood or adolescence
- classifications — range from mild to profound, depending on severity of deficits or level of support required
- causal factors
  - environmental
    - toxins such as lead or mercury
    - poverty
  - biological
    - Down syndrome
    - fetal alcohol syndrome
    - fragile X syndrome

other factors
- emotional intelligence
  - awareness of and ability to manage one's own emotions, self-motivation, empathy, and social skills
  - may be related to traditional intelligence but data is still being collected
- nature and nurture
  - identical twins reared together show a correlation of .86 between their IQs — correlation is not 1.00, so environment also has to play a part
  - heritability estimates apply *within* groups of people, not *between* groups, not to individuals, and only in a general sense — current heritability estimate is about .50

Reset

# Practice Quiz   How much do you remember?

*Pick the best answer.*

**1.** In Gardner's view, effective counseling psychologists and managers would likely be high in _____ intelligence.
  **a.** verbal/linguistic
  **b.** visual–spatial
  **c.** interpersonal
  **d.** intrapersonal

**2.** According to Sternberg, which type of intelligence has a low relationship to academic success and would be the most difficult to measure in the classroom?
  **a.** practical
  **b.** creative
  **c.** analytical
  **d.** verbal

**3.** Professor Becker designed an IQ test. To validate this test, the professor should be careful to do which of the following?
  **a.** Give the test at least twice to the same group to ensure accuracy.
  **b.** Select the people in the sample from the population of people for whom the test is designed.
  **c.** Select only university professors to take the test so that they can critique the questions on the test.
  **d.** Strive to make sure that the test measures what it is supposed to measure.

**4.** In terms of differing cultures, what should be the goal of every test designer?
  **a.** to create a test free of cultural bias
  **b.** to create a test that is culturally fair
  **c.** to create a test with no questions involving culture
  **d.** to create a series of culture-varied tests

**5.** In recent studies, what do some researchers argue is a more accurate means of gauging success in relationships and careers?
  **a.** intellectual intelligence
  **b.** emotional intelligence
  **c.** heredity studies
  **d.** stress surveys

**6.** Which of the following would be an example of a stereotype threat?
  **a.** Joaquim, who believes IQ tests are unfair to Hispanics, something that his IQ score seems to reflect
  **b.** Jasmine, who feels she must excel on her IQ test
  **c.** Tiana, who believes that all testing, no matter the type, is stereotypical and biased
  **d.** Malik, who believes that tests are equal but must excel so as not to be stereotyped by his friends

# Language

In Chapter Six we discussed how language can possibly affect our memory. For example, being asked "Did you see the car bump into the truck?" may prompt a slightly different memory than "Did you see the car smash into the truck?" In this section, we will examine language and how cognition can be affected by language.

## THE LEVELS OF LANGUAGE ANALYSIS

### 7.11 Identify the different elements and structure of language.

**Language** is a system for combining symbols (such as words) so that an infinite* number of meaningful statements can be made for the purpose of communicating with others. Language allows people not only to communicate with one another but also to represent their own internal mental activity. In other words, language is a very important part of how people think.

The structures of languages all over the world share common characteristics. They consist of the sounds that exist within a language, word meanings, word order, the rules for making words into other words, the meanings of sentences and phrases, and the rules for practical communication with others.

**GRAMMAR**   **Grammar** is the system of rules governing the structure and use of a language. According to famed linguist Noam Chomsky (Chomsky, 2006; Chomsky et al., 2002), humans have an innate ability to understand and produce language through a device he calls the *language acquisition device*, or *LAD*. He defined the LAD as an innate "program" that contained a *schema* for human language. The children matched the language they heard against this schema and, thus, language developed in a well-researched sequence (Chomsky, 1957, 1964, 1981, 1986). While humans may learn the *specific* language (English, Spanish, Mandarin, etc.) through the processes of imitation, reinforcement, and shaping, ⓛⓘⓝⓚ to Learning Objectives 5.5, 5.9, and 5.13, the complexities of the grammar of a language are, according to Chomsky, to some degree "wired in" to the developing brain. Recent research has supported Chomsky's ideas, with evidence of both hierarchical development of language comprehension and the underlying brain processes involved (Ding et al., 2015). ⓛⓘⓝⓚ to Learning Objective 2.13. The LAD "listens" to the language input of the infant's world and then begins to produce language sounds and eventually words and sentences in a pattern found across cultures. This pattern is discussed in greater detail in the next section. ⓛⓘⓝⓚ to Learning Objective 7.12. Grammar includes phonemes (the basic sounds of language), morphology (the study of the formation of words), rules for the order of words known as syntax, and pragmatics (the practical social expectations and uses of language).

**PHONEMES**   **Phonemes** are the basic units of sound in a language. The *a* in the word *car* is a very different phoneme from the *a* in the word *day*, even though it is the same letter of the alphabet. The difference is in how we say the sound of the *a* in each word. Phonemes are more than just the different ways in which we pronounce single letters, too. *Th, sh,* and *au* are also phonemes. Phonemes for different languages are also different, and one of the biggest problems for people who are trying to learn another language is the inability to both hear and pronounce the phonemes of that other language. Although infants are born with the ability to recognize all phonemes (Werker & Lalonde, 1988), after about 9 months, that ability has deteriorated, and the infant recognizes only the phonemes of the language to which the infant is exposed (Boyson-Bardies et al., 1989).

**MORPHEMES**   **Morphemes** are the smallest units of meaning within a language. For example, the word *playing* consists of two morphemes, *play* and *ing*.

**language**

a system for combining symbols (such as words) so that an unlimited number of meaningful statements can be made for the purpose of communicating with others.

**grammar**

the system of rules governing the structure and use of a language.

**phonemes**

the basic units of sound in language.

**morphemes**

the smallest units of meaning within a language.

---

*infinite: unlimited, without end.

**SYNTAX**   Syntax is a system of rules for combining words and phrases to form grammatically correct sentences. Syntax is quite important, as just a simple mix-up can cause sentences to be completely misunderstood. For example, "John kidnapped the boy" has a different meaning from "John, the kidnapped boy," although all four words are the same (Lasnik, 1990). Another example of the importance of syntax can be found in the lobby of a Moscow hotel across from a monastery: "You are welcome to visit the cemetery where famous composers, artists, and writers are buried daily except Thursday." So if people want to watch famous composers, artists, and writers being buried, they should not go to this monastery on Thursday.

**SEMANTICS**   Semantics are rules for determining the meaning of words and sentences. Sentences, for example, can have the same semantic meaning while having different syntax: "Johnny hit the ball" and "the ball was hit by Johnny."

**PRAGMATICS**   The **pragmatics** of language has to do with the practical aspects of communicating with others, or the social "niceties" of language. Simply put, pragmatics involves knowing things like how to take turns in a conversation, the use of gestures to emphasize a point or indicate a need for more information, and the different ways in which one speaks to different people (Yule, 1996). For example, adults speak to small children differently than they do to other adults by using simpler words. Both adults and children use higher-pitched voices and many repeated phrases when talking to infants; such child-directed speech plays an important role in the development of language in children. Part of the pragmatics of language includes knowing just what rhythm and emphasis to use when communicating with others, called *intonation*. When speaking to infants, adults and children are changing the inflection when they use the higher pitch and stress certain words differently than others. Some languages, such as Japanese, are highly sensitive to intonation, meaning that changing the stress or pitch of certain words or syllables of a particular word can change its meaning entirely (Beckman & Pierrehumbert, 1986). For example, the Japanese name Yoshiko should be pronounced with the accent or stress on the first syllable: YO-she-koh. This pronunciation of the name means "woman-child." But if the stress is placed on the second syllable (yo-SHE-ko), the name means "woman who urinates."

### DEVELOPMENT OF LANGUAGE

### 7.12   Explain how language develops.

The development of language is a very important milestone in the cognitive development of a child because language allows children to think in words rather than just images, to ask questions, to communicate their needs and wants to others, and to form concepts (L. Bloom, 1974; P. Bloom, 2000).

Language development in infancy is influenced by the language they hear, a style of speaking known as *child-directed speech* (the way adults and older children talk to infants and very young children, with higher-pitched, repetitious, sing-song speech patterns). Infants and toddlers attend more closely to this kind of speech, which creates a learning opportunity in the dialogue between caregiver and infant (Dominey & Dodane, 2004; Fernald, 1984, 1992; Küntay & Slobin, 2002). Other researchers are looking at the infant's use of gestures and signs (Behne et al., 2005; Lizskowski et al., 2006; Moll & Tomasello, 2007; Tomasello et al., 2007). Infants also seem to understand far more than they can produce, a phenomenon known as the *receptive-productive lag* (Stevenson et al., 1988). They may be able to only produce one or two words, but they understand much longer sentences from their parents and others.

There are several stages of language development that all children experience, no matter what culture they live in or what language they will learn to speak (Brown, 1973), as shown in **Table 7.4**.

Pragmatics involves the practical aspects of communicating. This young mother is talking and then pausing for the infant's response. In this way, the infant is learning about taking turns, an important aspect of language development. What kinds of games do adults play with infants that also aid the development of language?

**syntax**

the system of rules for combining words and phrases to form grammatically correct sentences.

**semantics**

the rules for determining the meaning of words and sentences.

**pragmatics**

aspects of language involving the practical ways of communicating with others, or the social "niceties" of language.

| **Table 7.4**   Stages of Language Development |
| --- |
| 1. **Cooing:** At around 2 months of age, babies begin to make vowel-like sounds. |
| 2. **Babbling:** At about 6 months, infants add consonant sounds to the vowels to make a babbling sound, which at times can almost sound like real speech. Deaf children actually decrease their babbling after 6 months while increasing their use of primitive hand signs and gestures (Petitto & Marentette, 1991; Petitto et al., 2001). |
| 3. **One-word speech:** Somewhere just before or around age 1, most children begin to say actual words. These words are typically nouns and may seem to represent an entire phrase of meaning. They are called *holophrases* (whole phrases in one word) for that reason. For example, a child might say "Milk!" and mean "I want some milk!" or "I drank my milk!" |
| 4. **Telegraphic speech:** At around a year and a half, toddlers begin to string words together to form short, simple sentences using nouns, verbs, and adjectives. "Baby eat," "Mommy go," and "Doggie go bye-bye" are examples of telegraphic speech. Only the words that carry the meaning of the sentence are used. |
| 5. **Whole sentences:** As children move through the preschool years, they learn to use grammatical terms and increase the number of words in their sentences, until by age 6 or so they are nearly as fluent as an adult, although the number of words they know is still limited when compared to adult vocabulary. |

## THE RELATIONSHIP BETWEEN LANGUAGE AND THOUGHT

### 7.13 Evaluate whether or not language influences how people think.

As with the different views on the relative importance of nature and nurture, researchers have long debated the relationship between language and thought. Does language actually influence thought, or does thinking influence language?

**TWO THEORIES ON THE RELATIONSHIP BETWEEN LANGUAGE AND THOUGHT**    Two very influential developmental psychologists, Jean Piaget and Lev Vygotsky, often debated the relationship of language and thought (Duncan, 1995). Piaget (1926, 1962) theorized that concepts preceded and aided the development of language. For example, a child would have to have a concept or mental schema for "mother" before being able to learn the word "mama." In a sense, concepts become the "pegs" upon which words are "hung." Piaget also noticed that preschool children seemed to spend a great deal of time talking to themselves—even when playing with another child. Each child would be talking about something totally unrelated to the speech of the other, in a process Piaget called *collective monologue.* Piaget believed that this kind of nonsocial speech was very egocentric (from the child's point of view only, with no regard for the listener) and that as the child became more socially involved and less egocentric, these nonsocial speech patterns would reduce.

Vygotsky, however, believed almost the opposite. He theorized that language actually helped develop concepts and that language could also help the child learn to control behavior—including social behavior (Vygotsky, 1962, 1978, 1987). For Vygotsky, the word helped form the concept: Once a child had learned the word "mama," the various elements of "mama-ness"—*warm, soft, food, safety,* and so on—could come together around that word. Vygotsky also believed that the "egocentric" speech of the preschool child was actually a way for the child to form thoughts and control actions. This "private speech" was a way for children to plan their behavior and organize actions so that their goals could be obtained. Since socializing with other children would demand much more self-control and behavioral regulation on the part of the preschool child, Vygotsky believed that private speech would actually increase as children became more socially active in the preschool years. This was, of course, the opposite of Piaget's assumption, and the evidence seems to bear out Vygotsky's view: Children, especially bright children, do tend to use more private speech when learning how to socialize with other children or when working on a difficult task (Berk, 1992; Berk & Spuhl, 1995; Bivens & Berk, 1990).

**LINGUISTIC RELATIVITY HYPOTHESIS**    The hypothesis that language shapes and influences thoughts was accepted by many theorists, with a few notable exceptions, such as Piaget. One of the best-known versions of this view is the Sapir-Whorf hypothesis (named for the two theorists who developed it, Edward Sapir and his student, Benjamin Lee Whorf). This hypothesis assumes that the thought processes and concepts within any culture are determined by the words of the culture (Sapir, 1921; Whorf, 1956). It has come to be known as the **linguistic relativity hypothesis**, meaning that thought processes and concepts are controlled by (relative to) language. That is, the words people use determine much of the way in which they think about the world around them.

One of the most famous examples used by Whorf to support this idea was that of the Inuits, Native Americans living in the Arctic. Supposedly, the Inuits have many more words for *snow* than do people in other cultures. One estimate was 23 different words, whereas other estimates have ranged in the hundreds. Unfortunately, this anecdotal evidence has turned out to be false, being more myth than reality (Pullum, 1991). In fact, English speakers also have many different words for snow (sleet, slush, powder, dusting, and yellow to name a few).

Is there evidence for the linguistic relativity hypothesis? Neither Sapir nor Whorf provided any scientific studies that would support their proposition. There have been numerous studies by other researchers, however. For example, in one study researchers assumed that a language's color names would influence the ability of the people who grew up with that language to distinguish among and perceive colors. The study found that basic color terms did directly influence color recognition memory (Lucy & Shweder, 1979). But an earlier series of studies of the perception of colors by Eleanor Rosch-Heider and others (Rosch-Heider, 1972; Rosch-Heider & Olivier, 1972) had already found just the opposite effect: Members of the Dani tribe, who have only two names for colors, were no different in their ability to perceive all of the colors than were the English speakers in the study. More recent studies (Davies et al., 1998a, 1998b; Laws et al., 1995; Pinker & Bloom, 1990) support Rosch-Heider's findings and the idea of a **cognitive universalism** (concepts are universal and influence the development of language) rather than linguistic relativity.

Other research suggests that although the linguistic relativity hypothesis may not work for fine perceptual discriminations such as those in the Rosch-Heider studies, it may be an appropriate explanation for concepts of a higher level. In one study, researchers showed pictures of two animals to preschool children (Gelman & Markman, 1986). The pictures were of a flamingo and a bat. The children were told that the flamingo feeds its baby mashed-up food but the bat feeds its baby milk. Then they were shown a picture of a blackbird (which looked more like the bat than the flamingo). Half of the children were told that the blackbird was a bird, while the other children were not. When asked how the blackbird fed its baby, the children who had been given the bird label were more likely to say that it fed its baby mashed-up food than were the children who were not given the label, indicating that the preschoolers were making inferences about feeding habits based on category membership rather than perceptual similarity—the word *bird* helped the children who were given that label to place the blackbird in its proper higher-level category.

Research continues in the investigation of relationships between language and thought and appears to support linguistic relativity and how language can shape our thoughts about space, time, colors, and objects (Boroditsky, 2001, 2009). Even our reasoning can be impacted, including making important decisions on such topics as how to manage crime (Thibodeau & Boroditsky, 2013, 2015). However, researchers do not always agree, and for some studies that offer support, there are others that reinterpret the data, fail to replicate, or offer critiques of the original studies, so findings are sometimes still in question (J. Y. Chen, 2007; January & Kako, 2007).

Psychologists cannot deny the influence of language on problem solving, cognition, and memory. Sometimes a problem can simply be worded differently to have the

Breakfast in an Ethiopian restaurant. What does "breakfast" food mean to you?

**linguistic relativity hypothesis**

the theory that thought processes and concepts are controlled by language.

**cognitive universalism**

theory that concepts are universal and influence the development of language.

solution become obvious, and memory (Ⓛ Ⓘ Ⓝ Ⓚ to Learning Objective 6.5) is certainly stored in terms of the semantics of language. Language can definitely influence the perception of others as well—"computer geek" and "software engineer" might be used to describe the same person, but one phrase is obviously less flattering, and the image brought to mind is different for the two terms. In the end, trying to determine whether language influences thoughts or thoughts influence language may be like trying to determine which came first, the chicken or the egg.

### ANIMAL STUDIES IN LANGUAGE

**7.14 Summarize the research on the ability of animals to communicate and use language.**

> 💬 I've heard that chimpanzees can be taught to use sign language. Is this for real, or are the chimps just performing tricks like the animals in the circus or the zoo?

There are really two questions about animals and language. The first is "Can animals communicate?" and the second is "Can animals use language?" The answer to the first question is a definite "Yes." Animals communicate in many ways. They use sounds such as the rattle of a rattlesnake or the warning growl of an angry dog. There are also physical behaviors, such as the "dance" of honeybees that tells the other bees where a source of pollen is (Gould & Gould, 1994). But the answer to the second question is more complicated, because language is defined as the use of symbols, and symbols are things that stand for something else. Words are symbols, and gestures can be symbols. But the gestures used by animals are instinctual, meaning they are controlled by the animal's genetic makeup. The honeybee doing the "dance" is controlled completely by instinct, as is the growling dog. In human language, symbols are used quite deliberately and voluntarily, not by instinct, and abstract symbols have no meaning until people assign meaning to them. (Although Chomsky's innate language acquisition device might lead some to think that language for humans is instinctual, it should be noted that the infant's production of speech sounds becomes quite deliberate within a short period of time.)

Can animals be taught to use symbols that are abstract? There have been attempts to teach animals (primates and dolphins) how to use sign language (as animals lack the vocal structure to form spoken words), but many of these attempts were simply not "good science." The most successful of these experiments (which is not without its critics as well) has been with Kanzi, a bonobo chimpanzee trained to press abstract symbols on a computer keyboard (Savage-Rumbaugh & Lewin, 1994). Kanzi actually was not the original subject of the study—his mother, Matata, was the chimp being trained. She did not learn many of the symbols, but Kanzi watched his mother use the keyboard and appeared to learn how to use the symbols through that observation. One estimate suggested Kanzi could understand about 150 spoken English words. Trainers who speak to him are not in his view, so he is not responding to physical cues or symbols. He has managed to follow correctly complex instructions up to the level of a 2-year-old child (Savage-Rumbaugh et al., 1998). A later report suggested Kanzi and his half-sister Pan-Banisha eventually acquired a working vocabulary of 480 symbols and understood up to 2,000 English words (Roffman et al., 2012)! However, aside from anecdotal reports based on video recordings, little to no data have been offered in published studies. One published study with Kanzi does suggest he makes sounds that seem to have consistent meaning across different situations (Taglialatela et al., 2003). Nearly 100 videotaped hours of Kanzi engaged in day-to-day activities were analyzed for these sounds. The researchers were able to identify

Dr. Sue Savage-Rumbaugh working with Kanzi, a bonobo chimpanzee.

four sounds that seemed to represent banana, grapes, juice, and the word *yes*. (However, remember that four sounds do not come close to making an entire language.)

Other studies, with dolphins (Herman et al., 1993) and with parrots (Pepperberg, 1998, 2007), have also met with some success. Is it real language? The answer seems to be a qualified "yes." The qualification is that none of the animals that have achieved success so far can compare to the level of language development of a 3-year-old human child (Pinker, 1995). However, linguists still debate whether these animals are truly learning language if they are not also learning how to use syntax—combining words into grammatically correct sentences as well as being able to understand the differences between sentences such as "The girl kissed the boy" and "The boy kissed the girl." As yet, there is no conclusive evidence that any of the animals trained in language have been able to master syntax (Demers, 1988; Johnson, 1995; Pinker, 1995).

## Concept Map L.O. 7.11, 7.12, 7.13, 7.14

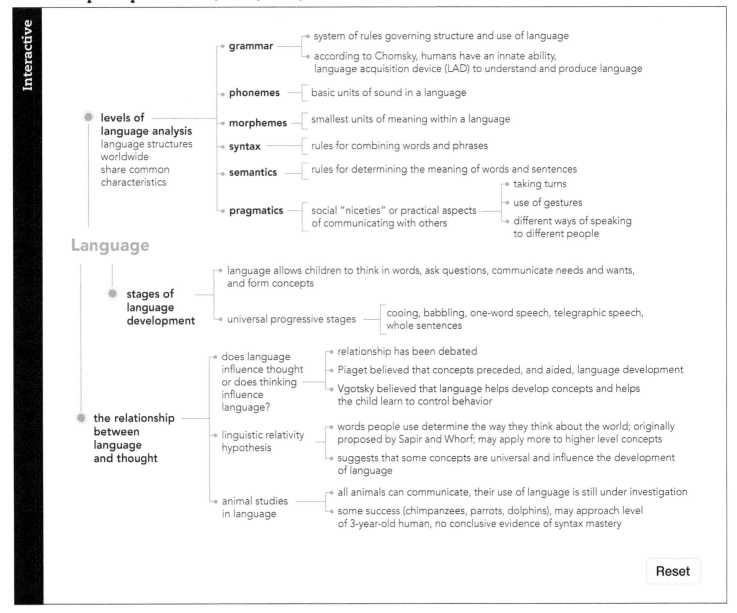

# Practice Quiz    How much do you remember?

*Pick the best answer.*

**1.** The basic units of sound in a language are known as
  **a.** grammar.          **c.** syntax.
  **b.** morphemes.        **d.** phonemes.

**2.** According to Noam Chomsky, what is a language acquisition device?
  **a.** an environmental entity that allows people to learn foreign languages
  **b.** a biological element of the brain that allows us to learn language
  **c.** a learning method that many can use to understand the language of infants and small children
  **d.** a part of the brain that develops during puberty that allows teens and adults to formulate questions and engage others

**3.** Researchers believe that up to the age of _____, individuals possess the ability to understand phonemes of all languages.
  **a.** 3 months          **c.** 2 years
  **b.** 9 months          **d.** 7 years

**4.** _____ believed that language helps develop concepts, whereas _____ believed that concepts must be developed first if language is to follow.
  **a.** Vygotsky; Piaget
  **b.** Chomsky; Sapir and Whorf
  **c.** Piaget; Rosch-Heider
  **d.** Sapir and Whorf; Vygotsky

**5.** "Daddy go bye-bye" is an example of _____.
  **a.** telegraphic speech
  **b.** babbling
  **c.** a holophrase
  **d.** cooing

# APA Goal 2: Scientific Inquiry and Critical Thinking

## A Cognitive Advantage for Bilingual Individuals?

*Addresses APA Learning Objectives 2.1: Use scientific reasoning to interpret psychological phenomena; and 2.3: Engage in innovative and integrative thinking and problem solving.*

In our growing, interconnected world, more and more of the population speaks more than one language (Bialystok et al., 2009). Individuals that speak a single language are *monolingual* and those that speak two are *bilingual*. Aside from enhanced communication, individuals who speak more than one language reportedly have greater cognitive reserves, are less prone to some age-related decreases in functioning, and are even less susceptible to some types of egocentric biases (Calvo et al., 2015; Rubio-Fernandez & Glucksberg, 2012).

Many studies suggest that bilingual people have other cognitive advantages as compared to monolingual people. The advantages stem from their ability to successfully manage the activities of more than one language, with some studies reporting changes in neuropsychological function and others reporting changes in the structure and connectivity of the brain (Hervais-Adelman et al., 2011; Kroll et al., 2014; Olulade et al., 2015; Pliatsikas et al., 2015). Those cognitive advantages extend beyond general language skills and are believed to result in better cognitive performance overall, and multiple enhanced executive functions, including better inhibitory control, better conflict monitoring, and more efficient mental set shifting (von Bastian et al., 2015).

However, despite many studies, over many years, not everyone agrees that bilingual individuals have such cognitive advantages. Some studies have failed to replicate previous results or reported either inconsistent or no benefits for those that are bilingual (Paap & Greenberg, 2013; von Bastian, et al., 2016). Additionally, others cite poor methodology, small samples, and even publication bias for positive results related to the bilingual cognitive advantage (de Bruin et al., 2015; Paap, 2014; Paap et al., 2014).

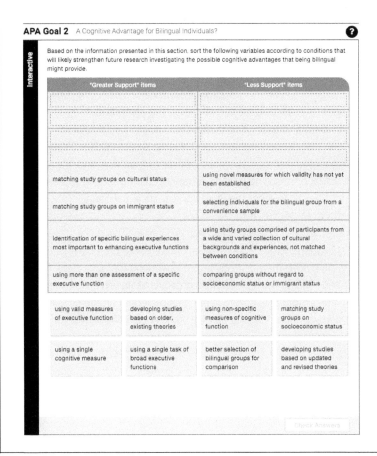

# Applying Psychology to Everyday Life
## Mental and Physical Exercises for Better Cognitive Health

**7.15  Identify some methods for improving your cognitive health.**

You may have heard the saying "use it or lose it" and likely think of it in terms of maintaining physical fitness. But it is not limited to that; in many regards, the saying applies as well to our ability to maintain cognitive fitness. However, just as there is a difference between physical activity and physical exercise, there is a difference in mental *activity* and mental *exercise*.

Quite a few computerized brain-training programs and devices have hit the market in the last few years. In addition, a lot of attention in the media has focused on the benefits of specific computer-based brain exercises you can do to improve your cognitive fitness. While some are more scientifically grounded and offer the possibility of real benefits, many more appear to be riding the current wave of interest and may not be useful. For some individuals, practicing certain mental skills through cognitive exercises appears to help with those same skills when tested later. In general, however, research has not identified any benefits that transfer to untrained areas (A. M. Owen et al., 2010). Just as being physically active in general will not make you an Olympic athlete, to tune up your cognitive fitness you may have to perform proper, focused cognitive exercises.

 Wait a minute! You just said most skills don't transfer.

That's correct, some do not, but just as in physical training, if you select the proper foundational exercises, you may be able to improve some higher-level cognitive functions.

In one study, it was found that for a group of individuals with schizophrenia, computerized cognitive exercises that placed increasing demands on auditory perception (a foundational skill) were beneficial (M. Fisher et al., 2009). Those same individuals later demonstrated significant progress in verbal working memory and global cognition tasks (higher-level skills). Although the cognitive exercise group originally received daily training for 10 weeks, when some participants were studied 6 months later, the researchers found that some of the gains were still evident and that gains overall were positively correlated with improved quality of life at the 6-month assessment point (Fisher et al., 2009). However, a more recent study has suggested that computerized attention, memory, and executive training for individuals with schizophrenia may improve performance on training tasks, but these improvements do not transfer to other measures or real-life situations (Gomar et al., 2015).

Clinical populations aside, some research suggests challenging, adaptive training in working memory may improve cognitive skills and fluid intelligence in both young and older adults (Au et al., 2015; Jaeggi et al., 2008; Karbach & Verhaeghen, 2014). Other researchers suggest training in working memory may improve *working memory capacity* on related tasks, but on measures of fluid intelligence, these improvements do not generalize (Harrison et al., 2013). As you can probably tell, there is still a lot of debate on the possible efficacy of cognitive training in general. Despite some studies being supportive of such efforts, conflicting findings suggest working memory training is not effective, and little evidence exists that any such training improves intelligence (Melby-Lervag & Hulme, 2016, 2015; Redick, 2015).

So while researchers continue to investigate the possible outcomes of cognitive training, what else can you do more generally to benefit your brain and mental health? Exercise! And this time, we are referring to physical exercise. Physical activity and specifically aerobic fitness has repeatedly been demonstrated to be associated with improved cognitive function across the life span. A physically active lifestyle and greater aerobic fitness has been implicated with better executive control and memory processes in preadolescent children (Chaddock et al., 2010; Hillman et al., 2009), better educational outcomes later in life and improved affect and visuospatial memory in young adults (Åberg et al., 2009; Stroth et al., 2009), increased hippocampal volume (associated with better memory) in elderly adults (Erickson et al., 2009), and as a useful intervention in a group of individuals at high risk of cognitive decline or impairment, especially for females in the group (Baker et al., 2010).

At least one possible benefit of regular aerobic activity is promoting or maintaining functional connectivity among key brain areas of the frontal, temporal, and parietal lobes (Voss et al., 2010). The increases in oxygen and blood flow to the brain play key roles. Other benefits include increased levels of mood-related neurotransmitters, including serotonin, norepinephrine, and dopamine, along with neurogenesis in specific brain areas including the hippocampus (Ratey & Hagerman, 2008). Increased myelination of hippocampal neurons has been found to occur after only 6 weeks of aerobic exercise in a group of middle-aged adults (Thomas et al., 2015). However, these results were temporary, returning to pre-exercise levels after 6 weeks of not exercising. In other words, keep moving!

So instead of "use it or lose it," perhaps a better saying to keep in mind is "what is good for the heart or body is also good for the mind."

### Questions for Further Discussion

1. Aside from those involving working memory, what other kinds of focused mental exercises might help keep the brain fit?

2. Should doctors suggest aerobic exercise for their patients interested in maintaining or improving their cognitive functions? What about psychologists working with individuals who have mood or anxiety disorders or clients with attention problems?

3. Based on this information, what might the implications be for schools that are reducing or eliminating their physical education requirements? What about college students who may experience a decrease in physical activity as compared to when they were in high school?

# Chapter Summary

## How People Think

- Thinking (cognition) is mental activity that occurs in the brain when information is being organized, stored, communicated, or processed.

### 7.1 Explain how mental images are involved in the process of thinking.

- Mental images represent objects or events and have a picture-like quality.

### 7.2 Describe how concepts and prototypes influence our thinking.

- Concepts are ideas that represent a class or category of events, objects, or activities.
- Prototypes are examples of a concept that more closely match the defining characteristics of that concept.

### 7.3 Identify some methods that people use to solve problems and make decisions.

- Problem solving consists of thinking and behaving in certain ways to reach a goal.
- Mechanical solutions include trial-and-error learning and rote solutions.
- Algorithms are a type of rote solution in which one follows step-by-step procedures for solving certain types of problems.
- A heuristic or "rule of thumb" is a strategy that narrows down the possible solutions for a problem.
- Insight is the sudden perception of a solution to a problem.

### 7.4 Identify three common barriers to successful problem solving.

- Functional fixedness is the tendency to perceive objects as having only the use for which they were originally intended and, therefore, failing to see them as possible tools for solving other problems.
- Confirmation bias is the tendency to search for evidence that confirms one's beliefs, ignoring any evidence to the contrary.

### 7.5 Recall some characteristics of creative, divergent thinking.

- Divergent thinking involves coming up with as many different answers as possible. This is a kind of creativity (combining ideas or behavior in new ways).
- Creative people are usually good at mental imagery and have knowledge on a wide range of topics, are unafraid to be different, value their independence, and are often unconventional in their work but not in other areas.

## Intelligence

### 7.6 Compare and contrast different theories on the nature of intelligence.

- Intelligence is the ability to understand the world, think rationally or logically, and use resources effectively when faced with challenges or problems.

- Spearman proposed general intelligence, or g factor, as the ability to reason and solve problems, whereas specific intelligence, or s factor, includes task-specific abilities in certain areas such as music, business, or art.
- Gardner proposed nine different types of intelligence, ranging from verbal, linguistic, and mathematical to interpersonal and intrapersonal intelligence.
- Sternberg proposed three types of intelligence: analytical, creative, and practical.
- The Cattell-Horn-Carroll (CHC) Theory of Intelligence includes general intelligence, or *g*, 16 broad abilities, and many narrow abilities within each broad area.
- Specific brain areas and brain functions have been tied to differences in intellectual ability, with some research indicating the frontal and parietal areas playing the most important roles.

### 7.7 Compare and contrast some methods of measuring intelligence.

- The Stanford-Binet Intelligence Test yields an IQ score that was once determined by dividing the mental age of the person by the chronological age and multiplying that quotient by 100 but now involves comparing a person's score to a standardized norm.
- The Wechsler Intelligence Tests yield four index scores derived from both verbal and nonverbal subtests and an overall score of intelligence.

### 7.8 Identify ways to evaluate the quality of a test.

- Standardization, validity, and reliability are all important factors in the construction of an intelligence test.
- Deviation IQs are based on the normal curve, defining different levels of intelligence based on the deviation of scores from a common mean.
- IQ tests are often criticized for being culturally biased.
- Neuropsychologists play an important role in the care of individuals with traumatic brain injury and other conditions in which brain functioning has been negatively impacted.
- Concussion, or mild traumatic brain injury, affects the lives of many athletes and military personnel.

### 7.9 Define intellectual disability, giftedness, and emotional intelligence.

- Intellectual disability is a neurodevelopmental condition in which IQ falls below 70 and adaptive behavior across conceptual, social, and practical domains of life is severely deficient for a person of a particular chronological age. Symptoms must also first be present during the developmental period.
- The four levels of intellectual disability are mild, moderate, severe, and profound. These are determined by the level of adaptive functioning and level of supports the individual needs in their daily life.
- Causes of intellectual disability include deprived environments as well as chromosome and genetic disorders and dietary deficiencies.

- Gifted persons are defined as those having IQ scores at the upper end of the normal curve (130 or above).
- Emotional intelligence involves being able to reach goals and engage in productive thinking through accurate awareness and effective management of our own emotions. It also involves our ability to understand what others feel.
- Terman conducted a longitudinal study that demonstrated that gifted children grow up to be successful adults for the most part.
- Terman's study has been criticized for a lack of objectivity because Terman became too involved in the lives of several of his participants, even to the point of intervening on their behalf.

**7.10  Evaluate the influence of heredity and environment on the development of intelligence.**

- Stronger correlations are found between IQ scores as genetic relatedness increases. Heritability of IQ is estimated at .50.
- In 1994, Herrnstein and Murray published *The Bell Curve*, in which they made widely criticized claims about the heritability of intelligence.

## Language

**7.11  Identify the different elements and structure of language.**

- Language is a system for combining symbols so that an infinite number of meaningful statements can be created and communicated to others.
- Grammar is the system of rules by which language is governed and includes the rules for using phonemes, morphemes, and syntax. Pragmatics refers to practical aspects of language.

**7.12  Explain how language develops.**

- The stages of language development are cooing, babbling, one-word speech (holophrases), telegraphic speech, and whole sentences.

**7.13  Evaluate whether or not language influences how people think.**

- Sapir and Whorf originally proposed that language controls and helps the development of thought processes and concepts, an idea that is known as the linguistic relativity hypothesis.
- Other researchers have found evidence that concepts are universal and directly influence the development of language, called the cognitive universalism viewpoint.

**7.14  Summarize the research on the ability of animals to communicate and use language.**

- Studies with chimpanzees, parrots, and dolphins have been somewhat successful in demonstrating that animals can develop a basic kind of language, including some abstract ideas.
- Controversy exists over the lack of evidence that animals can learn syntax, which some feel means that animals are not truly learning and using language.

## Applying Psychology to Everyday Life: Mental and Physical Exercises for Better Cognitive Health

**7.15  Identify some methods for improving your cognitive health.**

- While specific mental exercises (such as those involving working memory) may have some limited benefit, physical exercise promoting aerobic fitness is extremely important for optimal cognitive functioning.

# Test Yourself

*Pick the best answer.*

1. Researchers have found that it takes _____ to view a mental image that is larger or covers more distance than a smaller or more compact one.
   - **a.** longer
   - **b.** less time
   - **c.** the same amount of time
   - **d.** half the time

2. Research suggests we engage mental images in our mind _____ the way we engage or interact with physical objects.
   - **a.** a little like
   - **b.** much like
   - **c.** not at all like
   - **d.** randomly and completely different than

3. A psychologist asks people to envision a circle. Next he asks them to draw the circle they envisioned. When comparing the pictures, almost all circles look identical. The fact that a circle typically fits a specific and rigid set of rules is an example of a
   - **a.** formal concept.
   - **b.** natural concept.
   - **c.** fuzzy concept.
   - **d.** prototype.

4. Trial and error is sometimes referred to as a(n)
   - **a.** algorithm.
   - **b.** heuristic.
   - **c.** rule of thumb.
   - **d.** mechanical solution.

5. John and Karen bought a new house with an unfinished basement. To determine how they want to finish it, they lay down tape on the floor showing where walls will go and rooms will be. This process of problem solving is known as
   - **a.** representativeness heuristic.
   - **b.** trial and error.
   - **c.** working backward from the goal.
   - **d.** algorithms.

6. One day at work, Pauline's earring fell on the floor, and she was unable to find the back. To keep from losing her earring, Pauline reinserted it and used part of a pencil eraser to keep the earring in place. Using a pencil eraser as a temporary earring back showed that Pauline overcame
   - **a.** a mental set.
   - **b.** functional fixedness.
   - **c.** confirmation bias.
   - **d.** transformation bias.

7. Which of the following questions would be more likely to produce divergent thinking?
   a. "What is a clothes hanger?"
   b. "How do you spell clothes hanger?"
   c. "How many uses can you think of for a clothes hanger?"
   d. "What does a clothes hanger typically look like?"

8. Which type of intelligence, according to Howard Gardner, would most likely be present in farmers, landscapers, and biologists?
   a. naturalist
   b. visual/spatial
   c. existentialist
   d. movement

9. According to Sternberg, "book smarts" is another way of talking about which kind of intelligence?
   a. analytical
   b. creative
   c. practical
   d. emotional

10. Which of the following tests came first?
    a. The Wechsler tests
    b. The Stanford Binet
    c. The ACT
    d. Binet's mental ability test

11. Dr. Davenport gives all her classes 45 minutes to complete their psychology test regardless of if the class meets for 50 minutes, 75 minutes, or even 3 hours. Such a technique ensures test
    a. reliability.
    b. validity.
    c. norms.
    d. standardization.

12. In contrast to comparing mental age to chronological age, most modern tests of intelligence use _____.
    a. Stern's formula
    b. age-group comparison norms
    c. creativity assessments
    d. emotional assessments

13. The goal of all test developers is to _____ cultural bias in their intelligence tests.
    a. maximize
    b. eliminate
    c. minimize
    d. hide

14. Dr. Miller works with children who have grown up in poor socioeconomic conditions. Many of her clients come from homes that do not emphasize education or social involvement, and opportunities for advancement are practically nonexistent. Many are malnourished, have been exposed to a variety of environmental toxins, and have multiple infections without adequate or timely health care. What might these children be at risk for?
    a. intellectual disability
    b. genetic inhibition
    c. organically induced deprivation
    d. increased emotional intelligence

15. Dr. Thomas has found that William, her patient, has a defect in a gene on the X chromosome of his 23rd pair, which has resulted in a deficiency of a protein needed for William's brain development. William most likely suffers from
    a. Down syndrome.
    b. cretinism.
    c. fragile X syndrome.
    d. fetal alcohol syndrome.

16. In Terman's study of gifted children, mental health issues and relationship problems only occurred in those with IQs of
    a. 150 or higher.
    b. 180 or higher.
    c. 100 or lower.
    d. 45 or lower.

17. What might be the best predictor of why some people do not excel in school but essentially succeed in their life and career choices?
    a. cretinism
    b. phonemes
    c. one's intelligence quotient
    d. emotional intelligence

18. What does the Flynn effect theorize?
    a. Intelligence scores are steadily increasing in modernized countries.
    b. Intelligence scores are decreasing due to an overreliance on technology.
    c. Intelligence scores are relatively stable in contrast to improvement in our educational system.
    d. Intelligence scores are meaningless and should be abandoned.

19. Edward Sapir and Benjamin Whorf theorized that _____, a concept reflected in their linguistic relativity hypothesis.
    a. language shapes thoughts
    b. thoughts shape language
    c. language and thought develop independently
    d. language and thought influence each other

20. Cognitive universalism tends to _____ the linguistic relativity hypothesis.
    a. contradict
    b. support
    c. add further proof to
    d. mildly downplay

# 8 Development across the Life Span

How have you changed since your early teenage years? In what ways are you similar to other individuals of your age and in what ways are you different and unique?

After you have answered the question, watch the video to compare the answers of other students to yours.

▶ The response entered here will be saved to your notes and may be collected by your instructor if he/she requires it.

Watch the Video

## Why Study Human Development?

Beginning to understand how we come to be the people we are is a critical step in understanding ourselves as we are today and who we may become as we grow older. From the moment of conception, each of us is headed down a pathway of change, influenced by our biology, environment, and social interactions, to a final destination that is the same for all of us. The twists and turns of the pathway are what make each of us unique individuals. In this chapter, we'll look at the influences that help determine our developmental pathway through life.

# Learning Objectives

**8.1** Compare and contrast the special research methods used to study development.

**8.2** Explain the relationship between heredity and environmental factors in determining development.

**8.3** Summarize the role of chromosomes and genes in determining the transmission of traits and the inheritance of disorders.

**8.4** Explain the process of fertilization, including the twinning process.

**8.5** Describe the three stages of prenatal development.

**8.6** Describe the physical and sensory changes that take place in infancy and childhood.

**8.7** Compare and contrast two theories of cognitive development, and define autism spectrum disorder.

**8.8** Identify the development of personality, relationships, and self-concept in infancy and childhood.

**8.9** Describe the physical changes of puberty.

**8.10** Identify the cognitive and moral advances that occur in adolescence.

**8.11** Describe how the adolescent search for personal identity influences relationships with others.

**8.12** Identify the physical changes and health issues associated with adulthood.

**8.13** Describe how memory abilities change during adulthood.

**8.14** Apply Erikson's theory to some common psychosocial concerns of adulthood.

**8.15** Compare and contrast four theories of why aging occurs.

**8.16** Describe Kübler-Ross's theory of death and dying, and identify some criticisms of this theory.

**8.17** Compare and contrast some cross-cultural differences in views of death and dying.

# Studying Human Development

What is development? In the context of life, **human development** is the scientific study of the changes that occur in people as they age, from conception until death. This chapter will touch on almost all of the topics covered in the other chapters of this text, such as personality, cognition, biological processes, and social interactions. But here, all of those topics will be studied in the context of changes that occur as a result of the process of human development.

## RESEARCH DESIGNS

### 8.1 Compare and contrast the special research methods used to study development.

As briefly discussed in Chapter One, research in human development is affected by the problem of age. In any experiment, the participants who are exposed to the independent variable (the variable in an experiment that is deliberately manipulated by the experimenter) should be randomly assigned to the different experimental conditions. The challenge in developmental research is that the age of the people in the study should always be an independent variable, but people cannot be randomly assigned to different age groups.

There are some special designs that are used in researching age-related changes: the **longitudinal design**, in which one group of people is followed and assessed at different times as the group ages; the **cross-sectional design**, in which several different age groups are studied at one time; and the **cross-sequential design**, which is a combination of the longitudinal and cross-sectional designs (Baltes et al., 1988; Schaie & Willis, 2010).

The longitudinal design has the advantage of looking at real age-related changes as those changes occur in the same individuals. Disadvantages of this method are the lengthy amount of time, money, and effort involved in following participants over the years, as well as the loss of participants when they move away, lose interest, or die. The cross-sectional design has the advantages of being quick, relatively inexpensive, and easier to accomplish than the longitudinal design. Its main disadvantage is that the study no longer compares an individual to that same individual as he or she ages; instead, individuals of different ages are being compared to one another. Differences between age groups are often a problem in developmental research. For example, if comparing the IQ scores of 30-year-olds to 80-year-olds to see how aging affects intelligence, questions arise concerning the differing educational experiences and opportunities those two age groups have had that might affect IQ scores, in addition to any effects of aging. This is known as the **cohort effect**, the particular impact on development that occurs when a group of people share a common time period or common life experience (for example, having been born in the same time period or having gone through a specific historical event together). **Table 8.1** shows a comparison between examples of a longitudinal design, a cross-sectional design, and a cross-sequential design.

In studying human development, developmental psychologists have outlined many theories of how these age-related changes occur. There are some areas of controversy, however, and one of these is the issue of nature versus nurture.

## NATURE AND NURTURE

### 8.2 Explain the relationship between heredity and environmental factors in determining development.

**Nature** refers to heredity, the influence of inherited characteristics on personality, physical growth, intellectual growth, and social interactions. **Nurture** refers to the influence of the environment on all of those same things and includes parenting styles, physical

---

**human development**

the scientific study of the changes that occur in people as they age from conception until death.

**longitudinal design**

research design in which one participant or group of participants is studied over a long period of time.

**cross-sectional design**

research design in which several different participant age-groups are studied at one particular point in time.

**cross-sequential design**

research design in which participants are first studied by means of a cross-sectional design but are also followed and assessed longitudinally.

**cohort effect**

the impact on development occurring when a group of people share a common time period or common life experience.

**nature**

the influence of our inherited characteristics on our personality, physical growth, intellectual growth, and social interactions.

**nurture**

the influence of the environment on personality, physical growth, intellectual growth, and social interactions.

**Table 8.1** A Comparison of Three Developmental Research Designs

**Cross-Sectional Design**

| Different participants of various ages are compared at one point in time to determine age-related *differences*. | **Group One:** 20-year-old participants<br>**Group Two:** 40-year-old participants<br>**Group Three:** 60-year-old participants | Research done in 2014 |
| --- | --- | --- |

**Longitudinal Design**

| The same participants are studied at various ages to determine age-related *changes*. | **Study One:** 20-year-old participants<br>**Study Two:** Same participants at 40 years old<br><br>**Study Three:** Same participants are now 60 years old | Research done in 1974<br>Research done in 1994<br><br>Research done in 2014 |
| --- | --- | --- |

**Cross-Sequential Design**

| Different participants of various ages are compared at several points in time to determine both age-related *differences* and age-related *changes*. | **Study One:**<br>*Group One*: 20-year-old participants<br>*Group Two*: 40-year-old participants<br>**Study Two:**<br>*Group One*: Participants will be 25 years old<br>*Group Two*: Participants will be 45 years old | Research done in 2014<br><br><br>Research to be done in 2019 |
| --- | --- | --- |

surroundings, economic factors, and anything that can have an influence on development that does not come from within the person.

 💬 So is a person like Hitler born that way, or did something happen to make him the person he was?

How much of a person's personality and behavior is determined by nature and how much is determined by nurture? This is a key question, and the answer is quite complicated. It is also quite important: Are people like Hitler or Dzhokhar Tsarnaev (the youngest of the two brothers responsible for the bombings at the 2013 Boston Marathon) the result of bad genes, bad parenting, or life-altering experiences in childhood? How much of Stephen Hawking's genius is due to his genetic inheritance? What part did the parenting choices of his family play? Or are his cognitive abilities the unique combination of both hereditary and environmental influences? After many years of scientific research, most developmental psychologists now agree that the last possibility is the most likely explanation for most of human development: All that people are and all that people become is the product of an interaction between nature and nurture (Davis et al., 2012; Insel & Wang, 2010; Polderman et al., 2015; Ridley, 1999; Sternberg & Grigorenko, 2006). This does not mean that the nature versus nurture controversy no longer exists; for example, intelligence is still a "hot topic" with regard to how much is inherited and how much is learned. Some researchers and theorists assume a large genetic influence (Bouchard & Segal, 1985; Herrnstein & Murray, 1994; Jensen, 1969; Johnson et al., 2007; Kristensen & Bjerkedal, 2007), whereas many others believe that culture, economics, nutrition in early childhood, and educational opportunities have a greater impact (Gardner et al., 1996; Gould, 1996; Rose et al., 1984; Wahlsten, 1997).

*Behavioral genetics* is a field of study in which researchers try to determine how much of behavior is the result of genetic inheritance and how much is due to a person's experiences. As the video *Family and Twin Studies* explains, behavioral geneticists use a variety of methods to determine this, including family, twin, and adoption studies.

Genotype - Full
        hereditary
        Information

Phenotype -
Organisms Observed
        traits

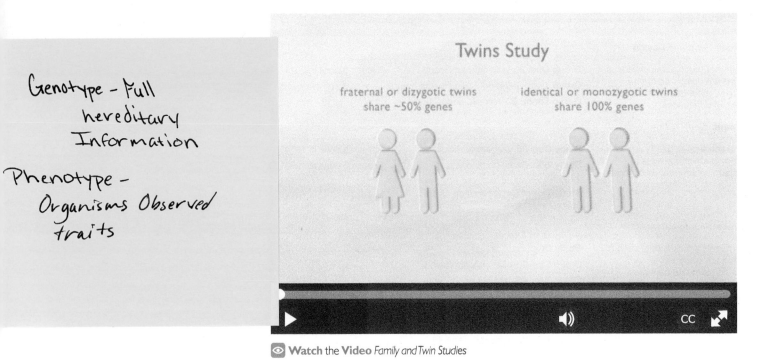

Twins Study

fraternal or dizygotic twins
share ~50% genes

identical or monozygotic twins
share 100% genes

👁 **Watch** the **Video** *Family and Twin Studies*

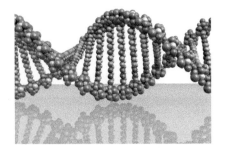

**Figure 8.1**   DNA Molecule
In this model of a DNA molecule, the two strands making up the sides of the "twisted ladder" are composed of sugars and phosphates. The "rungs" of the ladder that link the two strands are amines. Amines contain the genetic codes for building the proteins that make up organic life.

**genetics**
the science of inherited traits.

**DNA (deoxyribonucleic acid)**
special molecule that contains the genetic material of the organism.

**gene**
section of DNA having the same arrangement of chemical elements.

**chromosomes**
tightly wound strand of genetic material or DNA.

## THE BASIC BUILDING BLOCKS OF DEVELOPMENT

**8.3**  Summarize the role of chromosomes and genes in determining the transmission of traits and the inheritance of disorders.

Any study of the human life span must begin with looking at the complex material contained in the cells of the body that carries the instructions for life itself. After discussing the basic building blocks of life, we will discuss how the processes of conception and the development of the infant within the womb take place.

**CHROMOSOMES, GENES, AND DNA**   **Genetics** is the science of heredity. Understanding how genes transmit human characteristics and traits involves defining a few basic terms.

**DNA (deoxyribonucleic acid)** is a very special kind of molecule (the smallest particle of a substance that still has all the properties of that substance). DNA consists of two very long sugar–phosphate strands, each linked together by certain chemical elements called *amines* or *bases* arranged in a particular pattern. (See **Figure 8.1** for a representation of DNA.) The amines are organic structures that contain the genetic codes for building the proteins that make up organic life (hair coloring, muscle, and skin, for example) and that control the life of each cell. Each section of DNA containing a certain sequence (ordering) of these amines is called a **gene**. These genes are located on rod-shaped structures called **chromosomes**, which are found in the nucleus of a cell.

Humans have a total of 46 chromosomes in each cell of their bodies (with the exception of the egg and the sperm). Twenty-three of these chromosomes come from the mother's egg and the other 23 from the father's sperm. Most characteristics are determined by 22 such pairs, called the *autosomes*. The last pair determines the sex of the person. The two chromosomes of this pair are called the *sex chromosomes*. Two X-shaped chromosomes indicate a female, while an X and a Y indicate a male.

The 46 chromosomes can be arranged in pairs, with one member of each pair coming from the mother and the other member from the father. Let's consider just one of these pairs for the moment.

In this particular pair of chromosomes, assume that there is a gene influencing hair color on each chromosome. The observable color of the person's hair will be determined

Frank and Ernest

©1986 Thaves. Reprinted with permission. Newspaper dist. by NEA, Inc.

by those two genes, one gene from each parent. If both genes influence brown hair, the person will obviously have brown hair, right? And if both influence blond hair, the person's hair will be blond.

💬 But what if one gene influences brown hair and the other blond hair?

The answer lies in the nature of each gene. Some genes that are more active in influencing the trait are called **dominant**. A dominant gene will always be expressed in the observable trait, in this case, hair color. A person with a dominant gene influencing brown hair color will have brown hair, no matter what the other gene is, because brown is the most dominant of all the hair colors.

Some genes are less active in influencing the trait and will only be expressed in the observable trait if they are paired with another less active gene. These genes tend to recede, or fade, into the background when paired with a more dominant gene, so they are called **recessive**. Blond is the most recessive hair color and it will only show up as a trait if that person receives a blond-hair-color gene from each parent.

💬 What about red hair? And how come some people have a mixed hair color, like strawberry blond?

In reality, the patterns of genetic transmission of traits are usually more complicated. Almost all traits are influenced by more than one pair of genes in a process called *polygenic inheritance*. (*Polygenic* means "many genes.") Sometimes certain kinds of genes tend to group themselves with certain other genes, like the genes influencing blond hair and blue eyes. Other genes are so equally dominant or equally recessive that they combine their traits in the organism. For example, genes involved in blond hair and red hair are recessive. When a child inherits one of each from his or her parents, instead of one or the other influencing the child's hair color, the genes may blend together to form a strawberry-blond mix.

**GENETIC AND CHROMOSOME PROBLEMS** Several genetically determined disorders are carried by recessive genes. Diseases carried by recessive genes are inherited when a child inherits two recessive genes, one from each parent. Examples of disorders inherited in this manner are cystic fibrosis (a disease of the respiratory and digestive tracts), sickle-cell anemia (a blood disorder), Tay-Sachs disorder (a fatal neurological disorder), and phenylketonuria (PKU), in which an infant is born without the ability to break down phenylalanine, an amino acid controlling coloring of the skin and hair. If levels of phenylalanine build up, brain damage can occur; if untreated, it can result in severe intellectual disabilities. **Figure 8.2** illustrates a typical pattern of inheritance for dominant and recessive genes using the example of PKU.

**dominant**

referring to a gene that actively controls the expression of a trait.

**recessive**

referring to a gene that only influences the expression of a trait when paired with an identical gene.

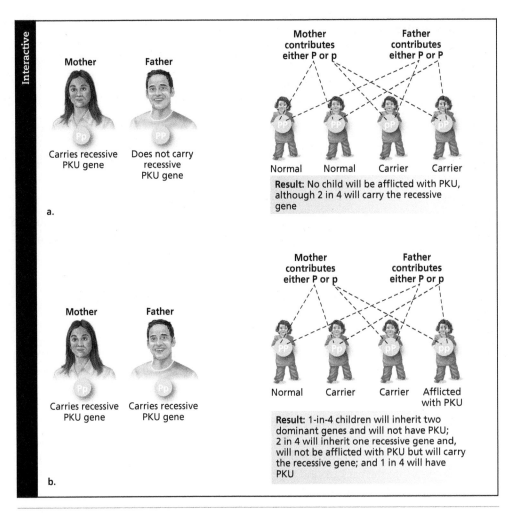

**Figure 8.2**   Dominant and Recessive Genes and PKU

This figure shows the variation of one or two parents carrying recessive genes and the result of this in their offspring. (a) If only one parent carries the PKU gene, their children might be carriers but will not have PKU. (b) Only if both parents are carriers of PKU, will a child have the 1-in-4 possibility of having PKU.

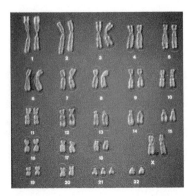

Down syndrome is a form of intellectual disability caused by an extra chromosome 21.

Sometimes the chromosome itself is the problem. Although each egg and each sperm are only supposed to have 23 chromosomes, in the creation of these cells a chromosome can end up in the wrong cell, leaving one cell with only 22 and the other with 24. If either of these cells survives to "mate," the missing or extra chromosome can cause mild to severe problems in development (American Academy of Pediatrics, 1995; Barnes & Carey, 2002; Centers for Disease Control and Prevention, 2009c; Gardner & Sutherland, 1996).

Examples of chromosome disorders include *Down syndrome*, a disorder in which there is an extra chromosome in what would normally be the 21st pair. Symptoms commonly include the physical characteristics of almond-shaped, wide-set eyes, intellectual disability, and the increased risk of organ failure later in life (Barnes & Carey, 2002; Hernandez & Fisher, 1996: Patel et al., 2015). Other chromosome disorders occur when there is an extra sex chromosome in the 23rd pair, such as *Klinefelter's syndrome*, in which the 23rd set of sex chromosomes is XXY, with the extra X producing a male with reduced masculine characteristics, enlarged breasts, obesity, and excessive height (Bock, 1993; Frühmesser & Kotzot, 2011); and *Turner's syndrome*, in which the 23rd pair is actually missing an X, so that the result is a lone X chromosome (Ranke & Saenger, 2001). These females tend to be very short, infertile, and sexually underdeveloped (American Academy of Pediatrics, 1995; Cramer et al., 2014; Hong et al., 2009; Rovet, 1993).

## Concept Map  L.O. 8.1, 8.2, 8.3

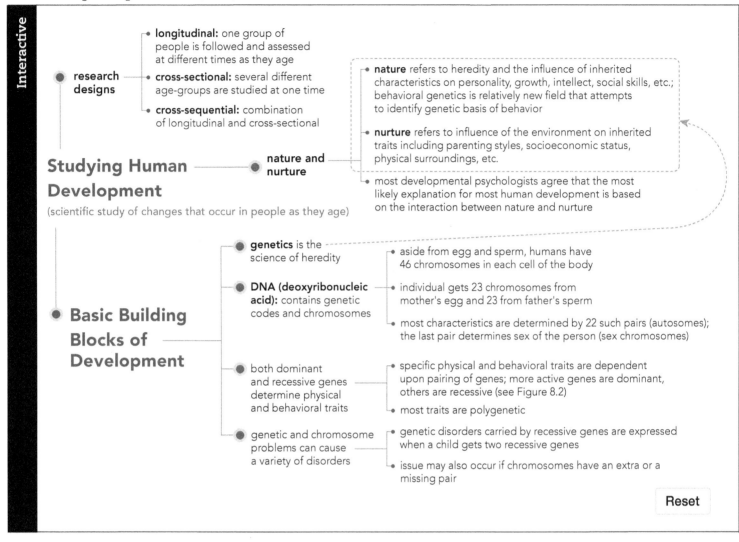

Interactive

**Studying Human Development**
(scientific study of changes that occur in people as they age)

- research designs
  - **longitudinal:** one group of people is followed and assessed at different times as they age
  - **cross-sectional:** several different age-groups are studied at one time
  - **cross-sequential:** combination of longitudinal and cross-sectional

- **nature and nurture**
  - **nature** refers to heredity and the influence of inherited characteristics on personality, growth, intellect, social skills, etc.; behavioral genetics is relatively new field that attempts to identify genetic basis of behavior
  - **nurture** refers to influence of the environment on inherited traits including parenting styles, socioeconomic status, physical surroundings, etc.
  - most developmental psychologists agree that the most likely explanation for most human development is based on the interaction between nature and nurture

**Basic Building Blocks of Development**

- **genetics** is the science of heredity
- **DNA (deoxyribonucleic acid):** contains genetic codes and chromosomes
  - aside from egg and sperm, humans have 46 chromosomes in each cell of the body
  - individual gets 23 chromosomes from mother's egg and 23 from father's sperm
  - most characteristics are determined by 22 such pairs (autosomes); the last pair determines sex of the person (sex chromosomes)
- both dominant and recessive genes determine physical and behavioral traits
  - specific physical and behavioral traits are dependent upon pairing of genes; more active genes are dominant, others are recessive (see Figure 8.2)
  - most traits are polygenetic
- genetic and chromosome problems can cause a variety of disorders
  - genetic disorders carried by recessive genes are expressed when a child gets two recessive genes
  - issue may also occur if chromosomes have an extra or a missing pair

Reset

# Practice Quiz    How much do you remember?

*Pick the best answer.*

1. In a _____ design, one group of people is followed and assessed at different times as the group ages.
   - **a.** longitudinal
   - **b.** cross-sectional
   - **c.** cross-sequential
   - **d.** cross-longitudinal

2. The cognitive and social changes students go through because they are born and grow up in an age of smartphones would be referred to as a(n)
   - **a.** experimental group.
   - **b.** control group.
   - **c.** dominance effect.
   - **d.** cohort effect.

3. Brandy has naturally blond hair. Based on this information, what do we know about Brandy's parents?
   - **a.** At least one of her parents has a recessive blond hair gene.
   - **b.** Each of her parents must have one recessive blond hair gene.
   - **c.** Each of her parents must have one dominant brown hair gene.
   - **d.** Neither of her parents has a recessive blond hair gene.

4. When sets of genes group together, the result can be multiple traits expressed as a single dominant trait. This is best explained by the process known as
   - **a.** dominant inheritance.
   - **b.** recessive inheritance.
   - **c.** polygenic inheritance.
   - **d.** amines.

5. Which of the following is a disorder resulting from recessive inheritance?
   - **a.** Turner's syndrome
   - **b.** Klinefelter's syndrome
   - **c.** cystic fibrosis
   - **d.** Down syndrome

6. Which disorder is characterized by having only one X chromosome in the 23rd pairing?
   - **a.** Tay-Sachs
   - **b.** Turner's syndrome
   - **c.** Klinefelter's syndrome
   - **d.** PKU

# Prenatal Development

From conception to the actual birth of the baby is a period of approximately 9 months, during which a single cell becomes a complete infant. It is also during this time that many things can have a positive or negative influence on the developing infant.

**ovum**

the female sex cell, or egg.

**fertilization**

the union of the ovum and sperm.

**zygote**

cell resulting from the uniting of the ovum and sperm.

**monozygotic twins**

identical twins formed when one zygote splits into two separate masses of cells, each of which develops into a separate embryo.

**dizygotic twins**

often called fraternal twins, occurring when two individual eggs get fertilized by separate sperm, resulting in two zygotes in the uterus at the same time.

**bioethics**

the study of ethical and moral issues brought about by new advances in biology and medicine.

## FERTILIZATION

**8.4**   **Explain the process of fertilization, including the twinning process.**

When an egg (also called an **ovum**) and a sperm unite in the process of **fertilization**, the resulting single cell will have a total of 46 chromosomes and is called a **zygote**. Normally, the zygote will begin to divide, first into two cells, then four, then eight, and so on, with each new cell also having 46 chromosomes, because the DNA molecules produce duplicates, or copies, of themselves before each division. (This division process is called *mitosis*.) Eventually, the mass of cells becomes a baby. Sometimes this division process doesn't work exactly this way, and twins or multiples are the result.

There are actually two kinds of twins (see **Figure 8.3**). Twins who are commonly referred to as "identical" are **monozygotic twins**, meaning that the two babies come from one (mono) fertilized egg (zygote). Early in the division process, the mass of cells splits completely—no one knows exactly why—into two separate masses, each of which will develop into a separate infant. The infants will be the same sex and have identical features because they each possess the same set of 46 chromosomes. The other type of twin is more an accident of timing and is more common in women who are older and who are from certain ethnic groups (Allen & Parisi, 1990; Bonnelykke, 1990; Imaizumi, 1998). A woman's body may either release more than one egg at a time or release an egg in a later ovulation period after a woman has already conceived once. If two eggs are fertilized, the woman may give birth to fraternal or **dizygotic twins** (two zygotes), or possibly triplets or some other multiple number of babies (Bryan & Hallett, 2001). This is also more likely to happen to women who are taking fertility drugs to help them get pregnant.

Pregnancies involving multiple babies are often very high risk and can be associated with premature birth and low birth weight, both factors in possible long-term disabilities in both physical and cognitive areas. Some of the babies may not survive, or doctors might actually recommend selective termination of some of the babies to increase the chances of survival for the remaining infants (Qin et al., 2015; Wilkinson et al., 2015). This is a concern of an area called **bioethics**, the study of ethical and moral issues brought about by new advances in biology and medicine and how those advances should influence policies and practices (Muzur, 2014; Qin et al., 2015).

For developmental psychologists, twins provide an important way to look at the contribution of nature and nurture to human development. Researchers may seek out genetically identical twins who have been separated at birth, looking at all the ways those twins are alike in spite of being raised in different environments. It should be noted that the environments in which children are raised within a particular culture are not necessarily that much different, so twin studies are not a perfect method. Researchers may also compare children who are adopted to their adoptive parents (an environmental influence) and to their biological parents (the genetic influences). Ⓛ Ⓘ Ⓝ Ⓚ **to** Learning Objective 13.12.

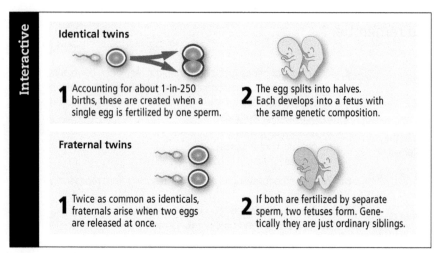

**Interactive**

**Identical twins**

**1** Accounting for about 1-in-250 births, these are created when a single egg is fertilized by one sperm.

**2** The egg splits into halves. Each develops into a fetus with the same genetic composition.

**Fraternal twins**

**1** Twice as common as identicals, fraternals arise when two eggs are released at once.

**2** If both are fertilized by separate sperm, two fetuses form. Genetically they are just ordinary siblings.

**Figure 8.3**   Monozygotic and Dizygotic Twins

Because identical twins come from one fertilized egg (zygote), they are called monozygotic. Fraternal twins, who come from two different fertilized eggs, are called dizygotic.

The time is coming when choosing the genetic traits of your child is going to be possible. What kinds of ethical and practical problems may arise from this development?

▶ The response entered here will be saved to your notes and may be collected by your instructor if he/she requires it.

Submit

## THREE STAGES OF DEVELOPMENT

### 8.5 Describe the three stages of prenatal development.

As you might imagine, the 9 months of a typical pregnancy involve a great many changes. While many people think in terms of trimesters (3-month periods), there are really three stages of pregnancy during which major aspects of development occur: the germinal period, the embryonic period, and the fetal period.

**THE GERMINAL PERIOD**  Once fertilization has taken place, the zygote begins dividing and moving down to the *uterus*, the muscular organ that will contain and protect the developing organism. This process takes about a week, followed by about a week during which the mass of cells, now forming a hollow ball, firmly attaches itself to the wall of the uterus. This 2-week period is called the **germinal period** of pregnancy. The *placenta* also begins to form during this period. The placenta is a specialized organ that provides nourishment and filters away the developing baby's waste products. The *umbilical cord* also begins to develop at this time, connecting the organism to the placenta.

💬 How does a mass of cells become a baby, with eyes, nose, hands, feet, and so on? How do all those different things come from the same original single cell?

During the germinal period, the cells begin to differentiate, or develop into specialized cells, in preparation for becoming all the various kinds of cells that make up the human body—skin cells, heart cells, and so on. Perhaps the most important of these cells are the *stem cells*, which stay in a somewhat immature state until needed to produce more cells. Researchers are looking into ways to use stem cells found in the umbilical cord to grow new organs and tissues for transplant or to repair neurological damage (Chen & Ende, 2000; Ding et al., 2015; Holden & Vogel, 2002; Lu & Ende, 1997). Ⓛ Ⓘ Ⓝ Ⓚ to Learning Objective 2.4.

**germinal period**
first 2 weeks after fertilization, during which the zygote moves down to the uterus and begins to implant in the lining.

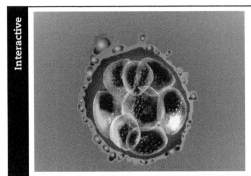
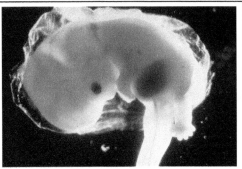
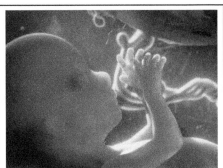

The three periods of pregnancy are the germinal period, lasting about 2 weeks, the embryonic period, from about 2 to 8 weeks, and the fetal period, which lasts from 8 weeks until the end of pregnancy.

**embryo**

name for the developing organism from 2 to 8 weeks after fertilization.

**embryonic period**

the period from 2 to 8 weeks after fertilization, during which the major organs and structures of the organism develop.

**critical periods**

times during which certain environmental influences can have an impact on the development of the infant.

**teratogen**

any factor that can cause a birth defect.

**fetal alcohol spectrum disorder (FASD)**

the physical and mental defects caused by consumption of alcohol during pregnancy.

**fetal period**

the time from about 8 weeks after conception until the birth of the baby.

**fetus**

name for the developing organism from 8 weeks after fertilization to the birth of the baby.

**THE EMBRYONIC PERIOD**   Once firmly attached to the uterus, the developing organism is called an **embryo**. The **embryonic period** will last from 2 weeks after conception to 8 weeks, and during this time the cells will continue to specialize and become the various organs and structures of a human infant. By the end of this period, the embryo is about 1 inch long and has primitive eyes, nose, lips, teeth, and little arms and legs, as well as a beating heart. Although no organ is fully developed or completely functional at this time, nearly all are "there."

**CRITICAL PERIODS**   As soon as the embryo begins to receive nourishment from the mother through the placenta, it becomes vulnerable to hazards such as diseases of the mother, drugs, and other toxins that can pass from the mother through the placenta to the developing infant. Because of this direct connection between mother and embryo and the fact that all major organs are in the process of forming, we can clearly see the effects of **critical periods**, times during which some environmental influences can have an impact—often devastating—on the development of the infant. The structural development of the arms and legs, for example, is only affected during the time that these limbs are developing (3 to 8 weeks), whereas the heart's structure is most affected very early in this period (2 to 6 weeks). Other physical and structural problems can occur with the central nervous system (2 to 5 weeks), eyes (3 to 8 weeks), and the teeth and roof of the mouth (about 7 to 12 weeks).

**PRENATAL HAZARDS**   Teratogens Any substance such as a drug, chemical, virus, or other factor that can cause a birth defect is called a **teratogen**. **Table 8.2** shows some common teratogens and their possible negative effects on the developing embryo.

One of the more common teratogens is alcohol. Consumption of alcohol during pregnancy, particularly during the critical embryonic period, can lead to **fetal alcohol spectrum disorder (FASD)**, a series of physical and mental defects including stunted growth, facial deformities, and brain damage (Dörrie et al., 2014; Esper & Furtado, 2014; Rangmar et al., 2015). Exposure to alcohol in early pregnancy is the leading known cause of intellectual disability (previously called mental retardation) in the Western hemisphere (Abel & Sokol, 1987; Caley et al., 2005). So how much alcohol is safe to drink while pregnant? The answer is clearly "none!"

**THE FETAL PERIOD: GROW, BABY, GROW**   The **fetal period** is a period of tremendous growth lasting from about 8 weeks after conception until birth. The length of the developing organism (now referred to as a **fetus**) increases by about 20 times, and its weight increases from about 1 ounce at 2 months to an average of a little over 7 pounds at birth. The organs, while accomplishing most of their differentiation in the embryonic period, continue to develop and become functional. At this time, teratogens will more likely

| Table 8.2 Common Teratogens | |
| --- | --- |
| **Teratogenic Agent** | **Effect on Development** |
| Measles, Mumps, and Rubella | Blindness, deafness, heart defects, brain damage |
| Marijuana | Irritability, nervousness, tremors; infant is easily disturbed, startled |
| Cocaine | Decreased height, low birth weight, respiratory problems, seizures, learning difficulties; infant is difficult to soothe |
| Alcohol | Fetal alcohol syndrome (intellectual disability, delayed growth, facial malformation), learning difficulties, smaller-than-normal heads |
| Nicotine | Miscarriage, low birth weight, stillbirth, short stature, intellectual disability, learning disabilities |
| Mercury | Intellectual disability, blindness |
| Vitamin A (high doses) | Facial, ear, central nervous system, and heart defects |
| Caffeine | Miscarriage, low birth weight |
| Toxoplasmosis | Brain swelling, spinal abnormalities, deafness, blindness, intellectual disability |
| High Water Temperatures | Increased chance of neural tube defects |

**SOURCES**: March of Dimes Foundation (2009); Organization of Teratology Information Specialists (2011); Shepard, T. H. (2001).

affect the physical functioning (physiology) of the organs rather than their structure. The functioning of the central nervous system, for example, is vulnerable throughout the fetal period, as are the eyes and the external sexual organs.

The last few months continue the development of fat and the growth of the body, until about the end of the 38th week. At 38 weeks, the fetus is considered full term. Most babies are born between 38 and 40 weeks. Babies born before 38 weeks are called *preterm* and may need life support to survive. If they are very premature, they may also experience problems later in life. This is especially true if the baby weighs less than 5½ pounds at birth. How early can an infant be born and still survive? The age of viability (the point at which it is possible for an infant to survive outside the womb) is between 22 and 26 weeks, with the odds of survival increasing from 10 percent at 22 weeks up to about 85 percent at 26 weeks (National Commission for the Protection of Human Subjects of Biomedical and Behavioral Research, 2006). Those odds will also increase if the infant is in a facility with advanced neonatal health care (Rysavy et al., 2015).

The most likely time for a *miscarriage, or spontaneous abortion*, is in the first 3 months, as the organs are forming and first becoming functional (Katz, 2007; Speroff et al., 1999). Some 15 to 20 percent of all pregnancies end in miscarriage, many so early that the mother may not have even known she was pregnant (Doubilet et al., 2013; Hill, 1998; Medical Economics Staff, 1994; Nelson et al., 2015). When a miscarriage occurs, it is most likely caused by a genetic defect in the way the embryo or fetus is developing that will not allow the infant to survive. In other words, there isn't anything that the mother did wrong or that could have been done to prevent the miscarriage.

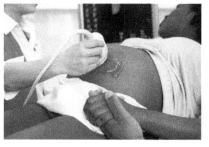

This pregnant woman is getting an ultrasound. Ultrasounds use high-frequency sound waves to create a picture, or sonogram, that allows doctors to see any physical deformities and make accurate measurements of gestational age without risk to the mother or the fetus.

## Concept Map L.O. 8.4, 8.5

Interactive

**fertilization, the zygote, and twinning**
- egg and sperm unite through process of fertilization, resulting in a single cell (zygote) that has 46 chromosomes
- through mitosis, zygote begins to divide, into two cells, then four, etc., until baby is formed
- alterations in mitosis can result in twins or multiples

**Prenatal Development**
from conception to birth of the baby is approximately 9 months in humans

**Prenatal Stages**

**germinal period**
(2-week period following fertilization)
- zygote continues dividing and moving toward the uterus; the placenta and umbilical cord also develop during this time
- cell differentiation is the process that results in specialized cells for all of the various parts of the body

**embryonic period**
(2 weeks after conception to 8 weeks)
- once attached to the uterus, developing organism is called an embryo
- cell specialization continues to occur, resulting in the preliminary versions of various organs
- embryo is vulnerable to hazards such as diseases and substances ingested by the mother as it receives nourishment through the placenta

**fetal period**
(from about 8 weeks to birth)
- developing organism now called a fetus; time of tremendous growth and development
- organs continue to develop and become fully functional
- full-term birth occurs around end of 38th week
- miscarriages (spontaneous abortions) are most likely to occur in the first 3 months

Reset

# Practice Quiz  How much do you remember?

*Pick the best answer.*

1. The first 2 weeks of pregnancy are called the _____ period.
   a. fetal
   b. embryonic
   c. placental
   d. germinal

2. Which of the following does NOT happen in the germinal period?
   a. dividing mass of cells travels to the uterus
   b. developing organs can be affected by toxins passing through the placenta
   c. mass of cells form a hollow ball
   d. cells begin to differentiate

3. The period of pregnancy that contains the clearest examples of critical periods is the _____ period.
   a. germinal
   b. embryonic
   c. fetal
   d. gestational

4. Intellectual disability and blindness are possible outcomes of the effects of _____ on the developing baby.
   a. alcohol
   b. caffeine
   c. cocaine
   d. mercury

# Infancy and Childhood Development

Infancy and early childhood are a time of rapid growth and development in the body, motor skills, cognitive abilities, and sensory systems.

## PHYSICAL DEVELOPMENT

**8.6 Describe the physical and sensory changes that take place in infancy and childhood.**

Immediately after birth, several things start to happen. The respiratory system begins to function, filling the lungs with air and putting oxygen into the blood. The blood now circulates only within the infant's system because the umbilical cord has been cut. Body temperature is now regulated by the infant's own activity and body fat (which acts as insulation) rather than by the amniotic fluid. The digestive system probably takes the longest to adjust to life outside the womb. This is another reason for the baby's excess body fat. It provides fuel until the infant is able to take in enough nourishment on its own. That is why most babies lose a little weight in the first week after birth.

How much can babies really do? Aren't they pretty much unaware of what's going on around them at first?

Surprisingly, babies can do a lot more than researchers used to believe they could. A lot of the early research on infants just after birth was done on babies who were still very drowsy from the general anesthesia that was administered to their mothers during the labor process. Drowsy babies don't tend to respond well, as one might imagine. Since those early days, researchers have developed ways of studying what infants cannot tell us in words. Two common methods are the use of *preferential looking* and *habituation*. Preferential looking assumes that the longer an infant spends looking at a stimulus, the more the infant prefers that stimulus over others (Fantz, 1961). Habituation is the tendency for infants (and adults) to stop paying attention to a stimulus that does not change. ⓁⒾⓃⓀ to Learning Objective 3.3. By exposing the infant to an unchanging sound or picture, for example, researchers can wait for the infant to habituate (look away) and then change the stimulus. If the infant reacts (dishabituates), the infant is capable of detecting that change (Columbo & Mitchell, 2009).

**REFLEXES**  Babies come into this world able to interact with it. Infants have a set of *innate* (existing from birth), involuntary behavior patterns called *reflexes*. Until a baby is capable of learning more complex means of interaction, reflexes help the infant survive. **Figure 8.4** shows five infant reflexes. Pediatricians use these and other reflexes to determine whether a newborn's nervous system is working properly.

Interactive

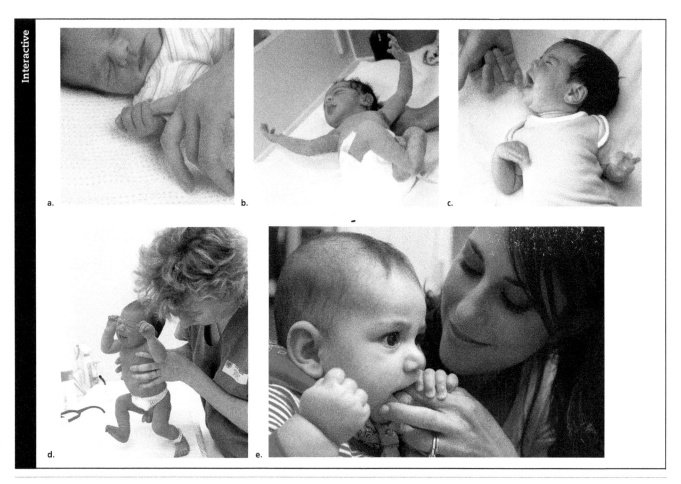

**Figure 8.4**   Five Infant Reflexes

Shown here are (a) grasping reflex; (b) startle reflex (also known as the Moro reflex); (c) rooting reflex (when you touch a baby's cheek, it will turn toward your hand, open its mouth, and search for the nipple); (d) stepping reflex; and (e) sucking reflex. These infant reflexes can be used to check the health of an infant's nervous system. If a reflex is absent or abnormal, it may indicate brain damage or some other neurological problem.

**MOTOR DEVELOPMENT: FROM CRAWLING TO A BLUR OF MOTION**   Infants manage a tremendous amount of development in motor skills from birth to about 2 years of age. **Figure 8.5** on the next page shows some of the major physical milestones of infancy. When looking at the age ranges listed, remember that even these ranges are averages based on large samples of infants. An infant may reach these milestones earlier or later than the average and still be considered to be developing normally.

**BRAIN DEVELOPMENT**   At birth, an infant's brain consists of more than 100 billion neurons. Rapid and extensive growth of these neurons occurs as the brain triples in weight from birth to age 3 years, with much of the increase caused by growth of new dendrites, axon terminals, and increasing numbers of synaptic connections (Nelson, 2011). Surprisingly, the development of the infant brain after birth involves a necessary loss of neurons called *synaptic pruning,* as unused synaptic connections and nerve cells are cleared away to make way for functioning connections and cells (Couperus & Nelson, 2006; Graven & Browne, 2008; Kozberg et al., 2013; Zhan et al. 2014). This process is similar to weeding your garden—you take out the weeds to make room for the plants that you want.

**BABY, CAN YOU SEE ME? BABY, CAN YOU HEAR ME? SENSORY DEVELOPMENT**

💬 I've heard that babies can't see or hear very much at birth. Is that true?

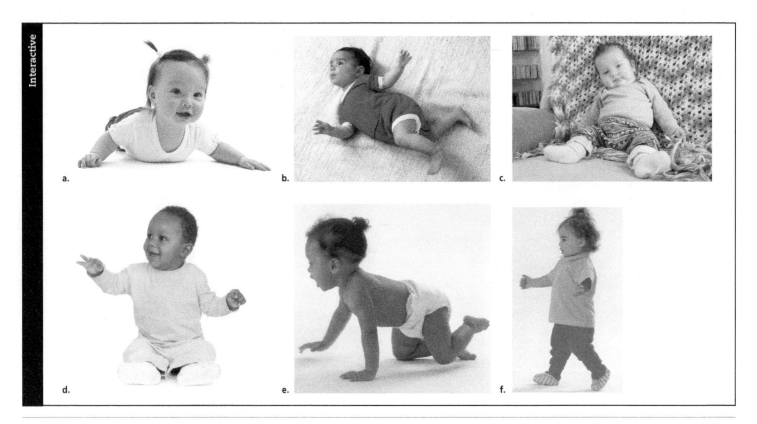

**Figure 8.5** Six Motor Milestones

Shown here are (a) raising head and chest—2 to 4 months, (b) rolling over—2 to 5 months, (c) sitting up with support—4 to 6 months, (d) sitting up without support—6 to 7 months, (e) crawling—7 to 8 months, and (f) walking—8 to 18 months. The motor milestones develop as the infant gains greater voluntary control over the muscles in its body, typically from the top of the body downward. This pattern is seen in the early control of the neck muscles and the much later development of control of the legs and feet.

Although most infant sensory abilities are fairly well developed at birth, some require a bit more time to reach "full power." By using techniques such as the habituation method discussed earlier, researchers have found that the sense of touch is the most well developed, which makes perfect sense when one realizes how much skin-to-womb contact the baby has had in the last months of pregnancy. The sense of smell is also highly developed. Breast-fed babies can actually tell the difference between their own mother's milk scent and another woman's milk scent within a few days after birth.

Taste is also nearly fully developed. At birth, infants show a preference for sweets (and human breast milk is very sweet) and by 4 months have developed a preference for salty tastes (which may come from exposure to the salty taste of their mother's skin). Sour and bitter, two other taste sensations, produce spitting up and the making of horrible faces (Ganchrow et al., 1983).

Hearing is functional before birth but may take a little while to reach its full potential after the baby is born. The fluids of the womb first must clear out of the auditory canals completely. From birth, newborns seem most responsive to high pitches, as in a woman's voice, and low pitches, as in a man's voice.

The least functional sense at birth is vision. The eye is quite a complex organ. **LINK** to Learning Objective 3.4. The rods, which see in black and white and have little visual acuity, are fairly well developed at birth, but the cones, which see color and provide sharpness of vision, will take about another 6 months to fully develop. So the newborn has relatively poor color perception when compared to sharply contrasting lights and darks until about 2 months of age (Adams, 1987) and has fairly "fuzzy" vision, much as a nearsighted person would have. The lens of the newborn stays fixed until the muscles that hold it in place mature. Until then the newborn is unable to shift what little focus it has from close to far. Thus, newborns actually have a fixed distance for clear vision of about 7–10 inches, which is the distance from the baby's face to the mother's face while nursing (Slater, 2000; von Hofsten et al., 2014).

Newborns also have visual preferences at birth, as discovered by researchers using preferential looking, measures of the time that infants spent looking at certain visual stimuli (Fantz, 1961). They found that infants prefer to look at complex patterns rather than simple ones, three dimensions rather than two, and that the most preferred visual stimulus was a human face. The fact that infants prefer human voices and human faces (DeCasper & Fifer, 1980; DeCasper & Spence, 1986; Fantz, 1964; Maurer & Young, 1983; Morii & Sakagami, 2015) makes it easier for them to form relationships with their care-givers and to develop language later on. Infants' preference for seeing things in three dimensions suggests that they possess depth perception. The following classic experiment provided evidence for that assumption.

# Classic Studies in Psychology
# The Visual Cliff

Eleanor Gibson and her fellow researcher, Michael Walk, wondered if infants could per-ceive the world in three dimensions, and so they devised a way to test babies for depth perception (Gibson & Walk, 1960). They built a special table (see **Figure 8.6**) that had a big drop on one side. The surface of the table on both the top and the drop to the floor were covered in a patterned tablecloth, so that the different size of the patterns would be a cue for depth (remember, in size constancy, if something looks smaller, people assume it is farther away from them). **LINK** to Learning Objective 3.14. The whole table was then covered by a clear glass top, so that a baby could safely be placed on or crawl across the "deep" side.

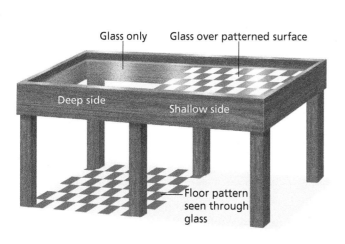
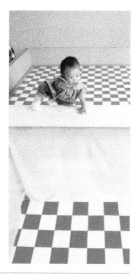

**Figure 8.6** The Visual Cliff Experiment

In the visual cliff experiment, the table has both a shallow and a "deep" side, with glass covering the entire table. When an infant looks down at the deep-appearing side, the squares in the design on the floor look smaller than the ones on the shallow side, forming a visual cue for depth. Notice that this little girl seems to be very reluctant to cross over the deep-appearing side of the table, gesturing to be picked up instead.

The infants tested in this study ranged from 6 to 14 months in age. They were placed on the middle of the table and then encouraged (usually by their mothers) to crawl over either the shallow side or the deep side. Most babies—81 percent—refused to crawl over the deep side, even though they could touch it with their hands and feel that it was solid. They were upset and seemed fearful when encouraged to crawl across. Gibson and Walk interpreted this as a very early sign of the concept of depth perception.

## Questions for Further Discussion

1. Does the fact that 19 percent of the infants did crawl over the deep side of the visual cliff necessarily mean that those infants could not perceive the depth?
2. What other factors might explain the willingness of the 19 percent to crawl over the deep side?
3. Are there any ethical concerns in this experiment?
4. Ducks aren't bothered by the visual cliff at all—why might that be?

## COGNITIVE DEVELOPMENT

### 8.7 Compare and contrast two theories of cognitive development, and define autism spectrum disorder.

By the time the average infant has reached the age of 1 year, it has tripled its birth weight and added about another foot to its height. The brain triples its weight in the first 2 years, reaching about 75 percent of its adult weight. By age 5, the brain is at 90 percent of its adult weight. This increase makes possible a tremendous amount of major advances in **cognitive development**, including the development of thinking, problem solving, and memory.

**PIAGET'S THEORY: FOUR STAGES OF COGNITIVE DEVELOPMENT** One of the three ways of examining the development of cognition that we will discuss in this chapter is found in the work of Jean Piaget. Early researcher Jean Piaget developed his theory from detailed observations of infants and children, most especially his own three children. Piaget made significant contributions to the understanding of how children think about the world around them; his theory shifted the commonly held view that children's thinking was that of "little adults" toward recognition that it was actually quite different from adult thinking. Piaget believed that children form mental concepts or **schemes** as they experience new situations and events. For example, if Sandy points to a picture of an apple and tells her child, "that's an apple," the child forms a scheme for "apple" that looks something like that picture. Piaget also believed that children first try to understand new things in terms of schemes they already possess, a process called *assimilation*. The child might see an orange and say "apple" because both objects are round. When corrected, the child might alter the scheme for apple to include "round" and "red." The process of altering or adjusting old schemes to fit new information and experiences is *accommodation* (Piaget, 1952, 1962, 1983).

Piaget also proposed that there are four distinct stages of cognitive development that occur from infancy to adolescence, as shown in **Table 8.3** (Piaget, 1952, 1962, 1983).

**THE SENSORIMOTOR STAGE** The **sensorimotor stage** is the first of Piaget's stages. It concerns infants from birth to age 2. In this stage, infants use their senses and motor abilities to learn about the world around them. At first, infants only have the involuntary reflexes present at birth to interact with objects and people. As their sensory and motor development progresses, they begin to interact deliberately with objects by grasping, pushing, tasting, and so on. Infants move from simple repetitive actions, such as grabbing their toes, to complex patterns, such as trying to put a shape into a sorting box.

**cognitive development**
the development of thinking, problem solving, and memory.

**schemes**
in this case, a mental concept formed through experiences with objects and events.

**sensorimotor stage**
Piaget's first stage of cognitive development, in which the infant uses its senses and motor abilities to interact with objects in the environment.

| Table 8.3 | Piaget's Stages of Cognitive Development | |
|---|---|---|
| **Stage** | **Age** | **Cognitive Development** |
| Sensorimotor | Birth to 2 years old | Children explore the world using their senses and ability to move. They develop object permanence and the understanding that concepts and mental images represent objects, people, and events. |
| Preoperational | 2 to 7 years old | Young children can mentally represent and refer to objects and events with words or pictures, and they can pretend. However, they can't conserve, logically reason, or simultaneously consider many characteristics of an object. |
| Concrete Operations | 7 to 12 years old | Children at this stage are able to conserve, reverse their thinking, and classify objects in terms of their many characteristics. They can also think logically and understand analogies but only about concrete events. |
| Formal Operations | 12 years old to adulthood | People at this stage can use abstract reasoning about hypothetical events or situations, think about logical possibilities, use abstract analogies, and systematically examine and test hypotheses. Not everyone can eventually reason in all these ways. |

By the end of the sensorimotor stage, infants have fully developed a sense of **object permanence**, the knowledge that an object exists even when it is not in sight. For example, the game of "peek-a-boo" is important in teaching infants that Mommy's smiling face is always going to be behind her hands. This is a critical step in developing language (and eventually abstract thought), as words themselves are symbols of things that may not be present. Symbolic thought, which is the ability to represent objects in one's thoughts with symbols such as words, becomes possible by the end of this stage, with children at 2 years old capable of thinking in simple symbols and planning out actions.

 💬 Why is it so easy for children to believe in Santa Claus and the Tooth Fairy when they're little?

**THE PREOPERATIONAL STAGE** The **preoperational stage** (ages 2–7) is a time of developing language and concepts. Children, who can now move freely about in their world, no longer have to rely only on senses and motor skills but now can ask questions and explore their surroundings more fully. Pretending and make-believe play become possible because children at this stage can understand, through symbolic thinking, that a line of wooden blocks can "stand in" for a train. They are limited, however, in several ways. They are not yet capable of logical thought—they can use simple mental concepts but are not able to use those concepts in a more rational, logical sense. They believe that everything is alive and has feelings just like their own, a quality called *animism,* so they might apologize to a chair for bumping it. They also tend to believe that what they see is literally true, so when children of this age see Santa Claus in a book, on television, or at the mall, Santa Claus becomes real to them. It doesn't occur to them to think about how Santa might get to every child's house in one night or why those toys he delivers are the same ones they saw in the store just last week.

Another limitation is **egocentrism**, the inability to see the world through anyone else's eyes but one's own. For the preoperational child, everyone else must see what the child sees, and what is important to the child must be important to everyone else. For example, 2-year-old Hiba, after climbing out of her crib for the third time, was told by her mother, "I don't want to see you in that living room again tonight!" So Hiba's next appearance was made with her hands over her eyes—if she couldn't see her mother, her

**object permanence**

the knowledge that an object exists even when it is not in sight.

**preoperational stage**

Piaget's second stage of cognitive development, in which the preschool child learns to use language as a means of exploring the world.

**egocentrism**

the inability to see the world through anyone else's eyes.

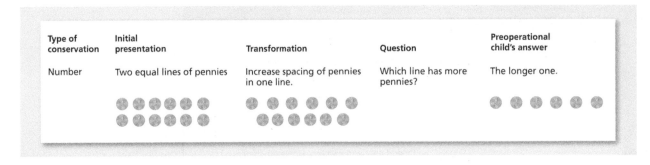

| Type of conservation | Initial presentation | Transformation | Question | Preoperational child's answer |
|---|---|---|---|---|
| Number | Two equal lines of pennies | Increase spacing of pennies in one line. | Which line has more pennies? | The longer one. |

**Figure 8.7**  Conservation Experiment

In this conservation task, pennies are laid out in two equal lines. When the pennies in the top line are spaced out, the child who cannot yet conserve will centrate on the top line and assume that there are actually more pennies in that line.

mother couldn't see *her*. Egocentrism is not the same as being egotistical or selfish—it would also be egocentric, but completely unselfish, if 4-year-old Jamal wants to give his grandmother an action figure for her birthday because that's what *he* would want.

Remember that children in this stage are also overwhelmed by appearances. A child who complains that his piece of pie is smaller than his brother's may be quite happy once his original piece is cut into two pieces—now he thinks he has "more" than his brother. He has focused only on the number of pieces, not the actual amount of the pie. Focusing only on one feature of some object rather than taking all features into consideration is called **centration**. In the coin example in **Figure 8.7**, children of this stage will focus (or center) on the *length* of the top line of coins only and ignore the *number* of coins. Centration is one of the reasons that children in this stage often fail to understand that changing the way something looks does not change its substance. The ability to understand that altering the appearance of something does not change its amount (as in the coin example), its volume, or its mass is called **conservation**.

Preoperational children fail at conservation not only because they *centrate* (focus on just one feature, such as the number of pieces of pie) but also because they are unable to "mentally reverse" actions. This feature of preoperational thinking is called **irreversibility**. For example, if a preoperational child sees liquid poured from a short, wide glass into a tall, thin glass, the child will assume that the second glass holds more liquid. This failure to

**centration**

in Piaget's theory, the tendency of a young child to focus only on one feature of an object while ignoring other relevant features.

**conservation**

in Piaget's theory, the ability to understand that simply changing the appearance of an object does not change the object's nature.

**irreversibility**

in Piaget's theory, the inability of the young child to mentally reverse an action.

👁 **Watch** the **Video** *Piaget's Concept of Conservation*

"conserve" (save) the volume of liquid as it takes on a different shape in the tall, thin glass is not only caused by the child's centration on the height of the liquid in the second glass but also by the inability of the child to imagine pouring the liquid back into the first glass and having it be the same amount again. Similar "reasoning" causes children of this age to assume that a ball of clay, when rolled out into a "rope" of clay, is now greater in mass.

**CONCRETE OPERATIONS** In the **concrete operations stage** (ages 7–12), children finally become capable of conservation and reversible thinking. Centration no longer occurs as children become capable of considering all the relevant features of any given object. They begin to think more logically about beliefs such as Santa Claus or the Tooth Fairy and to ask questions, eventually coming to their own more rational conclusions about these fantasies of early childhood. They are in school, learning all sorts of science and math, and are convinced that they know more than their parents at this point.

The major limitation of this stage is the inability to deal effectively with *abstract concepts*. Abstract concepts are those that do not have some physical, *concrete*, touchable reality. For example, "freedom" is an abstract concept. People can define it, they can get a good sense of what it means, but there is no "thing" that they can point to and say, "This is freedom." *Concrete concepts*, which are the kind of concepts understood by children of this age, are about objects, written rules, and real things. Children need to be able to see it, touch it, or at least "see" it in their heads to be able to understand it.

**FORMAL OPERATIONS** In the last of Piaget's stages, **formal operations** (age 12 to adulthood), abstract thinking becomes possible. Teenagers not only understand concepts that have no physical reality, but also they get deeply involved in hypothetical thinking, or thinking about possibilities and even impossibilities. "What if everyone just got along?" "If women were in charge of countries, would there be fewer wars?"

Piaget did not believe that everyone would necessarily reach formal operations, and studies show that only about half of all adults in the United States reach this stage (Sutherland, 1992). Adults who do not achieve formal operations tend to use a more practical, down-to-earth kind of intelligence that suits their particular lifestyle. Successful college students, however, need formal-operational thinking to succeed in their college careers, as most college classes require critical thinking, problem-solving abilities, and abstract thinking based on formal-operational skills (Powers, 1984).

Others have proposed another stage beyond formal operations, a relativistic thinking stage found in young adults, particularly those who have found their old ways of thinking in "black and white" terms challenged by the diversity they encounter in the college environment (LaBouvie-Vief, 1980, 1992; Perry, 1970). In this kind of thinking, young adults recognize that all problems cannot be solved with pure logic, and there can be multiple points of view for a single problem.

**EVALUATING PIAGET'S THEORY** Piaget saw children as active explorers of their surroundings, engaged in the discovery of the properties of objects and organisms within those surroundings. Educators have put Piaget's ideas into practice by allowing children to learn at their own pace, by "hands-on" experience with objects, and by teaching concepts that are at the appropriate cognitive level for those children (Brooks & Brooks, 1993). But Piaget's theory has also been criticized on several points. Some researchers believe that the idea of distinct stages of cognitive development is not completely correct and that changes in thought are more continuous and gradual rather than abruptly jumping from one stage to another (Courage & Howe, 2002; Feldman, 2003; Schwitzgebel, 1999; Siegler, 1996). Others point out that preschoolers are not as egocentric as Piaget seemed to believe (Flavell, 1999) and that object permanence exists much earlier than Piaget thought (Aguiar & Baillargeon, 2003; Baillargeon, 1986).

**VYGOTSKY'S THEORY: THE IMPORTANCE OF BEING THERE** Russian psychologist Lev Vygotsky's pioneering work in developmental psychology has had a profound influence

These concrete operational children, seen in a science class, have begun to think logically and are able to solve many kinds of problems that were not possible for them to solve while in the preoperational stage.

This girl is helping her younger brother learn to read a book. Vygotsky's view of cognitive development states that the help of skilled others aids in making cognitive advances such as this one.

**concrete operations stage**

Piaget's third stage of cognitive development, in which the school-age child becomes capable of logical thought processes but is not yet capable of abstract thinking.

**formal operations stage**

Piaget's last stage of cognitive development, in which the adolescent becomes capable of abstract thinking.

on school education in Russia, and interest in his theories continues to grow throughout the world (Bodrova & Leong, 1996; Duncan, 1995). Vygotsky wrote about children's cognitive development but differed from Piaget in his emphasis on the role of others in cognitive development (Vygotsky, 1934/1962, 1978, 1987). Whereas Piaget stressed the importance of the child's interaction with objects as a primary factor in cognitive development, Vygotsky stressed the importance of social and cultural interactions with other people, typically more highly skilled children and adults. Vygotsky believed that children develop cognitively when someone else helps them by asking leading questions and providing examples of concepts in a process called **scaffolding**. In scaffolding, the more highly skilled person gives the learner more help at the beginning of the learning process and then begins to withdraw help as the learner's skills improve (Rogoff, 1994).

Vygotsky also proposed that each developing child has a **zone of proximal development (ZPD)**, which is the difference between what a child can do alone versus what a child can do with the help of a teacher. For example, if Jenny can do fourth-grade math problems by herself but also can successfully work sixth-grade math problems with the help of a teacher, her ZPD is about 2 years, the difference between what she can do alone and what she can do with help. Suzi might be the same age as Jenny and just as skilled at working fourth-grade math problems (and might even score the same on a traditional IQ test), but if Suzi can only work up to fifth-grade math problems with the teacher's help, Suzi's ZPD is only about 1 year and is not as great as Jenny's. Both girls are smart, but Jenny could be seen as possessing a higher potential intelligence than Suzi. This might be a better way of thinking about intelligence: It [is no]t [wha]t you know (as measured by traditional tests), it's what you *can do*.

[Ot]her researchers have applied Vygotsky's social focus on learning to the develop[ment of] a child's memory for personal (autobiographical) events, finding evidence that [children] learn the culturally determined structures and purposes of personal stories from [the] conversations they have with their parents. This process begins with the parent [telling th]e story to the very young child, followed by the child repeating elements of the [story as] the child's verbal abilities grow. The child reaches the final stage at around age 5 [whe]n the child creates the personal story entirely—an excellent example of scaffolding [(Harley] et al., 1996; Fivush & Nelson, 2004; Nelson, 1993). Unlike Piaget, who saw a child's [speech t]o himself or herself as egocentric, Vygotsky thought that private speech was a way [for a c]hild to "think out loud" and advance cognitively. As adults, we still do this when [we talk] to ourselves to help solve a particular problem. Vygotsky's ideas have been put [into prac]tice in education through the use of cooperative learning, in which children work [togther] in groups to achieve a common goal, and in reciprocal teaching, in which teachers [lead stu]dents through the basic strategies of reading until the students themselves become [capable] of teaching the strategies to others. Chapter Seven details the stages of language development in infancy and childhood. (L I N K) to Learning Objective 7.12.

**AUTISM SPECTRUM DISORDER**   Before leaving the topic of cognitive development in infancy, let's briefly discuss a topic that has been making the news lately: the causes underlying autism spectrum disorder. Autism spectrum disorder (ASD) is a neurodevelopmental disorder that actually encompasses a whole range of previous disorders (with what may be an equally broad range of causes), which cause problems in thinking, feeling, language, and social skills in relating to others (American Psychiatric Association, 2013; Atladóttir et al., 2009; Johnson & Myers, 2007; Lai et al., 2015; Schuwerk et al., 2015).

*Theory of mind* is a term that refers to the ability to understand not only your own mental states, such as beliefs, intentions, and desires, but also to understand that other people have beliefs, intentions, and desires that may be different from yours (Baron-Cohen et al., 1985). Autism research suggests that one of the main problems for people with autism is that they do not possess a theory of mind, failing to understand that other people have their own points of view (Baron-Cohen et al., 1985; Kimhi, 2014; Korkmaz, 2011).

The exact causes of autism are not yet known, but rumors and misinformation about a possible cause of autism have been circulating on the Internet for many years

*Vygotsky -*
*Zone of proximal*
*development (ZPD)*

*Concept of difference*
*between what a child*
*can do alone*
*and what a child*
*can do w/ help*

**scaffolding**

process in which a more skilled learner gives help to a less skilled learner, reducing the amount of help as the less skilled learner becomes more capable.

**zone of proximal development (ZPD)**

Vygotsky's concept of the difference between what a child can do alone and what that child can do with the help of a teacher.

(Mitchell & Locke, 2015). The major source of misinformation began in 1998, when British gastroenterologist Dr. Andrew Wakefield published the results of two studies that seemed to link the MMR (measles, mumps, and rubella) vaccine to autism and bowel disease in children (Wakefield et al., 1998). Experts reviewed the quality of his research, and the studies were quickly denounced as inadequate and dangerous by autism specialists and others (Fitzpatrick, 2004; Judelsohn, 2007; Matthew & Dallery, 2007; Novella, 2007; Stratton et al., 2001a, 2001b). ⓛⓘⓝⓚ to Learning Objectives 1.8 and 1.9. Nevertheless, Wakefield's publication was followed by measles epidemics due to parents refusing the MMR inoculation for their children. The myth of a link persists, in spite of numerous studies that have consistently failed to show any link between the MMR vaccine and autism (Burns, 2010; Gilberg & Coleman, 2000; Johnson & Myers, 2007; Madsen et al., 2002; Mars et al., 1998; Taylor et al., 1999; Thompson et al., 2007). In 2004, the other authors listed on the study formally retracted the 1998 paper. In 2009, the final blow came to Wakefield's credibility when it was discovered that he had falsified his data, resulting in the revoking of his medical license in May of 2010 (Meikle & Bosley, 2010).

## PSYCHOSOCIAL DEVELOPMENT

### 8.8 Identify the development of personality, relationships, and self-concept in infancy and childhood.

The psychological and social development of infants and children involves the development of personality, relationships, and a sense of being male or female. Although these processes begin in infancy, they will continue, in many respects, well into adulthood.

 💬 Why are some children negative and whiny while others are sweet and good natured?

**TEMPERAMENT** One of the first ways in which infants demonstrate that they have different personalities (i.e., the long-lasting characteristics that make each person different from others) is in their **temperament**, the behavioral and emotional characteristics that are fairly well established at birth. Researchers (Chess & Thomas, 1986; Thomas & Chess, 1977) have identified three basic temperament styles of infants:

1. **Easy:** "Easy" babies are regular in their schedules of waking, sleeping, and eating and are adaptable to change. Easy babies are happy babies and when distressed are easily soothed.

2. **Difficult:** "Difficult" babies are almost the opposite of easy ones. Difficult babies tend to be irregular in their schedules and are very unhappy about change of any kind. They are loud, active, and tend to be crabby rather than happy.

3. **Slow to warm up:** This kind of temperament is associated with infants who are less grumpy, quieter, and more regular than difficult children but who are slow to adapt to change. If change is introduced gradually, these babies will "warm up" to new people and new situations.

Of course, not all babies will fall neatly into one of these three patterns—some children may be a mix of two or even all three patterns of behavior, as Chess and Thomas (1986) discovered. Even so, longitudinal research strongly suggests that these temperament styles last well into adulthood and are strongly influenced by heredity (Kagan, 1998; Kagan et al., 2007; Korn, 1984; Scarpa et al., 1995; Schwartz et al., 2010), although they are somewhat influenced by the environment in which the infant is raised. For example, a "difficult" infant who is raised by parents who are themselves very loud and active may not be perceived as difficult by the parents, whereas a child who is slow to warm up might be perceived as difficult if the parents themselves like lots of change and noise. The first infant is in a situation in which the "goodness of fit" of the infant's temperament to the parents'

**temperament**
the behavioral characteristics that are fairly well established at birth, such as "easy," "difficult," and "slow to warm up;" the enduring characteristics with which each person is born.

erament is very close, but the pare... ...t for that less active child (Ch... ... ...m an attachment, the important p...chos... ... ...on... ...on...

to ...

**ATTACHMENT** The emotional bond that forms between an infant and a primary caregiver is called **attachment**. Attachment is an extremely important development in the social and emotional life of the infant, usually forming within the first 6 months of the infant's life and showing up in a number of ways during the second 6 months, such as *stranger anxiety* (wariness of strangers) and *separation anxiety* (fear of being separated from the caregiver). Although attachment to the mother is usually the primary attachment, infants can attach to fathers and to other caregivers as well.

**ATTACHMENT STYLES** Mary Ainsworth (Ainsworth, 1985; Ainsworth et al., 1978) devised a special experimental design to measure the attachment of an infant to the caregiver; she called it the "Strange Situation" (exposing an infant to a series of leave-takings and returns of the mother and a stranger). Through this measurement technique, Ainsworth and another colleague identified four attachment styles:

1. **Secure:** Infants labeled as secure were willing to get down from their mother's lap soon after entering the room with their mothers. They explored happily, looking back at their mothers and returning to them every now and then (sort of like "touching base"). When the stranger came in, these infants were wary but calm as long as their mother was nearby. When the mother left, the infants got upset. When the mother returned, the infants approached her, were easily soothed, and were glad to have her back.

2. **Avoidant:** In contrast, avoidant babies, although somewhat willing to explore, did not "touch base." They did not look at the stranger or the mother and reacted very little to her absence or her return, seeming to have no interest or concern.

3. **Ambivalent:** The word *ambivalent* means to have mixed feelings about something. Ambivalent babies in Ainsworth's study were clinging and unwilling to explore, very upset by the stranger regardless of the mother's presence, protested mightily when the mother left, and were hard to soothe. When the mother returned, these babies would demand to be picked up but at the same time push the mother away or kick her in a mixed reaction to her return.

4. **Disorganized–disoriented:** In subsequent studies, other researchers (Main & Hesse, 1990; Main & Solomon, 1990) found that some babies seemed unable to decide just how they should react to the mother's return. These disorganized–disoriented infants would approach her but with their eyes turned away from her, as if afraid to make eye contact. In general, these infants seemed fearful and showed a dazed and depressed look on their faces.

It should come as no surprise that the mothers of each of the four types of infants also behaved differently from one another. Mothers of secure infants were loving, warm, sensitive to their infant's needs, and responsive to the infant's attempts at communication. Mothers of avoidant babies were unresponsive, insensitive, and coldly rejecting. Mothers of ambivalent babies tried to be responsive but were inconsistent and insensitive to the baby's actions, often talking to the infant about something totally unrelated to what the infant was doing at the time. Mothers of disorganized–disoriented babies were found to be abusive or neglectful in interactions with the infants.

Attachment is not necessarily the result of the behavior of the mother alone, however. The temperament of the infant may play an important part in determining the reactions of the mother (Goldsmith & Campos, 1982; Skolnick, 1986). For example, an infant with a difficult temperament is hard to soothe. A mother with this kind of infant might come to avoid unnecessary contact with the infant, as did the mothers of the avoidant babies in Ainsworth's studies.

Critics of Ainsworth's Strange Situation research focus on the artificial nature of the design and wonder if infants and mothers would behave differently in the more familiar

This toddler shows reluctance to explore her environment, instead clinging to her father's leg. Such clinging behavior, if common, can be a sign of an ambivalent attachment.

**attachment**

the emotional bond between an infant and the primary caregiver.

surroundings of home, even though Ainsworth's experimental observers also observed the infants and mothers in the home prior to the Strange Situation setting (Ainsworth, 1985). Other research has found results supporting Ainsworth's findings in home-based assessments of attachment (Blanchard & Main, 1979). Other studies have also found support for the concept of attachment styles and stability of attachment over the first 6 years of life (Lutkenhaus et al., 1985; Main & Cassidy, 1988; Owen et al., 1984; Wartner et al., 1994). Even adult relationships can be seen as influenced by the attachment style of the adult—those who are avoidant tend to have numerous shallow and brief relationships with different partners, whereas those who are ambivalent tend to have repeated breakups and makeups with the same person (Bartholomew, 1990; Hazan & Shaver, 1987; Schroeder, 2014).

**INFLUENCES ON ATTACHMENT**   As day care has become more widely acceptable and common, many parents have been concerned about the effect of day care on attachment. Psychologist Jay Belsky and colleagues (Belsky, 2005; Belsky & Johnson, 2005; Belsky et al., 2007) have studied the attachment of infants in day care and concluded that although higher quality of day care (small child-to-caregiver ratio, low turnover in caregivers, and caregivers educated in child-care techniques and theory) is important, especially for cognitive development, positive development including attachment was more clearly related to the quality of parenting that the infants and toddlers received at home.

Although there are some cultural differences in attachment—such as the finding that mothers in the United States tend to wait for a child to express a need before trying to fulfill that need, while Japanese mothers prefer to anticipate the child's needs (Rothbaum et al., 2000), attachment does not seem to suffer in spite of the differences in sensitivity. Evidence that similar attachment styles are found in other cultures demonstrates the need to consider attachment as an important first step in forming relationships with others, one that may set the stage for all relationships that follow (Agerup et al., 2015; Hu & Meng, 1996; Keromoian & Leiderman, 1986; Nievar et al., 2015; Posada et al., 2013; Stefanovic-Stanojevic et al., 2015). Before leaving the topic of attachment, let's take a look at one of the first studies that examined the key factors necessary for attachment.

## Classic Studies in Psychology
# Harlow and Contact Comfort

As psychologists began to study the development of attachment, they at first assumed that attachment to the mother occurred because the mother was associated with satisfaction of primary drives such as hunger and thirst. The mother is always present when the food (a primary reinforcer) is presented, so the mother becomes a secondary reinforcer capable of producing pleasurable feelings. (L)(I)(N) K to Learning Objective 5.5.

Psychologist Harry Harlow felt that attachment had to be influenced by more than just the provision of food. He conducted a number of studies of attachment using infant rhesus monkeys (Harlow, 1958). Noticing that the monkeys in his lab liked to cling to the soft cloth pad used to line their cages, Harlow designed a study to examine the importance of what he termed *contact comfort*, the seeming attachment of the monkeys to something soft to the touch.

He isolated eight baby rhesus monkeys shortly after their birth, placing each in a cage with two surrogate (substitute) "mothers." The surrogates were actually a block of wood covered in soft padding and terry cloth and a wire form, both heated from within. For half of the monkeys, the wire "mother" held the bottle from which they fed, while for the other half the soft "mother" held the bottle. Harlow then recorded the time each monkey spent with each "mother." If time spent with the surrogate is taken as an indicator of attachment, then learning theory would predict that the monkeys would spend more time with whichever surrogate was being used to feed them.

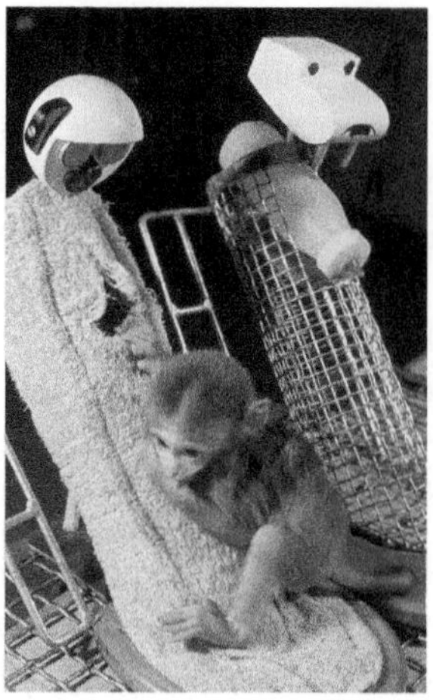

The wire surrogate "mother" provides the food for this infant rhesus monkey. But the infant spends all its time with the soft, cloth-covered surrogate. According to Harlow, this demonstrates the importance of contact comfort in attachment.

The results? Regardless of which surrogate was feeding them, all of the infant monkeys spent significantly more time with the soft, cloth-covered surrogate. In fact, all monkeys spent very little time with the wire surrogate, even if this was the one with the bottle. Harlow and his colleagues concluded that "contact comfort was an important basic affectional or love variable" (Harlow, 1958, p. 574).

Harlow's work represents one of the earliest investigations into the importance of touch in the attachment process and remains an important study in human development.

### Questions for Further Discussion

1. Even though the cloth surrogate was warm and soft and seemed to provide contact comfort, do you think that the monkeys raised in this way would behave normally when placed into contact with other monkeys? How might they react?
2. What might be the implications of Harlow's work for human mothers who feed their infants with bottles rather than breastfeeding?

**WHO AM I?: THE DEVELOPMENT OF THE SELF-CONCEPT** Infants begin life without understanding that they are separate from their surroundings and also from the other people in their social world. The **self-concept** is the image you have of yourself, and it is based on your interactions with the important people in your life. As infants experience the world around them, they slowly learn to separate "me" from both physical surroundings and the other people in their world.

One way to demonstrate a child's growing awareness of self is known as the rouge test. A spot of red rouge or lipstick is put on the end of the child's nose and the child is ...ed in front of a mirror. Infants from about 6 months to a little over a year will ...t to touch the image of the baby in the mirror, reacting as if to another child ...lam, 1972; Courage & Howe, 2002). In fact, some infants crawl or walk to the ...e of the mirror to look for the "other." But at about 15 to 18 months of age, the ...gins to touch his or her own nose when seeing the image in the mirror, indicat... ...areness that the image in the mirror is the infant's own (Nielsen et al., 2006). As ...grows, the self-concept grows to include gender ("I'm a boy" or "I'm a girl"), ...ppearances ("I have brown hair and blue eyes"), and in middle childhood, per... ...aits and group memberships (Stipek et al., 1990).

Self-concept
The image of oneself that develops from interactions w/ significant peoples in ones life

I've heard that you shouldn't pick a baby up every time it cries— ...at if you do, it might spoil the baby.

**...THEORY** Unfortunately, a lot of people have not only heard this advice but ...on it by frequently ignoring an infant's crying, which turns out to be a very ...or babies. When a baby under 6 months of age cries, it is an instinctive reac... ...to get the caregiver to tend to the baby's needs—hunger, thirst, pain, and even loneliness. Research has shown that babies whose cries are tended to consistently (that is, the infant is fed when hungry, changed when wet, and so on) in the early months are more securely attached at age 1 than those infants whose caregivers frequently allow the infants to cry when there is a need for attention—hunger, pain, or wetness, for example

**self-concept**
the image of oneself that develops from interactions with important significant people in one's life.

(Brazelton, 1992; Heinicke et al., 2000). Erik Erikson, a psychodynamic theorist who emphasized the importance of social relationships in the development of personality, would certainly disagree with letting a baby "cry it out," although allowing an infant who has been fed, changed, burped, and checked to cry on occasion will not damage attachment.

Erikson, who trained as a Freudian psychoanalyst but became convinced that social interactions were more important in development than Freud's emphasis on sexual development, believed that development occurred in a series of eight stages, with the first four of these stages occurring in infancy and childhood (Erikson, 1950; Erikson & Erikson, 1997). (Freud's stages of psychosexual development are covered in detail in a later chapter.) Ⓛ Ⓘ Ⓝ Ⓚ to Learning Objective 13.2. Each of Erikson's stages is an emotional *crisis*, or a kind of turning point, in personality, and the crisis in each stage must be successfully met for normal, healthy psychological development.

Erikson focused on the relationship of the infant and the child to significant ers in the immediate surroundings—parents and then later teachers and even pe **Table 8.4** summarizes the conflict in each of Erikson's eight stages and some of implications for future development (Erikson, 1950; Erikson & Erikson, 1997). For n look at the first four stages in particular.

Handwritten note:
① Trust v. Mistrust
② Autonomy v. Shame + Doubt
③ Initiative v. Guilt
④ Industry v. Inferiority
⑤ Identity v. Role Confusion
⑥ Intimacy v. Isolation
⑦ Generativity v. Stagnation
⑧ Ego Integrity v. Despair

**Table 8.4** Erikson's Psychosocial Stages of Development

| Stage | Developmental Crisis | Successful Dealing With Crisis | |
|---|---|---|---|
| 1. Infant Birth to 1 year old | Trust Versus Mistrust: Infants learn a basic sense of trust dependent upon how their needs are met. | If babies' needs for food, comf and affection are met, they dev a sense of trust in people and those needs to be met in future | |
| 2. Toddler 1 to 3 years old | Autonomy Versus Shame and Doubt: Toddlers begin to understand that they can control their own actions. | Toddlers who are successful in controlling their own actions de independence. | |
| 3. Preschool Age 3 to 5 years old | Initiative Versus Guilt: Preschool children learn to take responsibility for their own behavior as they develop self-control. | If preschoolers succeed in controlling their reactions and behavior, they feel capable and develop a sense of initiative. | If preschoolers fail in controlling their reactions and behavior, they feel irresponsible and anxious and develop a sense of guilt. |
| 4. Elementary School Age 5 to 12 years old | Industry Versus Inferiority: The school-aged child must learn new skills in both the academic world and the social world. They compare themselves to others to measure their success or failure. | When children feel they have succeeded at learning these skills, they develop a sense of industry, making them feel competent and improving their self-esteem. | When children fail or feel that they have failed in learning these skills, they feel inferior when compared to others. |
| 5. Adolescence 13 to early 20s | Identity Versus Role Confusion: Adolescents must decide who they are, what they believe, and what they want to be as an adult. | Adolescents who are able to define their values, goals, and beliefs will develop a stable sense of identity. | Adolescents who are unable to define themselves remain confused and may isolate themselves from others or try to be like everyone else instead of themselves. |
| 6. Early Adulthood 20s and 30s | Intimacy Versus Isolation: Young adults face the task of finding a person with whom they can share their identity in an ongoing, close, personal relationship. | Young adults who successfully find someone and share their identities will have a fulfilling relationship founded on psychological intimacy. | Young adults who are unable to find someone (often because they do not yet have a stable identity to share) will isolate themselves and may experience loneliness, even when involved in shallow relationships with others. |
| 7. Middle Adulthood 40s and 50s | Generativity Versus Stagnation: The focus of this task is to find a way to be a creative, productive person who is nurturing the next generation. | Adults who are able to focus on the next generation will be productive and creative, leaving a legacy for the future. | Adults who are unable to focus outside themselves will remain stagnated, self-centered, and feeling that they have not made a difference. |
| 8. Late Adulthood 60s and beyond | Ego Integrity Versus Despair: The task in this stage involves coming to terms with the end of life, reaching a sense of wholeness and acceptance of life as it has been. | Older adults who are able to come to terms with their lives, things they have done and left undone, and able to "let go" of regrets will have a sense of completion and will see death as simply the last stage of a full life. | Older adults who have not been able to achieve identity or intimacy or generativity, who cannot let go of their regrets, will feel a sense of having left things too late and see death as coming too soon. |

Derived from Erikson, 1950.

## Concept Map L.O. 8.6, 8.7, 8.8

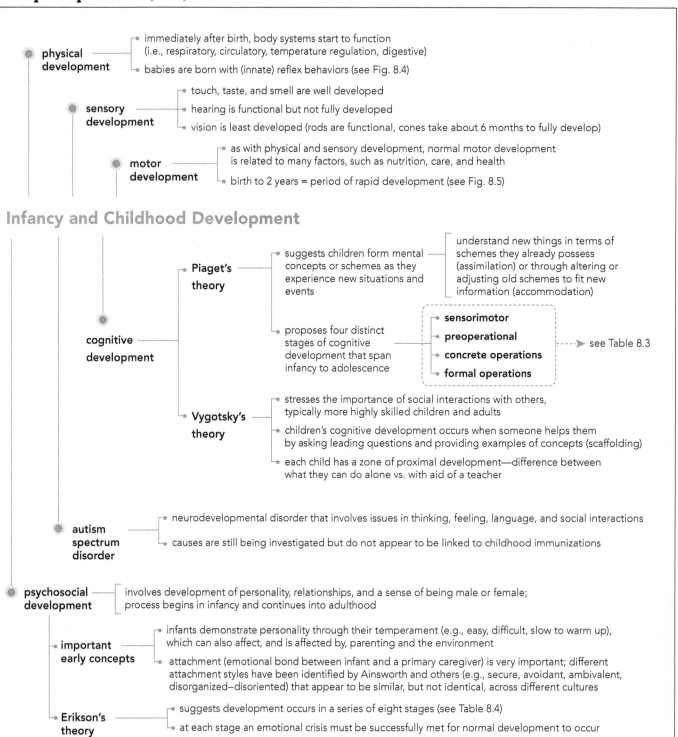

**Interactive**

**physical development**
- immediately after birth, body systems start to function (i.e., respiratory, circulatory, temperature regulation, digestive)
- babies are born with (innate) reflex behaviors (see Fig. 8.4)

**sensory development**
- touch, taste, and smell are well developed
- hearing is functional but not fully developed
- vision is least developed (rods are functional, cones take about 6 months to fully develop)

**motor development**
- as with physical and sensory development, normal motor development is related to many factors, such as nutrition, care, and health
- birth to 2 years = period of rapid development (see Fig. 8.5)

### Infancy and Childhood Development

**cognitive development**

**Piaget's theory**
- suggests children form mental concepts or schemes as they experience new situations and events → understand new things in terms of schemes they already possess (assimilation) or through altering or adjusting old schemes to fit new information (accommodation)
- proposes four distinct stages of cognitive development that span infancy to adolescence
  - sensorimotor
  - preoperational
  - concrete operations
  - formal operations
  - → see Table 8.3

**Vygotsky's theory**
- stresses the importance of social interactions with others, typically more highly skilled children and adults
- children's cognitive development occurs when someone helps them by asking leading questions and providing examples of concepts (scaffolding)
- each child has a zone of proximal development—difference between what they can do alone vs. with aid of a teacher

**autism spectrum disorder**
- neurodevelopmental disorder that involves issues in thinking, feeling, language, and social interactions
- causes are still being investigated but do not appear to be linked to childhood immunizations

**psychosocial development**
- involves development of personality, relationships, and a sense of being male or female; process begins in infancy and continues into adulthood

**important early concepts**
- infants demonstrate personality through their temperament (e.g., easy, difficult, slow to warm up), which can also affect, and is affected by, parenting and the environment
- attachment (emotional bond between infant and a primary caregiver) is very important; different attachment styles have been identified by Ainsworth and others (e.g., secure, avoidant, ambivalent, disorganized–disoriented) that appear to be similar, but not identical, across different cultures

**Erikson's theory**
- suggests development occurs in a series of eight stages (see Table 8.4)
- at each stage an emotional crisis must be successfully met for normal development to occur

Reset

# Practice Quiz   How much do you remember?

*Pick the best answer.*

1. One way researchers study newborn development involves measuring how long infants continue to focus upon a nonchanging stimulus. This technique is referred to as
   a. adaptation.
   b. habituation.
   c. longitudinal study.
   d. a cross-sectional design.

2. In which of Piaget's stages would a child be who has just developed the ability to conserve?
   a. sensorimotor
   b. preoperational
   c. concrete operations
   d. formal operations

3. Vygotsky defines _____ as the process of helping less as the learner improves at a given task.
   a. scaffolding
   b. habituation
   c. zone of proximal development
   d. metamemory

4. What kind of attachment, according to Ainsworth, is shown by a baby who clings to his or her mother, gets upset when the mother leaves, and demands to be picked up but at the same time kicks and pushes her away?
   a. secure
   b. avoidant
   c. ambivalent
   d. disorganized–disoriented

5. Studies by Harry Harlow showed that the most important element to developing attachment is
   a. feeding.
   b. physical contact.
   c. mental challenges.
   d. sleep.

6. According to Erikson, which stage results in a sense of independence because of one's ability to control their own actions?
   a. trust versus mistrust
   b. autonomy versus shame and doubt
   c. initiative versus guilt
   d. generativity versus stagnation

# APA Goal 2: Scientific Reasoning and Critical Thinking: The Facts About Immunizations

*Addresses APA Objective 2.1: Use scientific reasoning to interpret psychological phenomena; 2.3: Engage in innovative and integrative thinking and problem-solving.*

You'd think that by now, people would be well aware that immunizations do not cause autism or a host of other problems and that in fact immunization is a very good thing. Sadly, there is still a big problem with people failing to vaccinate their children against deadly diseases because they have been listening to the wrong people and reading the wrong information. In December of 2015, news outlets reported that an Australian elementary school (known for its tolerance of parents who do not want to vaccinate their children) had suffered an outbreak of chicken pox (Campbell, 2015). The school had only a 73 percent vaccination rate, compared to 92 percent in the surrounding community. At least 80 of the 320 students (roughly 25 percent) were affected, including some who had been vaccinated (they would get only mild cases of chicken pox, however). Because so many unvaccinated children attend the school, this particular population lost its "herd immunity"—the immunity a population gains over time as a significant majority of its members become immune to a particular disease (Plotkin et al., 2011).

Why do parents fail to vaccinate? Primarily, it's a failure of critical thinking. Think back to the Applying Psychology section of Chapter One of this text. (L)(I)(N)(K) to Learning Objective 1.12. The first criterion of critical thinking was "there are very few 'truths' that do not need to be subjected to testing." The link between vaccines and autism, for example, has been well studied and tested over many years, and the findings are clear: There is NO link (Burns, 2010; CDC, 2004, 2011, 2013; Gilberg & Coleman, 2000; Johnson & Myers, 2007; Madsen et al., 2002; Mars et al., 1998; Offit & Bell, 1998; Stratton et al., 2001a, 2001b; Taylor et al., 1999; Thompson et al., 2007).

But the people involved in the antivaccination movement get their information not from scientifically rigorous studies but from anecdotes and Internet blogs. The second criterion of critical thinking was: All evidence is not equal in quality. Testimonials, anecdotes, and the ravings of people on the Internet are not good evidence.

**APA Goal 2**   The Facts About Immunizations

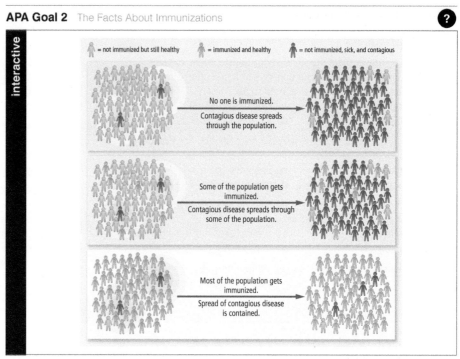

Herd immunity is a term that refers to the immunity of a population to a particular disease, typically because a majority of the population's members have acquired immunity through vaccination. As you can see from the diagram at the top, when a population does not have herd immunity, a disease carried by only a few people, or even one person, can spread throughout the whole population. This is what happened in the famous case of "Typhoid Mary," in which a woman who carried typhoid spread the disease to a large number of employers and their families. As more of a population gets immunized (middle diagram), the spread of disease begins to lessen. As most of the population gets immunized (bottom diagram), the spread of the disease is minimized—the "herd" is immune.

Another problem is the number of celebrities who have joined the antivaccination movement. These people have no real expertise, but they do have the ability to reach a lot of people and—unfortunately—some people are very willing to believe their favorite celebrity despite the lack of any authority on the subject at hand. The third criterion is one that is often forgotten: just because someone is considered to be an authority or to have a lot of expertise does not make everything that person claims automatically true, as the Wakefield disaster clearly demonstrated. The evidence is what is important, and in the case of immunizations, the evidence is clear: Vaccinate your children.

# Adolescence

**Adolescence** is the period of life from about age 13 to the early 20s, during which a young person is no longer physically a child but is not yet an independent, self-supporting adult. Although in the past, adolescence was always defined as the "teens," from ages 13 to 19, adolescence isn't necessarily determined by chronological age. It also concerns how a person deals with life issues such as work, family, and relationships. So although there is a clear age of onset, the end of adolescence may come earlier or later for different individuals.

## PHYSICAL DEVELOPMENT

### 8.9  Describe the physical changes of puberty.

💬 Isn't adolescence just the physical changes that happen to your body?

The clearest sign of the beginning of adolescence is the onset of **puberty**, the physical changes in both *primary sex characteristics* (growth of the actual sex organs such as the penis

**adolescence**

the period of life from about age 13 to the early 20s, during which a young person is no longer physically a child but is not yet an independent, self-supporting adult.

**puberty**

the physical changes that occur in the body as sexual development reaches its peak.

or the uterus) and *secondary sex characteristics* (changes in the body such as the development of breasts and body hair) that occur in the body as sexual development reaches its peak. ⓛⓘⓝⓚ to Learning Objective 10.1. Puberty occurs as the result of a complex series of glandular activities, stimulated by the "master gland" or the pituitary gland, when the proper genetically determined age is reached. The thyroid gland increases the rate of growth, and the adrenal glands and sex glands stimulate the growth of characteristics such as body hair, muscle tissue in males, and the menstrual cycle in girls, for example (Grumbach & Kaplan, 1990; Grumbach & Styne, 1998). Puberty often begins about 2 years after the beginning of the *growth spurt*, the rapid period of growth that takes place at around age 10 for girls and around age 12 for boys.

In addition to an increase in height, physical characteristics related to being male or female undergo rapid and dramatic change. In fact, the rate of growth and development in puberty approaches that of development in the womb. ⓛⓘⓝⓚ to Learning Objective 10.1.

After about 4 years, the changes of puberty are relatively complete. The development of the brain, however, continues well into the early 20s. In particular, the prefrontal cortex of the brain, which is responsible in part for impulse control, decision making, and the organization and understanding of information, does not complete its development until about age 25 years (Somerville et al., 2013). It is easy to understand, then, why adolescents may engage in risky behavior even when they know better.

## COGNITIVE DEVELOPMENT

**8.10** **Identify the cognitive and moral advances that occur in adolescence.**

💬 If I'm remembering correctly, teenagers should be in Piaget's formal operations stage. So why don't many teenagers think just like adults?

The cognitive development of adolescents is less visible than the physical development but still represents a major change in the way adolescents think about themselves, their peers and relationships, and the world around them.

**PIAGET'S FORMAL OPERATIONS REVISITED**    Adolescents, especially those who receive a formal high school education, may move into Piaget's final stage of formal operations, in which abstract thinking becomes possible. Teenagers begin to think about hypothetical situations, leading to a picture of what an "ideal" world would be like.

Piaget's theory has had a tremendous impact in the education of children and in stimulating research about children's cognitive development (Hopkins, 2011; Satterly, 1987). Children in different cultures usually come to understand the world in the way that Piaget described, although the age at which this understanding comes varies from one child to another.

Although headed into an adult style of thinking, adolescents are not yet completely free of egocentric thought. At this time in life, however, their egocentrism shows up in their preoccupation* with their own thoughts. They do a lot of introspection (turning inward) and may become convinced that their thoughts are as important to others as they are to themselves. Two ways in which this adolescent egocentrism emerges are the personal fable and the imaginary audience (Elkind, 1985; Galanaki, 2012; Lapsley et al., 1986; Rai et al., 2014; Vartanian, 2000).

In the **personal fable**, adolescents have spent so much time thinking about their own thoughts and feelings that they become convinced that they are special, one of a kind, and that no one else has ever had these thoughts and feelings before them. "You just don't understand me, I'm different from you" is a common feeling of teens. The personal fable is not without a dangerous side. Because they feel unique, teenagers may feel that they are somehow protected from the dangers of the world and so do not take the precautions that they should. This may result in an unwanted pregnancy, severe injury or death while racing in a car, drinking (or texting) and driving, and drug use, to name a few possibilities. "It can't happen to me, I'm special" is a risky but common thought.

The **imaginary audience** shows up as extreme self-consciousness in adolescents. They become convinced that *everyone is looking at them* and that they are always the center

Many adolescents feel that they are so unique, so special, that bad things just won't happen to them. This personal fable can cause some pretty risky behavior, like what this young man is doing.

**personal fable**

type of thought common to adolescents in which young people believe themselves to be unique and protected from harm.

**imaginary audience**

type of thought common to adolescents in which young people believe that other people are just as concerned about the adolescent's thoughts and characteristics as they themselves are.

---

*preoccupation: extreme or excessive concern with something.

**Example of a Moral Dilemma**

The ant worked long and hard over the summer to gather food for himself and his family. The grasshopper, who preferred to play and be lazy all summer, laughed at the ant for working so hard. The ant said, "you will be sorry this winter when you have no food." Sure enough, when winter came the very sorry grasshopper, cold and hungry, came to the ant and begged for food and shelter. Should the ant give food and shelter to the grasshopper?

**Figure 8.8** Example of a Moral Dilemma

of everyone else's world, just as they are the center of their own. This explains the intense self-consciousness that many adolescents experience concerning what others think about how the adolescent looks or behaves.

**MORAL DEVELOPMENT** Another important aspect in the cognitive advances that occur in adolescence concerns the teenager's understanding of "right" and "wrong." Harvard University professor Lawrence Kohlberg was a developmental psychologist who, influenced by Piaget and others, outlined a theory of the development of moral thinking through looking at how people of various ages responded to stories about people caught up in moral dilemmas (see **Figure 8.8** for an example of a dilemma). Kohlberg (1973) proposed three levels of moral development, or the knowledge of right and wrong behavior. These levels are summarized in **Table 8.5**, along with an example of each type of thinking. Although these stages are associated with certain age groups, adolescents and adults can be found at all three levels. For example, a juvenile delinquent tends to be preconventional in moral thinking.

Kohlberg's theory has been criticized as being male oriented and biased toward Western cultures, especially since he used only males in his studies (Gilligan, 1982; Snarey, 1985). Carol Gilligan (1982) proposed that men and women have different perspectives on morality: Men tend to judge as moral the actions that lead to a fair or just end, whereas women tend to judge as moral the actions that are nonviolent and hurt the fewest people. Earlier researchers did not find consistent support for gender differences in moral thinking (Walker, 1991), although more recent research suggests that males are more willing than females to accept the idea of committing a harmful actions when it is in the interest of the greater good (Friesdorf et al., 2015), a finding that seems to support Gilligan's proposal. Another criticism is that Kohlberg's assessment of moral development involves asking people what they think should be done in hypothetical moral dilemmas. What people say they will do and what people actually do when faced with a real dilemma are often two different things.

### PSYCHOSOCIAL DEVELOPMENT

**8.11** Describe how the adolescent search for personal identity influences relationships with others.

The development of personality and social relationships in adolescence primarily concerns the search for a consistent sense of self or personal identity.

**ERIKSON'S IDENTITY VERSUS ROLE CONFUSION** The psychosocial crisis that must be faced by the adolescent, according to Erikson, is that of **identity versus role confusion**.

**identity versus role confusion**
stage of personality development in which the adolescent must find a consistent sense of self.

| Table 8.5 | Kohlberg's Three Levels of Morality | |
|---|---|---|
| **Level of Morality** | **How Rules are Understood** | **Example** |
| **Preconventional morality** (very young children) | Morality of an action is based on the consequences; actions that get rewarded are right and those that earn punishment are wrong. | A child who takes money from a parent's wallet and does not get caught does not see that action as wrong. |
| **Conventional* morality** (older children, adolescents, and most adults) | An action is morally right if it conforms to the rules of the society and wrong if it does not. | A child scolds a parent for littering because there is a sign saying not to do so. |
| **Postconventional morality** (about one-fifth of the adult population) | Morality is now determined by the experiences and judgment of the person, even if that judgment disagrees with society's rules. | A husband helps his dying wife commit suicide to end her pain, even though society considers that action to be murder. |

*The term conventional refers to general standards or norms of behavior for a particular society, which will differ from one social group or culture to another.

In this stage, the teenager must choose from among many options for values in life and beliefs concerning things such as political issues, career options, and marriage (Feldman, 2003). From those options, a consistent sense of self must be found. Erikson believed that teens who have successfully resolved the conflicts of the earlier four stages are much better "equipped" to resist peer pressure to engage in unhealthy or illegal activities and find their own identity during the adolescent years. Those teens who are not as successful come into the adolescent years with a lack of trust in others, feelings of guilt and shame, low self-esteem, and dependency on others. Peer pressure is quite effective on teenagers who desperately want to "fit in" and have an identity of a certain sort and who feel that others will not want to be with them unless they conform to the expectations and demands of the peer group. They play the part of the model child for the parents, the good student for the teachers, and the "cool" juvenile delinquent to their friends and will be confused about which of the many roles they play really represents their own identity.

**PARENT–TEEN CONFLICT**   Even for the majority of adolescents who end up successfully finding a consistent sense of self, there will be conflicts with parents. Many researchers believe that a certain amount of "rebellion" and conflict is a necessary step in breaking away from childhood dependence on the parents and becoming a self-sufficient* adult (Bengston, 1970; Lynott & Roberts, 1997). Although many people think that these conflicts are intense and concern very serious behavior, the reality is that most parent–teen conflict is over trivial issues—hair, clothing, taste in music, and so on. On the really big moral issues, most parents and teens would be quite surprised to realize that they are in agreement (Giancola, 2006).

Can you see the effects of peer pressure in this picture? Most young people start smoking because their friends talk them into doing so, thinking it will make them seem more grown-up. What are some other choices that adolescents may make due to peer pressure?

## Concept Map  L.O. 8.9, 8.10, 8.11

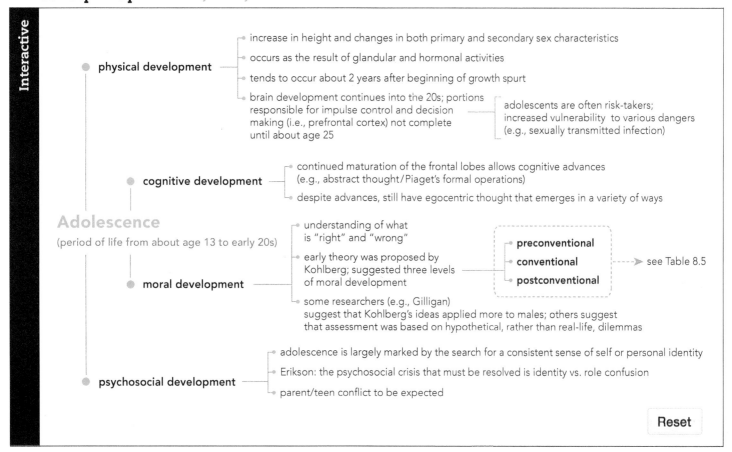

Interactive

**Adolescence**
(period of life from about age 13 to early 20s)

- **physical development**
  - increase in height and changes in both primary and secondary sex characteristics
  - occurs as the result of glandular and hormonal activities
  - tends to occur about 2 years after beginning of growth spurt
  - brain development continues into the 20s; portions responsible for impulse control and decision making (i.e., prefrontal cortex) not complete until about age 25
    - adolescents are often risk-takers; increased vulnerability to various dangers (e.g., sexually transmitted infection)

- **cognitive development**
  - continued maturation of the frontal lobes allows cognitive advances (e.g., abstract thought/Piaget's formal operations)
  - despite advances, still have egocentric thought that emerges in a variety of ways

- **moral development**
  - understanding of what is "right" and "wrong"
  - early theory was proposed by Kohlberg; suggested three levels of moral development
    - preconventional
    - conventional
    - postconventional
    - - - -> see Table 8.5
  - some researchers (e.g., Gilligan) suggest that Kohlberg's ideas applied more to males; others suggest that assessment was based on hypothetical, rather than real-life, dilemmas

- **psychosocial development**
  - adolescence is largely marked by the search for a consistent sense of self or personal identity
  - Erikson: the psychosocial crisis that must be resolved is identity vs. role confusion
  - parent/teen conflict to be expected

Reset

*self-sufficient: able to function without outside aid; capable of providing for one's own needs.

# Practice Quiz   How much do you remember?

*Pick the best answer.*

**1.** A change in the body of young boys such as the appearance and growth of body hair is considered
  **a.** a primary sex characteristic.
  **b.** a secondary sex characteristic.
  **c.** the final stage of puberty.
  **d.** a sign of postconventional morality.

**2.** "It can't happen to me. I'm special" is a common attitude found in adolescents who have developed
  **a.** a self-concept.     **c.** a personal fable.
  **b.** an imaginary audience.     **d.** a preconventional morality.

**3.** According to Kohlberg, about one-fifth of the adult population is at the _____ level of morality.
  **a.** preconventional     **c.** postconventional
  **b.** conventional     **d.** preliminary

**4.** According to Erikson, the task of the adolescent is to
  **a.** find a consistent sense of self.
  **b.** develop a sense of initiative.
  **c.** find intimacy with another.
  **d.** develop a sense of industry.

**5.** If Colin is going to argue and disagree with his parents, which of the following topics will he typically be arguing over?
  **a.** political beliefs
  **b.** religious beliefs
  **c.** social values
  **d.** his taste in clothes

# Adulthood and Aging

  When exactly does adulthood begin?

Adulthood can be thought of as the period of life from the early 20s until old age and death. Exactly when adulthood begins is not always easy to determine. In some cultures, adulthood is reached soon after puberty (Bledsoe & Cohen, 1993; Ocholla-Ayayo et al., 1993). Some people feel that it begins after graduation from high school, whereas others would say adulthood doesn't begin until after graduation from college. Others define it as the point when a person becomes totally self-sufficient with a job and a home separate from his or her parents. In that case, some people are not adults until their late 30s.

Many developmental psychologists now talk about **emerging adulthood** as a time from late adolescence through the 20s and referring to mainly those in developed countries who are childless, do not live in their own home, and are not earning enough money to be independent (Arnett, 2000, 2013; Azmitia et al., 2008; Greeson, 2013; Nelson et al., 2008). Decisions about identity, values, and the preparation for a career have begun to take longer and longer, and together with the downturn in the economy, many young people who would have been working and raising families a few decades ago now find that they cannot "leave the nest" so easily.

## PHYSICAL DEVELOPMENT: USE IT OR LOSE IT

**8.12** **Identify the physical changes and health issues associated with adulthood.**

Adulthood can also be divided into at least three periods: young adulthood, middle age, and late adulthood.

**PHYSICAL AGING** Physical changes in young adulthood are relatively minimal. The good news is that the 20s are a time of peak physical health, sharp senses, fewer insecurities, and mature cognitive abilities. The bad news is that even in the early 20s, the signs of aging are already beginning. Oil glands in the neck and around the eyes begin to malfunction, contributing to wrinkles in those areas near the end of the 20s and beginning of the 30s. The 30s may not bring noticeable changes, but vision and hearing are beginning to decline, and by around age 40, bifocal lenses may become necessary as

**emerging adulthood**

a time from late adolescence through the 20s referring to those who are childless, do not live in their own home, and are not earning enough money to be independent, mainly found in developed countries.

the lens of the eye hardens, becoming unable to change its shape to shift focus. Hearing loss may begin in the 40s and 50s but often does not become noticeable until the 60s or 70s, when hearing aids may become necessary.

In the 40s, while most adults are able to experience some security and stability without the worries and concerns of adolescence and young adulthood, physical aging continues: Skin begins to show more wrinkles, hair turns gray (or falls out), vision and hearing decline further, and physical strength may begin to decline (Frontera et al., 1991). In the 50s, these changes continue. Throughout middle age, weight may increase as the rate at which the body functions slows down but eating increases and less time is spent exercising. Height begins to decrease, with about half an inch of height lost for every 10 years past age 40, although people with the bone-loss disease osteoporosis may lose up to 8 inches or more (Cummings & Melton, 2002). Although sexual functioning usually does not decline in middle age, opportunities for sexual activity may be fewer than in the days of young adulthood (Hodson & Skeen, 1994; Kalra et al., 2011; Williams, 1995). Children, mortgages, and career worries can put a damper on middle-age romance.

Many people end up needing bifocals at some point in their 30s or 40s, as the lens hardens and loses its ability to visually accommodate to different distances of objects.

**MENOPAUSE**   In a woman's 40s, the levels of the female hormone estrogen decline as the body's reproductive system prepares to cease that function. Some women begin to experience "hot flashes," a sudden sensation of heat and sweating that may keep them awake at night. Interestingly, in some cultures, particularly those in which the diet contains high amounts of soy products, hot flashes are almost nonexistent (Cassidy et al., 1994; Lock, 1994). However, one study suggests soy intake is not a primary factor (Gold et al., 2013). The changes that happen at this time are called the *climacteric*, and the period of 5 to 10 years over which these changes occur is called *perimenopause*. At an average age of 51, most women will cease ovulation altogether, ending their reproductive years. The cessation of ovulation and the menstrual cycle is called **menopause** (Mishell, 2001). Many women look forward to the freedom from monthly menstruation and fear of unplanned pregnancies (Adler et al., 2000; Hvas, 2001; Leon et al., 2007).

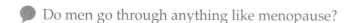

Do men go through anything like menopause?

Men also go through a time of sexual changes, but it is much more gradual and less dramatic than menopause. In males, **andropause** (Carruthers, 2001; Renneboog, 2012) usually begins in the 40s with a decline in several hormones, primarily testosterone (the major male hormone). Physical symptoms are also less dramatic but no less troubling: fatigue, irritability, possible problems in sexual functioning, and reduced sperm count. Males, however, rarely lose all reproductive ability.

**EFFECTS OF AGING ON HEALTH**   It is in middle age that many health problems first occur, although their true cause may have begun in the young adulthood years. Young adults may smoke, drink heavily, stay up late, and get dark tans, and the wear and tear that this lifestyle causes on their bodies will not become obvious until their 40s and 50s.

Some of the common health problems that may show up in middle age are high blood pressure, skin cancer, heart problems, arthritis, and obesity. High blood pressure can be caused by lifestyle factors such as obesity and stress but may also be related to hereditary factors (Rudd & Osterberg, 2002). Sleep problems, such as loud snoring and sleep apnea (in which breathing stops for 10 seconds or more), may also take their toll on physical health. There is some evidence that high blood pressure and apnea are linked, although the link very well may be the common factor of obesity (Nieto et al., 2000). Statistically, the four most frequent health-related causes of death in middle age (45 to 64 years of age) are cancer, followed closely by heart disease, chronic respiratory disease, and stroke for men (Centers for Disease Control [CDC], 2013a). For women in that age group, the results are slightly different: cancer, followed by heart disease as a much more distant second, chronic lung disease, and chronic liver disease (CDC, 2013b). Strokes were the fifth leading cause for women.

**menopause**

the cessation of ovulation and menstrual cycles and the end of a woman's reproductive capability.

**andropause**

gradual changes in the sexual hormones and reproductive system of middle-aged males.

## COGNITIVE DEVELOPMENT

### 8.13 Describe how memory abilities change during adulthood.

During this time, intellectual abilities do not decline overall, although speed of processing (or reaction time) does slow down. Compared to a younger adult, a middle-aged person may take a little longer to solve a problem. However, a middle-aged person also has more life experience and knowledge to bring to bear on a problem, which counters the lack of speed (Bugaiska et al., 2007; Migo et al., 2014). In one now-classic study (Salthouse, 1984), older typists were found to outperform younger typists, even though they typed more slowly than the younger subjects. The older typists, because of years of practice, had developed a skill of looking farther ahead in the document they were typing, so that they could type more continuously without looking back at the document. This allowed them to complete their typing more quickly than the younger typists.

This middle-aged woman works on a crossword puzzle. Mental exercises such as this are one way to keep the brain healthy and fit. What might be some other ways to exercise one's brain?

**CHANGES IN MEMORY**   Changes in memory ability are probably the most noticeable changes in middle-aged cognition. People find themselves having a hard time recalling a particular word or someone's name. This difficulty in retrieval is probably not evidence of a physical decline (or the beginning of Alzheimer's disease: ⓁⒾⓃⓀ to Learning Objective 6.13) but is more likely caused by the stresses a middle-aged person experiences and the sheer amount of information that a person of middle years must try to keep straight (Craik, 1994; Launer et al., 1995; Sands & Meredith, 1992). Some studies suggest that thinking about the positive events of the past aids the formation of newer memories—the areas of the brain that are linked to processing emotional content seem to have a strong connection to the areas of the brain responsible for memory formation (Addis et al., 2010, 2014; Madore & Schacter, 2016). Think positive!

**HOW TO KEEP YOUR BRAIN YOUNG**   People who exercise their mental abilities have been found to be far less likely to develop memory problems or even more serious senile dementias, such as Alzheimer's, in old age (Ball et al., 2002; Colcombe et al., 2003; Fiatarone, 1996). "Use it or lose it" is the phrase to remember. Working challenging crossword puzzles, for example, can be a major factor in maintaining a healthy level of cognitive functioning. Reading, having an active social life, going to plays, taking classes, and staying physically active can all have a positive impact on the continued well-being of the brain (Bosworth & Schaie, 1997; Cabeza et al., 2002; Hayes et al., 2015; Singh-Manoux et al., 2003).

## PSYCHOSOCIAL DEVELOPMENT

### 8.14 Apply Erikson's theory to some common psychosocial concerns of adulthood.

In adulthood, concerns involve career, relationships, family, and approaching old age. The late teens and early 20s may be college years for many, although other young people go to work directly from high school. The task of choosing and entering a career is very serious and a task that many young adults have difficulty accomplishing. A college student may change majors more than once during the first few years of college, and even after obtaining a bachelor's degree, many may either get a job in an unrelated field or go on to a different type of career choice in graduate school. Those who are working may also change careers several times (perhaps as many as five to seven times) and may experience periods of unemployment while between jobs.

**ERIKSON'S INTIMACY VERSUS ISOLATION: FORMING RELATIONSHIPS**   Erikson saw the primary task in young adulthood to be that of finding a mate. True **intimacy** is an emotional and psychological closeness that is based on the ability to trust, share, and care (an ability developed during the earlier stages such as trust versus mistrust) while still maintaining one's sense of self. ⓁⒾⓃⓀ to Learning Objective 12.13. Young adults who have difficulty trusting others and who are unsure of their own identities may find isolation instead of intimacy—loneliness, shallow relationships with others, and even

**intimacy**

an emotional and psychological closeness that is based on the ability to trust, share, and care, while still maintaining a sense of self.

a fear of real intimacy. For example, many marriages end in divorce within a few years, with one partner leaving the relationship—and even the responsibilities of parenting—to explore personal concerns and those unfinished issues of identity.

**ERIKSON'S GENERATIVITY VERSUS STAGNATION: PARENTING**   In middle adulthood, persons who have found intimacy can now turn their focus outward, toward others. Erikson saw this as parenting the next generation and helping them through their crises, a process he called **generativity**. Educators, supervisors, health-care professionals, doctors, and community volunteers might be examples of positions that allow a person to be generative.

Other ways of being generative include engaging in careers or some major life work that can become one's legacy to the generations to come. Those who are unable to focus outward and are still dealing with issues of intimacy or even identity are said to be *stagnated*. People who frequently hand the care of their children over to grandparents or other relatives so that they can go out and "have fun" may be unable to focus on anyone else's needs but their own.

💬 What kind of parent is the best parent—one who's really strict or one who's pretty easygoing?

Parenting children is a very important part of most people's middle adulthood. Diana Baumrind (1967) outlined three basic styles of parenting, each of which may be related to certain personality traits in the child raised by that style of parenting. The video *Parenting Styles* describes each of these parenting styles in more detail and explains why goodness of fit, or matching the parenting style to the child's needs, may be most important.

👁 Watch the Video *Parenting Styles*

**Authoritarian parenting** tends to be overly concerned with rules. This type of parent is stern, rigid, controlling, and uncompromising,* demands perfection, and has a tendency to use physical punishment. Children raised in this way are often insecure,

**generativity**
providing guidance to one's children or the next generation, or contributing to the well-being of the next generation through career or volunteer work.

**authoritarian parenting**
style of parenting in which parent is rigid and overly strict, showing little warmth to the child.

---

*uncompromising: not making or accepting any viewpoint other than one's own, allowing no other viewpoints.

timid, withdrawn, and resentful. As teenagers, they will very often rebel against parental authority in very negative and self-destructive ways, such as delinquency (criminal acts committed by minor children), drug use, or premarital sex (Baumrind, 1991, 2005; Sleddens et al., 2011).

**Permissive parenting** occurs when parents put very few demands on their children for behavior. **Permissive neglectful** parents simply aren't involved with their children, ignoring them and allowing them to do whatever they want, until it interferes with what the parent wants. At that point, this relationship may become an abusive one. **Permissive indulgent** parents seem to be too involved with their children, allowing their "little angels" to behave in any way they wish, refusing to set limits on the child's behavior or to require any kind of obedience. Children from both kinds of permissive parenting tend to be selfish, immature, dependent, lacking in social skills, and unpopular with peers (Baumrind, 1991, 2005; Dwairy, 2004; Sleddens et al., 2011).

**Authoritative parenting** involves combining firm limits on behavior with love, warmth, affection, respect, and a willingness to listen to the child's point of view. Authoritative parents are more democratic, allowing the child to have some input into the formation of rules but still maintaining the role of final decision maker. Punishment tends to be nonphysical, such as restrictions, time-out, or loss of privileges. Authoritative parents set limits that are clear and understandable, and when a child crosses the limits, they allow an explanation and then agree upon the right way to handle the situation. Children raised in this style of parenting tend to be self-reliant and independent (Baumrind, 1991, 2005; Dwairy, 2004; Sleddens et al., 2011; Sorkhabi, 2005; Underwood et al., 2009).

**ERIKSON'S EGO INTEGRITY VERSUS DESPAIR: DEALING WITH MORTALITY**   As people enter the stage known as late adulthood, life becomes more urgent as the realities of physical aging and the approaching end of life become harder and harder to ignore. Erikson (1980) believed that at this time, people look back on the life they have lived in a process called a life review. In the life review people must deal with mistakes, regrets, and unfinished business. If people can look back and feel that their lives were relatively full and are able to come to terms with regrets and losses, then a feeling of **ego integrity** or wholeness results. Integrity is the final completion of the identity, or ego. If people have many regrets and lots of unfinished business, they feel despair, a sense of deep regret over things that will never be accomplished because time has run out.

### THEORIES OF PHYSICAL AND PSYCHOLOGICAL AGING

**8.15**  **Compare and contrast four theories of why aging occurs.**

 💬 Why do people age? What makes us go through so many physical changes?

There are a number of theories of why people physically age. Some theories of physical aging point to biological changes in cellular structure, whereas others focus on the influence of external stresses on body tissues and functioning.

**CELLULAR-CLOCK THEORY**   One of the biologically based theories is the *cellular-clock theory* (Hayflick, 1977). In this theory, cells are limited in the number of times they can reproduce to repair damage. Evidence for this theory is the existence of *telomeres*, structures on the ends of chromosomes that shorten each time a cell reproduces (Martin & Buckwalter, 2001). When telomeres are too short, cells cannot reproduce and damage accumulates, resulting in the effects of aging. (Sounds almost like what happens when the warranty is up on a car, doesn't it?)

**WEAR-AND-TEAR THEORY**   The theory that points to outside influences such as stress, physical exertion, and bodily damage is known as the *wear-and-tear theory of aging*. In

---

**permissive parenting**

style of parenting in which parent makes few, if any, demands on a child's behavior.

**permissive neglectful**

permissive parenting in which parent is uninvolved with child or child's behavior.

**permissive indulgent**

permissive parenting in which parent is so involved that children are allowed to behave without set limits.

**authoritative parenting**

style of parenting in which parent combines warmth and affection with firm limits on a child's behavior.

**ego integrity**

sense of wholeness that comes from having lived a full life possessing the ability to let go of regrets; the final completion of the ego.

this theory, the body's organs and cell tissues simply wear out with repeated use and abuse. Damaged tissues accumulate and produce the effects of aging. *Collagen*, for example, is a natural elastic tissue that allows the skin to be flexible. As people age, the collagen "wears out," becoming less and less "stretchy" and allowing skin to sag and wrinkle (Cua et al., 1990; Kligman & Balin, 1989). (This process is not unlike what happens to the elastic in the waistband of one's underwear over time.)

**FREE-RADICAL THEORY** The *free-radical theory* is actually the latest version of the wear-and-tear theory in that it gives a biological explanation for the damage done to cells over time. *Free radicals* are oxygen molecules that have an unstable electron (negative particle). They bounce around the cell, stealing electrons from other molecules and increasing the damage to structures inside the cell. As people get older, more and more free radicals do more and more damage, producing the effects of aging (Hauck & Bartke, 2001; Knight, 1998).

💬 I've heard that most older people just want to be left alone and have some peace and quiet. Is that true?

**ACTIVITY THEORY** Activity theory (Havighurst et al., 1968) proposes that an elderly person adjusts more positively to aging when remaining active in some way. Even if a career must end, there are other ways to stay active and involved in life. Elderly people who volunteer at hospitals or schools, those who take up new hobbies or throw themselves full time into old ones, and those who maintain their friendships with others and continue to have social activities have been shown to be happier and live longer than those who withdraw themselves from activity. Contrary to the view of the elderly as voluntarily withdrawing from activities, the withdrawal of many elderly people is not voluntary at all; their lack of involvement is often because others simply stop inviting elderly people to social activities and including them in their lives.

One way to age successfully and maintain psychological health is to remain active and involved in life. This man is volunteering with grade-school students as a teacher's aide. This not only allows him to feel useful but also helps him to stay mentally alert and socially involved.

## STAGES OF DEATH AND DYING

### 8.16 Describe Kübler-Ross's theory of death and dying, and identify some criticisms of this theory.

There are several ways of looking at the process of dying. One of the more well-known theories is that of Elisabeth Kübler-Ross (Kübler-Ross, 1997), who conducted extensive interviews with dying persons and their caregivers.

Elisabeth Kübler-Ross theorized that people go through five stages of reaction when faced with death (Backer et al., 1994; Kübler-Ross, 1997). These stages are *denial*, in which people refuse to believe that the diagnosis of death is real; *anger*, which is really anger at death itself and the feelings of helplessness to change things; *bargaining*, in which the dying person tries to make a deal with doctors or even with God; *depression*, which is sadness from losses already experienced (e.g., loss of a job or one's dignity) and those yet to come (e.g., not being able to see a child grow up); and finally *acceptance*, when the person has accepted the inevitable* and quietly awaits death.

Obviously, some people do not have time to go through all of these stages or even go through them in the listed order (Schneidman, 1983, 1994). Some theorists do not agree with the stage idea, seeing the process of dying as a series of ups and downs, with hope on the rise at times and then falling, to be replaced by a rise in despair or disbelief (Corr, 1993; Maciejewski et al., 2007; Schneidman, 1983, 1994; Weisman, 1972). Still others question the idea of common reactions among dying people, stating that the particular disease or condition and its treatment, the person's personality before the terminal

**activity theory**

theory of adjustment to aging that assumes older people are happier if they remain active in some way, such as volunteering or developing a hobby.

---

*inevitable: something that cannot be avoided or escaped.

diagnosis, and other life history factors make the process of dying unique and unpredictable (Kastenbaum & Costa, 1977; Zlatin, 1995). The danger in holding too strictly to a stage theory is that people may feel there is a "right" way to face death and a "wrong" way, when in fact each person's dying process is unique. In fact, attitudes and rituals associated with death and the dying process vary from culture to culture, as discussed in the Applying Psychology section at the end of this chapter.

**THINKING CRITICALLY**

What are your thoughts on the need for closure in dealing with someone's death? Do you think it is always necessary?

▶ 
> The response entered here will be saved to your notes and may be
> collected by your instructor if he/she requires it.

Submit

---

## Concept Map L.O. 8.12, 8.13, 8.14, 8.15, 8.16

Interactive

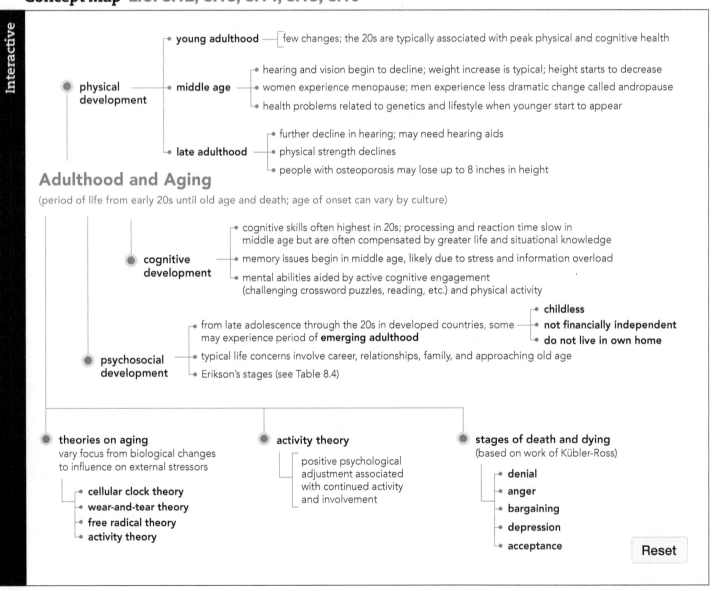

**physical development**

- **young adulthood** — few changes; the 20s are typically associated with peak physical and cognitive health
- **middle age**
  - hearing and vision begin to decline; weight increase is typical; height starts to decrease
  - women experience menopause; men experience less dramatic change called andropause
  - health problems related to genetics and lifestyle when younger start to appear
- **late adulthood**
  - further decline in hearing; may need hearing aids
  - physical strength declines
  - people with osteoporosis may lose up to 8 inches in height

## Adulthood and Aging
(period of life from early 20s until old age and death; age of onset can vary by culture)

**cognitive development**
- cognitive skills often highest in 20s; processing and reaction time slow in middle age but are often compensated by greater life and situational knowledge
- memory issues begin in middle age, likely due to stress and information overload
- mental abilities aided by active cognitive engagement (challenging crossword puzzles, reading, etc.) and physical activity

**psychosocial development**
- from late adolescence through the 20s in developed countries, some may experience period of **emerging adulthood**
  - **childless**
  - **not financially independent**
  - **do not live in own home**
- typical life concerns involve career, relationships, family, and approaching old age
- Erikson's stages (see Table 8.4)

**theories on aging**
vary focus from biological changes to influence on external stressors
- **cellular clock theory**
- **wear-and-tear theory**
- **free radical theory**
- **activity theory**

**activity theory**
- positive psychological adjustment associated with continued activity and involvement

**stages of death and dying**
(based on work of Kübler-Ross)
- denial
- anger
- bargaining
- depression
- acceptance

Reset

# Practice Quiz    How much do you remember?

*Pick the best answer.*

**1.** As Conrad has gotten older, he finds that it is becoming more difficult to remember certain words or the name of a new acquaintance. What is the most likely explanation for this change in memory?
   **a.** Alzheimer's disease
   **b.** the aging process
   **c.** stress
   **d.** heredity

**2.** According to Erikson, the primary task of early adulthood is
   **a.** completing your education.
   **b.** finding a mate.
   **c.** starting a career.
   **d.** taking care of aging parents.

**3.** According to Baumrind, which type of parent would most likely say, "Because I said so" or "It's my way or the highway!"
   **a.** authoritarian
   **b.** authoritative
   **c.** permissive neglectful
   **d.** permissive indulgent

**4.** Which theory of aging is compared to the limited number of repairs you can have before your car's warranty runs out?
   **a.** wear-and-tear theory
   **b.** cellular-clock theory
   **c.** free-radical theory
   **d.** activity theory

**5.** According to research, the reason many older people are no longer involved in their community is because
   **a.** they are not asked to take part.
   **b.** they quite often are unable to take part.
   **c.** they do not wish to be involved.
   **d.** they die.

**6.** What stage might terminally ill patients be in if they refuse to write a last will and testament because they believe that in doing so, they are admitting they will die?
   **a.** bargaining
   **b.** anger
   **c.** depression
   **d.** denial

## Applying Psychology to Everyday Life
## Cross-Cultural Views on Death

**8.17** **Compare and contrast some cross-cultural differences in views of death and dying.**

In the 1987 movie *The Princess Bride*, a character called Miracle Max says, "It just so happens that your friend here is only MOSTLY dead. There's a big difference between mostly dead and all dead. Mostly dead is slightly alive." As it turns out, that far-fetched idea of "mostly dead" is not unheard of in other cultures. While Westerners see a person as either dead or alive, in some cultures a person who, by Western standards, is clearly alive, is mourned as already dead—as is the case in many Native American cultures. Let's take a look at three diverse cultures and their views on death and dying, remembering to contrast them with what you know of death and funeral rites common in your own culture.

- In a wealthy Hindu family in India, the dying person is surrounded by family members, even while in the hospital. In addition, many visitors will attend to the dying person, creating a nearly constant flow of visitors in and out of the room. Once the person has passed away, preparations for the funeral period—which can take nearly 2 weeks—are begun. The body is not sent to a funeral home but rather is taken into the family home until the actual day of the funeral, where a cremation will take place. During the funeral preparation period, visitors and family stream in and out of the deceased's home, and an abundance of food—all vegetarian at this time—is prepared and eaten. Until the day of the funeral, mattresses are placed on the floor, and all but the very old and infirm are expected to sleep there; the body of the deceased is also placed on the floor. The family members themselves will eventually wash the body in preparation

The washed and wrapped body of a Hindu man is being carried to the crematorium by his family members.

for wrapping and the trip to the crematorium (Parkes et al., 1997). In Hinduism, it is believed that the dead person's soul will be reincarnated at either a higher level or a lower level of status, depending upon how the person lived his or her life.

- In the culture of the Northern Cheyenne Native American tribe, death is considered only the end of the physical body, while the self and one's Cheyenne nature will persist. The very old and the very young are said to be "close to the spirit," meaning that the infant has just come from the nonphysical world and the aged person is close to returning to it. The Cheyenne, like the Hindi, also believe in reincarnation, so many infants are seen to be the living embodiment of ancestors. Death itself is a long process, with various aspects of one's spirit leaving at different times. The first such "leaving" results in changes in the behavior and the mental activity of the dying person, but the person may still be able to walk and communicate. The second leads to loss of the senses, then consciousness, and finally, breathing. The very last essence to leave is the life principle, the first life given into an infant but the last to leave. This life principle stays in the skeleton until the bones begin to crumble into dust. Thus some Cheyenne believe that bones can become alive again (Strauss, 2004).

- In Navajo culture, a person who has died is believed to be in the underworld. Thus it is deemed possible for a dead person to visit the living; this is a feared situation, so the living try to avoid looking at the dead, and only a few people are permitted to touch or handle the body. A dying person is usually taken to a place removed from others, with only one or two very close relatives staying with the dying person—because to do so is to risk exposure to evil spirits. If a person dies in his or her own home, the home is destroyed—no one is allowed to live there afterward. At the time of death, two men prepare the body for burial, but prior to that ritual they must strip down to only their moccasins and then cover themselves in ashes, which serves to protect them from the evil spirits. The body is then washed and dressed. Two additional men dig the grave; only these four men will attend the burial, which is held as quickly as possible—usually the next day. The men carry the body on their shoulders to the grave, warning others to stay away from the area. The deceased is then buried along with all his or her belongings, the dirt is returned to the grave, and all footprints are swept away. Even the tools used to dig the grave are destroyed (Downs, 1984).

### Questions for Further Discussion

1. How has your own experience with death, if any, affected you and your outlook on life? What were the cultural trappings of the days leading up to the death and/or the funeral arrangements?

2. How do the customs of the wealthy Hindu family differ from those of the Cheyenne, and how are they alike? How do the two Native American cultures differ?

# Chapter Summary

## Studying Human Development

### 8.1 Compare and contrast the special research methods used to study development.

- Three special methods used in developmental research are the longitudinal design, the cross-sectional design, and the cross-sequential design.

### 8.2 Explain the relationship between heredity and environmental factors in determining development.

- Behavioral genetics is a field investigating the relative contributions to development of heredity (nature) and environment (nurture). Most developmental psychologists agree that development is a product of an interaction between nature and nurture.

**8.3** Summarize the role of chromosomes and genes in determining the transmission of traits and the inheritance of disorders.

- Dominant genes determine the expression of a trait, whereas recessive gene traits are only expressed when paired with another recessive gene influencing the same trait. Almost all traits are the result of combinations of genes working together in a process called polygenic inheritance.
- Chromosome disorders include Down syndrome, Klinefelter's syndrome, and Turner's syndrome, whereas genetic disorders include PKU, cystic fibrosis, sickle-cell anemia, and Tay-Sachs disease.

## Prenatal Development

**8.4** Explain the process of fertilization, including the twinning process.

- The fertilized egg cell is called a zygote and divides into many cells, eventually forming the baby.
- Monozygotic twins are formed when the zygote splits into two separate masses of cells, each of which will develop into a baby identical to the other.
- Dizygotic twins are formed when the mother's body releases multiple eggs and at least two are fertilized, or when another ovulation occurs even though the mother has already become pregnant.

**8.5** Describe the three stages of prenatal development.

- The germinal period is the first 2 weeks of pregnancy in which the dividing mass of cells moves into the uterus.
- The embryonic period begins at 2 weeks after conception and ends at 8 weeks. The vital organs and structures of the baby form during this period, making it a critical one when teratogens may adversely affect the development of those developing organs and structures.
- The fetal period is from the beginning of the 9th week until the birth of the baby. During the fetal period, tremendous growth occurs, length and weight increase, and organs continue to become fully functional.

## Infancy and Childhood Development

**8.6** Describe the physical and sensory changes that take place in infancy and childhood.

- Four critical areas of adjustment for the newborn are respiration, digestion, circulation, and temperature regulation.
- Infants are born with reflexes that help the infant survive until more complex learning is possible. These reflexes include sucking, rooting, Moro (startle), grasping, and stepping.
- The senses, except for vision, are fairly well developed at birth. Vision is blurry and lacking in full color perception until about 6 months of age. Gross and fine motor skills develop at a fast pace during infancy and early childhood.

**8.7** Compare and contrast two theories of cognitive development, and define autism spectrum disorder.

- Piaget's stages include the sensorimotor stage of sensory and physical interaction with the world, preoperational thought in which language becomes a tool of exploration, concrete operations in which logical thought becomes possible, and formal operations in which abstract concepts are understood and hypothetical thinking develops.
- Vygotsky believed that children learn best when being helped by a more highly skilled peer or adult in a process called scaffolding. The zone of proximal development is the difference between the mental age of tasks the child performs without help and those the child can perform with help.
- Autism spectrum disorder (ASD) is a neurode-velopmental disorder, which involves impairments in thinking, feeling, language, and social skills in relating to others.
- Parents and others who fear immunizing their children against dangerous diseases have failed to understand the basic principles of critical thinking.

**8.8** Identify the development of personality, relationships, and self-concept in infancy and childhood.

- The three basic infant temperaments are easy (regular, adaptable, and happy), difficult (irregular, nonadaptable, and irritable), and slow to warm up (need to adjust gradually to change).
- The four types of attachment are secure, avoidant (unattached), ambivalent (insecurely attached), and disorganized–disoriented (insecurely attached and sometimes abused or neglected).
- Harlow's classic research with infant rhesus monkeys demonstrated the importance of contact comfort in the attachment process, contradicting the earlier view that attachment was merely a function of associating the mother with the delivery of food.
- In trust versus mistrust, the infant must gain a sense of predictability and trust in caregivers or risk developing a mistrustful nature; in autonomy versus shame and doubt, the toddler needs to become physically independent.
- In initiative versus guilt, the preschool child is developing emotional and psychological independence; in industry versus inferiority, school-age children are gaining competence and developing self-esteem.

## Adolescence

**8.9** Describe the physical changes of puberty.

- Adolescence is the period of life from about age 13 to the early 20s during which physical development reaches completion.
- Puberty is a period of about 4 years during which the sexual organs and systems fully mature and during which secondary sex characteristics such as body hair, breasts, menstruation, deepening voices, and the growth spurt occur.

**8.10  Identify the cognitive and moral advances that occur in adolescence.**

- Adolescents engage in two kinds of egocentric thinking called the imaginary audience and the personal fable.
- Kohlberg proposed three levels of moral development: preconventional morality, conventional morality, and postconventional morality. Gilligan suggested that Kohlberg's ideas applied more to males.

**8.11  Describe how the adolescent search for personal identity influences relationships with others.**

- In Erikson's identity versus role confusion crisis, the job of the adolescent is to achieve a consistent sense of self from among all the roles, values, and futures open to him or her.

## Adulthood

**8.12  Identify the physical changes and health issues associated with adulthood.**

- Adulthood begins in the early 20s and ends with death in old age. It can be divided into young adulthood, middle adulthood, and late adulthood.
- The 20s are the peak of physical health; in the 30s the signs of aging become more visible, and in the 40s visual problems may occur, weight may increase, strength may decrease, and height begins to decrease.
- Women experience a physical decline in the reproductive system called the climacteric, ending at about age 50 with menopause, when a woman's reproductive capabilities are at an end. Men go through andropause, a less dramatic change in testosterone and other male hormones, beginning in the 40s.
- Many health problems such as high blood pressure, skin cancers, and arthritis begin in middle age, with the most common causes of death in middle age being heart disease, cancer, and stroke.

**8.13  Describe how memory abilities change during adulthood.**

- Reaction times slow down, but intelligence and memory remain relatively stable.

**8.14  Apply Erikson's theory to some common psychosocial concerns of adulthood.**

- Erikson's crisis of young adulthood is intimacy versus isolation, in which the young adult must establish an intimate relationship, usually with a mate.

- The crisis of middle adulthood is generativity versus stagnation, in which the task of the middle-aged adult is to help the next generation through its crises, either by parenting, mentoring, or a career that leaves some legacy to the next generation.
- Baumrind proposed three parenting styles: authoritarian (rigid and uncompromising), authoritative (consistent and strict but warm and flexible), and permissive (either indifferent and unconcerned with the daily activities of the child or indulgent and unwilling to set limits on the child).
- Erikson's final crisis is integrity versus despair, in which an older adult must come to terms with mortality.

**8.15  Compare and contrast four theories of why aging occurs.**

- Research strongly indicates that remaining active and involved results in the most positive adjustment to aging; this is a component of activity theory.
- The cellular-clock theory is based on the idea that cells only have so many times that they can reproduce; once that limit is reached, damaged cells begin to accumulate.
- The wear-and-tear theory of physical aging states that as time goes by, repeated use and abuse of the body's tissues cause it to be unable to repair all the damage.
- The free-radical theory states that oxygen molecules with an unstable electron move around the cell, damaging cell structures as they go.

**8.16  Describe Kübler-Ross's theory of death and dying, and identify some criticisms of this theory.**

- The five stages of reaction to death and dying are denial, anger, bargaining, depression, and acceptance.

## Applying Psychology to Everyday Life: Cross-Cultural Views on Death

**8.17  Compare and contrast some cross-cultural differences in views of death and dying.**

- In wealthy Hindu families, a dying person is surrounded by family and friends and then honored with a funeral process of nearly 2 weeks.
- In Northern Cheyenne culture, death is seen as part of the process of the life cycle and takes place in three stages.
- In Navajo culture, the dead are believed to move to the underworld, and contact with the body is strictly limited for fear of luring evil spirits to the world of the living.

# Test Yourself

*Pick the best answer.*

1. The thinking and attitudes of many who survived the Depression of the 1930s changed them for the rest of their lives. This would be an example of a
   a. cohort effect.
   b. cultural group.
   c. longitudinal group.
   d. cross-sequential group.

2. If a person has one gene influencing blue eyes but actually has brown eyes, blue eyes must be a _____ trait.
   a. dominant
   b. recessive
   c. sex-linked
   d. polygenic

3. In _____ syndrome, the 23rd pair of chromosomes consists of an XXY pairing, resulting in reduced masculine characteristics and excessive height.
   a. PKU
   b. Down
   c. Klinefelter's
   d. Turner's

4. Which of the following represents the fertilization process for monozygotic twins?
   a. One egg is fertilized by two different sperm.
   b. One egg splits and is then fertilized by two different sperm.
   c. One egg is fertilized by one sperm and then splits.
   d. Two eggs are fertilized by the same sperm.

5. What part of an infant's body is said to stay in an immature state until needed to produce more cells?
   a. uterus
   b. stem cells
   c. umbilical cord
   d. placenta

6. Based on today's science and medicine, when does the age of viability begin?
   a. between 8 and 12 weeks
   b. between 12 and 18 weeks
   c. between 22 and 26 weeks
   d. between 28 and 36 weeks

7. Dr. Kahn measures how long baby Lydia looks at a particular stimulus. The technique is known as
   a. preferential looking.
   b. dishabituation.
   c. habituation.
   d. stimulus discrimination.

8. At what age can the typical infant roll over?
   a. 2 months
   b. 5 weeks
   c. 8 months
   d. 12 months

9. Studies of the infant brain show signs of what scientists call synaptic pruning. What occurs during this process?
   a. The brain creates additional neural connections by removing parts of the surrounding bone.
   b. Unused synaptic connections and nerve cells are cleared out to make way for new cells.
   c. New cells work to "rewrite" old cells and ultimately change their functioning.
   d. New cells will not develop until the body makes sufficient physical space within the brain.

10. In which of Piaget's stages does the child become capable of understanding conservation?
    a. sensorimotor
    b. preoperational
    c. formal operations
    d. concrete operations

11. In which of Piaget's stages does the child become capable of abstract reasoning?
    a. sensorimotor
    b. preoperational
    c. formal operations
    d. concrete operations

12. Which infant temperament is associated with babies who are very regular in their schedules of sleeping and eating?
    a. Slow-to-warm-up
    b. Easy
    c. Difficult
    d. Anxious

13. In the Strange Situation, _____ babies would cry when their mother left the room but were happy upon her return.
    a. secure
    b. avoidant
    c. ambivalent
    d. disorganized–disoriented

14. What is a most likely explanation as to why teenagers and young adults may engage in risky and dangerous behavior?
    a. Such behavior is due to the tremendous pressure applied by peers.
    b. Such behavior is actually hereditary.
    c. Such behavior may be due to unbalanced levels of hormones in the body.
    d. Such behavior may be due to the incomplete development of the prefrontal cortex.

15. Samantha enters a classroom where two students are talking. When they stop their discussion, Samantha is certain they must have been talking about her. Such a belief is an example of
    a. the imaginary audience.
    b. the personal fable.
    c. abstract egocentrism.
    d. formal operations.

16. What cognitive changes occurring during middle adulthood are the most noticeable?
    a. Changes in memory begin to occur.
    b. Problem-solving skills diminish.
    c. Hearing begins to decline.
    d. Hair begins to turn gray.

17. Independence and self-reliance in the teenage years are most likely due to _____ parenting.
    a. authoritarian
    b. authoritative
    c. permissive neglectful
    d. permissive indulgent

18. The crisis of late adulthood, according to Erikson, is
    a. identity versus role confusion.
    b. generativity versus stagnation.
    c. intimacy versus isolation.
    d. integrity versus despair.

19. Which theory of aging states that unstable oxygen molecules tend to steal electrons as they bounce around, thus causing damage to surrounding cells?
    a. cellular-clock theory
    b. wear-and-tear theory
    c. free-radical theory
    d. activity theory

20. Kip is worried that he is losing his mind because he finds himself angry at a friend who died in an automobile accident. Based on Kübler-Ross's research, what might you tell him?
    a. Anger of this type is self-destructive and unhealthy.
    b. Anger is usually a mask to your true feelings of sadness.
    c. Anger toward a deceased individual is simply not normal and may require psychological counseling.
    d. Anger is a normal reaction to death and not a sign of mental illness.

# 9 Motivation and Emotion

As a busy college student, how do you stay motivated to succeed?
After you have answered the question, watch the video to compare the answers of other students to yours.

▶ The response entered here will be saved to your notes and may be collected by your instructor if he/she requires it.

👁 Watch the Video

# Why study motivation and emotion?

The study of motivation helps us understand not only why we do the things we do but also why our behaviors can change when our focus shifts or gets redirected. Emotions are a part of everything we do, affecting our relationships with others and our own health, as well as influencing important decisions. In this chapter, we will explore the motives behind our actions and the origins and influences of emotions.

# Learning Objectives

**9.1** Distinguish between intrinsic motivation and extrinsic motivation.

**9.2** Identify the key elements of the early instinct and drive-reduction approaches to motivation.

**9.3** Explain the characteristics of the three types of needs.

**9.4** Identify the key elements of the arousal and incentive approaches to motivation.

**9.5** Describe how Maslow's hierarchy of needs and self-determination theories explain motivation.

**9.6** Identify the physical and social factors that influence hunger.

**9.7** Recognize some of the factors that contribute to obesity.

**9.8** Describe the three elements of emotion.

**9.9** Distinguish among the common-sense, James-Lange, Cannon-Bard, and facial feedback theories of emotion.

**9.10** Identify the key elements in the cognitive arousal and cognitive-mediational theories of emotion.

**9.11** Summarize the five steps of the GTD method.

# Approaches to Understanding Motivation

Some people are content to sit and watch life pass them by, while others seem to need far more out of life. Some people want to do great things, while others are happy with more ordinary lives. What motivates people to do the things they do? What exactly is motivation?

## DEFINING MOTIVATION

### 9.1 Distinguish between intrinsic motivation and extrinsic motivation.

**Motivation** is the process by which activities are started, directed, and continued so that physical or psychological needs or wants are met (Petri, 1996). The word itself comes from the Latin word *movere*, which means "to move." Motivation is what "moves" people to do the things they do. For example, when a person is relaxing in front of the television and begins to feel hungry, the physical need for food might cause the person to get up, go into the kitchen, and search for something to eat. The physical need of hunger caused the action (getting up), directed it (going to the kitchen), and sustained the search (finding or preparing something to eat). Hunger is only one example, of course. Loneliness may lead to calling a friend or going to a place where there are people. The desire to get ahead in life motivates many people to go to college. Just getting out of bed in the morning is motivated by the need to keep a roof over one's head and food on the table by going to work.

There are different types of motivation. Sometimes people are driven to do something because of an external reward of some sort (or the avoidance of an unpleasant consequence, as when someone goes to work at a job to make money and avoid losing possessions such as a house or a car). Ⓛ Ⓘ Ⓝ Ⓚ to Learning Objective 5.5. In **extrinsic motivation**, a person performs an action because it leads to an outcome that is separate from the person (Lemos & Verissimo, 2014; Ryan & Deci, 2000). Other examples would be giving a child money for every A received on a report card, offering a bonus to an employee for increased performance, or tipping a server in a restaurant for good service. The child, employee, and server are motivated to work for the external or extrinsic rewards. In contrast, **intrinsic motivation** is the type of motivation in which a person performs an action because the act itself is fun, rewarding, challenging, or satisfying in some internal manner. Both outcome and level of effort can vary depending on the type of motivation. Psychologist Teresa Amabile (Amabile et al., 1976) found that children's creativity was affected by the kind of motivation for which they worked: Extrinsic motivation decreased the degree of creativity shown in an experimental group's artwork when compared to the creativity levels of the children in an intrinsically motivated control group. To learn more about the factors motivating your behavior, participate in the survey *What Motivates You?*

**motivation**

the process by which activities are started, directed, and continued so that physical or psychological needs or wants are met.

**extrinsic motivation**

type of motivation in which a person performs an action because it leads to an outcome that is separate from or external to the person.

**intrinsic motivation**

type of motivation in which a person performs an action because the act itself is rewarding or satisfying in some internal manner.

**Survey** WHAT MOTIVATES YOU

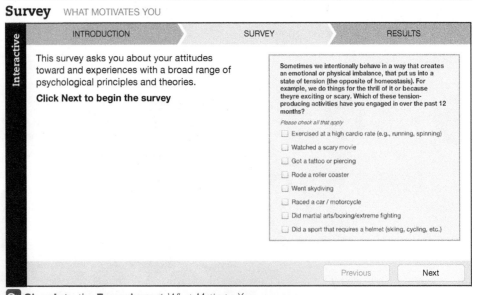

◉ **Simulate** the **Experiment** *What Motivates You*

## EARLY APPROACHES TO UNDERSTANDING MOTIVATION

**9.2** Identify the key elements of the early instinct and drive-reduction approaches to motivation.

Researchers and theorists began the serious study of motivation almost as soon as psychology became its own recognized field of study. As is often the case when first examining a topic such as this, there were many different areas of focus in those early days. As the decades have gone by, some approaches have fallen out of favor, some have been modified, and newer approaches have been developed. Let's take a look at some of the earlier theories.

**INSTINCTS AND THE EVOLUTIONARY APPROACH**   Early attempts to understand motivation focused on the biologically determined and innate patterns of behavior called **instincts** that exist in both people and animals. Just as animals are governed by their instincts to perform activities such as migrating, nest building, mating, and protecting their territory, evolutionary theorists proposed that human beings may also be governed by similar instincts (James, 1890; McDougall, 1908). For instance, according to these theorists, the human instinct to reproduce is responsible for sexual behavior, and the human instinct for territorial protection may be related to aggressive behavior.

William McDougall (1908) actually proposed a total of 18 instincts for humans, including curiosity, flight (running away), pugnacity (aggressiveness), and acquisition (gathering possessions). As the years progressed, psychologists added more and more instincts to the list until there were thousands of proposed instincts. However, none of these early theorists did much more than give names to these instincts. Although there were plenty of descriptions, such as "submissive people possess the instinct of submission," there was no attempt to explain why these instincts exist in humans, if they exist at all (Petri, 1996).

Instinct approaches have faded away because, although they could describe human behavior, they could not explain it. But these approaches did accomplish one important thing by forcing psychologists to realize that some human behavior is controlled by hereditary factors. This idea remains central in the study of human behavior today. For example, research on the genetics of both cognitive and behavioral traits suggests that hereditary factors can account for more than 50 percent of the variance in some aspects of human cognition, temperament, and personality; and much of this variance is due to the influence of multiple genes or hereditary factors, not just one (Kempf & Weinberger, 2009; Plomin et al., 1994; Plomin & Deary, 2015; Plomin & Spinath, 2004).

**DRIVE-REDUCTION THEORY**   The next approach to understanding motivation focuses on the concepts of needs and drives. A **need** is a requirement of some material (such as food or water) that is essential for survival of the organism. When an organism has a need, it leads to a psychological tension as well as a physical arousal that motivates the organism to act in order to fulfill the need and reduce the tension. This tension is called a **drive** (Hull, 1943).

**Drive-reduction theory** proposes just this connection between internal physiological states and outward behavior. In this theory, there are two kinds of drives. **Primary drives** are those that involve survival needs of the body such as hunger and thirst, whereas **acquired (secondary) drives** are those that are learned through experience or conditioning, such as the need for money or social approval or the need of recent former smokers to have something to put in their mouths. If this sounds familiar, it should. The concepts of primary and secondary reinforcers from Chapter Five are related to these drives. Primary reinforcers satisfy primary drives, and secondary reinforcers satisfy acquired, or secondary, drives. Ⓛ Ⓘ Ⓝ Ⓚ to Learning Objective 5.5.

This theory also includes the concept of **homeostasis**, or the tendency of the body to maintain a steady state. One could think of homeostasis as the body's version of a thermostat—thermostats keep the temperature of a house at a constant level, and homeostasis does the same thing for the body's functions. When there is a primary drive need, the body is in a state of imbalance. This stimulates behavior that brings the body back into balance, or

**instincts**

the biologically determined and innate patterns of behavior that exist in both people and animals.

**need**

a requirement of some material (such as food or water) that is essential for survival of the organism.

**drive**

a psychological tension and physical arousal arising when there is a need that motivates the organism to act in order to fulfill the need and reduce the tension.

**drive-reduction theory**

approach to motivation that assumes behavior arises from physiological needs that cause internal drives to push the organism to satisfy the need and reduce tension and arousal.

**primary drives**

those drives that involve needs of the body such as hunger and thirst.

**acquired (secondary) drives**

those drives that are learned through experience or conditioning, such as the need for money or social approval.

**homeostasis**

the tendency of the body to maintain a steady state.

homeostasis. For example, if Jarrod's body needs food, he feels hunger and the state of tension/arousal associated with that need. He will then seek to restore his homeostasis by eating something, which is the behavior stimulated to reduce the hunger drive (see **Figure 9.1**).

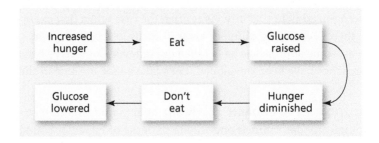

**Figure 9.1** Homeostasis

In homeostasis, the body maintains balance in its physical states. For example, this diagram shows how increased hunger (a state of imbalance) prompts a person to eat. Eating increases the level of glucose (blood sugar), causing the feelings of hunger to reduce. After a period without eating, the glucose levels become low enough to stimulate the hunger drive once again, and the entire cycle is repeated.

Although drive-reduction theory works well to explain the actions people take to reduce tension created by needs, it does not explain all human motivation. Why do people eat when they are not really hungry? People don't always seek to reduce their inner arousal either—sometimes they seek to increase it. Bungee-jumping, parachuting as recreation, rock climbing, and watching horror movies are all activities that increase the inner state of tension and arousal, and many people love doing these activities. Why would people do such things if they don't reduce some need or restore homeostasis? The answer is complex: There are different types of needs, different effects of arousal, different incentives, and different levels of importance attached to many forms of behavior. The following theories explore some of these factors in motivation.

(left) The human body needs water, especially when a person is working hard or under stress, as this man appears to be. Thirst is a survival need of the body, making it a primary drive, according to drive-reduction theory. What other kinds of needs might be primary drives?

(right) Some people are driven to do strenuous, challenging activities even when there is no physical need to do so. When a drive is acquired through learning, it is called an acquired or secondary drive. Fulfilling an acquired drive provides secondary reinforcement. What might this rock climber find reinforcing about scaling this steep cliff?

## DIFFERENT STROKES FOR DIFFERENT FOLKS: PSYCHOLOGICAL NEEDS

**9.3** Explain the characteristics of the three types of needs.

Obviously, motivation is about needs. Drive-reduction theory talks about needs, and other theories of motivation include the concept of needs. In many of these theories, most needs are the result of some inner physical drive (such as hunger or thirst) that demands to be satisfied, but other theories examine our psychological needs.

**MCCLELLAND'S THEORY: AFFILIATION, POWER, AND ACHIEVEMENT NEEDS**  Harvard University psychologist David C. McClelland (1961, 1987) proposed a theory of motivation that highlights the importance of three psychological needs not typically considered by the other theories: affiliation, power, and achievement.

According to McClelland, human beings have a psychological need for friendly social interactions and relationships with others. Called the **need for affiliation** (abbreviated as **nAff** in McClelland's writings), people high in this need seek to be liked by others and to be held in high regard by those around them. This makes high-affiliation people good team players, whereas a person high in achievement just might run over a few team members on the way to the top.

A second psychological need proposed by McClelland is the **need for power (nPow)**. Power is not about reaching a goal but about having control over other people. People high in this need would want to have influence over others and make an impact on them. They want their ideas to be the ones that are used, regardless of whether their ideas will lead to success. Status and prestige are important, so these people wear expensive clothes, live in expensive houses, drive fancy cars, and dine in the best restaurants. Whereas someone who is a high achiever may not need a lot of money to validate the achievement, someone who is high in the need for power typically sees the money (and cars, houses, jewelry, and other "toys") as the achievement—the one with the most toys wins.

The **need for achievement (nAch)** involves a strong desire to succeed in attaining goals, not only realistic ones but also challenging ones. People who are high in nAch look for careers and hobbies that allow others to evaluate them, because these high achievers also need to have feedback about their performance in addition to the achievement of reaching the goal. Although many of these people do become wealthy, famous, and publicly successful, others fulfill their need to achieve in ways that lead only to their own personal success, not material riches—they just want the challenge. Achievement motivation appears to be strongly related to success in school, occupational success, and the quality and amount of what a person produces (Collins et al., 2004; Gillespie et al., 2002; Hoferichter et al., 2015; Spangler, 1992).

Many people who are as wealthy as Kanye West and Kim Kardashian are continue to buy new houses, businesses, clothing, and cars (among other things) even though they do not need them. Such actions are examples of the need for power. How might this need for power be expressed in a person's relationships with others, such as a spouse, employee, or friend?

**need for affiliation (nAff)**

the need for friendly social interactions and relationships with others.

**need for power (nPow)**

the need to have control or influence over others.

**need for achievement (nAch)**

a need that involves a strong desire to succeed in attaining goals, not only realistic ones but also challenging ones.

### THINKING CRITICALLY

How might the three types of needs discussed in this section relate to the goals of many politicians? Would some needs be more important than others?

▶ The response entered here will be saved to your notes and may be collected by your instructor if he/she requires it.

Submit

💬 How do people get to be high achievers?

**PERSONALITY AND NACH: CAROL DWECK'S SELF-THEORY OF MOTIVATION**  According to motivation and personality psychologist Carol Dweck (Dweck, 1999; Nussbaum & Dweck, 2008), the need for achievement is closely linked to personality factors, including a person's view of how *self* (the beliefs a person holds about his or her own abilities and relationships with others) can affect the individual's perception of the success or

Many people are driven by a need to attain both realistic and challenging goals. This young girl seems eager to provide an answer to the teacher's question, and the teacher's positive feedback will help foster the girl's need for achievement.

failure of his or her actions. This concept is related to the much older notion of *locus of control*, in which people who assume that they have control over what happens in their lives are considered to be *internal* in locus of control, and those who feel that their lives are controlled by powerful others, luck, or fate are considered to be *external* in locus of control (A. P. MacDonald, 1970; Rotter, 1966).

Dweck has amassed a large body of empirical research, particularly in the field of education, to support the idea that people's "theories" about their own selves can affect their level of achievement motivation and their willingness to keep trying to achieve success in the face of failure (Dweck, 1986; Dweck & Elliott, 1983; Dweck & Leggett, 1988; Elliott & Dweck, 1988; Yeager et al., 2014). According to this research, people can form one of two belief systems about intelligence, which in turn affects their motivation to achieve. Those who believe intelligence is fixed and unchangeable often demonstrate an external locus of control when faced with difficulty, leading them to give up easily or avoid situations in which they might fail—often ensuring their own failure in the process (Dweck & Molden, 2008). They are prone to developing learned helplessness, the tendency to stop trying to achieve a goal because past failure has led them to believe that they cannot succeed. (L)(I)(N)(K) to Learning Objective 5.12. Their goals involve trying to "look smart" and to outperform others ("See, at least I did better than she did"). For example, a student faced with a big exam may avoid coming to class that day, even though that might mean getting an even lower score on a makeup exam. This does not mean that students with this view of intelligence are always unsuccessful. In fact, Dweck's research (1999) suggests that students who have had a long history of successes may be most at risk for developing learned helplessness after a big failure, precisely because their previous successes have led them to believe in their own fixed intelligence. For example, a child who had never earned anything less than an A in school who then receives his first C might become depressed and refuse to do any more homework, ensuring future failure.

The other type of person believes that intelligence is changeable and can be shaped by experiences and effort in small increases, or increments. These people also tend to show an internal locus of control, both in believing that their own actions and efforts will improve their intelligence and in taking control or increasing their efforts when faced with challenges (Dweck & Molden, 2008). They work at developing new strategies and get involved in new tasks, with the goal of increasing their "smarts." They are motivated to master tasks and don't allow failure to destroy their confidence in themselves or prevent them from trying again and again, using new strategies each time.

Based on this and other research, Dweck recommends that parents and teachers praise efforts and the methods that children use to make those efforts, not just successes or ability. Instead of saying, "You're right, how smart you are," the parent or teacher should say something such as, "You are really thinking hard" or "That was a very clever way to think about this problem." In the past, teachers and parents have been told that praise is good and criticism is bad—it might damage a child's self-esteem. Dweck believes that constructive criticism, when linked with praise of effort and the use of strategies, will be a better influence on the child's self-esteem and willingness to challenge themselves than endless praise that can become meaningless when given indiscriminately (Gunderson et al., 2013).

## AROUSAL AND INCENTIVE APPROACHES

### 9.4 Identify the key elements of the arousal and incentive approaches to motivation.

Another explanation for human motivation involves the recognition of yet another type of need, the need for stimulation. A **stimulus motive** is one that appears to be unlearned but causes an increase in stimulation. Examples would be curiosity, playing, and exploration. On the other hand, sometimes our motives for doing things involve the

**stimulus motive**

a motive that appears to be unlearned but causes an increase in stimulation, such as curiosity.

rewards or incentives we get when we act, such as eating food even when we are not hungry just because it tastes so good—an example of learned behavior.

**AROUSAL THEORY**    In **arousal theory**, people are said to have an optimal (best or ideal) level of tension. Task performances, for example, may suffer if the level of arousal is too high (such as severe test anxiety) or even if the level of arousal is too low (such as boredom). For many kinds of tasks, a moderate level of arousal seems to be best. This relationship between task performance and arousal has been explained by the **Yerkes-Dodson law** (Teigen, 1994; Yerkes & Dodson, 1908), although Yerkes and Dodson formulated the law referring to stimulus intensity, not arousal level (Winton, 1987).

Of special interest to both sports psychologists and social psychologists, this arousal effect appears to be modified by the difficulty level of the task: Easy tasks demand a somewhat "high–moderate" level for optimal performance, whereas difficult tasks require a "low–moderate" level. **Figure 9.2** shows this relationship in graphic form. A sports psychologist might work with an athlete to help them get "in the zone," where they are in that specific zone of arousal (not too low and not too high) and state of mental focus so as to maximize their athletic skills and performance. Social psychologists also examine the effect of the presence of other people on the facilitation or impairment of an individual's performance. (L)(I)(N)(K) to Learning Objective 12.1. For example, imagine someone in a classroom speaking to a classmate seated nearby. The act of speaking directly to another person is a fairly easy task for many people and is accomplished without any difficulty or errors. However, ask that same individual to stand, turn, and address the entire classroom of students, and all of a sudden his or her arousal level spikes; many individuals in a similar situation may find themselves unable to put words together well enough to form coherent sentences or to pronounce words correctly—in essence, they may become "tongue-tied," all because their arousal level has gotten too high.

Maintaining an optimal level of arousal, then, may involve reducing tension or creating it (Hebb, 1955). For example, husbands or wives who are underaroused may pick a fight with their spouse. Students who experience test anxiety (a high level of arousal) may seek out ways to reduce that anxiety to improve their test performance. Students who are not anxious at all may not be motivated to study well, thus lowering their test performance. Many arousal theorists believe that the optimal level of arousal for most people under normal circumstances is somewhere in the middle, neither too high nor too low.

 💬 If people are supposed to be seeking a level of arousal somewhere around the middle, why do some people love to do things like bungee-jumping?

Even though the average person might require a moderate level of arousal to feel content, there are some people who need less arousal and some who need more. The person who needs more arousal is called a **sensation seeker** (Lauriola et al., 2014; Zuckerman, 1979, 1994). Sensation seekers seem to need more complex and varied sensory experiences than do other people. The need does not always have to involve danger. For example, students who travel to other countries to study tend to score higher on scales of sensation seeking than do students who stay at home (Schroth & McCormack, 2000). Sensation seeking may be related to temperament. (L)(I)(N)(K) to Learning Objective 8.8. **Table 9.1** has some sample items from a typical sensation-seeking scale.

In one study (Putnam & Stifter, 2002), researchers found evidence of "sensation-seeking" behavior in children as young as age 2. In this study, 90 children were studied at the ages of 6, 12, 24, and 25 months. In a test of the youngest participants, the babies were shown two sets of toys: a block, a plate, and a cup; or a flashing light, a toy beeper, and a wind-up

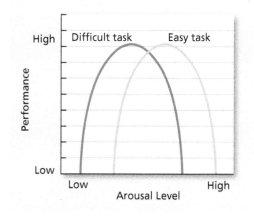

**Figure 9.2**  Arousal and Performance

The optimal level of arousal for task performance depends on the difficulty of the task. We generally perform easy tasks well if we are at a high–moderate level of arousal (green) and accomplish difficult tasks well if we are at a low–moderate level.

Does this look fun? If so, you may score relatively higher in sensation seeking.

**arousal theory**

theory of motivation in which people are said to have an optimal (best or ideal) level of tension that they seek to maintain by increasing or decreasing stimulation.

**Yerkes-Dodson law**

law stating that when tasks are simple, a higher level of arousal leads to better performance; when tasks are difficult, lower levels of arousal lead to better performance.

**sensation seeker**

someone who needs more arousal than the average person.

**Table 9.1**  Sample Items From the Zuckerman-Kuhlman Personality Questionnaire

| Scale Item | Sensation Seeking |
| --- | --- |
| I sometimes do "crazy" things just for fun. | High |
| I prefer friends who are excitingly unpredictable. | High |
| I am an impulsive person. | High |
| Before I begin a complicated job, I make careful plans. | Low |
| I usually think about what I am going to do before doing it. | Low |

**SOURCE:** Adapted from Zuckerman, M. (2002).

dragon. The first set was considered a low-intensity stimulus, whereas the second set was labeled a high-intensity stimulus. The infants who reached out for the toys more quickly and reached for the high-intensity toys in particular were high sensation seekers.

Is the tendency to be a sensation seeker something people have when they are born? Although it is tempting to think of 6-month-old children as having little in the way of experiences that could shape their personalities, the fact is that the first 6 months of life are full of experiences that might affect children's choices in the future. For example, a very young infant might, while being carried, stick a hand into some place that ends up causing pain. This experience might affect that infant's willingness in the future to put his or her hand in something else through the simple learning process of operant conditioning. **L I N K** to Learning Objective 5.5. In a longitudinal study taking place over about 4 years, researchers found that adolescents who played video games in which high risk taking is positively presented became more likely to engage in risky behavior and had increased scores on levels of sensation seeking (Hull et al., 2012).

The presence of other people may matter as well. Adolescents tend to make more risky decisions when in a group of peers than when alone, a phenomenon that is part of peer pressure (Albert et al., 2013; Chein et al., 2011; Smith et al., 2014; Willoughby et al., 2013). In one recent study (Silva et al., 2016), late-adolescent males (18 to 22 years of age) were given a battery of tests on decision making under three conditions: alone, in a group of four males of the same age, and in a group with three age-mates and one older male (25 to 30 years of age). When tested alone or in the group with the older male, the participants exhibited about the same level of risky behavior, but when tested in the group with same-age peers, they exhibited significantly greater risk taking. It would seem that the presence of just the one older male was enough to cancel out the risk-taking increase usually found in peer pressure situations.

### INCENTIVE APPROACHES

💬 Last Thanksgiving, I had eaten about all I could. Then my aunt brought out a piece of her wonderful pumpkin pie and I couldn't resist—I ate it, even though I was not at all hungry. What makes us do things even when we don't have the drive or need to do them?

**incentives**

things that attract or lure people into action.

**incentive approaches**

theories of motivation in which behavior is explained as a response to the external stimulus and its rewarding properties.

It's true that sometimes there is no physical need present, yet people still eat, drink, or react as if they did have a need. Even though that piece of pie was not necessary to reduce a hunger drive, it was very rewarding, wasn't it? And on past occasions, that pie was also delicious and rewarding, so there is anticipation of that reward now. The pie, in all its glorious promise of flavor and sweetness, becomes, in itself, an incentive to eat. **Incentives** are things that attract or lure people into action.

In **incentive approaches**, behavior is explained in terms of the external stimulus and its rewarding properties. These rewarding properties exist independently of any need or level of arousal and can cause people to act only upon the incentive. Thus, incentive theory is actually based, at least in part, on the principles of learning that were discussed in Chapter Five. ⓛⓘⓝⓚ to Learning Objective 5.5.

By itself, the incentive approach does not explain the motivation behind all behavior. Many theorists today see motivation as a result of both the "push" of internal needs or drives and the "pull" of a rewarding external stimulus. For example, sometimes a person may actually be hungry (the push) but choose to satisfy that drive by selecting a candy bar instead of a celery stick. The candy bar has more appeal to most people, and it, therefore, has more pull than the celery. (Frankly, to most people, just about anything has more pull than celery.)

## HUMANISTIC APPROACHES

### 9.5 Describe how Maslow's hierarchy of needs and self-determination theories explain motivation.

Some final approaches to the study of motivation are humanistic in nature. One of the classic humanistic approaches is that of Maslow, while a more modern approach is represented by self-determination theory.

**MASLOW'S HIERARCHY OF NEEDS**    The first humanistic theory is based on the work of Abraham Maslow (1943, 1987). As explained in the video *Maslow's Hierarchy of Needs*, Maslow proposed that there are several levels of needs that a person must strive to meet before achieving the highest level of personality fulfillment. According to Maslow, **self-actualization** is the point that is seldom reached—at which people have satisfied the lower needs and achieved their full human potential.

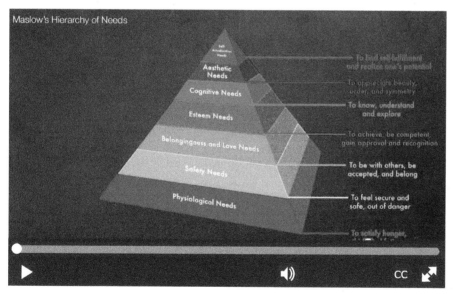

👁 **Watch** the **Video** *Maslow's Hierarchy of Needs*

These needs include both fundamental deficiency needs, such as the need for food or water, and growth needs, such as the desire for having friends or feeling good about oneself (Maslow, 1971; Maslow & Lowery, 1998). For a person to achieve self-actualization, which is one of the highest levels of growth needs, the primary, fundamental needs must first be fulfilled. **Figure 9.3** shows the typical way to represent Maslow's series of needs as a pyramid with the most basic needs for survival at the bottom and the highest needs at the top. This type of ranking is called a hierarchy.* The only need higher than self-actualization is transcendence, a search for spiritual meaning beyond one's immediate self, that Maslow added many years after his original hierarchy was formulated.

---

*hierarchy: a graded or ranked series.

**self-actualization**

according to Maslow, the point that is seldom reached at which people have sufficiently satisfied the lower needs and achieved their full human potential.

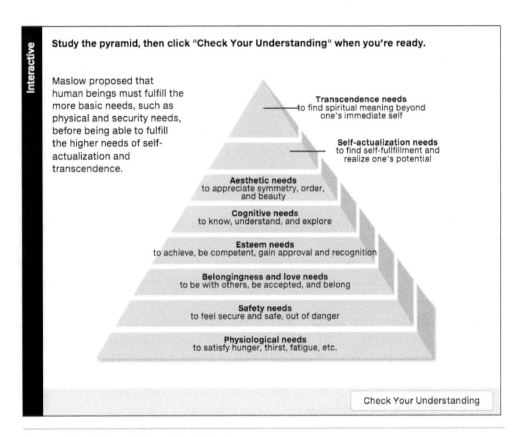

**Figure 9.3** Maslow's Hierarchy of Needs

Maslow proposed that human beings must fulfill the more basic needs, such as physical and security needs, before being able to fulfill the higher needs of self-actualization and transcendence.

People move up the pyramid as they go through life, gaining wisdom and the knowledge of how to handle many different situations. But a shift in life's circumstances can result in a shift down to a lower need. Moving up and down and then back up can occur frequently—even from one hour to the next. Times in a person's life in which self-actualization is achieved, at least temporarily, are called **peak experiences**. For Maslow, the process of growth and self-actualization is the striving to make peak experiences happen again and again.

  Does this theory apply universally?

Maslow's theory has had a powerful influence on the field of management (Heil et al., 1998) and has spawned new ideas and concepts of what might be an appropriate revised hierarchy. Ⓛ Ⓘ Ⓝ Ⓚ to Learning Objective B.7. In spite of this influence, Maslow's theory is not without its critics. There are several problems that others have highlighted, and the most serious is that there is little scientific support (Drenth et al., 1984). Like Sigmund Freud, Maslow developed his theory based on his personal observations of people rather than any empirically gathered observations or research. Although many people report that while they were starving, they could think of nothing but food, there is anecdotal evidence in the lives of many people, some of them quite well known, that the lower needs do not have to be satisfied before moving on to a higher need (Drenth et al., 1984). For example, artists and scientists throughout history have been known to deny their own physical needs while producing great works (a self-actualization need).

Maslow's work was also based on his studies of Americans. Cross-cultural research suggests that the order of needs on the hierarchy does not always hold true for other cultures, particularly those cultures with a stronger tendency than the culture

In the movie *The Martian*, Matt Damon's character is accidentally stranded on Mars and must find a way to survive for 4 years. His most important concern is how to produce enough food to survive that long, but he also makes recordings, needing to feel that someone might one day hear him. The need for companionship is a strong one once physical needs are met.

**peak experiences**

according to Maslow, times in a person's life during which self-actualization is temporarily achieved.

of the United States to avoid uncertainty, such as Greece and Japan. In those countries, security needs are much stronger than self-actualization needs in determining motivation (Hofstede, 1980; Hofstede et al., 2002). This means that people in those cultures value job security more than they do job satisfaction (holding an interesting or challenging job). In countries such as Sweden and Norway, which stress the quality of life as being of greater importance than what a person produces, social needs may be more important than self-actualization needs (Hofstede et al., 2002). (L)(I)(N)(K) to Learning Objective 13.13.

Other theorists (Alderfer, 1972; Kenrick et al., 2010) have developed and refined Maslow's hierarchy. Douglas Kenrick and colleagues have suggested a modification to Maslow's original hierarchy that encompasses aspects of evolutionary biology, anthropology, and psychology. Their modification incorporates dynamics between internal motives and environmental threats and opportunities (Kenrick et al., 2010). However, their revision has not been without critique and has spawned further contemplation. Some elements of Kenrick's theory have been challenged, including a questioning of its focus on evolutionary aspects instead of human cultural influences (Kesebir et al., 2010) and its removal of self-actualization from both the pinnacle of the pyramid and from the hierarchy altogether as a stand-alone motive (Peterson & Park, 2010). Just as there are many aspects to motivation, any revision or discussion of an appropriate hierarchy of needs will need to take into account a wide variety of opinions and viewpoints.

**SELF-DETERMINATION THEORY (SDT)**   Another theory of motivation that is similar to Maslow's hierarchy of needs is the **self-determination theory (SDT)** of Richard Ryan and Edward Deci (2000). In this theory, there are three inborn and universal needs that help people gain a complete sense of self and whole, healthy relationships with others. The three needs are *autonomy*, or the need to be in control of one's own behavior and goals (i.e., self-determination); *competence*, or the need to be able to master the challenging tasks of one's life; and *relatedness*, or the need to feel a sense of belonging, intimacy, and security in relationships with others. These needs are common in several theories of personality; the relatedness need is, of course, similar to Maslow's belongingness and love needs, and both autonomy and competence are important aspects of Erikson's theory of psychosocial personality development (Erikson, 1950, 1980). (L)(I)(N)(K) to Learning Objective 8.7.

Ryan, Deci, and their colleagues (Deci et al., 1994; Ryan & Deci, 2000) believe that satisfying these needs can best be accomplished if the person has a supportive environment in which to develop goals and relationships with others. Such satisfaction will not only foster healthy psychological growth but also increase the individual's intrinsic motivation (actions are performed because they are internally rewarding or satisfying). Evidence suggests that intrinsic motivation is increased or enhanced when a person feels not only competence (through experiencing positive feedback from others and succeeding at what are perceived to be challenging tasks) but also a sense of autonomy or the knowledge that his or her actions are self-determined rather than controlled by others (deCharms, 1968; Deci & Ryan, 1985; Evans, 2015; Hancox et al., 2015; Ryan et al., 2012; Silva et al., 2014).

Previous research has found a negative impact on intrinsic motivation when an external reward is given for the performance (Deci et al., 1999), while other studies find negative effects only for tasks that are not interesting in and of themselves (Cameron et al., 2001). When the task itself is interesting to the person (as might be an assignment that an instructor or manager has explained in terms of its importance and future value), external rewards may increase intrinsic motivation, at least in the short term. The bulk of current research seems to support this latter idea (Evans, 2015; Rigby et al., 2014; Silva et al., 2014). Researchers in this field are also using techniques such as fMRI to examine the role of the brain, particularly the ventromedial prefrontal cortex, in intrinsic and extrinsic motivation (Marsden et al., 2014; Murayama et al., 2015).

 But don't we sometimes do things for both kinds of motives?

How might this Japanese businessman be motivated differently than someone from another country and culture?

"That is the correct answer, Bill, but I'm afraid you don't win anything for it."

**self-determination theory (SDT)**

theory of human motivation in which the social context of an action has an effect on the type of motivation existing for the action.

There are usually elements of both intrinsic and extrinsic motives in many of the things people do. Most teachers, for example, work for money to pay bills (the extrinsic motive) but may also feel that they are helping young children become better adults in the future, which makes the teachers feel good about themselves (the intrinsic motive).

How universal are these three needs? Some cultures, such as the United States and Great Britain, are *individualistic*, stressing the needs of the individual over the group, independence, and self-reliance. Other cultures are collectivistic, such as those in Japan and China, and stress strong social ties, interdependence, and cooperation. Cross-cultural research indicates that even across such different cultures, the needs for autonomy, mastery, and belongingness are of similar importance (Chirkov, 2009; Chirkov et al., 2011; Ryan et al., 1999; Sheldon, 2012). The **APA Goal 2: Scientific Inquiry and Critical Thinking** feature looks at the effects of praise, a typical form of motivating achievement, across cultures.

## Concept Map L.O. 9.1, 9.2, 9.3, 9.4, 9.5

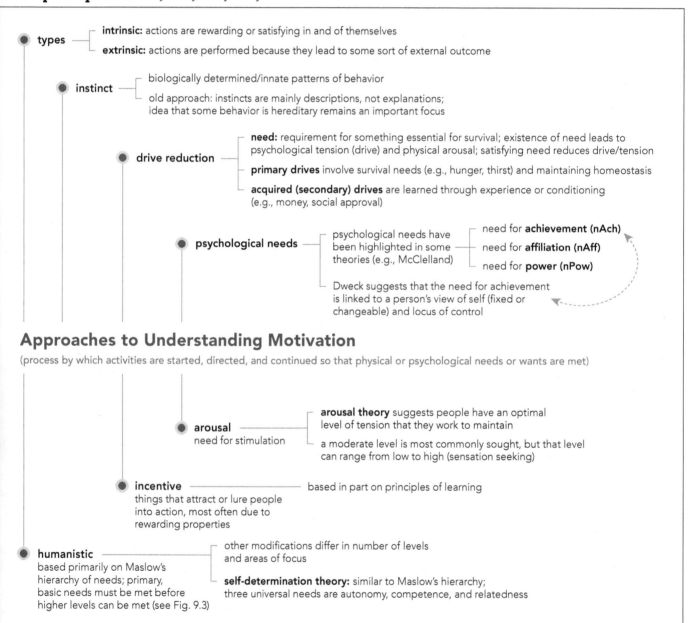

**Interactive**

- **types**
  - **intrinsic:** actions are rewarding or satisfying in and of themselves
  - **extrinsic:** actions are performed because they lead to some sort of external outcome

- **instinct**
  - biologically determined/innate patterns of behavior
  - old approach: instincts are mainly descriptions, not explanations; idea that some behavior is hereditary remains an important focus

- **drive reduction**
  - **need:** requirement for something essential for survival; existence of need leads to psychological tension (drive) and physical arousal; satisfying need reduces drive/tension
  - **primary drives** involve survival needs (e.g., hunger, thirst) and maintaining homeostasis
  - **acquired (secondary) drives** are learned through experience or conditioning (e.g., money, social approval)

- **psychological needs**
  - psychological needs have been highlighted in some theories (e.g., McClelland)
    - need for **achievement (nAch)**
    - need for **affiliation (nAff)**
    - need for **power (nPow)**
  - Dweck suggests that the need for achievement is linked to a person's view of self (fixed or changeable) and locus of control

## Approaches to Understanding Motivation

(process by which activities are started, directed, and continued so that physical or psychological needs or wants are met)

- **arousal**
  need for stimulation
  - **arousal theory** suggests people have an optimal level of tension that they work to maintain
  - a moderate level is most commonly sought, but that level can range from low to high (sensation seeking)

- **incentive**
  things that attract or lure people into action, most often due to rewarding properties
  — based in part on principles of learning

- **humanistic**
  based primarily on Maslow's hierarchy of needs; primary, basic needs must be met before higher levels can be met (see Fig. 9.3)
  - other modifications differ in number of levels and areas of focus
  - **self-determination theory:** similar to Maslow's hierarchy; three universal needs are autonomy, competence, and relatedness

Reset

# Practice Quiz How much do you remember?

*Pick the best answer.*

1. If a person carries out a behavior to receive an outcome that is separate from the person, this is known as
   a. intrinsic motivation.
   b. extrinsic motivation.
   c. drive-reduction motivation.
   d. instinctual motivation.

2. What motivational theory relies heavily on the concept of homeostasis?
   a. instinctual theory
   b. need for affiliation theory
   c. drive-reduction theory
   d. need for achievement theory

3. People high in the need for _____ want to be liked by others and are good team players.
   a. achievement
   b. affiliation
   c. power
   d. emotion

4. In terms of arousal and task difficulty, easy tasks typically demand a _____ level for optimal performance, whereas difficult tasks require a _____ level.
   a. high–moderate; low–moderate
   b. low–moderate; high–moderate
   c. either a high or low; medium
   d. low; low

5. In Maslow's theory, how often do people reach a point of self-actualization?
   a. Most people reach a state of self-actualization before they reach adulthood.
   b. Most people reach a state of self-actualization as they finish adolescence.
   c. Seldom, although there are times in a person's life when they are self-actualized at least temporarily.
   d. No one ever reaches the ultimate state. Our motivations express themselves in how we try to attain it.

6. In Ryan and Deci's self-determination theory, what is the key to achieving one's needs for autonomy, competence, and relatedness?
   a. an instinctual motivation
   b. support from others around you
   c. a motivation often driven by heredity
   d. a driving desire not to be a failure

## APA Goal 2: Scientific Inquiry and Critical Thinking: Cultural Differences in the Use of Praise as a Motivator

*Addresses APA Learning Objective 2.5: Incorporate sociocultural factors in scientific inquiry.*

In Western cultures, and particularly in the educational system of the United States, parents and children have been told to praise their children's achievements rather than using too much negative feedback and criticism (Trumbull & Rothstein-Fisch, 2011). The thinking behind this focus on positive reinforcement is that praise will boost a student's self-esteem, while excessive criticism will most likely do damage. In the individualistic culture of the United States, this does appear to work very well. But when the students are from a different cultural background, such as the more collectivistic Asian and Latin cultures, the story is quite different. What is sauce for the goose, you might say, is not always sauce for the gander.

In collectivistic cultures, it is more desirable to promote the welfare of the group rather than the individual. Students from these cultures who are singled out to receive praise, particularly in front of other classmates, may feel very uncomfortable to be "elevated" above their classmates. Instead of having the effect of motivating them to succeed, such praise might backfire, leading the student to underachieve so as to keep a lower profile, so to speak (Geary, 2001; Markus & Kitayama, 1991; Rothstein-Fisch & Trumbull, 2008; Trumbull & Rothstein-Fisch, 2011).

One study found that Latina students who were being taught English responded very negatively to the abundant praise given to them by their tutor, having been made uncomfortable by the positive reinforcement rather than bolstered by it (Geary, 2001; Trumbull

& Rothstein-Fisch, 2011). Other research found that, when compared to Canadian students, Japanese students were more critical of their own performances and more responsive to negative feedback (Heine et al., 2001). Contrary to what typical learning theory would predict, the benefits of positive reinforcement are not always as expected when dealing with very different cultural expectations.

---

**THINKING CRITICALLY**

Would the cultural differences in the effects of praise be likely to affect areas of daily life other than educational situations?

▶ | The response entered here will be saved to your notes and may be collected by your instructor if he/she requires it. |

[ Submit ]

---

# What, Hungry Again? Why People Eat

Satisfying hunger is one of our most primary needs. The eating habits of people today have become a major concern and a frequent topic of news programs, talk shows, and scientific research. Countless pills, supplements, and treatments are available to "help" people eat less and others to eat more. Eating is not only a basic survival behavior that reduces a primary drive; it is also a form of entertainment for many, and the attractive presentations and social environment of many eating experiences are a powerful incentive.

### PHYSIOLOGICAL AND SOCIAL COMPONENTS OF HUNGER

**9.6** **Identify the physical and social factors that influence hunger.**

 Why do we eat? What causes us to feel hungry in the first place?

There are actually several factors involved in the hunger drive. Walter Cannon (Cannon & Washburn, 1912) believed that stomach contractions, or "hunger pangs," caused hunger and that the presence of food in the stomach would stop the contractions and appease the hunger drive. Oddly enough, having an empty stomach is not the deciding factor in many cases. Although the stomach does have sensory receptors that respond to the pressure of the stretching stomach muscles as food is piled in and that send signals to the brain indicating that the stomach is full (Geliebter, 1988), people who have had their stomachs removed still get hungry (Janowitz, 1967).

**HORMONAL INFLUENCES**   One factor in hunger seems to be the insulin response that occurs after we begin to eat. **Insulin** and **glucagon** are hormones that are secreted by the pancreas to control the levels of fats, proteins, and carbohydrates in the whole body, including glucose (blood sugar). Insulin reduces the level of glucose in the bloodstream, for example, whereas glucagon increases the level. Insulin, normally released in greater amounts after eating has begun, causes a feeling of more hunger because of the drop in blood sugar levels. Carbohydrates, especially those that are simple or highly refined (such as table sugar, fruit drinks, white flour, and white bread or pasta), cause the insulin level to spike even more than other foods do because there

**insulin**

a hormone secreted by the pancreas to control the levels of fats, proteins, and carbohydrates in the body by reducing the level of glucose in the bloodstream.

**glucagon**

hormone that is secreted by the pancreas to control the levels of fats, proteins, and carbohydrates in the body by increasing the level of glucose in the bloodstream.

is such a large amount of glucose released by these foods at one time. High blood sugar leads to more insulin released, which leads to a low blood sugar level, increased appetite, and the tendency to overeat. That is the basic principle behind many of the diets that promote low carbohydrate intake. The proponents of these diets argue that if people control the carbohydrates, they can control the insulin reaction and prevent hunger cravings later on.

In recent years, a hormone called **leptin** has been identified as one of the factors that seems to control appetite. When released into the bloodstream, leptin signals the hypothalamus that the body has had enough food, reducing appetite and increasing the feeling of being full, or satiated. Genetic abnormalities in the receptors for leptin as well as leptin resistance may play an important role in obesity (Dubern & Clement, 2012; Pan et al., 2014).

**THE ROLE OF THE HYPOTHALAMUS**   The stomach and the pancreas are only two of the body parts involved in hunger. In Chapter Two, the role of the hypothalamus in controlling many kinds of motivational stimuli, including hunger, was seen as a result of its influence on the pituitary. But the hypothalamus itself has different areas, controlled by the levels of glucose and insulin in the body, which appear to control eating behavior.

The *ventromedial hypothalamus (VMH)* may be involved in stopping the eating response when glucose levels go up (Neary et al., 2004). In one study, rats whose VMH areas (located toward the bottom and center of the hypothalamus) were damaged would no longer stop eating—they ate and ate until they were quite overweight (Hetherington & Ranson, 1940). (See **Figure 9.4** for a picture of a rat with this kind of damage.) However, they did not eat everything in sight. They actually got rather picky, only overeating on food that appealed to them (Ferguson & Keesey, 1975; Parkinson & Weingarten, 1990). In fact, if all the food available to them was unappealing, they did not become obese and in some cases even lost weight.

Another part of the hypothalamus, located on the side and called the *lateral hypothalamus (LH)*, seems to influence the onset of eating when insulin levels go up (Neary et al., 2004). Damage to this area caused rats to stop eating to the point of starvation. They would eat only if force-fed and still lost weight under those conditions (Anand & Brobeck, 1951; Hoebel & Teitelbaum, 1966). Both of these areas of the hypothalamus are involved in the production of orexin-A, a neuropeptide (a small, protein-like molecule that neurons use to communicate) involved in appetite control (Li et al., 2014; Messina et al., 2014).

**WEIGHT SET POINT AND BASAL METABOLIC RATE**   Obviously, the role of the hypothalamus in eating behavior is complex. Some researchers (Leibel et al., 1995; Nisbett, 1972) believe that the hypothalamus affects the particular level of weight that the body tries to maintain, called the **weight set point**. Injury to the hypothalamus does raise or lower the weight set point rather dramatically, causing either drastic weight loss or weight gain.

Metabolism, the speed at which the body burns available energy, and exercise also play a part in the weight set point. Some people are no doubt genetically wired to have faster metabolisms, and those people can eat large amounts of food without gaining weight. Others have slower metabolisms and may eat a normal or even less-than-normal amount of food and still gain weight or have difficulty losing it (Bouchard et al., 1990; Higginson et al., 2016). (Some people swear they can gain weight just by *looking* at a piece of cake!) Regular, moderate exercise can help offset the slowing of metabolism and the increase in the weight set point that comes with it (Tremblay et al., 1999).

The rate at which the body burns energy when a person is resting is called the **basal metabolic rate (BMR)** and is directly tied to the set point. If a person's BMR decreases (as

**Figure 9.4**  Obese Laboratory Rat

The rat on the left has reached a high level of obesity because its ventromedial hypothalamus has been deliberately damaged in the laboratory. The result is a rat that no longer receives signals of being satiated, and so the rat continues to eat and eat and eat.

**leptin**

a hormone that, when released into the bloodstream, signals the hypothalamus that the body has had enough food and reduces the appetite while increasing the feeling of being full.

**weight set point**

the particular level of weight that the body tries to maintain.

**basal metabolic rate (BMR)**

the rate at which the body burns energy when the organism is resting.

it does in adulthood and with decreased activity levels), that person's weight set point increases if the same number of calories is consumed. **Figure 9.5** shows the changes in BMR of a typical woman and man as age increases from 10 to 80 years. Notice that the BMR decreases more dramatically as the age of the person increases. Adolescents typically have a very high BMR and activity level and, therefore, a lower weight set point, meaning they can eat far more than an adult of the same size and not gain weight. But when that adolescent becomes an adult, the BMR begins to decline. Adults should reduce the number of calories they consume and exercise most every day, but the tendency is to eat more and move less as income levels and job demands increase. Even if the eating habits of the teenage years are simply maintained, excessive weight gain is not far behind. (In some people, the excessive weight gain may be mostly "behind.")

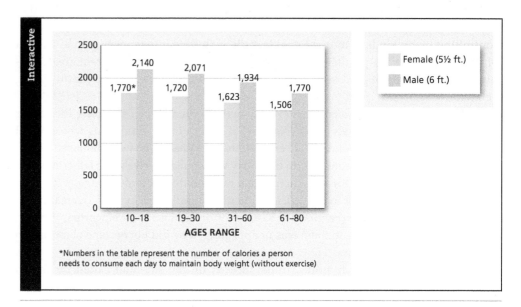

**Figure 9.5** Average BMR for a Female and Male

If you would like to calculate your own BMR, there are numerous Internet sites that allow a person to enter data such as height, age, weight, and activity level. The BMR is then automatically calculated according to a standard formula. Simply type "basal metabolic rate calculator" into your Web search engine to find these sites.

**SOCIAL COMPONENTS OF HUNGER** People often eat when they are not really hungry. There are all sorts of social cues that tell people to eat, such as the convention of eating breakfast, lunch, and dinner at certain times. A large part of that "convention" is actually the result of classical conditioning. **LINK** to Learning Objective 5.2. The body becomes conditioned to respond with the hunger reflex at certain times of the day; through association with the act of eating, those times of the day have become conditioned stimuli for hunger. Sometimes a person who has just eaten a late breakfast will still "feel" hungry at noon, simply because the clock says it's time to eat. People also respond to the appeal of food. How many times has someone finished a huge meal only to be tempted by that luscious-looking cheesecake on the dessert cart? To see whether you have any implicit preferences toward either healthy food or junk food, participate in the experiment *Implicit Association Test: Food.* **Simulate** the **Experiment,** *Implicit Association Test: Food*

Food can also be used in times of stress as a comforting routine, an immediate escape from whatever is unpleasant (Dallman et al., 2003). Rodin (1981, 1985) found that the insulin levels that create hunger may actually increase *before* food is eaten (similar to the way Pavlov's dogs began salivating before they received their food). Like getting hungry at a certain time of day, this physiological phenomenon may also be due to classical conditioning: In the past, eating foods with certain visual and sensory characteristics led to an insulin spike, and this pairing occurred so frequently that now just looking at or smelling the food produces the spike before the food is consumed (Stockhorst, 1999). This may explain why some people (who are called "externals" because of their tendency to focus on the external features of food rather than internal hunger) are far more responsive to these external signals—they produce far more insulin in response to the *anticipation* of eating than do nonexternals, or people who are less affected by external cues (Rodin, 1985).

Cultural factors and gender also play a part in determining hunger and eating habits. In one study, a questionnaire about eating habits was given to both men and women from the United States and Japan. Although no significant differences in what initiates eating existed for men in either culture, women in the United States were found to be much more likely to start eating for emotional reasons, such as depression. Japanese women were more likely to eat because of hunger signals or social demands (Hawks et al., 2003). In this same study, both men and women from the United States were more likely to eat while watching television or movies than were Japanese men and women. Both culture and gender must be taken into account when studying why and under what circumstances people eat.

### OBESITY

**9.7** **Recognize some of the factors that contribute to obesity.**

It would be nice if people all over the world ate just the amount of food that they needed and were able to maintain a healthy, normal weight. Unfortunately, that is not the case for many people. Some people weigh far more than they should, whereas others weigh far less.

Several maladaptive eating problems, including anorexia nervosa, bulimia nervosa, and binge-eating disorder, are classified as clinical (mental) disorders in the *Diagnostic and Statistical Manual of Mental Disorders, Fifth Edition*, or *DSM-5* (American Psychiatric Association, 2013), which is a listing of disorders and their symptoms used by psychological professionals to make a diagnosis. These disorders are discussed in a later chapter. (L I N K) to Learning Objective 14.11.

In this chapter, we look at the problem of obesity. Why do some people get so fat? Is it just overeating?

There are several factors that contribute to *obesity*, a condition in which the body weight of a person is 20 percent or more over the ideal body weight for that person's height. Actual definitions of obesity vary. Some definitions consider 20 to 30 percent to be overweight and limit obesity to 30 percent or more. Others state that men are obese at 20 percent over the ideal weight and women at 30 percent. However it is defined, a significant factor in obesity is heredity. There appear to be several sets of genes, some on different chromosomes, that influence a person's likelihood of becoming obese (Barsh et al., 2000). If there is a history of obesity in a particular family, each family member has a risk of becoming obese that is double or triple the risk of people who do not have a family history of obesity (Bouchard, 1997). Hormones also play a role, particularly leptin, which plays an important part in controlling appetite. Problems with leptin production or detection can lead to overeating (Friedman & Halaas, 1998), although this may not be the whole story. In a study in which leptin action was blocked in both obese and nonobese mice, there were no differences between the two groups in how much they ate or how much weight they gained, leading the researchers to conclude that impaired leptin activity may not be as important a cause of obesity as previously thought (Ottaway et al., 2015).

Certainly, another obesity factor is overeating. Around the world, as developing countries build stronger economies and their food supplies become stable, the rates of

(top) Cultural factors play an important part in why people eat. Women in Japan have been found to be motivated to eat by hunger and social demands, illustrated by the interaction during a meal at this family gathering.

(bottom) Women in the United States may eat because they are depressed or for other emotional reasons rather than just to appease hunger or as part of a social situation. Obviously, this woman does not need the social trappings of a bowl, dining table, and the company of others to motivate her eating habits—unless you count the cat.

This family is becoming more typical in the United States as obesity rates continue to rise. How much of the excess weight on each of these family members is caused by poor choices in diet and lack of exercise, and how much might be caused by inherited biological factors?

obesity increase dramatically and quickly (Barsh et al., 2000). Foods become more varied and enticing* as well, and an increase in variety is associated with an increase in eating beyond the physiological need to eat (Raynor & Epstein, 2001). In industrialized societies, when workers spend more hours in the workplace, there is less time available for preparing meals at home and more incentive to dine out (Chou et al., 2004). When the "dining out" choices include fast food and soft drinks, as is so often the case, obesity rates increase. In sum, as cultures become more industrialized and follow Western-culture lifestyles, negative aspects of those lifestyles, such as obesity, also increase. Over the last 20 years, rates of obesity in developing countries have tripled. Specifically, this is a trend in countries that have adopted the Western lifestyle of lower exercise rates and overeating—especially those foods that are cheap but high in fat and calories. In China, as well as many countries in the Middle East, Southeast Asia, and the Pacific Islands, 10 to 25 percent of children have been found to be overweight and another 2 to 10 percent are obese (Hawley et al., 2014; Hawley & McGarvey, 2015; Hossain et al., 2007).

Stress also contributes to obesity. One study found that female children of military personnel, for example, seem to be at a higher risk for eating disorders, including obesity, a risk that may be associated with higher rates of depression (Schvey et al., 2015). Related to stress is how much sleep we get, and sleep disturbances are also a factor in weight gain (Roane et al., 2015). ⓁⒾⓃⓀ to Chapter Four: *APA Goal 2: Scientific Inquiry and Critical Thinking: Weight Gain and Sleep.*

As mentioned earlier, metabolism slows down as people age. Aside from not changing the eating habits of their youth and lowering their intake, as they earn more income, people also often increase the amount of food they consume, thereby assuring a weight gain that may lead to obesity. The United States has the highest rate of obesity in the world: A third of its population is now obese (Flegal et al., 2012; Friedman, 2000, 2003; Marik, 2000; Mokdad et al., 2001; Ng et al., 2014; Ogden et al., 2014).

*enticing: attractive, desirable.

## Concept Map L.O. 9.6, 9.7

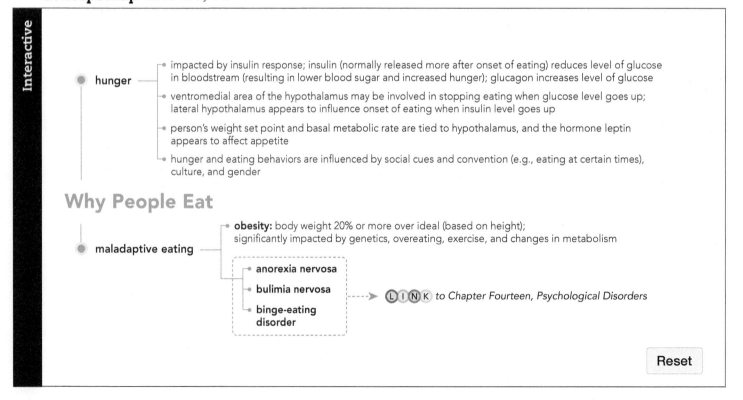

**Why People Eat**

- hunger
  - impacted by insulin response; insulin (normally released more after onset of eating) reduces level of glucose in bloodstream (resulting in lower blood sugar and increased hunger); glucagon increases level of glucose
  - ventromedial area of the hypothalamus may be involved in stopping eating when glucose level goes up; lateral hypothalamus appears to influence onset of eating when insulin level goes up
  - person's weight set point and basal metabolic rate are tied to hypothalamus, and the hormone leptin appears to affect appetite
  - hunger and eating behaviors are influenced by social cues and convention (e.g., eating at certain times), culture, and gender

- maladaptive eating
  - **obesity:** body weight 20% or more over ideal (based on height); significantly impacted by genetics, overeating, exercise, and changes in metabolism
  - anorexia nervosa
  - bulimia nervosa
  - binge-eating disorder

⟶ ⓁⒾⓃⓀ to Chapter Fourteen, *Psychological Disorders*

Reset

# Practice Quiz   How much do you remember?

*Pick the best answer.*

**1.** Damage to the _____ in rats can cause them to starve to
death, while damage to the _____ will cause them to eat and
eat and eat.
   **a.** pancreas; stomach
   **b.** liver; kidneys
   **c.** ventromedial hypothalamus; lateral hypothalamus
   **d.** lateral hypothalamus; ventromedial hypothalamus

**2.** If calorie intake stays the same, as the basal metabolic rate
decreases, the weight set point
   **a.** decreases.        **c.** stays the same.
   **b.** increases.        **d.** varies up and down.

**3.** Jermaine eats a late breakfast at 10:00 A.M. but finds he is hungry
at 11:30 A.M. when he typically eats lunch. What best explains his
hunger pains only 90 minutes after eating breakfast?
   **a.** heredity                    **c.** classical conditioning
   **b.** social pressure             **d.** self-actualization

**4.** In cultures in which Western lifestyles of eating and exercising
have been adopted, obesity rates have _____ over the
last 20 years.
   **a.** remained relatively stable   **c.** doubled
   **b.** decreased slightly           **d.** tripled

# Emotion

This chapter began with an overview of the motives that drive human behavior. But people
do more than just behave—they experience feelings during every human action. Human
beings are full of feelings, or emotions, and although emotions may be internal processes,
there are outward physical signs of what people are feeling. This section of the chapter
explores the world of human emotions and how those emotions are connected to both thinking and actions. Before we begin, take a moment to take the survey *How Do You Deal With
Your Emotions?* to learn more about how you identify, express, and manage your emotions.

**Survey**   HOW DO YOU DEAL WITH YOUR EMOTIONS?

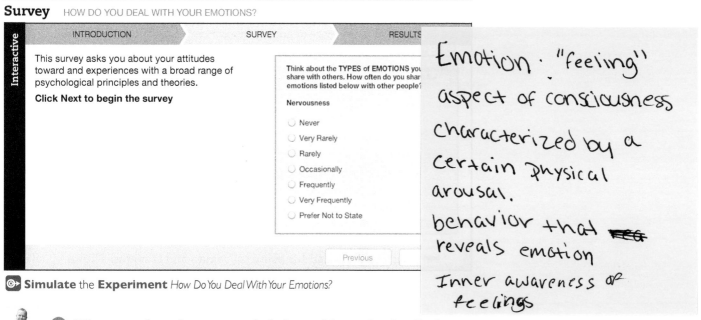

**Simulate** the **Experiment** *How Do You Deal With Your Emotions?*

💬 What part does the way we feel about things play in all of our
daily activities—what exactly causes feelings?

   Human beings are full of feelings, or emotions, and although emotions may be
internal processes, there are outward physical signs of what people are feeling.

## THE THREE ELEMENTS OF EMOTION

### 9.8  Describe the three elements of emotion.

The Latin root word *mot*, meaning "to move," is the source of both of the words we use in this
chapter over and over again—*motive* and *emotion*. **Emotion** can be defined as the "feeling"

**emotion**

the "feeling" aspect of consciousness,
characterized by a certain physical
arousal, a certain behavior that reveals
the emotion to the outside world, and
an inner awareness of feelings.

aspect of consciousness, characterized by three elements: a certain physical arousal, a certain behavior that reveals the feeling to the outside world, and an inner awareness of the feeling.

**THE PHYSIOLOGY OF EMOTION**  Physically, when a person experiences an emotion, an arousal is created by the sympathetic nervous system. Ⓛ Ⓘ Ⓝ Ⓚ to Learning Objective 2.5. The heart rate increases, breathing becomes more rapid, the pupils dilate, and the mouth may become dry. Think about the last time you were angry and then about the last time you were frightened. Weren't the physical symptoms pretty similar? Although facial expressions do differ among various emotional responses (Ekman, 1980; Ekman et al., 1969; Ekman & Friesen, 1978), emotions are difficult to distinguish from one another on the basis of physiological reactions alone. However, in the laboratory using devices to measure the heart rate, blood pressure, and skin temperature, researchers have found that different emotions may be associated with different physiological reactions: Sadness, anger, and fear are associated with greater increases in heart rate than is disgust; higher increases in skin conductance occur during disgust as compared to happiness; and anger is more often associated with vascular measures, such as higher diastolic blood pressure, as compared to fear (Larsen et al., 2008; Levenson, 1992; Levenson et al., 1992).

The polygraph test was originally designed as a kind of "lie detector" test in the early 1900s. The idea was that lying would produce different physiological reactions from telling the truth (Bell & Grubin, 2010; Iacono, 2001). This assumption has proven to be false: There is no specific, unique physiological reaction associated with lying versus telling the truth. There have been improvements added to the original polygraph test such as the use of questions about knowledge that only the police, the victim, and the suspect should know (Concealed Information Test, or CIT), but there is still a great deal of controversy over the validity of the results (Ben-Shakhar et al., 2015; Palmatier & Rovner, 2015; Vrij, 2015). While it may be a useful tool to convince suspects to confess to their crimes, it really only detects the physiological correlates of emotion in general, not lying in specific, and is not admissible as evidence of guilt or innocence in a courtroom in the United States.

Which parts of the brain are involved in various aspects of emotion? As discussed in Chapter Two, the *amygdala*, a small area located within the limbic system on each side of the brain, is associated with emotions such as fear and pleasure in both humans and animals (Breiter et al., 1997; Davis & Whalen, 2001; Fanselow & Gale, 2003; Hurlemann et al., 2010; Ritchey et al., 2011) and is also involved in the facial expressions of human emotions (Morris et al., 1998).

When portions of the amygdala are damaged in rats, the animals cannot be classically conditioned to fear new objects—they apparently cannot remember to be afraid (Nader et al., 2000; Fanselow & Gale, 2003). In humans, damage to the amygdala has been associated with similar effects (LaBar et al., 1995) and with impairment of the ability to interpret emotions from looking at the facial expressions of others (Adolphs & Tranel, 2003).

Much of what we know about the amygdala's role in emotion comes from the work of Joseph LeDoux and his many colleagues and students. The amygdala is a complex structure with many different nuclei and subdivisions, whose roles have been explored primarily through studies of fear conditioning (LeDoux & Phelps, 2008). Fear conditioning has been very helpful in relating behaviors to brain function because it results in stereotypical autonomic and behavioral responses. It is basically a classical conditioning procedure in which an auditory stimulus (conditioned stimulus) is paired with foot shock (unconditioned stimulus) to elicit autonomic and behavioral conditioned responses (LeDoux, 1996; LeDoux & Phelps, 2008).

LeDoux's work has provided many insights into the brain's processing of emotional information and the role of the amygdala. Emotional stimuli travel to the amygdala by both a fast, crude "low road" (subcortical) and a slower but more involved cortical "high road" (LeDoux, 1996, 2007; LeDoux & Phelps, 2008). (See **Figure 9.6**.) The direct route allows for quick responses to stimuli that are possibly dangerous, sometimes before we actually know what the stimuli are, but with the awareness provided by the indirect cortical route

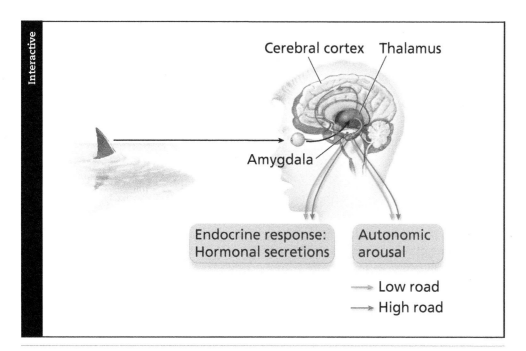

**Figure 9.6** The "Low Road" and "High Road"

When we are exposed to an emotion-provoking stimulus (such as a shark), the neural signals travel by two pathways to the amygdala. The "low road" is the pathway underneath the cortex and is a faster, simpler path, allowing for quick responses to the stimulus, sometimes before we are consciously aware of the nature of the stimulus. The "high road" uses cortical pathways and is slower and more complex, but it allows us to recognize the threat and, when needed, take more conscious control of our emotional responses. In this particular example, the low road shouts, "Danger!" and we react before the high road says, "It's a shark!"

(specifically, processing by the prefrontal cortex), we can override the direct route and take control of our emotional responses (LeDoux, 1996; LeDoux & Phelps, 2008; Öhman, 2008).

LeDoux's work also provides a mechanism for understanding psychological disorders related to anxiety or fear. Ⓛⓘⓝⓚ to Learning Objective 14.4. It is possible that the direct route may be the primary processing pathway for individuals with anxiety disorders and the indirect, cortical pathway is not able to override the processing initiated by the direct route. This would result in difficulty or inability to control our anxieties or the inability to extinguish fears we've already acquired (LeDoux, 1996; LeDoux & Phelps, 2008).

Besides the amygdala, other subcortical and cortical areas of the brain are involved in the processing of emotional information (Frank et al., 2014; Treadway et al., 2014). Research suggests that emotions may work differently depending on which side of the brain is involved. One area of investigation has been the frontal lobes. Researchers have found that positive emotions are associated with the left frontal lobe of the brain, whereas negative feelings such as sadness, anxiety, and depression seem to be a function of the right frontal lobe (R. J. Davidson, 2003; Garland et al., 2015; Geschwind & Iacoboni, 2007; Heilman, 2002). In studies in which the electrical activity of the brain has been tracked using an electroencephalograph, Ⓛⓘⓝⓚ to Learning Objective 2.9, left frontal lobe activation has been associated with pleasant emotions, while right frontal lobe activity has been associated with negative emotional states (R. J. Davidson, 2003). Furthermore, increased left frontal lobe activity has been found in individuals trained in meditation, and for the participants in this study, greater left frontal lobe activity was accompanied by a reduction in their anxiety as well as a boost in their immune system (Garland et al., 2015; R. J. Davidson et al., 2003).

The ability to interpret the facial expressions of others as a particular emotion also seems to be a function of one side of the brain more than the other. Researchers have found that when people are asked to identify the emotion on another person's face, the right hemisphere is more active than the left, particularly in women (Voyer & Rodgers, 2002). This difference begins weakly in childhood but increases in adulthood, with children being less able to identify negative emotions as well as they can positive emotions when compared to adults (Barth & Boles, 1999; Lane et al., 1995). This finding is consistent with early research that assigns the recognition of faces to the right hemisphere (Berent, 1977; Ellis, 1983).

Other types of emotional processing involve a variety of other brain areas. Have you ever been told to control your emotions? Different brain areas take primary roles based on the different ways you try to control your emotions, but there is a degree of overlap across several of the strategies. For example, some common strategies for regulating one's emotions include distraction, reappraisal, and controlling the influence of emotions on decision making. All three of these strategies take advantage of the lateral prefrontal cortex and anterior cingulate cortex and, as you might expect from the discussion before, the amygdala also comes into play (J. S. Beer, 2009).

However, distraction appears to be supported by activity in the anterior cingulate cortex, and reappraisal is supported by activity in the lateral orbitofrontal cortex; and both are accompanied by lower activity in the amygdala (J. S. Beer, 2009). Furthermore, distraction and reappraisal may engage more brain areas in general as compared to spontaneous control of emotions in decision making. Generally, brain areas associated with emotional control are the same brain areas responsible for control of nonemotional information (J. S. Beer, 2009; Buhle et al., 2014; Etkin et al., 2011).

**THE BEHAVIOR OF EMOTION: EMOTIONAL EXPRESSION**  How do people behave when in the grip of an emotion? There are facial expressions, body movements, and actions that indicate to others how a person feels. Frowns, smiles, and sad expressions combine with hand gestures, the turning of one's body, and spoken words to produce an understanding of emotion. People fight, run, kiss, and yell, along with countless other actions stemming from the emotions they feel.

Facial expressions can vary across different cultures, although some aspects of facial expression seem to be universal. (See **Figure 9.7** for some examples of universal

**Figure 9.7**  Facial Expressions of Emotion

Facial expressions appear to be universal. For example, these faces are consistently interpreted as showing (a) anger, (b) fear, (c) disgust, (d) happiness, (e) surprise, and (f) sadness by people of various cultures from all over the world. Although the situations that cause these emotions may differ from culture to culture, the expression of particular emotions remains strikingly the same.

facial expressions.) Charles Darwin (1898) was one of the first to theorize that emotions were a product of evolution and, therefore, universal—all human beings, no matter what their culture, would show the same facial expression because the facial muscles evolved to communicate specific information to onlookers. For example, an angry face would signal to onlookers that they should act submissively or expect a fight. Although Darwin's ideas were not in line with the behaviorist movement of the early and middle twentieth century, which promoted environment rather than heredity as the cause of behavior, other researchers have since found evidence that there is a universal nature to at least seven basic emotions, giving more support to the evolutionary perspective within psychology (Ekman, 1973; Ekman & Friesen, 1969, 1971). Ⓛ Ⓘ Ⓝ Ⓚ to Learning Objective 1.3. Even children who are blind from birth can produce the appropriate facial expressions for any given situation without ever having witnessed those expressions on others, which strongly supports the idea that emotional expressions have their basis in biology rather than in learning (Charlesworth & Kreutzer, 1973; Fulcher, 1942).

In their research, Ekman and Friesen found that people of many different cultures (including Japanese, European, American, and the Fore tribe of New Guinea) can consistently recognize at least seven facial expressions: anger, fear, disgust, happiness, surprise, sadness, and contempt (Ekman & Friesen, 1969, 1971). Although the emotions and the related facial expressions appear to be universal, exactly when, where, and how an emotion is expressed may be determined by the culture. **Display rules** that can vary from culture to culture (Ekman, 1973; Ekman & Friesen, 1969) are learned ways of controlling displays of emotion in social settings. For example, Japanese people have strict social rules about showing emotion in public situations—they simply do not show emotion, remaining cool, calm, and collected, at least on the *outside*. But if in a more private situation, as a parent scolding a child within the home, the adult's facial expression would easily be recognized as "angry" by people of any culture. The emotion is universal and the way it is expressed on the face is universal, but whether it is expressed or displayed depends on the learned cultural rules for displaying emotion.

Display rules are different between cultures that are *individualistic* (placing the importance of the individual above the social group) and those that are *collectivistic* (placing the importance of the social group above that of the individual). Whereas the culture of the United States is individualistic, for example, the culture of Japan is collectivistic. At least part of the difference between the two types of display rules may be due to these cultural differences (Edelmann & Iwawaki, 1987; Hofstede, 1980; Hofstede et al., 2002). Ⓛ Ⓘ Ⓝ Ⓚ to Learning Objective 13.13.

Display rules are also different for males and females. Researchers looking at the display rules of boys and girls found that boys are reluctant to talk about feelings in a social setting, whereas girls are expected and encouraged to do so (Polce-Lynch et al., 1998). With adults, researchers looking at the expression of anger in the workplace found that women are generally less willing than men to express negative emotions, although factors such as status complicate the findings somewhat (Domagalski & Steelman, 2007).

Crying is also an emotional behavior—we cry for many different reasons such as being sad, grieving, angry, or even happy. While most of us don't like to cry, many people seem to think that "a good cry" can make them feel better. Researchers in one study examined the effects of crying on mood both immediately after participants watched two emotionally charged films and after a delay (Gračanin et al., 2015). They found a fascinating difference between the people who cried and those who did not: While the mood of those who did not cry was not affected immediately, those who cried experienced a slight dip in mood immediately but an increase in positive mood after a delay. This may explain why many people claim to feel "better" after crying.

How might the display rules for this family differ if they were in a public place rather than at home?

**display rules**

learned ways of controlling displays of emotion in social settings.

**SUBJECTIVE EXPERIENCE: LABELING EMOTION** The third element of emotion is interpreting the subjective feeling by giving it a label: anger, fear, disgust, happiness, sadness, shame, interest, and so on. Another way of labeling this element is to call it the "cognitive element," because the labeling process is a matter of retrieving memories of previous similar experiences, perceiving the context of the emotion, and coming up with a solution—a label.

The label a person applies to a subjective feeling is at least in part a learned response influenced by their language and culture. Such labels may differ in people of different cultural backgrounds. For example, researchers in one study (J. L. Tsai et al., 2004) found that Chinese Americans who were still firmly rooted in their original Chinese culture were far more likely to use labels to describe their emotions that referred to bodily sensations (such as "dizzy") or social relationships (such as "friendship") than were more "Americanized" Chinese Americans and European Americans, who tended to use more directly emotional words (such as "liking" or "love").

In another study, even the subjective feeling of happiness showed cultural differences (Kitayama & Markus, 1994). In this study, Japanese students and students from the United States were found to associate a general positive emotional state with entirely different circumstances. In the case of the Japanese students, the positive state was more associated with friendly or socially engaged feelings. The students from the United States associated their positive emotional state more with feelings that were socially disengaged, such as pride. This finding is a further reflection of the differences between collectivistic and individualistic cultures. A major goal for psychologists engaged in cross-cultural research in emotions is to attempt to understand the meaning of other people's mental and emotional states without interpreting them incorrectly, or misleadingly, in the language or mindset of the researchers (Shweder et al., 2008).

### EARLY THEORIES OF EMOTION

**9.9** **Distinguish among the common-sense, James-Lange, Cannon-Bard, and facial feedback theories of emotion.**

  So which of the three elements is the most important?

In the early days of psychology, it was assumed that feeling a particular emotion led first to a physical reaction and then to a behavioral one. According to this viewpoint—we'll call it *the common-sense theory* of emotion—seeing a snarling dog in one's path causes the feeling of fear, which stimulates the body to arousal, followed by the behavioral act of running; that is, people are aroused because they are afraid. (See **Figure 9.8**.)

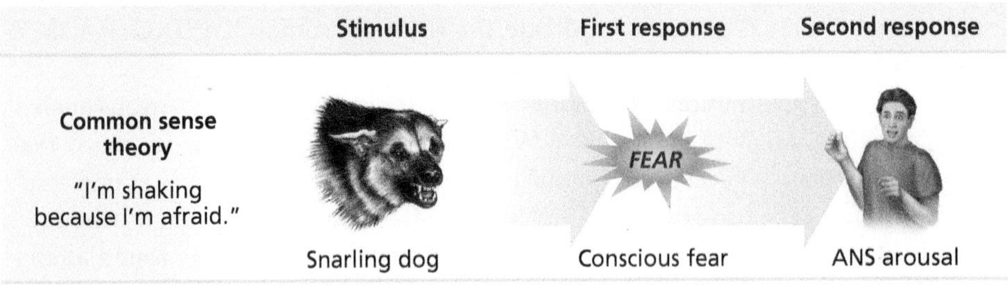

| | Stimulus | First response | Second response |
|---|---|---|---|
| **Common sense theory**<br>"I'm shaking because I'm afraid." | Snarling dog | FEAR<br>Conscious fear | ANS arousal |

**Figure 9.8** Common-Sense Theory of Emotion

In the common-sense theory of emotion, a stimulus (snarling dog) leads to an emotion of fear, which then leads to bodily arousal (in this case, indicated by shaking) through the autonomic nervous system (ANS).

**JAMES-LANGE THEORY OF EMOTION**   William James (1884, 1890, 1894), who was also the founder of the functionalist perspective in the early history of psychology, Ⓛ Ⓘ Ⓝ Ⓚ to Learning Objective 1.1, disagreed with the common-sense viewpoint. He believed that the order of the components of emotions was quite different. At nearly the same time, a physiologist and psychologist in Denmark, Carl Lange (1885), came up with an explanation of emotion so similar to that of James that the two names are used together to refer to the theory—the **James-Lange theory of emotion**. (See **Figure 9.9**.)

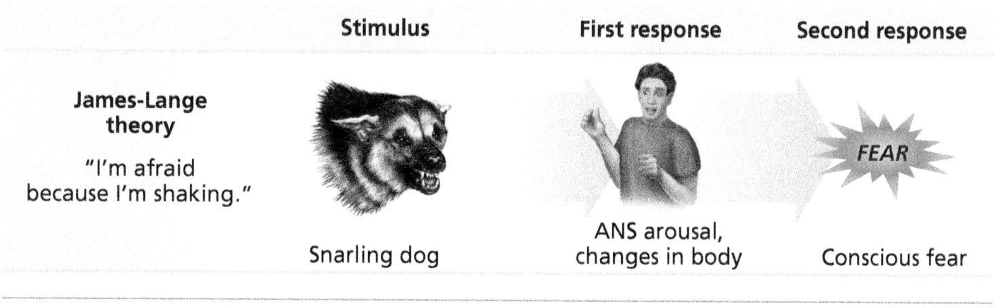

**Figure 9.9**   James-Lange Theory of Emotion

In the James-Lange theory of emotion, a stimulus leads to bodily arousal first, which is then interpreted as an emotion.

In this theory, a stimulus of some sort (for example, the large snarling dog) produces a physiological reaction. This reaction, which is the arousal of the "fight-or-flight" sympathetic nervous system (wanting to run), produces bodily sensations such as increased heart rate, dry mouth, and rapid breathing. James and Lange believed that the physical arousal led to the labeling of the emotion (fear). Simply put, "I am afraid because I am aroused," "I am embarrassed because my face is red," "I am nervous because my stomach is fluttering," and "I am in love because my heart rate increases when I look at her (or him)."

What about people who have spinal cord injuries that prevent the sympathetic nervous system from functioning? Although James-Lange would predict that these people should show decreased emotion because the arousal that causes emotion is no longer there, this does not in fact happen. Several studies of people with spinal cord injuries report that these people are capable of experiencing the same emotions after their injury as before, sometimes even more intensely (Bermond et al., 1991; Chwalisz et al., 1988).

**CANNON-BARD THEORY OF EMOTION**   Physiologists Walter Cannon (1927) and Philip Bard (1934) theorized that the emotion and the physiological arousal occur more or less at the same time. Cannon, an expert in sympathetic arousal mechanisms, did not feel that the physical changes caused by various emotions were distinct enough to allow them to be perceived as different emotions. Bard expanded on this idea by stating that the sensory information that comes into the brain is sent simultaneously (by the thalamus) to both the cortex and the organs of the sympathetic nervous system. The fear and the bodily reactions are, therefore, experienced at the same time—not one after the other. "I'm afraid and running and aroused!" (See **Figure 9.10**.)

This theory, known as the **Cannon-Bard theory of emotion**, also had its critics. Lashley (1938) stated that the thalamus would have to be pretty sophisticated to make sense of all the possible human emotions and relay them to the proper areas of the cortex and body. It would seem that other areas of the brain must be involved in processing emotional reactions. The studies of people with spinal cord injuries, which appear to suggest that emotions can be experienced without feedback from the sympathetic organs to the

**James-Lange theory of emotion**
theory in which a physiological reaction leads to the labeling of an emotion.

**Cannon-Bard theory of emotion**
theory in which the physiological reaction and the emotion are assumed to occur at the same time.

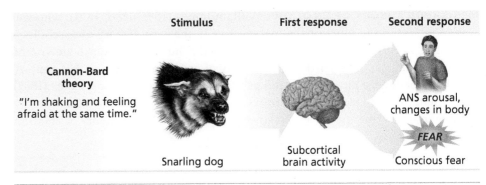

**Figure 9.10**  Cannon-Bard Theory of Emotion

In the Cannon-Bard theory of emotion, a stimulus leads to activity in the brain, which then sends signals to arouse the body and interpret the emotion at the same time.

cortex and were cited as a criticism of the James-Lange theory, seem at first to support the Cannon-Bard version of emotions: People do not need feedback from those organs to experience emotion. However, there is an alternate pathway that does provide feedback from these organs to the cortex; this is the *vagus nerve*, one of the cranial nerves (LeDoux, 1994). The existence of this feedback pathway makes the case for Cannon-Bard a little less convincing.

**THE FACIAL FEEDBACK HYPOTHESIS: SMILE, YOU'LL FEEL BETTER**    In his 1898 book *The Expression of the Emotions in Man and Animals*, Charles Darwin stated that facial expressions evolved as a way of communicating intentions, such as threat or fear, and that these expressions are universal within a species rather than specific to a culture. He also believed (as in the James-Lange theory) that when such emotions are expressed freely on the face, the emotion itself intensifies—meaning that the more one smiles, the happier one feels.

Psychologists proposed a theory of emotion that was consistent with much of Darwin's original thinking. Called the **facial feedback hypothesis**, this explanation assumes that facial expressions provide feedback to the brain concerning the emotion being expressed, which in turn not only intensifies the emotion but also actually *causes* the emotion (Buck, 1980; Ekman, 1980; Ekman & Friesen, 1978; Keillor et al., 2002). (See **Figure 9.11**.)

 💬 Does that mean that I don't smile because I'm happy—I'm happy because I smile?

As the old song goes, "put on a happy face" and yes, you'll feel happier, according to the facial feedback hypothesis. One study does cast some doubt on the validity of this

**facial feedback hypothesis**

theory of emotion that assumes that facial expressions provide feedback to the brain concerning the emotion being expressed, which in turn causes and intensifies the emotion.

**Figure 9.11**  Facial Feedback Theory of Emotion

In the facial feedback theory of emotion, a stimulus such as this snarling dog causes arousal and a facial expression. The facial expression then provides feedback to the brain about the emotion. The brain then interprets the emotion and may also intensify it.

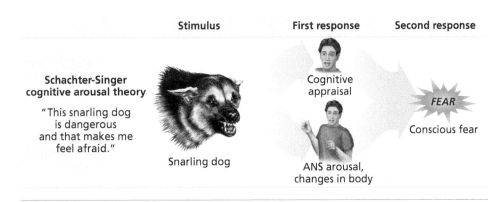

Stimulus          First response          Second response

Schachter-Singer
cognitive arousal theory

"This snarling dog
is dangerous
and that makes me
feel afraid."

Snarling dog

Cognitive
appraisal

*FEAR*

Conscious fear

ANS arousal,
changes in body

**Figure 9.12** Schachter-Singer Cognitive Arousal Theory of Emotion
Schachter and Singer's cognitive arousal theory is similar to the James-Lange theory but adds the element of cognitive labeling of the arousal. In this theory, a stimulus leads to both bodily arousal and the labeling of that arousal (based on the surrounding context), which leads to the experience and labeling of the emotional reaction.

The facial feedback hypothesis assumes that changing your own facial expression can change the way you feel. Smiling makes people feel happy, and frowning makes people feel sad. This effect seems to have an impact on the people around us as well. Is it hard for you to stay in a bad mood when the people around you are smiling and laughing?

hypothesis, however. If the facial feedback hypothesis is correct, then people who have facial paralysis on both sides of the face should be unable to experience emotions in a normal way. But a case study conducted on just such a person revealed that although she was unable to express emotions on her paralyzed face, she could respond emotionally to slides meant to stimulate emotional reactions, just as anyone else would (Keillor et al., 2002). Clearly, the question of how much the actual facial expression determines the emotional experience has yet to be fully answered.

### COGNITIVE THEORIES OF EMOTION

**9.10** **Identify the key elements in the cognitive arousal and cognitive-mediational theories of emotion.**

The early theories talked about the emotion and the physical reaction, but what about the mental interpretation of those components?

**COGNITIVE AROUSAL THEORY** In their **cognitive arousal theory (two-factor theory)**, Schachter and Singer (1962) proposed that two things have to happen before emotion occurs: the physical arousal and a labeling of the arousal based on cues from the surrounding environment. These two things happen at the same time, resulting in the labeling of the emotion. (See **Figure 9.12**.)

For example, if a person comes across a snarling dog while taking a walk, the physical arousal (heart racing, eyes opening wide) is accompanied by the thought (cognition) that this must be fear. Then and only then will the person experience the fear emotion. In other words, "I am aroused in the presence of a scary dog; therefore, I must be afraid." Evidence for this theory was found in what is now a classic experiment, described in the accompanying Classic Studies in Psychology.

## Classic Studies in Psychology
### The Angry/Happy Man

In 1962, Stanley Schachter and Jerome Singer designed an experiment to test their theory that emotions are determined by an interaction between the physiological state of arousal and the label, or cognitive interpretation, that a person places on the arousal.

**cognitive arousal theory (two-factor theory)**

theory of emotion in which both the physical arousal and the labeling of that arousal based on cues from the environment must occur before the emotion is experienced.

Male student volunteers were told that they were going to answer a questionnaire about their reactions to a new vitamin called Suproxin. In reality, they were all injected with a drug called epinephrine, which causes physical arousal in the form of increased heart rate, rapid breathing, and a reddened face—all responses that happen during a strong emotional reaction.

Each student then participated in one of two conditions. In one condition, a confederate* posing as one of the participants started complaining about the experimenter, tearing up his questionnaire and storming out. In the other condition, there was one man who acted more like he was very happy, almost giddy, and playing with some of the objects in the room. The "angry" man and the "happy" man in both conditions deliberately behaved in the two different ways as part of the experiment.

After both conditions had played out, participants in each of the two conditions were asked to describe their own emotions. The participants who had been exposed to the "angry" man interpreted their arousal symptoms as anger, whereas those exposed to the "happy" man interpreted their arousal as happiness. In all cases, the actual cause of arousal was the epinephrine and the physical symptoms of arousal were identical. The only difference between the two groups of participants was their exposure to the two different contexts. Schachter and Singer's theory would have predicted exactly these results: Physiological arousal has to be interpreted cognitively before it is experienced as a specific emotion.

Although this classic experiment stimulated a lot of research, much of that research has failed to find much support for the cognitive arousal theory of emotion (Reisenzein, 1983, 1994). But this theory did serve to draw attention to the important role that cognition plays in determining emotions. The role of cognition in emotion has been revisited in some more modern theories of emotion, as you will see in the remainder of the chapter.

## Questions for Further Discussion

1. How might observing the emotions of others under more normal circumstances (i.e., not in a drugged state) affect a person's own emotional state?

2. According to Schachter and Singer's theory, for your first date with a person, should you choose a happy movie or a sad one?

3. In this experiment, what was the independent variable manipulated by the experimenters? What was the dependent variable?

4. This experiment used deception, as the participants were not told the true nature of the injection they received. What kind of ethical problems might have arisen from this deception? What problems would the experimenters have had in getting this study approved by an ethics committee today?

**LAZARUS AND THE COGNITIVE-MEDIATIONAL THEORY OF EMOTION**   As mentioned in the Classic Studies in Psychology section, Schachter and Singer's (1962) study stressed the importance of cognition, or thinking, in the determination of emotions. One of the more modern versions of cognitive emotion theories is Lazarus's **cognitive-mediational theory** of emotion (1991). In this theory, the most important aspect of any emotional

**cognitive-mediational theory**

theory of emotion in which a stimulus must be interpreted (appraised) by a person in order to result in a physical response and an emotional reaction.

*confederate: someone who is cooperating with another person on some task.

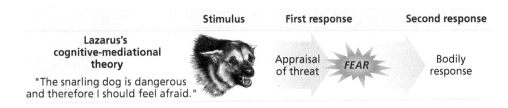

**Figure 9.13** Lazarus's Cognitive-Mediational Theory of Emotion

In Lazarus's cognitive-mediational theory of emotion, a stimulus causes an immediate appraisal (e.g., "The dog is snarling and not behind a fence, so this is dangerous"). The cognitive appraisal results in an emotional response, which is then followed by the appropriate bodily response.

experience is how the person interprets, or appraises, the stimulus that causes the emotional reaction. To *mediate* means to "come between," and in this theory, the cognitive appraisal mediates by coming between the stimulus and the emotional response to that stimulus.

For example, remember the person who encountered a snarling dog while walking through the neighborhood? According to Lazarus, the appraisal of the situation would come *before* both the physical arousal and the experience of emotion. If the dog is behind a sturdy fence, the appraisal would be something like "no threat." The most likely emotion would be annoyance, and the physical arousal would be minimal. But if the dog is not confined, the appraisal would more likely be "danger—threatening animal!" which would be followed by an increase in arousal and the emotional experience of fear. In other words, it's the *interpretation* of the arousal that results in the emotion of fear, not the labeling as in the Schachter-Singer model, and the interpretation comes first. (See **Figure 9.13**.)

Not everyone agrees with this theory, of course. Some researchers believe that emotional reactions to situations are so fast that they are almost instantaneous, which would leave little time for a cognitive appraisal to occur first (Zajonc, 1998). Others (Kihlstrom et al., 2000) have found that the human brain can respond to a physical threat before conscious thought enters the picture. And as addressed earlier, the amygdala can prompt emotional reactions before we are consciously aware of what we are responding to (LeDoux, 1996, 2007; LeDoux & Phelps, 2008).

💬 Which theory is right?

Human emotions are so incredibly complex that it might not be out of place to say that all of the theories are correct to at least some degree. In certain situations, the cognitive appraisal might have time to mediate the emotion that is experienced (such as falling in love), whereas in other situations, the need to act first and to think and feel later is more important. (See **Figure 9.14** on the next page.)

**THINKING CRITICALLY**

Which of these theories of emotion do you feel is most correct? Why?

▶ The response entered here will be saved to your notes and may be collected by your instructor if he/she requires it.

Submit

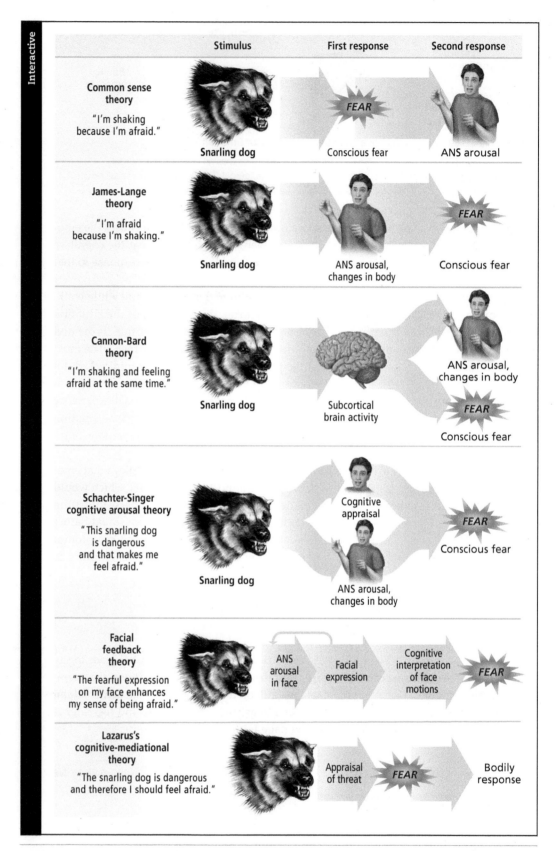

**Figure 9.14** Comparison of Theories of Emotion

These figures represent the six different theories of emotion as discussed in the text.

## Concept Map L.O. 9.8, 9.9, 9.10

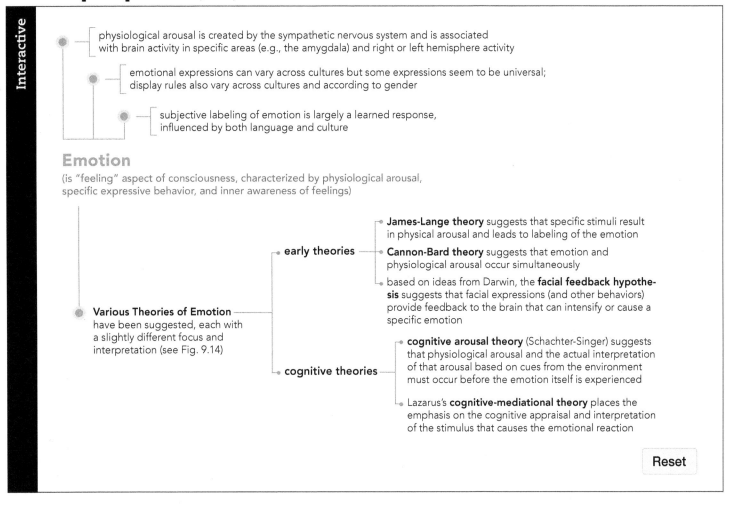

Interactive

- physiological arousal is created by the sympathetic nervous system and is associated with brain activity in specific areas (e.g., the amygdala) and right or left hemisphere activity
- emotional expressions can vary across cultures but some expressions seem to be universal; display rules also vary across cultures and according to gender
- subjective labeling of emotion is largely a learned response, influenced by both language and culture

**Emotion**
(is "feeling" aspect of consciousness, characterized by physiological arousal, specific expressive behavior, and inner awareness of feelings)

- **Various Theories of Emotion** have been suggested, each with a slightly different focus and interpretation (see Fig. 9.14)
  - **early theories**
    - **James-Lange theory** suggests that specific stimuli result in physical arousal and leads to labeling of the emotion
    - **Cannon-Bard theory** suggests that emotion and physiological arousal occur simultaneously
    - based on ideas from Darwin, the **facial feedback hypothesis** suggests that facial expressions (and other behaviors) provide feedback to the brain that can intensify or cause a specific emotion
  - **cognitive theories**
    - **cognitive arousal theory** (Schachter-Singer) suggests that physiological arousal and the actual interpretation of that arousal based on cues from the environment must occur before the emotion itself is experienced
    - Lazarus's **cognitive-mediational theory** places the emphasis on the cognitive appraisal and interpretation of the stimulus that causes the emotional reaction

Reset

# Practice Quiz How much do you remember?

*Pick the best answer.*

**1.** Which of the following is not one of the three elements of emotion?
**a.** Physical arousal **c.** Objective experience
**b.** Behavioral reaction **d.** Subjective experience

**2.** The phrase "I'm embarrassed because my face is red" is best explained by which theory of emotion?
**a.** Cannon-Bard **c.** Schachter-Singer
**b.** James-Lange **d.** common-sense theory of emotion

**3.** "I believe that emotions and physiological arousal tend to happen simultaneously." Which theorist would be responsible for making such a statement?
**a.** Walter Cannon or Philip Bard
**b.** William James or Carl Lange
**c.** Stanley Schachter or Jerome Singer
**d.** Sigmund Freud or Erik Erikson

**4.** One day at school, someone collides with you in the hall and knocks you down, causing you to be angry. However, when playing football with friends, if you get knocked down, you do not express anger. What theory best explains how we label each situation and choose the appropriate emotion to show?
**a.** James-Lange **c.** Cannon-Bard
**b.** Schachter-Singer **d.** facial feedback

**5.** In Schachter and Singer's classic study, participants who received epinephrine and were in the company of the "angry" research confederate interpreted their physiological arousal as __________, whereas those who were exposed to the "happy" confederate interpreted their arousal as __________.
**a.** anger; happiness **c.** happiness; happiness
**b.** happiness; anger **d.** anger; anger

**6.** Eileen smiles wherever she goes. She smiles a lot in the classroom, which in turn prompts her fellow students to smile, making them feel happier too. This effect is best explained by which of the following theories of emotion?
**a.** James-Lange **c.** Schachter-Singer
**b.** cognitive-mediational **d.** facial feedback

## Applying Psychology to Everyday Life
# When Motivation Is Not Enough

**9.11** **Summarize the five steps of the GTD method.**

Now that we have discussed a variety of ways in which behavior gets initiated or maintained, what can you do to make sure you complete the tasks you need to finish or address the commitments you've made? Many college students find it difficult to keep track of all of their class assignments and projects and to remember all of the things they are supposed to do—and when to do them. Keeping on task can be especially challenging when you might not be exactly thrilled about doing some of them in the first place. As such, if motivation is not enough to help you get things accomplished, what else can you do to ensure that you do what needs to be done?

There have been a variety of time- and task-management systems developed over the years, each with a slightly different focus on various aspects of motivation. One system suggests you should first identify key principles or important areas in your life (such as family, education, career, etc.); the next step is to sort your to-do list using those key categories, ranking your tasks by priority or in the order you need to do them. Finally, keep track of each item by plotting it on your calendar. This works for some people. For others it may sound like more steps than you want to do or feel you need to do.

The book *Getting Things Done: The Art of Stress-Free Productivity* by David Allen and his "Getting Things Done" (or GTD) methodology can provide a useful structure for a wide range of people who need help, well, in getting things done (Allen, 2001, 2008). Think about the number of college students that finish their first year of college with grades much lower than they expected. With a system like GTD, many may have improved chances of being more successful during their first year.

The GTD method consists of five stages of processing your "stuff" into actual outcomes, identifying "next actions" you can actually take to gain and maintain control of your tasks and commitments. The five stages of the GTD method are:

1. Capture anything and everything that has your attention, getting it out of your head and physically collected in one place. This place can be a folder, notebook, computer program, spreadsheet, a set of index cards, or the like.
2. Process and define what you can take action on and identify the next steps. For example, instead of "do my research paper," identify actionable next steps such as "pinpoint topic, collect articles, schedule meeting to discuss ideas with classmates," for example.
3. Organize information and reminders into categories or contexts, based on how and when you need them. For example, if you need to send an email or text message to your group partners, you probably need to have your phone or computer to do so; "phone" or "computer" might be a context that you use.
4. Complete weekly reviews of your projects, next actions, and new items. To get things done, you need to review what you need to do.
5. Do your next actions in the appropriate context or time frame for doing so.

Adapted from David Allen's *Getting Things Done: The Art of Stress-Free Productivity* (2001) and *Making It All Work* (2008).

In this discussion, we've only highlighted aspects of one specific approach for organizing and keeping on top of all those things you need to get done. There are a variety of time- and task-management systems and tools available, many more than we can cover in this textbook. **L I N K** to Learning Objective PIA.2. Watch the video *The GTD Method* to learn more. Finding an approach or strategy that works best for you will likely pay off, not only now while you are in school but also in areas of your personal and future professional

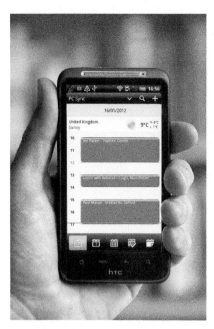

How do you keep track of all of your class assignments, appointments, and deadlines?

lives as well. Take some time now and investigate available strategies that will help you get organized and stay on track to meet your obligations in a timely manner. If you do, the next time you find that motivation and emotion are not enough to prompt you to get what you need done taken care of, you'll be glad you did.

👁 **Watch** the **Video** *The GTD Method*

Questions for Further Discussion

1. Aside from having a bunch of "lists" and possibly getting things done, what might be some specific personal benefits to keeping track of tasks and projects you have committed to?

2. What sort of personal barriers or roadblocks might you have to using a time- or task-management system?

# Chapter Summary

## Understanding Motivation

### 9.1 Distinguish between intrinsic motivation and extrinsic motivation.

• Motivation is the process by which activities are started, directed, and sustained so that physical and psychological needs are fulfilled.

• Intrinsic motivation occurs when people act because the act itself is satisfying or rewarding, whereas extrinsic motivation occurs when people receive an external reward (such as money) for the act.

### 9.2 Identify the key elements of the early instinct and drive-reduction approaches to motivation.

• Instinct approaches proposed that some human actions may be motivated by instincts, which are innate patterns of behavior found in both people and animals.

• Drive-reduction approaches state that when an organism has a need (such as hunger), the need leads to psychological tension that motivates the organism to act, fulfilling the need and reducing the tension.

• Primary drives involve needs of the body, whereas acquired (secondary) drives are those learned through experience. Homeostasis is the tendency of the body to maintain a steady state.

### 9.3 Explain the characteristics of the three types of needs.

• The need for affiliation is the desire to have friendly social interactions and relationships with others as well as the desire to be held in high regard by others.

• The need for power concerns having control over others, influencing them, and having an impact on them. Status and prestige are important to people high in this need.

- The need for achievement is a strong desire to succeed in achieving one's goals, both realistic and challenging.
- The self-theory of emotion links the need for achievement to the concept of locus of control. A belief in control over one's life leads to more attempts to achieve, even in the face of failure. Those who believe that they have little control over what happens to them are more likely to develop learned helplessness.

**9.4 Identify the key elements of the arousal and incentive approaches to motivation.**

- In arousal theory, a person has an optimal level of arousal to maintain. People who need more arousal than others are called sensation seekers.
- In the incentive approach, an external stimulus may be so rewarding that it motivates a person to act toward that stimulus even in the absence of a drive.

**9.5 Describe how Maslow's hierarchy of needs and self-determination theories explain motivation.**

- Maslow proposed a hierarchy of needs, beginning with basic physiological needs and ending with transcendence needs. The more basic needs must be met before the higher needs can be fulfilled.
- Self-determination theory (SDT) is a model of motivation in which three basic needs are seen as necessary to an individual's successful development: autonomy, competence, and relatedness.

## What, Hungry Again? Why People Eat

**9.6 Identify the physical and social factors that influence hunger.**

- The physiological components of hunger include signals from the stomach and the hypothalamus and the increased secretion of insulin.
- When the basal metabolic rate slows down, the weight set point increases and makes weight gain more likely.
- The social components of hunger include social cues for when meals are to be eaten, cultural customs and food preferences, and the use of food as a comfort device or as an escape from unpleasantness.
- Some people may be externals who respond to the anticipation of eating by producing an insulin response, increasing the risk of obesity.

**9.7 Recognize some of the factors that contribute to obesity.**

- There are genetic and hormonal factors that can influence obesity.
- Maladaptive eating may lead to obesity.
- A third of the population of the United States is obese.

## Emotion

**9.8 Describe the three elements of emotion.**

- Emotion is the "feeling" aspect of consciousness and includes physical, behavioral, and subjective (cognitive) elements.
- Physical arousal is tied to activation of the sympathetic nervous system.
- The amygdala plays a key role in emotional processing.

**9.9 Distinguish among the common-sense, James-Lange, Cannon-Bard, and facial feedback theories of emotion.**

- The common-sense theory of emotion states that an emotion is experienced first, leading to a physical reaction and then to a behavioral reaction.
- The James-Lange theory states that a stimulus creates a physiological response that then leads to the labeling of the emotion.
- The Cannon-Bard theory asserts that the physiological reaction and the emotion are simultaneous, as the thalamus sends sensory information to both the cortex of the brain and the organs of the sympathetic nervous system.
- In the facial feedback hypothesis, facial expressions provide feedback to the brain about the emotion being expressed on the face, intensifying the emotion.

**9.10 Identify the key elements in the cognitive arousal and cognitive-mediational theories of emotion.**

- In Schachter and Singer's cognitive arousal theory, both the physiological arousal and the actual interpretation of that arousal must occur before the emotion itself is experienced. This interpretation is based on cues from the environment.
- In the cognitive-mediational theory of emotion, the cognitive component of emotion (the interpretation) precedes both the physiological reaction and the emotion itself.

## Applying Psychology to Everyday Life: When Motivation Is Not Enough

**9.11 Summarize the five steps of the GTD method.**

- Time- or task-management systems can help you keep track of commitments and accomplish specific tasks and general goals.
- The stages of the Getting Things Done (GTD) method involve capturing, processing, organizing, reviewing, and doing the tasks you have committed to.
- Motivation and emotion are sometimes not enough to prompt human behavior.

# Test Yourself

*Pick the best answer.*

1. Eli enjoys woodcarving. Although none of his teenage friends are interested, he often spends hours creating several different pieces. His enjoyment of the task is all his own, and he rarely shows others his work. Many would call his motivation _____ in nature.
   a. instinctual
   b. arousal
   c. extrinsic
   d. intrinsic

2. Jasmine often requires her friends' approval when she buys new outfits. Her need is an example of a(n) _____ drive.
   a. primary
   b. acquired (secondary)
   c. innate
   d. instinctive

3. The approach to motivation that forced psychologists to consider the value of homeostasis in motivation was the _____ approach.
   a. arousal
   b. drive-reduction
   c. instinct
   d. incentive

4. Motivational theories such as _____ are physical in terms of their needs, while _____ is based on psychological motives.
   a. drive theory; instinctual theory
   b. biological theory; drive theory
   c. drive theory; McClelland's need theory
   d. need for power; drive theory

5. Dodi is always looking for new hobbies. He prefers exciting hobbies that will get him noticed. In his company, Dodi constantly asks for feedback from customers so he can know what he needs to do to be the best. Dodi is high in the need for _____.
   a. achievement
   b. affiliation
   c. power
   d. attention

6. An important component to Carol Dweck's theory of motivation is
   a. one's view of self.
   b. an understanding of classical conditioning and its impact on motivation.
   c. the importance of heredity in biological motivations.
   d. an understanding of emotions.

7. According to the arousal theory, people are typically motivated toward _____ point of arousal.
   a. the highest
   b. the optimal
   c. the easiest
   d. the quickest

8. According to Maslow, what is meant by a peak experience?
   a. that point, even for a moment, when someone reaches a state of self-actualization
   b. the point at which someone reaches transcendence
   c. the point at which someone begins to work through the hierarchy
   d. the point at which someone must descend back down the hierarchy to address a previous need which is no longer secure

9. Jacob believes he is in control of his own destiny. He feels he is secure in the friendships he has with others. However, he still feels the need to master many of the challenges in his own life and career. According to self-determination theory, which stage is Jacob still working to complete?
   a. autonomy
   b. competence
   c. relatedness
   d. affiliation

10. Leptin is a hormone involved in
    a. appetite control.
    b. metabolism control.
    c. digestion of fatty foods.
    d. neurotransmissions.

11. The structure in the brain that, when damaged, causes rats to eat and eat and eat is called the
    a. ventromedial pituitary.
    b. lateral hippocampus.
    c. ventromedial hypothalamus.
    d. lateral hypothalamus.

12. The level of weight the body tries to maintain is called the
    a. basal metabolic rate.
    b. weight set point.
    c. basal set point.
    d. weight metabolic rate.

13. Studies indicate that women from _____ are more likely to eat because their body tells them they are hungry.
    a. Hungary
    b. the United States
    c. Italy
    d. Japan

14. Since Dillon's family has a history of obesity, he has _____ of becoming obese compared to people without such a family history.
    a. the same risk
    b. double or triple the risk
    c. five times the risk
    d. less risk

15. LeDoux's work on the physiology involving emotions has focused on what part of the brain?
    a. thalamus
    b. hippocampus
    c. prefrontal cortex
    d. amygdala

16. Research on facial expressions has taught us that facial expressions are
    a. inherent to a region and therefore mean different things in different countries.
    b. inherent to a culture and therefore mean different things to different cultures.
    c. learned.
    d. universal.

17. What is meant by a display rule?
    a. an understanding of when and under what conditions emotions and feelings may be displayed within a culture
    b. an understanding of what behaviors can be expressed when someone is new to a situation
    c. an understanding of how children are to act in the presence of adults
    d. an understanding of how to hide emotions from others

18. What theory of emotion states that the emotion typically occurs before arousal and behavior?
    a. the original, or common-sense, theory
    b. Schachter and Singer's theory
    c. Cannon and Bard's theory
    d. James and Lange's theory

19. Which theory of emotion relies heavily on cognition and labeling?
    a. the original, or common-sense, theory
    b. Schachter and Singer's theory
    c. Cannon and Bard's theory
    d. James and Lange's theory

20. The first stage of David Allen's Getting Things Done (GTD) method is _____ anything and everything that has your attention.
    a. reviewing
    b. doing
    c. capturing
    d. organizing

# Sexuality and Gender

What are some cultural expectations for your gender? In what ways do you adhere to these gender roles and in what ways do you defy them?
After you have answered the question, watch the video to compare the answers of other students to yours.

▶ The response entered here will be saved to your notes and may be collected by your instructor if he/she requires it.

👁 Watch the Video

# Why study sexuality and gender?

Human sexual behavior is responsible for the reproduction of the human race, but it is also one of the most import-ant motivators of human behavior. Gender, the psychological identification of a person as masculine or feminine, affects not only how people think of themselves but also their relationships with others as friends, lovers, and coworkers and how those others think of them as well.

# Learning Objectives

**10.1** Distinguish between primary and secondary sex characteristics.

**10.2** Explain how sex characteristics develop.

**10.3** Identify the psychological, biological, environmental, and cultural influences on gender.

**10.4** Compare and contrast different views of how gender roles develop.

**10.5** Describe how men and women differ in thinking, social behavior, and personality.

**10.6** Identify the four stages of a sexual-response cycle.

**10.7** Summarize the findings of early and recent surveys of human sexual behavior.

**10.8** Identify some influences on the development of sexual orientation.

**10.9** Describe the causes and symptoms of some common sexually transmitted infections.

**10.10** Explain why the number of HIV and AIDS cases in Russia is increasing so dramatically.

# The Physical Side of Human Sexuality

Before discussing gender and gender identity, it may help to understand the physical structures of the human sexual system and the function of those structures. These structures differ for females and males and develop at different times in an individual's life. As you read this next section, keep in mind that physical sex characteristics are not the same as the experience of *gender*, the psychological aspects of identifying oneself as male or female. One's sex is about biology, but gender is a social expectation for behavior, an expectation that varies from culture to culture and that changes as societal views of acceptable and desirable behavior related to being perceived as male or female change.

## THE PRIMARY AND SECONDARY SEX CHARACTERISTICS

**10.1** **Distinguish between primary and secondary sex characteristics.**

The sexual organs include structures that are present at birth (called **primary sex characteristics**) and those that develop during *puberty*, the period of physiological change that takes place in the sexual organs and reproductive system during late middle childhood and adolescence (called **secondary sex characteristics**). ⓁⓘⓃⓚ to Learning Objective 8.9.

**THE PRIMARY SEX CHARACTERISTICS** Primary sex characteristics are directly involved in human reproduction. While not fully developed until puberty, these physical characteristics are present in the infant at birth. In the female, these characteristics include the **vagina** (the tube leading from the outside of the body to the opening of the womb), **uterus** (the womb), and *ovaries* (the female sex glands). In males, the primary sex characteristics include the **penis** (the organ through which males urinate and which delivers the male sex cells or sperm), the *testes* or *testicles* (the male sex glands), the **scrotum** (an external pouch that holds the testes), and the **prostate gland** (a gland that secretes most of the fluid that carries the sperm). (See **Figure 10.1**.)

**THE SECONDARY SEX CHARACTERISTICS** Secondary sex characteristics develop during puberty and are only indirectly involved in human reproduction. These characteristics serve to distinguish the male from the female and may act as attractants to members of the opposite sex, ensuring that sexual activity and reproduction will occur. They are also, in many cases, a physical necessity for reproduction.

FEMALE SECONDARY SEX CHARACTERISTICS In females, secondary sex characteristics include a growth spurt that begins at about ages 10 to 12 and finishes about 1 year following the first *menstrual cycle*, in which the blood and tissue lining of the uterus exit the body through the vagina if there is no pregnancy to support. This first cycle is known as **menarche** and occurs at an average age of about 12 in more developed countries such as the United States.

The earlier onset of menarche in more developed countries is associated with the availability of better health care and nutrition, and, along with an increase in height and weight compared to previous generations, is an example of a *secular trend*, a change or series of changes that takes place over a long period of time (Bellis et al., 2006; Roche, 1979). But better physical health is not the only factor in the decrease in age of menarche. Stress, in the form of marital strife, absentee fathers, and increasing rates of divorce also plays a part in speeding up the changes of puberty (Gluckman & Hansom, 2006; Parent et al., 2003). Some of the consequences of an earlier menarche (and an earlier production of sperm in boys, as well) include the possibility of pregnancy in children at a far younger age than previously thought possible (Wellings et al., 2001). Pregnancy in adolescence is not only hard on the young mothers physically but has negative social impact—poverty, child abuse and neglect, and a failure to continue in school, to name a few (Kirchengast, 2009).

Other changes include enlarged breasts about 2 years after the growth spurt, wider hips to allow the passage of the fetus through the pelvic bones, pubic hair, and

**primary sex characteristics**
sexual organs present at birth and directly involved in human reproduction.

**secondary sex characteristics**
sexual organs and traits that develop at puberty and are indirectly involved in human reproduction.

**vagina**
the tube that leads from the outside of a female's body to the opening of the womb.

**uterus**
the womb in which the baby grows during pregnancy.

**penis**
the organ through which males urinate and which delivers the male sex cells or sperm.

**scrotum**
external sac that holds the testes.

**prostate gland**
gland that secretes most of the fluid holding the male sex cells or sperm.

**menarche**
the first menstrual cycle, the monthly shedding of the blood and tissue that line the uterus in preparation for pregnancy when conception does not occur.

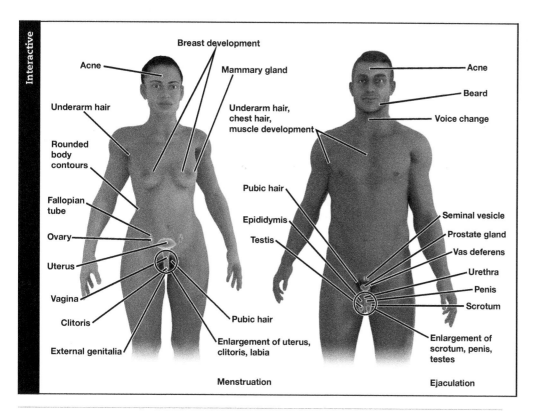

**Figure 10.1**   Male and Female Sexual Organs

These figures show the primary and secondary sexual characteristics of women and men. Primary sexual characteristics develop during the prenatal period, while secondary characteristics develop during puberty.

fat deposits on the buttocks and thighs. Some secondary sex characteristics also involve the growth and development of the primary sexual organs. In females, this occurs when the **mammary glands** in the breasts become capable of producing milk for an infant and when the menstrual cycle begins (Biro et al., 2013; Kreipe, 1992; Lee, 1995).

MALE SECONDARY SEX CHARACTERISTICS   The secondary sex characteristics of males include a deepening voice; emergence of facial, chest, and pubic hair; and the development of coarser skin texture. These changes are also accompanied by a large increase in height that continues beyond the growth spurt of the female. The male growth spurt occurs about 2 years later than the female growth spurt, but males continue to gain height until the late teens. Although the larynx (voice box) increases in size in both sexes, it increases so much in males that part of the tissue forming it becomes visible under the skin of the neck in a structure known as the Adam's apple. Primary sex characteristics also undergo changes during puberty, including the onset of the production of sperm (*spermarche*, occurring at a little over 14 years of age) and the growth of the penis and testes, which will eventually allow the male to function sexually and to reproduce (Kreipe, 1992; Lee, 1995; Song et al., 2015).

## THE DEVELOPMENT OF SEX CHARACTERISTICS

**10.2** **Explain how sex characteristics develop.**

💬 How does the person's body know which sexual characteristics to develop? Aren't some babies born with sex organs belonging to both sexes?

The primary sex characteristics develop as the embryo is growing in the womb as a result of the chromosomes contained within the embryonic cells as well as hormonal influences.

Puberty changes come about 2 years earlier for girls than for boys, including the growth spurt. The young people in this dancing couple are both 13 years old, but the physical difference in height is quite obvious.

**mammary glands**

glands within the breast tissue that produce milk when a woman gives birth to an infant.

At about 5 weeks of pregnancy, two organs called the *gonads* form in the embryo. Two sets of ducts (tubes) also develop next to the gonads, the Wolffian ducts (which can become the male sex organs) and the Müllerian ducts (which can become the female sex organs). At this point, the gonads are undifferentiated—neither fully male nor fully female—and the embryo could potentially become either male or female. The deciding factor is controlled by the chromosomes: If the chromosomes of the 23rd pair contain a Y chromosome, a gene on that Y chromosome causes the gonads to release *testosterone*, a male hormone or **androgen**. (Female hormones are called **estrogens**.) Testosterone causes the Wolffian ducts to develop into the male sex organs, while the Müllerian ducts deteriorate. If the 23rd pair of chromosomes contains two female or X chromosomes, the Y gene is absent so no testosterone is released, and the gonads will develop into the estrogen-secreting ovaries. The Müllerian ducts become the female sex organs while the Wolffian ducts deteriorate.

On rare occasions, an infant is born with sexual organs that are ambiguous—not clearly male or female. People with this condition are referred to as **intersex**, meaning "between the sexes," and represent about 1.7 percent of the population (Blackless et al., 2000; Dreger, 1998, 1999). It is very rare to find a person who truly has both ovary and testicle material in their body. More commonly, the development of the external genitals is affected by either chromosomes or the presence of hormones associated with the development of another sex at a critical time in the development of the fetus in the womb (Hutcheson & Snyder, 2004). A few of the possible hormonal abnormalities include androgen insensitivity (where someone who is genetically male is resistant to the male hormone androgen), congenital adrenal hyperplasia (several genetic conditions leading to limited production of hormones by the adrenal glands), and dihydrotestosterone deficiency, leading to a lack of a particular male hormone (Wiesemann et al., 2010; Wisniewski et al., 2000; Wolfe-Christensen et al., 2012). In these cases, a female clitoris might look more like a penis, or a penis might be so small as to resemble a clitoris. Many physicians, psychologists, and other experts now consider gender reassignment surgery performed on infants with intersex traits to be unnecessary (Wiesemann et al., 2010). Gender identity is not a biological concept, remember, and current thinking is in favor of allowing an intersex individual to make the decision about surgery once the person has determined a concept of gender. Surgery of this sort can lead to negative consequences for the ability to function sexually in later life (Creighton et al., 2001; Crouch et al., 2004; Kraus, 2015).

**androgens**

male hormones.

**estrogens**

female hormones.

**intersex**

modern term for a hermaphrodite, a person who possesses ambiguous sexual organs, making it difficult to determine actual sex from a visual inspection at birth.

## Concept Map  L.O. 10.1, 10.2

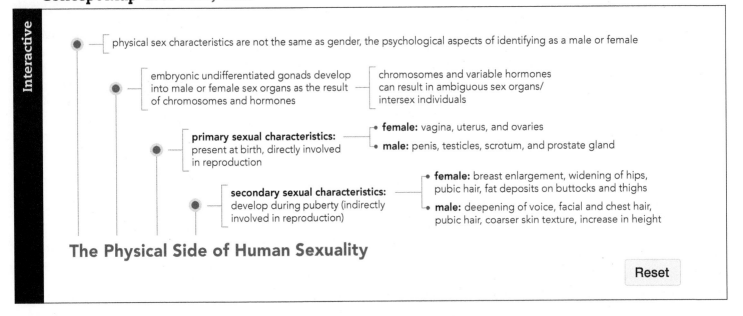

Interactive

- physical sex characteristics are not the same as gender, the psychological aspects of identifying as a male or female

- embryonic undifferentiated gonads develop into male or female sex organs as the result of chromosomes and hormones
  - chromosomes and variable hormones can result in ambiguous sex organs/intersex individuals

- **primary sexual characteristics:** present at birth, directly involved in reproduction
  - **female:** vagina, uterus, and ovaries
  - **male:** penis, testicles, scrotum, and prostate gland

- **secondary sexual characteristics:** develop during puberty (indirectly involved in reproduction)
  - **female:** breast enlargement, widening of hips, pubic hair, fat deposits on buttocks and thighs
  - **male:** deepening of voice, facial and chest hair, pubic hair, coarser skin texture, increase in height

### The Physical Side of Human Sexuality

Reset

# Practice Quiz    How much do you remember?

*Pick the best answer.*

**1.** The sex structures that develop during puberty are categorized as
   **a.** primary sex characteristics.
   **b.** secondary sex characteristics.
   **c.** either primary or secondary sex characteristics.
   **d.** primary or secondary sex characteristics based on the culture.

**2.** Which of the following is a secondary sex characteristic?
   **a.** uterus
   **b.** enlarging breasts
   **c.** penis
   **d.** ovaries

**3.** Which of the following is NOT associated with the embryo developing into a male:
   **a.** androgen
   **b.** Wolffian ducts
   **c.** Müllerian ducts
   **d.** testosterone

**4.** People who are intersex
   **a.** commonly have both ovaries and testes.
   **b.** are extremely rare—1 in a million births.
   **c.** have a mixture of male and female sexual characteristics.
   **d.** are people who suffer from gender dysphoria but are physically normal.

# The Psychological Side of Human Sexuality: Gender

Whereas sex can be defined as the physical characteristics of being male or female, **gender** is defined as the psychological aspects of being male or female. The expectations of a person's social group and culture, the development of the personality, and the sense of identity are all affected by the concept of gender.

## GENDER IDENTITY

**10.3** **Identify the psychological, biological, environmental, and cultural influences on gender.**

**Gender roles** are the culture's expectations for behavior of a person who is perceived as male or female, including attitudes, actions, and personality traits associated with a particular gender within that culture (Tobach, 2001; Unger, 1979). **Gender typing** is the process by which people learn their culture's preferences and expectations for male and female behavior. The process of developing a person's **gender identity** (a sense of being male or female) is influenced by both biological and environmental factors (in the form of parenting and other child-rearing behaviors), although which type of factor has greater influence is still controversial.

**PSYCHOLOGICAL INFLUENCES**    Gender identity, like physical sex, is also not always as straightforward as males who are masculine and females who are feminine. People's sense of gender identity does not always match their external appearance or even the sex chromosomes that determine whether they are male or female (Califia, 1997; Crawford & Unger, 2004; White, 2000). Such people are typically termed *transgender*. There are many famous people who are transgender, such as former Olympic athlete Caitlyn Jenner, actress Laverne Cox, and gay rights activist Chaz Bono.

Psychological issues, as well as biology and environment, have an influence on the concept of a person's gender identity. In a syndrome called *gender dysphoria*, a person experiences gender incongruence, feeling that he or she is occupying the body of the other gender, or some alternative gender that is not the same as their assigned gender, and has significant distress about the incongruence (American Psychiatric Association [APA], 2013). The last part of that definition is crucial: It is important to realize that many, and perhaps the majority, of transgender people have little or no distress about the changes they make and therefore do *not* have gender dysphoria (APA, 2013). In fact, once a person makes the change, he or she will typically feel more psychologically and emotionally grounded. Any distress will most likely come from those around the person who are unable or unwilling to accept the changes.

**gender**

the psychological aspects of being male or female.

**gender roles**

the culture's expectations for male or female behavior, including attitudes, actions, and personality traits associated with being male or female in that culture.

**gender typing**

the process of acquiring gender-role characteristics.

**gender identity**

the individual's sense of being male or female.

Although the causes of gender dysphoria are not fully understood, there is some evidence for both prenatal influences and early childhood experiences as causes (Stein, 1984; Ward, 1992; Zhou et al., 1995). While some people with this condition feel so strongly that they are the wrong gender that they have surgery to acquire primary and/or secondary sexual sex characteristics of the gender they feel they were always meant to be, many others prefer to receive hormone treatment only or to embrace their identity as it is. People who choose to alter themselves physically through surgery or hormonal treatments are generally termed *transsexuals*.

Many Native American tribes have long recognized the role of the male *winkte* (a contraction of the Lakota word *winyanktehca*, meaning "to be as a woman or two-souls person") in their societies. (Other tribes had different names, such as *berdache* or *nadleehe*, but the concept was the same.) These tribes traditionally were not only tolerant of such different individuals but also had important places for them in the social structure as caretakers of children, as cooks, and as menders and creators of clothing (VanderLaan et al., 2013). The winkte also performed certain rituals for bestowing luck upon a hunt (Medicine, 2002). Although some winkte (now often referred to as people with two spirits) may have been homosexual in orientation, many were not and would now be recognized as transgender. Unfortunately, as tribes have modernized and become more integrated into the larger European-dominated culture of the United States, the tolerant attitudes of other Native Americans toward the winkte and other two-spirit people have begun to be replaced with homophobic attitudes and aggressive behavior toward those who are different in this way (Gilley, 2006; Medicine, 2002).

In today's culture, being transgender is only beginning to become part of accepted gender identity, with many transgender individuals facing mockery, discrimination, and abuse, resulting in increased risk of stress-induced problems such as eating disorders and suicide (Diemer et al., 2015; Haas et al., 2014). Ⓛ Ⓘ Ⓝ Ⓚ to Learning Objective 14.9 and 14.11.

This is We-Wa, a Zuni berdache (the Zuni version of winkte). This photograph was taken near the end of the nineteenth century.

👁 **Watch** the **Video** *Transgender*

Another alternate gender condition is *couvade syndrome*, in which a man whose partner is pregnant may experience a kind of "sympathy pregnancy." For instance, he may feel physical pain while his wife is in labor. Men in Western cultures, as their roles as participating fathers have changed, have actually shown an increase in couvade experiences.

There are several possible explanations for couvade syndrome. Some view it as a psychiatric disorder—perhaps out of jealousy of the attention given to the pregnant wife.

Others note that it involves real biological changes. One study showed these men produce female hormones normally associated with the production of breast milk (Storey et al., 2000). It may be a way for some men to work through their feelings about impending fatherhood. Or it may be related to how emotionally sensitive they are, or prone to personal distress (Kazmierczak et al., 2013). Whatever the cause or causes, couvade syndrome remains a fascinating condition that seems to defy ordinary gender roles.

**BIOLOGICAL INFLUENCES**    Most researchers today would agree that biology has an important role in gender identity, at least in certain aspects of gender identity and behavior (Diamond & Sigmundson, 1997; Money, 1994; Reiner, 1999, 2000). In one study, 25 genetically male children who were born with ambiguous genitalia were surgically altered and raised as girls. Now, as older children and teenagers, they prefer male play activities such as sports. Fourteen of these children have openly declared themselves to be boys (Reiner, 2000; Reiner & Gearhart, 2004).

What are the biological influences on gender? Aside from the obvious external sexual characteristics of the genitals, there are also hormonal differences between men and women. Some researchers believe that exposure to these hormones during fetal development not only causes the formation of the sexual organs but also predisposes the infant to behavior that is typically associated with one gender or the other.

Gender appearance rigidity is a developmental stage many preschool age children seem to experience. Girls will insist upon wearing dresses, the frillier the better, even though only a few weeks ago they would happily wear pants. Boys begin to refuse to wear anything that might be considered "girlish." Researchers studying the prevalence of this behavior found that two thirds of the girls and nearly half of the boys went through a stage of rigid adherence to gender-typed clothing and toys, regardless of their parents' preferences for the same items (Halim et al., 2014). This observation held true in a diverse selection of children in the United States from both ethnically and economically diverse backgrounds. But is this rigidity stage due to biology or to environmental influences? Even if parents try not to influence their children's gender behavior, exposure to gender role stereotypes from other sources—the media, preschool, other children, teachers, and books, for example—is nearly impossible to control.

There have been several studies of infant girls who were exposed to androgens before birth (for example, some drugs to prevent miscarriages are male hormones). In these studies, the girls were found to be tomboys during early childhood—preferring to play with typically "boy" toys, wrestling and playing rough, and playing with boys rather than with other girls (Berenbaum & Snyder, 1995; Money & Mathews, 1982; Money & Norman, 1987). However, when these girls grew up, they became more typically "female" in their desire for marriage and motherhood, which many of these same researchers took as evidence that upbringing won out over the hormonal influences.

 💬 Was their early tomboy nature due to the influence of the male hormones?

This is difficult to prove, as the parents of these girls were told about their infants' exposure to male hormones during the pregnancy and may have formed assumptions about the effects of such masculinizing hormones on their children. It is entirely possible that these girls were simply allowed, or even encouraged, to be more "masculine" as small children because the parents were expecting them to be masculine. As these same girls grew older, they were exposed to the gender-role expectations of teachers, friends, and the media, which may have influenced them to become more like the feminine gender stereotype in contrast to their earlier "masculine" style of behavior. Some studies have attempted to investigate factors by researching the behavior of nonhuman animals. For instance, as the video *Gender Socialization* explains, male and female vervet monkeys appear to prefer typically "boy" and "girl" toys, such as trucks and dolls respectively, indicating a possible biological influence.

👁 **Watch** the **Video** *Gender Socialization*

Another study examined the way in which men and women respond to visual sexual stimuli and found that although men and women may report being equally aroused by erotic pictures, what happens in their brains is quite different (Hamann et al., 2004). Using a brain-scanning technique called *functional magnetic resonance imaging (fMRI)*, the researchers found that the amygdala and hypothalamus areas of the limbic system (areas involved in emotional and sexual responses) were more strongly active in men than in women who viewed the pictures. Ⓛ Ⓘ Ⓝ ⓀⓀ to Learning Objective 2.11. The researchers concluded that the male brain's enhanced reaction might be a product of natural selection, as early human males who could quickly recognize a sexually receptive female would have had a greater opportunity to mate and pass on their genes to their offspring.

**ENVIRONMENTAL INFLUENCES**   Even if the girls who were exposed to androgens prenatally were initially influenced by these hormones, it seems fairly clear that their later "reversion" to more feminine ways was at least somewhat influenced by the pressures of society. In most cultures, there are certain roles that males and females are expected to play (gender roles, in other words), and the pressure that can be brought to bear on a person who does not conform to these expectations can be tremendous. In most Western cultures, the pressure to be masculine is even greater for males than the pressure to be feminine is for girls. The term *tomboy* is not generally viewed as an insult, but there are no terms for a boy who acts in a feminine manner that are not insulting—*sissy*, for example, is not a nice term at all. And although studies of parents' influence on their children's gender typing show that both parents have an impact, they also show that the fathers are almost always more concerned about their sons showing male gender behavior than they are about their daughters showing female gender behavior (Kane, 2006; Lytton & Romney, 1991).

**THINKING CRITICALLY**

How do you believe men and women are portrayed in today's media? Strong? Weak? Inept and unable to take care of themselves? Is it different for television, commercials, or movies?

▶ | The response entered here will be saved to your notes and may be collected by your instructor if he/she requires it. |

Submit

**CULTURE AND GENDER**  A person's culture is also an environmental influence. Although initial cross-cultural studies suggested that cultural differences had little effect on gender roles (Best & Williams, 2001), more recent research suggests that in the past few decades, a change has occurred in cultures that are of different "personalities." Cultures that are more individualistic (those stressing independence and with loose ties among individuals) and have fairly high standards of living are becoming more nontraditional, especially for women in those cultures. Research has shown that more traditional views of gender seem to be held by collectivistic cultures (those stressing interdependence and with strong ties among individuals, especially familial ties) that have less wealth, although even in these cultures, women were more likely to be less traditional than men (Forbes et al., 2009; Gibbons et al., 1991; Li & Fung, 2015; Shafiro et al., 2003). Other studies have found that the most nontraditional ideas about gender roles and gender behavior are found in countries such as the Netherlands, Germany, Italy, and England, whereas the most traditional ideas predominate in African and Asian countries such as Nigeria, Pakistan, and Japan (Best, 2013; Best & Williams, 2001). The United States, often seen as very nontraditional by researchers, actually was somewhere in the middle in these studies, perhaps due to the large variation in subcultures that exists within this multicultural country. Environment, even in the form of culture, seems to play at least a partial and perhaps dominant role in gender behavior.

The *Gender and Sexuality Survey* asks you about your own views on gender and what factors influence gender roles.

Although Asian cultures are often more traditional in the roles that men and women play within society, even in these cultures gender roles are becoming more flexible, as this male preschool teacher in a Chinese classroom demonstrates. Why might gender roles in these traditional countries be changing?

**Survey**  GENDER AND SEXUALITY SURVEY

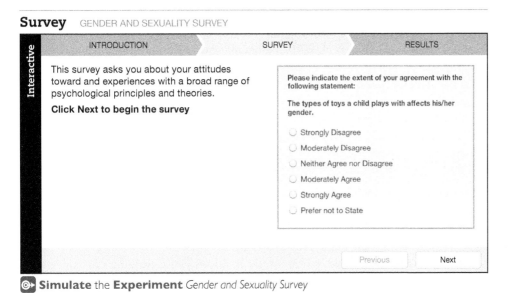

| INTRODUCTION | SURVEY | RESULTS |
| --- | --- | --- |

This survey asks you about your attitudes toward and experiences with a broad range of psychological principles and theories.

**Click Next to begin the survey**

Please indicate the extent of your agreement with the following statement:

The types of toys a child plays with affects his/her gender.

○ Strongly Disagree
○ Moderately Disagree
○ Neither Agree nor Disagree
○ Moderately Agree
○ Strongly Agree
○ Prefer not to State

Previous    Next

◉ **Simulate** the **Experiment** *Gender and Sexuality Survey*

GENDER-ROLE DEVELOPMENT

**10.4**  **Compare and contrast different views of how gender roles develop.**

How do children acquire the knowledge of their society or culture's gender-role expectations? How does that knowledge lead to the development of a gender identity? Although early psychodynamic theorists such as Freud (ⓁⒾⓃⓀ to Learning Objective 13.2) believed that children would learn their gender identities as a natural consequence of resolving the sexual conflicts of early childhood, many modern theorists focus on learning and cognitive processes for the development of gender identity and behavior.

**SOCIAL LEARNING THEORY**  Social learning theory, which emphasizes learning through observation and imitation of models, attributes* gender-role development to those processes. Children observe their same-sex parents behaving in certain ways and imitate that behavior. When the children imitate the appropriate gender behavior, they are reinforced with positive attention. Inappropriate gender behavior is either ignored or actively discouraged (Bussey & Bandura, 1999; Fagot & Hagan, 1991; Mischel, 1966; Wiggert et al., 2015).

As children develop the concept of gender, they begin to imitate the behavior of those they see as similar to themselves.

---

*attributes: explains as a cause.

Of course, parents are not the only gender-role models available to children. In addition to older brothers and sisters, family friends, teachers, and peers, children are exposed to male and female behavior on television and in other media. In fact, television, movies, video games, and children's books are often filled with very traditional male and female roles. In many books, doctors are males and nurses are female far more often than the other way around, for example. Although some children's books, television programs, and video games make a genuine effort to present males and females in nontypical occupations, there are far more that maintain traditional roles for men and women (Ivory, 2006; Miller & Summers, 2007; Wohn, 2011; Zosuls et al., 2011).

**GENDER SCHEMA THEORY**   A theory of gender-role development that combines social learning theory with cognitive development is called **gender schema theory** (Bem, 1987, 1993). In this theory based on the Piagetian concept of schemes (Ⓛ Ⓘ Ⓝ Ⓚ to Learning Objective 8.7), children develop a schema, or mental pattern, for being male or female in much the same way that they develop schemas for other concepts such as "dog," "bird," and "big." As their brains mature, they become capable of distinguishing among various concepts. For example, a "dog" might at first be anything with four legs and a tail, but as a child encounters dogs and other kinds of animals and is given instruction, "dog" becomes more specific and the schema for "dog" becomes well defined.

What are some of the ways in which this father may influence his sons' gender identities as they grow up?

In a similar manner, children develop a concept for "boy" and "girl." Once that schema is in place, children can identify themselves as "boy" or "girl" and will notice other members of that schema. They notice the behavior of other "boys" or "girls" and imitate that behavior. They play with their parents and pick up on differences in the behavior of fathers and mothers (Lindsey et al., 2010). Rather than being simple imitation and reinforcement, as in social learning theory, children acquire their gender-role behavior by organizing that behavior around the schema of "boy" or "girl." Evidence for this theory includes the finding that infants can discriminate between male and female faces and voices before age 1 (Martin, 2000), a sign that infants are already organizing the world into those two concepts, and in the sudden appearance rigidity that occurs in the preschool years, when boys may refuse to wear anything resembling pink and girls may only want to wear frilly dresses as they add those concepts to their gender schema (Halim et al., 2014).

**GENDER STEREOTYPING**   A **stereotype** is a concept that can be held about a person or group of people that is based on very superficial characteristics. A **gender stereotype** is a concept about males or females that assigns various characteristics to them on the basis of nothing more than being male or female.

The male gender stereotype generally includes the following characteristics: aggressive, logical, decisive, unemotional, insensitive, nonnurturing, impatient, and mechanically talented. The female stereotype typically includes these characteristics: illogical, changeable, emotional, sensitive, naturally nurturing, patient, and all thumbs when it comes to understanding machines. Notice that each of these stereotypes has both positive and negative characteristics, and also that all are based on society's opinions about men and women rather than actual biological differences.

Some researchers believe that accepting stereotyping of any kind, even positive stereotyping, can lead to **sexism**, or prejudice about males and females. In fact, some researchers (Glick & Fiske, 2001; Hammond et al., 2016) claim that acceptance of positive stereotypes can lead to **benevolent sexism**, prejudice that is more socially acceptable but still leads to men and women being treated unequally. Not all men are mechanically talented, nor are all women naturally nurturing, for example. A positive stereotype for men is that they are strong and protective of women, implying that women are weak and need protection, just as the positive female stereotype of natural nurturance of children implies that males cannot be nurturing. Such stereotypes, although somewhat "flattering" for the sex about whom they are held, can be harmful to the other sex. Any stereotype, whether negative or positive, continues to emphasize inequality between the genders and can lead to an increase in discrimination—definitely a harmful process.

**gender schema theory**

theory of gender identity acquisition in which a child develops a mental pattern, or schema, for being male or female and then organizes observed and learned behavior around that schema.

**stereotype**

a set of characteristics that people believe is shared by all members of a particular social category; a concept held about a person or group of people that is based on superficial, irrelevant characteristics.

**gender stereotype**

a concept held about a person or group of people that is based on being male or female.

**sexism**

prejudice about males and/or females leading to unequal treatment.

**benevolent sexism**

acceptance of positive stereotypes of males and females that leads to unequal treatment.

Can you think of examples of benevolent sexism in your own life?

▶ | The response entered here will be saved to your notes and may be
collected by your instructor if he/she requires it.

Submit

**ANDROGYNY**   Psychologist Sandra Bem (1975, 1981) has developed the concept of **androgyny** to describe a characteristic of people whose personalities reflect the characteristics of both males and females, regardless of gender. This allows them to be more flexible in everyday behavior and career choices. People who fall into the gender-role stereotypes, according to Bem, often find themselves limited in their choices for problem solving because of the stereotype's constraints on "proper" male or female behavior. An androgynous person, on the other hand, can make a decision based on the situation rather than on being masculine or feminine.

Actress Tilda Swinton has had a life-long interest in the concept of androgyny, and typically is seen dressed in an androgynous style.

For example, let's say that a man, through an unhappy circumstance, is left to raise his three small children. If he is a male who has "bought into" the male stereotype, he has no confidence in his ability to bring up these children by himself. He may rush into another relationship with a woman just to provide his children with a "mother." Similarly, a "traditional" female who is left without a husband might have difficulty in dealing with raising sons and with a task as simple as mowing the lawn. Researchers have found that when traditional males, traditional females, and androgynous people are compared in terms of the degree of depression they experience when their lives are filled with many negative events, the androgynous people report less than half the depression exhibited by traditional men and only a third of the depression felt by traditional women (Roos & Cohen, 1987). **Figure 10.2**

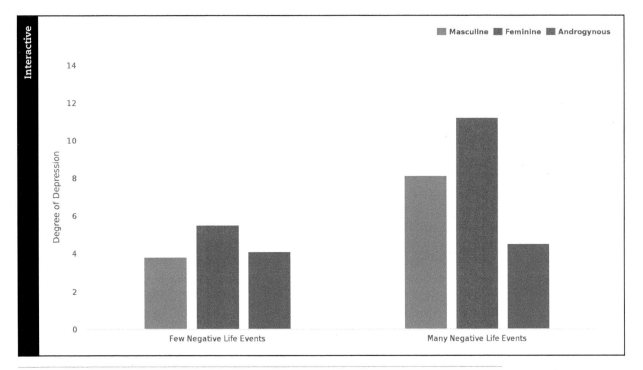

**Figure 10.2**   Depression as Influenced by Negative Life Events

The bar graph shows that men who are masculine and women who are feminine in their gender roles experience a significant increase in depression when they are exposed to an increased number of negative life events. The same is not true for people with an androgynous gender role. How might being androgynous allow a person to be more adaptable?

**androgyny**
characteristic of possessing the most positive personality characteristics of males and females regardless of actual sex.

shows the results of this study. Similar findings have been obtained by several subsequent studies, suggesting that androgyny may lead to better, more efficient and effective coping skills during times of stress (Cheng et al., 2014; Prakash, et al., 2010).

### GENDER DIFFERENCES

**10.5** **Describe how men and women differ in thinking, social behavior, and personality.**

Although there are clear biological differences in males and females, even to the point of affecting the size of certain structures in the brain (Swaab et al., 2012; Zilles & Amunts, 2012), what sort of differences exist in the behavior of males and females? Are those differences due to biology, socialization, or a combination of the two influences?

It was long believed that the difference between girls and boys in math skills was a function of biology, but research now shows that psychological and social issues are the more likely causes.

**COGNITIVE DIFFERENCES**   Researchers have long held that females score higher on tests of verbal abilities than do males but that males score higher on tests of mathematical skills and spatial skills (Diamond, 1991; Voyer et al., 1995). Early explanations of these differences in cognitive functioning involved physical differences in the way each sex used the two hemispheres of the brain as well as hormonal differences (Witelson, 1991). Other research, however, strongly suggests that psychological and social issues may be more responsible for these differences, as these differences have become less and less obvious (Hyde & Plant, 1995; Kimura, 1999; Miller & Halpern, 2014; Voyer et al., 1995; Watt, 2000). In particular, the supposed differences in math abilities between boys and girls have now been shown to be more the effect of girls' lack of confidence rather than any biological difference in the working of the brain (American Association of University Women, 1992, 1998; Else-Quest et al., 2010; Goetz et al., 2013; Guo et al., 2015; Sadker & Sadker, 1994). That the disparities (which are actually quite small) seem to be disappearing as society has begun to view the two genders as more equal in ability is taken as a sign that more equal treatment in society has reduced the gender difference.

"It's a guy thing."

**SOCIAL AND PERSONALITY DIFFERENCES**   The differences normally cited between men and women in the ways they interact with others and in their personality traits are often the result of stereotyped thinking about the sexes. It is difficult to demonstrate differences that are not caused by the way boys and girls are socialized as they grow up. Boys are taught to hold in their emotions, not to cry, to be "strong" and "manly." Girls are encouraged to form emotional attachments, be emotional, and be open about their feelings with others.

In communication, research suggests that when men talk to each other, they tend to talk about current events, sports, and other events. This has been called a "report" style of communication and seems to involve switching topics frequently, with attempts to dominate the conversation by certain members of the group. In contrast, women tend to use a "relate" style of communication with each other, revealing a lot about their private lives and showing concern and sympathy. They tend to interrupt each other less and let everyone participate in the conversation (Argamon et al., 2003; Coates, 1986; Pilkington, 1998; Swann, 1998). There seem to be similar differences in the way men and women use social media communication, such as Twitter (Cunha et al., 2014). Another study, using fMRI technology, found that men listen with the left hemisphere only, whereas women listen with both hemispheres, suggesting that women pay attention to the tone and emotion of statements as well as the content (Lurito et al., 2000). The existence of such differences does not necessarily mean that these differences are present at birth and influenced only by biology, however. Many experts caution that such differences in neurological functioning can be the result of sociocultural influences (Case & Oetama-Paul, 2015; Kaiser et al., 2009). And, contrary to what you may see in the popular press, human beings cannot simply be characterized as having a "female" versus a "male" brain (Joel et al., 2015).

## Concept Map L.O. 10.3, 10.4, 10.5

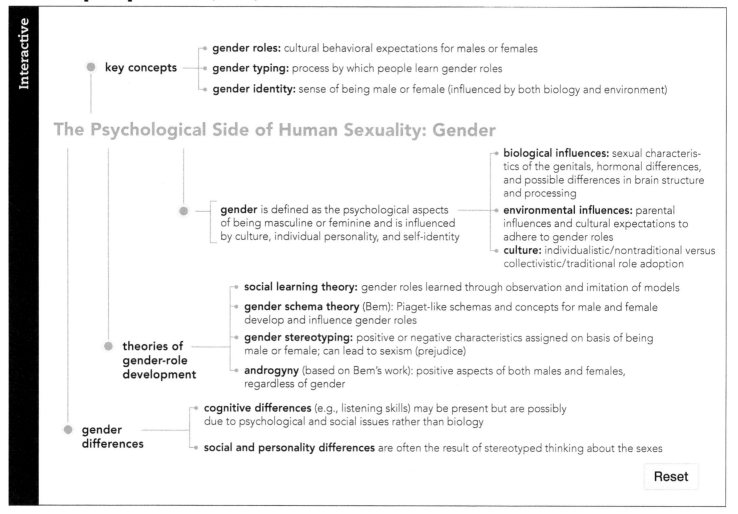

**Interactive**

**key concepts**
- **gender roles:** cultural behavioral expectations for males or females
- **gender typing:** process by which people learn gender roles
- **gender identity:** sense of being male or female (influenced by both biology and environment)

## The Psychological Side of Human Sexuality: Gender

**gender** is defined as the psychological aspects of being masculine or feminine and is influenced by culture, individual personality, and self-identity
- **biological influences:** sexual characteristics of the genitals, hormonal differences, and possible differences in brain structure and processing
- **environmental influences:** parental influences and cultural expectations to adhere to gender roles
- **culture:** individualistic/nontraditional versus collectivistic/traditional role adoption

**theories of gender-role development**
- **social learning theory:** gender roles learned through observation and imitation of models
- **gender schema theory** (Bem): Piaget-like schemas and concepts for male and female develop and influence gender roles
- **gender stereotyping:** positive or negative characteristics assigned on basis of being male or female; can lead to sexism (prejudice)
- **androgyny** (based on Bem's work): positive aspects of both males and females, regardless of gender

**gender differences**
- **cognitive differences** (e.g., listening skills) may be present but are possibly due to psychological and social issues rather than biology
- **social and personality differences** are often the result of stereotyped thinking about the sexes

Reset

# Practice Quiz   How much do you remember?

*Pick the best answer.*

**1.** The process by which people learn their culture's preferences and expectations for male and female behavior is called
   **a.** gender role.
   **b.** gender identity.
   **c.** gender typing.
   **d.** gender stereotyping.

**2.** People whose sense of gender identity does not match their external biological appearance are known as
   **a.** intersex.
   **b.** homosexual.
   **c.** hermaphrodites.
   **d.** transgender.

**3.** Alex sees his mother mixing ingredients for a cake. Later, Alex takes a bowl and spoon out of the cabinet and pretends to mix some imaginary ingredients. Of which theory of gender development would this be a good example?
   **a.** gender schema theory
   **b.** psychoanalytic theory
   **c.** gender-role theory
   **d.** social learning theory

**4.** Which theory of gender-role development places a heavy emphasis on the use of mental patterns?
   **a.** gender schema theory
   **b.** social learning theory
   **c.** psychoanalytic theory
   **d.** behavioral theory

**5.** Karl is often perceived as strong and tough, but he also has been known to be sincere and loving. Karla is warm and kind but is also independent and assertive when necessary. Bem would classify such behavior as examples of
   **a.** androgyny.
   **b.** benevolent sexism.
   **c.** schema error.
   **d.** negative stereotyping.

**6.** Studies show that women tend to use a _____ style to their conversation, while men use a _____ style.
   **a.** relate; report
   **b.** report; relate
   **c.** masculine; feminine
   **d.** androgynous; stereotypical

# Human Sexual Behavior

 💬 I've heard that men and women experience sex differently—is that true? What is different?

In 1957, gynecologist Dr. William Masters and psychologist Dr. Virginia Johnson began what would become a controversial* study of the human sexual response in 700 men and women volunteers (Masters & Johnson, 1966). At that time in history, human sexuality was still a relatively forbidden topic to all but young adults, who were exploring the concepts of "free love" and engaging in premarital sex far more openly than in the past. Masters and Johnson devised equipment that would measure the physical responses that occur during sexual activity. They used this equipment to measure physiological activity in both men and women volunteers who either were engaging in actual intercourse or masturbation. Although many conservative and religious people were outraged by this research, it remains one of the most important studies of the human sexual response.

## SEXUAL RESPONSE

### 10.6 Identify the four stages of a sexual-response cycle.

Masters and Johnson (1966) identified four stages of a sexual-response cycle in their groundbreaking research. Although these stages are similar in both men and women, there are some differences. Also, the transition between the stages is not necessarily as well defined as the descriptions of the stages might seem to describe, and the length of time spent in any one phase can vary from experience to experience and person to person.

**PHASE 1: EXCITEMENT**    This first phase is the beginning of sexual arousal and can last anywhere from 1 minute to several hours. Pulse rate increases, blood pressure rises, breathing quickens, and the skin may show a rosy flush, especially on the chest or breast areas. In women, the clitoris swells, the lips of the vagina open, and the inside of the vagina moistens in preparation for intercourse. In men, the penis becomes erect, the testes pull up, and the skin of the scrotum tightens. Nipples will harden and become more erect in both sexes, but especially in the female.

**PHASE 2: PLATEAU**    In the second phase of the sexual response, the physical changes that began in the first phase are continued. In women, the outer part of the vagina swells with increased amounts of blood to that area, while the clitoris retracts under the clitoral hood but remains highly sensitive. The outer lips of the vagina become redder in color. In men, the penis becomes more erect and may release a few drops of fluid. This phase may last only a few seconds to several minutes.

**PHASE 3: ORGASM**    The third phase is the shortest of the three stages and involves a series of rhythmic muscular contractions known as the **orgasm**. In women, this involves the muscles of the vaginal walls and can happen multiple times, lasting slightly longer than the orgasm experience of the male. The uterus also contracts, creating a pleasurable sensation. In men, the orgasmic contractions of the muscles in and around the penis trigger the release of **semen**, the fluid that contains the male sex cells, or sperm. Men typically have only one intense orgasm. Timing is also different for women and men, with women taking longer to reach orgasm than men and women requiring more stimulation to achieve orgasm.

**PHASE 4: RESOLUTION**    The final phase of the sexual response is **resolution**, the return of the body to its normal state before arousal began. The blood that congested the blood vessels in the various areas of the genitals recedes; the heart rate, blood pressure, and

**orgasm**

a series of rhythmic contractions of the muscles of the vaginal walls or the penis, also the third and shortest phase of sexual response.

**semen**

fluid released from the penis at orgasm that contains the sperm.

**resolution**

the final phase of the sexual response in which the body is returned to a normal state.

*controversial: leading to arguments or opposing viewpoints.

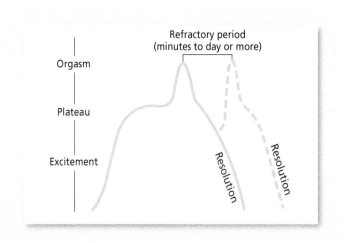

**Figure 10.3** The Male Sexual-Response Cycle

A male experiences sexual arousal (excitement), a plateau lasting a few seconds to a few minutes, orgasm, and then experiences a refractory period during which another orgasm is not yet possible. This refractory period can last for several minutes to several hours to a day or more and tends to increase in length with age. After the refractory period, a second orgasm is possible. Resolution, in which the body returns to its prearousal state, is last.

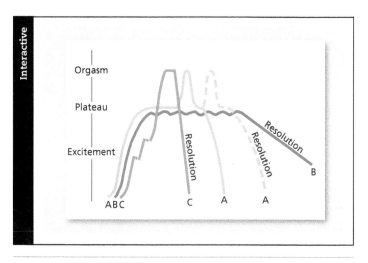

**Figure 10.4** The Female Sexual-Response Cycle

Women can experience several different patterns of sexual response. In Pattern A, a woman experiences excitement, a plateau, and orgasm in a manner similar to a man. Unlike a man, the woman does not have a refractory period and can experience several orgasms before entering resolution. In Pattern B, there is a longer plateau period but no orgasm, and in Pattern C, the woman goes from excitement to orgasm to a quick resolution without experiencing a plateau period.

breathing all reduce to normal levels during this phase. In women, the clitoris retracts, the color of the vaginal lips returns to normal, and the lips close once more. In men, the erection is lost, the testes descend, and the scrotal sac thins again. Also, men have a **refractory period** during which they cannot achieve another orgasm, lasting anywhere from several minutes to several hours for different individuals. The older the man gets, the longer the refractory period tends to extend. Women do not have a refractory period and in fact may achieve another series of orgasms if stimulation continues.

Read the Classic Studies in Psychology section that follows for a more detailed look at the historic Masters and Johnson study and to learn how this landmark research was accomplished. (See also **Figures 10.3** and **10.4**.)

**refractory period**

time period in males just after orgasm in which the male cannot become aroused to another orgasm.

## Classic Studies in Psychology

## Masters and Johnson's Observational Study of the Human Sexual Response

William Masters and Virginia Johnson pioneered the first direct observational study of human sexual behavior. Their study stirred up tremendous controversy in an era that feared that the study of human sexuality would undermine the structure of the family and society. Masters obtained permission from his department chair at the Washington University School of Medicine in St. Louis, Missouri, in 1954. He then assembled an advisory board composed of the police commissioner, a newspaper publisher, and several prominent religious leaders, in addition to the university's chancellor. Together, they accomplished a feat that seems incredible in today's media-driven world: They convinced the press to keep completely quiet about this research into human sexuality for the next 12 years (Kolodny, 2001).

Such research had to be conducted discreetly, as even Masters's choice of subjects was controversial. His initial studies in 1955 and 1956 were done

Dr. William Masters and Dr. Virginia Johnson examined human sexuality by measuring physiological responses in a laboratory. Their subjects were volunteers, many of whom were prostitutes, a fact that caused an uproar when their research became public.

entirely with prostitutes. He conducted interviews with them and observed them at work. Although this research was never published, he used the opportunity to think about what kind of instrumentation he would need to properly measure the sexual responses in a more controlled setting. Together with psychologist Virginia Johnson, Masters devised equipment that would allow them to measure sexual responses in humans in a laboratory setting. These machines were similar to a polygraph machine (a lie detector) but much more complex in their design and the particular physiological responses (for example, heart rate, body temperature) they measured. Masters and Johnson also used photography and direct observation in the laboratory settings, using prostitutes and other volunteers as subjects.

The publication of *Human Sexual Response* in 1966 was the result of the 12 years of research. Masters and Johnson became instant celebrities, and the book itself became a bestseller. This was the beginning of a partnership that lasted over 30 years. That partnership not only changed many people's attitudes about what was sexually normal but also challenged many sexual myths and created the field of sex therapy. Although direct observational studies can have the disadvantage of affecting the participant's behavior, the work of Masters and Johnson has remained some of the most important work in the field of human sexuality and is still used in sex therapy and sex education and by infertility and conception experts (Kolodny, 2001; Masters, Johnson, & Kolodny, 1995).

## Questions for Further Discussion

1. Would researchers today be able to convince the press (newspapers, magazines, and television) to keep research into human sexuality secret, as Masters did?
2. What problems with their research might have come from the fact that many of their participants were prostitutes?
3. In what ways might this kind of research be easier to conduct today?
4. In what ways might this kind of research be more difficult to conduct today?

## DIFFERENT TYPES OF SEXUAL BEHAVIOR

### 10.7 Summarize the findings of early and recent surveys of human sexual behavior.

While Masters and Johnson focused their research on the physiological responses that occur during the sexual act, other researchers had already been studying the different forms of sexual behavior. The study of sexual behavior is not the study of the sex act but rather when, with whom, and under what circumstances sexual acts take place. Although there were other attempts to study human sexual behavior before the mid-twentieth-century studies of Alfred Kinsey (Kinsey et al., 1948; Kinsey et al., 1953), his original work remains an important source of information concerning the different ways in which people engage in the sex act.

  What were the findings of the report?

**THE KINSEY STUDY** In 1948, Alfred Kinsey published a controversial report on the results of a massive survey of sexual behavior collected from 1938 forward (Kinsey et al., 1948). His findings concerning the frequency of behavior such as masturbation, anal sex, and premarital sex rocked many people, who were apparently not ready to believe that so many people had tried alternative sexual behaviors. Kinsey believed that sexual orientation was not an either/or situation in which one is either completely heterosexual or completely homosexual but instead that sexual orientation is on a continuum,* with

---

*continuum: a sequence of values, elements, or behavior that varies by small degrees.

some people falling at either extreme and some falling closer to the middle. The idea that there were many people who fit into that middle range of sexual orientation was shocking and, for many at that time, unbelievable.

Kinsey used highly trained interviewers who conducted face-to-face interviews with the participants, who were all male in the original study. A later survey was published in 1953 that dealt exclusively with females (Kinsey et al., 1953). The participants were volunteers supposedly from both rural and urban areas and from different socioeconomic, religious, and educational backgrounds. In reality, a large portion of the participants were well-educated, urban, young Protestants. In Kinsey's survey results, nearly half of the men but less than 20 percent of the women reported having bisexual experiences. More than three times as many men as women had intercourse by age 16 (21 percent versus 6 percent). Men were also more likely to report engaging in premarital sex, extramarital sex, and masturbation than were women. Ten percent of the men and 2 to 6 percent of the women answering the survey identified themselves as predominantly homosexual (Gebhard & Johnson, 1979/1998).

Although Kinsey's data are still quoted in many discussions of sexual behavior, his original surveys were far from perfect. As stated earlier, the participants were almost exclusively white, middle class, and college educated. Older people, those who lived in rural regions, and less educated people were not well represented. Some critics claimed that Kinsey gave far more attention to sexual behavior that was considered unusual or abnormal than he did to "normal" sexual behavior (Geddes, 1954). Also, Kinsey's surveys were no less susceptible to the exaggerations, falsifications, and errors of any method using self-report techniques. Finally, a face-to-face interview might cause some people being interviewed to be inhibited about admitting to certain kinds of sexual behavior, or others might exaggerate wildly, increasing the likelihood of inaccurate data.

Alfred Kinsey conducted many of his interviews face to face, as seen here. How might having to answer questions about one's sexual behavior be affected by Kinsey's presence?

**THE JANUS REPORT** In 1993, Dr. Samuel S. Janus and Dr. Cynthia L. Janus published the results of the first large-scale study of human sexual behavior since those of Kinsey and colleagues (1948) and Masters and Johnson (1966). This national survey, begun in 1983, sampled 3,000 people from all 48 mainland states. Survey respondents ranged in age from 18 to over 65 years old from all levels of marital status, educational backgrounds, and geographical regions in the United States.

Findings from the Janus Report (Janus & Janus, 1993) differed from Kinsey's findings, but not extremely so. For example, fewer men reported masturbating in the Janus Report than did in Kinsey's study (80 percent versus 92 percent), but the percentage of women reporting increased from 62 percent in Kinsey's survey to 70 percent in the Janus survey. Rates of premarital sex were about the same as in Kinsey's survey, but men in the Janus survey reported less extramarital sex than men in the Kinsey survey, while women's reporting of extramarital sex was the same in the two surveys. Percentages of both men and women in the Janus survey reporting as predominantly homosexual were also very similar to the earlier Kinsey study.

**THE NATIONAL SURVEY OF SEXUAL HEALTH AND BEHAVIOR** In 2010, researchers from the Center for Sexual Health Promotion at Indiana University produced the National Survey of Sexual Health and Behavior (NSSHB). Based on a nationally representative sample of 5,865 United States adolescents and adults ages 14 to 94, their research resulted in an extensive and comprehensive overview of sexual experiences and condom-use behaviors (Herbenick et al., 2010).

Of the males participating in the NSSHB and their sexual behaviors in the past month, 27.9 to 68.6 percent engaged in solo masturbation. Across age groups, the majority of males reported masturbating in the last year, with only 14- to 15-year-olds and 70+ age groups being the exception. For females, 20 percent engaged in solo masturbation during the past month. And other than those over 70 years, 40 to 72 percent of females did so in the past year, with the highest percentages in 18- to 49-year-olds (Herbenick et al., 2010).

The highest rates of vaginal intercourse were reported for both men and women across age groups associated with reproductive years. However, across the same age groups, a significant number of individuals also reported solo masturbation, masturbation with a partner, oral sex, and anal sex during the previous year (Herbenick et al., 2010). As noted by the researchers, sexual behavior during the reproductive years is not solely for reproductive purposes.

For most recent vaginal intercourse, 24.7 percent of adult men and 21.8 percent of adult women reported use of a condom. In adolescent males and females, the rates were 79.6 percent and 70.2 percent, respectively. Condom use appears to drop off significantly in early adulthood. Across all cohorts, condom use was more frequent when intercourse took place with a casual partner as compared to a relationship partner (Reece et al., 2010). Overall, the highest rates were reported during adolescence, were higher for men than for women, and higher among black and Hispanic individuals (Reece et al., 2010).

**EXPLAINING THE SURVEY FINDINGS** Why are men so much more sexually active than women, both before and during marriage? It may be in their genes. Evolutionary theory emphasizes that organisms will do what they must to maximize their chances of passing on their genetic material in their offspring, and that process is different for men and women. Robert Trivers proposed a theory of *parental investment* to explain the different sexual behavior of men and women (Trivers, 1972). Males of many species, including humans, do not have to invest a lot of time or effort into impregnating a female, so they are better off—genetically speaking—when they seek many sexual encounters with many sexual partners. Females, on the other hand, invest much more time and effort in reproducing: the pregnancy, feeding the infants, and so on. So females are better off being more selective about the males they choose for sex.

In real-life terms, this translates into men preferring women who are younger, prettier (immediate sexual attraction being the big draw), and therefore are likely to produce healthy, attractive offspring. Women are more likely to prefer men who are older (which means they will likely have more income and resources), hard workers, and loyal (Buss, 1989, 2007; Buss & Schmitt, 1993, 2011). Men are much more likely than women to have multiple sexual partners, even well into middle age, while women are more likely to have fewer partners over their lifetime (McBurney et al., 2005; Schutzwohl et al., 2009). This is true for both heterosexual and homosexual men and women (Peplau & Fingerhut, 2007). Men even think about sex differently, having more sexual fantasies than women and of a greater variety (Okami & Shackelford, 2001), as well as simply thinking about sex more often than women (Laumann et al., 1994). There is some evidence, however, that differences in mate preferences are much smaller in cultures or social groups in which there is greater gender equality, suggesting that many of the differences in mate preferences may be related to differences in gender roles rather than just biology (Zentner & Mitura, 2012).

Surveys of sexual behavior highlight the fact that age is not necessarily a barrier to being sexually active. One survey of more than 3,000 people aged 57 to 85 found that many people are sexually active well into their 80s (Lindau et al., 2007). In this survey, the most common barriers to sexual activity were health problems or lack of a partner rather than a lack of desire. Another survey of 1,939 Spanish people over the age of 65 found that just over 62 percent of men and 37 percent of women were sexually active, although the incidence of sexual inactivity did increase with age, with reasons for sexual inactivity being nearly equally distributed among "physically ill partner," "being widowed," and "lack of interest" (Palacios-Ceña et al., 2011).

Of course, surveys have their problems, as stated earlier. One possible problem might occur when asking the question, "At what age did you first have sex?" A study (Sanders et al., 2010) reports that not everyone means the same thing by the words "have sex" or "had sex." In a sample of people 18 to 96 years old, 30 percent did not consider oral sex to be sex. Many older men—nearly a fourth of those surveyed—did not consider penile–vaginal intercourse to be sex! Some thought it wasn't sex if there was no orgasm. There was simply little agreement among survey participants as to what "having sex" really means, and researchers examining sexual behavior through the survey method should be very aware of this possible confusion.

The technology we use every day may also have an impact on sexual behavior, as the APA Goal 2 feature in the next module illustrates.

## SEXUAL ORIENTATION

**10.8** **Identify some influences on the development of sexual orientation.**

The term **sexual orientation** refers to a person's sexual attraction and affection for members of either the opposite or the same sex. One of the more important questions that researchers are trying to answer is whether sexual orientation is the product of learning and experience or if it is biological in origin.

**CATEGORIES OF SEXUAL ORIENTATION**    As the video *Sexual Orientation: Definition and Prevalence* shows, there are a variety of sexual orientation categories that individuals may identify with, and getting reliable data can be challenging.

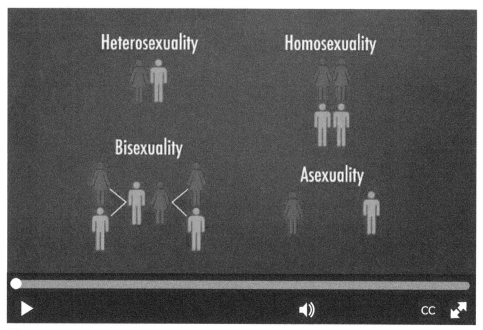

👁 **Watch** the **Video** *Sexual Orientation: Definition and Prevalence*

The most common sexual orientation is **heterosexual**, in which people are sexually attracted to members of the opposite physical sex, as in a man being attracted to a woman or vice versa. (The Greek word *hetero* means "other," so *heterosexual* means "other sexual" or attraction for the other sex.) Heterosexuality is a socially acceptable form of sexual behavior in all cultures.

It is difficult to get an accurate percentage for **homosexual** orientation, or sexual attraction to members of one's own sex. (The Greek word *homo* means "same.") The problem concerns the discrimination, prejudice, and mistreatment that homosexual people face in most cultures, making it more likely that a homosexual person will lie about his or her sexual orientation to avoid such negative treatment. A national survey estimates that about 1.8 percent of adult men and 1.5 percent of adult women aged 18 years and older consider themselves to be gay or lesbian, meaning that their sexual orientations are exclusively or predominantly homosexual (Ward et al., 2014).

**sexual orientation**

a person's sexual attraction to and affection for members of either the opposite or the same sex.

**heterosexual**

person attracted to the opposite sex.

**homosexual**

person attracted to the same sex.

Homosexuality is a sexual orientation that has faced discrimination and prejudice in many cultures.

 If people have had a homosexual experience as well as heterosexual ones, does that make them bisexual people?

A person who is **bisexual** may be either male or female and is attracted to both sexes. In the same national survey, only 0.4 percent of the men and 0.9 percent of the women considered themselves to be bisexual (Ward et al., 2014). (It should be noted that many people experiment with alternative sexual behavior before deciding upon their true sexual identity; one bisexual experience does not make a person bisexual any more than one homosexual experience makes a person homosexual.)

Bisexual people do not necessarily have relationships with both men and women during the same period of time and may vary in the degree of attraction to one sex or the other over time. Many bisexual individuals may not act on their desires but instead have a long-term monogamous relationship with only one partner.

There are also people who do not identify as heterosexual, homosexual, or bisexual but see themselves as *asexual*. Asexuality is a lack of sexual attraction to anyone, or a lack of interest in sexual activity (Prause et al., 2004). A study conducted in Great Britain indicated that about 1 percent of the British population identified as asexual (Bogaert, 2006). Obviously, sexual orientation is not as clearly defined as many people have assumed.

**DEVELOPMENT OF SEXUAL ORIENTATION**   Although heterosexuality may be socially acceptable across cultures, as stated earlier, there are various cultures in which homosexuality and bisexuality are not considered acceptable and in which people of those orientations have faced prejudice, discrimination, harassment, and much worse. Although attitudes in some of these cultures are beginning to change to more positive ones (Loftus, 2001; Pew Research Center, 2013; Tucker & Potocky-Tripodi, 2006), full acceptance of alternatives to heterosexuality is still a long way off. Try the experiment, *Implicit Association Test: Sexuality*, to learn what implicit preferences and prejudices you may hold toward both heterosexual and homosexual individuals. **◎→ Simulate the Experiment,** *Implicit Association Test: Sexuality*

Young people who are coming to terms with their identities and sexual orientation seem to have great difficulty when faced with being homosexual, bisexual, or transgender. These adolescents are at higher risk than their heterosexual peers for substance abuse, sexually risky behavior, eating disorders, suicidal thinking, and victimization by others (Coker et al., 2009; Kattari & Hasche, 2016; Ward et al., 2014; Zhao et al., 2010). When identification of one's sense of self as homosexual is paired with being another type of social minority (such as Asian American or Pacific Islander living in the United States), the stresses and pressures are compounded (Hahm & Adkins, 2009). In the cultures from which these young people's families originate, traditional values make homosexuality a dishonor and shame to the family.

 Is sexual orientation a product of the environment, biology, or both?

This is a very controversial issue for both heterosexual and homosexual people (Diamond, 1995). If homosexuality is a product of upbringing and environmental experiences, it can be assumed to be a behavior that can be changed, placing a burden of choice to be "normal" or "abnormal" squarely on the shoulders of homosexual people. If it is biological, either through genetic influences or hormonal influences during pregnancy, then it can be seen as a behavior that is no more a choice than whether the infant is born a male or a female. The implications of homosexuality as biological lead to some volatile* issues: If it is not a choice or a learned behavior pattern, then society will no longer be able to expect or demand that homosexual people change their sexual behavior or orientation. Homosexuality becomes an issue of diversity rather than socially unacceptable behavior. In a survey of college students (Elliott & Brantley, 1997), the majority of women reported knowing

**bisexual**

person attracted to both men and women.

---
*volatile: explosive.

they were gay or bisexual by their high school/college years, while the majority of men reported knowing they were gay or bisexual by junior high/high school.

In the past several decades, a large body of research in the areas of biological differences in the brains of heterosexual and homosexual males, genetic influences on sexual orientation, and even prenatal influences on sexual orientation has been amassed by various scientists. One of the earliest studies, for example, found that severe stress experienced by pregnant women during the second trimester of pregnancy (the time during which the sexual differences in genitalia are formed) results in a significantly higher chance of any male children becoming homosexual in orientation (Ellis et al., 1988). Another study found that homosexual men and heterosexual women respond similarly (and quite differently than heterosexual men) to a testosterone-based pheromone (glandular chemical) that is secreted in perspiration (Savic et al., 2005). In a recent study, researchers have found that while there has yet to be any actual gene found directly influencing the transmission of homosexuality, there are genetic "switches" that can be passed on and that may be the reason that homosexuality tends to run in families (Rice et al., 2012). These switches, called *epi-marks*, control when, where, and how much of the information contained in our genes is expressed. There are sex-specific epi-marks that control the sexual characteristics of the fetus during prenatal development. These sexual characteristics include not only physical sex organ development but also sexual identity and sexual partner preference. Normally epi-marks are created anew with each generation, but occasionally they remain to be passed on to the next generation. When that happens, they may cause the reverse of their intended effect, including a reverse of sexual orientation.

Birth order has also been the subject of research in this area, with studies suggesting that the more older brothers a man has, the more likely the younger man is to be homosexual in orientation (Blanchard, 2001; Currin et al., 2015; Kishida & Rahman, 2015; McConaghy et al., 2006). The hypothesis is that with each male birth, the mother of these males develops a kind of "antibody" effect against the Y chromosome, and these antibodies pass through the placenta and affect the sexual orientation of the later-born males. Even facial structure has been found to have some predictive value for sexual orientation (Skorska et al., 2015).

Finally, a neuroimaging study with heterosexual men and women and homosexual men and women found that the heterosexual men and homosexual women seemed neurologically similar when compared to homosexual men and heterosexual women, who were in turn neurologically similar to each other (Savic & Lindström, 2008). A more recent study of lateralization of the brain in homosexual men, heterosexual men, and heterosexual women found that the homosexual men were more similar in lateralization for recognizing facial emotions to heterosexual women than they were to heterosexual men (Rahman & Yusuf, 2015).

The evidence for genetic influences on sexual orientation is increasingly convincing. In studies of male and female homosexual people who have identical twins, fraternal twins, or adopted siblings, researchers found that 52 percent of the identical twin siblings were also gay, compared to 22 percent of the fraternal twins and only 11 percent of the adopted brothers and sisters (Bailey & Pillard, 1991). In a similar study with lesbian women only, 48 percent of identical twins were also gay compared to 16 percent of the fraternal twins and 6 percent of the adopted siblings (Bailey et al., 1993). Other research along similar lines has supported these findings (Bailey et al., 2000; Dawood et al., 2000:Ngun & Vilain, 2014; Sanders et al., 2015). However, these findings should be interpreted cautiously. Twin studies are difficult to conduct without the influence of environment on behavior. Even twins who are raised apart tend to be reared in similar environments, so that the influence of learning and experience on sexual orientation cannot be entirely ruled out.

Some research suggests that homosexuality may be transmitted by genes carried on the X chromosome, which is passed from mother to son but not from father to son. In 33 out of 40 homosexual brothers, Dean Hamer and colleagues (Hamer et al., 1993) found an area on the X chromosome (in a location called Xq28) that contains several hundred genes that the homosexual brothers had in common in every case, even though other genes on that chromosome were different. This was taken as evidence that the brothers had both inherited a set of genes, donated on the mother's X chromosome, that might be responsible for their sexual orientation. These findings have been supported in other research as well (Hu et al., 1994; Sanders et al., 2015; Turner, 1995).

One of the most common behavioral findings about male homosexuals has been that they are consistently "feminine" as children (Bailey & Zucker, 1995; Lippa, 2010). The Bailey and Zucker (1995) study found that about three fourths of homosexual male adults were "feminine" boys (defined as boys who were uninterested in sports or rough play, desired to be girls, or had a reputation as a "sissy"), a far greater rate than in the general population of males. The researchers interpreted these findings as further support for the biological foundations of sexual orientation. Of course, those differences in childhood behavior could also have been the result of attention and other forms of reinforcement from the social environment. It is a very difficult task to separate the environmental influences on any aspect of behavior from the biological ones. One thing is certain: The issue of what causes sexual orientation will continue to generate research and controversy for a long time to come.

## Concept Map L.O. 10.6, 10.7, 10.8

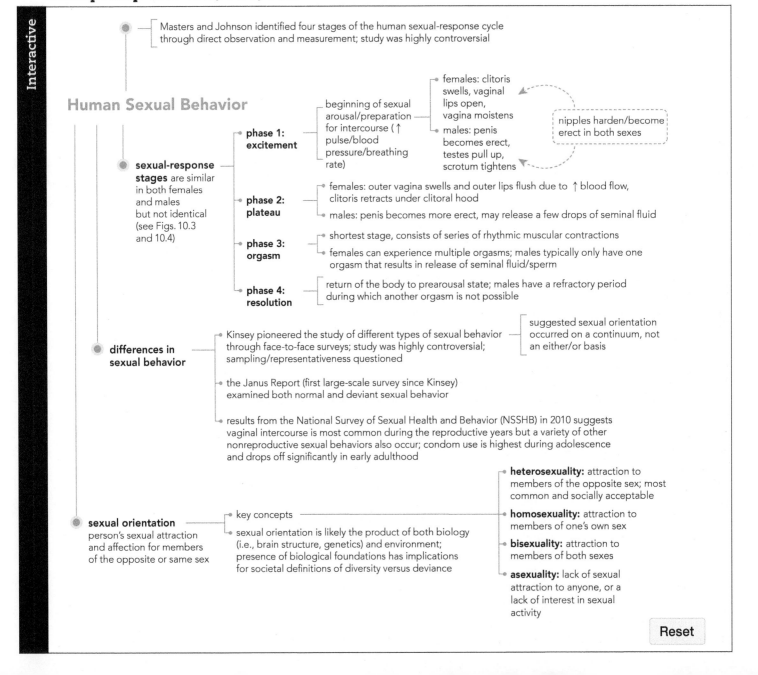

# Practice Quiz   How much do you remember?

*Pick the best answer.*

**1.** Which of the following is the first phase of the human sexual response cycle?
a. excitement      c. orgasm
b. plateau         d. resolution

**2.** Which phase of the sexual response is typically the shortest?
a. excitement      c. orgasm
b. plateau         d. resolution

**3.** In Kinsey's original data, approximately _____ of women reported being predominantly homosexual, while as many as _____ of men reported the same.
a. 6 percent; 21 percent      c. 2 percent; 22 percent
b. 6 to 14 percent; 46 percent   d. 2 to 6 percent; 10 percent

**4.** Which of the following was a criticism of Kinsey's research?
a. The study was incomplete.
b. The study asked poorly worded questions.
c. The study was rushed.
d. The study had a restricted sample.

**5.** Robert Trivers's theory of parental investment states that a _____ desire to engage in sex at an early age results from _____.
a. man's; social pressure
b. man's; evolution
c. woman's; biological concerns
d. woman's; psychological pressure

**6.** One study found that the major reason for decrease in sexual activity in later adulthood was primarily due to
a. a loss of interest in sex.
b. fewer opportunities to find an available partner.
c. a belief that sex and sexual fantasies in late adulthood was unhealthy.
d. a desire to channel energy into other tasks.

# APA Goal 2: Scientific Reasoning and Critical Thinking

*Addresses APA Learning Objectives 2.4: Interpret, design, and conduct basic psychological research; and 2.5: Incorporate sociocultural factors in scientific inquiry.*

### Sexting and Sex in Adolescents

For many people, it's hard to imagine being without a cell phone. Essentially a computer in your hand, we use them not just for making calls but also for surfing the Internet, watching movies, and dozens of other things—including, especially among the younger set, sending sexually explicit text messages and pictures to others. This phenomenon is called *sexting*. While sexting is certainly not limited to adolescents (think about the number of well-known public figures who have gotten themselves into hot water over sexting in recent years), a study suggests that sexting may now be a normal part of adolescent sexual development—and that it may have an impact on the frequency of adolescent sexual behavior as well.

As part of a six-year longitudinal study, researchers Dr. Jeff Temple and Dr. Hye Jeong Choi examined second- and third-year data from surveys of a group of ethnically diverse teens from Southeast Texas. These surveys were anonymous and asked the young people to answer questions about their sexting behavior (Temple & Choi, 2014). The questions about sexting were:

1. "Have you ever asked someone to send naked pictures of themselves to you?"
2. "Have you ever been asked to send a naked picture of yourself through text or e-mail?"
3. "Have you ever sent naked pictures of yourself to another through text or e-mail?"

Participants were also asked about their sexual behavior over the course of the study. If they responded "yes" to having had sexual intercourse, they were also asked about condom use, the number of sexual partners in the past year, and frequency of alcohol or drug use before sex.

The results: Adolescents who reported asking for a sext in their sophomore year (Question 1 above) were 4.55 times more likely to send a sext during their junior year when compared to those adolescents who reported never having asked for a sext. Those who reported having been asked to send a sext (Question 2 above) as sophomores were 5.35 times as likely to send a sext as juniors when compared to those who had not been asked.

Those adolescents who had sent sexts as sophomores were 1.32 times as likely to be sexually active in their junior years as those who had sent no sexts. Sexting was not, however, found to be related to later risky sexual behavior.

What conclusions about the relationship between sexting and sexual behavior can be drawn from the data? What social expectation does sexting seem to indicate?

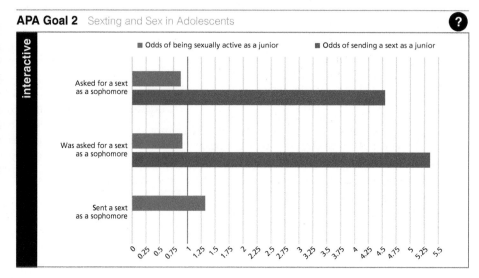

**APA Goal 2**  Sexting and Sex in Adolescents

**sexually transmitted infection (STI)**

an infection spread primarily through sexual contact.

These posters warning against sexually transmitted infections hang in a youth center in San Francisco, California. Adolescents often fail to take precautions against such infections and are becoming sexually active at younger ages, making them a high-risk group for STIs.

# Sexual Health

The health of the human sexual system can involve organic, sociocultural, and psychological influences, as well as a combination of these factors. While sexual dysfunctions (problems with the physical workings of the sex act or sexual functioning) will be discussed in detail in Chapter Fourteen, infectious conditions are the main concern in the following section. L I N K to Learning Objective 14.12.

## SEXUALLY TRANSMITTED INFECTIONS

**10.9** Describe the causes and symptoms of some common sexually transmitted infections.

One of the consequences of unprotected sexual contact is the risk of contracting a **sexually transmitted infection (STI)**, an infection spread primarily through sexual contact. **Table 10.1** lists some of the more common sexually transmitted infections and their causes. Some STIs affect the

| **Table 10.1** | Common Sexually Transmitted Infections | |
| --- | --- | --- |
| **STI** | **Cause** | **Symptoms** |
| Chlamydia | Bacterial infection that grows within the body's cells | Swollen testicles, discharge, burning during urination; women may experience no symptoms |
| Syphilis | Bacterial infection | Sores that appear on or in the genital area and can spread to other body parts and the brain |
| Gonorrhea | Bacterial infection that grows rapidly in warm, moist areas of the body (mouth, anus, throat, genitalia) | In men, a foul-smelling, cloudy discharge from the penis, burning upon urination; in women, inflamed cervix, light vaginal discharge |
| Genital Herpes | Herpes simplex virus | Sores on the genital area; itching, burning, throbbing, "pins-and-needles" sensations where sores are about to appear |
| Genital Warts | Human papillomavirus (HPV) | Warty growths on the genitalia |
| AIDS | Human immunodeficiency virus (HIV) | Severe malfunction and eventual breakdown of the immune system |

sex organs themselves, whereas others have broader and more life-threatening effects. The bacterial infections are quite treatable with antibiotics, but those caused by viruses are more difficult to treat and are often incurable. Even curable bacterial infections can cause serious problems if left untreated, and some bacterial infections are difficult to detect because the symptoms in at least one sex are not all that noticeable. For example, *chlamydia* is the most common STI and is easily treated, but it may go undetected in women because there are few symptoms or no symptoms noticed. If left untreated, chlamydia can cause *pelvic inflammatory disorder (PID)*, a condition that can damage the lining of the uterus and the fallopian tubes as well as the ovaries and other nearby structures. Ten percent of women in the United States will develop PID during their childbearing years (Miller & Graves, 2000).

On a positive note, there is now a vaccine for a group of STIs called human papillomaviruses, or HPVs. Some HPVs can cause cancer, so prevention is highly desirable. There are currently three vaccines approved for treatment that will prevent many of these viruses (Centers for Disease Control and Prevention, 2015).

Without a doubt, the one sexually transmitted infection that nearly everyone knows something about is **AIDS**, or **acquired immune deficiency syndrome**. AIDS is caused by a viral infection, specifically the *human immunodeficiency virus*, or *HIV*. A person who has HIV does not necessarily have AIDS but is at risk for developing AIDS in the future. HIV wears down the body's immune system, making the body vulnerable to "opportunistic" infections—infections caused by bacteria or viruses that, while harmless in a healthy immune system, will take hold when the immune system is weakened. When a person with HIV develops one of these types of infections or when their immune system's T-cell count goes below a certain level, the person is said to have AIDS (Folkman & Chesney, 1995).

 💬 I've heard a lot of stories about how people can get AIDS. What's the real story?

HIV can be transmitted to a person from anyone who has the infection, even if that person doesn't look sick. According to the Centers for Disease Control and Prevention (CDC) and World Health Organization (WHO), HIV may possibly be transmitted through:

- Having unprotected vaginal, oral, or anal sexual contact.
- Sharing a contaminated needle, syringe, or drug solution.
- Pregnancy, childbirth, and breastfeeding.
- Occupational exposure (accidental needle-stick injuries or exposure to contaminated blood or other body fluids).
- Blood transfusion or organ transplant (this is extremely rare in the United States).

Blood, vaginal fluid, semen, breast milk, and other bodily fluids containing blood are ways in which HIV is passed from the infected person to an uninfected person. However, unprotected vaginal or anal sex or sharing needles with an infected person are the most common ways HIV is transmitted in the United States (Centers for Disease Control and Prevention, 2010a, 2015). And while it is possible for a mother to transmit the virus to the baby during childbirth or breastfeeding, this is less common. Context is very important. In parts of Africa and other parts of the world, HIV–infected mothers are encouraged to breastfeed, especially if the mother is on antiretroviral (ARV) medications and the baby receives ARVs after birth, as the risk of the infant dying from unclean water or malnutrition is much greater than the risk of acquiring HIV through breastfeeding (World Health Organization, 2010, 2012).

Contrary to a lot of myths about HIV, there is no scientific proof or documented cases of HIV being passed through tears or ordinary saliva. Kissing an infected person will not result in transmission, although it is possible to transmit the virus through oral sex or, rarely, through deep kissing when there are open sores or bleeding gums in the mouth of either party. More troubling is the finding that HIV can be transmitted to children who are fed by mothers who have "prechewed" food (a practice that occurs in several countries and cultures, including that of the United States). This is not common, though, and HIV cannot normally be

These young men are attending a counseling session at a community-based AIDS clinic. They do not necessarily have AIDS; the purpose of this particular group is to help educate these men and others like them in ways to prevent HIV infections. With no cure as yet, prevention is the best defense against AIDS. Remember, AIDS can affect women and men of all sexual orientations.

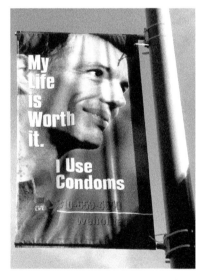

Not too many years ago, no one would have dared to advertise condoms in such a public manner. The only consequences of unsafe sex were unwanted pregnancies and serious, but not necessarily life-threatening, sexually transmitted infections. With the onslaught of the AIDS virus, safe sex has taken on a whole new meaning.

**Acquired Immune Deficiency Syndrome (AIDS)**

sexually transmitted viral disorder that causes deterioration of the immune system and eventually results in death due to complicating infections that the body can no longer fight.

transmitted through saliva; the women studied in this report all had sores or inflammations in their mouths, or the infants had cuts associated with teething in their mouths (Guar, 2008).

By the end of the year 2014, the number of estimated cases of AIDS in the United States had reached well over half a million people (Centers for Disease Control and Prevention, 2014). More than 1.2 million people in the United States are living with HIV, and nearly 13 percent of those people are unaware of their infection status. However, this number is probably a vast underestimate, as many HIV infections remain undiagnosed or unreported.

Treatments have improved greatly over the past decade, increasing the life expectancy of people with HIV or AIDS (Centers for Disease Control, 2013). Highly active antiretroviral therapy, or HAART for short, is a powerful "cocktail" of at least three and sometimes more medications aimed at reducing the virus in the blood so that it is no longer detectable. While it is not a cure, this treatment can delay progression from HIV to AIDS and improve immune system health (Cohen et al., 2011; Dieffenbach & Fauci, 2011).

In other cultures, AIDS is also taking a devastating toll. The most heavily hit areas in the world right now are the countries of sub-Saharan Africa, where an estimated 24.7 million people were living with HIV at the end of 2013—nearly three fourths of the total HIV infections in the world (Joint United Nations Programme on HIV/AIDS [UNAIDS], 2014). In 2013, 1.1 million people died from AIDS in these countries (UNAIDS, 2009). The Applying Psychology in Everyday Life section at the end of this chapter examines the course of AIDS in Russia—a region that is quickly becoming another AIDS "hot spot."

## Concept Map L.O. 10.9

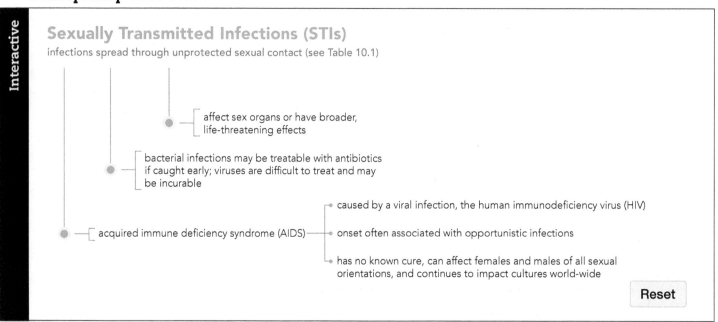

## Practice Quiz How much do you remember?

*Pick the best answer.*

1. Which of the following is NOT a sexually transmitted infection?
   a. syphilis
   b. gonorrhea
   c. candidiasis
   d. chlamydia

2. Which STI, if left untreated, can cause pelvic inflammatory disorder?
   a. syphilis
   b. gonorrhea
   c. candidiasis
   d. chlamydia

3. The human papillomavirus or HPV is the cause of _____ in both men and women.
   a. chlamydia
   b. syphilis
   c. genital warts
   d. AIDS

4. Which of the following ways can the human immunodeficiency virus be passed along to another person?
   a. kissing
   b. exposure to an infected person's tears
   c. exposure to an infected person's saliva
   d. exposure to an infected person's blood

# Applying Psychology to Everyday Life
## The AIDS Epidemic in Russia

**10.10** **Explain why the number of HIV and AIDS cases in Russia is increasing so dramatically.**

While sub-Saharan Africa is still the focal point of AIDS and HIV infections for now, Russia and several surrounding countries in Eastern Europe and Central Asia are quickly becoming the center for a new and rapidly expanding epidemic of AIDS. Within the last decade, the prevalence of HIV in Russia and these other areas has nearly doubled (AVERT, 2015; UNAIDS, 2009). By 2013, nearly 1.1 million people living in Eastern Europe and Central Asia are estimated to be infected with HIV, and both new infections and deaths have increased rapidly. Eighty-five percent of these people live in Russia and the Ukraine (AVERT, 2015).

What accounts for this horrific rise in AIDS cases? Drug users who often share needles are one cause. With the heavy opium-producing Afghanistan nearby, drug use is an ever-increasing problem in Russia and the surrounding region, with reports of more than half a million registered drug users and nearly 30,000 drug-related deaths each year (Hamers & Downs, 2003; RIA Novosti, 2010). Then there are the sex workers: prostitutes who are not only at risk because of the nature of their work but also because of their lack of education about the transmission of HIV and their own drug use (Baral et al., 2013; UNAIDS, 2008). Of course, the partners of these drug users and sex workers are also at risk. Nearly two-thirds of the infections in women are caused by heterosexual contact with husbands or male lovers (Federal Service for Surveillance of Consumer Rights Protection and Human Well-Being of the Russian Federation and UNAIDS, 2008).

Another group at risk are prisoners (AVERT, 2015; Dolan et al., 2007). The majority of the inmates were infected before entering the prison. Of note—one of the smallest groups responsible for the increase in AIDS and HIV infections is homosexual inmates (UNAIDS, 2008). Homosexuality in Russia and the surrounding areas was once punishable by death, so it is not so surprising that there are either fewer homosexual inmates in those countries or, at the very least, few who are willing to reveal themselves as homosexual persons.

Some researchers believe that between 2009 and 2015, Russia will experience its greatest number of AIDS–related deaths (Feshbach, 2008). Clearly, education about HIV and AIDS as well as a concerted effort to reduce the drug-using population, or, at the very least, giving them the tools necessary to reduce the risk of infection, must be a priority in the future—if there is to be one.

### Questions for Further Discussion

1. Are there other countries around the world that you think might be the next site of an HIV/AIDS epidemic?

2. How would you go about trying to educate people who do not understand how HIV is spread?

# Chapter Summary

## The Physical Side of Human Sexuality

### 10.1 Distinguish between primary and secondary sex characteristics.

- The female sexual organs present at birth are the primary sex characteristics consisting of vagina, uterus, and ovaries.

- The primary male sex characteristics are the penis, scrotum, testicles, and prostate gland.

### 10.2 Explain how sex characteristics develop.

- The female sexual organs that develop during puberty are secondary sex characteristics consisting of the growth spurt, onset of the menstrual cycle, breast development, widening hips, pubic hair, fat deposits, and further growth and development of the uterus, vagina, and ovaries.

- The secondary male sex characteristics are an enlarged larynx (Adam's apple), deepening voice, facial and chest hair, pubic hair, coarser skin texture, and a large increase in height.

## The Psychological Side of Human Sexuality: Gender

**10.3 Identify the psychological, biological, environmental, and cultural influences on gender.**

- Gender is the psychological aspect of being male or female.
- Gender roles are the culture's expectations for male and female behavior and personality.
- Gender typing is the process by which people in a culture learn the appropriate gender-role behavior.
- Gender identity is a person's sense of being male or female.
- Gender identities are formed by biological influences in the form of hormones and chromosomes as well as environmental influences in the form of parenting, surroundings, and culture, on the formation of gender identity.

**10.4 Compare and contrast different views of how gender roles develop.**

- Social learning theorists believe that gender identity is formed through reinforcement of appropriate gender behavior as well as imitation of gender models.
- Gender schema theorists believe that gender identity is a mental schema that develops gradually, influenced by the growth of the brain and organization of observed male or female behavior around the schema.
- Gender stereotyping occurs when people assign characteristics to a person based on the person's male or female status rather than actual characteristics.
- Androgyny describes people who do not limit themselves to the male or female stereotyped characteristics, instead possessing characteristics associated with both traditional masculine and feminine roles.

**10.5 Describe how men and women differ in thinking, social behavior, and personality.**

- Cognitive differences between men and women include a male advantage in mathematical and spatial skills and a female superiority in verbal skills. These differences are now less than they were previously.
- Males and females are socially taught to interact differently and express emotions differently. Men tend to talk with each other in a "report" style, whereas women tend to talk to each other in a "relate" style.

## Human Sexual Behavior

**10.6 Identify the four stages of a sexual-response cycle.**

- Masters and Johnson found four phases of human sexual response: arousal, plateau, orgasm, and resolution.

**10.7 Summarize the findings of early and recent surveys of human sexual behavior.**

- Alfred Kinsey conducted a series of sexual-behavior surveys in the late 1940s and early 1950s, revealing some highly controversial findings about the kinds of sexual behavior common among people in the United States, including homosexuality, premarital sex, and extramarital sex.

- In the mid-1990s, Janus and Janus published the results of a large-scale survey of sexual behavior in the United States. Their survey results did not differ widely from those of Kinsey, but they looked at many more types of sexual behavior and factors related to sexual behavior than did Kinsey's surveys.

- The results of the National Survey of Sexual Health and Behavior (NSSHB) was published in 2010. The results indicated that sexual behavior in the United States changes across the lifespan, with vaginal intercourse being most common in early to late adulthood. Masturbation is more common in younger and older individuals, and both oral and anal sex occur across different age cohorts. More men than women reported condom use, and overall, use was highest during adolescence.

**10.8 Identify some influences on the development of sexual orientation.**

- Research suggests that there are biological differences between heterosexual and homosexual persons and that there may be genetic influences as well.

## Sexual Health

**10.9 Describe the causes and symptoms of some common sexually transmitted infections.**

- Sexually transmitted infections can affect the sexual organs and the ability to reproduce and may result in pain, disfigurement, and even death.
- Some common bacterial sexually transmitted infections are chlamydia, syphilis, and gonorrhea. These infections are treatable with antibiotics.
- Viral sexually transmitted infections include genital herpes (caused by the herpes simplex virus that also causes cold sores) and genital warts (caused by the human papillomavirus). Neither can be cured, and both can lead to complications such as increased risk of cancer.
- Acquired immune deficiency syndrome (AIDS) is caused by a viral infection called human immunodeficiency virus (HIV) that is transmitted through an exchange of blood, vaginal fluid, semen, or breast milk. Having unprotected sex or sharing a needle with an infected person are the most common routes of transmission. HIV may also be transmitted through pregnancy, childbirth, breastfeeding a baby while infected, occupational exposure, or receiving contaminated blood or organ transplant.
- AIDS wears down the immune system, opening the body up to infections that, over time, will result in death.

## Applying Psychology to Everyday Life: The AIDS Epidemic in Russia

**10.10 Explain why the number of HIV and AIDS cases in Russia is increasing so dramatically.**

- Cases of both HIV infections and AIDS have dramatically increased due to increasing drug use, uneducated sex workers, and the spread of disease among prisoners.

# Test Yourself

*Pick the best answer.*

1. Primary sex characteristics
   a. include the development of pubic and ancillary hair.
   b. always begin their development during puberty.
   c. are typically the same for males and females.
   d. are directly involved in human reproduction.

2. What is the average age in the United States that menarche typically begins?
   a. 10          c. 13
   b. 12          d. 14

3. If the gonads within an embryo produce testosterone because of the presence of a Y gene on the sex chromosome, then the _____ will develop and the _____ will deteriorate.
   a. Müllerian ducts; Wolffian ducts
   b. Wolffian ducts; Müllerian ducts
   c. ovaries; testes
   d. testes; ovaries

4. An intersex person is
   a. a person who has sex with both men and women.
   b. another name for a homosexual.
   c. a person born with ambiguous sexual organs.
   d. another name for a heterosexual.

5. Annika's mother wants her daughter to grow up to become a mother of a large family. Such an expectation for Annika might be seen as an example of her
   a. gender role.          c. gender identity.
   b. gender typing.        d. gender constancy.

6. Darla shares with a close friend that she often feels a strong desire to be another gender and that it bothers her so much that she is having problems at work and in her social life. What is the term used to describe this?
   a. hermaphroditism       c. intersex
   b. transsexual           d. gender dysphoria

7. In social learning theory, gender identity results
   a. when a child learns that they are either a "girl" or a "boy."
   b. from observation and imitation.
   c. from biological changes that occurred before birth.
   d. from unconscious forces.

8. Jennifer's aunt tries to explain that running around with boys on the playground isn't "ladylike." Such a statement could be an example of
   a. androgyny.            c. role development.
   b. gender typing.        d. gender stereotyping.

9. Plateau occurs in
   a. Phase 1.              c. Phase 3.
   b. Phase 2.              d. Phase 4.

10. The refractory period is a time during which
    a. a woman cannot have another orgasm.
    b. a man cannot have another orgasm.
    c. a man begins to get sexually aroused.
    d. a woman cannot be aroused.

11. Which of the following studies was the most controversial for its method of gathering information?
    a. the Kinsey report
    b. the Janus report
    c. Masters and Johnson's study
    d. Savic's research on sexual orientation

12. The Kinsey report indicates that more than _____ as many men had intercourse by age 16 as did women.
    a. twice
    b. four times
    c. ten times
    d. three times

13. Parental investment theory seeks to explain
    a. why men have sex more often than women.
    b. why women are sexually attracted to men.
    c. why couples meet and remain together.
    d. why sexual activity diminishes in seniors.

14. Research on the epi-mark offers a _____ explanation to the existence of homosexuality.
    a. genetic               c. social
    b. psychological         d. behavioral

15. Some research suggests that a man is more likely to be homosexual if he has a lot of
    a. older sisters.        c. social support.
    b. older brothers.       d. testosterone.

16. Sexual health can be influenced by
    a. organic factors.
    b. organic and sociocultural factors.
    c. organic, psychological, and sociocultural factors.
    d. hereditary factors primarily.

17. Which of the following sexually transmitted infections can ultimately affect the brain?
    a. genital herpes        c. syphilis
    b. chlamydia             d. gonorrhea

18. Brandon has a couple of painful sores on his penis and experiences severe itching and burning in the surrounding area. Brandon probably has
    a. genital herpes.       c. syphilis.
    b. chlamydia.            d. gonorrhea.

19. Which of the following is a way in which HIV can be transmitted?
    a. through exposure to contaminated blood or other body fluids containing contaminated blood
    b. by sharing beverages with someone who is HIV positive
    c. by making contact with the tears of an HIV patient
    d. through hand holding, especially if the person with HIV is perspiring

20. Alicia is horrified to hear that her date from last night carries the human immunodeficiency virus. While they did not engage in sex, they did share a quick kiss at the end of the evening, hastened by her phone ringing in her apartment. Besides discussing her concerns with her date should they go out again, what precautions should Alicia take?
    a. She should see her doctor immediately, since kissing can cause the spread of HIV.
    b. She should see her doctor only if she begins to have symptoms.
    c. She should try to calm down, since stress helps transmit HIV.
    d. She should try not to worry, since kissing has not been proven to be a successful way to transmit HIV, and follow up with her doctor or other health care provider if she has concerns or questions.

# 11 Stress and Health

What are some common sources of stress in your life? How do you cope with or relieve stress?
After you have answered the question, watch the video to compare the answers of other students to yours.

▶ The response entered here will be saved to your notes and may be collected by your instructor if he/she requires it.

👁 Watch the Video

## Why study stress and health?

How are they related? Stress is not a rare experience but something that all people experience in varying degrees every day. This chapter will explore the sources of stress in daily life, the factors that can make the experience of stress easier or more difficult, and the ways that stress influences our physical and mental health. We'll finish by discussing various ways to cope with the stresses of everyday life as well as with the extraordinary experiences that arise in life that have the potential to induce stress.

# Learning Objectives

**11.1**  Distinguish between distress and eustress.

**11.2**  Identify three types of external events that can cause stress.

**11.3**  Identify psychological factors in stress.

**11.4**  Describe the stages of the general adaptation syndrome.

**11.5**  Explain how the immune system is impacted by stress.

**11.6**  Describe the branch of psychology known as health psychology.

**11.7**  Summarize Lazarus's cognitive appraisal approach to stress.

**11.8**  Explain how personality types and attitudes can influence people's reaction to stress.

**11.9**  Identify social and cultural factors that influence stress reactions.

**11.10**  Distinguish between problem-focused and emotion-coping strategies to stress.

**11.11**  Explain how a social-support system influences a person's ability to cope with stress.

**11.12**  Describe cultural differences in coping with stress.

**11.13**  Explain how religious beliefs can affect the ability to cope with stress.

**11.14**  Define mindfulness meditation and describe its use in coping with the effects of stress.

# Stress and Stressors

Life is really about change. Every day, each person faces some kind of challenge, big or small. Just deciding what to wear to work or school can be a challenge for some people, whereas others find the drive to the workplace or school the most challenging part of the day. There are decisions to be made and changes that will require that you adapt already-made plans. Sometimes there are actual threats to well-being—an accident, a fight with the boss, a failed exam, or the loss of a job, to name a few. All of these challenges, threats, and changes require people to respond in some way.

## THE RELATIONSHIP BETWEEN STRESS AND STRESSORS

### 11.1 Distinguish between distress and eustress.

**Stress** is the term used to describe the physical, emotional, cognitive, and behavioral responses to events that are appraised* as threatening or challenging.

Stress can show itself in many ways. Physical problems can include unusual fatigue, sleeping problems, frequent colds, and even chest pains and nausea. People under stress may behave differently, too: pacing, eating too much, crying a lot, smoking and drinking more than usual, or physically striking out at others by hitting or throwing things. Emotionally, people under stress experience anxiety, depression, fear, and irritability, as well as anger and frustration. Mental symptoms of stress include problems in concentration, memory, and decision making, and people under stress often lose their sense of humor.

  I feel like that most of the time!

Most people experience some degree of stress on a daily basis, and college students are even more likely to face situations and events that require them to make changes and adapt their behavior: Assigned readings, papers, studying for tests, juggling jobs, car problems, relationships, and dealing with deadlines are all examples of things that can cause a person to experience stress. Some people feel the effects of stress more than others because what is appraised as a threat by one person might be appraised as an opportunity by another. (For example, think of how you and your friends might respond differently to the opportunity to write a 10-page paper for extra credit in the last 3 weeks of the semester.) Stress-causing events are called **stressors**; they can come from within a person or from an external source and range from relatively mild to severe.

Events that can become stressors range from being stuck behind a person in the 10-items-or-less lane of the grocery store who has twice that amount to dealing with the rubble left after a tornado or a hurricane destroys one's home. Stressors can range from the deadly serious (hurricanes, fires, crashes, combat) to the merely irritating and annoying (delays, rude people, losing one's car keys). Stressors can even be imaginary, as when a couple puts off doing their income tax return, imagining that they will have to pay a huge tax bill, or when a parent imagines the worst happening to a teenage child who isn't yet home from an evening out.

Actually, there are two kinds of stressors: those that cause **distress**, which occurs when people experience unpleasant stressors, and those that cause *eustress*, which results from positive events that still make demands on a person to adapt or change. Marriage, a job promotion, and having a baby may all be positive events for most people, but they all require a great deal of change in people's habits, duties, and often lifestyle, thereby creating stress. Hans Selye (1936) originally coined the term *eustress* to describe the stress experienced when positive events require the body to adapt.

Taking a test is just one of many possible stressors in a college student's life. What aspects of college life have you found to be stressful? Do other students experience the same degree of stress in response to the same stressors?

**stress**

the term used to describe the physical, emotional, cognitive, and behavioral responses to events that are appraised as threatening or challenging.

**stressors**

events that cause a stress reaction.

**distress**

the effect of unpleasant and undesirable stressors.

---

*appraised: in this sense, evaluated or judged in terms of importance or significance.

In an update of Selye's original definition, researchers now define **eustress** as the optimal amount of stress that people need to promote health and well-being. The arousal theory, discussed in Chapter Nine, is based on the idea that a certain level of stress, or arousal, is actually necessary for people to feel content and function well (Zuckerman, 1994). (L)(I)(N)(K) to Learning Objective 9.4. That arousal can be viewed in terms of eustress. Many students are aware that experiencing a little anxiety or stress is helpful to them because it motivates them to study, for example. Without the arousal created by the impending exam, many students might not study very much or at all. In fact, as the video *Stress and Memory* describes, studies have shown that small amounts of stress may actually improve our memory. What about the student who is so stressed out that everything he's studied just flies right out of his head? Obviously, a high level of anxiety concerning an impending exam that actually interferes with the ability to study or to retrieve the information at exam time is distress. The difference is not only in the degree of anxiety but also in how the person interprets the exam situation. What is eustress for one person may be distress for another, and although both kinds of stress produce similar bodily reactions, a more positive interpretation of a stressor leads to more positive coping with that stressor (Fevre et al., 2006; Sarada & Ramkumar, 2014). A number of events, great and small, good and bad, can cause us to feel "stressed out." The next section looks at how life's big deals and little hassles contribute to our overall stress experience.

👁 **Watch** the **Video** *Stress and Memory*

## ENVIRONMENTAL STRESSORS: LIFE'S UPS AND DOWNS

**11.2** Identify three types of external events that can cause stress.

From the annoyingly loud next-door neighbor to major life changes, good or bad, stress is a fact of life. Let's take a look at the various causes of stress in everyday life.

**CATASTROPHES**   Losing one's home in a tornado is an example of a stressor called a **catastrophe**, an unpredictable event that happens on a large scale and creates tremendous amounts of stress and feelings of threat. Wars, hurricanes, floods, fires, airplane crashes, and other disasters are catastrophes. The terrorist-driven destruction of the World Trade Center in New York City on September 11, 2001, is a prime example of a catastrophe.

**eustress**

the effect of positive events, or the optimal amount of stress that people need to promote health and well-being.

**catastrophe**

an unpredictable, large-scale event that creates a tremendous need to adapt and adjust as well as overwhelming feelings of threat.

In one study, nearly 8 percent of the people living in the area near the attacks developed a severe stress disorder, and nearly 10 percent reported symptoms of depression even as late as 2 months after the attack (Galea et al., 2002). A study done 4 years later found a nearly 14 percent! increase in stress disorders as well as continued persistence of previously diagnosed stress disorders (Pollack et al., 2006). ⓛⓘⓝⓚ to Learning Objective 14.5. Other examples of catastrophes are the devastation caused by Hurricane Katrina on August 29, 2005, Hurricane ("Superstorm") Sandy on October 22–29, 2012, and in 2015, the earthquake that hit Nepal and the typhoon that hit China and the Philippines (Kessler et al., 2006; Stewart, 2012; Swenson & Marshall, 2005).

Some research suggests that the impact of catastrophic events can affect not only the people who experience the events directly but also any unborn children whose mothers are involved in the events. The prenatal stress can not only have short-term consequences such as premature birth but also long-term effects such as lower-than-normal intelligence levels and poor health behavior in adult life (Cao-Lei et al., 2014; Eriksson et al., 2014; Raposa et al., 2014; Witt et al., 2014).

**MAJOR LIFE CHANGES**    Thankfully, most people do not have to face the extreme stress of a catastrophe. But stress is present even in relatively ordinary life experiences and does not have to come from only negative events, such as job loss. Sometimes there are big events, such as marriage or going to college, that also require a person to make adjustments and changes—and adjustments and changes are really the core of stress, according to early researchers in the field (Holmes & Rahe, 1967).

**THE SOCIAL READJUSTMENT RATING SCALE (SRRS)**    Thomas Holmes and Richard Rahe (1967) believed that any life event that required people to change, adapt, or adjust their lifestyles would result in stress. Like Selye, they assumed that both negative events (such as getting fired) and positive events (such as getting a promotion) demand that a person adjust in some way, and so both kinds of events are associated with stress. Using a sample of nearly 400 people, Holmes and Rahe devised a scale to measure the amount of stress in a person's life by having that person add up the total "life change units" associated with each major event in their **Social Readjustment Rating Scale** (**SRRS**; see **Table 11.1**).

When an individual adds up the points for each event that has happened to him or her within the past 12 months (and counting points for repeat events as well), the resulting score can provide a good estimate of the degree of stress being experienced by that person. The researchers found that certain ranges of scores on the SRRS could be associated with increased risk of illness or accidents. (Note: Table 11.1 is not a complete listing of the original 43 events and associated life change units and should not be used to calculate a stress "score"! If you would like to calculate your SRRS score, try this free Web site: **http://www.stresstips.com/lifeevents.htm**.)

The risk of illness or accidents increases as the score increases. If a person's score is 300 or above, that person has a very high chance of becoming ill or having an accident in the near future (Holmes & Masuda, 1973). Illness includes not only physical conditions such as high blood pressure, ulcers, or migraine headaches but mental illness as well. In one study, researchers found that stressful life events of the kind listed in the SRRS were excellent predictors of the onset of episodes of major depression (Kendler & Prescott, 1999).

The SRRS was later revised (Miller & Rahe, 1997) to reflect changes in the ratings of the events in the 30 intervening years. Miller and Rahe found that overall stress associated with many of the items on the original list had increased by about 45 percent from the original 1967 ratings, citing changes in such issues as gender roles, economics, and social norms as possible reasons.

How can stress cause a person to have an accident? Many studies conducted on the relationship between stress and accidents in the workplace have shown that people under a lot of stress tend to be more distracted and less cautious and, therefore, place themselves at a greater risk for having an accident (Hansen, 1988; Sherry et al., 2003).

**Social Readjustment Rating Scale (SRRS)**

assessment that measures the amount of stress in a person's life over a 1-year period resulting from major life events.

| Table 11.1    Sample Items From the Social Readjustment Rating Scale (SRRS) | |
|---|---|
| **Major Life Event** | **Life Change Units** |
| Death of spouse | 100 |
| Divorce | 75 |
| Marital separation | 65 |
| Jail term | 63 |
| Death of a close family member | 63 |
| Personal injury or illness | 53 |
| Marriage | 50 |
| Dismissal from work | 47 |
| Marital reconciliation | 45 |
| Pregnancy | 40 |
| Death of close friend | 37 |
| Change to different line of work | 36 |
| Change in number of arguments with spouse | 36 |
| Major mortgage | 31 |
| Foreclosure of mortgage or loan | 30 |
| Begin or end school | 26 |
| Change in living conditions | 25 |
| Change in work hours or conditions | 20 |
| Change in residence/schools/recreation | 19 |
| Change in social activities | 18 |
| Small mortgage or loan | 17 |
| Vacation | 13 |
| Christmas | 12 |
| Minor violations of the law | 11 |

SOURCE: Adapted and abridged from Holmes & Rahe (1967).

*Interactive*

**THE COLLEGE UNDERGRADUATE STRESS SCALE (CUSS)**    The SRRS, as it was originally designed, seems more appropriate for adults who are already established in their careers. There are versions of the SRRS that use as life events some of those things more likely to be experienced by college students. One of these more recent versions is the **College Undergraduate Stress Scale** (**CUSS**; Renner & Mackin, 1998). This scale is quite different from Holmes and Rahe's original scale because the stressful events listed and rated include those that would be more common or more likely to happen to a college student. Some of the higher-stress items on the CUSS include rape, a close friend's death, contracting a sexually transmitted disease, as well as final exam week and flunking a class. Some of the lower stress items include peer pressure, homesickness, falling asleep in class, pressure to make high grades, and dating concerns.

 You mention that the CUSS has "falling asleep in class" as one of its items. How can falling asleep in class be stressful? It's what happens when the professor catches you that's stressful, isn't it?

Ah, but if you fall asleep in class, even if the professor doesn't catch on, you'll miss the lecture notes. You might then have to get the notes from a friend, find enough money

**College Undergraduate Stress Scale (CUSS)**

assessment that measures the amount of stress in a college student's life over a 1-year period resulting from major life events.

to pay for the copy machine, try to read your friend's handwriting, and so on—all stressful situations. Actually, all the events listed on both the SRRS and the CUSS are stressful not just because some of them are emotionally intense but also because there are so many little details, changes, adjustments, adaptations, frustrations, and delays that are caused by the events themselves. The death of a spouse, for example, rates 100 life change units because it requires the greatest amount of adjustment in a person's life. A lot of those adjustments are going to be the little details: planning the funeral, deciding what to do with the spouse's clothes and belongings, getting the notice in the obituaries, answering all of the condolence cards with a thank-you card, dealing with insurance and changing names on policies, and on and on and on. In other words, major life events create a whole host of hassles.

**HASSLES**  Although it's easy to think about big disasters and major changes in life as sources of stress, the bulk of the stress we experience daily actually comes from little frustrations, delays, irritations, minor disagreements, and similar small aggravations. These daily annoyances are called **hassles** (Lazarus, 1993; Lazarus & Folkman, 1984). Experiencing major changes in one's life is like throwing a rock into a pond: There will be a big splash, but the rock itself is gone. What is left behind are all the ripples in the water that came from the impact of the rock. Those "ripples" are the hassles that arise from the big event.

Lazarus and Folkman (1984) developed a *hassles scale* that has items such as "misplacing or losing things" and "troublesome neighbors." A person taking the test for hassles would rate each item in the scale in terms of how much of a hassle that particular item was for the person. The ratings range between 0 (no hassle or didn't occur) to 3 (extremely severe hassle). Whereas the major life events of Holmes and Rahe's scale (1967) may have a long-term effect on a person's chronic physical and mental health, the day-to-day minor annoyances, delays, and irritations that affect immediate health and well-being are far better predictors of short-term illnesses such as headaches, colds, backaches, and similar symptoms (Burks & Martin, 1985; DeLongis et al., 1988; Dunn et al., 2006). In one study, researchers found that among 261 participants who experienced headaches, scores on a scale measuring the number and severity of daily hassles were significantly better predictors of headaches than were scores on a life-events scale (Fernandez & Sheffield, 1996). The researchers also found that it was not so much the number of daily hassles that predicted headaches but rather the perceived severity of the hassles.

Research has indicated that hassles may also come from quite different sources depending on a person's developmental stage (Ellis et al., 2001). In this study, researchers surveyed 270 randomly selected people from ages 3 to 75. The participants were asked to check off a list of daily hassles and pleasures associated with having "bad days" and "good days," respectively, as well as ranking the hassles in terms of frequency and severity of impact. For children ages 3 to 5, getting teased was the biggest daily hassle. For children in the 6 to 10 age group, the biggest hassle was getting bad grades. Children 11 to 15 years old reported feeling pressured to use drugs, whereas older adolescents (ages 16 to 22)

Children in the preschool-age range find teasing by their peers to be the biggest daily hassle they experience. This boy may be upset because he has been teased by the other children. What other hassles might a child in this age range experience?

**hassles**

the daily annoyances of everyday life.

cited trouble at school or work. Adults found fighting among family members the greatest source of stress, whereas the elderly people in the study cited a lack of money.

In that same study, the researchers were somewhat surprised to find that elderly people were much more strongly affected by such hassles as going shopping, doctor's appointments, and bad weather than the children and younger adults were. It may be that while a young person may view going shopping as an opportunity to socialize, older adults find it threatening: Physically, they are less able to get to a place to shop and may have to rely on others to drive them and help them get around and, thus, may take much more time for shopping and doing errands than a younger person would. Mentally, shopping could be seen as threatening because of a lack of financial resources to pay for needed items. Even the need to make decisions might be seen as unpleasant to an older person.

## PSYCHOLOGICAL STRESSORS: WHAT, ME WORRY?

**11.3** Identify psychological factors in stress.

Although several specific stressors (such as marriage, car problems, etc.) have already been mentioned, the psychological reasons people find these events stressful fall into several categories.

**PRESSURE**   When there are urgent demands or expectations for a person's behavior coming from an outside source, that person is experiencing **pressure**. Pressure occurs when people feel that they must work harder or faster or do more, as when meeting a deadline or studying for final exams.

Time pressure is one of the most common forms of pressure. Although some people claim to "work well under pressure," the truth is that pressure can have a negative impact on a person's ability to be creative. Psychologist Teresa Amabile has gathered research within actual work settings strongly indicating that when time pressure is applied to workers who are trying to come up with creative, innovative ideas, creativity levels decrease dramatically—even though the workers may think they have been quite productive because of the effort they have made (Amabile et al., 2002).

**UNCONTROLLABILITY**   Another factor that increases a person's experience of stress is the degree of control that the person has over a particular event or situation. The less control a person has, the greater the degree of stress. Researchers in both clinical interviews and experimental studies have found that lack of control in a situation actually increases stress disorder symptoms (Breier et al., 1987; Henderson et al., 2012).

In studies carried out in a nursing home with the elderly residents as the participants, researchers Rodin and Langer (Langer & Rodin, 1976; Rodin & Langer, 1977) found that those residents who were given more control over their lives (e.g., being able to choose activities and their timing) were more vigorous, active, and sociable than those in the control group. Employees at mental health clinics who have more input into and control over policy changes experience less stress than those who believe themselves to have little control (Johnson et al., 2006). A more recent study found that retirees experience more happiness and less stress when retirement is by their choice and not forced upon them, regardless of whether the retirement was rapid or gradual (Calvo et al., 2009).

The stress-increasing effects of lack of control explain the relationship between unpredictability and stress as well. When potentially stressful situations are unpredictable, as in police work, the degree of stress experienced is increased. An unpredictable situation is one that is not controllable, which may at least partially explain the increase in stress (Zucchi et al., 2009). In one study, rats were either given an electric shock after a warning tone or given a shock with no warning. The rats receiving the unpredictable shocks developed severe stomach ulcers (Weiss, 1972).

Residents in retirement homes and nursing homes benefit both physically and psychologically when they can choose for themselves the activities in which they wish to participate, such as this exercise class. What are some other means of control residents might experience?

**pressure**

the psychological experience produced by urgent demands or expectations for a person's behavior that come from an outside source.

**FRUSTRATION**   **Frustration** occurs when people are blocked or prevented from achieving a desired goal or fulfilling a perceived need. As a stressor, frustration can be *external*, such as when a car breaks down, a desired job offer doesn't come through after all, or a theft results in the loss of one's belongings. Losses, rejections, failures, and delays are all sources of external frustration.

Obviously, some frustrations are minor and others are more serious. The seriousness of a frustration is affected by how important the goal or need actually is. A person who is delayed in traffic while driving to the mall to do some shopping just for fun will be less frustrated than a person who is trying to get to the mall before it closes to get that last-minute forgotten and important anniversary gift.

*Internal frustrations*, also known as *personal frustrations*, occur when the goal or need cannot be attained because of internal or personal characteristics. For example, someone who wants to be an astronaut might find that severe motion sickness prevents him or her from such a goal. If a man wants to be a professional basketball player but is only 5 feet tall and weighs only 85 pounds, he may find that he cannot achieve that goal because of his physical characteristics. A person wanting to be an engineer but who has no math skills would find it difficult to attain that goal.

When frustrated, people may use several typical responses. The first is *persistence*, or the continuation of efforts to get around whatever is causing the frustration. Persistence may involve making more intense efforts or changing the style of response. For example, anyone who has ever put coins into a vending machine only to find that the drink does not come out has probably (1) pushed the button again, more forcefully and (2) pushed several other buttons in an effort to get some kind of response from the machine. If neither of these strategies works, many people may hit or kick the machine itself in an act of aggression.

**Aggression**, or action meant to harm or destroy, is unfortunately another typical reaction to frustration. Early psychologists in the field of behaviorism proposed a connection between frustration and aggression, calling it the *frustration–aggression hypothesis* (Dollard et al., 1939; Miller et al., 1941). **LINK** to Learning Objective 12.15. Although they believed that some form of frustration nearly always precedes aggression, that does not mean that frustration *always* leads to aggression. In fact, aggression is a frequent and incessant response to frustration, but it is seldom the first response. In a reformulation of the frustration–aggression hypothesis, Berkowitz (1993) stated that frustration creates an internal "readiness to aggress" but that aggression will not follow unless certain external cues are also present. For example, if the human source of a person's frustration is far larger and stronger in appearance than the frustrated person, aggression is an unlikely outcome!

 Okay, so if the person who ticked you off is bigger than you—if aggression isn't possible—what can you do?

One could try to reason with the person who is the source of frustration. Reasoning with someone is a form of persistence. Trying to "get around" the problem is another way in which people can deal with frustration. Another possibility is to take out one's frustrations on less threatening, more available targets, in a process called **displaced aggression**. Anyone who has ever been frustrated by things that occurred at work or school and then later yelled at another person (such as a spouse, parent, child, etc.) has experienced displaced aggression. The person one really wants to strike out at is one's boss, the teacher, or whoever or whatever caused the frustration in

**frustration**

the psychological experience produced by the blocking of a desired goal or fulfillment of a perceived need.

**aggression**

actions meant to harm or destroy; behavior intended to hurt or destroy another person.

**displaced aggression**

taking out one's frustrations on some less threatening or more available target.

These parents are fighting in front of their obviously distressed daughter. In some instances, a child who experiences this kind of frustration might act out aggressively toward a sibling or a pet in a form of displaced aggression.

the first place. That could be dangerous, so the aggression is reserved for another less threatening or weaker target. For example, unemployment and financial difficulties are extremely frustrating, as they block a person's ability to maintain a certain standard of living and acquire desired possessions. In one study, male unemployment and single parenthood were the two factors most highly correlated to rates of child abuse (Gillham et al., 1998). Unemployment is also one of the factors correlated most highly with the murder of abused women, creating four times the risk of murder for women in abusive relationships (Campbell & Wolf, 2003). Both studies are examples of displaced aggression toward the weaker targets of children and women. Such targets often become *scapegoats*, or habitual targets of displaced aggression. Scapegoats are often pets, children, spouses, and even minority groups (who are seen as having less power). ⓁⒾⓃⓚ to Learning Objective 12.10.

Another possible reaction to frustration is **escape** or **withdrawal**. Escape or withdrawal can take the form of leaving, dropping out of school, quitting a job, or ending a relationship. Some people manage a psychological escape or withdrawal into apathy (ceasing to care about or act upon the situation), fantasy (which is only a temporary escape), or the use of drugs. Obviously the latter reaction can lead to even more problems. Others resort to what they see as the final escape: suicide.

**CONFLICT** Whenever you find yourself torn between two or more competing and incompatible desires, goals, or actions, you are in conflict. There are different forms of conflict, depending upon the nature of the incompatible desires, goals, or actions.

*Approach–Approach Conflict.* In an **approach–approach conflict**, a person experiences desire for two goals, each of which is attractive. Typically, this type of conflict, often called a "win–win situation," is relatively easy to resolve and does not involve a great deal of stress. Because both goals are desirable, the only stress involved is having to choose between them, acquiring one and losing the other. An example of this might be the need to choose between the chocolate cake or key lime pie for dessert or from among several good choices for a date to the prom. "Six on one hand, half a dozen on the other" is a phrase that sums up this conflict nicely.

*Avoidance–Avoidance Conflict.* **Avoidance–avoidance conflicts** are much more stressful. In this conflict, the choice is between two or more goals or events that are unpleasant. This type of conflict is so common that there are numerous phrases to symbolize it, for example, "caught between a rock and a hard place," "between the devil and the deep blue sea," "out of the frying pan into the fire," and "lose–lose situation." People who are fearful of dental procedures might face the conflict of suffering the pain of a toothache or going to the dentist. Because neither alternative is pleasant, many people avoid making a choice by delaying decisions (Tversky & Shafir, 1992). For example, given the choice of risky back surgery or living with the pain, some people would wait, hoping that the pain would go away on its own and relieve them of the need to make a choice.

*Approach–Avoidance Conflict.* **Approach–avoidance conflicts** are a bit different in that they only involve one goal or event. That goal or event may have both positive and negative aspects that make the goal appealing and yet unappealing at the same time. For example, marriage is a big decision to make for anyone and usually has both its attractive features, such as togetherness, sharing good times, and companionship, and also its negative aspects, such as disagreements, money issues, and mortgages. This is perhaps the most stressful of all of the types of conflict, causing many people to vacillate* or

**escape or withdrawal**
leaving the presence of a stressor, either literally or by a psychological withdrawal into fantasy, drug abuse, or apathy.

**approach–approach conflict**
conflict occurring when a person must choose between two desirable goals.

**avoidance–avoidance conflicts**
conflict occurring when a person must choose between two undesirable goals.

**approach–avoidance conflicts**
conflict occurring when a person must choose or not choose a goal that has both positive and negative aspects.

This couple has just purchased their first house, a rite of passage for many young couples. The decision to become a homeowner, with the "pulls" of privacy and earning equity and the "pushes" of mortgage payments and upkeep, is often an approach–avoidance conflict.

---

*vacillate: to go back and forth between one decision and another.

be unable to decide for or against the goal or event. The author of this text experienced a very stressful approach–avoidance conflict when deciding to write the book: On the one hand, there would be money, prestige, and the challenge of doing something new. On the other hand, a tremendous amount of effort and time would be required to write the text, which would take time and energy away from other areas of life. Another example is the offer of a promotion that would require a person to move to a city he or she doesn't like—more money and higher status but all the hassles of moving and living in a less-than-perfect place.

> 💬 What if I have to choose between two things, and each of them has good points and bad points?

*Multiple Approach–Avoidance Conflicts.* When the choice is between two goals that have both positive and negative elements to each goal, it is called a **double approach–avoidance conflict**. For example, what if a person had the choice of buying a house out in the country or in the city? The house in the country has its attractions: privacy, fresh air, and quiet. But there would be a long commute to one's job in the city. A house in the city would make getting to work a lot easier, but then there are the negative aspects of pollution, noise, and crowded city streets. Each choice has both good and bad points. This type of conflict also tends to lead to vacillation. Other examples of this type of conflict might be trying to decide which of two people one wants to date or which of two majors one should choose.

It is fairly common to face **multiple approach–avoidance conflicts** in daily life. In a multiple approach–avoidance conflict, one would have more than two goals or options to consider, making the decision even more difficult and stressful. For many college students, deciding on a specific school or a career major is actually this type of conflict.

See **Table 11.2** for a summary of these four types of conflicts.

**double approach–avoidance conflict**

conflict in which the person must decide between two goals, with each goal possessing both positive and negative aspects.

**multiple approach–avoidance conflicts**

conflict in which the person must decide between more than two goals, with each goal possessing both positive and negative aspects.

| Table 11.2 | Different Forms of Conflict | |
|---|---|---|
| **Conflict Type** | **Definition** | **Example** |
| **Approach–approach** | Must choose between two desirable goals. | You would like to go to both Italy and England, but you can only choose to go to one. |
| **Avoidance–avoidance** | Must choose between two undesirable goals. | You dislike both cleaning the bathroom and cleaning the kitchen but must choose one or the other. |
| **Approach–avoidance** | Must choose or not choose a goal that has both desirable and undesirable aspects. | You want to have a pet for the companionship but don't like the idea of cleaning up after it. |
| **Multiple approach–avoidance** | Must choose from among two or more goals, with each goal possessing both desirable and undesirable aspects. | You have to decide on a college. One close to home would be less expensive and closer to your friends but not as academically desirable. The one in another state would be academically challenging and would look much better when applying for jobs but is very expensive and far away from friends and family. |

Interactive

## Concept Map  **L.O. 11.1, 11.2, 11.3**

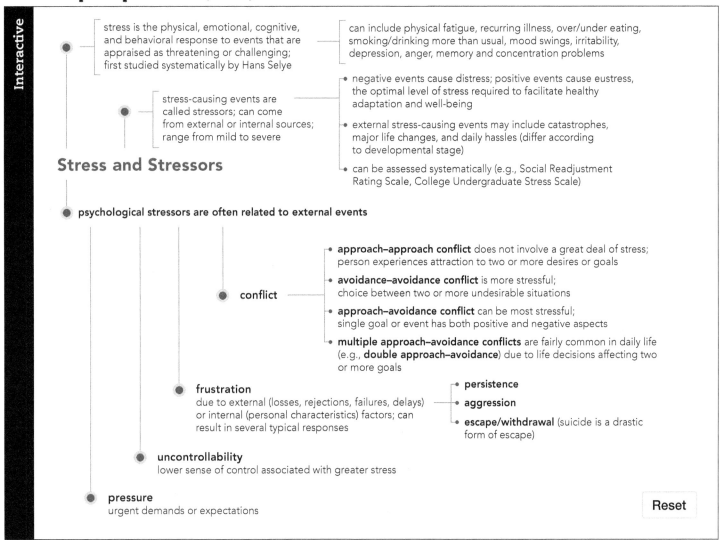

**Interactive**

stress is the physical, emotional, cognitive, and behavioral response to events that are appraised as threatening or challenging; first studied systematically by Hans Selye

can include physical fatigue, recurring illness, over/under eating, smoking/drinking more than usual, mood swings, irritability, depression, anger, memory and concentration problems

stress-causing events are called stressors; can come from external or internal sources; range from mild to severe

- negative events cause distress; positive events cause eustress, the optimal level of stress required to facilitate healthy adaptation and well-being
- external stress-causing events may include catastrophes, major life changes, and daily hassles (differ according to developmental stage)
- can be assessed systematically (e.g., Social Readjustment Rating Scale, College Undergraduate Stress Scale)

### Stress and Stressors

psychological stressors are often related to external events

**conflict**
- **approach–approach conflict** does not involve a great deal of stress; person experiences attraction to two or more desires or goals
- **avoidance–avoidance conflict** is more stressful; choice between two or more undesirable situations
- **approach–avoidance conflict** can be most stressful; single goal or event has both positive and negative aspects
- **multiple approach–avoidance conflicts** are fairly common in daily life (e.g., **double approach–avoidance**) due to life decisions affecting two or more goals

**frustration**
due to external (losses, rejections, failures, delays) or internal (personal characteristics) factors; can result in several typical responses
- **persistence**
- **aggression**
- **escape/withdrawal** (suicide is a drastic form of escape)

**uncontrollability**
lower sense of control associated with greater stress

**pressure**
urgent demands or expectations

Reset

# Practice Quiz    How much do you remember?

*Pick the best answer.*

**1.** Studies show that _____ is the optimal amount of stress that people need to positively promote their health and sense of well-being, which coincides with _____ theory.
- **a.** intensity; cognitive consistency
- **b.** distress; biological instinct
- **c.** eustress; arousal
- **d.** eustress; Maslow's

**2.** What does the Social Readjustment Rating Scale (SRRS) use to determine its results?
- **a.** The SRRS asks users to subjectively rate their stress level.
- **b.** The SRRS examines diet and family history to determine one's overall health risks.
- **c.** The SRRS records specific positive and negative life events to determine an individual's current level of stress.
- **d.** The SRRS looks exclusively at any catastrophes that a person has experienced.

**3.** Who, if anyone, would consider going shopping as a daily hassle and therefore stressful?
- **a.** adolescents
- **b.** those in their 20s and 30s
- **c.** senior citizens
- **d.** Hassles are stressful at any age, and studies do not find shopping to be a stressor or hassle at any age.

**4.** A retail store has announced to its employees that half of them will be laid off after a 2-week, random review of their personnel records. No current performance appraisals or individual interviews are being held. Over the next 2 weeks, many of the employees are arguing, fighting, and doing a poor job of taking care of their customers. What aspects of stress most likely started these behaviors?
- **a.** pressure and conflict
- **b.** uncontrollability and frustration
- **c.** pressure and frustration
- **d.** uncontrollability and conflict

**5.** Lisa wants the lead singing part in the next school musical, but by all accounts, she is not musically gifted in any way and has a rather unpleasant singing voice. Lisa may eventually realize her lack of singing ability is an _____ frustration.

**a.** internal

**b.** external

**c.** unacceptable

**d.** extrinsic

**6.** Marriage is sometimes perceived as a unique stressor. On one hand, you have many good aspects such as finding that special someone,

long-term commitment, and sometimes even combined incomes. On the other hand, there is a perceived loss of independence, a sense of finality, and the fear of "what if this isn't the right one?" Therefore, marriage may be seen as an example of a(n) _____ conflict.

**a.** approach–approach

**b.** avoidance–avoidance

**c.** approach–avoidance

**d.** double approach–avoidance

# Physiological Factors: Stress and Health

Chapter Two discussed in detail the function of the *autonomic nervous system* (ANS) the part of the human nervous system that is responsible for automatic, involuntary, and life-sustaining activities. The ANS consists of two divisions, the *parasympathetic* and the *sympathetic*. It is the sympathetic nervous system (the "fight-or-flight" system, Ⓛ Ⓘ Ⓝ Ⓚ to Learning Objective 2.5) that reacts when the human body is subjected to stress: Heart rate increases, digestion slows or shuts down, and energy is sent to the muscles to help deal with whatever action the stressful situation requires. The parasympathetic system returns the body to normal, day-to-day functioning after the stress is ended. Both systems, including many neural structures in the limbic system (Gianaros & Wager, 2015; Seo et al., 2014), figure prominently in a classic theory of the body's physiological reactions to stress, the general adaptation syndrome.

### THE GENERAL ADAPTATION SYNDROME

**11.4** Describe the stages of the general adaptation syndrome.

Endocrinologist Hans Selye was the founder of the field of research concerning stress and its effects on the human body. He studied the sequence of physiological reactions that the body goes through when adapting to a stressor. This sequence (see **Figure 11.1**) is called the **general adaptation syndrome (GAS)** and consists of three stages (Selye, 1956):

- **Alarm:** When the body first reacts to a stressor, the sympathetic nervous system is activated. The adrenal glands release hormones that increase heart rate, blood pressure, and the supply of blood sugar, resulting in a burst of energy. Reactions such as fever, nausea, and headache are common.

- **Resistance:** As the stress continues, the body settles into sympathetic division activity, continuing to release the stress hormones that help the body fight off, or resist, the stressor. The early symptoms of alarm lessen and the person or animal may actually feel better. This stage will continue until the stressor ends or the organism has used up all of its resources. Researchers have found that one of the hormones released under stress, noradrenaline (norepinephrine), actually seems to affect the brain's processing of pain, so that when under stress a person may experience a kind of analgesia (insensitivity to pain) if, for example, the person hits an arm or a shin (Delaney et al., 2007).

- **Exhaustion:** When the body's resources are gone, exhaustion occurs. Exhaustion can lead to the formation of stress-related diseases (e.g., high blood pressure or a weakened immune system) or the death of the organism if outside help is unavailable (Stein-Behrens et al., 1994). When the stressor ends, the parasympathetic division activates and the body attempts to replenish its resources.

Alarm and resistance are stages that people experience many times throughout life, allowing people to adapt to life's demands (Selye, 1976). It is the prolonged secretion of the stress hormones during the exhaustion stage that can lead to the most harmful effects of stress. It was this aspect of Selye's work that convinced other researchers of the connection between stress and certain *diseases of adaptation* as Selye termed them. The most common of these diseases are ulcers and high blood pressure.

**general adaptation syndrome (GAS)**

the three stages of the body's physiological reaction to stress, including alarm, resistance, and exhaustion.

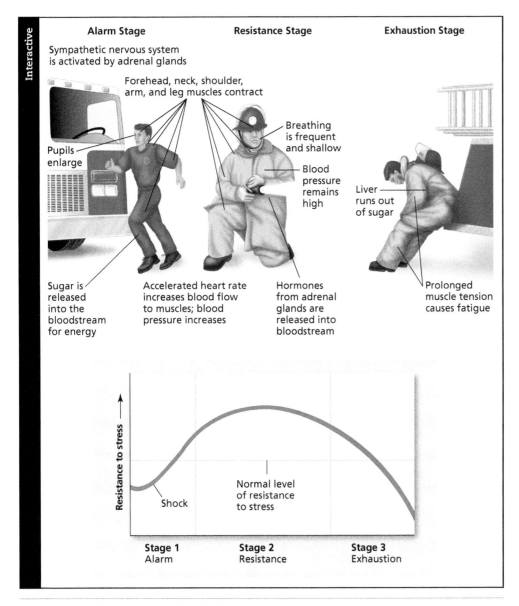

**Figure 11.1** General Adaptation Syndrome

The diagram at the top shows some of the physical reactions to stress in each of the three stages of the general adaptation syndrome. The graph at the bottom shows the relationship of each of the three stages to the individual's ability to resist a stressor. In the alarm stage, resistance drops at first as the sympathetic system quickly activates. But resistance then rapidly increases as the body mobilizes its defense systems. In the resistance stage, the body is working at a much increased level of resistance, using resources until the stress ends or the resources run out. In the exhaustion stage, the body is no longer able to resist, as resources have been depleted, and at this point disease and even death are possible.

## THE IMMUNE SYSTEM AND STRESS

**11.5** **Explain how the immune system is impacted by stress.**

As Selye first discovered, the **immune system** (the system of cells, organs, and chemicals in the body that responds to attacks on the body from diseases and injuries) is affected by stress. The field of **psychoneuroimmunology** concerns the study of the effects of psychological factors such as stress, emotions, thinking, learning, and behavior on the immune system (Ader, 2003; Cohen & Herbert, 1996; Kiecolt-Glaser, 2009; Kiecolt-Glaser et al., 1995, 1996, 2002). Researchers in this field have found that stress triggers the same response in the immune system that infection triggers (Maier & Watkins, 1998). Certain enzymes and other chemicals (including antibodies) are created by immune cells when the immune cells, or white blood

**immune system**

the system of cells, organs, and chemicals of the body that responds to attacks from diseases, infections, and injuries.

**psychoneuroimmunology**

the study of the effects of psychological factors such as stress, emotions, thoughts, and behavior on the immune system.

cells, encounter an infection in the body. The white blood cells surround the bacteria or other infectious material and release the chemicals and enzymes into the bloodstream. From there, these chemicals activate receptor sites on the *vagus nerve*, the longest nerve that connects the body to the brain. It is the activation of these receptor sites that signals the brain that the body is sick, causing the brain to respond by further activation of the immune system.

Stress activates this same system but starts in the brain rather than in the bloodstream. The same chemical changes that occur in the brain when it has been alerted by the vagus nerve to infection in the body occurred in laboratory animals when they were kept isolated from other animals or given electric shocks (Maier & Watkins, 1998). This has the effect of "priming" the immune system, allowing it to more successfully resist the effects of the stress, as in Selye's resistance stage of the GAS.

Hormones also play a part in helping the immune system fight the effects of stress. Researchers (Morgan et al., 2009) have found that a hormone called dehydroepiandrosterone (DHEA), known to provide antistress benefits in animals, also aids humans in stress toleration—perhaps by regulating the effects of stress on the hippocampus (part of the limbic system). Ⓛ Ⓘ Ⓝ Ⓚ to Learning Objective 2.11.

 💬 So stress actually increases the activity of the immune system? But then how does stress end up causing those diseases, like high blood pressure?

The positive effects of stress on the immune system only seem to work when the stress is not a continual, chronic condition. As stress continues, the body's resources begin to fail in the exhaustion phase of the general adaptation to stress (Kiecolt-Glaser et al., 1987, 1995, 1996; Prigerson et al., 1997). In one study, college students who were undergoing a stressful series of exams were compared to a group of similar students relaxing during a time of no classes and no exams (Deinzer et al., 2000). The exam group tested significantly lower for immune system chemicals that help fight off disease than did the relaxing control group, even as long as 14 days after the exams were over. The suppression of immune system functioning by stress apparently can continue even after the stress itself is over.

One reason that the early stress reaction is helpful but prolonged stress is not might be that the stress reaction, in evolutionary terms, is really only "designed" for a short-term response, such as running from a predator (Sapolsky, 2004). That level of intense bodily and hormonal activity isn't really meant to go on and on, as it does for human beings in the modern, stress-filled life we now know. Humans experience the stress reaction over prolonged periods of time and in situations that are not necessarily life-threatening, leading to a breakdown in the immune system. (See **Figure 11.2**)

While it is clear that stress affects the immune system and overall health, exactly why this occurs has been a topic of research. The *inflammatory response* happens when the tissues of the body are injured in some way—bacterial infections, heat, toxic substances, physical injury, and so on. Damaged cells release chemicals that then cause the blood vessels to leak fluids into surrounding tissues, and this causes swelling or inflammation. Believe it or not, this inflammation is an important part of the immune system's response to invading substances, serving to block access to other body tissues. Researchers are now finding that inflammation may actually be the means through which stress can

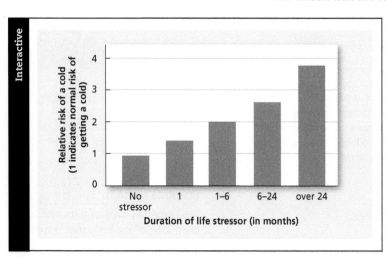

**Figure 11.2** Stress Duration and Illness

In this graph, the risk of getting a cold virus increases greatly as the months of exposure to a stressor increase. Although a stress reaction can be useful in its early phase, prolonged stress has a negative impact on the immune system, leaving the body vulnerable to illnesses such as a cold.

**SOURCE:** Cohen et al. (1998).

have its negative impact on health. One early study (Cohen et al., 1991) found that people under psychological stress are more likely to catch cold viruses than those who are not stressed. The researchers found that prolonged stress can cause the chemical that normally controls the inflammatory response, cortisol, to become less effective. This increases the inflammatory response, thus increasing the likelihood of getting a cold when exposed. In a more recent study (Cohen et al., 2012), the researchers found more evidence that prolonged stress was associated with a decrease in ability to regulate inflammation, and those higher levels of inflammation are associated with many diseases such as arthritis, heart disease, diabetes, and cancer (Hildreth, 2008; Pashkow, 2011; Rakoff-Nahoum, 2006).

**HEART DISEASE**   Of course, anything that can weaken the immune system can have a negative effect on other bodily systems. Stress has been shown to put people at a higher risk of **coronary heart disease (CHD)**, the buildup of a waxy substance called plaque in the arteries of the heart. Stress can affect the release of immune system chemicals such as cytokines, small proteins involved in the inflammatory process (Frostegård, 2013; Tian et al., 2014). Stress also affects the functioning of the liver, which is not activated while the sympathetic nervous system is aroused and does not have a chance to clear the fat and cholesterol from the bloodstream. This can lead to clogged arteries and eventually the possibility of heart attacks or strokes. In one study, middle-aged men were questioned about stress, diet, and lifestyle factors and were examined for biological risk factors for heart disease: obesity, high blood sugar, high triglycerides (a type of fatty acid found in the blood), and low levels of HDL or "good" cholesterol. (See **Figure 11.3**.) Stress and the production of stress hormones were found to be strongly linked to all four biological risk factors: The more stress the men were exposed to in their work environment and home lives, the more likely they were to exhibit these risk factors (Brunner et al., 2002).

Other studies have produced similar findings. One study looked at the heart health of people who suffered acute stress reactions after the 9/11 terrorist attacks and found a 53 percent increase in heart ailments over the 3 years following the attacks (Holman et al., 2008), whereas another large-scale study found that work stress is highly associated with an increased risk of coronary heart disease due to negative effects of stress on the ANS and glandular activity (Chandola et al., 2008). Recent studies have shown a clear relationship between stress in the workplace and an increased risk of coronary heart disease as well as depression, sleep disturbances, and unhealthy habits such as a lack of physical activity—none of which are good for coronary health (Emeny et al., 2012, 2013). Prolonged stress is simply not good for the heart.

**coronary heart disease (CHD)**
the buildup of a waxy substance called plaque in the arteries of the heart.

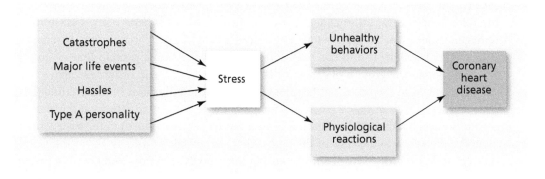

**Figure 11.3**   Stress and Coronary Heart Disease
The blue box on the left represents various sources of stress (Type A personality refers to someone who is ambitious, always working, and usually hostile). In addition to the physical reactions that accompany the stress reaction, an individual under stress may be more likely to engage in unhealthy behavior such as overeating, drinking alcohol or taking other kinds of drugs, avoiding exercise, and acting out in anger or frustration. This kind of behavior also contributes to an increased risk of coronary heart disease.

**DIABETES** Review the last paragraph, and it becomes obvious that weight problems may also become associated with stress. One chronic illness sometimes associated with excessive weight gain is *diabetes*, specifically **Type 2 diabetes** (Type 1 diabetes is an autoimmune disorder associated with failure of the pancreas to secrete enough insulin, necessitating medication, and is usually diagnosed before the age of 40). Type 2 diabetes is associated with excessive weight gain and occurs when pancreas insulin levels become less efficient as the body size increases. Insulin resistance has been linked by research to higher levels of the immune system's cytokines. Stress, as mentioned earlier, can increase the release of these cytokines (Tian et al., 2014). Type 2 diabetes can respond favorably to proper diet, exercise, and weight loss but may also require medication. Typically, it is associated with older adults, but with the rise in obesity among children, more cases of Type 2 diabetes in children are now occurring.

While controllable, diabetes is a serious disorder that has now been associated with an increased risk of Alzheimer's disease, although memory loss appears to be slower for diabetic Alzheimer patients than for nondiabetic Alzheimer's patients (Sanz et al., 2009). Several ongoing longitudinal studies strongly suggest that Type 2 diabetes not only is associated with mental decline in middle-aged individuals (Nooyens et al., 2010), but there is also indication that stress can compound the risk of that mental decline (Reynolds et al., 2010).

Research has continued to link high levels of stress with increased risk of diabetes. A 35-year study in Sweden monitored the health and stress factors of 7,500 men who began the study with no history of diabetes or coronary heart disease (Novak et al., 2013). Those men who reported experiencing permanent stress, related to home life and/or work life, had a 45 percent higher chance of developing diabetes compared to men who reported no stress or only periodic stress. Another study found that high levels of stress in the workplace can accurately predict who will develop diabetes, particularly in those people who had low levels of social support (Toker et al., 2012).

**CANCER** Cancer is not one disease but rather a collection of diseases that can affect any part of the body. Unlike normal cells, which divide and reproduce according to genetic instructions and stop dividing according to those same instructions, cancer cells divide without stopping. The resulting tumors affect the normal functioning of the organs and systems they invade, causing them to fail, eventually killing the organism.

Although stress itself cannot directly give a person cancer, stress can have a suppressing effect on the immune system, making the unchecked growth of cancer more likely (Le et al., 2016). In particular, an immune-system cell called a **natural killer (NK) cell** has as its main functions the suppression of viruses and the destruction of tumor cells (Chan et al., 2014; Herberman & Ortaldo, 1981). Stress has been shown to depress the release of natural killer cells, making it more difficult for the body's systems to fight cancerous growths (Chan et al., 2014; Zorilla et al., 2001). The hormone adrenaline is released under stress and has been found to interfere with a protein that normally would suppress the growth of cancer cells (Sastry et al., 2007). In other research, stress has been linked to the release of hormones such as adrenaline and noradrenaline that, over time, can cause mistakes (such as damage to the telomeres, structures at the ends of chromosomes that control the number of times a cell can reproduce) in the instructions given by the genes to the cells of the body. As these mistakes "pile up" over the years, cells can begin to grow out of control, causing the growth of tumors and possibly cancer (Kiecolt-Glaser et al., 2002).

Stress may impact the effectiveness of cancer treatments as well. In one study of mice implanted with human prostate cancer cells, treatment with a drug to destroy the cancer cells and prevent growth of tumors was effective when the mice were kept calm and stress free but failed miserably when the mice were stressed (Hassan et al., 2013).

One possible bit of positive news: Unlike the research linking stress at work to heart disease and diabetes, one study has found that work-related stress does not appear to be

**Type 2 diabetes**

disease typically occurring in middle adulthood when the body either becomes resistant to the effects of insulin or can no longer secrete enough insulin to maintain normal glucose levels.

**natural killer (NK) cell**

immune-system cell responsible for suppressing viruses and destroying tumor cells.

linked to developing cancer of the colon, lungs, breasts, or prostate (Heikkila et al., 2013). While 5 percent of more than 100,000 participants in the 12 years over which the study took place developed some form of cancer, there was no association between job-related stress and risk of cancer.

**OTHER HEALTH ISSUES**  Heart disease and cancer are not the only diseases affected by stress. Studies have shown that children in families experiencing ongoing stress are more likely to develop fevers with illness than are other children (Wyman et al., 2007). (Oddly enough, this same study showed that in children, stress actually seems to improve the function of their natural killer cells, just the opposite effect that is seen in adults.) A review of research and scientific literature (Cohen et al., 2007) found stress to be a contributing factor in a variety of human diseases and disorders, including heart disease, depression, and HIV/AIDS. Another longitudinal study's findings suggest that experiencing work-related stress in middle age may increase an individual's chances of developing both physical and mental disabilities in old age (Kulmala et al., 2013).

## HEALTH PSYCHOLOGY

**11.6** Describe the branch of psychology known as *health psychology*.

In the last three decades, people have become more aware of health issues and their relationship to what we do, what we eat, who we see, and how we think. A branch of psychology has begun to explore these relationships. **Health psychology** focuses on how our physical activities, psychological traits, and social relationships affect our overall health and rate of illnesses. (L)(I)(N)(K) to Learning Objective B.6. Psychologists who specialize in this field are typically clinical or counseling psychologists and may work with medical doctors in a hospital or clinic setting, although there are health psychologists who are primarily engaged in teaching and research. Some health psychologists focus on health and wellness issues in the workplace or public health issues such as disease prevention through immunizations or nutrition education. Others are more concerned with health-care programs that service all levels of the socioeconomic layers of society (Marks et al., 2005). Still others focus on the effects of stress on cognitive functioning, such as memory and attention (Aggarwal et al., 2014; Korten et al., 2014; Munoz et al., 2015; Olver et al., 2015). For more on the subject of health psychology, see the video *Health Psychology*.

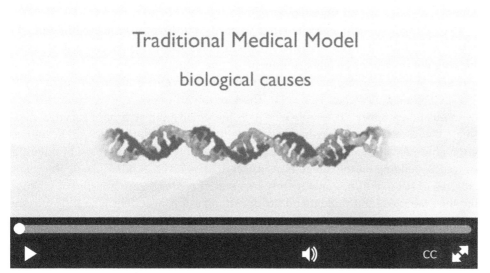

Traditional Medical Model — biological causes

Watch the Video *Health Psychology*

**health psychology**
area of psychology focusing on how physical activities, psychological traits, stress reactions, and social relationships affect overall health and rate of illnesses.

Health psychologists seek to understand how behavior (such as use of drugs, optimism, personality, or the type of food one eats) can affect a person's ability to fight off illnesses—or increase the likelihood of getting sick. They also want to know how factors like poverty, wealth, religion, social support, personality, and even one's ethnicity can affect health. *Clinical health psychology* is a subfield of health psychology focused on using the knowledge gained by researchers in the field to help promote healthy lifestyles, help people maintain their health and also to prevent or treat illnesses (Boll et al., 2002). Improving the health care system is another goal of clinical health psychologists. Health psychology also has connections to *behavioral psychology*, a field combining both medicine and psychology as well as numerous other scientific fields related to health issues (Christensen & Nezu, 2013; Miller, 1983). In this age of a new and intense focus on health care, health psychology is destined to become a more important force in future research. One important area in which health psychologists may focus is on the psychological effects of alternative medicines, as illustrated by the **APA Goal 2: Scientific Reasoning and Critical Thinking** feature.

## COGNITIVE FACTORS IN STRESS

### 11.7 Summarize Lazarus's cognitive appraisal approach to stress.

The physical effects of stress on the body and the immune system are only part of the picture of the influence of stress in daily life. Cognitive factors, such as how an individual interprets a stressful event, can affect the impact of stress.

Cognitive psychologist Richard Lazarus developed a cognitive view of stress called the *cognitive–mediational theory* of emotions, in which the way people think about and appraise a stressor is a major factor in how stressful that particular stressor becomes (Lazarus, 1991, 1999; Lazarus & Folkman, 1984). **L I N K** to Learning Objective 9.10. According to Lazarus, there is a two-step process in assessing the degree of threat or harm of a stressor and how one should react to that stressor (see **Figure 11.4**).

The first step in appraising a stressor is called **primary appraisal**, which involves estimating the severity of the stressor and classifying it as a threat (something that could be harmful in the future), a challenge (something to be met and defeated), or a harm or loss that has already occurred. If the stressor is appraised as a threat, negative emotions may arise that inhibit the person's ability to cope with the threat. For example, a student who has not read the text or taken good notes will certainly appraise an upcoming exam as threatening. If the stressor is seen as a challenge, however, it is possible to plan to meet that challenge, which is a more positive and less stressful approach. For example, the student who has studied and read and feels prepared is much more likely to appraise the upcoming exam as an opportunity to do well.

Perceiving a stressor as a challenge instead of a threat makes coping with the stressor (or the harm it may already have caused) more likely to be successful. Whereas perceiving the stressor as an embarrassment, or imagining future failure or rejection, is more likely to lead to increased stress reactions, negative emotions, and an inability to cope well (Folkman, 1997; Lazarus, 1993). Think positive!

In **secondary appraisal**, people who have identified a threat or harmful effect must estimate the resources that they have available for coping with the stressor. Resources might include social support, money, time, energy, ability, or any number of potential resources, depending on the threat. If resources are perceived as adequate or abundant, the degree of stress will be considerably less than if resources are missing or lacking. Using the example of the student and the upcoming exam, a student who feels that she has the time to study and the ability to understand the material in that time will feel much less distress than the student who has little time to study and doesn't feel that she understood all the content of the lectures covered on the exam.

An addition to the cognitive appraisal approach is the *cognitive reappraisal approach* (Jamieson et al., 2012, 2013). Researchers have found that instructing participants to

**primary appraisal**

the first step in assessing stress, which involves estimating the severity of a stressor and classifying it as either a threat or a challenge.

**secondary appraisal**

the second step in assessing a stressor, which involves estimating the resources available to the person for coping with the threat.

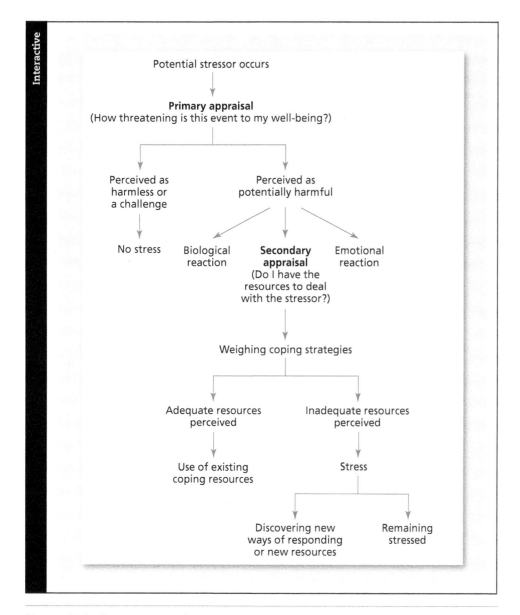

**Figure 11.4**   Responses to a Stressor

*Lazarus's Cognitive Appraisal Approach.* According to this approach, there are two steps in cognitively determining the degree of stress created by a potential stressor. Primary appraisal involves determining if the potential stressor is a threat. If it is perceived as a threat, secondary appraisal occurs in addition to the bodily and emotional reactions. Secondary appraisal involves determining the resources one has to deal with the stress, such as time, money, physical ability, and so on. Inadequate resources lead to increased feelings of stress and the possibility of developing new resources to deal with the stress.

reappraise their arousal while experiencing a stressor helped shift the negative effects of stress arousal to more positive effects. In one study (Jamieson et al., 2012), participants were told they were going to engage in a public-speaking task. Just before the task, participants were placed in three conditions: no instructions, a "placebo" instruction stating the best way of coping with stress was to ignore the source of stress, and an arousal-reappraisal condition in which they were given instructions that not only educated them about the reasons for physical arousal during stress and encouraged to interpret that arousal as a tool that would help them deal with the stress. For example, instead of seeing one's racing heart beat as a sign of fear, one could interpret it as the heart supplying blood to organs and tissues in preparation for dealing with the demands of the situation. The reappraisal participants were significantly less likely to look for cues of threat than were the other two groups. In a subsequent study (Jamieson et al., 2013), arousal reappraisal was found to help participants recover from stress as well, enabling them to return to normal physiological responses more quickly after stress when compared with participants who received no reappraisal instructions. Apparently, there's a big difference between feeling "excited" rather than "stressed."

## PERSONALITY FACTORS IN STRESS

**11.8** Explain how personality types and attitudes can influence people's reaction to stress.

Of course, how one cognitively assesses a stressor has a lot to do with one's personality, the unique and relatively stable ways in which people think, feel, and interact with others. People with certain kinds of personality traits—such as aggressiveness or a naturally high level of anxiety, for example—seem to create more stress for themselves than may exist in the actual stressor. Even as long ago as the early 1930s, psychologists have had evidence that personality characteristics are a major factor in predicting health. A longitudinal study begun in 1932 (Lehr & Thomae, 1987) found that personality was almost as important to longevity* as were genetic, physical, or lifestyle factors. Other researchers have found that people who live to be very old—into their 90s and even over 100 years—tend to be relaxed, easygoing, cheerful, and active. People who have the opposite personality traits, such as aggressiveness, stubbornness, inflexibility, and tenseness, typically do not live as long as the *average* life expectancy (Levy et al., 2002).

**PERSONALITY TYPES** Those positive and negative personality traits are some of the factors associated with two personality types that have been related to how people deal with stress and the influence of certain personality characteristics on coronary heart disease. (It should be noted that while personality is really far more complex than just a few "types," the following categories are simply handy, compact ways to refer to sets of associated traits.)

*Type A and Type B* In 1974, medical doctors Meyer Freidman and Ray Rosenman published a book titled *Type A Behavior and Your Heart*. The book was the result of studies spanning three decades of research into the influence of certain personality characteristics on coronary heart disease (Friedman & Kasanin, 1943; Friedman & Rosenman, 1959; Rosenman et al., 1975). Since then, numerous researchers have explored the link between what Friedman called Type A and Type B personalities.

**Type A** people are workaholics—they are very competitive, ambitious, hate to waste time, and are easily annoyed. They feel a constant sense of pressure and have a strong tendency to try to do several things at once. Often successful but frequently unsatisfied, they always seem to want to go faster and do more, and they get easily upset over small things. A typical Type A finds it difficult to relax and do nothing—Type A people take work with them on vacation, a laptop to the beach, and do business over the phone in the car.

In contrast, **Type B** people are not that competitive or driven, tend to be easygoing and slow to anger, and seem relaxed and at peace. Type B people are more likely to take a book to the beach to cover up their face than to actually read the book.

In 1961, the Western Collaborative Group Study (Rosenman et al., 1975) assessed 3,500 men and followed them for 8 years. For example, participants were asked to agree or disagree with statements such as "I can relax without guilt," in which strong agreement indicates a Type B personality. The results were that Type A men were three times more likely to develop heart disease than were Type B men. (See **Figure 11.5**)

"*He always times* 60 Minutes."

© The New Yorker Collection 1983 Mischa Richter from cartoonbank.com. All Rights Reserved.

**Type A personality**

person who is ambitious, time conscious, extremely hardworking, and tends to have high levels of hostility and anger as well as being easily annoyed.

**Type B personality**

person who is relaxed and laid-back, less driven and competitive than Type A, and slow to anger.

---

*longevity: how long people live

The Framingham Heart Study found that the risk of coronary heart disease for women who work and are also Type A is four times that of Type B working women (Eaker & Castelli, 1988). Other research has narrowed the key factors in Type A personality and heart disease to one characteristic: hostility* (Fredrickson et al., 2000; Matthews et al., 2004; Williams, 1999; Williams et al., 1980). Williams and his colleagues used the Minnesota Multiphasic Personality Inventory, a personality test that looks for certain characteristics that include the level of hostility. Ⓛ Ⓘ Ⓝ Ⓚ to Learning Objective 13.14. In this study, 424 patients who had undergone exploratory surgery for coronary heart disease were examined, and the presence of heart disease was related both to being Type A and to being hostile, with hostility being the more significant factor in the hardening of the arteries to the heart (Williams, 2001; Williams et al., 1980).

Numerous studies support the link between hostility and increased risk of coronary heart disease. A study of hostility levels and risk factors for heart disease in more than 4,000 young adults found that increases in hostility over a 5-year follow-up study were associated with a rise in high blood pressure, one of the major risk factors of heart disease (Markovitz et al., 1997). Another study of anger in young men and their risk for premature heart disease found that over a period of slightly more than three decades, the young men who had exhibited high levels of hostility in their youth were far more likely to develop premature cardiovascular disease, particularly heart attacks, than were those men who had lower levels of anger and hostility (Chang et al., 2002). Similar studies found that hostility in college-aged males and females was significantly related to increased risk of heart disease, particularly if levels of hostility rose in middle age (Brondolo et al., 2003; Siegler et al., 2003).

Even children may not escape the hostility–heart disease link. One study found that children and adolescents who scored high on assessments of hostility were more likely to show physical changes such as obesity, resistance to insulin, high blood pressure, and elevated levels of triglycerides 3 years after the initial measurements of hostility had been made (Raikkonen et al., 2003).

 💬 What about people who don't blow their top but try to keep everything "in" instead? Wouldn't that be bad for a person's health?

**TYPE C**  A third personality type was identified by researchers Temoshok and Dreher (1992) as being associated with a higher incidence of cancer. **Type C** people tend to be very pleasant and try to keep the peace but find it difficult to express emotions, especially negative ones. They tend to internalize their anger and often experience a sense of despair over the loss of a loved one or a loss of hope. They are often lonely. These personality characteristics are strongly associated with cancer, and people who have cancer and this personality type often have thicker cancerous tumors as well (Eysenck, 1994; Temoshok & Dreher, 1992). Just as the stress of hostility puts the cardiovascular systems of Type A people at greater risk, the internalized negative emotions of the Type C personality may increase the levels of harmful stress hormones, weaken the immune system, and slow recovery.

A word of caution here: "personality type" theories have come under criticism in recent years. Many consider them to be too simplistic—many people would not fall easily into one type or another. Nevertheless, many of the personality traits associated with these types do seem to be associated with stress and longevity. Many of the characteristics of the Type A personality, for example, fit the description of a major personality trait called *neuroticism*, the tendency to worry, be moody, and be emotionally intense.

*hostility: feelings of conflict, anger, and ill will that are long lasting.

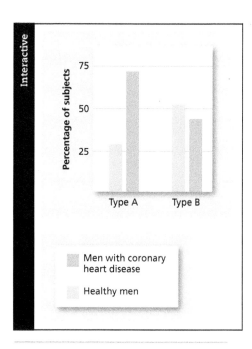

**Figure 11.5**  Personality and Coronary Heart Disease

The two bars on the left represent men with Type A personalities. Notice that within the Type A men, there are more than twice as many who suffer from coronary heart disease as those who are healthy. The two bars on the right represent men with Type B personalities. Far more Type B personalities are healthier than are Type A personalities, and there are far fewer Type B personalities with coronary heart disease when compared to Type A personalities.

**SOURCE:** Miller et al. (1991, 1996).

**Type C personality**

pleasant but repressed person, who tends to internalize his or her anger and anxiety and who finds expressing emotions difficult.

**L I N K** to Learning Objective 13.10. One recent longitudinal study's findings indicate that these characteristics are associated with an increased risk of an earlier death because people with these traits engage in poor health habits—poor diet, excessive drinking, smoking, and lack of exercise, to name a few (Mroczek et al., 2009).

**THE HARDY PERSONALITY**    Not all Type A people are prone to heart disease. Some people actually seem to thrive on stress instead of letting stress wear them down. These people have what is called the **hardy personality**, a term first coined by psychologist Suzanne Kobasa (1979). Hardy people (call them "Type H") differ from ordinary, hostile Type A people and others who suffer more ill effects due to stress in three ways:

- Hardy people have a deep sense of *commitment* to their values, beliefs, sense of identity, work, and family life.
- Hardy people also feel that they are in *control* of their lives and what happens to them.
- Hardy people tend to interpret events in primary appraisal differently than people who are not hardy. When things go wrong, they do not see a frightening problem to be avoided but instead a *challenge* to be met and answered.

Why would those three characteristics (often known as the three "Cs" of hardiness) lessen the negative impact of stress? Commitment makes a person more willing to make sacrifices and to deal with hardships than if commitment were lacking. Think about it: Have you ever had a job that you hated? Every little frustration and every snag was very stressful, right? Now think about doing something you love to do. The frustrations and snags that inevitably come with any endeavor just don't seem quite as bad when you are doing something you really want to do, do they?

As for control, uncontrollability is one of the major factors cited as increasing stress, as was discussed earlier in this chapter. Seeing events as challenges rather than problems also changes the level of stress experienced, a difference similar to that felt when riding a roller coaster: If riding the coaster is your own idea, it's fun; if someone makes you ride it, it's not fun.

The tendency for hardiness may even have genetic roots. Researchers have recently found that there seems to be a biochemical link between feeling miserable and an increased risk of death and that there may be a genetic variation in some individuals that actually severs that link, making that individual more biologically resilient or hardy (Cole et al., 2010).

The four personality types discussed so far could be summed up this way: If life gives you lemons,

- Type A people get enraged and throw the lemons back, having a minor heart attack while doing so.
- Type B people gather all the lemons and make lemonade.
- Type C people don't say anything but fume inside where no one can see.
- Type H people gather the lemons, make lemonade, sell it, turn it into a franchise business, and make millions. (Remember, laughing is good for you!)

**EXPLANATORY STYLE: OPTIMISTS AND PESSIMISTS**    In addition to personality type, there are other personal factors that have an influence on people's reactions to stressors. One of these factors is the attitude that people have toward the things that happen to them in life.

**Optimists** are people who always tend to look for positive outcomes. *Pessimists* seem to expect the worst to happen. For an optimist, a glass is half full, whereas for a pessimist, the glass is half empty. Researchers have found that optimism is associated with longer life and increased immune-system functioning. Mayo Clinic researchers conducted a longitudinal study of optimists and pessimists (as assessed by a scale) over a period of 30 years (Maruta et al., 2002). The results for pessimists were not good: They had a much higher death rate than did the optimists, more problems with physical and

TYPE Z BEHAVIOR

Type Z behavior
© The New Yorker Collection 1987 Donald Reilly from cartoonbank.com. All Rights Reserved.

**hardy personality**

a person who seems to thrive on stress but lacks the anger and hostility of the Type A personality.

**optimists**

people who expect positive outcomes.

emotional health, more pain, less ability to take part in social activities, and less energy than optimists. The optimists had a 50 percent lower risk of premature death and were more calm, peaceful, and happy than the pessimists (Maruta et al., 2002). Other studies link being optimistic to higher levels of helper T cells (immune system cells that direct and increase the functioning of the immune system) and higher levels of natural killer cells, the body's antivirus and anticancer cells (Segerstrom et al., 1998; Segerstrom & Sephton, 2010; Sin et al., 2015). Martin Seligman is a social learning psychologist who developed the concept of *learned helplessness,* Ⓛ Ⓘ Ⓝ Ⓚ to Learning Objective 5.12, and began the positive psychology movement. Seligman (2002) has outlined four ways in which optimism may affect how long a person lives:

1. Optimists are less likely to develop learned helplessness, the tendency to stop trying to achieve a goal that has been blocked in the past.

2. Optimists are more likely than pessimists to take care of their health by preventive measures (such as going to the doctor regularly, eating right, and exercising) because they believe that their actions make a difference in what happens to them. (Remember, this is a characteristic of hardy people as well.)

3. Optimists are far less likely than pessimists to become depressed, and depression is associated with mortality because of the effect of depression on the immune system.

4. Optimists have more effectively functioning immune systems than pessimists do, perhaps because they experience less psychological stress.

Seligman (1998) has also found that optimists are more successful in their life endeavors than pessimists are. Optimistic politicians win more elections, optimistic students get better grades, and optimistic athletes win more contests. For some advice on how to become more optimistic, see the Applying Psychology feature at the end of this chapter.

Regular exercise—whether alone or in the company of family and friends—increases the functioning of the immune system and helps give people a sense of control over their health. Having a sense of control decreases feelings of stress, which also helps the immune system function well.

## SOCIAL AND CULTURAL FACTORS IN STRESS: PEOPLE WHO NEED PEOPLE

**11.9** Identify social and cultural factors that influence stress reactions.

As stated earlier, much of the stress in everyday life comes from having to deal with other people and with the rules of social interaction. Overcrowding, for example, is a common source of stress. Overcrowding on our roadways, or traffic congestion, is one factor in aggressive driving behavior, which may escalate, or trigger in someone else, a disproportionate response or even *road rage* (AAA Foundation, 2009; Jeon et al., 2014). Road rage is a criminal act of assault by drivers against other drivers, which can result in serious injuries or even death. Two of the more prominent social factors in creating stressful living conditions are both economically based—poverty and job stress—while the third factor we will discuss has to do with the culture within which we live, work, and play.

**POVERTY** Living in poverty is stressful for many reasons. Lack of sufficient money to provide the basic necessities of life can lead to many stressors for both adults and children: overcrowding, lack of medical care, increased rates of disabilities due to poor prenatal care, noisy environments, increased rates of illness (such as asthma in childhood) and violence, and substance abuse (Aligne et al., 2000; Bracey, 1997; Evans & Kim, 2013; Leroy & Symes, 2001; Park et al., 2002; Renchler, 1993; Rouse, 1998; Schmitz et al., 2001).

**JOB STRESS** Even if a person has a job and is making an adequate salary, there are stresses associated with the workplace that add to daily stressors. Some of the typical sources of stress in the workplace include the workload,

Poverty can lead to many conditions that increase the degree of stress experienced by both adults and children. These children, for example, may face an increased risk of malnutrition, illness, and exposure to violence because of the conditions under which they must live.

a lack of variety or meaningfulness in work, lack of control over decisions, long hours, poor physical work conditions, racism, sexism, and lack of job security (Murphy, 1995).

Stress at work can result in the same symptoms as stress from any other source: headaches, high blood pressure, indigestion, and other physical symptoms; anxiety, irritability, anger, depression, and other psychological symptoms; and behavioral symptoms such as overeating, drug use, poor job performance, or changes in family relationships (Anschuetz, 1999; Chandola et al., 2006).

> 💬 There are times when I feel like I've just had it with school and all the work the teachers pile on—is that something like workplace stress?

One of the more serious effects of workplace stress is a condition called burnout. **Burnout** can be defined as negative changes in thoughts, emotions, and behavior as a result of prolonged stress or frustration, resulting in both mental and physical exhaustion (Bakker et al., 2014). In addition to exhaustion, symptoms of burnout are extreme dissatisfaction, pessimism, lowered job satisfaction, and a desire to quit. Although burnout is most commonly associated with job stress, college students can also suffer from burnout when the stresses of college life—term papers, exams, assignments, and the like—become overwhelming. The emotional exhaustion associated with burnout can be lessened when a person at risk of burnout is a member, within the work environment, of a social group that provides support and also the motivation to continue to perform despite being exhausted (Halbesleben & Bowler, 2007; Li et al., 2015).

**HOW CULTURE AFFECTS STRESS**  When a person from one culture must live in another culture, that person may experience a great deal of stress. *Acculturation* means the process of adapting to a new or different culture, often the dominant culture (Sam & Berry, 2010; Sodowsky et al., 1991). The stress resulting from the need to change and adapt to the dominant or majority culture is called **acculturative stress** (Berry & Kim, 1998; Berry & Sam, 1997). Some of the more obvious sources of acculturative stress include dealing with prejudice and discrimination.

The way in which a minority person chooses to enter into the majority culture can also have an impact on the degree of stress that person will experience (Berry & Kim, 1988; Ramos et al., 2015). One method is called *integration*, in which the individual tries to maintain a sense of the original cultural identity while also trying to form a positive relationship with members of the majority culture. For example, an integrated person will maintain a lot of original cultural traditions within the home and with immediate family members but will dress like the majority culture and adopt some of those characteristics as well. For people who choose integration, acculturative stress is usually low (Ramdhonee & Bhowon, 2012; Rudmin, 2003; Ward & Rana-Deuba, 1999).

In *assimilation*, the minority person gives up the old cultural identity and completely adopts the majority culture's ways. In the early days of the United States, many immigrants were assimilated into the mainstream American culture, even changing their names to sound more "American." Assimilation leads to moderate levels of stress, most likely due to the loss of cultural patterns and rejection by other members of the minority culture who have not chosen assimilation (LaFromboise et al., 1993; Lay & Nguyen, 1998; Rudmin, 2003).

*Separation* is a pattern in which the minority person rejects the majority culture's ways and tries to maintain the original cultural identity. Members of the minority culture refuse to learn the language of the dominant culture, and they live where others from their culture live, socializing only with others from their original culture. An example of this might be seen in many "Chinatown" areas across the United States, in which there are some residents who do not speak any English and who rarely go outside their

This Buddhist group is celebrating Songkran, the New Year, by performing their cultural ritual of pouring water over their elder's palms. Although they are wearing clothing typical of people living in Los Angeles, California, where the ceremony is taking place, they still maintain some of their former cultural traditions. This is a good example of integration.

**burnout**

negative changes in thoughts, emotions, and behavior as a result of prolonged stress or frustration, leading to feelings of exhaustion.

**acculturative stress**

stress resulting from the need to change and adapt a person's ways to the majority culture.

neighborhood. Separation results in a fairly high degree of stress, and that stress will be even higher if the separation is forced (by discrimination from the majority group) rather than voluntary (self-imposed withdrawal from the majority culture).

The greatest acculturative stress will most likely be experienced by people who have chosen to be *marginalized*, neither maintaining contact with their original culture nor joining the majority culture. They essentially live on the "margins" of both cultures without feeling or becoming part of either culture. Many Native Americans may feel marginalized, belonging neither to their original tribe of origin nor to the majority culture. Marginalized individuals do not have the security of the familiar culture of origin or the acceptance of the majority culture and may suffer a loss of identity and feel alienated from others (Roysircar-Sodowsky & Maestas, 2000; Rudmin, 2003). Obviously, marginalized people have little in the way of a social-support system to help them deal with both everyday stresses and major life changes.

## Concept Map L.O. 11.4, 11.5, 11.6, 11.7, 11.8, 11.9

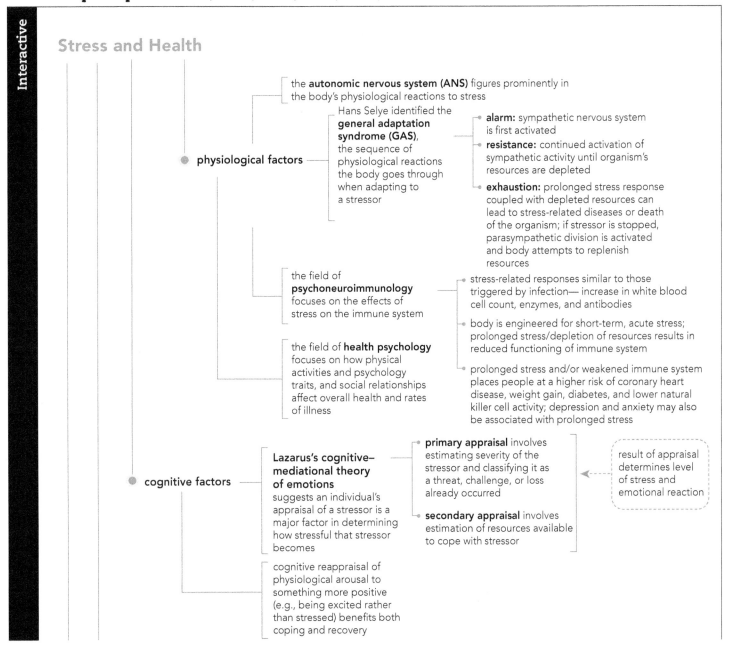

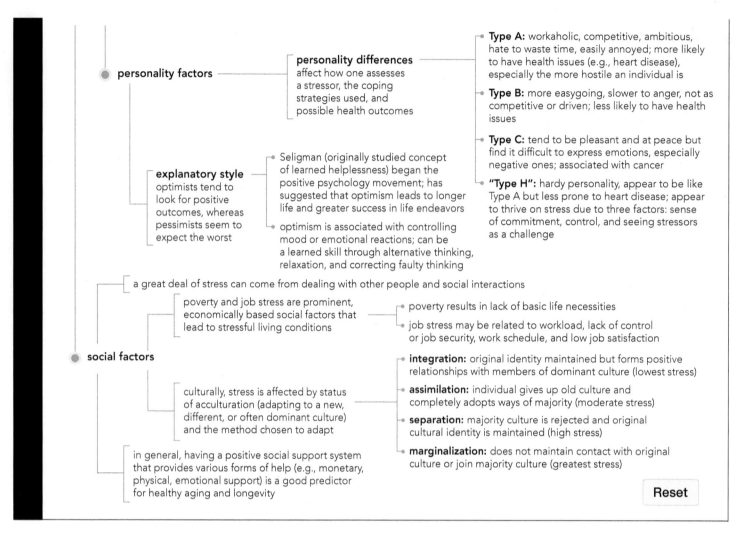

**personality factors** ──── **personality differences** affect how one assesses a stressor, the coping strategies used, and possible health outcomes

- **Type A:** workaholic, competitive, ambitious, hate to waste time, easily annoyed; more likely to have health issues (e.g., heart disease), especially the more hostile an individual is
- **Type B:** more easygoing, slower to anger, not as competitive or driven; less likely to have health issues
- **Type C:** tend to be pleasant and at peace but find it difficult to express emotions, especially negative ones; associated with cancer
- **"Type H":** hardy personality, appear to be like Type A but less prone to heart disease; appear to thrive on stress due to three factors: sense of commitment, control, and seeing stressors as a challenge

**explanatory style** optimists tend to look for positive outcomes, whereas pessimists seem to expect the worst

- Seligman (originally studied concept of learned helplessness) began the positive psychology movement; has suggested that optimism leads to longer life and greater success in life endeavors
- optimism is associated with controlling mood or emotional reactions; can be a learned skill through alternative thinking, relaxation, and correcting faulty thinking

**social factors**

- a great deal of stress can come from dealing with other people and social interactions
- poverty and job stress are prominent, economically based social factors that lead to stressful living conditions
    - poverty results in lack of basic life necessities
    - job stress may be related to workload, lack of control or job security, work schedule, and low job satisfaction
- culturally, stress is affected by status of acculturation (adapting to a new, different, or often dominant culture) and the method chosen to adapt
    - **integration:** original identity maintained but forms positive relationships with members of dominant culture (lowest stress)
    - **assimilation:** individual gives up old culture and completely adopts ways of majority (moderate stress)
    - **separation:** majority culture is rejected and original cultural identity is maintained (high stress)
    - **marginalization:** does not maintain contact with original culture or join majority culture (greatest stress)
- in general, having a positive social support system that provides various forms of help (e.g., monetary, physical, emotional support) is a good predictor for healthy aging and longevity

Reset

# Practice Quiz    How much do you remember?

*Pick the best answer.*

1. This stage of the general adaptation syndrome is accompanied by activation of the sympathetic nervous system.
   a. alarm
   b. resistance
   c. exhaustion
   d. termination

2. According to Richard Lazarus, when someone asks themselves, "How can I deal with this potentially harmful stressor?" the individual is focused on a _____ appraisal.
   a. primary
   b. secondary
   c. tertiary
   d. minimal

3. Greg rushes to an appointment, arriving 20 minutes early, while Aaron arrives with only minutes to spare. Slightly annoyed when Greg points this out, Aaron replies very casually, "Hey, I'm here." We might assume Greg has more of a _____ personality, while Aaron is more _____.
   a. Type A; Type B
   b. Type A; Type C
   c. Type B; Type C
   d. Type C; Type A

4. Olivia feels as if she is in control of her life and is committed to her goals. What final aspect of hardiness does she need to possess to be considered a hardy personality?
   a. being concerned when faced with problems
   b. exhibiting callousness in the face of threat
   c. being able to contain her anger
   d. seeing an event as a challenge rather than a problem

5. Devon is a full-time college student who has not taken a semester off in 3 years. He increasingly finds himself fatigued and stressed by the seemingly never-ending stream of papers, exams, and group projects. It has gotten to the point where he lacks the energy to work on his projects and puts little effort into his studying, figuring "What's the point?" What might Devon be experiencing?
   a. Devon is simply stressed. Nothing more.
   b. Devon is suffering from acculturative stress.
   c. Devon is suffering from burnout.
   d. Devon is suffering from eustress.

6. Joaquin moved from Nicaragua to the United States. He learned to speak and write English, changed his last name so that it would sound more "American," and no longer maintains any of his old culture's styles of dress or customs. Joaquin has used which method of entering the majority culture?
   a. integration
   b. assimilation
   c. separation
   d. marginalization

# APA Goal 2: Scientific Reasoning and Critical Thinking

## Homeopathy: An Illusion of Healing

*Addresses APA Objectives 2.1: Use scientific reasoning to interpret psychological phenomena; and 2.3: Engage in innovative and integrative thinking and problem solving.*

In the late nineteenth century, conventional medicine still made use of extremely questionable—and often harmful—practices such as bloodletting, purging (giving the patient enemas and substances meant to induce diarrhea and vomiting), and the use of mercury (Hall, 2014). It is no small wonder that many patients died. Into this arena came a doctor, Samuel Hahnemann, who truly wanted to find a safer way to treat his patients. The birth of the alternative medicine technique called **homeopathy**, the treatment of disease by introducing minute amounts of substances that would cause disease in larger doses, came from a series of events in Hahnemann's own experience. He took a dose of cinchona bark, used to treat malaria, and developed symptoms of malaria. From this one incident, he reasoned that if a substance causes a symptom of a disease in a healthy person, that substance can also be used to treat the same symptom in a sick person (Hahnemann, 1907; Hall, 2014). This was the first law of homeopathy, "like cures like." Notice that he is clearly making an assumption here based on one experience and no actual research whatsoever—remember the first criterion for critical thinking? "There are very few 'truths' that do not need to be subjected to testing." (L)(I)(N)(K) to Learning Objective 1.12.

His second law, the law of infinitesimals, came from the need to dilute his treatments to levels that would not actually cause symptoms, which he believed would make it not only safer but also more potent. Again, this was his belief, not a tested and carefully examined result of research. From these two laws the field of homeopathy was born, and even though famed nineteenth-century physician Oliver Wendell Holmes debunked the practice in the latter part of that century (Holmes, 1892), it is still going strong and has become big business.

There is ample evidence that homeopathy does not work (Ernst, 2002, 2012; Maddox et al., 1988; Sehon & Stanley, 2010; Shelton, 2004). The so-called substances that are supposed to effect a treatment are diluted to the extent that people using homeopathic remedies are simply using water, sugar pills, or glycerin—there is no effective medicine in these remedies at all. As Dr. Harriet Hall points out in her discussion of homeopathy in her column in *Skeptical Inquirer*, according to the reasoning used in homeopathy,

> If coffee keeps you awake, dilute coffee will put you to sleep. The more dilute, the stronger the effect. If you keep diluting it until there isn't a single molecule of coffee left, it will be even stronger. The water will somehow remember the coffee. If you drip that water onto a sugar pill and let the water evaporate, the water's memory will somehow be transferred to the sugar pill, and that memory of coffee will somehow enable it to function as a sleeping pill. (Hall, 2014).

Sounds pretty ridiculous when put that way, doesn't it? By the same reasoning, you don't need to fill your car's radiator with antifreeze because any water you put in must have at some point been in contact with ice, and all humans who have ever drunk water must be resistant to cholera, as all drinking water has at some point been tainted by that disease vector (Atwood, 2001). And while there are studies out there that

**homeopathy**
the treatment of disease by introducing minute amounts of substances that would cause disease in larger doses.

claim to have found support for the claims of homeopathy's effectiveness in treating diseases, systematic and scientific reviews of those studies have found numerous flaws in how that research was designed, conducted, and reported (Ernest, 2002, 2012). Plausible and likely explanations for their results were overlooked, such as the *placebo effect* (Ⓛ Ⓘ Ⓝ Ⓚ to Learning Objective 1.9), natural healing that has occurred as time has passed, the power of suggestion, and regression to the mean, which basically states that things tend to even out over the long run (Ⓛ Ⓘ Ⓝ Ⓚ to Learning Objective A.3). The fact is, people often don't look too closely at promised remedies for their ailments. That's really too bad, because a little critical thinking on their part could save them quite a bit of money.

### THINKING CRITICALLY

Many people have tried some pretty wild things to address things like acne, bad breath, hiccups, and other such maladies. What is the strangest thing you have ever tried to solve or cure such conditions? Did it work, and what prompted you to try it?

▶ The response entered here will be saved to your notes and may
be collected by your instructor if he/she requires it.

Submit

# Coping with Stress

💬 I have exams and my job and my relationship to worry about, so I feel pretty stressed out—how do people deal with all the stress they face every day?

So far, this chapter has talked about what stress is and the factors that can magnify the effects of stress, as well as the effects of stress on a person's physical health. Effectively dealing with stress involves increased awareness so changes can be made in factors that are actually controllable. Participate in the survey *Will This Survey Stress You Out?* to evaluate the level of stress in your life and what methods you use to cope with it.

**Survey**   WILL THIS SURVEY STRESS YOU OUT?

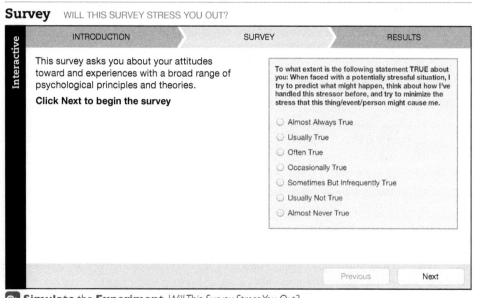

Ⓢ **Simulate** the **Experiment** *Will This Survey Stress You Out?*

**11.10** Distinguish between problem-focused and emotion-focused coping strategies to stress.

**Coping strategies** are actions that people can take to master, tolerate, reduce, or minimize the effects of stressors, and they can include both behavioral strategies and psychological strategies. While there are medications used for the treatment of stress-related problems, as well as nonmedical treatments such as hypnosis ( L I N K to Learning Objective 4.9) and meditation (discussed later in this chapter), let's take a look at some other methods for coping with stress.

**PROBLEM-FOCUSED COPING**   One type of coping strategy is to work on eliminating or changing the stressor itself. When people try to eliminate the source of a stress or reduce its impact through their own actions, it is called **problem-focused coping** (Folkman & Lazarus, 1980; Lazarus, 1993). For example, a student might have a problem understanding a particular professor. The professor is knowledgeable but has trouble explaining the concepts of the course in a way that this student can understand. Problem-focused coping might include talking to the professor after class, asking fellow students to clarify the concepts, getting a tutor, or forming a study group with other students who are also having difficulty to pool the group's resources.

**EMOTION-FOCUSED COPING**   Problem-focused coping can work quite well but is not the only method people can use. Most people use both problem-focused coping and **emotion-focused coping** to successfully deal with controllable stressful events (Eschenbeck et al., 2008; Folkman & Lazarus, 1980; Lazarus, 1993; Stowell et al., 2001). Emotion-focused coping is a strategy that involves changing the way a person feels or emotionally reacts to a stressor. This reduces the emotional impact of the stressor and makes it possible to deal with the problem more effectively. For example, the student who is faced with a professor who isn't easy to understand might share his concerns with a friend, talking it through until calm enough to tackle the problem in a more direct manner. Emotion-focused coping also works for stressors that are uncontrollable and for which problem-focused coping is not possible. Someone using emotion-focused coping may decide to view the stressor as a challenge rather than a threat, decide that the problem is a minor one, write down concerns in a journal, or even ignore the problem altogether.

  Ignore it? But won't that just make matters worse?

True, ignoring a problem is not a good strategy when there is something a person can actively do about solving the problem. But when it is not possible to change or eliminate the stressor, or when worrying about the stressor can be a problem itself, ignoring the problem is not a bad idea. Researchers working with people who had suffered heart attacks found that those people who worried about a future attack were more likely to suffer from symptoms of severe stress, such as nightmares and poor sleep (both factors that increase the risk of a future heart attack), than were the people who tried to ignore their worries (Ginzburg et al., 2003). L I N K to Learning Objective 14.5.

Using humor can also be a form of emotion-focused coping. A study on the effects of laughter found that laughter actually boosted the action of the immune system by increasing the work of natural killer cells (cells that attack viruses in the body). In this study, participants were shown a humor video for 1 hour. Blood samples were taken 10 minutes before the viewing, 30 minutes into the viewing, 30 minutes after viewing, and 12 hours after viewing the humor video. There were significant increases

An audience watches what is obviously a funny movie, one of the more popular choices for filmgoers. A large part of the success of such comedies can be attributed to the human need to laugh—laughter helps us cope with many of life's stresses.

**coping strategies**
actions that people can take to master, tolerate, reduce, or minimize the effects of stressors.

**problem-focused coping**
coping strategies that try to eliminate the source of a stress or reduce its impact through direct actions.

**emotion-focused coping**
coping strategies that change the impact of a stressor by changing the emotional reaction to the stressor.

in natural killer cell activity and nearly half a dozen other immune-system cells and systems, with some effects lasting the full 12 hours after the video ended (Berk et al., 2001).

In another study, researchers found that laughing can not only significantly *increase* levels of health-protecting hormones, but also just *looking forward* to a positive and humorous laughing experience can significantly *decrease* levels of potentially damaging hormones (Berk et al., 2008; Svebak et al., 2010). Other studies have found that repetitive, joyous laughter causes the body to respond as if receiving moderate exercise, which enhances mood and immune system activity, lowers both bad cholesterol and blood pressure, raises good cholesterol, decreases stress hormones, and even improves short-term memory in the elderly (Bains et al., 2012; Berk et al., 2009).

**Meditation** is a series of mental exercises meant to refocus attention and achieve a trancelike state of consciousness. Ⓛ Ⓘ Ⓝ Ⓚ to Learning Objective 4.1. Meditation can produce a state of relaxation that can aid in coping with the physiological reactions to a stressful situation. When properly meditating, brain waves change to include more theta and alpha waves (indicating deep relaxation), but little to no delta waves, which would indicate deep sleep (Lagopoulos et al., 2009).

Have you ever found yourself staring out into space or at some little spot on the wall or table, only to realize that your mind has been a complete blank for the last several minutes?

The state just described is really nothing more than **concentrative meditation**, the form of meditation best known to the general public. In concentrative meditation, the goal is to focus the mind on some repetitive or unchanging stimulus (such as a spot or the sound of one's own heart beating) so that the mind can forget daily hassles and problems and the body can relax. In fact, Herbert Benson (Benson, 1975; Benson et al., 1974a, 1974b) found that meditation produces a state of relaxation in which blood pressure is lowered, alpha waves (brain waves associated with relaxation) are increased, and the amounts of melatonin secreted at night (the hormone that helps induce sleep) are increased.

Research shows that meditation is a good way to relax and lower blood pressure in adolescents and adults, men and women, and both whites and African Americans (Barnes et al., 1997; Rainforth et al., 2007; Schneider et al., 1995; Wenneberg et al., 1997). Other research has suggested that meditation can reduce the levels of chronic pain (Brown & Jones, 2010; Kabat-Zinn et al., 1986), reduce the symptoms of anxiety, depression, and hostility (Kabat-Zinn et al., 1985), reduce the risk of heart disease (Schneider et al., 2012), and reduce stress levels in cancer patients (Speca et al., 2000). Reducing stress levels in cancer patients through meditation will increase the likelihood of recovery and reduce the incidence of recurrence. The *Applying Psychology to Everyday Life* section at the end of this chapter details the steps in a form of concentrative meditation based in Buddhist practices (but not tied to any particular religious beliefs) that can be easily learned and applied.

Meditation isn't the only way to relax, as reading a good book, taking a warm bath, or simply resting also produce relaxation. There are a couple of techniques recommended by experts to promote stress relief (Anspaugh et al., 2011; Mayo Clinic, 2016). One method is *progressive muscle relaxation*, in which you focus on tensing and then relaxing each of your muscle groups, usually beginning with the feet and working your way up the body. The purpose of this exercise is to help people recognize the difference between tense muscles and relaxed ones—we are often tensed up without realizing it. Another method is *visualization*, in which you use your imagination to "go" to a calm, peaceful place or situation, using as many of your senses as you can.

**meditation**

mental series of exercises meant to refocus attention and achieve a trancelike state of consciousness.

**concentrative meditation**

form of meditation in which a person focuses the mind on some repetitive or unchanging stimulus so that the mind can be cleared of disturbing thoughts and the body can experience relaxation.

## HOW SOCIAL SUPPORT AFFECTS COPING

**11.11** **Explain how a social-support system influences a person's ability to cope with stress.**

💬 I hear the term "social-support system" all the time now. Exactly what is it?

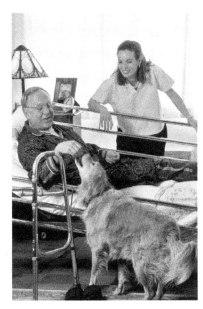

Coping with illness is always made easier when one has social support. Here, a man recovering in the hospital is visited by a volunteer and her dog. Animals are also a good source of social support, and people who have animals have been shown to recover from illnesses and stressors more quickly (Allen et al., 2002).

A **social-support system** is the network of friends, family members, neighbors, coworkers, and others who can offer help to a person in need. That help can take the form of advice, physical or monetary support, information, emotional support, love and affection, or companionship. Research has consistently shown that having a good social-support system is of critical importance in a person's ability to cope with stressors: People with good social-support systems are less likely to die from illnesses or injuries than those without such support (Kulik & Mahler, 1989, 1993). Breast cancer patients who have good social support tend to be better able to deal with pain and other symptoms of their disease (Kroenke et al., 2012). A good social support system also may promote better thinking: the more group ties a person has, the greater that person's cognitive health (Haslam et al., 2016).

Marriage, itself a form of social support, is a good predictor of healthy aging and longevity (Gardner & Oswald, 2004; Vaillant, 2002). Social support has been found to have a positive effect on the immune system (Holt-Lunstad et al., 2003); for example, it has been shown to improve the mental health and physical functioning of people who have *lupus*, a chronic inflammatory disease that can affect nearly any part of the body (Sutcliffe et al., 1999; M. M. Ward et al., 1999), as well as those with cancer and HIV (Carver & Antoni, 2004; Gonzalez et al., 2004). Thinking positively impacts health as well: In one recent study, people who experience warmer, more pleasant and upbeat emotions tend to have better health, and the researchers conclude that this connection is likely due to these people being able to make more social connections (Kok et al., 2013). The increased social-support network then has a positive effect on the health of these individuals.

Social support can make a stressor seem less threatening because people with such support know that there is help available. Having people to talk to about one's problems reduces the physical symptoms of stress—talking about frightening or frustrating events with others can help people think more realistically about the threat, for example, and talking with people who have had similar experiences can help put the event into perspective (Townsend et al., 2014). ⓛⓘⓝⓚ to Learning Objective 15.6. The negative emotions of loneliness and depression, which are less likely to occur with someone who has social support, can adversely affect one's ability to cope (Beehr et al., 2000; Weisse, 1992). The presence of multiple sources of support, such as friends, parents, and teachers, has been found to significantly decrease loneliness and social anxiety in adolescents (Cavanaugh & Buehler, 2016). Positive emotions, on the other hand, have a decidedly beneficial effect on health, helping people recover from stressful experiences more quickly and effectively (Tugade & Fredrickson, 2004). Positive emotions are more likely to occur in the presence of friends and family.

There is also a theory that gender makes a difference in coping with stress. While men are seen as dealing with stress by preparing to "fight or flee," women are more likely to resort to more socially oriented behavior. If there is an actual enemy, women may try to befriend that enemy and negate the threat, or if no actual enemy is available, they may seek out social support from family or friends (Taylor et al., 2000; Taylor, 2006). This *tend and befriend* theory may have a basis in a genetic difference between men and women. One study suggests that the SRY gene (a protein found only on the

**social-support system**

the network of family, friends, neighbors, coworkers, and others who can offer support, comfort, or aid to a person in need.

These people visiting a Mexican cemetery are honoring their loved ones who have passed away. The Day of the Dead is not only a celebration of the lives of those who have passed on but also a celebration for the living, who use this holiday to gain a sense of control over one of life's most uncontrollable events—death itself. What rituals or ceremonies do people of other cultures use to cope with death?

Y chromosome responsible for determining male sex characteristics) causes the fight-or-flight response (Lee & Harley, 2012). The researchers believe that women use a different genetic mechanism in coping with stress. As genetic research progresses, it will remain to be seen if this study's results will be supported.

### HOW CULTURE AFFECTS COPING

**11.12** **Describe cultural differences in coping with stress.**

Imagine this scene: You are driving out in the country when you come upon an elderly man working on a large wooden box, polishing it with great care. You stop to talk to the man and find out that the box is his own coffin, and he spends his days getting it ready, tending to it with great care. He isn't frightened of dying and doesn't feel strange about polishing his own coffin. How would you react?

If you were from the same rural area of Vietnam as the elderly man, you would probably think nothing strange is going on. For elderly people in the Vietnamese culture, thoughts of death and the things that go along with dying, such as a coffin, are not as stressful as they are to people from Western cultures. In fact, *stress* isn't all that common a term in Vietnamese society compared to Western societies (Phan & Silove, 1999).

Coping with stress in Vietnamese culture may include rituals, consulting a fortune-teller, or eating certain foods (Phan & Silove, 1999). In many Asian cultures, meditation is a common stress-relief tool, including the art of tai chi, a form of meditational exercise (Yip, 2002).

Other examples of cultural differences in coping: Thai children are twice as likely to use emotion-focused coping methods when facing powerful adults (doctors giving shots, angry teachers, etc.) than are children in the United States (McCarty et al., 1999). Adolescents in Northern Ireland, when compared to those in Colombia and Australia, tend to blame themselves when experiencing stress over social issues (e.g., fear of war, community violence) but also use more social/emotional support (Frydenberg et al., 2001). The Colombian youth used more problem-focused coping, as well as spiritual support and taking social action. Even within subcultures, there are different forms of coping: In interviews with Asian American, African American, and Hispanic American people living in New York after the September 11 terrorist attacks, researchers found that while both African American and Hispanic American people reported using church attendance and other forms of religious coping, Asian Americans reported using acceptance of the event as something out of their control (Constantine et al., 2005; Kuo, 2011). Cultures also vary in how much they engage their social network to help them cope.

Obviously, culture is an important factor in the kinds of coping strategies an individual may adopt and even in determining the degree of stress that is experienced. Mental health professionals should make an effort to include an assessment of a person's cultural background as well as immediate circumstances when dealing with adjustment problems due to stress.

### HOW RELIGION AFFECTS COPING

**11.13** **Explain how religious beliefs can affect the ability to cope with stress.**

A belief in a higher power can also be a source of great comfort in times of stress. There are several ways that religious beliefs can affect the degree of stress people experience and the ability to cope with that stress (Hill & Butter, 1995; Pargament, 1997).

First, most people who hold strong religious beliefs belong to a religious organization and attend regular religious functions, such as services at a synagogue, mosque, temple, or church. This membership can be a vital part of a person's social-support system. People do not feel alone in their struggle, both literally because of the people who surround them in their religious community and spiritually because of the intangible presence of their deity (Koenig et al., 1999).

Another way that religion helps people cope involves the rituals and rites that help people feel better about personal weaknesses, failures, or feelings of inadequacy (Koenig et al., 2001). These include rituals such as confession of sins or prayer services during times of stress. Religion can also increase the likelihood that a person will volunteer to help others and feel stronger and better in many ways. Finally, religious beliefs can give meaning to things that otherwise seem to have no meaning or purpose, such as viewing death as a pathway to a paradise or the destruction of one's home in a natural disaster as a reminder to place less attachment on material things.

Many religions also encourage healthy behavior and eating habits—eating wisely; limiting or forgoing the use of alcohol, tobacco, and other drugs; and sanctioning monogamous relationships. Some research even suggests that people with religious commitments live longer than those who have no such beliefs, although this is correlational research ( Ⓛ Ⓘ Ⓝ Ⓚ to Learning Objective 1.7) and should not be interpreted as concluding that religious belief causes longer life expectancies (Hummer et al., 1999; Koenig et al., 1999; Lambert et al., 2013; Strawbridge et al., 1997; Thoresen & Harris, 2002).

## THINKING CRITICALLY

What methods of stress reduction do you typically rely on? How effective do you believe them to be? Why?

▶
```
The response entered here will be saved to your notes and may be
collected by your instructor if he/she requires it.
```

Submit

## Concept Map L.O. 11.10, 11.11, 11.12, 11.13

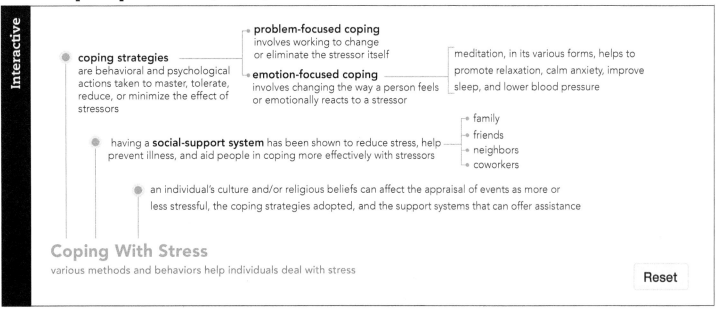

**Interactive**

- **coping strategies** are behavioral and psychological actions taken to master, tolerate, reduce, or minimize the effect of stressors
  - **problem-focused coping** involves working to change or eliminate the stressor itself
  - **emotion-focused coping** involves changing the way a person feels or emotionally reacts to a stressor — meditation, in its various forms, helps to promote relaxation, calm anxiety, improve sleep, and lower blood pressure

- having a **social-support system** has been shown to reduce stress, help prevent illness, and aid people in coping more effectively with stressors
  - family
  - friends
  - neighbors
  - coworkers

- an individual's culture and/or religious beliefs can affect the appraisal of events as more or less stressful, the coping strategies adopted, and the support systems that can offer assistance

**Coping With Stress**
various methods and behaviors help individuals deal with stress

Reset

# Practice Quiz    How much do you remember?

*Pick the best answer.*

1. Wanda explains that she ignores her problems when she feels she cannot control them or when she worries about them to the point of causing problems elsewhere in her life. What does the research say about using such an approach?
   a. This method can be somewhat harmful even if used only occasionally.
   b. This method is helpful only if you are a Type B personality.
   c. This method is fine when the stressor cannot be eliminated or worrying about the stressor causes problems.
   d. This method is dangerous, since a stressor really must be dealt with so as to feel better.

2. What does the research tell us about the effects of laughter on alleviating stress?
   a. Laughter can alleviate immediate stress, but the effects last only a few minutes.
   b. Laughter has been shown to help the immune system.
   c. Laughter in reality has little to no effect on one's overall stress level.
   d. Laughter can actually have a negative effect on the body.

3. Simply put, what type of stress reduction is tai chi, the focusing of the mind on specific movements of the body?
   a. optimism
   b. meditation
   c. personality type
   d. progressive muscle relaxation

4. Meditation, progressive muscle relaxation, and guided visualization are _____ coping strategies for stress.
   a. very effective
   b. basically ineffective
   c. emotion-focused
   d. problem-focused

5. What effect, if any, does religion have on one's stress?
   a. Religion has not been shown to effect one's stress.
   b. Religion can actually increase one's stress.
   c. Religion can help alleviate stress in young people but not in senior citizens.
   d. Religion can help people effectively cope with stress in multiple ways.

---

These people are practicing meditation. Meditation increases relaxation and helps lower blood pressure and muscle tension.

**mindfulness meditation**

A form of concentrative meditation in which the person purposefully pays attention to the present moment, without judgment or evaluation.

## Applying Psychology to Everyday Life
## Coping with Stress Through Mindfulness Meditation

**11.14**  **Define mindfulness meditation and describe its use in coping with the effects of stress.**

As mentioned in the discussion of meditation, there is a form of concentrative meditation called **mindfulness meditation**, based in Buddhist philosophy and sometimes called *shamatha* meditation. In this form of meditation, people deliberately and purposefully pay attention to the moment-by-moment "unfolding" of experience without judging or evaluating that experience (Hozel et al., 2011; Simkin & Black, 2014). Meditation in general and mindfulness meditation particularly has been found to help reduce stress, increase a sense of well-being, and improve emotional health (Creswell et al., 2014; Tang et al., 2015).

Some people think that meditation is nothing more than sitting around doing nothing, or even just another form of sleep. But learning to "sit around and do nothing" actually takes some practice—it's not as easy as you might think to be in your own head without thinking of dozens of other things.

Mindfulness meditation usually begins with the person sitting on a cushion with legs crossed or on a chair with the back straight. (The focus on a straight posture comes from the Buddhist idea that your energy "flows" better when you are sitting straight.) You should try to find a place that has a positive feeling for you, is quiet, and where you are not likely to be disturbed. Eyes are closed or focused down at a spot just a few inches from the end of your nose (this reduces distractions). Your attention should be focused on a bodily function such as the movement of the abdomen in and out as you breathe or on the sound and awareness of your breath as it moves through your nose. Your mind is probably going to try to wander at first, but that's okay—no judgment, remember? You just go back to focusing on the breathing. Not only does the breathing give you something on which to focus, it also relaxes you.

Typically short periods are best at first: 10 minutes of practice in this technique a day. As you get better at being aware of just what is going on at this moment in time, you'll become more aware of your thoughts, emotions, and actions at that moment.

### Questions for Further Discussion

1. What other benefits might there be from focusing on regular, rhythmic breathing?
2. What is the advantage to focusing on your own body's actions rather than an object or chant (such as a mantra)?

# Chapter Summary

## Stress and Stressors

### 11.1 Distinguish between distress and eustress.

- Stress is the physical, emotional, and behavioral responses that occur when events are identified as threatening or challenging.
- Stress that has a negative impact is called "distress." Eustress is the optimal amount of stress that people need to function well.

### 11.2 Identify three types of external events that can cause stress.

- Catastrophes are events such as floods or crashes that can result in high levels of stress.
- Major life changes create stress by requiring adjustments. Major life changes have an impact on chronic health problems and risk of accidents.
- Hassles are the daily frustrations and irritations that have an impact on day-to-day health.

### 11.3 Identify psychological factors in stress.

- Four sources of stress are pressure, uncontrollability, frustration, and conflict.
- Frustration, which can be internal or external, may result in persistence, aggression, displaced aggression, or withdrawal.

## Physiological Factors: Stress and Health

### 11.4 Describe the stages of the general adaptation syndrome.

- The autonomic nervous system consists of the sympathetic system, which responds to stressful events, and the parasympathetic system, which restores the body to normal functioning after the stress has ceased.
- The general adaptation syndrome is the body's reaction to stress and includes three stages of reaction: alarm, resistance, and exhaustion.

### 11.5 Explain how the immune system is impacted by stress.

- Stress causes the immune system to react as though an illness or invading organism has been detected, increasing the functioning of the immune system.

- As the stress continues or increases, the immune system can begin to fail.

### 11.6 Describe the branch of psychology known as *health psychology.*

- Health psychology focuses on the impact of physical and social activities as well as psychological traits on health and rates of illness.
- Clinical health psychology is a subfield in which knowledge is gained by researchers to promote health and wellness.

### 11.7 Summarize Lazarus's cognitive appraisal approach to stress.

- The cognitive appraisal approach states that how people think about a stressor determines, at least in part, how stressful that stressor will become.
- The first step in appraising a stressor is called primary appraisal, in which the person determines whether an event is threatening, challenging, or of no consequence. Threatening events are more stressful than those seen as challenging.
- The second step is secondary appraisal, in which the person assesses the resources available to deal with the stressor, such as time, money, and social support.

### 11.8 Explain how personality types and attitudes can influence people's reaction to stress.

- Type A personalities are ambitious, time-conscious, hostile, and angry workaholics who are at increased risk of coronary heart disease, primarily due to their anger and hostility.
- Type B personalities are relaxed and easygoing and have one third the risk of coronary heart disease as do Type A personalities if male and one fourth the risk if female and working outside the home.
- Type C personalities are pleasant but repressed, internalizing their negative emotions.
- Hardy people are hard workers who lack the anger and hostility of the Type A personality, instead seeming to thrive on stress.
- Optimists look for positive outcomes and experience far less stress than pessimists, who take a more negative view.

**11.9  Identify social and cultural factors that influence stress reactions.**

- Several social factors can be a source of stress or increase the effects of stress: poverty, stresses on the job or in the workplace, and entering a majority culture that is different from one's culture of origin.
- Burnout is a condition that occurs when job stress is so great that the person develops negative thoughts, emotions, and behavior as well as an extreme dissatisfaction with the job and a desire to quit.
- The four methods of acculturation are integration, assimilation, separation, and marginalization.
- Social-support systems are important in helping people cope with stress.

## Coping with Stress

**11.10  Distinguish between problem-focused and emotion-coping strategies to stress.**

- Problem-focused coping is used when the problem can be eliminated or changed so that it is no longer stressful or so that the impact of the stressor is reduced.
- Emotion-focused coping is often used with problem-focused coping and involves changing one's emotional reactions to a stressor.
- Meditation can produce a state of relaxation and reduce the physical reactions common to stressful situations.
- Concentrative meditation involves focusing inward on some repetitive stimulus, such as one's breathing.

**11.11  Explain how a social-support system influences a person's ability to cope with stress.**

- A social-support system is the network of friends, family members, neighbors, coworkers, and others who can offer help to a person in need. Having a social-support system has been shown to reduce stress, help prevent illness, and aid people in coping more effectively with stressors.

**11.12  Describe cultural differences in coping with stress.**

- Different cultures perceive stressors differently, and coping strategies will also vary from culture to culture.

**11.13  Explain how religious beliefs can affect the ability to cope with stress.**

- People with religious beliefs also have been found to cope better with stressful events.

## Applying Psychology to Everyday Life: Coping with Stress Through Mindfulness Meditation

**11.14  Define mindfulness meditation and describe its use in coping with the effects of stress.**

- Mindfulness meditation can help reduce the affects of stress and lead to improved psychological and physical health.
- The practice of mindfulness meditation includes maintaining an erect posture in a quiet area and focusing on one's breathing and the immediate moment-by-moment experience.

# Test Yourself

*Pick the best answer.*

**1.** Dean has a comprehensive final exam in three weeks that he is concerned about. His concerns prompt him to go ahead and start studying, and in doing so, he feels less worried as the exam approaches. In this example, the exam, Dean's concerns, and his behavior may be seen as an example of

_____.
  **a.** burnout          **c.** distress
  **b.** depression       **d.** eustress

**2.** Researchers today believe that eustress is based on _____ of motivation.
  **a.** Maslow's theory
  **b.** the arousal theory
  **c.** the biological theory
  **d.** the need for affiliation theory

**3.** Unpredictable, large-scale events that create a great deal of stress and feelings of threat are called
  **a.** major life events.     **c.** hassles.
  **b.** catastrophes.          **d.** major hassles.

**4.** A score above 300 on the SRRS would indicate a person has _____ of becoming ill or having an accident.
  **a.** a very high risk       **c.** a low risk
  **b.** an average risk        **d.** no risk

**5.** In addition to being emotionally intense, many items on both the SRRS and CUSS are stressful because they
  **a.** involve the most hassles.
  **b.** cause heart disease.
  **c.** turn into catastrophes.
  **d.** lead to mild stress disorder.

**6.** Research suggests the number and perceived severity of daily hassles are strong predictors of
  **a.** diabetes.     **c.** depression.
  **b.** headaches.    **d.** heart attacks.

**7.** Based on previous research, who is more likely to experience lack of money as the biggest daily hassle in their life?
  **a.** children       **c.** young adults
  **b.** adolescents    **d.** elderly people

**8.** Time pressure is often found to have a negative impact on
  **a.** creativity.    **c.** predictability.
  **b.** depression.    **d.** frustration.

**9.** Michael was cut from his high school basketball team. He told his friends that he was cut because the coach did not like him, but his close friends know Michael was cut because he hardly ever practiced. In this situation, Michael's excuse is an example of a(n) _____ frustration, while the fact he despises practicing is an example of a(n) _____ frustration.

   **a.** personal; external      **c.** internal; external
   **b.** external; personal      **d.** personal; internal

**10.** Kina's husband comes home from work angry because of an argument he had with his boss. Subsequently, Kina's husband begins yelling at her for no apparent reason. Ultimately, Kina finds herself yelling at their youngest child for apparently no good reason other than being frustrated. Kina is displaying

   **a.** escape.      **c.** displaced aggression.
   **b.** withdrawal.      **d.** projection.

**11.** Erica was very frustrated with her job and ultimately decided to quit. What do we call this method of handling frustration?

   **a.** This approach is called using a scapegoat.
   **b.** This is an example of an emotion-focused method.
   **c.** This approach is called escape or withdrawal.
   **d.** This approach is called ignoring.

**12.** Keenan is trying to decide if he should go on spring break with his friends to Las Vegas or with his other friends to Miami Beach, both of which he has enjoyed going to in the past. Keenan's situation is an example of a(n) _____ conflict.

   **a.** approach–approach
   **b.** avoidance–avoidance
   **c.** approach–avoidance
   **d.** multiple approach–avoidance

**13.** In which of Selye's stages is death a possible outcome?

   **a.** alarm      **c.** reaction
   **b.** resistance      **d.** exhaustion

**14.** According to Richard Lazarus, determining what can be done to deal with one's stress is an example of a _____ appraisal.

   **a.** primary      **c.** formal
   **b.** secondary      **d.** tertiary

**15.** Jolene rarely takes any work home, preferring to leave her work worries at the office. She is a bit carefree and not as ambitious as some of the other women in her office. Instead, Jolene likes to have a lot of leisure time whenever possible. She is also easygoing and doesn't lose her temper often, preferring to avoid conflict. Which of the following statements about Jolene is most likely TRUE?

   **a.** She is a Type A personality.
   **b.** She is a Type B personality.
   **c.** She is a Type C personality.
   **d.** Jolene's risk of coronary heart disease is high.

**16.** Azriel seems to thrive on stress and feels very much in control of his life. He would probably be labeled a _____ personality.

   **a.** Type A      **c.** Type C
   **b.** Type B      **d.** hardy

**17.** Huong has moved from China to the United States. While she dresses and acts like her American friends, she still has retained much of her cultural heritage and attends traditional Chinese dance classes on the weekends. This is an example of

   **a.** assimilation.      **c.** separation.
   **b.** integration.      **d.** marginalization.

**18.** Gary is having trouble with psychology and statistics. He goes to the school's academic help center for tutoring and spends extra time working on problems at home. Gary's method of coping is

   **a.** problem focused.      **c.** defensive focused.
   **b.** emotion focused.      **d.** internal.

**19.** To alleviate her stress, Jenny often closes her eyes and envisions herself on a quiet beach during sunset. This vision often helps her relax, especially before talking in front of a crowd. Such an approach is known as

   **a.** relaxation.      **c.** progressive muscle relaxation.
   **b.** concentrative meditation.      **d.** visualization.

**20.** Which of the following people may have the greatest ability to cope with stress?

   **a.** Mary, a very religious person who is involved in her community
   **b.** Carrie, who works hard but doesn't have any apparent hobbies or other interests
   **c.** Jeri, who has few friends and whose family lives far away from her
   **d.** Larry, who is highly driven to succeed

# 12 Social Psychology

How are your actions influenced by others? Are there certain actions or personal beliefs that you feel are consistent regardless of your social surroundings?

After you have answered the question, watch the video to compare the answers of other students to yours.

▶ The response entered here will be saved to your notes and may be collected by your instructor if he/she requires it.

👁 **Watch** the **Video**

# **Why study** social psychology?

If people lived in total isolation from other people, there would be no reason to study the effect that other people have on the behavior of individuals and groups. But human beings are social creatures—we live with others, work with others, and play with others. The people who surround us all of our lives have an impact on our beliefs and values, decisions and assumptions, and the way we think about ourselves and about other people in general. Why are some people prejudiced toward certain other people? Why do we obey some people but not others? What causes us to like, to love, or to hate others? The answers to all these questions and many more can be found in the study of social psychology.

# Learning Objectives

**12.1** Identify factors that influence people or groups to conform to the actions of others.

**12.2** Explain how our behavior is impacted by the presence of others.

**12.3** Compare and contrast three compliance techniques.

**12.4** Identify factors that make obedience more likely.

**12.5** Identify the three components of an attitude and how attitudes are formed.

**12.6** Describe how attitudes can be changed.

**12.7** Explain how people react when attitudes differ from behavior.

**12.8** Describe how people form impressions of others.

**12.9** Describe the process of explaining one's own behavior and the behavior of others.

**12.10** Distinguish between prejudice and discrimination.

**12.11** Describe theories of how prejudice is learned and how it can be overcome.

**12.12** Identify factors involved in interpersonal attraction.

**12.13** Describe the different types of love outlined in Sternberg's theory.

**12.14** Explain how aggressive behavior is determined by biology and learning.

**12.15** Identify the factors influencing why people help others.

**12.16** Define social neuroscience.

# Social Influence

Chapter One defined psychology as the scientific study of behavior and mental processes, including how people think and feel. The field of **social psychology** also looks at behavior and mental processes but includes as well the social world in which we exist, as we are surrounded by others to whom we are connected and by whom we are influenced in so many ways. It is the scientific study of how a person's behavior, thoughts, and feelings influence and are influenced by social groups.

Each of us lives in a world filled with other people. An infant is born into a world with adults who have an impact on the infant's actions, personality, and growth. Adults must interact with others on a daily basis. Such interactions provide ample opportunity for the presence of other people to directly or indirectly influence the behavior, feelings, and thoughts of each individual in a process called **social influence**. There are many forms of social influence. People can influence others to follow along with their own actions or thoughts, to agree to do things even when the person might prefer to do otherwise, and to be obedient to authorities. The mere presence of others, whether real or merely implied, can even influence the way people perform tasks successfully or unsuccessfully.

## CONFORMITY

### 12.1 Identify factors that influence people or groups to conform to the actions of others.

Have you ever noticed someone looking up at something? Did the urge to look up to see what that person was looking at become so strong that you actually found yourself looking up? This common practical joke always works, even when people suspect that it's a joke. It clearly demonstrates the power of **conformity**: changing one's own behavior to more closely match the actions of others.

In 1936, social psychologist Muzafer Sherif conducted a study in which participants were shown into a darkened room and exposed to a single point of light. Under those conditions, a point of light will seem to move because of tiny, involuntary movements of the eye. Ⓛ Ⓘ Ⓝ Ⓚ to Learning Objective 3.3. The participants were not told of this effect and reported the light moved anywhere from a few inches to several feet. When a confederate (a person chosen by the experimenter to deliberately manipulate the situation) also gave estimates, the original participants began to make estimates of motion that were more and more similar to those of the confederate (Sherif, 1936). This early experiment on conformity has been criticized because the judgments being made were ambiguous* (i.e., the light wasn't really moving, so any estimate within reason would sound good). Would participants be so easily swayed if the judgments were more specifically measurable and certain?

Solomon Asch (1951) conducted the first of his classic studies on conformity by having seven participants gather in a room. They were told that they were participating in an experiment on visual judgment. They were then shown a white card with only one line on it followed by another white card with three lines of varying lengths. The task was to determine which line on the second card was most similar to the line on the first card (see **Figure 12.1**).

In reality, only the next-to-the-last person in the group was a real participant. The others were all confederates who, after responding with the correct answer on a few trials, were instructed by the experimenter to start picking the same *incorrect* line from the comparison lines. Would the real participant, having heard the others pick what seemed to be the wrong answer, change to conform to the group's opinion? Surprisingly, the participants conformed to the group answer a little more than one third of the time. Asch also found that the number of confederates mattered: Conformity increased with each

**social psychology**

the scientific study of how a person's thoughts, feelings, and behavior influence and are influenced by social groups; area of psychology in which psychologists focus on how human behavior is affected by the presence of other people.

**social influence**

the process through which the real or implied presence of others can directly or indirectly influence the thoughts, feelings, and behavior of an individual.

**conformity**

changing one's own behavior to match that of other people.

---

*ambiguous: having no clear interpretation or able to be interpreted in many ways rather than just one way.

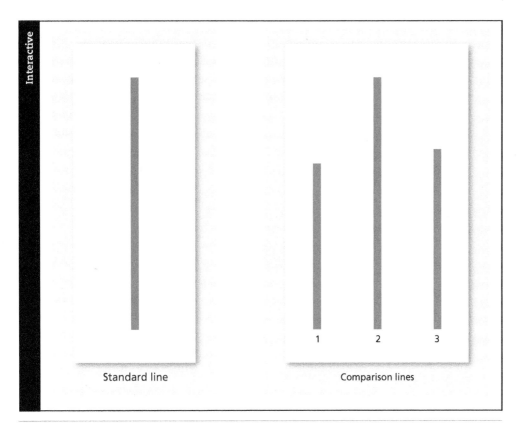

**Figure 12.1**  Stimuli Used in Asch's Study

Participants in Asch's famous study on conformity were first shown the standard line. They were then shown the three comparison lines and asked to determine which of the three was the standard line most similar. Which line would you pick? What if you were one of several people, and everyone who answered ahead of you chose line 3? How would that affect your answer?

**SOURCE:** Adapted from Asch (1956).

new confederate until there were four confederates; more than that did not increase the participants' tendency to conform (Asch, 1951). In a later experiment, Asch (1956) found that conformity greatly decreased if there was just one confederate who gave the correct answer—apparently, if participants knew that there was at least one other person whose answer agreed with their own, the evidence of their own eyes won out over the pressure to conform to the group.

Subsequent research in the United States has found less conformity among participants, perhaps suggesting that the Asch conformity effect was due to the more conforming nature of people in the era and culture of the United States in the 1950s (Lalancette & Standing, 1990; Nicholson et al., 1985; Perrin & Spencer, 1980, 1981). In other cultures, however, studies have found conformity effects similar to those in Asch's study (Neto, 1995). Still others have found even greater effects of conformity in collectivist cultures, such as Hong Kong, Japan, and Zimbabwe (Bond & Smith, 1996; Kim & Markus, 1999). This cultural difference may exist only when face-to-face contact is a part of the task, however. One study found that when the Asch judgment task is presented in an online format (participants were in communication but not able to see each other), the cultural difference disappears (Cinnirella & Green, 2007).

 💬 What about gender—are men or women more conforming?

Research shows that gender differences are practically nonexistent unless the situation involves behavior that is not private. If it is possible to give responses in private, conformity is no greater for women than for men, but if a public response is required, women do tend to show more conformity than men (Eagly, 1987; Eagly et al., 2000; Eagly & Carli, 2007). This effect may be due to the socialization that women receive in being agreeable and supportive; however, the difference in conformity is quite small.

Why do people feel the need to conform at all? One factor at work is *normative social influence*, the need to act in ways that we feel will let us be liked and accepted by others (Hewlin, 2009; Kaplan & Miller, 1987). We use the behavior and attitudes of other people as our "measuring stick" of what is "normal." We then judge how we are doing against that "norm." Have you ever laughed at a joke you really didn't get because everyone else was laughing? That's an example of normative social influence. Another factor at work is *informational social influence*, in which we take our cues for how to behave from other people when we are in a situation that is not clear or is ambiguous (Isenberg, 1986). In this case, the behavior of the people around us provides us with information about how we should act, and so we conform to their actions. Another possible explanation for some conforming behavior may involve individuals confusing their own behavior with the behavior of others, resulting in a kind of "mental averaging" of that behavior (Kim & Hommel, 2015).

## GROUP BEHAVIOR

### 12.2  Explain how our behavior is impacted by the presence of others.

Social influence is clearly seen in the behavior of people within a group, as Asch's classic study illustrated. But conformity is only one way in which a group can influence the behavior of an individual. Here are just a few others.

On April 20, 2010, an explosion occurred on the *Deepwater Horizon* oil drilling rig in the Gulf of Mexico. Oil flowed into the Gulf for 3 months, but the environmental impact will no doubt be felt for years. How might groupthink apply in this situation?

**THE HAZARDS OF GROUPTHINK**  Shortly after the terrorist attack on the World Trade Center in New York, President George W. Bush and his administration made the decision to invade Iraq. Although there were advisors who thought the action to be a mistake, no one person was willing to stand up to the rest of the group and challenge the group's decision and assumptions. Many now see this decision as a prime example of **groupthink**. Groupthink occurs when people within a group feel it is more important to maintain the group's cohesiveness than to consider the facts realistically (Hogg & Hains, 1998; Janis, 1972, 1982; Kamau & Harorimana, 2008; Schafer & Crichlow, 1996). Other examples include the sinking of the *Titanic* in 1912 (the group responsible for designing and building the ship assumed she was unsinkable and did not even bother to include enough lifeboats on board for all the passengers), the *Challenger* disaster of 1986 in which a part on the shuttle was known by a few to be unacceptable (but no one spoke up to delay the launch), the disastrous Bay of Pigs invasion of Cuba during the Kennedy administration, and the *Deepwater Horizon* oil explosion of 2010.

Why does groupthink happen? Social psychologist Irving Janis (1972, 1982), who originally gave this phenomenon its name, lists several "symptoms" of groupthink. For example, group members may come to feel that the group can do no wrong, is morally correct, and will always succeed, creating the illusion of invulnerability.* Group members also tend to hold stereotyped views of those who disagree with the group's opinions, causing members to think that those who oppose the group have no worthwhile opinions. They exert pressure on individual members to conform to group opinion, prevent those who might disagree from speaking up, and even censor themselves so that the group's mindset will not be disturbed in a "don't rock the boat" mentality. Self-appointed "mind guards" work to protect the leader of the group from contrary viewpoints. (See **Table 12.1**.)

Several things can be done to minimize the possibility of groupthink (Hart, 1998; McCauley, 1998; Moorhead et al., 1998). For example, leaders should remain impartial, and the entire group should seek the opinions of people outside the group. Any voting

**groupthink**

kind of thinking that occurs when people place more importance on maintaining group cohesiveness than on assessing the facts of the problem with which the group is concerned.

*invulnerability: quality of being unable to be attacked or harmed.

| Table 12.1 | Characteristics of Groupthink |
|---|---|
| **Characteristic** | **Description** |
| Invulnerability | Members feel they cannot fail. |
| Rationalization | Members explain away warning signs and help each other rationalize their decision. |
| Lack of introspection | Members do not examine the ethical implications of their decision because they believe that they cannot make immoral choices. |
| Stereotyping | Members stereotype their enemies as weak, stupid, or unreasonable. |
| Pressure | Members pressure each other not to question the prevailing opinion. |
| Lack of disagreement | Members do not express opinions that differ from the group consensus. |
| Self-deception | Members share in the illusion that they all agree with the decision. |
| Insularity | Members prevent the group from hearing disruptive but potentially useful information from people who are outside the group. |

SOURCE: Janis (1972, 1982).

should be done by secret ballots rather than by a show of hands, and it should be made clear that group members will be held responsible for decisions made by the group.

**THINKING CRITICALLY**

Can you think of a time when you conformed with the actions of a group of friends, even though you disagreed with their actions? Based on Asch's studies and studies on groupthink, what might have kept you from objecting?

► The response entered here will be saved to your notes and may be collected by your instructor if he/she requires it.

Submit

**GROUP POLARIZATION** Once called the "risky shift" phenomenon, **group polarization** is the tendency for members involved in a group discussion to take somewhat more extreme positions and suggest riskier actions when compared to individuals who have not participated in a group discussion (Bossert & Schworm, 2008; Moscovici & Zavalloni, 1969). A good example of group polarization can occur when a jury tries to decide on punitive damages during a civil trial: Studies have found that if members of a jury individually favored a relatively low amount of punitive damages before deliberation, after deliberation the amount usually lessened further. Similarly, if the individual jurors favored stiffer penalties, the deliberation process resulted in even higher penalties (MacCoun & Kerr, 1988). If information is provided in an online forum such as a social networking group, group polarization can become even more pronounced because group members are exposed to only the information fitting their worldview (Hansen et al., 2013). Group polarization is thought to be due to both normative social influence and informational social influence.

**SOCIAL FACILITATION AND SOCIAL LOAFING** Social influence can affect the success or failure of an individual's task performance within a group. The perceived difficulty of the task seems to determine the particular effect of the presence of others as well: If a task is perceived as easy, the presence of other people seems to improve performance. If the task is perceived as difficult, the presence of others actually has a negative effect on performance. The positive influence of others on performance is called **social facilitation**, whereas the negative influence is called **social impairment** (Aiello & Douthitt, 2001; Michaels et al., 1982; Zajonc, 1965).

In both social facilitation and social impairment, the presence of other people acts to increase arousal (Rosenbloom et al., 2007; Zajonc, 1965, 1968; Zajonc et al., 1970). Social facilitation occurs because the presence of others creates just enough increased arousal to improve

**group polarization**
the tendency for members involved in a group discussion to take somewhat more extreme positions and suggest riskier actions when compared to individuals who have not participated in a group discussion.

**social facilitation**
the tendency for the presence of other people to have a positive impact on the performance of an easy task.

**social impairment**
the tendency for the presence of other people to have a negative impact on the performance of a difficult task.

While the other people in this picture appear to be working, the man in the foreground seems to be engaged in a game on his phone. This is called social loafing. How do you think his colleagues who are working might feel about his behavior?

performance. But the presence of others when the task is difficult produces too high a level of arousal, resulting in impaired performance. ⓛⓘⓝⓚ to Learning Objective 9.4.

Interestingly, people who are lazy tend not to do as well when other people are also working on the same task, but they can do quite well when working on their own. This phenomenon is called **social loafing** (Karau & Williams, 1993, 1997; Latané et al., 1979; Suleiman & Watson, 2008). The reason for this is that it is easier for a lazy person (a "loafer") to hide laziness when working in a group of people, because it is less likely that the individual will be evaluated alone. But when the social loafer is working alone, the focus of evaluation will be on that person only. In that case, the loafer works harder because there is no one else to whom the work can be shifted.

Social loafing depends heavily on the assumption that personal responsibility for a task is severely lessened when working with a group of other people. One study suggests that although Americans may readily make that assumption, Chinese people, who come from a more interdependent cultural viewpoint, tend to assume that each individual within the group is still nearly as responsible for the group's outcome as the group at large (Menon et al., 1999). Chinese people may, therefore, be less likely to exhibit social loafing than are people in the United States.

**DEINDIVIDUATION**   Finally, when people are gathered in a group, there is often a tendency for each individual in the group to experience **deindividuation**, the lessening of their sense of personal identity and personal responsibility (Diener et al., 1980). This can result in a lack of self-control when in the group that would not be as likely to occur if the individual were acting alone. People in a crowd feel a degree of anonymity—being unknown and unidentified—and are more likely to act impulsively as a result. One only has to think about behavior of people in a riot or even the actions of groups like the Ku Klux Klan to see examples of deindividuation. The Stanford prison experiment, discussed later in this chapter, is an excellent study of deindividuation in action (Zimbardo, 1970, 1971; Zimbardo et al., 2000). Players in online games often play anonymously, and research results suggest that this anonymity results in greater deindividuation, leading to increased cheating and other deviant behavior online (Chen & Wu, 2013). It also allows *trolling*, which is the posting of deliberately inflammatory comments in online communities (Buckels et al., 2014). Online trolls would not be likely to say the things they post if they were not anonymous. In 2014, a harassment campaign against female gamers, and particularly a few female game developers, was begun using the Twitter hashtag #Gamergate (Chess & Shaw, 2015; Heron et al., 2014). The harassment included threats of rape and death threats by people hiding under the cloak of anonymity.

## COMPLIANCE

### 12.3 Compare and contrast three compliance techniques.

💬 I have a friend who watches all those infomercials on the shopping channels and buys stuff that isn't worth the money or that doesn't work like it's supposed to work. Why do people fall for pitches like that?

Marketing products is really very much a psychological process. In fact, the whole area of **consumer psychology** is devoted to figuring out how to get people to buy things that someone is selling. ⓛⓘⓝⓚ to Learning Objective B.7. But infomercials are not the only means by which people try to get others to do what they want them to do. **Compliance** occurs when people change their behavior as a result of another person or group asking or directing them to change. The person or group asking for the change in behavior typically doesn't have any real authority or power to command a change; when that authority does exist and behavior is changed as a result, it is called *obedience*, which is the topic of the next major section of this chapter.

A number of techniques that people use to get the compliance of others clearly show the relationship of compliance to the world of marketing, as they refer to techniques

**social loafing**
the tendency for people to put less effort into a simple task when working with others on that task.

**deindividuation**
the lessening of personal identity, self-restraint, and the sense of personal responsibility that can occur within a group.

**consumer psychology**
branch of psychology that studies the habits of consumers in the marketplace.

**compliance**
changing one's behavior as a result of other people directing or asking for the change.

that salespersons would commonly use. A common example of these techniques will also occur to anyone who has ever bought a car, as the video *Compliance Techniques* explains.

👁 **Watch** the **Video** *Compliance Techniques*

**FOOT-IN-THE-DOOR TECHNIQUE** A neighbor asks you to keep an eye on his house while he is on vacation. It's a small request, so you agree. Later that day the neighbor asks if you would kindly water his plants while he's gone. This is a little bit more involved and requires more of your time and energy—will you do it? If you are like most people, you probably will comply with this second, larger request.

When compliance with a smaller request is followed by a larger request, people are quite likely to comply because they have already agreed to the smaller one and they want to behave consistently with their previous response (Cialdini et al., 1995; Dillard, 1990, 1991; Freedman & Fraser, 1966; Meineri & Guéguen, 2008). This is called the **foot-in-the-door technique** because the first small request acts as an opener. (Door-to-door salespeople once literally stuck a foot in the door to prevent the occupant from shutting it so they could continue their sales pitch; hence the name.)

**DOOR-IN-THE-FACE TECHNIQUE** Closely related to the foot-in-the-door technique is its opposite: the **door-in-the-face technique** (Cialdini et al., 1975). In this method, the larger request comes first, which is usually refused. This is followed by a second smaller and more reasonable request that often gets compliance. An example of this would be if the neighbor first asked you to take care of his dog and cat in your home. After you refused to do so, the neighbor might ask if you would at least water his plants, which you would now be more likely to do. This technique may not be as effective with people who are abstract thinkers, however. You may remember the discussion concerning abstract versus concrete thinking in an earlier chapter. Ⓛ Ⓘ Ⓝ Ⓚ to Learning Objective 8.7. While a concrete thinker would look at an American flag and see the material and the red and white stripes, for example, an abstract thinker might look at the same flag and think about the concept of freedom. In one study, the door-in-the-face technique proved to be as effective as making a direct request for concrete thinkers, but abstract thinkers were less likely to comply with that technique (Henderson & Burgoon, 2013). This may be due to the tendency of abstract thinkers to have a more global perception of themselves when turning down the larger request as somewhat selfish, which then makes them more likely to also turn down the smaller request.

**LOWBALL TECHNIQUE** Another compliance technique, also common in the world of sales, is called the **lowball technique** (Bator & Cialdini, 2006; Burger & Petty, 1981; Weyant, 1996). In

**foot-in-the-door technique**

asking for a small commitment and, after gaining compliance, asking for a bigger commitment.

**door-in-the-face technique**

asking for a large commitment and being refused and then asking for a smaller commitment.

**lowball technique**

getting a commitment from a person and then raising the cost of that commitment.

this technique that is related to the foot-in-the-door technique, once a commitment is made, the cost of that commitment is increased. (In the sense used here, *cost* does not necessarily mean money; *cost* can also mean time, effort, or other kinds of sacrifices.) A common example of this is the way in which cable companies will advertise low prices in order to get people to sign up for their particular service. Once the service is established, the consumer is often unpleasantly surprised by the number of additional fees, surcharges, and taxes added onto the bill.

A more common example will occur to anyone who has ever bought a car. The commitment to buy the car at one low price is quickly followed by the addition of other costs: extended warranties, additional options, taxes and fees, and so on, causing the buyer to spend more money than originally intended.

**CULTURAL DIFFERENCES IN COMPLIANCE**   Cultural differences exist in people's susceptibility to these techniques. For the foot-in-the door technique in particular, research has shown that people in individualistic cultures (such as the United States) are more likely to comply with the second request than are people in collectivistic cultures (such as Japan). The research suggests that people in collectivistic cultures are not as concerned with being consistent with previous behavior because they are less focused on their inner motivation than are people in individualistic cultures, who are more concerned with their inner motives and consistency (Cialdini et al., 1999; Petrova et al., 2007). **L I N K** to Learning Objective 13.13.

The concept of compliance, along with conformity, also figures heavily in cult behavior, and both concepts can interfere with thinking critically about cult activities. The **APA Goal 2: Scientific Reasoning and Critical Thinking** feature has more information about cults.

### OBEDIENCE

#### 12.4 Identify factors that make obedience more likely.

There is a difference between the concepts of compliance, which is agreeing to change one's behavior because someone else asks for the change, and **obedience**, which is changing one's behavior at the direct order of an authority figure. A salesperson who wants a person to buy a car has no real power to force that person to buy, but an authority figure is a person with social power—such as a police officer, a teacher, or a work supervisor—who has the right to demand certain behavior from the people under the authority figure's command or supervision.

How far will people go in obeying the commands of an authority figure? What factors make obedience more or less likely? These are some of the questions that researchers have been investigating for many years. The answers to these questions became very important not only to researchers but also to people everywhere after the atrocities committed by the soldiers in Nazi Germany—soldiers who were "just following orders."

**MILGRAM'S SHOCKING RESEARCH**   In what is now a classic study, social psychologist Stanley Milgram set out to find answers to these questions. He was aware of Asch's studies of conformity and wondered how much impact social influence could have on a behavior that was more meaningful than judging the length of lines on cards. He designed what has become one of the most famous (even notorious\*) experiments in the history of psychology.

Through ads placed in the local newspaper, Milgram recruited people who were told that they would be participating in an experiment to test the effects of punishment on learning behavior (Milgram, 1963, 1974). Although there were several different forms of this experiment with different participants, the basic premise was the same: The participants believed that they had randomly been assigned to either the "teacher" role or the "learner" role, when in fact the learner was a confederate already aware of the situation. The task for the learner was a simple memory test for paired words.

The teacher was seated in front of a machine through which the shocks would be administered and the level of the shocks changed. (See **Figure 12.2**.) For each mistake made by the learner, the teacher was instructed to increase the level of shock by 15 volts. The learner (who was not actually shocked) followed a carefully arranged script by pounding on the wall and

**obedience**

changing one's behavior at the command of an authority figure.

\*notorious: widely and unfavorably known.

playing a series of recorded audio responses (sounds of discomfort, asking for the experiment to end, screaming) or remained silent as if unconscious—or dead. (See Figure 12.2 for samples similar to the scripted responses of the learner.) As the teachers became reluctant to continue administering the shocks, the experimenter in his authoritative white lab coat said, for example, "The experiment requires you to continue" or "You must continue" and reminded the teacher that the experimenter would take full responsibility for the safety of the learner.

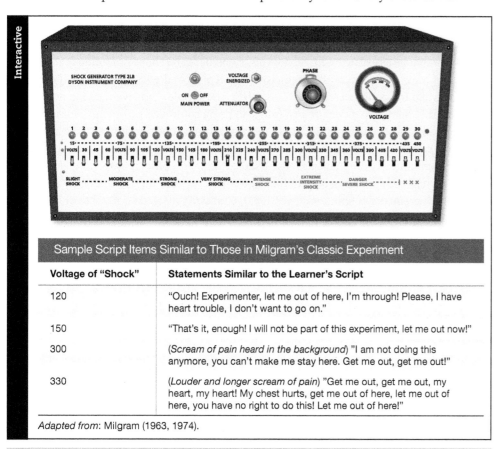

### Sample Script Items Similar to Those in Milgram's Classic Experiment

| Voltage of "Shock" | Statements Similar to the Learner's Script |
|---|---|
| 120 | "Ouch! Experimenter, let me out of here, I'm through! Please, I have heart trouble, I don't want to go on." |
| 150 | "That's it, enough! I will not be part of this experiment, let me out now!" |
| 300 | (*Scream of pain heard in the background*) "I am not doing this anymore, you can't make me stay here. Get me out, get me out!" |
| 330 | (*Louder and longer scream of pain*) "Get me out, get me out, my heart, my heart! My chest hurts, get me out of here, let me out of here, you have no right to do this! Let me out of here!" |

*Adapted from*: Milgram (1963, 1974).

**Figure 12.2**  Milgram's Classic Experiment

In Stanley Milgram's classic study on obedience, the participants were presented with a control panel like this one. Each participant ("teacher") was instructed to give electric shocks to another person (the "learner," who only pretended to be shocked by pounding on the wall and playing a recorded audiotape of grunts, protests, and screams). At what point do you think you would have refused to continue the experiment?

How many of the participants continued to administer what they believed were real shocks? Milgram surveyed psychiatrists, college students, and other adults prior to the experiments for their opinions on how far the participants would go in administering shocks. Everyone predicted that the participants would all refuse to go on at some point, with most believing that the majority of the participants would start refusing as soon as the learner protested—150 volts. None of those he surveyed believed that any participant would go all the way to the highest voltage.

So were they right? Far from it—in the first set of experiments, 65 percent of the teachers went all the way through the experiment's final 450-volt shock level, although many were obviously uncomfortable and begged to be allowed to stop. Of those teachers who did protest and finally stopped, not one of them quit before reaching 300 volts!

 💬 So what happened? Were those people sadists? Why would they keep shocking someone like that?

No one was more stunned than Milgram himself. He had not believed that his experiments would show such a huge effect of obedience to authority. These results do not appear to be some random "fluke" resulting from a large population of cruel people residing in the area. These experiments have been repeated at various times, in the United States and in other countries, and the percentage of participants who went all the way consistently remained between 61 and 66 percent (Blass, 1999; Slater et al., 2006).

 That's incredible—I just don't believe that I could do something like that to someone else.

**EVALUATION OF MILGRAM'S RESEARCH**   Researchers have looked for particular personality traits that might be associated with high levels of obedience but have not found any one trait or group of traits that consistently predicts who will obey and who will not in experiments similar to Milgram's original studies (Blass, 1991). The people who "went all the way" were not necessarily more dependent or susceptible to being controlled by others; they were simply people like most other people, caught in a situation of "obey or disobey" the authority. Some have suggested that Milgram's results may have been due to the same kind of foot-in-the-door technique of compliance as discussed earlier, with participants more likely to go on with each next demanding step of the experiment because they had already agreed to the smaller increments of shock (Gilbert, 1981). Gradually increasing the size of follow-up requests is helpful in changing behavior or attitudes, and participants may have actually come to see themselves as the type of person that follows the experimenter's instructions (Burger, 1999, 2009; Cialdini & Goldstein, 2004).

Milgram's research also raised a serious ethical question: How far should researchers be willing to go to answer a question of interest? Some have argued that the participants in Milgram's studies may have suffered damaged self-esteem and serious psychological stress from the realization that they were willing to administer shocks great enough to kill another person, just on the say-so of an experimenter (Baumrind, 1964). Milgram (1964) responded to the criticism by citing his follow-up study of the participants, in which he found that 84 percent of the participants were glad to have been a part of the experiment and only 1.3 percent said that they were sorry they had been in the experiment. A follow-up psychiatric exam 1 year later also found no signs of harm or trauma in the participants. Even so, most psychologists do agree that under the current ethical rules that exist for such research, this exact study would never be allowed to happen today. **(L) (I) (N) K** to Learning Objective 1.10.

There has been at least one attempt to replicate Milgram's study in recent years, although the shock was limited to only 150 volts (Burger, 2009). In that study, the confederates asked to end the study at 150 volts and the participants were asked whether they should continue or not. Regardless of their answer, the study was ended at that point. The results showed that the participants were only slightly less likely to obey than those in Milgram's study.

Other research has suggested that these studies may not actually examine "obedience" as most often portrayed. A follow-up study to the 2009 replication (Burger et al., 2011) found none of the participants continued with the experiment when the highest of the four prompts the experimenter used was reached. This was the only prompt readily seen as an actual order, "You have no other choice, you must go on." The more the prompts came across as an order, the less likely the teachers "obeyed" (Burger et al., 2011). Furthermore, it has been suggested that instead of obedience, the outcomes of the Milgram paradigm may be more about social identity. The participants identified themselves more in line with the experimenter than the learner and acted in a way that demonstrated their commitment to the larger scientific process rather than to the ordinary community (Reicher et al., 2012). Instead of blindly following orders, the participants were actively working to reach a goal established by the leader or, in this case, the experimenter. The people in this study and others may have obeyed because they came to believe that what they were doing was right—with help in developing that belief from the authority figure (Frimer et al., 2014; Haslam & Reicher, 2012; Reicher et al., 2012). They were decent people who did something terrible because they believed they were doing the right thing in the long run.

These possible reformulations will certainly offer social psychologists additional ways to further investigate the complex topic of obedience in the future.

## Concept Map  L.O. 12.1, 12.2, 12.3, 12.4

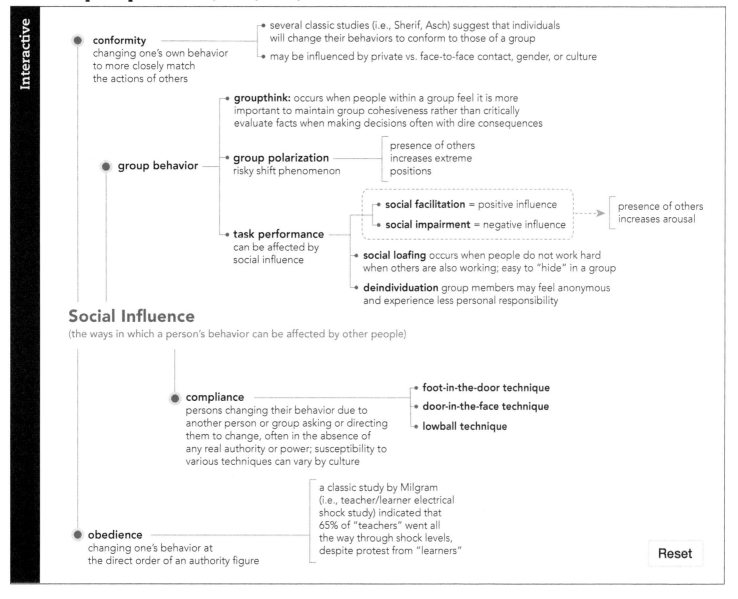

**Social Influence**

(the ways in which a person's behavior can be affected by other people)

- **conformity** — several classic studies (i.e., Sherif, Asch) suggest that individuals will change their behaviors to conform to those of a group
  - changing one's own behavior to more closely match the actions of others
  - may be influenced by private vs. face-to-face contact, gender, or culture

- **group behavior**
  - **groupthink:** occurs when people within a group feel it is more important to maintain group cohesiveness rather than critically evaluate facts when making decisions often with dire consequences
  - **group polarization** — presence of others increases extreme positions
    - risky shift phenomenon
  - **task performance** — **social facilitation** = positive influence / **social impairment** = negative influence → presence of others increases arousal
    - can be affected by social influence
  - **social loafing** occurs when people do not work hard when others are also working; easy to "hide" in a group
  - **deindividuation** group members may feel anonymous and experience less personal responsibility

- **compliance** — **foot-in-the-door technique** / **door-in-the-face technique** / **lowball technique**
  - persons changing their behavior due to another person or group asking or directing them to change, often in the absence of any real authority or power; susceptibility to various techniques can vary by culture

- **obedience** — a classic study by Milgram (i.e., teacher/learner electrical shock study) indicated that 65% of "teachers" went all the way through shock levels, despite protest from "learners"
  - changing one's behavior at the direct order of an authority figure

Reset

# Practice Quiz    How much do you remember?

*Pick the best answer.*

**1.** In Asch's study, conformity decreased when
  **a.** at least four confederates were present.
  **b.** at least one confederate agreed with the participant.
  **c.** the participant was a male.
  **d.** the participant had high self-esteem.

**2.** Which of the following would not be effective in minimizing groupthink?
  **a.** Caroline wants her team to openly vote by a show of hands either for or against her business plan.
  **b.** Karen openly invites input from all team members and even those outside her team.
  **c.** Annina reminds her team that everyone will be held responsible for the ultimate decision of her group.
  **d.** Juanita works hard to remain impartial to all ideas no matter what they are.

**3.** One of the keys to deindividuation is
  **a.** group polarization.      **c.** conformity.
  **b.** group protection.      **d.** anonymity.

**4.** Conner needs just $20 more to go out with his friends. He asks his mother for $50, but she tells him he can have $30 instead. In the end, Conner ended up with $10 more than he originally planned. What technique did Connor use?
  **a.** foot-in-the-door technique      **c.** lowball technique
  **b.** door-in-the-face technique      **d.** planned obedience

**5.** Follow-up research to Stanley Milgram's original study has found that _____ of "teachers" will deliver shocks up to the point of being lethal.
  **a.** less than 30 percent      **c.** 65 percent
  **b.** 40 percent      **d.** 80 percent

# APA Goal 2: Scientific Inquiry and Critical Thinking

## Cults and the Failure of Critical Thinking

*Addresses APA Learning Objective 2.3: Engage in innovative and integrative thinking and problem-solving.*

The term **cult** literally refers to any group of people with a particular religious or philosophical set of beliefs and identity. In the strictest sense of the word, the Roman Catholic Church and Protestantism are cults within the larger religion of Christianity. But most people associate the term *cult* with a negative connotation* : a group of people whose religious or philosophical beliefs and behavior are so different from that of mainstream organizations that they are viewed with suspicion and seen as existing on the fringes of socially acceptable behavior. Although many cults exist without much notice from more mainstream groups, at times members of cults have horrified the public with their actions, as was the case in 1997, when the followers of the Heaven's Gate cult, who believed that aliens in a spaceship were coming in the tail of the Hale-Bopp comet, committed suicide under the leadership of Marshall Applewhite. They believed that their souls would be taken up by the comet aliens. The splinter group calling itself ISIS in the Middle East is also an example of a cult, one that commits acts of extreme violence and destruction (Hassan, 2014).

Why would any person get so caught up in cult beliefs that suicide, and in some cases murder, becomes a desired behavior? What happened to their ability to think critically about ideas that, to those of us on the outside, seem obviously foolish and dangerous? The most likely targets of cult recruitment are people who are under a lot of stress, dissatisfied with their lives, unassertive, gullible, dependent, who feel a desire to belong to a group, and who are unrealistically idealistic ("We can solve all the world's problems if everyone will just love each other"; Langone, 1996). Young people rebelling against parental authority or trying to become independent of families are therefore prime targets.

Cult leaders have certain techniques for gaining compliance that are common to most cult organizations. The first step may be something called "love-bombing" by current cult members, who shower the recruits with affection and attention and claim to understand just how the potential cult members feel. Second, efforts are made to isolate the recruits from family and friends who might talk them out of joining. This is accomplished in part by keeping the recruits so busy with rigid rituals, ways of dress, meditations, and other activities that they do not allow the recruits time to think about what is happening. Third, cults also teach their members how to stop questioning thoughts or criticisms, which are typically seen as sins or extremely undesirable behavior. In other words, cults promote a high degree of conformity and compliance (Singer & Lalich, 1995; Zimbardo & Hartley, 1985).

Commitments to the cult are small at first, such as attending a music concert or some other cult function. (Notice that this is the foot-in-the-door technique.) Eventually, a major step is requested by the cult, such as quitting one's job, turning over money or property to the cult, or similar commitments. Leaving a cult is quite difficult, as members of the cult in good standing will often track down a "deserter." Actress Leah Remini has written a detailed and frank account of her struggles with Scientology and the difficulties of leaving that organization (Remini, 2015).

Cults have existed all through recorded history and will probably continue to exist in the future. Most cults do not pose a physical threat to their members or others, but the

**cult**
any group of people with a particular religious or philosophical set of beliefs and identity.

---

*connotation: the meaning of a word or concept that is more suggestive than directly stated.

examples of the followers of Jim Jones, Marshall Applewhite, David Koresh (the Waco, Texas, disaster in 1993), and ISIS clearly demonstrate that cults, like any group of people, can become deadly.

**APA Goal 2**  Cults and the Failure of Critical Thinking                                    ❓

**Interactive**

**Identify the method of persuasion used for each of the following possible statements from cult recruiters.**

We're having a performance by some friends tonight, why don't you come? There will be some good food and it'll be fun!

You are such a wonderful person, people in your life have not really appreciated you the way we do. We love you and will always be there for you.

Let's start our day with some meditation. Then I have some clothes you can try out, and we'll go to a lecture later on. The day is just packed with things to do right here!

Start Over      Check Answers

# Social Cognition

**Social cognition** focuses on the ways in which people think about other people and how those cognitions influence behavior toward those other people. In this section, we'll concentrate on how we perceive others and form our first impressions of them, as well as how we explain the behavior of others and ourselves.

## ATTITUDES

**12.5**  **Identify the three components of an attitude and how attitudes are formed.**

One area of social cognition concerns the formation and influence of attitudes on the behavior and perceptions of others. An **attitude** can be defined as a tendency to respond positively or negatively toward a certain idea, person, object, or situation (Triandis, 1971). This tendency, developed through people's experiences as they live and work with others, can affect the way they behave toward those ideas, people, objects, and situations and can include opinions, beliefs, and biases. In fact, attitudes influence the way people view these things *before* they've actually been exposed to them (Petty et al., 2003).

> 💬 What do you mean—how can an attitude have an effect on something that hasn't happened yet?

Attitudes are not something people have when they are born. They are learned through experiences and contact with others and even through direct instruction from parents, teachers, and other important people in a person's life. Because attitudes involve a positive or

**social cognition**

the mental processes that people use to make sense of the social world around them.

**attitude**

a tendency to respond positively or negatively toward a certain person, object, idea, or situation.

negative evaluation of things, it's possible to go into a new situation, meet a new person, or be exposed to a new idea with one's "mind already made up" to like or dislike, agree or disagree, and so on (Eagly & Chaiken, 1993; Petty et al., 2003; Petty & Briñol, 2015). For example, children are known for making up their minds about certain foods before ever tasting them, simply because the foods are "green." Those children may have tried a green food in the past and disliked it and now are predisposed* to dislike any green food whether they've tasted it or not.

**THE ABC MODEL OF ATTITUDES**  Attitudes are actually made up of three different parts, or components, as shown in **Figure 12.3**. These components should not come as a surprise to anyone who has been reading the other chapters in this text because, throughout the text, references have been made to personality and traits being composed of the ways people think, feel, and act. By using certain terms to describe these three things, psychologists have come up with a handy way to describe the three components of attitudes (Eagly & Chaiken, 1993, 1998; Fazio & Olson, 2003).

**AFFECTIVE COMPONENT**  The *affective component* of an attitude is the way a person feels toward the object, person, or situation. *Affect* is used in psychology to mean "emotions" or "feelings," so the affective component is the emotional component. For example, some people might feel that country music is fun and uplifting.

**BEHAVIOR COMPONENT**  The *behavior component* of an attitude is the action that a person takes in regard to the person, object, or situation. For example, a person who feels that country music is fun is likely to listen to a country music station, buy country music MP3s, or go to a country music concert.

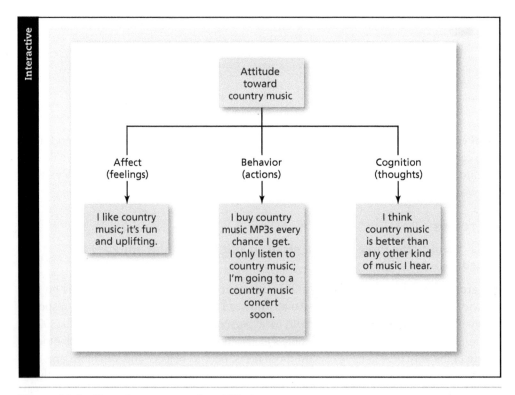

**Figure 12.3**  Three Components of an Attitude

Attitudes consist of the way a person feels and thinks about something, as well as the way the person chooses to behave. If you like country music, you are also likely to think that country music is good music. You are also more likely to listen to this style of music, buy this type of music, and even go to a performance. Each of the three components influences the other two.

---

*predisposed: referring to a tendency to respond in a particular way based on previous experience.

**COGNITIVE COMPONENT**  Finally, the *cognitive component* of an attitude is the way a person thinks about himself or herself, an object, or a situation. These thoughts, or cognitions, include beliefs and ideas about the focus of the attitude. For example, the country music lover might believe that country music is superior to other forms of music.

💬 So if you know what someone thinks or feels about something, you can predict what that person will do, right?

Oddly enough, attitudes turn out to be pretty poor predictors of actual behavior in a number of controlled research studies. The results of several decades of research indicate that what people say and what people do are often two very different things (van de Garde-Perik et al., 2008; Wicker, 1971). Studies have found that attitudes predict behavior only under certain conditions. For example, in one study, researchers found that a randomly chosen sample of people indicated in a survey that they believed in protecting the environment and would be willing to pay more for fruits and vegetables raised under environmentally friendly conditions. When the people of that same sample were studied for their actual buying habits, the only sample members who bought the ecofriendly fruit did so in grocery stores in areas of higher income levels. These consumers actually had the financial means to "put their money where their mouth was" (A. Clarke et al., 1999). Those members of the sample who did not live in a higher-income area gave what they probably saw as a socially desirable answer on the survey, but in practice, their lower income influenced their actual behavior—they did NOT buy the more expensive ecofriendly fruit.

Another factor in matching attitudes and behavior concerns how specific the attitude itself is. People may hold a general attitude about something without reflecting that attitude in their actual behavior. For example, doctors generally hold the attitude that people should do everything they can to protect their health and promote wellness, yet many doctors still smoke tobacco, fail to exercise, and often get too little sleep. But a very specific attitude, such as "exercise is important to my immediate health," will more likely be associated with the behavior of exercising (Ajzen, 2001; Ajzen & Fishbein, 2000). Even playing a simulation game in which players control a character within a fictional health care setting, making specific decisions about health behavior, has been shown to have a positive effect on attitudes toward health care in those players (Kaufman et al., 2015).

Some attitudes are stronger than others, and strong attitudes are more likely to predict behavior than weak ones. A person who quit smoking because of failing health might have a stronger attitude toward secondhand smoke than someone who quit smoking on a dare, for example. The importance, or salience*, of a particular attitude in a given situation also has an impact on behavior—the more important the attitude appears, the more likely the behavior will match the attitude. Someone who is antismoking might be more likely to confront a smoker breaking the rules in a hospital, for example, than they would a smoker outside the building (Eagly & Chaiken, 1998).

**ATTITUDE FORMATION**  Attitude formation is the result of a number of different influences with only one thing in common: They are all forms of learning.

**DIRECT CONTACT**  One way in which attitudes are formed is by direct contact with the person, idea, situation, or object that is the focus of the attitude. For example, a child who tries and dislikes brussels sprouts will form a negative attitude about brussels sprouts.

**DIRECT INSTRUCTION**  Another way attitudes are formed is through direct instruction, either by parents or some other individual. Parents may tell their children that smoking cigarettes is dangerous and unhealthy, for example.

While many people may believe in helping the environment by using organically grown products, one study found that only those with the money to buy these more expensive products did so.

*salience: importance or having the quality of being obvious or easily seen.

**INTERACTION WITH OTHERS**   Sometimes attitudes are formed because the person is around other people with that attitude. If a person's friends, for example, all hold the attitude that smoking is cool, that person is more likely to think that smoking is cool as well (Brenner, 2007; Eddy et al., 2000; Hill, 1990; Shean et al., 1994).

**VICARIOUS CONDITIONING (OBSERVATIONAL LEARNING)**   Many attitudes are learned through the observation of other people's actions and reactions to various objects, people, or situations. Just as a child whose mother shows a fear of dogs may develop a similar fear, Ⓛ Ⓘ Ⓝ Ⓚ to Learning Objective 5.3, a child whose mother or father shows a positive attitude toward classical music may grow into an adult with a similarly positive attitude.

Attitudes are not only influenced by other people in a person's immediate world but also by the larger world of the educational system (many attitudes may be learned in school or through reading books) and the mass media of social networking sites, magazines, television, and the movies—a fact of which advertisers and marketing experts are well aware (Gresham & Shimp, 1985; MacKenzie et al., 1986; Visser & Mirabile, 2004).

### ATTITUDE CHANGE: THE ART OF PERSUASION

**12.6**   **Describe how attitudes can be changed.**

 💬 Sometimes people learn attitudes that aren't necessarily good ones, right? So can attitudes change?

Because attitudes are learned, they are also subject to change with new learning. The world is full of people, companies, and other organizations that want to change people's attitudes. It's all about the art of **persuasion**, the process by which one person tries to change the belief, opinion, position, or course of action of another person through argument, pleading, or explanation.

Persuasion is not a simple matter. There are several factors that become important in predicting how successful any persuasive effort at attitude change might be. These factors include the following:

- Source: The *communicator* is the person delivering the message. There is a strong tendency to give more weight to people who are perceived as experts, as well as those who seem trustworthy, attractive, and similar to the person receiving the message (Eagly & Chaiken, 1975; O'Keefe, 2009; Petty & Cacioppo, 1986, 1996; Priester & Petty, 1995).

- Message: The actual message should be clear and well organized (Booth-Butterfield, 1996). It is usually more effective to present both sides of an argument to an audience that has not yet committed to one side or the other (Crowley & Hoyer, 1994; O'Keefe, 2009; Petty & Cacioppo, 1996; Petty et al., 2003). Messages that are directed at producing fear have been thought to be more effective if they produce only a moderate amount of fear and also provide information about how to avoid the fear-provoking consequences (Kleinot & Rogers, 1982; Meyrick, 2001; Petty, 1995; Rogers & Mewborn, 1976). More recent research suggests that fear messages with a higher amount of fear may be very effective when they not only provide information about how to avoid the consequences but also stress the severity of those consequences, particularly among women (Tannenbaum et al., 2015).

- Target Audience: The characteristics of the people who are the intended target of the message of persuasion are also important in determining the effectiveness of the message. The age of the audience members can be a factor, for example. Researchers have found that people who are in the young adult stage of the late teens to the mid-20s are more susceptible to persuasion than are older people (O'Keefe, 2009; Visser & Krosnick, 1998).

**persuasion**
the process by which one person tries to change the belief, opinion, position, or course of action of another person through argument, pleading, or explanation.

- Medium: The form through which a person receives a message is also important. For example, seeing and hearing a politician's speech on television may have a very different effect than simply reading about it in the newspaper or online. The visual impact of the television coverage is particularly important because it provides an opportunity for the source of the message to be seen as attractive, for example.

How easily influenced a person is will also be related to the way people tend to process information. In the **elaboration likelihood model** of persuasion (Briñol & Petty, 2015; Petty & Cacioppo, 1986), it is assumed that people either elaborate (add details and information) based on what they hear (the facts of the message), or they do not elaborate at all, preferring to pay attention to the surface characteristics of the message (length, who delivers it, how attractive the message deliverer is, etc.). Two types of processing are hypothesized in this model: **central-route processing**, in which people attend to the content of the message; and **peripheral-route processing**, a style of information processing that relies on peripheral cues (cues outside of the message content itself), such as the expertise of the message source, the length of the message, and other factors that have nothing to do with the message content. This style of processing causes people not to pay attention to the message itself but instead to base their decisions on those peripheral factors (Briñol & Petty, 2015; Petty & Cacioppo, 1986; Stiff & Mongeau, 2002). For example, the author once participated on a jury panel in which one woman voted "guilty" because the defendant had "shifty eyes" and not because of any of the evidence presented.

How the jurors in this courtroom interpret and process the information they are given will determine the outcome of the trial. Those who listen carefully to what is said by persons involved in the trial are using central-route processing. There may be some jurors, however, who are more affected by the appearance, dress, attractiveness, or tone of voice of the lawyers, defendant, and witnesses. When people are persuaded by factors other than the message itself, it is called peripheral-route processing.

### THINKING CRITICALLY

Imagine that you are asked to create a television commercial to sell a new product. Given what you know of the factors that effectively influence persuasion, how might you persuade a customer?

▶ | The response entered here will be saved to your notes and may be collected by your instructor if he/she requires it.

Submit

### COGNITIVE DISSONANCE: WHEN ATTITUDES AND BEHAVIOR CLASH

**12.7** Explain how people react when attitudes differ from behavior.

💬 As stated earlier, sometimes what people say and what they do are very different. I once pointed this out to a friend of mine who was behaving this way, and he got really upset over it. Why did he get so upset?

When adults find themselves doing things or saying things that don't match their idea of themselves as smart, nice, or moral, for example, they experience an emotional discomfort (and physiological arousal) known as **cognitive dissonance** (Aronson, 1997; Festinger, 1957; Kelly et al., 1997). When people are confronted with the knowledge that something they have done or said was dumb, immoral, or illogical, they suffer an inconsistency in cognitions. For example, they may have a cognition that says "I'm pretty smart" but also the cognition "That was a dumb thing to do," which causes a dissonance. (*Dissonance* is a term referring to an inconsistency or lack of agreement.)

When people experience cognitive dissonance, the resulting tension and arousal are unpleasant, and their motivation is to change something so that the unpleasant feelings

**elaboration likelihood model**
model of persuasion stating that people will either elaborate on the persuasive message or fail to elaborate on it and that the future actions of those who do elaborate are more predictable than those who do not.

**central-route processing**
type of information processing that involves attending to the content of the message itself.

**peripheral-route processing**
type of information processing that involves attending to factors not involved in the message, such as the appearance of the source of the message, the length of the message, and other noncontent factors.

**cognitive dissonance**
sense of discomfort or distress that occurs when a person's behavior does not correspond to that person's attitudes.

and tension are reduced or eliminated. There are three basic things that people can do to reduce cognitive dissonance:

1. Change their conflicting behavior to make it match their attitude.
2. Change their current conflicting cognition to justify their behavior.
3. Form new cognitions to justify their behavior.

Take the example of Larry, who is a college graduate and a cigarette smoker. On one hand, Larry is educated enough to know that cigarette smoking is extremely harmful, causing lung problems, cancer, and eventually death. On the other hand, Larry enjoys smoking, feeling that it calms him and helps him deal with stress—not to mention the fact that he's thoroughly addicted and finds it difficult to quit. His attitude (smoking is bad for you) doesn't match his behavior. Larry is experiencing cognitive dissonance and knows he needs to do something to resolve his dilemma.

If Larry chooses the first way of dealing with cognitive dissonance, he'll quit smoking, no matter how difficult it is (Option 1). As long as he is working at changing the conflicting behavior, his dissonance will be reduced. But what if he can't quit? He might decide that smoking isn't as bad as everyone says it is, which changes his original conflicting attitude (Option 2). He might also form a new attitude by deciding that if he smokes "light" cigarettes, he's reducing his risk enough to justify continuing smoking (Option 3).

In a classic experiment conducted at Stanford University by psychologist Leon Festinger and colleague James Carlsmith (1959), each male student volunteer was given an hour-long, very boring task of sorting wooden spools and turning wooden pegs. After the hour, the experimenters asked the participant to tell the female volunteer in the waiting room that the task was enjoyable. While half of the participants were paid only $1 to try to convince the waiting woman, the other participants were paid $20. (In the late 1950s, $20 was a considerable sum of money—the average income was $5,000, the average car cost $3,000, and gas was only 25 cents a gallon.)

At the time of this study, many researchers would have predicted that the more the participants were paid to lie, the more they would come to like the task, because they were getting more reinforcement ($20) for doing so. But what actually happened was that those participants who were paid only $1 for lying actually convinced themselves that the task was interesting and fun. The reason is cognitive dissonance: Participants who were paid only $1 experienced discomfort at thinking that they would lie to someone for only a dollar. Therefore, they must not be lying—the task really was pretty interesting, after all, and fun, too! Those who were paid more experienced no dissonance, because they knew exactly why they were lying—for lots of money—and the money was a sufficient amount to explain their behavior to their satisfaction. Although most people don't want to be thought of as liars, back then, getting paid enough money to fill the gas tank of one's car three or four times over was incentive enough to tell what probably seemed to be a harmless fib. Those who were paid only $1 had to change their attitude toward the task so that they would not really be lying and could maintain their self-image of honesty. (See **Figure 12.4**.)

There is evidence that cognitive dissonance occurs in children as young as 4 years of age, but the basic strategy for dealing with dissonance seems to be different for them than for older children and adults. Researchers compared the behavior of 4- and 6-year-old children by having them complete tasks to earn stickers (Benozio & Diesendruck, 2015). In one group, children of both ages had to work very hard to get stickers, while in another group, the tasks were very easy. The stickers they earned were also of two types, highly desirable (current cartoon characters) and unattractive (e.g., a plant sticker or a princess sticker for a boy). After earning 10 stickers each, the children were told they were going to play a game in which they had to decide how many stickers they wanted to give to a child they had seen in a video (a later variation had them giving stickers to a box to avoid possible social concerns). While both age groups gave away fewer of the attractive stickers, the 6-year-olds gave away far fewer unattractive stickers if they had been hard to

| Inducement | Attitude |
|---|---|
| $1 | +1.35 |
| $20 | − 0.5 |
| Control | − .45 |

*Based on a –5 to +5 scale, where –5 means "extremely boring" and +5 means "extremely interesting"

**Figure 12.4**  Cognitive Dissonance: Attitude Toward a Task

After completing a boring task, some participants were paid $1 and some $20 to convince others waiting to do the same task that the task was interesting and fun. Surprisingly, the participants who were paid only $1 seemed to change their own attitude toward the task, rating it as interesting, whereas those who were paid $20 rated the task no differently than a control group did.

**SOURCE:** Adapted from Festinger and Carlsmith (1959).

get. This suggests that the older children changed their cognition, with effort changing the desirability of the stickers, like the adults in the classic Festinger and Carlsmith (1959) study. But the younger children gave away significantly more unattractive stickers that were hard to earn compared to those that were easily earned, suggesting that they chose to change their conflicting behavior rather than their cognition. It may be that changing one's cognitions requires a little more brain maturation than the younger children possessed.

Cognitive dissonance theory has been challenged over the last 50 years by other possible explanations. Daryl Bem's *self-perception theory* says that instead of experiencing negative tension, people look at their own actions and then infer their attitudes from those actions (Bem, 1972). New research on dissonance still occurs, much of it focusing on finding the areas of the brain that seem to be involved when people are experiencing dissonance. These studies have found that the left frontal cortex (where language and much of our decision making occurs) is particularly active when people have made a decision that reduces dissonance and then acted upon that decision (Harmon-Jones, 2000, 2004, 2006; Harmon-Jones et al., 2008, 2011). Since reducing cognitive dissonance is mainly a function of people "talking" themselves into or out of a particular course of action, this neurological finding is not surprising. But researchers at Yale University have found surprising evidence for cognitive dissonance in both 4-year-old humans and capuchin monkeys—two groups that are not normally associated with having the developed higher-level mental abilities thought to be in use during the resolution of dissonance (Egan et al., 2007; Egan et al., 2010). Are monkeys and preschool humans more complex thinkers than we had assumed? Or are the cognitive processes used to resolve dissonance a lot simpler than previously indicated? Obviously, there are still questions to be answered with new research in cognitive dissonance.

## IMPRESSION FORMATION

### 12.8 Describe how people form impressions of others.

When one person meets another for the first time, it is the first opportunity either person will have to make initial evaluations and judgments about the other. That first opportunity is a very important one in **impression formation**, the forming of the first knowledge a person has about another person. Impression formation includes assigning the other person to a number of categories and drawing conclusions about what that person is likely to do—it's really all about prediction. In a sense, when first meeting another person, the observer goes through a process of concept formation similar to that discussed in Chapter Seven. Impression formation is another kind of social cognition.

There is a *primacy effect* in impression formation: The first time people meet someone, they form an impression of that person, often based on physical appearance alone, that persists even though they may later have other contradictory information about that person (DeCoster & Claypool, 2004; Lorenzo et al., 2010; Luchins, 1957; Macrae & Quadflieg, 2010). So the old saying is pretty much on target: First impressions do count.

**SOCIAL CATEGORIZATION**    One of the processes that occur when people meet someone new is the assignment of that person to some kind of category or group. This assignment is usually based on characteristics the new person has in common with other people or groups with whom the perceiver has had prior experience. This **social categorization** is mostly automatic and occurs without conscious awareness of the process (Macrae & Bodenhausen, 2000; Vernon et al., 2014). Although this is a natural process (human beings are just born categorizers, (L)(I)(N)(K) to Learning Objective 7.2), sometimes it can cause problems. When the characteristics used to categorize the person are superficial* ones that have become improperly attached to certain ideas, such as "red hair equals a bad temper," social categorization can result in a *stereotype*, a belief that a set of characteristics is shared by all members of a particular social category

*superficial: on the surface.

**impression formation**

the forming of the first knowledge that a person has concerning another person.

**social categorization**

the assignment of a person one has just met to a category based on characteristics the new person has in common with other people with whom one has had experience in the past.

At this job fair in Shanghai, China, thousands of applicants wait hopefully in line for an opportunity to get a job interview. Making a good first impression is important in any job interview situation, but when the competition numbers in the thousands, the people who will most likely get interviews are those who are neatly dressed and well groomed.

(Fiske, 1998). Stereotypes (although not always negative) are very limiting, causing people to misjudge what others are like and often to treat them differently as a result. Add the process of stereotyping to the primacy effect and it becomes easy to see how important first impressions really are. That first impression not only has more importance than any other information gathered about a person later on but may include a stereotype that is resistant to change as well (Hall et al., 2013; Hilton & von Hipple, 1996; Hugenberg & Bodenhausen, 2003).

 It sounds as though we'd be better off if people didn't use social categorization.

Social categorization does have an important place in the perception of others. It allows people to access a great deal of information that can be useful about others, as well as helping people remember and organize information about the characteristics of others (Macrae & Bodenhausen, 2000). The way to avoid falling into the trap of negatively stereotyping someone is to be aware of existing stereotypes and apply a little critical thinking: "Okay, so he's a guy with a lot of piercings. That doesn't mean that he's overly aggressive—it just means he has a lot of piercings."

**IMPLICIT PERSONALITY THEORIES**   The categories into which people place others are based on something called an **implicit personality theory**. Implicit personality theories are sets of assumptions that people have about how different types of people, personality traits, and actions are all related and form in childhood (Dweck et al., 1995; Erdley & Dweck, 1993; Plaks et al., 2005). For example, many people have an implicit personality theory that includes the idea that happy people are also friendly people and people who are quiet are shy. Although these assumptions or beliefs are not necessarily true, they do serve the function of helping organize *schemas*, or mental patterns that represent (in this case) what a person believes about certain "types" of people. (The concept of schema here is similar to the complex schemes proposed by Piaget. (L)(I)(N)(K) to Learning Objective 8.7.) Of course, the schemas formed in this way can easily become stereotypes when people have limited experience with others who are different from them, especially in superficial ways such as skin color or other physical characteristics (Levy et al., 1998).

There is a test designed to measure the implicit attitudes that make up one's implicit personality theory, called the Implicit Association Test, or IAT (Greenwald & Banaji, 1995; Greenwald et al., 1998). The test, taken by computer, measures the degree of association between certain pairs of concepts. For example, you might see the word "pleasant" on one side of the computer screen and the word "unpleasant" on the other side. In the middle would be another word that may be associated with one or the other of the two categories. You would be asked to sort the word into the appropriate category by pressing certain keys as quickly as you can. The computer measures reaction times, and it is the difference in reaction times over a series of similar comparisons that reveals implicit attitudes (Nosek et al., 2007). To try it out for yourself, participate in the experiment *Implicit Association Test: Prejudice.* ◉▸ **Simulate** the **Experiment** *Implicit Association Test: Prejudice*

Some evidence suggests that implicit personality theories may differ from culture to culture as well as from individual to individual. For example, one study found that Americans and Hong Kong Chinese people have different implicit personality theories about how much the personality of an individual is able to change. Whereas Americans assume that personality is relatively fixed and unchanging, Chinese people native to Hong Kong assume that personalities are far more changeable (Chiu et al., 1997).

**ATTRIBUTION**

**12.9** **Describe the process of explaining one's own behavior and the behavior of others.**

Another aspect of social cognition is the need people seem to have to explain the behavior of other people. Have you ever watched someone who was doing something you

**implicit personality theory**

sets of assumptions about how different types of people, personality traits, and actions are related to each other.

didn't understand? Chances are you were going through a number of possible explanations in your head: "Maybe he's sick, or maybe he sees something I can't see," and so on. It seems to be human nature to want to know why people do the things they do so that we know how to behave toward them and whom we might want to use as role models. If no obvious answer is available, people tend to come up with their own reasons. People also need an explanation for their own behavior. This need is so great that if an explanation isn't obvious, it causes the distress known as cognitive dissonance. The process of explaining both one's own behavior and the behavior of other people is called **attribution**.

**CAUSES OF BEHAVIOR**   Attribution theory was originally developed by social psychologist Fritz Heider (1958) as a way of not only explaining why things happen but also why people choose the particular explanations of behavior that they do. There are basically two kinds of explanations—those that involve an external cause and those that assume that causes are internal.

When the cause of behavior is assumed to be from external sources, such as the weather, traffic, educational opportunities, and so on, it is said to be a **situational cause**. The observed behavior is assumed to be caused by whatever situation exists for the person at that time. For example, if John is late, his lateness might be explained by heavy traffic or car problems.

On the other hand, if the cause of behavior is assumed to come from within the individual, it is called a **dispositional cause**. In this case, it is the person's internal personality characteristics that are seen as the cause of the observed behavior. Someone attributing John's behavior to a dispositional cause, for example, might assume that John was late because his personality includes being careless of his and other people's time.

There's an emotional component to these kinds of attributions as well. When people are happy in a marriage, for example, researchers have found that when a spouse's behavior has a positive effect, the tendency is to attribute it to an internal cause ("He did it because he wanted me to feel good"). When the effect is negative, the behavior is attributed to an external cause ("She must have had a difficult day"). But if the marriage is an unhappy one, the opposite attributions occur: "He is only being nice because he wants something from me" or "She's being mean because it's her nature to be crabby" (Fincham et al., 2000; Karney & Bradbury, 2000).

**FUNDAMENTAL ATTRIBUTION ERROR**

🗨 But what else determines which type of cause a person will use? For example, what determines how people explain the behavior of someone they don't already know or like?

The best-known attributional bias is the **fundamental attribution error**, which is the tendency for people observing someone else's actions to overestimate the influence of that person's internal characteristics on behavior and underestimate the influence of the situation. In explaining our own behavior, the tendency to use situational attributions instead of personal is called the *actor–observer* bias because we are the actor, not the observer. In other words, people tend to explain the actions of others based on what "kind" of person they are rather than looking for outside causes, such as social influences or situations (Blanchard-Fields et al., 2007; Harman, 1999; Jones & Harris, 1967; Leclerc & Hess, 2007; Weiner, 1985). (For example, people hearing about Milgram's "shock" study tend to assume that something is wrong with the "teachers" in the study rather than explaining their behavior within the circumstances of the situation.)

**attribution**

the process of explaining one's own behavior and the behavior of others.

**attribution theory**

the theory of how people make attributions.

**situational cause**

cause of behavior attributed to external factors, such as delays, the action of others, or some other aspect of the situation.

**dispositional cause**

cause of behavior attributed to internal factors such as personality or character.

**fundamental attribution error**

the tendency to overestimate the influence of internal factors in determining behavior while underestimating situational factors.

💬 But why do we do that? Why not assume an external cause for everyone?

When people are the actors, they are very aware of the situational influences on their own behavior. For example, Tardy John was actually the one driving to work, and he knows that heavy traffic and a small accident made him late to work—he was *there*, after all. But an outside observer of John's behavior doesn't have the opportunity to see all of the possible situational influences and has only John himself in focus and, thus, assumes that John's tardiness is caused by some internal personality flaw.

Other research has shown that when students are given an opportunity to make attributions about cheating, they make the fundamental attribution error and actor–observer bias: If others are cheating, it's because they are not honest people, but if the students themselves are cheating, it is because of the situation (Bogle, 2000).

Can the tendency to make these errors be reduced? There are several strategies for making errors in attribution less likely. One is to notice how many other people are doing the same thing. As a college professor, the author often has students who come in late. When it is only one student and it happens frequently, the assumption is that the student is not very careful about time (dispositional cause). But when a large number of students come straggling in late, the assumption becomes "there must be a wreck on the bridge," which is a situational attribution. In other words, if a lot of people are doing it, it is probably caused by an outside factor.

Another trick is to think about what you would do in the same situation. If you think that you might behave in the same way, the cause of behavior is probably situational. People should also make the effort of looking for causes that might not be obvious. If John were to look particularly stressed out, for example, the assumption might be that something stressed him out, and that "something" might have been heavy traffic.

Although the fundamental attribution error has been found in American culture (Jones & Harris, 1967), would the same error occur in a culture very different from that of America's, such as Japan's? This is the question asked by researchers Masuda and Kitayama (2004), who had both American and Japanese participants ask a target person to read a prewritten attitudinal statement. The participants were then asked to give their opinion on the target's real attitude. American participants made the classic error, assuming that the target's attitude matched the reading. The Japanese participants, however, assumed that the person's attitude might be different from the statement—the person might have been under social obligation to write the piece. Japanese society is a collectivistic culture, and a Japanese person might expect to write a paper to please a teacher or employer even though the paper's contents do not necessarily express the writer's attitudes. A summary of the research in cross-cultural differences in attribution provides further support for the idea that the fundamental attribution error is not a universal one (Peng et al., 2000). The work of Miller (1984) and many other researchers (Blanchard-Fields et al., 2007; Cha & Nam, 1985; Choi & Nisbett, 1998; Choi et al., 1999; Lee et al., 1996; Morris & Peng, 1994; Morris et al., 1995; Norenzayan et al., 1999) strongly suggests that in more interdependent, collectivistic cultures found in China, Hong Kong, Japan, and Korea, people tend to assume that external situational factors are more responsible for the behavior of other people than are internal dispositional factors—a finding that is exactly the reverse of the fundamental attribution error so common in the United States and other individualist Western cultures.

Even age is a factor in how likely someone is to fall prey to the fundamental attribution error. Several studies (Blanchard-Fields & Horhota, 2005; Follett & Hess, 2002; Leclerc & Hess, 2007) have found that older adults show a stronger bias toward attributing the actions of another to internal causes than do younger people.

One study has found that attribution of motive may also create conflict between groups (Waytz et al., 2014). The study compared Israelis and Palestinians in the Mideast as well as Republicans and Democrats in the United States. Obviously, these groups continue to experience a great deal of animosity, conflict, and an unwillingness to shift from long-held beliefs. Over the course of five studies, in which participants were asked to rate the motives of others for engaging in conflict, researchers found that each side felt that their side was motivated by love more than hate but that the other side's motivating force was hate. Calling this idea *motive attribution asymmetry*, the researchers suggest that this is at least one reason compromise and negotiation are so difficult to obtain—if the other side hates you, you believe them to be unreasonable and negotiations impossible.

## Concept Map L.O. 12.5, 12.6, 12.7, 12.8, 12.9

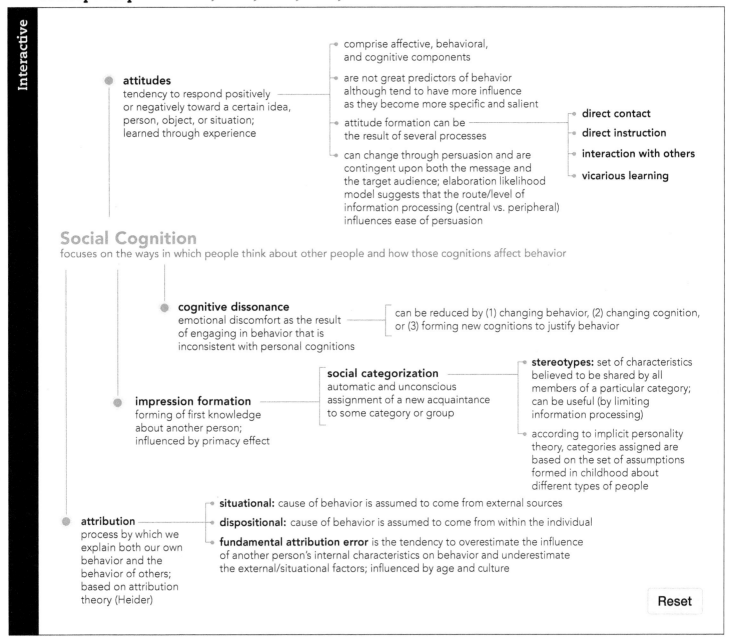

## Practice Quiz  How much do you remember?

*Pick the best answer.*

1. Which of the following represents the affective component of an attitude?
   a. "I love to go to the clubs—it makes me so happy!"
   b. "Tonight, we're going to that new club downtown."
   c. "It is interesting to watch people when I'm out at a club."
   d. "I'm going to wear a new outfit to the club tonight."

2. Erin hates snakes, even though she has never been bitten or been close to one. She developed her feelings by seeing how scared her mother was when she came across them in the garden or even when watching a movie or television show in which there was a snake. Erin's attitude toward snakes was most likely acquired through
   a. direct contact.
   b. direct instruction.
   c. interaction with others.
   d. vicarious conditioning.

**3.** One of your friends tells you, "I didn't like the environmental-awareness presentation today. First of all, it was too long, not to mention the person that gave it was drinking out of a polystyrene cup and drove away in a huge SUV." What kind of processing might your friend be using?
**a.** central-route processing
**b.** peripheral-route processing
**c.** cognitive-route processing
**d.** visual-route processing

**4.** Kohanna thinks that everyone who smiles must always be happy, and those people who are quiet must be naturally shy. Such assumptions are the basis for
**a.** stereotypes.
**b.** implicit personality theory.
**c.** attribution theory.
**d.** attitudes.

**5.** Caleb almost always shows up late for work. His friends attribute this to Caleb's laziness. This is an example of a _____ cause.
**a.** situational
**b.** dispositional
**c.** dispensational
**d.** superficial

**6.** How might someone who unknowingly is committing the fundamental attribution error explain Stanley Milgram's obedience study?
**a.** Subjects in that study were highly influenced by the power of Milgram and his team.
**b.** Subjects in that study desired a high degree of positive reinforcement.
**c.** Subjects in that study wanted to be part of Milgram's group.
**d.** Subjects in that study must have been the kind of people that like to hurt others.

# Social Interaction

Social influence and social cognition are two of three main areas included in the field of social psychology. The third major area has to do with social interactions with others, or the relationships between people, both casual and intimate. Social interactions include prejudice and discrimination, liking and loving, and aggression and prosocial behavior.

## PREJUDICE AND DISCRIMINATION

### 12.10 Distinguish between prejudice and discrimination.

We've seen how stereotypes, a set of characteristics that people believe is shared by all members of a particular social category or group, can be formed by using only superficial information about that person or group of people. When a person holds an unsupported and often negative stereotyped *attitude* about the members of a particular social group, it is called **prejudice**. The video *Are Stereotypes and Prejudices Inevitable?* explains the connection between stereotypes and prejudice.

**prejudice**

negative attitude held by a person about the members of a particular social group.

◉ **Watch** the **Video** *Are Stereotypes and Prejudices Inevitable?*

When prejudicial attitudes cause members of a particular social group to be treated differently than others in situations that call for equal treatment, it is called **discrimination**. Prejudice is the attitude, and discrimination is the behavior that can result from that attitude. Although laws can be made to minimize discriminatory behavior, it is not possible to have laws against holding certain attitudes. In other words, discrimination can be controlled and in some cases eliminated, but the prejudicial attitude that is responsible for the discrimination cannot be so easily controlled or eliminated.

**TYPES OF PREJUDICE AND DISCRIMINATION**    There are many kinds of prejudice. There are also many kinds of discrimination that occur as a result of prejudice. There's ageism, or prejudicial attitudes toward the elderly or teenagers (among others); sexism; racism, or prejudice toward those from different ethnic groups; prejudice toward those from different religions, those from different economic levels, those who are overweight, those who are too thin, or those who have a different sexual orientation. Prejudice can also vary in terms of what type of people or groups make the most likely targets. In any society, there will always be **in-groups** and **out-groups**, or "us" versus "them." The in-group is all the people with whom a particular person identifies and the out-groups are everyone else (Brewer, 2001; Hewstone et al., 2002; Tajfel & Turner, 1986). An example of this can be found in the Black Lives Matter movement that began as a Twitter campaign in 2013 in response to the acquittal of George Zimmerman in the shooting death of Trayvon Martin (Day, 2015). The formation of in-groups and out-groups begins in childhood (Ruble et al., 2004) and continues as children become adults.

Once an in-group is established, prejudice toward and discriminatory treatment of the out-group or groups soon follow, causing stress and possible negative impact on the health of the out-group members (Brewer, 2001; Forsyth et al., 2014). Members of the out-groups are usually going to become stereotyped according to some superficial characteristic, such as skin color or hair color, and getting rid of a stereotype once formed is difficult at best (Cameron et al., 2001; Hamilton & Gifford, 1976). *Microaggressions*, the seemingly minor insults and negative exchanges that members of the dominant culture often use toward minorities, add to the discriminatory treatment. Microaggressions are not as blatant as someone using a racial or gender-biased epithet, but are more subtle statements that might repeat a stereotyped idea or that minimize the reality of discrimination (Sue, 2010). For example, a professional woman who is told by a supervisor that she needs to change her hairstyle because it is unprofessional may be seen as experiencing microaggression from the supervisor.

**SCAPEGOATING**    Conflicts between groups are usually greater when there are other pressures or stresses going on, such as war, economic difficulties, or other misfortunes. When such pressures exist, the need to find a *scapegoat* becomes stronger. A scapegoat is a person or a group, typically a member or members of an out-group, who serves as the target for the frustrations and negative emotions of members of the in-group. (The term comes from the ancient Jewish tradition of sending a goat out into the wilderness with the symbolic sins of all the people on its head.)

Scapegoats are going to be the group of people with the least power, and the newest immigrants to any area are typically those who have the least power at that time. That is why many social psychologists believe that the rioting that took place in Los Angeles, California, in the spring of 1992 occurred in the areas it did. This was the time of the infamous Rodney King beating. Rodney King was an African American man who was dragged out of his car onto the street and severely beaten by four police officers. The beating was caught on tape by a bystander. At the trial, the officers were found not guilty of assault with a deadly weapon. This decision was followed by a series of violent riots (Knight, 1996). The puzzling thing about these riots is that the greatest amount of rioting

After the landmark 1954 Supreme Court decision (Brown v. the Board of Education of Topeka), schools in the United States began the process of integration, allowing African American students to attend school with white students. The desegregation laws were aimed at stopping discrimination, but attitudes of prejudice persisted then and, to some degree, still exist today. The courts can make laws against discrimination, but changing prejudicial attitudes is much more difficult.

The Black Lives Matter movement, begun in 2013, has become a force for advocating change, particularly in how black men are viewed by the police but also advocating a change to discriminatory treatment of all people.

**discrimination**

treating people differently because of prejudice toward the social group to which they belong.

**in-groups**

social groups with whom a person identifies; "us."

**out-groups**

social groups with whom a person does not identify; "them."

These Korean demonstrators were protesting the riots that followed the 1992 not-guilty verdict in the beating of Rodney King. The riots lasted 6 days, killing 42 people and damaging 700 buildings in mainly Korean and other Asian American neighborhoods. The Asian American population of Los Angeles, California, became scapegoats for aggression.

and violence did not take place in the neighborhoods of the mostly white police officers or in the African American neighborhoods. The rioting was greatest in the neighborhoods of the Asian Americans and Asians who were the most recent immigrants to the area. When a group has only recently moved into an area, as the Asians had, that group has the least social power and influence in that new area. So the rioters took out their frustrations *not* on the people seen as directly responsible for those frustrations but on the group of people with the least power to resist (Chang, 2004; Kim & Kim, 1999). After the events of September 11th, 2001, many Muslims living in predominantly non-Muslim countries may now be seen in a similar light, despite the fact that the atrocity was committed by one radical group.

## HOW PEOPLE LEARN AND OVERCOME PREJUDICE

**12.11** **Describe theories of how prejudice is learned and how it can be overcome.**

As we will see in the Classic Studies in Psychology section, even children are, under the right circumstances, prone to developing prejudiced attitudes. Exposure to the attitudes of parents, teachers, other children, and the various forms of media are just a few ways in which children can learn and develop prejudice.

**ORIGINS OF PREJUDICE**　Is all prejudice simply a matter of learning, or are there other factors at work? Several theories have been proposed to explain the origins and the persistence of prejudice. In **social cognitive theory** (using cognitive processes in relation to understanding the social world), prejudice is seen as an attitude that is formed as other attitudes are formed, through direct instruction, modeling, and other social influences on learning.

**REALISTIC CONFLICT THEORY**　The **realistic conflict theory** of prejudice states that increasing prejudice and discrimination are closely tied to an increasing degree of conflict between the in-group and the out-group when those groups are seeking a common resource, such as land or available jobs (Horowitz, 1985; Taylor & Moghaddam, 1994). Because the examples of this from history and modern times are so numerous, it is possible to list only a few: the conflict between the early Crusaders and the Muslims, between the Jewish people and the Germans, the hatred between the Irish Catholics and the Irish Protestants, and the conflict between the native population of you-name-the-country and the colonists who want that land. The section that follows is a classic study that illustrates how easily in-groups and out-groups can be formed and how quickly prejudice and discrimination follow.

**social cognitive theory**

referring to the use of cognitive processes in relation to understanding the social world.

**realistic conflict theory**

theory stating that prejudice and discrimination will be increased between groups that are in conflict over a limited resource.

# Classic Studies in Psychology
## Brown Eyes, Blue Eyes

In a small town in Iowa in 1968, a few days after the assassination of Dr. Martin Luther King, Jr., a second-grade teacher named Jane Elliott tried to teach her students a lesson in prejudice and discrimination. She divided her students into two groups, those with blue eyes and those with brown eyes.

On the first day of the lesson, the blue-eyed children were given special privileges, such as extra time at recess and getting to leave first for lunch. She also told the blue-eyed children that they were superior to the brown-eyed children, telling the brown-eyed children not to bother taking seconds at lunch because it would be wasted. She kept the blue-eyed children and the brown-eyed children apart (Peters, 1971).

Although Elliott tried to be critical of the brown-eyed out-group, she soon found that the blue-eyed children were also criticizing, belittling, and were quite vicious in their attacks on the brown-eyed children. By the end of the day, the blue-eyed children felt and acted superior, and the brown-eyed children were miserable. Even the lowered test scores of the brown-eyed children reflected their misery. Two days later, the brown-eyed children became the favored group, and the effects from the first two days appeared again but in reverse this time: The blue-eyed children began to feel inferior, and their test scores dropped.

The fact that test scores reflected the treatment received by the out-group is a stunning one, raising questions about the effects of prejudice and discrimination on the education of children who are members of stereotyped out-groups. That the children were so willing to discriminate against their own classmates, some of whom were their close friends before the experiment, is also telling. In his book about this classroom experiment, *A Class Divided*, Peters (1971) reported that the students who were part of the original experiment, when reunited 15 years later to talk about the experience, said that they believed that this early experience with prejudice and discrimination helped them become less prejudiced as young adults.

### Questions for Further Discussion

1. Is there anything about this experiment that you find disturbing?
2. How do you think adults might react in a similar experiment?
3. Are there any ethical concerns with what Elliott did in her classroom?
4. What kinds of changes might have occurred in the personalities and performances of the children if the experiment had continued for more than 2 days with each group?

**SOCIAL IDENTITY THEORY**   In **social identity theory**, three processes are responsible for the formation of a person's identity within a particular social group and the attitudes, concepts, and behavior that go along with identification with that group (Tajfel & Turner, 1986; Richard et al., 2015). The first process is *social categorization*, as discussed earlier in this chapter. Just as people assign categories to others (such as black, white, student, teacher, and so on) to help organize information about those others, people also assign themselves to social categories to help determine how they should behave. The second element of social identity theory is *identification*, or the formation of one's **social identity**. A social identity is the part of the self-concept that includes the view of oneself as a member of a particular social group within the social category—typically, the in-group. The third aspect of social identity theory is **social comparison**, Festinger's (1954) concept in which people compare themselves favorably to others to improve their own self-esteem: "Well, at least I'm better off than that person." Members of the out-group make handy comparisons. All three aspects of social identity form, at least in part, through interaction with a group, particularly a small group (Thomas et al., 2016).

With respect to prejudice, social identity theory helps explain why people feel the need to categorize or stereotype others, producing the in-group sense of "us versus them" that people adopt toward out-groups. Prejudice may result, at least in part, from the need to increase one's own self-esteem by looking down on others.

**STEREOTYPE VULNERABILITY**   As discussed previously, stereotypes are the widespread beliefs a person has about members of another group. Not only do stereotypes affect the way people perceive other people, but also stereotypes can affect the way people see themselves and their performance (Snyder et al., 1977). **Stereotype vulnerability** refers

**social identity theory**

theory in which the formation of a person's identity within a particular social group is explained by social categorization, social identity, and social comparison.

**social identity**

the part of the self-concept including one's view of self as a member of a particular social category.

**social comparison**

the comparison of oneself to others in ways that raise one's self-esteem.

**stereotype vulnerability**

the effect that people's awareness of the stereotypes associated with their social group has on their behavior.

Social comparison involves comparing yourself to others so that your self-esteem is protected. What do you think each of these young girls might be thinking?

### self-fulfilling prophecy

the tendency of one's expectations to affect one's behavior in such a way as to make the expectations more likely to occur.

Intergroup contact is one of the best ways to combat prejudice. When people have an opportunity to work together, as the students in this diverse classroom do, they get to know each other on common ground. Can you think of the first time you had direct contact with someone who was different from you? How did that contact change your viewpoint?

to the effect that a person's knowledge of another's stereotyped opinions can have on that person's behavior (Osborne, 2007; Steele, 1992, 1997). Research has shown that when people are aware of stereotypes that are normally applied to their own group by others, they may feel anxious about behaving in ways that might support that stereotype. This fear results in anxiety and self-consciousness that have negative effects on their performance in a kind of **self-fulfilling prophecy**, or the effect that expectations can have on outcomes.

Stereotype vulnerability is highly related to *stereotype threat*, in which members of a stereotyped group are made anxious and wary of any situation in which their behavior might confirm a stereotype (Abdou et al., 2016; Hartley & Sutton, 2013; Hyde & Kling, 2001; Steele, 1999). (**LINK** to Learning Objective 7.10.) In one study, researchers administered a difficult verbal test to both Caucasian and African American participants (Steele & Aronson, 1995). Half of the African American participants were asked to record their race on a demographic* question before the test, making them very aware of their minority status. Those participants showed a significant decrease in scores on the test when compared to the other participants, both African American and Caucasian, who did not answer such a demographic question. They had more incorrect answers, had slower response times, answered fewer questions, and demonstrated more anxiety when compared to the other participants (Steele & Aronson, 1995).

Similar effects of stereotype threat on performance have been found in women (Gonzales et al., 2002; Steele, 1997; Steele et al., 2002) and for athletes in academic settings (Yopyk & Prentice, 2005). A recent study did find that some people can overcome feelings of stereotype threat by identifying themselves with a different social identity, such as a woman who identifies herself with "college students" when taking a math exam rather than with "females," since the latter group is often stereotyped as being math deficient (Rydell & Boucher, 2010). This effect only held for those women with fairly high self-esteem, however.

**OVERCOMING PREJUDICE**  The best weapon against prejudice is education: learning about people who are different from you in many ways. The best way to learn about others is to have direct contact with them and to have the opportunity to see them as people rather than "as outsiders or strangers." *Intergroup contact* is very common in college settings, for example, where students and faculty from many different backgrounds live, work, and study together. Because they go through many of the same experiences (midterms, finals, and so on), people from these diverse** backgrounds find common ground to start building friendships and knowledge of each other's cultural, ethnic, or religious differences.

**EQUAL STATUS CONTACT**  Contact between social groups can backfire under certain circumstances, however, as seen in a famous study (Sherif et al., 1961) called the "Robber's Cave." In this experiment conducted at a summer camp called Robber's Cave, 22 white, well-adjusted, 11- and 12-year-old boys were divided into two groups. The groups each lived in separate housing and were kept apart from each other for daily activities. During the second week, after in-group relationships had formed, the researchers scheduled highly competitive events pitting one group against the other. Intergroup conflict quickly occurred, with name-calling, fights, and hostility emerging between the two groups.

---

*demographic: having to do with the statistical characteristics of a population.
**diverse: different, varied.

The third week involved making the two groups come together for pleasant, noncompetitive activities, in the hope that cooperation would be the result. Instead, the groups used the activities of the third week as opportunities for more hostility. It was only after several weeks of being forced to work together to resolve a series of crises (created deliberately by the experimenters) that the boys lost the hostility and formed friendships between the groups. When dealing with the crises, the boys were forced into a situation of **equal status contact**, in which they were all in the same situation with neither group holding power over the other. Equal status contact has been shown to reduce prejudice and discrimination, along with ongoing, positive cooperation. It appears that personal involvement with people from another group must be cooperative and occur when all groups are equal in terms of power or status to have a positive effect on reducing prejudice (Pettigrew & Tropp, 2000; Robinson & Preston, 1976).

**THE "JIGSAW CLASSROOM"** One possible way to help promote contact between people from different backgrounds occur in a cooperative fashion is to make success at a task dependent on the cooperation of each person in a group of people of mixed abilities or statuses. If each member of the group has information that is needed to solve the problem at hand, a situation is created in which people must depend on one another to meet their shared goals (Aronson et al., 1978). Ordinarily, school classrooms are not organized along these lines but are instead more competitive and, therefore, more likely to create conflict between people of different abilities and backgrounds.

In a **"jigsaw classroom,"** students have to work together to reach a specific goal. Each student is given a "piece of the puzzle," or information that is necessary for solving the problem and reaching the goal (Aronson et al., 1978; Clarke, 1994). Students then share their information with other members of the group. Interaction among diverse students is increased, making it more likely that those students will come to see each other as partners and form friendly relationships rather than labeling others as members of an out-group and treating them differently. This technique works at the college level as well as in the lower school grades (Johnson et al., 1991; Lord, 2001).

## INTERPERSONAL ATTRACTION

**12.12** Identify factors involved in interpersonal attraction.

Prejudice pretty much explains why people don't like each other. What does psychology say about why people like someone else? There are some "rules" for those whom people like and find attractive. Liking or having the desire for a relationship with someone else is called **interpersonal attraction**, and there's a great deal of research on the subject. (Who wouldn't want to know the rules?) Several factors are involved in the attraction of one person to another, including both superficial physical characteristics, such as physical beauty and proximity, as well as elements of personality.

**PHYSICAL ATTRACTIVENESS** When people think about what attracts them to others, one of the topics that usually arises is the physical attractiveness of the other person. Some research suggests that physical beauty is one of the main factors that influence individuals' choices for selecting people they want to know better, although other factors may become more important in the later stages of relationships (Eagly et al., 1991; Feingold, 1992; White, 1980).

**PROXIMITY—CLOSE TO YOU** The closer together people are physically, such as working in the same office building or living in the same dorm, the more likely they are to form a relationship. *Proximity* refers to being physically near someone else. People choose friends and lovers from the pool of people available to them, and availability depends heavily on proximity.

**equal status contact**
contact between groups in which the groups have equal status with neither group having power over the other.

**jigsaw classroom**
educational technique in which each individual is given only part of the information needed to solve a problem, causing the separate individuals to be forced to work together to find the solution.

**interpersonal attraction**
liking or having the desire for a relationship with another person.

One theory about why proximity is so important involves the idea of repeated exposure to new stimuli, sometimes called the *mere exposure effect*. The more people experience something, whether it is a song, a picture, or a person, the more they tend to like it. The phrase "it grew on me" refers to this reaction. When people are in physical proximity to each other, repeated exposure may increase their attraction to each other.

**BIRDS OF A FEATHER—SIMILARITY** Proximity does not guarantee attraction, just as physical attractiveness does not guarantee a long-term relationship. People tend to like being around others who are *similar* to them in some way. The more people find they have in common with others—such as attitudes, beliefs, and interests—the more they tend to be attracted to those others (Hartfield & Rapson, 1992; Moreland & Zajonc, 1982; Neimeyer & Mitchell, 1998). Similarity as a factor in relationships makes sense when seen in terms of validation of a person's beliefs and attitudes. When other people hold the same attitudes and beliefs and do the same kinds of actions, it makes a person's own concepts seem more correct or valid.

 💬 Isn't there a saying about "opposites attract"? Aren't people sometimes attracted to people who are different instead of similar?

There is often a grain of truth in many old sayings, and "opposites attract" is no exception. Some people find that forming a relationship with another person who has *complementary* qualities (characteristics in the one person that fill a need in the other) can be very rewarding (Carson, 1969; Schmitt, 2002). Research does not support this view of attraction, however. It is similarity, not complementarity, that draws people together and helps them stay together (Berscheid & Reis, 1998; McPherson et al., 2001).

**RECIPROCITY OF LIKING** Finally, people have a very strong tendency to like people who like them, a simple but powerful concept referred to as **reciprocity of liking**. In one experiment, researchers paired college students with other students (Curtis & Miller, 1986). Neither student in any of the pairs knew the other member. One member of each pair was randomly chosen to receive some information from the experimenters about how the other student in the pair felt about the first member. In some cases, target students were led to believe that the other students liked them and, in other cases, that the targets disliked them.

When the pairs of students were allowed to meet and talk with each other again, they were friendlier, disclosed more information about themselves, agreed with the other person more, and behaved in a warmer manner *if they had been told* that the other student liked them. The other students came to like these students better as well, so liking produced more liking.

The only time that liking someone does not seem to make that person like the other in return is if a person suffers from feelings of low self-worth. In that case, finding out that someone likes you when you don't even like yourself makes you question his or her motives. This mistrust can cause you to act unfriendly to that person, which makes the person more likely to become unfriendly to you in a kind of self-fulfilling prophecy (Murray et al., 1998).

**INTERPERSONAL RELATIONS ONLINE** No discussion of friendships and "liking" can be complete without some mention of the growing importance of social networking online. For example, which social network sites a college student selects may be related to racial identity and ethnic identity (Duggan et al., 2015). Facebook seems to be the most widely used platform regardless of one's racial or ethnic identity at 71 percent reported use. But when looking at other online platforms, white students prefer the interest/hobby-sharing site Pinterest, while Latino and African-American students prefer the photo-sharing site Instagram (Duggan et al., 2015).

**reciprocity of liking**

tendency of people to like other people who like them in return.

In China, the popular social networking site is Ozone, but Chinese users of this site spend less time on it, have fewer contacts, and seem to consider its use as less important when compared to users of Facebook in the United States (Jackson & Wang, 2013). When you consider the self-promotion focus of such social networking sites, it doesn't seem surprising that Chinese users, coming from a collectivistic cultural background that promotes connections with others over individual independence, would be less likely to use such a resource.

In another study, researchers found that young people who already experience positive social relationships use the online sites to enhance those same relationships, contrary to the stereotyped view that it would be the socially inept who would gravitate toward the anonymous nature of online networking (Mikami et al., 2010). In fact, those who are less well-adjusted either did not use social networking sites or used them in more negative ways: excessive bad language, hostile remarks, aggressive gestures, or posting of unflattering or suggestive photographs.

There may also be gender differences in how people organize their social networking. In a recent study, researchers found that females have more "friends," do more buying and selling, and are more likely to "friend" people who make the request than are males (Szell & Thurner, 2013). The study also found that females take fewer risks online than do males. Males talk to larger groups of contacts and are less likely to "friend" other males than females. They respond very quickly to females requesting a friendship.

### LOVE IS A TRIANGLE—ROBERT STERNBERG'S TRIANGULAR THEORY OF LOVE

**12.13** Describe the different types of love outlined in Sternberg's theory.

Dictionary definitions of love refer to a strong affection for another person due to kinship, personal ties, sexual attraction, admiration, or common interests.

> 💬 But those aren't all the same kind of relationships. I love my family and I love my friends, but in different ways.

Psychologists generally agree that there are different kinds of love. One psychologist, Robert Sternberg, outlined a theory of what he determined were the three main components of love and the different types of love that combinations of these three components can produce (Sternberg, 1986, 1988b, 1997a).

**THE THREE COMPONENTS OF LOVE**   According to Sternberg, love consists of three basic components: intimacy, passion, and commitment.

*Intimacy*, in Sternberg's view, refers to the feelings of closeness that one has for another person or the sense of having close emotional ties to another. Intimacy in this sense is not physical but psychological. Friends have an intimate relationship because they disclose things to each other that most people might not know, they feel strong emotional ties to each other, and they enjoy the presence of the other person.

*Passion* is the physical aspect of love. Passion refers to the emotional and sexual arousal a person feels toward the other person. Passion is not simply sex; holding hands, loving looks, and hugs can all be forms of passion.

*Commitment* involves the decisions one makes about a relationship. A short-term decision might be, "I think I'm in love." An example of a more long-term decision is, "I want to be with this person for the rest of my life."

**THE LOVE TRIANGLES**   A love relationship between two people can involve one, two, or all three of these components in various combinations. The combinations can produce seven different forms of love, as can be seen in the video *Attraction: Sternberg's Triangular Theory.*

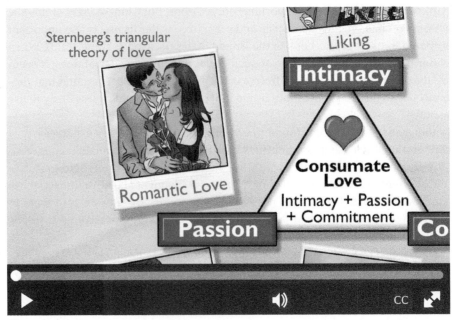

👁 **Watch** the **Video** *Attraction: Sternberg's Triangular Theory*

Two of the more familiar and more heavily researched forms of love from Sternberg's theory are romantic love and companionate love. When intimacy and passion are combined, the result is the more familiar **romantic love**, which is sometimes called passionate love by other researchers (Bartels & Zeki, 2000; Diamond, 2003; Hartfield, 1987). Romantic love is often the basis for a more lasting relationship. In many Western cultures, the ideal relationship begins with liking, then becomes romantic love as passion is added to the mix, and finally becomes a more enduring form of love as a commitment is made.

When intimacy and commitment are the main components of a relationship, it is called **companionate love**. In companionate love, people who like each other, feel emotionally close to each other, and understand one another's motives have made a commitment to live together, usually in a marriage relationship. Companionate love is often the binding tie that holds a marriage together through the years of parenting, paying bills, and lessening physical passion (Gottman & Krokoff, 1989; Steinberg & Silverberg, 1987). In many non-Western cultures, companionate love is seen as more sensible. Choices for a mate on the basis of compatibility are often made by parents or matchmakers rather than by the couple themselves (Duben & Behar, 1991; Hortaçsu, 1999; Jones, 1997; Thornton & HuiSheng, 1994).

Finally, when all three components of love are present, the couple has achieved *consummate love*, the ideal form of love that many people see as the ultimate goal. This is also the kind of love that may evolve into companionate love when the passion lessens during the middle years of a relationship's commitment.

### AGGRESSION

**12.14 Explain how aggressive behavior is determined by biology and learning.**

Unfortunately, violence toward others is another form of social interaction. When one person hurts or tries to destroy another person deliberately, either with words or with physical behavior, psychologists call it *aggression*. One common cause of aggressive behavior is frustration, which occurs when a person is prevented from reaching some desired goal. The concept of aggression as a reaction to frustration is known as the *frustration–aggression hypothesis* (Berkowitz, 1993; Miller et al., 1941). Many sources of frustration can lead to aggressive behavior. Pain, for example, produces negative

**romantic love**

type of love consisting of intimacy and passion.

**companionate love**

type of love consisting of intimacy and commitment.

sensations that are often intense and uncontrollable, leading to frustration and often aggressive acts against the nearest available target (Berkowitz, 1993). Loud noises, excessive heat, the irritation of someone else's cigarette smoke, and even awful smells can lead people to act out in an aggressive manner (Anderson, 1987; Rotton & Frey, 1985; Rotton et al., 1979; Zillmann et al., 1981).

Frustration is not the only source of aggressive behavior. Many early researchers, including Sigmund Freud (1930), believed that aggression was a basic human instinct, part of our death instinct. Famed sociobiologist Konrad Lorenz (1966) saw aggression as an instinct for fighting to promote the survival of our species. In evolutionary terms, those early humans who were most successful in protecting their territory, resources, and offspring were probably more aggressive and so survived to pass on their genetic material (Buss, 2009b; Cosmides & Tooby, 2013). But if aggression is an instinct present in all humans, it should occur in far more similar patterns across cultures than it does. Instinctual behavior, as often seen in animals, is not modifiable by environmental influences. Modern approaches include explanations of aggression as a biological phenomenon or a learned behavior.

**AGGRESSION AND BIOLOGY** There is some evidence that human aggression has, at least partially, a genetic basis. Studies of twins reared together and reared apart have shown that if one identical twin has a violent temper, the identical sibling will most likely also have a violent temper. This agreement between twins' personalities happens more often with identical twins than with fraternal twins (Miles & Carey, 1997; Rowe et al., 1999). It may be that, in some people, a gene or more likely a complex of genes influences a susceptibility to aggressive responses under the right environmental conditions.

As discussed in Chapter Two, certain areas of the brain seem to control aggressive responses. The frontal lobes, amygdala, and other structures of the limbic system, ⓛⓘⓝⓚ to Learning Objective 2.11, have been shown to trigger aggressive responses when stimulated in both animals and humans (Adams, 1968; Albert & Richmond, 1977; LaBar et al., 1995; Scott et al., 1997; Yang et al., 2010). Charles Whitman, the Texas Tower sniper, who in 1966 killed his mother and his wife and then shot and killed 12 more people before finally being killed by law enforcement officers, left a note asking for an examination of his brain. An autopsy did reveal a tumor that was pressing into his amygdala (Lavergne, 1997).

There are also chemical influences on aggression. Testosterone, a male sex hormone, has been linked to higher levels of aggression in humans (Archer, 1991). This may help explain why violent criminals tend to be young, male, and muscular. They typically have high levels of testosterone and low levels of serotonin, another important chemical found in the brain (Alexander et al., 1986; Brown & Linnoila, 1990; Coccaro & Kavoussi, 1996; Dabbs et al., 2001; Robins, 1996). Glutamate and serotonin, neurotransmitters found in the brain, may also play a part in aggressive behavior (Takahashi et al., 2015).

 💬 Don't some people get pretty violent after drinking too much? Does alcohol do something to those brain chemicals?

Alcohol does have an impact on aggressive behavior. Psychologically, alcohol acts to release inhibitions, making people less likely to control their behavior even if they are not yet intoxicated. Biologically, alcohol affects the functioning of many neurotransmitters and in particular is associated with a decrease in serotonin (Virkkunen & Linnoila, 1996). ⓛⓘⓝⓚ to Learning Objective 2.3. In one study, volunteers were asked to administer electric shocks to an unseen "opponent" in a study reminiscent of Milgram's shock experiment. The actual responses to the shock were simulated by a computer, although the volunteers believed that the responses were coming from a real person. The volunteers were told it was a test of reaction time and learning (Bushman, 1997). Volunteers participated

This photograph shows a "guard" searching a "prisoner" in Zimbardo's famous Stanford prison experiment. The students in the experiment became so deeply involved in their assigned roles that Zimbardo had to cancel the experiment after only 5 days—less than half the time originally scheduled for the study.

**social role**

the pattern of behavior that is expected of a person who is in a particular social position.

A U.S. soldier mistreats an Iraqi prisoner at the Abu Ghraib prison in Iraq. Investigators into alleged abuses at this prison found numerous sadistic and brutal acts committed by U.S. military personnel upon the prisoners.

both before consuming alcohol and after consuming alcohol. Participants were much more aggressive in administering stronger shocks after drinking.

**SOCIAL LEARNING EXPLANATIONS FOR AGGRESSION**  Although frustration, genetics, body chemicals, and even the effects of drugs can be blamed for aggressive behavior to some degree, much of human aggression is also influenced by learning. The social learning theory explanation for aggression states that aggressive behavior is learned (in a process called observational learning) by watching aggressive models get reinforced for their aggressive behavior (Bandura, 1980; Bandura et al., 1961). **LINK** to Learning Objective 5.13. Aggressive models can be parents, siblings, friends, or people on television or in computerized games.

**THE POWER OF SOCIAL ROLES**  Some evidence suggests that even taking on a particular *social role*, such as that of a soldier, can lead to an increase in aggressive behavior. A **social role** is the pattern of behavior that is expected of a person who is in a particular social position. For example, "doctor" is a social role that implies wearing a white coat, asking certain types of questions, and writing prescriptions, among other things. A deeply disturbing experiment was conducted by famed social psychologist Philip Zimbardo at Stanford University in 1971. The experiment was recorded on film from the beginning to its rather abrupt end. About 70 young men, most of whom were college students, volunteered to participate for 2 weeks. They were told that they would be randomly assigned the social role of either a guard or a prisoner in the experiment. The "guards" were given uniforms and instructions not to use violence but to maintain control of the "prison." The "prisoners" were booked at a real jail, blindfolded, and transported to the campus "prison," actually the basement of one of the campus buildings. On Day 2, the prisoners staged a revolt (not planned as part of the experiment), which was quickly crushed by the guards. The guards then became increasingly more aggressive, using humiliation to control and punish the prisoners. For example, prisoners were forced to clean out toilet bowls with their bare hands. The staff observing the experiment had to release five of the prisoners who became so upset that they were physically ill. The entire experiment was canceled on the sixth day (Zimbardo, 1971).

The conclusions of Zimbardo and his colleagues highlighted the influence that a social role, such as that of "guard," can have on perfectly ordinary people. Although history is full of examples of people behaving horribly to others while filling a particular role, one need not travel very far into the past to find an example.

During the war in Iraq in 2003, an army reserve general was suspended from duty while an investigation into reported prisoner abuses was conducted. Between October and December 2003, investigators found numerous cases of cruel, humiliating, and other startling abuses of the Iraqi prisoners by the army military police stationed at the prison of Abu Ghraib (Hersh, 2004). Among the cruelties reported were pouring cold water on naked detainees, beating them with a broom handle or chair, threatening them with rape, and one case of actually carrying out the threat. How could any normal person have done such things? The "guards" in the Stanford prison study were normal people, but the effect of putting on the uniform and taking on the social role of guard changed their behavior radically. Is it possible that a similar factor was at work at Abu Ghraib? The behavior of the guards at Abu Ghraib was not part of a formal, controlled study, so further research will be needed to determine to what degree the social roles at work in situations like this influence the kind of behavior seen in this real-life example.

No one can deny that abused children are exposed to powerful models of aggression. Unfortunately, the parents who abuse them are reinforced for their aggressive behavior when they get what they want from the child. No one can deny that there are people who were abused as children who then go on to become abusers. Contrary to popular belief, most children who suffer abuse do *not* grow up to become abusers themselves—in fact, only one third of abused children do so (Glaser et al., 2001; Kaufman & Zigler, 1993; Oliver, 1993). Instead of becoming the abuser, some abused children receive help in the form of counseling and/or removal from the abusive situation, overcoming the damage from their childhood, whereas others withdraw, isolating themselves rather than becoming abusive (Dodge et al., 1990).

There is some evidence, as discussed earlier in this chapter in regard to Milgram's obedience study, that the people in this study may have simply been decent people who did a terrible thing because they believed that the authority figure was doing a good thing overall (Frimer et al., 2014; Reicher et al., 2012).

 💬 I've heard that violent television programs can cause children to become more aggressive. How true is that?

**VIOLENCE IN THE MEDIA AND AGGRESSION**   Bandura's early study in which small children viewed a video of an aggressive model was one of the first attempts to investigate the effect of violence in the media on children's aggressive behavior (Bandura et al., 1963). Ⓛ Ⓘ Ⓝ Ⓚ to Learning Objective 5.13. Since then, researchers have examined the impact of television and other media violence on the aggressive behavior of children of various ages. The conclusions have all been similar: Children who are exposed to high levels of violent media are more aggressive than children who are not (Anderson et al., 2010; Baron & Reiss, 1985; Bushman & Huesmann, 2001, 2006; Centerwall, 1989; Geen & Thomas, 1986; Huesmann & Miller, 1994; Huesmann et al., 1997; Huesmann et al., 2003; Villani, 2001). These studies have found that there are several contributing factors involving the normal aggressive tendencies of the child, with more aggressive children preferring to watch more aggressive media, as well as the age at which exposure begins: The younger the child, the greater the impact. Parenting issues also have an influence, as the aggressive impact of television is lessened in homes where hostile behavior is not tolerated and punishment is not physical. Research has also demonstrated in a 1-year study of schoolchildren, parental monitoring of violent media decreased the likelihood of getting into a fight (Gentile & Bushman, 2012).

Violent video games have also come under fire as causing violent acting-out in children, especially young adolescents. The tragic shootings at schools all over the United States have, at least in part, been blamed on violent video games that the students seemed to be imitating. This was especially a concern in the Littleton, Colorado, shootings because the adolescent boys involved in those incidents had not only played a violent video game in which two shooters killed people who could not fight back but also had made a video of themselves in trench coats, shooting school athletes. This occurred less than a year before these same boys killed 13 of their fellow students at Columbine High School and wounded 23 others (Anderson & Dill, 2000). In one study, second-grade boys were allowed to play either an aggressive or a nonaggressive video game. After playing the game, the boys who had played the aggressive video game demonstrated more verbal and physical aggression both to objects around them and to their playmates while playing in a free period than did the boys who had played the nonaggressive video game (Irwin & Gross, 1995).

In a large meta-analysis of research (a careful statistical analysis of a large number of studies on a particular topic, able to more accurately measure the sizes of research effects than any one smaller study can measure) into the connection between violent media and aggressive behavior in children, social psychologist Craig Anderson and colleagues found clear and consistent evidence that even short-term exposure to violent media significantly increases the likelihood that children will engage in both physical and verbal aggression as well as aggressive thoughts and emotions (Anderson et al., 2003). Even larger, more recent studies have provided additional support (Anderson et al., 2010; Bushman & Huesman, 2006). While it should be noted there are some researchers that do not agree, with some questioning the measures of aggression being used, the analysis procedures, or finding different outcomes (Adachi & Willoughby, 2011; Ferguson, 2015; Ferguson & Kilburn, 2010), evidence appears to be strong that playing violent video games does correlate with increased aggression levels of the children who play them, both young children and adolescents (Anderson, 2003; Anderson & Bushman, 2001; Anderson et al., 2008; Bartlett et al., 2008; Ferguson et al., 2008; Przybylski et al., 2014). And while correlation does NOT prove causation—some researchers believe that we may be able to infer causation based on examination of the observed risk factors, outcomes, experimental studies of violent media exposure, and the positive effects of preventative measures (Bushman et al., 2016; (L) (I) (N) K to Learning Objective 1.7).

### PROSOCIAL BEHAVIOR

#### 12.15  Identify the factors influencing why people help others.

Another and far more pleasant form of human social interaction is prosocial behavior, or socially desirable behavior that benefits others rather than brings them harm.

**ALTRUISM**   One form of prosocial behavior that almost always makes people feel good about other people is altruism, or helping someone in trouble with no expectation of reward and often without fear for one's own safety. Although no one is surprised by the behavior of a mother who enters a burning house to save her child, some people are often surprised when total strangers step in to help, risking their own lives for people they do not know. Take the survey *Could You Be a Hero?* to learn more about your own tendencies to take risks to help others.

**Survey**    COULD YOU BE A HERO?

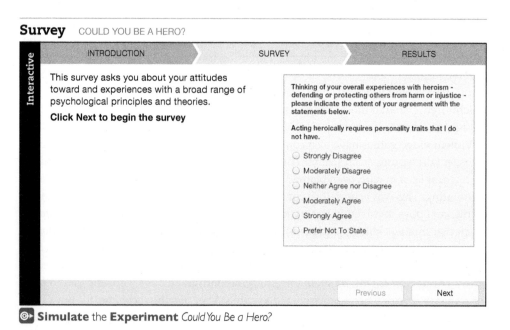

⊙ Simulate the Experiment *Could You Be a Hero?*

Sociobiologists, scientists who study the evolutionary and genetic bases of social organizations in both animals and humans, see altruistic behavior as a way of preserving one's genetic material, even at the cost of one's own life. This is why the males of certain species of spiders, for example, seem to willingly become "dinner" for the female mates they have just fertilized, ensuring the continuation of their genes through the offspring she will produce (Koh, 1996). It also explains the mother or father who risks life and limb to save a child.

But why do people risk their own lives to help total strangers? One answer may lie in the structure of the brain. Using brain-imaging techniques, researchers have found evidence that a brain region known as the temporoparietal junction (TPJ) is larger in

**prosocial behavior**

socially desirable behavior that benefits others.

**altruism**

prosocial behavior that is done with no expectation of reward and may involve the risk of harm to oneself.

individuals who make altruistic choices, particularly in the right hemisphere (Morishima et al., 2012). This area was also more active during decision making that involved a greater cost of helping the individual.

More importantly, why do people sometimes refuse to help when their own lives are not at risk?

**WHY PEOPLE WON'T HELP**  On March 13, 1964, at about 3:15 in the morning, Winston Mosely saw Catherine "Kitty" Genovese in the parking lot of her apartment complex, stabbed her, left, and then came back nearly half an hour later to rape and stab her to death in the entryway of the complex. Upon learning of the crime, a reporter for *The New York Times* wrote a story in which he claimed that at least 38 people heard or watched some part of the fatal attack from their apartment windows and that not one of these people called the police until after the attack was over (Delfiner, 2001; Gado, 2004; Rosenthal, 1964). This story outraged the public and has since become a symbol of bystander apathy.

In recent years, the truth of that fateful event has come to light, and the details may be more complex than originally reported. According to trial records, the two attacks occurred much closer in time than originally believed. At the first attack, a man shouted out his window "Leave that girl alone!" and Moseley fled. Another man supposedly called the police after that first attack, although there is no record of the call. The second attack took place in the entryway to the apartment complex—a far more sheltered area in which there could have been only a few witnesses. At this point, another witness, Sophia Farrar, told a friend to call the police while she went to Kitty Genovese's aid and held her until an ambulance arrived (Cook, 2014; Manning et al., 2007). Even though some did call for help and at least one came to Kitty's aid, there were several witnesses who still stood by and did nothing. One man, whose apartment door opened onto the entryway where the second attack occurred, cracked open his apartment door, saw the attack—and closed the door (Cook, 2014).

People were outraged by the apparent indifference and lack of sympathy for the poor woman's plight. Why did those people simply stand by and watch or listen? Social psychologists would explain that the lack of response to Kitty Genovese's screams for help was not due to indifference or a lack of sympathy but instead to the presence of other people.

Forty-three years later on June 23, 2007, 27-year-old LaShanda Calloway was stabbed to death during an argument in a convenience store. It took 2 minutes for someone to call 9-1-1. Surveillance video captured the attack, including the five shoppers who stepped over her bleeding form and continued shopping. One customer did stop—to take a picture of Ms. Calloway as she lay dying on the floor (Hegeman, 2007). When other people are present at the scene or are assumed to be present, individuals are affected by two basic principles of social psychology: the bystander effect and diffusion of responsibility.

The **bystander effect** refers to the finding that the likelihood of a bystander (someone observing an event and close enough to offer help) to help someone in trouble decreases as the number of bystanders increases. If only one person is standing by, that person is far more likely to help than if there is another person, and the addition of each new bystander decreases the possibility of helping behavior even more (Darley & Latané, 1968; Eagly & Crowley, 1986; Latané & Darley, 1969). In the case of Kitty Genovese, there were 38 "bystanders" at the windows of the apartment buildings, and none of them helped. There is some evidence that only six or seven people actually **saw** parts of the attack, while others heard what some interpreted as a lovers' quarrel. No one apparently witnessed the entire event from start to finish, and the greater part of the assault actually took place out of the hearing of any witnesses (Rasenberger, 2006). Still, not one person called the police.

Social psychologists Bibb Latané and John Darley conducted several classic experiments about the bystander effect. In one study, participants were filling out questionnaires in a room that began to fill with smoke. Some participants were alone in the room, whereas in another condition there were three participants in the room. In a third condition, one participant was in the room with two confederates of the experimenter, who were instructed to notice the smoke but ignore it afterward. In the "participant alone" condition, three fourths

**bystander effect**
referring to the effect that the presence of other people has on the decision to help or not help, with help becoming less likely as the number of bystanders increases.

of the participants left the room to report the smoke. In the "three participants" condition, only a little more than one third of the participants reported the smoke, whereas only one tenth of the participants who were in the room with confederates did so (**Figure 12.5**).

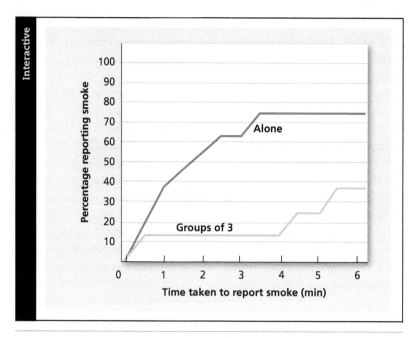

**Figure 12.5**   Elements Involved in Bystander Response

In a classic experiment, participants were filling out surveys as the room began to fill with smoke. As you can see in the accompanying graph, the time taken to report smoke and the percentage of people reporting smoke both depended on how many people were in the room at the time the smoke was observed. If a person was alone, he or she was far more likely to report the smoke and report it more quickly than when there were three people.

**SOURCE:** Latané & Darley (1969).

💬 But why does the number of bystanders matter?

Diffusion of responsibility is the phenomenon in which a person fails to take responsibility for either action or inaction because of the presence of other people who are seen to share the responsibility (Leary & Forsyth, 1987). Diffusion of responsibility is a form of attribution in which people explain why they acted (or failed to act) as they did because of others. Contrary to popular belief, bystanders who fail to act do not typically do so out of apathy (a lack of caring about the victim) but instead may care quite deeply. They do not act because of diffusion of responsibility, among other concerns (Glassman & Hadad, 2008). "I was just following orders," "Other people were doing it," and "There were a lot of people there, and I thought one of them would do something" are all examples of statements made in such situations. Kitty Genovese and LaShanda Calloway received no help because there were too many potential "helpers," and not one of the people listening to cries for help took the responsibility to intervene—they thought surely someone else was doing something about it.

**diffusion of responsibility**

occurring when a person fails to take responsibility for actions or for inaction because of the presence of other people who are seen to share the responsibility.

**FIVE DECISION POINTS IN HELPING BEHAVIOR**   What kind of decision-making process do people go through before deciding to help? What are the requirements for deciding when help is needed? Darley and Latané (1968) identified several cognitive decision points that a bystander must face before helping someone in trouble. These decision points, which are discussed in the video *Deciding to Help* and outlined in **Table 12.2**, are still considered useful more than 40 years later.

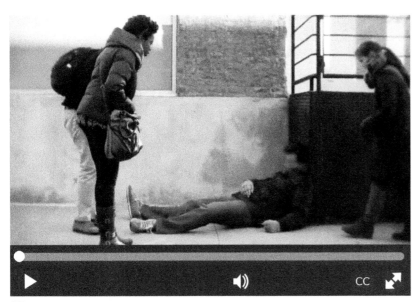

👁 **Watch** the **Video** *Deciding to Help*

Aside from the factors listed in the table, there are other influences on the decision to help. For example, the more ambiguity* in a situation, the less likely it will be defined as an emergency. (Remember, many of those who heard the attack on Kitty Genovese were not sure if it was a lovers' quarrel or not.) If there are other people nearby, especially if the situation is ambiguous, bystanders may rely on the actions of the others to help determine if the situation is an emergency or not. Since all the bystanders may be doing this, it is very likely that the situation will be seen as a nonemergency because no one is moving to help.

Another factor is the mood of the bystanders. People in a good mood are generally more likely to help than people in a bad mood, but oddly enough, they are not as likely to help if helping would destroy the good mood. Gender of the victim is also a factor, with women more likely to receive help than men if the bystander is male, but not if the bystander is female. Physically attractive people are more likely to be helped. Victims who look like "they deserve what is happening" are also less likely to be helped. For example, a man lying on the side of the street who is dressed in shabby clothing and appears to be drunk will be passed by, but if he is dressed in a business suit, people are more likely to stop and help. Racial and ethnicity differences between victim and bystander also decrease the probability of helping (Richards & Lowe, 2003; Tukuitonga & Bindman, 2002).

| **Table 12.2**  Help or don't Help: Five Decision Points | | |
|---|---|---|
| **Decision Point** | **Description** | **Factors Influencing Decision** |
| Noticing | Realizing that there is a situation that might be an emergency | Hearing a loud crash or a cry for help. |
| Defining an Emergency | Interpreting the cues as signaling an emergency | Loud crash is associated with a car accident; people are obviously hurt. |
| Taking Responsibility | Personally assuming the responsibility to act | A single bystander is much more likely to act than when others are present (Latané & Darley, 1969). |
| Planning a Course of Action | Deciding how to help and what skills might be needed | People who feel they have the necessary skills to help are more likely to help. |
| Taking Action | Actually helping | Costs of helping (e.g., danger to self) must not outweigh the rewards of helping. |

*Interactive*

*ambiguity: having the quality of being difficult to identify specific elements of the situation.

## Concept Map L.O. 12.10, 12.11, 12.12, 12.13, 12.14, 12.15

Interactive

### Social Interaction

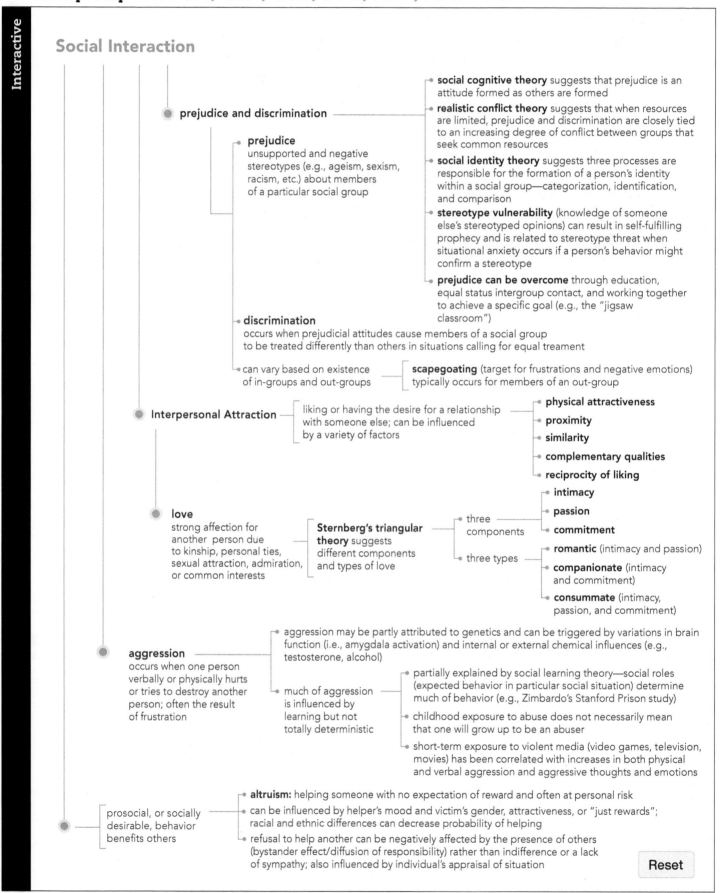

**prejudice and discrimination**

**prejudice**
unsupported and negative stereotypes (e.g., ageism, sexism, racism, etc.) about members of a particular social group

- **social cognitive theory** suggests that prejudice is an attitude formed as others are formed
- **realistic conflict theory** suggests that when resources are limited, prejudice and discrimination are closely tied to an increasing degree of conflict between groups that seek common resources
- **social identity theory** suggests three processes are responsible for the formation of a person's identity within a social group—categorization, identification, and comparison
- **stereotype vulnerability** (knowledge of someone else's stereotyped opinions) can result in self-fulfilling prophecy and is related to stereotype threat when situational anxiety occurs if a person's behavior might confirm a stereotype
- **prejudice can be overcome** through education, equal status intergroup contact, and working together to achieve a specific goal (e.g., the "jigsaw classroom")

**discrimination**
occurs when prejudicial attitudes cause members of a social group to be treated differently than others in situations calling for equal treatment

- can vary based on existence of in-groups and out-groups
  - **scapegoating** (target for frustrations and negative emotions) typically occurs for members of an out-group

**Interpersonal Attraction** — liking or having the desire for a relationship with someone else; can be influenced by a variety of factors
- **physical attractiveness**
- **proximity**
- **similarity**
- **complementary qualities**
- **reciprocity of liking**

**love**
strong affection for another person due to kinship, personal ties, sexual attraction, admiration, or common interests

**Sternberg's triangular theory** suggests different components and types of love
- three components
  - **intimacy**
  - **passion**
  - **commitment**
- three types
  - **romantic** (intimacy and passion)
  - **companionate** (intimacy and commitment)
  - **consummate** (intimacy, passion, and commitment)

**aggression**
occurs when one person verbally or physically hurts or tries to destroy another person; often the result of frustration

- aggression may be partly attributed to genetics and can be triggered by variations in brain function (i.e., amygdala activation) and internal or external chemical influences (e.g., testosterone, alcohol)

- much of aggression is influenced by learning but not totally deterministic
  - partially explained by social learning theory—social roles (expected behavior in particular social situation) determine much of behavior (e.g., Zimbardo's Stanford Prison study)
  - childhood exposure to abuse does not necessarily mean that one will grow up to be an abuser
  - short-term exposure to violent media (video games, television, movies) has been correlated with increases in both physical and verbal aggression and aggressive thoughts and emotions

prosocial, or socially desirable, behavior benefits others
- **altruism:** helping someone with no expectation of reward and often at personal risk
- can be influenced by helper's mood and victim's gender, attractiveness, or "just rewards"; racial and ethnic differences can decrease probability of helping
- refusal to help another can be negatively affected by the presence of others (bystander effect/diffusion of responsibility) rather than indifference or a lack of sympathy; also influenced by individual's appraisal of situation

Reset

# Practice Quiz    How much do you remember?

*Pick the best answer.*

1. Prejudice is about _____, while discrimination is about
   _____.
   a. beliefs; perceptions     c. behavior; attitudes
   b. perceptions; beliefs     d. attitudes; behavior

2. Jewell and Amie became friends while taking an evening class at
   the local community college. Jewell was later horrified to find out
   that Amie was actually a teacher at the college. Subsequently,
   Jewell stopped talking with Amie, thus ending their friendship.
   What theory of prejudice and discrimination might this be an
   example of?
   a. stereotype vulnerability theory
   b. in-group/out-group theory
   c. realistic conflict theory
   d. social cognitive theory

3. What does the research say about the concept of opposites attract?
   a. While it goes against the concept of similarity, it is real, and
      research can prove it.
   b. Opposites attract is really more an example of proximity,
      although studies show that opposites can be and often are
      attracted to one another.

   c. Research notes that opposites attract but is unable to explain
      why this happens.
   d. Studies do not support this idea but instead offer the explanation
      of complementary qualities.

4. According to Robert Sternberg's three components of love, which
   component addresses the physical aspects?
   a. intimacy       c. commitment
   b. passion        d. concern

5. When people are unable to reach a goal, frustration may result,
   which can ultimately turn into
   a. aggression.    c. confusion.
   b. pain.          d. depression.

6. Which of the following scenarios probably will not result in the
   bystander effect?
   a. You come across someone lying on a busy sidewalk in a large city.
   b. You see someone pass out at a concert.
   c. You drive past an automobile accident where a crowd has
      gathered.
   d. You come across someone lying on a walking path while you are
      walking alone at your local nature center.

---

## Applying Psychology to Everyday Life
### Peeking Inside the Social Brain

**12.16  Define social neuroscience.**

As scientists develop better techniques for studying the workings of the brain, researchers in many fields of psychology are able to find the neural bases for human behavior. Social psychology is no exception, and the study of how our bodies and brains work during social behavior is called **social neuroscience** (Cacioppo & Berntson, 1992). In the discussion of altruism, the temporoparietal junction, or TPJ, was named as one of the areas of the brain involved in prosocial behavior (Morishima et al., 2012). That research was accomplished with an fMRI, a brain-scanning technique that allows not only the structure but also the functioning of the living brain to be examined during various tasks and activities. **LINK** to Learning Objective 2.9.

The TPJ, located where the temporal and parietal lobes meet, is also a key neural structure involved in competitive behavior. Researchers pitted people against either a computer or another person and found that the TPJ is active when the person is trying to predict the actions of the human opponent but not the computer opponent (Carter et al., 2012). Research with nonhuman primates highlights the importance of the prefrontal cortex, the area of the brain at the very front of the large frontal lobes. The findings of that study suggest that primates make decisions about sharing behavior in three different parts of the prefrontal lobe (Chang et al., 2013). One can only guess that human sharing decisions are at least as complex, if not more so.

What all of these studies (and many, many more) mean is that there are specific structures and places in our brains for social interactions and decisions. It is important that we try to understand as much as we can about the "social brain" for many reasons, but chief among them is gaining an understanding of diseases and disorders

**social neuroscience**
the study of the relationship between biological systems and social processes and behavior.

which may be linked to the social areas of the brain (Adolphs, 2010). Consider autism, a developmental disorder than includes impaired social functioning, or Alzheimer's, Parkinson's, or Huntington's disease, all of which also have impaired social functioning. Many psychological disorders also involve abnormal social behavior—depression, the various personality disorders, and anxiety disorders, to name a few. Understanding how these malfunctions occur within the brain is a huge step on the road to changing that behavior. Where social psychologists once studied human interactions through observing outward behavior, social neuroscientists now study the most intimate workings of the social brain.

### Questions for Further Discussion

1. Can you think of other diseases or disorders which include disrupted social behavior?
2. What are the drawbacks of drawing parallels between nonhuman primate behavior and human behavior?

# Chapter Summary

- Social psychology is the scientific study of how a person's thoughts, feelings, and behavior are influenced by the real, imagined, or implied presence of other people.

## Social Influence

### 12.1 Identify factors that influence people or groups to conform to the actions of others.

- Asch used a set of comparison lines and a standard line to experiment with conformity, finding that subjects conformed to group opinion about one third of the time, increased as the number of confederates rose to four, and decreased if just one confederate gave the correct answer.
- Cross-cultural research has found that collectivistic cultures show more conformity than individualistic cultures. Gender differences do not exist in conformity unless the response is not private, in which case women are more conforming than men.

### 12.2 Explain how our behavior is impacted by the presence of others.

- Groupthink occurs when a decision-making group feels that it is more important to maintain group unanimity and cohesiveness than to consider the facts realistically. Minimizing groupthink involves holding group members responsible for the decisions made by the group.
- Group polarization occurs when members take somewhat more extreme positions and take greater risks as compared to those made by individuals.
- When the performance of an individual on a relatively easy task is improved by the presence of others, it is called social facilitation. When the performance of an individual on a relatively

difficult task is negatively affected by the presence of others, it is called social impairment.
- When a person who is lazy is able to work in a group of people, that person often performs less well than if the person were working alone, in a phenomenon called social loafing.
- Deindividuation occurs when group members feel anonymous and personally less responsible for their actions.

### 12.3 Compare and contrast three compliance techniques.

- Compliance occurs when a person changes behavior as a result of another person asking or directing that person to change.
- Three common ways of getting compliance from others are the foot-in-the-door technique, the door-in-the-face technique, and the lowball technique.

### 12.4 Identify factors that make obedience more likely.

- Obedience involves changing one's behavior at the direct order of an authority figure.
- Milgram did experiments in which he found that 65 percent of people obeyed an authority figure even if they believed they were hurting, injuring, or possibly killing another person with electric shock.

## Social Cognition

### 12.5 Identify the three components of an attitude and how attitudes are formed.

- Attitudes are tendencies to respond positively or negatively toward ideas, persons, objects, or situations.

- The three components of an attitude are the affective (emotional) component, the behavior component, and the cognitive component.
- Attitudes are often poor predictors of behavior unless the attitude is very specific or very strong.
- Direct contact with the person, situation, object, or idea can help form attitudes.
- Attitudes can be formed through direct instruction from parents or others.
- Interacting with other people who hold a certain attitude can help an individual form that attitude.
- Attitudes can also be formed through watching the actions and reactions of others to ideas, people, objects, and situations.

### 12.6 Describe how attitudes can be changed.

- Persuasion is the process by which one person tries to change the belief, opinion, position, or course of action of another person through argument, pleading, or explanation.
- The key elements in persuasion are the source of the message, the message itself, and the target audience.
- In the elaboration likelihood model, central-route processing involves attending to the content of the message itself, whereas peripheral-route processing involves attending to factors not involved in the message, such as the appearance of the source of the message, the length of the message, and other noncontent factors.

### 12.7 Explain how people react when attitudes differ from behavior.

- Cognitive dissonance is discomfort or distress that occurs when a person's actions do not match the person's attitudes.
- Cognitive dissonance is lessened by changing the conflicting behavior, changing the conflicting attitude, or forming a new attitude to justify the behavior.

### 12.8 Describe how people form impressions of others.

- Impression formation is the forming of the first knowledge a person has about another person.
- The primacy effect in impression formation means that the very first impression one has about a person tends to persist even in the face of evidence to the contrary.
- Impression formation is part of social cognition, or the mental processes that people use to make sense out of the world around them.
- Social categorization is a process of social cognition in which a person, upon meeting someone new, assigns that person to a category or group on the basis of characteristics the person has in common with other people or groups with whom the perceiver has prior experience.
- One form of a social category is the stereotype, in which the characteristics used to assign a person to a category are superficial and believed to be true of all members of the category.
- An implicit personality theory is a form of social cognition in which a person has sets of assumptions about different types of people, personality traits, and actions that are assumed to be related to each other.
- Schemas are mental patterns that represent what a person believes about certain types of people. Schemas can become stereotypes.

### 12.9 Describe the process of explaining one's own behavior and the behavior of others.

- Attribution is the process of explaining the behavior of others as well as one's own behavior.
- A situational cause is an explanation of behavior based on factors in the surrounding environment or situation.
- A dispositional cause is an explanation of behavior based on the internal personality characteristics of the person being observed.
- The fundamental attribution error is the tendency to overestimate the influence of internal factors on behavior while underestimating the influence of the situation.

## Social Interaction

### 12.10 Distinguish between prejudice and discrimination.

- Prejudice is a negative attitude that a person holds about the members of a particular social group. Discrimination occurs when members of a social group are treated differently because of prejudice toward that group.
- There are many forms of prejudice, including ageism, sexism, racism, and prejudice toward those who are too fat or too thin.
- In-groups are the people with whom a person identifies, whereas out-groups are everyone else at whom prejudice tends to be directed.
- Scapegoating refers to the tendency to direct prejudice and discrimination at out-group members who have little social power or influence. New immigrants are often the scapegoats for the frustration and anger of the in-group.

### 12.11 Describe theories of how prejudice is learned and how it can be overcome.

- Social cognitive theory views prejudice as an attitude acquired through direct instruction, modeling, and other social influences.
- Conflict between groups increases prejudice and discrimination according to realistic conflict theory.
- Social identity theory sees a person's formation of a social sense of self within a particular group as being due to three things: social categorization (which may involve the use of reference groups), social identity (the person's sense of belonging to a particular social group), and social comparison (in which people compare themselves to others to improve their own self-esteem).
- Stereotype vulnerability refers to the effect that a person's knowledge of the stereotypes that exist against his or her social group can have on that person's behavior.
- People who are aware of stereotypes may unintentionally come to behave in a way that makes the stereotype real in a self-fulfilling prophecy.

- Intergroup contact is more effective in reducing prejudice if the groups have equal status.
- Prejudice and discrimination can also be reduced when a super-ordinate goal that is large enough to override all other goals needs to be achieved by all groups.
- Prejudice and discrimination are reduced when people must work together to solve a problem because each person has an important key to solving the problem, creating a mutual interdependence. This technique used in education is called the "jigsaw classroom."

**12.12 Identify factors involved in interpersonal attraction.**

- Interpersonal attraction refers to liking or having the desire for a relationship with another person.
- People tend to form relationships with people who are in physical proximity to them.
- People are attracted to others who are similar to them in some way.
- People may also be attracted to people who are different from themselves, with the differences acting as a complementary support for areas in which each may be lacking.
- People tend to like other people who like them in return, a phenomenon called the reciprocity of liking.
- Use of a specific social networking site may be partially determined by racial identity and ethnic identity. The ways sites are used are influenced by both gender and the status of current social relationships.
- Love is a strong affection for another person due to kinship, personal ties, sexual attraction, admiration, or common interests.

**12.13 Describe the different types of love outlined in Sternberg's theory.**

- Sternberg states that the three components of love are intimacy, passion, and commitment.
- Romantic love is intimacy with passion, companionate love is intimacy with commitment, and consummate love contains all three components.

**12.14 Explain how aggressive behavior is determined by biology and learning.**

- Aggression is behavior intended to hurt or destroy another person in a way that may be physical or verbal. Frustration is a major source of aggression.

- Biological influences on aggression may include genetics, the amygdala and limbic system, and testosterone and serotonin levels.
- Social roles are powerful influences on the expression of aggression. Social learning theory states that aggression can be learned through direct reinforcement and through the imitation of successful aggression by a model.
- Studies have concluded that violent television, movies, and video games stimulate aggressive behavior, both by increasing aggressive tendencies and by providing models of aggressive behavior.

**12.15 Identify the factors influencing why people help others.**

- Prosocial behavior is behavior that is socially desirable and benefits others.
- Altruism is prosocial behavior in which a person helps someone else without expectation of reward or recognition, often without fear for his or her own safety.
- The bystander effect means that people are more likely to get help from others if there are one or only a few people nearby rather than a larger number. The more people nearby, the less likely it is that help will be offered.
- When others are present at a situation in which help could be offered, there is a diffusion of responsibility among all the bystanders, reducing the likelihood that any one person or persons will feel responsibility for helping.
- Researchers Latané and Darley found that people who were alone were more likely to help in an emergency than people who were with others.
- The five steps in making a decision to help are noticing, defining an emergency, taking responsibility, planning a course of action, and taking action.

## Applying Psychology to Everyday Life: Peeking inside the Social Brain

**12.16 Define social neuroscience.**

- Social neuroscience is the study of how biological processes influence social behavior. Studies use fMRI and other imaging techniques to discover areas of the brain involved in social actions.

# Test Yourself

*Pick the best answer.*

1. Saul admits that he conforms so as to be liked by others. This is known as
   a. compliance.
   b. obedience.
   c. informational social influence.
   d. normative social influence.

2. According to the text, in which of the following has groupthink been known to occur?
   a. presidential elections
   b. the fall of communism
   c. mass suicides by cults
   d. the sinking of the *Titanic*

3. Many businesses now require their employees to work in teams, believing that a group of four to five employees will accomplish more than four to five individuals working alone. This is an example of what concept?
   a. social facilitation
   b. social impairment
   c. social loafing
   d. social laziness

4. Maria was approached by her neighbor, who asked her to adopt three kittens that were abandoned by their mother. While Maria refused to take in three kittens, she did agree to adopt just one. What compliance technique did her neighbor use on Maria?
   a. foot-in-the-door
   b. door-in-the-face
   c. lowball
   d. double foot-in-the-door

5. Which of the following people would probably not be a prime candidate for membership in a cult?
   a. Lewis, who is mad at the world, especially his parents
   b. Leticia, who is open to new ideas and wants world peace and harmony among people
   c. Lauren, who is under a lot of stress and dissatisfied with her life
   d. Lawrence, who has only a high school diploma but tends to be independent and happy with his life

6. Follow-up studies to Stanley Milgram's research have suggested that a teacher's willingness to deliver potentially lethal shocks may be more a product of _____ than of obedience.
   a. conformity
   b. compliance
   c. social identity
   d. deindividuation

7. The public-service messages that encourage parents to sit down with their children and talk frankly about drugs are promoting which method of attitude formation?
   a. direct contact
   b. direct instruction
   c. vicarious conditioning
   d. observational learning

8. Researchers have found that a _____ degree of fear in a message makes it more effective, particularly when it is combined with _____.
   a. maximum; information about how to prevent the fearful consequences
   b. minimum; threats
   c. moderate; threats
   d. moderate; information about how to prevent the fearful consequences

9. Sandy was a juror in the trial for a man accused of stealing guns from a sporting-goods store. The defendant was not very well spoken and came from a very poor background, but Sandy listened carefully to the evidence presented and made her decision based on that. Sandy was using _____ processing.
   a. central-route
   b. peripheral-route
   c. cognitive-route
   d. visual-route

10. If LaShonda was experiencing a sense of cognitive dissonance between her attitude and behavior, which of the following would help her reduce that uncomfortable sensation?
    a. thinking constantly about the mismatch
    b. maintaining her existing attitude
    c. discussing the inconsistency with others
    d. changing her behavior

11. Gerard goes to a job interview dressed in patched blue jeans, a torn T-shirt, and sandals. His hair is uncombed, and he hasn't shaved in a few days. Obviously, Gerard knows nothing about
    a. cognitive dissonance.
    b. attitude formation.
    c. impression formation.
    d. groupthink.

12. If behavior is assumed to be caused by external characteristics, this is known as
    a. a situational cause.
    b. a dispositional cause.
    c. a fundamental attribution error.
    d. actor–observer bias.

13. Thomas likes to "hang with the guys." These people with whom Thomas identifies most strongly with are called a(n)
    a. referent group.
    b. in-group.
    c. out-group.
    d. "them" group.

14. The "Robber's Cave" experiment showed the value of _____ in combating prejudice.
    a. "jigsaw classrooms"
    b. equal-status contact
    c. subordinate goals
    d. stereotyping vulnerability

15. Vivian and Steve met at work. At first they were just friends, but over time, they found themselves falling in love—or, as Vivian tells her friends, "Steve just grew on me!" According to research in interpersonal attraction, the most likely explanation for their attraction is
    a. mere exposure.
    b. personal attractiveness.
    c. fate.
    d. reciprocity of liking.

16. According to Sternberg, a couple whose love is based on intimacy and passion but who are not yet committed to a long-term relationship are in the form of love called _____ love.
    a. companionate
    b. romantic
    c. affectionate
    d. consummate

17. The concept that aggression results from a social role is based on what psychological theory?
    a. humanistic
    b. learning
    c. psychoanalytical
    d. cognitive

18. To which two processes do most social psychologists attribute the failure of those around LaShanda Calloway to help her?
    a. bystander effect and altruism
    b. aggression and diffusion of responsibility
    c. altruism and diffusion of responsibility
    d. bystander effect and diffusion of responsibility

19. Cara knows that she can help people simply by dialing 9-1-1 on her cell phone if an emergency arises. Which step in the decision process for helping would Cara be at?
    a. noticing
    b. taking action
    c. taking responsibility
    d. planning a course of action

20. Which of the following would the field of social neuroscience be most likely to study?
    a. what parts of the brain influence social behavior
    b. how influential heredity is on social behavior
    c. what impact head trauma has on developing relationships
    d. what impact friends have in resolving conflicts

# Theories of Personality

In what ways are you similar to and different from your siblings? How has your personality been shaped by your environment? After you have answered the question, watch the video to compare the answers of other students to yours.

▶ | The response entered here will be saved to your notes and may be collected by your instructor if he/she requires it.

👁 Watch the Video

# Why study personality?

Personality is the sum total of who you are—your attitudes and reactions, both physical and emotional. It's what makes each person different from every other person in the world. How can any study of human behavior not include the study of who we are and how we got to be that way?

504

# Learning Objectives

**13.1** Explain how the mind and personality are structured, according to Freud.

**13.2** Distinguish among the five psychosexual stages of personality development.

**13.3** Describe how the neo-Freudians modified Freud's theory.

**13.4** Evaluate the influence of Freudian theory on modern personality theories.

**13.5** Compare and contrast the learning theories of Bandura and Rotter.

**13.6** Evaluate the strengths and limitations of the behavioral and social cognitive learning views of personality.

**13.7** Describe how humanists such as Carl Rogers explain personality.

**13.8** Evaluate the strengths and limitations of the humanistic view of personality.

**13.9** Describe early attempts to use traits to conceptualize personality.

**13.10** Identify the five trait dimensions of the five-factor model of personality.

**13.11** Evaluate the strengths and limitations of the trait view of personality.

**13.12** Explain how twin studies and adoption studies are used in the field of behavioral genetics.

**13.13** Summarize current research on the heritability of personality.

**13.14** Identify the advantages and disadvantages of using interviews, behavioral assessments, and personality inventories to measure personality.

**13.15** Identify the advantages and disadvantages of using projective personality tests.

**13.16** Identify some biological bases of personality.

# Psychodynamic Perspectives

**Personality** is the unique way in which each individual thinks, acts, and feels throughout life. Personality should not be confused with **character**, which refers to value judgments made about a person's morals or ethical behavior; nor should it be confused with *temperament*, the biologically innate and enduring characteristics with which each person is born, such as irritability or adaptability. Both character and temperament are vital parts of personality, however. Every adult personality is a combination of temperaments and personal history of family, culture, and the time during which they grew up (Kagan, 2010).

Personality is an area of psychology in which there are several ways to explain the characteristic behavior of human beings. Despite the investigation of personality reaching back to at least the fourth century BCE (Dumont, 2010), one reason no single explanation of personality exists is because personality is still difficult to measure precisely and scientifically, and different perspectives of personality have arisen. Overall these tend to examine the source of personality, such as individual behavioral tendencies or situational variables, both of which are influences that may be conscious or unconscious (Mischel & Shoda, 1995). Sources overlap and influence each other, such as the interaction of biological, developmental, social, and cultural factors. Some perspectives are influenced by early schools of thought in psychology, such as structuralism, functionalism, Gestalt, learning, or the cognitive perspective. Theories or perspectives may also be influenced by newer ideas from evolution, social adaptation, motivation, and information processing (Buss, 2009a, 2011; Higgins & Scholer, 2010; McAdams & Olson, 2010; Mischel & Shoda, 1995). From a foundational aspect, we will focus on several traditional perspectives in personality, starting with the work of Sigmund Freud.

Sigmund Freud (1856–1939) was the founder of the psychodynamic movement in psychology. Many of his patients sat or reclined on the couch above while he sat in a chair, listening to them and developing his psychoanalytic theory of personality.

## FREUD'S CONCEPTION OF PERSONALITY

**13.1** **Explain how the mind and personality are structured, according to Freud.**

It's hard to understand how Freud developed his ideas about personality unless we have some knowledge of the world in which he and his patients lived. He was born and raised in Europe during the Victorian Age, a time of sexual repression. People growing up in this period were told by their church that sex should take place only in the context of marriage and then only to make babies. To enjoy sexual intercourse was considered a sin. Men were understood to be unable to control their "animal" desires at times, and a good Victorian husband would father several children with his wife and then turn to a mistress for sexual comfort, leaving his virtuous* wife untouched. Women, especially those of the upper classes, were not supposed to have sexual urges. It is no wonder that many of Freud's patients were wealthy women with problems stemming from unfulfilled sexual desires or sexual repression. Freud's "obsession" with sexual explanations for abnormal behavior seems more understandable in light of his cultural background and that of his patients.

Freud came to believe that there were layers of consciousness in the mind. His belief in the influence of the unconscious mind on conscious behavior, published in *The Psychopathology of Everyday Life* (Freud, 1901), shocked the Victorian world.

**THE STRUCTURE OF THE MIND** Freud believed that the mind was divided into three parts: the preconscious, conscious, and unconscious (Freud, 1900). While no one really disagreed with the idea of a conscious mind in which one's current awareness exists or even of a preconscious mind containing memories, information, and events of which one can easily become aware, the **unconscious mind** (also called "the unconscious") was the

**personality**

the unique and relatively stable ways in which people think, feel, and behave.

**character**

value judgments of a person's moral and ethical behavior.

**unconscious mind**

level of the mind in which thoughts, feelings, memories, and other information are kept that are not easily or voluntarily brought into consciousness.

———————

*virtuous: morally excellent.

real departure for the professionals of Freud's day. Freud theorized that there is a part of the mind that remains hidden at all times, surfacing only in symbolic form in dreams and in some of the behavior people engage in without knowing why they have done so. Even when a person makes a determined effort to bring a memory out of the unconscious mind, it will not appear directly, according to Freud. Freud believed that the unconscious mind was the most important determining factor in human behavior and personality.

**FREUD'S DIVISIONS OF THE PERSONALITY**  Freud believed, based on observations of his patients, that personality itself could be divided into three parts, each existing at one or more levels of conscious awareness (see **Figure 13.1**). The way these three parts of the personality develop and interact with one another became the heart of his theory (Freud, 1923, 1933, 1940).

**ID: IF IT FEELS GOOD, DO IT**  The first and most primitive part of the personality, present in the infant, is the **id**. *Id* is a Latin word that means "it." The id is a completely unconscious, pleasure-seeking, amoral part of the personality that exists at birth, containing all of the basic biological drives: hunger, thirst, self-preservation, and sex, for example.

 Wait a minute—Freud thought babies have sex drives?

Yes, Freud thought babies have sex drives, which shocked and outraged his colleagues and fellow Victorians. By "sex drive" he really meant "pleasure drive," the need to seek out pleasurable sensations. People do seem to be pleasure-seeking creatures, and even infants seek pleasure from sucking and chewing on anything they can get into their

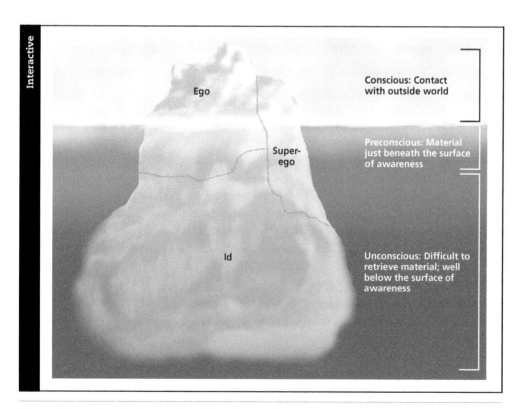

**Figure 13.1**  Freud's Conception of the Personality

This iceberg represents the three levels of the mind. The part of the iceberg visible above the surface is the conscious mind. Just below the surface is the preconscious mind, everything that is not yet part of the conscious mind. Hidden deep below the surface is the unconscious mind, feelings, memories, thoughts, and urges that cannot be easily brought into consciousness. While two of the three parts of the personality (ego and superego) exist at all three levels of awareness, the id is completely in the unconscious mind.

id
part of the personality present at birth and completely unconscious.

mouths. In fact, thinking about what infants are like when they are just born provides a good picture of the id. Infants are demanding, irrational, illogical, and impulsive. They want their needs satisfied immediately, and they don't care about anyone else's needs or desires. (A word of caution: The fact that infant behavior seems to fit Freud's concept of the id is not proof that the id exists. It simply means that Freud came up with the concept of the id to fit what he already knew about infants.)

Freud called this need for satisfaction the **pleasure principle**, which can be defined as the desire for immediate gratification of needs with no regard for the consequences. The pleasure principle can be summed up simply as "if it feels good, do it."

**EGO: THE EXECUTIVE DIRECTOR** People normally try to satisfy an infant's needs as quickly as possible. Infants are fed when hungry, changed when wet, and tended to whenever they cry. But as infants begin to grow, adults start denying them their every wish. There will be things they cannot touch or hold, and they must learn to wait for certain things, such as food. Freud would say that reality has reared its ugly head, and the id simply cannot deal with the reality of having to wait or not getting what it wants. Worse still would be the possibility of punishment as a result of the id's unrestrained actions.

According to Freud, to deal with reality, a second part of the personality develops called the **ego**. The ego, from the Latin word for "I," is mostly conscious and is far more rational, logical, and cunning than the id. The ego works on the **reality principle**, which is the need to satisfy the demands of the id only in ways that will not lead to negative consequences. This means that sometimes the ego decides to deny the id its desires because the consequences would be painful or too unpleasant.

For example, while an infant might reach out and take an object despite a parent's protests, a toddler with the developing ego will avoid taking the object when the parent says, "No!" to avoid punishment—but may go back for the object when the parent is not looking. A simpler way of stating the reality principle, then, is "if it feels good, do it, but only if you can get away with it."

 💬 If everyone acted on the pleasure principle, the world would be pretty scary. How does knowing right from wrong come into Freud's theory?

**SUPEREGO: THE MORAL WATCHDOG** Freud called the third and final part of the personality, the moral center of personality, the **superego**. The superego (also Latin, meaning "over the self") develops as a preschool-aged child learns the rules, customs, and expectations of society. The super ego contains the **conscience**, the part of the personality that makes people feel guilt, or *moral anxiety*, when they do the wrong thing. It is not until the conscience develops that children have a sense of right and wrong. (Note that the term *conscience* is a different word from *conscious*. They may look and sound similar, but they represent totally different concepts.)

**THE ANGEL, THE DEVIL, AND ME: HOW THE THREE PARTS OF THE PERSONALITY WORK TOGETHER** Anyone who has ever watched cartoons while growing up has probably seen these three parts of the personality shown in animated form—the id is usually a little devil, the superego an angel, and the ego is the person or animal caught in the middle, trying to decide what action to take. So the id makes demands, the superego puts restrictions on how those demands can be met, and the ego has to come up with a plan that will quiet the id but satisfy the superego. Sometimes the id or the superego does not get its way, resulting in a great deal of anxiety for the ego itself. This constant state of conflict is Freud's view of how personality works; it is only when the anxiety created by this conflict gets out of hand that disordered behavior arises. Note that despite the id being portrayed as the devil in the example, the id is not "evil"; it is concerned with survival and immediate gratification.

**pleasure principle**

principle by which the id functions; the desire for the immediate satisfaction of needs without regard for the consequences.

**ego**

part of the personality that develops out of a need to deal with reality; mostly conscious, rational, and logical.

**reality principle**

principle by which the ego functions; the satisfaction of the demands of the id only when negative consequences will not result.

**superego**

part of the personality that acts as a moral center.

**conscience**

part of the superego that produces guilt, depending on how acceptable behavior is.

The **psychological defense mechanisms** are ways of dealing with anxiety through unconsciously distorting one's perception of reality. These defense mechanisms were mainly outlined and studied by Freud's daughter, Anna Freud, who was a psychoanalyst (Benjafield, 1996; A. Freud, 1946). In order for the three parts of the personality to function, the constant conflict among them must be managed, and Freud assumed that the defense mechanisms were among the most important tools for dealing with the anxiety caused by this conflict. A list of the defense mechanisms, their definitions, and examples of each appears in **Table 13.1**.

## STAGES OF PERSONALITY DEVELOPMENT

**13.2** Distinguish among the five psychosexual stages of personality development.

💬 So the id exists at birth, but the other two parts of the personality develop later—how much later? When is personality finished?

Freud believed that personality development occurs in a series of **psychosexual stages** that are determined by the developing sexuality of the child. At each stage, a different *erogenous zone*, or area of the body that produces pleasurable feelings, becomes important and can become the source of conflicts. Conflicts that are not fully resolved can result in **fixation**, or getting "stuck" to some degree in a stage of development. The child may grow into an adult but will still carry emotional and psychological "baggage" from that earlier fixated stage.

**ORAL STAGE (FIRST 18 MONTHS)** The first stage is called the **oral stage** because the erogenous zone is the mouth. The conflict that can arise here, according to Freud, will be over weaning (taking the mother's breast away from the child, who will now drink from a cup). Weaning that occurs too soon or too late can result in too little or too much satisfaction of the child's oral needs, resulting in the activities and personality traits

**psychological defense mechanisms**

unconscious distortions of a person's perception of reality that reduce stress and anxiety.

**psychosexual stages**

five stages of personality development proposed by Freud and tied to the sexual development of the child.

**fixation**

disorder in which the person does not fully resolve the conflict in a particular psychosexual stage, resulting in personality traits and behavior associated with that earlier stage.

**oral stage**

the first stage in Freud's psychosexual stages, occurring in the first 18 months of life in which the mouth is the erogenous zone and weaning is the primary conflict.

### Table 13.1 The Psychological Defense Mechanisms

| Defense Mechanism and Definition | Example |
|---|---|
| **Denial:** refusal to recognize or acknowledge a threatening situation. | Renata refuses to acknowledge her son was killed during his recent military deployment. |
| **Repression:** "pushing" threatening or conflicting events or situations out of conscious memory. | Regan, who was sexually abused as a child, cannot remember the abuse at all. |
| **Rationalization:** making up acceptable excuses for unacceptable behavior. | "If I don't have breakfast, I can have that piece of cake later on without hurting my diet." |
| **Projection:** placing one's own unacceptable thoughts onto others, as if the thoughts belonged to them and not to oneself. | Maria is attracted to her sister's husband but denies this and believes the husband is attracted to her. |
| **Reaction formation:** forming an emotional reaction or attitude that is the opposite of one's threatening or unacceptable actual thoughts. | Kyle is unconsciously attracted to Cian but outwardly voices an extreme hatred of homosexuals. |
| **Displacement:** expressing feelings that would be threatening if directed at the real target onto a less threatening substitute target. | Sandra gets reprimanded by her boss and goes home to angrily pick a fight with her husband. |
| **Regression:** falling back on childlike patterns as a way of coping with stressful situations. | Four-year-old Blaine starts wetting his bed after his parents bring home a new baby. |
| **Identification:** trying to become like someone else to deal with one's anxiety. | Samantha really admires Emily, the most popular girl in school, and tries to copy her behavior and dress. |
| **Compensation (substitution):** trying to make up for areas in which a lack is perceived by becoming superior in some other area. | Ethan is not good at athletics, so he puts all of his energies into becoming an academic scholar. |
| **Sublimation:** turning socially unacceptable urges into socially acceptable behavior. | Ryder, who is very aggressive, becomes a mixed martial arts fighter. |

associated with an orally fixated adult personality: overeating, drinking too much, chain smoking, talking too much, nail biting, gum chewing, and a tendency to be either too dependent and optimistic (when the oral needs are overindulged) or too aggressive and pessimistic (when the oral needs are denied).

**ANAL STAGE (18 TO 36 MONTHS)**   As the child becomes a toddler, Freud believed that the erogenous zone moves from the mouth to the anus, because he also believed that children got a great deal of pleasure from both withholding and releasing their feces at will. This stage is, therefore, called the **anal stage**.

Obviously, Freud thought that the main area of conflict here is toilet training, the demand that the child use the toilet at a particular time and in a particular way. This invasion of reality is part of the process that stimulates the development of the ego during this stage. Fixation in the anal stage, from toilet training that is too harsh, can take one of two forms. The child who rebels openly will refuse to go in the toilet and, according to Freud, translate in the adult as an *anal expulsive personality*, someone who sees messiness as a statement of personal control and who is somewhat destructive and hostile. Some children, however, are terrified of making a mess and rebel passively—refusing to go at all or retaining the feces. No mess, no punishment. As adults, they are stingy, stubborn, and excessively neat. This type is called the *anal retentive personality*.

**PHALLIC STAGE (3 TO 6 YEARS)**   As the child grows older, the erogenous zone shifts to the genitals. Children have discovered the differences between the sexes by now, and most have also engaged in perfectly normal self-stimulation of the genitals, or masturbation. One can only imagine the horror of the Victorian parent who discovered a child engaged in masturbation. People of that era believed that masturbation led to all manner of evils, including mental illness.

This awakening of sexual curiosity and interest in the genitals is the beginning of what Freud termed the **phallic stage**. (The word *phallic* comes from the Greek word *phallos* and means "penis.") Freud believed that when boys realized that the little girl down the street had no penis, they developed a fear of losing the penis called *castration anxiety*, while girls developed *penis envy* because they were missing a penis. If this seems an odd focus on male anatomy, remember the era—the Western world at that time was very male oriented and male dominated. Fortunately, nearly all psychoanalysts have long since abandoned the concept of penis envy (Horney, 1939, 1973; Slipp, 1993). The conflict in the phallic stage centers on the awakening sexual feelings of the child. Freud essentially believed that boys develop both sexual attraction to their mothers and jealousy of their fathers during this stage, a phenomenon called the **Oedipus complex**. (Oedipus was a king in a Greek tragedy who unknowingly killed his father and married his mother.)

The sexual attraction is not that of an adult male for a female but more of a sexual curiosity that becomes mixed up with the boy's feelings of love and affection for his mother. Of course, his jealousy of his father leads to feelings of anxiety and fears that his father, a powerful authority figure, might get angry and do something terrible—remember that castration anxiety? To deal with this anxiety, two things must occur by the time the phallic stage ends. The boy will *repress* his sexual feelings for his mother and *identify* with his father. (*Identification* is one of the defense mechanisms used to combat anxiety.) The boy tries to be just like his father in every way, taking on the father's behavior, mannerisms, values, and moral beliefs as his own, so that Daddy won't be able to get angry with the boy. Girls go through a similar process called the **Electra complex** with their father as the target of their affections and their mother as the rival. The result of identification is the development of the superego, the internalized moral values of the same-sex parent.

What happens when things go wrong? If a child does not have a same-sex parent with whom to identify, or if the opposite-sex parent encourages the sexual attraction,

For females, chastity belts like this were occasionally used to prevent intercourse or masturbation. The openings allowed for urination and defecation, but their size and design, such as metal teeth in this one, did not allow for intercourse or masturbation to easily take place.

**anal stage**

the second stage in Freud's psychosexual stages, occurring from about 18 to 36 months of age, in which the anus is the erogenous zone and toilet training is the source of conflict.

**phallic stage**

the third stage in Freud's psychosexual stages, occurring from about 3 to 6 years of age, in which the child discovers sexual feelings.

**Oedipus complex/Electra complex**

situation occurring in the phallic stage in which a child develops a sexual attraction to the opposite-sex parent and jealousy of the same-sex parent. Males develop an Oedipus complex whereas females develop an Electra complex.

fixation can occur. Fixation in the phallic stage usually involves immature sexual attitudes as an adult. People who are fixated in this stage, according to Freud, will often exhibit promiscuous* sexual behavior and be very vain. The vanity is seen as a cover-up for feelings of low self-worth arising from the failure to resolve the complex, and the lack of moral sexual behavior stems from the failure of identification and the inadequate formation of the superego. Additionally, men with this fixation may be "mama's boys" who never quite grow up, and women with this fixation may look for much older father figures to marry.

**LATENCY STAGE (6 YEARS TO PUBERTY)** Remember that by the end of the phallic stage, children have pushed their sexual feelings for the opposite sex into the unconscious in another defensive reaction, repression. From age 6 to the onset of puberty, children will remain in this stage of hidden, or *latent*, sexual feelings, so this stage is called **latency**. In this stage, children grow and develop intellectually, physically, and socially but not sexually. This is the age at which boys play only with boys, girls play only with girls, and each thinks the opposite sex is pretty awful.

**GENITAL STAGE (PUBERTY ON)** When puberty does begin, the sexual feelings that were once repressed can no longer be ignored. Bodies are changing and sexual urges are once more allowed into consciousness, but these urges will no longer have the parents as their targets. Instead, the focus of sexual curiosity and attraction will become other adolescents, celebrities, and other objects of adoration. Since Freud tied personality development into sexual development, the **genital stage** represented the final process in Freud's personality theory, as well as the entry into adult social and sexual behavior.

### THE NEO-FREUDIANS

**13.3** Describe how the neo-Freudians modified Freud's theory.

At first Freud's ideas were met with resistance and ridicule by the growing community of doctors and psychologists. Eventually, a number of early psychoanalysts, objecting to Freud's emphasis on biology and particularly on sexuality, broke away from a strict interpretation of psychoanalytic theory, instead altering the focus of **psychoanalysis** (the term Freud applied to both his explanation of the workings of the unconscious mind and the development of personality and the therapy he based on that theory) to the impact of the social environment. Ⓛ Ⓘ Ⓝ Ⓚ to Learning Objective 1.2. At the same time, they retained many of Freud's original concepts such as the id, ego, superego, and defense mechanisms. These early psychoanalysts became the **neo-Freudians**, or "new" Freudian psychoanalysts. This section briefly covers some of the more famous neo-Freudians.

**JUNG** Carl Gustav Jung ("YOONG") disagreed with Freud about the nature of the unconscious mind. Jung believed that the unconscious held much more than personal fears, urges, and memories. He believed that there was not only a **personal unconscious**, as described by Freud, but a **collective unconscious** as well (Jung, 1933).

According to Jung, the collective unconscious contains a kind of "species" memory, memories of ancient fears and themes that seem to occur in many folktales and cultures. These collective, universal human memories were called **archetypes** by Jung. There are many archetypes, but two of the more well-known are the *anima/animus* (the feminine side of a man/the masculine side of a woman) and the *shadow* (the dark side of personality, called the "devil" in Western cultures). The side of one's personality that is shown to the world is termed the *persona*.

**ADLER** Alfred Adler was also in disagreement with Freud over the importance of sexuality in personality development. Adler (1954) developed the theory that as young,

---

*promiscuous: having sexual relations with more than one partner.

**latency**

the fourth stage in Freud's psychosexual stages, occurring during the school years, in which the sexual feelings of the child are repressed while the child develops in other ways.

**genital stage**

the final stage in Freud's psychosexual stages; from puberty on, sexual urges are allowed back into consciousness and the individual moves toward adult social and sexual behavior.

**psychoanalysis**

an insight therapy based on the theory of Freud, emphasizing the revealing of unconscious conflicts; Freud's term for both the theory of personality and the therapy based on it.

**neo-Freudians**

followers of Freud who developed their own competing psychodynamic theories.

**personal unconscious**

Jung's name for the unconscious mind as described by Freud.

**collective unconscious**

Jung's name for the memories shared by all members of the human species.

**archetypes**

Jung's collective, universal human memories.

helpless children, people all develop feelings of inferiority when comparing themselves to the more powerful, superior adults in their world. The driving force behind all human endeavors, emotions, and thoughts for Adler was not the seeking of pleasure but the seeking of superiority. The defense mechanism of *compensation*, in which people try to overcome feelings of inferiority in one area of life by striving to be superior in another area, figured prominently in Adler's theory (see Table 13.1).

Adler (1954) also developed a theory that the birth order of a child affected personality. Firstborn children with younger siblings feel inferior once those younger siblings get all the attention and often overcompensate by becoming overachievers. Middle children have it slightly easier, getting to feel superior over the dethroned older child while dominating younger siblings. They tend to be very competitive. Younger children are supposedly pampered and protected but feel inferior because they are not allowed the freedom and responsibility of the older children. Although some researchers have found evidence to support Adler's birth order theory (Stein, 2001; Sulloway, 1996), and some have even linked birth order to career choices (Leong et al., 2001; Watkins & Savickas, 1990), other researchers point to sloppy methodology and the bias of researchers toward the birth order idea (Beer & Horn, 2001; Freese et al., 1999; Ioannidis, 1998).

**HORNEY** Karen Horney (horn-EYE) disagreed with Freudian views about the differences between males and females and most notably with the concept of penis envy. She countered with her own concept of "womb envy," stating that men felt the need to compensate for their lack of child-bearing ability by striving for success in other areas (Burger, 1997).

Rather than focusing on sexuality, Horney focused on the **basic anxiety** created in a child born into a world that is so much bigger and more powerful than the child. While people whose parents gave them love, affection, and security would overcome this anxiety, others with less secure upbringings would develop **neurotic personalities** and maladaptive ways of dealing with relationships. Some children, according to Horney, try to deal with their anxiety by moving toward people, becoming dependent and clingy. Others move against people, becoming aggressive, demanding, and cruel. A third way of coping would be to move away from people by withdrawing from personal relationships.

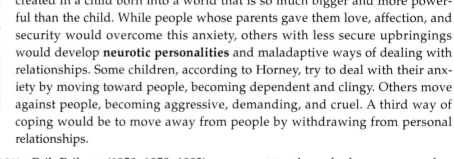

Of the three ways children deal with anxiety according to Horney, which way do you think this child might be using?

**ERIKSON** Erik Erikson (1950, 1959, 1982) was an art teacher who became a psychoanalyst by studying with Anna Freud. He also broke away from Freud's emphasis on sex, preferring instead to emphasize the social relationships that are important at every stage of life. Erikson's eight psychosocial stages are discussed in detail in Chapter Eight. (L)(I)(N)K to Learning Objective 8.8.

 💬 It sounds as if all of these theorists became famous by ditching some of Freud's original ideas. Is Freud even worth studying anymore?

**basic anxiety**

anxiety created when a child is born into the bigger and more powerful world of older children and adults.

**neurotic personalities**

personalities typified by maladaptive ways of dealing with relationships in Horney's theory.

**CURRENT THOUGHTS ON FREUD AND THE PSYCHODYNAMIC PERSPECTIVE**

**13.4 Evaluate the influence of Freudian theory on modern personality theories.**

Although Freud's original psychoanalytic theory seems less relevant in today's sexually saturated world, many of his concepts have remained useful and still form a basis for many modern personality theories, as well as the psychodynamic perspective. The idea of the defense mechanisms has had some research support and has remained useful in clinical psychology as a way of describing people's defensive behavior and irrational thinking. The concept of an unconscious mind also has some research support.

What aspects of psychodynamic theory do you think still have relevance in today's world? Was there one neo-Freudian whose theory appealed to you, and if so, why?

> ▶ | The response entered here will be saved to your notes and may be collected by your instructor if he/she requires it.

Submit

As strange as the idea of an unconscious mind that guides behavior must have seemed to Freud's contemporaries, modern researchers have had to admit that there are influences on human behavior that exist outside of normal conscious awareness. Although much of this research has taken place in the area of hypnosis and subliminal perception (Borgeat & Goulet, 1983; Bryant & McConkey, 1989; Kihlstrom, 1987, 1999, 2001), other researchers have looked at the concept of implicit memory and implicit learning (Frensch & Runger, 2003). **LINK** to Learning Objective 6.5.

This might be a good time to point out a very important fact about Freud's theory: He did no experiments to arrive at his conclusions about personality. His theory is based on his own observations (case studies) of numerous patients. Basing his suppositions on his patients' detailed memories of their childhoods and life experiences, he interpreted their behavior and reminiscences to develop his theory of psychoanalysis. He felt free to interpret what his patients told him of their childhoods as fantasy or fact, depending on how well those memories fit in with his developing theory. For example, many of Freud's patients told him that they were sexually abused by fathers, brothers, and other close family members. Freud was apparently unable to accept these memories as real and decided that they were fantasies, making them the basis of the Oedipal conflict. He actually revised his original perceptions of his patients' memories of abuse as real in the face of both public and professional criticism from his German colleagues (Masson, 1984).

Freud based much of his diagnoses of patients' problems on the interpretations of dreams (**LINK** to Learning Objective 4.7) and the results of the patient's free association (talking about anything without fear of negative feedback). These "sources" of information are often criticized as being too ambiguous and without scientific support for the validity of his interpretations. The very ambiguity of these sources of information allowed Freud to fit the patient's words and recollections to his own preferred interpretation, as well as increasing the possibility that his own suggestions and interpretations, if conveyed to the patient, might alter the actual memories of the patient, who would no doubt be in a very suggestible state of mind during therapy (Grünbaum, 1984).

Another criticism of Freud's theory concerns the people upon whose dreams, recollections, and comments the theory of psychoanalysis was based. Freud's clients were almost all wealthy Austrian women living in the Victorian era of sexual repression. Critics state that basing his theory on observations made with such a demographically limited group of clients promoted his emphasis on sexuality as the root of all problems in personality, as women of that social class and era were often sexually frustrated. Freud rarely had clients who did not fit this description, and so his theory is biased in terms of sexual frustrations (Robinson, 1993).

Although most professionals today view Freud's theory with a great deal of skepticism, his influence on the modern world cannot be ignored. Freudian concepts have had an impact on literature, movies, and even children's cartoons. People who have never taken a course in psychology are familiar with some of Freud's most basic concepts, such as the defense mechanisms. He was also one of the first theorists to emphasize the importance of childhood experiences on personality development—in spite of the fact that he did not work extensively with children.

It has only been in the last several decades that people have had the necessary tools to examine the concepts of the unconscious mind. One can only wonder how Freud might have changed his theory in light of what is known about the workings of the human brain and the changes in society that exist today.

## Concept Map L.O. 13.1, 13.2, 13.3, 13.4

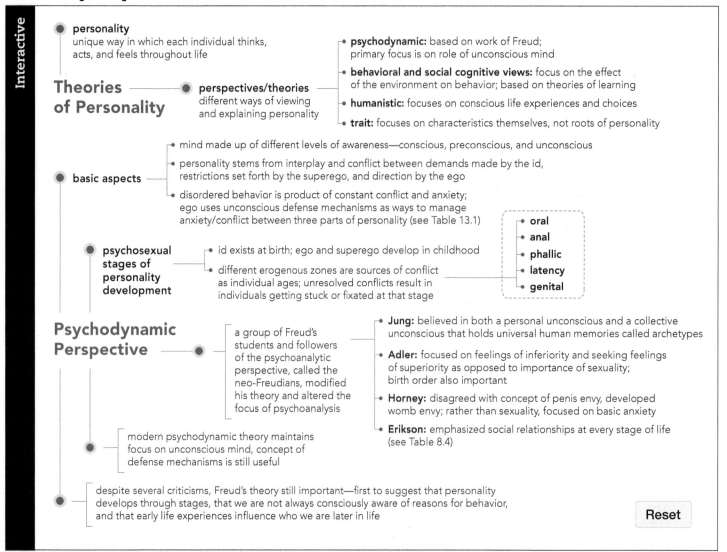

**Interactive**

- **personality**
  unique way in which each individual thinks, acts, and feels throughout life

**Theories of Personality**
- **perspectives/theories** different ways of viewing and explaining personality
  - **psychodynamic:** based on work of Freud; primary focus is on role of unconscious mind
  - **behavioral and social cognitive views:** focus on the effect of the environment on behavior; based on theories of learning
  - **humanistic:** focuses on conscious life experiences and choices
  - **trait:** focuses on characteristics themselves, not roots of personality

- **basic aspects**
  - mind made up of different levels of awareness—conscious, preconscious, and unconscious
  - personality stems from interplay and conflict between demands made by the id, restrictions set forth by the superego, and direction by the ego
  - disordered behavior is product of constant conflict and anxiety; ego uses unconscious defense mechanisms as ways to manage anxiety/conflict between three parts of personality (see Table 13.1)

- **psychosexual stages of personality development**
  - id exists at birth; ego and superego develop in childhood
  - different erogenous zones are sources of conflict as individual ages; unresolved conflicts result in individuals getting stuck or fixated at that stage
    - oral
    - anal
    - phallic
    - latency
    - genital

**Psychodynamic Perspective**
- a group of Freud's students and followers of the psychoanalytic perspective, called the neo-Freudians, modified his theory and altered the focus of psychoanalysis
  - **Jung:** believed in both a personal unconscious and a collective unconscious that holds universal human memories called archetypes
  - **Adler:** focused on feelings of inferiority and seeking feelings of superiority as opposed to importance of sexuality; birth order also important
  - **Horney:** disagreed with concept of penis envy, developed womb envy; rather than sexuality, focused on basic anxiety
  - **Erikson:** emphasized social relationships at every stage of life (see Table 8.4)

- modern psychodynamic theory maintains focus on unconscious mind, concept of defense mechanisms is still useful

- despite several criticisms, Freud's theory still important—first to suggest that personality develops through stages, that we are not always consciously aware of reasons for behavior, and that early life experiences influence who we are later in life

Reset

# Practice Quiz   How much do you remember?

*Pick the best answer.*

**1.** If you are asked to describe your best friends by explaining how they act, typically feel, and what they think about, you would be describing their
   **a.** temperament.          **c.** personality.
   **b.** character.              **d.** mood.

**2.** According to Freud, the _____ mind was the most important determining factor in human behavior and personality.
   **a.** preconscious          **c.** conscience
   **b.** conscious              **d.** unconscious

**3.** According to Freud, which part of the personality is totally buried within each individual?
   **a.** ego                    **c.** id
   **b.** superego               **d.** conscience

**4.** The awakening of sexual curiosity and interest in the genitals is the beginning of what Freud termed the
   **a.** oral stage.            **c.** phallic stage.
   **b.** anal stage.            **d.** latency stage.

**5.** Many of Tao's friends like to dress up on Halloween as devils, vampires, and zombies. According to Carl Jung's theory, what archetype is being expressed?
   **a.** anima                  **c.** persona
   **b.** animus                 **d.** shadow

**6.** Which neo-Freudian believed personality was mostly a product of dealing with anxieties during childhood?
   **a.** Karen Horney           **c.** Carl Jung
   **b.** Erik Erikson           **d.** Alfred Adler

# The Behavioral and Social Cognitive View of Personality

At the time that Freud's theory was shocking the Western world, another psychological perspective was also making its influence known. In Chapter Five the theories of classical and operant conditioning were discussed in some detail. *Behaviorists* (researchers who use the principles of conditioning to explain the actions and reactions of both animals and humans) and *social cognitive theorists* (researchers who emphasize the influence of social and cognitive factors on learning) have a very different view of personality.

## LEARNING THEORIES

**13.5** **Compare and contrast the learning theories of Bandura and Rotter.**

For the behaviorist, personality is nothing more than a set of learned responses or **habits** (DeGrandpre, 2000; Dollard & Miller, 1950). In the strictest traditional view of Watson and Skinner, everything a person or animal does is a response to some stimulus that has been either conditioned, or reinforced in some way.

 💬 So how does a pattern of rewarding certain behavior end up becoming part of some kind of personality pattern?

Think about how a traditional behaviorist might explain a shy personality. Beginning in childhood, a person might be exposed to a parent with a rather harsh discipline style (stimulus). Avoiding the attention of that parent would result in fewer punishments and scoldings, so that avoidance response is negatively reinforced—the "bad thing" or punishment is avoided by keeping out of sight and quiet. Later, that child might generalize that avoidance response to other authority figures and adults, such as teachers. In this way, a pattern (habit) of shyness would develop.

Of course, many learning theorists today do not use only classical and operant conditioning to explain the development of the behavior patterns referred to as personality. **Social cognitive learning theorists**, who emphasize the importance of both the influences of other people's behavior and of a person's own expectancies on learning, hold that observational learning, modeling, and other cognitive learning techniques can lead to the formation of patterns of personality. Ⓛ Ⓘ Ⓝ Ⓚ to Learning Objective 5.12.

One of the more well-researched learning theories that includes the concept of cognitive processes as influences on behavior is the social cognitive theory of Albert Bandura. In the **social cognitive view**, behavior is governed not just by the influence of external stimuli and response patterns but also by cognitive processes such as anticipating, judging, and memory as well as learning through the imitation of models. In fact, you might remember Bandura's work with observation learning and imitation of models from his Bobo doll study. Ⓛ Ⓘ Ⓝ Ⓚ to Learning Objective 5.13.

**BANDURA'S RECIPROCAL DETERMINISM AND SELF-EFFICACY** Bandura (1989) believes that three factors influence one another in determining the patterns of behavior that make up personality: the environment, the behavior itself, and personal or cognitive factors that the person brings into the situation from earlier experiences (see **Figure 13.2**). These three factors each affect the other two in a reciprocal, or give-and-take, relationship. Bandura calls this relationship **reciprocal determinism**.

Take a look at Figure 13.2. The environment includes the actual physical surroundings, the other people who may or may not be present, and the potential for reinforcement in those surroundings. The intensity and frequency of the behavior will not only be influenced by the environment but will also have an impact on that environment.

**habits**
in behaviorism, sets of well-learned responses that have become automatic.

**social cognitive learning theorists**
theorists who emphasize the importance of both the influences of other people's behavior and of a person's own expectancies on learning.

**social cognitive view**
learning theory that includes cognitive processes such as anticipating, judging, memory, and imitation of models.

**reciprocal determinism**
Bandura's explanation of how the factors of environment, personal characteristics, and behavior can interact to determine future behavior.

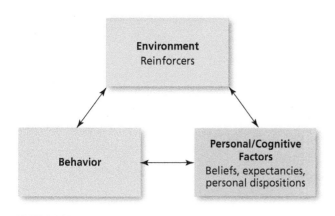

**Figure 13.2** Reciprocal Determinism

In Bandura's model of reciprocal determinism, three factors influence behavior: the environment, which consists of the physical surroundings and the potential for reinforcement; the person (personal/cognitive characteristics that have been rewarded in the past); and the behavior itself, which may or may not be reinforced at this particular time and place.

**self-efficacy**

individual's expectancy of how effective his or her efforts to accomplish a goal will be in any particular circumstance.

**locus of control**

the tendency for people to assume that they either have control or do not have control over events and consequences in their lives.

According to Rotter, what would be the most likely form of locus of control experienced by this young woman?

The person brings into the situation previously reinforced responses (personality, in other words) and mental processes such as thinking and anticipating.

Here's how this might work: Richard walks into a classroom filled with other students, but no teacher is present at this time. (This is the *environment*.) Part of Richard's *personal* characteristics includes the desire to have attention from other people by talking loudly and telling jokes, which has been very rewarding to him in the past (past reinforcements are part of his cognitive processes, or expectancies of future rewards for his behavior). Also in the past, he has found that he gets more attention when an authority figure is not present. His *behavior* will most likely be to start talking and telling jokes, which will continue if he gets the reaction he expects from his fellow students. If the teacher walks in (the *environment* changes), his behavior will change. If the other students don't laugh, his behavior will change. In the future, Richard might be less likely to behave in the same way because his expectations for reward (a cognitive element of his *personal* variables) are different.

One of the more important personal variables that Bandura talks about is **self-efficacy**, a person's expectancy of how effective his or her efforts to accomplish a goal will be in any particular circumstance (Bandura, 1998). (Self-efficacy is not the same concept as *self-esteem*, which is the positive values a person places on his or her sense of worth.)

People's sense of self-efficacy can be high or low, depending on what has happened in similar circumstances in the past (success or failure), what other people tell them about their competence, and their own assessment of their abilities. For example, if Fiona has an opportunity to write an extra-credit paper to improve her grade in psychology, she will be more likely to do so if her self-efficacy is high: She has gotten good grades on such papers in the past, her teachers have told her that she writes well, and she knows she can write a good paper. According to Bandura, people high in self-efficacy are more persistent and expect to succeed, whereas people low in self-efficacy expect to fail and tend to avoid challenges (Bandura, 1998).

**ROTTER'S SOCIAL LEARNING THEORY: EXPECTANCIES**   Julian Rotter (1966, 1978, 1981, 1990) devised a theory based on a basic principle of motivation derived from Thorndike's law of effect: People are motivated to seek reinforcement and avoid punishment. He viewed personality as a relatively stable set of *potential* responses to various situations. If in the past a certain way of responding led to a reinforcing or pleasurable consequence, that way of responding would become a pattern of responding, or part of the "personality" as learning theorists see it.

One very important pattern of responding in Rotter's view became his concept of **locus of control**, the tendency for people to assume that they either have control or do not have control over events and consequences in their lives. Ⓛⓘⓝⓚ to Learning Objective 9.3. People who assume that their own actions and decisions directly affect the consequences they experience are said to be *internal* in locus of control, whereas people who assume that their lives are more controlled by powerful others, luck, or fate are *external* in locus of control (MacDonald, 1970; Rotter, 1966). Rotter associated people high in internal locus of control with the personality characteristics of high achievement motivation (the will to succeed in any attempted task). Those who give up too quickly or who attribute events in their lives to external causes can fall into patterns of learned helplessness and depression (Abramson et al., 1978, 1980; Gong-Guy & Hammen, 1980).

Like Bandura, Rotter (1978, 1981) also believed that an interaction of factors would determine the behavioral patterns that become personality for an individual. For Rotter, there are two key factors influencing a person's decision to act in a certain way given a particular situation: expectancy and reinforcement value. **Expectancy** is fairly similar to Bandura's concept of self-efficacy in that it refers to the person's subjective feeling that a particular behavior will lead to a reinforcing consequence. A high expectancy for success is similar to a high sense of self-efficacy and is also based on past experiences with successes and failures. *Reinforcement value* refers to an individual's preference for a particular reinforcer over all other possible reinforcing consequences. Things or circumstances that are particularly appealing to us have a higher reinforcement value than other possible reinforcers.

#### CURRENT THOUGHTS ON THE BEHAVIORAL AND SOCIAL COGNITIVE LEARNING VIEWS

**13.6** **Evaluate the strengths and limitations of the behavioral and social cognitive learning views of personality.**

Behaviorism as an explanation of the formation of personality has its limitations. The classic theory does not take mental processes into account when explaining behavior, nor does it give weight to social influences on learning. The social cognitive view of personality, unlike traditional behaviorism, does include social and mental processes and their influence on behavior. Unlike psychoanalysis, the concepts in this theory can and have been tested under scientific conditions (Backenstrass et al., 2008; Bandura, 1965; Catanzaro et al., 2000; DeGrandpre, 2000; Domjan et al., 2000; Skinner, 1989). Some of this research has investigated how people's expectancies can influence their control of their own negative moods. Although some critics think that human personality and behavior are too complex to explain as the result of cognitions and external stimuli interacting, others point out that this viewpoint has enabled the development of therapies based on learning theory that have become effective in changing undesirable behavior. ⓁⒾⓃⓀ to Learning Objective 15.4.

**expectancy**

a person's subjective feeling that a particular behavior will lead to a reinforcing consequence.

---

## Concept Map   L.O. 13.5, 13.6

**Interactive**

- for behaviorists, personality is a set of learned responses and habits, gained through classical and operant conditioning

- social cognitive learning theorists emphasize both the influences of other people's behavior and of a person's own expectancies on learning; observational learning, modeling, and other cognitive learning techniques influence personality

  - **Bandura:** concept of self-efficacy; believed three factors were important: the environment, the behavior itself, and personal or cognitive experiences from earlier experiences; each affect the other two in a reciprocal way—reciprocal determinism (see Figure 13.2)

    - in Bandura's **social cognitive view**, both learning (individual and through imitation of models) and cognitive processes (such as anticipation, judgment, and memory) are important

  - **Rotter:** theory based on principles of motivation derived from Thorndike's law of effect; personality is set of potential responses to various situations, including one's locus of control (internal vs. external), sense of expectancy, and preference for particular reinforcers.

**Behavioral and Social Cognitive Learning Perspectives**

Reset

# Practice Quiz    How much do you remember?

*Pick the best answer.*

1. According to the behavioral theory, personality primarily consists of
   a. unconscious forces.
   b. learned responses.
   c. biologically driven traits.
   d. personal choices.

2. Albert Bandura considers _____ as a person's expectancy of how effective his or her efforts to accomplish a goal will be in any particular circumstance.
   a. self-image
   b. self-esteem
   c. self-awareness
   d. self-efficacy

3. You have walked in late to class, and your psychology professor is explaining how one personality theorist sees personality as a relatively stable set of potential responses to various situations. You know immediately that your professor is talking about the theories of
   a. Julian Rotter.
   b. B. F. Skinner.
   c. Albert Bandura.
   d. John Watson.

4. Nina appreciates compliments about her new photography business but really values constructive criticism, as she can then address particular issues. According to Julian Rotter, Nina has a(n)
   a. strong self-concept.
   b. real self.
   c. internal locus of control.
   d. external locus of control.

# The Third Force: Humanism and Personality

As first discussed in Chapter One, in the middle of the twentieth century the pessimism of Freudian psychodynamic theory with its emphasis on conflict and animalistic needs, together with the emphasis of behaviorism on external control of behavior, gave rise to a third force in psychology: the *humanistic perspective*.

## CARL ROGERS AND THE HUMANISTIC PERSPECTIVE

**13.7  Describe how humanists such as Carl Rogers explain personality.**

The **humanistic perspective**, led by psychologists such as Carl Rogers and Abraham Maslow, wanted psychology to focus on the things that make people uniquely human, such as subjective emotions and the freedom to choose one's own destiny. As Maslow's theory was discussed more fully in Chapter Nine, in this chapter the discussion of the humanistic view of personality will focus on the theory of Carl Rogers. A brief overview of the humanistic perspective is also offered in the video *Humanistic Personality Theory*.

**humanistic perspective**
the "third force" in psychology that focuses on those aspects of personality that make people uniquely human, such as subjective feelings and freedom of choice.

**self-actualizing tendency**
the striving to fulfill one's innate capacities and capabilities.

**self-concept**
the image of oneself that develops from interactions with important significant people in one's life.

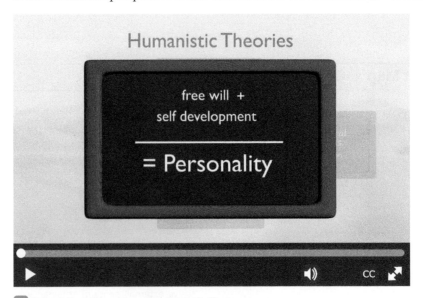

Humanistic Theories

free will + self development

= Personality

👁 **Watch** the **Video** *Humanistic Personality Theory*

"It's always 'Sit,' 'Stay,' 'Heel'—never 'Think,' 'Innovate,' 'Be yourself.'"
© The New Yorker Collection 1990 Peter Steiner from cartoonbank.com. All Rights Reserved.

Both Maslow and Rogers (1961) believed that human beings are always striving to fulfill their innate capacities and capabilities and to become everything that their genetic potential will allow them to become. This striving for fulfillment is called the **self-actualizing tendency**. An important tool in human self-actualization is the development of an image of oneself, or the **self-concept**. The self-concept is based on what people are told by others and how the sense of **self** is reflected in the words and actions of important people in one's life, such as parents, siblings, coworkers, friends, and teachers.

**REAL AND IDEAL SELF**    Two important components of the self-concept are the *real self* (one's actual perception of characteristics, traits, and abilities that form the basis of the striving for self-actualization) and the *ideal self* (the perception of what one should be or would like to be). The ideal self primarily comes from important, significant others in a person's life, especially our parents when we are children. Rogers believed that when the real self and the ideal self are very close or similar to each other, people feel competent and capable, but when there is a mismatch between the real self and ideal self, anxiety and neurotic behavior can be the result. (See **Figure 13.3**.)

The two halves of the self are more likely to match if they aren't that far apart at the start. When a person has a realistic view of the real self, and the ideal self is something that is actually attainable, there usually isn't a problem of a mismatch. It is when a person's view of self is distorted or the ideal self is impossible to attain that problems arise. Once again, how the important people (who can be either good or bad influences) in a person's life react to the person can greatly impact the degree of agreement, or congruence, between real and ideal selves. However, as an individual develops, they look less to others for approval and disapproval and more within themselves to decide if they are living in a way that is satisfying to them (Rogers, 1951, 1961).

**CONDITIONAL AND UNCONDITIONAL POSITIVE REGARD**    Rogers defined **positive regard** as warmth, affection, love, and respect that come from the significant others (parents, admired adults, friends, and teachers) in people's experience. Positive regard is vital to people's ability to cope with stress and to strive to achieve self-actualization. Rogers believed that **unconditional positive regard**, or love, affection, and respect with no strings attached, is necessary for people to be able to explore fully all that they can achieve and become. Unfortunately, some parents, spouses, and friends give **conditional positive regard**, which is love, affection, respect, and warmth that depend, or seem to depend, on doing what those people want.

Here is an example: As a freshman, Sasha was thinking about becoming a math teacher, a computer programmer, or an elementary school teacher. Karen, also a freshman, already knew that she was going to be a doctor. Whereas Sasha's parents had told her that what she wanted to become was up to her and that they would love her no matter what, Karen's parents had made it very clear to her as a small child that they expected her to become a doctor. She was under the very strong impression that if she tried to choose any other career, she would lose her parents' love and respect. Sasha's parents were giving her unconditional positive regard, but Karen's parents (whether they intended to do so or not) were giving her conditional positive regard. Karen was obviously not as free as Sasha to explore her potential and abilities.

For Rogers, a person who is in the process of self-actualizing, actively exploring potentials and abilities and experiencing a match between the real self and ideal self, is a **fully functioning person**. Fully functioning people are in touch with their own feelings and abilities and are able to trust their innermost urges and intuitions (Rogers, 1961). To become fully functioning, a person needs unconditional positive regard. In Rogers's view, Karen would not have been a fully functioning person.

Ideal self    Real self

Congruence = Match = Harmony

Ideal self    Real self

Incongruence = Mismatch = Anxiety

**Figure 13.3**    Real and Ideal Selves

According to Rogers, the self-concept includes the real self and the ideal self. The real self is a person's actual perception of traits and abilities, whereas the ideal self is the perception of what a person would like to be or thinks he or she should be. When the ideal self and the real self are very similar (matching), the person experiences harmony and contentment. When there is a mismatch between the two selves, the person experiences anxiety and may engage in neurotic behavior.

**self**

an individual's awareness of his or her own personal characteristics and level of functioning.

**positive regard**

warmth, affection, love, and respect that come from significant others in one's life.

**unconditional positive regard**

referring to the warmth, respect, and accepting atmosphere created by the therapist for the client in person-centered therapy; positive regard that is given without conditions or strings attached.

**conditional positive regard**

positive regard that is given only when the person is doing what the providers of positive regard wish.

**fully functioning person**

a person who is in touch with and trusting of the deepest, innermost urges, and feelings.

These proud parents are giving their daughter unconditional positive regard.

 💬 What kind of people are considered to be fully functioning? Is it the same thing as being self-actualized?

Although the two concepts are highly related, there are some subtle differences. Self-actualization is a goal that people are always striving to reach, according to Maslow (1987). ⓁⒾⓃⓀ to Learning Objective 9.5. In Rogers's view, only a person who is fully functioning is capable of reaching the goal of self-actualization. To be fully functioning is a necessary step in the process of self-actualization. Maslow (1987) listed several people who he considered to be self-actualized people: Albert Einstein, Mahatma Gandhi, and Eleanor Roosevelt, for example. These were people who Maslow found to have the self-actualized qualities of being creative, autonomous, and unprejudiced. In Rogers's view, these same people would be seen as having trusted their true feelings and innermost needs rather than just going along with the crowd.

## CURRENT THOUGHTS ON THE HUMANISTIC VIEW OF PERSONALITY

**13.8** Evaluate the strengths and limitations of the humanistic view of personality.

Humanistic views of personality paint a very rosy picture. Some critics believe that the picture is a little too rosy, ignoring the more negative aspects of human nature. For example, would humanistic theory easily explain the development of sociopathic personalities who have no conscience or moral nature? Or could a humanist explain the motivation behind terrorism?

Some aspects of humanistic theory are difficult to test scientifically, and it has been suggested this viewpoint could be considered more a philosophical view of human behavior than a psychological explanation. Despite the challenges, how people view themselves continues to be central to many aspects of psychology and the study of personality (Leary & Toner, 2015). Overall, humanistic theory's greatest impact has been in the development of therapies designed to promote self-growth and to help people better understand themselves and others. For example, when viewed through the lens of psychotherapy and therapist variables, there appears to be a consistent relationship between Rogers's ideas of unconditional positive regard and the level of therapist empathy perceived by clients, positively contributing to improvements in clients' self-evaluation and improving clients' relationships with others (Watson et al., 2014). ⓁⒾⓃⓀ to Learning Objective 15.3.

Some of the premises of positive psychology have their roots in humanistic psychology. The term "positive psychology" was first used by Maslow in 1954 when he stressed the need for psychology to focus on human potential rather than on problems (Maslow, 1954). And some have pointed out that related views go back to the work of William James and beyond (Froh, 2004; Taylor, 2001). However, the field of positive psychology itself has emerged more recently and strives to understand how human beings prosper during difficult times and focuses on the science of subjective, individual, and group factors that foster positive experiences (Seligman & Csikszentmihalyi, 2000). There has been debate between the two fields, primarily on the choice of research approaches and some philosophical nuances, but nonetheless, positive psychology shares many facets with humanism and other areas in psychology in its focus on human potential, identification of strengths, and the positive aspects of what it means to be a human (Mahoney, 2005; Seligman, 2005; Snyder & Lopez, 2005; Waterman, 2013).

## Concept Map L.O. 13.7, 13.8

Interactive

### Humanistic Perspective
(referred to as the third force in psychology; based largely on work of Rogers and Maslow)

- **Rogers:** believed that humans are always striving to fulfill their innate capacities and capabilities (self-actualizing tendency)
- **self-concept** is based on an individual's view of his or her real self and ideal self; when close/similar, people feel capable and competent; when there is mismatch, anxiety and neurotic behavior can occur
- **self-actualization** is facilitated through positive regard, especially unconditional positive regard
- when there is congruence between real and ideal selves, one is considered to be fully functioning and capable of reaching the goal of self-actualization

Reset

## Practice Quiz How much do you remember?

*Pick the best answer.*

1. In Rogers's viewpoint, what is the striving to fulfill innate capacities and needs called?
   a. functioning fully
   b. self-actualizing tendency
   c. real self
   d. self-concept

2. What did Carl Rogers mean by the term "fully functioning person"?
   a. Someone who is working to discover his or her real self.
   b. Someone who is working to discover his or her ideal self.
   c. Someone who is experiencing a match between his or her real and ideal self and who is also trusting of their innermost intuitions and urges.
   d. Someone who has discovered his or her self-efficacy.

3. Which of the following statements concerning the self-concept is false?
   a. It is based on what people are told by others.
   b. It is a reflection of the sense of self in the words and actions of others.
   c. It is an important tool in human self-actualization.
   d. It is formed based solely on what a person believes about himself or herself.

4. Karen's parents told her that they expected her to become a doctor, like her father and grandfather before her. They told her that if she chose any other career, they would no longer support her or respect her choice. According to Rogers, Karen's parents were giving her
   a. unconditional positive regard.
   b. conditional positive regard.
   c. unconditional negative regard.
   d. conditional negative regard.

## Trait Theories: Who Are You?

The theories discussed so far attempt to explain how personality develops or how factors within or external to the individual influence personality. These theories may also provide psychologists and other professionals with hints as to how personality may be changed. However, not all personality theories have the same goals.

### ALLPORT AND CATTELL: EARLY ATTEMPTS TO LIST AND DESCRIBE TRAITS

**13.9** Describe early attempts to use traits to conceptualize personality.

**Trait theories** are less concerned with the explanation for personality development and changing personality than they are with describing personality and predicting behavior based on that description. A **trait** is a consistent, enduring way of thinking, feeling, or behaving, and trait theories attempt to describe personality in terms

**trait theories**

theories that endeavor to describe the characteristics that make up human personality in an effort to predict future behavior.

**trait**

a consistent, enduring way of thinking, feeling, or behaving.

## Trait Theories

| | |
|---|---|
| Reserved | Outgoing |
| Concrete thinker | Abstract thinker |
| Easily upset | Emotionally stable |
| Submissive | Dominant |
| Serious | Happy-go-lucky |
| Rule defying | Conscientious |
| Shy | Bold |
| Tough-minded | Sensitive |
| Trusting | Suspicious |
| Practical | Imaginative |
| Forthright | Shrewd |
| Self-assured | Apprehensive |
| Conservative | Experimenting |
| Group-dependent | Self-sufficient |
| Undisciplined | Controlled |
| Relaxed | Tense |

👁 **Watch** the **Video** *Trait Theories of Personality*

of a person's traits. The video *Trait Theories of Personality* describes this perspective in more detail.

**ALLPORT**   One of the earliest attempts to list and describe the traits that make up personality can be found in the work of Gordon Allport (Allport & Odbert, 1936). Allport and his colleague H. S. Odbert literally scanned the dictionary for words that could be traits, finding about 18,000, then paring that down to 200 traits after eliminating synonyms. Allport believed (with no scientific evidence, however) that these traits were literally wired into the nervous system to guide one's behavior across many different situations and that each person's "constellation" of traits was unique. (In spite of Allport's lack of evidence, behavioral geneticists have found support for the heritability of personality traits, and these findings are discussed in the next section of this chapter.)

**CATTELL AND THE 16PF**   Two hundred traits is still a very large number of descriptors. How might an employer be able to judge the personality of a potential employee by looking at a list of 200 traits? A more compact way of describing personality was needed. Raymond Cattell (1990) defined two types of traits as *surface traits* and *source traits*. **Surface traits** are like those found by Allport, representing the personality characteristics easily seen by other people. **Source traits** are those more basic traits that underlie the surface traits. For example, shyness, being quiet, and disliking crowds might all be surface traits related to the more basic source trait of **introversion**, a tendency to withdraw from excessive stimulation.

Using a statistical technique that looks for groupings and commonalities in numerical data called *factor analysis*, Cattell identified 16 source traits (Cattell, 1950, 1966), and although he later determined that there might be another 7 source traits to make a total of 23 (Cattell & Kline, 1977), he developed his assessment questionnaire, *The Sixteen Personality Factor (16PF) Questionnaire* (Cattell, 1995), based on just 16 source traits (see **Figure 13.4**). These 16 source traits are seen as trait dimensions, or continuums, in which there are two opposite traits at each end with a range of possible degrees for each trait measurable along the dimension. For example, someone scoring near the "reserved" end of the "reserved/outgoing" dimension would be more introverted than someone scoring in the middle or at the opposite end.

**surface traits**
aspects of personality that can easily be seen by other people in the outward actions of a person.

**source traits**
the more basic traits that underlie the surface traits, forming the core of personality.

**introversion**
dimension of personality in which people tend to withdraw from excessive stimulation.

**Figure 13.4**  Cattell's Self-Report Inventory

The personality profiles of individuals working in various occupations may be characterized by using such tools as Cattell's 16PF self-report inventory. For example, airline pilots versus writers. Airline pilots, when compared to writers, tend to be more conscientious, relaxed, self-assured, and far less sensitive. Writers, on the other hand, were more imaginative and better able to think abstractly.
Based on Cattell (1973).

## MODERN TRAIT THEORIES: THE BIG FIVE

**13.10**  Identify the five trait dimensions of the five-factor model of personality.

Sixteen factors are still quite a lot to discuss when talking about someone's personality. Later researchers attempted to reduce the number of trait dimensions to a more manageable number, with several groups of researchers arriving at more or less the same five trait dimensions (Botwin & Buss, 1989; Jang et al., 1998; McCrae & Costa, 1996). These five dimensions have become known as the **five-factor model**, or the **Big Five** (see **Table 13.2**), and represent the core description of human personality—that is, the only dimensions necessary to understand what makes us tick.

As shown in the table, these five trait dimensions can be remembered by using the acronym OCEAN, in which each of the letters is the first letter of one of the five dimensions of personality.

- **Openness** can best be described as a person's willingness to try new things and be open to new experiences. People who try to maintain the status quo and who don't like to change things would score low on openness.

- **Conscientiousness** refers to a person's organization and motivation, with people who score high in this dimension being those who are careful about being places on time and careful with belongings as well. Someone scoring low on this dimension, for example, might always be late to important social events or borrow belongings and fail to return them or return them in poor condition.

- **Extraversion** is a term first used by Carl Jung (1933), who believed that all people could be divided into two personality types: **extraverts** and **introverts**. Extraverts are outgoing and sociable, whereas introverts are more solitary and dislike being the center of attention.

- **Agreeableness** refers to the basic emotional style of a person, who may be easygoing, friendly, and pleasant (at the high end of the scale) or grumpy, crabby, and hard to get along with (at the low end).

- **Neuroticism** refers to emotional instability or stability. People who are excessive worriers, overanxious, and moody would score high on this dimension, whereas those who are more even-tempered and calm would score low.

**five-factor model (Big Five)**
model of personality traits that describes five basic trait dimensions.

**extraverts**
people who are outgoing and sociable.

**introverts**
people who prefer solitude and dislike being the center of attention.

Robert McCrae and Paul Costa proposed that these five traits are not interdependent. In other words, knowing someone's score on extraversion would not give any information about scores on the other four dimensions, allowing for a tremendous amount of variety in personality descriptions.

Beyond descriptions of personality, there is a good deal of support for the predictive power of the five-factor model as well. These traits predict many different outcomes in life, such as how we feel about ourselves, our physical and mental health, success in school and work, and various aspects of social behavior (Ozer & Benet-Martinez, 2006). For example, aspects of the five-factor model have been linked to cognition. In older adults, openness is positively related to an individual's general level of cognitive ability. It is also positively related to verbal ability, episodic memory, and fluid intelligence (Curtis et al., 2015). In contrast, individuals lower in conscientiousness but higher in neuroticism appear to be at greater risk for Alzheimer's disease (Terracciano et al., 2014).

**Table 13.2** The Big Five

| High Scorer Characteristics | Factor (Ocean) | Low Scorer Characteristics |
|---|---|---|
| Creative, artistic, curious, imaginative | Openness (O) | Conventional, down-to-earth, uncreative, nonconforming |
| Organized, reliable, neat, ambitious | Conscientiousness (C) | Unreliable, lazy, careless, negligent, spontaneous |
| Talkative, optimistic, sociable, affectionate | Extraversion (E) | Reserved, comfortable being alone, stays in the background |
| Good-natured, trusting, helpful | Agreeableness (A) | Rude, uncooperative, irritable, aggressive, competitive |
| Worrying, insecure, anxious, temperamental | Neuroticism (N) | Calm, secure, relaxed, stable |

**SOURCE:** Adapted from McCrae & Costa (1990).

#### CURRENT THOUGHTS ON THE TRAIT PERSPECTIVE

**13.11** **Evaluate the strengths and limitations of the trait view of personality.**

Some theorists have cautioned that personality traits will not always be expressed in the same way across different situations. Walter Mischel, a social cognitive theorist, has emphasized that there is a **trait–situation interaction** in which the particular circumstances of any given situation are assumed to influence the way in which a trait is expressed (Mischel & Shoda, 1995). An outgoing extravert, for example, might laugh, talk to strangers, and tell jokes at a party. That same person, if at a funeral, would still talk and be open, but the jokes and laughter would be less likely to occur. However, the five-factor model provides a dimensional approach to classifying personality structure (as opposed to a categorical approach), which is consistent with possible alternative approaches to diagnosing personality disorders discussed in the most recent edition of the *Diagnostic and Statistical Manual of Mental Disorders* (*DSM-5*; American Psychiatric Association, 2013). **LINK** to Learning Objective 14.3.

The components of the five-factor model are the topic of many studies. For example, openness has been linked to intellect as a related trait, leading some five-factor researchers to use the label *Openness/Intellect* to recognize both subfactors (Allen & DeYoung, 2016). Both appear to be related to cognitive exploration, with individuals higher in *Openness/Intellect* displaying a greater ability and tendency to pursue, understand, and make use of information than those lower in the construct (DeYoung et al., 2014). When examined further as a compound trait, *Openness* appears to be associated with verbal intelligence, and *Intellect* appears to be associated with general intelligence, nonverbal intelligence, and verbal intelligence (DeYoung et al., 2014). **LINK** to Learning Objective 7.6.

Although regional variations exist, cross-cultural research from 56 countries has found evidence of these five trait dimensions in all primary cultural regions of the world

**trait–situation interaction**

the assumption that the particular circumstances of any given situation will influence the way in which a trait is expressed.

(Schmitt et al., 2007). Furthermore, it appears these dimensions are evident or recognizable not only in most languages and cultures, they are also consistent when assessed by either self-ratings or observers (Allik et al., 2013; McCrae & Terracciano, 2005). This cultural commonality raises the question of the origins of the Big Five trait dimensions: Are child-rearing practices across all those cultures similar enough to result in these five aspects of personality, or could these five dimensions have a genetic component that transcends cultural differences? The next section will discuss the evidence for a genetic basis of the Big Five. The Applying Psychology section at the end of the chapter will highlight research into insights about these dimensions offered by brain imaging and personality neuroscience.

## Concept Map   L.O. 13.9, 13.10, 13.11

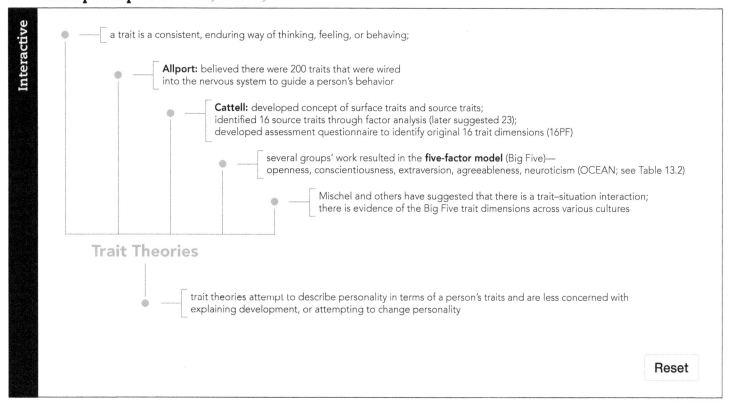

**Interactive**

- a trait is a consistent, enduring way of thinking, feeling, or behaving;

  - **Allport:** believed there were 200 traits that were wired into the nervous system to guide a person's behavior

    - **Cattell:** developed concept of surface traits and source traits; identified 16 source traits through factor analysis (later suggested 23); developed assessment questionnaire to identify original 16 trait dimensions (16PF)

      - several groups' work resulted in the **five-factor model** (Big Five)— openness, conscientiousness, extraversion, agreeableness, neuroticism (OCEAN; see Table 13.2)

        - Mischel and others have suggested that there is a trait–situation interaction; there is evidence of the Big Five trait dimensions across various cultures

**Trait Theories**

- trait theories attempt to describe personality in terms of a person's traits and are less concerned with explaining development, or attempting to change personality

Reset

# Practice Quiz    How much do you remember?

*Pick the best answer.*

**1.** Trait theories are less concerned with _____ and more concerned with _____.
   **a.** changing personality; predicting personality
   **b.** describing personality; explaining personality development
   **c.** predicting personality; changing personality
   **d.** predicting behavior; changing personality

**2.** A colleague at work is asked to describe you to the new manager. Most likely, the traits they will use in their description are examples of
   **a.** common traits.       **c.** source traits.
   **b.** cardinal traits.      **d.** surface traits.

**3.** Cattell's research and use of factor analysis essentially scaled down many, many different ways of describing aspects of personality into _____ source traits.
   **a.** 10       **c.** 5
   **b.** 16       **d.** 2

**4.** In the Big Five theory of personality, "E" stands for
   **a.** empathy.       **c.** external.
   **b.** energy.        **d.** extraversion.

# Personality: Genetics and Culture

 What about genetics? How much of our personality is inherited?

When was the last time you were around a lot of family members other than your own? Was it a reunion? Or maybe when meeting your significant other's family for the first time? Did you notice any commonalities in the way different family members interacted, spoke, or behaved? This section will explore the "nature" side of personality, or the degree that some of our personality is linked to our parents and close relations.

## THE BIOLOGY OF PERSONALITY: BEHAVIORAL GENETICS

### 13.12 Explain how twin studies and adoption studies are used in the field of behavioral genetics.

The field of **behavioral genetics** is devoted to the study of just how much of an individual's personality is due to inherited traits. Animal breeders have known for a long time that selective breeding of certain animals with specific desirable traits can produce changes not only in size, fur color, and other physical characteristics but also in the temperament of the animals (Isabel, 2003; Trut, 1999). As stated earlier in this chapter, temperament consists of the characteristics with which each person is born and is, therefore, determined by biology to a great degree. If the temperaments of animals can be influenced by manipulating patterns of genetic inheritance, then it is only one small step to assume that at least those personality characteristics related to temperament in human beings may also be influenced by heredity.

Animal breeders have an advantage over those who are studying the influence of genes in human behavior. Those who breed animals can control the mating of certain animals and the conditions under which those animals are raised. Human research cannot ethically or practically develop that degree of control and so must fall back on the accidental "experiments" of nature and opportunity, studies of twins and adopted persons.

**behavioral genetics**

field of study devoted to discovering the genetic bases for personality characteristics.

James Edward Lewis, and James Arthur Springer, otherwise known as the "Jim" twins, pictured here with Lewis's adoptive mother. Although separated shortly after birth and reunited at age 39, they exhibited many similarities in personality and personal habits. Although genetics may explain some of these similarities, what other factors might also be at work?

**TWIN STUDIES**   The difference between monozygotic (identical) and dizygotic (fraternal) twins was discussed in Chapter Eight. (L)(I)(N)(K) to Learning Objective 8.4. As discussed previously, identical twins share 100 percent of their genetic material, having come from one fertilized egg originally, whereas fraternal twins share only about 50 percent of their genetic material, as any other pair of siblings would. By comparing identical twins to fraternal twins, especially when twins can be found who were not raised in the samve environment, researchers can begin to find evidence of possible genetic influences on various traits, including personality. (See **Figure 13.5**.)

Many people have heard the story of the "Jim" twins, James Arthur Springer and James Edward Lewis, identical twins separated just after birth. At age 39, Springer and Lewis were the first set of twins studied by University of Minnesota psychologist Thomas Bouchard, who examined the differences and similarities between identical and fraternal twins raised apart from each other (Bouchard et al., 1990).

The two Jims were remarkably similar. They shared interests in mechanical drawing and carpentry, they smoked and drank the same amount, and they even both divorced women named Linda before marrying women named Betty. It is easy to attribute these similarities to their shared genetics. But Springer and Lewis were both raised in Ohio by parents from relatively similar socioeconomic backgrounds—how much of their similarity to each other might be due to those conditions?

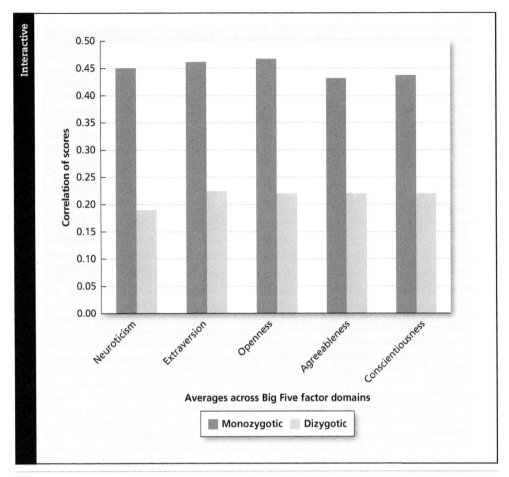

**Figure 13.5**  Personalities of Identical and Fraternal Twins

Identical and fraternal twins differ in the way they express the Big Five personality factors. In a recent study, data from 696 twin pairs suggest identical twins have a correlation of about 45 percent for self-ratings across each of the Big Five factor domains, whereas fraternal twins have a correlation of about 22 percent. These findings give support to the idea that some aspects of personality are genetically based.
Based on: Kandler et al. (2010)

The results of the Minnesota twin study have revealed that identical twins are more similar than fraternal twins or unrelated people in intelligence, leadership abilities, the tendency to follow rules, and the tendency to uphold traditional cultural expectations (Bouchard, 1997; Finkel & McGue, 1997). They are also more alike with regard to nurturance,* empathy,** assertiveness (Neale et al., 1986), and aggressiveness (Miles & Carey, 1997). This similarity holds even if the twins are raised in separate environments.

**ADOPTION STUDIES**   Another tool of behavioral geneticists is to study adopted children and their adoptive and birth families. If studying genetically identical twins raised in different environments can help investigators understand the genetic influences on personality, then studying *unrelated* people who are raised in the *same* environment should help investigators discover the influence of environment. By comparing adopted children to their adoptive parents and siblings and, if possible, to their biological parents who have not raised them, researchers can uncover some of the shared and nonshared environmental and genetic influences on personality.

Adoption studies have confirmed what twin studies have shown: Genetic influences account for a great deal of personality development, regardless of shared or

---

*nurturance: affectionate care and attention.
**empathy: the ability to understand the feelings of others.

nonshared environments (Hershberger et al., 1995; Loehlin et al., 1985; Loehlin et al., 1998). Through this kind of study, for example, a genetic basis has been suggested for shyness (Plomin et al., 1988) and aggressiveness (Brennan et al., 1997).

**CURRENT FINDINGS ON THE HERITABILITY OF PERSONALITY**

**13.13** Summarize current research on the heritability of personality.

One important aspect of genetic studies is the concept of *heritability*, or how much some trait within a population can be attributed to genetic influences, and the extent individual genetic variation impacts differences in observed behavior. ⓛ ⓘ ⓝ ⓚ to Learning Objectives 7.10 and 8.3. Several studies have found that the five personality factors of the five-factor model have nearly a 50 percent rate of heritability across several cultures (Bouchard, 1994; Herbst et al., 2000; Jang et al., 1996; Loehlin, 1992; Loehlin et al., 1998). Personality's relationship to psychopathology is also being investigated via genetic techniques (Plomin & Spinath, 2004). Together with the results of the Minnesota twin study and other research (Lubinski, 2000; Lykken & Tellegen, 1996; Plomin, 1994), the studies of genetics and personality seem to indicate that variations in personality traits are about 25 to 50 percent inherited (Jang et al., 1998). This also means that environmental influences apparently account for about half of the variation in personality traits as well.

Although the five factors have been found across several cultures, this does not mean that different cultures do not have an impact on personality. For more on this topic, see the Classic Studies in Psychology section that follows.

## Classic Studies in Psychology
## Geert Hofstede's Four Dimensions of Cultural Personality

In the early 1980s, organizational management specialist Geert Hofstede conducted a massive study into the work-related values of employees of IBM, a multinational corporation (Hofstede, 1980; Hofstede et al., 2002). The study surveyed workers in 64 countries across the world. Hofstede analyzed the data collected from this survey and found four basic dimensions of personality along which cultures differed.

1. **Individualism/collectivism:** *Individualistic cultures* tend to have loose ties between individuals, with people tending to look after themselves and their immediate families only. Members of such cultures have friends based on shared activities and interests and may belong to many different loosely organized social groups. Autonomy,* change, youth, security of the individual, and equality are all highly valued. In contrast, in a *collectivistic culture*, people are from birth deeply tied into very strong in-groups, typically extended families that include grandparents, aunts and uncles, and cousins. Loyalty to the family is highly stressed, and the care of the family is placed before the care of the individual. Group membership is limited to only a few permanent groups that have tremendous influence over the individual. The values of this kind of culture are duty, order, tradition, respect for the elderly, group security, and respect for the group status and hierarchy.** Whereas the United States and Great Britain are examples of individualistic cultures, Japan, China, Korea, Mexico, and Central America are much more collectivistic.

2. **Power distance:** This dimension refers to the degree to which the less powerful members of a culture accept and even expect that the power within the culture is held in the hands of a select few rather than being more evenly distributed. Countries such

---

*autonomy: the quality of being self-directed or self-controlled.
**hierarchy: in this sense, a body of persons in authority over others.

as the Philippines, Mexico, many Arab countries, and India were found to be high in such expectations, whereas countries such as Austria, Sweden, Australia, Great Britain, and the United States were low in power distance.

3. **Masculinity/femininity:** Referring to how a culture distributes the roles played by men and women within the culture, this dimension varies more for the men within a culture than for the women. "Masculine" cultures are assertive and competitive, although more so for men than for women, and "feminine" cultures are more modest and caring. Both men and women in "feminine" countries have similar, caring values, but in "masculine" countries, the women are not quite as assertive and competitive as the men, leading to a greater difference between the sexes in masculine countries. Japan, Austria, Venezuela, Italy, Switzerland, Mexico, Ireland, Jamaica, the United States, Great Britain, and Germany were found to be masculine countries, whereas Sweden, Norway, the Netherlands, Denmark, Costa Rica, Yugoslavia, Finland, Chile, Portugal, Thailand, and Guatemala were ranked as more feminine.

4. **Uncertainty avoidance:** Some cultures are more tolerant of uncertainty, ambiguity,* and unstructured situations. Cultures that do not tolerate such uncertainty and lack of structure tend to have strict rules and laws, with lots of security and safety measures, and tend toward a philosophical/religious belief of One Truth (and "we have it!"). Cultures that are more accepting of uncertainty are more tolerant of different opinions and have fewer rules. They tend to allow many different religious beliefs to exist side by side and are less anxious and emotional than people in uncertainty-avoiding countries. Uncertainty-avoiding countries include Greece, Portugal, Guatemala, Uruguay, Belgium, El Salvador, Japan, Yugoslavia, and Peru, whereas those that are more tolerant of uncertainty include Singapore, Jamaica, Denmark, Sweden, Hong Kong, Ireland, Great Britain, Malaysia, India, Philippines, the United States, Canada, and Indonesia.

Note that the Big Five personality dimensions of Costa and McCrae (2000) are not necessarily in competition with Hofstede's dimensions. Hofstede's dimensions are cultural personality traits, whereas those of the Big Five refer to individuals.

### Questions for Further Discussion

1. Was your own culture listed for any of these dimensions? If so, do you agree with the personality dimension assigned to your culture?

2. If your culture was not listed for a personality dimension, where do you think your culture would fall on that dimension?

---

## Concept Map **L.O. 13.12, 13.13**

*Interactive*

### Personality and Behavioral Genetics

- behavioral genetics studies how much of an individual's personality is due to inherited traits
- identical twins are more similar than fraternal twins or unrelated people in many facets of personality
- adoption studies of twins have confirmed that genetic influences account for a great deal of personality development, regardless of shared or nonshared environments
- personality factors of the five-factor model have nearly a 50 percent rate of heritability across cultures; variations in personality are about 25 to 50 percent inherited

Reset

---

*ambiguity: the quality of being uncertain and indistinct.

# Practice Quiz How much do you remember?

*Pick the best answer.*

1. What is a major shortcoming in the field of behavioral genetics in terms of their studies on human personality traits?
   a. Behavioral geneticists are unable to conduct controlled research studies on human subjects.
   b. Behavioral geneticists are unable to scientifically validate anything.
   c. Behavioral geneticists are unable to conduct studies on animals, only on humans.
   d. Behavioral geneticists conduct their studies by looking at single individuals over a long period of time, thus slowing the rate at which they can gather data.

2. Which of the following traits or characteristics were NOT found to be more similar in identical twins when compared to fraternal twins in the Minnesota twin study?
   a. intelligence
   b. leadership
   c. tendency to divorce
   d. empathy

3. What, if anything, have adoption studies taught us regarding the relationship between heredity and personality?
   a. Adoption studies are a new area of study and have yet to offer any information on the effects of heredity on personality.
   b. Adoption studies have confirmed that personality can be strongly influenced by genetics.
   c. Adoption studies have not supported many behavioral genetics studies, thus questioning the idea that personality can be influenced by genetics.
   d. Adoption studies have resulted in conflicting findings, with some strongly supporting the influence of heredity on personality while others suggest that heredity has no influence whatsoever.

4. Several studies have found nearly a _____ percent rate of heritability across several cultures with respect to the five-factor model of personality.
   a. 20
   b. 30
   c. 40
   d. 50

# APA Goal 2: Scientific Inquiry and Critical Thinking

## Personality, Family, and Culture

*Addresses APA Learning Objective 2.5: Incorporate sociocultural factors in scientific inquiry.*

Imagine this: You and your family immigrated to the United States when you were very young. Your life, as much as you can remember, has been in the United States. You speak English as your primary language, although your mother and father work hard to maintain the family's cultural heritage and still speak their native language at home. Your mother and father have worked hard to create a safe home, valuing hard work, dedication, and self-reliance.

You are now starting college, and money is tight. Although you have saved money, your family has limited resources to assist you with the newfound challenges of paying for tuition, books, and supplies, all while balancing the demands of home, your part-time job, and keeping your grades up. In short, times are tough.

Your college has started a food pantry for students in need. Although it took a while, you decided to stop by to look at the offerings. The pantry has both prepared and fresh foods, including fruit and vegetables. Although your individual personality acknowledges that external assistance is sometimes necessary, your father and mother would never visit the food pantry, much less accept anything from one.

What challenges might this present to your sense of self?

How might you resolve any conflicts?

This Critical Thinking feature was based in part on the experiences of an actual college student. To learn more about campus food pantries and how some college students are using them, read or listen to the story on NPR, *Campus Food Pantries For Hungry Students On The Rise*, http://n.pr/1R56pSw.

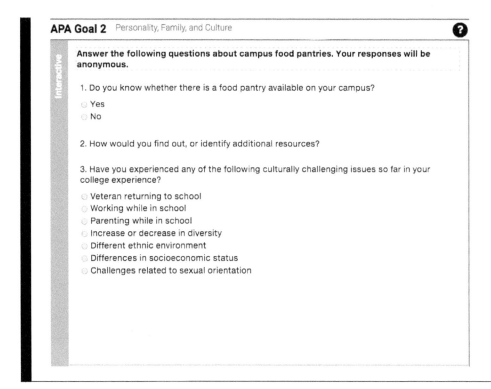

**APA Goal 2**  Personality, Family, and Culture  ❓

Interactive

**Answer the following questions about campus food pantries. Your responses will be anonymous.**

1. Do you know whether there is a food pantry available on your campus?

○ Yes
○ No

2. How would you find out, or identify additional resources?

3. Have you experienced any of the following culturally challenging issues so far in your college experience?

○ Veteran returning to school
○ Working while in school
○ Parenting while in school
○ Increase or decrease in diversity
○ Different ethnic environment
○ Differences in socioeconomic status
○ Challenges related to sexual orientation

# Assessment of Personality

💬 With all the different theories of personality, how do people find out what kind of personality they have?

The methods for measuring or assessing personality vary according to the theory of personality used to develop those methods, as one might expect. However, most psychological professionals doing a personality assessment on a client do not necessarily tie themselves down to one theoretical viewpoint only, preferring to take a more *eclectic* view of personality. The eclectic view is a way of choosing the parts of different theories that seem to best fit a particular situation rather than using only one theory to explain a phenomenon. In fact, looking at behavior from multiple perspectives can often bring insights into a person's behavior that would not easily come from taking only one perspective. Many professionals will not only use several different perspectives but also several of the assessment techniques that follow. Even so, certain methods are more commonly used by certain kinds of theorists, as can be seen in **Table 13.3**.

Personality assessments may also differ in the purposes for which they are conducted. For example, sometimes a researcher may administer a personality test of some sort to participants in a research study so that the participants may be classified according to certain personality traits. There are tests available to people who simply want to learn more about their own personalities. Finally, clinical and counseling psychologists, psychiatrists, and other psychological professionals use these personality assessment tools in the diagnosis of disorders of personality. ⓁⒾⓃⓀ to Learning Objective 14.15.

INTERVIEWS, BEHAVIORAL ASSESSMENTS, AND PERSONALITY INVENTORIES

**13.14** **Identify the advantages and disadvantages of using interviews, behavioral assessments, and personality inventories to measure personality.**

As covered in the last section, the methods for measuring or assessing personality vary according to the theory of personality used to develop those methods. They also vary

| Table 13.3 Who Uses What Method? | |
|---|---|
| **Type of Assessment** | **Most Likely Used by...** |
| Interviews | Psychoanalysts, humanistic therapists |
| Projective Tests | Psychoanalysts |
|   Rorschach | |
|   Thematic Apperception Test | |
| Behavioral Assessments | Behavioral and social cognitive therapists |
|   Direct observation | |
|   Rating scales | |
|   Frequency counts | |
| Personality Inventories | Trait theorists |
|   Sixteen Personality Factor Questionnaire (16PF) | |
|   Neuroticism/Extraversion/Openness Personality Inventory (NEO-PI-3) | |
|   Myers-Briggs Type Indicator (MBTI) | |
|   Eysenck Personality Questionnaire (EPQ) | |
|   Keirsey Temperament Sorter II | |
|   California Psychological Inventory (CPI) | |
|   Minnesota Multiphasic Personality Inventory, Version II, Restructured Form (MMPI-2-RF) | |

according to their response format and the type of data they provide. We will first examine a variety of methods that provide test takers a more structured response format, with the aim of getting data that are more objective.

**BEHAVIORAL ASSESSMENTS** Behaviorists do not typically want to "look into the mind." Because behaviorists assume that personality is merely habitually learned responses to stimuli in the environment, the preferred method for a behaviorist would be to watch that behavior unfold in the real world.

In **direct observation**, the psychologist observes the client engaging in ordinary, everyday behavior, preferably in the natural setting of home, school, or workplace, for example. A therapist who goes to the classroom and observes that tantrum behavior only happens when a child is asked to do something involving fine motor abilities (like drawing or writing) might be able to conclude that the child has difficulty with those skills and throws a tantrum to avoid the task.

Other methods often used by behavioral therapists and other assessors are rating scales and frequency counts. In a **rating scale**, a numerical rating is assigned, either by the assessor or by the client, for specific behaviors (Nadeau et al., 2001). In a **frequency count**, the assessor literally counts the frequency of certain behaviors within a specified time limit. Educators make use of both rating scales and frequency counts to diagnose behavioral problems such as attention-deficit/hyperactivity disorder (ADHD) and aspects of personality such as social-skill level through the various grade levels.

**INTERVIEWS** Some therapists ask questions and note down the answers in a survey process called an **interview**. ⓛ ⓘ ⓝ ⓚ to Learning Objective 1.6. This type of interview, unlike a job interview, may be *unstructured* and flow naturally from the beginning dialogue between the client and the psychologist. Other professionals may use a *semistructured* interview, which has specific questions, and, based on the individual's responses, guidance for follow-up items, similar to a decision tree or flow diagram.

 💬 So an interview is a kind of self-report process?

Yes. When psychologists interview clients, clients must report on their innermost feelings, urges, and concerns—all things that only they can directly know.

**direct observation**

assessment in which the professional observes the client engaged in ordinary, day-to-day behavior in either a clinical or natural setting.

**rating scale**

assessment in which a numerical value is assigned to specific behavior that is listed in the scale.

**frequency count**

assessment in which the frequency of a particular behavior is counted.

**interview**

method of personality assessment in which the professional asks questions of the client and allows the client to answer, either in a structured or unstructured fashion.

**PERSONALITY INVENTORIES**   Trait theorists are typically more interested in personality descriptions. They tend to use an assessment known as a **personality inventory**, a questionnaire that has a standard list of questions and only requires certain specific answers, such as "yes," "no," and "can't decide." The standard nature of the questions (everyone gets the same list) and the lack of open-ended answers make these assessments far more objective and reliable than projective tests (a more subjective form of assessment discussed in a later section of this chapter), although they are still a form of self-report (Garb et al., 1998).

**THE MMPI-2-RF**   By far the most common personality inventory is the *Minnesota Multiphasic Personality Inventory, Version II, Restructured Form* or *MMPI-2-RF*, which specifically tests for abnormal behavior and thinking patterns in personality and psychopathology (Ben-Porath & Tellegen, 2011; Butcher & Rouse, 1996; Butcher et al., 2000, 2001). The current questionnaire consists of 338 statements such as "I am often very tense" or "I believe I am being plotted against." The person taking the test must answer "true," "false," or "cannot say." The MMPI-2-RF has 12 higher-order and clinical scales, 10 validity scales, and numerous scales for specific problems (e.g., family problems, aggression, anxiety, etc.). Each scale tests for a particular kind of behavior or way of thinking. The thinking and behavior patterns include relatively mild personality problems such as excessive worrying and shyness as well as more serious disorders such as schizophrenia and depression. (L)(I)(N)(K) to Learning Objectives 14.10 and 14.13.

Besides assessment of personality or psychopathology, the MMPI-2-RF is also useful for other purposes. In addition to being a valuable tool for mental health settings, it has also been used for vocational guidance and job screening. For specific jobs in high-risk settings, something more involved than simply providing a resume and job application and possibly participating in an interview is likely to be required to identify the most successful applicants. For example, in conjunction with other requirements of the application process, research has supported the use of the MMPI-2-RF in screening potential police officers (Tarescavage et al., 2015).

 💬 How can you tell if a person is telling the truth on a personality inventory?

*Validity scales*, which are built into any well-designed psychological inventory, are intended to indicate whether a person taking the inventory is responding honestly. Responses to certain items on the test will indicate if people are trying to make themselves look better or worse than they are, for example, and certain items are repeated throughout the test in a slightly different form, so that anyone trying to "fake" the test will have difficulty responding to those items consistently (Butcher et al., 2001). For example, if one of the statements is "I am always happy" and a person responds "true" to that statement, the suspicion would be that this person is trying to look better than he or she really is. If several of the validity scale questions are answered in this way, the conclusion is that the person is not being honest. In fact, some validity scales are so good that even experts have a hard time pretending to have symptoms of specific disorders. For example, a group of mental health professionals, with both expertise and significant experience in assessing and treating major depression, were unable to successfully fake major depression on the MMPI-2 (Bagby et al., 2000).

**OTHER COMMON INVENTORIES**   Another common personality inventory is Cattell's 16PF, described earlier in this chapter. Costa and McCrae have further revised their *Revised Neuroticism/Extraversion/Openness Personality Inventory (NEO-PI-R)*, which is based on the five-factor model of personality traits and still being published. The newest version is the NEO-PI-3, which has been made easier to read for use with adolescents and has new norms (McCrae et al., 2005; McCrae, Martin, et al., 2005). You can answer select questions from the NEO-PI for yourself by completing the experiment

**personality inventory**
paper-and-pencil or computerized test that consists of statements that require a specific, standardized response from the person taking the test.

*IPIP Neo Personality Inventory*. NOTE: This is not a brief experiment; allow enough time to answer 122 items. ◉ **Simulate** the **Experiment,** *IPIP Neo Personality Inventory*

Another inventory in common use is the *Myers-Briggs Type Indicator (MBTI)*, which is based on the ideas of Carl Jung and looks at four personality dimensions: the *sensing/intuition* (S/N) dimension, the *thinking/feeling* (T/F) dimension, the *introversion/extraversion* (I/E) dimension, and the *perceiving/judging* (P/J) dimension. These four dimensions can differ for each individual, resulting in 16 ($4 \times 4$) possible personality types: ISTJ, ISTP, ISFP, ISFJ, and so on (Briggs & Myers, 1998). The Myers-Briggs is often used to assess personality to help people know the kinds of careers for which they may best be suited. However, despite the widespread use of the MBTI in business and vocational counseling, it has some significant limitations. The assessment has been questioned for both its validity and its reliability, and it has been suggested that more robust assessments be used, especially in employee selection and assignment situations (Pittenger, 2005). ⓛⓘⓝⓚ to Learning Objective 7.8

Other common personality tests include the Eysenck Personality Questionnaire (Eysenck & Eysenck, 1993), the Keirsey Temperament Sorter II (Keirsey, 1998), and the California Psychological Inventory (Gough, 1995).

### EVALUATING BEHAVIORAL ASSESSMENTS, INTERVIEWS, AND PERSONALITY INVENTORIES

We have discussed a variety of structured assessment techniques aimed at providing objective responses and data. Each of these has advantages and disadvantages. For example, the same problems that exist with self-report data (such as surveys) exist with interviews. Clients can lie, distort the truth, misremember, or give what they think is a socially acceptable answer instead of true information. Interviewers themselves can be biased, interpreting what the client says in light of their own belief systems or prejudices. Freud certainly did this when he refused to believe that his patients had actually been sexually molested as children, preferring to interpret that information as a fantasy instead of reality (Russell, 1986).

Another problem with interviews is something called the **halo effect**, which is a tendency to form a favorable or unfavorable impression of someone at the first meeting, so that all of a person's comments and behavior after that first impression will be interpreted to agree with the impression—positively or negatively. The halo effect can happen in any social situation, including interviews between a psychological professional and a client. First impressions really do count, and people who make a good first impression because of clothing, personal appearance, or some other irrelevant* characteristic will seem to have a "halo" hanging over their heads—they can do no wrong after that (Lance et al., 1994; Thorndike, 1920). (Sometimes the negative impression is called the "horn effect.")

Problems with behavioral assessments can include the observer effect (when a person's behavior is affected by being watched) and observer bias, which can be controlled by having multiple observers and correlating their observations with each other. ⓛⓘⓝⓚ to Learning Objective 1.6. As with any kind of observational method, there is no control over the external environment. A person observing a client for a particular behavior may not see that behavior occur within the observation time—much as some car problems never seem to show up when the mechanic is examining the car.

The advantage of personality inventories over interviews and projective tests (discussed in the next section) is that inventories are standardized (i.e., everyone gets exactly the same questions and the answers are scored in exactly the same way). In fact, responses to inventories are often scored on a computer. Observer bias and bias of interpretation are typically not possible. Across different scoring programs, though, there may be some variability in the diagnostic suggestions provided by the computerized scoring (Pant et al., 2014). In general, the validity and reliability of personality inventories are generally recognized as being greatly superior to those of projective tests (Anastasi & Urbina, 1997; Lilienfeld et al., 2000; Wood et al., 2010).

**halo effect**

tendency of an interviewer to allow positive characteristics of a client to influence the assessments of the client's behavior and statements.

---

*irrelevant: not applying to the case or example at hand.

There are some problems, however. The validity scales, for example, are a good check against cheating, but they are not perfect. Some people are still able to modify their response patterns and respond in what they feel are more socially appropriate ways (Anastasi & Urbina, 1997; Hicklin & Widiger, 2000). Despite the best intentions of the test creators, individual responses to specific questions may also vary, as questions may be interpreted in different ways by different individuals (Lilienfeld et al., 2015), and are very likely to be subject to cultural influences (Kagan, 2010). Other problems have to do with human nature itself: Some people may develop a habit of picking a particular answer rather than carefully considering the statement, whereas others may simply grow tired of responding to all those statements and start picking answers at random.

### THINKING CRITICALLY

Should employers require prospective employees to take a personality test? Why or why not? Would such a requirement make more sense in certain professions, and, if so, what professions might those be?

▶ | The response entered here will be saved to your notes and may be collected by your instructor if he/she requires it.

Submit

### PROJECTIVE TESTS

**13.15** **Identify the advantages and disadvantages of using projective personality tests.**

Have you ever tried to see "shapes" in the clouds? You might see a house where another person might see the same cloud as a horse. The cloud isn't really either of those things but can be *interpreted* as one or the other, depending on the person doing the interpretation. That makes a cloud an ambiguous stimulus—one that is capable of being interpreted in more than one way.

In just this way, psychoanalysts (and a few other psychologists) show their clients ambiguous visual stimuli and ask the clients to tell them what they see. The hope is that the client will project unconscious concerns onto the visual stimulus, revealing them to the examiner. Tests using this method are called **projective tests**. Such tests are performance based and can be used to explore a client's personality or used as a diagnostic tool to uncover problems in personality.

◉ **Watch** the **Video** *Projective Tests*

**THE RORSCHACH INKBLOTS** One of the more well-known projective tests is the **Rorschach inkblot test**, developed in 1921 by Swiss psychiatrist Hermann Rorschach

**projective tests**

personality assessments that present ambiguous visual stimuli to the client and ask the client to respond with whatever comes to mind.

**Rorschach inkblot test**

projective test that uses 10 inkblots as the ambiguous stimuli.

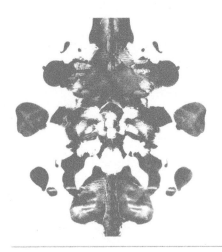

**Figure 13.6** Rorschach Inkblot Example

A facsimile of a Rorschach inkblot. A person being tested is asked to tell the interviewer what he or she sees in an inkblot similar to the one shown. Answers are neither right nor wrong but may reveal unconscious concerns. What do you see in this inkblot?

**Figure 13.7** Thematic Apperception Test Example

A sample from the Thematic Apperception Test (TAT). When you look at this picture, what story does it suggest to you? Who is the person? Why is he climbing a rope?

**Thematic Apperception Test (TAT)**

projective test that uses 20 pictures of people in ambiguous situations as the visual stimuli.

**subjective**

referring to concepts and impressions that are only valid within a particular person's perception and may be influenced by biases, prejudice, and personal experiences.

(ROR-shok). There are 10 inkblots, 5 in black ink on a white background and 5 in colored inks on a white background. (See **Figure 13.6** for an image similar to a Rorschach-type inkblot.)

People being tested are asked to look at each inkblot and simply say whatever it might look like to them. Using predetermined categories and responses commonly given by people to each picture (Exner, 1980), psychologists score responses on key factors, such as reference to color, shape, figures seen in the blot, and response to the whole or to details.

Rorschach tested thousands of inkblots until he narrowed them down to the 10 in use today. They are still used to describe personality, diagnose mental disorders, and predict behavior (Watkins et al., 1995; Weiner, 1997). However, along with the use of other projective techniques in general, their use is controversial given questions about some scoring methods and overall validity (Lilienfeld et al., 2000).

**THE TAT**  First developed in 1935 by psychologist Henry Murray and his colleagues (Morgan & Murray, 1935), the **Thematic Apperception Test (TAT)** consists of 20 pictures, all black and white, that are shown to a client. The client is asked to tell a story about the person or people in the picture, who are all deliberately drawn in ambiguous situations (see **Figure 13.7**). Again, the story developed by the client is interpreted by the psychoanalyst, who looks for revealing statements and projection of the client's own problems onto the people in the pictures.

These are only two of the more well-known projective tests. Other types of projective tests include the Sentence Completion test, Draw-A-Person, and House-Tree-Person. In the Sentence Completion test, the client is given a series of sentence beginnings, such as "I wish my mother ..." or "Almost every day I feel ..." and asked to finish the sentence, whereas in the Draw-A-Person and House-Tree-Person, the client is asked to draw the named items.

💬 But how can anyone know if the interpretation is correct? Isn't there a lot of room for error?

**PROBLEMS WITH PROJECTIVE TESTS**  Projective tests are by their nature very **subjective** (valid only within the person's own perception), and interpreting the answers of clients is almost an art. It is certainly not a science and is not known for its accuracy. Problems lie in the areas of reliability and validity. In Chapter Seven, *reliability* was defined as the tendency of a test to give the same score every time it is administered to the same person or group of people, and *validity* was defined as the ability of the test to measure what it is intended to measure. 🅛🅘🅝🅚 to Learning Objective 7.8. Projective tests, with no standard grading scales, have both low reliability and low validity (Gittelman-Klein, 1978; Lilienfeld, 1999; Lilienfeld et al., 2000; Wood et al., 1996). A person's answers to the Rorschach, for example, might be quite different from one day to the next, depending on the person's mood and what scary movie might have been on television the previous night.

Projective tests may sound somewhat outdated, but many psychologists and psychiatrists still use this type of testing (McGrath & Carroll, 2012). Some psychologists believe that the latest versions of these tests and others like them still have practical use and some validity (Choca, 2013; Meyer & Kurtz, 2006; Weiner, 2013), especially when a client's answers on these tests are used as a starting point for digging deeper into the client's recollections, concerns, and anxieties.

## Concept Map  L.O. 13.14, 13.15

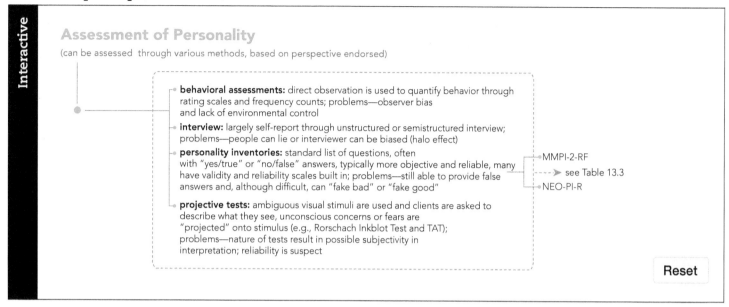

## Practice Quiz  How much do you remember?

*Pick the best answer.*

**1.** Which of the following is an example of a halo effect?
  **a.** Terrance unknowingly tends to rate his new client's behavior slightly higher during testing after noticing the client is wearing a class ring from his own alma mater.
  **b.** James tends to distrust all instructors, regardless if they are new or if he has had them for multiple classes.
  **c.** Madeline always seems to like the last person she interviews for a job because she remembers the most about them.
  **d.** Aileen provided her diagnosis only after conducting her own assessment and compiling information from two of her professional colleagues.

**2.** Frequency counts and rating scales are especially helpful in assessing
  **a.** internal thought processes.
  **b.** observable behaviors.
  **c.** self-efficacy.
  **d.** personal values.

**3.** Which of the following personality assessments might be best suited for objectively identifying abnormal patterns of behavior or thinking?
  **a.** Personal interview
  **b.** MBTI
  **c.** MMPI-2-RF
  **d.** TAT

**4.** What is the function of a validity scale?
  **a.** to determine if a person is giving an accurate response
  **b.** to determine how a subject really feels
  **c.** to help better explain the results of a personality test
  **d.** to offer a diagnosis of abnormal behavior plus a positive therapeutic treatmen

## Applying Psychology to Everyday Life
## Biological Bases of Personality

**13.16 Identify some biological bases of personality.**

In 1796, Dr. Franz Joseph Gall, a German physician, developed a theory of personality traits based on the shape of a person's skull. This theory became very popular in the nineteenth century and was known as *phrenology*. Gall believed that certain areas of the brain were responsible for certain aspects of personality and that the skull itself would bulge out according to which of these traits were dominant (Finger, 1994; Simpson, 2005). As psychology became a scientific area of its own, nonscience-based ideas such as phrenology were soon relegated to the realm of pseudoscience.

How odd, then, that a study by Dr. Colin DeYoung and colleagues (DeYoung et al., 2010) seems to suggest that there are indeed certain areas of the brain associated with certain personality traits. Specifically, DeYoung and colleagues believe they have evidence for the biological seat of four of the Big Five: extraversion, neuroticism, agreeableness, and conscientiousness.

In their study, 116 volunteers answered a questionnaire about their Big Five personality traits. The participants were then subjected to a structural magnetic resonance imaging technique for identifying the volume of specific areas of the brain. One participant was found to be near the group average for personality traits, and that individual's brain image was used as a reference image to which the other participants' scans were compared.

The trait of *extraversion* was associated with a higher volume in the medial orbitofrontal cortex (underside of the frontal lobe, directly above the eyes). This area of the brain is associated with recognizing the value of rewarding information. *Neuroticism* was associated with lower brain volume in several areas responding to threat, punishment, and negative emotions. Reduced volumes were found in the dorsomedial prefrontal cortex (toward the top and middle of the prefrontal cortex) and in the left posterior hippocampus. Neuroticism was also associated with higher brain volume in the middle cingulate cortex (cortical component of limbic system), associated with error detection and response to pain. Areas of the brain associated with the intentions of actions and mental states of others were correlated to *agreeableness*, with the area of the posterior cingulate cortex showing a greater volume in individuals high in that trait and a lesser volume in the left superior temporal sulcus. *Conscientiousness* seemed associated with the left lateral prefrontal cortex, an area located on the side of the frontal lobes involved in planning, working memory, and voluntary control of behavior. (The researchers did look at areas that might be associated with the fifth of the Big Five traits, *openness*, but failed to find any significant differences.)

The advances in personality neuroscience, coupled with better understanding of brain function and brain processes, have also led to new and revised theories of personality. For example, Dr. DeYoung has developed the *Cybernetic Big Five Theory* (DeYoung, 2015). This theory looks at personality through traits that are related to variations in brain structure and also through *characteristic adaptations*, or how someone's life circumstances influence their individual goals, strategies, and personal interpretations (DeYoung, 2015).

Despite the advances offered through personality neuroscience, some researchers urge caution. Some studies have been with small samples. To counterbalance this, researchers need to take advantage of meta-analysis techniques to attempt to synthesize the results of hundreds of smaller studies, as well as conduct studies with larger sample sizes (Yarkoni, 2015). Additional studies and meta-analyses will continue to help us understand the links between personality and the physical structure and functioning of the brain. No skull bulges needed!

## Questions for Further Discussion

1. We use personality assessments to make predictions about employment, marriage, and stability, among other things. What might it mean for the future if a brain scan becomes part of personality assessment?

2. If personality traits are so closely linked with brain structure, what does that say about the plasticity of personality? Are people able to change their traits? Their behavior?

# Chapter Summary

## Theories of Personality

- Personality is the unique way individuals think, feel, and act. It is different from character and temperament but includes those aspects.
- Four traditional perspectives in the study of personality are the psychodynamic, behavioristic (including social cognitive theory), humanistic, and trait perspectives.

## Psychodynamic Perspectives

### 13.1 Explain how the mind and personality are structured, according to Freud.

- The three divisions of the mind are the conscious, preconscious, and unconscious. The unconscious can be revealed in dreams.
- The three parts of the personality are the id, ego, and superego.
- The id works on the pleasure principle and the ego works on the reality principle.
- The superego is the moral center of personality, containing the conscience, and is the source of moral anxiety.
- The conflicts between the demands of the id and the rules and restrictions of the superego lead to anxiety for the ego, which uses defense mechanisms to deal with that anxiety.

### 13.2 Distinguish among the five psychosexual stages of personality development.

- The personality develops in a series of psychosexual stages: oral (id dominates), anal (ego develops), phallic (superego develops), latency (period of sexual repression), and genital (sexual feelings reawaken with appropriate targets).
- The Oedipus and Electra complexes (sexual "crushes" on the opposite-sex parent) create anxiety in the phallic stage, which is resolved through identification with the same-sex parent.
- Fixation occurs when conflicts are not fully resolved during a stage, resulting in adult personality characteristics reflecting childhood inadequacies.

### 13.3 Describe how the neo-Freudians modified Freud's theory.

- The neo-Freudians changed the focus of psychoanalysis to fit their own interpretation of the personality, leading to the more modern version known as the psychodynamic perspective.
- Jung developed a theory of a collective unconscious.
- Adler proposed feelings of inferiority as the driving force behind personality and developed birth order theory.
- Horney developed a theory based on basic anxiety and rejected the concept of penis envy.
- Erikson developed a theory based on social rather than sexual relationships, covering the entire life span.

### 13.4 Evaluate the influence of Freudian theory on modern personality theories.

- Current research has found support for the defense mechanisms and the concept of an unconscious mind that can influence conscious behavior, but other concepts cannot be scientifically researched.

## The Behavioral and Social Cognitive View of Personality

### 13.5 Compare and contrast the learning theories of Bandura and Rotter.

- Behaviorists define personality as a set of learned responses or habits.
- The social cognitive view of personality includes the concept of reciprocal determinism, in which the environment, characteristics of the person, and the behavior itself all interact.
- Self-efficacy is a characteristic in which a person perceives a behavior as more or less effective based on previous experiences, the opinions of others, and perceived personal competencies.
- Locus of control is a determinant of personality in which one either assumes that one's actions directly affect events and reinforcements one experiences or that such events and reinforcements are the result of luck, fate, or powerful others.
- Personality, in the form of potential behavior patterns, is also determined by an interaction between one's expectancies for success and the perceived value of the potential reinforcement.

### 13.6 Evaluate the strengths and limitations of the behavioral and social cognitive learning views of personality.

- Traditional behavioral personality theory has scientific support but is criticized as being too simplistic.
- The social cognitive theory of Bandura and social learning theory of Rotter account for the influences of individual cognitive processes and social influences on personality.

## The Third Force: Humanism and Personality

### 13.7 Describe how humanists such as Carl Rogers explain personality.

- Humanism developed as a reaction against the negativity of psychoanalysis and the deterministic nature of behaviorism.
- Carl Rogers proposed that self-actualization depends on proper development of the self-concept.
- The self-concept includes the real self and the ideal self. When these two components do not match or agree, anxiety and disordered behavior result.
- Unconditional positive regard from important others in a person's life helps the formation of the self-concept and the congruity of the real and ideal selves, leading to a fully functioning person.

### 13.8 Evaluate the strengths and limitations of the humanistic view of personality.

- Some aspects of humanistic theory are not easy to evaluate through research.
- Despite noted challenges, humanistic theory approaches have been effective in therapy situations. The theory has also led to therapies promoting self-growth and increased understanding of self and others.

## Trait Theories: Who Are You?

### 13.9 Describe early attempts to use traits to conceptualize personality.

- Trait theorists describe personality traits in order to predict behavior.
- Allport first developed a list of about 200 traits and believed that these traits were part of the nervous system.
- Cattell reduced the number of traits to between 16 and 23 with a computer method called factor analysis.

### 13.10 Identify the five trait dimensions of the five-factor model of personality.

- Several researchers have arrived at five trait dimensions that have research support across cultures, called the Big Five or five-factor model. The five factors are openness, conscientiousness, extraversion, agreeableness, and neuroticism.
- Traits may be used to predict a variety of life outcomes, including occupations, success in school and work, physical health, and mental health.
- Specific traits appear to be related to different aspects of cognition and intelligence.

### 13.11 Evaluate the strengths and limitations of the trait view of personality.

- Some researchers believe the expression of some traits will differ based on situation or context.
- Factors continue to be researched. For example, some five-factor researchers use the label *Openness/Intellect* to recognize potentially different aspects of cognition and intelligence.

## Personality: Genetics and Culture

### 13.12 Explain how twin studies and adoption studies are used in the field of behavioral genetics.

- Behavioral genetics is a field of study of the relationship between heredity and personality.
- Studies with both identical and fraternal twins, those either raised together or raised apart, assist researchers in investigating the role of genetics and environment on the development of personality.
- Adoption studies of twins or nontwin siblings also provide valuable information.

### 13.13 Summarize current research on the heritability of personality.

- Studies of twins and adopted children have found support for a genetic influence on many personality traits, including intelligence, leadership abilities, traditionalism, nurturance, empathy, assertiveness, neuroticism, and extraversion.
- Cross-cultural research has found support for the five-factor model of personality traits in a number of different cultures.
- Future research will explore the degree to which child-rearing practices and heredity may influence the five personality factors.

## Assessment of Personality

### 13.14 Identify the advantages and disadvantages of using interviews, behavioral assessments, and personality inventories to measure personality.

- Interviews are used primarily by psychoanalysts and humanists and can include structured or unstructured interviews. Disadvantages of interviews can include the halo effect and bias of the interpretation on the part of the interviewer.
- Behavioral assessments are primarily used by behaviorists and include direct observation of behavior, rating scales of specific behavior, and frequency counts of behavior. Behavioral assessments have the disadvantage of the observer effect, which causes an observed person's behavior to change, and observer bias on the part of the person doing the assessment.
- Personality inventories are typically developed by trait theorists and provide a detailed description of certain personality traits. The NEO-PI-3 is based on the five-factor model, whereas the MMPI-2-RF is designed to detect abnormal personality.
- Personality inventories include validity scales to prevent minimization or exaggeration of symptoms, or "faking bad," but such measures are not perfect.

### 13.15 Identify the advantages and disadvantages of using projective personality tests.

- Projective tests are based on the defense mechanism of projection and are used by psychoanalysts. Projective tests include the Rorschach inkblot test and the Thematic Apperception Test.
- Projective tests can be useful in finding starting points to open a dialogue between therapist and client but have been criticized for being low in reliability and validity.

## Applying Psychology to Everyday Life: Biological Bases of Personality

### 13.16 Identify some biological bases of personality.

- Personality neuroscience is a growing area of research, and brain structure differences associated with some aspects of the Big Five dimensions of personality have been identified using structural MRI.

# Test Yourself

*Pick the best answer.*

1. If you are describing characteristics of your child such as irritability or adaptability, psychologists would say you are not describing their personality but rather their
   a. character.
   b. consciousness.
   c. mood.
   d. temperament.

2. According to Freud, the _____ works off of the pleasure principle, while the _____ is often perceived as the executive director of your personality.
   a. id; ego
   b. ego; superego
   c. superego; id
   d. superego; ego

3. You are shocked to hear that two of your coworkers who seemingly hated one another are now getting married. According to Freud, what defense mechanism best explains their prior behavior?
   a. projection
   b. reaction formation
   c. repression
   d. regression

4. Four-year-old Brandon has watched his father as he has mowed the lawn. This year, Brandon has asked for a lawn mower of his own for his birthday. Freud would say that Brandon is beginning the process of _____ as a way of resolving his Oedipal conflict.
   a. compensation
   b. identification
   c. sublimation
   d. denial

5. Your professor explains how all females have an inner masculine side that adds to their personality. This concept is known as a(n)
   a. anima.
   b. animus.
   c. shadow.
   d. source trait.

6. According to Adler, firstborn children with younger siblings tend to be
   a. overachieving.
   b. competitive.
   c. pampered.
   d. filled with feelings of inferiority.

7. Karen Horney's study of one's personality focused on
   a. anxiety during childhood.
   b. biological changes during adolescence.
   c. trait-based characteristics that were present in infancy.
   d. environmental influences through adulthood.

8. Candice believes that fate will help her find the right man with whom to live her life. According to Rotter, she has a(n)
   a. external locus of control.
   b. internal locus of control.
   c. strong self-efficacy.
   d. perceived sense of control.

9. Keisha works hard at her job because she believes it will increase her chances for a promotion. According to Julian Rotter's theory, her effort is an example of what he calls
   a. reinforcement value.
   b. expectancy.
   c. archetypes.
   d. latency stage.

10. What is a primary advantage of the social-cognitive view of personality over the psychodynamic view?
    a. The social cognitive view tries to explain how people become the people they are.
    b. The social cognitive view stresses the importance of early childhood in personality development.
    c. The social cognitive view is fully able to explain all the complexities of human behavior.
    d. The social cognitive view has concepts that can be tested scientifically.

11. Which perspective of psychology focuses on the role of each person's conscious life experiences and choices in personality development?
    a. trait
    b. behavior
    c. humanistic
    d. psychodynamic

12. An old motto of the U.S. Army was, "Be all you can be." This concept fits well with Carl Rogers's theory of
    a. unconditional positive regard.
    b. empathy.
    c. self-actualizing tendency.
    d. the real versus the ideal self.

13. According to Rogers, a mismatch between the real and ideal self
    a. typically motivates individuals to close the gap.
    b. can result in anxiety and neurotic behavior.
    c. causes one to better understand their unconscious motives.
    d. causes an increase in unconditional positive regard.

14. Dr. Hill is constantly late for meetings. She often arrives to her classes 5 to 10 minutes late and leaves students waiting at her door during office hours for up to 30 minutes. Using the five-factor model, which dimension would show a very low score for Dr. Hill?
    a. self-sufficiency
    b. openness
    c. agreeableness
    d. conscientiousness

15. To explain an individual's personality, trait theorists would look to
    a. early childhood emotional traumas.
    b. the kind of love, warmth, and affection given to the person by his or her parents.
    c. the early experiences of rewards and punishments for certain behavior.
    d. the constellation of personality characteristics possessed by the person.

16. Studies of the heritability of personality traits have found
    a. little evidence to support the belief that personality can be passed on by genetics.
    b. evidence to support the belief that personality can be passed on by genetics but only in highly developed countries.
    c. strong evidence to support some personality traits can be passed on by genetics.
    d. strong evidence that personality is passed on exclusively by genetics.

17. As examples of what might be required as parts of specific projective tests, the _____ asks clients to look at a picture and tell a story while the _____ asks clients to report everything they see in an ambiguous figure.
    a. Rorschach; Thematic Apperception Test
    b. MMPI-2-RF; Thematic Apperception Test
    c. MMPI-2-RF; NEO-PI-3
    d. Thematic Apperception Test; Rorschach

18. Which type of assessment would be the most reliable?
    a. subjective test
    b. projective test
    c. personality inventory
    d. observational study

19. The _____ is based on the five-factor model, while _____ is based on the work of Raymond Cattell.
    a. NEO-PI-3; 16PF
    b. MBTI; NEO-PI-3
    c. MMPI-2-RF; MBTI
    d. 16PF; MMPI-2-RF

20. Personality neuroscience is an emerging field offering evidence of a possible relationship between various aspects of personality with
    a. brain structure and function.
    b. the structure and function of individual neurons.
    c. skull shape and size.
    d. neuroticism.

# 14 Psychological Disorders

Have you ever questioned if someone's way of thinking or acting was normal? How do you know if a behavior is normal or abnormal?

After you have answered the question, watch the video to compare the answers of other students to yours.

▶ The response entered here will be saved to your notes and may be collected by your instructor if he/she requires it.

👁 Watch the Video

# Why study abnormal behavior and mental processes?

Because it is all around us, which raises many questions: How should one react? What should be done to help? What kind of person develops a mental illness? Could this happen to someone close to you? The key to answering these questions is to develop an understanding of just what is meant by abnormal behavior and thinking and the different ways in which thinking and behavior can depart from the "normal" path.

# Learning Objectives

**14.1** Explain how our definition of abnormal behavior and thinking has changed over time.

**14.2** Identify models used to explain psychological disorders.

**14.3** Describe how psychological disorders are diagnosed and classified.

**14.4** Identify different types of anxiety disorders and their symptoms.

**14.5** Describe obsessive-compulsive disorder and stress-related disorders.

**14.6** Identify potential causes of anxiety, trauma, and stress disorders.

**14.7** Differentiate among dissociative amnesia, dissociative fugue, and dissociative identity disorder.

**14.8** Summarize explanations for dissociative disorders.

**14.9** Describe different disorders of mood, including major depressive disorder and bipolar disorders.

**14.10** Compare and contrast behavioral, social cognitive, and biological explanations for depression and other disorders of mood.

**14.11** Identify the symptoms and risk factors associated with anorexia nervosa, bulimia nervosa, and binge-eating disorder.

**14.12** Describe types of sexual dysfunction and explain how they may develop.

**14.13** Distinguish between the positive and negative symptoms of schizophrenia.

**14.14** Evaluate the biological and environmental influences on schizophrenia.

**14.15** Classify different types of personality disorders.

**14.16** Identify potential causes of personality disorders.

**14.17** Identify some ways to overcome test anxiety.

# What Is Abnormality?

💬 I've heard people call the different things other people do "crazy" or "weird." How do psychologists decide when people are really mentally ill and not just a little odd?

Exactly what is meant by the term *abnormal behavior*? When is thinking or a mental process *maladaptive*? Abnormal or maladaptive as compared to what? Who gets to decide what is normal and what is not? Has the term always meant what it means now?

## CHANGING CONCEPTIONS OF ABNORMALITY

**14.1** **Explain how our definition of abnormal behavior and thinking has changed over time.**

The study of abnormal behavior and psychological dysfunction is called **psychopathology**. Defining abnormality is a complicated process, and our view of what is abnormal has changed significantly over time.

**A VERY BRIEF HISTORY OF PSYCHOLOGICAL DISORDERS**  Dating from as early as 3000 BCE, archaeologists have found human skulls with small holes cut into them, holes made while the person was still alive. Many of the holes show evidence of healing, meaning that the person survived the process. Although *trephining*, or cutting holes into the skull of a living person, is still done today to relieve pressure of fluids on the brain, in ancient times the reason may have had more to do with releasing the "demons" possessing the poor victim (Gross, 1999).

A Greek physician named Hippocrates (460–377 BCE) challenged that belief with his assertion that illnesses of both the body and the mind were the result of imbalances in the body's vital fluids, or *humors*. Although he was not correct, his was the first recorded attempt to explain abnormal thinking or behavior as due to some biological process.

Moving forward in time, people of the Middle Ages believed in spirit possession as one cause of abnormality. The treatment of choice was a religious one: *exorcism*, or the formal casting out of the demon through a religious ritual (Lewis, 1995). During the Renaissance, belief in demonic possession (in which the possessed person was seen as a victim) gave way to a belief in witchcraft, and mentally ill persons were most likely called witches and put to death.

Fast forward to the present day, where psychological disorders are often viewed from a *medical model*, in that they can be diagnosed according to various symptoms and have an *etiology\**, *course*, and *prognosis* (Kihlstrom, 2002). In turn, psychological disorders can be treated, and like many physical ailments, some may be "cured," whereas other psychological disorders will require lifelong attention. And while numerous perspectives in psychology are not medical in nature, the idea of diagnosis and treatment of symptoms bridges many of them. This chapter will focus on the types of psychological disorders and some of their possible causes. We will focus more on psychological treatment and therapies in the next chapter, Ⓛ Ⓘ Ⓝ Ⓚ to Chapter Fifteen: Psychological Therapies.

**HOW CAN WE DEFINE WHAT IS ABNORMAL?**  Defining abnormal behavior, abnormal thinking, or abnormality is not as simple as it might seem at first. The easy way out is to say that abnormal behavior is behavior that is not normal, abnormal thinking is thinking that is not normal, but what does that mean? It's complicated, as you'll see by considering different criteria for determining abnormality. Before we explore different criteria for identifying abnormality and mental illness, take a moment to reflect on your own beliefs in the survey *Are You Normal*?

These human skull casts show signs of trephining, a process in which holes were cut into the skulls of a living person, perhaps to release "demons" that were making the person's behavior or thinking odd or disturbed. Some who were treated in this way must have survived, as some of the holes show evidence of healing.

**SOURCE:** New York Public Library/Science Source.

**psychopathology**

the study of abnormal behavior and psychological dysfunction.

---

*etiology—the origin, cause, or set of causes for a disorder.

**Survey** ARE YOU NORMAL?

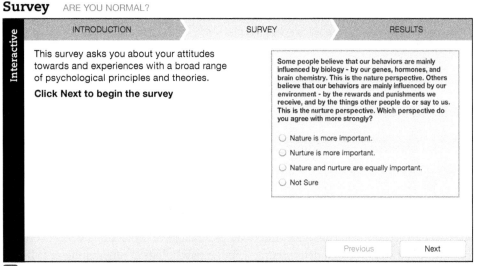

Simulate the **Experiment** *Are You Normal?*

**STATISTICAL OR SOCIAL NORM DEVIANCE** One way to define *normal* and *abnormal* is to use a statistical definition. Frequently occurring behavior would be considered normal, and behavior that is rare would be abnormal. Or how much behavior or thinking deviates from the norms of a society. For example, refusing to wear clothing in a society that does not permit nudity would likely be rare and be seen as abnormal. But deviance (variation) from social norms is not always labeled as negative or abnormal. For instance, a person who decides to become a monk and live in a monastery in the United States would be exhibiting unusual behavior, and certainly not what the society considers a standard behavior, but it wouldn't be a sign of abnormality.

The **situational context** (the social or environmental setting of a person's behavior) can also make a difference in how behavior or thinking is labeled. For example, if a man comes to a therapist complaining of people listening in on his phone conversations and spying on all his activities, the therapist's first thought might be that the man is suffering from thoughts of persecution. But if the man then explains that he is in a witness protection program, the complaints take on an entirely different and quite understandable tone.

**SUBJECTIVE DISCOMFORT** One sign of abnormality is when the person experiences a great deal of **subjective discomfort**, or emotional distress while engaging in a particular behavior or thought process. A woman who suffers from a fear of going outside her house, for example, would experience a great deal of anxiety when trying to leave home and distress over being unable to leave. However, all thoughts or behavior that might be considered abnormal do not necessarily create subjective discomfort in the person having them or committing the act—a serial killer, for example, does not experience emotional distress after taking someone's life, and some forms of disordered behavior involve showing no emotions at all.

**INABILITY TO FUNCTION NORMALLY** Thinking or behavior that does not allow a person to fit into society or function normally can also be labeled abnormal. These may be termed **maladaptive**, meaning that the person finds it hard to adapt to the demands of day-to-day living. Maladaptive thinking or behavior may initially help a person cope but has harmful or damaging effects. For example, a woman who cuts herself to relieve anxiety does experience initial relief but is harmed by the action. Maladaptive thinking and behavior are key elements in the definition of abnormality.

Have you ever questioned if someone was talking to herself and then discovered she was on the phone? What are some other public behaviors that may vary by context or situation?

**situational context**
the social or environmental setting of a person's behavior.

**subjective discomfort**
emotional distress or emotional pain.

**maladaptive**
anything that does not allow a person to function within or adapt to the stresses and everyday demands of life.

In today's growing technological age, can you think of any new criteria that should be considered in defining abnormal behavior or thinking?

▶ | The response entered here will be saved to your notes and may be collected by your instructor if he/she requires it. |

Submit

## A WORKING DEFINITION OF ABNORMALITY

 So how do psychologists decide what is abnormal?

To get a clear picture of abnormality, it is often necessary to take all of the factors just discussed into account. Psychologists and other psychological professionals must consider several different criteria when determining whether psychological functioning or behavior is abnormal (at least two of these criteria must be met to form a diagnosis of abnormality):

1.  Is the thinking or behavior unusual, such as experiencing severe panic when faced with a stranger or being severely depressed in the absence of any stressful life situations?

2.  Does the thinking or behavior go against social norms? (And keep in mind that social norms change over time—e.g., homosexuality was once considered a psychological disorder rather than a variation in sexual orientation.)

3.  Does the behavior or psychological function cause the person significant subjective discomfort?

4.  Is the thought process or behavior maladaptive, or does it result in an inability to function?

5.  Does the thought process or behavior cause the person to be dangerous to self or others, as in the case of someone who tries to commit suicide or who attacks other people without reason?

Abnormal thinking or behavior that includes at least two of these five criteria is perhaps best classified by the term **psychological disorder**, which is defined as any pattern of behavior or psychological functioning that causes people significant distress, causes them to harm themselves or others, or harms their ability to function in daily life.

Before moving on, it is important to clarify how the term *abnormality* is different from the term *insanity*. Only psychological professionals can diagnose disorders and determine the best course of treatment for someone who suffers from mental illness. Lawyers and judges are sometimes charged with determining how the law should address crimes committed under the influence of mental illness. Psychologists and psychiatrists determine whether certain thinking or behavior is abnormal, but they do not decide whether a certain person is insane. In the United States, *insanity* is not a psychological term; it is a legal term used to argue that a mentally ill person who has committed a crime should not be held responsible for his or her actions because that person was unable to understand the difference between right and wrong at the time of the offense. This argument is called the *insanity defense*.

## MODELS OF ABNORMALITY

**14.2** Identify models used to explain psychological disorders.

 What causes psychological disorders?

**psychological disorder**

any pattern of behavior or thinking that causes people significant distress, causes them to harm others, or harms their ability to function in daily life.

Recognition of abnormal behavior and thinking depends on the "lens," or perspective, from which it is viewed. Different perspectives determine how the disordered behavior or thinking is explained. And as we will see in Chapter Fifteen, those same perspectives influence how psychological disorders are treated.

**THE BIOLOGICAL MODEL: MEDICAL CAUSES FOR PSYCHOLOGICAL DISORDERS**   The **biological model** proposes that psychological disorders have a biological or medical cause (Gamwell & Tomes, 1995). This model explains disorders such as anxiety, depression, and schizophrenia as caused by faulty neurotransmitter systems, genetic problems, brain damage and dysfunction, or some combination of those causes. For example, as you may recall from the discussion of trait theory and the five-factor theory of personality traits, (L)(I)(N)K to Learning Objectives 13.10, 13.11, a growing body of evidence suggests that basic personality traits are as much influenced by genetic inheritance as they are by experience and upbringing, even across cultures (Bouchard, 1994; Herbst et al., 2000; Jang et al., 1996; Loehlin, 1992; Loehlin et al., 1998). One of the Big Five factors was neuroticism, for example, and it is easy to see how someone who scores high in neuroticism would be at greater risk for anxiety-based disorders.

**THE PSYCHOLOGICAL MODELS**   Although biological explanations of psychological disorders are influential, they are not the only ways or even the first ways in which disorders are explained. Several different theories of personality were discussed in Chapter Thirteen. These theories of personality can be used to describe and explain the formation of not only personality but disordered thinking, behavior, and abnormal personality as well.

**PSYCHODYNAMIC VIEW: HIDING PROBLEMS**   For instance, the psychodynamic model, based on the work of Freud and his followers, (L)(I)(N)K to Learning Objectives 13.3, 13.4, explains disordered thinking and behavior as the result of repressing one's threatening thoughts, memories, and concerns in the unconscious mind (Carducci, 1998). These repressed thoughts and urges try to resurface, and disordered functioning develops as a way of keeping the thoughts repressed. According to this view, a woman who has unacceptable thoughts of sleeping with her brother-in-law might feel "dirty" and be compelled to wash her hands every time those thoughts threaten to become conscious, ridding herself symbolically of the "dirty" thoughts.

**BEHAVIORISM: LEARNING PROBLEMS**   Behaviorists, who define personality as a set of learned responses, have no trouble explaining disordered behavior as being learned just like normal behavior (Skinner, 1971; Watson, 1913). For example, when Emma was a small child, a spider dropped onto her leg, causing her to scream and react with fear. Her mother made a big fuss over her, giving her lots of attention. Each time Emma saw a spider after this, she screamed again, drawing attention to herself. Behaviorists would say that Emma's fear of the spider was classically conditioned, and her screaming reaction was positively reinforced by all the attention. (L)(I)(N)K to Learning Objectives 5.2 and 5.5.

**COGNITIVE PERSPECTIVE: THINKING PROBLEMS**   **Cognitive psychologists,** who study the way people think, remember, and mentally organize information, see maladaptive functioning as resulting from illogical thinking patterns (Mora, 1985). A cognitive psychologist might explain Emma's fear of spiders as distorted thinking: "All spiders are vicious and will bite me, and I will die!" Emma's particular thinking patterns put her at a higher risk of depression and anxiety than those of a person who thinks more logically.

**THE SOCIOCULTURAL PERSPECTIVE**   What's normal in one culture may be abnormal in another culture. In the **sociocultural perspective** of abnormality, abnormal thinking or behavior (as well as normal) is seen as the product of behavioral shaping within the context of family influences, the social group to which one belongs, and the culture within which the family and social group exist. In particular, cultural differences in abnormal thoughts or actions must be addressed when psychological professionals are attempting to assess and treat members of a culture different from that of the professional. **Cultural relativity** is a term that refers to the need to consider the unique characteristics of the

**biological model**

model of explaining thinking or behavior as caused by biological changes in the chemical, structural, or genetic systems of the body.

**cognitive psychologists**

psychologists who study the way people think, remember, and mentally organize information.

**sociocultural perspective**

perspective that focuses on the relationship between social behavior and culture; in psychopathology, perspective in which abnormal thinking and behavior (as well as normal) is seen as the product of learning and shaping within the context of the family, the social group to which one belongs, and the culture within which the family and social group exist.

**cultural relativity**

the need to consider the unique characteristics of the culture in which behavior takes place.

culture in which the person with a disorder was nurtured to be able to correctly diagnose and treat the disorder (Castillo, 1997). For example, in most traditional Asian cultures, mental illness is often seen as a shameful thing that brings disgrace to one's family. It may be seen as something inherited and, therefore, something that would hurt the marriage chances of other family members, or it may be seen as stemming from something the family's ancestors did wrong in the past (Ritts, 1999; Ying, 1990). This leads many Asian people suffering from disorders that would be labeled as depression or even schizophrenia to report bodily symptoms rather than emotional or mental ones, because bodily ailments are more socially acceptable (Fedoroff & McFarlane, 1998; Lee, 1995; Ritts, 1999).

The conceptualization of culture and its influences on psychological function and disorders has been explained by three concepts: **cultural syndromes**, *cultural idioms of distress*, and *cultural explanations or perceived cause* (American Psychiatric Association, 2013). Cultural syndromes may or may not be recognized as an illness within the culture but are nonetheless recognizable as a distinct set of symptoms or characteristics of distress. Cultural idioms of distress refer to terms or phrases used to describe suffering or distress within a given cultural context. And cultural explanations or perceived cause are culturally defined ways of explaining the source or cause of symptoms or illness (American Psychiatric Association, 2013).

It is important to take into account other background and influential factors such as socioeconomic status and education level. Another area of awareness should be primary language and, if applicable, degree of acculturation (adapting to or merging with another culture). Psychosocial functioning has been part of the diagnostic process for some time now, but traditionally, greater attention has been paid to specifically identifying symptoms of pathology rather than focusing on the environmental factors that influence an individual's overall level of functioning (Ro & Clark, 2009). For example, in one study, college students of Mexican heritage with migrant farming backgrounds reported more symptoms of anxiety and depression as compared to nonmigrant college students of Mexican heritage (Mejía & McCarthy, 2010). The nature of migrant farming poses different stressors than those faced by nonmigrant families.

A migrant farming background has been found to be related to increased symptoms of anxiety and depression among college students of Mexican heritage when compared to those without a migrant background.

**cultural syndromes**

sets of particular symptoms of distress found in particular cultures, which may or may not be recognized as an illness within the culture.

**biopsychosocial model**

perspective in which abnormal thinking or behavior is seen as the result of the combined and interacting forces of biological, psychological, social, and cultural influences.

**BIOPSYCHOSOCIAL PERSPECTIVE: ALL OF THE ABOVE** In recent years, the biological, psychological, and sociocultural influences on abnormality are no longer seen as independent causes. Instead, these influences interact with one another to cause the various forms of disorders. For example, a person may have a genetically inherited tendency for a type of disorder, such as anxiety, but may not develop a full-blown disorder unless the family and social environments produce the right stressors at the right time in development. We will see later how this idea specifically applies to a theory of schizophrenia. How accepting a particular culture is of a specific disorder will also play a part in determining the exact degree and form that disorder might take. This is known as the **biopsychosocial model** of disorder, which has become a very influential way to view the connection between mind and body.

### DIAGNOSING AND CLASSIFYING DISORDERS

**14.3** Describe how psychological disorders are diagnosed and classified.

Have you ever asked a young child, or remember from being one yourself, "what's wrong?" when they reported not feeling well? If so, you likely received a variety of answers describing their tummy ache, ouchie, or booboo. And in turn, you may have not known exactly what was wrong due to differences in their descriptive language and yours, especially when you could not see where or why they were hurting. The same applies to understanding and treating psychological disorders. Having a common set of terms and systematic way of describing psychological and behavioral symptoms is vital to not only correct identification and diagnosis but also in communication among and between psychological professionals and other health-care providers.

**THE DSM-5** One international resource is the World Health Organization's (WHO's) *International Classification of Diseases* (ICD), currently in its tenth edition (*ICD-10*). In the United States, the prevalent resource to help psychological professionals diagnose psychological disorders has been the *Diagnostic and Statistical Manual of Mental Disorders* (*DSM*), first published in 1952. The *DSM* has been revised multiple times as our knowledge and ways of thinking about psychological disorders have changed. The most recent version, which was released in 2013, is the *Diagnostic and Statistical Manual of Mental Disorders, Fifth Edition* (*DSM-5*; American Psychiatric Association, 2013). It also includes changes in organization of disorders, modifications in terminology used to describe disorders and their symptoms, and discusses the possibility of dimensional assessments for some disorders in future versions of the manual. The *DSM* has been useful in providing clinicians with descriptions and criteria for diagnosing mental disorders, but it has not been without its share of controversy, as the video *Diagnosing and Classifying Disorders: The DSM-5* explains.

👁 **Watch** the **Video** *Diagnosing and Classifying Disorders: The DSM -5*

The *DSM-5* describes about 250 different psychological disorders. Each disorder is described in terms of its symptoms, the typical path the disorder takes as it progresses, and a checklist of specific criteria that must be met in order for the diagnosis of that disorder to be made. Whereas previous editions of the manual divided disorders and relevant facts about the person being diagnosed along five different categories, or axes, the *DSM-5* uses a single axis for all disorders, with provisions for also noting significant and relevant facts about the individual (American Psychiatric Association, 2013).

A few of the 20 categories of disorders that can be diagnosed include depressive disorders, anxiety disorders, schizophrenia spectrum and other psychotic disorders, feeding and eating disorders, and neurodevelopmental disorders such as ADHD (American Psychiatric Association, 2013). Other categories include personality disorders, intellectual disability, trauma- and stressor-related disorders, and obsessive-compulsive and related disorders.

While the diagnosis of psychological disorders into categories, based on signs and symptoms, has been the prevalent approach for many years, it is not the only way to think about psychological disorders. In fact, continuing advances in neuroimaging, genetics, and cognitive science have led the National Institute of Mental Health (NIMH) to call for a change in the way we think about and study disorders through the launch of their Research Domain Criteria (RDoC) project. This project promotes research that incorporates all of these advances, as well as other types of information, to provide a knowledge base for a new system of classifying psychological disorders (Insel, 2013). The RDoC research matrix is a framework consisting of several domains, each containing certain measurable and related ideas or constructs. For example, one domain is "negative valence systems" and

**Figure 14.1 RDoC Research Matrix Example**
Hypothetical application of the RDoC approach. Individuals with a variety of symptom-based anxiety disorders are
examined with different methods, and across different areas of investigation, to identify specific data-based clusters and categories for diagnosis.

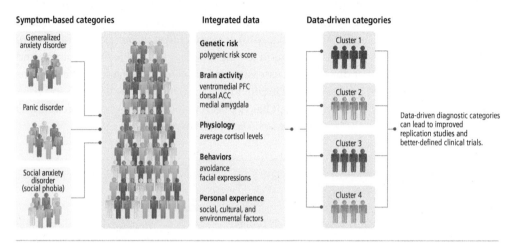

**Figure 14.1**   RDoC Research Matrix Example

**SOURCE**: Based on and adapted from Insel & Cuthbert, 2015, and information from the RDoC Matrix,
http://www.nimh.nih.gov/research-priorities/rdoc/constructs/rdoc-matrix.shtml

contains the constructs fear, anxiety, and loss, among others. The purpose of the matrix is
to provide a means by which disorders may be better conceptualized and measured, based
on more modern research approaches in genetics and neuroscience in addition to those of
the behavioral sciences (Cuthbert, 2014; Insel & Cuthbert, 2015; see **Figure 14.1**).

## HOW COMMON ARE PSYCHOLOGICAL DISORDERS?

 💬 That sounds like a lot of possible disorders, but most people
don't get these problems, right?

Actually, psychological disorders are more common than most people might think.
Estimates of prevalence can vary based on the survey methodology, groups used, and the
questions being asked. For example, different analyses of data from the same survey suggest that anywhere from 26.2 to 32.4 percent of American adults over age 18 suffer from a
mental disorder (Harvard Medical School, Department of Health Care Policy, 2007; Kessler
et al., 2005). More recently, data from the *National Survey on Drug Use and Health* reveals
about 43.6 million American adults over age 18, or 18.1 percent, experienced some kind of
mental illness in 2014 (excluding developmental and substance use disorders). Fortunately,
the same survey revealed only about 4.1 percent of American adults had a serious mental
disorder (Center for Behavioral Health Statistics and Quality, 2015). Overall, it
appears that more than 1 in 5 American adults experience a psychological disorder in any given year.

Statistically, mental disorders are one of the leading causes of disability in
the United States and Canada (National Institute of Mental Health, 2010). In fact,
it is quite common for people to suffer from more than one mental disorder at a
time, such as a person with depression who also has a substance-abuse disorder
or a person with an anxiety disorder who also suffers from sleep disorders. For
example, in 2014, of the 20.2 million American adults that had a substance use
disorder, approximately 39.1 percent met criteria for another psychological disorder (Center for Behavioral Health Statistics and Quality, 2015). **Table 14.1** has
percentages of selected psychological disorders in the United States. Please note
the most recent *National Survey on Drug Use and Health* data does not provide
prevalence information for all of the different disorders. The data in this table is
based on earlier estimates.

Statistically speaking, about one out of every five of the people
in this crowd probably suffers from some form of psychological
disorder.

**Table 14.1**  Yearly Occurrence of Psychological Disorders in the United States

| CATEGORY OF DISORDER | SPECIFIC DISORDER | PERCENTAGE OF U.S. POPULATION AND NUMBER AFFECTED* |
|---|---|---|
| Bipolar and Depressive disorders | All types | 9.5% or 22.3 million |
| | Major depressive disorder | 6.7% or 15.7 million |
| | Persistent depressive disorder (dysthymia) | 1.5% or 3.5 million |
| | Bipolar disorder | 2.6% or 6.1 million |
| Anxiety, Obsessive-Compulsive, and Trauma-Related disorders | All types | 18.1% or 42.5 million |
| | Specific phobia | 8.7% or 20.4 million |
| | Social anxiety disorder (social phobia) | 6.8% or 16 million |
| | Panic disorder | 2.7% or 6.3 million |
| | Agoraphobia | 0.8% or 1.9 million |
| | Generalized anxiety disorder | 3.1% or 7.3 million |
| | Obsessive-compulsive | 1% or 2.3 million |
| | disorder | 3.5% or 8.2 million |
| | Posttraumatic stress disorder | |
| Schizophrenia | All types | 1.1% or 2.6 million |

*Percentage of adults over age 18 affected annually and approximate number within the population based on 2010 United States Census data.
Adapted from National Institute of Mental Health (2016). Table uses terminology from both the *DSM-IV* and *DSM-5* (American Psychiatric Association, 2000, 2013).

**THE PROS AND CONS OF LABELS**  With its lists of disorders and their corresponding symptoms, the *DSM-5* helps psychological professionals diagnose patients and provide those patients with labels that explain their conditions. In the world of psychological diagnosis and treatment, labels like *depression, anxiety*, and *schizophrenia* can be very helpful: They make up a common language in the mental health community, allowing psychological professionals to communicate with each other clearly and efficiently. Labels establish distinct diagnostic categories that all professionals recognize and understand, and they help patients receive effective treatment.

However, labels can also be dangerous—or, at the very least, overly prejudicial. In 1972, researcher David Rosenhan asked healthy participants to enter psychiatric hospitals and complain that they were hearing voices. All of the participants, whom Rosenhan called "pseudopatients," were admitted into the hospitals and diagnosed with either schizophrenia or manic depression (now called bipolar disorder). Once the pseudopatients were admitted, they stopped pretending to be ill and acted as they normally would, but the hospital staff's interpretation of the pseudopatients' normal behavior was skewed by the label of mental illness. For example, hospital workers described one pseudopatient's relatively normal relationships with family and friends as evidence of a psychological disorder, and another pseudopatient's note-taking habits were considered to be a pathological behavior. The pseudopatients had been diagnosed and labeled, and those labels stuck, even when actual symptoms of mental illness disappeared. Rosenhan concluded that psychological labels are long-lasting and powerful, affecting not only how other people see mental patients but how patients see themselves (Rosenhan, 1973).

Before describing the various categories and types of disorders, here is a word of caution: It's very easy to see oneself in these disorders. Medical students often become convinced that they have every one of the symptoms for some rare, exotic disease they have been studying. Psychology students studying abnormal behavior can also become convinced that they have some mental disorder, a problem that can be called "psychology student's syndrome." The problem is that so many psychological disorders are really ordinary variations in human behavior taken to an extreme. For example, some people are natural-born worriers. They look for things that can go wrong around every corner. That doesn't make them disordered—it makes them pessimistic worriers. Remember, it doesn't become a disorder until the worrying causes them significant distress, causes them to harm themselves or others, or harms their ability to function in everyday life. So if you start "seeing" yourself or even your friends and family in any of the following discussions, don't panic—all of you are *probably* okay.

## Concept Map L.O. 14.1, 14.2, 14.3

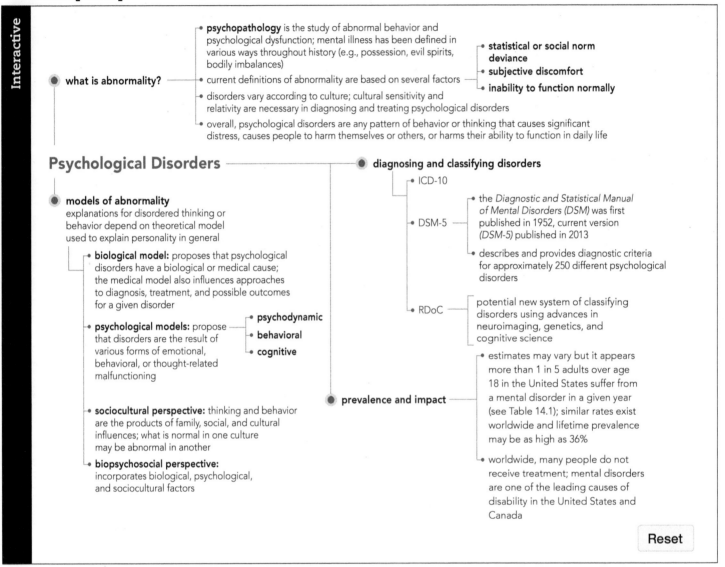

**Interactive**

**what is abnormality?**

- **psychopathology** is the study of abnormal behavior and psychological dysfunction; mental illness has been defined in various ways throughout history (e.g., possession, evil spirits, bodily imbalances)
- current definitions of abnormality are based on several factors
  - statistical or social norm deviance
  - subjective discomfort
  - inability to function normally
- disorders vary according to culture; cultural sensitivity and relativity are necessary in diagnosing and treating psychological disorders
- overall, psychological disorders are any pattern of behavior or thinking that causes significant distress, causes people to harm themselves or others, or harms their ability to function in daily life

## Psychological Disorders

**models of abnormality**
explanations for disordered thinking or behavior depend on theoretical model used to explain personality in general

- **biological model:** proposes that psychological disorders have a biological or medical cause; the medical model also influences approaches to diagnosis, treatment, and possible outcomes for a given disorder
- **psychological models:** propose that disorders are the result of various forms of emotional, behavioral, or thought-related malfunctioning
  - **psychodynamic**
  - **behavioral**
  - **cognitive**
- **sociocultural perspective:** thinking and behavior are the products of family, social, and cultural influences; what is normal in one culture may be abnormal in another
- **biopsychosocial perspective:** incorporates biological, psychological, and sociocultural factors

**diagnosing and classifying disorders**

- ICD-10
- DSM-5
  - the *Diagnostic and Statistical Manual of Mental Disorders (DSM)* was first published in 1952, current version *(DSM-5)* published in 2013
  - describes and provides diagnostic criteria for approximately 250 different psychological disorders
- RDoC
  - potential new system of classifying disorders using advances in neuroimaging, genetics, and cognitive science

**prevalence and impact**

- estimates may vary but it appears more than 1 in 5 adults over age 18 in the United States suffer from a mental disorder in a given year (see Table 14.1); similar rates exist worldwide and lifetime prevalence may be as high as 36%
- worldwide, many people do not receive treatment; mental disorders are one of the leading causes of disability in the United States and Canada

Reset

# Practice Quiz    How much do you remember?

*Pick the best answer.*

**1.** How would the Greek physician Hippocrates have typically dealt with someone suffering from mental illness?
 **a.** He would have made a hole in the patient's skull to release the pressure, a process known today as trephining.
 **b.** He would focus on correcting the imbalance of bodily fluids, or humors.
 **c.** He would have someone conduct the religious ritual known as an exorcism.
 **d.** He would have tried to understand the person's unconscious and the forces at work there.

**2.** Lisa has just been fired from her new job for consistently arriving 2 hours late for work. Lisa tries to explain that she must often drive back home to ensure that all the doors are locked and that no appliances have been left on. Lisa's condition is abnormal from the _____ definition.
 **a.** maladaptive
 **b.** situational context
 **c.** social deviance
 **d.** subjective discomfort

**3.** In the United States, "insanity" is a term typically used by
 **a.** psychologists.
 **b.** psychiatrists.
 **c.** the social work system.
 **d.** the legal system.

**4.** Elliot became widowed after nearly 40 years of marriage. He has convinced himself that no one will ever love him again. His irrational thinking has caused him to suffer from depression, and he rarely leaves his house. What perspective might best explain his behavior?
 **a.** psychodynamic
 **b.** cognitive
 **c.** behavioral
 **d.** biological

**5.** Which of the following concepts is not specifically associated with the *DSM-5* examination of culture-related disorders?
 **a.** cultural syndrome
 **b.** cultural idioms of distress
 **c.** cultural explanations or perceived cause
 **d.** cultural binding

# Disorders of Anxiety, Trauma, and Stress: What, Me Worry?

In this section, we will examine disorders in which the most dominant symptom is excessive or unrealistic anxiety. In addition to anxiety disorders, we will also address disorders that many people associate with anxiety symptoms, including obsessive-compulsive disorder, posttraumatic stress disorder, and acute stress disorders. These were classified as anxiety disorders in previous editions of the *DSM*. However, they now fall under different categories in the *DSM-5*. Obsessive-compulsive disorder now falls in the category of "Obsessive-Compulsive and Related Disorders," while posttraumatic stress disorder and acute stress disorder are found under "Trauma- and Stressor-Related Disorders" (American Psychiatric Association, 2013).

## ANXIETY DISORDERS

**14.4** **Identify different types of anxiety disorders and their symptoms.**

The category of **anxiety disorders** includes disorders in which the most dominant symptom is excessive or unrealistic anxiety. Anxiety can take very specific forms, such as a fear of a specific object, or it can be a very general emotion, such as that experienced by someone who is worried and doesn't know why.

 💬 But doesn't everybody have anxiety sometimes? What makes it a disorder?

Everyone does have anxiety, and some people have a great deal of anxiety at times. When talking about anxiety disorders, the anxiety is either excessive—greater than it should be given the circumstances—or unrealistic. If final exams are coming up and a student hasn't studied enough, that student's anxiety is understandable and realistic. But a student who has studied, has done well in all the exams, and is very prepared and still worries *excessively* about passing is showing an unrealistic amount of anxiety. For more about test anxiety, see the Applying Psychology to Everyday Life section in this chapter. **Free-floating anxiety** is the term given to anxiety that seems to be unrelated to any realistic and specific, known factor, and it is often a symptom of an anxiety disorder (Freud, 1977).

**PHOBIC DISORDERS: WHEN FEARS GET OUT OF HAND** One of the more specific anxiety disorders is a **phobia**, an irrational, persistent fear of something. The "something" might be an object or a situation or may involve social interactions. For example, many people would feel fear if they suddenly came upon a live snake as they were walking and would take steps to avoid the snake. Although those same people would not necessarily avoid a *picture* of a snake in a book, a person with a phobia of snakes would. Avoiding a live snake is rational; avoiding a picture of a snake is not.

**SOCIAL ANXIETY DISORDER (SOCIAL PHOBIA)** **Social anxiety disorder** (also called *social phobia*) involves a fear of interacting with others or being in a social situation and is one of the most common phobias people experience (Kessler et al., 2012). People with social anxiety disorder are afraid of being evaluated in some negative way by others, so they tend to avoid situations that could lead to something embarrassing or humiliating. They are very self-conscious as a result. Common types of social phobia are stage fright, fear of public speaking, and fear of urinating in a public restroom. Not surprisingly, people with social phobias often have a history of being shy as children (Sternberger et al., 1995).

**SPECIFIC PHOBIAS** A **specific phobia** is an irrational fear of some object or specific situation, such as a fear of dogs or a fear of being in small, enclosed spaces (**claustrophobia**). Other specific phobias include a fear of injections (*trypanophobia*), fear of dental work (*odontophobia*), fear of blood (*hematophobia*), fear of washing and bathing (*ablutophobia*), and fear of heights (**acrophobia**).

**anxiety disorders**

class of disorders in which the primary symptom is excessive or unrealistic anxiety.

**free-floating anxiety**

anxiety that is unrelated to any specific and known cause.

**phobia**

an irrational, persistent fear of an object, situation, or social activity.

**social anxiety disorder (social phobia)**

fear of interacting with others or being in social situations that might lead to a negative evaluation.

**specific phobia**

fear of objects or specific situations or events.

**claustrophobia**

fear of being in a small, enclosed space.

**acrophobia**

fear of heights.

Many people get nervous when they have to speak in front of an audience. Fear of public speaking is a common social phobia. Can you remember a time when you experienced a fear like this?

**AGORAPHOBIA**  A third type of phobia is **agoraphobia**, a Greek name that literally means "fear of the marketplace." It is the fear of being in a place or situation from which escape is difficult or impossible if something should go wrong (American Psychiatric Association, 2013). Furthermore, the anxiety is present in more than one situation. Someone is diagnosed with agoraphobia if they feel anxiety in at least two of five possible situations such as using public transportation like a bus or plane, being out in an open space such as on a bridge or in a parking lot, being in an enclosed space such as a grocery store or movie theatre, standing in line or being in a crowd like at a concert, or being out of the home alone (American Psychiatric Association, 2013).

💬 If a person has agoraphobia, it might be difficult to even go to work or to the store, right?

Exactly. People with specific phobias can usually avoid the object or situation without too much difficulty, and people with social phobias may simply avoid jobs and situations that involve meeting people face to face. But people with agoraphobia cannot avoid their phobia's source because it is simply being outside in the real world. A severe case of agoraphobia can make a person's home a prison, leaving the person trapped inside unable to go to work, shop, or engage in any kind of activity that requires going out of the home.

**PANIC DISORDER**  Fourteen-year-old Dariya was sitting in science class watching a film. All of a sudden, she started feeling really strange. Her ears seemed to be stuffed with cotton and her vision was very dim. She was cold, had broken out in a sweat, and felt extremely afraid for no good reason. Her heart was racing, and she immediately became convinced that she was dying. A friend sitting behind her saw how pale she had become and tried to ask her what was wrong, but Dariya couldn't speak. She was in a state of panic and couldn't move.

Dariya's symptoms are the classic symptoms of a **panic attack**, a sudden onset of extreme panic with various physical symptoms: racing heart, rapid breathing, a sensation of being "out of one's body," dulled hearing and vision, sweating, and dry mouth (Kumar & Oakley-Browne, 2002). Many people who have a panic attack think that they are having a heart attack and can experience pain as well as panic, but the symptoms are caused by the panic, not by any actual physical disorder. Psychologically, the person having a panic attack is in a state of terror, thinking that this is it, death is happening, and many people may feel a need to escape. The attack happens without warning and quite suddenly. Although some panic attacks can last as long as half an hour, some last only a few minutes, with most attacks peaking within 10 to 15 minutes.

Having a panic attack is not that unusual, especially for adolescent girls and young adult women (Eaton et al., 1994; Hayward et al., 1989, 2000; Kessler et al., 2007). Researchers have also found evidence that cigarette smoking greatly increases the risk of panic attacks in adolescence, young adulthood, and middle adulthood (Bakhshaie et al., 2016; Johnson et al., 2000; Zvolensky et al., 2003). Regardless, it is only when panic attacks occur more than once or repeatedly and cause persistent worry or changes in behavior that they become a **panic disorder**. Many people try to figure out what triggers a panic attack and then do their best to avoid the situation if possible. If driving a car sets off an attack, they don't drive. If being in a crowd sets off an attack, they don't go where crowds are.

**GENERALIZED ANXIETY DISORDER**

 💬 What about people who are just worriers? Can that become a disorder?

Remember free-floating anxiety? That's the kind of anxiety that has no known specific source and may be experienced by people with **generalized anxiety disorder**, in which excessive anxiety and worries (apprehensive expectations) occur more days than not for at

**agoraphobia**
fear of being in a place or situation from which escape is difficult or impossible.

**panic attack**
sudden onset of intense panic in which multiple physical symptoms of stress occur, often with feelings that one is dying.

**panic disorder**
disorder in which panic attacks occur more than once or repeatedly, and cause persistent worry or changes in behavior.

**generalized anxiety disorder**
disorder in which a person has feelings of dread and impending doom along with physical symptoms of stress, which lasts 6 months or more.

**Table 14.2** Anxiety Disorders and their Symptoms

| Anxiety Disorder | Definition | Examples/Symptoms |
|---|---|---|
| Social Anxiety Disorder | Fear of interacting with others or being in social situations that might lead to a negative evaluation | Stage fright, fear of public speaking, fear of urinating in public, fear of eating with other people |
| Specific Phobias | Fear of objects or specific situations or events | Fears of animals, the natural environment such as thunder storms, blood injections/injury, specific situations such as flying |
| Agoraphobia | Fear of being in a place or situation from which escape is difficult or impossible | Using public transportation, open spaces, enclosed spaces, being in a crowd |
| Panic Disorder | Disorder in which panic attacks occur more than once or repeatedly and cause persistent worry or changes in behavior | Various physical symptoms: racing heart, dizziness, rapid breathing, dulled senses, along with uncontrollable feelings of terror |
| Generalized Anxiety Disorder | Disorder in which a person has feelings of dread and impending doom along with physical symptoms of stress, which lasts 6 months or more | Tendency to worry about situations, people, or objects that are not really problems, tension, muscle aches, sleeping problems, problems concentrating |

least 6 months. People with this disorder may also experience anxiety about a number of events or activities (such as work or school performance). These feelings of anxiety have no particular source that can be pinpointed, nor can the person control the feelings even if an effort is made to do so.

People with this disorder are just plain worriers (Ruscio et al., 2001). They worry *excessively* about money, their children, their lives, their friends, the dog, as well as things no one else would see as a reason to worry. They feel tense, edgy, get tired easily, and may have trouble concentrating. They have muscle aches, they experience sleeping problems, and they are often irritable—all signs of stress. Generalized anxiety disorder is often found occurring with other anxiety disorders and depression.

### OTHER DISORDERS RELATED TO ANXIETY

**14.5** Describe obsessive-compulsive disorder and stress-related disorders.

As discussed earlier, despite anxiety being a common symptom, the following disorders are no longer classified as anxiety disorders in the *DSM-5*. *Obsessive-compulsive disorder* now falls in the category of "Obsessive-Compulsive and Related Disorders," while *posttraumatic stress disorder* and *acute stress disorder* are found under "Trauma- and Stressor-Related Disorders" (American Psychiatric Association, 2013).

**OBSESSIVE-COMPULSIVE DISORDER** Sometimes people get a thought running through their head that just won't go away, like when a song gets stuck in one's mind. If that particular thought causes a lot of anxiety, it can become the basis for an **obsessive-compulsive disorder**, or OCD. OCD is a disorder in which intruding* thoughts that occur again and again (obsessions, such as a fear that germs are on one's hands) are followed by some repetitive, ritualistic behavior or mental acts (compulsions, such as repeated hand washing, counting, etc.). The compulsions are meant to lower the anxiety caused by the thought (Soomro, 2001).

💬 I knew someone who had just had a baby, and she spent the first few nights home with the baby checking it to see if it was breathing—is that an obsessive-compulsive disorder?

Everyone waited as Allen figured out how much the meal had cost per bite.

**obsessive-compulsive disorder**
disorder in which intruding, recurring thoughts or obsessions create anxiety that is relieved by performing a repetitive, ritualistic behavior or mental act (compulsion).

---
*intruding: forcing one's way in; referring to something undesirable that enters awareness.

No, many parents check their baby's breathing often at first. Everyone has a little obsessive thinking on occasion or some small ritual that makes them feel better. The difference is whether a person *likes* to perform the ritual (but doesn't *have* to) or feels *compelled* to perform the ritual and feels extreme anxiety if unable to do so. You may wash your hands a time or two after picking up garbage, but it is entirely different if you *must* wash them a *thousand times* to prevent getting sick. The distress caused by a failure or an inability to successfully complete the compulsion is a defining feature of OCD.

**ACUTE STRESS DISORDER (ASD) AND POSTTRAUMATIC STRESS DISORDER (PTSD)**
Both general and specific stressors were discussed in Chapter Eleven: Stress and Health. Two trauma- and stressor-related disorders—*acute stress disorder* and *posttraumatic stress disorder*—are related to exposure to significant and traumatic stressors. The trauma, severe stress, and anxiety experienced by people after 9/11, Hurricane Katrina, the April 2013 Boston Marathon bombings, the 2015 terrorist attacks in Paris and earthquake in Nepal, and the 2016 attacks in Brussels, Orlando, and Nice can lead to **acute stress disorder (ASD)**. The symptoms of ASD often occur immediately after the traumatic event and include anxiety, dissociative symptoms (such as emotional numbness/lack of responsiveness, not being aware of surroundings, dissociative amnesia), recurring nightmares, sleep disturbances, problems in concentration, and moments in which people seem to "relive" the event in dreams and flashbacks for as long as 1 month following the event. One published study gathered survey information from Katrina evacuees at a major emergency shelter and found that 62 percent of those sampled met the criteria for having acute stress disorder (Mills et al., 2007).

When the symptoms associated with ASD last for more than 1 month, the disorder is then called **posttraumatic stress disorder (PTSD)**. In the same study (Mills et al., 2007), researchers concluded that it was likely that anywhere from 38 to 49 percent of all the evacuees sampled were at risk of developing PTSD that would still be present 2 years after the disaster. Furthermore, whereas the onset of ASD often occurs immediately after the traumatic event, the symptoms of PTSD may not occur until 6 months or later after the event (American Psychiatric Association, 2013). Treatment of these stress disorders may involve psychotherapy and the use of drugs to control anxiety. ⓁⒾⓃⓀ to Learning Objectives 15.10, 15.13. The video *PTSD: The Memories We Don't Want* describes PTSD in more detail.

What stressors and types of trauma might refugees fleeing war-torn countries experience?

**acute stress disorder (ASD)**

a disorder resulting from exposure to a major stressor, with symptoms of anxiety, dissociation, recurring nightmares, sleep disturbances, problems in concentration, and moments in which people seem to "relive" the event in dreams and flashbacks for as long as 1 month following the event.

**posttraumatic stress disorder (PTSD)**

a disorder resulting from exposure to a major stressor, with symptoms of anxiety, dissociation, nightmares, poor sleep, reliving the event, and concentration problems, lasting for more than 1 month; symptoms may appear immediately, or not occur until 6 months or later after the traumatic event.

**Symptoms of PTSD**
re-experiencing
avoidance
hypervigilance

👁 **Watch** the **Video** *PTSD: The Memories We Don't Want*

Researchers have found that women have almost twice the risk of developing PTSD as do men and that the likelihood increases if the traumatic experience took place before the woman was 15 years old (Breslau et al., 1997, 1999). However, female and male veterans tend to have similar symptoms of PTSD, at least for military-related stressors (King et al., 2013). Children may also suffer different effects from stress than do adults. Severe PTSD has been linked to a decrease in the size of the hippocampus in children with the disorder (Carrion et al., 2007). The hippocampus is important in the formation of new long-term declarative memories (Ⓛ Ⓘ Ⓝ Ⓚ to Learning Objectives 2.11, 6.5, 6.12), and this may have a detrimental effect on learning and the effectiveness of treatments for these children. Changes in the connections between different brain areas, especially those involved in regulating fear, also likely impair possible recovery efforts (Keding & Herringa, 2015).

Some life experiences lend themselves to people experiencing traumatic events. For example, the rate of PTSD (self-reported) among combat-exposed military personnel has tripled since 2001 (Smith et al., 2008). One study of older veterans over a 7-year period (Yaffe et al., 2010) found that those with PTSD were also more likely to develop dementia (10.6 percent risk) when compared to those without PTSD (only 6.6 percent risk). Increased levels of stress can make things worse. The risk of developing dementia appears to be

Anxiety disorders affect children as well as adults.

more than 75 percent higher for veterans that were prisoners of war (POWs) than veterans that were not (Meziab et al., 2014).

Last, individuals with ASD and PTSD likely perceive the world around them differently. A study of assault and motor vehicle accident survivors treated in a South London, UK, emergency room suggested individuals with ASD or PTSD were more likely to identify trauma-related pictures than neutral pictures, as compared to trauma survivors not diagnosed with ASD or PTSD. Furthermore, such preferential processing of trauma-related information may be more strongly primed in individuals with PTSD (Kleim et al., 2012) and is supported by fMRI studies demonstrating heightened brain processing in areas associated with associative learning and priming in individuals with PTSD (Sartory et al., 2013). Ⓛ Ⓘ Ⓝ Ⓚ to Learning Objective 6.5.

## CAUSES OF ANXIETY, TRAUMA, AND STRESS DISORDERS

### 14.6 Identify potential causes of anxiety, trauma, and stress disorders.

Different perspectives on how personality develops offer different explanations for these disorders. For example, the psychodynamic model sees anxiety as a kind of danger signal that repressed urges or conflicts are threatening to surface (Freud, 1977). A phobia is seen as a kind of displacement, in which the phobic object is actually only a symbol of whatever the person has buried deep in his or her unconscious mind—the true source of the fear. A fear of knives might mean a fear of one's own aggressive tendencies, or a fear of heights may hide a suicidal desire to jump.

**BEHAVIORAL AND COGNITIVE FACTORS** Behaviorists believe that anxious behavioral reactions are learned. They see phobias, for example, as nothing more than classically conditioned fear responses, as was the case with "Little Albert" (Rachman, 1990; Watson & Rayner, 1920). Ⓛ Ⓘ Ⓝ Ⓚ to Learning Objective 5.3. Cognitive psychologists see anxiety disorders as the result of illogical, irrational thought processes. One way in which people with anxiety disorders show irrational thinking (Beck, 1976, 1984) is through **magnification**, or the tendency to "make mountains out of molehills" by interpreting situations as being far more harmful, dangerous, or embarrassing than they

**magnification**

the tendency to interpret situations as far more dangerous, harmful, or important than they actually are.

actually are. In panic disorder, for example, a person might interpret a racing heartbeat as a sign of a heart attack instead of just a momentary arousal.

Cognitive-behavioral psychologists may see anxiety as related to another distorted thought process called **all-or-nothing thinking**, in which a person believes that his or her performance must be perfect or the result will be a total failure. **Overgeneralization** (a single negative event interpreted as a never-ending pattern of defeat), jumping to conclusions without facts to support that conclusion, and **minimization** (giving little or no emphasis to one's successes or positive events and traits) are other examples of irrational thinking. In a recent study with firefighters, a profession with repeated exposure to trauma, research suggests cognitive flexibility in regulating emotions according to the demands of particular situations can protect someone from developing PTSD symptoms (Levy-Gigi et al., 2016).

**BIOLOGICAL FACTORS**  Growing evidence exists that biological factors contribute to anxiety disorders. Several disorders, including generalized anxiety disorder, panic disorders, phobias, and OCD, tend to run in families, pointing to a genetic basis for these disorders. Furthermore, genetic factors in PTSD seem to influence both the risk of developing the disorder and the likelihood individuals may be involved in potentially dangerous situations (Hyman & Cohen, 2013). Functional neuroimaging studies, (LINK) to Learning Objective 2.9, have revealed that the amygdala, an area of the limbic system, is more active in phobic people responding to pictures of spiders than in nonphobic people (LeDoux, 2003; Rauch et al., 2003) and also more active in individuals with PTSD and social anxiety disorder, suggesting excessive conditioning and exaggerated responses to stimuli that would typically elicit minimal fear-related responses (Hyman & Cohen, 2013). (LINK) to Learning Objectives 2.11, 6.12, and 9.8. Structural neuroimaging studies have also been helpful, (LINK) to Learning Objective 2.9, in that specific brain areas have been associated with a variety of anxiety disorders, namely reductions of gray matter in the parts of the right ventral anterior cingulate gyrus (at the bottom and front of the right cingulate gyrus) and left inferior frontal gyrus (Shang et al., 2014). In a study of individuals across six different psychological disorders, reductions in gray matter were found in the dorsal anterior (at the top and front) cingulate gyrus and both the left and right insula (Goodkind et al., 2015).

**CULTURAL VARIATIONS**  Anxiety disorders are found around the world, although the particular form the disorder takes might be different in various cultures. For example, in some Latin American cultures, anxiety can take the form of *ataque de nervios*, or "attack of nerves," in which the person may have fits of crying, shout uncontrollably, experience sensations of heat, and become very aggressive, either verbally or physically. These attacks usually come after some stressful event such as the death of a loved one (American Psychiatric Association, 2013). Several syndromes that are essentially types of phobias are specific to certain cultures. For example, *koro*, found primarily in China and a few other South Asian and East Asian countries, involves a fear that one's genitals are shrinking (Pfeiffer, 1982), and *taijin kyofusho* (TKS), found primarily in Japan, involves excessive fear and anxiety, but in this case it is the fear that one will do something in public that is socially inappropriate or embarrassing, such as blushing, staring, or having an offensive body odor (Kirmayer, 1991). Panic disorder occurs at similar rates in adolescents and adults in the United States and parts of Europe but is found less often in Asian, African, and Latin American countries. Within the United States, Native Americans have significantly higher rates, whereas Latinos, African Americans, Caribbean blacks, and Asian Americans have significantly lower rates as compared to non-Latino whites (American Psychiatric Association, 2013).

**all-or-nothing thinking**
the tendency to believe that one's performance must be perfect or the result will be a total failure.

**overgeneralization**
distortion of thinking in which a person draws sweeping conclusions based on only one incident or event and applies those conclusions to events that are unrelated to the original; the tendency to interpret a single negative event as a neverending pattern of defeat and failure.

**minimization**
distortions of thinking in which a person blows a negative event out of proportion to its importance (magnification) while ignoring relevant positive events (minimization).

## Concept Map L.O. 14.4, 14.5, 14.6

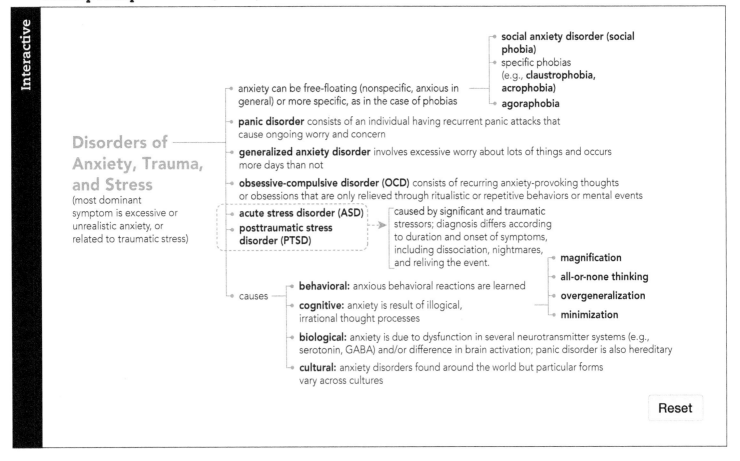

**Interactive**

**Disorders of Anxiety, Trauma, and Stress**
(most dominant symptom is excessive or unrealistic anxiety, or related to traumatic stress)

- anxiety can be free-floating (nonspecific, anxious in general) or more specific, as in the case of phobias
  - social anxiety disorder (social phobia)
  - specific phobias (e.g., **claustrophobia, acrophobia**)
  - **agoraphobia**
- **panic disorder** consists of an individual having recurrent panic attacks that cause ongoing worry and concern
- **generalized anxiety disorder** involves excessive worry about lots of things and occurs more days than not
- **obsessive-compulsive disorder (OCD)** consists of recurring anxiety-provoking thoughts or obsessions that are only relieved through ritualistic or repetitive behaviors or mental events
- **acute stress disorder (ASD)**
- **posttraumatic stress disorder (PTSD)**
  - caused by significant and traumatic stressors; diagnosis differs according to duration and onset of symptoms, including dissociation, nightmares, and reliving the event.
- causes
  - **behavioral:** anxious behavioral reactions are learned
  - **cognitive:** anxiety is result of illogical, irrational thought processes
    - **magnification**
    - **all-or-none thinking**
    - **overgeneralization**
    - **minimization**
  - **biological:** anxiety is due to dysfunction in several neurotransmitter systems (e.g., serotonin, GABA) and/or difference in brain activation; panic disorder is also hereditary
  - **cultural:** anxiety disorders found around the world but particular forms vary across cultures

Reset

# Practice Quiz How much do you remember?

*Pick the best answer.*

**1.** Who is most likely to be diagnosed with a phobic disorder?
- **a.** Brianne, who is afraid of snakes after nearly being bitten while running
- **b.** Calista, who is afraid of snakes after watching a documentary on poisonous snakes found in her region
- **c.** Jennifer, who is morbidly afraid of snakes and refuses to even look at a picture of a snake
- **d.** Both Calista and Jennifer's behavior would qualify as a phobic disorder.

**2.** Amelia has recently given birth to her first child. She mentions that she often goes into her baby's bedroom to check if he is still breathing. Would this qualify as an obsessive-compulsive disorder (OCD)?
- **a.** If Amelia continues to carry out this behavior for more than 1 or 2 days, this would qualify as an OCD.
- **b.** If Amelia and her husband both carry out this behavior, then it would qualify as an OCD.
- **c.** If Amelia enjoys frequently checking to see that her baby is breathing, then this would qualify as an OCD.
- **d.** As long as Amelia is not compelled to check on her baby and does not suffer from severe anxiety if she is unable to do so, then this is not an OCD.

**3.** Sandy took part in the April 2013 Boston Marathon, where two bombs were detonated near the finish line, killing three spectators. For approximately 2 weeks after the marathon, Sandy was unable to sleep or concentrate and often found herself reliving the moment she heard the bombs explode. What disorder might Sandy be diagnosed with?
- **a.** acute stress disorder
- **b.** posttraumatic stress disorder
- **c.** phobic disorder
- **d.** panic disorder

**4.** Melanie has just received an exam grade in her psychology class. She earned a grade of 89 percent, which is a B. All of her work during the semester thus far has earned A grades, and she is very upset about the exam score. "This is the worst thing that could possibly have happened," she laments to her best friend, Keesha, who just rolls her eyes. A cognitive psychologist would suggest that Melanie is employing the cognitive distortion called _____.
- **a.** all-or-nothing thinking
- **b.** overgeneralization
- **c.** magnification
- **d.** minimization

# Dissociative Disorders: Altered Identities

Just as there is sometimes overlap of symptoms between different diagnoses, various disorders can be related to similar circumstances or phenomena. As already discussed, exposure to trauma is a key component to ASD and PTSD, and both may include symptoms of dissociation. Dissociation plays a more prominent role in the dissociative disorders, where the dissociative symptoms encompass many aspects of everyday life and not just memories of the traumatic events themselves or the time around them (American Psychiatric Association, 2013).

**dissociative disorders**

disorders in which there is a break in conscious awareness, memory, the sense of identity, or some combination.

**dissociative identity disorder (DID)**

disorder occurring when a person seems to have two or more distinct personalities within one body.

## TYPES OF DISSOCIATIVE DISORDERS

### 14.7 Differentiate among dissociative amnesia, dissociative fugue, and dissociative identity disorder.

**Dissociative disorders** involve a break, or dissociation, in consciousness, memory, or a person's sense of identity. This "split" is easier to understand when thinking about how people sometimes drive somewhere and then wonder how they got there—they don't remember the trip at all. This sort of "automatic pilot" driving happens when the route is familiar and frequently traveled. One part of the conscious mind was thinking about work, school, or whatever was uppermost in the mind, while lower centers of consciousness were driving the car, stopping at signs and lights, and turning when needed. This split in conscious attention is very similar to what happens in dissociative disorders. The difference is that in these disorders, the dissociation is much more pronounced and involuntary.

**DISSOCIATIVE AMNESIA AND FUGUE: WHO AM I AND HOW DID I GET HERE?**  In *dissociative amnesia*, the individual cannot remember personal information such as one's own name or specific personal events—the kind of information contained in episodic long-term memory. **LINK** to Learning Objective 6.5. Dissociative amnesia may sound like retrograde amnesia, but it differs in its cause. In retrograde amnesia, the memory loss is typically caused by a physical injury, such as a blow to the head. In dissociative amnesia, the cause is psychological rather than physical. The "blow" is a mental one, not a physical one. The reported memory loss is usually associated with a stressful or emotionally traumatic experience, such as rape or childhood abuse (Chu et al., 1999; Kirby et al., 1993), and cannot be easily explained by simple forgetfulness. It can be a loss of memory for only one small segment of time, or it can involve a total loss of one's past personal memories. For example, a soldier might be able to remember being in combat but cannot remember witnessing a friend get killed, or a person might forget his or her entire life. These memories usually resurface, sometimes quickly and sometimes after a long delay. Dissociative amnesia can occur with or without *fugue*. The Latin word *fugere* means "flight" and is the word from which the term *fugue* is taken. A *dissociative fugue* occurs when a person suddenly travels away from home (the flight) and afterwards cannot remember the trip or even personal information such as identity. The individual may become confused about identity, sometimes even taking on a whole new identity in the new place (Nijenhuis, 2000). Such flights usually take place after an emotional trauma and are more common in times of disasters or war.

An apparent case of dissociative amnesia and fugue. Edward Lighthart, or as he preferred, John Doe, was found in Seattle, Washington in 2009. During the interview when this photo was taken, Doe reported memories were slowly trickling back during the nearly seven weeks since he walked out of a Seattle park with no idea of who he was and how he got there. News reports indicated he was found later that same year in Las Vegas, New Mexico, again without knowing who he was or how he got there.

**DISSOCIATIVE IDENTITY DISORDER: HOW MANY AM I?**  Perhaps the most controversial dissociative disorder is **dissociative identity disorder**

(DID), formerly known as multiple personality disorder. In this disorder, a person seems to experience at least two or more distinct personalities existing in one body. There may be a "core" personality, who usually knows nothing about the other personalities and is the one who experiences "blackouts" or losses of memory and time. Fugues are common in dissociative identity disorder, with the core personality experiencing unsettling moments of "awakening" in an unfamiliar place or with people who call the person by another name (Kluft, 1984).

With the publication of several famous books and movies made from those books, dissociative identity disorder became well known to the public. Throughout the 1980s, psychological professionals began to diagnose this condition at an alarming rate—"multiple personality," as it was then known, had become the "fad" disorder of the late twentieth century, according to some researchers (Aldridge-Morris, 1989; Boor, 1982; Cormier & Thelen, 1998; Showalter, 1997). Although the diagnosis of dissociative identity disorder has been a point of controversy and scrutiny, with many (but not all) professionals doubting the validity of previous diagnoses, some believe otherwise.

Some research suggests DID is not only a valid diagnostic category, it may co-occur in other disorders, such as individuals with *borderline personality disorder*, and may possibly be characterized by specific variations in brain functioning (Dorahy et al., 2014; Ross et al., 2014; Schlumpf et al., 2014). Dissociative symptoms and features can also be found in other cultures. The trancelike state known as *amok* in which a person suddenly becomes highly agitated and violent (found in Southeast Asia and Pacific Island cultures) is usually associated with no memory for the period during which the "trance" lasts (Hagan et al., 2015; Suryani & Jensen, 1993). However, despite their occurrence, in some cultures dissociative symptoms in and of themselves are not always perceived as a source of stress or a problem (van Duijl et al., 2010).

## CAUSES OF DISSOCIATIVE DISORDERS

**14.8** Summarize explanations for dissociative disorders.

Psychodynamic theory sees the repression of threatening or unacceptable thoughts and behavior as a defense mechanism at the heart of all disorders, and the dissociative disorders in particular seem to have a large element of repression—motivated forgetting—in them. In the psychodynamic view, loss of memory or disconnecting one's awareness from a stressful or traumatic event is adaptive in that it reduces the emotional pain (Dorahy, 2001).

Cognitive and behavioral explanations for dissociative disorders are connected: The person may feel guilt, shame, or anxiety when thinking about disturbing experiences or thoughts and start to avoid thinking about them. This "thought avoidance" is negatively reinforced by the reduction of the anxiety and unpleasant feelings and eventually will become a habit of "not thinking about" these things. This is similar to what many people do when faced with something unpleasant, such as an injection or a painful procedure such as having a root canal. They "think about something else." In doing that, they are deliberately not thinking about what is happening to them at the moment, and the experience of pain is decreased. People with dissociative disorders may simply be better at doing this sort of "not thinking" than other people are.

Also, consider the positive reinforcement possibilities for a person with a dissociative disorder: attention from others and help from professionals. Shaping may also play a role in the development of some cases of dissociative identity disorder. The therapist may unintentionally pay more attention to a client who talks about "feeling like someone else," which may encourage the client to report more such feelings and even elaborate on them.

There are some possible biological sources for dissociations as well. Researchers have found that people with *depersonalization/derealization disorder* (a dissociative disorder in which people feel detached and disconnected from themselves, their bodies, and their surroundings) have lower brain activity in the areas responsible for their sense of body awareness than do people without the disorder (Simeon et al., 2000). Others have found evidence that people with dissociative identity disorders show significant differences in brain activity, as evidenced by PET and fMRI, when different "personalities" are present (Reinders et al., 2001; Schlumpf et al., 2014; Tsai et al., 1999). It is also possible individuals with DID may be more elaborative when forming memories and are better at memory recall as a result (García-Campayo et al., 2009).

## Concept Map L.O. 14.7, 14.8

*Interactive*

**Dissociative Disorders**
(involve a dissociation in consciousness, memory, or sense of identity, often associated with extreme stress or trauma)

- **dissociative amnesia:** one cannot remember personal information; may involve a dissociative fugue in that the person takes a sudden trip and also cannot remember the trip

- **dissociative identity disorder:** person seems to experience at least two or more distinct personalities; validity of actual disorder has been topic of debate

- causes
  - **psychodynamic:** repressed thoughts and behavior is primary defense mechanism and reduces emotional pain
  - **cognitive and behavioral:** trauma-related thought avoidance is negatively reinforced by reduction in anxiety and emotional pain
  - **biological:** support for brain activity differences in body awareness has been found in individuals with depersonalization/derealization disorder

Reset

# Practice Quiz   How much do you remember?

*Pick the best answer.*

1. What is the major difference between dissociative amnesia and retrograde amnesia?
   a. Retrograde amnesia patients often suffer from some form of physical brain trauma.
   b. Individuals suffering from dissociative amnesia often have a history of memory loss that seems to be hereditary.
   c. Those suffering from dissociative amnesia have prior damage to the brain, which in turn causes memory loss.
   d. Retrograde amnesia patients often have suffered from painful psychological trauma.

2. Franklin wakes up on a cot in a homeless shelter in another town. He doesn't know where he is or how he got there, and he's confused when people say he has been calling himself Anthony. This is most likely an episode of dissociative
   a. amnesia.
   c. identity disorder.
   b. amnesia with fugue.
   d. multiple personality.

3. Dr. Cowden believes that Jamison's dissociation disorder may be due to his apparent enhanced ability to think about things other than those associated with his traumatic childhood. What psychological perspective is Dr. Cowden applying?
   a. psychodynamic perspective
   b. biological perspective
   c. cognitive/behavioral perspective
   d. evolutionary perspective

4. Dissociative symptoms and features can be found in many different cultures. For example, in Southeast Asian and Pacific Islander cultures, people sometimes experience a trancelike state called _____ that is associated with increased agitation and violent tendencies.
   a. "TKS"        c. amok
   b. koro         d. susto

# Disorders of Mood: The Effect of Affect

When was the last time you felt down and sad? Or maybe a period of excitement or jubilation? Did these come about as the result of normal, day-to-day events or circumstances and change accordingly? Imagine how the experience of such feelings would impact your life if they lasted for much longer periods of time, were much more persistent across life events, and if you were unable to identify the source or cause for such emotions. That is often the case when someone experiences a disordered mood.

## MAJOR DEPRESSIVE DISORDER AND BIPOLAR DISORDERS

**14.9** **Describe different disorders of mood, including major depressive disorder and bipolar disorders.**

In psychological terms, the word **affect** is used to mean "emotion" or "mood." **Mood disorders** are disturbances in emotion and are also referred to as affective disorders. Although the range of human emotions runs from deep, intense sadness and despair to extreme happiness and elation, under normal circumstances people stay in between those extremes—neither too sad nor too happy but content (see **Figure 14.1**). It is when stress or some other factor pushes a person to one extreme or the other that mood disorders can result. Mood disorders can be relatively mild or moderate (straying only a short distance from the "average"), or they can be extreme (existing at either end of the full range). While we will examine disorders of mood together here, note that in the *DSM-5*, disorders of mood can be found under "Bipolar and Related Disorders" or "Depressive Disorders."

**MAJOR DEPRESSIVE DISORDER**  When a deeply depressed mood comes on fairly suddenly and either seems to be too severe for the circumstances or exists without any external cause for sadness, it is called **major depressive disorder**. Major depression would fall at the far extreme of sadness on Figure 14.1. People suffering from major depressive disorder are depressed for most of every day, take little or no pleasure in any activities, feel tired, have trouble sleeping or sleep too much, experience changes in appetite and significant weight changes, experience excessive guilt or feelings of worthlessness, and have trouble concentrating. Some people with this disorder also suffer from delusional thinking and may experience hallucinations. Most of these symptoms occur on a daily basis, lasting for the better part of the day (American Psychiatric Association, 2013).

 Some people with depression may have thoughts of death or suicide, including suicide attempts. Death by suicide is the most serious negative outcome for the person with depression. It is now the second leading cause of death among young people from 15 to 34 years of age in the United States, and more than 90 percent of suicides are associated with a psychological disorder, with depression being the most likely cause (Centers for Disease Control and Prevention, 2015; Hyman & Cohen, 2013). If you or someone you know is thinking about suicide, confidential assistance is available from the National Suicide Prevention Lifeline, 1-800-273-TALK (8255).

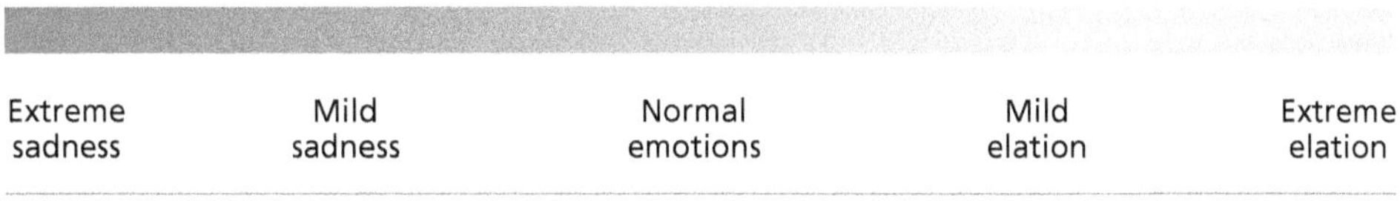

**affect**
in psychology, a term indicating "emotion" or "mood."

**mood disorders**
disorders in which mood is severely disturbed.

**major depressive disorder**
severe depression that comes on suddenly and seems to have no external cause, or is too severe for current circumstances.

| Extreme sadness | Mild sadness | Normal emotions | Mild elation | Extreme elation |
|---|---|---|---|---|

**Figure 14.2**  The Range of Emotions

Most people experience a range of emotions over the course of a day or several days, such as mild sadness, calm contentment, or mild elation and happiness. A person with a disorder of mood experiences emotions that are extreme and, therefore, abnormal.

Major depressive disorder is the most common of the diagnosed disorders of mood and is 1.5 to 3 times more likely in women than it is in men (American Psychiatric Association, 2013). This is true even across various cultures (Kessler et al., 2012; Seedat et al., 2009). Many possible explanations have been proposed for this gender difference, including the different hormonal structure of the female system (menstruation, hormonal changes during and after pregnancy, menopause, etc.) and different social roles played by women in the culture (Blehar & Oren, 1997). Research has found little support for hormonal influences in general, instead finding that the role of hormones and other biological factors in depression is unclear. Furthermore, studies have found that the degree of differences between male and female rates of depression is decreasing and is nonexistent in college students and single adults, leading some to conclude that gender roles and social factors such as marital status, career type, and number of children may have more importance in creating the gender difference than biological differences do (McGrath et al., 1992; Nolen-Hoeksema, 1990; Seedat et al., 2009; Weissman & Klerman, 1977). Women also tend to ruminate, or repeatedly focus more on negative emotions, more than men, and this may also be a contributing factor for reported gender differences in prevalence rates for both depression and anxiety (Krueger & Eaton, 2015; Nolen-Hoeksema, 2012).

Some people find that they only get depressed at certain times of the year. In particular, depression seems to set in during the winter months and goes away with the coming of spring and summer. *Seasonal affective disorder (SAD)* is a mood disorder that is caused by the body's reaction to low levels of light present in the winter months (Partonen & Lonnqvist, 1998). Despite the use of this term, recent research suggests there may not be a valid category of depression that varies by season and raise questions about the continued use of this diagnosis (Traffanstedt et al., 2016).

**BIPOLAR DISORDERS**   Major depressive disorder is sometimes referred to as a *unipolar disorder* because the emotional problem exists at only one end, or "pole," of the emotional range. When a person experiences periods of mood that can range from severe depression to **manic** episodes (excessive excitement, energy, and elation), that person is said to suffer from a type of **bipolar disorder** (American Psychiatric Association, 2013). However, while an individual may experience periods of mood at the two extremes, in some instances the individual may only experience mood that spans from normal to manic and may or may not experience episodes of depression, called *bipolar I disorder*. In the manic episodes, the person is extremely happy or euphoric* without any real cause to be so happy. Restlessness, irritability, an inability to sit still or remain inactive, and seemingly unlimited energy are also common. The person may seem silly to others and can become aggressive when not allowed to carry out the grand (and sometimes delusional) plans that may occur in mania. Speech may be rapid and jump from one topic to another. Oddly, people in the manic state are often very creative until their lack of organization renders their attempts at being creative useless (Blumer, 2002; McDermott, 2001; Rothenberg, 2001). In *bipolar II disorder*, spans of normal mood are interspersed with episodes of major depression and episodes of *hypomania*, a level of mood that is elevated but at a level below or less severe than full mania (American Psychiatric Association, 2013).

 That sounds almost like a description of an overactive child—can't sit still, can't concentrate—are the two disorders related?

The answer to that question is actually part of an ongoing controversy. There does seem to be a connection between attention-deficit/hyperactivity disorder (ADHD) and the onset of bipolar disorder in adolescence (Carlson et al., 1998), but only a small

**manic**
having the quality of excessive excitement, energy, and elation or irritability.

**bipolar disorder**
periods of mood that may range from normal to manic, with or without episodes of depression (bipolar I disorder), or spans of normal mood interspersed with episodes of major depression and episodes of hypomania (bipolar II disorder).

*euphoric: having a feeling of vigor, well-being, or high spirits.

percentage of children with ADHD go on to develop bipolar disorder. Recent evidence has found significantly higher rates of ADHD among relatives of individuals with bipolar disorder and a higher prevalence of bipolar disorder among relatives of individuals with ADHD (Faraone et al., 2012). The symptoms of bipolar disorder include irrational thinking and other manic symptoms that are not present in ADHD (Geller et al., 1998). Confusion between the two disorders arises because hyperactivity (excessive movement and an inability to concentrate) is a symptom of both disorders. In one study, researchers compared children diagnosed with both bipolar disorder and ADHD to children diagnosed with ADHD only on measures of academic performance and a series of neurological tests (Henin et al., 2007). They found that the two groups responded in very similar ways, showing the same deficits in information-processing abilities, with only one exception: The children with both disorders performed more poorly on one measure of processing speed when compared to children with only ADHD. The researchers concluded that the neurological deficits often observed in children with bipolar disorder are more likely to be due to the ADHD than to the bipolar disorder itself. Children with bipolar disorder also seem to suffer from far more severe emotional and behavioral problems than those with ADHD (Ferguson-Noyes, 2005; McDougall, 2009).

CAUSES OF DISORDERED MOOD

**14.10** **Compare and contrast behavioral, social cognitive, and biological explanations for depression and other disorders of mood.**

Explanations of depression and other disorders of mood come from the perspectives of behavioral, social cognitive, and biological theories as well as genetics.

Behavioral theorists link depression to learned helplessness (Seligman, 1975, 1989), whereas social cognitive theorists point to distortions of thinking such as blowing negative events out of proportion and minimizing positive, good events (Beck, 1976, 1984). **LINK** to Learning Objective 5.12. In the social cognitive view, depressed people continually have negative, self-defeating thoughts about themselves, which depress them further in a downward spiral of despair. Learned helplessness has been linked to an increase in such self-defeating thinking and depression in studies with people who have experienced uncontrollable, painful events (Abramson et al., 1978, 1980). This link does not necessarily mean that negative thoughts *cause* depression; it may be that depression increases the likelihood of negative thoughts (Gotlib et al., 2001). One study found that when comparing adolescents who were depressed to those who were not, the depressed group faced risk factors specifically associated with the social cognitive environment, such as being female or a member of an ethnic minority, living in poverty, regular use of drugs (including tobacco and alcohol), and engaging in delinquent behavior (Costello et al., 2008). In contrast, those in the nondepressed group of adolescents were more likely to come from two-parent households; had higher self-esteem; and felt connected to parents, peers, and school. Clearly, learned helplessness in the face of discrimination, prejudice, and poverty may be associated with depression in these adolescents. Research has also found that when therapists focus on helping clients change their way of thinking, depression improves significantly when compared to therapy that focuses only on changing behavior; these results lend support to the cognitive explanation of distorted thinking as the source of depression (Strunk et al., 2010).

Biological explanations of disordered mood focus on the effects of brain chemicals such as serotonin, norepinephrine, and dopamine; drugs used to treat depression and mania typically affect the levels of these three neurotransmitters, either alone or in combination (Cohen, 1997; Cummings & Coffey, 1994; Ruhe et al., 2007). And as with other psychological disorders, neuroimaging continues to provide information regarding possible brain areas associated with mood. Gray matter loss has been found in individuals with a history of neglect or physical, emotional, or sexual abuse, in brain areas associated with mood, regulation of emotional behaviors, and attention (Lim et al., 2014). One recent investigation across different psychological disorders found variations in gray matter loss in several brain regions. Think back to the coverage of different brain areas in Chapter Two. In addition to the reductions found in the dorsal anterior cingulate and bilateral insular cortex across disorders, there was greater loss in the hippocampus and amygdala in depressed individuals (Goodkind, et al., 2015). Another investigation has found that baseline thickness of cortical gray matter in the right medial orbitofrontal and right precentral areas of the frontal lobe, the left anterior cingulate, and bilateral areas of insular cortex predicted future onset of major depression in a group of 33 adolescent females (Foland-Ross et al., 2015). For subcortical structures, researchers have found smaller volumes in the caudate, part of the basal ganglia, for individuals with major depressive disorder (MDD) and bipolar disorder (BD) as compared to controls, but individuals with MDD had greater volume in the ventral diencephalon, an area that includes the hypothalamus, than both controls and individuals with BD (Sacchet et al., 2015). Functional neuroimaging has also found dysfunction in many of these brain areas, with some being more active and others less active as compared to controls, and to complicate it even further, the direction of altered activity may be different in youth than in adults with depression (Miller et al., 2015; Su et al., 2014).

Genes also play a part in these disorders. The fact that the more severe mood disorders are not a reaction to some outside source of stress or anxiety but rather seem to come from within the person's own body, together with the tendency of mood disorders to appear in genetically related individuals at a higher rate, suggests rather strongly that inheritance may play a significant part in these disorders (Barondes, 1998; Farmer, 1996). It is possible that some mood disorders share a common gene, but actual rates vary. For example, genetic risks are higher in bipolar disorder as compared to unipolar depression (Hyman & Cohen, 2013; McMahon et al., 2010). More than 65 percent of people with bipolar disorder have at least one close relative with either bipolar disorder or major depression (Craddock et al., 2005; National Institute of Mental Health Genetics Workgroup, 1998; Sullivan et al., 2000). Twin studies have shown that if one identical twin has either major depression or bipolar disorder, the chances that the other twin will also develop a mood disorder are about 40 to 70 percent (Muller-Oerlinghausen et al., 2002).

## Concept Map L.O. 14.9, 14.10

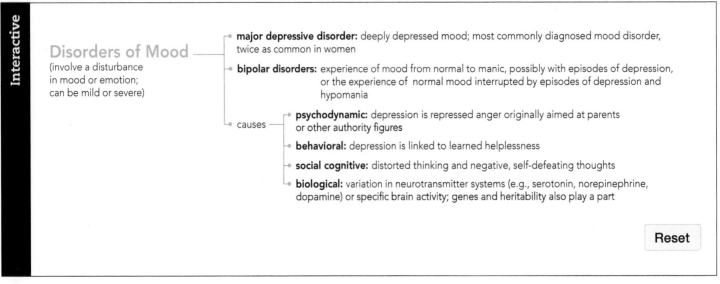

**Interactive**

**Disorders of Mood**
(involve a disturbance in mood or emotion; can be mild or severe)

- **major depressive disorder:** deeply depressed mood; most commonly diagnosed mood disorder, twice as common in women
- **bipolar disorders:** experience of mood from normal to manic, possibly with episodes of depression, or the experience of normal mood interrupted by episodes of depression and hypomania
- **causes**
  - **psychodynamic:** depression is repressed anger originally aimed at parents or other authority figures
  - **behavioral:** depression is linked to learned helplessness
  - **social cognitive:** distorted thinking and negative, self-defeating thoughts
  - **biological:** variation in neurotransmitter systems (e.g., serotonin, norepinephrine, dopamine) or specific brain activity; genes and heritability also play a part

Reset

# Practice Quiz How much do you remember?

*Pick the best answer.*

**1.** Jorge finds himself feeling depressed most of the day. He is constantly tired yet he sleeps very little. He has feelings of worthlessness that have come on suddenly and seemingly have no basis in reality. What might Jorge be diagnosed with?
**a.** seasonal affective disorder
**b.** acute depressive disorder
**c.** major depressive disorder
**d.** bipolar disorder

**2.** Studies have suggested the increased rates of major depressive disorder in women may have a basis in _____
**a.** gender roles, social factors, and emotional processing.
**b.** hormonal differences.
**c.** biological differences.
**d.** heredity.

**3.** What disorder seems to hold an association with bipolar disorder?
**a.** dysthymia
**b.** cyclothymia
**c.** phobic disorder
**d.** ADHD

**4.** Biological explanations of disordered mood have focused on the effects of several different brain chemicals, and medications used to treat these disorders are designed to work on these various neurotransmitter systems. Which of the following is not one of the chemicals that has been implicated in mood disorders?
**a.** serotonin
**b.** dopamine
**c.** norepinephrine
**d.** melatonin

# Eating Disorders and Sexual Dysfunction

Thus far we have talked about disorders that have primarily focused on mood, anxiety, stress, and trauma. We will now shift to disorders of a slightly different type and will first examine eating disorders and then sexual dysfunction.

## EATING DISORDERS

### 14.11 Identify the symptoms and risk factors associated with anorexia nervosa, bulimia nervosa, and binge-eating disorder.

There are a variety of disorders that relate to the intake of food, or in some cases non-nutritive substances, or in the elimination of bodily waste. These are found in the *DSM-5* under "Feeding and Eating Disorders."

**TYPES OF EATING DISORDERS** We will specifically examine three eating disorders: *anorexia nervosa, bulimia nervosa, and binge-eating disorder.*

**ANOREXIA NERVOSA** **Anorexia nervosa**, often called **anorexia**, is a condition in which a person (typically young and female) reduces eating to the point that their body weight is significantly low, or less than minimally expected. For adults, this is likely a body mass index (BMI; weight in kilograms/height in meters$^2$) less than 18.5 (American Psychiatric Association, 2013). Hormone secretion becomes abnormal, especially in the thyroid and adrenal glands. The heart muscles become weak and heart rhythms may alter. Other physical effects of anorexia may include diarrhea, loss of muscle tissue, loss of sleep, low blood pressure, and lack of menstruation in females.

Some individuals with anorexia will eat in front of others (whereas individuals with bulimia tend to binge eat as secretly as possible) but then force themselves to throw up or take large doses of laxatives. They are often obsessed with exercising and with food—cooking elaborate meals for others while eating nothing themselves. They have extremely distorted body images, seeing fat where others see only skin and bones.

**BULIMIA NERVOSA** **Bulimia nervosa**, often called **bulimia**, is a condition in which a person develops a cycle of "binging," or overeating enormous amounts of food at one sitting, and then using inappropriate methods for avoiding weight gain (American Psychiatric Association, 2013). Most individuals with bulimia engage in "purging" behaviors, such as deliberately vomiting after the binge or misuse of laxatives, but some may not, using other inappropriate methods to avoid weight gain such as fasting the day or two after the binge or engaging in excessive exercise (American Psychiatric Association, 2013). There are some similarities to anorexia: The victims are usually

**anorexia nervosa (anorexia)**
a condition in which a person reduces eating to the point that their body weight is significantly low, or less than minimally expected. In adults, this is likely associated with a BMI 18.5.

**bulimia nervosa (bulimia)**
a condition in which a person develops a cycle of "binging," or overeating enormous amounts of food at one sitting, and then using unhealthy methods to avoid weight gain.

This young model is not merely thin; by medical standards, she is probably at a weight that would allow her to be labeled as having anorexia. The "thin is in" mentality that dominates the field of fashion design models is a major contributor to the Western cultural concept of very thin women as beautiful and desirable. The model pictured here is a far cry from the days of sex symbol Marilyn Monroe, who was rumored to be a size 12.

**binge-eating disorder**

a condition in which a person overeats, or binges, on enormous amounts of food at one sitting, but unlike bulimia nervosa, the individual does not then purge or use other unhealthy methods to avoid weight gain.

female, are obsessed with their appearance, diet excessively, and believe themselves to be fat even when they are quite obviously not fat. But individuals with bulimia are typically a little older than individuals with anorexia at the onset of the disorder—early 20s rather than early puberty. Individuals with bulimia often maintain a normal weight, making the disorder difficult to detect. The most obvious difference between the two conditions is that the individual with bulimia will eat, and eat to excess, binging on huge amounts of food—an average of 3,500 calories in a single binge and as much as 50,000 calories in one day (Humphries, 1987; Mitchell et al., 1981; Oster, 1987). A typical binge may include a gallon of ice cream, a package of cookies, and a gallon of milk—all consumed as quickly as possible.

 But wait a minute—if individuals with bulimia are so concerned about gaining weight, why do they binge at all?

The binge itself may be prompted by an anxious or depressed mood, social stressors, feelings about body weight or image, or intense hunger after attempts to diet. The binge continues due to a lack of or impairment in self-control once the binge begins. The individual is unable to control when to stop eating or how much to eat. Eating one cookie while trying to control weight can lead to a binge—after all, since the diet is completely blown, why not go all out? This kind of thought process is another example of the cognitive distortion of all-or-nothing thinking.

One might think that bulimia is not as damaging to the health as anorexia. After all, the individual with bulimia is in no danger of starving to death. But bulimia comes with many serious health consequences: severe tooth decay and erosion of the lining of the esophagus from the acidity of the vomiting, enlarged salivary glands, potassium, calcium, and sodium imbalances that can be very dangerous, damage to the intestinal tract from overuse of laxatives, heart problems, fatigue, and seizures (Berg, 1999).

**BINGE-EATING DISORDER** **Binge-eating disorder** also involves uncontrolled binge eating but differs from bulimia primarily in that individuals with binge-eating disorder do not purge or use other inappropriate methods for avoiding weight gain (American Psychiatric Association, 2013).

**CAUSES OF EATING DISORDERS** The causes of anorexia, bulimia, and binge-eating disorder are not yet fully understood, but the greatest risk factor appears to be someone being an adolescent or young adult female (Keel & Forney, 2013). Increased sensitivity to food and its reward value may play a role in bulimia and binge-eating disorder, while fear and anxiety may become associated with food in anorexia nervosa, with altered activity or functioning of associated brain structures in each (Friedrich et al., 2013; Kaye et al., 2009; Kaye et al., 2013). Research continues to investigate genetic components for eating disorders, as they account for 40 to 60 percent of the risk for anorexia, bulimia, and binge-eating disorder, and although several genes have been implicated, the exact ones to focus on have not yet been identified (Trace et al., 2013; Wade et al., 2013).

Although many researchers have believed eating disorders, especially anorexia, are cultural syndromes that only show up in cultures obsessed with being thin (as many Western cultures are), eating disorders are also found in non-Western cultures (Miller & Pumariega, 1999). What differs between Western and non-Western cultures is the rate at which such disorders appear. For example, Chinese and Chinese American women are far less likely to suffer from eating disorders than are non-Hispanic white women (Pan, 2000). Why wouldn't Chinese American women be more likely to have eating disorders after being exposed to the Western cultural obsession with thinness? Pan (2000) assumes that whatever Chinese cultural factors "protect" Chinese women from developing eating disorders may also still have a powerful influence on Chinese American women.

One problem with studying anorexia and bulimia in other cultures is that the behavior of starving oneself may be seen in other cultures as having an entirely different purpose than in Western cultures. One key component of anorexia, for example, is a fear of being fat, a fear that is missing in many other cultures. Yet women in those cultures have starved themselves for other socially recognized reasons: religious fasting or unusual ideas about nutrition (Castillo, 1997).

Anorexia and bulimia have also been thought to occur only rarely in African American women, but that characterization seems to be changing. Researchers are seeing an increase in anorexia and bulimia among young African American women of all socioeconomic levels (Crago et al., 1996; Mintz & Betz, 1988; Pumariega & Gustavson, 1994). Eating disorders are present in males, and as compared to females, adolescent males may be more likely to be diagnosed with anorexia than with bulimia. They may also be more likely to have had a previous diagnosis of ADHD (Welch et al., 2015). There is also a high rate of eating disorders among transgender individuals (Diemer et al., 2015; Haas et al., 2014). If clinicians and doctors are not aware that these disorders can affect more than the typical white, young, middle-class to upper-middle-class woman, important signs and symptoms of eating disorders in non-white or non-Western people may allow these disorders to go untreated until it is too late.

## THINKING CRITICALLY

How might the proliferation of various media and the Internet affect the development of eating disorders in cultures not previously impacted by them?

▶ | The response entered here will be saved to your notes and may be
collected by your instructor if he/she requires it.

Submit

**TREATMENT OF EATING DISORDERS** What can be done to treat eating disorders? If the weight loss due to anorexia is severe (40 percent or more below expected normal weight), dehydration, severe chemical imbalances, and possibly organ damage may result. Hospitalization should occur before this dangerous point is reached. In the hospital the individual's physical needs will be treated, even to the point of force-feeding in extreme cases. Psychological counseling will also be part of the hospital treatment, which may last from 2 to 4 months. Those individuals with anorexia who are not so severely malnourished as to be in immediate danger can be treated outside of the hospital setting. Psychological treatment strategies might include supportive clinical management, interpersonal therapy, cognitive-behavioral therapy, group therapy, or family-based therapy (Hay, 2013). **LINK** to Learning Objective 15.6. The prognosis for full recovery is not as hopeful as it should be; only 40 to 60 percent of all individuals with anorexia who receive treatment will make a recovery. For some individuals with anorexia who do gain weight, the damage already done to the heart and other body systems may still be so great that an early death is a possibility (Neumarker, 1997). Overall, the estimated mortality rate in anorexia is highest among all of the eating disorders and much higher than any other psychological disorder (Arcelus et al., 2011).

Treatment of bulimia can involve many of the same measures taken to treat anorexia. In addition, the use of antidepressant medications can be helpful, especially those that affect serotonin levels such as the SSRIs (Mitchell et al., 2013). The prognosis for recovery of the individual with bulimia is somewhat more hopeful than that of anorexia. Therapist-led cognitive-behavioral therapy is the best empirically supported therapy, and there is developing evidence for some guided self-help approaches (Hay, 2013). A cognitive therapist is very direct, forcing clients to see how their beliefs do not stand up when considered in "the light of day" and helping them form new, more constructive ways of thinking about themselves and their behavior. (L I N K) to Learning Objective 15.5. Treatment of binge-eating disorder may use some of the same strategies used for anorexia and bulimia, with the added issue of weight loss management in those with obesity.

### SEXUAL DYSFUNCTIONS AND PROBLEMS

**14.12** **Describe types of sexual dysfunction and explain how they may develop.**

A **sexual dysfunction** is a problem with sexual functioning, or with the actual physical workings of the sex act. Sexual dysfunctions involve problems in three possible areas of sexual activity: sexual interest, arousal, and response.

 How common are problems like these—aren't they pretty rare?

Results of surveys from around the globe suggest that about 40 to 45 percent of women and 20 to 30 percent of men have at least one sexual dysfunction, and the rate increases as we age (Lewis et al., 2010). In fact, the figures may actually be higher than those reported. As stated in Chapter One, one of the hazards of doing survey research is that people don't always tell the truth ((L I N K) to Learning Objective 1.6). If a person is going to lie about sexual problems, the most likely lie (or distorted truth) would probably be to deny or minimize such problems.

There are a variety of physical sexual dysfunctions included in the *DSM-5*. Sexual desire or arousal disorders include *female sexual interest/arousal disorder* and *male hypoactive sexual desire disorder*. Disorders related to the physical act of intercourse include *erectile disorder* and *genito-pelvic pain/penetration disorder*. And last, disorders related to the timing or inability to reach orgasm include *premature (early) ejaculation, female orgasmic disorder*, and *delayed ejaculation* (American Psychiatric Association, 2013). Watch the video *Sexual Problems and Dysfunction* for more information on some of these disorders.

👁 **Watch** the **Video** *Sexual Problems and Dysfunction*

**sexual dysfunction**
a problem in sexual functioning.

Some sexual dysfunctions stem from physical sources, known *organic factors*. Others can be caused by purely *sociocultural factors*, or *psychological factors*. However, body and mind influence each other's functioning, and these categories are not mutually exclusive (Lewis et al., 2010).

Organic factors include physical problems such as illnesses, side effects from medication, the effects of surgeries, physical disabilities, and even the use of illegal and legal drugs, such as cocaine, alcohol, and nicotine. Chronic illnesses such as diabetes, cancer, or strokes also belong in this category of factors.

Sociocultural influences on sexual attitudes and behavior also exist and may be a source of psychological stress leading to sexual dysfunction. In the United States and some other Western cultures, people may have experienced instruction from their parents (both direct and indirect teaching) that actually influenced them to form negative attitudes toward sex and sexual activities, such as masturbation.

Psychological stressors also include individual psychological problems, such as low self-esteem, anxiety over performance of the sex act, depression, self-consciousness about one's body image, anxiety disorders, or a history of previous sexual abuse or assault. Another source of psychological stress leading to sexual dysfunctions is the relationship between the two sexual partners. The sexual dysfunction may be only an outward symptom of an underlying problem with the relationship.

For all of the sexual dysfunctions, treatment can include medication, psychotherapy, hormone therapy, stress reduction, sex therapy, and behavioral training. Still commonly used today, Masters and Johnson (1970) recommended a technique called *sensate focus* for treatment of premature ejaculation, in which each member of a couple engages in a series of exercises meant to focus attention on his or her own sensual experiences during various stages of sexual arousal and activity. Male erectile disorder is now commonly treated with drug therapy (Kukula et al., 2014).

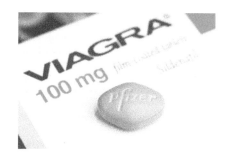

There are a variety of drugs aimed at treating male erectile disorder.

## Concept Map L.O. 14.11, 14.12

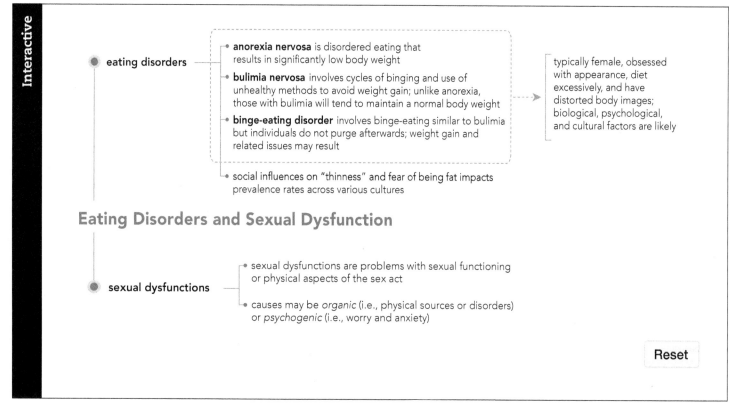

**Interactive**

- **eating disorders**
  - **anorexia nervosa** is disordered eating that results in significantly low body weight
  - **bulimia nervosa** involves cycles of binging and use of unhealthy methods to avoid weight gain; unlike anorexia, those with bulimia will tend to maintain a normal body weight
  - **binge-eating disorder** involves binge-eating similar to bulimia but individuals do not purge afterwards; weight gain and related issues may result

  typically female, obsessed with appearance, diet excessively, and have distorted body images; biological, psychological, and cultural factors are likely

  - social influences on "thinness" and fear of being fat impacts prevalence rates across various cultures

### Eating Disorders and Sexual Dysfunction

- **sexual dysfunctions**
  - sexual dysfunctions are problems with sexual functioning or physical aspects of the sex act
  - causes may be *organic* (i.e., physical sources or disorders) or *psychogenic* (i.e., worry and anxiety)

Reset

# Practice Quiz    How much do you remember?

*Pick the best answer.*

1. Olivia is a teenager who has been diagnosed with anorexia nervosa. What percentage of individuals with anorexia that receive treatment make a recovery?
   a. 40 to 60 percent
   b. 70 to 80 percent
   c. 80 to 90 percent
   d. approximately 95 percent

2. Which of the following characteristics best describes differences between bulimia nervosa and anorexia nervosa?
   a. Individuals with anorexia do not have as severe health risks as individuals with bulimia have.
   b. Individuals with bulimia may have a normal body weight, whereas those with anorexia tend to be severely under their expected body weight.
   c. Individuals with anorexia have been known to binge like those with bulimia on occasion.
   d. Anorexia tends to occur in early adulthood, while bulimia often starts in early adolescence.

3. Researchers believe that 40 to 60 percent of the risk for anorexia, bulimia, and binge-eating disorder is due to
   a. genetic factors.
   b. hormonal factors.
   c. environmental factors.
   d. psychological factors.

4. What is a major cause of sexual dysfunction?
   a. stress
   b. paraphilias
   c. heredity
   d. economic status

5. Surveys suggest that about _____ percent of women and _____ percent of men have at least one sexual dysfunction.
   a. 10; 25
   b. 40 to 45; 20 to 30
   c. 80; 50
   d. 10 to 20; 30 to 40

# Schizophrenia: Altered Reality

Once known as *dementia praecox*, a Latin-based term meaning "out of one's mind before one's time," *schizophrenia* was renamed by Eugen Bleuler, a Swiss psychiatrist, to better illustrate the division (*schizo-*) within the brain (*phren*) among thoughts, feelings, and behavior that seems to take place in people with this disorder (Bleuler, 1911; Möller & Hell, 2002). Because the term literally means "split mind," it has often been confused with dissociative identity disorder, which was at one time called "split personality."

### SYMPTOMS OF SCHIZOPHRENIA

**14.13** **Distinguish between the positive and negative symptoms of schizophrenia.**

Today, **schizophrenia** is described as a long-lasting **psychotic** disorder (involving a severe break with reality), in which there is an inability to distinguish what is real from fantasy as well as disturbances in thinking, emotions, behavior, and perception. The disorder typically arises in the late teens or early 20s, affects both males and females, and is consistent across cultures.

Schizophrenia includes several different kinds of symptoms. Disorders in thinking are a common symptom and are called **delusions**. Although delusions are not prominent in everyone with schizophrenia, they are the symptom that most people associate with this disorder. Delusions are false beliefs about the world that the person holds and that tend to remain fixed and unshakable even in the face of evidence that disproves the delusions. Common schizophrenic delusions include *delusions of persecution*, in which people believe that others are trying to hurt them in some way; *delusions of reference*, in which people believe that other people, television characters, and even books are specifically talking to them; *delusions of influence*, in which people believe that they are being controlled by external forces, such as the devil, aliens, or cosmic forces; and *delusions of grandeur* (or *grandiose delusions*), in which people are convinced that they are powerful people who can save the world or have a special mission (American Psychiatric Association, 2013).

Delusional thinking alone is not enough to merit a diagnosis of schizophrenia, as other symptoms must be present (American Psychiatric Association, 2013). Speech disturbances are common: People with schizophrenia will make up words, repeat words or

**schizophrenia**

severe disorder in which the person suffers from disordered thinking, bizarre behavior, hallucinations, and inability to distinguish between fantasy and reality.

**psychotic**

refers to an individual's inability to separate what is real and what is fantasy.

**delusions**

false beliefs held by a person who refuses to accept evidence of their falseness.

sentences persistently, string words together on the basis of sounds (called *clanging*, such as "come into house, louse, mouse, mouse and cheese, please, sneeze"), and experience sudden interruptions in speech or thought. Thoughts are significantly disturbed as well, with individuals with schizophrenia having a hard time linking their thoughts together in a logical fashion, and in advanced schizophrenia, they may express themselves in a meaningless and jumbled mixture of words and phrases sometimes referred to as a *word salad*. Attention is also a problem for many people with schizophrenia. They seem to have trouble "screening out" information and stimulation that they don't really need, causing them to be unable to focus on information that is relevant (Asarnow et al., 1991; Luck & Gold, 2008).

People with schizophrenia may also have **hallucinations**, in which they hear voices or see things or people that are not really there. Hearing voices is actually more common and one of the key symptoms in making a diagnosis of schizophrenia (Kuhn & Nasar, 2001; Nasar, 1998). Hallucinations involving touch, smell, and taste are less common but also possible. Emotional disturbances are also a key feature of schizophrenia. **Flat affect** is a condition in which the person shows little or no emotion. Emotions can also be excessive and/or inappropriate—a person might laugh when it would be more appropriate to cry or show sorrow, for example. The person's behavior may also become disorganized and extremely odd. The person may not respond to the outside world and either doesn't move at all, maintaining often odd-looking postures for hours on end, or moves about wildly in great agitation. Both extremes, either wildly excessive movement or total lack thereof, are referred to as **catatonia**.

Another way of describing symptoms in schizophrenia is to group them by the way they relate to normal functioning. **Positive symptoms** appear to reflect an excess or distortion of normal functions, such as hallucinations and delusions. **Negative symptoms** appear to reflect a decrease of normal functions, such as poor attention or lack of affect (American Psychiatric Association, 2013). According to the American Psychiatric Association (2013), at least two or more of the following symptoms must be present frequently for at least 1 month to diagnose schizophrenia: delusions, hallucinations, disorganized speech, negative symptoms, and grossly disorganized or catatonic behavior, and at least one of the two symptoms has to be delusions, hallucinations, or disorganized speech. The video *Positive and Negative Symptoms of Schizophrenia* summarizes the key positive and negative symptoms of the disorder.

Dr. John Nash is a famous mathematician who won the Nobel Prize for mathematics in 1994. His fame, however, is more due to the fact that Nash once suffered from a form of schizophrenia in which he experienced delusions of persecution. He at one time believed that aliens were trying to contact him through the newspaper (delusions of reference). His life story and remarkable recovery from schizophrenia are portrayed in the 2001 movie *A Beautiful Mind*, which starred Russell Crowe as Nash.

**hallucinations**
false sensory perceptions, such as hearing voices that do not really exist.

**flat affect**
a lack of emotional responsiveness.

**catatonia**
disturbed behavior ranging from statue-like immobility to bursts of energetic, frantic movement, and talking.

**positive symptoms**
symptoms of schizophrenia that are excesses of behavior or occur in addition to normal behavior; hallucinations, delusions, and distorted thinking.

**negative symptoms**
symptoms of schizophrenia that are less than normal behavior or an absence of normal behavior; poor attention, flat affect, and poor speech production.

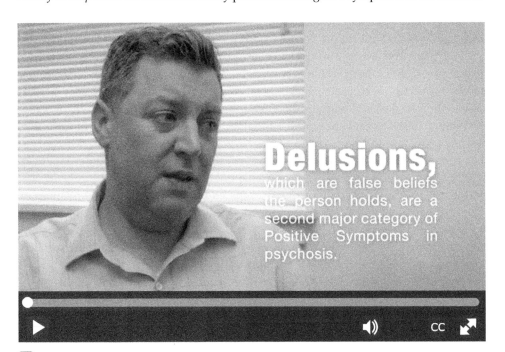

👁 **Watch** the **Video** *Positive and Negative Symptoms of Schizophrenia*

Schizophrenia and depression have been suggested as possible diagnoses that may have been applicable for Mary Todd Lincoln, the wife and widow of President Abraham Lincoln. However, she reportedly experienced a variety of medical conditions that could also explain aspects of her eccentric behavior, personality, and mood changes.

## CAUSES OF SCHIZOPHRENIA

**14.14** **Evaluate the biological and environmental influences on schizophrenia.**

When trying to explain the cause or causes of schizophrenia, biological models and theories prevail, as it appears to be most likely caused by a combination of genetic and environmental factors. This is captured by the neurodevelopmental model, or neurodevelopmental hypothesis, of schizophrenia (Rapoport et al., 2005; Rapoport et al., 2012). Biological explanations of schizophrenia have generated a significant amount of research pointing to genetic origins, prenatal influences such as the mother experiencing viral infections during pregnancy, inflammation in the brain, chemical influences (dopamine, GABA, glutamate, and other neurotransmitters), and brain structural defects (frontal lobe defects, deterioration of neurons, and reduction in white matter integrity) as the causes of schizophrenia (Brown & Derkits, 2010; Cardno & Gottesman, 2000; Gottesman & Shields, 1982; Harrison, 1999; Kety et al., 1994; Nestor et al., 2008; Rijsdijk et al., 2011; Söderlund et al., 2009). Dopamine was first suspected when amphetamine users began to show schizophrenia-like psychotic symptoms. One of the side effects of amphetamine usage is to increase the release of dopamine in the brain. Drugs used to treat schizophrenia decrease the activity of dopamine in areas of the brain responsible for some of the positive symptoms. However, it is not that simple. The prefrontal cortex (an area of the brain involved in planning and organization of information) of people with schizophrenia has been shown to produce lower levels of dopamine than normal (Harrison, 1999), resulting in attention deficits (Luck & Gold, 2008) and poor organization of thought, negative symptoms of the disorder.

Further support for a biological explanation of schizophrenia comes from studies of the incidence of the disorder across different cultures. If schizophrenia were caused mainly by environmental factors, the expectation would be that rates of schizophrenia would vary widely from culture to culture. There is some variation for immigrants and children of immigrants, but about 7 to 8 individuals out of 1,000 will develop schizophrenia in their lifetime, regardless of the culture (Saha et al., 2005).

Family, twin, and adoption studies have provided strong evidence that genes are a major means of transmitting schizophrenia. The highest risk for developing schizophrenia if one has a blood relative with the disorder is faced by monozygotic (identical) twins, who share 100 percent of their genetic material, with a risk factor of about 50 percent (Cardno & Gottesman, 2000; Gottesman & Shields, 1976, 1982; Gottesman et al., 1987). Dizygotic twins, who share about 50 percent of their genetic material, have about a 17 percent risk, the same as a child with one parent with schizophrenia. As genetic relatedness decreases, so does the risk (see **Figure 14.3**). Twin studies are not perfect tools, however; identical twins share the same womb but are not necessarily exposed to the same exact prenatal or postnatal environments, causing some to urge caution in interpreting the 50 percent figure; and even twins reared apart are often raised in similar childhood environments (Davis et al., 1995).

Adoption studies also support the genetic basis of schizophrenia (Sullivan, 2005; Tienari et al., 2004). In one study, the biological and adoptive relatives of adoptees with schizophrenia were compared to a control group of adoptees without schizophrenia but from similar backgrounds and conditions (Kety et al., 1994). The adoptees with schizophrenia had relatives with schizophrenia but *only among their biological relatives.* When the prevalence of schizophrenia was compared between the biological relatives of the adoptees with schizophrenia and the biological relatives of the control group, the rate of the disorder in the relatives of the group with schizophrenia was 10 times higher than in the control group (Kety et al., 1994). It appears the strongest genetic risk may be associated with a gene that plays a role in synaptic pruning during development. In individuals with schizophrenia that have this gene, this process appears to go awry during adolescence, leading to the removal of too many connections between neurons (Sekar et al., 2016).

💬 There's something I don't understand. If one identical twin has the gene and the disorder, shouldn't the other one always have it, too? Why is the rate only 50 percent?

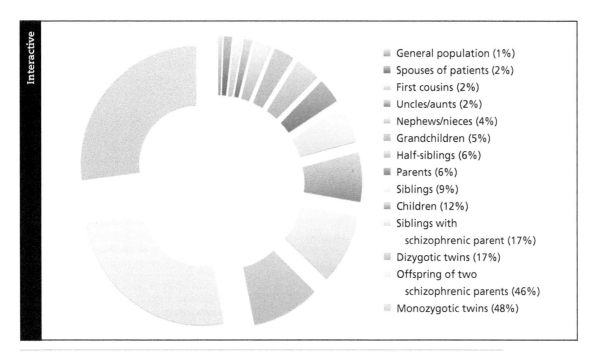

Interactive

- General population (1%)
- Spouses of patients (2%)
- First cousins (2%)
- Uncles/aunts (2%)
- Nephews/nieces (4%)
- Grandchildren (5%)
- Half-siblings (6%)
- Parents (6%)
- Siblings (9%)
- Children (12%)
- Siblings with schizophrenic parent (17%)
- Dizygotic twins (17%)
- Offspring of two schizophrenic parents (46%)
- Monozygotic twins (48%)

**Figure 14.3** Genetics and Schizophrenia

This chart shows a definite pattern: The greater the degree of genetic relatedness, the higher the risk of schizophrenia in individuals related to each other. The only individual to carry a risk even close to that of identical twins (who share 100 percent of their genes) is a person who is the child of two parents with schizophrenia.

Based on Gottesman (1991).

If schizophrenia were entirely controlled by genes, identical twins would indeed both have the disorder at a risk of 100 percent, not merely 50 percent. Obviously, there is some influence of environment on the development of schizophrenia. One model that has been proposed is the **stress-vulnerability model**, which assumes that persons with the genetic "markers" for schizophrenia have a physical vulnerability to the disorder but will not develop schizophrenia unless they are exposed to environmental or emotional stress at critical times in development, such as puberty (Harrison, 1999; Weinberger, 1987). That would explain why only one twin out of a pair might develop the disorder when both carry the genetic markers for schizophrenia—the life stresses for the affected twin were different from those of the one who remained healthy. The immune system is activated during stress, and one recent study has found that in recent-onset schizophrenia (the early stages of the disorder), the brain's immune system secretes high levels of an inflammation-fighting substance, indicating a possible infection (Söderlund et al., 2009). This leads to the possibility that schizophrenia might one day be treatable with anti-inflammatory medications.

Both structural and functional neuroimaging have provided information about how schizophrenia affects the brain, or how the brain operates in an individual with schizophrenia. In one study, researchers using *diffusion tensor imaging* (DTI), **L I N K** to Learning Objective 2.9, in addition to other neurological testing, found that, when compared to healthy control participants, participants with schizophrenia showed structural differences in two particular areas of the brain (Nestor et al., 2008). Specifically, a white matter tract called the cingulum bundle (CB) that lies under the cingulate gyrus and links part of the limbic system, and another that links the frontal lobe to the temporal lobe, were found to have significantly less myelin coating on the axons of the neurons within the bundle. This makes these areas of the brain less efficient in sending neural

**stress-vulnerability model**

explanation of disorder that assumes a biological sensitivity, or vulnerability, to a certain disorder will result in the development of that disorder under the right conditions of environmental or emotional stress.

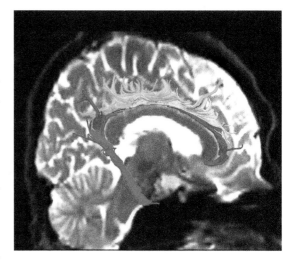

Nestor et al. (2008) used diffusion tensor imaging to investigate schizophrenia. Two of the brain areas examined were the cingulum bundle (CB, consisting of fibers underlying the cingulate gyrus linking parts of the limbic system) and the uncinate fasciculus (UF, neural fibers linking the frontal lobe to the temporal lobe). The cingulum bundle is depicted in the image above. For individuals with schizophrenia, both the CB and UF fiber pathways were found to have neurons with significantly less myelin, making them less efficient in information transfer and resulting in decreased memory and decision-making ability. Image courtesy of Dr. Paul Nestor.

messages to other cells, resulting in decreased memory and decision-making ability. Examination of differences in functional connectivity between brain areas is providing new information about schizophrenia and its symptoms (Schilbach et al., 2016; Shaffer et al., 2015). Measuring cortical thickness and tracking changes in the volume of gray matter and white matter is also providing valuable information about the abnormal patterns of brain development in schizophrenia and other disorders (Gogtay et al., 2008; Gogtay & Thompson, 2010; Goldman et al., 2009; Goodkind et al., 2015).

## Concept Map L.O. 14.13, 14.14

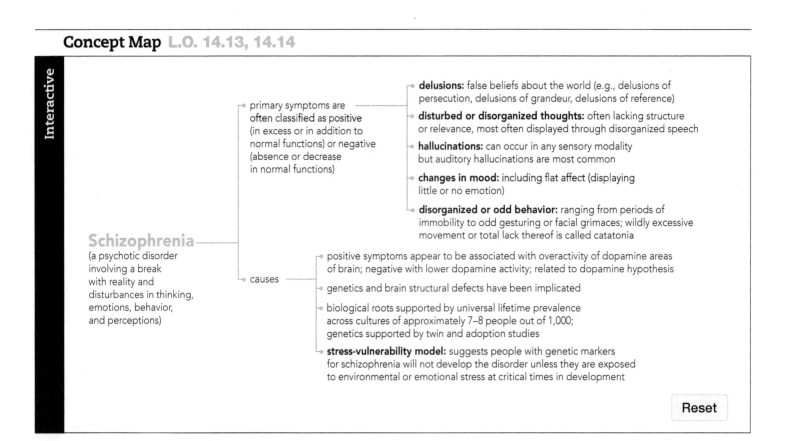

## Practice Quiz How much do you remember?

*Pick the best answer.*

1. David believes that characters in a popular science fiction show are secretly sending him messages. This would be an example of a delusion of
a. persecution.
b. reference.
c. influence.
d. grandeur.

2. Dr. Haldol has several patients with schizophrenia who appear to exhibit excessive or distorted characteristics in relation to what one might consider normal functioning. Specific symptoms include varied hallucinations and multiple delusions. According to the *DSM-5*, these are referred to as
a. flat affect.
b. positive symptoms.
c. negative symptoms.
d. catatonia.

3. Charles has suffered from schizophrenia for many years and now resides in a group treatment facility. One day a nurse approaches him and quietly tells him that his sister, who has been fighting cancer for many months, died that morning. Charles has no appreciable facial reaction, and in a very monotone voice says, "okay." The nurse is not surprised by Charles's lack of response to the awful news, because she knows that _____ is one symptom often seen in those suffering from schizophrenia.
a. clang associations
b. echolalia
c. flat affect
d. perseveration

4. Neuroimaging studies examining potential causes of schizophrenia have discovered that an area of the brain called the _____ appears to have significantly less myelin coating on the axons of its neurons in people with schizophrenia compared to those without the condition.
a. cingulum bundle
b. striate nuclei
c. putamen
d. lateral geniculate nucleus of the thalamus

# Personality Disorders: I'm Okay, It's Everyone Else Who's Weird

*Personality disorders* are a little different from other psychological disorders in that the disorder does not affect merely one aspect of the person's life, such as a higher-than-normal level of anxiety or a set of distorted beliefs, but instead affects the entire life adjustment of the person. The disorder is the personality itself, not one aspect of it. However, despite personality disorders affecting the entire person, current research suggests they are not always life-long in nature as once believed.

## CATEGORIES OF PERSONALITY DISORDERS

**14.15** Classify different types of personality disorders.

In **personality disorder**, a person has an excessively rigid, maladaptive pattern of behavior and ways of relating to others (American Psychiatric Association, 2013). This rigidity and the inability to adapt to social demands and life changes make it very difficult for the individual with a personality disorder to fit in with others or have relatively normal social relationships. The *DSM-5* lists 10 primary types of personality disorder across three basic categories (American Psychiatric Association, 2013): those in which the people are seen as odd or eccentric by others (Paranoid, Schizoid, Schizotypal), those in which the behavior of the person is very dramatic, emotional, or erratic (Antisocial, Borderline, Histrionic, Narcissistic), and those in which the main emotion is anxiety or fearfulness (Avoidant, Dependent, Obsessive-Compulsive). These categories are labeled Cluster A, Cluster B, and Cluster C, respectively.

**ANTISOCIAL PERSONALITY DISORDER** One of the most well researched of the personality disorders is **antisocial personality disorder (ASPD)**. People with ASPD are literally "against society." The antisocial person may habitually break the law, disobey rules, tell lies, and use other people without worrying about their rights or feelings. The person with ASPD may be irritable or aggressive. These individuals may not keep promises or other obligations and are consistently irresponsible. They may also seem indifferent or able to rationalize taking advantage of or hurting others. Typically they borrow money or belongings and don't bother to repay the debt or return the items, they are impulsive, they don't keep their commitments either socially or in their jobs, and they tend to be very selfish, self-centered, and manipulative. There is a definite gender difference in ASPD, with many more males diagnosed with this disorder than females (American Psychiatric Association, 2013).

**BORDERLINE PERSONALITY DISORDER** People with **borderline personality disorder (BLPD)** have relationships with other people that are intense and relatively unstable. They are impulsive, have an unstable sense of self, and are intensely fearful of abandonment. Life goals, career choices, friendships, and even sexual behavior may change quickly and dramatically. Close personal and romantic relationships are marked by extreme swings from idealization to demonization. Periods of depression are not unusual, and some may engage in excessive spending, drug abuse, or suicidal behavior (suicide attempts may be part of the manipulation used against others in a relationship). Emotions are often inappropriate and excessive, with a pattern of self-destructiveness, chronic loneliness, and disruptive anger in close relationships (American Psychiatric Association, 2013). The frequency of this disorder in women is nearly three times greater than in men (American Psychiatric Association, 2013).

**personality disorders**

disorders in which a person adopts a persistent, rigid, and maladaptive pattern of behavior that interferes with normal social interactions.

**antisocial personality disorder (ASPD)**

disorder in which a person uses other people without worrying about their rights or feelings and often behaves in an impulsive or reckless manner without regard for the consequences of that behavior.

**borderline personality disorder (BLPD)**

maladaptive personality pattern in which the person is moody, unstable, lacks a clear sense of identity, and often clings to others with a pattern of self-destructiveness, chronic loneliness, and disruptive anger in close relationships.

## CAUSES OF PERSONALITY DISORDERS

### 14.16 Identify potential causes of personality disorders.

Cognitive-behavioral theorists talk about how specific behavior can be learned over time through the processes of reinforcement, shaping, and modeling. More cognitive explanations involve the belief systems formed by the personality disordered persons, such as the paranoia, extreme self-importance, and fear of being unable to cope by oneself of the paranoid, narcissistic, and dependent personalities, for example.

There is some evidence of genetic factors in personality disorders (Reichborn-Kjennerud, 2008). Close biological relatives of people with disorders such as antisocial, schizotypal, and borderline are more likely to have these disorders than those who are not related (American Psychiatric Association, 2013; Kendler et al., 2006; Reichborn-Kjennerud et al., 2007; Torgersen et al., 2008). Adoption studies of children whose biological parents had antisocial personality disorder show an increased risk for that disorder in those children, even though raised in a different environment by different people (American Psychiatric Association, 2013). A longitudinal study has linked the temperaments of children at age 3 to antisocial tendencies in adulthood, finding that those children with lower fearfulness and inhibitions were more likely to show antisocial personality characteristics in a follow-up study at age 28 (Glenn et al., 2007).

Other causes of personality disorders have been suggested. Antisocial personalities are emotionally unresponsive to stressful or threatening situations when compared to others, which may be one reason that they are not afraid of getting caught (Arnett et al., 1997; Blair et al., 1995; Lykken, 1995). This unresponsiveness seems to be linked to lower than normal levels of stress hormones in antisocial persons (Fairchild et al., 2008; Lykken, 1995).

Disturbances in family relationships and communication have also been linked to personality disorders and, in particular, to antisocial personality disorder (Benjamin, 1996; Livesley, 1995). Childhood abuse, neglect, overly strict parenting, overprotective parenting, and parental rejection have all been put forth as possible causes, making the picture of the development of personality disorders a complicated one. It is safe to say that many of the same factors (genetics, social relationships, and parenting) that help create ordinary personalities also create disordered personalities.

## Concept Map L.O. 14.15, 14.16

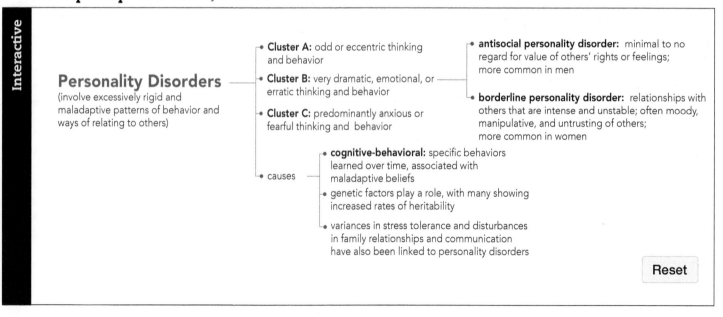

**Interactive**

**Personality Disorders** (involve excessively rigid and maladaptive patterns of behavior and ways of relating to others)

- **Cluster A:** odd or eccentric thinking and behavior
- **Cluster B:** very dramatic, emotional, or erratic thinking and behavior
  - **antisocial personality disorder:** minimal to no regard for value of others' rights or feelings; more common in men
  - **borderline personality disorder:** relationships with others that are intense and unstable; often moody, manipulative, and untrusting of others; more common in women
- **Cluster C:** predominantly anxious or fearful thinking and behavior
- causes
  - **cognitive-behavioral:** specific behaviors learned over time, associated with maladaptive beliefs
  - genetic factors play a role, with many showing increased rates of heritability
  - variances in stress tolerance and disturbances in family relationships and communication have also been linked to personality disorders

Reset

# Practice Quiz   How much do you remember?

*Pick the best answer.*

**1.** Which of the following is not an accurate portrayal of antisocial personality disorder?
   **a.** Most people with this disorder are female.
   **b.** Most people with this disorder are male.
   **c.** People with this disorder suffer little or no guilt for their criminal acts.
   **d.** People with this disorder are consistently irresponsible and don't keep commitments.

**2.** Studies show that _____ personality disorders occur more frequently in women while _____ personality disorders happen more often in men.
   **a.** antisocial; borderline
   **b.** borderline; schizotypal
   **c.** schizotypal; antisocial
   **d.** borderline; antisocial

**3.** One suggested physiological cause of antisocial personality disorder is that people with this condition have:
   **a.** lack of appropriate short-term memory related to ethical and moral rules, caused by deficient function in the hippocampus.
   **b.** lower-than-normal levels of stress hormones.
   **c.** increased synaptic pruning in the prefrontal cortex.
   **d.** heightened sensitivity to external stimuli in the amygdala

**4.** Due to the types and degree of emotions often experienced by people with borderline personality disorder, their personal relationships are often characterized by _____.
   **a.** periods of domestic bliss
   **b.** long-term stability
   **c.** intense emotions, impulsivity, and relative instability
   **d.** long periods of boredom

## APA Goal 2: Scientific Inquiry and Critical Thinking

## Learning More: Psychological Disorders

*Addresses APA Learning Objective 2.2: Demonstrate psychology information literacy.*

We have covered several areas of research that have prompted various levels of controversy, and for various reasons. You have read about the possible comorbidity of ADHD and bipolar disorders in children. You have also read about genetics research in psychological disorders. How might this knowledge impact your personal behavior or thinking about the disorders themselves or the people they affect? While these topics can certainly raise multiple ethical questions, consider each of them from a psychological information and literacy perspective.

What information would you want to know as the parent of a child with ADHD or bipolar disorder? If you are the spouse or partner of someone with a psychological disorder, how might the knowledge of genetic contributions impact decisions to have children, or what might you want to be mindful of in the children you already have?

Several research studies have been cited and summarized in this chapter. If you wanted to look beyond your text, what sources of information would be most useful to you in trying to learn more about a possible disorder or the contribution of genetics? Where would you find or obtain those sources? What would you look for in each? What are some characteristics of objective data, as opposed to personal reports? Do you know how to interpret a graph or chart? How do you determine if the information is relevant? Can it be generalized to your current situation?

After reviewing the questions raised in the last paragraph above, identify at least two information sources you would pursue and what data would you want to get from them.

▶ | The response entered here will be saved to your notes and may
be collected by your instructor if he/she requires it.

Submit

# Applying Psychology to Everyday Life
## Taking the Worry Out of Exams

**14.17**   **Identify some ways to overcome test anxiety.**

Imagine this scenario: You sit down to take your midterm exam, feeling that you are prepared and ready. Once you get the test in front of you, well, maybe you start to feel just a bit more nervous, your hands get sweaty, your stomach may ache; and when you look at the first question—your mind becomes a complete blank!

These are a few of the common symptoms of *test anxiety*, the personal experience of possible negative consequences or poor outcomes on an exam or evaluation, accompanied by a cluster of cognitive, affective, and behavioral symptoms (Zeidner & Matthews, 2005). Cognitive symptoms may consist of worrying excessively about an exam, expecting to do poorly no matter how hard you study, or even finding it hard to start studying in the first place. Then, while taking the test, you might find you do not understand certain directions or questions, "go blank" when looking at the items, or feel like you cannot concentrate on the exam in front of you because your mind keeps wandering. *Affective* or emotional symptoms may include body tension and heightened physiological arousal including sweaty palms, upset stomach, difficulty breathing, and the like, prior to and/or during the exam. *Behavioral* aspects may include procrastination, deficient study skills, or avoiding studying altogether.

While not a clinical disorder, test anxiety has caused countless students considerable stress and agony over the years. Remember "psychology student's syndrome"? You may not really have any of the psychological disorders we've discussed in this chapter, but chances are good that you *have* experienced test anxiety a time or two. It is often easier to address milder forms of anxiety *before* they escalate, and the main intent of this section is to help you achieve that.

So what can you do if you experience test anxiety and want to get your worrying under control? First, determine why you want to do well on the test in the first place. Do you really want to demonstrate your understanding of the material, or are you hoping just to pass? Try to find an internal motivation to do well on the exam rather than simply relying on extrinsic reasons. Even if you are taking a test in a subject you don't necessarily enjoy, try to identify something you want to accomplish, and get your focus off the goal of simply earning a passing grade.

Second, develop some type of strategy for controlling both your cognitive state and behavior before and during the exam. Review the study tips we presented in the Psychology in Action section of this book. Ⓛ Ⓘ Ⓝ Ⓚ to Learning Objective PIA.5. As mentioned there, if you are well prepared, you are less likely to worry. Avoid cramming and take advantage of the additive effects of distributed practice. Refer to that information and review suggestions that will help you manage your tasks and your time. Schedule regular study sessions and avoid or limit distractions (email, phone, text messages, television, noisy roommates, and the like may seem to provide welcome escapes from studying, but they will only keep you from your intended goal). You've read the chapter on memory (or at least you should have!) and now know that spacing out your study and using meaningful, elaborative rehearsal over multiple study periods is going to yield much better results than an all-out cramming marathon the night before an exam. Ⓛ Ⓘ Ⓝ Ⓚ to Learning Objectives 6.5, 6.10 and 6.11.

The way you approach an exam can have a significant impact on the testing experience and how you manage yourself during that exam (Davis et al., 2008). Instead of focusing on how nervous you are and how sure you are that you aren't going to be able to remember anything, turn that thinking around and recognize how much energy you have going into the exam (Dundas et al., 2009). Positive self-talk can be very valuable in this kind of situation (and is a good example of cognitive therapy at work). A recent study demonstrated that competence-priming (imagining a person who is successful at a related task) lowered the relationship between test anxiety and test performance (Lang & Lang, 2010). Additionally, instead of focusing on the whole exam, take control and address one question at a time, first answering the questions you know—that will build your confidence and help you progress through the test. Also control your body; try to stay relaxed and breathe normally. If you get distracted, consciously redirect yourself back to the next question. Before you know it, you will have completed the entire exam—whew!

### Questions for Further Discussion

1. Have you ever experienced test anxiety? What methods did you use to get your worrying under control?

2. What factors, other than the ones listed here, might influence the anxiety one feels when taking an exam?

# Chapter Summary

## What Is Abnormality?

**14.1 Explain how our definition of abnormal behavior and thinking has changed over time.**

- Psychopathology is the study of abnormal behavior and psychological dysfunction.

- In ancient times, holes were cut in an ill person's head to let out evil spirits in a process called trephining. Hippocrates believed that mental illness came from an imbalance in the body's four humors, whereas in the early Renaissance period the mentally ill were labeled as witches.

- Abnormality can be characterized as thinking or behavior that is statistically rare, deviant from social norms, causes subjective discomfort, does not allow day-to-day functioning, or causes a person to be dangerous to self or others.

- In the United States, *insanity* is a legal term, not a psychological term.

**14.2 Identify models used to explain psychological disorders.**

- In biological models of abnormality, the assumption is that mental illnesses are caused by chemical or structural malfunctions in the nervous system.

- Psychodynamic theorists assume that abnormal thinking and behavior stem from repressed conflicts and urges that are fighting to become conscious.

- Behaviorists see abnormal behavior or thinking as learned.

- Cognitive theorists see abnormal behavior as coming from irrational beliefs and illogical patterns of thought.

- The sociocultural perspective conceptualizes all thinking and behavior as the product of learning and shaping of behavior within the context of family, social group, and culture.

- Cultural relativity refers to the need to consider the norms and customs of another culture when diagnosing a person from that culture with a disorder.

- The biopsychosocial model views abnormal thinking and behavior as the sum result of biological, psychological, social, and cultural influences.

**14.3 Describe how psychological disorders are diagnosed and classified.**

- *The Diagnostic and Statistical Manual of Mental Disorders, Fifth Edition (DSM-5)* is a manual of psychological disorders and their symptoms.

- More than one fifth of all adults over age 18 suffer from a mental disorder in any given year.

- Diagnoses provide a common language for health care providers, but they may also predispose providers to think about their patients in particular ways.

- In contrast to categorical approaches to diagnosis, research is building related to dimensional assessment of psychopathology across brain, behavior, cognitive, and genetic factors.

## Disorders of Anxiety, Trauma, and Stress: What, Me Worry?

**14.4 Identify different types of anxiety disorders and their symptoms.**

- Anxiety disorders are all disorders in which the most dominant symptom is excessive and unrealistic anxiety.

- Phobias are irrational, persistent fears. Three types of phobias are social anxiety disorder (social phobia), specific phobias, and agoraphobia.

- Panic disorder is the sudden and recurrent onset of intense panic for no reason, with all the physical symptoms that can occur in sympathetic nervous system arousal.

- Generalized anxiety disorder is a condition of intense and unrealistic anxiety that lasts 6 months or more.

**14.5 Describe obsessive-compulsive disorder and stress-related disorders.**

- Obsessive-compulsive disorder consists of an obsessive, recurring thought that creates anxiety and a compulsive, ritualistic, and repetitive behavior or mental action that reduces that anxiety.

- Significant and traumatic stressors can lead to acute stress disorder or posttraumatic stress disorder. The diagnosis differs according to duration and onset but includes symptoms of anxiety, dissociation, nightmares, and reliving the event.

**14.6 Identify potential causes of anxiety, trauma, and stress disorders.**

- Psychodynamic explanations of anxiety and related disorders point to repressed urges and desires that are trying to come into consciousness, creating anxiety that is controlled by the abnormal behavior.

- Behaviorists state that disordered behavior is learned through both operant conditioning and classical conditioning techniques.

- Cognitive psychologists believe that excessive anxiety comes from illogical, irrational thought processes.

- Biological explanations of anxiety-related disorders include chemical imbalances in the nervous system, in particular serotonin and GABA systems.

- Genetic transmission may be responsible for anxiety-related disorders among related persons.

## Dissociative Disorders: Altered Identities

**14.7 Differentiate among dissociative amnesia, dissociative fugue, and dissociative identity disorder.**

- Dissociative disorders involve a break in consciousness, memory, or both. These disorders include dissociative amnesia, with or without fugue, and dissociative identity disorder.

**14.8** Summarize explanations for dissociative disorders.

• Psychodynamic explanations point to repression of memories, seeing dissociation as a defense mechanism against anxiety.

• Cognitive and behavioral explanations see dissociative disorders as a kind of avoidance learning. Biological explanations point to lower-than-normal activity levels in the areas of the brain responsible for body awareness.

## Disorders of Mood: The Effect of Affect

**14.9** Describe different disorders of mood, including major depressive disorder and bipolar disorders.

• Mood disorders, also called affective disorders, are severe disturbances in emotion.

• Major depressive disorder has a fairly sudden onset and is extreme sadness and despair, typically with no obvious external cause. It is the most common of the mood disorders and is more common in women than in men.

• Bipolar disorders are characterized by shifts in mood that may range from normal to manic, with or without episodes of depression (bipolar I disorder) or spans of normal mood interspersed with episodes of major depression and hypomania (bipolar II disorder).

**14.10** Compare and contrast behavioral, social cognitive, and biological explanations for depression and other disorders of mood.

• Learning theories link depression to learned helplessness.

• Cognitive theories see depression as the result of distorted, illogical thinking.

• Biological explanations of mood disorders look at the function of serotonin, norepinephrine, and dopamine systems in the brain.

• Mood disorders are more likely to appear in genetically related people, with higher rates of risk for closer genetic relatives.

## Eating Disorders and Sexual Dysfunction

**14.11** Identify the symptoms and risk factors associated with anorexia nervosa, bulimia nervosa, and binge-eating disorder.

• Maladaptive eating problems include anorexia nervosa, bulimia nervosa, and binge-eating disorder.

• Genetics, increased sensitivity to the rewarding value of food, or food-related anxiety, altered brain function, and being female contribute to risk of being diagnosed with an eating disorder.

**14.12** Describe types of sexual dysfunction and explain how they may develop.

• Sexual dysfunctions are problems with sexual functioning. They may be caused by physical problems, interpersonal or sociocultural issues, or psychological problems and can affect sexual interest, arousal, and response.

• These dysfunctions include female sexual interest/arousal disorder, male hypoactive sexual desire disorder, erectile disorder, genito-pelvic pain/penetration disorder, premature (early) ejaculation, female orgasmic disorder, and delayed ejaculation.

## Schizophrenia: Altered Reality

**14.13** Distinguish between the positive and negative symptoms of schizophrenia.

• Schizophrenia is a split among thoughts, emotions, and behavior. It is a long-lasting psychotic disorder in which reality and fantasy become confused.

• Symptoms of schizophrenia include delusions (false beliefs about the world), hallucinations, emotional disturbances, attentional difficulties, disturbed speech, and disordered thinking.

• Positive symptoms are excesses of behavior associated with increased dopamine activity in some parts of the brain, whereas negative symptoms are deficits in behavior associated with decreased dopamine activity in other parts of the brain.

**14.14** Evaluate the biological and environmental influences on schizophrenia.

• Biological explanations for schizophrenia focus on dopamine, structural defects in the brain, and genetic influences. Rates of risk of developing schizophrenia increase drastically as genetic relatedness increases, with the highest risk faced by an identical twin whose twin sibling has schizophrenia.

## Personality Disorders: I'm Okay, It's Everyone Else Who's Weird

**14.15** Classify different types of personality disorders.

• Personality disorders are extremely rigid, maladaptive patterns of behavior that prevent a person from normal social interactions and relationships.

• The *DSM-5* lists 10 primary types of personality disorders across three broad categories.

• In antisocial personality disorder, a person consistently violates the rights of others.

• In borderline personality disorder, a person is clingy, moody, unstable in relationships, and suffers from problems with identity.

**14.16** Identify potential causes of personality disorders.

• Cognitive-learning theorists see personality disorders as a set of learned behavior that has become maladaptive—bad habits learned early on in life. Belief systems of the personality-disordered person are seen as illogical.

• Biological relatives of people with personality disorders are more likely to develop similar disorders, supporting a genetic basis for such disorders.

• Biological explanations look at the lower-than-normal stress hormones in antisocial personality disordered persons as responsible for their low responsiveness to threatening stimuli.

• Other possible causes of personality disorders may include disturbances in family communications and relationships, childhood abuse, neglect, overly strict parenting, overprotective parenting, and parental rejection.

## Applying Psychology to Everyday Life: Taking the Worry Out of Exams

**14.17 Identify some ways to overcome test anxiety.**

• Test anxiety is the personal experience of possible negative consequences or poor outcomes on an exam or evaluation.

• Some ways to deal with test anxiety are to find an internal motivation, develop strategies for studying and controlling your emotional reactions, and focus on the positive rather than the negative.

# Test Yourself

*Pick the best answer.*

1. What was the most likely reason that someone would perform an exorcism?
   a. to relieve fluid pressure on the brain
   b. to look into the brain to see what was wrong
   c. to release evil spirits
   d. to restore balance to the body's humors

2. In 1972, a jet carrying a rugby team from Peru crashed high in the snow-covered Andes Mountains. Many of the players survived for more than 2 months by eating the remains of those who died. Psychologists justified their cannibalism because that was the only way they could have survived so long without food. By what definition might their behavior best be classified?
   a. statistical
   b. subjective discomfort
   c. maladaptive
   d. situational context

3. Which of the following is an example of cultural relativity?
   a. Dr. Han believes that the voices his patient is hearing stem from a biological instead of a psychological cause.
   b. While Dr. Howard believes that hypnosis is the best way to understand all disorders, his approach is not shared by his colleagues.
   c. While Dr. Akido knows that his patient, Aki, believes her anxiety has a biological explanation, in learning more about her family of origin, he suspects it has a psychological cause.
   d. Dr. Roland uses a behavioral approach to treat all his clients who are younger than age 10.

4. How many axes does the *DSM-5* use to aid mental health professionals in making a diagnosis?
   a. one
   b. two
   c. four
   d. five

5. *Trypanophobia*, also known as a fear of receiving an injection, is an example of
   a. obsession.
   b. social phobia.
   c. anxiety attack.
   d. specific phobia.

6. Aaron hates to go to restaurants for fear that he will be seated in the far back of the restaurant and be unable to get out in case of an emergency. This may be a symptom of
   a. social phobia.
   b. specific phobia.
   c. agoraphobia.
   d. claustrophobia.

7. Ria experienced a sudden attack of intense fear when she was boarding a plane with her friends to fly to Mexico for spring break. Ria's heart raced, she became dizzy, and she was certain she would die in a plane crash if she boarded the plane. Subsequently she did not go on her trip, and the plane arrived safely in Mexico 3 hours later. Ria experienced
   a. a depressive episode.
   b. a panic attack.
   c. panic disorder.
   d. agoraphobia.

8. Dr. Kirby has been meeting with 9-year-old Loren, whose family lost everything in a tornado. In her initial visit, Loren was diagnosed with acute stress disorder. During a 2-month follow-up with Dr. Kirby, Loren is still exhibiting many of the same symptoms. What should Dr. Kirby do?
   a. Dr. Kirby will revise Loren's diagnosis from ASD to posttraumatic stress disorder.
   b. Dr. Kirby will revise Loren's diagnosis from ASD to generalized anxiety disorder.
   c. Dr. Kirby will continue treatment for acute stress disorder for at least 6 months.
   d. Dr. Kirby should tell Loren she is cured so as to speed her recovery.

9. Survivors of natural disasters like Hurricane Sandy in 2012 may experience higher incidences of
   a. bipolar disorder.
   b. posttraumatic stress disorder.
   c. personality disorders.
   d. schizophrenia.

10. Calvin is terribly worried that his college education was wasted when he doesn't get his dream job. Furthermore, Calvin believes he ruined his future when he did poorly in his job interview. Calvin explains, "I had to ace the interview. It had to be perfect, and it wasn't!" How might a cognitive-behavioral psychologist classify this distorted thought process?
    a. magnification
    b. overgeneralization
    c. all-or-nothing thinking
    d. minimization

11. Dissociative amnesia is different from retrograde amnesia because
    a. dissociative amnesia is typically psychological in origin.
    b. retrograde amnesia has been shown to not actually exist.
    c. dissociative amnesia is caused by a physical blow to the head.
    d. retrograde amnesia is caused by psychological trauma.

12. Depersonalization/derealization disorder is a type of dissociative disorder that has been found to have possible _____ foundations for the experience of detachment.
    a. biological
    b. psychodynamic
    c. behavioral
    d. cognitive

13. Which type of depression is the most common type of mood disorder?
    a. bipolar disorder
    b. mania
    c. seasonal affective disorder
    d. major depressive disorder

14. Behavioral theorists link depression to _____, whereas social cognitive theorists point to _____.
    a. distortions in thinking; learned helplessness
    b. biological abnormalities; distortions in thinking
    c. unconscious forces; learned helplessness
    d. learned helplessness; distortions in thinking

**15.** Individuals with bulimia often rationalize that since they have had a single treat, their diet is ruined and therefore they might as well go ahead and eat excessively. Such irrational thinking is an example of the cognitive distortion known as
**a.** overgeneralization.
**b.** all-or-nothing thinking.
**c.** magnification.
**d.** minimization.

**16.** Binge-eating disorder is different from bulimia in that individuals with binge-eating disorder
**a.** typically eat much smaller portions before purging the food.
**b.** do not typically purge the food they eat.
**c.** only purge their food after several binge sessions.
**d.** often resort to anorexic methods to rid themselves of the food they have eaten.

**17.** Sexual dysfunctions and problems can be caused by
**a.** organic factors.
**b.** organic and sociocultural factors.
**c.** organic, psychological, and sociocultural factors.
**d.** hereditary factors primarily.

**18.** On your first call as a paramedic, you enter the house of a man who has covered his walls and ceiling in aluminum foil to protect his brain from the thought-controlling rays of the government. This is an example of a _____ delusion.
**a.** persecution
**b.** reference
**c.** influence
**d.** grandeur

**19.** Rodney has been diagnosed with schizophrenia. He rarely smiles and often shows little emotion in any situation. Psychologists refer to this characteristic as
**a.** catatonia.
**b.** flat affect.
**c.** positive symptoms.
**d.** negative symptoms.

**20.** What neurotransmitter was first believed to be the cause of schizophrenia?
**a.** GABA
**b.** serotonin
**c.** epinephrine
**d.** dopamine

**21.** Colleen found herself attracted to her psychology instructor. She would frequently go by his office just to be near him. When he didn't respond to her advances, Colleen eventually told him that she had thoughts of killing herself so that he would spend time trying to counsel her. What personality disorder best describes Colleen's thinking and behavior?
**a.** borderline personality disorder
**b.** schizoid personality disorder
**c.** schizotypal personality disorder
**d.** antisocial personality disorder

# Psychological Therapies

What information might be most useful for someone interested in pursuing a particular therapy or treatment for a psychological disorder?
After you have answered the question, watch the video to compare the answers of other students to yours.

▶ | The response entered here will be saved to your notes and may be collected by your instructor if he/she requires it.

◉ Watch the Video

# Why study therapies for psychological disorders?

There are almost as many therapy methods as there are disorders. Correctly matching the type of therapy to the disorder can mean the difference between a cure and a crisis. It is important to know the choices available for treatment and how they relate to the different kinds of disorders so that an informed decision can be made and the best possible outcome can be achieved for mental health and wellness.

# Learning Objectives

**15.1** Describe how the treatment of psychological disorders has changed throughout history.

**15.2** Describe the basic elements of Freud's psychoanalysis and psychodynamic approaches today.

**15.3** Identify the basic elements of the humanistic therapies known as person-centered therapy and Gestalt therapy.

**15.4** Explain how behavior therapists use classical and operant conditioning to treat disordered behavior.

**15.5** Summarize the goals and basic elements of cognitive and cognitive-behavioral therapies.

**15.6** Compare and contrast different forms of group therapy.

**15.7** Identify the advantages and disadvantages of group therapy.

**15.8** Summarize the research on the effectiveness of psychotherapy.

**15.9** Identify factors that influence the effectiveness of therapy.

**15.10** Categorize types of drugs used to treat psychological disorders.

**15.11** Explain how electroconvulsive therapy and psychosurgery are used to treat psychological disorders.

**15.12** Identify some of the newer technologies being used to treat psychological disorders.

**15.13** Describe how virtual reality can be used in psychotherapy.

# Treatment of Psychological Disorders: Past to Present

**15.1** Describe how the treatment of psychological disorders has changed throughout history.

As discussed in Chapter Fourteen, although psychological or social causes might have been identified for some disorders, until the late 1700s, people suffering severe mental illnesses were sometimes thought to be possessed by demons or evil spirits, and the "treatments" to rid the person of these spirits were severe and deadly. Even within the last 200 years, a period of supposedly more "enlightened" awareness, the mentally ill did not always receive humane* treatment.

> 💬 I've seen movies about mental hospitals, and they didn't look like great places to be in even now—how bad was it back then? What did people do with relatives who were ill that way?

The first truly organized effort to do something with mentally ill persons began in England in the middle of the sixteenth century. Bethlehem Hospital in London (later known as "Bedlam") was converted into an asylum (a word meaning "place of safety") for the mentally ill. In reality, the first asylums were little more than prisons where the mentally ill were chained to their beds. "Treatments" consisted of bloodletting (which more often than not led to death or the need for lifelong care for the patient), beatings, ice baths in which the person was submerged until passing out or suffering a seizure, and induced vomiting in a kind of spiritual cleansing (Hunt, 1993). This cleansing or purging was meant to rid the body of physical impurities so that the person's mind and soul could function more perfectly.

It was not until 1793 that efforts were made to treat the mentally ill with kindness and guidance—known as "moral treatment"—rather than beating them or subjecting them to the harsh physical purging that had been commonplace. It was at this time that Philippe Pinel personally unchained the inmates at La Bicêtre Asylum in Paris, France, beginning the movement of humane treatment of the mentally ill (Brigham, 1844; Curtis, 1993).

Today, we can group the primary approaches to **therapy** (treatment methods aimed at making people feel better and function more effectively) into two broad categories. One category is based primarily in psychological theory and techniques; people tell the therapist about their problems, and the therapist listens and tries to help them understand those problems or assists them in changing the behaviors related to the problem. The other category uses medical interventions to bring the symptoms under control. Although we can separate treatments into these two larger categories, in actual practice, many effective treatment strategies or treatment plans combine facets of both. Just as there is no one single "cause" of a disorder (Maxmen et al., 2009), different psychological treatments are often used in tandem or combined with biomedical interventions. Furthermore, many psychology professionals do not limit themselves to a single technique and are **eclectic**, using more than one treatment approach or technique to best meet the needs of the people they are working with. The fields of clinical psychology and counseling psychology are diverse, and professionals have a wide variety of educational and training experiences. Ⓛ Ⓘ Ⓝ Ⓚ to Learning Objective B.5.

**Psychotherapy** typically involves an individual, couple, or small group of individuals working directly with a therapist and discussing their concerns or problems. The goal of most psychotherapy is to help both mentally healthy and psychologically disordered persons understand themselves better (Goin, 2005; Wolberg, 1977). Because understanding

In this famous painting by French artist Robert Fleury, French psychiatrist Dr. Philippe Pinel orders the chains removed from patients at a Paris asylum for insane women. Pinel was one of the first psychiatrists to recommend humane treatment of the mentally ill.

**therapy**

treatment methods aimed at making people feel better and function more effectively.

**eclectic**

approach to therapy that results from combining elements of several different approaches or techniques.

**psychotherapy**

therapy for mental disorders in which a person with a problem talks with a psychological professional.

---

*humane: marked by compassion, sympathy, or consideration for humans (and animals).

of one's motives and actions is called *insight*, therapies aimed mainly at this goal are called **insight therapies**. A therapy that is directed more at changing behavior than providing insights into the reasons for that behavior is called **action therapy**. Many psychological professionals use a combination of insight and action therapeutic* methods.

The other main type of therapy uses some biological treatment in the form of a medical procedure to bring about changes in the person's disordered behavior. **Biomedical therapies** include the use of drugs, surgical methods, electric shock treatments, and noninvasive stimulation techniques. It is important to understand that biomedical therapy often eliminates or alleviates the symptoms of a disorder, while psychotherapy addresses issues associated with the disorder, and when used together, these two types of therapy facilitate** each other (Maxmen et al., 2009). For example, when medications are needed, individuals taking the proper medications are going to benefit more from psychotherapy, as their symptoms will be better controlled. Furthermore, psychotherapy, not medication, is going to help them better understand what the symptoms of their disorder are and facilitate adjustment, other coping strategies, and proactive ways of addressing the disorder or its related outcomes (Maxmen et al., 2009).

The National Institute of Mental Health's (NIMH) Research Domain Criteria (RDoC) project was introduced in Chapter 14. ⓁⒾⓃⓀ to Learning Objective 14.3. Goals of the RDoC project are consistent with attempts to classify psychological disorders along dimensions of brain, cognitive, and behavioral functioning. Instead of simply identifying someone with depression as having a "mental disorder," a psychological professional might be able to better understand the respective cluster of symptoms and features as a subset of disrupted functions and be better able to identify more effective treatment strategies (Insel & Cuthbert, 2015). There are also attempts to identify common factors that bridge a variety of diagnoses. Such "transdiagnostic" factors may include internalizing versus externalizing types of symptoms or brain areas shared by a variety of disorders (Goodkind et al., 2015; Krueger & Eaton, 2015). Overall, these approaches have a lot of potential to improve both diagnostic and treatment approaches in the future.

**insight therapies**

therapies in which the main goal is helping people to gain insight with respect to their behavior, thoughts, and feelings.

**action therapy**

therapy in which the main goal is to change disordered or inappropriate behavior directly.

**biomedical therapies**

therapies that directly affect the biological functioning of the body and brain; therapies for mental disorders in which a person with a problem is treated with biological or medical methods to relieve symptoms.

## Concept Map L.O. 15.1

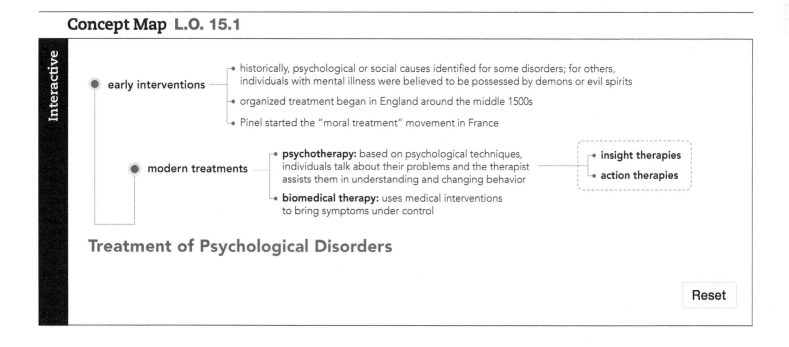

**Interactive**

- **early interventions**
  - historically, psychological or social causes identified for some disorders; for others, individuals with mental illness were believed to be possessed by demons or evil spirits
  - organized treatment began in England around the middle 1500s
  - Pinel started the "moral treatment" movement in France

- **modern treatments**
  - **psychotherapy:** based on psychological techniques, individuals talk about their problems and the therapist assists them in understanding and changing behavior
    - insight therapies
    - action therapies
  - **biomedical therapy:** uses medical interventions to bring symptoms under control

**Treatment of Psychological Disorders**

Reset

---

*therapeutic: providing or assisting in a cure.
**facilitate: to assist, make possible, or make easier.

# Practice Quiz   How much do you remember?

*Pick the best answer.*

1. One of the first therapists to begin a movement towards the humane treatment of patients was
   **a.** Robert Fleury.
   **b.** Philippe Pinel.
   **c.** Sigmund Freud.
   **d.** Josef Breuer.

2. Psychotherapies that attempt to increase the understanding of a client's motives are known as _____ therapies.
   **a.** insight
   **b.** action
   **c.** biomedical
   **d.** psychoanalytic

3. DeWayne has decided to seek psychotherapy for some personal difficulties he has been having. While on the telephone with one possible clinician, he asks her to describe the kind of treatment approach that she uses with clients. "I don't limit myself to a single theory or approach," the therapist answers. "Instead I operate in a(n) _____ fashion, integrating various treatment approaches based on the specific needs of each client."
   **a.** eclectic
   **b.** Gestalt
   **c.** supratheoretical
   **d.** atheoretical

4. Which of the following is *not* one of the main types of therapy noted by your textbook that helps people improve their overall functioning?
   **a.** Insight therapy
   **b.** Action therapy
   **c.** Biomedical therapy
   **d.** Regressive therapy

---

# Insight Therapies: Psychodynamic and Humanistic Approaches

We'll begin our discussion of psychotherapy with two types of insight therapies: psychodynamic therapy and humanistic therapy. While these approaches use different methods, they both strive to gain an understanding of one's motives and actions.

## PSYCHOTHERAPY BEGINS: FREUD'S PSYCHOANALYSIS

**15.2  Describe the basic elements of Freud's psychoanalysis and psychodynamic approaches today.**

 💬 So what exactly happens in psychoanalysis? I've heard lots of stories about it, but what's it really like?

In a sense, Freud took the sixteenth-century method of physical cleansing to a different level. Instead of a physical purge, cleansing for Freud meant removing all the "impurities" of the unconscious mind that he believed were responsible for his patients' psychological and nervous disorders. (Freud was a medical doctor and referred to the people who came to him for help as "patients.") The impurities of the unconscious mind were considered to be disturbing thoughts, socially unacceptable desires, and immoral urges that originated in the id, the part of the personality that is itself unconscious and driven by basic needs for survival and pleasure. **LINK** to Learning Objective 13.1.

**PSYCHOANALYSIS**   Freud believed that his patients used these unconscious thoughts to prevent anxiety, and as such, the thoughts would not be easily brought into conscious awareness. Freud designed a therapy technique to help his patients feel more relaxed, open, and able to explore their innermost feelings without fear of embarrassment or rejection. This method was called *psychoanalysis*, and it is an insight therapy that emphasizes revealing the unconscious conflicts, urges, and desires that are assumed to cause disordered emotions and behavior (Freud, 1904a, 1904b; Mitchell & Black, 1996). This is the original reason for the couch in Freud's version of psychoanalysis; people lying on the couch were more relaxed and would, Freud thought, feel more dependent and childlike, making it easier for them to "get at" those early childhood memories. An additional plus was that he could sit behind the patients at the head of the couch and take notes. Without the patients being able to see his reactions to what they said, they remained unaffected by his reactions.

*"Why do you think you cross the road?"*

"Why do you think you cross the road?"
© The New Yorker Collection 1990 Arnie Levin from cartoonbank.com. All Rights Reserved.

Freud also made use of two techniques to try to reveal the repressed information in his patients' unconscious minds. These techniques were the interpretation of dreams and allowing patients to talk freely about anything that came to mind.

**DREAM INTERPRETATION** *Dream interpretation*, or the analysis of the elements within a patient's reported dream, formed a large part of Freud's psychoanalytic method. Ⓛ Ⓘ Ⓝ Ⓚ to Learning Objective 4.7. Freud believed that repressed material often surfaced in dreams, although in symbolic form. The *manifest content* of the dream was the actual dream and its events, but the **latent content** was the hidden, symbolic meaning of those events that would, if correctly interpreted, reveal the unconscious conflicts that were creating the nervous disorder (Freud, 1900).

**FREE ASSOCIATION** The other technique for revealing the unconscious mind was a method originally devised by Freud's coworker, Josef Breuer (Breuer & Freud, 1895). Breuer encouraged his patients to freely say whatever came into their minds without fear of being negatively evaluated or condemned. As the patients talked, they began to reveal things that were loosely associated with their flow of ideas, often revealing what Breuer felt were hidden, unconscious concerns. Freud adopted this method of **free association**, believing that repressed impulses and other material were trying to "break free" into consciousness and would eventually surface using this technique.

**RESISTANCE AND TRANSFERENCE** Other components of Freud's original psychoanalytic method were **resistance** (the point at which the patient becomes unwilling to talk about certain topics) and **transference** (when the therapist becomes a symbol of a parental authority figure from the past). Therapists can also experience *countertransference*, in which the therapist has a transference reaction to the patient. This reaction might not always be to the benefit of the patient. As in all of the therapeutic approaches, peer and professional supervision helps therapists recognize potential issues in providing effective therapy.

**EVALUATION OF PSYCHOANALYSIS AND PSYCHODYNAMIC APPROACHES** Freud's original theory, on which he based his interpretations of his patients' revelations, has been criticized as having several flaws, which were discussed in Chapter Thirteen. These included the lack of scientific research to support his claims, his unwillingness to believe some of the things revealed by his patients when those revelations did not fit into his view of the world, and his almost obsessive need to assume that problems with sex and sexuality were at the heart of nearly every nervous disorder.

Few psychoanalysts today still use Freud's original methods, which could take years to produce results. The couch is gone, and the *client* (a term used to support the active role of the person seeking help and to avoid implying "sickness," as might result when using the term *patient*) may sit face to face with the therapist. The client may also stand or walk about. Rather than remaining quiet until the client says something revealing, the modern psychoanalyst is far more **directive**, asking questions, suggesting helpful behavior, and giving opinions and interpretations earlier in the relationship, which helps speed up the therapeutic process. Today's psychoanalysts also focus less on the id as the motivator of behavior, instead looking more at the ego or sense of self as the motivating force behind all actions, and some more on basic relationship issues, including the relationship between the therapist and client (McWilliams, 2016; Prochaska & Norcross, 2014). Some psychoanalysts also focus on the process of transference more than on other typical aspects of traditional psychoanalysis, leading to the more general method called **psychodynamic therapy**. Psychodynamic therapy is typically shorter in duration than traditional psychoanalysis. Watch the video *Psychodynamic Therapy* to learn more about the history and practice of this therapy.

**latent content**

the symbolic or hidden meaning of dreams.

**free association**

psychoanalytic technique in which a patient was encouraged to talk about anything that came to mind without fear of negative evaluations.

**resistance**

occurring when a patient becomes reluctant to talk about a certain topic, by either changing the subject or becoming silent.

**transference**

in psychoanalysis, the tendency for a patient or client to project positive or negative feelings for important people from the past onto the therapist.

**directive**

therapy in which the therapist actively gives interpretations of a client's statements and may suggest certain behavior or actions.

**psychodynamic therapy**

a newer and more general term for therapies based on psychoanalysis with an emphasis on transference, shorter treatment times, and a more direct therapeutic approach.

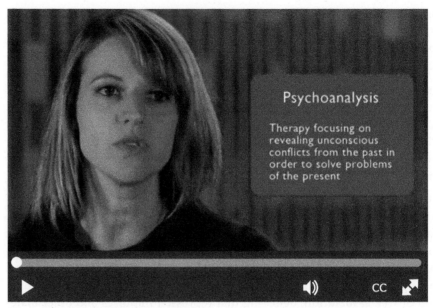

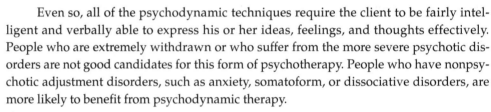

👁 **Watch** the **Video** *Psychodynamic Therapy*

Even so, all of the psychodynamic techniques require the client to be fairly intelligent and verbally able to express his or her ideas, feelings, and thoughts effectively. People who are extremely withdrawn or who suffer from the more severe psychotic disorders are not good candidates for this form of psychotherapy. People who have nonpsychotic adjustment disorders, such as anxiety, somatoform, or dissociative disorders, are more likely to benefit from psychodynamic therapy.

**INTERPERSONAL PSYCHOTHERAPY** Interpersonal psychotherapy (IPT) is a psychotherapy developed to address depression. It is an insight therapy focusing on relationships of the individual with others and the interplay between mood and the events of everyday life (Bleiberg & Markowitcz, 2008). It is based on the interpersonal theories of Adolph Meyer and Harry Stack Sullivan along with the attachment theory of John Bowlby and focuses on interpersonal relationships and functioning (Bleiberg & Markowitcz, 2008). It is one of the few theories derived from psychodynamic thinking that does have some research support for its effectiveness in treating depression, particularly when combined with medication (Mufson et al., 2004; Reynolds et al., 1999). Despite its origins, IPT is not considered to be a psychodynamic therapy, as it combines aspects of humanistic and cognitive-behavioral therapies, making it truly eclectic.

**HUMANISTIC THERAPY: TO ERR IS HUMAN**

**15.3** **Identify the basic elements of the humanistic therapies known as person-centered therapy and Gestalt therapy.**

Unlike psychodynamic therapists, humanistic theorists do not focus on unconscious, hidden conflicts. Instead, humanists focus on conscious, subjective experiences of emotion and people's sense of self, as well as the more immediate experiences in their daily lives rather than early childhood experiences of the distant past (Cain & Seeman, 2001; Rowan, 2001; Schneider et al., 2001). Ⓛ Ⓘ Ⓝ Ⓚ to Learning Objective 1.3. Humanistic therapy emphasizes the importance of the choices made by individuals and the potential to change one's behavior. The two most common therapy styles based on humanistic theory are Carl Rogers's person-centered therapy and Fritz Perls's Gestalt therapy; both are primarily insight therapies.

**TELL ME MORE: ROGERS'S PERSON-CENTERED THERAPY** Chapter Thirteen discussed the basic elements of Rogers's theory of personality, which emphasizes the sense of self (Rogers, 1961). To sum it up quickly, Rogers proposed that everyone has a *real self* (how people see their actual traits and abilities) and an *ideal self* (how people think they should be). The more closely the real and ideal selves match up, the happier and more well-adjusted the person. To have these two self-concepts match, people need to receive *unconditional positive regard*, which is

Psychotherapy often takes place one on one, with a client and therapist exploring various issues together to achieve deeper insights or to change undesirable behavior.

**interpersonal psychotherapy (IPT)**

form of therapy for depression which incorporates multiple approaches and focuses on interpersonal problems.

love, warmth, respect, and affection without any conditions attached. If people think that there are conditions put on the love and affection they receive, their ideal selves will be determined by those conditions and become more difficult to achieve, resulting in a mismatch of selves and unhappiness.

 💬 So the key to getting over unhappiness would be to get the real and ideal selves closer together? How does a therapist do that?

Rogers believed that the goal of the therapist should be to provide the unconditional positive regard that has been absent from the troubled person's life and to help the person recognize the discrepancies between the real and ideal selves. He also believed that the person would actually have to do most of the work, talking out problems and concerns in an atmosphere of warmth and acceptance from the therapist, so he originally called the people in this therapy relationship "clients" instead of "patients," to put the therapeutic relationship on a more equal footing. As a result, Rogers's therapy is very **nondirective** because the person actually does all the real work, with the therapist merely acting as a sounding board. However, therapists may help individuals redirect or reallocate their attention to focus on feelings not fully processed previously (Prochaska & Norcross, 2009). Later, the term *client* was changed to the even more neutral term *person*. His therapy is now called **person-centered therapy** because the person is truly the center of the process.

**BASIC ELEMENTS** Rogers (1961) saw three key elements as being necessary in any successful person–therapist relationship.

- **Authenticity** The therapist must show **authenticity** in a genuine, open, and honest response to the individual. It is easier for some professionals to "hide" behind the role of the therapist, as was often the case in psychoanalysis. In person-centered therapy, the therapist has to be able to tolerate a person's differences without being judgmental.

- **Unconditional Positive Regard** Another key element of person-centered therapy is the warm, accepting, completely uncritical atmosphere that the therapist must create for the people they work with. Having respect for an individual and their feelings, values, and goals, even if they are different from those of the therapist, is called **unconditional positive regard**.

- **Empathy** Last, the therapist needs to be able to see the world through the eyes of the person they are working with. The therapist has to be able to acknowledge what people are feeling and experiencing by using a kind of understanding called **empathy**. This involves listening carefully and closely to what individuals are saying and trying to feel what they feel. Therapists must also avoid getting their own feelings mixed up with their clients' feelings (e.g., countertransference).

A person-centered therapist typically responds in a way that seeks clarification and demonstrates attempts to understand the experience of the individual. **Reflection** refers to a technique therapists use to allow clients to continue to talk and have insights without the interference of the therapist's interpretations and possible biases. Reflection is literally a kind of mirroring of clients' statements. Here's an example from one of Rogers's own therapy sessions with a client (Meador & Rogers, 1984, p. 143):

> CLIENT: I just ain't no good to nobody, never was, and never will be.
> ROGERS: Feeling that now, hm? That you're just no good to yourself, no good to anybody. Never will be any good to anybody. Just that you're completely worthless, huh?—Those really are lousy feelings. Just feel that you're no good at all, hm?
> CLIENT: Yeah.

**MOTIVATIONAL INTERVIEWING** A variation of person-centered therapy is *motivational interviewing*, or MI (Miller & Rollnick, 2002), which has been described by Hal Arkowitz and William R. Miller as "client-centered therapy with a twist" (p. 4). In contrast to person-centered therapy, MI has specific goals, to reduce ambivalence about change and

A Rogerian person-centered therapist listens with calm acceptance to anything the client says. A sense of empathy with the client's feelings is also important.

**nondirective**

therapy style in which the therapist remains relatively neutral and does not interpret or take direct actions with regard to the client, instead remaining a calm, nonjudgmental listener while the client talks.

**person-centered therapy**

a nondirective insight therapy based on the work of Carl Rogers in which the client does all the talking and the therapist listens.

**authenticity**

the genuine, open, and honest response of the therapist to the client.

**unconditional positive regard**

referring to the warmth, respect, and accepting atmosphere created by the therapist for the client in person-centered therapy; positive regard that is given without conditions or strings attached.

**empathy**

the ability of the therapist to understand the feelings of the client.

**reflection**

therapy technique in which the therapist restates what the client says rather than interpreting those statements.

to increase intrinsic motivation to bring that change about (Arkowitz & Miller, 2008). As originally conceived, the four principles of MI were to express empathy, develop discrepancy between the client's present behaviors and values, roll with resistance, and support the client's self-efficacy (Miller & Rollnick, 2002). While still true to its foundations, MI has recently been updated and now consists of four broad processes: *engaging* with the client to develop a therapeutic working alliance, *focusing* on the goals and direction of counseling, *evoking* and eliciting the client's motivation to change, and when the client is ready to change, *planning* how to implement change (Miller & Arkowitz, 2015; Miller & Rollnick, 2013). The idea of resistance has been recast, with a focus on differentiating *sustain talk*, conversations reinforcing no change, from *change talk*, conversations leading to improvement (Corbett, 2016; Miller & Rollnick, 2013). Although it was originally developed and validated as effective for addictive disorders, it has also been useful in the treatment of anxiety and mood disorders (Arkowitz & Miller, 2008; Barlow et al., 2013), with applications to both health and mental health increasing (Corbett, 2016).

**GESTALT THERAPY**    Another therapy based on humanistic ideas is called **Gestalt therapy**. The founder of this therapeutic method is Fritz Perls, who believed that people's problems often stemmed from hiding important parts of their feelings from themselves. If some part of a person's personality, for example, is in conflict with what society says is acceptable, the person might hide that aspect behind a false "mask" of socially acceptable behavior. As happens in Rogers's theory when the real and ideal selves do not match, in Gestalt theory the person experiences unhappiness and maladjustment when the inner self does not match the mask (Perls, 1951, 1969).

💬 That sounds pretty much like the same thing, only with slightly different words. How is Gestalt therapy different from person-centered therapy?

The two therapy types are similar because they are both based in humanism. But whereas person-centered therapy is nondirective, allowing the client to talk out concerns and eventually come to insights with only minimal guidance from the therapist, Gestalt therapists are very directive, often confronting clients about the statements they have made. This means that a Gestalt therapist does more than simply reflect back clients' statements; instead, a Gestalt therapist actually leads clients through a number of planned experiences, with the goal of helping clients to become more aware of their own feelings and take responsibility for their own choices in life, both now and in the past. These experiences might include a dialogue that clients have with their own conflicting feelings in which clients actually argue both sides of those feelings. Clients may talk with an empty chair to reveal their true feelings toward the person represented by the chair or take on the role of a parent or other person with whom they have a conflict so that the clients can see things from the other person's point of view. The Gestalt therapist pays attention to body language as well as to the events going on in the client's life at the time of therapy. Unlike psychoanalysis, which focuses on the *hidden past*, Gestalt therapy focuses on the *denied past*. Gestalt therapists do not talk about the unconscious mind. They believe everything is conscious but that it is possible for some people to simply refuse to "own up" to having certain feelings or to deal with past issues. By looking at the body language, feelings both stated and unstated, and the events in the life of the client, the therapist gets a *gestalt*—a whole picture—of the client.

**EVALUATION OF THE HUMANISTIC THERAPIES**    Humanistic therapies have been used to treat psychological disorders, help people make career choices, deal with workplace problems, and counsel married couples. Person-centered therapy in particular can be a very "hands-off" form of therapy because it is so nondirective: Most often, there's nothing that the therapist says that the client has not already said, so the therapist runs a lower risk of misinterpretation. However, omission or not reflecting some things back might be a source of error.

In Gestalt therapy, it is not unusual to find a client talking to an empty chair. The chair represents some person from the past with whom the client has unresolved issues, and this is the opportunity to deal with those issues.

**Gestalt therapy**

form of directive insight therapy in which the therapist helps clients to accept all parts of their feelings and subjective experiences, using leading questions and planned experiences such as role-playing.

As noted in Chapter Thirteen, how people view themselves is central to many approaches in psychology (Leary & Toner, 2015). Many therapeutic approaches benefit from humanistic influences, namely the importance of the client–therapist relationship, including Rogers's concepts of unconditional positive regard and how much empathy clients perceive in the therapist (Angus et al., 2014; Goldfried, 2007; Watson et al., 2014). Humanistic therapies have some of the same drawbacks as Freudian psychoanalysis and other forms of modern psychodynamic therapy. Much of the research on this approach, at least the earlier studies, relied heavily on case studies. Also, people must be intelligent, verbal, and able to express their thoughts, feelings, and experiences in a logical manner. This makes humanistic therapies a somewhat less practical choice for treating the more serious mental disorders such as schizophrenia, at least as a first line of treatment. However, the data from a collection of studies are promising and suggest that humanistic therapy approaches may be beneficial for individuals with schizophrenia and other psychotic disorders (Elliott et al., 2013). Furthermore, humanistic approaches are associated with large pre–post client changes that are maintained for a significant period of time, appear to be statistically equivalent to other approaches for some conditions, and have demonstrated positive effects for some in particular, such as moderate depression, perinatal depression, and interpersonal and relationship problems (Angus et al., 2014; Elliott et al., 2013).

## Concept Map L.O. 15.2, 15.3

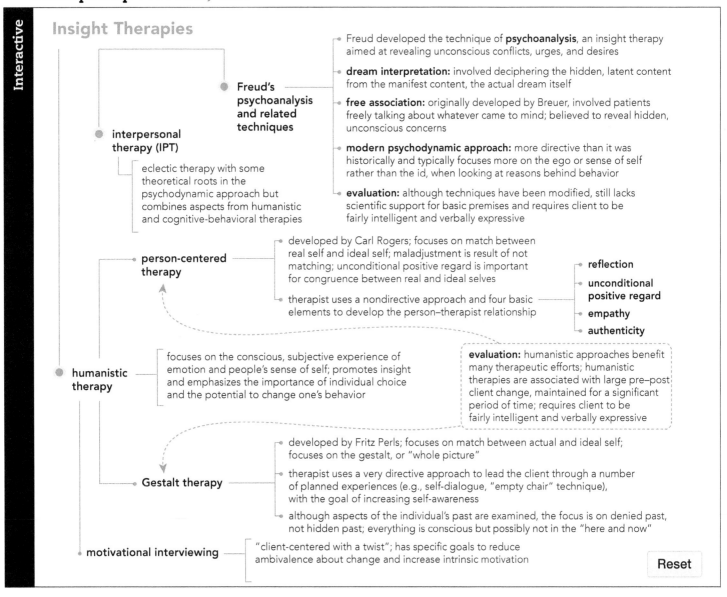

**Insight Therapies**

*Interactive*

- Freud developed the technique of **psychoanalysis**, an insight therapy aimed at revealing unconscious conflicts, urges, and desires
- **dream interpretation:** involved deciphering the hidden, latent content from the manifest content, the actual dream itself
- **free association:** originally developed by Breuer, involved patients freely talking about whatever came to mind; believed to reveal hidden, unconscious concerns
- **modern psychodynamic approach:** more directive than it was historically and typically focuses more on the ego or sense of self rather than the id, when looking at reasons behind behavior
- **evaluation:** although techniques have been modified, still lacks scientific support for basic premises and requires client to be fairly intelligent and verbally expressive

**Freud's psychoanalysis and related techniques**

**interpersonal therapy (IPT)**
- eclectic therapy with some theoretical roots in the psychodynamic approach but combines aspects from humanistic and cognitive-behavioral therapies

**person-centered therapy**
- developed by Carl Rogers; focuses on match between real self and ideal self; maladjustment is result of not matching; unconditional positive regard is important for congruence between real and ideal selves
- therapist uses a nondirective approach and four basic elements to develop the person–therapist relationship
  - reflection
  - unconditional positive regard
  - empathy
  - authenticity

**humanistic therapy**
- focuses on the conscious, subjective experience of emotion and people's sense of self; promotes insight and emphasizes the importance of individual choice and the potential to change one's behavior
- **evaluation:** humanistic approaches benefit many therapeutic efforts; humanistic therapies are associated with large pre–post client change, maintained for a significant period of time; requires client to be fairly intelligent and verbally expressive

**Gestalt therapy**
- developed by Fritz Perls; focuses on match between actual and ideal self; focuses on the gestalt, or "whole picture"
- therapist uses a very directive approach to lead the client through a number of planned experiences (e.g., self-dialogue, "empty chair" technique), with the goal of increasing self-awareness
- although aspects of the individual's past are examined, the focus is on denied past, not hidden past; everything is conscious but possibly not in the "here and now"

**motivational interviewing**
- "client-centered with a twist"; has specific goals to reduce ambivalence about change and increase intrinsic motivation

Reset

# Practice Quiz    How much do you remember?

*Pick the best answer.*

1. Although the term may apply to many therapies, "transference" is typically associated with _____ therapies.
   a. behavioral
   b. humanistic
   c. biomedical
   d. psychodynamic

2. Motivational interviewing is an alternative therapy to what therapeutic approach?
   a. psychodynamic therapy
   b. Gestalt therapy
   c. humanistic therapy
   d. group therapy

3. Dr. Ellington is directive in his approach with clients. He pays close attention to body language and often focuses on a client's denied past. What type of therapeutic approach is Dr. Ellington using?
   a. humanistic approach
   b. Gestalt approach
   c. group approach
   d. behavioral approach

4. Which of the following cases would a humanistic approach probably be LEAST effective in treating?
   a. Leilani, a university professor who has feelings of inadequacy
   b. Kayla, a professional musician who feels worthless and suffers from depression
   c. Miranda, a corporate executive who suffers from marked delusions and active auditory hallucinations
   d. Felicia, a homemaker who suffers from the traumatic memories of her abusive childhood

## Action Therapies: Behavior Therapies and Cognitive Therapies

While insight therapies strive to understand the motives behind one's behavior, action therapies are focused on changing the behavior itself. In behavior therapies, the goal is to change behavior through the use of learning techniques, while cognitive therapies strive to change maladaptive thoughts.

### BEHAVIOR THERAPIES: LEARNING ONE'S WAY TO BETTER BEHAVIOR

**15.4** **Explain how behavior therapists use classical and operant conditioning to treat disordered behavior.**

The last chapter talked about how behaviorists have a very different way of looking at abnormality—it's all learned. So do behaviorists do any kind of therapy?

That's right—the basic concept behind behaviorism is that all behavior, whether "normal" or "abnormal," is learned through the same processes of classical and operant conditioning. Unlike the psychodynamic and humanistic therapies, **behavior therapies** are action based rather than insight based. Their aim is to change behavior through the use of the same kinds of learning techniques that people (and animals) use to learn any new responses. The abnormal or undesirable behavior is not seen as a symptom of anything else but rather is the problem itself. Learning created the problem, and new learning can correct it (Onken et al., 1997; Skinner, 1974; Sloan & Mizes, 1999).

**THERAPIES BASED ON CLASSICAL CONDITIONING**    Classical conditioning is the learning of involuntary responses by pairing a stimulus that normally causes a particular response with a new, neutral stimulus. After enough pairings, the new stimulus will also cause the response to occur. ⓁⒾⓃⓀ to Learning Objectives 5.2 and 5.3. Through classical conditioning, old and undesirable automatic responses can be replaced by desirable ones. There are several techniques that have been developed using this type of learning to treat disorders such as phobias, anxiety disorders, and obsessive-compulsive disorder.

**behavior therapies**

action therapies based on the principles of classical and operant conditioning and aimed at changing disordered behavior without concern for the original causes of such behavior.

Using learning techniques to change undesirable behavior and increase desirable behavior has a long history (Hughes, 1993; Lovaas, 1987; Lovaas et al., 1966). Originally called *behavior modification*, the more recent adaptation of these techniques is *applied behavior analysis*. The newer term better highlights the need for a functional analysis of the behavior to be modified, which is then followed by the use of conditioning techniques to modify the behavior. Watch the video *Behavioral Therapy* to learn more about the use of these techniques.

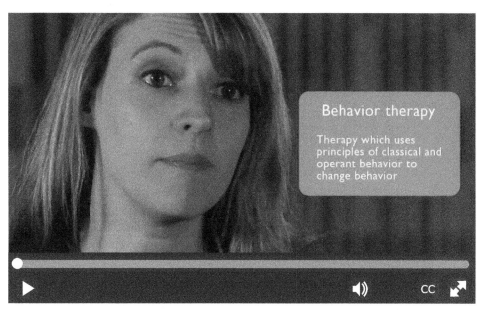

👁 **Watch** the **Video** *Behavioral Therapy*

**SYSTEMATIC DESENSITIZATION**   **Systematic desensitization**, in which a therapist guides the client through a series of steps meant to reduce fear and anxiety, is normally used to treat phobic disorders and consists of a three-step process. First, the client must learn to relax through deep muscle relaxation training. Next, the client and the therapist construct a list, beginning with the object or situation that causes the least fear to the client, eventually working up to the object or situation that produces the greatest degree of fear. Finally, under the guidance of the therapist, the client begins with the first item on the list that causes minimal fear and looks at it, thinks about it, or actually confronts it, all while remaining in a relaxed state. By pairing the old conditioned stimulus (the fear object) with a new relaxation response that is incompatible* with the emotions and physical arousal associated with fear, the person's fear is reduced and relieved. The person then proceeds to the next item on the list of fears (called a *hierarchy of fears*) until the phobia is gone (see **Table 15.1**). It is even possible to use a computer-generated virtual reality technique for desensitization (Rothbaum et al., 1995).

**AVERSION THERAPY**   Another way to use classical conditioning is to reduce the frequency of undesirable behaviors, such as smoking or overeating, by teaching the client to pair an aversive (unpleasant) stimulus with the stimulus that results in the undesirable response in a process called **aversion therapy**. For example, someone who wants to stop smoking might go to a therapist who uses a *rapid-smoking* technique, in which the client is allowed to smoke but must take a puff on the cigarette every 5 or 6 seconds. As nicotine is a poison, such rapid smoking produces nausea and dizziness, both unpleasant effects.

**systematic desensitization**

behavior technique used to treat phobias, in which a client is asked to make a list of ordered fears and taught to relax while concentrating on those fears.

**aversion therapy**

form of behavioral therapy in which an undesirable behavior is paired with an aversive stimulus to reduce the frequency of the behavior.

---

*incompatible: referring to two or more things that cannot exist together or at the same time.

| Table 15.1 Fear Hierarchy | |
|---|---|
| **Situation** | **Fear Level** |
| Being bitten by a rabbit | 100 |
| Petting a rabbit on the head | 90 |
| Petting a rabbit on the back | 80 |
| Holding a rabbit | 70 |
| Touching a rabbit held by someone else | 60 |
| Seeing someone I trust hold a rabbit | 50 |
| Being in a room with a rabbit | 40 |
| Thinking about petting a rabbit | 30 |
| Looking at pictures of rabbits | 20 |
| Watching the movie *Hop* | 10 |

Items are ranked by level of fear from most fearful, Fear = 100, to least fearful, Fear = 0.

 Could you use aversion therapy to help someone with a phobia?

Because phobias are already very unpleasant, aversive conditioning is not the most useful method of therapy. But although desensitization remains one of the more common therapies for phobias, it does not always bring quick results.

**EXPOSURE THERAPIES** Behavioral techniques that introduce the client to situations, under carefully controlled conditions, which are related to their anxieties or fears are called **exposure therapies**. Exposure can be accomplished through a variety of routes and is intended to promote new learning. It can be *in vivo* ("in life"), where the client is exposed to the actual anxiety-related stimulus; *imaginal*, where the client visualizes or imagines the stimulus; and even *virtual*, where virtual reality (VR) technology is used (Najavits, 2007). (For more on virtual reality in psychology, see the Applying Psychology to Everyday Life section at the end of this chapter.)

For example, if Chang-sun has social anxiety disorder (fairly rare for Korean males, at a lifetime prevalence of only about 0.1 percent; Sadock et al., 2007), for in vivo exposure he might have to attend a social event; for imaginal exposure he might be asked to visualize himself attending a social event; and for virtual exposure, Chang-sun might experience a social event, such as attending a dinner party, through VR technology.

Exposure methods can introduce the feared stimulus gradually or quite suddenly. A gradual, or *graded*, exposure involves the client and therapist developing a fear hierarchy as in systematic desensitization: Exposure begins at the least feared event and progresses through to the most feared, similar to desensitization. If the exposure is rapid and intense, it begins with the most feared event and is called **flooding** (Gelder, 1976; Olsen, 1975). Flooding is used under very controlled conditions and, like graded exposure, produces extinction of the conditioned fear response by preventing an escape or avoidance response (e.g., Chang-sun would not be allowed to leave the party).

*Eye-movement desensitization and reprocessing*, or EMDR, is an exposure-based therapy sometimes used in the treatment of PTSD. As originally formulated, it involves very brief and repeated imaginal flooding, cognitive reprocessing and desensitization of the fearful event, and rapid eye movements or other bilateral stimulation (Shapiro, 2001, 2012). However, it is a somewhat controversial therapy, as it evolved from the founder's personal observation, not psychological theory or modification of techniques for other disorders, and research has suggested the eye movements or other bilateral stimulation serve little to no purpose (Lilienfeld et al., 2015; Resick et al., 2008).

**exposure therapies**
behavioral techniques that expose individuals to anxiety- or fear-related stimuli, under carefully controlled conditions, to promote new learning.

**flooding**
technique for treating phobias and other stress disorders in which the person is rapidly and intensely exposed to the fear-provoking situation or object and prevented from making the usual avoidance or escape response.

A primary exposure-based treatment for PTSD is *prolonged exposure* (PE), which involves both exposure and components of *cognitive-behavioral therapy*. ⓁⒾⓃⓀ to Learning Objective 15.5. The approach involves four primary components: education about PTSD and common trauma reactions, learning to breathe in a relaxing and calming way, repeated *in vivo* exposure to safe activities, objects, situations, or places that are causing the person anxiety, and repeated, prolonged imaginal exposure to memories associated with the trauma (Foa et al., 2007). As with many other treatments for trauma, a primary goal of treatment is to help individuals approach memories and stimuli they fear or avoid to overcome their anxiety and to process the emotions associated with the trauma (Foa et al., 2007; Ruzek et al., 2014). Preliminary research suggests PE and successful remission of PTSD may lead to changes in brain structures associated with the positive changes, such as the anterior cingulate cortex (Helpman et al., 2016).

*Exposure and response prevention* (EX/RP), or exposure and ritual prevention, is one of the most effective strategies for treating OCD (Bornheimer, 2015; Fisher & Wells, 2005; Lilienfeld et al., 2013; Strauss et al., 2015). Grounded in behavioral theory and the core component of exposure, like PE, it also has features of cognitive-behavioral therapy. ⓁⒾⓃⓀ to Learning Objective 15.5. In short, it encourages individuals with OCD to gradually and regularly expose themselves to the things that trigger their obsessive thoughts but not to engage in their typical compulsive act or process (Strauss et al., 2015). In addition to adults with OCD, it has also been demonstrated to be effective with youth (Kircanski & Peris, 2015).

**THERAPIES BASED ON OPERANT CONDITIONING**   Operant conditioning techniques include reinforcement, extinction, shaping, and modeling to change the frequency of voluntary behavior. ⓁⒾⓃⓀ to Learning Objectives 5.8, 5.9, 5.13, and 5.14. In the treatment of psychological disorders, the goal is to reduce the frequency of undesirable behavior and increase the frequency of desirable responses.

One of the advantages of using operant conditioning to treat a problem behavior is that results are usually quickly obtained rather than having to wait through years of more insight-oriented forms of therapy. When bringing the behavior under control (rather than finding out why it occurs in the first place) is the goal, operant and other behavioral techniques are very practical. There's an old joke about a man whose fear of things hiding under his bed is cured by a behavioral therapist in one night. The therapist simply cut the legs off the bed.

MODELING   **Modeling**, or learning through the observation and imitation of a model, is discussed in Chapter Five. The use of modeling as a therapy is based on the work of Albert Bandura, which states that a person with specific fears or someone who needs to develop social skills can learn to do so by watching someone else (the model) confront those fears or demonstrate the needed social skills (Bandura et al., 1969). In **participant modeling**, a model demonstrates the desired behavior in a step-by-step, gradual process. The client is encouraged by the therapist to imitate the model in the same gradual, step-by-step manner (Bandura, 1986; Bandura et al., 1974). The model can be a person actually present in the same room with the client or someone viewed on video. For example, a model might first approach a dog, then touch the dog, then pet the dog, and finally hug the dog. A child (or adult) who fears dogs would watch this process and then be encouraged to repeat the steps that the model demonstrated.

Behavioral therapists can give parents or others advice and demonstrations on how to carry out behavioral techniques. Once a person knows what to do, modeling is a fairly easy technique. Modeling has been effective in helping children with dental fears (Klorman et al., 1980; Ollendick & King, 1998), social withdrawal (O'Connor, 1972), phobias (Hintze, 2002), and while interacting with LEGO© play materials, to facilitate improved social skills in children with autism spectrum disorder (LeGoff, 2004).

**modeling**
learning through the observation and imitation of others.

**participant modeling**
technique in which a model demonstrates the desired behavior in a step-by-step, gradual process while the client is encouraged to imitate the model.

**USING REINFORCEMENT** *Reinforcement* is the strengthening of a response by following it with some pleasurable consequence (positive reinforcement) or the removal of an unpleasant stimulus (negative reinforcement). Reinforcement of both types can form the basis for treatment of people with behavioral problems.

In a *token economy*, objects known as *tokens* can be traded for food, candy, treats, or special privileges. Clients earn tokens for behaving correctly or accomplishing behavioral goals and can later exchange those tokens for things that they want. They may also lose tokens for inappropriate behavior. This trading system is a token economy. ⓛⓘⓝⓚ to Learning Objective 5.9. Token economies have also been used successfully in modifying the behavior of relatively disturbed persons in mental institutions, such as people with schizophrenia or depressed persons (Dickerson et al., 1994; Glynn, 1990; McMonagle & Sultana, 2002).

Another method based on the use of reinforcement involves making a **contingency contract** with the client (Salend, 1987). This contract is a formal agreement between therapist and client (or teacher and student, or parent and child) in which both parties' responsibilities and goals are clearly stated. Such contracts are useful in treating specific problems such as drug addiction (Talbott & Crosby, 2001), educational problems (Evans & Meyer, 1985; Evans et al., 1989), and eating disorders (Brubaker & Leddy, 2003). Monetary contingency contracts may be useful in weight-loss programs (Sykes-Muskett et al., 2015). Because the stated tasks, penalties, and reinforcements are clearly stated and consistent, both parties are always aware of the consequences of acting or failing to act within the specifications of the contract, making this form of behavioral treatment fairly effective. Consistency is one of the most effective tools in using both rewards and punishments to mold behavior. ⓛⓘⓝⓚ to Learning Objectives 5.6, 5.7.

**USING EXTINCTION** *Extinction* involves the removal of a reinforcer to reduce the frequency of a particular response. In modifying behavior, operant extinction often involves removing one's attention from the person when that person is engaging in an inappropriate or undesirable behavior. With children, this removal of attention may be a form of **time-out**, in which the child is removed from the situation that provides reinforcement (Kazdin, 1980). In adults, a simple refusal by the other persons in the room to acknowledge the behavior is often successful in reducing the frequency of that behavior.

**BEHAVIORAL ACTIVATION** *Behavioral activation* is an operant-based intervention that has been used successfully with depression. Individuals with depression may limit their involvement with others or the typical activities they would normally engage in. This avoidant behavior limits their opportunities to be positively reinforced through social activities or pleasant experiences. Behavioral activation involves reintroducing individuals to their regular environments and routines as one way to increase opportunities for positive reinforcement (Dimidjian et al., 2006; Ekers et al., 2014; Forman, n.d.). Therapists work with their clients to schedule activities through daily activity monitoring, activity scheduling, and a variety of other ways to restore an environment that increases the likelihood of activation behavior, decreases avoidant and depressive behavior, and increases positive reinforcement (Manos et al., 2010; Puspitasari et al., 2013).

**EVALUATION OF BEHAVIOR THERAPIES** Behavior therapies may be more effective than other forms of therapy in treating specific behavioral problems, such as bed-wetting, overeating, drug addictions, and phobic reactions (Burgio, 1998; Wetherell, 2002). Some problems do not respond as well overall to behavioral treatments, although improvement of specific symptoms can be achieved (Glynn, 1990; McMonagle & Sultana, 2002). While EX/RP is often a successful treatment for OCD, some associated cognitive symptoms, such as deficits in executive functioning, may

---

**contingency contract**

a formal, written agreement between the therapist and client (or teacher and student) in which goals for behavioral change, reinforcements, and penalties are clearly stated.

**time-out**

an extinction process in which a person is removed from the situation that provides reinforcement for undesirable behavior, usually by being placed in a quiet corner or room away from possible attention and reinforcement opportunities.

Contingency contracts are useful for establishing a variety of desired behaviors. When used effectively, explicit expectations and consistency of implementation are key factors that lead to their success.

interfere with the use of this approach (Snyder et al., 2015). Bringing symptoms under control is an important step in allowing a person to function normally in the social world, and behavior therapies are a relatively quick and efficient way to eliminate or greatly reduce such symptoms. However, some behavioral paradigms are not simple to establish or continually implement, and steps have to be taken so adaptive behaviors can be maintained and generalized to other situations and environments, such as the family and the individual's culture (Prochaska & Norcross, 2014). Others are easier to implement and may in fact not require extensive training to be successful. For example, behavioral activation is an effective intervention for depression that is relatively simple to implement, even by nonspecialists, and it has been shown to be either comparable or superior to antidepressant medication in the short term and superior to cognitive therapies (Dimidjian et al., 2006; Ekers et al., 2014). Furthermore, EX/RP for OCD, PE for PTSD, and other exposure-based approaches may possibly be enhanced, such as by using two fear-provoking stimuli at the same time to facilitate learning during exposure (Culver et al., 2015).

### COGNITIVE THERAPIES: THINKING IS BELIEVING

**15.5** **Summarize the goals and basic elements of cognitive and cognitive-behavioral therapies.**

**Cognitive therapy** (Beck, 1979; Freeman et al., 1989) was developed by Aaron T. Beck and is focused on helping people change their ways of thinking. Rather than focusing on the behavior itself, the cognitive therapist focuses on the distorted thinking and unrealistic beliefs that lead to maladaptive behavior (Hollon & Beck, 1994), especially those distortions relating to depression (Abela & D'Allesandro, 2002; McGinn, 2000). The goal is to help clients test, in a more objective, scientific way, the truth of their beliefs and assumptions, as well as their attributions concerning both their own behavior and the behavior of others in their lives. (L I N K) to Learning Objective 12.9. Then they can recognize thoughts that are distorted and negative and replace them with more positive, helpful thoughts. Because the focus is on changing thoughts rather than gaining deep insights into their causes, this kind of therapy is primarily an action therapy.

### BECK'S COGNITIVE THERAPY

  What are these unrealistic beliefs?

Cognitive therapy focuses on the distortions of thinking. (L I N K) to Learning Objective 13.5. Here are some of the more common distortions in thought that can create negative feelings and unrealistic beliefs in people:

- **Arbitrary inference:** This refers to "jumping to conclusions" without any evidence. Arbitrary means to decide something based on nothing more than personal whims. Example: "Suzy canceled our lunch date—I'll bet she's seeing someone else!"

- **Selective thinking:** In selective thinking, the person focuses only on one aspect of a situation, leaving out other relevant facts that might make things seem less negative. Example: Peter's teacher praised his paper but made one comment about needing to check his punctuation. Peter assumes that his paper is lousy and that the teacher really didn't like it, ignoring the other praise and positive comments.

- **Overgeneralization:** Here a person draws a sweeping conclusion from one incident and then assumes that the conclusion applies to areas of life that have nothing to do with the original event. Example: "I got yelled at by my boss. My boyfriend is going to break up with me and kick me out of the apartment—I'll end up living in a van down by the river."

**cognitive therapy**

therapy in which the focus is on helping clients recognize distortions in their thinking and replacing distorted, unrealistic beliefs with more realistic, helpful thoughts.

"It's been almost 5 minutes and Madison has still not yet said yes to my request to follow her on Instagram. She must not like me......"

How many times have you jumped to a conclusion without first examining the actual evidence, or getting the whole story?

• **Magnification and minimization:** Here a person blows bad things out of proportion while not emphasizing good things. Example: A student who has received good grades on every other exam believes that the C she got on the last quiz means she's not going to succeed in college.

• **Personalization:** In personalization, an individual takes responsibility or blame for events that are not really connected to the individual. Example: When Sandy's husband comes home in a bad mood because of something that happened at work, she immediately assumes that he is angry with her.

A cognitive therapist tries to get clients to look at their beliefs and test them to see how accurate they really are. The first step is to identify an illogical or unrealistic belief, which the therapist and client do in their initial talks. Then the client is guided by the therapist through a process of asking questions about that belief, such as "When did this belief of mine begin?" or "What is the evidence for this belief?"

💬 Don't those questions sound like critical thinking, which was discussed in Chapter One?

Cognitive therapy really is critical thinking applied to one's own thoughts and beliefs. Just as cognitive psychology grew out of behaviorism, **LINK** to Learning Objectives 1.3 and 1.4, therapies using cognitive methods have behavioral elements within them as well, leading to the term **cognitive-behavioral therapy (CBT)**.

Cognitive behavioral therapy (CBT)

Therapy focusing on changing illogical thinking and techniques to change behavior

👁 **Watch** the **Video** *Cognitive-Behavioral Therapy*

CBT focuses on the present rather than the past (like behaviorism) but also assumes that people interact with the world with more than simple, automatic reactions to external stimuli. People observe the world and the people in the world around them, make assumptions and inferences* based on those observations or cognitions, and then decide how to respond (Rachman & Hodgson, 1980). CBT also assumes that disorders come from illogical, irrational cognitions and that changing the thinking patterns to more rational, logical ones will relieve the symptoms of the disorder, making it an action therapy. CBT has three basic elements: cognitions affect behavior, cognitions

**cognitive-behavioral therapy (CBT)**
action therapy in which the goal is to help clients overcome problems by learning to think more rationally and logically, which in turn will impact their behavior.

_____

*inferences: conclusions drawn from observations and facts.

can be changed, behavior change can result from cognitive change (Dobson & Block, 1988). Cognitive-behavioral therapists may also use any of the tools that behavioral therapists use to help clients alter their actions. The three basic goals of any cognitive-behavioral therapy follow.

1. Relieve the symptoms and help clients resolve the problems.

2. Help clients develop strategies that can be used to cope with future problems.

3. Help clients change the way they think from irrational, self-defeating thoughts to more rational, self-helping, positive thoughts.

**ELLIS AND RATIONAL EMOTIVE BEHAVIOR THERAPY (REBT)**   Albert Ellis proposed a version of CBT called **rational emotive behavior therapy (REBT)**, in which clients are taught a way to challenge their own irrational beliefs with more rational, helpful statements (Ellis, 1997, 1998). Here are some examples of irrational beliefs:

- Everyone should love and approve of me (if they don't, I am awful and unlovable).

- When things do not go the way I wanted and planned, it is terrible, and I am, of course, going to get very disturbed. I can't stand it!

 💬 But I've felt that way at times. Why are these statements so irrational?

Notice that these statements have one thing in common: It's either all or nothing. Can a person really expect the love and affection of every single person? Is it realistic to expect things to work as planned every time? Rational emotive behavioral therapy is about challenging these types of "my way or nothing" statements, helping people realize that life can be good without being "perfect." In REBT, therapists take a very directive role, challenging the client when the client makes statements like those listed earlier, assigning homework, using behavioral techniques to modify behavior, and arguing with clients about the rationality of their statements.

**EVALUATION OF COGNITIVE AND COGNITIVE-BEHAVIORAL THERAPIES**   Cognitive and cognitive-behavioral therapies are less expensive than the typical insight therapy because they are comparatively short-term therapies. As in behavior therapy, clients do not have to dig too deep for the hidden sources of their problems. Instead, cognitive-based therapies get right to the problems themselves, helping clients deal with their symptoms more directly. In fact, one of the criticisms of these therapies as well as behavior therapies is that they treat the symptom, not the cause. However, it should be noted that in the cognitive viewpoint, the maladaptive thoughts are seen as the cause of the problems, not merely the symptoms. There is also an element of potential bias because of the therapist's opinions as to which thoughts are rational and which are not (Westen, 2005).

Nevertheless, cognitive and cognitive-behavioral therapies have considerable success in treating many types of disorders, including insomnia, depression, stress disorders, eating disorders, anxiety disorders, personality disorders, and even—in addition to other forms of therapy—some types of schizophrenia (Barlow et al., 2007; Beck, 2007; Clark et al., 1989, 2009; DeRubeis et al., 1999; Holcomb, 1986; Jay & Elliot, 1990; Kendall, 1983; Kendall et al., 2008; McGinn, 2000; Meichenbaum, 1996; Mueser et al., 2008; Resick et al., 2008; Savard et al., 2014; Trauer et al., 2015; Turk et al., 2008; Young et al., 2008). As an offshoot of behaviorism, the learning principles that are the basis of cognitive-behavioral therapies are considered empirically sound (Barlow et al., 2007; Masters et al., 1987). For a summary of the various types of psychotherapies discussed up to this point, see **Table 15.2**.

**rational emotive behavior therapy (REBT)**

cognitive-behavioral therapy in which clients are directly challenged in their irrational beliefs and helped to restructure their thinking into more rational belief statements.

**Table 15.2**   Characteristics of Psychotherapies

| Type of Therapy (Key People) | Goal | Methods |
|---|---|---|
| Psychodynamic therapy (Freud) | Insight | Aims to reveal unconscious conflicts through dream interpretation, free association, resistance and transference |
| Humanistic therapy<br>    Person-centered therapy (Rogers) | Insight | Nondirective therapy; client does most of the talking; key elements are authenticity, unconditional positive regard, and empathy |
|     Gestalt therapy (Perls) | | Directive therapy; therapist uses leading questions and role playing to help client accept all parts of their feelings and experiences |
| Behavior therapy (Watson, Jones, Skinner, Bandura) | Action | Based on principles of classical and operant conditioning; aimed at changing behavior without concern for causes of behavior |
| Cognitive therapy (Beck)<br>    CBT (various professionals) | Action | Aims to help clients overcome problems by learning to think more rationally and logically |
|     REBT (Ellis) | | Clients are challenged in their irrational beliefs and helped to restructure their thinking |

## Concept Map L.O. 15.4, 15.5

**behavior therapies**
action-based therapies operating on the premise that all behaviors, both normal and abnormal, are learned; applied behavior analysis involves functional analysis and learning techniques to increase desirable behaviors and decrease undesirable behaviors

- techniques based on classical conditioning—pairing of stimuli
  - systematic desensitization
  - aversion therapy
  - exposure therapies: expose individual to anxiety-provoking stimulus in real or imagined form, in a gradual or sudden (flooding) manner
- techniques based on operant conditioning—reinforcement, extinction, shaping, and modeling
  - participant modeling
  - token economies (reinforcement)
  - contingency contracting (reinforcement)
  - time-out (extinction)
- evaluation: more effective than others for specific behavioral problems (e.g., bed-wetting, overeating, drug addictions, phobic reactions)

## Action Therapies

**cognitive therapies**
action-based therapies that focus on helping people change their ways of thinking; emphasis on identifying distorted and unrealistic beliefs that lead to maladaptive behavior and problem emotions and then replacing them with more-positive, helpful thoughts

- Beck's cognitive therapy identifies several common distortions
  - arbitrary inference (jumping to conclusions)
  - selective thinking
  - overgeneralization
  - magnification and minimization
  - personalization
- cognitive-behavioral therapy (CBT) uses cognitive methods that have behavioral elements within them as well
- rational emotive behavior therapy (REBT) was developed by Albert Ellis; teaches clients to challenge their own irrational beliefs with more rational, helpful statements
- evaluation: typically shorter and less expensive than insight therapies; treating the symptom, not the cause, is both a feature and a criticism; especially effective for many disorders, including depression, anxiety disorders, and personality disorders

Reset

# Practice Quiz   How much do you remember?

*Pick the best answer.*

1. Behavior-based therapies are _____ based, while psycho-dynamic and humanistic therapies are _____ based.
   a. insight; action
   b. action; insight
   c. rationale; medically
   d. medically; action

2. Dr. Kali works with clients to help them learn deep relaxation. Next, he has them list their fears from least to most anxiety provoking. Finally, Dr. Kali slowly exposes his clients to each of their fears and assists them in gaining control of their anxiety. His approach is best known as
   a. aversion therapy.
   b. systematic desensitization.
   c. flooding.
   d. fear therapy.

3. Dr. Williams uses exposure-based therapies to treat many of her patients. Client A is actually confronted with the situation that causes her anxiety, while Client B is asked to think about and visualize the frightening situation. Client A's treatment method would be described as _____, while client B's treatment method is _____.
   a. virtual; in vivo
   b. imaginal; virtual
   c. in vivo; imaginal
   d. virtual; in vivo

4. Which of the following therapies has been successful across multiple settings in the establishment of desirable behaviors and modification of problem behaviors?
   a. token economies
   b. aversion therapy
   c. systematic desensitization
   d. flooding

5. Nicole's therapist tells her that she is applying arbitrary inference to her thinking, which ultimately is causing her to be depressed. Which of the following is an example of Nicole's arbitrary inference?
   a. Nicole maximizes the bad things she experiences while minimizing the good aspects of life.
   b. Nicole tends to jump to conclusions with little or no evidence to support her beliefs.
   c. Nicole focuses strictly on a single negative event while ignoring less negative aspects.
   d. Nicole tends to overgeneralize a single bad event and assume all things about her life are failing.

# Group Therapies: Not Just for the Shy

An alternative to individual therapy, in which the client and the therapist have a private, one-on-one session, is **group therapy**, in which a group of clients with similar problems gathers together to discuss their problems under the guidance of a single therapist (Yalom, 1995).

In family therapy, a therapist will often meet with the entire family in the effort to identify what aspects of the family dynamic is contributing to a problem, such as conflict between different family members.

## TYPES OF GROUP THERAPIES

**15.6** **Compare and contrast different forms of group therapy.**

Group therapy can be accomplished in several ways. The therapist may use either an insight or cognitive-behavioral style, although person-centered, Gestalt, and behavior therapies seem to work better in group settings than psychodynamic and cognitive-behavioral therapies (Andrews, 1989).

In addition to the variations in the style of therapy, the group structure can also vary. There may be small groups formed of related persons or other groups of unrelated persons that meet without the benefit of a therapist. Their goal is to share their problems and provide social and emotional support for each other.

**FAMILY COUNSELING**   One form of group therapy is **family counseling** or **family therapy**, in which all of the members of a family who are experiencing some type of problem—marital problems, problems in child discipline, or sibling rivalry, for example—are seen by the therapist as a group. The therapist may also meet with one or more family members individually at times, but the real work in opening the lines of communication among family members is accomplished in the group setting (Frankel & Piercy, 1990; Pinsof & Wynne, 1995). The family members may include grandparents, aunts and uncles, and in-laws as well as the core family. This is because family therapy focuses on the family as a whole unit or system of interacting "parts." No one person is seen as "the problem" because all members of the family system are part of the problem: They are experiencing it, rewarding it, or by their actions or inactions causing it to occur in the first place.

The goal in family therapy, then, is to discover the unhealthy ways in which family members interact and communicate with one another and change those ways to healthier,

**group therapy**
form of therapy or treatment during which a small group of clients with similar concerns meet together with a therapist to address their issues.

**family counseling (family therapy)**
a form of group therapy in which family members meet together with a counselor or therapist to resolve problems that affect the entire family.

In self-help groups, the person or persons leading a group are not specialists or therapists but just members of the group. They often have the same problem as all of the other people in the room, which is the strength of this type of program—people may be more likely to trust and open up to someone who has struggled as they have.

more productive means of interaction. Family therapists work not only with families but also with couples who are in a committed relationship, with the goal of improving communication, helping the couple to learn better ways of solving their problems and disagreements, and increasing feelings of intimacy and emotional closeness (Christensen et al., 1995; Heavey et al., 1993).

**SELF-HELP GROUPS** Many people may feel that a therapist who has never had, for example, a drug problem would be unable to truly understand their situation; and they may also feel that someone who has experienced addiction and beaten it is more capable of providing real help. Therapists are also often in short supply, and they charge a fee for leading group-therapy sessions. These are reasons some people choose to meet with others who have problems similar to their own, with no therapist in charge. Called **self-help groups** or **support groups**, these groups are usually formed around a particular problem. Some examples of self-help groups are Alcoholics Anonymous, Overeaters Anonymous, and Narcotics Anonymous, all of which have groups meeting all over the country at almost any time of the day or night. There are countless smaller support groups for nearly every condition imaginable, including anxiety, phobias, having a parent with dementia, having difficult children, depression, and dealing with stress—to name just a few. The advantages of self-help groups are that they are free and provide the social and emotional support that a group session can provide (Bussa & Kaufman, 2000). Self-help groups do not have leaders but instead have people who volunteer monthly or weekly to lead individual meetings. So the person who is in charge of organizing the meetings is also a member of the group, with the same problem as all the other members.

### EVALUATION OF GROUP THERAPY

**15.7** Identify the advantages and disadvantages of group therapy.

Group therapy can provide help to people who might be unable to afford individual psychotherapy. Because the therapist can see several clients at one time, this type of therapy is usually less expensive than individual therapy. It also allows an opportunity for both the therapist and the person to see how that person interacts with others.

Another advantage of group therapy is that it offers social and emotional support from people who have problems that are similar or nearly identical to one's own. This advantage is an important one; studies have shown that breast cancer patients who were part of a group-therapy process had much higher survival and recovery rates than those who received only individual therapy or no psychotherapy (Fawzy et al., 1993; Spiegel et al., 1989). Another study found that adolescent girls in Africa, suffering from depression due to the stresses of the war in Uganda, experienced significant reductions in depression when treated with group therapy (Bolton et al., 2007).

Group therapy is not appropriate for all situations, and there can be disadvantages. Clients must share the therapist's time during the session. People who are not comfortable in social situations or who have trouble speaking in front of others may not find group therapy as helpful as those who are more verbal and social by nature. In addition, since the therapist is no longer the only person to whom secrets and fears are revealed, some people may be reluctant to speak freely. An extremely shy person may initially have great difficulty speaking up in a group setting, but cognitive-behavioral group therapy can be effective for social anxiety disorder (Heimberg & Becker, 2002; Turk et al., 2008). People with psychiatric disorders involving paranoia that is not well controlled, such as schizophrenia, may not be able to tolerate group-therapy settings.

A survey and comparison of the effectiveness of both individual and group therapy found that group therapy is only effective if it is long term and that it is more effective

**self-help groups (support groups)** a group composed of people who have similar problems and who meet together without a therapist or counselor for the purpose of discussion, problem solving, and social and emotional support.

when used to promote skilled social interactions rather than as an attempt to decrease the more bizarre symptoms of delusions and hallucinations (Evans et al., 2000). It is also important to note that group therapy can be used in combination with individual and biomedical therapies.

## Concept Map L.O. 15.6, 15.7

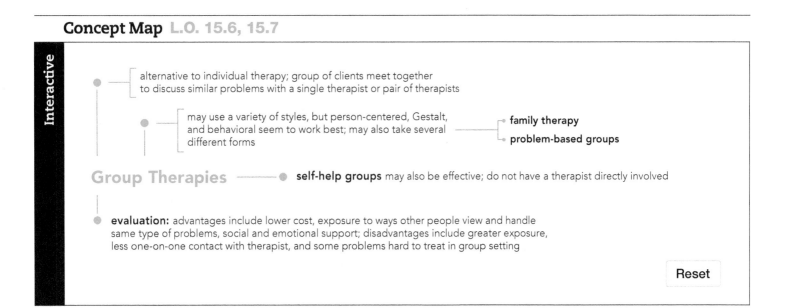

**Interactive**

- alternative to individual therapy; group of clients meet together to discuss similar problems with a single therapist or pair of therapists

- may use a variety of styles, but person-centered, Gestalt, and behavioral seem to work best; may also take several different forms
  - family therapy
  - problem-based groups

**Group Therapies** — **self-help groups** may also be effective; do not have a therapist directly involved

- **evaluation:** advantages include lower cost, exposure to ways other people view and handle same type of problems, social and emotional support; disadvantages include greater exposure, less one-on-one contact with therapist, and some problems hard to treat in group setting

Reset

## Practice Quiz    How much do you remember?

*Pick the best answer.*

1. Which of the following may be an effective option for some concerns if there isn't a therapist available in your local community?
   **a.** family therapy
   **b.** group therapy
   **c.** self-help group
   **d.** psychodynamic therapy

2. Erika and William, along with their children Maximillian and Stella, are all seeing a psychologist to help work through some difficulties that have been occurring in their home. From time to time, their therapist opts to work with one of them instead of all four at once. This group of individuals is receiving _____ therapy.
   **a.** family therapy
   **b.** group therapy
   **c.** self-help group
   **d.** psychodynamic therapy

3. Catherine runs a weekly meeting of Alcoholics Anonymous, and several dozen members come every week. In addition, each week some new members show up to see what the group is all about, and some members who were there the previous week

do not return. Which of the following is most likely true about Catherine?
   **a.** Catherine has probably never experienced a substance-related problem herself.
   **b.** Catherine is probably a licensed psychologist.
   **c.** Catherine is probably a licensed psychiatrist.
   **d.** Catherine has likely experienced some problems with alcohol in her past and is probably not a professional therapist.

4. Which of the following is *not* a noted advantage of group psychotherapy?
   **a.** Group therapy is less expensive than individual psychotherapy.
   **b.** Group therapy offers social support from people facing similar challenges.
   **c.** Group therapy is appropriate for anyone, so it is more "available" to those with personal struggles.
   **d.** Group therapy offers emotional support from people facing similar challenges.

# Does Psychotherapy Really Work?

There sure are a lot of psychotherapies, but do any of them really work?

In the 1950s, Hans Eysenck did one of the earliest studies of the effectiveness of therapy. His conclusion: that the people receiving psychotherapy did not recover at any higher rate than those who had no psychotherapy and that the passage of time alone could account for all recovery.

## STUDIES OF EFFECTIVENESS

### 15.8 Summarize the research on the effectiveness of psychotherapy.

Eysenck's classic survey created a major controversy within the world of clinical and counseling psychology. Other researchers began their own studies to find evidence that would contradict Eysenck's findings. One such effort reviewed studies that the researchers considered to be well controlled and concluded that the psychotherapies did not differ from one another in effectiveness (Luborsky et al., 1975). Of course, that can mean either that the psychotherapies were all equally effective or that they were all equally ineffective. (Reminder—many psychological professionals take an eclectic approach, using more than one psychotherapy technique.)

Studies that do not use empirical* procedures but instead try to determine if the clients who have been helped by the therapy in general are plagued by problems such as experimenter bias (the therapist expects the therapy to work and is also the one assessing the progress of the client), the inaccuracies of self-report information, and the same placebo-effect expectations cited by Shapiro and Shapiro (Seligman, 1995; Wampold, 1997). Ⓛ Ⓘ Ⓝ Ⓚ to Learning Objective 1.9.

Surveys have shown that people who have received psychotherapy believe that they have been helped more often than not (*Consumer Reports*, 1995; Hunsley et al., 2014; Kotkin et al., 1996). The *Consumer Reports* research was a survey of the magazine's readers in which those who had been or were currently clients in psychotherapy rated the effectiveness of the therapy they received. Here are the findings from a summary of this and several other similar surveys (Lambert & Ogles, 2004; Seligman, 1995; Thase, 1999):

THE SEVEN DWARFS AFTER THERAPY

"William, Chris, Ben, Richard, Neal, Jason, Roger"

- An estimated 75 to 90 percent of people feel that psychotherapy has helped them.
- The longer a person stays in therapy, the greater the improvement.

Other studies have found that some psychotherapies are more effective for certain types of disorders (Clarkin et al., 2007; Hollon et al., 2002) but that no one psychotherapy is the most effective or works for every type of problem. Overall the evidence for psychotherapy is strong, and data support its efficacy with different age groups, across a broad range of disorders, and with clients from a variety of backgrounds and orientations (American Psychological Association, 2013; Campbell et al., 2013; Chorpita et al., 2011).

Although psychotherapy is usually accomplished by the client or clients speaking face to face with the therapist, other modalities of therapy or counseling are available using various forms of technology. While some interventions are phone based or use email, others have fallen under the general term of *cybertherapy*, but *Internet-based, online therapy, online counseling, e-therapy, web-based*, and *distance counseling* are some other terms referring to psychotherapy or mental health interventions that are offered remotely and primarily via the Internet. Although this method of delivery may have the advantages of lower or minimal cost, availability of therapy opportunities for those unable to get to a therapist easily (such as people living in a remote or rural area), access to support groups online, and relative anonymity, there are risks.

Just as with face-to-face interventions, clients need to make sure the therapist has appropriate training and credentials in psychotherapy. Therapists should also have

*empirical: capable of being verified or disproved by observation or experiment.

training and experience with distance counseling and be able to address the relative risks and benefits of distance counseling, including what steps to take when the counselor is not available (American Counseling Association, 2014; Jencius, 2015). The web and other forms of technology can offer other challenges as well. Clients and counselors alike should be mindful of the prevalence of social media and avoid "personal virtual relationships" (American Counseling Association, 2014; Jencius, 2015; Kaplan, 2016). Just as counselors and clients avoid multiple relationships to maintain professional boundaries, with the widespread use of social media, even greater attention is likely required to avoid the blurring of any personal and professional boundaries (Kaplan, 2016).

## CHARACTERISTICS OF EFFECTIVE THERAPY

**15.9** **Identify factors that influence the effectiveness of therapy.**

💬 So how does a person with a problem know what kind of therapist to go to? How do you pick a good one?

It can sometimes be hard to determine if you or someone you know needs professional help and, if so, where to find it. The video *Finding a Therapist if You Need One* offers some advice.

👁 **Watch** the **Video** *Finding a Therapist if You Need One*

As discussed before, many psychological professionals today take an eclectic view of psychotherapy, using a combination of methods or switching methods to fit the particular client's needs or specific problems.

**COMMON FACTORS APPROACH**   The *common factors approach* in psychotherapy is a modern approach to eclecticism and focuses on those factors common to successful outcomes from different forms of therapy (Norcross, 2005). These factors are seen as the source of the success rather than specific differences among therapies. The most important common factor of a successful psychotherapy may be the relationship between the client and the therapist, known as the **therapeutic alliance**. This relationship should be caring, warm, and accepting and be characterized by empathy, mutual

**therapeutic alliance**

the relationship between therapist and client that develops as a warm, caring, accepting relationship characterized by empathy, mutual respect, and understanding.

respect, and understanding. Therapy should also offer clients a *protected setting* in which to release emotions and reveal private thoughts and concerns and should help clients understand why they feel the way they do and provide them with ways to feel better. Other common factors in therapy effectiveness are *opportunity for catharsis* (relieving pent-up emotions), *learning and practice of new behaviors*, and *positive experiences* for the client (Norcross, 2005).

**EVIDENCE-BASED TREATMENT**  An ongoing area of research in psychology is related to identifying those treatments and other aspects of treatment that work best for specific disorders. Some treatments may not only be ineffective for certain disorders, some treatments or alternative therapies may even prove to be dangerous or harmful. Especially in light of managed health care and tight budgets, clients benefit through *evidence-based practice.* Empirically supported or **evidence-based treatment** (EBT) refers to techniques or interventions that have produced desired outcomes, or therapeutic change in controlled studies (Barlow et al., 2013; Kazdin, 2008). Evidence-based practice includes systematic reviews of relevant and valid information that ranges from assessment to intervention (American Psychological Association, 2005, 2013; Hunsley & Mash, 2008; Kazdin, 2008; Nathan & Gorman, 2007). Some examples of evidence-based, or empirically supported, treatments are exposure therapies, cognitive-behavioral, and cognitive processing for PTSD (Ehlers et al., 2010; Hajcak & Starr, n.d.; Najavits, 2007; Resick et al., 2008), cognitive-behavioral treatment for panic disorder with agoraphobia (Barlow et al., 2007; Craske & Barlow, 2008), cognitive-behavioral group therapy for social anxiety disorder (Turk et al., 2008), cognitive therapy for depression (Young et al., 2008), antipsychotic drugs for schizophrenia (Sharif et al., 2007), and interpersonal psychotherapy for depression (Bleiberg & Markowitcz, 2008). For additional information, Division 12 of the American Psychological Association maintains an excellent resource on research-supported treatments, https://www.div12.org/psychological-treatments/treatments/.

**NEUROIMAGING OF PSYCHOTHERAPY**  A growing body of research is focused on the potential uses of neuroimaging in evaluating psychological treatments. These studies are looking at the structural and functional changes that occur as the result of treatment, those that occur during treatment, and the potential identification of personalized treatment options for someone with a given disorder. While it will be quite some time before such approaches may be feasible and broadly available for individual consumers, if ever, it is still an exciting area of investigation and one that will likely improve treatment options for many. Broadly speaking, there is support for psychotherapy altering activity in brain areas associated with negative emotion, emotion regulation, fear, and reward (Fournier & Price, 2014). Neuroimaging has also been used to illustrate how individuals with major depressive disorder respond to either psychological or pharmacological treatment based on pretreatment brain activity. In one study, depressed individuals with hypometabolism in the insula responded best with cognitive-behavioral therapy, while individuals with hypermetabolism in the insula responded best to antidepressant medication (McGrath et al., 2013).

**evidence-based treatment**

also called empirically supported treatment, refers to interventions, strategies, or techniques that have been found to produce therapeutic and desired changes during controlled research studies.

**CULTURAL, ETHNIC, AND GENDER CONCERNS IN PSYCHOTHERAPY**  Consider the following situation (adapted from Wedding, 2004).

> *K. is a 24-year-old Korean American. She lived with her parents, who were both born and reared in Korea before moving to the United States as adults. She came to a therapist because she was depressed and unhappy with her lack of independence. Her father was angry about her plans to marry a non-Korean. Her therapist*

*immediately began assertiveness training and role playing to prepare K. to deal with her father. The therapist was disappointed when K. failed to keep her second appointment.*

This example of an actual case demonstrates a problem that exists in the therapist–client relationship for many clients when the ethnicity or culture of the client is different from that of the therapist. This cultural difference makes it difficult for therapists to understand the exact nature of their clients' problems and for clients to benefit from therapies that do not match their needs (Matsumoto, 1994; Moffic, 2003; Wedding, 2004). The values of different cultures and ethnic groups are not universally the same. How, for example, could a female therapist who is white, from an upper-middle-class family, and well educated understand the problems of a Hispanic adolescent boy from a poor family living in substandard housing if she did not acknowledge the differences between them? In this case, gender, ethnicity, and economic background of client and therapist are all vastly different.

In the case of K., for example, the therapist mistakenly assumed that the key to improving K.'s situation was to make her more assertive and independent from her family, particularly her father. This Western idea runs counter to Korean cultural values. Korean culture stresses interdependence, not independence. The family comes first, obedience to one's elders is highly valued, and "doing one's own thing" is not acceptable. K.'s real problem may have been her feelings of guilt about her situation and her father's anger. She may have wanted help in dealing with her family situation and her feelings about that situation, not help in becoming more independent.

For therapy to be effective, the client must continue in treatment until a successful outcome is reached. K. never came back after the first session. One of the problems that can occur when the culture or ethnic backgrounds of the client and therapist are mismatched, as in K.'s case, is that the therapist may project his or her values onto the client, failing to achieve true empathy with the client's feelings or even to realize what the client's true feelings are, thus causing the client to drop out of therapy. Studies of such situations have found that members of minority racial or ethnic groups drop out of therapy at a significantly higher rate than the majority-group clients (Brown et al., 2003; Cooper et al., 2003; Flaherty & Adams, 1998; Fortuna et al., 2010; Sue, 1977, 1992; Sue et al., 1994; Vail, 1976; Vernon & Roberts, 1982).

Traditional forms of psychotherapy, developed mainly in Western, individualistic cultures, may need to be modified to fit the more collectivistic, interdependent cultures. For example, Japanese psychologist Dr. Shigeru Iwakabe has pointed out that the typical "talking cure" practiced by many psychotherapists—including psychodynamic and humanistic therapists—may have to be altered to a nontalking cure and the use of nonverbal tasks (like drawing) due to the reluctance of many traditional Japanese people to talk openly about private concerns (Iwakabe, 2008).

 💬 Are differences in gender that important? For example, do women prefer female therapists, but men would rather talk to another man?

Research on gender and therapist–client relationships varies. When talking about white, middle-class clients, it seems that both men and women prefer a female therapist (Jones et al., 1987). But African-American clients were more likely to drop out of therapy if the therapist was the *same* sex as the client (Vail, 1976); male Asian clients seemed to prefer a male therapist; and female Asian clients stayed in therapy equally long with either male or female therapists (Flaherty & Adams, 1998; Flaskerud, 1991).

How might the establishment of an effective therapeutic relationship be impacted when the client and therapist are from different ethnic or cultural backgrounds?

Multiple barriers to effective psychotherapy exist when the culture or ethnic backgrounds of client and therapist are different (Sue & Sue, 2016):

- **Culture-bound values.** Including being individual centered versus other (or others) centered, verbal/emotional/behavioral expressiveness, communication patterns from client to counselor, insight, self-disclosure, scientific empiricism, and distinctions between mental and physical functioning (Sue & Sue, 2016). Differing cultural values can cause therapists to fail at forming an empathetic relationship (Sattler, 1977; Wedding, 2004).

- **Class-bound values.** Social class including impact of poverty and therapeutic class bias, adherence to time schedules, ambiguous approach to problems, looking for long-range goals (Sue & Sue, 2016). Clients from impoverished backgrounds may have values and experiences that the therapist cannot understand (Wedding, 2004).

- **Language.** Use of standard English, emphasis on verbal communication (Sue & Sue, 2016). Speaking different languages becomes a problem in understanding what both client and therapist are saying and in psychological testing (Betancourt & Jacobs, 2000; Lewis, 1996).

- **"American" cultural assumptions.** Particular values differ, and "American" values cannot be assumed. Differences can occur as related to identity, relationships, role of the family (individualism versus collectivism, nuclear family versus extended family), relationships with nature, time orientation, relationships with others, and activity (doing versus being; Sue & Sue, 2016).

- **Communication style.** Both verbal and nonverbal communication can differ between cultures and ethnicities. *Communication style* has a huge impact on what is actually said, referring to things like the physical distance between the client and therapist, the use of gestures, eye contact, and use of personal space (Sue & Sue, 2016). People in some cultures are content with long periods of silence whereas others are not, direct eye contact is desirable in some cultures and offensive in others, and even facial expressions of emotion vary. For example, smiling to express happiness may be commonplace in U.S. society, whereas in some Chinese and Japanese individuals, restraint of facial expressions may be more common (Sue & Sue, 2016).

The American Psychiatric Association (2013) has included information for psychology professionals concerning cultural issues and culture syndromes. Ⓛ Ⓘ Ⓝ Ⓚ to Learning Objective 14.2. All therapists need to make an effort to become aware of cultural differences, syndromes, and possible gender issues. Sociopolitical issues should also be examined (Sue & Sue, 2016). There is great value in learning characteristics about different groups, but in doing so, therapists need to remain mindful of not using that information to overgeneralize and stereotype the people they are working with (Sue & Sue, 2016).

## THINKING CRITICALLY

Which of the forms of psychotherapy discussed so far would probably work best for a client who has commitment issues in relationships? Why?

▶ The response entered here will be saved to your notes and may be collected by your instructor if he/she requires it.

Submit

## Concept Map L.O. 15.8, 15.9

Interactive

effectiveness is not easy to study due to different theories, techniques, time frames for success, etc.; tendency of some therapists to be eclectic (using variety of techniques) is also a challenge

common factors approach: focuses on those factors common to successful outcomes from different forms of therapy

clients benefit through evidence-based practice, or empirically validated treatment—identification of treatments and other aspects of treatment that work best for specific disorders

where effective, greater success is often tied to the relationship between the therapist and client (therapeutic alliance), a sense of safety, and longer time in therapy

cultural, ethnic, and gender concerns should also be examined; these factors can affect not only the therapeutic alliance but also identification of actual problem(s) and treatment options

**Does Psychotherapy Work?**

Reset

## Practice Quiz    How much do you remember?

*Pick the best answer.*

**1.** Dr. Cavendish is trying to establish what is known as a therapeutic alliance with her clients. What specifically should she do to accomplish this goal?
   **a.** She should work to better understand the disorder that she is treating.
   **b.** She should be more confrontational in her approach so as to make clients aware of their difficulties.
   **c.** She should be more empathetic and caring when working with her clients.
   **d.** She should openly consult with others on all cases to ensure quality therapeutic treatment.

**2.** Research shows that African American clients prefer a therapist _____ while Asian men prefer a _____ therapist.
   **a.** of the opposite sex; male
   **b.** of the same sex; female
   **c.** of the same culture; Hispanic
   **d.** who is female; White

**3.** What do studies show about the overall effectiveness of cybertherapy?
   **a.** It is a fad, and studies indicate that cybertherapy is relatively ineffective.
   **b.** Cybertherapy can be effective for people who otherwise might be unable to get to a therapist.
   **c.** Studies indicate that many clients who use chat rooms as part of their cybertherapy often stop showing up after 1 or 2 sessions.
   **d.** There currently are not enough studies to indicate whether cybertherapy is or is not effective.

**4.** _____ refers to techniques or interventions that have produced desired outcomes, or therapeutic change in controlled studies.
   **a.** Client-friendly
   **b.** Insurance-approved
   **c.** Clinically valid
   **d.** Evidence-based treatment

## APA Goal 2: Scientific Inquiry and Critical Thinking

### Does It Work? Psychological Treatment

*Addresses APA Learning Objective 2.4: Interpret, design, and conduct basic psychological research.*

Now that you have learned about a variety of treatment options for psychological disorders, how would you design an experiment to study the effects of Treatments A and B for Disorder X?

There are numerous problems with studying the effectiveness of psychotherapy. Controlled studies can be done using an experimental group of people who receive a particular psychotherapy and a comparison group of people who are put on a waiting list, but this is less than ideal. The comparison group is not getting the attention from the therapist, for one thing, and so there would be no placebo-effect expectations about getting better because of therapy (Shapiro & Shapiro, 1997). Also, not all therapies take the same amount of time to be effective. For example, psychoanalysis, even in its short form, takes longer than a behavioral therapy. In a short-term study, behavioral therapy would obviously look more effective. Action therapies such as behavior therapy measure the success of the therapy differently than do insight therapies; in a behavioral therapy the reduction of the undesired behavior is easy to objectively measure, but gaining insights and feelings of control, self-worth, self-esteem, and so on are not as easily evaluated (Shadish et al., 2002).

Let's assume your research hypothesis is something like, "Treatment A will be more effective than Treatment B for Disorder X, and both Treatment A and B will be more effective than no treatment for Disorder X." How would you evaluate these treatments? What kind of research methods would you use to be able to speak to cause-and-effect relationships? How are you going to operationalize the treatments and their effects? What data will you need to confirm your hypothesis?

For example, let's assume Treatment A consists of ten 50-minute sessions of one-on-one cognitive-behavioral therapy with a psychologist. Treatment B consists of ten Internet-based, self-study modules based on cognitive-behavioral therapy, each requiring approximately 45 minutes to complete. Although progression through the sessions will be monitored by a psychologist, there will not be any direct interaction with a psychology professional.

Based on the information presented, what data do you need and how will you collect it? You will likely want to make sure you have individuals that have similar symptoms of Disorder X, and if possible, do not have any other disorders. What do you need to keep in mind as you populate your treatment groups and a comparison group? Preferably, these groups need to be close to identical in terms of demographics, including age, level of education, socioeconomic status, gender, and so on. Will you randomly assign individuals to each of the three groups? Where will you get your participants? How many individuals do you need in each group? Ideally, you would have 30 or more people in each group. Groups should contain approximately the same amount of people. Ⓛ Ⓘ Ⓝ Ⓚ to Learning Objectives A.1, A.5.

Assume you find that either Treatment A or Treatment B has a positive effect on the symptoms of Disorder X. Following the study, how do you accommodate the individuals that were in the comparison group? One way is to offer treatment to the people in the comparison group at the conclusion of the original study. What if the hypothesis is confirmed and Treatment A is more effective than Treatment B? Which treatment do you offer to the comparison group, or do you give them a choice? In this case, you may want to offer both and allow them to choose, explaining the benefits of each and letting the individual decided which they prefer.

Regardless of the outcomes of the study, how might you share the results with other psychology professionals? How might you share the information with the public? With students taking an introduction to general psychology class? Would the manner in which you share the information differ based on the hypothesis being confirmed versus some other finding or combination of findings?

# Biomedical Therapies

Just as a therapist trained in psychoanalysis is more likely to use that technique, a therapist whose perspective on personality and behavior is biological will most likely turn to medical techniques to manage disordered behavior. Even psychotherapists who are not primarily biological in orientation may combine psychotherapy with medical treatments that are supervised by a medical doctor working with the psychologist. As medical doctors, psychiatrists are almost inevitably biological in perspective and, thus, use *biomedical therapies* (directly affecting the biological functioning of the body and brain) in addition to any psychotherapy technique they may favor. The biomedical therapies fall into several approaches and may consist of drug therapy, shock therapy, surgical treatments, or noninvasive stimulation techniques.

## PSYCHOPHARMACOLOGY

15.10 **Categorize types of drugs used to treat psychological disorders.**

The use of drugs to control or relieve the symptoms of a psychological disorder is called **psychopharmacology**. Although these drugs are sometimes used alone, they are more often combined with some form of psychotherapy and are more effective as a result (Kearney & Silverman, 1998; Keller et al., 2000). There are four basic categories of drugs used to treat psychotic disorders, anxiety disorders, the manic phase of mood disorders, and depression.

**ANTIPSYCHOTIC DRUGS** Drugs used to treat psychotic symptoms, such as hallucinations, delusions, and bizarre behavior, are called **antipsychotic drugs**. These drugs can be classified into two categories, the classical, or *typical antipsychotics*, and newer *atypical antipsychotics*. The first of the typical antipsychotics to be developed was *chlorpromazine*. The first-generation antipsychotics caused "neurolepsis," or psychomotor slowing and reduced emotionality, and thus were referred to as *neuroleptics* due to the neurological side effects they produced (Julien et al., 2011; Preston et al., 2008; Stahl, 2013). **Table 15.3** lists several typical and atypical antipsychotic drugs and their side effects.

Typical antipsychotic drugs work by blocking certain dopamine receptors in the brain, namely the D2 receptor, thereby reducing the effect of dopamine in synaptic transmission (Julien et al., 2011; Preston et al., 2008; Stahl, 2013). However, because they block more pathways in the dopamine system than are involved in psychosis, with prolonged use they tend to cause problems. Such problems include movement disorders similar to those in Parkinson's disease, sometimes called *extrapyramidal symptoms*, and others such as *tardive dyskinesia*. Tardive dyskinesia is a syndrome caused by long-term treatment and can even persist when typical antipsychotic medications are no longer used. The syndrome is characterized by the person making facial and tongue movements such as repeatedly sticking their tongue out, grimacing, or constant chewing, or causing repetitive

**psychopharmacology**
the use of drugs to control or relieve the symptoms of psychological disorders.

**antipsychotic drugs**
drugs used to treat psychotic symptoms such as delusions, hallucinations, and other bizarre behavior.

**Table 15.3** Types of Drugs Used in Psychopharmacology

| Classification | Treatment Areas | Side Effects | Examples |
|---|---|---|---|
| Antipsychotic: Typical antipsychotic | Positive (excessive) symptoms such as delusions or hallucinations | Motor problems, tardive dyskinesia | Chlorpromazine, droperidol, haloperidol |
| Antipsychotic: Atypical antipsychotic | Positive and some negative symptoms of psychoses | Fewer than typical antipsychotic; clozapine may cause serious blood disorder | Risperidone, clozapine, aripiprazole |
| Antianxiety: Minor Tranquilizers | Symptoms of anxiety and phobic reactions | Slight sedative effect; potential for physical dependence | Alprazolam, lorazepam, diazepam |
| Antimanic | Manic behavior | Potential for toxic buildup | Lithium, anticonvulsant drugs |
| Antidepressants: MAOIs | Depression | Weight gain, constipation, dry mouth, dizziness, headache, drowsiness, insomnia, some sexual arousal disorders | Iproniazid, isocarboxazid, phenelzine sulfite, tranylcypromine sulfate |
| Antidepressants: Tricyclics | Depression | Skin rashes, blurred vision, lowered blood pressure, weight loss | Imipramine, desipramine, amitriptyline, doxepin |
| Antidepressants: SSRIs | Depression | Nausea, nervousness, insomnia, diarrhea, rash, agitation, some sexual arousal problems | Fluoxetine, sertraline, paroxetine |

involuntary jerks or dance-like movements of the arms and legs (Julien et al., 2011; Preston et al., 2008; Stahl, 2013).

The atypical antipsychotics may also suppress dopamine but to a much greater degree in the one dopamine pathway that seems to cause psychotic problems. These drugs also block or partially block certain serotonin receptors, resulting in fewer negative side effects and occasionally some improvement in the negative symptoms of schizophrenia (Julien et al., 2011; Preston et al., 2008; Stahl, 2013). Despite their effectiveness, the atypical antipsychotics may also have unwanted side effects, such as weight gain, diabetes, blood lipid level changes, or changes in the electrical rhythms of the heart (Julien et al., 2011). One of these, clozapine, can cause a potentially fatal reduction in the white blood cells of the body's immune system in a very small percentage of people. For this reason, the blood of patients on clozapine is closely monitored, and it is not considered to be a first choice when selecting treatment options but is used more often when other antipsychotic drugs are ineffective (Stahl, 2013).

Newer classes of atypical antipsychotics include *partial dopamine agonists* that affect the release of dopamine rather than blocking its receptors in the brain and other agents that have agonistic or antagonistic properties for dopamine and serotonin (Stahl, 2013). (An *agonist* facilitates, whereas an *antagonist* blocks or reduces effects.) Drugs are also being investigated that are linked to the actions of *glutamate*. (L)(I)(N)K to Learning Objective 2.3.

 How long do people generally have to take these antipsychotic medications?

In some cases, a person might have a psychotic episode that lasts only a few months or a few years and may need drug treatment only for that time. But in most cases, especially in schizophrenia that starts in adolescence or young adulthood, the medication must be taken for the rest of the person's life. Long-term use of antipsychotics, particularly the older typical drugs, has been associated with a decrease in cognitive functioning such as impaired memory and sedation, possibly due to the chemical actions of the drugs themselves. The hope for newer atypical antipsychotics is that they will not only produce fewer negative side effects but also have less impact on the cognitive processes of those persons taking these drugs (Julien et al., 2011; Stahl, 2013).

**ANTIANXIETY DRUGS** The traditional **antianxiety drugs** are the minor tranquilizers or *benzodiazepines* such as Xanax, Ativan, and Valium. All of these drugs have a sedative effect and, in the right dose, can start to relieve symptoms of anxiety within 20 to 30 minutes of taking the drug by mouth (Preston et al., 2008). Although many side effects are possible, the main concern in using these drugs is their potential for addiction as well as abuse in the form of taking larger doses to "escape" (National Institute on Drug Abuse [NIDA], 2002).

**MOOD-STABILIZING DRUGS** For many years, the treatment of choice for bipolar disorder and episodes of mania has been *lithium*, a metallic chemical element that in its salt form (lithium carbonate) evens out both the highs and the lows of bipolar disorder. It is generally recommended that treatment with lithium continue at maintenance levels in people with recurring bipolar disorder. Lithium affects the way sodium ions in neuron and muscle cells are transported, although it is not clear exactly how this affects mood. Side effects typically disappear quickly, although the use of lithium has been associated with weight gain. Diet needs to be controlled when taking lithium because lowered levels of sodium in the diet can cause lithium to build up to toxic levels, as can any substance that removes water from the body such as the caffeine in sodas, tea, and coffee.

Anticonvulsant drugs, normally used to treat seizure disorders, have also been used to treat mania. Examples are carbamazepine, valproic acid (Depakote), and lamotrigine. These drugs can be as effective in controlling mood swings as lithium and can also be used in combination with lithium treatments (Bowden et al., 2000; Thase & Sachs, 2000). Some atypical antipsychotics work as mood stabilizers and may be used alone or in conjunction with anticonvulsant medications (Julien et al., 2011; Preston et al., 2008; Stahl, 2013).

**ANTIDEPRESSANT DRUGS** As is so often the case in scientific discoveries, the first types of drugs used in the treatment of depression were originally developed to treat other disorders. Iproniazid, for example, was used to treat tuberculosis symptoms in the early 1950s and was found to have a positive effect on mood, becoming the first modern **antidepressant** (López-Muñoz & Alamo, 2009). This drug became the first of the *monoamine oxidase inhibitors* (MAOIs), a class of antidepressants that blocks the activity of an enzyme called monoamine oxidase. Monoamine oxidase is the brain's "cleanup worker" because its primary function is to break down the neurotransmitters norepinephrine, serotonin, and dopamine—the three neurotransmitters most involved in control of mood. Under normal circumstances, the excess neurotransmitters are broken down *after* they have done their "job" in mood control. In depression, these neurotransmitters need more time to do their job, and the MAOIs allow them that time by inhibiting the enzyme's action.

Some common MAOIs in use today are isocarboxazid (Marplan), phenelzine sulfate (Nardil), and tranylcypromine sulfate (Parnate). These drugs can produce some unwanted side effects, although in most cases the side effects decrease or disappear with continued treatment: weight gain, constipation, dry mouth, dizziness, headache, drowsiness or insomnia, and sexual arousal disorders are possible. People taking MAOIs in general should also be careful about eating certain smoked, fermented, or pickled foods, drinking certain beverages, or taking some other medications due to a risk of severe high blood pressure in combination with consumption of these items, although there are a

**antianxiety drugs**
drugs used to treat and calm anxiety reactions, typically minor tranquilizers.

**antidepressant**
drugs used to treat depression and anxiety.

couple of MAOIs that do not require any dietary restrictions (Stahl, 2013). And while these precautions are very important, certain drug–drug interactions may be more common and sometimes even lethal, so individuals taking MAOIs should work closely with their health-care professionals to monitor adverse drug interactions (Julien et al., 2011; Preston et al., 2008; Stahl, 2013).

The second category of antidepressant drug to be developed is called the *tricyclic antidepressants*. These drugs were discovered in the course of developing treatments for schizophrenia (López-Muñoz & Alamo, 2009). Tricyclics, so called because of their molecular structure consisting of three rings (cycles), increase the activity of serotonin and norepinephrine in the nervous system by inhibiting their reuptake into the synaptic vesicles of the neurons. (L I N K) to Learning Objective 2.3. Some common tricyclics are imipramine (Tofranil), desipramine (Norpramin, Pertofrane), amitriptyline (Elavil), and doxepin (Sinequan, Adapin). Side effects of these drugs, which may also decrease over the course of treatment, are very similar to those of the MAOIs but can also include skin rashes, blurred vision, lowered blood pressure, and weight gain (Julien et al., 2011; Preston et al., 2008; Stahl, 2013).

The effect of the MAOIs and the tricyclics on the action of the three critical neurotransmitters led researchers to try to develop drugs that would more specifically target the critical neural activity involved in depression with fewer negative side effects. This led to the development of the *selective serotonin reuptake inhibitors* (SSRIs), drugs that inhibit the reuptake process of only serotonin. This causes fewer side effects while still providing effective antidepressant action, making these drugs relatively safe when compared to the older antidepressants. But like the other two classes of antidepressants, the SSRIs may take from 2 to 6 weeks to produce effects. Some of the better-known SSRIs are fluoxetine (Prozac), sertraline (Zoloft), and paroxetine (Paxil). Other classes of antidepressants have been or are being investigated, including *serotonin-norepinephrine reuptake inhibitors* (SNRIs), *serotonin partial agonist/reuptake inhibitors* (SPARIs), *norepinephrine-dopamine reuptake inhibitors* (NDRIs), *selective norepinephrine reuptake inhibitors* (NRIs), and *serotonin antagonist/reuptake inhibitors* (SARIs).

There is also research examining the potential use of subanesthetic doses of *ketamine* as an antidepressant due to its apparent ability to have immediate antidepressant effects and reduction of suicidal thoughts (Stahl, 2013). The effects are not permanent, but its effects can come on within a few hours and last for several days and up to a week in some individuals (DiazGranados, Ibrahim, Brutsche, Ameli, et al., 2010; DiazGranados, Ibrahim, Brutsche, Newberg, et al., 2010; Zarate et al., 2006; Zarate et al., 2012). In addition to rapid effects, it appears to also facilitate synaptogenesis and reverse some of the neuronal effects of chronic stress (Duman & Aghajanian, 2012). Drugs that act like ketamine are being investigated for potential use as antidepressants. Ketamine itself is an anesthetic, sometimes abused due to its dissociative and hallucinogenic effects (e.g., "Special K" or "K"), or used in cases of sexual assault.

Concerns have arisen that children and teenagers taking newer antidepressant medications may have an increased risk of suicide versus those not receiving treatment. Recent meta-analyses have provided conflicting information, with some data suggesting an increased risk for suicide while other data do not support an increased risk (Gibbons et al., 2012; Hetrick et al., 2012). Where there is an increased risk, it is possible depressive symptoms are being addressed while suicidal thoughts and behavior are not reduced. Regardless, caution is urged, especially in children and teens being treated with newer antidepressant medications.

With regard to other uses for antidepressant medication, in the last several years the use of the benzodiazepines to treat anxiety has declined, and physicians and therapists have begun to prescribe antidepressant drugs to treat anxiety and related disorders such as panic disorder, obsessive-compulsive disorder, and post traumatic stress disorder. Although the antidepressants take from 3 to 5 weeks to show any effect, they are not as subject to abuse as the minor tranquilizers and have fewer of the same side effects.

At what age do you think children and/or teenagers should be able to decide if they will take medications to treat abnormal psychological functioning or behavior?

▶ | The response entered here will be saved to your notes and may be collected by your instructor if he/she requires it.

Submit

Overall, many psychological professionals today believe that combining psychotherapy with medical therapies—particularly drug therapy—is a more effective approach to treating many disorders. A person dealing with major depressive disorder may be given an antidepressant drug to alleviate symptoms but may also still need to talk about what it's like to deal with their symptoms and with needing the medication. Psychotherapy combined with antidepressant medication therapy is more effective in treating major depressive disorder than medication therapy alone and possibly better than psychotherapy alone (Craighead & Dunlop, 2014). However, cognitive-behavioral therapy in combination with drug therapy may not be more effective, as it may have a larger impact than some other approaches, leaving less room for improvement (Craighead & Dunlop, 2014). Individuals with such disorders as schizophrenia also benefit from combined approaches, with strategies ranging from family- and community support-based programs to individual or group-based cognitive-behavioral therapy proving to be valuable conjunctive therapies to psychopharmacological treatment (Stahl, 2013). However, at least for individuals with major depressive disorder, combined treatment should not be the default, as some individuals may respond effectively to only one treatment modality, and there are increased monetary costs for combined treatments (Craighead & Dunlop, 2014).

### ECT AND PSYCHOSURGERY

**15.11** **Explain how electroconvulsive therapy and psychosurgery are used to treat psychological disorders.**

As addressed at the beginning of the chapter, psychological disorders have been treated in a variety of ways, via a variety of medical means, and some treatments have been better options than others. Unfortunately, some methods were used indiscriminately, were ineffective, or caused more harm than good. That has changed, and current alternative biomedical options are effective options when other strategies have not been successful, and they are sometimes the best option.

**ELECTROCONVULSIVE THERAPY** Many people are—well—*shocked* to discover that **electroconvulsive therapy (ECT)** is still in use to treat cases of severe depression. ECT involves the delivery of an electric shock to either one side or both sides of a person's head, resulting in a seizure or convulsion of the body and the release of a flood of neurotransmitters in the brain (American Psychiatric Association [APA] Committee on Electroconvulsive Therapy, 2001). The result is an almost immediate improvement in mood, and ECT is used not only in severe cases of depression that have not responded to drug treatments or psychotherapy or where the side effects of medication are not acceptable but also in the treatment of several other severe disorders, such as schizophrenia and severe mania, that are not responding to alternate treatments (APA Committee on Electroconvulsive Therapy, 2001; Pompili et al., 2013).

In the 1930s, doctors actually were researching the possible uses of inducing seizures in treating schizophrenia, although the seizures were induced through means of

**electroconvulsive therapy (ECT)** form of biomedical therapy to treat severe depression in which electrodes are placed on either one or both sides of a person's head and an electric current is passed through the electrodes that is strong enough to cause a seizure or convulsion.

a drug (camphor) in those early experiments. It was Italian researchers Cerletti and Bini who first used electricity to induce a seizure in a man with schizophrenia, who fully recovered after only 11 such treatments (Endler, 1988; Fink, 1984; Shorter, 1997). Soon doctors were using ECT on every kind of severe mental disorder. In those early days, no anesthesia was used because the shock was severe enough to result in a loss of consciousness (most of the time). Broken bones, bitten tongues, and fractured teeth were not untypical "side effects."

Today's ECT is far more controlled and humane. It is only used to treat severe disorders, and written and informed consent is required in most states. ECT has been found to be most useful for severe depression that has not responded to medications or psychotherapy and in cases where suicide is a real possibility or has already been attempted. ECT works more quickly than antidepressant medications, so it can play an important role in helping prevent suicide attempts (APA Committee on Electroconvulsive Therapy, 2001). Although relationships to clinical symptoms are not yet clear, it has also been shown to increase the volume of gray matter and increase cortical thickness in some areas of the brain, including the hippocampus and amygdala, areas involved in emotion and memory (Bouckaert et al., 2015; Sartorius et al., 2015). **L I N K** to Learning Objective 2.11. Despite the results and these findings, ECT should not be considered a "cure." It is a way to get a person suffering from severe depression into a state of mind that is more receptive to other forms of therapy or psychotherapy. Relapse is very possible in individuals receiving ECT, and maintenance or continuation therapies are an important treatment strategy to pursue (Nordenskjold et al., 2011; Petrides et al., 2011).

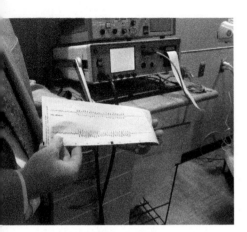

Brain activity is monitored before, during, and after an electroconvulsive treatment (ECT). ECT consists of applying an electric shock to one or both sides of the head to induce a seizure. The result is rapid improvement in mood. It has been shown to be most effective in treating severe depression that has not responded to other treatments, or where the side effects of other treatments cannot be tolerated.

💬 What are some of the side effects? Wasn't there something from an earlier chapter about this therapy affecting memory?

ECT does have several negative side effects, some of which last longer than others. Memory is definitely affected, as ECT disrupts the consolidation process and prevents the formation of long-term memories. **L I N K** to Learning Objective 6.12. This causes both retrograde amnesia, the loss of memories for events that happen close to the time of the treatment, and anterograde amnesia, the rapid forgetting of new material (APA Committee on Electroconvulsive Therapy, 2001; Lisanby et al., 2000; Weiner, 2000). The retrograde effects can extend to several months before and a few weeks after treatment, and the older memories may return with time, whereas the anterograde amnesia is more temporary, clearing up in a few weeks after treatment. When ECT is used today, every effort is made to reduce as many side effects as possible. The modern patient is given muscle relaxants to reduce the effects of the convulsion as well as a very short-term anesthetic. There are even ECT approaches that use *ultrabrief* pulses, which appear to have fewer cognitive side effects but not the same level of therapeutic results as other methods (Tor et al., 2015). Despite its efficacy, the utilization of ECT in general is not uniform. In the United States, racial differences in the use of ECT appear to be present, with African Americans with depression less likely to pursue or receive ECT treatment as compared to white Americans, and the overall use of ECT in general appears to be declining (Case, Bertollo, Laska, Price et al., 2013; Case, Bertollo, Laska, Siegel, et al., 2012).

**PSYCHOSURGERY**   Just as surgery involves cutting into the body, **psychosurgery** involves cutting into the brain to remove or destroy brain tissue for the purpose of relieving symptoms of mental disorders. One of the earliest and best-known psychosurgical techniques is the **prefrontal lobotomy**, in which the connections of the prefrontal cortex to other areas of the brain are severed. The lobotomy was developed in 1935 by Portuguese neurologist Dr. Antonio Egas Moniz, who was awarded the Nobel Prize in medicine for his contribution to psychosurgery (Cosgrove & Rauch, 1995;

**psychosurgery**

surgery performed on brain tissue to relieve or control severe psychological disorders.

**prefrontal lobotomy**

psychosurgery in which the connections of the prefrontal cortex to other areas of the brain are severed.

Freeman & Watts, 1937). Walter Freeman and James W. Watts modified Moniz's technique and developed a procedure called the *transorbital lobotomy*, during which an instrument resembling an ice pick, called a leucotome, was inserted through the back of the eye socket and into the brain to sever the brain fibers. It was this technique that became widely used, and unfortunately sometimes overused, in the pursuit of relief for so many people suffering from mental illness.

> 💬 But I thought lobotomies left most people worse off than before—didn't it take away their emotions or something?

Although it is true that some of the early lobotomy patients did seem less agitated, anxious, and delusional, it is also true that some early patients did not survive the surgery (about 6 percent died, in fact), and others were left with negative changes in personality: apathy, lack of emotional response, intellectual dullness, and childishness, to name a few. Fortunately, the development of antipsychotic drugs, beginning with chlorpromazine, together with the results of long-term studies that highlighted serious side effects of lobotomies, led to the discontinuation of lobotomies as a psychosurgical technique (Cosgrove & Rauch, 1995; Swayze, 1995). In the last decades lobotomies were used, some famous recipients (and the disorders for which the procedure was performed) were Rosemary Kennedy, sister of John F. Kennedy (mild intellectual disability), and Rose Williams, sister of playwright Tennessee Williams (schizophrenia).

> 💬 Are there any psychosurgical techniques in use today since the lobotomy is no longer used?

The woman on the left is Rosemary Kennedy, sister of President John F. Kennedy. The man on the right is her father, U.S. Ambassador to Great Britain Joseph Kennedy. About 6 years after this photograph was taken, Rosemary, who had mild intellectual disability and whose behavior had become difficult to control, was subjected to a transorbital lobotomy. The results were disastrous, and she remained institutionalized until her death on January 7, 2005.

The lobotomy is gone, but there is a different and more modern technique called **bilateral anterior cingulotomy**, in which magnetic resonance imaging, ⓛⓘⓝⓚ to Learning Objective 2.9, is used to guide an electrode to a specific area of the brain called the cingulate gyrus. This area connects the frontal lobes to the limbic system, which controls emotional reactions. By running a current through the electrode, a very small and specific area of brain cells can be destroyed. This process is called *lesioning*. ⓛⓘⓝⓚ to Learning Objective 2.8. Cingulotomies are relatively rare and only used as a last resort, but they have been shown to be effective in some cases of major depressive disorder and obsessive-compulsive disorder that have not responded to any other therapy techniques (Nuttin et al., 2014). Because this is deliberate brain damage and quite permanent, all other possible treatments must be exhausted before it will be performed and, unlike the early days of lobotomies, it can be performed only with the patient's full and informed consent (Nuttin et al., 2014). Given that not all individuals respond positively to this invasive procedure, current research efforts are ongoing to better predict who will respond to this treatment versus those that may not (Banks et al., 2015).

**EMERGING TECHNIQUES**

**15.12** **Identify some of the newer technologies being used to treat psychological disorders.**

Some newer noninvasive techniques for effecting changes in the brain were discussed in Chapter Two, including repetitive transcranial magnetic stimulation (rTMS), in which magnetic pulses are applied to the cortex, and transcranial direct current stimulation (tDCS), which uses scalp electrodes to pass very-low-amplitude direct currents to the brain. These new and exciting strategies are being evaluated as possible treatment options for a variety of psychological disorders or in assisting researchers to better understand

**bilateral anterior cingulotomy**
psychosurgical technique in which an electrode wire is inserted into the anterior cingulate gyrus, with the guidance of magnetic resonance imaging, to destroy a very small portion of that brain area with electric current.

Deep brain stimulation (DBS) is an invasive procedure, and sometimes used when all other treatment options have failed. It involves the implantation of a pulse generator, a device that will send electric stimulation to specific areas of the brain.

the brain mechanisms underlying them, including PTSD, depression, stroke, spinal cord injuries, and ADHD, along with many others (Adeyemo et al., 2012; Benito et al., 2012; Boggio, Rocha, et al., 2009; Cristancho et al., 2013; Helfrich et al., 2012; Nitsche et al., 2009).

Another technique highlighted in Chapter Two is deep brain stimulation (DBS). And while rTMS and tDCS are noninvasive, DBS is not and is used when other approaches have failed. DBS is being evaluated as a treatment modality for both depression and OCD (Denys et al., 2010; Holtzheimer et al., 2012), with some evidence that DBS may also improve some neuropsychological functions in depressed individuals (Moreines et al., 2014). Exciting research is investigating the use of DBS for individuals with chronic anorexia nervosa who have not responded well to other treatments, with initial results suggesting some individuals have improved body mass index (BMI), mood, and anxiety symptoms after DBS treatment (Lipsman et al., 2013). Pilot studies and initial investigations are also examining the potential use of DBS in chronic obesity (Val-Laillet et al., 2015; Whiting et al., 2013).

## Concept Map L.O. 15.10, 15.11, 15.12

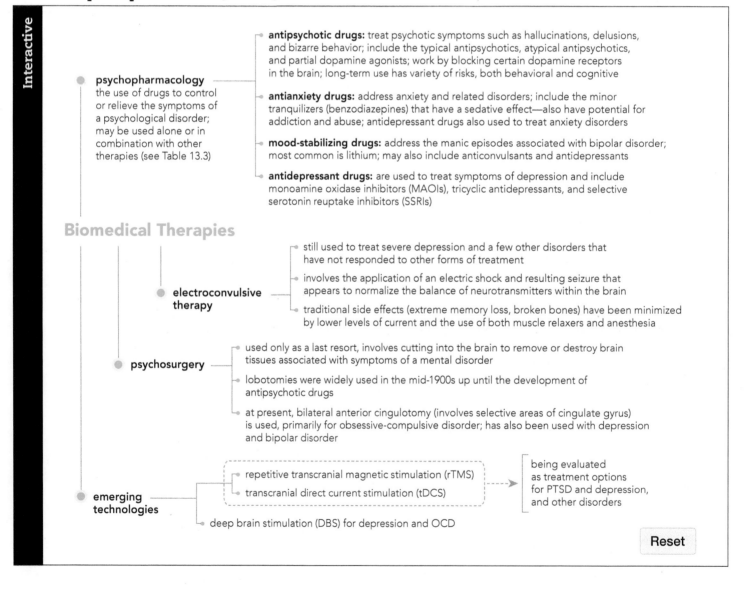

Interactive

**psychopharmacology** the use of drugs to control or relieve the symptoms of a psychological disorder; may be used alone or in combination with other therapies (see Table 13.3)

**antipsychotic drugs:** treat psychotic symptoms such as hallucinations, delusions, and bizarre behavior; include the typical antipsychotics, atypical antipsychotics, and partial dopamine agonists; work by blocking certain dopamine receptors in the brain; long-term use has variety of risks, both behavioral and cognitive

**antianxiety drugs:** address anxiety and related disorders; include the minor tranquilizers (benzodiazepines) that have a sedative effect—also have potential for addiction and abuse; antidepressant drugs also used to treat anxiety disorders

**mood-stabilizing drugs:** address the manic episodes associated with bipolar disorder; most common is lithium; may also include anticonvulsants and antidepressants

**antidepressant drugs:** are used to treat symptoms of depression and include monoamine oxidase inhibitors (MAOIs), tricyclic antidepressants, and selective serotonin reuptake inhibitors (SSRIs)

**Biomedical Therapies**

**electroconvulsive therapy**
- still used to treat severe depression and a few other disorders that have not responded to other forms of treatment
- involves the application of an electric shock and resulting seizure that appears to normalize the balance of neurotransmitters within the brain
- traditional side effects (extreme memory loss, broken bones) have been minimized by lower levels of current and the use of both muscle relaxers and anesthesia

**psychosurgery**
- used only as a last resort, involves cutting into the brain to remove or destroy brain tissues associated with symptoms of a mental disorder
- lobotomies were widely used in the mid-1900s up until the development of antipsychotic drugs
- at present, bilateral anterior cingulotomy (involves selective areas of cingulate gyrus) is used, primarily for obsessive-compulsive disorder; has also been used with depression and bipolar disorder

**emerging technologies**
- repetitive transcranial magnetic stimulation (rTMS)
- transcranial direct current stimulation (tDCS)
→ being evaluated as treatment options for PTSD and depression, and other disorders
- deep brain stimulation (DBS) for depression and OCD

Reset

# Practice Quiz    How much do you remember?

*Pick the best answer.*

1. Why are antidepressants taking the place of many antianxiety drugs in the treatment of anxiety disorders?
   **a.** Antidepressants are more cost effective.
   **b.** Antianxiety drugs may be addictive and have more side effects.
   **c.** Antianxiety drugs are becoming less effective.
   **d.** Antianxiety drugs are actually no longer available.

2. Prolonged use of antipsychotic medication can lead to a side effect called _____, which is characterized by involuntary facial and tongue movements (e.g., grimacing, constant chewing), or repetitive involuntary jerks or dance-like movements of the arms and legs.
   **a.** agranulocytosis
   **b.** tardive dyskinesia
   **c.** synesthesia
   **d.** neuromalignant disorder

3. Today's electroconvulsive shock therapy is often quite useful in the treatment of
   **a.** dissociative identity disorder.
   **b.** schizophrenia.
   **c.** mild anxiety.
   **d.** severe depression.

4. A new therapeutic technique known as deep brain stimulation (DBS) is showing promise in the treatment of
   **a.** anorexia nervosa where other treatments have failed.
   **b.** phobias.
   **c.** personality disorders.
   **d.** mania.

---

## Applying Psychology to Everyday Life
# Virtual Reality Therapies

**15.13** **Describe how virtual reality can be used in psychotherapy.**

*Virtual reality* is a software-generated, three-dimensional simulated environment. Imagine yourself playing a video game, but instead of viewing your character on the screen in front of you, you are immersed in the visual and auditory world created by the game designers, seeing and hearing through the eyes and ears of your character. While playing a video game in this manner might be a lot of fun, there are some very practical uses of virtual reality (VR) for treating psychological disorders.

One of the main uses of VR as a therapy incorporates exposure therapy of some form. Exposure therapy involves preventing a person with a phobia, for example, from avoiding the presentation of the phobic object—preventing the typical avoidance response and eventually resulting in extinction of the conditioned fear. Using VR ensures that the person being treated cannot avoid exposure, as the sight and sound of the animal, open spaces, or whatever the phobia involves is always right in front of him or her. For example, one study examined the use of exposure therapy

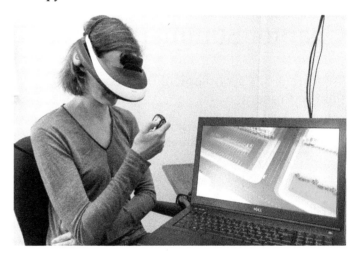

Virtual reality can be used to expose patients to phobic objects and situations, including scenarios that someone with acrophobia (fear of heights) may find distressing.

using VR technology with specific phobia of small animals, namely spiders and cockroaches (Botella et al., 2016). Participants wore VR goggles and were able to interact with the spiders or cockroaches virtually. The control group participants were exposed to real spiders or cockroaches. After the VR and *in vivo* exposure treatments, both conditions resulted in significant improvements (Botella et al., 2016).

Posttraumatic stress disorder (PTSD) is another mental health issue benefiting from the use of VR psychotherapy. Cases of this disorder are rising (and with the world events discussed in Chapter Fourteen and other such stressors, psychologists expect the number of PTSD cases to continue to rise), and traditional treatments are not always effective. Although still a relatively new area of research, evidence suggests virtual reality psychotherapy may be as effective as traditional exposure methods in the treatment of PTSD and may especially be appealing for clients that do not want to pursue traditional exposure methods or techniques (Goncalves et al., 2012; Motraghi et al., 2015). Another advantage is the more vivid and realistic imagery possible with VR, especially for patients who are asked to "imagine" the scenarios that disturb them who may not be highly skilled in visualization. Think also of the portability of VR: There are currently handheld VR devices that eventually could be used to deliver therapy for PTSD, for example, to survivors of earthquakes, tsunamis, hurricanes, and other massive disasters around the world.

VR psychotherapy has been effective for many soldiers experiencing symptoms of PTSD.

Questions for Further Discussion

1. What other disorders can you think of that might benefit from virtual reality psychotherapy?

2. Can you think of any disadvantages to this method of therapy?

# Chapter Summary

## Treatment of Psychological Disorders: Past to Present

**15.1 Describe how the treatment of psychological disorders has changed throughout history.**

- Mentally ill people began to be confined to institutions called asylums in the mid-1500s. Treatments were harsh and often damaging.
- Philippe Pinel became famous for demanding that the mentally ill be treated with kindness, personally unlocking the chains of inmates at Bicêtre Asylum in Paris, France.
- Psychotherapy involves a person talking to a psychological professional about the person's problems.
- Psychotherapy for the purpose of gaining understanding into one's motives and actions is called insight therapy, whereas psychotherapy aimed at changing disordered behavior directly is called action therapy.
- Biomedical therapy uses a medical procedure to bring about changes in behavior.

## Insight Therapies: Psychodynamic and Humanistic Approaches

**15.2 Describe the basic elements of Freud's psychoanalysis and psychodynamic approaches today.**

- Sigmund Freud developed a treatment called psychoanalysis that focused on releasing a person's hidden, repressed urges and concerns from the unconscious mind.

- Psychoanalysis uses interpretation of dreams, free association, positive and negative transference, and resistance to help patients reveal their unconscious concerns.
- Freud's original therapy technique is criticized for its lack of scientific research and his own personal biases that caused him to misinterpret much of what his patients revealed.
- Modern psychodynamic therapists have modified the technique so that it takes less time and is much more direct, and they do not focus on the id and sexuality as Freud did.

**15.3 Identify the basic elements of the humanistic therapies known as person-centered therapy and Gestalt therapy.**

- Humanistic therapies focus on the conscious mind and subjective experiences to help clients gain insights.
- Person-centered therapy is very nondirective, allowing the client to talk through problems and concerns while the therapist provides a supportive background.
- The three basic elements of person-centered therapy are authenticity of the therapist in the client's perception, unconditional positive regard given to the client by the therapist, and the empathy of the therapist for the client.
- Gestalt therapy is more directive, helping clients become aware of their feelings and take responsibility for their choices in life.
- Gestalt therapists try to help clients deal with things in their past that they have denied and will use body language and other nonverbal cues to understand what clients are really saying.
- Humanistic therapies are also not based in experimental research and work best with intelligent, highly verbal persons.

## Action Therapies: Behavior Therapies and Cognitive Therapies

**15.4** **Explain how behavior therapists use classical and operant conditioning to treat disordered behavior.**

- Behavior therapies are action therapies that do not look at thought processes but instead focus on changing the abnormal or disordered behavior itself through classical or operant conditioning.

- Classical conditioning techniques for changing behavior include systematic desensitization, aversion therapy, and various exposure therapies.

- Therapies based on operant conditioning include modeling, reinforcement and the use of token economies, extinction, and behavioral activation.

- Behavior therapies can be effective in treating specific problems, such as bed wetting, drug addictions, and phobias, and can help improve some of the more troubling behavioral symptoms associated with more severe disorders.

**15.5** **Summarize the goals and basic elements of cognitive and cognitive-behavioral therapies.**

- Cognitive therapy is oriented toward teaching clients how their thinking may be distorted and helping clients see how inaccurate some of their beliefs may be.

- Some of the cognitive distortions in thinking include arbitrary inference, selective thinking, overgeneralization, magnification and minimization, and personalization.

- Cognitive-behavioral therapies are action therapies that work at changing a person's illogical or distorted thinking.

- The three goals of cognitive-behavioral therapies are to relieve the symptoms and solve the problems, to develop strategies for solving future problems, and to help change irrational, distorted thinking.

- Rational emotive behavior therapy is a directive therapy in which the therapist challenges clients' irrational beliefs, often arguing with clients and even assigning them homework.

- Although CBT has seemed successful in treating depression, stress disorders, and anxiety, it is criticized for focusing on the symptoms and not the causes of disordered behavior.

## Group Therapies: Not Just for the Shy

**15.6** **Compare and contrast different forms of group therapy.**

- Group therapy can be accomplished using many styles of psychotherapy and may involve treating people who are all part of the same family, as in family counseling.

- Group therapy can also be accomplished without the aid of a trained therapist in the form of self-help or support groups composed of other people who have the same or similar problems.

- Group therapy is most useful to persons who cannot afford individual therapy and who may obtain a great deal of social and emotional support from other group members.

**15.7** **Identify the advantages and disadvantages of group therapy.**

- Group therapy has the advantages of low cost, exposure to other people with similar problems, social interaction with others, and social and emotional support from people with similar disorders or problems. It has also been demonstrated to be very effective for people with social anxiety.

- Disadvantages of group therapy can include the need to share the therapist's time with others in the group, the lack of a private setting in which to reveal concerns, and the inability of people with severe disorders to tolerate being in a group.

## Does Psychotherapy Really Work?

**15.8** **Summarize the research on the effectiveness of psychotherapy.**

- Eysenck's early survey of client improvement seemed to suggest that clients would improve as time passed, with or without therapy.

- Surveys of people who have received therapy suggest that psychotherapy is more effective than no treatment at all.

- Surveys reveal that 75 to 90 percent of people who receive therapy report improvement, the longer a person stays in therapy the better the improvement, and psychotherapy works as well alone as with drugs.

- Some types of psychotherapy are more effective for certain types of problems, and no one psychotherapy method is effective for all problems.

- Effective therapy should be matched to the particular client and the particular problem, there should exist a therapeutic alliance between therapist and client, and a protected setting in which clients can release emotions and reveal private thoughts is essential.

- When the culture, ethnic group, or gender of the therapist and the client differs, misunderstandings and misinterpretations can occur due to differences in cultural/ethnic values, socioeconomic differences, gender roles, and beliefs.

- Barriers to effective psychotherapy exist when the backgrounds of client and therapist differ and include language, cultural values, social class, and nonverbal communication.

- Cybertherapy is therapy that is offered on the Internet and offers options for people who cannot otherwise get to a therapist.

**15.9** **Identify factors that influence the effectiveness of therapy.**

- Most therapies benefit through the establishment of an effective, working, therapeutic alliance between the professional and the client.

- Treatment approaches that have the greatest research support are referred to as evidence based or empirically supported treatments.

- Neuroimaging is being used to potentially identify the mechanisms and outcomes of effective treatment.

## Biomedical Therapies

**15.10** **Categorize types of drugs used to treat psychological disorders.**

- Biomedical therapies include the use of drugs, induced convulsions, and surgery to relieve or control the symptoms of mental disorders.

- Antipsychotic drugs are used to control delusions, hallucinations, and bizarre behavior and include the typical antipsychotics, atypical antipsychotics, and partial dopamine agonists.

- Antianxiety drugs are used to treat anxiety and related disorders and include the benzodiazepines and certain antidepressant drugs.

- Antimanic drugs are used to treat bipolar disorder and include lithium and certain anticonvulsant drugs.

- Antidepressant drugs are used in the treatment of depression and include monoamine oxidase inhibitors (MAOIs), tricyclic antidepressants, and selective serotonin reuptake inhibitors (SSRIs).

**15.11** **Explain how electroconvulsive therapy and psychosurgery are used to treat psychological disorders.**

- Electroconvulsive therapy, or ECT, is used to treat severe depression, bipolar disorder, and schizophrenia and involves the use of a muscle relaxant, a short-term anesthetic, and induction of a seizure under controlled conditions.

- One of the earliest psychosurgeries was the prefrontal lobotomy, in which the front part of the frontal lobe was cut away from the back part of the brain, producing effects ranging from a disappearance of symptoms to a lack of emotional response and dulling of mental functions.

- Modern psychosurgery includes the bilateral cingulotomy, used to treat major depression, bipolar disorders, and certain forms of obsessive-compulsive disorder that have not responded to other forms of treatment.

**15.12** **Identify some of the newer technologies being used to treat psychological disorders.**

- Emerging technologies for treatment of psychological disorders include repetitive transcranial magnetic stimulation (rTMS), transcranial direct current stimulation (tDCS), and deep brain stimulation (DBS).

## Applying Psychology to Everyday Life: Virtual Reality Therapies

**15.13** **Describe how virtual reality can be used in psychotherapy.**

- Virtual reality therapy is a computer-based simulation of environments that can be used to treat disorders such as phobias and PTSD with less risk than that of actual exposure to anxiety-provoking stimuli.

- Virtual reality therapy is particularly useful as a delivery system for exposure therapy.

# Test Yourself

*Pick the best answer.*

1. Clara is going to a therapist to gain a better understanding of why she has self-destructive relationships with all her friends. This type of therapy is known as _____ therapy.
   a. insight
   b. action
   c. behavioral
   d. biomedical

2. The hidden meaning of a dream is the _____ content, according to Freud.
   a. repressed
   b. latent
   c. manifest
   d. sexual

3. Through the use of _____, a person-centered therapist conveys they are trying to understand the experience of the person they are working with.
   a. reflection
   b. unconditional positive regard
   c. empathy
   d. authenticity

4. What differentiates motivational interviewing from person-centered therapy?
   a. Motivational interviewing has specific goals of reducing ambivalence about change and increasing intrinsic motivation to bring changes about, while traditional person-centered therapy does not.
   b. Motivational interviewing focuses on unconscious motives, while traditional person-centered therapy focuses on the self.
   c. Motivational interviewing allows the client to talk about anything they wish, while traditional person-centered therapy is more direct.
   d. Motivational interviewing is a behavioral therapeutic technique, while person-centered therapy is a biomedical therapy.

5. Which of the following clients would probably get the least benefit from a humanistic therapy?
   a. Colin, who is bright but confused about self-image
   b. Cole, who is very talkative and open in discussing feelings
   c. Colleen, who enjoys exploring the inner workings of the mind
   d. Cody, who has a hard time putting thoughts and feelings into words in a logical manner

6. To overcome her fear of balloons, because of the loud sound they might suddenly make should they pop, Bella must sit in a room filled with balloons while the therapist pops each one. After a while, Bella realizes that her fear is unjustified and even begins to pop balloons herself. This technique is known as
   a. systematic desensitization.
   b. aversion therapy.
   c. flooding.
   d. extinction.

7. Megan's daughter Kayla was afraid of dogs. Megan took Kayla to a therapist to help her overcome her fear but was surprised when the therapist brought a dog into the room. At first Kayla was asked to watch from across the room as the therapist showed her

how to approach and pet the dog and not grab its tail. Eventually, Kayla was asked to come over and mimic the behavior she had observed. After just a few sessions, Kayla was no longer fearful of dogs. What technique did the therapist use with Kayla?
- **a.** virtual exposure
- **b.** aversion therapy
- **c.** flooding
- **d.** participant modeling

8. Maria sat down with her daughter, Zoe, and together wrote out a list of things that Zoe was expected to do each day and the rewards she would get if she accomplished them, as well as the penalties she would face if she did not do them. This is most like which technique?
- **a.** token economy
- **b.** time-out
- **c.** extinction
- **d.** contingency contracting

9. For both children and adults, and for many undesirable behaviors, the use of _____ or some form of "time-out" can be quite effective.
- **a.** arbitrary inference
- **b.** extinction
- **c.** positive reinforcement
- **d.** negative reinforcement

10. Stephan gets a text message from his girlfriend saying that she will have to work overtime tonight. Stephan immediately assumes his girlfriend is seeing someone else at work. Beck would say that Stephan has engaged in what type of distorted thinking?
- **a.** arbitrary inference
- **b.** selective thinking
- **c.** overgeneralization
- **d.** personalization

11. Devin's wife comes home angry from her job, and he immediately assumes that he has done something wrong. Such irrational thinking is an example of
- **a.** overgeneralization.
- **b.** personalization.
- **c.** arbitrary inference.
- **d.** selective thinking.

12. Latanya tends to blow negative events out of proportion to their importance (magnification) while ignoring relevant positive events (minimization). What therapeutic technique may work best to help Latanya?
- **a.** group therapy
- **b.** virtual therapy
- **c.** bilateral anterior cingulotomy
- **d.** rational emotive behavior therapy (REBT)

13. Which therapy style requires the therapist to actively confront a client's irrational beliefs?
- **a.** person-centered
- **b.** frontal lobotomy
- **c.** rational emotive behavior therapy (REBT)
- **d.** cognitive restructuring

14. Family therapy is a form of group therapy in which
- **a.** nonprofessionals lead a selected group of family members with similar concerns.
- **b.** the entire family participates, as no one person is seen as the problem.

- **c.** family members meet to single out the individual that is causing problems in the family dynamic.
- **d.** psychology professionals treat their own family members.

15. If Dr. Phelps uses an eclectic approach to her work as a therapist, what specifically is she doing?
- **a.** Dr. Phelps tends to rely on the unconscious as the source for all therapeutic treatments.
- **b.** Dr. Phelps tends to rely on a behavioral approach in the treatment of her clients.
- **c.** Dr. Phelps uses only the newest and most innovative approaches to treating her clients.
- **d.** Dr. Phelps uses one or a combination of any number of therapeutic treatments depending on the situation.

16. With regard to treatment of psychological disorders, many psychological professionals believe medications work best in combination with
- **a.** electroconvulsive therapy.
- **b.** psychotherapy.
- **c.** psychosurgery.
- **d.** deep brain stimulation.

17. Typical antipsychotic drugs work by blocking what neurotransmitter?
- **a.** norepinephrine
- **b.** serotonin
- **c.** dopamine
- **d.** epinephrine

18. Bradley has been on an antipsychotic drug for many years to control his schizophrenia. He has developed repetitive, involuntary jerks and movements of the face, lips, legs, and body. These side effects make up a syndrome known as
- **a.** the "Thorazine shuffle."
- **b.** neurolepsis.
- **c.** tardive dyskinesia.
- **d.** psychotic syndrome.

19. As part of the medical treatment trial she is participating in for severe and suicidal depression, Kierra was given _____, which is being investigated due to its seemingly immediate, although short-term, effects.
- **a.** ketamine
- **b.** lithium
- **c.** valproic acid
- **d.** paroxetine

20. In bilateral anterior cingulotomy,
- **a.** the front of the brain is cut away from the back.
- **b.** a thin wire electrode is used to destroy a small area of brain tissue.
- **c.** an electric shock is used to stimulate certain areas of the brain.
- **d.** a drug is injected into the brain to destroy a large area of brain tissue.

# Statistics in Psychology

## Why study statistics?

Psychology is a science, and scientists must have ways of describing, summarizing, and analyzing the numerical data gathered through systematic observation and experimentation. Statistics allow researchers to do all of these things in a meaningful, logical fashion.

---

## Learning Objectives

**A.1** Explain why statistics are important to psychologists and psychology majors.

**A.2** Describe the types of tables and graphs that represent patterns in data.

**A.3** Identify three measures of central tendency and explain how they are impacted by the shape of the distribution.

**A.4** Identify the types of statistics used to examine variations in data.

**A.5** Describe how inferential statistics can be used to determine if differences in sets of data are large enough to be due to something other than chance variation.

**A.6** Explain how statistics are used to predict one score from another.

---

## What Are Statistics?

**A.1** **Explain why statistics are important to psychologists and psychology majors.**

Many students in psychology wonder why the field uses such seemingly complicated mathematics. The answer is easy. Psychologists base their field on research findings. Data are collected, and they have to be analyzed. *Statistics* is the field that gives us the tools to do that.

Psychologists have to be able to do two things with the data they collect. The first is to summarize the information from a study or experiment. The second is to make judgments and decisions about the data. We are interested if groups differ from each other. We are also interested in how one group of variables is related to another.

**Statistics** is the branch of mathematics that is concerned with the collection and interpretation of data from samples (Agresti & Finlay, 1997; Aron et al., 2005). A **sample** is a group of people selected, usually randomly, from a larger population of people. If you asked what the average height of teenage males was, and you calculated the average from just your high school, that average would be a statistic.

Statistical analysis is a way of trying to account for the error that exists in almost any body of data. Psychology is only one of many fields that use the following types of statistics.

**statistics**
branch of mathematics concerned with the collection and interpretation of numerical data.

**sample**
group of subjects selected from a larger population of subjects, usually selected randomly.

In this appendix we will take a look at describing data—seeing if groups differ from each other and seeing if two variables are related to each other. Those are the basic ideas of psychological statistics. The more advanced techniques are just bigger and better versions of these ideas. Many psychology students sometimes panic at the thought of taking statistics. However, it is crucial to the field and not really that hard if you put your mind to it and don't freeze yourself up. Why is it so important? Even if you are not the kind of psychologist who uses statistics on a daily basis, all psychologists have to be able to read and understand the research others are doing, and understanding what the statistical analyses of that research is really saying is crucial. Here's a practical hint: Students with good research and statistical skills are much more employable and make more money than those who don't try to master research skills. It's nice to care about people, but you need all the skills you can get in today's world. Statistics and research design is one really profitable set of skills.

# Practice Quiz    How much do you remember?

*Pick the best answer.*

1. _____ is the branch of mathematics that is concerned with the collection and interpretation of data from samples.
   a. Statistics
   b. Psychometrics
   c. Probabilities
   d. Coefficients

2. What is the primary advantage of using statistical analysis in a research study?
   a. It allows you to confirm the hypotheses that were set forth when you started the research.
   b. It allows you to attempt to account for any of the error that exists in virtually any body of data.

   c. It allows you to demonstrate that you, as the researcher, are competent to examine and interpret the results of your research.
   d. It allows you to get your research proposal approved by an Institutional Review Board and, later, allows your research to be published.

3. Which of the following is the underlying question of any psychological research statistics?
   a. Is behavior determined by "nature" or "nurture"?
   b. Do people want to be "good" or "bad" in their general behaviors?
   c. Is there a singular commonality that underlies all behaviors?
   d. Are groups different from each other, and are two variables related to each other?

# Descriptive Statistics

**Descriptive statistics** are a way of organizing numbers and summarizing them so that they can be understood. There are two main types of descriptive statistics:

- **Measures of Central Tendency.**    Measures of central tendency are used to summarize the data and give you one score that seems typical of your sample.

- **Measures of Variability.**    Measures of variability are used to indicate how spread out the data are. Are they tightly packed or are they widely dispersed?

The actual descriptive statistics are best understood after we explain the concept of a frequency distribution.

One way psychologists get started in a research project is to look at their data, but just looking at a list of numbers wouldn't do much good. So we make a graph or chart. Then we can look for patterns.

**descriptive statistics**

a way of organizing numbers and summarizing them so that patterns can be determined.

**frequency distribution**

a table or graph that shows how often different numbers or scores appear in a particular set of scores.

**FREQUENCY DISTRIBUTIONS**

**A.2** **Describe the types of tables and graphs that represent patterns in data.**

A **frequency distribution** is a table or graph that shows how often different numbers, or scores, appear in a particular set of scores. For example, let's say that you have a sample of 30 people, the size of some psychology classes. You ask them how many glasses of water they drink each day. You could represent the answers as shown in **Table A.1**.

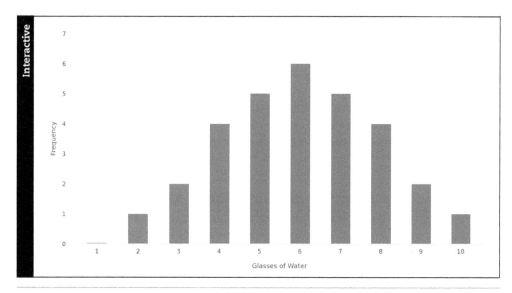

| Table A.1 | A Frequency Distribution |
| --- | --- |
| **Number of Glasses Per Day** | **Number of People Out of 30 (Frequency)** |
| 1 | 0 |
| 2 | 1 |
| 3 | 2 |
| 4 | 4 |
| 5 | 5 |
| 6 | 6 |
| 7 | 5 |
| 8 | 4 |
| 9 | 2 |
| 10 | 1 |

**Figure A.1**   A Histogram

Histograms, or bar graphs, provide a visual way to look at data from frequency distributions. In this graph, for example, the height of the bars indicates that most people drink between four and eight glasses of water (represented by the five highest bars in the middle of the graph).

Just by looking at this table, it is clear that typical people drink between four and eight glasses of water a day.

Tables can be useful, especially when dealing with small sets of data. Sometimes a more visual presentation gives a better "picture" of the patterns in a data set, and that is when researchers use graphs to plot the data from a frequency distribution. One common graph is a **histogram**, or a bar graph. **Figure A.1** shows how the same data from Table A.1 would look in a bar graph. Another type of graph used in frequency distributions is the **polygon**, a line graph. **Figure A.2** shows the same data in a polygon graph.

**THE NORMAL CURVE**   Frequency polygons allow researchers to see the shape of a set of data easily. For example, the number of people drinking glasses of water in **Figure A.2** is easily seen to be centered about six glasses (central tendency) but drops

**histogram**

a bar graph showing a frequency distribution.

**polygon**

line graph showing a frequency distribution.

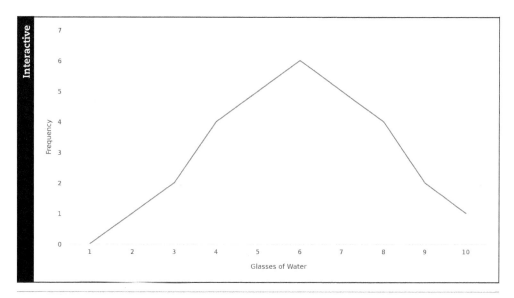

**Figure A.2**   A Polygon

A polygon is a line graph that can represent the data in a frequency distribution in much the same way as a bar graph but allows the shape of the data set to be easily viewed.

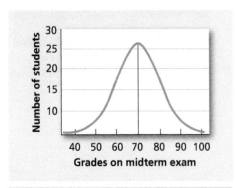

**Figure A.3**  The Normal Curve

The normal curve, also known as the bell curve because of its unique shape, is often the way in which certain characteristics such as intelligence or weight are represented in the population. The highest point on the curve typically represents the average score in any distribution.

**skewed distribution**

frequency distribution in which most of the scores fall to one side or the other of the distribution.

**positively skewed**

a distribution of scores in which scores are concentrated in the low end of the distribution.

**negatively skewed**

a distribution of scores in which scores are concentrated in the high end of the distribution.

off below four glasses and above eight glasses a day (variability). Our frequency polygon has a high point, and the frequency decreases on both sides.

A common frequency distribution of this type is called the **normal curve**. It has a very specific shape and is sometimes called the *bell curve*. Look at **Figure A.3**. This curve is almost a perfect normal curve, and many things in life are not that perfect. The normal curve is used as a model for many things that are measured, such as intelligence, height, or weight, but even those measures only come close to a perfect distribution (provided large numbers of people are measured). One of the reasons that the normal curve is so useful is that it has very specific relationships to measures of central tendency and a measurement of variability, known as the standard deviation.

**OTHER DISTRIBUTION TYPES: SKEWED AND BIMODAL**   Distributions aren't always normal in shape. Some distributions are described as *skewed*. This occurs when the distribution is not even on both sides of a central score with the highest frequency (like in our example). Instead, the scores are concentrated toward one side of the distribution. For example, what if a study of people's water-drinking habits in a different class revealed that most people drank around seven to eight glasses of water daily, with no one drinking more than eight? The frequency polygon shown in **Figure A.4** reflects this very different distribution.

In this case, scores are piled up in the high end, with most people drinking seven or eight glasses of water a day. The graphs in **Figure A.5** show a **skewed distribution**. Skewed distributions are called positively or negatively skewed, depending on where the scores are concentrated. A concentration in the high end would be called **negatively skewed**. A concentration in the low end would be called **positively skewed**. The direction of the extended tail determines whether it is positively (tail to right) or negatively (tail to left) skewed. Here's an example. What do you think about the distribution of heights of Hobbits (the little guys from *The Lord of the Rings*) and NBA basketball players (who are usually tall)? Might not these frequency distributions of height in **Figure A.5** be appropriate?

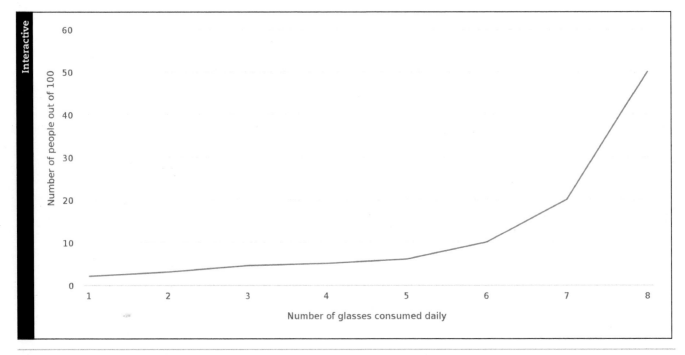

**Figure A.4**  A Frequency Polygon

Skewed distributions are those in which the most frequent scores occur at one end or the other of the distribution, as represented by this frequency polygon, in which most people are seen to drink at least seven to eight glasses of water each day.

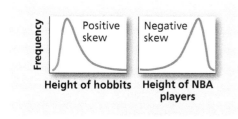

**Figure A.5**   Skewed Distribution

These frequency polygons show how distributions can be skewed in two different directions. The graph on the left represents the frequency of heights among Hobbits (the little people from the fantasy *The Lord of the Rings*) and is positively skewed because the long "tail" goes to the right, or positive direction. The graph on the right shows the frequency of heights among NBA basketball players and is negatively skewed—the tail points to the left.

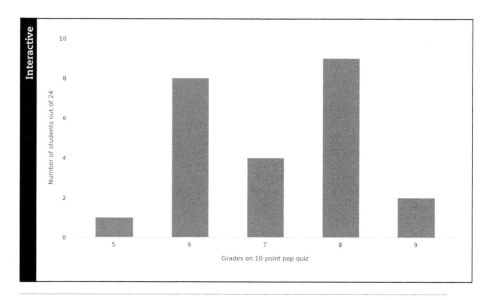

**Figure A.6**   A Bimodal Distribution

When a distribution is bimodal, it means that there are two high points instead of just one. For example, in the pop-quiz scores represented on this graph, there are two "most frequent" scores—6 and 8. This most likely represents two groups of students, with one group being less successful than the other.

Some frequency polygons show two high points rather than just one (see **Figure A.6**) and are called **bimodal distributions**. In this example, we have a distribution of scores from a 10-point pop quiz, and we see that one group of students seemed to do well and one group didn't. Bimodal distributions usually indicate that you have two separate groups being graphed in one polygon. What would the distribution of height for men and women look like?

## MEASURES OF CENTRAL TENDENCY

**A.3 Identify three measures of central tendency and explain how they are impacted by the shape of the distribution.**

A frequency distribution is a good way to look at a set of numbers, but there's still a lot to look at—isn't there some way to sum it all up? One way to sum up numerical data is to find out what a "typical" score might be, or some central number around which all the others seem to fall. This kind of summation is called a **measure of central tendency**, or the number that best represents the central part of a frequency distribution. There are three different measures of central tendency: the mean, the median, and the mode.

**MEAN**   The most commonly used measure of central tendency is the **mean**, the arithmetic average of a distribution of numbers. That simply indicates that you add up all the numbers in a particular set and then divide them by how many numbers there are. This is usually the way teachers get the grade point average for a particular student, for example. If Rochelle's grades on the tests she has taken so far are 86, 92, 87, and 90, then the teacher would add $86 + 92 + 87 + 90 = 355$, and then divide 355 by 4 (the number of scores) to get the mean, or grade point average, of 88.75. Here is the formula for the mean:

$$\text{Mean} = \Sigma X/N$$

**bimodal distributions**
frequency distribution in which there are two high points rather than one.

**measure of central tendency**
numbers that best represent the most typical score of a frequency distribution.

**mean**
the arithmetic average of a distribution of numbers.

What does this mean?

- $\Sigma$ is a symbol called sigma. It is a Greek letter and it is also called the summation sign.
- $X$ represents a score. Rochelle's grades are represented by $X$.
- $\Sigma X$ means add up or sum all the $X$ scores or $\Sigma X = 86 + 92 + 37 + 90 = 355$.
- $N$ means the number of scores. In this case, there are four grades.
- We then divide the sum of the scores ($\Sigma X$) by $N$ to get the mean or

$$\text{Mean} = \Sigma X/N = \frac{355}{4} = 88.75$$

The mean is a good way to find a central tendency if the set of scores clusters around the mean with no extremely different scores that are either far higher or far lower than the mean.

You may hear or read about a concept called "regression to the mean." This is a concept that describes the tendency for measurements of a variable to even out over the course of the measurements (Stigler, 1997). If a measurement is fairly high at first, subsequent measurements will tend to be closer to the mean, the average measurement, for example. This is one of the reasons that researchers want to replicate measurements many times rather than relying on the first results, which could cause them to draw incorrect conclusions from the data.

**MEDIAN**

> 💬 I remember that sometimes my teacher would "curve" the grades for a test, and it was always bad when just one person did really well and everyone else did lousy—is that what you mean about extremely different scores?

Yes, the mean doesn't work as well when there are extreme scores, as you would have if only two students out of an entire class had a perfect score of 100 and everyone else scored in the 70s or lower. If you want a truer measure of central tendency in such a case, you need one that isn't affected by extreme scores. The **median** is just such a measure. A median is the score that falls in the middle of an *ordered* distribution of scores. Half of the scores will fall above the median, and half of the scores will fall below it. If the distribution contains an odd number of scores, it's just the middle number, but if the number of scores is even, it's the average of the two middle scores. The median is also the 50th percentile. Look at **Table A.2** for an example of the median.

The mean IQ of this group would be 114.6, but the median would be 101 (the average between Evan with 102 and Fethia with 100, the average of the two middle numbers). This may not look like much of a difference, but it's really a change of about 13.6 IQ points—a big difference. Also, think about measures of income in a particular area. If most people earn around $35,000 per year in a particular area, but there are just a few extremely wealthy people in the same area who earn $1,000,000 a year, a mean of all the annual incomes would no doubt make the area look like it was doing much better than it really is economically. The median would be a more accurate measure of the central tendency of such data.

**median**

the middle score in an ordered distribution of scores, or the mean of the two middle numbers; the 50th percentile.

| Table A.2 | Intelligence Test Scores For 10 People | | | | | | | | | |
|---|---|---|---|---|---|---|---|---|---|---|
| **Name** | **Allison** | **Ben** | **Carol** | **Denise** | **Evan** | **Fethia** | **George** | **Hal** | **Inga** | **Jay** |
| *IQ* | 160 | 150 | 139 | 102 | 102 | 100 | 100 | 100 | 98 | 95 |

**MODE**   The **mode** is another measure of central tendency, in which the most frequent score is taken as the central measure. In the numbers given in Table A.2, the mode would be 100 because that number appears more times in the distribution than any other. Three people have that score. This is the simplest measure of central tendency and is also more useful than the mean in some cases, especially when there are two sets of frequently appearing scores. For example, suppose a teacher notices that on the last exam the scores fall into two groups, with about 15 students making a 95 and another 14 students making a 67. The mean *and* the median would probably give a number somewhere between those two scores—such as 80. That number tells the teacher a lot less about the distribution of scores than the mode would because, in this case, the distribution is **bimodal**—there are two very different yet very frequent scores. (Refer to Figure A.6 for another example.)

**MEASURES OF CENTRAL TENDENCY AND THE SHAPE OF THE DISTRIBUTION**   When the distribution is normal or close to it, the mean, median, and mode are the same or very similar. There is no problem. When the distribution is not normal, then the situation requires a little more explanation.

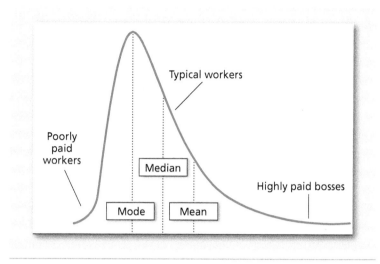

**Figure A.7**   Positively Skewed Distribution

In a skewed distribution, the high scores on one end will cause the mean to be pulled toward the tail of the distribution, making it a poor measure of central tendency for this kind of distribution. For example, in this graph, many workers make very little money (represented by the mode), while only a few workers make a lot of money (the tail). The mean in this case would be much higher than the mode because of those few high scores distorting the average. In this case, the median is a much better measure of central tendency because it tends to be unaffected by extremely high or extremely low scores such as those in this distribution.

**SKEWED DISTRIBUTIONS**   If the distribution is skewed, then the mean is pulled in the direction of the tail of the distribution. The mode is still the highest point, and the median is between the two. Let's look at an example. In **Figure A.7** we have a distribution of salaries at a company. A few people make a low wage, most make a mid-level wage, and the bosses make a lot of money. This gives us a positively skewed distribution with the measures of central tendency placed as in the figure. As mentioned earlier, with such a distribution, the median would be the best measure of central tendency to report. If the distribution were negatively skewed (tail to the left), the order of the measures of central tendency would be reversed.

**BIMODAL DISTRIBUTIONS**   If you have a bimodal distribution, then none of the measures of central tendency will do you much good. You need to discover why you appear to have two groups in your one distribution.

### MEASURES OF VARIABILITY

**A.4** **Identify the types of statistics used to examine variations in data.**

Descriptive statistics can also determine how much the scores in a distribution differ, or vary, from the central tendency of the data. These **measures of variability** are used to discover how "spread out" the scores are from each other. The more the scores cluster around the central scores, the smaller the measure of variability will be, and the more widely the scores differ from the central scores, the larger this measurement will be.

There are two ways that variability is measured. The simpler method is by calculating the **range** of the set of scores, or the difference between the highest score and the lowest score in the set of scores. The range is somewhat limited as a measure of variability

**mode**
the most frequent score in a distribution of scores.

**bimodal**
condition in which a distribution has two modes.

**measures of variability**
measurement of the degree of differences within a distribution or how the scores are spread out.

**range**
the difference between the highest and lowest scores in a distribution.

when there are extreme scores in the distribution. For example, if you look at Table A.2, the range of those IQ scores would be 160 – 95, or 65. But if you just look at the numbers, you can see that there really isn't that much variation except for the three highest scores of 139, 150, and 160.

The other measure of variability that is commonly used is the one that is related to the normal curve, the **standard deviation**. This measurement is simply the square root of the average squared difference, or deviation, of the scores from the mean of the distribution. The mathematical formula for finding the standard deviation looks complicated, but it is really nothing more than taking each individual score, subtracting the mean from it, squaring that number (because some numbers will be negative and squaring them gets rid of the negative value), and adding up all of those squares. Then this total is divided by the number of scores, and the square root of that number is the standard deviation. In the IQ example, it would go like this:

$$\text{Standard Deviation Formula } SD = \sqrt{[\Sigma(X - M)^2/N]}$$

The mean ($M$) of the 10 IQ scores is 114.6. To calculate the standard deviation, we

1. Subtract the mean from each score to get a deviation score $\rightarrow (X - M)$
2. Square each deviation score $\rightarrow (X - M)^2$
3. Add them up. Remember that's what the sigma ($\Sigma$) indicates $\rightarrow \Sigma(X - M)^2$
4. Divide the sum of the squared deviation by $N$ (the number of scores) $\rightarrow \Sigma(X - M)^2/N$
5. Take the square root ($\sqrt{}$) of the sum for our final step. $\sqrt{[\Sigma(X - M)^2/N]}$
6. The process is laid out in **Table A.3**.

The standard deviation is equal to 23.5. What that tells you is that this particular group of data deviates, or varies, from the central tendencies quite a bit—there are some very different scores in the data set or, in this particular instance, three noticeably different scores.

**Table A.3**  Finding the Standard Deviation

| Score | Deviation from The Mean ($X \pm M$) | Squared Deviation |
|---|---|---|
| 160.00 | 45.40 | 2,061.16 |
| | (ex. 160 − 114.60 = 45.40) | ($45.40^2$ = 2,061.16) |
| 150.00 | 35.4 | 1,253.16 |
| 139.00 | 24.4 | 595.36 |
| 102.00 | −12.60 | 158.76 |
| 102.00 | −12.60 | 158.76 |
| 100.00 | −14.60 | 213.16 |
| 100.00 | −14.60 | 213.16 |
| 100.00 | −14.60 | 213.16 |
| 98.00 | −16.60 | 275.56 |
| 95.00 | −19.60 | 384.16 |
| Sum of Scores ($\Sigma X$) = 1,146.00 Mean = $(\Sigma X)/N$ = 1,146/10 = 114.60 | ($\Sigma X - M$) = 0.00 | $\Sigma(X - M)^2$ = 5,526.40 Standard Deviation = $\sqrt{[\Sigma(X - M)^2/N]}$ = $\sqrt{5,526.40/10}$ = 23.5 |

**standard deviation**

the square root of the average squared deviations from the mean of scores in a distribution; a measure of variability.

This procedure may look very complicated. Let us assure you that computers and inexpensive calculators can figure out the standard deviation simply by entering the numbers and pressing a button. No one does a standard deviation by hand anymore.

How does the standard deviation relate to the normal curve? Let's look at the classic distribution of IQ scores. It has a mean of 100 and a standard deviation of 15 as set up by the test designers. It is a bell curve. With a true normal curve, researchers know exactly what percentage of the population lies under the curve between each standard deviation from the mean. For example, notice that in the percentages in **Figure A.8**, one standard deviation above the mean has 34.13 percent of the population represented by the graph under that section. These are the scores between the IQs of 100 and 115. One standard deviation below the mean (−1) has exactly the same percent, 34.13, under that section—the scores between 85 and 100. This means that 68.26 percent of the population falls within one standard deviation from the mean, or one average "spread" from the center of the distribution. For example, "giftedness" is normally defined as having an IQ score that is two standard deviations *above* the mean. On the Wechsler Intelligence Scales, this means having an IQ of 130 or greater because the Wechsler's standard deviation is 15. But if the test a person took to determine giftedness was the Stanford-Binet Fourth Edition (the previous version of the test), the IQ score must have been 132 or greater because the standard deviation of that test was 16, not 15. The current version, the Stanford-Binet Fifth Edition, was published in 2003, and it now has a mean of 100 and a standard deviation of 15 for composite scores.

Although the "tails" of this normal curve seem to touch the bottom of the graph, in theory they go on indefinitely, never touching the base of the graph. In reality, though, any statistical measurement that forms a normal curve will have 99.72 percent of the population it measures falling within three standard deviations either above or below the mean. Because this relationship between the standard deviation and the normal curve does not change, it is always possible to compare different test scores or sets of data that come close to a normal curve distribution. This is done by computing a **z score**, which indicates how many standard deviations you are away from the mean. It is calculated by subtracting the mean from your score and dividing by the standard deviation. For example, if you had an IQ of 115, your z score would be 1.0. If you had an IQ of 70, your z score would be −2.0. So on any exam, if you had a positive z score, you did relatively well. A negative z score means you didn't do as well. The formula for a z score is:

$$Z = (X - M)/SD$$

**z score**

a statistical measure that indicates how far away from the mean a particular score is in terms of the number of standard deviations that exist between the mean and that score.

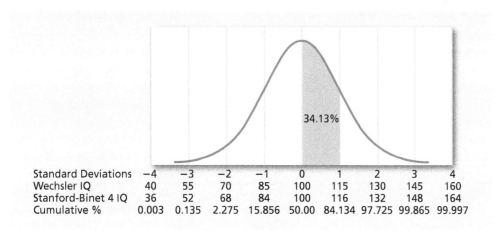

| Standard Deviations | −4 | −3 | −2 | −1 | 0 | 1 | 2 | 3 | 4 |
|---|---|---|---|---|---|---|---|---|---|
| Wechsler IQ | 40 | 55 | 70 | 85 | 100 | 115 | 130 | 145 | 160 |
| Stanford-Binet 4 IQ | 36 | 52 | 68 | 84 | 100 | 116 | 132 | 148 | 164 |
| Cumulative % | 0.003 | 0.135 | 2.275 | 15.856 | 50.00 | 84.134 | 97.725 | 99.865 | 99.997 |

**Figure A.8** IQ Normal Curve

Scores on intelligence tests are typically represented by the normal curve. The dotted vertical lines each represent one standard deviation from the mean, which is always set at 100. For example, an IQ of 116 on the Stanford-Binet Fourth Edition (Stanford-Binet 4) represents one standard deviation above the mean, and the area under the curve indicates that 34.13 percent of the population falls between 100 and 116 on that test. The Stanford-Binet Fifth Edition was published in 2003 and it now has a mean of 100 and a standard deviation of 15 for composite scores.

# Practice Quiz    How much do you remember?

*Pick the best answer.*

1. Dr. Kopelowoski has just given an examination to his Introduction to Psychology class. Because this is a class of more than 500 students, it would be difficult for him to assess the results looking at each score one at a time. If he wants to know how many students earned an A, a B, and so on, which of the following might be the best for him to program his computer to provide?
   a. A measure of central tendency
   b. A mean
   c. A frequency distribution
   d. A correlation coefficient

2. Because of its very specific shape, a "normal" distribution is also often described as a _____ curve.
   a. bell
   b. positively skewed
   c. negatively skewed
   d. multimodal

3. Aaron has just received his grade on the third exam of his chemistry class. He earned a 90 on this test. He is happy because his grades have been steadily increasing since the start of the term. On the first exam he earned an 80, and on the second exam he earned an 85. Which of the following represents the approximate mean of the three exam scores?
   a. 80
   b. 85
   c. 88
   d. 255

4. Which of the following would be most useful if you want to know how many standard deviations from the mean a single score in a data set falls?
   a. A *t*-score
   b. A *z* score
   c. A deviation coefficient
   d. A variance determination

# Inferential Statistics

Descriptive methods of statistics are useful for organizing and summarizing numbers or scores. But what method is useful when it comes to comparing sets of numbers or scores to see if there are differences between them that are great enough to be caused by something other than chance variation?

**LOOKING AT DIFFERENCES: STATISTICAL SIGNIFICANCE**

**A.5  Describe how inferential statistics can be used to determine if differences in sets of data are large enough to be due to something other than chance variation.**

**Inferential statistics** consist of statistical techniques that allow researchers to determine the difference between results of a study that are meaningful and those that are merely due to chance variations. Inferential statistics also allow researchers to draw conclusions, or make *inferences*, about the results of research and about whether those results are only true for the specific group of animals or people involved in the study or whether the results can be applied to, or *generalized* to, the larger population from which the study participants were selected.

For example, in the Cheryan (Cheryan et al., 2009) study of the difference in male and female students' attitudes toward computer science when exposed to environments that were either stereotypically masculine or nonstereotypical, there were a lot of variables that simply could not be controlled completely, even with random assignment of participants to the two conditions. **LINK** to Learning Objective 1.1. For example, there was no guarantee that random assignment would account for the interfering effects of female participants who might have really liked the science fiction toys, posters, and pizza they saw in one of the test conditions. Maybe any difference found between the males and females was due to pure luck or chance and not to the variables under study.

In any analysis that compares two or more sets of data, there's always the possibility of error in the data that comes either from within the group (all participants in one group, for example, will not be exactly like each other) or differences between groups (the experimental group and the control group are formed with different people, so there

**inferential statistics**

statistical analysis of two or more sets of numerical data to reduce the possibility of error in measurement and to determine if the differences between the data sets are greater than chance variation would predict.

are differences between the two groups that have nothing to do with the manipulations of the experimenter). When researchers want to know if the differences they find in the data that come from studies like the Cheryan experiment are large enough to be caused by the experimental manipulation and *not* just by the chance differences that exist within and between groups, they have to use a kind of statistical technique that can take those chance variations into account. These kinds of statistical analysis use inferential statistics.

Inferential statistical analysis also allows researchers to determine how much confidence they should have in the results of a particular experiment. As you might remember, results from other kinds of studies that look for relationships—observations, surveys, and case studies—are often analyzed with descriptive statistics, especially correlations. But experiments look for *causes* of relationships, and researchers want to have some evidence that the results of their experiments really mean what they think they mean.

There are many different kinds of inferential statistical methods. The method that is used depends on the design of the experiment, such as the number of independent and dependent variables or the number of experimental groups. All inferential statistics have one thing in common—they look for differences in group measurements that are **statistically significant**. Statistical significance is a way to test differences to see how likely those differences are to be real and not just caused by the random variations in behavior that exist in everything animals and people do.

For example, in a classic study investigating the effects of intrinsic versus extrinsic motivation on children's creativity, Dr. Teresa Amabile's 1982 study showed that the collages of the children who were promised prizes (an extrinsic reward) were judged to be less creative than those of the children who created collages just for fun. Ⓛ Ⓘ Ⓝ K to Learning Objective 9.1. But was that difference between the creativity scores of the two groups a real difference, or was it merely due to chance variations in the children's artistic creations? Dr. Amabile used an inferential test on her results that told her that the difference was too big to be just chance variations, which means her results were *significant*—they were most likely to be real differences. How likely? Tests of significance give researchers the probability that the results of their experiment were caused by chance and not by their experimental manipulation. For example, in one test called a *t*-test, the scores of the children's artwork would have been placed into a formula that would result in a single number ($t$) that evaluates the probability that the difference between the two group means is due to pure chance or luck. That number would be compared to a value that exists in a table of possible $t$ values, which tells researchers the probability that the result is due to chance or luck. If the number obtained by the calculation is bigger than the value in the table, there will be a probability associated with that number in the table. The probability, symbolized by the letter $p$, will tell researchers the probability that the difference was due to chance. In Dr. Amabile's case, the probability was $p < 0.05$, which means the probability that the results were due to chance alone was less than 5 out of 100. Another way of stating the same result is that Dr. Amabile could be 95 percent certain that her results were real and not due to chance. Dr. Amabile would, thus, report that the study found a **significant difference**, which means a difference thought not to be due to chance.

There are several statistical techniques to test if groups are different from each other. Here are some common ones you might encounter if you read journal articles.

- *t*-test—determines if two means are different from each other.
- *F*-test or analysis of variance—determines if three or more means are different from each other. Can also evaluate more than one independent variable at a time.
- chi-square—compares frequencies of proportions between groups to see if they are different. For example, the proportion of women hired at a company is too low and might indicate discrimination. *Chi* is pronounced like the beginning of the word *kite*. Don't say "chee." It will be ugly.

**statistically significant**
referring to differences in data sets that are larger than chance variation would predict.

**t-test**
type of inferential statistical analysis typically used when two means are compared to see if they are significantly different.

**significant difference**
a difference between groups of numerical data that is considered large enough to be due to factors other than chance variation.

If you do take a statistics course, you will find out that most analyses are done by computers, and you don't have to manually go through the long formulas.

We've already talked about the correlation coefficient. Let's see how psychologists can predict one variable from another by using it.  (L I N K) to Learning Objective 1.9.

### THE CORRELATION COEFFICIENT

**A.6** **Explain how statistics are used to predict one score from another.**

A *correlation* is a measure of the relationship between two or more variables. For example, if you wanted to know if scores on the SAT are related to grade point average, you could get SAT scores and GPAs from a group of people and enter those numbers into a mathematical formula, which will produce a number called the **correlation coefficient**. The correlation coefficient represents the direction of the relationship and its strength. Chapter One discusses correlation in more detail and also emphasizes that correlation does not allow the assumption that one variable causes the other.

💬 Is the formula for the correlation coefficient really complicated?

Actually, the definitional formula for finding a correlation coefficient is not very complicated. Here it is:

$$r = \frac{\Sigma Z_x Z_y}{n}$$

The $r$ is the correlation coefficient, the number representing the strength and direction of the relationship between the two variables. $Z_x$ and $Z_y$ are the z scores for each score. If you remember, the z score tells you how many standard deviations a score is away from the mean. You would calculate the $Z_x$ and $Z_y$ for each subject, multiply, and add them up. Then divide by the number of subjects. There is a very complicated-looking formula based on the raw scores.

$$r = \frac{\Sigma XY - \frac{\Sigma X \, \Sigma Y}{N}}{\sqrt{\left(\Sigma X^2 - \frac{(\Sigma X)^2}{N}\right)\left(\Sigma Y^2 - \frac{(\Sigma Y)^2}{N}\right)}}$$

Don't worry. You can do all this work on inexpensive calculators or on computers using common statistical programs or spreadsheets. Let's take the following example of two sets of scores, one on a test of drawing ability with scores from 1 (poor) to 5 (excellent) and the other on a test of writing ability using the same scale (see **Table A.4**).

If we plugged our data set into our calculator or spreadsheet, we would find that $r$ (the correlation coefficient) equals 0.86. That would indicate a fairly strong correlation. If you continue studies in statistics, you will find out how to see if the correlation coefficient we calculated is statistically significant or, if you recall, not due to just dumb luck when we picked our subjects. In our case, the $r$ is very significant and would happen by chance only 1 in 100 times!

Remember that the correlation coefficient has values that range between +1.0 and −1.0. The closer the $r$ is to these values, the stronger the relationship. A positive $r$ means a positive relationship, whereas a negative $r$ means a negative relationship. (L I N K) to Learning Objective 1.9; see Figure 1.3.

Our example had us trying to see if two scores were related. It is also possible to see if three or more scores are related with various techniques. The most common one is called multiple regression.

**correlation coefficient**

a number that represents the strength and direction of a relationship existing between two variables; number derived from the formula for measuring a correlation.

| Table A.4  Drawing and Writing Ability Test Scores | Drawing (X) | Writing (Y) |
|---|---|---|
| Student 1 | 3 | 5 |
| Student 2 | 1 | 2 |
| Student 3 | 2 | 3 |
| Student 4 | 4 | 4 |
| Student 5 | 1 | 3 |
| Student 6 | 4 | 6 |
| Student 7 | 2 | 3 |
| Student 8 | 3 | 4 |
| Student 9 | 5 | 5 |
| Student 10 | 1 | 2 |

# Practice Quiz    How much do you remember?

*Pick the best answer.*

1. _____ statistics consist of techniques that allow researchers to determine the difference between results of a study that are meaningful and those that are merely due to chance variations.
   a. Inferential
   b. Parametric
   c. Predictive
   d. Descriptive

2. Andrew is conducting a test in which he has three different participant groups, and he wants to analyze the variance among the three groups. In other words, he wants to know whether the means of each group are significantly different from each other. Which of the following would he want to calculate?
   a. A z-test
   b. A t-test
   c. An F-test
   d. A chi-square test

3. Bailey is conducting a correlational study that examines the frequency with which it rains in her town and the atmospheric pressure at noon on each day. When she is done, she calculates a correlation coefficient that will summarize the relationship between these two variables. This coefficient is going to be summarized by the lowercase letter _____.
   a. $c$
   b. $r$
   c. $p$
   d. $e$

4. If a researcher wants to demonstrate that their findings depict a significant difference between participant groups, which of the following statistical statements would need to be made?
   a. $p \leq 0.05$
   b. $r = \pm 1.00$
   c. $t \geq 2.50$
   d. $z \leq 100$

# Chapter Summary

## What Are Statistics?

### A.1 Explain why statistics are important to psychologists and psychology majors.

- Statistics is a branch of mathematics that involves the collection, description, and interpretation of numerical data.
- Students who understand the process of research and the statistical methods used in research are more desirable to many university and business institutions than those who lack such skills.

## Descriptive Statistics

- Descriptive statistics are ways of organizing numbers and summarizing them so that they can be understood.

### A.2 Describe the types of tables and graphs that represent patterns in data.

- Frequency distributions are tables or graphs that show the patterns in a set of scores and can be a table, a bar graph or histogram, or a line graph or polygon.
- The normal curve is a special frequency polygon that is symmetrical and has the mean, median, and mode as the highest point on the curve.

### A.3 Identify three measures of central tendency and explain how they are impacted by the shape of the distribution.

- Measures of central tendency are ways of finding numbers that best represent the center of a distribution of numbers and include the mean, median, and mode.

**A.4** Identify the types of statistics used to examine variations in data.

- Measures of variability provide information about the differences within a set of numbers and include the range and the standard deviation.

## Inferential Statistics

**A.5** Describe how inferential statistics can be used to determine if differences in sets of data are large enough to be due to something other than chance variation.

- Inferential statistics involves statistical analysis of two or more sets of numerical data to reduce the possibility of error in measurement and determine statistical significance of the results of research.

**A.6** Explain how statistics are used to predict one score from another.

- The correlation coefficient is a number that represents the strength and direction of a relationship existing between two variables.

# Test Yourself

*Pick the best answer.*

**1.** Polygons and histograms are examples of
 **a.** frequency distributions.
 **b.** correlations.
 **c.** inferential statistics.
 **d.** mode.

**2.** If a chart shows that more than 80 percent of the students received either an A or B in the class, one would describe the chart as
 **a.** normal distribution.
 **b.** positively skewed.
 **c.** negatively skewed.
 **d.** bell shaped.

**3.** Your psychology instructor posts the results of the midterm on a histogram chart. On the chart, you see a high frequency of Bs and a high frequency of Ds. How else might you describe the results?
 **a.** This is a normal curve.
 **b.** This chart is skewed and bimodal.
 **c.** This chart is a typical bell-shaped chart.
 **d.** This chart is incapable of expressing an accurate picture of the results.

**4.** The mean, median, and mode are all measures of
 **a.** correlations.
 **b.** inferential statistics.
 **c.** variability.
 **d.** central tendency.

**5.** Imagine that the following is a set of grades from your class's first psychology exam: 71, 71, 71, 73, 75, 76, 81, 86, 97. What is the median score?
 **a.** 71
 **b.** 75
 **c.** 9
 **d.** 700

**6.** Imagine that the following is a set of grades from your first psychology exam: 71, 71, 71, 73, 75, 76, 81, 86, 97. What is the mode?
 **a.** 71
 **b.** 75
 **c.** 9
 **d.** 700

**7.** In the normal curve,
 **a.** the mean, median, and mode are all on the highest point of the curve.
 **b.** the mean is on the highest point, while the median and mode are on either side of the mean.
 **c.** the median is on the highest point, while the mean and mode are on either side of the median.
 **d.** the standard deviation is located at the highest point of the curve.

**8.** _____ is a way of organizing numbers and summarizing them so that they can be understood, whereas _____ allows researchers to draw conclusions about the results of research.
 **a.** Descriptive statistics; inferential statistics
 **b.** Inferential statistics; descriptive statistics
 **c.** Correlational research; mean statistics
 **d.** Inferential statistics; mean, medium, and mode

**9.** Dr. White finds that the results of his *t*-test are significant at $p < 0.05$. That means that he can be
 **a.** reasonably assured that the results are not due to chance.
 **b.** reasonably assured that the results are due to chance.
 **c.** 5 percent certain that the results are not due to chance.
 **d.** 95 percent certain that the results are not due to chance.

**10.** Your best friend tells you he got a correlational score of 14.6 from the research he conducted. What can you infer from his finding?
 **a.** Your friend's research shows only a small correlation since 14.6 is close to zero.
 **b.** Your friend's research shows a positive score in 14.6, and therefore a positive relationship exists.
 **c.** Your friend's research is inconclusive. You need more than a correlational score of 14.6 to know if there is any statistical significance.
 **d.** Your friend's analysis is flawed. Correlational scores only range from −1.00 to +1.00.

# Applied Psychology and Psychology Careers

## Why study applied psychology?

Many different kinds of psychologists study or work in many different fields. Whereas early psychologists were still discovering the processes that govern the human mind, today's psychologists are more often applying information and principles gained from research to people in the real world. Why study careers in psychology? With so many different areas of focus, a career in psychology can be varied and exciting. There is much more to psychology than helping people who have mental health problems.

Professor John Gambon of Ozarks Technical and Community College in Springfield, Missouri, begins his class like any other. After a few minutes, two students rush in and each throw two water balloons at the professor. As they run out, they yell something about fried eggs. Professor Gambon, soaked from the balloons, asks his students to write down everything they just saw, including what was said. After a few minutes, he gathers up the paperwork and invites his two balloon-throwing accomplices back into the room.

As he reads the papers of his students, many realize that they made mistakes in identifying the perpetrators. Quite often, students mismatch hair color, height, facial features, and even the clothes that each was wearing. What's more, nearly 90 percent claim that they heard the two men yell, "That was for last Friday!" When students are shown the truth, many are shocked at their overall inaccuracy at identifying the two men.

Work such as this is not new to Professor Gambon. He has worked as a consultant in several trials where the issue of accurately identifying someone has been brought into question. His cases include several homicides, assault, breaking and entering, and armed robbery.

His demonstrations show the overall unreliability of eyewitness identification, as outlined by psychologist Elizabeth Loftus. (L)(I)(N)(K) to Learning Objective 6.7. The kind of issues that influence an eyewitness's accuracy include the presence of a weapon (people tend to look at a weapon more than the physical attributes of the assailant), time of day, fatigue, and the amount of time between the crime and when they are required to recall it. Clearly, there are flaws inherent in eyewitness identification.

Forensic psychology is just one of many areas in which psychological principles can be applied to issues and concerns of everyday life. This appendix will look at several areas of applied psychology, as well as the types of careers that are open to someone who studies psychology today.

## Learning Objectives

B.1     Define applied psychology.

B.2     Describe different types of psychological professionals and identify their educational background and training.

B.3     List the kinds of careers that are available to someone with a master's degree in psychology.

B.4   List the kinds of careers that are available to someone with a bachelor's degree in psychology.

B.5   Describe some areas of specialization in psychology.

B.6   Describe how psychology interacts with other career fields.

B.7   Explain the fields of industrial/organizational psychology and human factors psychology.

B.8   Describe how the I/O field has evolved throughout its history.

B.9   Identify techniques used by sports psychologists.

# What Is Applied Psychology?

### B.1  Define applied psychology.

The term **applied psychology** refers to using findings from psychological research to solve real-world problems. The psychological professional, who might be a psychiatrist, a psychologist, or even a psychiatric social worker (as described later in this appendix), may do testing or use some other type of assessment and then describe a plan of action intended to solve whatever problem is of concern. As is evident in the opening comments about John Gambon, you can see that his training in psychology and his specialized knowledge enabled him to testify in court as an expert witness. This is a practical application of psychological tools to a real problem—the professional literally "applies" psychology.

> It seems to me that psychology could be useful in a lot of different areas, not just education. In fact, wasn't that what all those "Applying Psychology" sections at the end of each chapter were about?

Every chapter in this text (and even this appendix) does end with some application of psychology to the real world. The field of applied psychology isn't just one field but rather a lot of different areas that all share the common goal of using psychology in a practical way. A large number of areas can be considered applied psychology, including one of the broadest areas of psychology: clinical and counseling psychology. For example, health psychologists examine the effects of stress on physical as well as mental health; educational and school psychologists look for ways to improve student learning and apply the findings to the classroom; sports psychologists help athletes prepare themselves mentally for competition; human factors psychologists deal with the way people and machines interact; forensic psychologists deal with psychological issues within the legal system; and industrial/organizational (I/O) psychologists deal with the work environment. In addition, environmental psychologists examine the interaction of people with their surroundings at work, in social settings, and in schools, homes, and other buildings. Those surroundings include not just the physical structures but also the particular population of people who live, work, and play in those surroundings. Other psychologists look at the factors that influence people to buy certain products, analyze the best ways to market a product, and examine the buying habits of the typical consumer.

This appendix includes information on the different roles of psychological professionals and the type of education required for many professions, along with a brief overview of many of the specialized areas in psychology. The remainder of this appendix briefly explores how psychology can be used in practical ways in several different areas of life: the environment, law, education, the military, sports, and the world of work.

**applied psychology**
the use of psychological concepts in solving real-world problems.

# Practice Quiz   How much do you remember?

*Pick the best answer.*

1. The term _____ psychology refers to using findings from psychological research to solve real-world problems.
   a. applied
   b. practical
   c. pragmatic
   d. academic

2. Which of the following types of psychologists might be most interested in dealing with the work environment?
   a. A vocational psychologist
   b. A health psychologist
   c. A psychiatric social worker
   d. An industrial/organizational psychologist

3. Charlotte has designed a new type of gearshift to be used in automobiles with an automatic transmission. Before she proposes it to the major car manufacturers, she wants to make sure that it will be more advantageous for people who drive such cars. With which of the following types of psychologist would Charlotte most want to consult about her design?
   a. An environmental psychologist
   b. An industrial/organizational psychologist
   c. A human-factors psychologist
   d. A machinery psychologist

# Psychology as a Career

When most people think of psychology as a potential career, they assume certain things about the profession: For example, to help people with their problems one has to be a psychologist, all psychologists are doctors, and all psychologists counsel mentally ill people. None of these assumptions are completely true.

## TYPES OF PSYCHOLOGICAL PROFESSIONALS

**B.2** **Describe different types of psychological professionals and identify their educational background and training.**

There are several types of professionals who work in psychology. These professionals have different training with different focuses and may have different goals.

**PSYCHIATRIC SOCIAL WORKERS**   A *psychiatric social worker* is trained in the area of social work and usually possesses a master of social work (M.S.W.) degree and may be licensed in the state in which he or she works as a licensed clinical social worker (LCSW). These professionals focus more on the social conditions that can have an impact on mental disorders, such as poverty, overcrowding, stress, and drug abuse. They may administer psychotherapy (talking with clients about their problems) and often work in a clinical setting where other types of psychological professionals are available.

**PSYCHIATRISTS**   A *psychiatrist* has a medical doctorate (M.D. or D.O.) degree and is a physician who specializes in the diagnosis and treatment of psychological disorders. Like any other medical doctor who may specialize in emergency medicine, treating the diseases of the elderly, treating infants and children, or any other special area of medicine, psychiatrists are able to write prescriptions and perform medical procedures on their patients. They simply have special training in the diagnosis and treatment of disorders that are considered to be mental disorders, such as schizophrenia, depression, or extreme anxiety. Because they are medical doctors, they tend to have a biopsychological perspective on the causes of and treatments for such disorders.

**PSYCHOLOGISTS**   A *psychologist* doesn't have a medical degree but instead undergoes intense academic training, learning about many different areas of psychology before choosing an area in which to specialize. Psychologists typically have either a doctor of philosophy (Ph.D.) or doctor of psychology (Psy.D.) degree. (People who hold a master of science or M.S. degree are not usually called psychologists except in a few states. They can be called therapists or counselors, or they may be teachers or researchers.)

What's the difference between a Ph.D. and a Psy.D.?

Psychologists specialize in many different areas and work in many different settings.

The Ph.D. is a type of degree that usually indicates the highest degree of learning available in almost any subject area—psychology, the study of languages, education, philosophy, the sciences, and many others. It is typically very research oriented, and earning the degree usually requires a previous master's degree in addition to coursework for the doctorate itself, as well as a dissertation—a scholarly work of research in the area of focus that is as long as a book and may even be published as a book.

The Psy.D. is a type of degree developed in the late 1970s that is focused less on research and more on the practical application of psychological principles (Peterson, 1976, 1982). In addition to academic coursework such as that required for the Ph.D., this degree may require a major paper instead of a dissertation, with the difference being that the paper is not a report of research designed and conducted by the student but is rather a large-scale term paper. Each year of a Psy.D. program will also require the student to participate in a *practicum*, an actual experience with observing and eventually conducting therapy and treatments under supervision.

Unlike psychiatrists, psychologists typically cannot prescribe medicines or perform medical procedures. Some states are seeking legislative changes to allow psychologists to prescribe psychotropic medications if they receive special education in the use of prescription drugs. Such privileges were first pursued by the U.S. military. The reasoning behind this move, for which the American Psychological Association has been lobbying since 1984, involves both cost and the delay in receiving mental health services. If a person sees a psychologist and then has to go to a psychiatrist for medical prescriptions, the cost can be prohibitive. There are also fewer psychiatrists in some states than in others, causing long waits for mental health services from those doctors—delays that can sometimes lead to an increase in suicide rates for patients who are not getting the help they need. Although some psychologists in the military or Indian Health Service can already prescribe, as of May 2016, only four states and one territory (New Mexico, Louisiana, Illinois, Iowa, and Guam) have successfully afforded prescription privileges to psychologists.

Some psychologists provide counseling or therapy and use a variety of techniques and approaches. (L)(I)(N)K to Learning Objectives 15.2–15.7. However, many psychologists do no counseling at all. There are psychologists who only engage in assessment, those who teach at colleges or universities, those who do only research in those same institutions or for industries, and those who do a combination of teaching and research (and some that do a combination of teaching, research, and counseling or clinical practice). Other psychologists are involved in designing equipment and workplaces, developing educational methods, or working as consultants to businesses and the court system. As of 2013 in the United States, the number of active psychologists appears to be stable, with a growing number of females and an increase in diversity, although representation from racial/ethnic minority groups is not as high as the overall or general doctoral/professional workforce (American Psychological Association, 2015).

Although becoming a psychologist requires a doctorate degree of some kind, many career fields can benefit from a 4-year college degree in psychology as the basis of that career or going on to obtain a master's degree in psychology.

### CAREERS WITH A MASTER'S DEGREE IN PSYCHOLOGY

**B.3** **List the kinds of careers that are available to someone with a master's degree in psychology.**

While individuals earning a master's degree in psychology are not typically able to engage in the same level of independent research or practice of psychology as someone with a doctoral degree, they can still work in a variety of areas, both within and beyond the field of psychology. They may work directly under the supervision of a doctoral psychologist if engaged in clinical, counseling, or school psychology or engaged in assessment. Others work outside of the field in jobs requiring research or analysis skills and work in health, industry, or government areas.

For those interested in counseling or providing therapy, many states allow individuals with master's degrees and prerequisite training and supervision experiences to become licensed to provide unsupervised counseling and therapy. Titles may vary by state, but some of the areas and titles associated with licensed master's-level work include licensed marriage and family therapist (LMFT), licensed professional counselor (LPC), licensed mental health counselor (LMHC), or licensed clinical social worker (LCSW). These individuals may work in a larger organization or work independently in private practice. Beyond these areas, some individuals with a master's degree in psychology become certified or licensed to serve as school counselors at various levels and may work in an elementary, middle, or high school.

## CAREERS WITH A BACHELOR'S DEGREE IN PSYCHOLOGY

**B.4** **List the kinds of careers that are available to someone with a bachelor's degree in psychology.**

Although people earning only the baccalaureate (bachelor's) degree in psychology cannot be called psychologists or provide therapy in a private practice, there are many career fields open to such a person. More than 1 million bachelor's degrees in psychology have been awarded since 1970, and since 2000 the number has increased each year (Landrum, 2009; Snyder & Dillow, 2010). A bachelor's degree in psychology can be highly flexible and adaptable to many different kinds of careers (Landrum, 2009; Landrum & Davis, 2007; Schwartz, 2000). While surveys by both the American Psychological Association and others reveal many may work in health-related or social fields, individuals with a bachelor's degree in psychology may be employed in research development or research management, administration, business, education and teaching, professional services, sales, or management (Grocer & Kohout, 1997; Landrum, 2009).

Many people with a bachelor's degree in psychology work in health-related or social fields, such as this social worker who is working with a mother and child.

Other possible careers include marketing researcher, social worker, and communications specialist (Landrum & Davis, 2007; Schwartz, 2000). With its emphasis on critical thinking and empirical observation, psychology trains people for a variety of potential workplace environments and requirements. Psychology is an excellent major even if you intend to do graduate work in some other career: Business, law, child care, teaching, and management are only a few of the areas that relate to psychology.

## AREAS OF SPECIALIZATION

**B.5** **Describe some areas of specialization in psychology.**

💬 You said that some psychologists teach or do research. What kind of research do they do?

There are many different areas in which psychologists may focus their energies. They conduct experiments, surveys, observations, and so on to gather more information for their particular field of interest, to find support for current theories, or to develop new ones. Let's look at some of the areas in which psychologists may specialize.

**CLINICAL PSYCHOLOGY** Even though not all psychologists do counseling or therapy, many psychologists do. **Clinical psychology** is the most similar of the areas to psychiatry in that professionals with this focus traditionally work with individuals with more serious forms of mental illness. It is also the area of specialization with the largest number of psychologists. Clinical psychologists, like psychiatrists, diagnose and treat psychological disorders in people. However, the clinical psychologist cannot prescribe drugs or

**clinical psychology**

area of psychology in which the psychologists diagnose and treat people with psychological disorders that may range from mild to severe.

medical therapies (with the exceptions discussed earlier, of course) but instead relies on listening or observing the client's problems, possibly administering psychological tests, and then providing explanations for the client's behavior and feelings or directing the client in specific actions to make positive changes in his or her life.

**COUNSELING PSYCHOLOGY**  **Counseling psychology** is similar to clinical psychology in that this type of psychologist diagnoses and treats problems. The difference is that a counseling psychologist usually works with relatively healthy people who have less severe forms of mental illness or problems, such as adjustment to college, marriage, family life, work problems, and so on. As of 2008, nearly 73 percent of surveyed psychologists currently providing health services identified themselves as clinical psychologists or counseling psychologists (Michalski et al., 2010). (L)(I)(N)K to Learning Objective 1.4.

**DEVELOPMENTAL PSYCHOLOGY**  **Developmental psychology** is an area that focuses on the study of change, or development. Developmental psychologists are interested in changes in the way people think, in how people relate to others, and in the ways people feel over the entire span of life. These psychologists work in academic settings such as colleges and universities and may do research in various areas of development. They do not provide therapy. (L)(I)(N)K to Learning Objective 8.1.

**EXPERIMENTAL PSYCHOLOGY**  **Experimental psychology** encompasses several different areas such as learning, memory, thinking, perception, motivation, and language. The focus of these psychologists, however, is on doing research and conducting studies and experiments with both people and animals in these various areas. They tend to work in academic settings, especially in large universities. (L)(I)(N)K to Learning Objective 1.4

**SOCIAL PSYCHOLOGY**  *Social psychology* is an area that focuses on how human behavior is affected by the presence of other people. For example, social psychologists explore areas such as prejudice, attitude change, aggressive behavior, and interpersonal attraction. Although most social psychologists work in academic settings teaching and doing research, some work in federal agencies and big business doing practical (applied) research. In fact, many social psychologists are experimental psychologists who perform their experiments in real-world settings rather than the laboratory to preserve the natural reactions of people. When people are in an artificial setting, they often behave in self-conscious ways, which is not the behavior the researcher wishes to study. (L)(I)(N)K to Learning Objective 12.1

**PERSONALITY PSYCHOLOGY**  **Personality psychology** focuses on the differences in personality among people. These psychologists may look at the influence of heredity on personality. They study the ways in which people are both alike and different. They look at the development of personality and do personality assessment. They may be involved in forming new theories of how personality works or develops. Personality psychologists work in academic settings, doing research and teaching. (L)(I)(N)K to Learning Objective 13.1

**PHYSIOLOGICAL PSYCHOLOGY**  **Physiological psychology** is an area that focuses on the study of the biological bases of behavior. Many professionals now refer to this area as *behavioral neuroscience* or *biopsychology*. Physiological psychologists study the brain, nervous system, and the influence of the body's chemicals, such as hormones and the chemicals in the brain, on human behavior. They study the effects of drug use and possible genetic influences on some kinds of abnormal and normal human behavior, such as schizophrenia or aspects of intelligence. Most physiological psychologists, like experimental psychologists, work in an academic setting. (L)(I)(N)K to Learning Objective 2.1.

**NEUROPSYCHOLOGY**  **Neuropsychology** is an area within the field of psychology in which professionals explore the relationships between the brain systems and behavior. Neuropsychologists may be engaged in research or more focused on the assessment,

---

**counseling psychology**

area of psychology in which the psychologists help people with problems of adjustment.

**developmental psychology**

area of psychology in which the psychologists study the changes in the way people think, relate to others, and feel as they age.

**experimental psychology**

area of psychology in which the psychologists primarily do research and experiments in the areas of learning, memory, thinking, perception, motivation, and language.

**personality psychology**

area of psychology in which the psychologists study the differences in personality among people.

**physiological psychology**

area of psychology in which the psychologists study the biological bases of behavior.

**neuropsychology**

area of psychology in which psychologists specialize in the research or clinical implications of brain-behavior relationships.

diagnosis, treatment, and/or rehabilitation of individuals with various neurological, medical, neurodevelopmental, or psychiatric conditions (National Academy of Neuropsychology, 2001). (L I N K) to Learning Objective 7.8.

**COMPARATIVE PSYCHOLOGY** Comparative psychology is an area that focuses exclusively on animals and animal behavior. By comparing and contrasting animal behavior with what is already known about human behavior, comparative psychologists can contribute to the understanding of human behavior by studying animals. Research in animal behavior also helps people learn how to treat animals more humanely and coexist with the animals in a common environment. Comparative psychologists might work in animal laboratories in a university or may do observation and studies of animals in the animals' natural habitats.

Psychologists in these areas may do research that is directed at discovering basic principles of human behavior (basic research), or they may engage in research designed to find solutions to practical problems of the here and now (applied research). (L I N K) to Learning Objective 1.4. There are many other areas in which psychologists may specialize that focus almost exclusively on applied research. These areas are those most often associated with applied psychology.

### PSYCHOLOGY BEYOND THE CLASSROOM

**B.6** Describe how psychology interacts with other career fields.

Individuals working in psychology can serve in important roles in many different fields. Some are extensions of the areas of specialization just covered. Other fields are well suited due to the general and sometimes specific skills psychology professionals can provide.

**PSYCHOLOGY AND HEALTH** *Health psychology* focuses on the relationship of human behavior patterns and stress reactions to physical health with the goal of improving and helping maintain good health while preventing and treating illness. For example, a health psychologist might design a program to help people lose weight or stop smoking. Stress-management techniques are also a major focus of this area. Health psychologists may work in hospitals, clinics, medical schools, health agencies, academic settings, or private practice.

In one study (Kerwin et al., 2010), researchers found an association between obesity in older women and a decline in memory functioning in those women. This finding was particularly true for women carrying the excess weight around their hips (pear shapes) and less so for women carrying the excess weight around their waists (apple shapes). The study controlled for other health variables, such as diabetes, heart disease, and stroke. This is a good example of the kind of research that health psychologists conduct. Other areas studied by health psychologists include the influence of optimistic attitudes on the progress of disease, the link between mental distress and health, and the promotion of wellness and hope in an effort to prevent illness. (L I N K) to Learning Objectives 11.5, 11.6.

**PSYCHOLOGY AND EDUCATION** *Educational psychology* is concerned with the study of human learning. As educational psychologists come to understand some of the basic aspects of learning, they develop methods and materials for aiding the process of learning. For example, educational psychologists helped design the phonics method of teaching children to read. This type of psychologist may have a doctorate of education (Ed.D.) rather than a Ph.D. and typically works in academic settings.

What types of research might an educational psychologist conduct? The August 2016 issue of *Journal of Educational Psychology* included articles on the impact of teacher emotional exhaustion on student educational outcomes, developmental changes in working memory and math achievement, kindergarten readiness as predictors of Grade 2–5 achievement in Latino children, and evaluation of a school-based intervention for reducing posttraumatic symptoms and multicultural intolerance during times of political violence—just to name a few.

This woman is a health psychologist. Through the use of a storybook, she is helping this young patient learn more about his medical condition and address some of his fears.

**comparative psychology**

area of psychology in which the psychologists study animals and their behavior for the purpose of comparing and contrasting it to human behavior.

**educational psychology**

area of psychology in which the psychologists are concerned with the study of human learning and development of new learning techniques.

School psychologists often administer tests to assess a child's level of achievement, intelligence, or psychological well-being.

**School psychology** is related to but not at all the same as educational psychology. Whereas educational psychologists may do research and develop new learning techniques, school psychologists may take the results of that research or those methods and apply them in the actual school system. School psychologists work directly with children in the school setting. They do testing and other forms of assessment to place children in special programs or to diagnose educational problems such as dyslexia or attention-deficit/hyperactivity disorder. They may act as consultants to teachers, parents, and educational administrators. Counseling students is actually a relatively small part of the job of a school psychologist, although counseling takes a much bigger role when tragedies strike a school. When traumatic events such as the unexpected and tragic death of a classmate or even larger-scale tragedies such as the numerous school shootings of the past decade take place, school psychologists are often called on to offer help and counseling to students.

**PSYCHOLOGY AND SPORTS**  **Sports psychology** is a relatively new and fast-growing field in which the main focus is on helping athletes and others involved in sports activities prepare mentally rather than just physically for participation in sports. The idea behind this field is that a superior physical performance is not enough to guarantee success; rather, the mind must be prepared for the activity by setting clear short-term goals, holding positive thoughts, using visualization of the goal, stopping negative thoughts, and other techniques based primarily in the cognitive perspective. For example, a sports psychologist might have a golfer who has been having trouble with the accuracy of his drives perform visualization exercises, mentally seeing himself hit the ball down the fairway again and again. Sports psychologists work in athletic organizations and may have a private practice or do consulting work. (For more on the techniques used in sports psychology, see the Applying Psychology to Everyday Life section at the end of this appendix.)

**PSYCHOLOGY AND THE MILITARY**  Within the military, psychologists work in a variety of areas ranging from assessment, teaching, management, and research to the provision of mental health services. The variety of psychologists in this field may include clinical, counseling, experimental, I/O, or human factors, among others, and may reflect any specialty area in the field of psychology. In short, they apply psychological skills to human issues in military environments, working with both military personnel and their families (American Psychological Association, Division 19, 2016). One poignant example, the rise of suicides in the armed forces associated with the conflicts in Iraq and Afghanistan, has placed demands on both the military and military families at a level not seen before (Berman et al., 2010).

**PSYCHOLOGY AND THE LAW**  Psychologists have often been involved in the world of legal matters in various ways. Social psychologists often do research in the areas of criminal behavior and may consult with attorneys or other agents of the court system on such topics as witness credibility, jury selection, and the kind of influences that exist for decision-making processes. Developmental psychologists may become involved in determining the accuracy of and influences on the testimony of children and adolescents, as well as the needs of children caught up in a custody battle between divorced or divorcing parents. Cognitive psychologists may become expert witnesses on the accuracy of memory and eyewitness testimony or ways to determine the truth or falsehood of statements made by witnesses or defendants. Clinical psychologists may deliver their services directly to incarcerated prisoners or may conduct assessments of intelligence and/or mental status to determine whether a person charged with a crime should stand trial.

**school psychology**

area of psychology in which the psychologists work directly in the schools, doing assessments, educational placement, and diagnosing educational problems.

**sports psychology**

area of psychology in which the psychologists help athletes and others to prepare themselves mentally for participation in sports activities.

All of the forms of psychological involvement in legal matters mentioned here can be considered as part of the growing field of **forensic psychology**. Forensic psychology is the practice of psychology related to the legal system, and it involves examining criminal evidence and aiding law enforcement investigations into criminal activities. Some forensic psychologists provide information and advice to officials in the legal system, such as lawyers or judges; some act as expert witnesses (like Professor John Gambon in the opening story); some actually diagnose and treat criminals within the prison system; and others may administer psychological tests to criminal defendants. Forensic psychologists may aid either the prosecution or the defense in a trial by helping determine which potential jurors would be the best or worst choices. This type of professional may do consulting work in addition to maintaining a regular private practice in clinical or counseling psychology or may work entirely within the justice system as a police psychologist or a full-time jury expert, for example.

**PSYCHOLOGY AND THE COMMUNITY**   **Community psychology** is an area that focuses on both individuals and their community. This field is often concerned with issues at various levels, including individual, group, neighborhood, and organizational. It is an area that focuses on promoting health and preventing common societal issues across all levels. Community psychology aims to understand human behavior in context and recognizes the role of human diversity in promoting change. Advocacy is a key role for individuals in this area as they work to promote social justice, or practices and policies that directly impact aspects of life such as equal opportunity for all people, prevention of violence, and active citizenship. Community psychologists are involved in a variety of life activities and may be engaged in promoting mental health, physical health, educational interventions, or work policies.

**PSYCHOLOGY AND THE ENVIRONMENT**   Another broad area in which psychological principles can be applied to solve practical problems is the area of managing the environment. **Environmental psychology** is an area that focuses on the relationship between human behavior and the environment in which the behavior takes place, such as an office, store, school, dormitory, or hospital. Because the concern of researchers in this field deals directly with behavior in a particular setting, research is always conducted in that setting rather than in a laboratory. Environmental psychologists may work with other professionals such as urban or city planners, economists, engineers, and architects, helping those professionals plan the most efficient buildings, parks, housing developments, or plants.

**forensic psychology**

area of psychology concerned with people in the legal system, including psychological assessment of criminals, jury selection, and expert witnessing.

**community psychology**

area of psychology in which psychologists serve at various levels including individual, group, and community, focusing on promoting social welfare and preventing social problems.

**environmental psychology**

area of psychology in which the focus is on how people interact with and are affected by their physical environments.

# Practice Quiz   How much do you remember?

*Pick the best answer.*

**1.** Dr. Saschi works at a hospital and is regularly called to the emergency room to assist with patients who are having acute mental health crises. She often prescribes psychotropic medications to help these patients get stabilized. Which of the following degrees has Dr. Saschi most likely earned?
   **a.** An Ed.D.          **c.** An M.D.
   **b.** A Ph.D.           **d.** A Psy.D.

**2.** Rochelle has earned a master's degree but decided not to pursue her doctorate. She does, however, want to provide counseling and therapy to clients but does not want to be supervised for her entire career. After several years of training and appropriate supervision, she has achieved a degree that, in her state, will allow her to have this career. Which of the following would not likely be a title that Rochelle may now hold?
   **a.** LCP (Licensed Children's Psychologist)
   **b.** LPC (Licensed Professional Counselor)
   **c.** LMHC (Licensed Mental Health Counselor)
   **d.** LMFT (Licensed Marriage and Family Therapist)

**3.** _____ psychologists are primarily interested in changes in the way people think, in how people relate to others, and in the ways people feel over the entire span of life. They often work in academic settings, such as colleges and universities, and may do research in various areas. They do not generally provide therapy.
   **a.** Counseling          **c.** Sociocultural
   **b.** Developmental       **d.** Environmental

**4.** Dr. Kandlend has spent his entire career working with chimpanzees, studying the ways that their behavioral profiles are both similar to and different from those of human beings. Dr. Kandlend is probably a _____ psychologist.
   **a.** physiological        **c.** forensic
   **b.** zoological           **d.** comparative

# Psychology and Work

Work is a tremendous part of many people's lives. People often spend more time at work than they do with their families or in social activities. One of the largest branches of applied psychology focuses on how psychology can help people in management, productivity, morale, and many other areas of the world of work.

## WHAT ARE INDUSTRIAL/ORGANIZATIONAL PSYCHOLOGY AND HUMAN FACTORS PSYCHOLOGY?

**B.7** Explain the fields of industrial/organizational psychology and human factors psychology.

**Industrial/organizational (I/O) psychology** is concerned with the relationships between people and their work environments. I/O psychologists may help in personnel selection, administer job performance assessments, design work schedules that help workers adjust to new time periods of work hours with less difficulty, or design new work areas to increase morale and productivity. Psychologists in this field may study the behavior of entire organizations. They are often hired by corporations and businesses to deal with the hiring and assessment of employees. They may research and develop ways for workers to be more efficient and productive. They may work in business, government agencies, and academic settings. **Table B.1** briefly lists some of the areas of specialization.

A specific kind of I/O specialist, called a *human factors engineer*, focuses on ergonomics, or designing machines, furniture, and other devices that people have to use so that those devices are the most practical, comfortable, and logical for human use. **Human factors psychology** consists of these researchers and designers who study the way humans and machines interact with each other. They may work directly in the companies involved in the design of appliances, airplane controls, and the operation of computers or other mechanical devices. For example, recall a recent iPhone® commercial about how your thumb can reach all parts of the screen. Or have you ever seen an ergonomic chair? Most likely a human factors engineer was involved in the design or testing of these products.

Psychologists working in I/O settings apply psychological principles and theories to the workplace. For example, Maslow's humanistic theory and hierarchy of needs (Ⓛ Ⓘ Ⓝ Ⓚ to Learning Objective 9.5) has had a powerful influence on the field of management (Heil et al., 1998). Douglas McGregor, in his

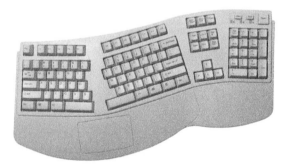

Human factors psychologists design machines that are more practical and comfortable for people to use. For example, this keyboard is designed to reduce the risk of pain in the wrists and increase accuracy in typing.

**industrial/organizational (I/O) psychology**

area of psychology concerned with the relationships between people and their work environment.

**human factors psychology**

area of industrial/organizational psychology concerned with the study of the way humans and machines interact with each other.

| **Table B.1** Areas in I/O Psychology | |
| --- | --- |
| **Areas in Industry** | **Areas in Organizations** |
| Job analysis | Social behavior of work teams |
| Job evaluation and compensation | Job satisfaction |
| Characteristics critical to effective management | Personality characteristics critical to job performance |
| Personnel recruiting, selection, and placement | Relationships between management and workers |
| Occupational training | Leadership characteristics and training |
| Examination of working conditions | Consumer psychology |
| Interviewing and testing | Motivational concerns |
| Performance appraisal and feedback | Conflict management |

explanations of two different styles of management (McGregor, 1960), relates the older and less productive "Theory X" (workers are unmotivated and need to be managed and directed) to Maslow's lower needs and the newer, more productive style of management called "Theory Y" (workers want to work and want that work to be meaningful) to the higher needs.

## THE HISTORY OF INDUSTRIAL/ORGANIZATIONAL PSYCHOLOGY AND THE FIELD TODAY

**B.8** **Describe how the I/O field has evolved throughout its history.**

Industrial/organizational psychology got its start near the beginning of the twentieth century with the work of Walter D. Scott, a former student of famed physiologist and founder of the first psychological laboratory Wilhelm Wundt. Scott applied psychological principles to hiring, management, and advertising techniques (Schultz & Schultz, 2004). He also wrote one of the first books about the application of psychology to industry and advertising, called *The Theory and Practice of Advertising* (Scott, 1908). Another early figure in the newly developing field of industrial/organizational psychology was Hugo Munsterberg, a psychologist also trained by Wundt, who conducted research on such varied topics as the power of prayer and eyewitness testimony (Hothersall, 1995). Munsterberg wrote a book about eyewitness testimony called *On the Witness Stand* (1907) and later wrote *Psychology and Industrial Efficiency* (1913).

The I/O field became important during World War I when the army needed a way to test the intelligence of potential recruits. Psychologist Robert Yerkes, who would later become known for his groundbreaking research in comparative psychology while working with the great apes, developed the Army Alpha and Army Beta tests. The Army Alpha test was used with applicants who were able to read, whereas the Army Beta test was administered to applicants who were illiterate (McGuire, 1994; Yerkes, 1921).

In the mid-1920s, a series of studies conducted by Elton Mayo for the Western Electric Company (Franke & Kaul, 1978; Parsons, 1992; Roethlisberger & Dickson, 1939) broadened the field. These were the first studies to view the workplace as a social system rather than as just a production line. Instead of treating workers as simply other pieces of equipment, these studies suggested that allowing workers some input into the decision-making process not only improved worker morale* but also reduced workers' resistance to changes in the workplace. These studies led the way for others to examine how management of employees and production could be improved. For example, Google® is one of the leaders in creating a rewarding work environment and providing various perks to its employees. It was selected as *Fortune* magazine's top company to work for in both 2012 and 2013 ("Best Companies to Work For 2013 – *Fortune*"). From free gourmet food, to an on-site laundry and dry cleaners, and both indoor and outdoor recreation facilities, Google works to create an intimate environment for its employees (Mangalindan, 2012). Management theories and strategies may also be applied to other kinds of settings such as schools, colleges, and universities. Yet another setting I/O psychologists are currently involved in is working with NASA for the planned 2030 trip to Mars (Novotney, 2013, March). I/O psychologists are researching ways to improve team selection and training for the astronauts who will have to endure a longer and further space voyage than anyone ever has, a trip that will take close to 3 years. Promotion of resiliency, adaptability, and group cohesion are some of the areas being investigated, especially in light of the lack of privacy and cramped quarters they will be living in.

---

*morale: a sense of common purpose, enthusiasm, confidence, and loyalty.

# Practice Quiz    How much do you remember?

*Pick the best answer.*

1. Dr. Irish is an industrial/organizational psychologist who has just been hired by a major electronics production company. His job there will include many different responsibilities. Which of the following is not likely to be high on his list of responsibilities?
   a. Helping workers visualize their performance.
   b. Helping select personnel
   c. Administering job performance assessments
   d. Designing new work areas to increase morale and productivity

2. Which of the following would a human factors psychologist have the most input in designing?
   a. A new ergonomic chair that reduces muscle fatigue in the legs and back
   b. A new smartphone application that allows you to track your spending

   c. A book of recipes for single parents who do not have a lot of time to cook
   d. A list of maps that will show college students the closest stores that offer various products

3. One of the earliest industrial/organization psychologists, _____, was a student of famed researcher Wilhelm Wundt and wrote a book entitled *The Theory and Practice of Advertising*.
   a. Keith Engelhorn
   b. William James
   c. Walter D. Scott
   d. Robert Yerkes

---

## Applying Psychology to Everyday Life
### Techniques Used by Sports Psychologists

**B.9  Identify techniques used by sports psychologists.**

Many athletes become frustrated when their performance seems to be less than it could be or when they reach some "roadblock" on their way to achieving new goals. The techniques that follow are designed to help athletes get around the roadblocks and get the most out of their performance. The same techniques are also helpful in the careers of acting, musical performance, professional speaking, teaching, or any career in which there is an element of performance in front of others.

1. *Visualization.*    In this technique, athletes try to "see" their performance in their minds as if watching from the sidelines before actually doing it.
2. *Imagery/mental rehearsal.*    Similar to visualization, imagery can be used to mentally rehearse the desired performance. Instead of visualizing oneself as if from the sidelines, however, imagery/mental rehearsal involves actually "seeing" and "feeling" the performance in one's mind from one's own viewpoint. This helps prepare the muscles that will be used for action.
3. *Distraction desensitization.*    Athletes can be trained to ignore distractions, such as the shouts of spectators.
4. *Thought stopping.*    People often have negative thoughts about things that might happen: "I'm going to miss it, I just know it!" is a good example of a negative, self-defeating thought. Sports psychologists train athletes to stop such thoughts in the making, replacing them with more positive thoughts: "I can do this. I've done it before and it was easy."
5. *Confidence training.*    Another thing that sports psychologists do is try to build confidence and self-esteem in the athletes who come to them for help. Lack of confidence in one's own abilities is a major roadblock.
6. *Focus training.*    Athletes can also be trained to focus attention, often through the use of hypnosis, concentrative meditation, or similar psychological techniques.
7. *Relaxation training.*    Athletes can be trained to use special breathing methods, tension and relaxation of muscles, and other strategies for relaxation to reduce anxiety and tension before a performance.
8. *Autogenic training.*    Autogenic essentially means "from within the self." In the sense used here, autogenic training involves helping athletes learn about their physiological responses

to stress. Once they have learned how their bodies react, athletes can gain control over these responses, such as learning to slow one's heart rate or to lower anxiety.

9. *Fostering realistic goals and expectations.*    Sports psychologists try to teach athletes that although setting goals is important, setting unrealistic goals can lead to burnout, frustration, and feelings of failure. Sports psychologists try to help athletes modify their expectations and goals to be more realistic.

10. *Fostering team unity.*    Sports psychologists may also work with entire teams of athletes, helping them become a unit that works as one single "organism" while still providing support for each individual athlete.

### Questions for Further Discussion

1. What are some other occupations in which people might benefit from using some of these techniques?

2. Are there factors outside of the game itself that might interfere with fostering team unity?

The sports psychologist on the right is helping Red Sox player David Ortiz work through his frustration at being injured during the game.

# Chapter Summary

## What Is Applied Psychology?

### B.1  Define applied psychology.

- Applied psychology refers to using psychological principles and research to solve problems in the real world.

## Psychology as a Career

### B.2  Describe different types of psychological professionals and identify their educational background and training.

- Different types of psychological professionals vary by level of education and training. Examples include psychiatrists, psychiatric social workers, and psychologists.
- Psychologists hold either a Ph.D. or Psy.D. degree.

### B.3  List the kinds of careers that are available to someone with a master's degree in psychology.

- Individuals with a master's degree may work under the supervision of a doctoral-level psychology professional, practice independently if licensed, or work in private or educational settings.

### B.4  List the kinds of careers that are available to someone with a bachelor's degree in psychology.

- Education, statistical consulting, administration and other business occupations, as well as health services are examples of careers that a person with a bachelor's degree in psychology might enter.

### B.5  Describe some areas of specialization in psychology.

- Areas of specialization include clinical and counseling psychology, developmental, experimental, social, personality, and physiological psychology, neuropsychology, and comparative psychology.

### B.6  Describe how psychology interacts with other career fields.

- Health psychology is an area in which the goal is to discover relationships between human behavior, including stress factors, and physical health, with the intention of preventing and treating ill health.
- Educational psychologists study the processes of human learning to develop new techniques and methods, whereas school psychologists apply those methods in the school, administer assessments, recommend placement, and provide counseling and diagnosis of educational problems.
- Sports psychologists help athletes prepare themselves mentally for participation in sports.
- Psychologists working in the military represent almost all subfields of psychology and work with both military personnel and their families in military environments.
- Psychologists may act as expert witnesses for legal matters, help in jury selection, provide clinical services to defendants or prisoners, or produce personality profiles of various types of criminals in the field of forensic psychology.
- Community psychologists help solve social issues and work to promote health for individuals and for the larger community in which people live.
- Environmental psychology looks at the relationship between human behavior and the physical environment in which that behavior takes place.

## Psychology and Work

### B.7  Explain the fields of industrial/organizational psychology and human factors psychology.

- Industrial/organizational psychology is concerned with how people function in and are affected by their work environments.

• Human factors is a type of I/O psychology in which the focus is on the way humans and machines interact with each other, designing or helping design the machines used by people in various science and industrial settings.

**B.8  Describe how the I/O field has evolved throughout its history.**

• The I/O field began in the twentieth century with the application of psychological principles to hiring, management, and advertising.

## Applying Psychology to Everyday Life: Techniques Used by Sports Psychologists

**B.9  Identify techniques used by sports psychologists.**

• Sports psychologists use many techniques to help athletes better their performances, including visualization, imagery, thought stopping, confidence training, relaxation training, and fostering team unity.

# Test Yourself

*Pick the best answer.*

1. Which of the following professionals has a medical degree?
   a. clinical psychologist
   b. psychiatrist
   c. psychiatric social worker
   d. counseling psychologist

2. Elaine has always wanted to be a psychologist. She dreams of helping people with their problems and wants to become "Dr. Elaine." However, she is not interested in conducting scientific research or in becoming a medical doctor. What type of degree would be best for Elaine to pursue?
   a. a master's degree in psychology
   b. a Ph.D.
   c. a Psy.D.
   d. a master's degree in social work

3. Dr. Troxell conducts scientific studies on topics such as the power of prejudice, attitude change, aggressive behavior, and interpersonal attraction in teenagers. Dr. Troxell's area of specialization is most likely in _____ psychology.
   a. social
   b. personality
   c. comparative
   d. developmental

4. Dr. Cavendish is a _____ psychologist who conducts experiments using animals as her subjects. Her focus of study includes animal learning, memory, and even language.
   a. experimental
   b. comparative
   c. developmental
   d. social

5. What type of psychologist would be most likely to put together an antibullying program for middle school students?
   a. experimental
   b. clinical
   c. forensic
   d. educational

6. In working with a professional athlete, what aspects of performance might a sports psychologist likely focus on?
   a. strength and agility training
   b. focus and relaxation
   c. memory and motivation
   d. perceptual and problem solving

7. Dr. Lewis studies the topic of crowding. She often wonders why people can feel crowded in an elevator that has 8–10 people in it but not at a large sporting event where more than 2,000 people are present. What is Dr. Lewis's specialty?
   a. developmental
   b. physiological
   c. social
   d. environmental

8. Which type of psychologist is most concerned with maximizing job satisfaction in night-shift employees?
   a. industrial/organizational
   b. clinical
   c. forensic
   d. environmental

9. Suzanne is working to redesign the controls for a new type of plane so that pilots can tell the difference between instruments in the dark just by the way each control feels. Suzanne is probably a(n) _____ psychologist.
   a. industrial/organizational
   b. human factors
   c. experimental
   d. military

10. Thought stopping, mental rehearsal, and focus training are some of the tools of the _____ psychologist.
   a. experimental
   b. clinical
   c. sports
   d. military

# Glossary

**absolute threshold** the lowest level of stimulation that a person can consciously detect 50 percent of the time the stimulation is present.

**accommodation** as a monocular cue of depth perception; the brain's use of information about the changing thickness of the lens of the eye in response to looking at objects that are close or far away.

**acculturative stress** stress resulting from the need to change and adapt a person's ways to the majority culture.

**acquired (secondary) drives** those drives that are learned through experience or conditioning, such as the need for money or social approval.

**acrophobia** fear of heights.

**action potential** the release of the neural impulse, consisting of a reversal of the electrical charge within the axon.

**action therapy** therapy in which the main goal is to change disordered or inappropriate behavior directly.

**activation-information-mode model (AIM)** revised version of the activation-synthesis explanation of dreams in which information that is accessed during waking hours can have an influence on the synthesis of dreams.

**activation-synthesis hypothesis** premise that states that dreams are created by the higher centers of the cortex to explain the activation by the brain stem of cortical cells during REM sleep periods.

**activity theory** theory of adjustment to aging that assumes older people are happier if they remain active in some way, such as volunteering or developing a hobby.

**acute stress disorder (ASD)** a disorder resulting from exposure to a major stressor, with symptoms of anxiety, dissociation, recurring nightmares, sleep disturbances, problems in concentration, and moments in which people seem to "relive" the event in dreams and flashbacks for as long as 1 month following the event.

**adaptive theory** theory of sleep proposing that animals and humans evolved sleep patterns to avoid predators by sleeping when predators are most active.

**adolescence** the period of life from about age 13 to the early 20s, during which a young person is no longer physically a child but is not yet an independent, self-supporting adult.

**adrenal glands** endocrine glands located on top of each kidney that secrete more than 30 different hormones to deal with stress, regulate salt intake, and provide a secondary source of sex hormones affecting the sexual changes that occur during adolescence.

**aerial (atmospheric) perspective** monocular depth perception cue; the haziness that surrounds objects that are farther away from the viewer, causing the distance to be perceived as greater.

**affect** in psychology, a term indicating "emotion" or "mood."

**afferent (sensory) neuron** a neuron that carries information from the senses to the central nervous system.

**afterimages** images that occur when a visual sensation persists for a brief time even after the original stimulus is removed.

**aggression** actions meant to harm or destroy; behavior intended to hurt or destroy another person.

**agonists** chemical substances that mimic or enhance the effects of a neurotransmitter on the receptor sites of the next cell, increasing or decreasing the activity of that cell.

**agoraphobia** fear of being in a place or situation from which escape is difficult or impossible.

**agreeableness** the emotional style of a person that may range from easygoing, friendly, and likeable to grumpy, crabby, and unpleasant.

**AIDS or acquired immune deficiency syndrome** sexually transmitted viral disorder that causes deterioration of the immune system and eventually results in death due to complicating infections that the body can no longer fight.

**alcohol** the chemical resulting from fermentation or distillation of various kinds of vegetable matter.

**algorithms** very specific, step-by-step procedures for solving certain types of problems.

**all-or-none** referring to the fact that a neuron either fires completely or does not fire at all.

**all-or-nothing thinking** the tendency to believe that one's performance must be perfect or the result will be a total failure.

**alpha waves** brain waves that indicate a state of relaxation or light sleep.

**altered state of consciousness** state in which there is a shift in the quality or pattern of mental activity as compared to waking consciousness.

**altruism** prosocial behavior that is done with no expectation of reward and may involve the risk of harm to oneself.

**amphetamines** stimulants that are synthesized (made) in laboratories rather than being found in nature.

**amygdala** brain structure located near the hippocampus, responsible for fear responses and memory of fear.

**anal stage** the second stage in Freud's psychosexual stages, occurring from about 18–36 months of age, in which the anus is the erogenous zone and toilet training is the source of conflict.

**analytical intelligence** the ability to break problems down into component parts, or analysis, for problem solving.

**androgens** male hormones.

**androgyny** characteristic of possessing the most positive personality characteristics of males and females regardless of actual sex.

**andropause** gradual changes in the sexual hormones and reproductive system of middle-aged males.

**anorexia nervosa (anorexia)** a condition in which a person reduces eating to the point that their body weight is significantly low, or less than minimally expected. In adults, this is likely associated with a BMI < 18.5.

**antagonists** chemical substances that block or reduce a cell's response to the action of other chemicals or neurotransmitters.

**anterograde amnesia** loss of memory from the point of injury or trauma forward, or the inability to form new long-term memories.

**antianxiety drugs** drugs used to treat and calm anxiety reactions, typically minor tranquilizers.

**antidepressant drugs** drugs used to treat depression and anxiety.

**antipsychotic drugs** drugs used to treat psychotic symptoms such as delusions, hallucinations, and other bizarre behavior.

**antisocial personality disorder (ASPD)** disorder in which a person uses other people without worrying about their rights or feelings and often behaves in an impulsive or reckless manner without regard for the consequences of that behavior.

**anxiety disorders** class of disorders in which the primary symptom is excessive or unrealistic anxiety.

**applied behavior analysis (ABA)** modern term for a form of functional analysis and behavior modification that uses a variety of behavioral techniques to mold a desired behavior or response.

**applied psychology** the use of psychological concepts in solving real-world problems.

**applied research** research focused on finding practical solutions to real-world problems.

**approach–approach conflict** conflict occurring when a person must choose between two desirable goals.

**approach–avoidance conflict** conflict occurring when a person must choose or not choose a goal that has both positive and negative aspects.

**arbitrary inference** distortion of thinking in which a person draws a conclusion that is not based on any evidence.

**archetypes** Jung's collective, universal human memories.

**arousal theory** theory of motivation in which people are said to have an optimal (best or ideal) level of tension that they seek to maintain by increasing or decreasing stimulation.

**association areas** areas within each lobe of the cortex responsible for the coordination and interpretation of information, as well as higher mental processing.

**attachment** the emotional bond between an infant and the primary caregiver.

**attitude** a tendency to respond positively or negatively toward a certain person, object, idea, or situation.

**attribution** the process of explaining one's own behavior and the behavior of others.

**attribution theory** the theory of how people make attributions.

**auditory canal** short tunnel that runs from the pinna to the eardrum.

**auditory nerve** bundle of axons from the hair cells in the inner ear.

**authenticity** the genuine, open, and honest response of the therapist to the client.

**authoritarian parenting** style of parenting in which parent is rigid and overly strict, showing little warmth to the child.

**authoritative parenting** style of parenting in which parent combines warmth and affection with firm limits on a child's behavior.

**autobiographical memory** the memory for events and facts related to one's personal life story.

**automatic encoding** tendency of certain kinds of information to enter long-term memory with little or no effortful encoding.

**autonomic nervous system (ANS)** division of the PNS consisting of nerves that control all of the involuntary muscles, organs, and glands.

**availability heuristic** estimating the frequency or likelihood of an event based on how easy it is to recall relevant information from memory or how easy it is for us to think of related examples.

**aversion therapy** form of behavioral therapy in which an undesirable behavior is paired with an aversive stimulus to reduce the frequency of the behavior.

**avoidance–avoidance conflict** conflict occurring when a person must choose between two undesirable goals.

**axon** tubelike structure of a neuron that carries the neural message from the cell body to the axon terminals for communication with other cells.

**axon terminals** enlarged ends of axonal branches of the neuron, specialized for communication between cells.

**basal metabolic rate (BMR)** the rate at which the body burns energy when the organism is resting.

**basic anxiety** anxiety created when a child is born into the bigger and more powerful world of older children and adults.

**basic research** research focused on adding information to the scientific knowledge base.

**behavioral genetics** field of study devoted to discovering the genetic bases for personality characteristics.

**behaviorism** the science of behavior that focuses on observable behavior only.

**behavior modification or applied behavior analysis** the use of learning techniques to modify or change undesirable behavior and increase desirable behavior.

**behavior therapies** action therapies based on the principles of classical and operant conditioning and aimed at changing disordered behavior without concern for the original causes of such behavior.

**benevolent sexism** acceptance of positive stereotypes of males and females that leads to unequal treatment.

**benzodiazepines** drugs that lower anxiety and reduce stress.

**beta waves** smaller and faster brain waves, typically indicating mental activity.

**bilateral anterior cingulotomy** psychosurgical technique in which an electrode wire is inserted into the anterior cingulate gyrus, with the guidance of magnetic resonance imaging, to destroy a very small portion of that brain area with electric current.

**bimodal** condition in which a distribution has two modes.

**bimodal distribution** frequency distribution in which there are two high points rather than one.

**binge-eating disorder** a condition in which a person overeats, or binges, on enormous amounts of food at one sitting, but unlike bulimia nervosa, the individual does not then purge or use other unhealthy methods to avoid weight gain.

**binocular cues** cues for perceiving depth based on both eyes.

**binocular disparity** binocular depth perception cue; the difference in images between the two eyes, which is greater for objects that are close and smaller for distant objects.

**bioethics** the study of ethical and moral issues brought about by new advances in biology and medicine.

**biofeedback** using feedback about biological conditions to bring involuntary responses, such as blood pressure and relaxation, under voluntary control.

**biological model** model of explaining thinking or behavior as caused by biological changes in the chemical, structural, or genetic systems of the body.

**biological preparedness** referring to the tendency of animals to learn certain associations, such as taste and nausea, with only one or few pairings due to the survival value of the learning.

**biological psychology or behavioral neuroscience** branch of neuroscience that focuses on the biological bases of psychological processes, behavior, and learning.

**biomedical therapies** therapies that directly affect the biological functioning of the body and brain; therapies for mental disorders in which a person with a problem is treated with biological or medical methods to relieve symptoms.

**biopsychological perspective** perspective that attributes human and animal behavior to biological events occurring in the body, such as genetic influences, hormones, and the activity of the nervous system.

**biopsychosocial model** perspective in which abnormal thinking or behavior is seen as the result of the combined and interacting forces of biological, psychological, social, and cultural influences.

**bipolar disorder** periods of mood that may range from normal to manic, with or without episodes of depression (bipolar I disorder), or spans of normal mood interspersed with episodes of major depression and episodes of hypomania (bipolar II disorder).

**bisexual** person attracted to both men and women.

**blind spot** area in the retina where the axons of the three layers of retinal cells exit the eye to form the optic nerve; insensitive to light.

**borderline personality disorder (BLPD)** maladaptive personality pattern in which the person is moody, unstable, lacks a clear sense of identity, and often clings to others with a pattern of self-destructiveness, chronic loneliness, and disruptive anger in close relationships.

**bottom-up processing** the analysis of the smaller features to build up to a complete perception.

**brightness constancy** the tendency to perceive the apparent brightness of an object as the same even when the light conditions change.

**Broca's aphasia** condition resulting from damage to Broca's area, causing the affected person to be unable to speak fluently, to mispronounce words, and to speak haltingly.

**bulimia nervosa (bulimia)** a condition in which a person develops a cycle of "bingeing," or overeating enormous amounts of food at one sitting, and then using unhealthy methods to avoid weight gain.

**burnout** negative changes in thoughts, emotions, and behavior as a result of prolonged stress or frustration, leading to feelings of exhaustion.

**bystander effect** referring to the effect that the presence of other people has on the decision to help or not help, with help becoming less likely as the number of bystanders increases.

**caffeine** a mild stimulant found in coffee, tea, and several other plant-based substances.

**Cannon–Bard theory of emotion** theory in which the physiological reaction and the emotion are assumed to occur at the same time.

**case study** study of one individual in great detail.

**catastrophe** an unpredictable, large-scale event that creates a tremendous need to adapt and adjust as well as overwhelming feelings of threat.

**catatonia** disturbed behavior ranging from statue-like immobility to bursts of energetic, frantic movement and talking.

**central nervous system (CNS)** part of the nervous system consisting of the brain and spinal cord.

**central-route processing** type of information processing that involves attending to the content of the message itself.

**centration** in Piaget's theory, the tendency of a young child to focus only on one feature of an object while ignoring other relevant features.

**cerebellum** part of the lower brain located behind the pons that controls and coordinates involuntary, rapid, fine motor movement and may have some cognitive functions.

**cerebral hemispheres** the two sections of the cortex on the left and right sides of the brain.

**cerebrum** the upper part of the brain consisting of the two hemispheres and the structures that connect them.

**character** value judgments of a person's moral and ethical behavior.

**chromosome** tightly wound strand of genetic material or DNA.

**circadian rhythm** a cycle of bodily rhythm that occurs over a 24-hour period.

**classical conditioning** learning to make an involuntary response to a stimulus other than the original, natural stimulus that normally produces the response.

**claustrophobia** fear of being in a small, enclosed space.

**clinical psychology** area of psychology in which the psychologists diagnose and treat people with psychological disorders that may range from mild to severe.

**closure** a Gestalt principle of perception; the tendency to complete figures that are incomplete.

**cocaine** a natural drug derived from the leaves of the coca plant.

**cochlea** snail-shaped structure of the inner ear that is filled with fluid.

**cognitive arousal theory (two-factor theory)** theory of emotion in which both the physical arousal and the labeling of that arousal based on cues from the environment must occur before the emotion is experienced.

**cognitive–behavioral therapy (CBT)** action therapy in which the goal is to help clients overcome problems by learning to think more rationally and logically, which in turn will impact their behavior.

**cognitive development** the development of thinking, problem solving, and memory.

**cognitive dissonance** sense of discomfort or distress that occurs when a person's behavior does not correspond to that person's attitudes.

**cognitive-mediational theory** theory of emotion in which a stimulus must be interpreted (appraised) by a person in order to result in a physical response and an emotional reaction.

**cognitive neuroscience** study of the physical changes in the brain and nervous system during thinking.

**cognitive perspective** modern perspective in psychology that focuses on memory, intelligence, perception, problem solving, and learning.

**cognitive perspective** in classical conditioning, modern theory in which conditioning is seen to occur because the conditioned stimulus provides information or an expectancy about the coming of the unconditioned stimulus.

**cognitive psychologists** psychologists who study the way people think, remember, and mentally organize information.

**cognitive therapy** therapy in which the focus is on helping clients recognize distortions in their thinking and replacing distorted, unrealistic beliefs with more realistic, helpful thoughts.

**cognitive universalism** theory that concepts are universal and influence the development of language.

**cohort effect** the impact on development occurring when a group of people share a common time period or common life experience.

**collective unconscious** Jung's name for the memories shared by all members of the human species.

**College Undergraduate Stress Scale (CUSS)** assessment that measures the amount of stress in a college student's life over a 1-year period resulting from major life events.

**community psychology** area of psychology in which psychologists serve at various levels including individual, group, and community, focusing on promoting social welfare and preventing social problems.

**companionate love** type of love consisting of intimacy and commitment.

**comparative psychology** area of psychology in which the psychologists study animals and their behavior for the purpose of comparing and contrasting it to human behavior.

**compensation (substitution)** defense mechanism in which a person makes up for inferiorities in one area by becoming superior in another area.

**compliance** changing one's behavior as a result of other people directing or asking for the change.

**computed tomography (CT)** brain-imaging method using computer-controlled X-rays of the brain.

**concentrative meditation** form of meditation in which a person focuses the mind on some repetitive or unchanging stimulus so that the mind can be cleared of disturbing thoughts and the body can experience relaxation.

**concept map** an organized visual representation of knowledge consisting of concepts and their relationships to other concepts.

**concepts** ideas that represent a class or category of objects, events, or activities.

**concrete operations stage** Piaget's third stage of cognitive development, in which the school-age child becomes capable of logical thought processes but is not yet capable of abstract thinking.

**conditional positive regard** positive regard that is given only when the person is doing what the providers of positive regard wish.

**conditioned emotional response (CER)** emotional response that has become classically conditioned to occur to learned stimuli, such as a fear of dogs or the emotional reaction that occurs when seeing an attractive person.

**conditioned response (CR)** in classical conditioning, a learned response to a conditioned stimulus.

**conditioned stimulus (CS)** in classical conditioning, a previously neutral stimulus that becomes able to produce a conditioned response after pairing with an unconditioned stimulus.

**conditioned taste aversion** development of a nausea or aversive response to a particular taste because that taste was followed by a nausea reaction, occurring after only one association.

**cones** visual sensory receptors found at the back of the retina, responsible for color vision and sharpness of vision.

**confirmation bias** the tendency to search for evidence that fits one's beliefs while ignoring any evidence that does not fit those beliefs.

**conformity** changing one's own behavior to match that of other people.

**conscience** part of the superego that produces guilt, depending on how acceptable behavior is.

**conscientiousness** the care a person gives to organization and thoughtfulness of others; dependability.

**consciousness** a person's awareness of everything that is going on around him or her at any given time.

**conservation** in Piaget's theory, the ability to understand that simply changing the appearance of an object does not change the object's nature.

**consolidation** the changes that take place in the structure and functioning of neurons when a memory is formed.

**constructive processing** referring to the retrieval of memories in which those memories are altered, revised, or influenced by newer information.

**consumer psychology** branch of psychology that studies the habits of consumers in the marketplace.

**contiguity** a Gestalt principle of perception; the tendency to perceive two things that happen close together in time as being related.

**contingency contract** a formal, written agreement between the therapist and client (or teacher and student) in which goals for behavioral change, reinforcements, and penalties are clearly stated.

**continuity** a Gestalt principle of perception; the tendency to perceive things as simply as possible with a continuous pattern rather than with a complex, broken-up pattern.

**continuous reinforcement** the reinforcement of each and every correct response.

**control group** subjects in an experiment who are not subjected to the independent variable and who may receive a placebo treatment.

**conventional morality** second level of Kohlberg's stages of moral development in which the child's behavior is governed by conforming to the society's norms of behavior.

**convergence** binocular depth perception cue; the rotation of the two eyes in their sockets to focus on a single object, resulting in greater convergence for closer objects and lesser convergence if objects are distant.

**convergent thinking** type of thinking in which a problem is seen as having only one answer, and all lines of thinking will eventually lead to that single answer, using previous knowledge and logic.

**coping strategies** actions that people can take to master, tolerate, reduce, or minimize the effects of stressors.

**coronary heart disease (CHD)** the buildup of a waxy substance called plaque in the arteries of the heart.

**corpus callosum** thick band of neurons that connects the right and left cerebral hemispheres.

**correlation** a measure of the relationship between two variables.

**correlation coefficient** a number that represents the strength and direction of a relationship existing between two variables; number derived from the formula for measuring a correlation.

**cortex** outermost covering of the brain consisting of densely packed neurons, responsible for higher thought processes and interpretation of sensory input.

**counseling psychology** area of psychology in which the psychologists help people with problems of adjustment.

**creative intelligence** the ability to deal with new and different concepts and to come up with new ways of solving problems.

**creativity** the process of solving problems by combining ideas or behavior in new ways.

**critical periods** times during which certain environmental influences can have an impact on the development of the infant.

**critical thinking** making reasoned judgments about claims.

**cross-sectional design** research design in which several different participant age groups are studied at one particular point in time.

**cross-sequential design** research design in which participants are first studied by means of a cross-sectional design but are also followed and assessed longitudinally.

**cult** any group of people with a particular religious or philosophical set of beliefs and identity.

**cultural relativity** the need to consider the unique characteristics of the culture in which behavior takes place.

**cultural syndromes** sets of particular symptoms of distress found in particular cultures, which may or may not be recognized as an illness within the culture.

**curve of forgetting** a graph showing a distinct pattern in which forgetting is very fast within the first hour after learning a list and then tapers off gradually.

**cybertherapy** psychotherapy that is offered on the Internet. Also called online, Internet, or Web therapy or counseling.

**dark adaptation** the recovery of the eye's sensitivity to visual stimuli in darkness after exposure to bright lights.

**decay** loss of memory due to the passage of time, during which the memory trace is not used.

**decision making** process of cognition that involves identifying, evaluating, and choosing among several alternatives.

**declarative (explicit) memory** type of long-term memory containing information that is conscious and known.

**deindividuation** the lessening of personal identity, self-restraint, and the sense of personal responsibility that can occur within a group.

**delta waves** long, slow brain waves that indicate the deepest stage of sleep.

**delusions** false beliefs held by a person who refuses to accept evidence of their falseness.

**dendrites** branchlike structures of a neuron that receive messages from other neurons.

**denial** psychological defense mechanism in which the person refuses to acknowledge or recognize a threatening situation.

**dependent variable** variable in an experiment that represents the measurable response or behavior of the subjects in the experiment.

**depressants** drugs that decrease the functioning of the nervous system.

**depth perception** the ability to perceive the world in three dimensions.

**descriptive statistics** a way of organizing numbers and summarizing them so that patterns can be determined.

**developmental psychology** area of psychology in which the psychologists study the changes in the way people think, relate to others, and feel as they age.

**deviation IQ scores** a type of intelligence measure that assumes that IQ is normally distributed around a mean of 100 with a standard deviation of about 15.

**diffusion** process of molecules moving from areas of high concentration to areas of low concentration.

**diffusion of responsibility** occurs when a person fails to take responsibility for actions or for inaction because of the presence of other people who are seen to share the responsibility.

**directive** therapy in which the therapist actively gives interpretations of a client's statements and may suggest certain behavior or actions.

**direct observation** assessment in which the professional observes the client engaged in ordinary, day-to-day behavior in either a clinical or natural setting.

**discrimination** treating people differently because of prejudice toward the social group to which they belong.

**discriminative stimulus** any stimulus, such as a stop sign or a doorknob, that provides the organism with a cue for making a certain response in order to obtain reinforcement.

**displaced aggression** taking out one's frustrations on some less threatening or more available target.

**displacement** redirecting feelings from a threatening target to a less threatening one.

**display rules** learned ways of controlling displays of emotion in social settings.

**dispositional cause** cause of behavior attributed to internal factors such as personality or character.

**dissociation** divided state of conscious awareness.

**dissociative disorders** disorders in which there is a break in conscious awareness, memory, the sense of identity, or some combination.

**dissociative identity disorder (DID)** disorder occurring when a person seems to have two or more distinct personalities within one body.

**distress** the effect of unpleasant and undesirable stressors.

**distributed practice** spacing the study of material to be remembered by including breaks between study periods.

**disuse** another name for decay, assuming that memories that are not used will eventually decay and disappear.

**divergent thinking** type of thinking in which a person starts from one point and comes up with many different ideas or possibilities based on that point.

**dizygotic twins** often called fraternal twins, occurring when two individual eggs get fertilized by separate sperm, resulting in two zygotes in the uterus at the same time.

**DNA (deoxyribonucleic acid)** special molecule that contains the genetic material of the organism.

**dominant** referring to a gene that actively controls the expression of a trait.

**door-in-the-face technique** asking for a large commitment and being refused and then asking for a smaller commitment.

**double approach–avoidance conflict** conflict in which the person must decide between two goals, with each goal possessing both positive and negative aspects.

**double-blind study** study in which neither the experimenter nor the subjects know if the subjects are in the experimental or the control group.

**drive** a psychological tension and physical arousal arising when there is a need that motivates the organism to act in order to fulfill the need and reduce the tension.

**drive-reduction theory** approach to motivation that assumes behavior arises from physiological needs that cause internal drives to push the organism to satisfy the need and reduce tension and arousal.

**drug tolerance** the decrease of the response to a drug over repeated uses, leading to the need for higher doses of drug to achieve the same effect.

**echoic memory** auditory sensory memory, lasting only 2 to 4 seconds.

**eclectic** approach to therapy that results from combining elements of several different approaches or techniques.

**educational psychology** area of psychology in which the psychologists are concerned with the study of human learning and development of new learning techniques.

**efferent (motor) neuron** a neuron that carries messages from the central nervous system to the muscles of the body.

**ego** part of the personality that develops out of a need to deal with reality; mostly conscious, rational, and logical.

**egocentrism** the inability to see the world through anyone else's eyes.

**ego integrity** sense of wholeness that comes from having lived a full life, possessing the ability to let go of regrets; the final completion of the ego.

**eidetic imagery** the ability to access a visual memory for 30 seconds or more.

**elaboration likelihood model** model of persuasion stating that people will either elaborate on the persuasive message or fail to elaborate on it and that the future actions of those who do elaborate are more predictable than those who do not.

**elaborative rehearsal** a way of increasing the number of retrieval cues for information by connecting new information with something that is already well known.

**electroconvulsive therapy (ECT)** form of biomedical therapy to treat severe depression in which electrodes are placed on either one or both sides of a person's head and an electric current is passed through the electrodes that is strong enough to cause a seizure or convulsion.

**electroencephalogram (EEG)** a recording of the electrical activity of large groups of cortical neurons just below the skull, most often using scalp electrodes.

**electroencephalograph** machine designed to record the electroencephalogram.

**embryo** name for the developing organism from 2 weeks to 8 weeks after fertilization.

**embryonic period** the period from 2 to 8 weeks after fertilization, during which the major organs and structures of the organism develop.

**emerging adulthood** a time from late adolescence through the 20s referring to those in who are childless, do not live in their own home, and are not earning enough money to be independent, mainly found in developed countries.

**emotion** the "feeling" aspect of consciousness, characterized by a certain physical arousal, a certain behavior that reveals the emotion to the outside world, and an inner awareness of feelings.

**emotional intelligence** the awareness of and ability to manage one's own emotions to facilitate thinking and attain goals, as well as the ability to understand emotions in others.

**emotion-focused coping** coping strategies that change the impact of a stressor by changing the emotional reaction to the stressor.

**empathy** the ability of the therapist to understand the feelings of the client.

**encoding** the set of mental operations that people perform on sensory information to convert that information into a form that is usable in the brain's storage systems.

**encoding failure** failure to process information into memory.

**encoding specificity** the tendency for memory of information to be improved if related information (such as surroundings or physiological state) that is available when the memory is first formed is also available when the memory is being retrieved.

**endocrine glands** glands that secrete chemicals called hormones directly into the bloodstream.

**environmental psychology** area of psychology in which the focus is on how people interact with and are affected by their physical environments.

**enzymatic degradation** process by which the structure of a neurotransmitter is altered so it can no longer act on a receptor.

**episodic memory** type of declarative memory containing personal information not readily available to others, such as daily activities and events.

**equal status contact** contact between groups in which the groups have equal status with neither group having power over the other.

**escape or withdrawal** leaving the presence of a stressor, either literally or by a psychological withdrawal into fantasy, drug abuse, or apathy.

**estrogens** female hormones.

**eustress** the effect of positive events, or the optimal amount of stress that people need to promote health and well-being.

**evidence-based treatment** also called empirically supported treatment; refers to interventions, strategies, or techniques that have been found to produce therapeutic and desired changes during controlled research studies.

**evolutionary perspective** perspective that focuses on the biological bases of universal mental characteristics that all humans share.

**excitatory synapse** synapse at which a neurotransmitter causes the receiving cell to fire.

**expectancy** a person's subjective feeling that a particular behavior will lead to a reinforcing consequence.

**experiment** a deliberate manipulation of a variable to see if corresponding changes in behavior result, allowing the determination of cause-and-effect relationships.

**experimental group** subjects in an experiment who are subjected to the independent variable.

**experimental psychology** area of psychology in which the psychologists primarily do research and experiments in the areas of learning, memory, thinking, perception, motivation, and language.

**experimenter effect** tendency of the experimenter's expectations for a study to unintentionally influence the results of the study.

**exposure therapies** behavioral techniques that expose individuals to anxiety- or fear-related stimuli under carefully controlled conditions to promote new learning.

**extinction** the disappearance or weakening of a learned response following the removal or absence of the unconditioned stimulus (in classical conditioning) or the removal of a reinforcer (in operant conditioning).

**extraversion** dimension of personality referring to one's need to be with other people.

**extraverts** people who are outgoing and sociable.

**extrinsic motivation** type of motivation in which a person performs an action because it leads to an outcome that is separate from or external to the person.

**facial feedback hypothesis** theory of emotion that assumes that facial expressions provide feedback to the brain concerning the emotion being expressed, which in turn causes and intensifies the emotion.

**family counseling (family therapy)** a form of group therapy in which family members meet together with a counselor or therapist to resolve problems that affect the entire family.

**fertilization** the union of the ovum and sperm.

**fetal alcohol spectrum disorder (FASD)** the physical and mental defects caused by consumption of alcohol during pregnancy.

**fetal period** the time from about 8 weeks after conception until the birth of the baby.

**fetus** name for the developing organism from 8 weeks after fertilization to the birth of the baby.

**figure–ground** the tendency to perceive objects, or figures, as existing on a background.

**five-factor model (Big Five)** model of personality traits that describes five basic trait dimensions.

**fixation** disorder in which the person does not fully resolve the conflict in a particular psychosexual stage, resulting in personality traits and behavior associated with that earlier stage.

**fixed interval schedule of reinforcement** schedule of reinforcement in which the interval of time that must pass before reinforcement becomes possible is always the same.

**fixed ratio schedule of reinforcement** schedule of reinforcement in which the number of responses required for reinforcement is always the same.

**flashbulb memories** type of automatic encoding that occurs because an unexpected event has strong emotional associations for the person remembering it.

**flat affect** a lack of emotional responsiveness.

**flooding** technique for treating phobias and other stress disorders in which the person is rapidly and intensely exposed to the fear-provoking situation or object and prevented from making the usual avoidance or escape response.

**foot-in-the-door technique** asking for a small commitment and, after gaining compliance, asking for a bigger commitment.

**forensic psychology** area of psychology concerned with people in the legal system, including psychological assessment of criminals, jury selection, and expert witnessing.

**formal operations stage** Piaget's last stage of cognitive development, in which the adolescent becomes capable of abstract thinking.

**free association** psychoanalytic technique in which a patient was encouraged to talk about anything that came to mind without fear of negative evaluations.

**free-floating anxiety** anxiety that is unrelated to any specific and known cause.

**frequency count** assessment in which the frequency of a particular behavior is counted.

**frequency distribution** a table or graph that shows how often different numbers or scores appear in a particular set of scores.

**frequency theory** theory of pitch that states that pitch is related to the speed of vibrations in the basilar membrane.

**frontal lobes** areas of the brain located in the front and top, responsible for higher mental processes and decision making as well as the production of fluent speech.

**frustration** the psychological experience produced by the blocking of a desired goal or fulfillment of a perceived need.

**fully functioning person** a person who is in touch with and trusting of the deepest, innermost urges and feelings.

**functional fixedness** a block to problem solving that comes from thinking about objects in terms of only their typical functions.

**functionalism** early perspective in psychology associated with William James, in which the focus of study is how the mind allows people to adapt, live, work, and play.

**functional magnetic resonance imaging (fMRI)** MRI-based brain-imaging method that allows for functional examination of brain areas through changes in brain oxygenation.

**fundamental attribution error** the tendency to overestimate the influence of internal factors in determining behavior while underestimating situational factors.

**gender** the psychological aspects of being male or female.

**gender identity** the individual's sense of being male or female.

**gender roles** the culture's expectations for male or female behavior, including attitudes, actions, and personality traits associated with being male or female in that culture.

**gender schema theory** theory of gender identity acquisition in which a child develops a mental pattern, or schema, for being male or female and then organizes observed and learned behavior around that schema.

**gender stereotype** a concept held about a person or group of people that is based on being male or female.

**gender typing** the process of acquiring gender-role characteristics.

**gene** section of DNA having the same arrangement of chemical elements.

**general adaptation syndrome (GAS)** the three stages of the body's physiological reaction to stress, including alarm, resistance, and exhaustion.

**generalized anxiety disorder** disorder in which a person has feelings of dread and impending doom along with physical symptoms of stress, which lasts 6 months or more.

**generativity** providing guidance to one's children or the next generation, or contributing to the well-being of the next generation through career or volunteer work.

**genetics** the science of inherited traits.

**genital stage** the final stage in Freud's psychosexual stages; from puberty on, sexual urges are allowed back into consciousness and the individual moves toward adult social and sexual behavior.

**germinal period** first 2 weeks after fertilization, during which the zygote moves down to the uterus and begins to implant in the lining.

**Gestalt psychology** early perspective in psychology focusing on perception and sensation, particularly the perception of patterns and whole figures.

**Gestalt therapy** form of directive insight therapy in which the therapist helps clients accept all parts of their feelings and subjective experiences, using leading questions and planned experiences such as role playing.

**g factor** the ability to reason and solve problems, or general intelligence.

**gifted** the 2 percent of the population falling on the upper end of the normal curve and typically possessing an IQ of 130 or above.

**glial cells** cells that provide support for the neurons to grow on and around, deliver nutrients to neurons, produce myelin to coat axons, clean up waste products and dead neurons, influence information processing, and, during prenatal development, influence the generation of new neurons.

**glucagon** hormone that is secreted by the pancreas to control the levels of fats, proteins, and carbohydrates in the body by increasing the level of glucose in the bloodstream.

**gonads** sex glands; secrete hormones that regulate sexual development and behavior as well as reproduction.

**grammar** the system of rules governing the structure and use of a language.

**group polarization** the tendency for members involved in a group discussion to take somewhat more extreme positions and suggest riskier actions when compared to individuals who have not participated in a group discussion.

**group therapy** form of therapy or treatment during which a small group of clients with similar concerns meet together with a therapist to address their issues.

**groupthink** kind of thinking that occurs when people place more importance on maintaining group cohesiveness than on assessing the facts of the problem with which the group is concerned.

**habits** in behaviorism, sets of well-learned responses that have become automatic.

**habituation** tendency of the brain to stop attending to constant, unchanging information.

**hallucinations** false sensory perceptions, such as hearing voices that do not really exist.

**hallucinogenics** drugs including hallucinogens and marijuana that produce hallucinations or increased feelings of relaxation and intoxication.

**hallucinogens** drugs that cause false sensory messages, altering the perception of reality.

**halo effect** tendency of an interviewer to allow positive characteristics of a client to influence the assessments of the client's behavior and statements.

**hardy personality** a person who seems to thrive on stress but lacks the anger and hostility of the Type A personality.

**hassles** the daily annoyances of everyday life.

**health psychology** area of psychology focusing on how physical activities, psychological traits, stress reactions, and social relationships affect overall health and rate of illnesses.

**heritability** degree to which the changes in some trait within a population can be considered to be due to genetic influences; the extent to which individual genetic differences affect individual differences in observed behavior; in IQ, proportion of change in IQ within a population that is caused by hereditary factors.

**heroin** narcotic drug derived from opium that is extremely addictive.

**hertz (Hz)** cycles or waves per second, a measurement of frequency.

**heterosexual** person attracted to the opposite sex.

**heuristic** an educated guess based on prior experiences that helps narrow down the possible solutions for a problem. Also known as a "rule of thumb."

**higher-order conditioning** occurs when a strong conditioned stimulus is paired with a neutral stimulus, causing the neutral stimulus to become a second conditioned stimulus.

**hindsight bias** the tendency to falsely believe, through revision of older memories to include newer information, that one could have correctly predicted the outcome of an event.

**hippocampus** curved structure located within each temporal lobe, responsible for the formation of long-term declarative memories.

**histogram** a bar graph showing a frequency distribution.

**homeopathy** the treatment of disease by introducing minute amounts of substances that would cause disease in larger doses.

**homeostasis** the tendency of the body to maintain a steady state.

**homosexual** person attracted to the same sex.

**hormones** chemicals released into the bloodstream by endocrine glands.

**human development** the scientific study of the changes that occur in people as they age from conception until death.

**human factors psychology** area of industrial/organizational psychology concerned with the study of the way humans and machines interact with each other.

**humanistic perspective** the "third force" in psychology that focuses on those aspects of personality that make people uniquely human, such as subjective feelings and freedom of choice.

**hypnosis** state of consciousness in which the person is especially susceptible to suggestion.

**hypothalamus** small structure in the brain located below the thalamus and directly above the pituitary gland, responsible for motivational behavior such as sleep, hunger, thirst, and sex.

**hypothesis** tentative explanation of a phenomenon based on observations.

**iconic memory** visual sensory memory, lasting only a fraction of a second.

**identification** defense mechanism in which a person tries to become like someone else to deal with anxiety.

**identity versus role confusion** stage of personality development in which the adolescent must find a consistent sense of self.

**id** part of the personality present at birth and completely unconscious.

**imaginary audience** type of thought common to adolescents in which young people believe that other people are just as concerned about the adolescent's thoughts and characteristics as they themselves are.

**immune system** the system of cells, organs, and chemicals of the body that responds to attacks from diseases, infections, and injuries.

**implicit personality theory** sets of assumptions about how different types of people, personality traits, and actions are related to each other.

**impression formation** the forming of the first knowledge that a person has concerning another person.

**incentive approaches** theories of motivation in which behavior is explained as a response to the external stimulus and its rewarding properties.

**incentives** things that attract or lure people into action.

**independent variable** variable in an experiment that is manipulated by the experimenter.

**industrial/organizational (I/O) psychology** area of psychology concerned with the relationships between people and their work environment.

**infantile amnesia** the inability to retrieve memories from much before age 3.

**inferential statistics** statistical analysis of two or more sets of numerical data to reduce the possibility of error in measurement and to determine if the differences between the data sets are greater than chance variation would predict.

**information-processing model** model of memory that assumes the processing of information for memory storage is similar to the way a computer processes memory in a series of three stages.

**in-groups** social groups with whom a person identifies; "us."

**inhibitory synapse** synapse at which a neurotransmitter causes the receiving cell to stop firing.

**insight** the sudden perception of relationships among various parts of a problem, allowing the solution to the problem to come quickly.

**insight therapies** therapies in which the main goal is helping people gain insight with respect to their behavior, thoughts, and feelings.

**insomnia** the inability to get to sleep, stay asleep, or get a good quality of sleep.

**instinctive drift** tendency for an animal's behavior to revert to genetically controlled patterns.

**instincts** the biologically determined and innate patterns of behavior that exist in both people and animals.

**insulin** a hormone secreted by the pancreas to control the levels of fats, proteins, and carbohydrates in the body by reducing the level of glucose in the bloodstream.

**intellectual disability (intellectual developmental disorder)** condition in which a person's behavioral and cognitive skills exist at an earlier developmental stage than the skills of others who are the same chronological age; may also be referred to as developmentally delayed. This condition was formerly known as mental retardation.

**intelligence** the ability to learn from one's experiences, acquire knowledge, and use resources effectively in adapting to new situations or solving problems.

**intelligence quotient (IQ)** a number representing a measure of intelligence, resulting from the division of one's mental age by one's chronological age and then multiplying that quotient by 100.

**interneuron** a neuron found in the center of the spinal cord that receives information from the afferent neurons and sends commands to the muscles through the efferent neurons. Interneurons also make up the bulk of the neurons in the brain.

**interpersonal attraction** liking or having the desire for a relationship with another person.

**interpersonal therapy (IPT)** form of therapy for depression that incorporates multiple approaches and focuses on interpersonal problems.

**intersexed, intersexual** modern term for a hermaphrodite, a person who possesses ambiguous sexual organs, making it difficult to determine actual sex from a visual inspection at birth.

**interview** method of personality assessment in which the professional asks questions of the client and allows the client to answer, in either a structured or unstructured fashion.

**intimacy** an emotional and psychological closeness that is based on the ability to trust, share, and care, while still maintaining a sense of self.

**intrinsic motivation** type of motivation in which a person performs an action because the act itself is rewarding or satisfying in some internal manner.

**introversion** dimension of personality in which people tend to withdraw from excessive stimulation.

**introverts** people who prefer solitude and dislike being the center of attention.

**irreversibility** in Piaget's theory, the inability of the young child to mentally reverse an action.

**James-Lange theory of emotion** theory in which a physiological reaction leads to the labeling of an emotion.

**"jigsaw classroom"** educational technique in which each individual is given only part of the information needed to solve a problem, causing the separate individuals to be forced to work together to find the solution.

**just noticeable difference (jnd or the difference threshold)** the smallest difference between two stimuli that is detectable 50 percent of the time.

**kinesthesia** the awareness of body movement.

**language** a system for combining symbols (such as words) so that an unlimited number of meaningful statements can be made for the purpose of communicating with others.

**latency** the fourth stage in Freud's psychosexual stages, occurring during the school years, in which the sexual feelings of the child are repressed while the child develops in other ways.

**latent content** the symbolic or hidden meaning of dreams.

**latent learning** learning that remains hidden until its application becomes useful.

**law of effect** law stating that if an action is followed by a pleasurable consequence, it will tend to be repeated, and if followed by an unpleasant consequence, it will tend not to be repeated.

**learned helplessness** the tendency to fail to act to escape from a situation because of a history of repeated failures in the past.

**learning** any relatively permanent change in behavior brought about by experience or practice.

**learning/performance distinction** referring to the observation that learning can take place without actual performance of the learned behavior.

**leptin** a hormone that, when released into the bloodstream, signals the hypothalamus that the body has had enough food and reduces the appetite while increasing the feeling of being full.

**lesioning** insertion of a thin, insulated electrode into the brain through which an electrical current is sent, destroying the brain cells at the tip of the wire.

**levels-of-processing model** model of memory that assumes information that is more "deeply processed," or processed according to its meaning rather than just the sound or physical characteristics of the word or words, will be remembered more efficiently and for a longer period of time.

**light adaptation** the recovery of the eye's sensitivity to visual stimuli in light after exposure to darkness.

**limbic system** a group of several brain structures located primarily under the cortex and involved in learning, emotion, memory, and motivation.

**linear perspective** monocular depth perception cue; the tendency for parallel lines to appear to converge on each other.

**linguistic relativity hypothesis** the theory that thought processes and concepts are controlled by language.

**locus of control** the tendency for people to assume that they either have control or do not have control over events and consequences in their lives.

**longitudinal design** research design in which one participant or group of participants is studied over a long period of time.

**long-term memory (LTM)** the system of memory into which all the information is placed to be kept more or less permanently.

**lowball technique** getting a commitment from a person and then raising the cost of that commitment.

**LSD (lysergic acid diethylamide)** powerful synthetic hallucinogen.

**magnetic resonance imaging (MRI)** brain-imaging method using radio waves and magnetic fields of the body to produce detailed images of the brain.

**magnification** the tendency to interpret situations as far more dangerous, harmful, or important than they actually are.

**magnification and minimization** distortions of thinking in which a person blows a negative event out of proportion to its importance (magnification) while ignoring relevant positive events (minimization).

**maintenance rehearsal** practice of saying some information to be remembered over and over in one's head in order to maintain it in short-term memory.

**major depressive disorder** severe depression that comes on suddenly and seems to have no external cause, or is too severe for current circumstances.

**maladaptive** anything that does not allow a person to function within or adapt to the stresses and everyday demands of life.

**mammary glands** glands within the breast tissue that produce milk when a woman gives birth to an infant.

**manic** having the quality of excessive excitement, energy, and elation or irritability.

**marijuana** mild hallucinogen (also known as "pot" or "weed") derived from the leaves and flowers of a particular type of hemp plant.

**MDMA (Ecstasy or X)** designer drug that can have both stimulant and hallucinatory effects.

**mean** the arithmetic average of a distribution of numbers.

**measure of central tendency** numbers that best represent the most typical score of a frequency distribution.

**measures of variability** measurement of the degree of differences within a distribution or how the scores are spread out.

**median** the middle score in an ordered distribution of scores, or the mean of the two middle numbers; the 50th percentile.

**meditation** mental series of exercises meant to refocus attention and achieve a trancelike state of consciousness.

**medulla** the first large swelling at the top of the spinal cord, forming the lowest part of the brain, which is responsible for life-sustaining functions such as breathing, swallowing, and heart rate.

**memory** an active system that receives information from the senses, puts that information into a usable form, and organizes it as it stores it away, and then retrieves the information from storage.

**memory trace** physical change in the brain that occurs when a memory is formed.

**menarche** the first menstrual cycle, the monthly shedding of the blood and tissue that line the uterus in preparation for pregnancy when conception does not occur.

**menopause** the cessation of ovulation and menstrual cycles and the end of a woman's reproductive capability.

**mental images** mental representations that stand for objects or events and have a picturelike quality.

**mental set** the tendency for people to persist in using problem-solving patterns that have worked for them in the past.

**microsleeps** brief sidesteps into sleep lasting only a few seconds.

**mindfulness meditation** a form of concentrative meditation in which the person purposefully pays attention to the present moment, without judgment or evaluation.

**minimization** the tendency to give little or no importance to one's successes or positive events and traits.

**mirror neurons** neurons that fire when an animal or person performs an action and also when an animal or person observes that same action being performed by another.

**misinformation effect** the tendency of misleading information presented after an event to alter the memories of the event itself.

**mode** the most frequent score in a distribution of scores.

**modeling** learning through the observation and imitation of others.

**monocular cues (pictorial depth cues)** cues for perceiving depth based on one eye only.

**monozygotic twins** identical twins formed when one zygote splits into two separate masses of cells, each of which develops into a separate embryo.

**mood disorders** disorders in which mood is severely disturbed.

**morphemes** the smallest units of meaning within a language.

**morphine** narcotic drug derived from opium, used to treat severe pain.

**motion parallax** monocular depth perception cue; the perception of motion of objects in which close objects appear to move more quickly than objects that are farther away.

**motivation** the process by which activities are started, directed, and continued so that physical or psychological needs or wants are met.

**motor cortex** rear section of the frontal lobe, responsible for sending motor commands to the muscles of the somatic nervous system.

**motor pathway** nerves coming from the CNS to the voluntary muscles, consisting of efferent neurons.

**Müller-Lyer illusion** illusion of line length that is distorted by inward-turning or outward-turning corners on the ends of the lines, causing lines of equal length to appear to be different.

**multiple approach-avoidance conflict** conflict in which the person must decide between more than two goals, with each goal possessing both positive and negative aspects.

**myelin** fatty substances produced by certain glial cells that coat the axons of neurons to insulate, protect, and speed up the neural impulse.

**narcolepsy** sleep disorder in which a person falls immediately into REM sleep during the day without warning.

**natural killer (NK) cell** immune-system cell responsible for suppressing viruses and destroying tumor cells.

**nature** the influence of our inherited characteristics on our personality, physical growth, intellectual growth, and social interactions.

**need** a requirement of some material (such as food or water) that is essential for survival of the organism.

**need for achievement (nAch)** a need that involves a strong desire to succeed in attaining goals, not only realistic ones but also challenging ones.

**need for affiliation (nAff)** the need for friendly social interactions and relationships with others.

**need for power (nPow)** the need to have control or influence over others.

**negatively skewed** a distribution of scores in which scores are concentrated in the high end of the distribution.

**negative reinforcement** the reinforcement of a response by the removal, escape from, or avoidance of an unpleasant stimulus.

**negative symptoms** symptoms of schizophrenia that are less than normal behavior or an absence of normal behavior; poor attention, flat affect, and poor speech production.

**neo-Freudians** followers of Freud who developed their own competing psychodynamic theories.

**nerves** bundles of axons coated in myelin that travel together through the body.

**nervous system** an extensive network of specialized cells that carries information to and from all parts of the body.

**neurofeedback** form of biofeedback using brain-scanning devices to provide feedback about brain activity in an effort to modify behavior.

**neuron** the basic cell that makes up the nervous system and that receives and sends messages within that system.

**neuroplasticity** the ability within the brain to constantly change both the structure and function of many cells in response to experience or trauma.

**neuropsychology** area of psychology in which psychologists specialize in the research or clinical implications of brain–behavior relationships.

**neuroscience** a branch of the life sciences that deals with the structure and function of neurons, nerves, and nervous tissue.

**neuroticism** degree of emotional instability or stability.

**neurotic personalities** personalities typified by maladaptive ways of dealing with relationships in Horney's theory.

**neurotransmitter** chemical found in the synaptic vesicles that, when released, has an effect on the next cell.

**neutral stimulus (NS)** in classical conditioning, a stimulus that has no effect on the desired response prior to conditioning.

**nicotine** the active ingredient in tobacco.

**nightmares** bad dreams occurring during REM sleep.

**night terrors** relatively rare disorder in which the person experiences extreme fear and screams or runs around during deep sleep without waking fully.

**nondeclarative (implicit) memory** type of long-term memory including memory for skills, procedures, habits, and conditioned responses. These memories are not conscious but are implied to exist because they affect conscious behavior.

**nondirective** therapy style in which the therapist remains relatively neutral and does not interpret or take direct actions with regard to the client, instead remaining a calm, nonjudgmental listener while the client talks.

**non-REM (NREM) sleep** any of the stages of sleep that do not include REM.

**normal curve** a special frequency polygon, shaped like a bell, in which the scores are symmetrically distributed around the mean, and the mean, median, and mode are all located on the same point on the curve, with scores decreasing as the curve extends from the mean.

**nurture** the influence of the environment on personality, physical growth, intellectual growth, and social interactions.

**obedience** changing one's behavior at the command of an authority figure.

**objective introspection** the process of examining and measuring one's own thoughts and mental activities.

**object permanence** the knowledge that an object exists even when it is not in sight.

**observational learning** learning new behavior by watching a model perform that behavior.

**observer bias** tendency of observers to see what they expect to see.

**observer effect** tendency of people or animals to behave differently from normal when they know they are being observed.

**obsessive-compulsive disorder** disorder in which intruding, recurring thoughts or obsessions create anxiety that is relieved by performing a repetitive, ritualistic behavior or mental act (compulsion).

**occipital lobe** section of the brain located at the rear and bottom of each cerebral hemisphere containing the primary visual centers of the brain.

**Oedipus complex/Electra complex** situation occurring in the phallic stage in which a child develops a sexual attraction to the opposite-sex parent and jealousy of the same-sex parent. Males develop an Oedipus complex, whereas females develop an Electra complex.

**olfaction (olfactory sense)** the sensation of smell.

**olfactory bulbs** two bulb-like projections of the brain located just above the sinus cavity and just below the frontal lobes that receive information from the olfactory receptor cells.

**openness** one of the five factors; willingness to try new things and be open to new experiences.

**operant** any behavior that is voluntary and not elicited by specific stimuli.

**operant conditioning** the learning of voluntary behavior through the effects of pleasant and unpleasant consequences to responses.

**operationalization** specific description of a variable of interest that allows it to be measured.

**opiates** a class of opium-related drugs that suppress the sensation of pain by binding to and stimulating the nervous system's natural receptor sites for endorphins.

**opium** substance derived from the opium poppy from which all narcotic drugs are derived.

**opponent-process theory** theory of color vision that proposes visual neurons (or groups of neurons) are stimulated by light of one color and inhibited by light of another color.

**optimists** people who expect positive outcomes.

**oral stage** the first stage in Freud's psychosexual stages, occurring in the first 18 months of life, in which the mouth is the erogenous zone and weaning is the primary conflict.

**orgasm** a series of rhythmic contractions of the muscles of the vaginal walls or the penis; also the third and shortest phase of sexual response.

**out-groups** social groups with whom a person does not identify; "them."

**ovaries** the female gonads or sex glands.

**overgeneralization** distortion of thinking in which a person draws sweeping conclusions based on only one incident or event and applies those conclusions to events that are unrelated to the original; the tendency to interpret a single negative event as a never-ending pattern of defeat and failure.

**overlap (interposition)** monocular depth perception cue; the assumption that an object that appears to be blocking part of another object is in front of the second object and closer to the viewer.

**ovum** the female sex cell, or egg.

**oxytocin** hormone released by the posterior pituitary gland that is involved in reproductive and parental behaviors.

**pancreas** endocrine gland; controls the levels of sugar in the blood.

**panic attack** sudden onset of intense panic in which multiple physical symptoms of stress occur, often with feelings that one is dying.

**panic disorder** disorder in which panic attacks occur more than once or repeatedly and cause persistent worry or changes in behavior.

**parallel distributed processing (PDP) model** a model of memory in which memory processes are proposed to take place at the same time over a large network of neural connections.

**parasympathetic division (eat-drink-and-rest system)** part of the ANS that restores the body to normal functioning after arousal and is responsible for the day-to-day functioning of the organs and glands.

**parietal lobes** sections of the brain located at the top and back of each cerebral hemisphere containing the centers for touch, temperature, and body position.

**partial reinforcement effect** the tendency for a response that is reinforced after some, but not all, correct responses to be very resistant to extinction.

**participant modeling** technique in which a model demonstrates the desired behavior in a step-by-step, gradual process while the client is encouraged to imitate the model.

**participant observation** a naturalistic observation in which the observer becomes a participant in the group being observed.

**PCP** synthesized drug now used as an animal tranquilizer that can cause stimulant, depressant, narcotic, or hallucinogenic effects.

**peak experiences** according to Maslow, times in a person's life during which self-actualization is temporarily achieved.

**penis** the organ through which males urinate and which delivers the male sex cells or sperm.

**perception** the method by which the sensations experienced at any given moment are interpreted and organized in some meaningful fashion.

**perceptual set (perceptual expectancy)** the tendency to perceive things a certain way because previous experiences or expectations influence those perceptions.

**peripheral nervous system (PNS)** all nerves and neurons that are not contained in the brain and spinal cord but that run through the body itself.

**peripheral-route processing** type of information processing that involves attending to factors not involved in the message, such as the appearance of the source of the message, the length of the message, and other noncontent factors.

**permissive indulgent** permissive parenting in which parent is so involved that children are allowed to behave without set limits.

**permissive neglectful** permissive parenting in which parent is uninvolved with child or child's behavior.

**permissive parenting** style of parenting in which parent makes few, if any, demands on a child's behavior.

**personal fable** type of thought common to adolescents in which young people believe themselves to be unique and protected from harm.

**personality** the unique and relatively stable ways in which people think, feel, and behave.

**personality disorders** disorders in which a person adopts a persistent, rigid, and maladaptive pattern of behavior that interferes with normal social interactions.

**personality inventory** paper-and-pencil or computerized test that consists of statements that require a specific, standardized response from the person taking the test.

**personality psychology** area of psychology in which the psychologists study the differences in personality among people.

**personalization** distortion of thinking in which a person takes responsibility or blame for events that are unconnected to the person.

**personal unconscious** Jung's name for the unconscious mind as described by Freud.

**person-centered therapy** a nondirective insight therapy based on the work of Carl Rogers in which the client does all the talking and the therapist listens.

**persuasion** the process by which one person tries to change the belief, opinion, position, or course of action of another person through argument, pleading, or explanation.

**phallic stage** the third stage in Freud's psychosexual stages, occurring from about 3 to 6 years of age, in which the child discovers sexual feelings.

**phobia** an irrational, persistent fear of an object, situation, or social activity.

**phonemes** the basic units of sound in language.

**physical dependence** condition occurring when a person's body becomes unable to function normally without a particular drug.

**physiological psychology** area of psychology in which the psychologists study the biological bases of behavior.

**pineal gland** endocrine gland located near the base of the cerebrum; secretes melatonin.

**pinna** the visible part of the ear.

**pitch** psychological experience of sound that corresponds to the frequency of the sound waves; higher frequencies are perceived as higher pitches.

**pituitary gland** gland located in the brain that secretes human growth hormone and influences all other hormone-secreting glands (also known as the master gland).

**placebo effect** the phenomenon in which the expectations of the participants in a study can influence their behavior.

**place theory** theory of pitch that states that different pitches are experienced by the stimulation of hair cells in different locations on the organ of Corti.

**pleasure principle** principle by which the id functions; the desire for the immediate satisfaction of needs without regard for the consequences.

**polygon** line graph showing a frequency distribution.

**pons** the larger swelling above the medulla that relays information from the cortex to the cerebellum, and that plays a part in sleep, dreaming, left–right body coordination, and arousal.

**population** the entire group of people or animals in which the researcher is interested.

**positively skewed** a distribution of scores in which scores are concentrated in the low end of the distribution.

**positive regard** warmth, affection, love, and respect that come from significant others in one's life.

**positive reinforcement** the reinforcement of a response by the addition or experiencing of a pleasurable stimulus.

**positive symptoms** symptoms of schizophrenia that are excesses of behavior or occur in addition to normal behavior; hallucinations, delusions, and distorted thinking.

**positron emission tomography (PET)** brain-imaging method in which a radioactive sugar is injected into the subject and a computer compiles a color-coded image of the activity of the brain.

**postconventional morality** third level of Kohlberg's stages of moral development in which the person's behavior is governed by moral principles that have been decided on by the individual and that may be in disagreement with accepted social norms.

**posttraumatic stress disorder (PTSD)** a disorder resulting from exposure to a major stressor, with symptoms of anxiety, dissociation, nightmares, poor sleep, reliving the event, and concentration problems, lasting for more than 1 month; symptoms may appear immediately or not occur until 6 months or later after the traumatic event.

**practical intelligence** the ability to use information to get along in life and become successful.

**pragmatics** aspects of language involving the practical ways of communicating with others, or the social "niceties" of language.

**preconventional morality** first level of Kohlberg's stages of moral development, in which the child's behavior is governed by the consequences of the behavior.

**prefrontal lobotomy** psychosurgery in which the connections of the prefrontal cortex to other areas of the brain are severed.

**prejudice** negative attitude held by a person about the members of a particular social group.

**preoperational stage** Piaget's second stage of cognitive development, in which the preschool child learns to use language as a means of exploring the world.

**pressure** the psychological experience produced by urgent demands or expectations for a person's behavior that come from an outside source.

**primacy effect** tendency to remember information at the beginning of a body of information better than the information that follows.

**primary appraisal** the first step in assessing stress, which involves estimating the severity of a stressor and classifying it as either a threat or a challenge.

**primary drives** those drives that involve needs of the body such as hunger and thirst.

**primary reinforcer** any reinforcer that is naturally reinforcing by meeting a basic biological need, such as hunger, thirst, or touch.

**primary sex characteristics** sexual organs present at birth and directly involved in human reproduction.

**proactive interference** memory problem that occurs when older information prevents or interferes with the learning or retrieval of newer information.

**problem-focused coping** coping strategies that try to eliminate the source of a stress or reduce its impact through direct actions.

**problem solving** process of cognition that occurs when a goal must be reached by thinking and behaving in certain ways.

**projection** psychological defense mechanism in which unacceptable or threatening impulses or feelings are seen as originating with someone else, usually the target of the impulses or feelings.

**projective tests** personality assessments that present ambiguous visual stimuli to the client and ask the client to respond with whatever comes to mind.

**proprioception** awareness of where the body and body parts are located in relation to each other in space and to the ground.

**prosocial behavior** socially desirable behavior that benefits others.

**prostate gland** gland that secretes most of the fluid holding the male sex cells or sperm.

**prototype** an example of a concept that closely matches the defining characteristics of the concept.

**proximity** a Gestalt principle of perception; the tendency to perceive objects that are close to each other as part of the same grouping; physical or geographical nearness.

**psychiatric social worker** a social worker with some training in therapy methods who focuses on the environmental conditions that can have an impact on mental disorders, such as poverty, overcrowding, stress, and drug abuse.

**psychiatrist** a physician who specializes in the diagnosis and treatment of psychological disorders.

**psychoactive drugs** chemical substances that alter thinking, perception, and memory.

**psychoanalysis** an insight therapy based on the theory of Freud, emphasizing the revealing of unconscious conflicts; Freud's term for both the theory of personality and the therapy based on it.

**psychodynamic perspective** modern version of psychoanalysis that is more focused on the development of a sense of self and the discovery of motivations behind a person's behavior other than sexual motivations.

**psychodynamic therapy** a newer and more general term for therapies based on psychoanalysis with an emphasis on transference, shorter treatment times, and a more direct therapeutic approach.

**psychological defense mechanisms** unconscious distortions of a person's perception of reality that reduce stress and anxiety.

**psychological dependence** the feeling that a drug is needed to continue a feeling of emotional or psychological well-being.

**psychological disorder** any pattern of behavior or thinking that causes people significant distress, causes them to harm others, or harms their ability to function in daily life.

**psychologist** a professional with an academic degree and specialized training in one or more areas of psychology.

**psychology** scientific study of behavior and mental processes.

**psychoneuroimmunology** the study of the effects of psychological factors such as stress, emotions, thoughts, and behavior on the immune system.

**psychopathology** the study of abnormal behavior and psychological dysfunction.

**psychopharmacology** the use of drugs to control or relieve the symptoms of psychological disorders.

**psychosexual stages** five stages of personality development proposed by Freud and tied to the sexual development of the child.

**psychosurgery** surgery performed on brain tissue to relieve or control severe psychological disorders.

**psychotherapy** therapy for mental disorders in which a person with a problem talks with a psychological professional.

**psychotic** refers to an individual's inability to separate what is real and what is fantasy.

**puberty** the physical changes that occur in the body as sexual development reaches its peak.

**punishment** any event or object that, when following a response, makes that response less likely to happen again.

**punishment by application** the punishment of a response by the addition or experiencing of an unpleasant stimulus.

**punishment by removal** the punishment of a response by the removal of a pleasurable stimulus.

**random assignment** process of assigning subjects to the experimental or control groups randomly, so that each subject has an equal chance of being in either group.

**range** the difference between the highest and lowest scores in a distribution.

**rapid eye movement (REM) sleep** stage of sleep in which the eyes move rapidly under the eyelids and the person is typically experiencing a dream.

**rating scale** assessment in which a numerical value is assigned to specific behavior that is listed in the scale.

**rational emotive behavior therapy (REBT)** cognitive behavioral therapy in which clients are directly challenged in their irrational beliefs and helped to restructure their thinking into more rational belief statements.

**rationalization** psychological defense mechanism in which a person invents acceptable excuses for unacceptable behavior.

**reaction formation** psychological defense mechanism in which a person forms an opposite emotional or behavioral reaction to the way he or she really feels to keep those true feelings hidden from self and others.

**realistic conflict theory** theory stating that prejudice and discrimination will be increased between groups that are in conflict over a limited resource.

**reality principle** principle by which the ego functions; the satisfaction of the demands of the id only when negative consequences will not result.

**recall** type of memory retrieval in which the information to be retrieved must be "pulled" from memory with very few external cues.

**recency effect** tendency to remember information at the end of a body of information better than the information that precedes it.

**receptor sites** three-dimensional proteins on the surface of the dendrites or certain cells of the muscles and glands, which are shaped to fit only certain neurotransmitters.

**recessive** referring to a gene that only influences the expression of a trait when paired with an identical gene.

**reciprocal determinism** Bandura's explanation of how the factors of environment, personal characteristics, and behavior can interact to determine future behavior.

**reciprocity of liking** tendency of people to like other people who like them in return.

**recognition** the ability to match a piece of information or a stimulus to a stored image or fact.

**reflection** therapy technique in which the therapist restates what the client says rather than interpreting those statements.

**reflex** an involuntary response, one that is not under personal control or choice.

**reflex arc** the connection of the afferent neurons to the interneurons to the efferent neurons, resulting in a reflex action.

**refractory period** time period in males just after orgasm in which the male cannot become aroused to another orgasm.

**regression** psychological defense mechanism in which a person falls back on childlike patterns of responding in reaction to stressful situations.

**reinforcement** any event or stimulus that, when following a response, increases the probability that the response will occur again.

**reinforcers** any events or objects that, when following a response, increase the likelihood of that response occurring again.

**relative size** monocular depth perception cue; perception that occurs when objects that a person expects to be of a certain size appear to be small and are, therefore, assumed to be much farther away.

**reliability** the tendency of a test to produce the same scores again and again each time it is given to the same people.

**REM behavior disorder** a rare disorder in which the mechanism that blocks the movement of the voluntary muscles fails, allowing the person to thrash around and even get up and act out nightmares.

**REM rebound** increased amounts of REM sleep after being deprived of REM sleep on earlier nights.

**replicate** in research, repeating a study or experiment to see if the same results will be obtained in an effort to demonstrate reliability of results.

**representativeness heuristic** assumption that any object (or person) sharing characteristics with the members of a particular category is also a member of that category.

**representative sample** randomly selected sample of subjects from a larger population of subjects.

**repression** psychological defense mechanism in which the person refuses to consciously remember a threatening or unacceptable event, instead pushing those events into the unconscious mind.

**resistance** occurring when a patient becomes reluctant to talk about a certain topic by either changing the subject or becoming silent.

**resolution** the final phase of the sexual response in which the body is returned to a normal state.

**resting potential** the state of the neuron when not firing a neural impulse.

**restorative theory** theory of sleep proposing that sleep is necessary to the physical health of the body and serves to replenish chemicals and repair cellular damage.

**reticular formation (RF)** an area of neurons running through the middle of the medulla and the pons and slightly beyond that is responsible for general attention, alertness, and arousal.

**retrieval** getting information that is in storage into a form that can be used.

**retrieval cue** a stimulus for remembering.

**retroactive interference** memory problem that occurs when newer information prevents or interferes with the retrieval of older information.

**retrograde amnesia** loss of memory from the point of some injury or trauma backward, or loss of memory for the past.

**reuptake** process by which neurotransmitters are taken back into the synaptic vesicles.

**reversible figures** visual illusions in which the figure and ground can be reversed.

**rods** visual sensory receptors found at the back of the retina, responsible for noncolor sensitivity to low levels of light.

**romantic love** type of love consisting of intimacy and passion.

**Rorschach inkblot test** projective test that uses 10 inkblots as the ambiguous stimuli.

**sample** group of subjects selected from a larger population of subjects, usually selected randomly.

**scaffolding** process in which a more skilled learner gives help to a less skilled learner, reducing the amount of help as the less skilled learner becomes more capable.

**scheme** in this case, a mental concept formed through experiences with objects and events.

**schizophrenia** severe disorder in which the person suffers from disordered thinking, bizarre behavior, hallucinations, and inability to distinguish between fantasy and reality.

**school psychology** area of psychology in which the psychologists work directly in the schools, doing assessments, educational placement, and diagnosing educational problems.

**scientific approach** system of gathering data so that bias and error in measurement are reduced.

**scrotum** external sac that holds the testes.

**secondary appraisal** the second step in assessing a stressor, which involves estimating the resources available to the person for coping with the threat.

**secondary reinforcer** any reinforcer that becomes reinforcing after being paired with a primary reinforcer, such as praise, tokens, or gold stars.

**secondary sex characteristics** sexual organs and traits that develop at puberty and are indirectly involved in human reproduction.

**selective attention** the ability to focus on only one stimulus from among all sensory input.

**selective thinking** distortion of thinking in which a person focuses on only one aspect of a situation while ignoring all other relevant aspects.

**self** an individual's awareness of his or her own personal characteristics and level of functioning.

**self-actualization** according to Maslow, the point that is seldom reached at which people have sufficiently satisfied the lower needs and achieved their full human potential.

**self-actualizing tendency** the striving to fulfill one's innate capacities and capabilities.

**self-concept** the image of oneself that develops from interactions with important significant people in one's life.

**self-determination theory (SDT)** theory of human motivation in which the social context of an action has an effect on the type of motivation existing for the action.

**self-efficacy** individual's expectancy of how effective his or her efforts to accomplish a goal will be in any particular circumstance.

**self-fulfilling prophecy** the tendency of one's expectations to affect one's behavior in such a way as to make the expectations more likely to occur.

**self-help groups (support groups)** a group composed of people who have similar problems and who meet together without a therapist or counselor for the purpose of discussion, problem solving, and social and emotional support.

**semantic memory** type of declarative memory containing general knowledge, such as knowledge of language and information learned in formal education.

**semantic network model** model of memory organization that assumes information is stored in the brain in a connected fashion, with concepts that are related stored physically closer to each other than concepts that are not highly related.

**semantics** the rules for determining the meaning of words and sentences.

**semen** fluid released from the penis at orgasm that contains the sperm.

**sensation** the process that occurs when special receptors in the sense organs are activated, allowing various forms of outside stimuli to become neural signals in the brain.

**sensation seeker** someone who needs more arousal than the average person.

**sensorimotor stage** Piaget's first stage of cognitive development, in which the infant uses its senses and motor abilities to interact with objects in the environment.

**sensory adaptation** tendency of sensory receptor cells to become less responsive to a stimulus that is unchanging.

**sensory conflict theory** an explanation of motion sickness in which the information from the eyes conflicts with the information from the vestibular senses, resulting in dizziness, nausea, and other physical discomfort.

**sensory memory** the very first system in memory, in which raw information from the senses is held for a very brief period of time.

**sensory pathway** nerves coming from the sensory organs to the CNS consisting of afferent neurons.

**serial position effect** tendency of information at the beginning and end of a body of information to be remembered more accurately than information in the middle of the body of information.

**sexism** prejudice about males and/or females leading to unequal treatment.

**sexual dysfunction** a problem in sexual functioning.

**sexually transmitted infection (STI)** an infection spread primarily through sexual contact.

**sexual orientation** a person's sexual attraction to and affection for members of either the opposite or the same sex.

**s factor** the ability to excel in certain areas, or specific intelligence.

**shape constancy** the tendency to interpret the shape of an object as being constant, even when its shape changes on the retina.

**shaping** the reinforcement of simple steps in behavior through successive approximations that lead to a desired, more complex behavior.

**short-term memory (STM)** the memory system in which information is held for brief periods of time while being used.

**significant difference** a difference between groups of numerical data that is considered large enough to be due to factors other than chance variation.

**similarity** a Gestalt principle of perception; the tendency to perceive things that look similar to each other as being part of the same group.

**single-blind study** study in which the subjects do not know if they are in the experimental or the control group.

**situational cause** cause of behavior attributed to external factors, such as delays, the action of others, or some other aspect of the situation.

**situational context** the social or environmental setting of a person's behavior.

**size constancy** the tendency to interpret an object as always being the same actual size, regardless of its distance.

**skewed distribution** frequency distribution in which most of the scores fall to one side or the other of the distribution.

**skin senses** the sensations of touch, pressure, temperature, and pain.

**sleep apnea** disorder in which the person stops breathing for 10 seconds or more.

**sleep deprivation** any significant loss of sleep, resulting in problems in concentration and irritability.

**sleep paralysis** the inability of the voluntary muscles to move during REM sleep.

**sleepwalking (somnambulism)** occurring during deep sleep, an episode of moving around or walking around in one's sleep.

**social anxiety disorder (social phobia)** fear of interacting with others or being in social situations that might lead to a negative evaluation.

**social categorization** the assignment of a person one has just met to a category based on characteristics the new person has in common with other people with whom one has had experience in the past.

**social cognition** the mental processes that people use to make sense of the social world around them.

**social cognitive theory** referring to the use of cognitive processes in relation to understanding the social world.

**social cognitive theory of hypnosis** theory that assumes that people who are hypnotized are not in an altered state but are merely playing the role expected of them in the situation.

**social cognitive view** learning theory that includes cognitive processes such as anticipating, judging, memory, and imitation of models.

**social comparison** the comparison of oneself to others in ways that raise one's self-esteem.

**social facilitation** the tendency for the presence of other people to have a positive impact on the performance of an easy task.

**social identity** the part of the self-concept including one's view of self as a member of a particular social category.

**social identity theory** theory in which the formation of a person's identity within a particular social group is explained by social categorization, social identity, and social comparison.

**social impairment** the tendency for the presence of other people to have a negative impact on the performance of a difficult task.

**social influence** the process through which the real or implied presence of others can directly or indirectly influence the thoughts, feelings, and behavior of an individual.

**social loafing** the tendency for people to put less effort into a simple task when working with others on that task.

**social neuroscience** the study of the relationship between biological systems and social processes and behavior.

**social psychology** the scientific study of how a person's thoughts, feelings, and behavior influence and are influenced by social groups; area of psychology in which psychologists focus on how human behavior is affected by the presence of other people.

**Social Readjustment Rating Scale (SRRS)** assessment that measures the amount of stress in a person's life over a 1-year period resulting from major life events.

**social role** the pattern of behavior that is expected of a person who is in a particular social position.

**social-support system** the network of family, friends, neighbors, coworkers, and others who can offer support, comfort, or aid to a person in need.

**sociocultural perspective** perspective that focuses on the relationship between social behavior and culture; in psychopathology, perspective in which abnormal thinking and behavior (as well as normal) is seen as the product of learning and shaping within the context of the family, the social group to which one belongs, and the culture within which the family and social group exist.

**soma** the cell body of the neuron responsible for maintaining the life of the cell.

**somatic nervous system** division of the PNS consisting of nerves that carry information from the senses to the CNS and from the CNS to the voluntary muscles of the body.

**somatosensory cortex** area of cortex at the front of the parietal lobes responsible for processing information from the skin and internal body receptors for touch, temperature, and body position.

**somesthetic senses** the body senses consisting of the skin senses, the kinesthetic and proprioceptive senses, and the vestibular senses.

**source traits** the more basic traits that underlie the surface traits, forming the core of personality.

**spatial neglect** condition produced most often by damage to the parietal lobe association areas of the right hemisphere, resulting in an inability to recognize objects or body parts in the left visual field.

**specific phobia** fear of objects or specific situations or events.

**spinal cord** a long bundle of neurons that carries messages between the body and the brain and is responsible for very fast, lifesaving reflexes.

**spontaneous recovery** the reappearance of a learned response after extinction has occurred.

**sports psychology** area of psychology in which the psychologists help athletes and others prepare themselves mentally for participation in sports activities.

**standard deviation** the square root of the average squared deviations from the mean of scores in a distribution; a measure of variability.

**statistically significant** referring to differences in data sets that are larger than chance variation would predict.

**statistics** branch of mathematics concerned with the collection and interpretation of numerical data.

**stem cells** special cells found in all the tissues of the body that are capable of becoming other cell types when those cells need to be replaced due to damage or wear and tear.

**stereotype** a set of characteristics that people believe is shared by all members of a particular social category; a concept held about a person or group of people that is based on superficial, irrelevant characteristics.

**stereotype threat** condition in which being made aware of a negative performance stereotype interferes with the performance of someone that considers himself or herself part of that group.

**stereotype vulnerability** the effect that people's awareness of the stereotypes associated with their social group has on their behavior.

**stimulants** drugs that increase the functioning of the nervous system.

**stimulatory hallucinogenics** drugs that produce a mixture of psychomotor stimulant and hallucinogenic effects.

**stimulus discrimination** the tendency to stop making a generalized response to a stimulus that is similar to the original conditioned stimulus because the similar stimulus is never paired with the unconditioned stimulus.

**stimulus generalization** the tendency to respond to a stimulus that is only similar to the original conditioned stimulus with the conditioned response.

**stimulus motive** a motive that appears to be unlearned but causes an increase in stimulation, such as curiosity.

**storage** holding on to information for some period of time.

**stress** the term used to describe the physical, emotional, cognitive, and behavioral responses to events that are appraised as threatening or challenging.

**stressors** events that cause a stress reaction.

**stress-vulnerability model** explanation of disorder that assumes a biological sensitivity, or vulnerability, to a certain disorder will result in the development of that disorder under the right conditions of environmental or emotional stress.

**structuralism** early perspective in psychology associated with Wilhelm Wundt and Edward Titchener, in which the focus of study is the structure or basic elements of the mind.

**subjective** referring to concepts and impressions that are only valid within a particular person's perception and may be influenced by biases, prejudice, and personal experiences.

**subjective discomfort** emotional distress or emotional pain.

**sublimation** channeling socially unacceptable impulses and urges into socially acceptable behavior.

**superego** part of the personality that acts as a moral center.

**surface traits** aspects of personality that can easily be seen by other people in the outward actions of a person.

**sympathetic division (fight-or-flight system)** part of the ANS that is responsible for reacting to stressful events and bodily arousal.

**synapse (synaptic gap)** microscopic fluid-filled space between the axon terminal of one cell and the dendrites or soma of the next cell.

**synaptic vesicles** saclike structures found inside the synaptic knob containing chemicals.

**synesthesia** disorder in which the signals from the various sensory organs are processed in the wrong cortical areas, resulting in the sense information being interpreted as more than one sensation.

**syntax** the system of rules for combining words and phrases to form grammatically correct sentences.

**systematic desensitization** behavior technique used to treat phobias, in which a client is asked to make a list of ordered fears and taught to relax while concentrating on those fears.

**temperament** the behavioral characteristics that are fairly well established at birth, such as "easy," "difficult," and "slow to warm up"; the enduring characteristics with which each person is born.

**temporal lobes** areas of the cortex located along the side of the brain, starting just behind the temples, containing the neurons responsible for the sense of hearing and meaningful speech.

**teratogen** any factor that can cause a birth defect.

**testes (testicles)** the male gonads or sex glands.

**texture gradient** monocular depth perception cue; the tendency for textured surfaces to appear to become smaller and finer as distance from the viewer increases.

**thalamus** part of the limbic system located in the center of the brain, this structure relays sensory information from the lower part of the brain to the proper areas of the cortex and processes some sensory information before sending it to its proper area.

**Thematic Apperception Test (TAT)** projective test that uses 20 pictures of people in ambiguous situations as the visual stimuli.

**therapeutic alliance** the relationship between therapist and client that develops as a warm, caring, accepting relationship characterized by empathy, mutual respect, and understanding.

**theory** a general explanation of a set of observations or facts.

**therapy** treatment methods aimed at making people feel better and function more effectively.

**theta waves** brain waves indicating the early stages of sleep.

**thinking (cognition)** mental activity that goes on in the brain when a person is organizing and attempting to understand information and communicating information to others.

**thyroid gland** endocrine gland found in the neck; regulates metabolism.

**time-out** an extinction process in which a person is removed from the situation that provides reinforcement for undesirable behavior, usually by being placed in a quiet corner or room away from possible attention and reinforcement opportunities.

**token economy** the use of objects called tokens to reinforce behavior in which the tokens can be accumulated and exchanged for desired items or privileges.

**top-down processing** the use of preexisting knowledge to organize individual features into a unified whole.

**trait** a consistent, enduring way of thinking, feeling, or behaving.

**trait–situation interaction** the assumption that the particular circumstances of any given situation will influence the way in which a trait is expressed.

**trait theories** theories that endeavor to describe the characteristics that make up human personality in an effort to predict future behavior.

**transduction** the process of converting outside stimuli, such as light, into neural activity.

**transference** in psychoanalysis, the tendency for a patient or client to project positive or negative feelings for important people from the past onto the therapist.

**trial and error (mechanical solution)** problem-solving method in which one possible solution after another is tried until a successful one is found.

**triarchic theory of intelligence** Sternberg's theory that there are three kinds of intelligence: analytical, creative, and practical.

**trichromatic theory** theory of color vision that proposes three types of cones: red, blue, and green.

*t-test* type of inferential statistical analysis typically used when two means are compared to see if they are significantly different.

**Type 2 diabetes** disease typically occurring in middle adulthood when the body either becomes resistant to the effects of insulin or can no longer secrete enough insulin to maintain normal glucose levels.

**Type A personality** person who is ambitious, time conscious, extremely hardworking, and tends to have high levels of hostility and anger as well as being easily annoyed.

**Type B personality** person who is relaxed and laid back, less driven and competitive than Type A, and slow to anger.

**Type C personality** pleasant but repressed person, who tends to internalize his or her anger and anxiety and who finds expressing emotions difficult.

**unconditional positive regard** referring to the warmth, respect, and accepting atmosphere created by the therapist for the client in person-centered therapy; positive regard that is given without conditions or strings attached.

**unconditioned response (UCR)** in classical conditioning, an involuntary and unlearned response to a naturally occurring or unconditioned stimulus.

**unconditioned stimulus (UCS)** in classical conditioning, a naturally occurring stimulus that leads to an involuntary and unlearned response.

**unconscious mind** level of the mind in which thoughts, feelings, memories, and other information are kept that are not easily or voluntarily brought into consciousness.

**uterus** the womb in which the baby grows during pregnancy.

**vagina** the tube that leads from the outside of a female's body to the opening of the womb.

**validity** the degree to which a test actually measures what it's supposed to measure.

**variable interval schedule of reinforcement** schedule of reinforcement in which the interval of time that must pass before reinforcement becomes possible is different for each trial or event.

**variable ratio schedule of reinforcement** schedule of reinforcement in which the number of responses required for reinforcement is different for each trial or event.

**vestibular sense** the awareness of the balance, position, and movement of the head and body through space in relation to gravity's pull.

**vicarious conditioning** classical conditioning of an involuntary response or emotion by watching the reaction of another person.

**visual accommodation** the change in the thickness of the lens as the eye focuses on objects that are far away or close.

**volley principle** theory of pitch that states that frequencies from about 400 Hz to 4,000 Hz cause the hair cells (auditory neurons) to fire in a volley pattern, or take turns in firing.

**waking consciousness** state in which thoughts, feelings, and sensations are clear and organized and the person feels alert.

**weight set point** the particular level of weight that the body tries to maintain.

**Wernicke's aphasia** condition resulting from damage to Wernicke's area, causing the affected person to be unable to understand or produce meaningful language.

**withdrawal** physical symptoms that can include nausea, pain, tremors, crankiness, and high blood pressure, resulting from a lack of an addictive drug in the body systems.

**working memory** an active system that processes the information in short-term memory.

**Yerkes-Dodson law** law stating that when tasks are simple, a higher level of arousal leads to better performance; when tasks are difficult, lower levels of arousal lead to better performance.

**zone of proximal development (ZPD)** Vygotsky's concept of the difference between what a child can do alone and what that child can do with the help of a teacher.

*z* **score** a statistical measure that indicates how far away from the mean a particular score is in terms of the number of standard deviations that exist between the mean and that score.

**zygote** cell resulting from the uniting of the ovum and sperm.

# References

AAA Foundation. (2009, April). Aggressive driving: Research update. Retrieved from https://www.aaafoundation.org/sites/default/files/Aggressive Driving Research Update 2009.pdf

Abadinsky, H. (1989). *Drug abuse: An introduction*. Chicago: Nelson-Hall Series in Law, Crime, and Justice.

Abbott, L., Nadler, J., & Rude, R. K. (1994). Magnesium deficiency in alcoholism: Possible contribution to osteoporosis and cardiovascular disease in alcoholics. *Alcoholism, Clinical & Experimental Research, 18*(5), 1076–1082.

Abdou, C. M., Fingerhut, A. W., Jackson, J. S., & Wheaton, F. (2016). Healthcare stereotype threat in older adults in the health and retirement study. *American Journal of Preventive Medicine, 50*(2), 191–198. doi: 10.1016/j.amepre.2015.07.034

Abel, E. L., & Sokol, R. J. (1987). Incidence of fetal alcohol syndrome and economic impact of FAS-related anomalies: Drug alcohol syndrome and economic impact of FAS-related anomalies. *Drug and Alcohol Dependency, 19*(1), 51–70.

Abel, G. G., & Osborn, C. A. (1992). The paraphilias: The extent and nature of sexually deviant and criminal behavior. In J. M. W. Bradford (Ed.), *Psychiatric Clinics of North America, 15*(3) (pp. 675–687). Philadelphia: W. B. Saunders Company.

Abela, J. R. Z., & D'Allesandro, D. U. (2002). Beck's cognitive theory of depression: The diathesis-stress and causal mediation components. *British Journal of Clinical Psychology, 41*, 111–128.

Åberg, M. A., Pedersen, N. L., Torén, K., Svartengren, M., Bäckstrand, B., Johnsson, T., Cooper-Kuhn, C. M., Åberg, N. D., Nilsson, M., & Kuhn, H. G. (2009). Cardiovascular fitness is associated with cognition in young adulthood. *Proceedings of the National Academy of Sciences, 106*(49), 20906–20911.

Abramson, L. Y., Garber, J., & Seligman, M. E. P. (1980). Learned helplessness in humans: An attributional analysis. In J. Garber & M. E. P. Seligman (Eds.), *Human Helplessness* (pp. 3–34). New York: Academic Press.

Abramson, L. Y., Seligman, M. E. P., & Teasdale, J. D. (1978). Learned helplessness in humans: Critique and reformulation. *Journal of Abnormal Psychology, 87*, 49–74.

Acheson, D. J., MacDonald, M. C., & Postle, B. R. (2010). The interaction of concreteness and phonological similarity in verbal working memory. *Journal of Experimental Psychology: Learning, Memory and Cognition, 36*(1), 17–36.

Adachi, P. J. C., & Willoughby, T. (2011). The effect of video game competition and violence on aggressive behavior: Which characteristic has the greatest influence? *Psychology of Violence, 1*(4), 259–274. doi: 10.1037/a0024908

Adam, K. (1980). Sleep as a restorative process and a theory to explain why. *Progressive Brain Research, 53*, 289–305.

Adams, D. B. (1968). The activity of single cells in the midbrain and hypothalamus of the cat during affective defense behavior. *Archives Italiennes de Biologie, 106*, 243–269.

Adams, R. J. (1987). An evaluation of colour preferences in early infancy. *Infant Behaviour and Development, 10*, 143–150.

Addis, D. R., Giovanello, K. S., Vu, M. A., & Schacter, D. L. (2014). Age-related changes in prefrontal and hippocampal contributions to relational encoding. *NeuroImage, 84*, 19–26.

Addis, D. R., Leclerc, C. M., Muscatell, K., & Kensinger, E. A. (2010). There are age-related changes in neural connectivity during the encoding of positive, but not negative, information. *Cortex, 46*, 9.

Ader, R. (2003). Conditioned immunomodulation: Research needs and directions. *Brain, Behavior, and Immunity, 17*(1), 51–57.

Adeyemo, B. O., Simis, M., Macea, D. D., & Fregni, F. (2012). Systematic review of parameters of stimulation, clinical trial design characteristics, and motor outcomes in non-invasive brain stimulation in stroke. *Frontiers in Psychiatry, 3*, 88. doi: 10.3389/fpsyt.2012.00088

Adler, A. (1954). *Understanding human nature*. New York: Greenburg Publisher.

Adler, S. R., Fosket, J. R., Kagawa-Singer, M., McGraw, S. A., Wong-Kim, E., Gold, E., & Sternfeld, B. (2000). Conceptualizing menopause and midlife: Chinese American and Chinese women in the U.S. *Maturitas, 35*(1), 11–23.

Adolphs, R. (2010). Conceptual challenges and directions for social neuroscience. *Neuron, 65*(6), 752–767.

Adolphs, R., Gosselin, F., Buchanan, T. W., Tranel, D., Schyns, P., & Damasio, A. R. (2005). A mechanism for impaired fear recognition after amygdala damage. *Nature, 433*, 68–72.

Adolphs, R., & Tranel, D. (2003). Amygdala damage impairs emotion recognition from scenes only when they contain facial expressions. *Neuropsychologia, 41*, 1281–1289.

Afifi, T. O., Mota, N. P., Dasiewicz, P., MacMillan, H. L., & Sareen, J. (2012). Physical punishment and mental disorders: Results from a nationally representative US sample. *Pediatrics, 130*(2), 184–192. doi: 10.1542/peds.2011-2947

Agerup, T., Lydersen, S., Wallander, J., & Sund, A. M. (2015). Associations between parental attachment and course of depression between adolescence and young adulthood. *Child Psychiatry and Human Development, 46*, 632–642.

Aggarwal, N. T., Wilson, R. S., Beck, T. L., Rajan, K. B., de Leon, C. F. M., Evans, D. A., & Everson-Rose, S. A. (2014). Perceived stress and change in cognitive function among adults aged 65 and older. *Psychosomatic Medicine, 76*, 80–85.

Agresti, A., & Finlay, B. (1997). *Statistical Methods for the Social Sciences*, New Jersey: Prentice Hall.

Aguiar, A., & Baillargeon, R. (2003). Perseverative responding in a violation-of-expectation task in 6.5-month-old infants. *Cognition, 88*(3), 277–316.

Ahlskog, J. E. (2003). Slowing Parkinson's disease progression: Recent dopamine agonist trials. *Neurology, 60*(3), 381–389.

Ahn, W. (1998). Why are different features central for natural kinds and artifacts? The role of causal status in determining feature centrality. *Cognition, 69*, 135–178.

Aiello, J. R., & Douthitt, E. A. (2001). Social facilitation from Triplett to electronic performance monitoring. *Group Dynamics: Theory, Research, and Practice, 5*(3), 163–180.

Ainsworth, M. D. S. (1985). Attachments across the life span. *Bulletin of the New York Academy of Medicine, 61*, 792–812.

Ainsworth, M. D. S., Blehar, M. C., Waters, E., & Wall, S. (1978). *Patterns of attachment: A study of the strange situation*. Hillsdale, NJ: Erlbaum.

Aitchison, J. (1992). Good birds, better birds, and amazing birds: The development of prototypes. In P. J. Arnaud & H. Béjoint (Eds.), *Vocabulary and applied linguistics* (pp. 71–84). London: Macmillan.

Ajzen, I. (2001). Nature and operation of attitudes. *Annual Review of Psychology, 52*, 27–58.

Ajzen, I., & Fishbein, M. (2000). Attitudes and the attitude–behavior relation: Reasoned and automatic processes. In W. Stroebe & M. Hewstone (Eds.), *European review of social psychology* (pp. 1–33). New York: John Wiley & Sons.

Åkerstedt, T., Hallvig, D., Nund, A., Fors, C., Schwarz, J., & Kecklund, G. (2013). Having to stop driving at night because of dangerous sleepiness—awareness, physiology and behavior. *Journal of Sleep Research, 22*(4), 380–388.

Akil, M., Kolachana, B. S., Rothmond, D. A, Hyde, T. M, Weinberger, D. R, & Kleinman, J. E. (2003). Catechol-o-methyltransferase genotype and dopamine regulation in the human brain. *Journal of Neuroscience, 23*(6), 2008–2013.

Albert, D., Chein, J., & Steinberg, L. (2013). The teenage brain: Peer influences on adolescent decision making. *Current Directions in Psychological Science, 22*, 114–120.

Albert, D. J., & Richmond, S. E. (1977). Reactivity and aggression in the rat: Induction by alpha–adrenergic blocking agents injected ventral to anterior septum but not into lateral septum. *Journal of Comparative and Physiological Psychology, 91*, 886–896 [DBA] *Physiology and Behavior, 20*, 755–761.

Alderfer, C. P. (1972). *Existence, relatedness and growth: Human needs in organisational settings*. New York: Free Press.

Aldridge-Morris, R. (1989). *Multiple personality: An exercise in deception*. Hillsdale, NJ: Erlbaum.

Alexander, G., DeLong, M. R., & Strick, P. L. (1986). Parallel organization of functionally segregated circuits linking basal ganglia and cortex. *Annual Review of Neuroscience, 9*, 357–381.

Aligne, C. A., Auinger, P., Byrd, R. S., & Weitzman, M. (2000). Risk factors for pediatric asthma contributions of poverty, race, and urban residence. *American Journal of Respiratory Critical Care Medicine, 162*(3), 873–877.

Alkon, D. (1989). Memory storage and neural systems. *Scientific American, 261*(1), 42–50.

Allen, D. (2001). *Getting things done: the art of stress-free productivity*. New York: Viking Adult.

Allen, D. (2008). *Making it all work*. New York: Viking Adult.

Allen, F. (1994). *Secret formula*. New York: HarperCollins.

Allen, G., & Parisi, P. (1990). Trends in monozygotic and dizygotic twinning rates by maternal age and parity. Further analysis of Italian data, 1949–1985, and rediscussion of U.S. data, 1964–1985. *Acta Genetic Medicine & Gemellology, 39*, 317–328.

Allen, G. E. (2006). *Intelligence tests and immigration to the United States, 1900–1940*. Hoboken, NJ: John Wiley and Sons.

Allen, K., Blascovich, J., & W. Mendes. (2002). Cardiovascular reactivity and the presence of pets, friends, and spouses: The truth about cats and dogs. *Psychosomatic Medicine, 64*, 727–739.

Allen, T. A., & DeYoung, C. G. (2016). Personality neuroscience and the five factor model. In T. A. Widiger (Ed.), *Oxford handbook of the five factor model*. New York, NY: Oxford University Press. http://www.oxfordhandbooks.com/view/10.1093/oxfordhb/9780199352487.001.0001/oxfordhb-9780199352487-e-26

Allik, J., Realo, A., & McCrae, R. R. (2013). Univerality of the five-factor model of personality. In T. A. Widiger & P. T. Costa (Eds.), *Personality disorders and the five-factor model of personality* (3rd ed., pp. 61–74). Washington, DC: American Psychological Association.

Alloway, T. P., Rajendran, G., & Archibald, L. (2009). Working memory in children with developmental disorders. *Journal of Learning Disabilities, 42*(4), 372–382.

Alloy, L. B., & Clements, C. M. (1998). Hopelessness theory of depression: Tests of the symptom component. *Cognitive Therapy and Research, 22,* 303–335.

Allport, G. W., & Odbert, H. S. (1936). Trait names: A psycho-lexical study. *Psychological Monographs, 47*(1), i.

Alm, H., & Nilsson, L. (1995). The effects of a mobile telephone conversation on driver behaviour in a car following situation. *Accident Analysis and Prevention, 27*(5), 707–715.

Alz.org®: Alzheimer's Association. (2015). Alzheimer's myths. Retrieved from http://www.alz.org/alzheimers_disease_myths_about_alzheimers.asp

Alzheimer's Association. (2010). Alzheimer's disease facts and figures. *Alzheimer's & Dementia, 6,* 4–54.

Alzheimer's Association. (2015). Alzheimer's disease facts and figures. *Alzheimer's & Dementia, 11*(3), 332–420.

Amabile, T., DeJong, W., & Lepper, M. R. (1976). Effects of externally imposed deadlines on subsequent intrinsic motivation. *Journal of Personality and Social Psychology, 34,* 92–98.

Amabile, T., Hadley, C. N., & Kramer, S. J. (2002). Creativity under the gun. *Harvard Business Review, 80*(8), 52–60.

Amaral, D. G., & Strick, P. L. (2013). The organization of the central nervous system. In E. R. Kandel, J. H. Schwartz, T. M. Jessell, S. A. Siegelbaum, & A. J. Hudspeth (Eds.), *Principles of neural science* (5th ed., pp. 337–355). USA: McGraw-Hill.

Amariglio, R. E., Donohue, M. C., Marshall, G. A., Rentz, D. M., Salmon, D. P., Ferris, S. H., . . . Alzheimer's Disease Cooperative, S. (2015). Tracking early decline in cognitive function in older individuals at risk for Alzheimer disease dementia: The Alzheimer's disease cooperative study cognitive function instrument. *JAMA Neurology, 72*(4), 446–454. doi: 10.1001/jamaneurol.2014.3375

Amat, J., Aleksejev, R. M., Paul, E., Watkins, L. R., & Maier, S. F. (2010). Behavioral control over shock blocks behavioral and neurochemical effects of later social defeat. *Neuroscience, 165*(4), 1031–1038. doi: 10.1016/j.neuroscience.2009.11.005

Amat, J., Baratta, M. V., Paul, E., Bland, S. T., Watkins, L. R., & Maier, S. F. (2005). Medial prefrontal cortex determines how stressor controllability affects behavior and dorsal raphe nucleus. *Nature Neuroscience, 8*(3), 365–371.

American Academy of Pediatrics. (1995). Health supervision for children with Turner syndrome. *Pediatrics, 96*(6), 1166–1173.

American Association of University Women. (1992). *How schools shortchange girls.* Washington, DC: AAUW Educational Foundation, The Wellesley College Center for Research on Women.

American Association of University Women. (1998). *Separated by sex: A critical look at single-sex education for girls.* Washington, DC: AAUW Educational Foundation, The Wellesley College Center for Research on Women.

American Counseling Association. (2014). 2014 ACA code of ethics. Retrieved from http://www.counseling.org/docs/ethics/2014-aca-code-of-ethics.pdf

American Psychiatric Association. (2000). *Diagnostic and statistical manual of mental disorders* (4th ed., Text Revision). Washington, DC: Author.

American Psychiatric Association. (2013). *Diagnostic and statistical manual of mental disorders* (5th ed.). Washington, DC: Author.

American Psychiatric Association Committee on Electroconvulsive Therapy. (2001). *The practice of electroconvulsive therapy: Recommendations for treatment, training, and privileging,* (2nd ed.). Washington, DC: Author.

American Psychological Association. (2002). Ethical principles of psychologists and code of conduct. *American Psychologist, 57,* 1060–1073.

American Psychological Association (2005). Policy statement on evidence-based practice in psychology. Retrieved September 22, 2010, from http://www.apa.org/practice/guidelines/evidence-based.pdf

American Psychological Association, Division 19. (2010). Society for Military Psychology. Retrieved from http://www.apadivision19.org/about.htm

American Psychological Association. (2013). Recognition of psychotherapy effectiveness. *Psychotherapy, 50*(1), 102–109. doi: 10.1037/a0030276

American Psychological Association. (2014). How many psychology doctorates are awarded by U.S. institutions? News from APA's Center for Workforce Studies. *Monitor on Psychology, 45*(7), 13.

American Psychological Association. (2015). *Demographics of the U.S. psychology workforce: Findings from the American Community Survey.* Washington, DC: Author.

Amsterdam, B. (1972). Mirror self-image reactions before age two. *Developmental Psychobiology, 5*(4), 297–305. doi:10.1002/dev.420050403

Anand, B. K., & Brobeck, J. R. (1951). Hypothalamic control of food intake in rats and cats. *Yale Journal of Biological Medicine, 24,* 123–146.

Anastasi, A., & Urbina, S. (1997). *Psychological testing* (7th ed.). Upper Saddle River, NJ: Prentice-Hall.

Anderson, C. A. (1987). Temperature and aggression: Effects on quarterly, yearly, and city rates of violent and nonviolent crime. *Journal of Personality and Social Psychology, 52*(6), 1161–1173.

Anderson, C. A. (2003). Video games and aggressive behavior. In D. Ravitch & J. P. Viteritti (Eds.), *Kid stuff: Marketing sex and violence to America's children* (p. 157). Baltimore/London: The Johns Hopkins University Press.

Anderson, C. A., Berkowitz, L., Donnerstein, E., Huesmann, L. R., Johnson, J. D., Linz, D., Malamuth, N. M., & Wartella, E. (2003). The influence of media violence on youth. *Psychological Science in the Public Interest, 4*(3), 81–110.

Anderson, C. A., & Bushman, B. J. (2001). Effects of violent video games on aggressive behavior, aggressive cognition, aggressive affect, physiological arousal, and prosocial behavior: A meta–analytic review of the scientific literature. *Psych Science, 12*(5), 353–359.

Anderson, C. A., Bushman, B. J., Donnerstein, E., Hummer, T. A., & Warburton, W. (2015). SPSSI research summary on media violence. *Analyses of Social Issues and Public Policy, 15*(1), 4–19.

Anderson, C. A., & Dill, K. E. (2000). Video games and aggressive thoughts, feelings, and behavior in the laboratory and in life. *Journal of Personality and Social Psychology, 78*(4), 772–790.

Anderson, C. A., Sakamoto, A., Gentile, D., Ihori, N., Shibuya, A., Yukawa, S., Naito, M., & Kobayashi, K. (2008). Longitudinal effects of violent video games on aggression in Japan and the United States, *Pediatrics, 122*(5), e1067–e1072.

Anderson, C. A., Shibuya, A., Ihori, N., Swing, E. L., Bushman, B. J., Sakamoto, A., . . . Saleem, M. (2010). Violent video game effects on aggression, empathy, and prosocial behavior in Eastern and Western countries: A meta-analytic review. *Psychological Bulletin, 136*(2), 151–173. doi: 10.1037/a0018251

Anderson, L. W., Krathwohl, D. R., Airasian, P. W., Cruikshank, K. A., Mayer, R. E., Pintrich, P. R., Raths, J., & Wittrock, M. C. (Eds.). (2001). *A taxonomy for learning, teaching, and assessing—A revision of Bloom's Taxonomy of Educational Objectives.* New York: Addison Wesley Longman.

Anderson, M. C., & Neely, J. H. (1996). Interference and inhibition in memory retrieval. In E. L. Bjork & R. A. Bjork (Eds.). *Handbook of perception and cognition, Memory,* (2nd ed.), 237–313. San Diego, CA: Academic Press.

Andrews, J. D. W. (1989). Integrating visions of reality: Interpersonal diagnosis and the existential vision. *American Psychologist, 44,* 803–817.

Angus, L., Watson, J. C., Elliott, R., Schneider, K., & Timulak, L. (2014). Humanistic psychotherapy research 1990–2015: From methodological innovation to evidence-supported treatment outcomes and beyond. *Psychotherapy Research, 25*(3), 330–347. doi: 10.1080/10503307.2014.989290

Anschuetz, B. L. (1999). The high cost of caring: Coping with workplace stress. *The Journal, the Newsletter of the Ontario Association of Children's Aid Societies, 43*(3), 1–63.

Anspaugh, D., Hamrick, M., & Rosato, F. (2011). Coping with and managing stress. In D. Anspaugh, M. Hamrick, and F. Rosato (Eds.), *Wellness: Concepts and applications* (8th ed., pp. 307–340). New York: McGraw-Hill.

Antonakis, J. (2004). On why "emotional intelligence" will not predict leadership effectiveness beyond IQ or the "Big Five": An extension and rejoinder. *Organizational Analysis, 12*(2), 171–182.

Antony, J. W., Gobel, E. W., O'Hare, J. K., Reber, P. J., & Paller, K. A. (2012). Cued memory reactivation during sleep influences skill learning. *Nature Neuroscience, 15*(8), 1114–1116. doi: 10.1038/nn.3152

Antuono, P. G., Jones, J. L., Wang, Y., & Li, S. (2001). Decreased glutamate [plus] glutamine in Alzheimer's disease detected in vivo with (1)H-MRS at 0.5 T. *Neurology, 56*(6), 737–742.

Apps, M. A. J., Lesage, E., & Ramnani, N. (2015). Vicarious reinforcement learning signals when instructing others. *The Journal of Neuroscience, 35*(7), 2904–2913.

Arcelus, J., Mitchell, A. J., Wales, J., & Nielsen, S. (2011). Mortality rates in patients with anorexia nervosa and other eating disorders: A meta-analysis of 36 studies. *Archives of General Psychiatry, 68*(7), 724–731. doi: 10.1001/archgenpsychiatry.2011.74

Archer, J. (1991). The influence of testosterone on human aggression. *British Journal of Psychology, 82,* 1–28.

Argamon, S., Koppel, M., Fine, J., & Shimoni, A. (2003, August). Gender, genre, and writing style in formal written texts. *Text, 23*(3), 321–346.

Arkowitz, H., & Miller, W. R. (2008). Learning, applying, and extending motivational interviewing. In H. Arkowitz, H. A. Westra, W. R. Miller, & S. Rollnick (Eds.). *Motivational interviewing in the treatment of psychological disorders* (pp. 1–25). New York: Guilford Press.

Armstrong, R. (1997). When drugs are used for rape. *Journal of Emergency Nursing, 23*(4), 378–381.

Arnett, J. J. (2000). Emerging adulthood. A theory of development from the late teens through the twenties. *American Psychologist, 55*(5), 469–480.

Arnett, J. J., (2013). The evidence of Generation We and against Generation Me. *Emerging Adulthood, 1*(1), 5–10.

Arnett, P. A., Smith, S. S., & Newman, J. P. (1997). Approach and avoidance motivation in psychopathic criminal offenders during passive avoidance. *Journal of Personality and Social Psychology, 72*(6), 1413–1428.

Arns, M., de Ridder, S., Strehl, U., Breteler, M., & Coenen, A. (2009). Efficacy of neurofeedback treatment in ADHD: The effects on inattention, impulsivity and hyperactivity: A meta-analysis. *Clinical EEG and Neuroscience, 40*(3), 180–189.

Arns, M., van der Heijden, K. B., Arnold, L. E., & Kenemans, J. L. (2013). Geographic variation in the prevalence of attention-deficit/hyperactivity disorder: The sunny perspective. *Biological Psychiatry* (74(8): 585–590). doi: 10.1016/j.biopsych.2013.02.010

Aron, A., Aron, E., & Coups, E. (2005). *Statistics for the behavioral and social sciences: Brief course.* (4th ed.). Upper Saddle River, NJ: Prentice-Hall.

Aronson, E. (1997). Back to the future. Retrospective review of Leon Festinger's—A theory of cognitive dissonance. *American Journal of Psychology, 110,* 127–137.

Aronson, E., Blaney, N., Stephan, C., Sikes, J., & Snapp, M. (1978). *The jigsaw classroom.* Beverly Hills, CA: Sage.

Arora, S., Ashrafian, H., Davis, R., Athanasiou, T., Darzi, A., & Sevdalis, N. (2010). Emotional intelligence in medicine: A systematic review through the context of the ACGME competencies. *Medical Education, 44*(8), 749–764. doi: 10.1111/j.1365-2923.2010.03709.x

Asarnow, L. D., McGlinchey, E., & Harvey, A. G. (2015). Evidence for a possible link between bedtime and change in body mass index. *Sleep, 38*(10), 1523–1527.

Asarnow, R. F., Granholm, E., & Sherman, T. (1991). Span of apprehension in schizophrenia. In H. A. Nasrallah (Ed.), *Handbook of Schizophrenia*, Vol. 5. In S. R. Steinhauer, J. H. Gruzelie, & J. Zubin (Eds.), *Neuropsychology, psychophysiology and information processing* (pp. 335–370). Amsterdam: Elsevier.

Asch, S. E. (1951). Effects of group pressure upon the modification and distortion of judgement. In H. Guetzkow (Ed.), *Groups, leadership and men*. Pittsburgh: Carnegie Press.

Asch, S. E. (1956). Studies of independence and conformity: A minority of one against a unanimous majority. *Psychological Monographs, 70* (Whole no. 416).

Aserinsky, E., & Kleitman, N. (1953). Regularly occurring periods of eye motility, and concomitant phenomena, during sleep. *Science, 118,* 273–274.

Ash, M. G. (1998). *Gestalt psychology in German culture, 1890–1967: Holism and the quest for objectivity.* Cambridge: Cambridge University Press.

Asp, E., & Tranel, D. (2013). False tagging theory. In D. T. Stuss & R. T. Knight (Eds.), *Principles of frontal lobe function* (pp. 383–416). New York, NY: Oxford University Press.

Atkinson, R. C., & Shiffrin, R. M. (1968). Human memory: A proposed system and its control processes. In K. W. Spence & J. T. Spence (Eds.). *The psychology of learning and motivation* (Vol. 2, pp. 89–105). New York: Academic Press.

Atladóttir, H. O., Pedersen, M. G., Thorsen, C., Mortensen, P. B., Deleuran, B., Eaton, W. W., & Parner, E. T. (2009). Association of family history of autoimmune diseases and autism spectrum disorders. *Pediatrics, 124*(2), 687–694.

Aton, S., Seibt, J., Dumoulin, M., Jha, S. K., Steinmetz, N., Coleman, T., Naidoo, N., & Frank, M. G. (2009). Mechanisms of sleep-dependent consolidation of cortical plasticity. *Neuron, 61*(3), 454–466.

Atwood, K. C. (2001). Homeopathy and critical thinking. *The Scientific Review of Alternative Medicine, 5*(3), 149–151.

Au, J., Sheehan, E., Tsai, N., Duncan, G. J., Buschkuehl, M., & Jaeggi, S. M. (2015). Improving fluid intelligence with training on working memory: A meta-analysis. *Psychonomic Bulletin & Review, 22*(2), 366–377. doi: 10.3758/s13423-014-0699-x

AVERT: AVERTing HIV and AIDS. (2015). HIV and AIDS in Eastern Europe & Central Asia. Retrieved from http://www.avert.org/professionals/hiv-around-world/eastern-europe-central-asia

Azmitia, M., Syed, M., & Radmacher, K. (2008). On the intersection of personal and social identities: Introduction and evidence from a longitudinal study of emerging adults. In M. Azmitia, M. Syed, & K. Radmacher (Eds.), *The intersections of personal and social identities. New Directions for Child and Adolescent Development, 120,* 1–16. San Francisco: Jossey-Bass.

Babiloni, C., Vecchio, F., Buffo, P., Buttiglione, M., Cibelli, G., & Rossini, P. M. (2010). Cortical responses to consciousness of schematic emotional facial expressions: A high-resolution EEG study. *Human Brain Mapping, 8,* 8.

Backenstrass, M., Pfeiffer, N., Schwarz, T., Catanzaro, S. J., & Mearns, J. (2008). Reliability and validity of the German version of the Generalized Expectancies for Negative Mood Regulation (NMR) Scale. *Diagnostica, 54,* 43–51.

Backer, B., Hannon, R., & Russell, N. (1994). *Death and dying: Understanding and care* (2nd ed.). Albany, NY: Delmar.

Baddeley, A. D. (1986). *Working memory.* London/New York: Oxford University Press.

Baddeley, A. D. (1988). Cognitive psychology and human memory. *Trends in Neurosciences, 11,* 176–181.

Baddeley, A. D. (1996). Exploring the central executive. *Quarterly Journal of Experimental Psychology, 49A,* 5–28.

Baddeley, A. D. (2003). Working memory: Looking back and looking visual forward. *Nature Reviews Neuroscience, 4*(10), 829–839.

Baddeley, A. D. (2012). Working memory: Theories, models, and controversies. *Annual Review of Psychology, 63*(1), 1–29. doi: 10.1146/annurev-psych-120710-100422

Baddeley, A. D., & Hitch, G. (1974). Working memory. In G. A. Bower (Ed.), *The psychology of learning and motivation, 8* (pp. 47–89). New York: Academic Press.

Baddeley, A. D., & Larson, J. D. (2007). The phonological loop unmasked? A comment on the evidence for a "perceptual-gestural" alternative. *Quarterly Journal of Experimental Psychology, 60*(4), 497–504.

Baehr, E. K., Revelle, W., & Eastman, C. I. (2000). Individual difference in the phase amplitude of the human circadian temperature rhythm: With an emphasis on morningness-eveningness. *Journal of Sleep Research, 9,* 117–127.

Baer, D. M., Wolf, M. M., & Risley, T. R. (1968). Some current dimensions of applied behavior analysis. *Journal of Applied Behavior Analysis, 1,* 91–97.

Bagby, R. M., Nicholson, R. A., Buis, T., & Bacchiochi, J. R. (2000). Can the MMPI-2 validity scales detect depression feigned by experts? *Assessment, 7*(1), 55–62.

Bahrick, H. (1984). Fifty years of second language attrition: Implications for programmatic research. *Modern Language Journal, 68,* 105–118.

Bahrick, H. P., Hall, L. K., & Berger, S. A. (1996, September). Accuracy and distortion in memory for high school grades. *Psychological Science, 7,* 265–271.

Bailey, J., Dunne, M. P., & Martin, N. G. (2000). Genetic and environmental influences on sexual orientation and its correlates in an Australian twin sample. *Journal of Personality and Social Psychology Volume, 78*(3), 524–536.

Bailey, J. M., & Pillard, R. C. (1991). A genetic study of male sexual orientation. *Archives of General Psychiatry, 48,* 1089–1096.

Bailey, J. M., Pillard, R. C., Neale, M. C., & Agyei, Y. (1993). Heritable factors influence sexual orientation in women. *Archives of General Psychiatry, 50,* 217–223.

Bailey, J. M., & Zucker, K. J. (1995). Childhood sex-typed behavior and sexual orientation: A conceptual analysis and quantitative review. *Developmental Psychology, 31,* 43–55.

Baillargeon, R. (1986). Representing the existence and the location of hidden objects: Object permanence in 6- and 8-month-old infants. *Cognition, 23,* 21–41.

Bains, G. S., Berk, L., Deshpande, P., Pawar, P., Daher, N., Lohman, E., Petrofsky, J., & Schwab, E. (2012). Effectiveness of humor on short term memory function in elderly subjects. *The Journal of the Federation of American Societies for Experimental Biology, 26,* lb834.

Baker, L. D., Frank, L. L., Foster-Schubert, K., Green, P. S., Wilkinson, C. W., McTiernan, A., Plymate, S. R., Fishel, M. A., Watson, G. S., Cholerton, B. A., Duncan, G. E., Mehta, P. D., & Craft, S. (2010). Effects of aerobic exercise on mild cognitive impairment: A controlled trial. *Archives of Neurology, 67*(1), 71–79.

Bakker, A. B., Demerouti, E., & Sanz-Vergel, A. I. (2014). Burnout and work engagement: The JD-R approach. *Annual Review of Organizational Psychology and Organizational Behavior, 1,* 389–411.

Bakhshaie, J., Zvolensky, M. J., & Goodwin, R. D. (2016). Cigarette smoking and the onset and persistence of panic attacks during mid-adulthood in the United States: 1994–2005. *Journal of Clinical Psychiatry, 77*(1), e21–24. doi: 10.4088/JCP.14m09290

Ball, K., Berch, D. B., Helmers, K. F., Jobe, J. B., Leveck, M. D., Marsiske, M., Morris, J. N., Rebok, G. W., Smith, D. M., Tennstedt, S. L., Unverzagt, F. W., & Willis, S. L. (2002). Advanced Cognitive Training for Independent and Vital Elderly Study Group. Effects of cognitive training interventions with older adults: A randomized controlled trial. *Journal of the American Medical Association, 288,* 2271–2281.

Ball, T. M., Stein, M. B., & Paulus, M. P. (2014). Toward the application of functional neuroimaging to individualized treatment for anxiety and depression. *Depression and Anxiety, 31*(11), 920–933. doi: 10.1002/da.22299

Baltes, P. B., Reese, H. W., & Nesselroade, J. R. (1988). *Introduction to research methods, life-span developmental psychology.* Hillsdale, NJ: Lawrence Erlbaum

Bandura, A. (1965). Influence of models' reinforcement contingencies on the acquisition of imitative responses. *Journal of Social Psychology, 1,* 589–595.

Bandura, A. (1980). The social learning theory of aggression. In R. A. Falk & S. S. Kim (Eds.), *The war system: An interdisciplinary approach* (p. 146). Boulder, CO: Westview Press.

Bandura, A. (1986). *Social foundations of thought and action: A social cognitive theory.* Englewood Cliffs, NJ: Prentice Hall.

Bandura, A. (1989). Human agency in social cognitive theory. *American Psychologist, 44,* 1175–1184.

Bandura, A. (1998). Exploration of fortuitous determinants of life paths. *Psychological Inquiry, 9,* 95–99.

Bandura, A., Blanchard, E. B., & Ritter, B. (1969). Relative efficacy of desensitization and modeling approaches for inducing behavioral, affective, and attitudinal changes. *Journal of Personality and Social Psychology, 13,* 173–199.

Bandura, A., Jeffrey, R. W., & Wright, C. L. (1974). Efficacy of participant modeling as a function of response induction aids. *Journal of Abnormal Psychology, 83,* 56–64.

Bandura, A., & Rosenthal, T. L. (1966). Vicarious classical conditioning as a functioning of arousal level. *Journal of Personality and Social Psychology, 3,* 54–62.

Bandura, A., Ross, D., & Ross, S. A. (1961). Transmission of aggression through imitation of aggressive models. *Journal of Abnormal and Social Psychology, 63,* 575–582.

Bandura, A., Ross, D., & Ross, S. A. (1963). Imitation of film-mediated aggressive models. *Journal of Abnormal and Social Psychology, 66,* 3–11.

Banerjee, A., & Chaudhury, S. (2010). Statistics without tears: Populations and samples. *Industrial Psychiatry Journal, 19*(1), 60–65.

Banks, G. P., Mikell, C. B., Youngerman, B. E., Henriques, B., Kelly, K. M., Chan, A. K., . . . Sheth, S. A. (2015). Neuroanatomical characteristics associated with response to dorsal anterior cingulotomy for obsessive-compulsive disorder. *JAMA Psychiatry, 72*(2), 127–135. doi: 10.1001/jamapsychiatry.2014.2216

Baral, S., Todd, C. S., Aumakhan, B., Lloyd, J., Delegchoimbol, A., & Sabin, K. (2013). HIV among female sex workers in the Central Asian Republics, Afghanistan, and

Mongolia: Contexts and convergence with drug use. *Drug and Alcohol Dependence, 132*(1), 13–16.

Bard, P. (1934). On emotional expression after decortication with some remark on certain theoretical views. *Psychological Review, 41,* 309–329, 424–449.

Bargh, J. A., Chen, M., & Burrows, C. (1996). Automaticity of social behavior: Direct effects of trait construct and stereotype activation on action. *Journal of Personality & Social Psychology, 71*(2), 230–244.

Bargh, J. A., Schwader, K. L., Hailey, S. E., Dyer, R. L., & Boothby, E. J. (2012). Automaticity in social-cognitive processes. *Trends in Cognitive Sciences, 16*(12), 593–605.

Barkley, R. A., Murphy, K. R., & Fischer, M. (2008). *ADHD in adults: What the science says.* New York: Guilford Press.

Barlow, D. H., Allen, L. B., & Basden, S. L. (2007). Psychological treatments for panic disorders, phobias, and generalized anxiety disorder. In P. E. Nathan & J. M. Gorman (Eds.), *A guide to treatments that work* (3rd ed., pp. 351–394). New York: Oxford University Press.

Barlow, D. H., Bullis, J. R., Comer, J. S., & Ametaj, A. A. (2013). Evidence-based psychological treatments: An update and a way forward. *Annual Review of Clinical Psychology, 9,* 1–27. doi: 10.1146/annurev-clinpsy-050212-185629

Barnes, A. M., & Carey, J. C. (2002, January). Common problems of babies with trisomy 18 or 13. Rochester, NY, *Support Organization for Trisomy 18, 13, and Related Disorders,* January 11, New York: Soft Publications.

Barnes, V., Schneider, R., Alexander, C., & Staggers, F. (1997). Stress, stress reduction, and hypertension in African Americans: An updated review. *Journal of the National Medical Association, 89*(7), 464–476.

Barnyard, P., & Grayson, A. (1996). *Introducing psychological research.* London: MacMillan Press.

Baron, J. N., & Reiss, P. C. (1985). Same time, next year: Aggregate analyses of the mass media and violent behavior. *American Sociological Review, 50,* 347–363.

Baron-Cohen, S., Leslie, A. M., & Frith, U. (1985). Does the autistic child have a "theory of mind"? *Cognition, 21*(1), 3744.

Barondes, S. H. (1998). *Mood genes: Hunting for origins of mania and depression.* New York: W. H. Freeman.

Barsalou, L. W. (1992). *Cognitive psychology: An overview for cognitive scientists.* Hillsdale, NJ: Lawrence Erlbaum.

Barsh, G. S., Farooqi, I. S., & O'Rahilly, S. (2000). Genetics of body-weight regulation. *Nature, 404,* 644–651.

Bartels, A., & Zeki, S. (2000). The neural basis of romantic love. *NeuroReport, 11,* 3829–3834.

Barth, J. M., & Boles, D. B. (1999, September,). *Positive relations between emotion recognition skills and right hemisphere processing.* Paper presented at the 11th Annual Convention of the American Psychological Society, Denver, CO.

Bartholomew, K. (1990). Avoidance of intimacy: An attachment perspective. *Journal of Social and Personal Relationships, 7,* 147–178.

Bartlett, C., Harris, R., & Bruey, C. (2008). The effect of the amount of blood in a violent video game on aggression, hostility, and arousal. *Journal of Experimental Social Psychology, 44*(3), 539–546.

Bartlett, F. C. (1932). *Remembering: A study in experimental ad social psychology.* Cambridge, UK: Cambridge University Press.

Bartlett, N. R. (1965). Dark and light adaptation. In C. H. Graham (Ed.), *Vision and visual perception* (185–207). New York: John Wiley & Sons

Bartol, T. M., Bromer, C., Kinney, J., Chirillo, M. A., Bourne, J. N., Harris, K. M., & Sejnowski, T. J. (2015). Nanoconnectomic upper bound on the variability of synaptic plasticity. *Elife, 4.* doi: 10.7554/eLife.10778

Barton, M. E., & Komatsu, L. K. (1989). Defining features of natural kinds and artifacts. *Journal of Psycholinguistic Research, 18,* 433–447.

Bartoshuk, L. M. (1993). The biological basis for food perception and acceptance. *Food Quality and Preference, 4*(1/2), 21–32.

Bartoshuk, L. M., Duffy, V. B., Hayes, J. E., Moskowitz, H. R., & Snyder, D. J. (2006). Psychophysics of sweet and fat perception in obesity: Problems, solutions and new perspectives. *Philosophical transactions of the Royal Society of London. Series B, Biological sciences, 361*(1471), 1137–1148.

Bartoshuk, L. M., Fast, K., & Snyder, D. J. (2005). Differences in our sensory worlds. *Current Directions in Psychological Science, 14*(3), 122–125.

Bartz, J. A., Lydon, J. E., Kolevzon, A., Zaki, J., Hollander, E., Ludwig, N., & Bolger, N. (2015). Differential effects of oxytocin on agency and communion for anxiously and avoidantly attached individuals. *Psychological Science, 26*(8), 1177–1186. doi: 10.1177/0956797615580279

Bartz, J. A., Zaki, J., Bolger, N., Hollander, E., Ludwig, N. N., Kolevzon, A., & Ochsner, K. N. (2010). Oxytocin selectively improves empathic accuracy. *Psychological Science, 21*(10), 1426–1428. doi: 10.1177/0956797610383439

Bartz, J. A., Zaki, J., Bolger, N., & Ochsner, K. N. (2011). Social effects of oxytocin in humans: Context and person matter. *Trends in Cognitive Sciences, 15*(7), 301–309. doi: 10.1016/j.tics.2011.05.002

Basadur, M., Pringle, P., & Kirkland, D. (2002). Crossing cultures: Training effects on the divergent thinking attitudes of Spanish-speaking South American managers. *Creativity Research Journal, 14*(3, 4), 395–408.

Basner M., Rao, H., Goel, N., & Dinges, D. F. (2013). Sleep deprivation and neurobehavioral dynamics. *Current Opinion in Neurobiology.* doi: 10.1016/j.conb.2013.02.008

Basten, U., Hilger, K., & Fiebach, C. J. (2015). Where smart brains are different: A quantitative meta-analysis of functional and structural brain imaging studies on intelligence. *Intelligence, 51,* 10–27. doi: 10.1016/j.intell.2015.04.009

Bastien, C. H., Morin, C. M., Ouellet, M., Blais, F. C., Bouchard, S. (2004). Cognitive-behavioral therapy for insomnia: Comparison of individual therapy, group therapy, and telephone consultations. *Journal of Consulting and Clinical Psychology, 72*(4), 653–659.

Bateman, R. J., Xiong, C., Benzinger, T. L., Fagan, A. M., Goate, A., Fox, N. C., . . . Dominantly Inherited Alzheimer, N. (2012). Clinical and biomarker changes in dominantly inherited Alzheimer's disease. *New England Journal of Medicine, 367*(9), 795–804. doi: 10.1056/NEJMoa1202753

Bator, R. J., & Cialdini, R. B. (2006). The nature of consistency motivation: Consistency, aconsistency, and anticonsistency in a dissonance paradigm. *Social Influence, 1,* 208–233.

Baumann, O., Borra, R. J., Bower, J. M., Cullen, K. E., Habas, C., Ivry, R. B., . . . Sokolov, A. A. (2015). Consensus paper: The role of the cerebellum in perceptual processes. *Cerebellum (London, England), 14*(2), 197–220. doi: 10.1007/s12311-014-0627-7

Baumeister, D., Tojo, L. M., & Tracy, D. K. (2015). Legal highs: Staying on top of the flood of novel psychoactive substances. *Therapeutic Advances in Psychopharmacology, 5*(2), 97–132.

Baumgart, M., Snyder, H. M., Carrillo, M. C., Fazio, S., Kim, H., & Johns, H. (2015). Summary of the evidence on modifiable risk factors for cognitive decline and dementia: A population-based perspective. *Alzheimer's & Dementia, 11*(6), 718–726.

Baumrind, D. (1964). Some thoughts on ethics of research: After reading Milgram's "Behavioral Study of Obedience." *American Psychologist, 19,* 421–423.

Baumrind, D. (1967). Child care practices anteceding three patterns of preschool behavior. *Genetic Psychology Monograph, 75,* 43–88.

Baumrind, D. (1991). The influence of parenting style on adolescent competence and substance abuse. *Journal of Early Adolescence, 11*(1), 56–95.

Baumrind, D. (1997). Necessary distinctions. *Psychological Inquiry, 8,* 176–182.

Baumrind, D. (2005). Patterns of parental authority and adolescent autonomy. In J. Smetana (Ed.), *New directions for child development: Changes in parental authority during adolescence* (pp. 61–69). San Francisco: Jossey-Bass.

Bayliss, D. M., Baddeley, J. C., & Gunn, D. M. (2005). The relationship between short-term memory and working memory: Complex span made simple? *Memory, 13*(3–4), 414–421.

Beardsley, T. (1995, January). For whom the bell curve really tolls. *Scientific American,* 14–17.

Beauchamp, G. K., & Mennella, J. A. (2011). Flavor perception in human infants: Development and functional significance. *Digestion, 83* (Suppl 1), 1–6. doi: 10.1159/000323397

Bechtel, W., & Abrahamsen, A. (2002). *Connectionism and the mind: Parallel processing, dynamics, and evolution in networks* (2nd ed.). Oxford, UK: Basil Blackwell.

Beck, A. T. (1976). *Cognitive therapy and the emotional disorders.* New York: International Universities Press.

Beck, A. T. (1979). *Cognitive therapy and the emotional disorders.* New York: Penguin Books.

Beck, A. T. (1984). Cognitive approaches to stress. In C. Lehrer & R. L. Woolfolk (Eds.), *Clinical guide to stress management,* pp. 255–305. New York: Guilford Press.

Beck, H. P., & Irons, G. (2011). Finding Little Albert: A seven-year search for psychology's lost boy. *The Psychologist, 25,* 180–181.

Beck, H. P., Levinson, S., & Irons, G. (2009). Finding Little Albert: A journey to John B. Watson's infant laboratory. *American Psychologist, 64*(7), 605–614. doi: 10.1037/a0017234

Beck, J. S. (2007). Cognitive therapy for personality disorders. Retrieved November 17, 2010, from http://www.academyofct.org/Library/InfoManage/Guide.asp?FolderID=196.

Beckman, M., & Pierrehumbert, J. (1986). Intonational structure in English and Japanese. *Phonology Year Book III,* 15–70.

Beehr, T. A., Jex, S. M., Stacy, B. A., & Murray, M. A. (2000). Work stressors and coworker support as predictors of individual strain and job performance. *Journal of Organizational Behavior, 21*(4), 391–405.

Beer, J. M., & Horn, J. M. (2001). The influence of rearing order on personality development within two adoption cohorts. *Journal of Personality, 68,* 789–819.

Beer, J. S. (2009). The neural basis of emotion regulation: Making emotion work for you and not against you. In M. S. Gazzaniga (Ed.), *The Cognitive Neurosciences* (pp. 961–972). Cambridge, MA: The MIT Press.

Behne, T., Carpenter, M., & Tomasello, M. (2005). One-year-olds comprehend the communicative intentions behind gestures in a hiding game. *Developmental Science, 8,* 492–499.

Békésy, G. V. (1960). *Experiments in Hearing* (E. G. Wever, Trans.). New York: McGraw-Hill Book Company.

Bell, B. G., & Grubin, D. (2010). Functional magnetic resonance imaging may promote theoretical understanding of the polygraph test. *Journal of Forensic Psychiatry and Psychology, 21*(1), 52–65.

Bellis, M. A., Downing, J., & Ashton, J. A. (2006). Adults at 12? Trends in puberty and their public health consequences. *Journal of Epidemiology and Community Health, 60,* 910–911. doi: 10.1136/jech.2006.049379

Belsky, J. (2005). Differential susceptibility to rearing influence: An evolutionary hypothesis and some evidence. In B. Ellis & D. Bjorklund (Eds.), *Origins of the social mind: Evolutionary psychology and child development* (pp. 139–163). New York: Guilford.

Belsky, J., & Johnson, C. D. (2005). Developmental outcome of children in day care. In J. Murph, S. D. Palmer, & D. Glassy (Eds.), *Health in child care: A manual for health professionals* (4th ed., pp. 81–95). Elks Grove Village, IL: American Academy of Pediatrics.

Belsky, J., Vandell, D., Burchinal, M., Clarke-Stewart, K. A., McCartney, K., Owen, M., & NICHD Early Child Care Research Network. (2007). Are there long-term effects of early child care? *Child Development, 78,* 681–701.

Bem, D. J. (1972). Self-perception theory. In L. Berkowitz (Ed.), *Advances in experimental social psychology* (Vol. 6, pp. 1–62). New York: Academic Press.

Bem, S. L. (1975). Sex role adaptability: The consequence of psychological androgyny. *Journal of Personality and Social Psychology, 31,* 634–643.

Bem, S. L. (1981). Gender schema theory: A cognitive account of sex typing. *Psychological Review, 88,* 354–364.

Bem, S. L. (1987). Gender schema theory and the romantic tradition. In P. Shaver & C. Hendrick (Eds.), *Review of personality and social psychology* (Vol. 7, pp. 251–271). Newbury Park, CA: Sage.

Bem, S. L. (1993). Is there a place in psychology for a feminist analysis of the social context? *Feminism & Psychology, 3,* 247–251.

Bengston, V. L. (1970). The generation gap. *Youth and Society, 2,* 7–32.

Benito, J. M., Kumru, H. P., Murillo, N. P., Costa, U. P., Medina, J. P., Tormos, J. M. P., . . . Vidal, J. P. (2012). Motor and gait improvement in patients with incomplete spinal cord injury induced by high-frequency repetitive transcranial magnetic stimulation. *Topics in Spinal Cord Injury Rehabilitation, 18*(2), 106–112. doi: 10.1310/sci1802-106

Ben-Porath, Y. S., & Tellegen, A. (2011). *Mmpi-2-RF (Minnesota Multiphasic Personality Inventory-2 Restructured Form): Manual for administration, scoring, and interpretation.* Minneapolis: University of Minnesota Press.

Ben-Shakhar, G., Garner, M., Iacono, W., Meijer, E., & Verschuere, B. (2015). Preliminary process theory does not validate the comparison question test: A comment on Palmatier and Rovner (2015). *International Journal of Psychophysiology, 95*(1),16–19.

Benjafield, J. J. G. (1996). *A history of psychology.* Boston: Allyn and Bacon.

Benjamin, S. L. (2005). An interpersonal theory of personality disorders. In J. F. Clarkin & M. F. Lenzenweger (Eds.), *Major theories of personality disorder,* 157–230. New York: Guilford Press.

Benowitz, N. L. (1988). Pharmacologic aspects of cigarette smoking and nicotine addiction. *New England Journal of Medicine, 319,* 1318–1330.

Benozio, A., & Diesendruck, G. (2015). From effort to value: Preschool children's alternative to effort justification. *Psychological Science, 26*(9), 1423–1429. doi: 10.1177/0956797615589585

Benson, H. (1975). *The relaxation response.* New York: Morrow.

Benson, H., Beary, J., & Carol, M. (1974a). The relaxation response. *Psychiatry, 37,* 37–46.

Benson, H., Rosner, B. A., Marzetta, B. R., & Klemchuk, H. M. (1974b). Decreased blood pressure in pharmacologically treated hypertensive patients who regularly elicited the relaxation response. *Lancet, 1*(7852), 289–291.

Benton, D., & Parker P. (1998). Breakfast, blood glucose and cognition. *American Journal of Clinical Nutrition, 67*(4), 772S–778S.

Berenbaum, S. A., & Snyder, E. (1995). Early hormonal influences on childhood sex-typed activity and playmate preferences: Implications for the development of sexual orientation. *Developmental Psychology, 31,* 31–42.

Berent, S. (1977). Functional asymmetry of the human brain in the recognition of faces. *Neuropsychologia, 15,* 829–831.

Berg, F. (1999). Health risks associated with weight loss and obesity treatment programs. *Journal of Social Issues, 55*(2), 277–297.

Bergmann, O., Liebl, J., Bernard, S., Alkass, K., Yeung, M. S., Steier, P., . . . Frisen, J. (2012). The age of olfactory bulb neurons in humans. *Neuron, 74*(4), 634–639. doi: 10.1016/j.neuron.2012.03.030

Berk, L., Prowse, M., Petrofsky, J. S., Batt, J., Laymon, M., Bains, G., Daher, N., Tan, S., & Berk, D. (2009, May). *Laughercise: Health benefits similar of exercise lowers cholesterol and systolic blood pressure.* Presented at the Association for Psychological Science 21st Annual Convention, San Francisco, CA.

Berk, L. E. (1992). Children's private speech: An overview of theory and the status of research. In R. M. Diaz & L. E. Berk (Eds.), *Private speech: From social interaction to self-regulation* (pp. 17–53). Hillsdale, NJ: Erlbaum.

Berk, L. E., & Spuhl, S. T. (1995). Maternal interaction, private speech, and task performance in preschool children. *Early Childhood Research Quarterly, 10,* 145–169.

Berk, L. S., Felten, D. L., Tan, S. A., Bittman, B. B., & Westengard, J. (2001). Modulation of neuroimmune parameters during the eustress of humor-associated mirthful laughter. *Alternative Therapy Health Medicines, 7*(2), 62–72, 74–76.

Berk L.S., Tan, S. A., & Berk, D. (2008, April). *Cortisol and catecholamine stress hormone decrease is associated with the behavior of perceptual anticipation of mirthful laughter.* Presented at the 121st Annual Meeting of the American Physiological Society, San Diego, CA.

Berkowitz, L. (1993). *Aggression: Its causes, consequences and control.* New York: McGraw-Hill.

Berlin, L. J., Ispa, J. M., Fine, M. A., Malone, P. S., Brooks-Gunn, J., Brady-Smith, C., Ayoub, C., & Bai, Y. (2009). Correlates and consequences of spanking and verbal punishment for low-income white, African American, and Mexican American toddlers. *Child Development, 80*(5), 1403–1420.

Berman, A., Bradley, J. C., Carroll, B., Certain, R. D., Gabrelcik, J. C., Green, R., . . . & Werbel, A. (2010). *The challenge and the promise: Strengthening the force, preventing suicide and saving lives. Final report of the Department of Defense task force on the prevention of suicide by members of the armed forces,* pp. 41–44. Washington, DC.

Bermond, B., Nieuwenhuyse, B., Fasotti, L., & Schuerman, J. (1991). Spinal cord lesions, peripheral feedback, and intensities of emotional feelings. *Cognition and Emotion, 5,* 201–220.

Bernat, E., Shevrin, H., & Snodgrass, M. (2001). Subliminal visual oddball stimuli evoke a P300 component. *Clinical Neurophysiology, 112,* 159–171.

Berry, J. A., Cervantes-Sandoval, I., Chakraborty, M., & Davis, R. L. (2015). Sleep facilitates memory by blocking dopamine neuron-mediated forgetting. *Cell, 161*(7), 1656–1667.

Berry, J. W., & Kim, U. (1998). Acculturation and mental health. In P. R. Dasen, J. W. Berry, & N. Sartorius (Eds.), *Health and cross-cultural psychology: Toward applications* (pp. 207–236). Newbury Park, CA: Sage.

Berry, J. W., & Sam, D. L. (1997). Acculturation and adaptation. In J. W. Berry, M. H. Segall, & C. Kagitcibasi (Eds.), *Handbook of cross-cultural psychology, Vol. 3: Social behaviour and applications* (2nd ed., pp. 291–326). Boston: Allyn & Bacon.

Berscheid, E., & Reis, H. T. (1998). Attraction and close relationships. In D. T. Gilbert & S. T. Fiske & G. Lindzey (Eds.), *The handbook of social psychology, Vol. 2* (4th ed., pp. 193–281), New York: McGraw-Hill.

Berteretche, M. V., Dalix, A. M., Cesar d'Ornano, A. M., Bellisle, F., Khayat, D., & Faurion, A. (2004). Decreased taste sensitivity in cancer patients under chemotherapy. *Supportive Care in Cancer, 12*(8), 571–576.

Berthiller, J., Straif, K., Boniol, M., Voirin, N., Behnaim-Luzon, V., Ayoub, W. B., Dari, I., Laouamri, S., Hamdi-Cherif, M., Bartal, M., Ayed, F. B., & Sasco, A. J. (2008). Cannabis smoking and risk of lung cancer in men: A pooled analysis of three studies in Maghreb. *Journal of Thoracic Oncology, 3*(12), 1398–1403.

Bertram, L., & Tanzi, R. E. (2005). The genetic epidemiology of neurodegenerative disease. *The Journal of Clinical Investigation, 115*(6), 1449–1457.

Best, D. L. (2013). African perspectives on gender development. In T. M. S. Tchombe, A. B. Nsamenang, H. Keller, & M. Fülöp (Eds.), *Cross-cultural psychology: An Africa-centric perspective* (pp. 149–161). Limbe, Cameroon; Gainesville, FL: Design House; Bukhum Communications.

Best, D. L., & Williams, J. E. (2001). Gender and culture. In D. Matsumoto (Ed.), *The handbook of culture and psychology* (pp. 195–212). New York: Oxford University Press.

Betancourt, J. R., & Jacobs, E. A. (2000). Language barriers to informed consent and confidentiality: The impact on women's health. *Journal of American Medical Women's Association, 55,* 294–295.

Beyer, B. K. (1995). *Critical thinking.* Bloomington, IN: Phi Delta Kappa Educational Foundation.

Beyreuther, K., Biesalski, H. K., Fernstrom, J. D., Grimm, P., Hammes, W. P., Heinemann, U., Kempski, O., Stehle, P., Steinhart, H., & Walker, R. (2007). Consensus meeting: Monosodium glutamate, an update. *European Journal of Clinical Nutrition, 61,* 304–313.

Bialystok, E., Craik, F. I., Green, D. W., & Gollan, T. H. (2009). Bilingual minds. *Psychological Science in the Public Interest, 10*(3), 89–129. doi: 10.1177/1529100610387084

Bieniek, K. F., Ross, O. A., Cormier, K. A., Walton, R. L., Soto-Ortolaza, A., Johnston, A. E., . . . Dickson, D. W. (2015). Chronic traumatic encephalopathy pathology in a neurodegenerative disorders brain bank. *Acta Neuropathol, 130*(6), 877–889. doi: 10.1007/s00401-015-1502-4

Binder, J. R., Desai, R. H., Graves, W. W., & Conant, L. L. (2009). Where is the semantic system? A critical review and meta-analysis of 120 functional neuroimaging studies. *Cerebral Cortex, 19*(12), 2767–2796.

Binet, A., & Simon, T. (1916). *The development of intelligence in children.* Baltimore: Williams & Wilkins.

Bird, C. M., Keidel, J. L., Ing, L. P., Horner, A. J., & Burgess, N. (2015). Consolidation of complex events via reinstatement in posterior cingulate cortex. *Journal of Neuroscience, 35*(43), 14426–14434.

Birks, J., & Evans, J. G. (2009). Ginkgo biloba for cognitive impairment and dementia. *The Cochrane Database of Systematic Reviews* 1, CD003120. doi: 10.1002/14651858.CD003120.pub3

Biro, F. M., Greenspan, L. C., Galvez, M. P., Pinney, S. M., Teitelbaum, S., Windham, G. C., Deardorff, J., Herrick, R. L., Succop, P. A., Hiatt, R. A., Kushi, L. H., & Wolff, M. S. (2013). Onset of breast development in a longitudinal cohort. *Pediatrics, 132*(6), 1019.

Bivens, J. A., & Berk, L. E. (1990). A longitudinal study of the development of elementary school children's private speech. *Merill-Palmer Quarterly, 36,* 443–463.

Bjork, R. A., & Bjork, E. L. (1992). A new theory of disuse and an old theory of stimulus fluctuation. In A. Healy, S. Kosslyn, & R. Shiffrin (Eds.), *From learning processes to cognitive processes: Essays in honor of William K. Estes* (Vol. 2, pp. 35–67). Hillsdale, NJ: Erlbaum.

Bjork, R. A., & Whitten, W. B. (1974). Recency-sensitive retrieval processes in long-term free recall. *Cognitive Psychology, 6*, 173–189.

Blackless, M., Charuvastra, A., Derryck, A., Fausto-Sterling, A., Lauzanne, K., & Lee, E. (2000). How sexually dimorphic are we? Review and synthesis. *American Journal of Human Biology, 12*, 151–166.

Blackmon, L. R., Batton, D. G., Bell, E. F., Engle, W. A., Kanto, W. P., Martin, G. I., Rosenfeld, W. N., Stark, A. R., & Lemons, J. A. (Committee on Fetus and Newborn). (2003). *Apnea, sudden infant death syndrome, and home monitoring. Pediatrics, 111*(4), 914–917.

Blair, R. J. R., Sellars, C., Strickland, I., Clark, F., Williams, A. O., Smith, M., & Jones, L. (1995). Emotion attributions in the psychopath. *Personality and Individual Differences, 19*(4), 431–437.

Blanchard, M., & Main, M. (1979). Avoidance of the attachment figure and social-emotional adjustment in day-care infants. *Developmental Psychology, 15*, 445–446.

Blanchard, R. (2001). Fraternal birth order and the maternal immune hypothesis of male homosexuality. *Hormones and Behavior, 40*(2), 105–114.

Blanchard-Fields, F., Chen, Y., Horhota, M., & Wang, M. (2007). Cultural differences in the relationship between aging and the correspondence bias. *Journals of Gerontology Series B: Psychological Sciences and Social Sciences, 62*(6), 362–365.

Blanchard-Fields, F., & Horhota, M. (2005). Age differences in the correspondence bias: When a plausible explanation matters. *Journals of Gerontology Series B: Psychological Sciences and Social Sciences, 60*(5), 259–267.

Blass, T. (1991). Understanding behavior in the Milgram obedience experiment: The role of personality, situations, and their interactions. *Journal of Personality and Social Psychology, 60*, 398–413.

Blass, T. (1999). The Milgram paradigm after 35 years: Some things we now know about obedience to authority. *Journal of Applied Social Psychology, 25*, 955–978.

Bledsoe, C. H., & Cohen, B. (1993). *Social dynamics of adolescent fertility in sub-Saharan Africa.* Washington, DC: National Academy Press.

Blehar, M. C., & Oren, D. A. (1997). Gender differences in depression. *Medscape General Medicine, 1*(2). Retrieved June 27, 2004, from http://www.medscape.com/viewarticle/719236

Bleiberg, K. L., & Markowitcz, J. C. (2008). Interpersonal psychotherapy for depression. In D. H. Barlow (Ed.), *Clinical handbook of psychological disorders* (pp. 306–327). New York: Guilford Press.

Bleuler, E. (1911, reissued 1950). *Dementia praecox or the group of schizophrenias.* New York: International Universities Press.

Block, N. (2005). Two neural correlates of consciousness. *Trends in Cognitive Sciences, 9*, 41–89.

Bloom, B. S. (Ed.). (1956) Taxonomy of educational objectives, the classification of educational goals—Handbook I: Cognitive domain. New York: McKay.

Bloom, L. (1974). Talking, understanding and thinking. In R. Schiefelbusch & L. L. Lloyd (Eds.), *Language perspectives: Acquisition, retardation and intervention.* New York: Macmillan.

Bloom, P. (2000). *How children learn the meaning of words.* Cambridge, MA: MIT Press.

Blumenfeld, H. (2010). *Neuroanatomy through clinical cases* (2nd ed.). Sunderland, MA: Sinauer Associates, Inc.

Blumer, D. (2002). The illness of Vincent van Gogh. *American Journal of Psychiatry, 159*(4), 519–526.

Bock, R. (1993, August). *Understanding Klinefelter syndrome: A guide for XXY males and their families.* NIH Publication No. -93-3202. National Institutes of Health, Office of Research Reporting. Washington, DC: Retrieved August 10, 2010, from http://www.nichd.nih.gov/publications/pubs/klinefelter.cfm

Bodrova, E., & Leong, D. J. (1996). *Tools of the mind: The Vygotskian approach to early childhood education.* Englewood Cliffs, NJ: Prentice Hall.

Bogaert, A. F. (2006). Toward a conceptual understanding of asexuality. *Review of General Psychology, 10*, 241–250.

Boggio, P. S., Campanha, C., Valasek, C. A., Fecteau, S., Pascual-Leone, A., & Fregni, F. (2010). Modulation of decision-making in a gambling task in older adults with transcranial direct current stimulation. *The European Journal of Neuroscience, 31*(3), 593–597.

Boggio, P. S., Fregni, F., Valasek, C., Ellwood, S., Chi, R., Gallate, J., Pascual-Leone, A. & Snyder, A. (2009). Temporal lobe cortical electrical stimulation during the encoding and retrieval phase reduces false memories. *PLoS One, 4*(3), e4959.

Boggio, P. S., Rocha, M., Oliveira, M. O., Fecteau, S., Cohen, R. B., Campanha, C., Ferreira-Santos, E., Meleiro, A., Corchs, F., Zaghi, S., Pascual-Leone, A., & Fregni, F. (2009). Noninvasive brain stimulation with high-frequency and low-intensity repetitive transcranial magnetic stimulation treatment for posttraumatic stress disorder. *The Journal of Clinical Psychiatry, 29*, 29.

Bogle, K. D. (2000). Effect of perspective, type of student, and gender on the attribution of cheating. *Proceedings of the Oklahoma Academy of Science, 80*, 91–97.

Boll, T. J., Johnson, S. B., Perry, N., & Roszensky, R. H. (2002). Handbook of Clinical Health Psychology. Washington, DC: American Psychological Association.

Bolton, P., Bass, J., Betancourt, T., Speelman, L., Onyango, G., Clougherty, K. F., Neugebauer, R., Murray, L., & Verdeli, H. (2007). Interventions for depression symptoms among adolescent survivors of war and displacement in northern Uganda. *Journal of Medical Association, 298*, 519–527.

Bond, R. A., & Smith, P. B. (1996). Culture and conformity: A meta-analysis of studies using Asch's (1952, 1956) line judgment task. *Psychological Bulletin, 119*, 111–137.

Bondarenko, L. A. (2004). Role of methionine in nocturnal melatonin peak in the pineal gland. *Bulletin of Experimental Biological Medicine, 137*(5), 431–432.

Bonnelykke, B. (1990). Maternal age and parity as predictors of human twinning. *Acta Genetic Medicine & Gemellology, 39*, 329–334.

Boor, M. (1982). The multiple personality epidemic: Additional cases and inferences regarding diagnosis, etiology, dynamics, and treatment. *Journal of Nervous and Mental Disease, 170*, 302–304.

Booth-Butterfield, S. (1996). Message characteristics. *Steve's primer of practical persuasion and influence.* Retrieved August 2, 2004, from http://www.austincc.edu/colangelo/1311/persuasivecharacteristics.htm

Borgeat, F., & Goulet, J. (1983, June). Psychophysiological changes following auditory subliminal suggestions for activation and deactivation. *Perceptual & Motor Skills, 56*(3), 759–766.

Borgelt, L. M., Franson, K. L., Nussbaum, A. M., & Wang, G. S. (February 2013). The pharmacologic and clinical effects of medical cannabis. *Pharmacotherapy (Review) 33*(2), 195–209. doi: 10.1002/phar.1187

Borges, M. A., Stepnowsky, M. A., & Holt, L. H. (1977). Recall and recognition of words and pictures by adults and children. *Bulletin of the Psychonomic Society, 9*, 113–114.

Bornheimer, L. A. (2015). Exposure and response prevention as an evidence-based treatment for obsessive–compulsive disorder: Considerations for social work practice. *Clinical Social Work Journal, 43*(1), 38–49.

Boroditsky, L. (2001). Does language shape thought? Mandarin and English speakers' conceptions of time. *Cognitive Psychology, 43*(1), 1–22.

Boroditsky, L. (2009). How does our language shape the way we think? In M. Brockman (Ed.), *What's next? Dispatches on the future of science* (pp. 116–129). New York: Vintage.

Bossert, W., & Schworm, W. (2008). A class of two-group polarization measures. *Journal of Public Economic Theory, Association for Public Economic Theory, 10*(6), 1169–1187.

Bosworth, H. B., & Schaie, K. W. (1997). The relationship of social environment, social networks, and health outcomes in the Seattle Longitudinal Study: Two analytical approaches. *Journals of Gerontology Series B: Psychological Sciences and Social Sciences, 52*(5), 197–205.

Botella, C., Perez-Ara, M. A., Breton-Lopez, J., Quero, S., Garcia-Palacios, A., & Banos, R. M. (2016). In vivo versus augmented reality exposure in the treatment of small animal phobia: A randomized controlled trial. *PLoS One, 11*(2), e0148237. doi: 10.1371/journal.pone.0148237

Botwin, M. D., & Buss, D. M. (1989). The structure of act data: Is the Five-Factor Model of personality recaptured? *Journal of Personality and Social Psychology, 56*, 988–1001.

Bouchard, C., Tremblay, A., Nadeau, A., Dussault, J., Despres, J. P., Theriault, G., Lupien, P. J., Serresse, O., Boulay, M. R., & Fournier, G. (1990). Long-term exercise training with constant energy intake. 1: Effect on body composition and selected metabolic variables. *International Journal on Obesity, 14*(1), 57–73.

Bouchard, T. (1994). Genes, environment, and personality. *Science, 264*, 1700–1701.

Bouchard, T. J., Jr. (1997). Whenever the twain shall meet. *The Science, 37*(5), 52–57.

Bouchard, T. J., & Segal, N. L. (1985). Environment and IQ. In B. B. Wolman (Ed.), *Handbook of intelligence: Theories, measurements, and applications* (pp. 391–464). New York: John Wiley.

Bouckaert, F., De Winter, F. L., Emsell, L., Dols, A., Rhebergen, D., Wampers, M., . . . Vandenbulcke, M. (2015). Grey matter volume increase following electroconvulsive therapy in patients with late life depression: A longitudinal MRI study. *Journal of Psychiatry & Neuroscience, 40*(5), 140322. doi: 10.1503/jpn.140322

Boutwell, B. B., Franklin, C. A., Barnes, J. C., & Beaver, K. M. (2011). College students more likely to be lawbreakers if spanked as children. *Aggressive Behavior, 37*(6), 559.

Bowden, C. L., Calabrese, J. R., McElroy, S. L., Gyulai, L., Wassef, A., Petty, F., Pope, H. G., Jr., Chou, J. C., Keck, P. E., Jr., Rhodes, L. J., Swann, A. C., Hirschfeld, R. M., & Wozniak, P. J. (2000). For the Divalproex Maintenance Study Group. A randomized, placebo-controlled 12-month trial of divalproex and lithium in treatment of outpatients with bipolar I disorder. *Archives of General Psychiatry, 57*(5), 481–489.

Bowers, K. S., & Woody, E. Z. (1996). Hypnotic amnesia and the paradox of intentional forgetting. *Journal of Abnormal Psychology, 105*, 381–390.

Bowman, E. S. (1996). Delayed memories of child abuse: Part II: An overview of research findings relevant to understanding their reliability and suggestibility. *Dissociation: Progress in the Dissociative Disorders, 9*, 232–243.

Boxer, P., Groves, C. L., & Docherty, M. (2015). Video games do indeed influence children and adolescents' aggression, prosocial behavior, and academic performance: A clearer reading of Ferguson. *Perspectives on Psychological Science, 10*(5), 671–673. doi: 10.1177/1745691615592239

Boyd, C. H., & Peeler, C. M. (May, 2004). *Highlighting vs note taking: A comparison of students' performance on tests.* Poster presented at 16th Annual Convention of the American Psychological Society, Chicago, IL, USA.

Boyd, L. A., & Winstein, C. J. (2004). Cerebellar stroke impairs temporal but not spatial accuracy during implicit motor learning. *Neurorehabilitation and Neural Repair, 18*(3), 134–143.

Boyson-Bardies, B., deHalle, P., Sagart, L., & Durand, C. (1989). A cross-linguistic investigation of vowel formats in babbling. *Journal of Child Language, 16*, 1–17.

Bracey, G. (1997). A few facts about poverty. *Phi Delta Kappan, 79*, 163–164.

Braun, S. R. (1996). *Buzz: the science and lore of alcohol and caffeine.* New York: Oxford University Press.

Brazelton, T. B. (1992). *Touchpoints: Your child's emotional and behavioral development.* Reading, MA: Addison-Wesley.

Brecher, M., Wang, B. W., Wong, H., & Morgan, J. P. (1988). Phencyclidine and violence: Clinical and legal issues. *Journal of Clinical Psychopharmacology, 8*, 397–401.

Breedlove, S. M. (2010). Minireview: Organizational hypothesis: instances of the fingerpost. *Endocrinology, 151*(9), 4116–4122. doi: 10.1210/en.2010-0041

Breier, A., Albus, M., Pickar, D., Zahn, T. P., Wolkowitz, O. M., & Paul, S. M. (1987). Controllable and uncontrollable stress in humans: Alterations in mood, neuroendocrine and psychophysiological function. *American Journal of Psychiatry, 144*, 1419–1425.

Breiter, H. C., Gollub, R. L., Weisskoff, R. M., Kennedy, D. N., Makris, N., Berke, J. D., Goodman, J. M., Kantor, H. L., Gastfriend, D. R., Riorden, J. P., Mathew, R. T., Rosen, B. R., & Hyman, S. E. (1997). Acute effects of cocaine on human brain activity and emotion. *Neuron, 19*(3), 591–611.

Breland, K., & Breland, M. (1961). The misbehavior of organisms. *American Psychologist, 16*, 681–684.

Bremmer, J. D. (2005). *Brain imaging handbook.* New York: W. W. Norton.

Brennan, J. F. (2002). *History and systems of psychology* (6th ed.). Upper Saddle River, NJ: Prentice Hall.

Brennan, P. A., Raine, A., Schulsinger, F., Kirkegaard-Sorensen, L., Knop, J., Hutchings, B., Rosenberg, R., & Mednick, S. A. (1997). Psychophysiological protective factors for male subjects at high risk for criminal behavior. *American Journal of Psychiatry, 154*, 853–855.

Brenner, J. (2007, August). Parental impact on attitude formation—A siblings study on worries about immigration. *Ruhr Economic Paper No. 22.* Retrieved from Social Science Research Network (SSR) at http://ssrn.com/abstract=1012110

Breslau, N., Chilcoat, H. D., Kessler, R. C., Peterson, E. L., & Lucia, V. C. (1999). Vulnerability to assaultive violence: Further specification of the sex difference in posttraumatic stress disorder. *Psychological Medicine, 29*, 813–821.

Breslau, N., Davis, G. C., Andreski, P., & Peterson, E. L. (1997). Sex differences in posttraumatic stress disorder. *Archives of General Psychiatry, 54*(11), 1044–1048.

Breslow, R. A., Dong, C., & White, A. (2015). Prevalence of alcohol-interactive prescription medication use among current drinkers: United States, 1999 to 2010. *Alcoholism, Clinical and Experimental Research, 39*(2), 371–379.

Breuer, J., & Freud, S. (1895). *Studies on hysteria (cathartic method). Special Edition, 2,* 1–309.

Brewer, M. B. (2001). Ingroup identification and intergroup conflict: When does in-group love become outgroup hate? In R. D. Ashmore, L. Jussim, & D. Wilder (Eds.), *Social identity, intergroup conflict, and conflict reduction.* New York: Oxford University Press.

Brick, J. (2003). The characteristics of alcohol: Chemistry, use and abuse. In J. Brick (Ed.), *Handbook of the medical consequences of alcohol and drug abuse* (pp. 1–11). New York: Haworth Medical Press.

Briem, V., & Hedman, L. R. (1995). Behavioural effects of mobile telephone use during simulated driving. *Ergonomics, 38*, 2536–2562.

Briggs, K. C., & Myers, I. B. (1998). *The Myers-Briggs Type Indicator-Form M.* Palo Alto, CA: Consulting Psychologists Press.

Brigham, A. (1844). Asylums exclusively for the incurably insane. Classic article in *The American Journal of Psychiatry, 151*, 50–70.

Bright, S. (2013, April). *Not for human consumption: New and emerging drugs in Australia.* Prevention Research, Melbourne: Australian Drug Foundation.

Briñol, P., & Petty, R. E. (2015). Elaboration and validation processes: Implications for mass media attitude change. *Media Psychology, 18*, 267–291.

Broadbent, D. (1958). *Perception and communication.* Elmsford, NY: Pergamon.

Brodrick, J., & Mitchell, B. G. (2015). Hallucinogen persisting perception disorder and risk of suicide. *Journal of Pharmacy Practice, 29*(4), 431–434. Published online before print January 27. doi: 10.1177/0897190014566314.

Brondolo, E., Rieppi, R., Erickson, S. A., Bagiella, E., Shapiro, P. A., McKinley, P., & Sloan, R. P. (2003). Hostility, interpersonal interactions, and ambulatory blood pressure. *Psychosomatic Medicine, 65*, 1003–1011.

Bronkhorst, A. W. (2000). The cocktail party phenomenon: A review on speech intelligibility in multiple-talker conditions. *Acta Acustica united with Acustica, 86*, 117–128. Retrieved from http://eaa-fenestra.org/products/acta-acustica/most-cited/acta_86_2000_Bronkhorst.pdf

Brooks, J. G., & Brooks, M. G. (1993). *In search of understanding: The case for constructivist classrooms.* Alexandria, VA: The Association for Supervision and Curriculum Development.

Brouwers, S. A., Van de Vijver, F. J. R., & Van Hemert, D. A. (2009). Variation in Raven's Progressive Matrices scores across time and place. *Learning and Individual Differences, 19*(3), 330–338. doi: 10.1016/j.lindif.2008.10.006

Brown, A. S., & Derkits, E. J. (2010). Prenatal infection and schizophrenia: A review of epidemiologic and translational studies. *The American Journal of Psychiatry, 167*(3), 261–280. doi: 10.1176/appi.ajp.2009.09030361

Brown, C., Taylor, J., Green, A., Lee, B. E., Thomas, S. B., & Ford, A. (2003). *Managing depression in African Americans: Consumer and provider perspectives.* (Final Report to Funders). Pittsburgh: Mental Health Association of Allegheny County.

Brown, C. A., & Jones, A. K. P. (2010). Meditation experience predicts less negative appraisal of pain: Electrophysiological evidence for the involvement of anticipatory neural responses. *Pain.* doi: 10.1016/j.pain.2010.04.017

Brown, G., Lawrence, T. B., & Robinson, S. L. (2005). Territoriality in management organizations. *Academy of Management Review, 30*(3), 577–594.

Brown, G. L., & Linnoila, M. I. (1990). CSF serotonin metabolite (5–HIAA) studies in depression, impulsivity, and violence. *Journal of Clinical Psychiatry, 51*(4), 31–43.

Brown, J. (1958). Some tests of the decay theory of immediate memory. *Quarterly Journal of Experimental Psychology, 10*, 12–21.

Brown, P. K., & Wald, G. (1964). Visual pigments in single rods and cones of the human retina. *Science, 144*, 45.

Brown, R. (1973). *A first language: The early stages.* Cambridge, MA: Harvard University Press.

Brown, R., & McNeill, D. (1966). The "tip of the tongue" phenomenon. *Journal of Verbal Learning & Verbal Behavior, 5*(4), 325–337.

Browne, D. (2004). Do dolphins know their own minds? *Biology & Philosophy, 19*, 633–653.

Browne, M. N., & Keeley, S. M. (2009). *Asking the right questions: A guide to critical thinking* (9th ed.). Upper Saddle River, NJ: Pearson Prentice-Hall.

Broyles, S. (2006). Subliminal advertising and the perpetual popularity of playing to people's paranoia. *Journal of Consumer Affairs, 40*(2), 392–406.

Brubaker, D. A., & Leddy, J. J. (2003). Behavioral contracting in the treatment of eating disorders. *The Physician and Sportsmedicine, 31*(9), 15–26.

Brunner, E. J., Hemingway, H., Walker, B., Page, M., Clarke, P., Juneja, M., Shipley, M. J., Kumari, M., Andrew, R., Seckl, J. R., Papadopoulos, A., Checkley, S., Rumley, A., Lowe, G. D., Stansfeld, S. A., & Marmot, M. G. (2002). Adrenocortical, autonomic and inflammatory causes of the metabolic syndrome: Nested case-control study. *Circulation, 106*, 2659–2665.

Bryan, E. B., & Hallett, F. (2001). *Guidelines for professionals. Twins and triplets: The first five years and beyond.* London: Multiple Births Foundation.

Bryan, J., & Freed, F. (1982). Corporal punishment: Normative data and sociological and psychological correlates in a community college population. *Journal of Youth and Adolescence, 11*(2), 77–87.

Bryant, R. A., & McConkey, K. M. (1989). Hypnotic blindness: A behavioral and experimental analysis. *Journal of Abnormal Psychology, 98*, 71–77.

Buccino, G., Binkofski, F., Fink, G. R., Fadiga, L., Fogassi, L., Gallese, V., Seitz, R. J., Zilles, K., Rizzolatti, G., & Freund, H. J. (2001). Action observation activates premotor and parietal areas in a somatotopic manner: An fMRI study. *European Journal of Neuroscience, 13*(2), 400–404.

Buccino, G., Binkofski, F., & Riggio, L. (2004). The mirror neuron system and action recognition. *Brain and Language, 89*(2), 370–376.

Bucher, B. D., & Lovaas, O. I. (1967). Use of aversive stimulation in behavior modification. In M. R. Jones (Ed.), *Miami Symposium on the Prediction of Behavior 1967: Aversive Stimulation,* 77–145. Coral Gables: University of Miami Press.

Buck, L. B., & Bargmann, C. I. (2013). Smell and taste: The chemical senses. In E. R. Kandel, J. H. Schwartz, T. M. Jessell, S. A. Siegelbaum, & A. J. Hudspeth (Eds.), *Principles of neural science* (5th ed., pp. 712–735). New York: McGraw-Hill.

Buck, R. (1980). Nonverbal behavior and the theory of emotion: The facial feedback hypothesis. *Journal of Personality and Social Psychology, 38*, 811–824.

Buckels, E. E., Trapnell, P. D., & Paulhus, D. L. (2014). Trolls just want to have fun. *Personality and Individual Differences, 67*, 97–102.

Bugaiska, A., Clarys, D., Jarry, C., Taconnat, L., Tapia, G., Vanneste, S., & Isingring, M. (2007). The effect of aging in recollective experience: The processing speed and executive functioning hypothesis. *Consciousness and Cognition, 16*(4), 797–808.

Buhle, J. T., Silvers, J. A., Wager, T. D., Lopez, R., Onyemekwu, C., Kober, H., Weber, J., & Ochsner, K. N. (2014). Cognitive reappraisal of emotion: A meta-analysis of human neuroimaging studies. *Cerebral Cortex, 24*(11), 2981–2993.

Bullock, T. H., Bennett, M. V., Johnston, D., Josephson, R., Marder, E., & Fields, R. D. (2005). Neuroscience. The neuron doctrine, redux. *Science, 310*(5749), 791–793.

Burger, J. M. (1997). *The psychoanalytic approach: Neo-Freudian theory, application, and assessment. Personality* (4th ed.). Pacific Grove, CA: Brooks/Cole.

Burger, J. M. (1999). The foot-in-the-door compliance procedure: A multiple-process analysis and review. *Personality and Social Psychology Review, 3*(4), 303–325. doi: 10.1207/s15327957pspr0304_2

Burger, J. M. (2009). Replicating Milgram: Would people still obey today? *American Psychologist, 64*(1), 1–11. doi: 10.1037/a0010932

Burger, J. M., Girgis, Z. M., & Manning, C. C. (2011). In their own words: Explaining obedience to authority through an examination of participants' comments. *Social Psychological and Personality Science, 2*, 460–466. doi: 10.1177/1948550610397632

Burger, J. M., & Petty, R. E. (1981). The low-ball compliance technique: Task or person commitment? *Journal of Personality and Social Psychology, 40*, 492–500.

Burgio, K. L. (1998). Behavioral vs. drug treatment for urge urinary incontinence in older women: A randomized controlled trial. *Journal of the American Medical Association, 280*, 1995–2000.

Burguière, E., Monteiro, P., Guoping, F., & Graybiel, A. M. (2013). Optogenetic stimulation of lateral orbitofronto-striatal pathway suppresses compulsive behaviors. *Science, 340*(6137), 1243–1246. doi: 10.1126/science.1232380

Burke, D. M., MacKay, D. G., Worthley, J. S., & Wade, E. (1991). On the tip of the tongue: What causes word finding failures in young and older adults. *Journal of Memory and Language, 30*, 542–579.

Burks, N., & Martin, B. (1985). Everyday problems and life change events: Ongoing versus acute sources of stress. *Journal of Human Stress, 11*, 27–35.

Burns, J. F. (2010, May 24). British medical council bars doctor who linked vaccine with autism. *New York Times*.

Bush, G., Frazier, J. A., Rauch, S. L., Seidman, L. J., Whalen, P. J., Jenike, M. A., Rosen, B. R., & Biederman, J. (1999). Anterior cingulate cortex dysfunction in attention-deficit/hyperactivity disorder revealed by fMRI and the Counting Stroop. *Biological Psychiatry, 45*(12), 1542–1552.

Bush, G., Spencer, T. J., Holmes, J., Shin, L. M., Valera, E. M., Seidman, L. J., Biederman, J. (2008). Functional magnetic resonance imaging of methylphenidate and placebo in attention-deficit/hyperactivity disorder during the Multi-Source Interference Task. *Archives of General Psychiatry, 65*(1), 102–114.

Bushey, D., Tononi, G., & Cirelli, C. (2011). Sleep and synaptic homeostasis: Structural evidence in Drosophila. *Science, 332*(6037), 1576–1581.

Bushman, B. J. (1997). Effects of alcohol on human aggression: Validity of proposed explanations. In M. Galanter (Ed.), *Recent developments in alcoholism. Vol. 1: Alcohol and violence—Epidemiology, neurobiology, psychology, family issues* (pp. 227–243). New York: Plenum Press.

Bushman, B. J., & Huesmann, L. R. (2001). Effects of televised violence on aggression. In D. G. Singer & J. L. Singer (Eds.), *Handbook of children and the media* (Ch. 11, pp. 223–254). Thousand Oaks, CA: Sage.

Bushman, B. J., & Huesman, L. R. (2006). Short-term and long-term effects of violent media on aggression in children and adults. *Archives of Pediatrics & Adolescent Medicine, 160*, 348–352. doi: 10.1001/archpedi.160.4.348

Bushman, B. J., Newman, K., Calvert, S. L., Downey, G., Dredze, M., Gottfredson, M., . . . Webster, D. W. (2016). Youth violence: What we know and what we need to know. *American Psychologist, 71*(1), 17–39. doi: 10.1037/a0039687

Buss, D. M. (1989). Sex differences in human mate preferences: Evolutionary hypotheses testing in 37 cultures. *Behavioral and Brain Sciences, 12*, 1–49.

Buss, D. M. (2007). The evolution of human mating. *Acta Psychologica Sinica, 39*(3), 502–512.

Buss, D. M. (2009a). How can evolutionary psychology successfully explain personality and individual differences? *Perspectives on Psychological Science, 4*(4), 359–366. doi: 10.1111/j.1745-6924.2009.01138.x

Buss, D. M. (2009b). The multiple adaptive problems solved by human aggression. *Behavioral and Brain Sciences, 32*, 271–272.

Buss, D. M. (2011). Personality and the adaptive landscape: The role of individual differences in creating and solving social adaptive problems. In D. M. Buss & P. H. Hawley (Eds.), *The evolution of personality and individual differences*. New York: Oxford University Press.

Buss, D. M., Larsen, R. J., Westen, D., & Semmelroth, J. (1992). Sex differences in jealousy: Evolution, physiology, and psychology. *Psychological Science, 3*, 251–255.

Buss, D., & Schmitt, D. (1993). Sexual strategies theory: An evolutionary perspective on human mating. *Psychological Review, 100*(2), 204–232. doi: 10.1037/0033-295X.100.2.204

Buss, D., & Schmitt, D. (2011). Evolutionary psychology and feminism. *Sex Roles, 64*(9–10), 768–787. doi: 10.1007/s11199-011-9987-3

Bussa, B., & Kaufman, C. (2000). What can self-help do? *The Journal of the California Alliance of the Mentally Ill, 2*(2), 34–45.

Bussey, K., & Bandura, A. (1999). Social cognitive theory of gender development and differentiation. *Psychological Review, 106*(4), 676–713.

Butcher, J. N., Graham, J. R., Ben-Poarth, Y. S., Tellegen, A., Dahlstrom, W. G., & Kaemmer, B. (2001). *Minnesota Multiphasic Personality Inventory-2. Manual for administration, scoring, and interpretation* (Rev. ed.). Minneapolis, MN: University of Minnesota Press.

Butcher, J. N., & Rouse, S. V. (1996). Personality: Individual differences and clinical assessment. *Annual Review of Psychology, 47*, 87–111.

Butcher, J. N., Rouse, S. V., & Perry, J. N. (2000). Empirical description of psychopathology in therapy clients: Correlates of MMPI-2 scales. In J. N. Butcher (Ed.), *Basic sources on the MMPI-2* (pp. 487–500). Minneapolis, MN: University of Minnesota Press.

Cabeza, R., Anderson, N. D., Locantore, J. K., & McIntosh, A. R. (2002). Aging gracefully: Compensatory brain activity in high-performing older adults. *NeuroImage, 17*(3), 1394–1402.

Cabeza, R., & Nyberg, L. (2000). Imaging cognition II: An empirical review of 275 PET and fMRI studies. *Journal of Cognitive Neuroscience, 12*(1), 1–47.

Cacioppo, J. T. (2013). Psychological science in the 21st century. *Teaching of Psychology, 40*, 304–309.

Cacioppo, J. T., & Berntson, G. G. (1992). Social psychological contributions to the decade of the brain: Doctrine of multilevel analysis. *American Psychologist, 47*, 1019–1028.

Cain, D., & Seeman, J. (Eds.). (2001). *Humanistic psychotherapies: Handbook of research and practice*. Washington, DC: APA Publications.

Cajal, S. R. y. (1995). *Histology of the nervous system of man and vertebrates* (translated from the French by Neely Swanson and Larry W. Swanson ed.). New York, NY: Oxford University Press.

Caldji, C., Tannenbaum, B., Sharma, S., Francis, D., Plotsky, P. M., & Meaney, M. J. (1998). Maternal care during infancy regulates the development of neural systems mediating the expression of fearfulness in the rat. *Proceedings of the National Academy of Sciences of the United States of America, 95*, 5335–5340.

Caley, L. M., Kramer, C., & Robinson, L. K. (2005). Fetal alcohol spectrum disorder. *The Journal of School Nursing, 21*(3), 139–146.

Califia, P. (1997). *Sex changes: The politics of transgenderism*. San Francisco: Cleis Press.

Calvo, E. Haverstick, K., & Sass, S. A. (2009). Gradual retirement, sense of control, and retirees' happiness. *Research on Aging, 31*, 112–135.

Calvo, N., Garcia, A. M., Manoiloff, L., & Ibanez, A. (2015). Bilingualism and cognitive reserve: A critical overview and a plea for methodological innovations. *Frontiers in Aging Neuroscience, 7*, 1–17. doi: 10.3389/fnagi.2015.00249

Camacho, E. M., Verstappen, S. M., Chipping, J., & Symmons, D. P. (2013). Learned helplessness predicts functional disability, pain and fatigue in patients with recent-onset inflammatory polyarthritis. *Rheumatology (Oxford), 52*(7), 1233–1238. doi: 10.1093/rheumatology/kes434

Cameron, J., Banko, K. M., & Pierce, W. D. (2001). Pervasive negative effects of rewards on intrinsic motivation: The myth continues. *The Behavior Analyst, 24*, 1–44.

Cameron, J. A., Alvarez, J. M., Ruble, D. N., & Fuligni, A. J. (2001). Children's lay theories about ingroups and outgroups: Reconceptualizing research on prejudice. *Personality and Social Psychology Review, 5*, 118–128.

Cami, J., Farre, M., Mas, M., Roset, P. N., Poudevida, S., Mas, A., San, L., & de la Torre, R. (2000). Human pharmacology of 3,4-methylenedioxymethamphetamine ("ecstasy"): Psychomotor performance and subjective effects. *Journal of Clinical Psychopharmacology, 20*, 455–466.

Campbell, A. (2015). 80 children get chicken pox at school with low vaccination rate. Huffpost Healthy Living, 12/10/2015. Retrieved from http://www.huffingtonpost.com/entry/chicken-pox-low-vaccination-outbreak_5669d5d4e4b0f290e5227559

Campbell, J. C., & Wolf, A. D. (2003). Risk factors for femicide in abusive relationships: Results from a multisite case control study. *American Journal of Public Health, 93*(7).

Campbell, L. F., Norcross, J. C., Vasquez, M. J. T., & Kaslow, N. J. (2013). Recognition of psychotherapy effectiveness: The APA resolution. *Psychotherapy, 50*(1), 98–101. doi: 10.1037/a0031817

Cannon, W. B. (1927). The James-Lange theory of emotion: A critical examination and an alternative theory. *American Journal of Psychology, 39*, 10–124.

Cannon, W. B., & Washburn, A. L. (1912). An explanation of hunger. *American Journal of Physiology, 29*, 444–454.

Cao-Lei, L., Massart, R., Suderman, M. J., Machnes, Z., Elgbeili, G., Laplante, D. P., & King, S. (2014). DNA methylation signatures triggered by prenatal maternal stress exposure to a natural disaster: Project Ice Storm. *PLoS ONE, 9*, e107653.

Cardinali, D. P., Scacchi Bernasconi, P. A., Reynoso, R., Reyes Toso, C. F., & Scacchi, P. (2013). Melatonin may curtail the metabolic syndrome: Studies on initial and fully established fructose-induced metabolic syndrome in rats. *International Journal of Molecular Sciences, 14*(2), 2502–2514.

Cardno, A. G., & Gottesman, I. I. (2000). Twin studies of schizophrenia: From bow-and-arrow concordances to Star Wars Mx and functional genomics. *American Journal of Medical Genetics, 97*(1), 12–17. doi: 10.1002/(SICI)1096-8628(200021)97:1<12::AID-AJMG3>3.0.CO;2-U [pii]

Carducci, B. (1998). *The psychology of personality*. Pacific Grove, CA: Brooks/Cole Publishing Co.

Carey, B. (2009, December 21). Building a search engine of the brain, slice by slice. *New York Times*. Retrieved June 10, 2010, from http://www.nytimes.com/2009/12/22/health/22brain.html?ref=henry_gustav_molaison

Carlsen, A. (2013, March 18). Some people really can taste the rainbow [Web log post]. Retrieved from http://www.npr.org/blogs/thesalt/2013/03/12/174132392/synesthetes-really-can-taste-the-rainbow

Carlson, G. A., Jensen, P. S., & Nottelmann, E. D. (Eds.). (1998). Current issues in childhood bipolarity [Special issue]. *Journal of Affective Disorders, 51*, 1–5.

Carnot, M. J., Dunn, B., Cañas, A. J., Graham, P., & Muldoon, J. (2001). Concept Maps vs. Web Pages for Information Searching and Browsing. Manuscript in preparation. Institute for Human and Machine Cognition.

Carpenter, P. A., Just, M. A., & Shell, P. (1990). What one intelligence test measures: A theoretical account of the processing in the Raven Progressive Matrices test. *Psychological Review, 97*(3), 404–431.

Carr, E. G., & Lovaas, O. I. (1983). Contingent electric shock as a treatment for severe behavior problems. In S. Axelrod & J. Apsche (Eds.), *The effects of punishment on human behavior* (pp. 221–245). New York: Academic Press.

Carrion, V. G., Weems, C. F., & Reiss, A. L. (2007). Stress predicts brain changes in children: A pilot longitudinal study on youth stress, posttraumatic stress disorder, and the hippocampus. *Pediatrics, 119*(3), 509–516.

Carruthers, M. (2001). A multifactorial approach to understanding andropause. *Journal of Sexual and Reproductive Medicine, 1*, 69–74.

Carskadon, M. A., & Dement, W. C. (2005). Normal human sleep overview. In M. H. Kryger, T. Roth, & W. C. Dement (Eds.), *Principles and practice of sleep medicine* (4th ed., pp. 13–23). Philadelphia: Elsevier/Saunders.

Carskadon, M. A., & Dement, W. C. (2011). Normal human sleep: An overview. In M. H. Kryger, T. Roth, & W. C. Dement (Eds.), *Principles and practice of sleep medicine*, pp. 16–26. St. Louis, MO: Elsevier Saunders.

Carson, R. C. (1969). *Interaction concepts of personality.* Chicago: Aldine.

Carter, C., Bishop, J., & Kravits, S. L. (2005). *Keys to success: Building successful intelligence for college, career, and life* (5th ed.). Englewood Cliffs, NJ: Prentice Hall.

Carter, R. M., Bowling, D. L., Reeck, C., & Huettel, S. (2012). A distinct role of the temporal-parietal junction in predicting socially guided decisions. *Science, 337*(6090), 109–111.

Carver, C. S., & Antoni, M. H. (2004). Finding benefit in breast cancer during the year after diagnosis predicts better adjustment 5 to 8 years after diagnosis. *Health Psychology, 26*, 595–598.

Carver, L. J., & Bauer, P. J. (2001). The dawning of a past: The emergence of long-term explicit memory in infancy. *Journal of Experimental Psychology: General, 130*, 726–745.

Case, B. G., Bertollo, D. N., Laska, E. M., Price, L. H., Siegel, C. E., Olfson, M., & Marcus, S. C. (2013). Declining use of electroconvulsive therapy in United States general hospitals. *Biological Psychiatry, 73*(2), 119–126. doi: 10.1016/j.biopsych.2012.09.005

Case, B. G., Bertollo, D. N., Laska, E. M., Siegel, C. E., Wanderling, J. A., & Olfson, M. (2012). Racial differences in the availability and use of electroconvulsive therapy for recurrent major depression. *Journal of Affective Disorders, 136*(3), 359–365. doi: 10.1016/j.jad.2011.11.026

Case, S. S., & Oetama-Paul, A. J. (2015). Brain biology and gendered discourse. *Applied Psychology: An International Review, 64*, 338–378. doi: 10.1111/apps.12040

Cassidy, A., Bingham, S., & Setchell, K. D. R. (1994). Biological effects of a diet of soy protein rich in isoflavones on the menstrual cycle of premenopausal women. *American Journal of Clinical Nutrition, 60*, 333–340.

Castillo, R. J. (1997). Eating disorders. In R. J. Castillo (Ed.), *Culture and mental illness: A client-centered approach* (p. 152). Pacific Grove, CA: Brooks/Cole.

Catanzaro, S. J., Wasch, H. H., Kirsch, I., & Mearns, J. (2000). Coping-related expectancies and dispositions as prospective predictors of coping responses and symptoms: Distinguishing mood regulation expectancies, dispositional coping, and optimism. *Journal of Personality, 68*, 757–788.

Cattell, R. B. (1950). *Personality: A systematic, theoretical, and factual study.* New York: McGraw-Hill.

Cattell, R. B. (Ed.). (1966). *Handbook of multivariate experimental psychology.* Chicago: Rand McNally.

Cattell, R. B. (1973). *Personality and mood by questionnaire.* San Francisco: Jossey-Bass.

Cattell, R. B. (1990). Advances in Cattellian personality theory. In L. A. Pervin (Ed.), *Handbook of personality: Theory and research* (pp. 101–110). New York: Guilford.

Cattell, R. B. (1994). *Sixteen Personality Factor Questionnaire* (5th ed.). Champaign, IL: Institute for Personality and Ability Testing, Inc.

Cattell, R. B. (1995). Personality structure and the new fifth edition of the 16PF. *Educational & Psychological Measurement, 55*(6), 926–937.

Cattell, R. B., & Kline, P. (1977). *The scientific analysis of personality and motivation.* New York: Academic Press.

Cavanaugh, A. M., & Buehler, C. (2016). Adolescent loneliness and social anxiety: The role of multiple sources of support. *Journal of Social and Personal Relationships, 33*(2), 149–170.

Cave, K. R., & Kim, M. (1999). Top-down and bottom-up attentional control: On the nature of interference from a salient distractor. *Perception & Psychophysics, 61*, 1009–1023.

Center for Behavioral Health Statistics and Quality. (2015). Behavioral health trends in the United States: Results from the 2014 National Survey on Drug Use and Health: (HHS Publication No. SMA 15-4927, NSDUH Series H-50). Retrieved from http://www.samhsa.gov/data/

Centers for Disease Control and Prevention. (2004). Cigarette smoking among adults United States, 2002. *Morbidity and Mortality Weekly Report, 53*(20), 427–431.

Centers for Disease Control and Prevention (CDC). (2004). *Parents' guide to childhood immunization.* Atlanta, GA: U.S. Department of Health and Human Services, Public Health Service.

Centers for Disease Control and Prevention (CDC). (2009). Down syndrome. Retrieved June 19, 2010, from www.cdc.gov/ncbddd/birthdefects/DownSyndrome.htmCenters for Disease Control and Prevention (CDC). (2010). How tobacco smoke causes disease: The biology and behavioral basis for smoking-attributable disease: A report of the Surgeon General. Retrieved from the Internet March 27, 2013, from http://www.cdc.gov/tobacco/data_statistics/sgr/2010/index.htm

Centers for Disease Control and Prevention (CDC). (2010a). HIV transmission. Divisions of HIV/AIDS Prevention. Retrieved from http://www.cdc.gov/hiv/resources/qa/transmission.htm

Centers for Disease Control and Prevention (CDC). (2011). FastStats: Alcohol use. Retrieved from the Internet March 27, 2013, from http://www.cdc.gov/nchs/fastats/alcohol.htm

Centers for Disease Control and Prevention (CDC). (2011). Vaccines & immunizations: Some common misconceptions. Retrieved April 26, 2013, from http://www.cdc.gov/vaccines/vac-gen/6mishome.htm

Centers for Disease Control and Prevention (CDC). (2013a). *Leading causes of death in males United States.* Atlanta, GA: U.S. Department of Health and Human Services, Public Health Service.

Centers for Disease Control and Prevention (CDC). (2013a). HIV basics: HIV transmission. Divisions of HIV/AIDS Prevention. Retrieved from http://www.cdc.gov/hiv/basics/transmission.html

Centers for Disease Control and Prevention (CDC). (2013b). *Leading causes of death in females United States.* Atlanta, GA: U.S. Department of Health and Human Services, Public Health Service.

Centers for Disease Control and Prevention (CDC). (2013b, Feburary). *HIV Surveillance Report, 2011.* Divisions of HIV/AIDS Prevention, Centers for Disease Control and Prevention Retrieved from http://www.cdc.gov/hiv/library/reports/surveillance/index.html.

Centers for Disease Control and Prevention (CDC). (2014). HIV Surveillance Report 2014 (Vol. 26). National Center for Chronic Disease Prevention and Health Promotion. Atlanta, Georgia. Retrieved from http://www.cdc.gov/hiv/library/reports/surveillance/

Centers for Disease Control and Prevention (CDC). (2015). HIV basics: HIV transmission. Divisions of HIV/AIDS Prevention. Retrieved from http://www.cdc.gov/hiv/basics/transmission.html

Centers for Disease Control and Prevention (CDC). (2015). HPV vaccines: Vaccinating your preteen or teen. National Center for Preparedness, Detection, and Control of Infectious Diseases. U. S. Department of Health & Human Services. Retrieved from http://www.cdc.gov/hpv/parents/vaccine.html

Centers for Disease Control and Prevention. (2015). *Suicide: Facts at a glance.* Retrieved from http://www.cdc.gov/violenceprevention/pdf/suicide-datasheet-a.pdf

Centers for Disease Control and Prevention (CDC). (2015a). Fact sheets: Alcohol use and your health. Atlanta, GA: CDC. Retrieved from http://www.cdc.gov/alcohol/fact-sheets/alcohol-use.htm

Centers for Disease Control and Prevention (CDC). (2015b). Smoking & tobacco use: Current cigarette smoking among adults in the United States. Office on Smoking and Health, National Center for Chronic Disease Prevention and Health Promotion. Atlanta, GA, CDC. Retrieved from http://www.cdc.gov/tobacco/data_statistics/fact_sheets/adult_data/cig_smoking/index.htm#national

Centers for Disease Control and Prevention (CDC). (2015c). *Vital signs: Today's heroin epidemic.* Atlanta, GA: CDC. Retrieved from http://www.cdc.gov/vitalsigns/heroin/

Centers for Disease Control and Prevention. (2015d). Injury prevention & control: Motor vehicle safety: Distracted driving. Retrieved from http://www.cdc.gov/motorvehiclesafety/distracted_driving/

Centerwall, B. S. (1989). Exposure to television as a risk factor for violence. *American Journal of Epidemiology, 129*, 643–652.

Cepeda, N. J., Pashler, H., Vul, E., Wixted, J. T., & Rohrer, D. (2006). Distributed practice in verbal recall tasks: A review and quantitative synthesis. *Psychological Bulletin, 132*, 354–380.

Cermak, L., & Craik, F. (1979). *Levels of processing in human memory.* Hillsdale, NJ: Erlbaum.

Cha, J. H., & Nam, K. D. (1985). A test of Kelley's cube theory of attribution: A cross-cultural replication of McArthur's study. *Korean Social Science Journal, 12*, 151–180.

Chaddock, L., Hillman, C. H., Buck, S. M., & Cohen, N. J. (2010). Aerobic fitness and executive control of relational memory in preadolescent children. *Medicine and Science in Sports and Exercise.* doi: 10.1249/MSS.0b013e3181e9af48

Chahua, M., Sanchez-Niubo, A., Torrens, M., Sordo, L., Bravo, M. J., Brugal, M. T., & Domingo-Salvany, A. (2015). Quality of life in a community sample of young cocaine and/or heroin users: The role of mental disorders. *Quality of Life Research: An International Journal of Quality of Life Aspects of Treatment, Care, and Rehabilitation, 24*(9), 2129–2137.

Chan, C. J., Smyth, M. J., & Martinet, L. (2014). Molecular mechanisms of natural killer cell activation in response to cellular stress. *Cell Death and Differentiation, 21*, 5–14.

Chandola, T., Britton, A., Brunner, E., Hemingway, H., Malik, M., Kumari, M., Badrick, E., Kivimaki, M., & Marmot, M. (2008). Work stress and coronary heart disease: What are the mechanisms? *European Heart Journal.* doi:10.1093/eurheartj/ehm584

Chandola, T., Brunner, E., & Marmot, M. (2006). Chronic stress at work and the metabolic syndrome: Prospective study. *British Medical Journal, 332*, 521–525.

Chang, A.-M., Aeschbach, D., Duffy, J. F., & Czeisler, C. A. (2015). Evening use of light-emitting eReaders negatively affects sleep, circadian timing, and next-morning alertness. *Proceedings of the National Academy of Sciences of the United States of America, 112*(4), 1232–1237.

Chang, E. (2004). As Los Angeles burned, Korean America was born: Community in the twenty-first century. *Amerasia Journal, 30*(1), vii–ix.

Chang, P. P., Ford, D. E., Meoni, L. A., Wang, N., & Klag, M. J. (2002). Anger in young men and subsequent premature cardiovascular disease: The precursors study. *Archives of Internal Medicine, 162*, 901–906.

Chang, S. W., Gariépy, J. F., & Platt, M. L. (2013). Neuronal reference frames for social decisions in primate frontal cortex. *Nature Neuroscience, 16*, 243–250.

Charlesworth, W. R., & Kreutzer, M. A. (1973). Facial expression of infants and children. In P. Ekman (Ed.), *Darwin and facial expression: A century of research in review.* New York: Academic.

Chee, M. W. L., & Choo, W. C. (2004, April 24–May 1). Functional imaging of working memory following 24 hours of total sleep deprivation. *Program and abstracts of the 56th Annual Meeting of the American Academy of Neurology.* San Francisco.

Chein, J., Albert, D., O'Brien, L., Uckert, K., & Steinberg, L. (2011). Peers increase adolescent risk taking by enhancing activity in the brain's reward circuitry. *Developmental Science, 14*, F1–F10.

Chen, J. Y. (2007). Do Chinese and English speakers think about time differently? Failure of replicating Boroditsky (2001). *Cognition, 104*(2), 427–436.

Chen, L. Y., Rex, C. S., Sanaiha, Y., Lynch, G., & Gall, C. M. (2010). Learning induces neurotrophin signaling at hippocampal synapses. *Proceedings of the National Academy of Sciences, USA, 107*(15), 7030–7035.

Chen, R., & Ende, N. (2000). The potential for the use of mononuclear cells from human umbilical cord blood in the treatment of amyotrophic lateral sclerosis in SOD1 mice. *Journal of Medicine, 31*, 21–31.

Chen, V. H. H., & Wu, Y. (2013). Group identification as a mediator of the effect of players' anonymity on cheating in online games. *Behaviour & Information Technology, 34*(7), 658–667. doi: 10.1080/0144929X.2013.843721

Chen, Y., Huang, X., Zhang, Y.-W., Rockenstein, E., Bu, G., Golde, T. E., Masliah, E., & Xu, H. (2012). Alzheimer's β-Secretase (BACE1) regulates the cAMP/PKA/CREB pathway independently of β-Amyloid. *Journal of Neuroscience, 32*(33), 11390. doi: 10.1523/JNEUROSCI.0757-12.2012

Cheng, C., Lau, H.-P. B., & Chan, M.-P. S. (2014). Coping flexibility and psychological adjustment to stressful life changes: A meta-analytic review. *Psychological Bulletin, 140*(6), 1582–1307.

Cherry, E. C. (1953). Some experiments on the recognition of speech, with one and with two ears. *Journal of the Acoustical Society of America, 25*(5), 975–979.

Cheryan, S., Plaut, V., Davis, P., & Steele, C. (2009). Ambient belonging: How stereotypical cues impact gender participation in computer science. *Journal of Personality and Social Psychology, 97*(6), 1045–1060.

Cheryan, S., Plaut, V. C., Handron, C., & Hudson, L. (2013). The stereotypical computer scientist: Gendered media representations as a barrier to inclusion for women. *Sex Roles: A Journal of Research, 69*, 58–71.

Cheryan, S., Siy, J. O., Vichayapai, M., Drury, B. J., & Kim, S. (2011). Do female and male role models who embody STEM stereotypes hinder women's anticipated success in STEM? *Social Psychological and Personality Science, 2*, 656–664.

Chess, S., & Shaw, A. (2015). A conspiracy of fishes, or, How we learned to stop worrying about #GamerGate and embrace hegemonic masculinity. *Journal of Broadcasting & Electronic Media, 59*(1), 208–220.

Chess, S., & Thomas, A. (1986). *Temperament in clinical practice.* New York: Guilford Press.

Chesterton, L. S., Barlas, P., Foster, N. E., Baxter, G. D., & Wright, C. C. (2003). Gender differences in pressure pain threshold in healthy humans. *Pain, 101*, 259–266.

Cheyne, J. A. (2003). Sleep paralysis and the structure of waking-nightmare hallucinations. *Dreaming, 13*(3), 163–179.

Chidester, D. (2003). *Salvation and suicide: Jim Jones, the Peoples Temple, and Jonestown* (Rev. ed.). Bloomington, IN: Indiana University Press.

Chinn, A. B., & Trujillo, K. A. (1996). Drugs and the brain: A World Wide Web tutorial in neuropsychopharmacology. *Society for Neuroscience Abstracts, 22*, 246.

Chirkov, V. I. (2009). A cross-cultural analysis of autonomy in education: A self-determination theory perspective. *Theory and Research in Education, 7*(2), 253–262.

Chirkov, V. I., Lebedeva, N. M., Molodtsova, I., & Tatarko, A. (2011). Social capital, motivational autonomy, and health behavior: A comparative study of Canadian and Russian youth. In D. Chadee & A. Kosti (Eds.), *Social psychological dynamics* (pp. 211–241). Trinidad: University of West Indies Press.

Chiu, C., Hong, Y., & Dweck, C. S. (1997). Lay dispositionism and implicit theories of personality. *Journal of Personality and Social Psychology, 73*, 19–30.

Choca, J. P. (2013). *The Rorschach inkblot test: An interpretive guide for clinicians.* Washington, DC, US: American Psychological Association.

Choi, I., & Nisbett, R. E. (1998). Situational salience and cultural differences in the correspondence bias and in the actor–observer bias. *Personality and Social Psychology Bulletin, 24*, 949–960.

Choi, I., Nisbett, R. E., & Norenzayan, A. (1999). Causal attribution across cultures: Variation and universality. *Psychological Bulletin, 125*, 47–63.

Chomsky, N. (1957). *Syntactic structures.* The Hague: Mouton.

Chomsky, N. (1964). *Current issues in linguistic theory.* The Hague: Mouton.

Chomsky, N. (1981). Principles and parameters in syntactic theory. In N. Hornstein & D. Lightfoot (Eds.), *Explanation in linguistics: The logical problem of language acquisition*, 32–75. London: Longman.

Chomsky, N. (1986). *Knowledge of language: Its nature, origin and use.* New York: Praeger.

Chomsky, N. (2006). *Language and mind* (3rd ed.). New York: Cambridge University Press.

Chomsky, N., Belletti, A., & Rizzi, L. (2002). *On nature and language.* New York: Cambridge University Press.

Chorpita, B. F., Daleiden, E. L., Ebesutani, C., Young, J., Becker, K. D., Nakamura, B. J., . . . Starace, N. (2011). Evidence-based treatments for children and adolescents: An updated review of indicators of efficacy and effectiveness. *Clinical Psychology Science and Practice, 18*, 154–172. doi: 10.1111/j.1468-2850.2011.01247.x

Chou, S. Y., Grossman, M., & Saffer, H. (2004). An economic analysis of adult obesity: Results from the behavioral risk factor surveillance system. *Journal of Health Economics, 23*, 565–587.

Christensen, A., Jacobson, N. S., & Babcock, J. C. (1995). Integrative behavioral couple therapy. In N. S. Jacobson & A. S. Gurman (Eds.), *Clinical handbook of couple therapy* (pp. 31–64). New York: Norton.

Christensen, A. J., & Nezu, A. M. (2013). Behavioral medicine and clinical health psychology: Introduction to the special issue. *Journal of Consulting and Clinical Psychology, 81*(2), 193–195.

Chu, J. A., Frey, L. M., Ganzel, B. L., & Matthews, J. A. (1999). Memories of childhood abuse: Dissociation, amnesia, and corroboration. *American Journal of Psychiatry, 156*, 749–755.

Chwalisz, K., Diener, E., & Gallagher, D. (1988). Autonomic arousal feedback and emotional experience: Evidence from the spinal cord injured. *Journal of Personality and Social Psychology, 54*, 820–828.

Cialdini, R. B., & Goldstein, N. J. (2004). Social influence: Compliance and conformity. *Annual Review of Psychology, 55*, 591–621. doi: 10.1146/annurev.psych.55.090902.142015

Cialdini, R. B., Trost, M. R., & Newsom, J. T. (1995). Preference for consistency: The development of a valid measure and the discovery of surprising behavioral implications. *Journal of Personality and Social Psychology, 69*, 318–328.

Cialdini, R., Vincent, J., Lewis, S., Catalan, J., Wheeler, D., & Darby, B. (1975). Reciprocal concessions procedure for inducing compliance: The door–in–the–face technique. *Journal of Personality and Social Psychology, 31*, 206–215.

Cialdini, R., Wosinska, W., Barrett, D., Butner, J., & Gornik–Durose, M. (1999). Compliance with a request in two cultures: The differential influence of social proof and commitment/consistency on collectivists and individualists. *Personality and Social Psychology Bulletin, 25*, 1242–1253.

Ciardiello, A. (1998). Did you ask a good question today? Alternative cognitive and metacognitive strategies. *Journal of Adolescent & Adult Literacy, 42*, 210–219.

Cinnirella, M., & Green, B. (2007). Does "cyber-conformity" vary cross-culturally? Exploring the effect of culture and communication medium on social conformity. *Computers in Human Behavior, 23*(4), 2011–2025.

Cirelli, C. (2012). Brain plasticity, sleep and aging. *Gerontology, 58*: 441–445.

Clancy, S. A., McNally, R. J., Schacter, D. L., Lenzenweger, M. F., & Pitman, R. K. (2002). Memory distortion in people reporting abduction by aliens. *Journal of Abnormal Psychology, 111*(3), 455–461.

Clark, A. (1991). *Microcognition: Philosophy, cognitive science, and parallel distributed processing.* Cambridge, MA: MIT Press, reprint edition (1989).

Clark, D. A., Beck, A. T., & Brown, G. (1989). Cognitive mediation in general psychiatric outpatients: A test of the content-specificity hypothesis. *Journal of Personality and Social Psychology, 56*, 958–964.

Clark, D. A., Hollifield, M., Leahy, R. L., & Beck, J. S. (2009). Theory of cognitive therapy. In G. Gabbard, J. S. Beck, & J. Wright (Eds.), *Textbook of psychotherapeutic treatments in psychiatry* (pp. 165–200). Washington, DC: American Psychiatric Press.

Clarke, A., Harvey, M. L., & Kane, D. J. (1999). *Attitudes and behavior: Are produce consumers influenced by eco-labels?* Paper presented at a National Conference on Eco-labels, "Making Change in the Marketplace," October 22–23, 1998. Retrieved August 1, 2004, from http://www.ssi.nrcs.usda.gov/ssienvpsy/nrcs/ecolabel.pdf

Clarke, A. R., Barry, R. J., McCarthy, R., Selikowitz, M., Johnstone, S. J., Hsu, C. I., Croft, R. J. (2007). Coherence in children with Attention-Deficit/Hyperactivity Disorder and excess beta activity in their EEG. *Clinical Neurophysiology, 118*(7), 1472–1479.

Clarke, J. (1994). Pieces of the puzzle: The jigsaw method. In S. Sharan (Ed.), *Handbook of cooperative learning methods* (pp. 34–50). Westport, CT: Greenwood Press.

Clarkin, J. F., Levy, K. N., Lenzenweger, M. F., & Kernberg, O. F. (2007). Evaluating three treatments for borderline personality disorder: A multiwave study. *American Journal of Psychiatry, 164*(6), 922–928.

Coates, J. (1986). *Women, men, and language.* New York: Longman.

Coccaro, E. F., & Kavoussi, R. J. (1996). Neurotransmitter correlates of impulsive aggression. In D. M. Stoff & R. B. Cairns (Eds.), *Aggression and violence* (pp. 67–86). Mahwah, NJ: Lawrence Erlbaum.

Cohen, L. J. (1997). Rational drug use in the treatment of depression. *Pharmacotherapy, 17*, 45–61.

Cohen, M. S., Chen, Y. Q., McCauley, M., Gamble, T., Hosseinipour, M. C., Kumarasamy, N., . . . Fleming, T. R. (2011). Prevention of HIV-1 infection with early antiretroviral therapy. *New England Journal of Medicine, 365*, 493–505.

Cohen, N. J., Eichenbaum, R., Decedo, J. C., & Corkin, S. (1985). Preserved learning capacity in amnesia: Evidence for multiple memory systems. In L. S. Squire & N. Butters (Eds.), *Neuropsychology of memory*, pp. 83–103. New York: Guilford Press.

Cohen, S., Frank, E., Doyle, B. J., Skoner, D. P., Rabin, B. S., & Gwaltney, J. M. (1998). Types of stressors that increase susceptibility to the common cold. *Health Psychology, 17,* 214–223.

Cohen, S., & Herbert, T. B. (1996). Health psychology: Psychological factors and physical disease from the perspective of human psychoneuroimmunology. *Annual Review of Psychology, 47,* 113–142.

Cohen, S., Janicki-Deverts, D., Doyle, W. J., Miller, G. E., Frank, E. Rabin, B. S., & Turner, R. B. (2012). Chronic stress, glucocorticoid receptor resistance, inflammation, and disease risk. *Proceedings of the National Academy of Sciences of the United States of America, 109*(16), 5995–5999.

Cohen, S., Janicki-Deverts, D., & Miller, G. E. (2007). Psychological stress and disease. *Journal of the American Medical Association, 298*(14), 1685–1687.

Cohen, S., Tyrrell, D. A., & Smith, A. P. (1991). Psychological stress and susceptibility to the common cold. *New England Journal of Medicine, 325,* 606–612.

Coker, T., Austin, S., & Schuster, M. (2009). The health and health care of lesbian, gay, and bisexual adolescents. *Annual Review of Public Health, 31,* 457–477.

Colcombe, S. J., Erickson, K. I., Raz, N., Webb, A. G., Cohen, N. J., McAuley, E., & Kramer, A. F. (2003). Aerobic fitness reduces brain tissue loss in aging humans. *Journal of Gerontology Series A: Biological Sciences and Medical Sciences, 58,* 176–180.

Cole, S. W., Arevalo, J. M. G., Takahashi, R., Sloan, E. K., Lutgendorf, S. K., Sood, A. K., Sheridan, J. F., & Seeman, T. E. (2010). Computational identification of gene-social environment interaction oat the human IL6 locus. *Proceedings of the National Academy of Sciences of the United States of America.* Retrieved September 27, 2010, from http://www.pnas.org/content/107/12/5681.full.

Colligan, J. (1983). Musical creativity and social rules in four cultures. *Creative Child and Adult Quarterly, 8,* 39–44.

Collin, S. H. P., Milivojevic, B., & Doeller, C. F. (2015). Memory hierarchies map onto the hippocampal long axis in humans. *Nature Neuroscience, 18,* 1562–1564.

Collins, A. M., & Loftus, E. F. (1975). A spreading activation theory of semantic processing. *Psychological Review, 82,* 407–428.

Collins, A. M., & Quillian, M. R. (1969). Retrieval time from semantic memory. *Journal of Verbal Learning and Verbal Behaviour, 8,* 240–247.

Collins, C. J., Hanges, P. J., & Locke, E. A. (2004). The relationship of achievement motivation to entrepreneurial behavior: A meta-analysis. *Human Performance, 17*(1), 95–117.

Colom, R., Privado, J., García, L. F., Estrada, E., Cuevas, L., & Shih, P.-C. (2015). Fluid intelligence and working memory capacity: Is the time for working on intelligence problems relevant for explaining their large relationship? *Personality and Individual Differences, 79,* 75–80. doi: 10.1016/j.paid.2015.01.051

Colom, R., Shih, P. C., Flores-Mendoza, C., & Quiroga, M. A. (2006). The real relationship between short-term memory and working memory. *Memory, 14*(7), 804–813.

Columbo, J., & Mitchell, D. W. (2009). Infant visual habituation. *Neurobiology of Learning and Memory, 92*(2), 225–234.

Committee on Animal Research and Ethics. (2004). Research with animals in psychology. Retrieved October 12, 2004, from www.apa.org/science/animal2.html

Cone-Wesson, B. (2005). Prenatal alcohol and cocaine exposure: Influences on cognition, speech, language, and hearing. *Journal of Communication Disorders, 38*(4), 279–302.

Connor, S., Tenorio, G., Clandinin, M. T., & Sauv, Y. (2012). DHA supplementation enhances high-frequency, stimulation-induced synaptic transmission in mouse hippocampus. *Applied Physiology, Nutrition, and Metabolism, 37*(5), 880–887. doi: 10.1139/h2012-062

Conrad, R., & Hull, A. J. (1964). Information, acoustic confusion, and memory span. *British Journal of Psychology, 55,* 429–432.

Constantine, M. G., Alleyne, V. L., Caldwell, L. D., McRae, M. B., & Suzuki, M. B. (2005). Coping responses of Asian, Black, and Latino/Latina New York City residents following the September 11, 2001 terrorist attacks against the United States. *Cultural Diversity & Ethnic Minority, 11,* 293–308.

*Consumer Reports.* (1995, November). Mental health: Does psychotherapy help? 734–739.

Conway, M. A., Cohen, G., & Stanhope, N. (1992). Very long-term memory for knowledge acquired at school and university. *Applied Cognitive Psychology, 6,* 467–482.

Cook, K. (2014). *Kitty Genovese: The murder, the bystanders, the crime that changed America.* New York: W. W. Norton & Co.

Cook, M., & Mineka, S. (1989). Observational conditioning of fear to fear-relevant versus fear-irrelevant stimuli in rhesus monkeys. *Journal of Abnormal Psychology, 98*(4), 448–459.

Coolidge, F. L. (2006). *Dream interpretation as a psychotherapeutic technique.* London: Radcliffe.

Cooper, C., Li, R., Lyketsos, C., & Livingston, G. (2013). Treatment for mild cognitive impairment: Systematic review. *The British Journal of Psychiatry, 203*(4), 255–264.

Cooper, L. A., Gonzales, J. J., Gallo, J. J., Rost, K. M., Meredith, L. S., Rubenstein, L. V., Wang, N. Y., & Ford, D. E. (2003). The acceptability of treatment for depression among African-American, Hispanic, and White primary care patients. *Medical Care, 41*(4), 479–489.

Corballis, M. C. (2009). The evolution and genetics of cerebral asymmetry. *Philosophical Transactions of the Royal Society B: Biological Sciences, 364*(1519), 867–879. doi: 10.1098/rstb.2008.0232

Corbett, G. (2016). Motivational interviewing. In I. Marini & M. A. Stebnicki (Eds.), *The professional counselor's desk reference* (2nd ed., pp. 235–239). New York: Springer Publishing.

Corbetta, M., Kincade, M. J., Lewis, C., Snyder, A. Z., & Sapir, A. (2005). Neural basis and recovery of spatial attention deficits in spatial neglect. *Nature Neuroscience, 8,* 1603–1610.

Cormier, J. F., & Thelen, M. H. (1998). Professional skepticism of multiple personality disorder. *Professional Psychology: Research and Practice, 29,* 163–167.

Corr, C. A. (1993). Coping with dying: Lessons that we should and should not learn from the work of Elisabeth Kübler-Ross. *Death Studies, 17,* 69–83.

Cosgrove, G. R., & Rauch, S. L. (1995). Psychosurgery. *Neurosurgery Clinics of North America, 6,* 167–176.

Cosmides, L., & Tooby, J. (2013). Evolutionary psychology: New perspectives on cognition and motivation. *Annual Review of Psychology, 64,* 201–229.

Costa, P. T., Jr., & McCrae, R. R. (2000). The Revised NEO Personality Inventory (NEO PI-R). In S. R. Briggs, J. Cheek & E. M. Donahue (Eds.), *Handbook of personality inventories,* pp. 410–413. New York: Plenum.

Costello, D. M., Swendsen, J., Rose, J. S., & Dierker, L. C. (2008). Risk and protective factors associated with trajectories of depressed mood from adolescence to early adulthood. *Journal of Consulting and Clinical Psychology, 76*(2), 173–183.

Couperus, J. W., & Nelson, C. A. (2006). Early brain development and plasticity. In K. McCartney & D. Phillips (Eds.), *The Blackwell handbook of early childhood development* (pp. 85–105). Oxford, UK: Blackwell Press.

Courage, M. L., & Howe, M. L. (2002). From infant to child: The dynamics of cognitive change in the second year of life. *Psychological Bulletin, 128,* 250–277.

Cowan, N. (1988). Evolving conceptions of memory storage, selective attention, and their mutual constraints within the human information processing system. *Psychological Bulletin, 104,* 163–191.

Cowan, N. (2001). The magical number 4 in short-term memory: A reconsideration of mental storage capacity. *Behavioral and Brain Sciences, 24,* 97–185.

Cowan, N., Elliott, E. M., Saults, J. S., Morey, C. C., Mattox, S., Hismjatullina, A., & Conway, A. R. A. (2005). On the capacity of attention: Its estimation and its role in working memory and cognitive aptitudes. *Cognitive Psychology, 51*(1), 42–100.

Craddock, N., O'Donovan, M. C., & Owen, M. J. (2005). The genetics of schizophrenia and bipolar disorder: Dissecting psychosis. *Journal of Medical Genetics, 42,* 288–299.

Crago, M. B., Shisslak, C. M., & Estes, L. S. (1996). Eating disturbances among American minority groups: A review. *International Journal of Eating Disorders, 19,* 239–248.

Craighead, W. E., & Dunlop, B. W. (2014). Combination psychotherapy and antidepressant medication treatment for depression: For whom, when, and how. *Annual Review of Psychology, 65,* 267–300. doi: 10.1146/annurev.psych.121208.131653

Craik, F. I. M. (1970). The fate of primary memory items in free recall. *Journal of Verbal Learning and Verbal Behavior, 9,* 143–148.

Craik, F. I. M. (1994). Memory changes in normal aging. *Current Directions in Psychological Science, 3*(5), 155–158.

Craik, F. I. M., & Lockhart, R. S. (1972). Levels of processing. A framework for memory research. *Journal of Verbal Learning and Verbal Behaviour, 11,* 671–684.

Craik, F. I. M., & Tulving, E. (1975). Depth of processing and the retention of words in episodic memory. *Journal of Experimental Psychology: General, 104,* 268–294.

Cramer, J. W., Bartz, P. J., Simpson, P. M., & Zangwill, S. D. (2014). The spectrum of congenital heart disease and outcomes after surgical repair among children with Turner syndrome: A single-center review. *Pediatric Cardiology, 35,* 253.

Craske, M. G., & Barlow, D. H. (2008). Panic disorder and agoraphobia. In D. H. Barlow (Ed.), *Clinical handbook of psychological disorders* (pp. 1–64). New York: Guilford Press.

Crawford, M., & Unger, R. (2004). *Women and gender: A feminist psychology* (4th ed.). Boston: McGraw-Hill.

Creed, M., Pascoli, V. J., & Lüscher, C. (2015). Refining deep brain stimulation to emulate optogenetic treatment of synaptic pathology. *Science, 347*(6222), 659–664. doi: 10.1126/science.1260776

Creighton, S. M., Minto, C. L., & Woodhouse, C. (2001). Long term sexual function in intersex conditions with ambiguous genitalia. *Journal of Pediatric & Adolescent Gynecology, 14,* 141–142.

Creswell, J. D., Pacilio, L. E., Lindsay, E. K., & Brown, K. W. (2014). Brief mindfulness meditation training alters psychological and neuroendocrine responses to social evaluative stress. *Psychoneuroendocrinology, 44,* 1–12.

Crick, F., & Koch, C. (1990). Towards a neurobiological theory of consciousness. *Seminars in the Neurosciences, 2,* 263–275.

Crick, F., & Koch, C. (2003). A framework for consciousness. *Nature Neuroscience, 6,* 119–127.

Cristancho, M. A., Helmer, A., Connolly, R., Cristancho, P., & O'Reardon, J. P. (2013). Transcranial magnetic stimulation maintenance as a substitute for maintenance electroconvulsive therapy: A case series. *J ECT, 29*(2), 106–108. doi: 10.1097/YCT.0b013e31827a70ba

Critchfield, T. S., Haley, R., Sabo, B., Colbert, J., & Macropoulis, G. (2003). A half century of scalloping in the work habits of the United States Congress. *Journal of Applied Behavior Analysis, 36*(4), 465–486.

Crouch, N. S., Minto, C. L., Liao, L.-M., Woodhouse, C. R. J., & Creighton, S. M. (2004). Genital sensation after feminizing genitoplasty for congenital adrenal hyperplasia: A pilot study *British Journal of Urology International, 93,* 135–138.

Crowley, A. E., & Hoyer, W. D. (1994). An integrative framework for understanding two-sided persuasion. *Journal of Consumer Research, 20,* 561–574.

Csikszentmihalyi, M. (1996). *Creativity: Flow and the psychology of discovery and invention.* New York: Harper Perennial.

Csikszentmihalyi, M. (1997). *Finding flow: The psychology of engagement with everyday life.* New York: Basic Books.

Cua, A. B., Wilhelm, K. P., & Maibach, H. I. (1990). Elastic properties of human skin: Relation to age, sex and anatomical region. *Archives of Dermatology Research, 282,* 283–288.

Cuellar, N. G., Whisenant, D., & Stantoon, M. P. (2015). Hypnic jerks: A scoping literature review. *Sleep Medicine Clinics, 10*(3), 393–401.

Culver, N. C., Vervliet, B., & Craske, M. G. (2015). Compound extinction: Using the Rescorla-Wagner model to maximize exposure therapy effects for anxiety disorders. *Clinical Psychological Science, 3*(3), 335–348. doi: 10.1177/2167702614542103

Cummings, J. L., & Coffey C. E. (1994). Neurobiological basis of behavior. In C. E. Coffey & J. L. Cummings (Eds.), *Textbook of geriatric neuropsychiatry* (pp. 72–96). Washington, DC: American Psychiatric Press.

Cummings, S. R., & Melton, L. J., III. (2002). Epidemiology and outcomes of osteoporotic fractures. *Lancet, 359*(9319), 1761–1767.

Cunha, E., Magno, G., Gonçalves, M. A., Cambraia, C., & Almeida, V. (2014). He votes or she votes? Female and male discursive strategies in Twitter political hashtags. *PLoS ONE 9*(1), (e87041. doi: 10.1371/journal.pone.0087041

Currin, J. M., Gibson, L., & Hubach, R. D. (2015). Multidimensional assessment of sexual orientation and the fraternal birth order effect. *Psychology of Sexual Orientation and Gender Diversity, 2,* 113–122.

Curtis, R. C., & Miller, K. (1986). Believing another likes or dislikes you: Behaviors making the beliefs come true. *Journal of Personality and Social Psychology, 51,* 284–290.

Curtis, R. G., Windsor, T. D., & Soubelet, A. (2015). The relationship between Big-5 personality traits and cognitive ability in older adults—A review. *Aging, Neuropsychology, and Cognition: A Journal on Normal and Dysfunctional Development, 22*(1), 42–71. doi: 10.1080/13825585.2014.888392

Curtis, R. H. (1993). *Great lives: Medicine.* New York: Charles Scribner's Sons Books for Young Readers.

Cuthbert, B. N. (2014). The RDoC framework: Facilitating transition from icd/dsm to dimensional approaches that integrate neuroscience and psychopathology. *World Psychiatry, 13*(1), 23–35. doi: http://doi.org/10.1002/wps.20087

Czeisler, C. A. (1995). The effect of light on the human circadian pacemaker. In D. J. Chadwick & K. Ackrill (Eds.), *Circadian clocks and their adjustment* (pp. 254–302). West Sussex, England: John Wiley & Sons.

Czeisler, C. A., Moore-Ede, M. C., & Coleman, R. M. (1982). Rotating shift work schedules that disrupt sleep are improved by applying circadian principles. *Science, 217,* 460–463.

Czeisler, C. A., Weitzman, E. D., Moore-Ede, M. C., Zimmerman, J. C., & Knauer, R. S. (1980). Human sleep: Its duration and organization depend on its circadian phase. *Science, 210,* 1264–1267.

Dabbs, J. M., Jr., Bernieri, F. J., Strong, R. K., Campo, R., & Milun, R. (2001). Going on stage: Testosterone in greetings and meetings. *Journal of Research in Personality, 35,* 27–40.

Dahl, R. E., & Lewin, D. S. (2002). Pathways to adolescent health: Sleep regulation and behavior. *Journal of Adolescent Health, 31,* 175–184.

Daiello, L. A., Gongvatana, A., Dunsiger, S., Cohen, R. A., & Ott, B. R. (2014). Association of fish oil supplement use with preservation of brain volume and cognitive function. *Alzheimer's & Dementia, 11*(2), 226–235.

Dalenberg, C. J. (1996). Accuracy, timing and circumstances of disclosure in therapy of recovered and continuous memories of abuse. *The Journal of Psychiatry and Law, 24*(2), 229–275.

Dallman, M., Pecoraro, N., Akana, S., la Fleur, S. E., Gomez, F., Houshyar, H., Bell, M. E., Bhatnagar, S., Laugero, K. D., & Manalo, S. (2003). Chronic stress and obesity: A new view of "comfort food." *Proceedings of the National Academy of Sciences, USA, 100*(20), 11696–11701.

Daly, M., Wilson, M., & Weghorst, S. J. (1982). Male sexual jealousy. *Ethology and Sociobiology, 3,* 11–27.

Damasio, H., Grabowski, T., Frank, R., Galaburda, A. M., & Damasion, A. R. (1994). The return of Phineas Gage: Clues about the brain from the skull of a famous patient. *Science, 264,* 1102–1105.

Dani, J., Burrill, C., & Demmig-Adams, B. (2005). The remarkable role of nutrition in learning and behavior. *Nutrition & Food Science, 35*(4), 258–263.

Darley, J. M., & Latané, B. (1968). Bystander intervention in emergencies: Diffusion of responsibility. *Journal of Personality and Social Psychology, 8,* 377–383.

Darvill, T., Lonky, E., Reihman, J., Stewart, P., & Pagano, J. (2000). Prenatal exposure to PCBs and infant performance on the Fagan test of infant intelligence. *Neurotoxicology, 21*(6), 1029–1038.

Darwin, C. (1859). *The origin of species by means of natural selection.* London: John Murray.

Darwin, C. (1898). *The expression of the emotions in man and animals.* New York: D. Appleton.

Daum, I., & Schugens, M. M. (1996). On the cerebellum and classical conditioning. *Current Directions in Psychological Science, 5,* 58–61.

Davidson, R. J. (2003). Affective neuroscience and psychophysiology: Toward a synthesis. *Psychophysiology, 40*(5), 655–665.

Davidson, R. J., Kabat-Zinn, J., Schumacher, J., Rosenkranz, M., Muller, D., Santorelli, S., . . . Sheridan, J. (2003). Alterations in brain and immune function produced by mindfulness meditation. *Psychosomatic Medicine, 65,* 564–570.

Davidson, R. J., Putman, K. M., & Larson, C. L. (2000). Dysfunction in the neural circuitry of emotion regulation—A possible prelude to violence. *Science, 289,* 591–594.

Davies, I. R. L., Laws, G., Corbett, G. G., & Jerrett, D. J. (1998a). Cross-cultural differences in colour vision: Acquired "colour blindness" in Africa. *Personality and Individual Differences, 25,* 1153–1162.

Davies, I. R. L., Sowden, P., Jerrett, D. T., Jerrett, T., & Corbett, G. G. (1998b). A cross-cultural study of English and Setswana speakers on a colour triads task: A test of the Sapir-Whorf hypothesis. *British Journal of Psychology, 89,* 1–15.

Davis, C. J., Harding, J. W., & Wright, J. W. (2003). REM sleep deprivation induced deficits in the latency-to-peak induction and maintenance of longterm potentiation within the CA1 region of hippocampus. *Brain Research, 973,* 293–297.

Davis, H. A., DiStefano, C., & Schutz, P. A. (2008). Identifying patterns of appraising tests in first-year college students: Implications for anxiety and emotion regulation during test taking. *Journal of Educational Psychology, 100*(4), 942–960. doi: 10.1037/a0013096

Davis, J. O., Phelps, J. A., & Bracha, H. S. (1995). Prenatal development of monozygotic twins and concordance for schizophrenia. *Schizophrenia Bulletin, 21,* 357–366.

Davis, K. F., Parker, K. P., & Montgomery, G. (2004). Sleep in infants and young children: Part 1: Normal sleep. *Journal of Pediatric Healthcare, 18*(2), 65–71.

Davis, M., & Whalen, P. J. (2001). The amygdala: Vigilance and emotion. *Molecular Psychiatry, 6,* 13–34.

Davis, O. S. P., Haworth, C. M. A., Lewis, C. M., & Plomin, R. (2012). Visual analysis of geocoded twin data puts nature and nurture on the map. *Molecular Psychiatry, 17,* 867–874. doi: 10.1038/mp.2012.68

Dawood, K., Pillard, R. C., Horvath, C., Revelle, W., & Bailey, J. M. (2000). Familial aspects of male homosexuality. *Archives of Sexual Behavior, 29*(2), 155.

Day, E. (2015). #BlackLivesMatter: The birth of a new civil rights movement. The Guardian, Sunday July 19, 2015. Retrieved from http://www.theguardian.com/world/2015/jul/19/blacklivesmatter-birth-civil-rights-movement

Dean, G., & Kelly, I. W. (2000). Does astrology work? Astrology and skepticism 1975–2000. In P. Kurtz (Ed.), *Skepticism: A 25 Year Retrospective* (pp. 191–207). Amherst, NY: Prometheus Books.

Dêbiec, J., Díaz-Mataix, L., Bush, D. E. A., Doyère, V., & LeDoux, J. E. (2010). The amygdala encodes specific sensory features of an aversive reinforcer. *Nature Neuroscience, 13,* 536–537.

de Bruin, A., Treccani, B., & Della Sala, S. (2015). Cognitive advantage in bilingualism: An example of publication bias? *Psychological Science, 26*(1), 99–107. doi: 10.1177/0956797614557866

De Camp, J. E. (1917). The influence of color on apparent weight. A preliminary study. *Journal of Experimental Psychology: General, 2*(5), 347–370. doi: dx.doi.org/10.1037/h0075903

DeCasper, A. J., & Fifer, W. P. (1980). Of human bonding: Newborns prefer their mothers' voices. *Science, 208,* 1174–1176.

DeCasper, A. J., & Spence, M. J. (1986). Prenatal maternal speech influence on newborns' perception of sounds. *Infant Behaviour and Development, 9,* 133–150.

deCharms, R. (1968). *Personal causation.* New York: Academic Press.

Deci, E. L., Eghrari, H., Patrick, B. C., & Leone, D. R. (1994). Facilitating internalization: The self-determination theory perspective. *Journal of Personality, 62,* 119–142.

Deci, E. L., Koestner, R., & Ryan, R. M. (1999). A meta-analytic review of experiments examining the effects of extrinsic rewards on intrinsic motivation. *Psychological Bulletin, 125,* 627–668.

Deci, E. L., & Ryan, R. M. (1985). *Intrinsic motivation and self-determination in human behavior.* New York: Plenum.

DeCoster, J., & Claypool, H. M. (2004). A meta-analysis of priming effects on impression formation supporting a general model of informational biases. *Personality and Social Psychology Review, 8*(1), 2–27.

Deger, M., Helias, M., Rotter, S., & Diesmann, M. (2012). Spike-timing dependence of structural plasticity explains cooperative synapse formation in the neocortex. *PLoS Computational Biology, 8*(9), e1002689. doi: 10.1371/journal.pcbi.1002689

DeGrandpre, R. J. (2000). A science of meaning: Can behaviorism bring meaning to psychological science? *American Psychologist, 55,* 721–739.

Deinzer, R., Kleineidam, C. H., Winkler, R., Idel, H., & Bachg, D. (2000). Prolonged reduction of salivary immunoglobulin A (sIgA) after a major academic exam. *International Journal of Psychophysiology, 37,* 219–232.

Delagrange, P., & Guardiola-Lemaitre, B. (1997). Melatonin, its receptors, and relationships with biological rhythm disorders. *Clininical Neuropharmacology, 20,* 482–510.

Delaney, A. J., Crane, J. W., & Sah, P. (2007). Noradrenaline modulates transmission at a central synapse by a presynaptic mechanism. *Neuron, 56*(6), 880–892.

Delfiner, R. (2001, November 16). Kitty left at death's door. *New York Post.*

DeLongis, A., Lazarus, R. S., & Folkman, S. (1988). The impact of daily stress on health and mood: Psychological and social resources as mediators. *Journal of Personality and Social Psychology, 54*(3), 486–495.

Dement, W. C. (1960). The effect of dream deprivation. *Science, 131,* 1705–1707.

Dement, W. C. (1974). Some must watch while some must sleep. San Francisco: W. H. Freeman.

Dement, W. C., Henry, P., Cohen, H., & Ferguson, J. (1969). Studies on the effect of REM deprivation in humans and animals. In K. H. Pribram (Ed.), *Mood, states, and mind.* Baltimore: Penguin.

Demers, R. A. (1988). Linguistics and animal communication. In F. J. Newmeyer (Ed.), *Language form and language function* (pp. 314–335). Cambridge, MA: MIT Press.

Dempster, F. N., & Farris, R. (1990). The spacing effect: Research and practice. *Journal of Research and Development in Education 23*(2), 97–101.

Deng, L. X., Deng, P., Ruan, Y., Xu, Z. C., Liu, N. K., Wen, X., . . . Xu, X. M. (2013). A novel growth-promoting pathway formed by GDNF-overexpressing Schwann cells promotes propriospinal axonal regeneration, synapse formation, and partial recovery of function after spinal cord injury. *The Journal of Neuroscience, 33*(13), 5655–5667. doi: 10.1523/jneurosci.2973-12.2013

Dennett, D. C. (1991). *Consciousness explained.* New York: Little, Brown.

Denys, D., Mantione, M., Figee, M., van den Munckhof, P., Koerselman, F., Westenberg, H., . . . Schuurman, R. (2010). Deep brain stimulation of the nucleus accumbens for treatment-refractory obsessive-compulsive disorder. *Archives of General Psychiatry, 67*(10), 1061–1068. doi: 10.1001/archgenpsychiatry.2010.122

Deregowski, J. B. (1969). Perception of the two-pronged trident by two- and three-dimensional perceivers. *Journal of Experimental Psychology, 82,* 9–13.

DeRubeis, R. J., Gelfand, L. A., Tang, T. Z., & Simons, A. D. (1999). Medications versus cognitive behavior therapy for severely depressed outpatients: Mega-analysis of four randomized comparisons. *American Journal of Psychiatry, 156*(7), 1007–1013.

De Valois, R. L., & Jacobs, G. H. (1968). Primate color vision. *Science, 162,* 553–540.

DeYoung, C. G. (2015). Cybernetic Big Five theory. *Journal of Research in Personality, 56,* 33–58. doi: 10.1016/j.jrp.2014.07.004

DeYoung, C. G., Hirsh, J. B., Shane, M. S., Papademetris, X., Rajeevan, N., & Gray, J. R. (2010). Testing predictions from personality neuroscience: Brain structure and the Big Five. *Psychological Science, 21*(6), 820–828.

DeYoung, C. G., Quilty, L. C., Peterson, J. B., & Gray, J. R. (2014). Openness to experience, intellect, and cognitive ability. *Journal of Personality Assessment, 96*(1), 46–52. doi: 10.1080/00223891.2013.806327

Diamond, L. M. (2003). What does sexual orientation orient? A biobehavioral model distinguishing romantic love and sexual desire. *Psychological Review, 110,* 173–192.

Diamond, M. (1995). Biological aspects of sexual orientation and identity. In L. Diamant & R. McAnulty (Eds.), *The psychology of sexual orientation, behavior, and identity: A handbook* (pp. 45–80). Westport, CT: Greenwood Press.

Diamond, M. C. (1991). Hormonal effects on the development of cerebral lateralization. *Psychoneuroendocrinology, 16,* 121–129.

Diamond, M., & Sigmundson, H. K. (1997). Sex reassignment at birth. Long-term review and clinical implications. *Archives of Pediatric Adolescent Medicine, 151*(3), 298–304.

DiazGranados, N., Ibrahim, L. A., Brutsche, N. E., Ameli, R., Henter, I. D., Luckenbaugh, D. A., . . . Zarate, C. A., Jr. (2010). Rapid resolution of suicidal ideation after a single infusion of an N-methyl-D-aspartate antagonist in patients with treatment-resistant major depressive disorder. *The Journal of Clinical Psychiatry, 71*(12), 1605–1611. doi: 10.4088/JCP.09m05327blu

DiazGranados, N., Ibrahim, L., Brutsche, N. E., Newberg, A., Kronstein, P., Khalife, S., . . . Zarate, C. A., Jr. (2010). A randomized add-on trial of an N-methyl-D-aspartate antagonist in treatment-resistant bipolar depression. *Archives of General Psychiatry, 67*(8), 793–802. doi: 10.1001/archgenpsychiatry.2010.90

Dickens, W. T., & Flynn, J. R. (2001 April). Heritability estimates vs. large environmental effects: The IQ paradox resolved. *Psychological Review, 108*(2), 346–369.

Dickerson, F., Ringel, N., Parente, F., & Boronow, J. (1994). Seclusion and restraint, assaultiveness, and patient performance in a token economy. *Hospital and Community Psychiatry, 45,* 168–170.

Dickinson, T. (2015). Exploring the drugs/violence nexus among active offenders: Contributions from the St. Louis School. *Criminal Justice Review, 40*(1), 67–86.

Dieffenbach, C. W., & Fauci, A. S. (2011). Thirty years of HIV and AIDS: Future challenges and opportunities. *Annuals of Internal Medicine, 11*(154), 766–771.

Diemer, E. W., Grant, J. D., Munn-Chernoff, M. A., Patterson, D. A., & Duncan, A. E. (2015). Gender identity, sexual orientation, and eating-related pathology in a national sample of college students. *Journal of Adolescent Health, 57*(2), 144–149. doi: 10.1016/j.jadohealth.2015.03.003

Diener, E., Lusk, R., DeFour, D., & Flax, R. (1980). Deindividuation: Effects of group size, density, number of observers, and group member similarity on self-consciousness and disinhibited behavior. *Journal of Personality and Social Psychology, 39,* 449–459.

Dillard, J. (1990). Self-inference and the foot-in-the-door technique: Quantity of behavior and attitudinal mediation. *Human Communication Research, 16,* 422–447.

Dillard, J. (1991). The current status of research on sequential–request compliance techniques. *Personality and Social Psychology Bulletin, 17,* 282–288.

Dimidjian, S., Hollon, S. D., Dobson, K. S., Schmaling, K. B., Kohlenberg, R. J., Addis, M. E., . . . Jacobson, N. S. (2006). Randomized trial of behavioral activation, cognitive therapy, and antidepressant medication in the acute treatment of adults with major depression. *Journal of Consulting and Clinical Psychology, 74*(4), 658–670. doi: 10.1037/0022-006X.74.4.658

Ding, D. C., Chang, Y. H., Shyu, W. C., & Lin, S. Z. (2015). Human umbilical cord mesenchymal stem cells: A new era for stem cell therapy. *Cell Transplantaton, 14*(3), 339–347.

Ding, M., Bhupathiraju, S. N., Chen, M., van Dam, R. M., & Hu, F. B. (2014). Caffeinated and decaffeinated coffee consumption and risk of Type 2 diabetes: A systematic review and a dose-response meta-analysis. *Diabetes Care, 37*(2), 569–586.

Ding, M., Satija, A., Bhupathiraju, S. N., Hu, Y., Sun, Q., Han, J., Lopez-Garcia, E., Willett, W., van Dam, R. M., & Hu, F. B. (2015). Association of coffee consumption with total and cause-specific mortality in three large prospective cohorts. *Circulation National Heart Association, 132,* 2305–2315.

Ding, N., Melloni, L., Zhang, H., Tian, X., & Poeppel, D. (2015). Cortical tracking of hierarchical linguistic structures in connected speech. *Nature Neuroscience, 19*(1), 158–164. doi: 10.1038/nn.4186

Dinges, D. F. (1995). An overview of sleepiness and accidents. *Journal of Sleep Research, 4*(2), 4–14.

Dobson, K. S., & Block, L. (1988). Historical and philosophical bases of the cognitive-behavioral therapies. In K. S. Dobson (Ed.), *Handbook of cognitive-behavioral therapies* (pp. 3–38). New York: Guilford Press.

Dodge, K. A., Bates, J. E., & Pettit, G. S. (1990). Mechanisms in the cycle of violence. *Science, 250,* 1678–1683.

Dolan, K., Kite, B., Black, E., Aceijas, C., & Stimson, G. V. (2007). HIV in prison in low-income and middle-income countries. *The Lancet: Infectious Diseases, 7*(1), 32–41.

Dolcos, F., LaBar, K. S., Cabeza, R., & Purves, D. (2005). Remembering one year later: Role of the amygdala and the medial temporal lobe memory system in retrieving emotional memories. *Proceedings of the National Academy of Sciences, USA.* doi: 10.1073/pnas.0409848102

Dollard, J., Doob, L. W., Miller, N. E., Mowrer, O. H., & Sears, R. R. (1939). *Frustration and aggression.* New Haven, CT: Yale University Press.

Dollard, J., & Miller, N. F. (1950). *Personality and psychotherapy.* New York: McGraw-Hill.

Domagalski, T. A., & Steelman, L. A. (2007). The impact of gender and organizational status on workplace anger expression. *Management Communication Quarterly, 20*(3), 297–315.

Domhoff, G. W. (1996). *Finding meaning in dreams: A quantitative approach.* New York: Plenum Publishing.

Domhoff, G. W. (2005). The content of dreams: Methodologic and theoretical implications. In M. Kryger, T. Roth, & W. Dement (Eds.), *Principles and practices of sleep medicine* (4th ed., pp. 522–534). Philadelphia: Saunders.

Domhoff, G. W., & Schneider, A. (2008). Similarities and differences in dream content at the cross-cultural, gender, and individual levels. *Consciousness and Cognition, 17,* 1257–1265.

Dominey, P. F., & Dodane, C. (2004). Indeterminacy in language acquisition: The role of child-directed speech and joint attention. *Journal of Neurolinguistics, 17*(2–3), 121–145.

Domjan, M., Cusato, B., & Villarreal, R. (2000). Pavlovian feed-forward mechanisms in the control of social behavior. *Behavioral and Brain Sciences, 23,* 235–282.

Donaldson, Z. R., & Young, L. J. (2008). Oxytocin, vasopressin, and the neurogenetics of sociality. *Science, 322*(5903), 900–904. doi: 10.1126/science.1158668

Donohue, S. E., James, B., Eslick, A. N., & Mitroff, S. R. (2012). Cognitive pitfall! Videogame players are not immune to dual-task costs. *Attention, Perception, & Psychophysics, 74*(5), 803–809. doi: 10.3758/s13414-012-0323-y

Donovan, J. J., & Radosevich, D. R. (1999). A meta-analytic review of the distribution of practice effect: Now you see it, now you don't. *Journal of Applied Psychology, 84,* 795–805.

Dorahy, M. J. (2001). Dissociative identity disorder and memory dysfunction: The current state of experimental research and its future directions. *Clinical Psychology Review, 21*(5), 771–795.

Dorahy, M. J., Brand, B. L., Sar, V., Kruger, C., Stavropoulos, P., Martinez-Taboas, A., . . . Middleton, W. (2014). Dissociative identity disorder: An empirical overview. *Australian and New Zealand Journal of Psychiatry, 48*(5), 402–417. doi: 10.1177/0004867414527523

Dörrie, N., Föcker, M., Freunscht, I., & Hebebrand, J. (2014). Fetal alcohol spectrum disorders. *European Child & Adolescent Psychiatry, 23,* 863–875.

Doubilet, P. M., Benson, C. B., Bourne, T., & Blaivas, M. (2013). Diagnostic criteria for nonviable pregnancy early in the first trimester. The New England Journal of Medicine, 369(15),1443–1451.

Dove, A. (1971). The "Chitling" Test. In L. R. Aiken Jr. (Ed.), *Psychological and educational testings.* Boston: Allyn and Bacon.

Downs, J. F. (1984). *The Navajo.* Prospect Heights, IL: Waveland Press, International.

Dreger, A. D. (1998). "Ambiguous sex"—or ambivalent medicine? Ethical issues in the treatment of intersexuality. *Hastings Center Report, 28*(3), 24–35.

Dreger, A. D. (1999). *Intersex in the age of ethics*. Hagerstown, MD: University Publishing Groups.

Drenth, P. J., Thierry, H., Willems, P. J., & de Wolff, C. J. (1984). *Handbook of work and organizational psychology*. Chichester, England: John Wiley and Sons.

Druckman, D., & Bjork, R. A. (Eds.). (1994). *Learning, remembering, believing: Enhancing human performance.* (Study conducted by the National Research Council). Washington, DC: National Academy Press.

Du, L., Shan, L., Wang, B., Li, H., Xu, Z., Staal, W. G., & Jia, F. (2015). A pilot study on the combination of applied behavior analysis and bumetanide treatment for children with autism. *Journal of Child and Adolescent Psychopharmacology, 25*(7), 585–588.

Duben, A., & Behar, C. (1991). *Istanbul households: Marriage, family and fertility 1880–1940.* Cambridge, NY: Cambridge University Press.

Dubern, B., & Clement, K. (2012). Leptin and leptin receptor-related monogenic obesity. *Biochimie, 94*(10), 2111–2115.

Dubowitz, H., & Bennett, S. (2007). Physical abuse and neglect of children. *Lancet, 369*(9576), 1891–1899.

Duckworth, A. L., Quinn, P. D., Lynam, D. R., Loeber, R., & Stouthamer-Loeber, M. (2011). Role of test motivation in intelligence testing. *Proceedings of the National Academy of Sciences, 108*(19), 7716–7720. doi: 10.1073/pnas.1018601108

Duckworth, A. L., & Seligman, M. E. P. (2005). Self-discipline outdoes IQ in predicting academic performance of adolescents. *Psychological Science, 16*(12), 939–944. doi: 10.1111/j.1467-9280.2005.01641.x

Dudai, Y. (2004). The neurobiology of consolidations, or, how stable is the engram? *Annual Review of Psychology, 55,* 51–86.

Duggan, M., Ellilson, N. B., Lampe, C., Lenhart, A., & Madden, M. (2015). Demographics of key social networking platforms. Pew Research Center: Social Media Update 2014. Retrieved from http://www.pewinternet.org/2015/01/09/demographics-of-key-social-networking-platforms-2/

Duker, P. C., & Seys, D. M. (1996). Long-term use of electrical aversion treatment with self-injurious behaviors. *Research in Developmental Disabilities, 17,* 293–301.

Duman, R. S., & Aghajanian, G. K. (2012). Synaptic dysfunction in depression: Potential therapeutic targets. *Science, 338*(6103), 68–72. doi: 10.1126/science.1222939

Dumont, F. (2010). *A history of personality psychology.* New York: Cambridge University Press.

Duncan, R. M. (1995). Piaget and Vygotsky revisited: Dialogue or assimilation? *Developmental Review, 15,* 458–472.

Dundas, I., Wormnes, B. R., & Hauge, H. (2009). Making exams a manageable task. *Nordic Psychology, 61*(1), 26–41.

Dunn, J. C., Whelton, W. J., & Sharpe, D. (2006). Maladaptive perfectionism, hassles, coping, and psychological distress in university professors. *Journal of Counseling Psychology, 53*(4), 511–523.

Durrant, J., & Ensom, R. (2012). Physical punishment of children: Lessons from 20 years of research. *Canadian Medical Association Journal, 184*(12), 1373–1377. doi: 10.1503/cmaj.101314

Durrant, M. (Ed.). (1993). *Aristotle's De anima in focus.* London: Routledge.

Durso, F., Rea, C., & Dayton, T. (1994). Graph-theoretic confirmation of restructuring during insight. *Psychological Science, 5,* 94–98.

Durston, S. (2003). A review of the biological bases of ADHD: What have we learned from imaging studies? *Mental Retardation and Developmental Disabilities Research Reviews, 9,* 184–195.

Dwairy, M. (2004). Parenting styles and mental health of Palestinian-Arab adolescents in Israel. *Transcultural Psychiatry, 41*(2), 233–252.

Dweck, C. (1986). Motivational processes affecting learning. *American Psychologist, 41*(10), 1040–1048.

Dweck, C., & Elliott, E. (1983). Achievement motivation. In P. Mussen (Ed.), *Handbook of child psychology: Vol. 4. Socialization, personality, and social development* (pp. 643–691). New York: Wiley.

Dweck, C. S. (1999). *Self-theories: Their role in motivation, personality and development.* Philadelphia: Psychology Press.

Dweck, C. S., Chiu, C., & Hong, Y. (1995). Implicit theories and their role in judgments and reactions: A world from two perspectives. *Psychological Inquiry, 6,* 267–285.

Dweck, C. S., & Leggett, E. L. (1988). A social-cognitive approach to motivation and personality. *Psychological Review, 95,* 256–273.

Dweck, C. S., & Molden, D. C. (2008). Self-theories: The construction of free will. In J. Baer, J. C. Kaufman, & R. F. Baumeister (Eds.), *Are we free? Psychology and free will* (pp. 44–64). New York: Oxford University Press.

Dykens, E. M., Hodapp, R. M., & Leckman, J. F. (1994). *Behavior and development in fragile X syndrome.* Thousand Oaks, CA: Sage.

Eagleman, D. M. (2001). Visual illusions and neurobiology. *Nature reviews: Neuroscience, 2*(12), 920–926.

Eagly, A. H. (1987). *Sex difference in social behavior: A social-role interpretation.* Hillsdale, NJ: Lawrence Erlbaum.

Eagly, A. H., Ashmore, R. D., Makhijani, M. G., & Longo, L. C. (1991). What is beautiful is good, but . . . : A meta-analytic review of the physical attractiveness stereotype. *Psychological Bulletin, 110,* 109–128.

Eagly, A. H., & Carli, L. L. (2007). *Through the labyrinth: The truth about how women become leaders.* Boston: Harvard Business School Press.

Eagly, A.H., & Chaiken, S. (1975). An attribution analysis of the effect of communicator characteristics on opinion change: The case of communicator attractiveness. *Journal of Personality and Social Psychology, 37,* 136–144.

Eagly, A. H., & Chaiken, S. (1993). *The psychology of attitudes.* Fort Worth, TX: Harcourt Brace.

Eagly, A. H., & Chaiken, S. (1998). Attitude structure and function. In D. T. Gilbert, S. T. Fiske, & G. Lindzey (Eds.), *The handbook of social psychology* (4th ed., pp. 269–322). New York: McGraw-Hill.

Eagly, A.H., & Crowley, M. (1986). Gender and helping behavior: A meta-analytic review of the social psychological literature. *Psychological Bulletin, 100,* 283–308.

Eagly, A. H., Wood, W., & Diekman, A. B. (2000). Social role theory of sex differences and similarities: A current appraisal. In T. Eckes & H. M. Trautner (Eds.), *The developmental social psychology of gender* (pp. 123–174). Mahwah, NJ: Lawrence Erlbaum.

Eaker, E. D., & Castelli, W. P. (1988). Type A behavior and mortality from coronary disease in the Framingham Study. *New England Journal of Medicine, 319,* 1480–1481.

Eastern Virginia Medical School (2009, May 5). Texting while driving can be deadly, study shows. *ScienceDaily.* Retrieved May 5, 2010, from http://www.sciencedaily.com/releases/2009/05/090504094434.htm

Eaton, W. W., Kessler, R. C., Wittchen, H. U., & Magee, W. J. (1994). Panic and panic disorder in the United States. *American Journal of Psychiatry, 151*(3), 413–420.

Ebbinghaus, H. (1885). *Memory: A contribution to experimental psychology.* New York: Dover Publications.

Ebbinghaus, H. (1913). *Memory: A contribution to experimental psychology.* New York: Teachers College Press. (Translated from the 1885 German original.)

Eddy, J., Fitzhugh, E., & Wang, M. (2000). Smoking acquisition: Peer influence and self-selection. *Psychological Reports, 86,* 1241–1246.

Edelmann, R. J., & Iwawaki, S. (1987). Self-reported expression of embarrassment in five European cultures. *Psychologia: An International Journal of Psychology, 30,* 205–216.

Edlund, J. E., Heider, J. D., Scherer, C. R., Farc, M.-M., & Sagarin, B. J. (2006). Sex differences in jealousy in response to actual infidelity. *Evolutionary Psychology, 4,* 462–470.

Edwards, C., Mukherjee, S., Simpson, L., Palmer, L. J., Almeida, O. P., & Hillman, D. R. (2015). Depressive symptoms before and after treatment of obstructive sleep apnea in men and women. *Journal of Clinical Sleep Medicine, 11*(9), 1029–1038. doi: 10.5664/jcsm.5020

Egan, L. C., Bloom, P., & Santos, L. R. (2010). Choice-induced preferences in the absence of choice: Evidence from a blind two choice paradigm with young children and capuchin monkeys. *Journal of Experimental Social Psychology, 46*(1), 204–207.

Egan, L. C., Santos, L. R., & Bloom, P. (2007). The origins of cognitive dissonance. Evidence from children and monkeys. *Psychological Science, 18*(11), 978–983.

Ehlers, A., Bisson, J., Clark, D. M., Creamer, M., Pilling, S., Richards, D., Schnurr, P. P., Turner, S., & Yule, W. (2010). Do all psychological treatments really work the same in posttraumatic stress disorder? *Clinical Psychology Review, 30*(2), 269–276.

Eich, E., & Metcalfe, J. (1989). Mood dependent memory for internal vs. external events. *Journal of Experimental Psychology: Learning, Memory and Cognition, 15,* 443–455.

Eiden, R. D., McAuliffe, S., Kachadourian, L., Coles, C., Colder, C., & Schuetze, P. (2009). Effects of prenatal cocaine exposure on infant reactivity and regulation. *Neurotoxicology and Teratology, 31,* 60–68.

Ekers, D., Webster, L., Van Straten, A., Cuijpers, P., Richards, D., & Gilbody, S. (2014). Behavioural activation for depression; an update of meta-analysis of effectiveness and sub group analysis. *PLoS One, 9*(6), e100100. doi: 10.1371/journal.pone.0100100

Ekman, P. (1973). Darwin and cross-cultural studies of facial expression. In P. Ekman (Ed.), *Darwin and facial expression: A century of research in review.* New York: Academic Press.

Ekman, P. (1980). Asymmetry in facial expression. *Science, 209,* 833–834.

Ekman, P., & Friesen, W. (1969). The repertoire of nonverbal behavior: Categories, origins, usage, and coding. *Semiotica, 1,* 49–98.

Ekman, P., & Friesen, W. (1971). Constants across cultures in the face and emotion. *Journal of Personality and Social Psychology, 17*(2), 124–129.

Ekman, P., & Friesen, W. V. (1978). *The facial action coding system.* Palo Alto, CA: Consulting Psychologists Press.

Ekman, P., Sorensen, E. R., & Friesen, W. V. (1969). Pan-cultural elements in facial displays of emotion. *Science, 164,* 86–88.

Elkind, D. (1985). Egocentrism redux. *Developmental Review, 5,* 218–226.

Ellenbogen, J. M., Payne, J. D., & Stickgold, R. (2006). The role of sleep in declarative memory consolidation: Passive, permissive, active or none? *Current Opinions in Neurobiology, 16,* 716–722.

Elliott, E., & Dweck, C. (1988). Goals: An approach to motivation and achievement. *Journal of Personality and Social Psychology, 54,* 5–12.

Elliott, L., & Brantley, C. (1997). *Sex on campus: The naked truth about the real sex lives of college students.* New York: Random House.

Elliott, R., Greenberg, L. S., Watson, J., Timulak, L., & Freire, E. (2013). Research on humanistic-experiential psychotherapies. In M. J. Lambert (Ed.), *Bergin & Garfield's handbook of psychotherapy and behavior change* (6th ed., pp. 495–538). New York: Wiley.

Ellis, A. (1997). *The practice of rational emotive behavior therapy.* New York: Springer.

Ellis, A. (1998). *The Albert Ellis reader: A guide to well-being using rational emotive behavior therapy.* Secaucus, NJ: Carol Publishing Group.

Ellis, H. D. (1983). The role of the right hemisphere in face perception. In A. W. Young (Ed.), *Functions of the right cerebral hemisphere* (pp. 33–64). London: Academic Press.

Ellis, J. G., & Barclay, N. L. (2014). Cognitive behavior therapy for insomnia: State of the science or a stated science? *Sleep Medicine, 15*(8), 849–850.

Ellis, L., Ames, M. A., Peckham, W., & Burke, D. (1988). Sexual orientation of human offspring may be altered by severe maternal stress during pregnancy. *The Journal of Sex Research, 25*, 152–157.

Ellis, L. K., Gay, P. E., & Paige, E. (2001). *Daily pleasures and hassles across the lifespan.* Poster presented at the September annual meeting of the American Psychological Association, San Francisco, CA.

Elmenhorst, D., Kroll, T., Matusch, A., & Bauer, A. (2012). Sleep deprivation increases cerebral serotonin 2a receptor binding in humans. *Sleep, 35*(12), 1615–1623. doi: 10.5665/sleep.2230

Else-Quest, N., Shibley Hyde, J., Linn, M. C. (2010). Cross-national patterns of gender differences in mathematics: A meta-analysis. *Psychological Bulletin, 136*(1), 103–127.

Emeny, R. T., Lacruz, M-E., Baumert, J., Zierer, A., von Eisenhart Rothe, A., Autenrieth, C., Herder, C., . . . Ladwig, K-H. (2012). Job strain associated CRP is mediated by leisure time physical activity: Results from the MONICA/KORA study. *Brain, Behaviour and Immunity, 26*, 1077–1084.

Emeny, R. T., Zierer, A., Lacruz, M-E., Baumert, J., Herder, C., Gornitzka, G., . . . Ladwig, K-H. (2013). Job strain–associated inflammatory burden and long-term risk of coronary events: Findings from the MONICA/KORA Augsburg case-cohort study. *Psychosomatic Medicine, 75*(3), 317–325.

Endler, N. S. (1988). The origins of electroconvulsive therapy (ECT). *Convulsive Therapy, 4*, 5–23.

Engle, R. W., & Kane, M. J. (2004). Executive attention, working memory capacity, and a two-factor theory of cognitive control. *The Psychology of Learning and Motivation, 44*, 145–199.

Enns, J. T., & Coren, S. (1995). The box alignment illusion: An orientation illusion induced by pictorial depth. *Perception & Psychophysics, 57*, 1163–1174.

Ephraim, P. L., Wegener, S. T., MacKenzie, E. J., Dillingham, T. R., & Pezzin, L. E. (2005). Phantom pain, residual limb pain and back pain in persons with limb loss: Results of a national survey. *Archives of Physical Medicine and Rehabilitation, 86*, 1910–1919.

Epping-Jordan, M., Waltkins, S. S., Koob, G. F., & Markou, A. (1998). Dramatic decreases in brain reward function during nicotine withdrawal. *Nature, 393*, 76–79.

Erdley, C. A., & Dweck, C. S. (1993). Children's implicit personality theories as predictors of their social judgments. *Child Development, 64*, 863–878.

Erickson, K. I., Prakash, R. S., Voss, M. W., Chaddock, L., Hu, L., Morris, K. S., & Kramer, A. F. (2009). Aerobic fitness is associated with hippocampal volume in elderly humans. *Hippocampus, 19*(10), 1030–1039.

Erikson, E. H. (1950). *Childhood and society.* New York: Norton.

Erikson, E. H. (1959). Growth and crises of the healthy personality. *Psychological Issues, 1*, 50–100.

Erikson, E. H. (1980). Elements of a psychoanalytic theory of psychosocial development. In S. Greenspan & G. Pollock (Eds.), *The course of life* (Vol. 1, pp. 11–61). Washington, DC: U.S. Dept. of Health and Human Services.

Erikson, E. H. (1982). *The life cycle completed.* New York: Norton.

Erikson, E. H., & Erikson, J. M. (1997). *The life cycle completed.* New York: Norton.

Eriksson, M., Räikkönen, K., & Eriksson, J. G. (2014). Early life stress and later health outcomes—findings from the Helsinki Birth Cohort Study. *American Journal of Human Biology, 26*, 111–116.

Eriksson, P., Ankarberg, E., Viberg, H., & Fredriksson, A. (2001). The developing cholinergic system as target for environmental toxicants, nicotine and polychlorinated biphenyls (PCBs): Implications for neurotoxicological processes in mice. *Neurotoxicity Research, 3*(1), 37–51.

Ernst, A., Alkass, K., Bernard, S., Salehpour, M., Perl, S., Tisdale, J., . . . Frisen, J. (2014). Neurogenesis in the striatum of the adult human brain. *Cell, 156*(5), 1072–1083. doi: 10.1016/j.cell.2014.01.044

Ernst, A., & Frisen, J. (2015). Adult neurogenesis in humans—common and unique traits in mammals. *PLoS Biology, 13*(1), e1002045. doi: 10.1371/journal.pbio.1002045

Ernst, E. (2002). A systematic review of systematic reviews of homeopathy. *British Journal of Clinical Pharmacology, 54*, 577–582.

Ernst, E. (2012). Homeopathy: A critique of current clinical research. *Skeptical Inquirer, 36*(6). Retrieved from http://www.csicop.org/si/show/homeopathy_a_critique_of_current_clinical_research/

Eschenbeck, H., Kohlmann, C.-W., & Lohaus, A. (2008). Gender differences in coping strategies in children and adolescents. *Journal of Individual Differences, 28*(1), 18–26.

Eskenazi, B., Bradman, A., & Castorina, R. (1999). Exposures of children to organophosphate pesticides and their potential adverse health effects. *Environmental Health Perspectives, 107*(Suppl. 3), 409–419.

Esper, L. H., & Furtado, E. F. (2014). Identifying maternal risk factors associated with fetal alcohol spectrum disorders: A systematic review. *European Child & Adolescent Psychiatry, 23*, 877–889.

Etkin, A., Egner, T., & Kalisch, R. (2011). Emotional processing in anterior cingulate and medial prefrontal cortex. *Trends in Cognitive Sciences, 15*(2), 85–93.

European Monitoring Centre for Drugs and Drug Addiction (EMCDDA). (2015). *New psychoactive substances in Europe—An update from the EU Early Warning System.* Lisbon: Author.

Evans, D., Hodgkinson, B., O'Donnell, A., Nicholson, J., & Walsh, K. (2000). The effectiveness of individual therapy and group therapy in the treatment of schizophrenia. *Best Practice, 5*(3), 1–54.

Evans, G. W., & Kim, P. (2013). Childhood poverty, chronic stress, self-regulation, and coping. *Child Development Perspectives, 7*(1), 43–48.

Evans, I. M., & Meyer, L. H. (1985). *An educative approach to behavior problems: A practical decision model for interventions with severely handicapped learners.* Baltimore: Paul H. Brookes.

Evans, P. (2015). Self-determination theory: An approach to motivation in music education. *Musicae Scientiae, 19*(1), 65–83.

Evans, W. H., Evans, S. S., & Schmid, R. E. (1989). *Behavior and instructional management: An ecological approach.* Boston: Allyn and Bacon.

Everson, S. (1995). Psychology. In J. Barnes (Ed.), *The Cambridge companion to Aristotle* (pp. 168–194). Cambridge, England: Cambridge University Press.

Exner, J. E. (1980). But it's only an inkblot. *Journal of Personality Assessment, 44*, 562–577.

Eysenck, H. J. (1994). *Test your IQ.* Toronto: Penguin Books.

Eysenck, H. J., & Eysenck, S. B. G. (1993). *Eysenck personality questionnaire* (Rev. ed.). London: Hodder & Stoughton Educational.

Fagot, B. I., & Hagan, R. (1991). Observations of parent reactions to sex-stereotyped behaviours: Age and sex effects. *Child Development, 62*, 617–628.

Fairchild, G., Van Goozen, S. H., Stollery, S. J., & Goodyer, I. M. (2008). Fear conditioning and affective modulation of the startle reflex in male adolescents with early-onset or adolescence-onset conduct disorder and healthy control subjects. *Biological Psychiatry 63*(3), 279–285.

Fan, Q., Davis, N., Anderson, A. W., & Cutting, L. E. (2014). Thalamo-cortical connectivity: What can diffusion tractography tell us about reading difficulties in children? *Brain Connectivity, 4*(6), 428–439. doi: 10.1089/brain.2013.0203

Fanselow, M. S., & Gale, G. D. (2003). The amygdala, fear, and memory. *Annals of the New York Academy of Sciences, 985*, 125–134.

Fantz, R. L. (1961). The origin of form perception. *Scientific American, 204*, 66–72.

Fantz, R. L. (1964). Visual experience in infants: Decreased attention to familiar patterns relative to novel ones. *Science, 146*, 668–670.

Faraone, S. V., Biederman, J., & Wozniak, J. (2012). Examining the comorbidity between attention deficit hyperactivity disorder and bipolar I disorder: A meta-analysis of family genetic studies. *The American Journal of Psychiatry, 169*(12), 1256–1266. doi: 10.1176/appi.ajp.2012.12010087

Farmer, A. E. (1996). The genetics of depressive disorders. *International Review of Psychiatry, 8*(4), 369–372.

Farmer, L. M., Le, B. N., & Nelson, D. J. (2013). CLC-3 chloride channels moderate long-term potentiation at Schaffer collateral-CA1 synapses. *The Journal of Physiology, 591*(Pt 4), 1001–1015. doi: 10.1113/jphysiol.2012.243485

Farthing, W. (1992). *The psychology of consciousness.* Upper Saddle River, NJ: Prentice-Hall.

Faucett, J., Gordon, N., & Levine, J. (1994). Differences in postoperative pain severity among four ethnic groups. *Journal of Pain Symptom Management, 9*, 383–389.

Fawzy, F. I., Fawzy, N. W., Hyun, C. S., Elashoff, R., Guthrie, D., Fahey, J. L., & Morton, D. L. (1993). Malignant melanoma effects of an early structured psychiatric intervention, coping, and affective state on recurrence and survival 6 years later. *Archives of General Psychiatry, 50*(9), 681–689.

Fazel-Rezai, R., & Peters, J. F. (2005). P300 wave feature extraction: Preliminary results, in *Proceedings of the 18th Annual Canadian Conference on Electrical and Computer Engineering (CCECE '05,* pp. 390–393). Saskatoon, Saskatchewan, Canada.

Fazio, R. H., & Olson, M. A. (2003). Attitudes: Foundations, functions, and consequences. In M. A. Hogg & J. Cooper (Eds.), *The Handbook of Social Psychology* (pp. 139–160). London: Sage.

Fechner, G. T. (1860). *Elemente der Psykophysik.* Leipzig: Breitkopf und Härtel.

Federal Service for Surveillance of Consumer Rights Protection and Human Well-Being of the Russian Federation and UNAIDS. (2008). *Country progress report of the Russian Federation on the implementation of the declaration of commitment on HIV/AIDS.* Adopted at the 26th United Nations General Assembly Special Session, June 2001. Moscow, Russia: UNAIDS.

Fedoroff, I. C., & McFarlane, T. (1998). Cultural aspects of eating disorders. In S. S. Kazarian & D. R. Evans (Eds.), *Cultural clinical psychology: Theory, research and practice* (pp. 152–176). New York: Oxford University Press.

Feingold, A. (1992). Good-looking people are not what we think. *Psychological Bulletin, 111*, 304–341.

Feldman, D. H. (2003). Cognitive development in childhood. In R. M. Lerner, M. A. Easterbrooks, J. Mistry, and I. B. Weiner. (Eds.), *Handbook of psychology: Developmental psychology* (Vol. 6, pp. 195–201). New York: Wiley.

Ferenczi, E. A., Zalocusky, K. A., Liston, C., Grosenick, L., Warden, M. R., Amatya, D., . . . Deisseroth, K. (2016). Prefrontal cortical regulation of brainwide circuit dynamics and reward-related behavior. *Science, 351*(6268). doi: 10.1126/science.aac9698

Ferguson, C. J. (2015). Do Angry Birds make for angry children? A meta-analysis of video game influences on children's and adolescents' aggression, mental health, prosocial behavior, and academic performance. *Perspectives on Psychological Science, 10*(5), 646–666. doi: 10.1177/1745691615592234

Ferguson, C. J., & Kilburn, J. (2010). Much ado about nothing: The misestimation and overinterpretation of violent video game effects in Eastern and Western nations: Comment on Anderson et al. (2010). *Psychological Bulletin, 136*(2), 174–178; discussion 182–177. doi: 10.1037/a0018566

Ferguson, C. J., Rueda, S., Cruz, A., Ferguson, D., & Fritz, S. (2008). Violent video games and aggression: Causal relationship or byproduct of family violence and intrinsic violence motivation? *Criminal Justice and Behavior, 35*(3), 311–332.

Ferguson, J. N., Aldag, J. M., Insel, T. R., & Young, L. J. (2001). Oxytocin in the medial amygdala is essential for social recognition in the mouse. *The Journal of Neuroscience, 21*(20), 8278–8285.

Ferguson, N. B., & Keesey, R. E. (1975). Effect of a quinine-adulterated diet upon body weight maintenance in male rats with ventromedial hypothalamic lesions. *Journal of Comparative Physiological Psychology, 89*(5), 478–488.

Ferguson-Noyes, N. (2005). Bipolar disorder in children. *Advanced Nurse Practitioner, 13*, 35.

Fernald, A. (1984). The perceptual and affective salience of mothers' speech to infants. In L. Feagans, C. Garvey, & R. Golinkoff (Eds.), *The origins and growth of communication,* 5–29. Norwood, NJ: Ablex.

Fernald, A. (1992) Human maternal vocalizations to infants as biologically relevant signals: An evolutionary perspective. In J. H. Barkow, L. Cosmides, & J. Tooby (Eds.), *The adapted mind: Evolutionary psychology and the generation of culture,* 391–448. New York: Oxford University Press.

Fernandez, E., & Sheffield, J. (1996). Relative contributions of life events versus daily hassles to the frequency and intensity of headaches. *Headache, 36*(10), 595–602.

Feroah, T. R., Sleeper, T., Brozoski, D., Forder, J., Rice, T. B., & Forster, H. V. (2004). *Circadian slow wave sleep and movement behavior are under genetic control in inbred strains of rat.* Paper presented at the American Physiological Society Annual Conference, April 17–21, 2004, Washington, DC.

Feshbach, M. (2008, August 13), What's in a number? A new projection by Pokrovskiy's Center for HIV prevention and treatment and some consequences for Russia, Johnson's Russia List. Retrieved June 17, 2010, from http://www.cdi.org/russia/johnson/2008-153-36.cfm.

Festinger, L. (1954). A theory of social comparison processes. *Human Relations, 7,* 117–140.

Festinger, L. (1957). *A theory of cognitive dissonance.* Stanford, CA: Stanford University Press.

Festinger, L., & Carlsmith, J. (1959). $1/$20 experiment: Cognitive consequences of forced compliance. *Journal of Abnormal and Social Psychology, 58*(2), 203–210.

Fevre, M. L., Kolt, G. S., & Matheny, J. (2006). Eustress, distress and their interpretation in primary and secondary occupational stress management interventions: Which way first? *Journal of Managerial Psychology, 21*(6), 547–565.

Fiatarone, M. (1996). Physical activity and functional independence in aging. *Research Quarterly for Exercise & Sport, 67,* 70–75.

Fields, R. D. (2014). Neuroscience. Myelin—more than insulation. *Science, 344*(6181), 264–266. doi: 10.1126/science.1253851

Fincham, F. D., Harold, G. T., & Gano-Phillips, S. (2000). The longitudinal association between attributions and marital satisfaction: Direction of effects and role of efficacy expectations. *Journal of Family Psychology, 14,* 267–285.

Finger, S. (1994). *Origins of neuroscience: A history of explorations into brain function.* New York: Oxford University Press.

Fink, M. (1984). Meduna and the origins of convulsive therapy. *American Journal of Psychiatry, 141,* 1034–1041.

Finke, C., Esfahani, N. E., & Ploner, C. J. (2012). Preservation of musical memory in an amnesic professional cellist. *Current Biology, 22*(15), R59.

Finke, R. (1995). Creative realism. In S. Smith, T. Ward & R. Finke (Eds.), *The creative cognition approach* (pp. 301–326). Cambridge, MA.: Cambridge University Press.

Finkel, D., & McGue, M. (1997). Sex differences and nonadditivity in heritability of the Multidimensional Personality Questionnaire scales. *Journal of Personality and Social Psychology, 72,* 929–938.

Fioriti, L., Myers, C., Huang, Y. Y., Li, X., Stephan, J. S., Trifilieff, P., . . . Kandel, E. R. (2015). The persistence of hippocampal-based memory requires protein synthesis mediated by the prion-like protein cpeb3. *Neuron, 86*(6), 1433–1448. doi: 10.1016/j.neuron.2015.05.021

Fischl, B., Liu, A., & Dale, A. M. (2001). Automated manifold surgery: Constructing geometrically accurate and topologically correct models of the human cerebral cortex. *IEEE Transactions on Medical Imaging, 20,* 70–80.

Fisher, M., Holland, C., Merzenich, M. M., & Vinogradov, S. (2009). Using neuroplasticity-based auditory training to improve verbal memory in schizophrenia. *The American Journal of Psychiatry, 166*(7), 805–811.

Fisher, P. L., & Wells, A. (2005). How effective are cognitive and behavioral treatments for obsessive–compulsive disorder? A clinical significance analysis. *Behaviour Research and Therapy, 43*(12), 1543–1558. doi: http://dx.doi.org/10.1016/j.brat.2004.11.007

Fisher, R., Salanova, V., Witt, T., Worth, R., Henry, T., Gross, R., & Graves, N. (2010). Electrical stimulation of the anterior nucleus of thalamus for treatment of refractory epilepsy. *Epilepsia, 17,* 17.

Fiske, S. T. (1998). Stereotyping, prejudice, and discrimination. In D. T. Gilbert & S. T. Fiske (Eds.), *The handbook of social psychology* (4th ed., Vol. 2, pp. 357–411). New York: McGraw-Hill.

Fitzpatrick, M. (2004). *MMR and autism.* New York: Routledge.

Fivush, R., Haden, C., & Reese, E. (1996). Remembering, recounting, and reminiscing: The development of autobiographical memory in social context. In D. C. Rubin (Ed.), *Remembering our past: Studies in autobiographical memory* (pp. 341–359). New York: Cambridge University Press.

Fivush, R., & Nelson, K. (2004). Culture and language in the emergence of autobiographical memory. *Psychological Science, 15*(9), 573.

Flaherty, J. A., & Adams, S. A. (1998). Therapist–patient race and sex matching: Predictors of treatment duration. *Psychiatric Times, 15*(1), 1–4.

Flanagan, D. P., & Dixon, S. G. (2013). The Cattell-Horn-Carroll theory of cognitive abilities. In C. R. Reynolds, K. J. Vannest, & E. Fletcher-Janzen (Eds.), *Encyclopedia of special education* (pp. 368–382). Hoboken, NJ: John Wiley & Sons.

Flaskerud, J. H. (1991). Effects of an Asian client–therapist language, ethnicity and gender match on utilization and outcome of therapy. *Community Mental Health Journal, 27,* 31–42.

Flavell, J. H. (1999). Cognitive development: Children's knowledge about the mind. *Annual Review of Psychology, 50,* 21–45.

Flegal, K. M., Carroll, M. D., & Ogden, C. L. (2012). Prevalence of obesity and trends in the distribution of body mass index among US adults, 1999–2010. *Journal of the American Medical Association, 307*(5), 491–497.

Fleming, M. F., & Barry, K. L. (1992). Clinical overview of alcohol and drug disorders. In M. F. Fleming & K. L. Barry (Eds.), *Addictive disorders,* 3–21. St. Louis: Mosby Year Book.

Flemons, W. W. (2002). Obstructive sleep apnea. *New England Journal of Medicine, 347,* 498–504.

Flinker, A., Korzeniewska, A., Shestyuk, A. Y., Franaszczuk, P. J., Dronkers, N. F., Knight, R. T., & Crone, N. E. (2015). Redefining the role of Broca's area in speech. *Proceedings of the National Academy of Sciences of the United States of America, 112*(9), 2871–2875. doi: 10.1073/pnas.1414491112

Flint, J., & Munafò, M. (2014). Schizophrenia: Genesis of a complex disease. *Nature, 511,* 412–413. doi: 10.1038/nature13645

Flor, H., Elbert, T., Knecht, S., Wienbruch, C., Pantev, C., Birbaumer, N., . . . Taub, E. (1995). Phantom-limb pain as a perceptual correlate of cortical reorganization following arm amputation. *Nature, 375*(6531), 482–484. doi: 10.1038/375482a0

Floresco, S. B. (2015). The nucleus accumbens: An interface between cognition, emotion, and action. *Annual Review of Psychology, 66,* 25–52. doi: 10.1146/annurev-psych-010213-115159

Flynn, J. R. (2009). *What is intelligence? Beyond the Flynn effect.* New York: Cambridge University Press.

Foa, E. B., Hembree, E. A., & Rothbaum, B. O. (2007). *Prolonged exposure therapy for PTSD: Emotional processing of traumatic experiences, therapist guide.* New York: Oxford University Press.

Foland-Ross, L. C., Sacchet, M. D., Prasad, G., Gilbert, B., Thompson, P. M., & Gotlib, I. H. (2015). Cortical thickness predicts the first onset of major depression in adolescence. *International Journal of Developmental Science, 46,* 125–131. doi: 10.1016/j.ijdevneu.2015.07.007

Folkard, S., Arendt, J., & Clark, M. (1993). Can melatonin improve shift workers' tolerance of the night shift? Some preliminary findings. *Chronobiology International: The Journal of Biological and Medical Rhythm Research, 10*(5), 315–320.

Folkard, S., Lombardi, D. A., & Spencer, M. B. (2006). Estimating the circadian rhythm in the risk of occupational injuries and accidents. *Chronobiology International: The Journal of Biological and Medical Rhythm Research, 23*(6), 1181–1192.

Folkard, S., Lombardi, D. A., & Tucker, P. (2005). Shiftwork: Safety, sleepiness, and sleep. *Industrial Health, 43*(1), 20–23.

Folkard, S., & Tucker, P. (2003). Shift work, safety, and productivity. *Medicine, 53,* 95–101.

Folkman, S. (1997). Positive psychological states and coping with severe stress. *Social Science and Medicine, 45,* 1207–1221.

Folkman, S., & Chesney, M. A. (1995). Coping with HIV infection. In M. Stein & A. Baum (Eds.), *Perspectives in behavioral medicine* (pp. 115–133). Hillsdale, NJ: Lawrence Erlbaum.

Folkman, S., & Lazarus, R. S. (1980). An analysis of coping in a middle-aged community sample. *Journal of Health and Social Behavior, 21*(3), 219–239.

Follett, K. J., & Hess, T. M. (2002). Aging, cognitive complexity, and the fundamental attribution error. *Journals of Gerontology Series B: Psychological Sciences and Social Sciences, 57,* 312–323.

Forbes, G., Zhang, X., Doroszewicz, K., & Haas, K. (2009). Relationships between individualism-collectivism, gender, and direct or indirect aggression: a study in China, Poland, and the U.S. *Aggressive Behavior, 35*(1), 24–30.

Forman, E. (n.d.). Behavioral activation for depression. Retrieved from http://www.div12.org/psychological-treatments/disorders/depression/behavioral-activation-for-depression/

Fornito, A., Yucel, M., & Pantelis, C. (2009). Reconciling neuroimaging and neuropathological findings in schizophrenia and bipolar disorder. *Current Opinion in Psychiatry*, 22(3), 312–319.

Forster, S., & Lavie, N. (2016). Establishing the attention-distractibility trait. *Psychological Science*, 27(2), 203–212. doi: 10.1177/0956797615617761

Forsyth, J., Schoenthaler, A., Chaplin, W. F., Ogedegbe, G., & Ravenell, J. (2014). Perceived discrimination and medication adherence in black hypertensive patients: The role of stress and depression. *Psychosomatic Medicine*, 76, 229–236.

Fortuna, L. R., Alegria, M., & Gao, S. (2010). Retention in depression treatment among ethnic and racial minority groups in the United States. *Depression and Anxiety*, 27(5), 485–494. doi: 10.1002/da.20685

*Fortune*. (2013). Best companies to work for 2013. Retrieved May 30, 2013, from http://money.cnn.com/magazines/fortune/best-companies/

Foulkes, D. (1982). *Children's dreams*. New York: Wiley.

Foulkes, D., & Schmidt, M. (1983). Temporal sequence and unit comparison composition in dream reports from different stages of sleep. *Sleep*, 6, 265–280.

Fournier, J. C., & Price, R. B. (2014). Psychotherapy and neuroimaging. *Focus (Am Psychiatr Publ)*, 12(3), 290–298. doi: 10.1176/appi.focus.12.3.290

Fox, M. C., & Mitchum, A. L. (2013). A knowledge-based theory of rising scores on "culture-free" tests. *Journal of Experimental Psychology: General*, 142(3), 979–1000. doi: 10.1037/a0030155

Frank, D. W., Dewitt, M., Hudgens-Haney, M., Schaeffer, D. J., Ball, B. H., Schwarz, N. F., Hussein, A. A., Smart, L. M., & Sabatinelli, D. (2014). Emotion regulation: Quantitative meta-analysis of functional activation and deactivation. *Neuroscience and Biobehavioral Reviews*, 45, 202–211.

Frank, M. G., & Benington, J. (2006). The role of sleep in brain plasticity: Dream or reality? *The Neuroscientist*, 12: 477–488.

Franke, R. H., & Kaul, J. D. (1978). The Hawthorne experiments: First statistical interpretation. *American Sociological Review*, 43, 623–643.

Frankel, B. R., & Piercy, F. P. (1990). The relationship among selected supervisor, therapist, and client behaviors. *Journal of Marital and Family Therapy*, 16, 407–421.

Franklin, D. (1990). Hooked: Why isn't everyone an addict? *In Health*, 4(6), 38–52.

Fredrickson, B. L., Maynard, K. E., Helms, M. J., Haney, T. L., Siegler, I. C., & Barefoot, J. C. (2000). Hostility predicts magnitude and duration of blood pressure response to anger. *Journal of Behavioral Medicine*, 23, 229–243.

Freedman, J., & Fraser, S. (1966). Compliance without pressure: The foot-in-the-door technique. *Journal of Personality and Social Psychology*, 4, 195–202.

Freeman, A., Simon, K. M., Beutler, L. E., & Arkowitz, H. (Eds.). (1989). *Comprehensive handbook of cognitive therapy*. New York: Plenum Press.

Freeman, J. (2001). *Gifted children grown up*. London: David Fulton.

Freeman, W., & Watts, J. W. (1937). Prefrontal lobotomy in the treatment of mental disorders. *Southern Medical Journal*, 30, 23–31.

Freese, J., Powell, B., & Steelman, L. C. (1999). Rebel without a cause or effect: Birth order and social attitudes. *American Sociological Review*, 64, 207–231.

Frenda, S. J., Patihis, L., Loftus, E. F., Lewis, H. C., & Fenn, K. M. (2014). Sleep deprivation and false memories. *Psychological Science*, 25(9), 1674–1681.

Frensch, P. A., & Runger, D. (2003). Implicit learning. *Current Directions in Psychological Science*, 12, 13–18.

Freud, A. (1946). *The ego and the mechanisms of defense*. American Edition, New York: I.U.P.

Freud, S. (1900). *The interpretation of dreams*. S.E., 4–5. (cf. J. Crick, Trans., 1999). London: Oxford University Press.

Freud, S. (1901). *The psychopathology of everyday life*. S.E., 6, 1–290.

Freud, S. (1904a). *Psychopathology of everyday life*. New York: Macmillan; London: Fisher Unwin.

Freud, S. (1904b). Freud's psycho-analytic procedure. S.E., 7, 249–254.

Freud, S. (1923). The ego and the id. S.E., 19, 12–66.

Freud, S. (1930). *Civilization and its discontents*. New York: Jonathon Cape and Co.

Freud, S. (1933). *New introductory lectures on psycho-analysis*. London: Hogarth.

Freud, S. (1940). Splitting of the ego in the process of defence. *International Journal of Psychoanalysis*, 22, 65 [1938], S.E., 23, 275–278.

Freud, S. (1977). *Inhibitions, symptoms and anxiety. Standard edition of the complete works of Sigmund Freud*. New York: W. W. Norton.

Fridlund, A. J., Beck, H. P., Goldie, W. D., & Irons, G. (2012). Little Albert: A neurologically impaired child. *History of Psychology*, 15(4), 302–327.

Friedman, J. M. (2000). Obesity in the new millennium. *Nature*, 404, 632–634.

Friedman, J. M. (2003). A war on obesity, not the obese. *Science*, 299(5608), 856–858.

Friedman, J. M., & Halaas, J. L. (1998). Leptin and the regulation of body weight in mammals. *Nature*, 395, 763.

Friedman, M., & Kasanin, J. D. (1943). Hypertension in only one of identical twins. *Archives of Internal Medicine*, 72, 767–774.

Friedman, M., & Rosenman, R. H. (1959). Association of specific behavior pattern with blood and cardiovascular findings. *Journal of the American Medical Association*, 169, 1286–1296.

Friederich, H.-C., Wu, M., Simon, J. J., & Herzog, W. (2013). Neurocircuit function in eating disorders. *International Journal of Eating Disorders*, 46(5), 425–432. doi: 10.1002/eat.22099

Friesdorf, R., Conway, P., & Gawronski, B. (2015). Gender differences in responses to moral dilemmas: A process dissociation analysis. *Personality and Social Psychology Bulletin*, 41(5), 696–713.

Frimer, J. A., Gaucher, D., & Schaefer, N. K. (2014). Political conservatives' affinity for obedience to authority is loyal, not blind. *Personality and Social Psychology Bulletin*, 40(9), 1205–1214. doi: 10.1177/0146167214538672

Froh, J. J. (2004). The history of positive psychology: Truth be told. *NYS Psychologist*, 16(3), 18–20.

Frontera, W. R., Hughes, V. A., Lutz, K. J., & Evans, W. J. (1991). A cross-sectional study of muscle strength and mass in 45- to 78-year-old men and women. *Journal of Applied Physiology*, 71, 644–650.

Frostegård, J. (2013). Immunity, atherosclerosis and cardiovascular disease. *BMC Medicine*, 11, 117. doi: 10.1186/1741-7015-11-117

Frühmesser, A., & Kotzot, D. (2011). Chromosomal variants in Klinefelter syndrome. *Sexual Development*, 5(3), 109–123.

Frydenberg, E., Lewis, R., Ardila, R., Cairns, E., & Kennedy, G. (2001). Adolescent concern with social issues: An exploratory comparison between Australian, Colombian and North Irish students. *Journal of Peace Psychology*, 7, 59–76.

Fulcher, J. S. (1942). "Voluntary" facial expression in blind and seeing children. *Archives of Psychology*, 38, 1–49.

Furumoto, L. (1979). Mary Whiton Calkins (1863–1930): Fourteenth president of the American Psychological Association. *Journal of the History of Behavioral Sciences*, 15, 346–356.

Furumoto, L. (1991). From "paired associates" to a psychology of self: The intellectual odyssey of Mary Whiton Calkins. In A. Kimble, M. Wertheimer, & C. White (Ed.), *Portraits of pioneers in psychology* (pp. 57–72). Washington, DC: American Psychological Association.

Gable, R. S. (2004). Acute toxic effects of club drugs. *Journal of Psychoactive Drugs*, 36(1), 303–313.

Gado, M. (2004). A cry in the night: The Kitty Genovese murder. *Court TV's Crime Library: Criminal Minds and Methods*. Retrieved August 2, 2004, from www.crimelibrary.com/serial_killers/predators/kitty_genovese/1.html?sect=2.

Galanaki, E. P. (2012). The imaginary audience and the personal fable: A test of Elkind's theory of adolescent egocentrism. *PSYCH*, 3(6), 457–466.

Galante, M., & Zeveloff, J. (2012). Harvard is investigating 125 undergrads in massive cheating scandal. *Business Insider*, August 30. Retrieved from http://www.businessinsider.com/harvard-cheating-scandal-2012-8

Gale, J. T., Shields, D. C., Ishizawa, Y., & Eskkandar, E. N. (2016). Reward and reinforcement activity in the nucleus accumbens during learning. *Frontiers of Behavioral Neuroscience*, 15(1), 114.

Galea, S., Resnick, H., Kilpatrick, D., Bucuvalas, M., Gold, J., & Vlahov, D. (2002, March 28). Psychological sequelae of the September 11 terrorist attacks in New York City. *New England Journal of Medicine*, 346(13), 982–987.

Gallagher, R. P. (2009). National Survey of Counseling Center Directors, 2009. *The American College Counseling Association (ACCA)*. Retrieved from http://www.iacsinc.org/2009%20National%20Survey.pdf

Gallistel, C. R., & Matzel, L. D. (2013). The neuroscience of learning: Beyond the Hebbian synapse. *Annual Review of Psychology*, 64, 169–200.

Gamwell, L., & Tomes, N. (1995). *Madness in America: Cultural and medical perspectives of mental illness before 1914*. Ithaca, NY: Cornell University Press.

Ganchrow, J. R., Steiner, J. E., & Munif, D. (1983). Neonatal facial expressions in response to different qualities and intensities of gustatory stimuli. *Infant Behavior Development*, 6, 473–478.

Gandhi, A. V., Mosser, E. A., Oikonomou, G., & Prober, D. A. (2015). Melatonin is required for the circadian regulation of sleep. *Neuron*, 85, 1193–1199.

Ganis, G., Thompson, W. L., & Kosslyn, S. M. (2004). Brain areas underlying visual mental imagery and visual perception: An fMRI study. *Cognitive Brain Research*, 20(2), 226–241.

Garb, H. N., Florio, C. M., & Grove, W. M. (1998). The validity of the Rorschach and the Minnesota Multiphasic Personality Inventory: Results from metaanalyses. *Psychological Science*, 9, 402–404.

Garcia, J., Brett, L. P., & Rusiniak, K. W. (1989). Limits of Darwinian conditioning. In S. B. Klein & R. R. Mowrer (Eds.), *Contemporary learning theories: Instrumental conditioning theory and the impact of biological constraints on learning* (pp. 237–275). Hillsdale, NJ: Erlbaum.

Garcia, J., & Koelling, R. A. (1966). Relation of cue to consequence in avoidance learning. *Psychonomic Science*, 4, 123.

García-Campayo, J., Fayed, N., Serrano-Blanco, A., & Roca, M. (2009). Brain dysfunction behind functional symptoms: Neuroimaging and somatoform, conversive, and dissociative disorders. *Current Opinion in Psychiatry*, 22(2), 224–231.

Gardner, E. P., & Johnson, K. O. (2013). Sensory coding. In E. R. Kandel, J. H. Schwartz, T. M. Jessell, S. A. Siegelbaum, & A. J. Hudspeth (Eds.), *Principles of neural science* (5th ed., pp. 449–474). New York: McGraw-Hill.

Gardner, H. (1993a). *Creating minds: An anatomy of creativity seen through the lives of Freud, Einstein, Picasso, Stravinsky, Eliot, Graham, and Ghandi.* New York: Basic Books.

Gardner, H. (1993b). *Multiple intelligences: The theory in practice.* New York: Basic Books.

Gardner, H. (1998). Are there additional intelligences? The case for naturalist, spiritual, and existential intelligences. In J. Kane (Ed.), *Education, information, and transformation* (pp. 111–131). Upper Saddle River, NJ: Merrill-Prentice Hall.

Gardner, H. (1999a). *Intelligence reframed: Multiple intelligences for the 21st century.* New York: Basic Books.

Gardner, H. (1999b, February). Who owns intelligence? *Atlantic Monthly*, 67–76.

Gardner, H., Kornhaber, M. L., & Wake, W. K. (1996). *Intelligence: Multiple perspectives.* Orlando, FL: Harcourt Brace & Co.

Gardner, H., & Moran, S. (2006). The science in multiple intelligences: A response to Lynn Waterhouse. *Educational Psychologist*, 41, 227–232.

Gardner, J., & Oswald, A. J. (2004). How is mortality affected by money, marriage, and stress? *Journal of Health Economics*, 23(6), 1181–1207.

Gardner, R. J. M., & Sutherland, G. R. (1996). Chromosome abnormalities and genetic counseling. *Oxford Monographics on Medical Genetics No. 29.* New York: Oxford University Press.

Garland, E. L., Geschwind, N., Peeters, F., & Wichers, M. (2015). Mindfulness training promotes upward spirals of positive affect and cognition: Multilevel and autoregressive latent trajectory modeling analyses. *Frontiers in Psychology*, 6, 15.

Garnier-Dykstra, L. M., Caldeira, K. M., Vincent, K. B., O'Grady, K. E., & Arria, A. M. (2012). Nonmedical use of prescription stimulants during college: Four-year trends in exposure opportunity, use, motives, and sources. *Journal of American College Health*, 60(3), 226–234. doi: 10.1080/07448481.2011.589876

Gazzaniga, M. S. (2006). *The ethical brain: The science of our moral dilemmas.* New York: HarperCollins.

Gazzaniga, M. S. (2009). *Human: The science behind what makes us unique.* New York: Harper Perennial.

Geary, J. P. (2001). *Bridging culture through school counseling: Theoretical understanding and practical solutions* (Unpublished master's thesis). California State University, Northridge.

Gebhard, P. H., & Johnson, A. B. (1979/1998). *The Kinsey data: Marginal tabulations of 1938–1963 interviews conducted by the Institute for Sex Research.* Philadelphia: W. B. Saunders.

Geddes, D. P. (Ed.). (1954). *An analysis of the Kinsey reports.* New York: New American Library.

Geen, R. G., & Thomas, S. L. (1986). The immediate effects of media violence on behavior. *Journal of Social Issues*, 42, 7–27.

Geier, J., Bernáth, L., Hudák, M., & Sára, L. (2008). Straightness as the main factor of the Hermann grid illusion. *Perception*, 37(5), 651–665.

Gelder, M. (1976). Flooding. In T. Thompson & W. Dockens (Eds.), *Applications of behavior modification* (pp. 250–298). New York: Academic Press.

Geliebter, A. (1988). Gastric distension and gastric capacity in relation to food intake in humans. *Physiological Behavior*, 44, 665–668.

Geller, A. I., Shehab, N., Weidle, N. J., Lovegrove, M. C., Wolpert, B. J., Timbo, B. B., Mozersky, R. P., & Budnitz, D. S. (2015). Emergency department visits for adverse events related to dietary supplements. *New England Journal of Medicine*, 373, 1531–1540.

Geller, B., Williams, M., Zimerman, B., Frazier, J., Beringer, L., & Warner, K. L. (1998). Prepubertal and early adolescent bipolarity differentiate from ADHD by manic symptoms, grandiose delusions, ultra-rapid or ultradian cycling. *Journal of Affective Disorders*, 51(2), 81–91.

Gelman, S. A., & Markman, E. M. (1986). Categories and induction in young children. *Cognition*, 23, 183–209.

Gentile, D. A. (2015). What is a good skeptic to do? The case for skepticism in the media violence discussion. *Perspectives on Psychological Science*, 10(5), 674–676. doi: 10.1177/1745691615592238

Gentile, D. A., & Bushman, B. J. (2012). Reassessing media violence effects using a risk and resilience approach to understanding aggression. *Psychology of Popular Media Culture*, 1(3), 138–151. doi: 10.1037/a0028481

Gershoff, E. T. (2000). The short- and long-term effects of corporal punishment on children: A meta-analytical review. In D. Elliman & M. A. Lynch, *The physical punishment of children* (pp. 196–198).

Gershoff, E. T. (2002). Corporal punishment by parents: Effects on children and links to physical abuse. *Child Law Practice*, 21(10), 154–157.

Gershoff, E. T. (2010). More harm than good: A summary of scientific research on the intended and unintended effects of corporal punishment on children. *Law and Contemporary Problems*, 73(31), 31–56.

Geschwind, D. H., & Iacoboni, M. (2007). Structural and functional asymmetries of the frontal lobes. In B. L. Miller & J. K. Cummings (Eds.), *The human frontal lobes* (2nd ed., pp. 68–91). New York: Guilford Press.

Ghaziri, J., Tucholka, A., Larue, V., Blanchette-Sylvestre, M., Reyburn, G., Gilbert, G., . . . Beauregard, M. (2013). Neurofeedback training induces changes in white and gray matter. *Clinical EEG and Neuroscience*, 44(4), 265–272. doi: 10.1177/1550059413476031

Giachero, M., Calfa, G. D., & Molina, V. A. (2015). Hippocampal dendritic spines remodeling and fear memory are modulated by gabaergic signaling within the basolateral amygdala complex. *Hippocampus*, 25(5), 545–555. doi: 10.1002/hipo.22409

Gianaros, P. J., & Wager, T. D. (2015). Brain-body pathways linking psychological stress and physical health. *Current Directions in Psychological Science*, 24, 313–321.

Giancola, F. (2006). The generation gap: More myth than reality. *Human Resource Planning*, 29(4), 32–37.

Gibbons, J. L., Stiles, D. A., & Shkodriani, G. M. (1991). Adolescents' attitudes toward family and gender roles: An international comparison. *Sex Roles*, 25, 625–643.

Gibbons, R. D., Brown, C. H., Hur, K., Davis, J., & Mann, J. J. (2012). Suicidal thoughts and behavior with antidepressant treatment: Reanalysis of the randomized placebo-controlled studies of fluoxetine and venlafaxine. *Archives of General Psychiatry*, 69(6), 580–587. doi: 10.1001/archgenpsychiatry.2011.2048

Gibson, E. J., & Walk, R. D. (1960). The "visual cliff." *Scientific American*, 202, 67–71.

Giedd, J. N., Raznahan, A., Alexander-Bloch, A., Schmitt, E., Gogtay, N., & Rapoport, J. L. (2015). Child psychiatry branch of the National Institute of Mental Health longitudinal structural magnetic resonance imaging study of human brain development. *Neuropsychopharmacology*, 40(1), 43–49. doi: 10.1038/npp.2014.236

Gilberg, C., & Coleman, M. (2000). *The biology of the autistic syndromes* (3rd ed.). London: Mac Keith Press.

Gilbert, S. J. (1981). Another look at the Milgram obedience studies: The role of the graduated series of shocks. *Personality and Social Psychology Bulletin*, 7(4), 690–695.

Gill, S. T. (1991). Carrying the war into the never-never land of psi. *Skeptical Inquirer*, 15(1), 269–273.

Gillen-O'Neel, C., Huynh, V. W., & Fuligni, A. J. (2012). To study or to sleep? The academic costs of extra studying at the expense of sleep. *Child Development*, 84(1), 133–142.

Gillespie, M. A., Kim, B. H., Manheim, L. J., Yoo, T., Oswald, F. L., & Schmitt, N. (2002, June). The development and validation of biographical data and situational judgment tests in the prediction of college student success. Presented in A. M. Ryan (Chair), *Beyond g: Expanding thinking on predictors of college success.* Symposium conducted at the 14th Annual Convention of the American Psychological Society, New Orleans, LA.

Gilley, B. J. (2006). Chapter three: "Adapting to homophobia among Indians." In Brian Joseph Gilley (Ed.), *Becoming two-spirit: Gay identity and social acceptance in Indian Country* (pp. 51–86). Lincoln: University of Nebraska Press.

Gillham, B., Tanner, G., Cheyne, B., Freeman, I., Rooney, M., & Lambie, A. (1998). Unemployment rates, single parent density, and indices of child poverty: Their relationship to different categories of child abuse and neglect. *Child Abuse and Neglect*, 22(2), 79–90.

Gilligan, C. (1982). *In a different voice: Psychological theory and women's development.* Cambridge, MA: Harvard University Press.

Gillund, G., & Shiffrin, R. M. (1984). A retrieval model for both recognition and recall. *Psychological Review*, 91, 1–67.

Gilmour, J., & Skuse, D. (1999). A case-comparison study of the characteristics of children with a short stature syndrome induced by stress (hyperphagic short stature) and a consecutive series of unaffected "stressed" children. *Journal of Child Psychology and Psychiatry and Allied Disciplines*, 40(6), 969–978.

Ginzburg, K., Solomon, Z., Koifman, B., Keren, G., Roth, A., Kriwisky, M., . . . Bleich, A. (2003). Trajectories of post-traumatic stress disorder following myocardial infarction: A prospective study. *Journal of Clinical Psychiatry*, 64(10), 1217–1223.

Gittelman-Klein, R. (1978). Validity in projective tests for psychodiagnosis in children. In R. L. Spitzer & D. F. Klein (Eds.), *Critical issues in psychiatric diagnosis* (pp. 141–166). New York: Raven Press.

Glangetas, C., Fois, G. R., Jalabert, M., Lecca, S., Valentinova, K., Meye, F. J., . . . Georges, F. (2015). Ventral subiculum stimulation promotes persistent hyperactivity of dopamine neurons and facilitates behavioral effects of cocaine. *Cell Symposia: Aging and MetabolismL Cell Reports*, 13(10), 2287–2296.

Glaser, M., Kolvin, I., Campbell, D., Glasser, A., Leitch, I., & Farrelly, S. (2001). Cycle of child sexual abuse: links between being a victim and becoming a perpetrator. *British Journal of Psychiatry*, 179, 482–494.

Glassman, W. E., & Hadad, M. (2008). Chapter eight: Perspectives on social behaviour, altruism and bystander behavior. In William E. Glassman & Marilyn Hadad (Eds.), *Approaches to Psychology* (pp. 399–401). London: Open University Press.

Glenn, A. L., Raine, A., Mednick, S. A., & Venables, P. (2007). Early temperamental and psychophysiological precursors of adult psychopathic personality. *Journal of Abnormal Psychology*, 116(3), 508–518.

Glick, P., & Fiske, S. (2001). An ambivalent alliance: Hostile and benevolent sexism as complementary justifications for gender inequality. *American Psychologist*, 56, 109–118.

Gluckman, P. D., & Hanson, M. A. (2006). Evolution, development and timing of puberty. *Trends in Endocrinology and Metabolism*, 17(1), 7–12.

Glucksman, M. L. (2006). Psychoanalytic and psychodynamic education in the 21st century. *Journal of American Academy of Psychoanalysis*, 34, 215–22.

Glynn, S. M. (1990). Token economy approaches for psychiatric patients: Progress and pitfalls over 25 years. *Behavior Modification*, 14, 383–407.

Godden, D. R., & Baddeley, A. D. (1975). Context-dependent memory in two natural environments: On land and underwater. *British Journal of Psychology*, 66, 325–331.

Goetz, T., Bieg, M., Lüdtke, O., Pekrun, R., & Hall, N. C. (2013). Do girls really experience more anxiety in mathematics? *Psychological Science*, 24(10), 2079–2087.

Gogtay, N., Lu, A., Leow, A. D., Klunder, A. D., Lee, A. D., Chavez, A., . . . Thompson, P. M. (2008). Three-dimensional brain growth abnormalities in childhood-onset schizophrenia visualized by using tensor-based morphometry. *Proceedings of the National Academy of Sciences, USA, 105*(41), 15979–15984.

Gogtay, N., & Thompson, P. M. (2010). Mapping gray matter development: Implications for typical development and vulnerability to psychopathology. *Brain and Cognition, 72*(1), 6–15.

Goin, M. K. (2005). Practical psychotherapy: A current perspective on the psychotherapies. *Psychiatric Services, 56*(3), 255–257.

Gold, E. B., Leung, K., Crawford, S. L., Huang, M. H., Waetjen, L. E., & Greendale, G. A. (2013). Phytoestrogen and fiber intakes in relation to incident vasomotor symptoms: Results from the Study of Women's Health Across the Nation. *Menopause, 20*(3), 305–314. doi: 10.1097/GME.0b013e31826d2f43

Goldfried, M. R. (2007). What has psychotherapy inherited from Carl Rogers? *Psychotherapy: Theory, Research, Practice, Training, 44*(3), 249–252. doi: 10.1037/0033-3204.44.3.249

Goldman, A. L., Pezawas, L., Mattay, V. S., Fischl, B., Verchinski, B. A., Chen, Q., Weinberger, D. R., & Meyer-Lindenberg, A. (2009). Widespread reductions of cortical thickness in schizophrenia and spectrum disorders and evidence of heritability. *Archives of General Psychiatry, 66*(5), 467–477.

Goldman-Rakic, P. S. (1998). The prefrontal landscape: Implications of functional architecture for understanding human mentation and the central executive. In A. C. Roberts, T. W. Robbins, & L. Weiskrantz (Eds.), *The prefrontal cortex: Executive and cognitive functions* (pp. 87–102). Oxford, UK: Oxford University Press.

Goldsmith, H. H., & Campos, J. (1982). Toward a theory of infant temperament. In R. Emde & R. Harmon (Eds.), *The development of attachment and affiliative systems: Psychobiological aspects* (pp. 161–193). New York: Plenum Press.

Goleman, D. (1982). Staying up: The rebellion against sleep's gentle tyranny. *Psychology Today, 3,* 24–35.

Goleman, D. (1995). *Emotional intelligence: Why it can matter more than IQ.* New York: Bantam Books.

Gomar, J. J., Valls, E., Radua, J., Mareca, C., Tristany, J., Del Olmo, F., . . . Cognitive Rehabilitation Study, G. (2015). A multisite, randomized controlled clinical trial of computerized cognitive remediation therapy for schizophrenia. *Schizophrenia Bulletin, 41*(6), 1387–1396. doi: 10.1093/schbul/sbv059

Goncalves, R., Pedrozo, A. L., Coutinho, E. S., Figueira, I., & Ventura, P. (2012). Efficacy of virtual reality exposure therapy in the treatment of PTSD: A systematic review. *PLoS One, 7*(12), e48469. doi: 10.1371/journal.pone.0048469

Gong-Guy, E., & Hammen, C. (1980). Causal perceptions of stressful events in depressed and nondepressed outpatients. *Journal of Abnormal Psychology, 89,* 662–669.

Gonsalves, B., Reber, P. J., Gitelman, D. R., Parrish, T. B., Mesulam, M. M., & Paller, K. A. (2004). Neural evidence that vivid imagining can lead to false remembering. *Psychological Science, 15,* 655–660.

Gonzales, P. M., Blanton, H., & Williams, K. J. (2002). The effects of stereotype threat and double–minority status on the test performance of Latino women. *Personality and Social Psychology Bulletin, 28*(5), 659–670.

Gonzalez, J. S., Penedo, F. J., Antoni, M. H., Durán, R. E., Fernandez, M. I., McPherson-Baker, S., . . . Schneiderman, N. (2004). Social support, positive states of mind, and HIV treatment adherence in men and women living with HIV/AIDS. *Health Psychology, 23*(4), 413–418.

Goodglass, H., Kaplan, E., & Barresi, B. (2001). *The assessment of aphasia and related disorders* (3rd ed.). Baltimore: Lippincott, Williams & Wilkins.

Goodkind, M., Eickhoff, S. B., Oathes, D. J., Jiang, Y., Chang, A., Jones-Hagata, L. B., . . . Etkin, A. (2015). Identification of a common neurobiological substrate for mental illness. *JAMA Psychiatry, 72*(4), 305–315. doi: 10.1001/jamapsychiatry.2014.2206

Goodman, E. S. (1980). Margaret Floy Washburn (1871–1939) first woman Ph.D. in psychology. *Psychology of Women Quarterly, 5,* 69–80.

Goossens, L., van Roekel, E., Verhagen, M., Cacioppo, J. T., Cacioppo, S., Maes, M., & Boomsma, D. I. (2015). The genetics of loneliness: Linking evolutionary theory to genome-wide genetics, epigenetics, and social science. *Perspectives on Psychological Science, 10*(2), 213–226. doi: 10.1177/1745691614564878

Gordon, A. J., Conley, J. W., Gordon, J. M. (2013). Medical consequences of marijuana use: A review of current literature. *Current Psychiatry Reports (Review) 15*(12), 419. doi: 10.1007/s11920-013-0419-7

Gosselin, R. E., Smith, R. P., Hodge, H. C., & Braddock, J. E. (1984). *Clinical toxicology of commercial products* (5th ed.). Sydney, Australia: Williams & Wilkins.

Gotlib, I. H., Sivers, H., Canli, T., Kasch, K. L., & Gabrieli, J. D. E. (2001, November). Neural activation in depression in response to emotional stimuli. In I. H. Gotlib (Chair), *New directions in the neurobiology of affective disorders.* Symposium conducted at the annual meeting of the Society for Research in Psychopathology, Madison, WI.

Gottesman, I. I. (1991). *Schizophrenia genesis: The origins of madness.* New York: Freeman.

Gottesman, I. I., McGuffin, P., & Farmer, A. E. (1987). Clinical genetics as clues to the "Real" genetics of schizophrenia (A decade of modest gains while playing for time). *Schizophrenia Bulletin, 13,* 23–47.

Gottesman, I. I., & Shields, J. (1976). A critical review of recent adoption, twin and family studies of schizophrenia: Behavioural genetics perspectives. *Schizophrenia Bulletin, 2,* 360–401.

Gottesman, I., & Shields, J. (1982). *Schizophrenia: The epigenetic puzzle.* New York: Cambridge University Press.

Gottman, J. M., & Krokoff, L. J. (1989). Marital interaction and satisfaction: A longitudinal view. *Journal of Consulting and Clinical Psychology, 57,* 47–52.

Gotz, M., Sirko, S., Beckers, J., & Irmler, M. (2015). Reactive astrocytes as neural stem or progenitor cells: In vivo lineage, in vitro potential, and genome-wide expression analysis. *Glia, 63*(8), 1452–1468. doi: 10.1002/glia.22850

Gough, H. G. (1995). *California Psychological Inventory* (3rd ed.). Palo Alto, CA: Consulting Psychologist-Press.

Gould, J. L., & Gould, C. G. (1994). *The animal mind.* New York: Scientific American Library.

Gould, S. J. (1981). *The mismeasure of man.* New York: Norton.

Gould, S. J. (1996). *The mismeasure of man.* New York: W. W. Norton.

Gračanin, A., Vingerhoets, A. J. J. M., Kardum, I., Zupčić, M., Šantek, M., & Šimić, M. (2015). Why crying does and sometimes does not seem to alleviate mood: A quasi-experimental study. *Motivation and Emotion, 39*(6), 953–960. doi: 10.1007/s11031-015-9507-9.

Graf, W. D., Nagel, S. K., Epstein, L. G., Miller, G., Nass, R., & Larriviere, D. (2013). Pediatric neuroenhancement: Ethical, legal, social, and neurodevelopmental implications. *Neurology, 80*(13), 1251–1260. doi: 10.1212/WNL.0b013e318289703b

Grandjean, P., Weihe, P., White, R. F., Debes, F., Araki, S., Yokoyama, K., Murata, K., Sorensen, N., Dahl, R., & Jorgensen, P. J. (1997). Cognitive deficit in 7-year-old children with prenatal exposure to methylmercury. *Neurotoxicology and Teratology, 19*(6), 417–428.

Graven, S. N., & Browne, J. V. (2008). Sleep and brain development: The critical role of sleep in fetal and early neonatal brain development. *Newborn & Infant Nursing Review, 8,* 173–179.

Greeley, A. (1987). Mysticism goes mainstream. *American Health, 1,* 47–49.

Green, D. M., & Swets, J. A. (1966). *Signal detection theory and psychophysics.* New York: Wiley.

Greenwald, A. G., & Banaji, M. R. (1995). Implicit social cognition: Attitudes, self-esteem, and stereotypes. *Psychological Review, 102,* 4–27.

Greenwald, A. G., McGhee, D. E., & Schwartz, J. K. L. (1998). Measuring individual differences in implicit cognition: The Implicit Association Test. *Journal of Personality and Social Psychology, 74,* 1464–1480.

Greer, G. R., Grob, C. S., & Halberstadt, A. L. (2014). PTSD symptom reports of patients evaluated for the New Mexico medical cannabis program. *Journal of Psychoactive Drugs, 46*(1), 73. doi: 10.1080/02791072.2013.873843

Greeson, J. (2013). Foster youth & the transition to adulthood: The theoretical & conceptual basis for natural mentoring. *Emerging Adulthood, 1*(1), 40–51.

Gregory, R. L. (1990). *Eye and brain, the psychology of seeing.* Princeton, NJ: Princeton University Press.

Gresham, L. G., & Shimp, T. A. (1985). Attitude toward the advertisement and brand attitudes: A classical conditioning prospective. *Journal of Advertising, 14*(1), 10–17, 49.

Griggs, E. M., Young, E. J., Rumbaugh, G., & Miller, C. A. (2013). MicroRNA-182 regulates amygdala-dependent memory formation. *Journal of Neuroscience, 33*(4), 1734. doi: 10.1523/JNEUROSCI.2873-12.2013

Griggs, R. A. (2015). Coverage of the Phineas Gage story in introductory psychology textbooks: Was Gage no longer Gage? *Teaching of Psychology, 42*(3), 195–202. doi: 10.1177/0098628315587614

Grimbos, T., Dawood, K., Burriss, R. P., Zucker, K. J., & Puts, D. A. (2010). Sexual orientation and the second to fourth finger length ratio: A meta-analysis in men and women. *Behavioral Neuroscience, 124*(2), 278–287. doi: 10.1037/a0018764

Grocer, S., & Kohout, J. (1997). *The 1995 APA survey of 1992 baccalaureate recipients.* Washington, DC: American Psychological Association.

Gross, C. G. (1999). A hole in the head. *The Neuroscientist, 5,* 263–269.

Grumbach, M. M., & Kaplan, S. L. (1990). The neuroendocrinology of human puberty: An ontogenetic perspective. In M. M. Grumbach, P. C. Sizonenko, & M. L. Aubert (Eds.), *Control of the onset of puberty* (pp. 1–6). Baltimore: Williams & Wilkins.

Grumbach, M. M., & Styne, D. M. (1998). Puberty: Ontogeny, neuroendocrinology, physiology, and disorders. In J. D. Wilson, D. W. Foster, H. M. Kronenberg, & P. R. Larsen (Eds.), *Williams textbook of endocrinology* (9th ed. pp. 1509–1625). Philadelphia: W. B. Saunders.

Grünbaum, A. (1984). *The foundations of psychoanalysis: A philosophical critique.* Berkeley, CA: University of California Press.

Guar, A., Dominguez, K., Kalish, M., Rivera-Hernandez, D., Donohoe, M., & Mitchell, C. (2008, February). *Practice of offering a child pre-masticated food: An unrecognized possible risk factor for HIV transmission.* Paper presented at the 15th Conference on Retroviruses and Opportunistic Infections, Boston, MA.

Guilford, J. P. (1967). *The nature of human intelligence.* New York: McGraw-Hill.

Gunderson, E. A., Gripshover, S. J., Romero, C., Dweck, C. S., Goldin-Meadow, S., & Levine, S. C. (2013). Parent praise to 1- to 3-year-olds predicts children's motivational frameworks 5 years later. *Child Development,* ePub ahead of print, *84*(5), 1526–1541. doi: 10.1111/cdev.12064

Guo, J., Marsh, H. W., Parker, Pl. D., Morin, A. J. S., & Yeung, A. S. (2015). Expectancy-value in mathematics, gender and socioeconomic background as predictors of achievement and aspirations: A multi-cohort study. *Learning and Individual Differences, 37*, 161–168.

Gurung, R. A. (2003). Pedagogical aids and student performance. *Teaching of Psychology, 30*, 92–95.

Gurung, R. A. (2004). Pedagogical aids: Learning enhancers or dangerous detours? *Teaching of Psychology, 31*(3), 164–166.

Guskiewicz, K. M., Marshall, S. W., Bailes, J., McCrea, M., Harding, H. P., Jr., Matthews, A., . . . Cantu, R. C. (2007). Recurrent concussion and risk of depression in retired professional football players. *Medicine and Science in Sports and Exercise, 39*(6), 903–909.

Guthrie, R. V. (2004). *Even the rat was white: A historical view of psychology.* Boston: Allyn & Bacon.

Haas, A. P., Rodgers, P. L., & Herman, J. L. (2014). Suicide attempts among transgender and gender non-conforming adults: Findings of the National Transgender Discrimination Survey. *American Foundation for Suicide Prevention and Williams Institute,* UCLA School of Law.Retrieved from http://williamsinstitute.law.ucla.edu/wp-content/uploads/AFSP-Williams-Suicide-Report-Final.pdf.

Haass, C., Lemere, C. A., Capell, A., Citron, M., Seubert, P., Schenk, D., . . . Selkoe, D. J. (1995). The Swedish mutation causes early-onset Alzheimer's disease by β-secretase cleavage within the secretory pathway. *Nature Medicine, 1*, 1291–1296. doi:10.1038/nm1295-1291

Haber, R. N. (1979). Twenty years of haunting eidetic imagery: Where's the ghost? *The Behavioral and Brain Sciences, 2*, 583–619.

Hagan, C. R., Podlogar, M. C., & Joiner, T. E. (2015). Murder-suicide: Bridging the gap between mass murder, amok, and suicide. *Journal of Aggression, Conflict and Peace Research, 7*(3), 179–186.

Hahm, H. C., & Adkins, C. (2009). A model of Asian and Pacific Islander sexual minority acculturation. *Journal of LGBT Youth, 6*, 155–173.

Hahn, J., Wang, X., & Margeta, M. (2015). Astrocytes increase the activity of synaptic glun2b nmda receptors. *Frontiers in Cellular Neuroscience, 9*, 117. doi: 10.3389/fncel.2015.00117

Hahnemann, S. (1907). Indications of the homeopathic employment of medicines in ordinary practice. Hufeland's Journal (Journal der praktischen Azneikunde und Wundarzneykuns), Tome II, Parts 3 and 4.

Hajcak, G., & Starr, L. (n.d.). Posttraumatic stress disorder. Retrieved from http://www.div12.org/psychological-treatments/disorders/post-traumatic-stress-disorder/

Haj-Dahmane, S., & Shen, R.-Y. (2014). Chronic stress impairs α1-adrenoceptor-induced endocannabinoid-dependent synaptic plasticity in the dorsal raphe nucleus. *Journal of Neuroscience, 34*(44), 14560. doi: 10.1523/JNEUROSCI.1310-14.2014

Halbesleben, J. R. B., & Bowler, W. M. (2007). Emotional exhaustion and job performance: The mediating role of motivation. *Journal of Applied Psychology, 91*, 93–106.

Halim, M. L., Ruble, D. N., Tamis-LeMonda, C. S., Zosuls, K. M., Lurye, L. E., & Greulich, F. K. (2014). Pink frilly dresses and the avoidance of all thing "girly": Children's appearance rigidity and cognitive theories of gender development. *Developmental Psychology, 50*(4), 1091–1101.

Hall, A. P., & Henry, J. A. (2006). Acute toxic effects of 'Ecstasy' (MDMA) and related compounds: Overview of pathophysiology and clinical management. *British Journal of Anaesthesia, 96*(6), 678–685.

Hall, C. (1966). Studies of dreams collected in the laboratory and at home. *Institute of Dream Research Monograph Series* (No. 1). Santa Cruz, CA: Privately printed.

Hall, C. S. (1953). A cognitive theory of dreams. The Journal of General Psychology, 49, 273–282. Abridged version in M. F. DeMartino (Ed.). (1959). *Dreams and personality dynamics* (pp. 123–134). Springfield, IL: Charles C. Thomas.

Hall, H. (2014). An intro to homeopathy. *Skeptical Inquirer, 38*(5), 54–58. Retrieved from http://www.csicop.org/si/show/an_introduction_to_homeopathy/

Hall, J. A., Pennington, N., & Lueders, A. (2013). Impression management and formation on Facebook: A lens model approach. *New Media & Society, 16*(6), 958. doi: 10.1177/1461444813495166

Hall, W., & Degenhardt, L. (2009). Adverse health effects of non-medical cannabis use. *Lancet, 374*, 1383–1391.

Hamann, S., Herman, R. A., Nolan, C. L., & Wallen, K. (2004). Men and women differ in amygdale response to visual sexual stimuli. *Nature Neuroscience, 7*(4), 411–419.

Hamer, D. H., Hu, S., Magnuson, V. L., Hu, N., & Pattatucci, A. M. L. (1993). A linkage between DNA markers on the X chromosome and male sexual orientation. *Science, 261*, 321–327.

Hamers, F. F., & Downs, A. M. (2003, March). HIV in central and eastern Europe. *Lancet, 362*, 9362.

Hamilton, D. L., & Gifford, R. K. (1976). Illusory correlation in interpersonal perception: A cognitive basis of stereotypic judgments. *Journal of Experimental Social Psychology, 12*, 392–407.

Hammond, M. D., Overall, N. C., & Cross, E. J. (2016). Internalizing sexism within close relationships: Perceptions of intimate partners' benevolent sexism promote women's endorsement of benevolent sexism. *Journal of Personality and social Psychology, 110*(2), 214–238.

Hampton, J. A. (1998). Similarity-based categorization and fuzziness of natural categories. *Cognition, 65*, 137–165.

Hancox, J., Ntoumanis, N., Thogersen-Ntoumani, C., & Quested, E. (2015). Self-determination theory. In *Essentials of motivation & behaviour change* (pp. 68–85). Brussels: EuropeActive.

Handel, S. (1989). *Listening: An introduction to the perception of auditory events.* Cambridge, MA: MIT Press.

Hansen, C. P. (1988). Personality characteristics of the accident involved employee. *Journal of Business and Psychology, 2*(4), 346–365.

Hansen, P. G., Hendricks, V. F., & Rendsvig, R. K. (2013). Infostorms. *Metaphilosophy, 44*(3), 301. doi: 10.1111/meta.12028

Harlow, H. F. (1958). The nature of love. *American Psychologist, 13*, 573–685.

Harlow, J. M. (1848). Passage of an iron rod through the head. *Boston Medical and Surgical Journal, 39*, 389–393.

Harlow, J. M. (1868). Recovery from the passage of an iron bar through the head. *Publications of the Massachusetts Medical Society, 2*, 327–347.

Harman, G. (1999). Moral philosophy meets social psychology: Virtue ethics and the fundamental attribution error. *Proceedings of the Aristotelian Society, 1998–99, 99,* 315–331.

Harmon-Jones, E. (2000). Cognitive dissonance and experienced negative affect: Evidence that dissonance increases experienced negative affect even in the absence of aversive consequences. *Personality and Social Psychology Bulletin, 26*, 1490–1501.

Harmon-Jones, E. (2004). Insights on asymmetrical frontal brain activity gleaned from research on anger and cognitive dissonance. *Biological Psychology, 67*, 51–76.

Harmon-Jones, E. (2006). Integrating cognitive dissonance theory with neurocognitive models of control. *Psychophysiology, 43*, S16.

Harmon-Jones, E., Harmon-Jones, C., Serra, R., & Gable, P. A. (2011). The effect of commitment on relative left frontal cortical activity: Tests of the action-based model of dissonance. *Personality and Social Psychology Bulletin, 37*(3), 395–408. doi: 10.1177/0146167210397059

Harmon-Jones, E., Harmon-Jones, C., Fearn, M., Sigelman, J. D., & Johnson, P. (2008). Action orientation, relative left frontal cortical activation, and spreading of alternatives: A test of the action-based model of dissonance. *Journal of Personality and Social Psychology, 94*(1), 1–15.

Harris, B. (2011). Letting go of Little Albert: Disciplinary memory, history, and the uses of myth. *Journal of the History of the Behavioral Sciences, 47*(1), 1–17. doi: 10.1002/jhbs.20470

Harrison, P. J. (1999). The neuropathology of schizophrenia: A critical review of the data and their interpretation. *Brain, 122*, 593–624.

Harrison, T. L., Shipstead, Z., Hicks, K. L., Hambrick, D. Z., Redick, T. S., & Engle, R. W. (2013). Working memory training may increase working memory capacity but not fluid intelligence. *Psychological Science.* doi: 10.1177/0956797613492984

Hart, P. (1998). Preventing groupthink revisited: Evaluating and reforming groups in government. *Organizational Behavior & Human Decision Processes, 73*(2–3), 306–326.

Hartfield, E. (1987). Passionate and companionate love. In R. J. Sternberg & M. L. Barnes (Eds.), *The psychology of love* (pp. 191–217). New Haven, CT: Yale University Press.

Hartfield, E., & Rapson, R. L. (1992). Similarity and attraction in intimate relationships. *Communication Monographs, 59*, 209–212.

Hartley, B. L., & Sutton, R. M. (2013). A stereotype threat account of boys' academic underachievement. *Child Development, 84*(5), 1716–1733. doi: 10.1111/cdev.12079

Harvard Medical School, Department of Health Care Policy. (2007). *National comorbidity survey: 12-month prevalence of DSM-IV/WMH-CICI disorders by sex and cohort.* Retrieved from http://www.hcp.med.harvard.edu/ncs/ftpdir/NCS-R_12-month_Prevalence_Estimates.pdf

Harvey, A. R., Lovett, S. J., Majda, B. T., Yoon, J. H., Wheeler, L. P. G., & Hodgetts, S. I. (2015). Neurotrophic factors for spinal cord repair: Which, where, how and when to apply, and for what period of time? *Brain Research, 1619*, 36–71. doi: http://dx.doi.org/10.1016/j.brainres.2014.10.049

Hassan, S., Karpova, Y., Baiz, D., Yancey, D., Pullikuth, A., Flores, A., Register, T., Cline, J. M., D'Agostino, R., Danial, N., Datta, S. R., & Kulik, G. (2013). Behavioral stress accelerates prostate cancer development in mice. *Journal of Clinical Investigation, 123*(2), 874–886. doi:10.1172/JCI63324

Hasin, D. S., Wall, M., Keyes, K. M., Cerdá, M., Schulenberg, J., O'Malley, P. M., . . . Feng, T. (2015). Medical marijuana laws and adolescent marijuana use in the USA from 1991 to 2014: Results from annual, repeated cross-sectional surveys. *The Lancet, 2*(7), 601–608. doi: 10.1016/S2215-0366(15)00217-5

Haslam, C., Cruwys, T., Milne, M., Kan, C.-H., & Haslam, S. A. (2016). Group ties protect cognitive health by promoting social identification and social support. *Journal of Aging and Health, 28*(2), 244–266.

Haslam, S. A., & Reicher, S. D. (2012). Contesting the "nature" of conformity: What Milgram and Zimbardo's studies really show. *Public Library of Science (PLoS) Biology, 10*(11), e1001426. doi: 10.1370/journal.pbio.1001426

Hassan, S. (2014). ISIS is a cult that uses terrorism: A fresh new strategy. The WorldPost: The Huffington Post, October 21, 2014. Retrieved from http://www.huffingtonpost.com/steven-hassan/isis-is-a-cult-that-uses-_b_6023890.html

Hauck, S. J., & Bartke, A. (2001). Free radical defenses in the liver and kidney of human growth hormone transgenic mice. *Journal of Gerontology and Biological Science, 56*, 153–162.

Havighurst R. J., Neugarten B. L., & Tobin S. N. S. (1968). Disengagement and patterns of aging. In B. L. Neugarten (Ed.), *Middle age and aging: A reader in social psychology* (pp. 161–172). Chicago: University of Chicago Press.

Hawks, S. R., Madanat, H. N., Merrill, R. M., Goudy, M. B., & Miyagawa, T. (2003). A cross-cultural analysis of "motivation for eating" as a potential factor in the emergence of global obesity: Japan and the United States. *Health Promotion International, 18*(2), 153–162.

Hawley, N. L., & McGarvey, S. T. (2015). Obesity and diabetes in Pacific Islanders: The current burden and the need for urgent action. *Current Diabetes Reports, 15*(5), 29.

Hawley, N., L., Minster, R. L., Weeks, D. E., Viali, S., Reupena, M. S., Sun, G., Cheng, H., Deka, R., & Mcgarvey, S. T. (2014). Prevalence of adiposity and associated cardiometabolic risk factors in the Samoan genome-wide association study. *American Journal of Human Biology: The Official Journal of the Human Biology Council, 26*(4), 491–501.

Hay, P. (2013). A systematic review of evidence for psychological treatments in eating disorders: 2005–2012. *International Journal of Eating Disorders, 46*(5), 462–469. doi: 10.1002/eat.22103

Hayes, J. P., Bigler, E. D., & Verfaellie, M. (2016). Traumatic brain injury as a disorder of brain connectivity. *Journal of the International Neuropsychological Society, 22*(*Special Issue 02*), 120–137. doi: doi:10.1017/S1355617715000740

Hayes, S. M., Alosco, M. L., Hayes, J. P., Cadden, M., Peterson, K. M., Allsup, K., . . . Verfaellie, M. (2015). Physical activity is positively associated with episodic memory in aging. *Journal of the International Neuropsychological Society, 21*(10), 780.

Hayflick, L. (1977). The cellular basis for biological aging. In C. E. Finch & L. Hayflick (Eds.), *Handbook of biology of aging* (p. 159). New York: Van Nostrand Reinhold.

Hayward, C., Killen, J. D., Kraemer, H. C., & Taylor, C. B. (2000). Predictors of panic attacks in adolescents. *Journal of the American Academy of Child and Adolescent Psychiatry, 39*(2), 207–214.

Hayward, C., Killen, J. D., & Taylor, C. B. (1989). Panic attacks in young adolescents. *American Journal of Psychiatry, 146*(8), 1061–1062.

Hazan, C., & Shaver, P. (1987). Romantic love conceptualized as an attachment process. *Journal of Personality and Social Psychology, 52*, 511–524.

Hazrati, L. N., Tartaglia, M. C., Diamandis, P., Davis, K. D., Green, R. E., Wennberg, R., . . . Tator, C. H. (2013). Absence of chronic traumatic encephalopathy in retired football players with multiple concussions and neurological symptomatology. *Frontiers in Human Neuroscience, 7*, 222. doi: 10.3389/fnhum.2013.00222

Heavey, C. L., Layne, C., & Christensen, A. (1993). Gender and conflict structure in marital interaction: A replication and extension. *Journal of Consulting and Clinical Psychology, 61*, 16–27.

Hebb, D. O. (1955). Drives and the CNS (Conceptual Nervous System). *Psychological Review, 62*, 243–254.

Hecker, T., Hermenau, K., Isele, D., & Elbert, T. (2014). Corporal punishment and children's externalizing problems: A cross-sectional study of Tanzanian primary school–aged children. *Child Abuse & Neglect, 38*(5), 884–892.

Hegeman, R. (2007). "Police: Shoppers stepped over victim." Associated Press, July 4. http://abcnews.go.com/US/wireStory?id=3342724.

Heider, F. (1958). *The psychology of interpersonal relations*. New York: John Wiley & Sons.

Heikkila, K., Nyberg, S. T., Theorell, T., Fransson, E. I., Alfredsson, L., Bjorner, J. B., . . . Kivimaki, M. (2013). Work stress and risk of cancer: Meta-analysis of 5700 incident cancer events in 116 000 European men and women. *BMJ, 346*(Feb07 1), f165. doi: 10.1136/bmj.f165

Heil, G., Maslow, A., & Stephens, D. (1998). *Maslow on management*. New York: John Wiley and Sons.

Heilman, K. M. (2002). *Matter of mind: A neurologist's view of brain-behavior relationships*. New York: Oxford University Press.

Heilman, K.M., Watson, R., & Valenstein, E. (1993). Neglect and related disorders. In K. Heilman & E. Valenstein (Eds.), *Clinical neuropsychology*. New York: Oxford University Press.

Heimberg, R. G., & Becker, R. E. (2002). *Cognitive-behavioral group therapy for social phobia: Basic mechanisms and clinical strategies*. New York: Guilford Press.

Heimer, L. (1995). *The human brain and spinal cord: Functional neuroanatomy and dissection guide*. New York, NY: Springer-Verlag.

Heine, S., Kitayama, S., & Lehman. D. (2001). Cultural differences in self-evaluation: Japanese readily accept negative self-relevant information. *Journal of Cross-Cultural Psychology, 32*(4), 434–443.

Heinicke, C. M., Goorsky, M., Moscov, S., Dudley, K., Gordon, J., Schneider, C., & Guthrie, D. (2000). Relationship-based intervention with at-risk mothers: Factors affecting variations in outcome. *Infant Mental Health Journal, 21*, 133–155.

Heinrich, B. (2000). Testing insight in ravens. In C. Heyes & L. Huber (Eds.), *The evolution of cognition*, 289–305. Cambridge, MA: MIT Press.

Helfrich, C., Pierau, S. S., Freitag, C. M., Roeper, J., Ziemann, U., & Bender, S. (2012). Monitoring cortical excitability during repetitive transcranial magnetic stimulation in children with ADHD: A single-blind, sham-controlled TMS-EEG study. *PLoS One, 7*(11), e50073. doi: 10.1371/journal.pone.0050073

Helms, J. E. (1992). Why is there no study of cultural equivalence in standardized cognitive ability testing? *American Psychologist, 47*(9), 1083–1101.

Helpman, L., Papini, S., Chhetry, B. T., Shvil, E., Rubin, M., Sullivan, G. M., . . . Neria, Y. (2016). PTSD remission after prolonged exposure treatment is associated with anterior cingulate cortex thinning and volume reduction. *Depression and Anxiety*, n/a-n/a. doi: 10.1002/da.22471

Henderson, M. D., & Burgoon, E. M. (2013). Why the door-in-the-face technique can sometimes backfire: A construal-level account. *Social Psychological and Personality Science, 5*(4), 475–483. doi: 10.1177/1948550613506719

Henderson, R. K., Snyder, H. R., Gupta, T., & Banich, M. T. (2012). When does stress help or harm? The effects of stress controllability and subjective stress response on Stroop performance. *Frontiers in Psychology, 3*, 179.

Henin, A., Mick, E., Biederman, J., Fried, R., Wozniak, J., Faraone, S. V., . . . Doyle, A. E. (2007). Can bipolar disorder-specific neuropsychological impairments in children be identified? *Journal of Consulting and Clinical Psychology, 75*(2), 210–220.

Henningfield., J. E., Clayton, R., & Pollin, W. (1990). Involvement of tobacco in alcoholism and illicit drug use. *British Journal of Addition, 85*, 279–292.

Henningfield, J. E., Cohen, C., & Slade, J. D. (1991). Is nicotine more addictive than cocaine? *British Journal of Addiction, 86*, 565–569.

Herbenick, D., Reece, M., Sanders, S. A., Schick, V., Dodge, B., & Fortenberry, J. D. (2010). Sexual behavior in the united states: Results from a national probability sample of males and females ages 14 to 94. *Journal of Sexual Medicine, 7*(Suppl 5), 255–265.

Herberman, R. B., & Ortaldo, J. R. (1981). Natural killer cells: Their role in defenses against disease. *Science, 214*, 24–30.

Herbst, J. H., Zonderman, A. B., McCrae, R. R., & Costa, P. T., Jr. (2000). Do the dimensions of the Temperament and Character Inventory map a simple genetic architecture? Evidence from molecular genetics and factor analysis. *American Journal of Psychiatry, 157*, 1285–1290.

Herman, L. M., Pack, A. A., & Morrell-Samuels, P. (1993). Representational and conceptual skills of dolphins. In H. L. Roitblatt, L. M. Herman, & P. E. Nachtigall (Eds.), *Language and communication: Comparative perspectives*. Hillsdale, NJ: Erlbaum.

Hernandez, D., & Fisher, E. M. (1996). Down syndrome genetics: Unravelling a multifactorial disorder. *Human Molecular Genetics, 5*, 1411–1416.

Heron, M. J., Belford, P., & Goker, A. (2014). Sexism in the circuitry. *ACM SIGCAS Computers and Society: Association for Computing Machinery, 44*(4), 18–29.

Herrnstein, R. J., & Murray, C. (1994). *The bell curve: The reshaping of American life by differences in intelligence*. New York: Free Press.

Hersh, S. M. (2004, May 10). Annals of national security: Torture at Abu Ghraib. *The New Yorker*.

Hershberger, S. L., Plomin, R., & Pedersen, N. L. (1995, October). Traits and metatraits: Their reliability, stability, and shared genetic influence. *Journal of Personality and Social Psychology, 69*(4), 673–685.

Hervais-Adelman, A. G., Moser-Mercer, B., & Golestani, N. (2011). Executive control of language in the bilingual brain: Integrating the evidence from neuroimaging to neuropsychology. *Frontiers in Psychology, 2*, 234. doi: 10.3389/fpsyg.2011.00234

Herxheimer, A., & Petrie, K. J. (2001). Melatonin for preventing and treating jet lag. *Cocharane Database of Systematic Reviews* (1), CD 001520.

Heslegrave, R. J., & Rhodes. W. (1997). Impact of varying shift schedules on the performance and sleep in air traffic controllers. *Sleep Research, 26*, 198.

Hetherington, A. W., & Ranson, S. W. (1940). Hypothalamic legions and adiposity in rats. *Anatomical Records, 78*, 149–172.

Hetrick, S. E., McKenzie, J. E., Cox, G. R., Simmons, M. B., & Merry, S. N. (2012). Newer generation antidepressants for depressive disorders in children and adolescents. *Cochrane Database of Systematic Reviews (Online), 11*, CD004851. doi: 10.1002/14651858.CD004851.pub3

Hewlin, P. F. (2009). Wearing the cloak: Antecedents and consequences of creating facades of conformity. *Journal of Applied Psychology, 94*(3), 727–741.

Hewstone, M., Rubin, M., & Willis, H. (2002). Intergroup bias. *Annual Review of Psychology, 53*, 575–604.

Heyes, C. M. (1998). Theory of mind in nonhuman primates. *Behavior and Brain Science, 21*, 101–148.

Hicklin, J., & Widiger, T. A. (2000). Convergent validity of alternative MMPI-2 personality disorder scales. *Journal of Personality Assessment, 75*(3), 502–518.

Higgins, E. T., & Scholer, A. A. (2010). When is personality revealed? A motivated cognition approach. In O. P. John, R. W. Robins, & L. A. Pervin (Eds.), *Handbook of personality: Theory and research* (pp. 182–207). New York: Guilford Press.

Higginson, A. D., McNamara, J. M., & Houston, A. I. (2016). Fatness and fitness: Exposing the logic of evolutionary explanations for obesity. *Proceedings of Biological Sciences, 283*(1822), 20152443.

Hildreth, C. J. (2008). Inflammation and diabetes. *The Journal of the American Medical Association, 300*(21), 2476.

Hilgard E. R. (1965). *Hypnotic susceptibility*. New York: Harcourt, Brace & World.

Hilgard, E. R. (1991). A neodissociation interpretation of hypnosis. In S. J. Lynn & J. W. Rhue (Eds.), *Theories of hypnosis* (pp. 83–104). New York: Guilford Press.

Hilgard, E. R., & Hilgard, J. R. (1994). *Hypnosis in the relief of pain* (Rev. ed.). New York: Brunner/Mazel.

Hill, D. (1990). Causes of smoking in children. In B. Durston & K. Jamrozik, *Smoking and health 1990—The global war. Proceedings of the 7th World Conference on Smoking and Health*, 1–5 April. Perth: Health Department of Western Australia, 205–209.

Hill, E. S., Vasireddi, S. K., Wang, J., Bruno, A. M., & Frost, W. N. (2015). Memory formation in tritonia via recruitment of variably committed neurons. Current Biology, 25(22), 2879–2888.

Hill, J. A. (1998). Miscarriage risk factors and causes: What we know now. *OBG Management*, 10, 58–68.

Hill, P. C., & Butter E. M. (1995). The role of religion in promoting physical health. *Journal of Psychology and Christianity*, 14(2), 141–155.

Hillman, C. H., Pontifex, M. B., Raine, L. B., Castelli, D. M., Hall, E. E., & Kramer, A. F. (2009). The effect of acute treadmill walking on cognitive control and academic achievement in preadolescent children. *Neuroscience*, 159(3), 1044–1054.

Hilton, J. L., & von Hippel, W. (1996). Stereotypes. *Annual Review of Psychology*, 47, 237–271.

Hilts, P. J. (1998, August 2). Is nicotine addictive? It depends on whose criteria you use. *New York Times*, p. C3.

Hines, T. (2003). *Pseudoscience and the paranormal: A critical examination of the evidence.* Amherst, NY: Prometheus.

Hintze, J. M. (2002). Interventions for fears and anxiety problems. In M. R. Shinn, H. R. Walker, & G. Stoner (Eds.), *Interventions for academic and behavior problems II: Preventive and remedial approaches* (pp. 939–954). Bethesda, MD: National Association of School Psychologists.

Hirshkowitz, M., Whiton, K., Albert, S. M., Alessi, C., Bruni, O., DonCarlos, L., . . . Hillard, P. J. A. (2015). National Sleep Foundation's sleep time duration recommendations: Methodology and results summary. *Sleep Health: Journal of the National Sleep Foundation*, 1(1), 40–43. Available at http://www.sleephealthjournal.org/article/S2352-7218%2815%2900015-7/abstract

Hirst, W., & Phelps, E. A. (2016). Flashbulb memories. *Current Directions in Psychological Science*, 25(1), 36–41.

Hirvonen, J., Goodwin, R. S., Li, C.-T., Terry, G. E., Zoghbi, S. S., Morse, C., . . . Innis, R. B. (2011). Reversible and regionally selective downregulation of brain cannabinoid CB1 receptors in chronic daily cannabis smokers. *Molecular Psychiatry*, 17(6), 642–649. doi: 10.1038/mp.2011.82

Hnasko, T. S., Chuhma, N., Zhang, H., Goh, G. Y., Sulzer, D., Palmiter, R. D., . . . Edwards, R. H. (2010). Vesicular glutamate transport promotes dopamine storage and glutamate corelease in vivo. *Neuron*, 65, 643–656.

Hobson, J. A. (1988). *The dreaming brain.* New York: Basic Books.

Hobson, J. A., & McCarley, R. (1977). The brain as a dream state generator: An activation-synthesis hypothesis of the dream process. *American Journal of Psychiatry*, 134, 1335–1348.

Hobson, J. A., Pace-Schott, E., & Stickgold, R. (2000). Dreaming and the brain: Towards a cognitive neuroscience of conscious states. *Behavioral and Brain Sciences*, 23(6), 793–1121.

Hochman, J. (1994). Buried memories challenge the law. *National Law Journal*, 1, 17–18.

Hodges, J. R. (1994). Retrograde amnesia. In A. Baddeley, B. A. Wilson, & F. Watts (Eds.), *Handbook of memory disorders* (pp. 81–107). New York: Wiley.

Hodgson, B. (2001). *In the arms of Morpheus: The tragic history of laudanum, morphine, and patent medicines.* New York: Firefly Books.

Hodson, D. S., & Skeen, P. (1994). Sexuality and aging: The hammerlock of myths. *The Journal of Applied Gerontology*, 13, 219–235.

Hoebel, B. G., & Teitelbaum, P. (1966). Weight regulation in normal and hypothalamic hyperphagic rats. *Journal of Comparative Physiological Psychology*, 61, 189–193.

Hoeft, F., Gabrieli, J. D. E., Whitfield-Gabrieli, S., Haas, B. W., Bammer, R., Menon, V., & Spiegel, D. (2012). Functional brain basis of hypnotizability. *Archives of General Psychiatry*, 69(10), 1064.

Hoffrage, U., Hertwig, R., & Gigerenzer, G. (2000). Hindsight bias: A by-product of knowledge updating? *Journal of Experimental Psychology: Learning, Memory, and Cognition*, 26, 566–581.

Hoferichter, F., Raufelder, D., & Eid, M. (2015). Socio-motivational moderators—two sides of the same coin? Testing the potential buffering role of socio-motivational relationships on achievement drive and test anxiety among German and Canadian secondary school students. *Frontiers in Psychology*, 6, 1675.

Hofstede, G. H. (1980). *Culture's consequences, international differences in work-related values.* Beverly Hills, CA: Sage.

Hofstede, G. J., Pedersen, P. B., & Hofstede, G. H. (2002). *Exploring culture: Exercises, stories, and synthetic cultures.* Yarmouth, ME: Intercultural Press.

Hogg, M. A., & Hains, S. C. (1998). Friendship and group identification: A new look at the role of cohesiveness in groupthink. *European Journal of Social Psychology*, 28(1), 323–341.

Holahan, C. K., & Sears, R. R. (1996). *The gifted group at later maturity.* Stanford, CA: Stanford University Press.

Holcomb, W. R. (1986). Stress inoculation therapy with anxiety and stress disorders of acute psychiatric patients. *Journal of Clinical Psychology*, 42, 864–872.

Holden, C., & Vogel, G. (2002). Plasticity: Time for a reappraisal? *Science*, 296, 2126–2129.

Hollon, S. D., & Beck, A. T. (1994). Cognitive and cognitive-behavioral therapies. In A. E. Bergin & and S. L. Garfield (Eds.), *Handbook of psychotherapy and behavior change* (4th ed., p. 428). Chichester, UK: John Wiley & Sons.

Hollon, S. D., These, M., & Markowitz, J. (2002). Treatment and prevention of depression. *Psychological Science in the Public Interest*, 3, 39–77.

Holman, E. A., Silver, R. C., Poulin, M., Andersen, J., Gil-Rivas, V., & McIntosh, D. N. (2008). Terrorism, acute stress, and cardiovascular health: A 3-year national study following the September 11th attacks. *Archives of General Psychiatry*, 65, 73–80.

Holm-Denoma, J. M., Joiner, T. E., Vohs, K. D., & Heatherton, T. F. (2008). The "freshman fifteen" (the "freshman five" actually): Predictors and possible explanations. *Health Psychology*, 27(1), S3–9. doi: 10.1037/0278-6133.27.1.S3

Holmes, O. W. (1892). Preface to "Homeopathy and its Kindred Delusions." Medical Essays, vol. X of The Standard Edition of The Works of Oliver Wendell Holmes, xiii, pp. 6–70. Boston: Houghton Mifflin.

Holmes, T. H., & Masuda, M. (1973). Psychosomatic syndrome: When mothers-in-law or other disasters visit, a person can develop a bad, bad cold. *Psychology Today*, 5(11), 71–72, 106.

Holmes, T. H., & Rahe, R. H. (1967). The Social Readjustment Rating Scale. *Journal of Psychosomatic Research II*, 213–218.

Holroyd, J. (1996). Hypnosis treatment of clinical pain: Understanding why hypnosis is useful. *International Journal of Clinical and Experimental Hypnosis*, 44, 33–51.

Holt-Lunstad, J., Uchino, B. N., Smith, T. W., Cerny, C. B., & Nealey-Moore, J. B. (2003). Social relationships and ambulatory blood pressure: Structural and qualitative predictors of cardiovascular function during everyday social interactions. *Health Psychology*, 22, 388–397.

Holtzheimer, P. E., Kelley, M. E., Gross, R. E., Filkowski, M. M., Garlow, S. J., Barrocas, A., . . . Mayberg, H. S. (2012). Subcallosal cingulate deep brain stimulation for treatment-resistant unipolar and bipolar depression. *Archives of General Psychiatry*, 69(2), 150–158. doi: 10.1001/archgenpsychiatry.2011.1456

Hong, D., Scaletta-Kent, J., & Kesler, S. (2009). Cognitive profile of Turner syndrome. *Developmental Disabilities Research Reviews*, 15(4), 270–278. doi: 10.1002/ddrr.79

Hood, D. C. (1998). Lower-level visual processing and models of light adaptation. *Annual Review of Psychology*, 49, 503–535.

Hopfinger, J. B., Buonocore, M. H., & Mangun, G. R. (2000). The neural mechanisms of top-down attentional control. *Nature Neuroscience*, 3, 284–291.

Hopkins, J. R. (2011). The enduring influence of Jean Piaget. *Observer*, 24(10), 35–36. Retrieved from http://www.psychologicalscience.org/index.php/publications/observer/2011/december-11/jean-piaget.html

Horikawa, T., Tamaki, M., Miyawaki, Y., & Kamitani, Y. (2013). Neural decoding of visual imagery during sleep. *Science*, 340(6132), 639–642.

Horne, J. A., & Staff, C. H. (1983). Exercise and sleep: Body heating effects. *Sleep*, 6, 36–46.

Horney, K. (1939). *New ways in psychoanalysis.* New York: W. W. Norton.

Horney, K. (1967/1973). *Feminine psychology.* New York: W. W. Norton.

Hornung, J. P. (2012). Raphe nuclei. In J. K. Mai & G. Paxinos (Eds.), *The human nervous system* (pp. 642–685). London, UK: Academic Press.

Horowitz, D. L. (1985). *Ethnic groups in conflict.* Berkeley: University of California Press.

Hortaçsu, N. (1999). The first year of family and couple initiated marriages of a Turkish sample: A longitudinal investigation. *International Journal of Psychology*, 34(1), 29–41.

Hossain, P., Kawar, B., & El Nahas, M. (2007). Obesity and diabetes in the developing world—A growing challenge. *New England Journal of Medicine*, 356(9), 973.

Hothersall, D. (1995). *History of psychology.* New York: McGraw-Hill, Inc.

Hovland, C. I. (1937). The generalization of conditioned responses. I. The sensory generalization of conditioned responses with varying frequencies of tone. *Journal of General Psychology*, 17, 125–48.

Hozel, B., Lazar, S., Gard, T., Schulman-Olivier, Z., Vago, R., & Ott, U. (2011). How does mindfulness meditation work? Proposing mechanisms of action from a conceptual and neural perspective. *Perspectives on Psychological Science* 6(6), 537–559.

Hsu, B., Cumming, R. G., Waite, L. M., Blyth, F. M., Naganathan, V., Couteur, D. G. L., . . . Handelsman, D. J. (2015). Longitudinal relationships between reproductive hormones and cognitive decline in older men: The Concord Health and Ageing in Men project. *The Journal of Clinical Endocrinology & Metabolism*, 100(6), 2223–2230. doi: doi:10.1210/jc.2015-1016

Hu, P., & Meng, Z. (August, 1996). *An examination of infant–mother attachment in China.* Poster session presented at the meeting of the International Society for the Study of Behavioral Development, Quebec City, Quebec, Canada.

Hu, S., Pattatucci, A. M. L., Patterson, C., Li, L., Fulker, D. W., Cherny, S. S., . . . Hamer, D. H. (1994). Linkage between sexual orientation and chromosome Xq28 in males but not in females. *Nature Genetics*, 11, 248–256.

Hu, S., & Stern, R. M. (1999). Retention of adaptation to motion sickness eliciting stimulation. *Aviation, Space, and Environmental Medicine*, 70, 766–768.

Hu, X., Pornpattananangkul, N., & Rosenfeld, J. P. (2013). N200 and P300 as orthogonal and integrable indicators of distinct awareness and recognition processes in memory detection. *Psychophysiology*, 50(5), 454–464. doi: 10.1111/psyp.12018

Huang, J. Y., & Bargh, J. A. (2014). The selfish goal: Autonomously operating motivational structures as the proximate cause of human judgment and behavior. *Behavioral and Brain Sciences, 37*(2), 121–135.

Huang, Y., Li, Y., Chen, J., Zhou, H., & Tan, S. (2015). Electrical stimulation elicits neural stem cells activation: New perspectives in CNS repair. *Frontiers in Human Neuroscience, 9*, 586. doi: 10.3389/fnhum.2015.00586

Hubbard, E. M., & Ramachandran, V. S. (2005). Neurocognitive mechanisms of synesthesia. *Neuron, 48*(3), 509–520. doi: 10.1016/j.neuron.2005.10.012

Hubel, D. H., & Wiesel, T. N. (1959). Receptive fields of single neurons in the cat's striate cortex. *The Journal of Physiology, 148*, 574–591.

Huesmann, L. R., & Eron, L. (1986). *Television and the aggressive child: A cross-national comparison.* Hillsdale, NJ: Erlbaum.

Huesmann, L. R., & Miller, L. S. (1994). Long-term effects of repeated exposure to media violence in childhood. In L. R. Huesmann (Ed.), *Aggressive behavior: Current perspectives* (pp. 153–183). New York: Plenum Press.

Huesmann, L. R., Moise, J. F., & Podolski, C. L. (1997). The effects of media violence on the development of antisocial behavior. In D. M. Stoff, J. Breiling, & J. D. Maser (Eds.), *Handbook of antisocial behavior* (pp. 181–193). New York: John Wiley.

Huesmann, L. R., Moise-Titus, J., Podolski, C. L., & Eron, L. D. (2003). Longitudinal relations between children's exposure to TV violence and their aggressive and violent behavior in young adulthood: 1977–1992. *Developmental Psychology, 39*(2), 201–221.

Hugenberg, K., & Bodenhausen, G. V. (2003). Facing prejudice: Implicit prejudice and the perception of facial threat. *Psychological Science, 14*, 640–643.

Hughes, J. (1993). Behavior therapy. In T. R. Kratochwill & R. J. Morris (Eds.), *Handbook of psychotherapy with children and adolescents* (pp. 185–220). Boston: Allyn and Bacon.

Hughes, S. M., Harrison, M. A., & Gallup, G. G., Jr. (2007). Sex differences in romantic kissing among college students: An evolutionary perspective. *Evolutionary Psychology, 5*(3), 612–631.

Hull, C. L. (1943). *Principles of behavior.* New York: Appleton-Century.

Hull, J. G., Draghici, A. M., & Sargent, J. D. (2012). A longitudinal study of risk-glorifying video games and reckless driving. *Psychology of Popular Media Culture, 1*(4), 244–253. doi: 10.1037/a0029510

Hummer, R. A., Rogers, R. G., Nam, C. B., & Ellison, C. G. (1999). Religious involvement and U.S. adult mortality. *Demography, 36*(2), 273–285.

Humphries, L. L. (1987). Bulimia: Diagnosis and treatment. *Comprehensive Therapy, 13*, 12–15.

Hunsley, J., Elliott, K., & Therrien, Z. (2014). The efficacy and effectiveness of psychological treatments for mood, anxiety, and related disorders. *Canadian Psychology, 55*(3), 161–176.

Hunsley, J., & Mash, E. J. (2008). Developing criteria for evidence-based assessment: An introduction to assessments that work. In J. Hunsley & E. J. Mash (Eds.), *A guide to assessments that work* (3rd ed.). pp. 3–14. New York: Guilford Press.

Hunt, E. (2001). Multiple views of multiple intelligence. [Review of Intelligence reframed: Multiple intelligence in the 21st century.] *Contemporary Psychology, 46*, 5–7.

Hunt, M. (1993). *The story of psychology.* New York: Doubleday.

Hurlemann, R., Patin, A., Onur, O. A., Cohen, M. X., Baumgartner, T., Metzler, S., . . . Kendrick, K. M. (2010). Oxytocin enhances amygdala-dependent, socially reinforced learning and emotional empathy in humans. *Journal of Neuroscience, 301*, 4999–5007. doi: 10.1523/JNEUROSCI.553809.2010

Hurley, D. (1989). The search for cocaine's methadone. *Psychology Today, 23*(7/8), 54.

Hurley, S., & Nudds, M. (Eds.). (2006). *Rational animals?* Oxford, UK: Oxford University Press.

Hurvich, L. M., & Jameson, D. (1957). An opponent-process theory of color vision. *Psychological Review, 64*, 384–404.

Hutcheson, J., & Snyder, H. M. (2004). Ambiguous genitalia and intersexuality. *eMedicine Journal, 5*(5). Retrieved November 17, 2004, from http://author.emedicine.com/PED/topic1492.htm

Hvas, L. (2001). Positive aspects of menopause: A qualitative study. *Maturitas 39*(1), 11–17.

Hyde, J. S., & Kling, K. C. (2001). Women, motivation, and achievement. *Psychology of Women Quarterly, 25*, 264–378.

Hyde, J. S., & Plant, E. A. (1995). Magnitude of psychological gender differences. *American Psychologist, 50*, 159–161.

Hygge, S. A., & Öhman, A. (1976). The relation of vicarious to direct instigation and conditioning of electrodermal responses. *Scandanavian Journal of Psychology, 17*(1), 217–222.

Hyman, I. E., Jr. (1993). Imagery, reconstructive memory, and discovery. In B. Roskos-Ewoldsen, M. J. Intons-Peterson, & R. E. Anderson (Eds.), *Imagery, creativity, and discovery: A cognitive perspective* (pp. 99–121). The Netherlands: Elsevier Science.

Hyman, I. E., Gilstrap, L. L., Decker, K., & Wilkinson, C. (1998). Manipulating remember and know judgements of autobiographical memories. *Applied Cognitive Psychology, 12*, 371–386

Hyman, I. E., Jr., & Loftus, E. F. (1998). Errors in autobiographical memories. *Clinical Psychology Review, 18*, 933–947.

Hyman, I. E., Jr., & Loftus, E. F. (2002). False childhood memories and eyewitness memory errors. In M. L. Eisen, J. A. Quas, & G. S. Goodman (Eds.), *Memory and suggestibility in the forensic interview* (pp. 63–84). Mahwah, NJ: Erlbaum.

Hyman, S. E., & Cohen, J. D. (2013). Disorders of mood and anxiety. In E. R. Kandel, J. H. Schwartz, T. M. Jessell, S. A. Siegelbaum, & A. J. Hudspeth (Eds.), *Principles of neural science* (5th ed., pp. 1402–1424). USA: McGraw-Hill.

Iacoboni, M., Woods, R. P., Brass, M., Bekkering, H., Mazziotta, J. C., & Rizzolatti, G. (1999). Cortical mechanisms of human imitation. *Science, 286*, 2526–2528.

Iacono, W. G. (2001). Forensic "lie detection": Procedures without scientific basis. *Journal of Forensic Psychology Practice, 1*(1), 75–86.

Iber, C., Ancoli-Israel, S., Chesson Jr., A. L., & Quan, S. F. (2007). *The AASM Manual for the scoring of sleep and associated events: Rules, terminology and technical specifications.* Westchester, IL: American Academy of Sleep Medicine

Imaizumi, Y. (1998). A comparative study of twinning and triplet rates in 17 countries, 1972–1996. *Acta Genetic Medicine & Gemellology, 47*, 101–114.

Insel, T. R. (2013, Apr. 25). Transforming diagnosis. Retrieved from http://www.nimh.nih.gov/about/director/2013/transforming-diagnosis.shtml

Insel, T. R., & Cuthbert, B. N. (2015). Brain disorders? Precisely. *Science, 348*(6234), 499–500.

Insel, T. R., & Wang, P. S. (2010). Rethinking mental illness. *The Journal of the American Medical Association, 303*(19). 1970–1971.

Ioannidis, J. P. A. (1998, January 28). Effect of the statistical significance of results on the time to completion and publication of randomized efficacy trials. *Journal of the American Medical Association, 279*, 281–286.

Irwin, A. R., & Gross, A. M. (1995). Cognitive tempo, violent video games, and aggressive behavior in young boys. *Journal of Family Violence, 10*(3), 337–350.

Irwin, M., Cole, J., & Nicassio, P. (2006). Comparative meta-analysis of behavioral intervention for insomnia and their efficacy in middle aged adults and in older adults 55+ years of age. *Health Psychology, 25*, 3–14.

Isabel, J. (2003). *Genetics: An introduction for dog breeders.* Loveland, CO: Alpine.

Isenberg, D. J. (1986). Group polarization: A critical review and meta-analysis. *Journal of Personality and Social Psychology, 50*(6), 1141–1151.

Ivory, J. D. (2006). Still a man's game: Gender representation in online reviews of video games. *Mass Communication & Society, 9*(1), 103–114.

Iwakabe, S. (2008). Psychotherapy integration in Japan. *Journal of Psychotherapy Integration, 18*(1), 103–125.

Iwamoto, E. T., & Martin, W. (1988). A critique of drug self-administration as a method for predicting abuse potential of drugs. *National Institute on Drug Abuse Research Monograph, 1046*, 81457–81465.

Izard, C. (1988). Emotion-cognition relationships and human development. In C. Izard, J. Kagan, & R. Zajonc (Eds.), *Emotions, cognition, and behavior.* New York: Cambridge University Press.

Jackson, L. A., & Wang, J.-L. (2013). Cultural differences in social networking site use: A comparative study of China and the United States. *Computers in Human Behavior, 29*(3), 910. doi: 10.1016/j.chb.2012.11.024

Jackson, M. L., Gunzelmann, G., Whitney, P., Hinson, J. M., Belenky, G., Rabat, A., & Van Dongen, H. P. (2013). Deconstructing and reconstructing cognitive performance in sleep deprivation. *Sleep Medicine Reviews, 17*(3), 215–225. doi: 10.1016/j.smrv.2012.06.007

Jackson, T., Iezzi, T., Gunderson, J., Fritch, A., & Nagasaka, T. (2002). Gender differences in pain perception: The mediating role of self-efficacy beliefs. *Sex Roles, 47*, 561–568.

Jacobson, S. G., Cideciyan A. V., Regunath, G., Rodriguez, F. J., Vandenburgh, K., Sheffield, V. C., & Stone, E. M. (1995). Night blindness in Sorsby's fundus dystrophy reversed by vitamin A. *Nature Genetics, 11*, 27–32.

Jaeggi, S. M., Buschkuehl, M., Jonides, J., & Perrig, W. J. (2008). Improving fluid intelligence with training on working memory. *Proceedings of the National Academy of Sciences, USA, 105*(19), 6829–6833.

Jamal, A., Homa, D. M., O'Connor, E., Babb, S. D., Caraballo, R. S., Singh, T., . . . King, R. A. (2015). Current cigarette smoking among adults—United States, 2005–2014. *Centers for Disease Control and Prevention: Morbidity and mortality weekly report (MMWR), 64*(44), 1233–1240.

James, W. (1884). What is an emotion? *Mind, 9*, 188–205.

James, W. (1890, 2002). *The principles of psychology (Vols. 1 and 2).* Cambridge, MA: Harvard University Press.

James, W. (1890). *Principles of psychology.* New York: Henry Holt.

James, W. (1894). The physical basis of emotion. *Psychological Review, 1*, 516–529.

Jameson, M., Diehl, R., & Danso, H. (2007). Stereotype threat impacts college athletes' academic performance. *Current Research in Social Psychology, 12*(5), 68–79

Jamieson, J. P., Nock, M. K., & Mendes, W. B. (2012). Mind over matter: Reappraising arousal improves cardiovascular and cognitive responses to stress. *Journal of Experimental Psychology: General, 141*(3), 417–422.

Jamieson, J. P., Nock, M. K., & Mendes, W. B. (2013). Changing the conceptualization of stress in social anxiety disorder: Affective and physiological consequences. *Clinical Psychological Science, 1*, 363–374.

Jang, K. L., Livesley, W. J., & Vernon, P. A. (1996). Heritability of the Big Five personality dimensions and their facets: A twin study. *Journal of Personality, 64*, 577–591.

Jang, K. L., McCrae, R. R., Angleitner, A., Riemann, R., & Livesley, W. J. (1998). Heritability of facet-level traits in a cross-cultural twin sample: Support for a hierarchical model of personality. *Journal of Personality and Social Psychology, 74*, 1556–1565.

Janis, I. (1972). *Victims of groupthink.* Boston: Houghton-Mifflin.

Janis, I. (1982). *Groupthink* (2nd ed.). Boston: Houghton-Mifflin.

Janos, P. M. (1987). A fifty-year follow-up of Terman's youngest college students and IQ-matched agemates. *Gifted Child Quarterly, 31*, 55–58.

Janowitz, H. D. (1967). Role of gastrointestinal tract in the regulation of food intake. In C. F. Code (Ed.), *Handbook of physiology: Alimentary canal, Section 6, Volume 1.* Washington, DC: American Physiological Society.

January, D., & Kako, E. (2007). Re-evaluating evidence for linguistic relativity: Reply to Boroditsky (2001). *Cognition, 104*(2), 417–426.

Janus, S. S., & Janus, C. L. (1993). *The Janus report on sexual behavior.* New York: John Wiley & Sons.

Jay, S. M., & Elliot, C. H. (1990). A stress inoculation program for parents whose children are undergoing medical procedures. *Journal of Consulting and Clinical Psychology, 58*, 799–804.

Jehn, K., Northcraft, G., & Neale, M. (1999). Why differences make a difference: A field study of diversity, conflict, and performance in workgroups. *Administrative Science Quarterly, 44*, 741–763.

Jencius, M. (2015). Technology, social media, and online counseling. In B. Herlihy & G. Corey (Eds.), *ACA ethical standards casebook* (7th ed., pp. 245–258). Alexandria, VA: American Counseling Association.

Jensen, A. R. (1969). How much can we boost IQ and scholastic achievement? *Harvard Educational Review, 39*, 1–123.

Jensen, M. P., Gertz, K. J., Kupper, A. E., Braden, A. L., Howe, J. D., Hakimian, S., & Sherlin, L. H. (2013). Steps toward developing an EEG biofeedback treatment for chronic pain. *Applied Psychophysiology and Biofeedback.* doi: 10.1007/s10484-013-9214-9

Jeon, M., Walker, B. N., & Gable, T. M. (2014). Anger effects on driver situation awareness and driving performance. *MIT Press Journals: Presence, 23*(1), 71–89.

Joel, D., Berman, Z., Tavor, I., Wexler, N., Gaber, O., Stein, Y., . . . Assaf, Y. (2015). Sex beyond the genitalia: The human brain mosaic. *Proceedings of the National Academy of Sciences of the United States of America, 112*(50), 15468–15473. doi: 10.1073/pnas.1509654112

Johnson, C. P., & Myers, S. M. (Council on Children with Disabilities). (2007). Identification and evaluation of children with autism spectrum disorders. *Pediatrics, 120*(5), 1183–1215.

Johnson, D., Johnson, R., & Smith, K. (1991). *Active learning: Cooperation in the college classroom.* Edna, MN: Interaction Book Company.

Johnson, G. (1995, June 6). Chimp talk debate: Is it really language? *New York Times.*

Johnson, J., Cohen, P., Pine, D. S., Klein, D. F., Kasen, S., & Brook, J. S. (2000). Association between cigarette smoking and anxiety disorders during adolescence and early adulthood. *Journal of the American Medical Association, 284*(18), 2348–2351.

Johnson, M. E., Brems, C., Mills, M. E., Neal, D. B., & Houlihan, J. L. (2006). Moderating effects of control on the relationship between stress and change. *Administration and Policy in Mental Health and Mental Health Services Research, 33*(4), 499–503.

Johnson, R. M., Fairman, B., Gilreath, T., Xuan, Z., Rothman, E. F., Parnham, T. C., & Furr-Holden, D. M. (2015). Past 15-year trends in adolescent marijuana use: Differences by race/ethnicity and sex. *Drug and Alcohol Dependence,* doi: 10.1016/j.drugalcdep.2015.08.025

Johnson, W., Bouchard, T. J., Jr., McGue, M., Segal, N. L., Tellegen, A., Keyes, M., & Gottesman, I. I. (2007). Genetic and environmental influences on the Verbal-Perceptual-Image Rotation (VPR) model of the structure of mental abilities in the Minnesota Study of Twins Reared Apart. *Intelligence, 35*(6), 542–562.

Johnston, L. D., O'Malley, P. M., Bachman, J. G., Schulenberg, J. E. (2007). *Monitoring the Future national survey results on drug use, 1975–2006: Vol. 1. Secondary school students 2006.* Bethesda, MD: National Institute on Drug Abuse; September 2007.

Jones, E. E., & Harris, V. A. (1967). The attribution of attitudes. *Journal of Experimental Social Psychology, 3*, 1–24.

Jones, E. J., Krupnick, J. L., & Kerig, P. K. (1987). Some gender effects in a brief psychotherapy. *Psychotherapy, 24*, 336–352.

Jones, G. W. (1997). Modernization and divorce: Contrasting trends in Islamic Southeast Asia and the West. *Population and Development Review, 23*(1), 95–113.

Jones, M. C. (1924). A laboratory study of fear: The case of Peter. *Pedagogical Seminary, 31*, 308–315.

Jones, M. K., & Menzies, R. G. (1995). The etiology of fear of spiders. *Anxiety, Stress and Coping, 8*, 227–234.

Josephson Institute Center for Youth Ethics. (2012). *The ethics of American youth: 2012.* Retrieved from https://charactercounts.org/programs/reportcard/2012/installment_report-card_honesty-integrity.html

Judelsohn, R. G. (2007, November/December). Vaccine safety: Vaccines are one of public health's great accomplishments. *Skeptical Inquirer, 31*(6), 32–35. Retrieved June 13, 2010, from http://www.csicop.org/si/show/vaccine_safety_vaccines_are_one_of_public_healthrsquos_great_accomplishment/

Julien, R. M., Advokat, C. D., & Comaty, J. E. (2011). *A primer of drug action: A comprehensive guide to the actions, uses, and side effects of psychoactive drugs* (12th ed.). New York: Worth Publishers.

Junco, R., & Cotton, S. R. (2012). No A 4 U: The relationship between multitasking and academic performance. *Computers & Education, 59*, 505–514.

Jung, C. (1933). *Modern man in search of a soul.* New York: Harcourt Brace.

Jung, R. E., & Haier, R. J. (2007). The parieto-frontal integration theory (P-FIT) of intelligence: Converging neuroimaging evidence. *Behavioral and Brain Sciences, 30*(2), 135–154; discussion 154–187. doi: 10.1017/S0140525X07001185

Kabat-Zinn, J., Lipworth, L., & Burney, R. (1985). The clinical use of mindfulness meditation for the self-regulation of chronic pain. *Journal of Behavioral Medicine, 8*, 163–190.

Kabat-Zinn, J., Lipworth, L., Burney, R., & Sellers, W. (1986). Four year follow-up of a meditation-based program for the self regulation of chronic pain: Treatment outcomes and compliance. *Clinical Journal of Pain, 2*, 159–173.

Kable, J. A., Coles, C. D., Lynch, M. E., & Platzman, K. (2008). Physiological responses to social and cognitive challenges in 8-year-olds with a history of prenatal cocaine exposure. *Developmental Psychobiology, 50*(3), 251–265.

Kagan, J. (1998). *Galen's prophecy: Temperament in human nature.* New York: Basic Books.

Kagan, J. (2010). *The temperamental thread.* New York: Dana Press.

Kagan, J., Snidman, N., Kahn, V., & Towsley, S. (2007). The preservation of two infant temperaments into adolescence. *SRCD Monographs, 72*(2), 76–80.

Kahan, M., & Sutton, N. (1998). Overview: Methadone treatment for the opioid-dependent patient. In B. Brands & J. Brands (Eds.), *Methadone maintenance: A physician's guide to treatment* (pp. 1–15). Toronto, ON: Addiction Research Foundation.

Kahneman, D. (2011). *Thinking, fast and slow.* New York: Farrar, Straus and Giroux.

Kahneman, D., Slovic, P., & Tversky, A. (1982). *Judgment under uncertainty: Heuristics and biases.* New York: Cambridge University Press.

Kahneman, D., & Tversky, A. (1973). On the psychology of prediction. *Psychological Review, 80*, 237–251.

Kail, R., & Hall, L. K. (2001). Distinguishing short-term memory from working memory. *Memory & Cognition, 29*(1), 1–9.

Kaiser, A., Haller, S., Schmitz, S., & Nitsch, C. (2009). On sex/gender related similarities and difference in fMRI language research. *Brain Research Reviews, 61*, 49–59.

Kakko, J., Svanborg, K. D., Kreek, M. J., & Heilig, M. (2003). 1-year retention and social function after buprenorphine-associated relapse prevention treatment for heroin dependence in Sweden: A randomised, placebo-controlled trial. *Lancet, 361*, 662–668.

Kales, A., Soldatos, C., Bixler, E., Ladda, R. L., Charney, D. S., Weber, G., & Schweitzer, P. K. (1980). Hereditary factors in sleepwalking and night terrors. *British Journal of Psychiatry, 137*, 111–118.

Kalra, G., Subramanyam, A., & Pinto, C. (2011). Sexuality: desire, activity and intimacy in the elderly. *Indian Journal of Psychiatry, 53*(4), 300–306.

Kamau, C., & Harorimana, D. (2008). Does knowledge sharing and withholding of information in organizational committees affect quality of group decision making? *Proceedings of the 9th European Conference on Knowledge Management* (pp. 341–348). Reading, PA: Academic.

Kamin, L. J. (1995, February). Behind the curve. *Scientific American*, 99–103.

Kandel, E. R. (2012). The molecular biology of memory: cAMP, PKA, CRE, CREB-1, CREB-2, and CPEB. *Molecular Brain, 5*(14). doi: 10.1186/1756-6606-5-14

Kandel, E. R., & Schwartz, J. H. (1982). Molecular biology of learning: Modulation of transmitter release. *Science, 218*, 433–443.

Kandel, E. R., & Siegelbaum, S. A. (2013). Cellular mechanisms of implicit memory storage and the biological basis of individuality. In E. R. Kandel, J. H. Schwartz, T. M. Jessell, S. A. Siegelbaum, & A. J. Hudspeth (Eds.), *Principles of neural science* (5th ed., pp. 1461–1486). USA: McGraw-Hill.

Kandler, C., Riemann, R., Spinath, F. M., & Angleitner, A. (2010). Sources of variance in personality facets: A multiple-rater twin study of self–peer, peer–peer, and self–self (dis)agreement. *Journal of Personality, 78*(5), 1565–1594. doi: 10.1111/j.1467-6494.2010.00661.x

Kane, W. (2006). "No way my boys are going to be like that!" Parents' responses to children's gender nonconformity. *Gender & Society, 20*, 149–176.

Kaplan, D. M. (2016). Raising the bar: New concepts in the 2014 ACA code of ethics. In I. Marini & M. A. Stebnicki (Eds.), *The professional counselor's desk reference* (2nd ed., pp. 37–42). New York: Springer Publishing.

Kaplan, M. F., & Miller, C. E. (1987). Group decision making and normative versus informational influence: Effects of type of issue and assigned decision rule. *Journal of Personality and Social Psychology, 53*(2), 306–313.

Karantzoulis, S., & Galvin, J. E. (2011). Distinguishing Alzheimer's disease from other major forms of dementia. *Expert Review of Neurotherapeutics, 11*(11), 1579–1591.

Karau, S. J., & Williams, K. D. (1993). Social loafing: A meta-analytic review and theoretical integration. *Journal of Personality and Social Psychology, 65*, 681–706.

Karau, S. J., & Williams, K. D. (1997). The effects of group cohesiveness on social loafing and social compensation. *Group Dynamics: Theory, Research and Practice, 1*, 156–168.

Karbach, J., & Verhaeghen, P. (2014). Making working memory work: A meta-analysis of executive-control and working memory training in older adults. *Psychological Science, 25*(11), 2027–2037. doi: 10.1177/0956797614548725

Karl, A., Birbaumer, N., Lutzenberger, W., Cohen, L. G., & Flor, H. (2001). Reorganization of motor and somatosensory cortex in upper extremity amputees with phantom limb pain. *The Journal of Neuroscience, 21*(10), 3609–3618.

Karney, B. R., & Bradbury, T. N. (2000). Attributions in marriage: State or trait? A growth curve analysis. *Journal of Personality and Social Psychology, 78*, 295–309.

Karpicke, J. D. (2012). Retrieval-based learning: Active retrieval promotes meaningful learning. *Current Directions in Psychological Science, 21*(3), 157–163. doi: 10.1177/0963721412443552

Karpicke, J. D., & Blunt, J. R. (2011). Retrieval practice produces more learning than elaborative studying with concept mapping. *Science*, doi: 10.1126scoemce/1199327.

Kastenbaum, R., & Costa, P. T., Jr. (1977). Psychological perspective on death. *Annual Review of Psychology, 28*, 225–249.

Kattari, S. K., & Hasche, L. (2016). Difference across age groups in transgender and gender non-conforming people's experiences of health care discrimination, harassment, and victimization. *Journal of Aging and Health, 28*(2), 258–306.

Katz, V. L. (2007). Spontaneous and recurrent abortion: Etiology, diagnosis, treatment. In V. L. Katz, G. M. Lentz, R. A. Lobo, & D. M. Gershenson (Eds.), *Comprehensive Gynecology* (5th ed.). Philadelphia: Mosby Elsevier

Kaufman, G., Flanagan, M., Seidman, M., & Wien, S. (2015). "Replay health": An experiential role-playing sport for modeling healthcare decisions, policies, and outcomes. *Games for Health Journal, 4*(4), 295–304. doi: 10.1089/g4h.2014.0134

Kaufman, J., & Zigler, E. (1993). The intergenerational transmission of abuse is overstated. In R. J. Gelles & D. R. Loseke (Eds.), *Current controversies on family violence.* Newbury Park, CA: Sage.

Kaye, W. H., Fudge, J. L., & Paulus, M. (2009). New insights into symptoms and neurocircuit function of anorexia nervosa. *Nature Reviews Neuroscience, 10*(8), 573–584. doi: 10.1038/nrn2682

Kaye, W. H., Wierenga, C. E., Bailer, U. F., Simmons, A. N., & Bischoff-Grethe, A. (2013). Nothing tastes as good as skinny feels: The neurobiology of anorexia nervosa. *Trends in Neurosciences, 36*(2), 110–120. doi: 10.1016/j.tins.2013.01.003

Kazdin, A. E. (1980). Acceptability of time out from reinforcement procedures for disruptive behavior. *Behavior Therapy, 11*(3), 329–344.

Kazdin, A. E. (2008). Evidence-based treatment and practice: New opportunities to bridge clinical research and practice, enhance the knowledge base, and improve patient care. *American Psychologist, 63*(3), 146–159. doi: 10.1037/0003-066x.63.3.146

Kazmierczak, M., Kielbratowska, B., & Pastwa-Wojciechowska, B. (2013). Couvade syndrome among polish expectant fathers. *Medical Science Monitor, 19*, 132–138. doi: 10.12659/msm.883791

Kearney, C. A., & Silverman, W. K. (1998). A critical review of pharmacotherapy for youth with anxiety disorders: Things are not as they seem. *Journal of Anxiety Disorders, 12*, 83–102.

Keel, P. K., & Forney, K. J. (2013). Psychosocial risk factors for eating disorders. *The International Journal of Eating Disorders, 46*(5), 433–439. doi: 10.1002/eat.22094

Keding, T. J., & Herringa, R. J. (2015). Abnormal structure of fear circuitry in pediatric post-traumatic stress disorder. *Neuropsychopharmacology, 40*(3), 537–545. doi: 10.1038/npp.2014.239

Keillor, J., Barrett, A., Crucian, G., Kortenkamp, S., & Heilman, K. (2002). Emotional experience and perception in the absence of facial feedback. *Journal of the International Neuropsychological Society, 8*(1), 130–135.

Keirsey, D. (1998). *Please understand me ii: Temperament character intelligence.* Del Mar, CA: Prometheus Nemesis Book Company.

Keith, T. Z., & Reynolds, M. R. (2010). Cattell-Horn-Carroll abilities and cognitive tests: What we've learned from 20 years of research. *Psychology in the Schools.* doi: 10.1002/pits.20496

Keller, M. B., McCullough, J. P., Klein, D. N., Arnow, B., Dunner, D., Gelenberg, A., Markowitz, J. C., Nemeroff, C. B., Russell, J. M., Thase, M. E., Trivedi, M. H., & Zajecka, J. (2000). A comparison of nefazodone, the cognitive behavioral-analysis system of psychotherapy, and their combination for the treatment of chronic depression. *New England Journal of Medicine, 342*(20), 1462–1470.

Kellermann, T., Regenbogen, C., De Vos, M., Mößnang, C., Finkelmeyer, A., & Habel, U. (2012). Effective connectivity of the human cerebellum during visual attention. *The Journal of Neuroscience, 32*(33), 11453–11460. doi: 10.1523/jneurosci.0678-12.2012

Kelly, I. (1980). The scientific case against astrology. *Mercury, 10*(13), 135.

Kelly, J. A., McAuliffe, T. L., Sikkema, K. J., Murphy, D. A., Somlai, A. M., Mulry, G., . . . Fernandez, M. I. (1997). Reduction in risk behavior among adults with severe mental illness who learned to advocate for HIV prevention. *Psychiatric Services, 48*(10), 1283–1288.

Kempf, L., & Weinberger, D. R. (2009). Molecular genetics and bioinformatics: An outline for neuropsychological genetics. In T. E. Goldberg & D. R. Weinberger (Eds.), *The genetics of cognitive neuroscience* (pp. 3–26). Cambridge, MA: MIT Press.

Kendall, P. (1983). Stressful medical procedures: Cognitive-behavioral strategies for stress management and prevention. In D. Meichenbaum & M. Jaremko (Eds.), *Stress reduction and prevention.* (pp. 159–190). New York: Plenum Press.

Kendall, P. C., Hudson, J. L., Gosch, E., Flannery-Schroeder, E., & Suveg, C. (2008). Cognitive-behavioral therapy for anxiety disordered youth: A randomized clinical trial evaluating child and family modalities. *Journal of Consulting and Clinical Psychology, 76*(2), 282–297.

Kendler, K. S. (1985). Diagnostic approaches to schizotypal personality disorders: A historical perspective. *Schizophrenia Bulletin, 11*, 538–553.

Kendler, K. S., Czajkowski, N., Tambs, K., Torgersen, S., Aggen, S. H., Neale, M. C., & Reichborn-Kjennerud, T. (2006). Dimensional representations of DSM-IV cluster A personality disorders in a population-based sample of Norwegian twins: A multivariate study. *Psychological Medicine, 36*(11), 1583–1591. doi: 10.1017/s0033291706008609

Kendler, K. S., & Prescott, C. A. (1999). A population-based twin study of lifetime major depression in men and women. *Archives of General Psychiatry, 56*(1), 39–44.

Kenny, A. (1968). Mind and body, In *Descartes: A study of his philosophy* (p. 279). New York: Random House.

Kenny, A. (1994). Descartes to Kant. In A. Kenny (Ed.), *The Oxford history of western philosophy* (pp. 107–192). Oxford, England: Oxford University Press.

Kenrick, D. T., Griskevicius, V., Neuberg, S. L., & Schaller, M. (2010). Renovating the pyramid of needs: Contemporary extensions built upon ancient foundations. *Perspectives on Psychological Science, 5*(3), 292–314.

Kensinger, E. A., Shearer, D. K., Locascio, J. J., Growdon, J. H., & Corkin, S. (2003). Working memory in mild Alzheimer's disease and early Parkinson's disease. *Neuropsychology, 17*(2), 230–239.

Keromoian, R., & Leiderman, P. H. (1986). Infant attachment to mother and child caretaker in an East African community. *International Journal of Behavioral Development, 9*, 455–469.

Kerwin, D. R., Zhang, Y., Kotchen, J. M., Espeland, M. A., Van Horn, L., McTigue, K. M., . . . Hoffmann, R. (2010). The cross-sectional relationship between body mass index, waist–hip ratio, and cognitive performance in postmenopausal women enrolled in the women's health initiative. *Journal of the American Geriatric Society, 58*, 1427–1432. [Article first published online July 14, 2010]. doi: 10.1111/j.1532-5415.2010.02969.x

Kesebir, S., Graham, J., & Oishi, S. (2010). A theory of human needs should be human-centered, not animal-centered. *Perspectives on Psychological Science, 5*(3), 315–319.

Kessler, R. C., Chiu, W. T., Demler, O., & Walters, E. E. (2005). Prevalence, severity, and comorbidity of twelve-month DSM-IV disorders in the national comorbidity survey replication (NCS-R). *Archives of General Psychiatry, 62*(6), 617–627. doi: 10.1001/archpsyc.62.6.617

Kessler, R. C., Chiu, W. T., Jin, R., Ruscio, A. M., Shear, K., & Walters, E. E. (2007). The epidemiology of panic attacks, panic disorder, and agoraphobia in the National Comorbidity Survey replication. *Archives of General Psychiatry, 63*(4), 415–424. doi: 10.1001/archpsyc.63.4.415

Kessler, R. C., Galea, S., Jones, R. T., Parker, H. A., & Hurricane Katrina Community Advisory Group. (2006). Mental illness and suicidality after Hurricane Katrina. *Bulletin of the World Health Organization, 84*(12), 930–939.

Kessler, R. C., Petukhova, M., Sampson, N. A., Zaslavsky, A. M., & Wittchen, H. U. (2012). Twelve-month and lifetime prevalence and lifetime morbid risk of anxiety and mood disorders in the United States. *International Journal of Methods in Psychiatric Research, 21*(3), 169–184. doi: 10.1002/mpr.1359

Kettenmann, H., & Ransom, B. R. (Eds.). (2013). *Neuroglia.* New York, NY: Oxford University Press.

Kety, S. S., Wender, P. H., Jacobsen, B., Ingham, L. J., Jansson, L., Faber, B., & Kinney, D. K. (1994). Mental illness in the biological and adoptive relatives of schizophrenic adoptees. *Archives of General Psychiatry, 51*, 442–455.

Kiecolt-Glaser, J. K. (2009). Psychoneuroimmunology: Psychology's gateway to the biomedical future. *Perspectives on Psychological Science, 4*(4), 367.

Kiecolt-Glaser, J. K., Fisher, L. D., Ogrocki, P., Stout, J. C., Speicher, C. E., & Glaser, R. (1987). Marital quality, marital disruption, and immune function. *Psychosomatic Medicine, 49*, 13–34.

Kiecolt-Glaser, J. K., Glaser, R., Gravenstein, S., Malarkey, W. B., & Sheridan, J. (1996). Chronic stress alters the immune response to influenza virus vaccine in older adults. *Proceedings of the National Academy of Sciences, USA, 93*(7), 3043–3047.

Kiecolt-Glaser, J. K., Marucha, P. T., Malarkey, W. B., & Marcado, A. M. (1995). Slowing of wound healing by psychological stress. *Lancet, 346*, 1194–1196.

Kiecolt-Glaser, J. K., McGuire, L., Robles, T., & Glaser, R. (2002). Psychoneuroimmunology: Psychological influences on immune function and health. *Journal of Consulting and Clinical Psychology, 70*, 537–547.

Kihlstrom, J. F. (1985). Hypnosis. *Annual Review of Psychology, 36*, 385–418.

Kihlstrom, J. F. (1987). The cognitive unconscious. *Science, 237*, 1445–1452.

Kihlstrom, J. F. (1999). Conscious and unconscious cognition. In R. J. Sternberg (Ed.), *The nature of cognition* (pp. 173–203). Cambridge, MA: MIT Press.

Kihlstrom, J. F. (2001). Hypnosis and the psychological unconscious. In Howard S. Friedman (Ed.), *Assessment and therapy: Specialty articles from the encyclopedia of mental health* (pp. 215–226). San Diego, CA: Academic Press.

Kihlstrom, J. F. (2002a). Memory, autobiography, history. *Proteus: A Journal of Ideas, 19*(2), 1–6.

Kihlstrom, J. F. (2002b). To honor Kraepelin . . .: From symptoms to pathology in the diagnosis of mental illness. In L. E. Beutler & M. L. Malik (Eds.), *Rethinking the DSM: A psychological perspective* (pp. 279–303). Washington, DC: American Psychological Association.

Kihlstrom, J., Mulvaney, S., Tobias, B., & Tobis, I. (2000). The emotional unconscious. In E. Eich, J. Kihlstrom, G. Bower, J. Forgas, & P. Niedenthal (Eds.), *Cognition and emotion* (pp. 30–86). New York: Oxford University Press.

Kim, D., & Hommel, B. (2015). An event-based account of conformity. *Psychological Science, 26*(4), 484. doi: 10.1177/0956797614568319

Kim, H., & Markus, H. R. (1999). Deviance or uniqueness, harmony or conformity? A cultural analysis. *Journal of Personality and Social Psychology, 77*, 785–800.

Kim, K. C., & Kim, S. (1999). The multiracial nature of Los Angeles unrest in 1992. In Kwang Chung Kim (Ed.), *Koreans in the Hood: Conflict with African Americans* (pp. 17–38). Baltimore, MD: Johns Hopkins University Press.

Kimhi, Y. (2014). Theory of mind abilities and deficits in autism spectrum disorders. *Topics in Language Disorders, 34*(4), 329–343.

Kimura, D. (1999). *Sex and cognition.* Cambridge, MA: MIT Press.

Kimura, R., Mactavish, E., Yang, J., Westaway, D., & Jhamandas, J. H. (2012). Beta amyloid-induced depression of hippocampal long-term potentiation is mediated through the amylin receptor. *Journal of Neuroscience, 32*(48), 17401–17406. doi: 10.1523/%u200BJNEUROSCI.3028-12.2012

King, M. W., Street, A. E., Gradus, J. L., Vogt, D. S., & Resick, P. A. (2013). Gender differences in posttraumatic stress symptoms among OEF/OIF veterans: An item response theory analysis. *Journal of Traumatic Stress, 26*(2), 175–183. doi: 10.1002/jts.21802

Kinsey, A. C., Pomeroy, W. B., & Martin, C. E. (1948). *Sexual behavior in the human male.* Philadelphia: W. B. Saunders.

Kinsey, A. C., Pomeroy, W. B., Martin, C. E., & Gebhard, P. H. (1953). *Sexual behavior in the human female.* New York: W. B. Saunders.

Kirby, J. S., Chu, J. A., & Dill, D. L. (1993). Correlates of dissociative symptomatology in patients with physical and sexual abuse histories. *Comprehensive Psychiatry, 34*, 250–263.

Kircanski, K., & Peris, T. S. (2015). Exposure and response prevention process predicts treatment outcome in youth with OCD. *Journal of Abnormal Child Psychology, 43*(3), 543–552. doi: 10.1007/s10802-014-9917-2

Kirchengast, S. (2009). Teenage-pregnancies—a biomedical and a sociocultural approach to a current problem. *Current Women's Health Reviews, 5*, 1–7.

Kirmayer, L. J. (1991). The place of culture in psychiatric nosology: *Taijin kyofusho* and the *DSM-III-TR. Journal of Nervous and Mental Disease, 179*, 19–28.

Kirsch, I. (2000). The response set theory of hypnosis. *American Journal of Clinical Hypnosis, 42* (3/42), 4, 274–292.

Kirsch, I., & Lynn, S. J. (1995). The altered state of hypnosis: Changes in the theoretical landscape. *American Psychologist, 50*, 846–858.

Kishida, M., & Rahman, O. (2015). Fraternal birth order and extreme right-handedness as predictors of sexual orientation and gender nonconformity in men. *Archives of Sexual Behavior, 44*, 1493–1501.

Kitamura, T., Saitoh, Y., Takashima, N., Murayama, A., Niibori, Y., Ageta, H., . . . Inokuchi, K. (2009). Adult neurogenesis modulates the hippocampus-dependent period of associative fear memory. *Cell, 139*(4), 814–827.

Kitayama, S., & Markus, H. R. (1994). Introduction to cultural psychology and emotion research. In S. Kitayama & H. R. Markus (Eds.), *Emotion and culture: Empirical studies of mutual influence* (pp. 1–22). Washington, DC: American Psychological Association.

Klaver, C. C., Wolfs, R. C., Vingerling, J. R., Hofman, A., & de Jong, P. T. (1998). Age-specific prevalence and causes of blindness and visual impairment in an older population: The Rotterdam Study. *Archives of Ophthalmology, 116*, 653–658.

Kleim, B., Ehring, T., & Ehlers, A. (2012). Perceptual processing advantages for trauma-related visual cues in post-traumatic stress disorder. *Psychological Medicine, 42*(1), 173–181. doi: 10.1017/s0033291711001048

Klein, N., & Kemper, K. J. (2016). Integrative approaches to caring for children with autism. Current Problems in Pediatric and Adolescent Health Care, E-pub ahead of print. doi: 10.1016/j.cppeds.2015.12.004

Klein, R. G., Mannuzza, S., Olazagasti, M. A., Roizen, E., Hutchison, J. A., Lashua, E. C., & Castellanos, F. X. (2012). Clinical and functional outcome of childhood attention-deficit/hyperactivity disorder 33 years later. *Archives of General Psychiatry, 69*(12), 1295–1303. doi: 10.1001/archgenpsychiatry.2012.271

Klein, S. B., & Mowrer, R. R. (1989). *Contemporary learning theories: Pavlovian conditioning and the status of traditional learning theory.* Hillsdale, NJ: Lawrence Erlbaum.

Kleinot, M. C., & Rogers, R. W. (1982). Identifying effective components of alcohol misuse prevention programs. *Journal of Studies on Alcohol, 43*, 802–811.

Kligman, A. M., & Balin, A. K. (1989). Aging of human skin. In A. K. Balin & A. M. Kligman (Eds.), *Aging and the skin* (pp. 1–42). New York: Raven Press.

Klorman, R., Hilpert, P. L., Michael, R., LaGana, C., & Sveen, O. B. (1980). Effects of coping and mastery modeling on experienced and inexperienced pedodontic patients' disruptiveness. *Behavior Therapy, 11*, 156–168.

Kluft, R. P. (1984). Introduction to multiple personality disorder. *Psychiatric Annals, 14*, 19–24.

Klüver, H., & Bucy, P. C. (1939). Preliminary analysis of functions of the temporal lobes in monkeys. *Archives of Neurological Psychiatry, 42*, 979–1000.

Knecht, S., Dräger, B., Deppe, M., Bobe, L., Lohmann, H., Flöel, A., . . . Henningsen, H. (2000). Handedness and hemispheric language dominance in healthy humans. *Brain, 123*(12), 2512–2518. doi: 10.1093/brain/123.12.2512

Knight, A. (1996). *The life of the law: The people and cases that have shaped our society, from King Alfred to Rodney King.* New York: Crown Publishing Group.

Knight, J. A. (1998). Free radicals: Their history and current status in aging and disease. *Annals of Clinical and Laboratory Science, 28*, 331–346.

Kobasa, S. (1979). Stressful life events, personality, and health: An inquiry into hardiness. *Journal of Personality and Social Psychology, 37*(1), 1–11.

Koberda, J. L. (2015). Application of Z-score LORETA neuro-feedback in therapy of epilepsy. *Journal of Neurology and Neurobiology, 1*(1), e101.

Koch, C., & Mormann, F. (2010). The neurobiology of consciousness. In G. Mashour (Ed.), *Consciousness, awareness, and anesthesia* (pp. 24–46). New York: Cambridge University Press.

Koenig, H. G., Hays, J. C., Larson, D. B., George, L. K., Cohen, H. J., McCullough, M. E., . . . Blazer, D. G. (1999). Does religious attendance prolong survival? A six-year follow-up study of 3,968 older adults. *Journal of Gerontology, 54A*, M370–M377.

Koenig, H. G., McCullough, M. E., & Larson, D. B. (2001). *Handbook of religion and health.* Oxford, UK: Oxford University Press.

Koester, J., & Siegelbaum, S. A. (2013). Membrane potential and the passive electrical properties of the neuron. In E. R. Kandel, J. H. Schwartz, T. M. Jessell, S. A. Siegelbaum, & A. J. Hudspeth (Eds.), *Principles of neural science* (5th ed., pp. 148–171), New York: McGraw-Hill.

Koh, J. K. (1996). A guide to common Singapore spiders. *BP Guide to Nature* series. Singapore: Singapore Science Center.

Kohlberg, L. (1973). Continuities in childhood and adult moral development revisited. In P. Baltes & K. W. Schaie (Eds.), *Life-span development psychology: Personality and socialization.* San Diego, CA: Academic Press.

Köhler, W. (1925, 1992). *Gestalt psychology: An introduction to new concepts in modern psychology (reissue).* New York: Liveright.

Kok, B. E., Coffey, K. A., Cohn, M. A., Catalino, L. I., Vacharkulksemsuk, T., Algoe, S. B., . . . Fredrickson, B. L. (2013). How positive emotions build physical health: Perceived positive social connections account for the upward spiral between positive emotions and vagal tone. *Psychological Science, 24*(5), ePub ahead of print. doi: 10.1177/0956797612470827

Kolodny, R. C. (2001, August). In memory of William H. Masters. *Journal of Sex Research.*

Kompanje, E. J. (2008). "The devil lay upon her and held her down." Hypnagogic hallucinations and sleep paralysis described by the Dutch physician Isbrand van Diemerbroeck (1609–1674). *Journal of Sleep Research, 17*(4), 464–467.

Konowal, N. M., Van Dongen, H. P. A., Powell, J. W., Mallis, M. M., & Dinges, D. F. (1999). Determinants of microsleeps during experimental sleep deprivation. *Sleep, 22* (Suppl. 1), 328.

Koob, G. F., & Le Moal, M. (2005). Plasticity of reward neurocircuitry and the 'dark side' of drug addiction. *Nature Neuroscience, 8*(11), 1442–1444.

Korkmaz, B. (2011). Theory of mind and neurodevelopmental disorders of childhood. *Pediatric Research, 69*, 101R–108R.

Korn, S. (1984). Continuities and discontinuities in difficult/easy temperament: Infancy to young adulthood. *Merrill Palmer Quarterly, 30*, 189–199.

Korten, N., Sliwinski, M. J., Comijs, H. C., & Smyth, J. M. (2014). Mediators of the relationship between life events and memory functioning in a community sample of adults. *Applied Cognitive Psychology, 28*, 626–633.

Kosslyn, S. M. (1983). Mental imagery. In Z. Rubin (Ed.), *The psychology of being human.* New York: Harper & Row.

Kosslyn, S. M., Alpert, N. M., Thompson, W. L., Maljkovic, V., Weise, S. B., Chabris, C. F., . . . Buonano, F. S. (1993). Visual mental imagery activates topographically organized visual cortex: PET investigations. *Journal of Cognitive Neuroscience, 5*, 263–287.

Kosslyn, S. M., Ball, T. M., & Reiser, B. J. (1978). Visual images preserve metric spatial information: Evidence from studies of image scanning. *Journal of Experimental Psychology: Human Perception and Performance, 4*, 47–60.

Kosslyn, S. M., Ganis, G., & Thompson, W. L. (2001). Neural foundations of imagery. *Nature Reviews Neuroscience, 2*, 635–642.

Kosslyn, S. M., Pascual-Leone, A., Felician, O., Camposano, S., Keenan, J. P., Thompson, W. L., . . . Alpert, N. M. (1999). The role of area 17 in visual imagery: Convergent evidence from PET and rTMS. *Science 284*, 167–170.

Kosslyn, S. M., Thompson, W. L., Wraga, M. J., & Alpert, N. M. (2001). Imagining rotation by endogenous and exogenous forces: Distinct neural mechanisms for different strategies. *Neuroreport, 12*, 2519–2525.

Kotkin, M., Daviet, C., & Gurin, J. (1996). The *Consumer Reports* mental health survey. *American Psychologist, 51*(10), 1080–1082.

Kovacs, K., Lajtha, A., & Sershen, H. (2010). Effect of nicotine and cocaine on neurofilaments and receptors in whole brain tissue and synaptoneurosome preparations. *Brain Research Bulletin, 82*(1–2), 109–117.

Kozberg, M., Chen, B. R., De Leo, S. E., Bouchard, M. B., & Hillman, E. M. C. (2013). Resolving the transition from negative to positive blood oxygen level-dependent responses in the developing brain. *Proceedings of the National Academy of Sciences of the United States of America (PNAS).* Published online ahead of print, February 20, 2013. doi: 10.1073/pnas.1212785110

Kraha, A., & Boals, A. (2014). Why so negative? Positive flashbulb memories for a personal event. *Memory, 22*(4), 442–449.

Kratofil, P. H., Baberg, H. T., & Dimsdale, J. E. (1996). Self-mutilation and severe self-injurious behavior associated with amphetamine psychosis. *General Hospital Psychiatry, 18*, 117–120.

Kraus, C. (2015). Classifying intersex in DSM-5: Critical reflections on gender dysphoria. *Archives of Sexual Behavior, 44*(5), 1147–1163.

Kreipe, R. E. (1992). Normal somatic adolescent growth and development. In E. McAnarney, R. E. Kreipe, D. Orr, & G. Comerci (Eds.), *Textbook of adolescent medicine* (pp. 44–68). Philadelphia: W. B. Saunders & Co.

Kriegstein, A., & Alvarez-Buylla, A. (2009). The glial nature of embryonic and adult neural stem cells. *Annual Review of Neuroscience, 32*(1), 149–184.

Kristensen, P., & Bjerkedal, T. (2007). Explaining the relation between birth order and intelligence. *Science, 316*(5832), 1717.

Kroenke, C. H., Quesenberry, C., Kwan, M. L., Sweeney, C., Castillo, A., & Caan, B. J. (2012). Social networks, social support, and burden in relationships, and mortality after breast cancer diagnosis in the Life After Breast Cancer Epidemiology (LACE) study. *Breast Cancer Research and Treatment, 137*(1), 261. doi: 10.1007/s10549-012-2253-8

Kroll, J. F., Bobb, S. C., & Hoshino, N. (2014). Two languages in mind: Bilingualism as a tool to investigate language, cognition, and the brain. *Current Directions in Psychological Science, 23*(3), 159–163. doi: 10.1177/0963721414528511

Krueger, R. F., & Eaton, N. R. (2015). Transdiagnostic factors of mental disorders. *World Psychiatry, 14*(1), 27–29. doi: http://doi.org/10.1002/wps.20175

Krüttner, S., Stepien, B., Noordermeer, J. N., Mommaas, M. A., Mechtler, K., Dickson, B. J., & Keleman, K. (2012). Drosophila CPEB Orb2A mediates memory independent of its RNA-binding domain. *Neuron, 76*(2), 383. doi: 10.1016/j.neuron.2012.08.028

Kryger, M., Lavie, P., & Rosen, R. (1999). Recognition and diagnosis of insomnia. *Sleep, 22*, S421–S426.

Kübler-Ross, E. (1997). *The wheel of life: A memoir of living and dying*. New York: Touchstone.

Kuhl, B. A., Dudukovic, N. M., Kahn, I., & Wagner, A. D. (2007). Decreased demands on cognitive control reveal the neural processing benefits of forgetting. *Nature Neuroscience, 10*(7), 908–914.

Kuhn, H. W., & Nasar, S. (Eds.). (2001). *The essential John Nash*. Princeton, NJ: Princeton University Press.

Kukula, K. C., Jackowich, R. A., & Wassersug, R. J. (2014). Eroticization as a factor influencing erectile dysfunction treatment effectiveness. *International Journal of Impotence Research, 26*(1), 1–6. doi: 10.1038/ijir.2013.29

Kulik, J. A., & Mahler, H. I. M. (1989). Social support and recovery from surgery. *Health Psychology, 8*, 221–238.

Kulik, J. A., & Mahler, H. I. M. (1993). Emotional support as a moderator of adjustment and compliance after coronary bypass surgery: A longitudinal study. *Journal of Behavioral Medicine, 16*, 45–63.

Kulmala, J., von Bonsdorff, M. B., Stenholm, S., Tormakangas, T., von Bonsdorff, M. E., Nygard, C-H., . . . Rantanen, T. (2013). Perceived stress symptoms in midlife predict disability in old age: A 28-year prospective cohort study. *The Journals of Gerontology Series A: Biological Sciences and Medical Sciences*, doi: 10.1093/Gerona/gls339

Kumar, S., & Oakley-Browne, M. (2002). Panic disorder. *Clinical Evidence, 7*, 906–912.

Küntay, A., & Slobin, D. I. (2002). Putting interaction back into child language: Examples from Turkish. *Psychology of Language and Communication, 6*, 5–14.

Kuo, B. C. H. (2011). Culture's consequences on coping: Theories, evidences, and dimensionalities. *Journal of Cross-Cultural Psychology, 42*, 1084. doi: 10.1177/0022022110381126

Kupfer, D. J., & Reynolds, C. F., III. (1997). Management of insomnia. *New England Journal of Medicine, 336*(5), 341–346.

Kurdziel, L., Duclos, K., & Spencer, R. M. C. (2013). Sleep spindles in midday naps enhance learning in preschool children. *Proceedings of the National Academy of Sciences, 110*(43), 17267–17272.

Kuriki, I., Ashida, H., Murakami, I., & Kitaoka, A. (2008). Functional brain imaging of the Rotating Snakes illusion by fMRI. *Journal of Vision, 8*(10), 16 11–10.

Kvavilashvili, L., Mirani, J., Schlagman, S., Foley, K., & Dornbrot, D. E. (2009). Consistency of flashbulb memories of September 11 over long delays: Implications for consolidation and wrong time slice hypotheses. *Journal of Memory and Language, 61*(4), 556–572.

LaBar, K. S., LeDoux, J. E., Spencer, D. D., & Phelps, E. A. (1995). Impaired fear conditioning following unilateral temporal lobectomy to humans. *Journal of Neuroscience, 15*, 6846–6855.

LaBerge, D. (1980). Unitization and automaticity in perception. In J. H. Flowers (Ed.), *Nebraska Symposium on Motivation* (pp. 53–71). Lincoln: University of Nebraska Press.

Labkovsky, E., & Rosenfeld, J. P. (2014). A novel dual probe complex trial protocol for detection of concealed information. *Psychophysiology, 51*(11), 1122–1130. doi: 10.1111/psyp.12258

Labouvie-Vief, G. (1980). Beyond formal operations: Uses and limits of pure logic in lifespan development. *Human Development, 23*, 114–146.

Labouvie-Vief, G. (1992). A neo-Piagetian perspective on adult cognitive development. In R. Sternberg & C. Berg (Eds.), *Intellectual development* (pp. 197–228). Cambridge, UK: Cambridge University Press.

Lacayo, A. (1995). Neurologic and psychiatric complications of cocaine abuse. *Neuropsychiatry, Neuropsychology, and Behavioral Neurology, 8*(1), 53–60.

LaFromboise, T., Coleman, H. L. K., & Gerton J. (1993). Psychological impact of biculturalism: Evidence and theory. *Psychological Bulletin, 114*, 395–412.

Lagopoulos, J., Xu, J., Rasmussen, I., Vik, A., Malhi, G. S., Eliassen, C. F., . . . Ellingsen, Ø. (2009). Increased theta and alpha EEG activity during nondirective meditation. *The Journal of Alternative and Complementary Medicine, 15*(11), 1187.

Lai, M.-C., Lombardo, M. V., Auveung, B., Chakrabarti, B., & Baron-Cohen, S. (2015). Sex/gender differences and autism: Setting the scene for future research. Journal of the American Academy of Child & Adolescent Psychiatry, 54, 11–24.

Lal, S. (2002). Giving children security: Mamie Phipps Clark and the radicalization of child psychology. *American Psychologist, 57*(1), 20–28.

Lalancette, M.-F., & Standing, L. G. (1990). Asch fails again. *Social Behavior and Personality, 18*(1), 7–12.

Lambert, M. J., & Ogles, B. M. (2004). The efficacy and effectiveness of psychotherapy. In M. J. Lambert (Ed.), *Handbook of psychotherapy and behavior change* (5th ed.) (pp. 139–193). New York: Wiley.

Lambert, N., Fincham, F. D., Dewall, N. C., Pond, R., & Beach, S. R. (2013). Shifting toward cooperative tendencies and forgiveness: How partner-focused prayer transforms motivation. *Personal Relationships, 20*(1), 184. doi: 10.1111/j.1475-6811.2012.01411.x

Lana-Peixoto, Marco A. (2014). Complex visual hallucinations in mentally healthy people. *Arquivos de Neuro-Psiquiatria, 72*(5), 331–332. https://dx.doi.org/10.1590/0004-282X20140050.

Lance, C. J., LaPointe, J. A., & Fisicaro, S. (1994). Tests of three causal models of halo rater error. *Organizational Behavior and Human Decision Performance, 57*, 83–96.

Landrum, R. E. (2009). *Finding jobs with a psychology bachelor's degree*. Washington, DC: American Psychological Association.

Landrum, R. E., & Davis, S. F. (2007). *The psychology major: Career options and strategies for success* (3rd ed.) Upper Saddle River, NJ: Prentice Hall.

Lane, R. D., Kivley, L. S., DuBois, M. A. Shamasundara, P., & Schwartz, G. E. (1995). Levels of emotional awareness and the degree of right hemisphere dominance in the perception of facial emotion. *Neuropsychologia, 33*, 525–538.

Laney, C., & Loftus, E. F. (2013). Recent advances in false memory research. South African *Journal of Psychology, 43*(2), 137–146.

Lang, J. W. B., & Lang, J. (2010). Priming competence diminishes the link between cognitive test anxiety and test performance. *Psychological Science, 21*(6), 811–819.

Lange, C. (1885). The emotions. Reprinted in C. G. Lange & W. James (Eds.), *The emotions*. New York: Harner.

Langer, E. J., & Rodin, J. (1976). The effects of enhanced personal responsibility for the aged: A field experiment in an institutional setting. *Journal of Personality and Social Psychology, 34*, 191–198.

Langone, M. C. (1996). Clinical update on cults. *Psychiatric Times, 13*(7), 1–3.

Lanphear, B. P., Dietrich, K., Auinger, P., & Cox, C. (2000). Cognitive deficits associated with blood lead concentrations <10 micrograms/dL in U.S. children and adolescents. *Public Health Reports, 115*(6), 521–529.

Lapsley, D. K., Milstead, M., Quintana, S. M., Flannery, D., & Buss, R. R. (1986). Adolescent egocentrism and formal operations: Tests of a theoretical assumption. *Developmental Psychology, 22*, 800–807.

Larsen, J. T., Berntson, G. G., Poehlmann, K. M., Ito, T. A., & Cacioppo, J. T. (2008). The psychophysiology of emotion. In M. Lewis, J. M. Haviland-Jones, & L. F. Barrett (Eds.), *Handbook of emotions* (3rd ed., pp. 180–195). New York: Guilford Press.

Larzelere, R. (1986). Moderate spanking: Model or deterrent of children's aggression in the family? *Journal of Family Violence, 1*(1), 27–36.

Lashley, K. S. (1938). The thalamus and emotion. *The Psychological Review, 45*, 21–61.

Lasnik, H. (1990). Metrics and morphophonemics in early English verse. *University of Connecticut Working Papers in Linguistics* (Vol. 3, pp. 29–40). Storrs: University of Connecticut.

Latané, B., & Darley, J. M. (1969). Bystander "apathy." *American Scientist, 57*(2), 244–268.

Latané, B., Williams, K., & Harkins, S. (1979). Many hands make light the work: The causes and consequences of social loafing. *Journal of Personality & Social Psychology, 37*(6), 822–832.

Laumann, E. O., Gagnon, J. H., Michael, R. T., & Michaels, S. (1994). *The social organization of sexuality: Sexual practices in the United States* (pp. 77–145). Chicago: University of Chicago Press.

Launer, L., Masaki, K., Petrovitch, H., Foley, D., & Havlik, R. (1995). The association between midlife blood pressure levels and late-life cognitive function. *Journal of the American Medical Association, 272*(23), 1846–1851.

Lauriola, M., Panno, A., Levin, I. P., & Lejuez, C. W. (2014). Individual differences in risky decision making: A meta-analysis of sensation seeking and impulsivity with the balloon alalogue risk task. *Journal of Behavioral Decision Making, 27*(1), 20–36.

Lavergne, G. M. (1997). *A sniper in the tower: The true story of the Texas Tower massacre*. New York: Bantam.

Laviolette, S. R., Lauzon, N. M., Bishop, S. F., Sun, N., & Tan, H. (2008). Dopamine signaling through D1-like versus D2-like receptors in the nucleus accumbens core versus shell differentially modulates nicotine reward sensitivity. *Journal of Neuroscience*, August 6, 28(32), 8025–8033.

Laws, G., Davies, I., & Andrews, C. (1995). Linguistic structure and nonlinguistic cognition: English and Russian blues compared. *Language and Cognitive Processes, 10*, 59–94.

Laws, K. R., & Kokkalis, J. (2007). Ecstasy (MDMA) and memory function: A meta-analytic update. *Human Psychopharmacology: Clinical and Experimental, 22*(6), 381–88. doi: 10.1002/hup.857

Laws, K. R., Sweetnam, H., & Kondel, T. K. (2012). Is ginkgo biloba a cognitive enhancer in healthy individuals? A meta-analysis. *Human Psychopharmacology: Clinical and Experimental, 27*(6), 527–533.

Lay, C., & Nguyen, T. T. I. (1998). The role of acculturation-related and acculturation non-specific daily hassles: Vietnamese-Canadian students and psychological distress. *Canadian Journal of Behavioural Science, 30*(3), 172–181.

Lazarus, R. S. (1991). *Emotion and adaptation.* New York: Oxford University Press.

Lazarus, R. S. (1993). From psychological stress to the emotions: A history of changing outlooks. *Annual Review of Psychology, 44*, 1–22.

Lazarus, R. S. (1999). *Stress and emotion: A new synthesis.* New York: Springer.

Lazarus, R. S., & Folkman, S. (1984). *Stress, appraisal and coping.* New York: Springer.

Le, C. P., Nowell, C. J., Kim-Fuchs, C., Botteri, E., Hiller, J. G., Ismail, H., . . . Sloan, E. K. (2016). Chronic stress in mice remodels lymph vasculature to promote tumor cell dissemination. *Nature Communications, 7*, Article 10634. doi: 10.1038/ncomms10634

Lee, J., & Harley, V. R. (2012). The male fight-flight response: A result of SRY regulation of catecholamines? *Bioessays, 34*(6), 454–457.

Leary, M. R., & Forsyth, D. R. (1987). Attributions of responsibility for collective endeavors. *Review of Personality and Social Psychology, 8*, 167–188.

Leary, M. R., & Toner, K. (2015). Self-processes in the construction and maintenance of personality. In M. Mikulincer & P. R. Shaver (Eds.), *APA handbook of personality and social psychology: Vol. 4. Personality processes and individual differences* (pp. 447–467). Washington, DC: American Psychological Association.

Leask, J., Haber, R. N., & Haber, R. B. (1969). Eidetic imagery in children: II. Longitudinal and experimental results. *Psychonomic Monograph Supplements, 3*, 25–48.

Leccese, A. P., Pennings, E. J. M., & De Wolff, F. A. (2000). *Combined use of alcohol and psychotropic drugs. A review of the literature.* Leiden, The Netherlands: Academisch Ziekenhuis Leiden (AZL).

Leclerc, C. M., & Hess, T. M. (2007). Age differences in the bases for social judgments: Tests of a social expertise perspective. *Experimental Aging Research, 33*(1), 95–120.

LeDoux, J. E. (1994). Emotion, memory and the brain. *Scientific American, 270*, 32–39.

LeDoux, J. E. (1996). *The emotional brain: The mysterious underpinnings of emotional life.* New York: Simon & Schuster.

LeDoux, J. E. (2003). The emotional brain, fear, and the amygdala. *Cellular and Molecular Neurobiology, 23*(4–5), 727–738.

LeDoux, J. E. (2007). The amygdala. *Current Biology, 17*(20), R868–R874.

LeDoux, J. E., & Damasio, A. R. (2013). Emotions and feelings. In E. R. Kandel, J. H. Schwartz, T. M. Jessell, S. A. Siegelbaum, & A. J. Hudspeth (Eds.), *Principles of neural science* (5th ed., pp. 1079–1094). New York: McGraw-Hill.

LeDoux, J. E., & Phelps, E. A. (2008). Emotional networks in the brain. In M. Lewis, J. M. Haviland-Jones, & L. F. Barrett (Eds.), *Handbook of emotions* (3rd ed., pp. 159–179). New York: Guilford Press.

Lee, F., Hallahan, M., & Herzog, T. (1996). Explaining real life events: How culture and domain shape attributions. *Personality and Social Psychology Bulletin, 22*, 732–741.

Lee, M., & Shlain, B. (1986). *Acid dreams: The complete social history of LSD: The CIA, the sixties, and beyond.* New York: Grove Press.

Lee, P. A. (1995). Physiology of puberty. In K. L. Becker (Ed.), *Principles and practice of endocrinology and metabolism* (pp. 822–830). Philadelphia: J. B. Lippincott.

Lee, S. H., Kim, E. Y., Kim, S., & Bae, S. M. (2010). Event-related potential patterns and gender effects underlying facial affect processing in schizophrenia patients. *Neuroscience Research, 7, 7.*

Lee, S. J., Altschul, I., & Gershoff, E. T. (2013). Does warmth moderate longitudinal associations between maternal spanking and child aggression in early childhood? *Developmental Psychology, 49*(11), 2017–2028.

LeGoff, D. B. (2004). Use of Lego© as a therapeutic medium for improving social competence. *Journal of Autism and Developmental Disorders, 34*(5), 557–571.

Lehnert, B. (2007). Joint wave-particle properties of the individual photon. *Progress in Physics, 4*(10), 104–108.

Lehr, U., & Thomae, H. (1987). Patterns of psychological aging. *Results from the Bonne Aging Longitudinal Study (BOLSA).* Stuttgart, Germany: Enke.

Leibel, R. L., Rosenbaum, M., & Hirsch, J. (1995). Changes in energy expenditure resulting from altered body weight. *The New England Journal of Medicine, 332*, 621–628.

Lemos, M. S., & Verissimo, L. (2014). The relationships between intrinsic motivation, extrinsic motivation, and achievement, along elementary school. *Procedia: Social and Behavioral Sciences, 112*, 930–938.

Leon, P., Chedraui, P., Hidalgo, L., & Ortiz, F. (2007). Perceptions and attitudes toward the menopause among middle-aged women from Guayaquil, Ecuador. *Maturitas, 57*(3), 233–238.

Leong, F. T. L., Hartung, P. J., Goh, D., & Gaylor, M. (2001). Appraising birth order in career assessment: Linkages to Holland's and Super's models. *Journal of Career Assessment, 9*, 25–39.

LePort, A. K., Mattfeld, A. T., Dickinson-Anson, H., Fallon, J. H., Stark, C. E., Kruggel, F., Cahill, L., & McGaugh, J. L. (2012). Behavioral and neuroanatomical investigation of Highly Superior Autobiographical Memory (HSAM). *Neurobiology of Learning and Memory, 98*(1), 78. doi: 10.1016/j.nlm.2012.05.002

Lerner, A. G., Gelkopf, M., Skladman, I., Oyffe, I., Finkel, B., Sigal, M., & Weizman, A. (2002). Flashback and hallucinogen persisting perception disorder: Clinical aspects and pharmacological treatment approach. *The Israel Journal of Psychiatry and Related Sciences, 39*(2), 92–99.

Leroy, C., & Symes, B. (2001). Teachers' perspectives on the family backgrounds of children at risk. *McGill Journal of Education, 36*(1), 45–60.

Leslie, M. (2000, July/August). The vexing legacy of Louis Terman. *Stanford Magazine.* Retrieved August 12, 2010, from http://www.stanfordalumni.org/news/magazine/2000/julaug/articles/terman.html

Levenson, R. W. (1992). Autonomic nervous system differences among emotions. *Psychological Sciences, 3*, 23–27.

Levenson, R. W., Ekman, P., Heider, K., & Friesen, W. V. (1992). Emotion and autonomic nervous system activity in the Minangkabau of West Sumatra. *Journal of Personality and Social Psychology, 62*, 972–988.

Levesque, R. J. R. (2014). Opiates. In R. J. R. Levesque (Ed.), *Encyclopedia of Adolescence* (p. 1941). New York: Springer.

Levy, B. R., Slade, M. D., Kunkel, S. R., & Kasl, S. V. (2002). Longevity increased by positive self-perceptions of aging. *Journal of Personality and Social Psychology, 83*, 261–269.

Levy, S. R., Stroessner, S. J., & Dweck, C. S. (1998). Stereotype formation and endorsement: The role of implicit theories. *Journal of Personality and Social Psychology, 74*(6), 1421–1436. http://dx.doi.org/10.1037/0022-3514.74.6.1421

Levy-Gigi, E., Bonanno, G. A., Shapiro, A. R., Richter-Levin, G., Keri, S., & Sheppes, G. (2016). Emotion regulatory flexibility sheds light on the elusive relationship between repeated traumatic exposure and posttraumatic stress disorder symptoms. *Clinical Psychological Science, 4*(1), 28–39. doi: 10.1177/2167702615577783

Lewis, D. K. (1996, June). A cross-cultural model for psychotherapy: Working with the African-American client. *Perspectives on Multiculturalism and Cultural Diversity, VI*(2).

Lewis, D. M., Russell, E. M., Al-Shawaf, L., & Buss, D. M. (2015). Lumbar curvature: A previously undiscovered standard of attractiveness. *Evolution and Human Behavior, 36*(5), 345–350. doi: 10.1016/j.evolhumbehav.2015.01.007

Lewis, J. R. (1995). *Encyclopedia of afterlife beliefs and phenomenon.* Detroit, MI: Visible Ink Press.

Lewis, R. W., Fugl-Meyer, K. S., Corona, G., Hayes, R. D., Laumann, E. O., Moreira, E. D., Jr., . . . Segraves, T. (2010). Definitions/epidemiology/risk factors for sexual dysfunction. *The Journal of Sexual Medicine, 7*(4pt2), 1598–1607. doi: 10.1111/j.1743-6109.2010.01778.x

Li, J., Hu, Z., & de Lecea, L. (2014). The hypcretins/orexins: Integrators of multiple psychological functions. *British Journal of Pharmacology, 171*(2), 332–350.

Li, L., Ruan, H., & Yuan, W.-J. (2015). The relationship between social support and burnout among ICU nurses in Shanghai: A cross-sectional study. *Chinese Nursing Research, 2*(2–3), 45–50.

Li, X., & Fung, A. L.-C. (2015). Reactive and proactive aggression in mainland Chinese secondary school students. *Journal of Social Work, 15*(3), 297–316.

Libbrecht, N., Lievens, F., Carette, B., & Cote, S. (2014). Emotional intelligence predicts success in medical school. *Emotion, 14*(1), 64–73. doi: 10.1037/a0034392

Liechti, M. E., & Vollenweider, F. X. (2001). Which neuroreceptors mediate the subjective effects of MDMA in humans? A summary of mechanistic studies. *Human Psychopharmacology, 16*: 589–598.

Light, K. R, Kolata, S., Wass, C., Denman-Brice, A., Zagalsky, R., & Matzel, L. D. (2010). Working memory training promotes general cognitive abilities in genetically heterogeneous mice. *Current Biology, 20*(8), 777–782.

Lilienfeld, S. O. (1999). Projective measures of personality and psychopathology: How well do they work? *Skeptical Inquirer, 23*(5), 32–39.

Lilienfeld, S. O., Lynn, S. J., & Lohr, J. M. (2004). Science and pseudoscience in clinical psychology: Initial thoughts, reflections, and considerations. In S. O. Lilienfeld, S. J. Lynn, & J. M. Lohr (Eds.), *Science and pseudoscience in clinical psychology* (p. 2). New York: Guilford Press.

Lilienfeld, S. O., Lynn, S. J., & Lohr, J. M. (2015). *Science and pseudoscience in clinical psychology* (2nd ed.). New York: The Guilford Press.

Lilienfeld, S. O., Ritschel, L. A., Lynn, S. J., Cautin, R. L., & Latzman, R. D. (2013). Why many clinical psychologists are resistant to evidence-based practice: Root causes and constructive remedies. *Clinical Psychology Review, 33*(7), 883–900. doi: 10.1016/j.cpr.2012.09.008

Lilienfeld, S. O., Sauvigné, K. C., Lynn, S. J., Cautin, R. L., Latzman, R. D., & Waldman, I. D. (2015). Fifty psychological and psychiatric terms to avoid: A list of inaccurate, misleading, misused, ambiguous, and logically confused words and phrases. *Frontiers in Psychology, 6*, 1100. doi: 10:3389/fpsyg.2015.01100

Lilienfeld, S. O., Wood, J. M., & Garb, H. N. (2000). The scientific status of projective techniques. *Psychological Science in the Public Interest, 1*(2), 27–66. doi: 10.1111/1529-1006.002

Lim, J., Choo, W. C., & Chee, M. W. L. (2007). Reproducibility of changes in behavior and fMRI activation associated with sleep deprivation in a working memory task. *Sleep, 30*, 61–70.

Lim, L., Radua, J., & Rubia, K. (2014). Gray matter abnormalities in childhood maltreatment: A voxel-wise meta-analysis. *American Journal of Psychiatry, 171*(8), 854–863. doi: http://dx.doi.org/10.1176/appi.ajp.2014.13101427

Lim, M. M., & Young, L. J. (2006). Neuropeptidergic regulation of affiliative behavior and social bonding in animals. *Hormones and Behavior, 50*(4), 506–517. doi: 10.1016/j.yhbeh.2006.06.028

Lim, Y. Y., Ellis, K. A., Pietrzak, R. H., Ames, D., Darby, D., Harrington, K., . . . Maruff, P. (2012). Stronger effect of amyloid load than APOE genotype on cognitive decline in healthy older adults. *Neurology, 79*(16), 1645. doi: 10.1212/WNL.0b013e31826e9ae6

Lin, C. S., Lyons, J. L., & Berkowitz, F. (2007). Somatotopic identification of language-SMA in language processing via fMRI. *Journal of Scientific and Practical Computing 1*(2), 3–8.

Lin, P. J., & Schwanenflugel, P. J. (1995). Cultural familiarity and language factors in the structure of category knowledge. *Journal of Cross-Cultural Psychology, 26*, 153–168.

Lin, P. J., Schwanenflugel, P. J., & Wisenbaker, J. M. (1990). Category typicality, cultural familiarity, and the development of category knowledge. *Developmental Psychology, 26*, 805–813.

Lindau, S. T., Schumm, P., Laumann, E. O., Levinson, W., O'Muircheartaigh, C. A., & Waite, L. J. (2007). A study of sexuality and health among older adults in the United States. *New England Journal of Medicine, 357*(8), 762–764.

Lindemann, B. (1996). Taste reception. *Physiological Review, 76*, 719–766.

Lindsey, E. W., Cremeens, P. R., & Caldera, Y. M. (2010). Gender differences in mother–toddler and father–toddler verbal initiations and responses during a caregiving and play context. *Sex Roles, 62*(11–12), 746–759.

Lippa R. A. (2010). Sex differences in personality traits and gender-related occupational preferences across 53 nations: Testing evolutionary and social-environmental theories. *Archives of Sexual Behavior, 39*, 619–636.

Lipsman, N., Woodside, D. B., Giacobbe, P., Hamani, C., Carter, J. C., Norwood, S. J., . . . Lozano, A. M. (2013). Subcallosal cingulate deep brain stimulation for treatment-refractory anorexia nervosa: A phase 1 pilot trial. *Lancet, 381*(9875), 1361–1370. doi: 10.1016/s0140-6736(12)62188-6

Lisanby, S. H., Maddox, J. H., Prudic, J., Devanand, D. P., & Sackeim, H. A. (2000). The effects of electroconvulsive therapy on memory of autobiographical and public events. *Archives of General Psychiatry, 57*, 581–590.

Livesley, J. W. (Ed.). (1995). *The DSM-IV Personality disorders*. New York: Guilford Press.

Lizskowski, U., Carpenter, M., Striano, T., & Tomasello, M. (2006). 12- and 18-month-olds point to provide information for others. *Journal of Cognition and Development, 7*, 173–187.

Lo Bue, A., Salvaggio, A., Insalaco, G., & Marrone, O. (2014). Extreme REM rebound during continuous positive airway pressure titration for obstructive sleep apnea in a depressed patient. *Case Reports in Medicine, 2014*, 292181. doi: 10.1155/2014/292181

Lock, M. (1994). Menopause in cultural context. *Experimental Gerontology, 29*(3–4), 307–317.

Loehlin, J. C. (1992). *Genes and environment in personality development*. Newbury Park, CA: Sage.

Loehlin, J. C., McCrae, R. R., Costa, P. T., Jr., & John, O. P. (1998). Heritabilities of common and measure-specific components of the Big Five personality factors. *Journal of Research in Personality, 32*, 431–453.

Loehlin, J. C., Willerman, L., & Horn, J. M. (1985). Personality resemblances in adoptive families when the children are late-adolescent or adult. *Journal of Personality and Social Psychology, 48*, 376–392.

Loftus, E. (1975). Leading questions and the eyewitness report. *Cognitive Psychology, 7*, 560–572.

Loftus, E. (1987, June 29). Trials of an expert witness. *Newsweek, 109*: 10–11.

Loftus, E. F., & Loftus, G. R. (1980). On the permanence of stored information in the human brain. *American Psychologist, 35*, 409–420.

Loftus, E. F., Miller, D. G., & Burns H. J. (1978). Semantic integration of verbal information into a visual memory. *Journal of Experimental Psychology: Human Learning, 4*, 19–31.

Loftus, J. (2001). America's liberalization in attitudes toward homosexuality, 1973 to 1998. *American Sociological Review, 66*(5), 762–782.

Loo, S. K., Hale, T. S., Macion, J., Hanada, G., McGough, J. J., McCracken, J. T., & Smalley, S. L. (2009). Cortical activity patterns in ADHD during arousal, activation and sustained attention. *Neuropsychologia, 47*(10), 2114–2119.

López-Muñoz, F., & Alamo, C. (2009). Monoaminergic neurotransmission: The history of the discovery of antidepressants from 1950s until today. *Current Pharmaceutical Design, 15*, 1563–1586.

Lord, T. R. (2001). 101 reasons for using cooperative learning in biology teaching. *The American Biology Teacher, 63*(1), 30–38.

Lorenz, K. (1966). *On Aggression*. (Marjorie Kerr Wilson, Trans.) New York: Harcourt, Brace & World, Inc.

Lorenzo, G. L., Biesanz, J. C., & Human, L. J. (2010). What is beautiful is good and more accurately understood: Physical attractiveness and accuracy in first impressions of personality. *Psychological Science, 21*, 1777–1782.

Lovaas, O. I. (1964). Cue properties of words: The control of operant responding by rate and content of verbal operants. *Child Development, 35*, 245–256.

Lovaas, O. I. (1987). Behavioral treatment and normal educational and intellectual functioning in young autistic children. *Journal of Consulting and Clinical Psychology, 55*, 3–9.

Lovaas, O. I., Berberich, J. P., Perloff, B. F., & Schaffer, B. (1966). Acquisition of imitative speech by schizophrenic children. *Science, 151*, 705–707.

Lu, S., & Ende, N. (1997). Potential for clinical use of viable pluripotent progenitor cells in blood bank stored human umbilical cord blood. *Life Sciences, 61*, 1113–1123.

Lubinski, D. (2000). Scientific and social significance of assessing individual differences: "Sinking shafts at a few critical points." *Annual Review of Psychology, 51*, 405–444.

Luborsky, L., Singer, B., & Luborsky, L. (1975). Comparative studies of psychotherapies: Is it true that "everyone has won and all must have prizes"? *Archives of General Psychiatry, 32*, 995–1008.

Luchins, A. S. (1957). Primacy-recency in impression formation. In C. Hovland (Ed.), *The order of presentation in persuasion* (pp. 33–40, 55–61). New Haven, CT: Yale University Press.

Luck, S. J., & Gold, J. M. (2008). The construct of attention in schizophrenia. *Biological Psychiatry, 64*(1), 34–39.

Lucy, J. A., & Shweder, R. A. (1979). Whorf and his critics: Linguistic and nonlinguistic influences on color memory. *American Anthropologist, 81*, 581–615.

Luria, A. R. (1965). Two kinds of motor perseveration in massive injury of the frontal lobes. *Brain, 88*, 1–10.

Luria, A. R. (1968). *The mind of a mnemonist*. New York: Basic Books.

Lurito, J. T., Dzemidzic, M., Mathews, V. P., Lowe, M. J., Kareken, D. A., Phillips, M. D., & Wang, Y. (2000). Comparison of hemispheric lateralization using four language tasks. *Neuroimage, 11*, S358.

Lutkenhaus, P., Grossmann, K. E., & Grossman, K. (1985). Infant–mother attachment at twelve months and style of interaction with a stranger at the age of three years. *Child Development, 56*, 1538–1542.

Ly, M., Adluru, N., Destiche, D. J., Lu, S. Y., Oh, J. M., Hoscheidt, S. M., . . . Bendlin, B. B. (2016). Fornix microstructure and memory performance is associated with altered neural connectivity during episodic recognition. *Journal of the International Neuropsychological Society, 22(Special Issue 2)*, 191–204. doi: doi:10.1017/S1355617715001216

Lykken, D. T. (1995). *The antisocial personalities*. Hillsdale, NJ: Laurence Erlbaum.

Lykken, D. T., & Tellegen, A. (1996). Happiness is a stochastic phenomenon. *Psychological Science, 7*, 186–189.

Lynn, S. J., Laurence, J. R., & Kirsch, I. (2015). Hypnosis, suggestion, and suggestibility: An integrative model. *The American Journal of Clinical Hypnosis, 57*(3), 314–329.

Lynott, P. P., & Roberts, R. (1997). The developmental stake hypothesis and changing perceptions of intergenerational relations, 1971–1985. *The Gerontologist, 37*, 394–405.

Lytton, H., & Romney, D. M. (1991). Parents' sex-differentiated socialization of boys and girls: A meta-analysis. *Psychological Bulletin, 109*, 267–296.

Lyznicki, J. M., Doege, T. C., Davis, R. M., & Williams, M. A. (Council on Scientific Affairs, American Medical Association). (1998). Sleepiness, driving, and motor-vehicle crashes. *Journal of the American Medical Association, 279*(23), 1908–1913.

Ma, J., Han, Y., Grogan-Kaylor, A., Delva, J., & Castillo, M. (2012). Corporal punishment and youth externalizing behavior in Santiago, Chile. *Child Abuse & Neglect, 36*(6), 481–490. doi: 10.1016/j.chiabu.2012.03.006

MacCoun, R. J., & Kerr, N. L. (1988). Asymmetric influence in mock jury deliberation: Jurors' bias for leniency. *Journal of Personality and Social Psychology, 54*, 21–33.

MacDonald, A. P. (1970). Internal-external locus of control and the practice of birth control. *Psychological Reports, 27*, 206.

MacDonald, D., Kabani, N., Avis, D., & Evens, A. C. (2000). Automated 3D extraction of inner and outer surfaces of cerebral cortex from MRI. *NeuroImage, 12*, 340–356.

Macdonald, I., Amos, J., Crone, T., Wereley, S. (2010, May 21). The measure of an oil disaster. [Electronic version]. *New York Times*. Retrieved June 9, 2010, from http://www.nytimes.com/2010/05/22/opinion/22macdonald.html

Maciejewski, P. K., Zhang, B., Block, S. D., & Prigerson, H. G. (2007). An empirical examination of the stage theory of grief. *The Journal of the American Medical Association, 297*(7), 716–723. doi:10.1001/jama.297.7.716

Mack, J. E. (1994). *Abduction*. New York: Scribner.

MacKenzie, S. B., Lutz, R. J., & Belch, G. E. (1986, May). The role of attitude toward the ad as a mediator of advertising effectiveness: A test of competing explanations. *Journal of Marketing Research, 23*, 130–143.

Macknik, S. L., King, M., Randi, J., Robbins, A., Teller, Thompson, J., & Martinez-Conde, S. (2008). Attention and awareness in stage magic: Turning tricks into research. *Nature Reviews: Neuroscience, 9*(11), 871–879.

Macknik, S. L., & Martinez-Conde, S. (2009). Real magic: Future studies of magic should be grounded in neuroscience. *Nature reviews: Neuroscience, 10*(3), 241–241.

MacLeod, C. M. (1998). Directed forgetting. In J. M. Golding & C. M. MacLeod (Eds.), *Intentional forgetting: Interdisciplinary approaches* (pp. 1–57). Mahwah, NJ: Erlbaum.

Macmillan, M. (2000). *An odd kind of fame: Stories of Phineas Gage.* Cambridge, MA: The MIT Press.

Macmillan, M., & Lena, M. L. (2010). Rehabilitating Phineas Gage. *Neuropsychological Rehabilitation, 20*(5), 641–658. doi: 10.1080/09602011003760527

Macmillan, N. A., & Creelman, C. D. (1991). *Detection theory: A user's guide.* Cambridge, UK; New York: Cambridge University Press.

Macquet, P., & Franck, G. (1996). Functional neuroanatomy of human rapid eye movement sleep and dreaming. *Nature, 383,* 163–166.

Macrae, C. N., & Bodenhausen, G. V. (2000). Social cognition: Thinking categorically about others. *Annual Review of Psychology, 51,* 93–120.

Macrae, C. N., & Quadflieg, S. (2010). Perceiving people. In S. Fiske, D. T. Gilbert, & G. Lindzey (Eds.), *The handbook of social psychology* (5th ed., pp. 428–463). New York: McGraw-Hill.

Maddox, J., Randi, J., & Stewart, W.W. (1988). "High-dilution" experiments a delusion. *Nature, 334*(6181), 368.

Madore, K. P., & Schacter, D. L. (2016). Remembering the past and imagining the future: Selective effects of an episodic specificity induction on detail generation. *The Quarterly Journal of Experimental Psychology, 69,* 285–298. doi: 10.1080/17470218.2014.999097

Madras, B. K. (2014). Dopamine challenge reveals neuroadaptive changes in marijuana abusers. *Proceedings of the National Academy of Sciences, 111*(33), 11915–11916. doi: 10.1073/pnas.1412314111

Madsen, K. M., Hviid, A., Vestergaard, M., Schendel, D., Wohlfahrt, J., Thorsen, P., . . . Melbye, M. (2002). A population-based study of measles, mumps, rubella vaccine and autism. *New England Journal of Medicine, 347,* 1477–1482.

Mahoney, M. J. (2005). Constructivism and positive psychology. In C. R. Snyder & S. J. Lopez (Eds.), *Handbook of positive psychology* (pp. 745–750). New York: Oxford University Press.

Mahowald, M. W., & Schenck, C. H. (1996). NREM sleep parasomnias. *Neurologic Clinics, 14,* 675–696.

Mahowald, M. W., Schenck, C. H., & Bornemann, M. A. (2005). Sleep-related violence. *Current Neurology and Neuroscience Reports, 5,* 153–158.

Mahr, I., Bambico, F. R., Mechawar, N., & Nobrega, J. N. (2013). Stress, serotonin, and hippocampal neurogenesis in relation to depression and antidepressant effects. *Neuroscience and Behavioural Reviews, 38,* 173–192. doi: 10.1016/j.neubiorev.2013.11.009

Maier, S. F., Amat, J., Baratta, M. V., Paul, E., & Watkins, L. R. (2006). Behavioral control, the medial prefrontal cortex, and resilience. *Dialogues in Clinical Neuroscience, 8*(4), 397–406.

Maier, S. F., & Watkins, L. R. (1998). Cytokines for psychologists: Implications of bidirectional immune-to-brain communication for understanding behavior, mood, and cognition. *Psychological Review, 105,* 83–107.

Maier, S. F., & Watkins, L. R. (2005). Stressor controllability and learned helplessness: The roles of the dorsal raphe nucleus, serotonin, and corticotropin-releasing factor. *Neuroscience & Biobehavioral Reviews, 29*(4–5), 829–841.

Main, M., & Cassidy, J. (1988). Categories of response to reunion with the parent at age 6: Predictable from infant attachment classifications and stable over a 1 month period. *Developmental Psychology, 24,* 415–426.

Main, M., & Hesse, E. (1990). Parents' unresolved traumatic experiences are related to infant disorganized attachment status; Is frightened and/or frightening parental behaviour the linking mechanism? In M. T. Greenberg, D. Cicchetti, & E. M. Cummings (Eds.), *Attachment in the preschool years: Theory, research and intervention* (pp. 161–182). Chicago: University of Chicago Press.

Main, M., & Solomon, J. (1990). Procedures for identifying infants as disorganized/disoriented during the Ainsworth Strange Situation. In M. T. Greenberg, D. Cicchetti, & E. M. Cummings (Eds.), *Attachment in the preschool years: Theory, research and intervention* (pp. 121–160). Chicago: University of Chicago Press.

Makin, T. R., Scholz, J., Henderson Slater, D., Johansen-Berg, H., & Tracey, I. (2015). Reassessing cortical reorganization in the primary sensorimotor cortex following arm amputation. *Brain, 138*(Pt 8), 2140–2146. doi: 10.1093/brain/awv161

Maletic, V., Robinson, M., Oakes, T., Iyengar, S., Ball, S. G., & Russell, J. (2007). Neurobiology of depression: An integrated view of key findings. *The International Journal of Clinical Practice, 61*(12), 2030–2040.

Mancuso, C., Siciliano, R., Barone, E., & Preziosi, P. (2011). Natural substance and Alzheimer's disease: From preclinical studies to evidence-based medicine. *Biochimica et Biophysica Acta (BBA), 1822*(5), 616–624.

Mandler, G. (1967). Organization and memory. In K. W. Spence & J. T. Spence (Eds.), *The psychology of learning and motivation* (Vol. 1, pp. 327–372). New York: Academic Press.

Mangalindan, J. P. (2012). Google: The king of perks – CNN Money. Retrieved May 30, 2013, from http://money.cnn.com/galleries/2012/technology/1201/gallery.best-companies-google-perks.fortune/index.html

Manning, R., Levine, M., & Collins, A. (2007). The Kitty Genovese murder and the social psychology of helping: The parable of the 38 witnesses. *American Psychologist, 62*(6), 555–562. doi:10.1037/0003-066X.62.6.555

Manos, R. C., Kanter, J. W., & Busch, A. M. (2010). A critical review of assessment strategies to measure the behavioral activation model of depression. *Clinical Psychology Review, 30*(5), 547–561. doi: 10.1016/j.cpr.2010.03.008

Mantoan, L., Eriksson, S. H., Nisbet, A. P., & Walker, M. C. (2013). Adult-onset NREM parasomnia with hypnopompic hallucinatory pain: A case report. *Sleep, 36*(2), 287–290.

Manusov, V., & Patterson, M. L. (Eds.). (2006). *The Sage handbook of nonverbal communication.* Thousand Oaks, CA: Sage.

Maquet, P., Schwartz, S., Passingham, R., & Frith, C. (2003). Sleep-related consolidation of a visuomotor skill: Brain mechanisms as assessed by functional magnetic resonance imaging. *The Journal of Neuroscience, 23*(4), 1432.

March of Dimes Foundation. (2009). Pregnancy & Newborn Health Education Center. Quick reference fact sheet: Birth defects. Retrieved from http://208.74.202.108/printableArticles/4439_1206.asp

Marcus, G. F. (2001). *The algebraic mind: Integrating connectionism and cognitive science (learning, development, and conceptual change).* Cambridge, MA: MIT Press.

Maren, S., & Fanselow, M. S. (1996). The amygdala and fear conditioning: Has the nut been cracked? *Neuron, 16,* 237–240.

Margolin, S., & Kubic, L. S. (1944). An apparatus for the use of breath sounds as a hypnogogic stimulus. *American Journal of Psychiatry, 100,* 610.

Marik, P. E. (2000). Leptin, obesity, and obstructive sleep apnea. *Chest, 118,* 569–571.

Markovitz, J. H., Lewis, C. E., Sanders, P. W., Tucker, D., & Warnock, D. G. (1997). Relationship of diastolic blood pressure with cyclic GMP excretion among young adults (the CARDIA study): Influence of a family history of hypertension. *Journal of Hypertension, 15*(9), 955–962.

Marks, D. F., Murray, M., Evans, B., Willig, C., Sykes, C. M., & Woodall, C. (2005). *Health Psychology: Theory, research & practice* (pp. 3–25). London: Sage.

Markus, H. R., & Kitayama, S. (1991). Culture and the self: Implications for cognition, emotion, and motivation. *Psychological Review, 98,* 224–253.

Mars, A. E., Mauk, J. E., & Dowrick, P. (1998). Symptoms of pervasive developmental disorders as observed in prediagnostic home videos of infants and toddlers. *Journal of Pediatrics, 132,* 500–504.

Marsden, K. E., Ma, W. J., Deci, E. L., Ryan, R. M., & Chiu, P. H. (2014). Diminished neural responses predict enhanced intrinsic motivation and sensitivity to external incentive. *Cognitive, Affective, Behavioral Neuroscience, 15,* 276–286. doi: 10.3758/s13415-014-0324-5

Martin, C. L. (2000). Cognitive theories of gender development. In T. Eckes & H. M. Trautner (Eds.), *The developmental social psychology of gender* (pp. 91–121). Mahwah, NJ: Lawrence Erlbaum.

Martin, J. A., & Buckwalter, J. J. (2001). Telomere erosion and senescence in human articular cartilage chondrocytes. *Journal of Gerontology and Biological Science, 56*(4), 172–179.

Martin, L. (2004). Can sleepwalking be a murder defense? Retrieved October 19, 2004, from http://www.lakesidepress.com/pulmonary/Sleep/sleep-murder.htm

Martín, R., Bajo-Grañeras, R., Moratalla, R., Perea, G., & Araque, A. (2015). Circuit-specific signaling in astrocyte-neuron networks in basal ganglia pathways. *Science, 349*(6249), 730–734. doi: 10.1126/science.aaa7945

Martinussen, R., Hayden J., Hogg-Johnson, S., & Tannock, R. (2005). A meta-analysis of working memory components in children with Attention-Deficit/Hyperactivity Disorder. *Journal of the American Academy of Child & Adolescent Psychiatry, 44*(4), 377–384.

Martyn, A. C., De Jaeger, X., Magalhaes, A. C., Kesarwani, R., Goncalves, D. F., Raulic, S., . . . Prado, V. F. (2012). Elimination of the vesicular acetylcholine transporter in the forebrain causes hyperactivity and deficits in spatial memory and long-term potentiation. *Proceedings of the National Academy of Sciences, 109*(43), 17651–17656. doi: 10.1073/pnas.1215381109

Maruta, T., Colligan, R. C., Malinchoc, M., & Offord, K. P. (2002, August). Optimism-pessimism assessed in the 1960s and self-reported health status 30 years later. *Mayo Clinic Proceedings, 77,* 748–753.

Maslow, A. (1943). A theory of human motivation. *Psychological Review, 50,* 370–396.

Maslow, A. (1971). *The farther reaches of human nature.* New York: Viking Press.

Maslow, A. (1987). *Motivation and personality* (3rd ed.). New York: Harper & Row.

Maslow, A. H. (1954). *Motivation and personality.* New York: Harper & Row.

Maslow, A., & Lowery, R. (Ed.). (1998). *Toward a psychology of being* (3rd ed.). New York: Wiley & Sons.

Massaro, D. W., & Cowan, N. (1993). Information processing models: Microscopes of the mind. *Annual Review of Psychology, 44,* 383–426.

Masson, J. M. (1984). *The assault on truth: Freud's suppression of the seduction theory.* New York: Farrar, Straus & Giroux.

Master, A., Cheryan, S., & Meltzoff, A. N. (2015). Computing whether she belongs: Stereotypes undermine girls' interest and sense of belonging in computer science. *Journal of Educational Psychology, 108*(3), 424–437. doi: 10.1037/edu0000061

Masters, J. C., Burish, T. G., Holton, S. D., & Rimm, D. C. (1987). *Behavior therapy: Techniques and empirical finding.* San Diego, CA: Harcourt Brace Jovanovich.

Masters, W. H., & Johnson, V. E. (1966). *Human sexual response.* Boston: Little, Brown.

Masters, W. H., & Johnson, V. E. (1970). *Human sexual inadequacy.* Boston: Little, Brown.

Masters, W. H., Johnson, V. E., & Kolodny, R. (1995). *Human sexuality* (5th ed.). New York: HarperCollins.

Masuda, T., & Kitayama, S. (2004). Perceiver-induced constraint and attitude attribution in Japan and the U.S.: A case for the cultural dependence of the correspondence bias. *Journal of Experimental Social Psychology, 40*, 409–416.

Meikle, J., & Boseley, S. (2010, May 24). MMR row doctor Andrew Wakefield struck off register. *The Guardian* (London). Retrieved April 26, 2013, from http://www.guardian.co.uk/society/2010/may/24/mmr-doctor-andrew-wakefield-struck-off

Meineri, S., & Guéguen N. (2008). An application of the foot-in-the-door strategy in the environmental field. *European Journal of Social Sciences, 7,* 71–74.

Mejía, O. L., & McCarthy, C. J. (2010). Acculturative stress, depression, and anxiety in migrant farmwork college students of Mexican heritage. *International Journal of Stress Management, 17*(1), 1–20.

Melby-Lervag, M., & Hulme, C. (2013). Is working memory training effective? A meta-analytic review. *Developmental Psychology, 49*(2), 270–291. doi: 10.1037/a0028228

Melby-Lervag, M., & Hulme, C. (2016). There is no convincing evidence that working memory training is effective: A reply to Au et al. (2014) and Karbach and Verhaeghen (2014). *Psychonomic Bulletin & Review, 23*(1), 324–330. doi: 10.3758/s13423-015-0862-z

Melzack, R., & Wall, P. D. (1965). Pain mechanisms: A new theory. *Science, 150,* 971–979.

Melzack, R., & Wall, P. D. (1996). *The challenge of pain.* London: Penguin Books.

Mendez, M. F., & Fras, I. A. (2011). The false memory syndrome: Experimental studies and comparison to confabulations. *Medical Hypotheses, 76*(4), 492–496. doi: 10.1016/j.mehy.2010.110.33

Mennella, J. A., & Trabulsi, J. C. (2012). Complementary foods and flavor experiences: Setting the foundation. *Ann Nutr Metab, 60 Suppl 2,* 40–50. doi: 10.1159/000335337

Menon, T., Morris, M., Chiu, C. Y., & Hong, Y. I. (1999). Culture and the construal of agency: Attribution to individual versus group dispositions. *Journal of Personality and Social Psychology, 76,* 701–727.

Merikle, M. P. (2001). Subliminal perception. In A. E. Kazdin (Ed.), *Encyclopedia of Psychology* (Vol. 7, pp. 497–499). New York: Oxford University Press.

Mervis, C. B., & Rosch, E. (1981). Categorization of natural objects. *Annual Review of Psychology, 32,* 89–115.

Mesgarani, N., & Chang, E. F. (2012). Selective cortical representation of attended speaker in multi-talker speech perception. *Nature, 485,* 233–236. doi: 10.1038/nature11020

Messina, G., Dalia, C., Tafuri, D., Monda, V., Palmieri, F., Dato, A., . . . Monda, M. (2014). Orexin-A controls sympathetic activity and eating behavior. *Frontiers in Psychology, 5,* 997.

Meyer, G. J., & Kurtz, J. E. (2006). Advancing personality assessment terminology: Time to retire 'objective' and 'projective' as personality test descriptors. *Journal of Personality Assessment, 87*(3), 223–225. doi: 10.1207/s15327752jpa8703_01

Meyer, J. S. (2013). 3,4-methylenedioxymethamphetamine (MDMA): Current perspectives". *Substance Abuse Rehabilitation, 4,* 83–99. doi: 10.2147/SAR.S37258

Meyrick, J. (2001). Forget the blood and gore: An alternative message strategy to help adolescents avoid cigarette smoking. *Health Education, 101*(3), 99–107.

Meziab, O., Kirby, K. A., Williams, B., Yaffe, K., Byers, A. L., & Barnes, D. E. (2014). Prisoner of war status, posttraumatic stress disorder, and dementia in older veterans. *Alzheimer's & Dementia, 10*(3 Suppl), S236–241. doi: 10.1016/j.jalz.2014.04.004

Michaels, J. W., Blommel, J. M., Brocato, R. M., Linkous, R. A., & Rowe, J. S. (1982). Social facilitation and inhibition in a natural setting. *Replications in Social Psychology, 2,* 21–24.

Michalski, D., Kohout, J., Wicherski, M., & Hart, B. (2011). 2009 Doctorate Employment Survey (Table 3). Washington, DC: American Psychological Association. Retrieved from https://www.apa.org/workforce/publications/09-doc-empl/report.pdf

Michalski, D., Mulvey, T., & Kohoout, J. (2010). *2008 American Psychological Association survey of psychology health service providers.* Retrieved April 5, 2010, from http://www.apa.org/workforce/publications/08-hsp/report.pdf

Micoulaud-Franchi, J. A., Lanteaume, L., Pallanca, O., Vion-Dury, J., & Bartolomei, F. (2014). Biofeedback and drug-resistant epilepsy: Back to an earlier treatment? *Revue Neurologique, 170*(3), 187–196.

Migo, E. M., Quamme, J. R., Holmes, S., Bendell, A., Norman, K. A., Mayes, A. R., & Montaldi, D. (2014). Individual difference in forced-choice recognition memory: Partitioning contributions of recollection and familiarity. *Wharterly Journal of Experimental Psychology, 67*(11), 2189–2206.

Mikami, A. Y., Szwedo, D. E., Allen, J. P., Evans, M. A., & Hare, A. L. (2010). Adolescent peer relationships and behavior problems predict young adults' communication on social networking websites. *Developmental Psychology, 46,* 46–56.

Miles, D. R., & Carey, G. (1997). Genetic and environmental architecture of human aggression. *Journal of Personality and Social Psychology, 72,* 207–217.

Milgram, S. (1963). Behavioral study of obedience. *The Journal of Abnormal and Social Psychology, 67*(4), 371–378. doi: 10.1037/h0040525

Milgram, S. (1964). Issues in the study of obedience: A reply to Baumrind. *American Psychologist, 19,* 848–852.

Milgram, S. (1974). *Obedience to authority: An experimental view.* New York: Harper & Row.

Miller, C. H., Hamilton, J. P., Sacchet, M. D., & Gotlib, I. H. (2015). Meta-analysis of functional neuroimaging of major depressive disorder in youth. *JAMA Psychiatry, 72*(10), 1045–1053. doi: 10.1001/jamapsychiatry.2015.1376

Miller, D. I., & Halpern, D. F. (2014). The new science of cognitive sex differences. *Trends in Cognitive sciences, 18*(1), 37–45.

Miller, G. (2009). Neuropathology. A late hit for pro football players. *Science, 325*(5941), 670–672.

Miller, G. (2013). Neuroscience. The promise and perils of oxytocin. *Science, 339*(6117), 267–269. doi: 10.1126/science.339.6117.267

Miller, G. A. (1956). The magical number seven, plus or minus two: Some limits on our capacity for processing information. *Psychological Review, 63,* 81–97.

Miller, J. G. (1984). Culture and the development of everyday social explanation. *Journal of Personality and Social Psychology, 46,* 961–978.

Miller, K. E., & Graves, J. C. (2000). Update on the prevention and treatment of sexually transmitted diseases. *American Family Physician, 61,* 379–386.

Miller, M., & Rahe, R. H. (1997). Life changes scaling for the 1990s. *Journal of Psychosomatic Research, 43*(3), 279–292.

Miller, M. E., & Bowers, K. S. (1993). Hypnotic analgesia: Dissociated experience or dissociated control? *Journal of Abnormal Psychology, 102,* 29–38.

Miller, M. K., & Summers, A. (2007). Gender differences in video game characters' roles, appearances, and attire as portrayed in video game magazines. *Sex Roles, 57*(9–10), 733–742.

Miller, M. N., & Pumariega, A. (1999). Culture and eating disorders. *Psychiatric Times, 16*(2), 1–4.

Miller, N. E. (1983). Behavioral medicine: Symbiosis between laboratory and clinic. *Annual Review of Psychology, 34,* 1–31.

Miller, N. E., Sears, R. R., Mowrer, O. H., Doob, L. W., & Dollard, J. (1941). The frustration-aggression hypothesis. *Psychological Review, 48,* 337–342.

Miller, T. Q., Smith, T. W., Turner, C. W., Guijarro, M. L., & Hallet, A. J. (1996). A meta-analytic review of research on hostility and physical health. *Psychological Bulletin, 119,* 322–348.

Miller, T. Q., Turner, C. W., Tindale, R. S., Posavac, E. J., & Dugoni, B. L. (1991). Reasons for the trend toward null findings in research on Type A behavior. *Psychological Bulletin, 110,* 469–485.

Miller, W. R., & Arkowitz, H. (2015). Learning, applying, and extending motivational interviewing. In H. Arkowitz, W. R. Miller, & S. Rollnick (Eds.), *Motivational interviewing in the treatment of psychological problems* (2nd ed.). New York: The Guilford Press.

Miller, W. R., & Rollnick, S. (2002). *Motivational interviewing: Preparing people for change* (2nd ed.). New York: Guilford Press.

Miller, W. R., & Rollnick, S. (2013). *Motivational interviewing: Helping people change* (3rd ed.). New York: The Guilford Press.

Mills, M. A., Edmondson, D., & Park, C. L. (2007). Trauma and stress response among Hurricane Katrina evacuees. *American Journal of Public Health, 97*(1), 116–123.

Milner, B., Corkin, S., & Teuber, H. L. (1968). Further analysis of the hippocampal syndrome: 14-year follow-up study of H. M. *Neuropsychologia, 6,* 215–234.

Milner, J. (1992, January). Risk for physical child abuse: Adult factors. *Violence Update,* pp. 9–11.

Mintz, L. B., & Betz, N. E. (1988). Prevalence and correlates of eating disordered behaviors among undergraduate women. *Journal of Counseling Psychology, 35,* 463–471.

Miocinovic, S., Somayajula, S., Chitnis, S., & Vitek, J. L. (2013). History, applications, and mechanisms of deep brain stimulation. *JAMA Neurology, 70*(2), 163–171. doi: 10.1001/2013.jamaneurol.45

Mischel, W. (1966). A social learning view of sex differences in behaviour. In E. E. Maccoby (Ed.), *The development of sex differences* (pp. 56–81). Stanford, CT: Stanford University Press.

Mischel, W., & Shoda, Y. (1995). A cognitive-affective system theory of personality: Reconceptualizing situations, dispositions, dynamics, and invariances in personality structure. *Psychological Review, 102*(2), 246–268.

Mishell, D. R. (2001). Menopause. In M. A. Stenchever W. Droegemueller, A. L. Herbst, and D. R. Mishell. (Eds.), *Comprehensive gynecology* (4th ed., pp. 1217–1258). St. Louis, MO: Mosby.

Missonnier, P., Hasler, R., Perroud, N., Herrmann, F. R., Millet, P., Richiardi, J., . . . Baud, P. (2013). EEG anomalies in adult ADHD subjects performing a working memory task. *Neuroscience, 241,* 135–146. doi: 10.1016/j.neuroscience.2013.03.011

Mitchell, G. E., & Locke, K. D. (2015). Lay beliefs about autism spectrum disorder among the general public and childcare providers. *Autism, 19,* 553–561.

Mitchell, J. E., Pyle, R. L., Eckert, E. D. (1981). Frequency and duration of binge-eating episodes in patients with bulimia. *American Journal of Psychiatry, 138,* 835–836.

Mitchell, J. E., Roerig, J., & Steffen, K. (2013). Biological therapies for eating disorders. *International Journal of Eating Disorders, 46*(5), 470–477. doi: 10.1002/eat.22104

Mitchell, S. A., & Black, M. J. (1996). *Freud and beyond: A history of modern psychoanalytic thought* [Reprint ed.]. New York: HarperCollins.

Miyatake, A., Morimoto Y., Oishi, T., Hanasaki, N., Sugita, Y., Iijima, S., . . . Yamamura, Y. (1980). Circadian rhythm of serum testosterone and its relation to sleep: Comparison with the variation in serum luteinizing hormone, prolactin, and cortisol in normal men. *Journal of Clinical Endocrinology and Metabolism, 51*(6), 1365–1371.

Moffic, H. S. (2003). Seven ways to improve "cultural competence." *Current Psychiatry, 2*(5), 78.

Mogil, J. S. (1999). The genetic mediation of individual differences in sensitivity to pain and its inhibition. *Proceedings of the National Academy of Sciences, USA, 96*(14), 7744–7751.

Mohammadzaheri, F., Koegel, L. K., Rezaei, M., & Bakhshi, E. (2015). A randomized clinical trial comparison between pivotal response treatment (PRT) and adult-driven applied behavior analysis (ABA) intervention on disruptive behaviors in public school children with autism. *Journal of Autism and Developmental Disorders, 45*(9), 2899–2907.

Mokdad, A. H., Bowman, B. A., Ford, E. S., Dietz, W. H., Vinicor, F., Bales, V. S., & Marks, J. S. (2001). Prevalence of obesity, diabetes, and obesity related health risk factors. *Journal of the American Medical Association, 289*, 76–79.

Moldofsky, H. (1995). Sleep and the immune system. *International Journal of Immunopharmacology, 17*(8), 649–654.

Moll, H., & Tomasello, M. (2007). How 14- and 18-month-olds know what others have experienced. *Developmental Psychology, 43*, 309–317.

Möller, A., & Hell, D. (2002). Eugen Bleuler and forensic psychiatry. *International Journal of Law and Psychiatry, 25*, 351–360.

Molloy, K., Griffiths, T. D., Chait, M., & Lavie, N. (2015). Inattentional deafness: Visual load leads to time-specific suppression of auditory evoked responses. *Journal of Neuroscience, 35*(49), 16046–16054. doi: 10.1523/JNEUROSCI.2931-15.2015

Molofsky, A. V., Krencik, R., Ullian, E. M., Tsai, H. H., Deneen, B., Richardson, W. D., . . . Rowitch, D. H. (2012). Astrocytes and disease: A neurodevelopmental perspective. *Genes & Development, 26*(9), 891–907. doi: 10.1101/gad.188326.112

Money, J. (1994). *Sex errors of the body and related syndromes.* Baltimore: Paul H. Brookes.

Money, J., & Mathews, D. (1982). Prenatal exposure to virilizing progestins: An adult follow-up study of 12 women. *Archives of Sexual Behavior, 11*(1), 73–83.

Money, J., & Norman, B. F. (1987). Gender identity and gender transposition: Longitudinal outcome study of 24 male hermaphrodites assigned as boys. *Journal of Sex and Marriage Therapy, 13*, 75–79.

Montgomery, C., & Fisk, J. E. (2008). Ecstasy-related deficits in the updating component of executive processes. *Human Psychopharmacology, 23*(6), 495–511.

Moody, R., & Perry, P. (1993). *Reunions: Visionary encounters with departed loved ones.* London: Little, Brown.

Moore, T. E. (1988). The case against subliminal manipulation. *Psychology and Marketing, 5*, 297–316.

Moore, T. H., Zammit, S., Lingford-Hughes, A., Barnes, T. R., Jones, P. B., Burke, M., & Lewis, G. (2007). Cannabis use and risk of psychotic or affective mental health outcomes: A systematic review. *Lancet, 370*, 293–294, 319–328.

Moore-Ede, M. C., Sulzman, F. M., & Fuller, C. A. (1982). *The clocks that time us.* Cambridge, MA: Harvard University Press.

Moorhead, G., Neck, C. P., & West, M. S. (1998). The tendency toward defective decision making within self-managing teams: The relevance of groupthink for the 21st century. *Organizational Behavior & Human Decision Processes, 73*(2–3), 327–351.

Mora, G. (1985). History of psychiatry. In H. I. Kaplan & B. J. Sadock (Eds.), *Comprehensive textbook of psychiatry* (pp. 2034–2054). Baltimore: Williams & Wilkins.

Moreines, J. L., McClintock, S. M., Kelley, M. E., Holtzheimer, P. E., & Mayberg, H. S. (2014). Neuropsychological function before and after subcallosal cingulate deep brain stimulation in patients with treatment-resistant depression. *Depression and Anxiety, 31*(8), 690–698. doi: 10.1002/da.22263

Moreland, R. L., & Zajonc, R. B. (1982). Exposure effects in person perceptions: Familiarity, similarity, and attraction. *Journal of Experimental Social Psychology, 18*(5), 395–415.

Morgan, C. A., Rasmusson, A., Pietrzak, R. H., Coric, V., Southwick, S. M. (2009). Relationships among plasma dehydroepiandrosterone and dehydroepiandrosterone sulfate, cortisol, symptoms of dissociation, and objective performance in humans exposed to underwater navigation stress. *Biological Psychiatry, 66*(4), 334–340.

Morgan, C. D., & Murray, H. A. (1935). A method for investigating fantasies: The Thematic Apperception Test. *Archives of Neurology and Psychiatry, 34*, 298–306.

Morii, M., & Sakagami, T. (2015). The effect of gaze-contingent stimulus elimination on preference judgments. *Frontiers in Psychology, 6*, 1351.

Morin, C. M., Bootzin, R. R., Buysse, D. J., Edinger, J. D., Espie, C. A., & Lichstein, K. L. (2006). Psychological and behavioral treatment of insomnia: Update of the recent evidence (1998–2004). *Sleep, 29*(11), 1398–1414.

Morishima, Y., Schunk, D., Bruhin, A., Ruff, C. C., & Fehr, E. (2012). Linking brain structure and activation in temporoparietal junction to explain the neurobiology of human altruism. *Neuron, 75*(1), 73–79. doi: 10.1016/j.neuron.2012.05.021

Morita, K., Morishima, M., Sakai, K., & Kawaguchi, Y. (2013). Dopaminergic control of motivation and reinforcement learning: A closed-circuit account for reward-oriented behavior. *The Journal of Neuroscience, 33*(20), 8866–8890.

Morris, H., & Wallach, J. (2014). From PCP to MXE: A comprehensive review of the non-medical use of dissociative drugs. *Drug Testing and Analysis, 6*(7–8), 614–632. doi: 10.1002/dta.1620. PMID 24678061

Morris, J. S., Friston, K. J., Buche, L. C., Frith, C. D., Young, A. W., Calder, A. J., & Dolan, R. J. (1998). A neuromodulatory role for the human amygdala in processing emotional facial expressions. *Brain, 121*, 47–57.

Morris, M., Nisbett, R. E., & Peng, K. (1995). Causal understanding across domains and cultures. In D. Sperber, D. Premack, & A. J. Premack (Eds.), *Causal cognition: A multidisciplinary debate* (pp. 577–612). Oxford, UK: Oxford University Press.

Morris, M. W., & Peng, K. (1994). Culture and cause: American and Chinese attributions social and physical events. *Journal of Personality and Social Psychology, 67*, 949–971.

Morris, S. (2009, November 20). Devoted husband who strangled wife in his sleep walks free from court. Retrieved April 9, 2010, from http://www.guardian.co.uk/uk/2009/nov/20/brian-thomas-dream-strangler-tragedy

Morrow, C. E., Culbertson, J. L., Accornero, V. H., Xue, L., Anthony, J. C., & Bandstra, E. S. (2006). Learning disabilities and intellectual functioning in school-aged children with prenatal cocaine exposure. *Developmental Neuropsychology, 30*(3), 905–931.

Moruzzi, G., & Magoun, H. W. (1949). Brainstem reticular formation and activation of the EEG. *Electroencephalographs in Clinical Neurophysiology, 1*, 455–473.

Moscovici, S., & Zavalloni, M. (1969). The group as a polarizer of attitudes. *Journal of Personality and Social Psychology 12*, 125–135.

Mostert, J. C., Shumskaya, E., Mennes, M., Onnink, A. M., Hoogman, M., Kan, C. C., . . . Norris, D. G. (2016). Characterising resting-state functional connectivity in a large sample of adults with ADHD. *Progress in Neuro-Psychopharmacology & Biological Psychiatry, 67*, 82–91. doi: 10.1016/j.pnpbp.2016.01.011

Motraghi, T. E., Seim, R. W., Meyer, E. C., & Morissette, S. B. (2014). Virtual reality exposure therapy for the treatment of posttraumatic stress disorder: A methodological review using consort guidelines. *Journal of Clinical Psychology, 70*(3), 197–208. doi: 10.1002/jclp.22051

Mowat, F. (1988). *Woman in the mists: The story of Dian Fossey and the mountain gorillas of Africa.* New York: Warner Books.

Mroczek, D. K., Spiro, A., & Turiano, N. A. (2009). Do health behaviors explain the effect of neuroticism on mortality? Longitudinal findings from the VA Normative Aging Study. *Journal of Research in Personality, 43*(4), 653.

Mueller, K., Moller, H. E., Horstmann, A., Busse, F., Lepsien, J., Bluher, M., . . . Pleger, B. (2015). Physical exercise in overweight to obese individuals induces metabolic- and neurotrophic-related structural brain plasticity. *Frontiers in Human Neuroscience, 9*, 372. doi: 10.3389/fnhum.2015.00372

Mueser, K. T., Rosenberg, St. D., Xie, H., Jankowski, M. K., Bolton, E. E., Lu, E., . . . Wolfe, R. (2008). A randomized controlled trial of cognitive-behavioral treatment for posttraumatic stress disorder in severe mental illness. *Journal of Consulting and Clinical Psychology, 76*(2), 259–271.

Mufson, L. H., Dorta, K. P., Olfson, M., Weissman, M. M., & Hoagwood, K. (2004). Effectiveness research: Transporting interpersonal psychotherapy for depressed adolescents (IPT-A) from the lab to school-based health clinics. *Clinical Child and Family Psychology Review, 7*(4), 251–261.

Muhlberger, A., Herrmann, M. J., Wiedemann, G. C., Ellgring, H., & Pauli, P. (2001). Repeated exposure of flight phobics to flights in virtual reality. *Behaviour Research and Therapy, 39*(9), 1033–1050.

Mukamel, R., Ekstrom, A. D., Kaplan, J., Iacoboni, M., & Fried, I. (2010). Single-neuron responses in humans during execution and observation of actions. *Current Biology, 20*, 750–756.

Muller-Oerlinghausen, B., Berghofer, A., & Bauer, M. (2002). Bipolar disorder. *Lancet, 359*, 241–247.

Munoz, E., Sliwinski, M. J., Scott, S. B., & Hofer, S. (2015). Global perceived stress predicts cognitive change among older adults. *Psychology and Aging, 30*, 487–499.

Münsterberg, H. (1908). *On the witness stand.* New York: Clark, Boardman.

Münsterberg, H. (1913). *Psychology and industrial efficiency.* Boston & New York: Houghton Mifflin.

Murayama, K., Matsumoto, M., Izuma, K., Sugiura, A., Ryan, R. M., Deci, E. L., & Matsumoto, K. (2015). How self-determined choice facilitates performance: A key role of the ventromedial prefrontal cortex. *Cerebral Cortex, 25*, 1241–1251. doi: 10.1093/cercor/bht317

Murdock, B. B., Jr. (1962). The serial position effect in free recall. *Journal of Experimental Psychology, 64*, 482–488.

Murphy, C. C., Boyle, C., Schendel, D., Decouflé, P., & Yeargin-Allsopp, M. (1998). Epidemiology of mental retardation in children. *Mental Retardation and Developmental Disabilities Research Reviews, 4*, 6–13.

Murphy, L. R. (1995). Managing job stress: An employee assistance/human resource management partnership. *Personnel Review, 24*(1), 41–50.

Murray, S. L., Holmes, J. G., MacDonald, G., & Ellsworth, P. C. (1998). Through the looking glass darkly? When self-doubts turn into relationship insecurities. *Journal of Personality and Social Psychology, 75*, 1459–1480.

Muter, P. (1978). Recognition failure of recallable words in semantic memory. *Memory & Cognition, 6*(1), 9–12.

Muthuraman, M., Fleischer, V., Kolber, P., Luessi, F., Zipp, F., & Groppa, S. (2016). Structural brain network characteristics can differentiate CIS from early RRMS. *Frontiers in Neuroscience, 10*, 14. doi: 10.3389/fnins.2016.00014

Muzur, A. (2014). The nature of bioethics revisited: A comment on Tomislav Bracanović. *Developing World Bioethics, 14*: 109–110. doi: 10.1111/dewb.12008.

Nadeau, K. G., Quinn, P., & Littman, E. (2001). *AD/HD self-rating scale for girls.* Springfield, MD: Advantage Books.

Nagahara, T., Saitoh, T., Kutsumura, N., Irukayama-Tomobe, Y., Ogawa, Y., Kuroda, D., . . . Nagase, H. (2015). Design and synthesis of non-peptide, selective orexin receptor 2 agonists. *Journal of Medicinal Chemistry*, 58(20), 7931. doi: 10.1021/acs.jmedchem.5b00988

Nairne J. S. (2015). Adaptive memory: Novel findings acquired through forward engineering. In D. S. Lindsay, C. M. Kelley, A. P. Yonelinas, & H. L. Roediger (Eds.). *Remembering: Attributions, processes, and control in human memory*. New York: Psychology Press.

Naitoh, P., Kelly, T. L., & Englund, C. E. (1989). *Health effects of sleep deprivation* (Naval Health Research Centre, Rep. No. 89–46), San Diego, CA: NHRC.

Najavits, L. M. (2007). Psychosocial treatments for postraumatic stress disorder. In P. E. Nathan & J. M. Gorman (Eds.), *A guide to treatments that work* (3rd ed., pp. 513–530). New York: Oxford University Press.

Naqvi, R., Liberman, D., Rosenberg, J., Alston, J., & Straus, S. (2013). Preventing cognitive decline in healthy older adults. *Canadian Medical Association Journal*, 185(10) 881–885,

Nasar, S. (1998). *A beautiful mind: A biography of John Forbes Nash, Jr., winner of the Nobel Prize in economics 1994*. New York: Simon & Schuster.

Nathan, P. E., & Gorman, J. M. (2007). *Psychosocial treatments for postraumatic stress disorder* (3rd ed.). New York: Oxford University Press.

National Academy of Neuropsychology. (May, 2001). NAN definition of a clinical neuropsychologist [Electronic version]. Retrieved April 13, 2010, from http://www.nanonline.org/NAN/Files/PAIC/PDFs/NANPositionDefNeuro.pdf

National Center for Health Statistics. (2015). Deaths: Final data for 2013. *National Vital Statistics Report*, 64(2), 1–119. Hyattsville, MD. Retrieved from www.cdc.gov/nchs/data/nvsr/nvsr64/nvsr64_02.pd

National Collegiate Athletic Association (2002). 2002 NCAA graduation rates report. Retrieved September 21, 2007, from NCAA—The National Collegiate Athletic Association: The online resource for the National Collegiate Athletic Association Web site: Retrieved from http://web1.ncaa.org/web_files/grad_rates/2002/index.html

National Commission for the Protection of Human Subjects of Biomedical and Behavioral Research. (2006). Fetal viability and death: United States. Retrieved April 26, 2013, from https://scholarworks.iupui.edu/bitstream/handle/1805/583/OS76-127_VII.pdf?sequence=1

National Institute of Mental Health (NIMH). (2010). The numbers count: Mental disorders in America. Retrieved from http://www.nimh.nih.gov/health/publications/the-numbers-count-mental-disorders-in-america/index.shtml

National Institute of Mental Health. (2013). Statistics Retrieved May 14, 2013, from http://www.nimh.nih.gov/statistics/index.shtml

National Institute of Mental Health. (2016). Statistics. Retrieved from http://www.nimh.nih.gov/statistics/index.shtml

National Institute of Mental Health (NIMH) Genetics Workgroup. (1998). *Genetics and mental disorders* (NIH Publication No. 98-4268). Rockville, MD: National Institute of Mental Health.

National Institute of Neurological Disorders and Stroke. (2015). NINDS sleep apnea information page. Retrieved from http://www.ninds.nih.gov/disorders/sleep_apnea/sleep_apnea.htm

National Institute on Alcohol Abuse and Alcoholism (NIAAA). (2016). Alcohol facts and statistics. Retrieved from http://pubs.niaaa.nih.gov/publications/AlcoholFacts&Stats/AlcoholFacts&Stats.htm

National Institute on Drug Abuse (NIDA). (2002). Research report series—Prescription drugs: Abuse and addiction. National Institutes of Health (NIH). Retrieved July 19, 2008, from www.drugabuse.gov/ResearchReports/Prescription/prescription5.html

National Institute on Drug Abuse. (2016). NIDA DrugFacts: Hallucinogens. Retrieved January 18 from https://www.drugabuse.gov/publications/drugfacts/hallucinogens

National Institute on Drug Abuse. (2016). NIDA DrugFacts: Hallucinogens. Retrieved from https://www.drugabuse.gov/publications/drugfacts/hallucinogens

National Institutes of Health; National Heart, Lung and Blood Institute. (2011). *Your guide to healthy sleep*. NIH Publication No. 06-5271.

National Safety Council. (2015). Annual estimate of cell phone crashes 2013. Retrieved from http://www.nsc.org/DistractedDrivingDocuments/Cell-Phone-Estimate-Summary-2013.pdf

National Sleep Foundation. (2009). Can't sleep? What to know about insomnia. Retrieved May 5, 2010, from http://www.sleepfoundation.org/article/sleep-related-problems/insomnia-and-sleep

Neale, M. C., Rushton, J. P., & Fulker, D. W. (1986). The heritability of items from the Eysenck Personality Questionnaire. *Personality and Individual Differences*, 7, 771–779.

Neary, N. M., Goldstone, A. P., & Bloom, S. R. (2004). Appetite regulations: From the gut to the hypothalamus. *Clinical Endocrinology*, 60(2), 153–160.

Ne'eman, R., Perach-Barzilay, N., Fischer-Shofty, M., Atias, A., & Shamay-Tsoory, S. G. (2016). Intranasal administration of oxytocin increases human aggressive behavior. *Hormones and Behavior*. doi: http://dx.doi.org/10.1016/j.yhbeh.2016.01.015

Neimark, J. (1996). The diva of disclosure, memory researcher Elizabeth Loftus. *Psychology Today*, 29(1), 48–80.

Neimeyer, R. A., & Mitchell, K. A. (1998). Similarity and attraction: A longitudinal study. *Journal of Social and Personality Relationships*, 5, 131–148.

Neisser, U. (1982). Snapshots or benchmarks? In U. Neisser (Ed.), *Memory observed: Remembering in natural contexts* (pp. 43–48). San Francisco: W. H. Freeman.

Neisser, U., Boodoo, G., Bouchard, T. J., Boykin, A. W., Brody, N., Ceci, S. J., . . . Urbina, S. (1996). Intelligence: Knowns and unknowns. *American Psychologist*, 51, 77–101.

Neisser, U., & Harsch, N. (1992). Phantom flashbulbs: False recollections of hearing the news about *Challenger*. In E. Winograd & U. Neisser (Eds.), *Affect and accuracy in recall: Studies of "flashbulb memories"* (pp. 9–31). New York: Cambridge University Press.

Nelson, C. A. (2011). Brain development and behavior. In A. M. Rudolph, C. Rudolph, L. First, G. Lister, & A. A. Gershon (Eds.), *Rudolph's pediatrics* (22nd ed.). New York: McGraw-Hill.

Nelson, D. B., Hanlon, A. L., Wu, G., Liu, C., & Fredricks, D. N. (2015). First trimester levels of BV-associated bacteria and risk of miscarriage among women early in pregnancy. *Maternal and Child Health Journal*, 19(12), 2682–2687.

Nelson, K. (1993). The psychological and social origins of autobiographical memory. *Psychological Science*, 4, 7–14.

Nelson, L. J., Padilla-Walker, L. M., Badger, S., Barry, C. M., Carroll, J., & Madsen, S. (2008). Associations between shyness and internalizing behaviors, externalizing behaviors, and relationships during emerging adulthood. *Journal of Youth and Adolescence*, 37, 605–615.

Nestor, P. G., Kubicki, M., Niznikiewicz, M., Gurrera, R. J., McCarley, R. W., & Shenton, M. E. (2008). Neuropsychological disturbance in schizophrenia: A diffusion tensor imaging study. *Neuropsychology*, 22(2), 246–254.

Neto, F. (1995). Conformity and independence revisited. *Social Behavior and Personality*, 23(3), 217–222.

Neumarker, K. (1997). Mortality and sudden death in anorexia nervosa. *International Journal of Eating Disorders*, 21, 205–212.

Neville, H. J., & Bavelier, D. (2000). Specificity and plasticity in neurocognitive development in humans. In M. S. Gazzaniga (Ed.), *The New Cognitive Neurosciences* (2nd ed., pp. 83–99). Cambridge, MA: MIT Press.

Ng, M., Fleming, T., Robinson, M., Thomson, B., Graetz, N., Margono, C., . . . & Gakidou, E. (2014). Global, regional, and national prevalence of overweight and obesity in children and adults during 1980–2013: A systematic analysis for the Global Burden of Disease Study 2013. *The Lancet*, 384(9945), 766–781.

Ngun, T. C., & Vilain, E. (2014). The biological basis of human sexual orientation: Is there a role for epigenetics? *Advances in Genetics*, 86, 167–184. doi: 10.1016/B978-0-12-800222-3.00008-5

Nicholson, N., Cole, S., & Rocklin, T. (1985). Conformity in the Asch situation: A comparison between contemporary British and U.S. students. *British Journal of Social Psychology*, 24, 59–63.

Nickell, J. 1995. Crop circle mania wanes: An investigative update. *Skeptical Inquirer*, 19(3), 41–43.

Nickerson, R. S., & Adams, J. J. (1979). Long-term memory for a common object. *Cognitive Psychology*, 11, 287–307.

Niedermeyer, E. (2005). Historical aspects. In E. Niedermeyer & F. Lopes da Silva (Eds.), *Electroencephalography: Basic principles, clinical applications, and related fields* (5th ed., pp. 1–15). Philadelphia: Lippincott, Williams & Wilkins.

Nielsen, M., Suddendorf, T., & Slaughter, V. (2006). Mirror self-recognition beyond the face. *Child Development*, 77(1), 176–185. doi: 10.1111/j.1467-8624.2006.00863.x

Nieto, F., Young, T. B., Lind, B. K., Shahar, E., Samet, J. M., Redline, S., . . . Pickering, T. G. (2000). Association of sleep-disordered breathing, sleep apnea, and hypertension in a large, community-based study. *Journal of the American Medical Association*, 283(14), 1829–1836.

Nievar, M. A., Moske, A. K., Johnson, D. J., & Chen, Q. (2015). Parenting practices in preschool leading to later cognitive competencies: A family stress model. *Early Education and Development*, 25, 318–337.

Nigg, J. T. (2006). *What causes ADHD? Understanding what goes wrong and why*. New York, NY: The Guilford Press.

Nigg, J. T. (2010). Attention-Deficit/Hyperactivity Disorder: Endophenotypes, structure, and etiological pathways. *Current Directions in Psychological Science*, 19(1), 24–29.

Nigg, J. T., Elmore, A. L., Natarajan, N., Friderici, K. H., & Nikolas, M. A. (2016). Variation in an iron metabolism gene moderates the association between blood lead levels and attention-deficit/hyperactivity disorder in children. *Psychological Science*, 27(2), 257–269. doi: 10.1177/0956797615618365

Nihei, Y., Takahashi, K., Koto, A., Mihara, B., Morita, Y., Isozumi, K., . . . Suzuki, N. (2012). REM sleep behavior disorder in Japanese patients with Parkinson's disease: A multicenter study using the REM sleep behavior disorder screening questionnaire. *Journal of Neurology*, 259(8), 1606–1612.

Nijenhuis, E. R. (2000). Somatoform dissociation: Major symptoms of dissociative disorders. *Journal of Trauma and Dissociation*, 1(4), 7–29.

Nikolajsen, L., & Jensen, T. S. (2001). Phantom limb pain. *British Journal of Anaesthesia*, 87, 107–116.

Nisbett, R. E. (1972). Hunger, obesity, and the ventromedial hypothalamus. *Psychological Review*, 79, 433–453.

Nisbett, R. E., Aronson, J., Blair, C., Dickens, W., Flynn, J., Halpern, D. F., & Turkheimer, E. (2012). Intelligence: New findings and theoretical developments. *American Psychologist, 67*(2), 130–159. doi: 10.1037/a0026699

Nitsche, M. A., Boggio, P. S., Fregni, F., & Pascual-Leone, A. (2009). Treatment of depression with transcranial direct current stimulation (tDCS): A review. *Experimental Neurology, 219*(1), 14–19.

Nokia, M. S., Lensu, S., Ahtiainen, J. P., Johansson, P. P., Koch, L. G., Britton, S. L., & Kainulainen, H. (2016). Physical exercise increases adult hippocampal neurogenesis in male rats provided it is aerobic and sustained. *Journal of Physiology.* doi: 10.1113/JP271552

Nolen-Hoeksema, S. (1990). *Sex differences in depression.* Palo Alto, CA: Stanford University Press.

Nolen-Hoeksema, S. (2012). Emotion regulation and psychopathology: The role of gender. *Annual Review of Clinical Psychology, 8,* 161–187. doi: 10.1146/annurev-clinpsy-032511-143109

Nooyens, A. C. J., Baan, C. A., Spijkerman, A. M. W., & Verschuren, W. M. M. (2010). *Type 2 diabetes mellitus and cognitive decline in middle-aged men and women—The Doetinchem Cohort Study.* American Diabetes Association: Diabetes Care.

Norcross, J. C. (2005). A primer on psychotherapy integration. In J. C. Norcross & M. R. Goldfried (Eds.), *Handbook of psychotherapy integration* (2nd ed., pp. 3–23). New York: Oxford University Press.

Nordenskjold, A., von Knorring, L., & Engstrom, I. (2011). Predictors of time to relapse/recurrence after electroconvulsive therapy in patients with major depressive disorder: A population-based cohort study. *Depression Research and Treatment, 2011,* 470985. doi: 10.1155/2011/470985

Norenzayan, A., Choi, I., & Nisbett, R. E. (1999). Eastern and Western perceptions of causality for social behavior: Lay theories about personalities and situations. In D. A. Prentice & D. T. Miller (Eds.), *Cultural divides* (pp. 239–272). New York: Russell Sage Foundation.

Norrbrink Budh, C., Lund, I., Hultling, C., Levi, R., Werhagen, L., Ertzgaard, P., & Lundeberg, T. (2003). Gender-related differences in pain in spinal cord injured individuals. *Spinal Cord, 41,* 122–128.

Nosek, B. A., Greenwald, A. G., & Banaji, M. R. (2007). The Implicit Association Test at age 7: A methodological and conceptual review. In J. A. Bargh (Ed.), *Automatic processes in social thinking and behavior* (pp. 265–292). New York: Psychology Press.

Nosek, B. A., Spies, J. R., & Motyl, M. (2012). Scientific utopia: Ii. Restructuring incentives and practices to promote truth over publishability. *Perspectives on Psychological Science, 7*(6), 615–631. doi: 10.1177/1745691612459058

Nosich, G. M. (2008). *Learning to think things through: A guide to critical thinking across the curriculum* (3rd ed., pp. 2–16). Upper Saddle River, NJ: Prentice-Hall.

Novak, J. D. (1995). Concept maps to facilitate teaching and learning. *Prospects, 25,* 95–11.

Novak, M., Björck, L., Giang, K. W., Heden-Ståhl, C., Wilhelmsen, L., & Rosengren, A. (2013). Perceived stress and incidence of Type 2 diabetes: A 35-year follow-up study of middle-aged Swedish men. *Diabetic Medicine, 30*(1), e8. doi: 10-1111/dme.12037

Novella, S. (2007, November/December). The Anti-Vaccination Movement. *Skeptical Inquirer.* Retrieved May 21, 2010, from http://www.csicop.org/si/show/anti-vaccination_movement/www.guardian.co.uk/science/2007/feb/24/badscience.uknews

Novotney, A. (2013, March). I/O psychology goes to Mars. *Monitor on Psychology, 44*(3), 38.

Nussbaum, A. D., & Dweck, C. S. (2008). Defensiveness vs. remediation: Self-theories and modes of self-esteem maintenance. *Personality and Social Psychology Bulletin, 34,* 599–612.

Nuttin, B., Wu, H., Mayberg, H., Hariz, M., Gabriels, L., Galert, T., . . . Schlaepfer, T. (2014). Consensus on guidelines for stereotactic neurosurgery for psychiatric disorders. *Journal of Neurology, Neurosurgery, & Psychiatry, 85*(9), 1003–1008. doi: 10.1136/jnnp-2013-306580

Nyberg, L., & Tulving, E. (1996). Classifying human long-term memory: Evidence from converging dissociations. *European Journal of Cognitive Psychology, 8*(2), 163–183.

Oberman, L. M., & Ramachandran, V. S. (2007). The simulating social mind: The role of simulation in the social and communicative deficits of autism spectrum disorders, *Psychological Bulletin, 133,* 310–327.

Ocholla-Ayayo, A. B. C., Wekesa, J. M., & Ottieno, J. A. M. (1993). *Adolescent pregnancy and its implications among ethnic groups in Kenya.* In International Population Conference, Montreal, Canada: International Union for the Scientific Study of Population, 1: 381–395.

Ochsner, K., & Kosslyn, S. M. (1994). Mental imagery. In V. S. Ramaschandran (Ed.), *Encyclopedia of human behavior.* New York: Academic Press.

Ocklenburg, S., Beste, C., & Gunturkun, O. (2013). Handedness: A neurogenetic shift of perspective. *Neuroscience and Biobehavioral Reviews, 37*(10 Pt 2), 2788–2793. doi: 10.1016/j.neubiorev.2013.09.014

O'Connor, R. D. (1972). Relative efficacy of modeling, shaping, and the combined procedures for modification of social withdrawal. *Journal of Abnormal Psychology, 79,* 327–334.

Offit, P. A., & Bell, L. M. (1998). *What every parent should know about vaccines.* New York: Macmillan.

Ogden, C. L., Carroll, M. D., Kit, B. K., & Flegal, K. (2014). Prevalence of childhood and adult obesity in the United States, 2011–2012. *The Journal of the American Medical Association, 311*(8), 806–814.

Ohayon, M. M., Priest, R. G., Caulet, M., & Guilleminault, C. (1996). Hypnagogic and hypnopompic hallucinations: pathological phenomena? *British Journal of Psychiatry, 169,* 459–67.

Öhman, A. (2008). Fear and anxiety. In M. Lewis, J. M. Haviland-Jones & L. F. Barrett (Eds.), *Handbook of emotion* (3rd ed., pp. 709–729). New York: Guiford Press.

Okami, P., & Shackelford, T. K. (2001). Human sex differences in sexual psychology and behavior. *Annual Review of Sex Research, 12,* 186–241.

O'Keefe, D. J. (2009). Theories of persuasion. In R. L. Nabi & M. B. Oliver (Eds.), *The Sage handbook of media processes and effects* (pp. 277–278). Los Angeles: Sage.

Olin, B. R., (Ed.). (1993). Central nervous system drugs, sedatives and hypnotics, barbiturates. In *Facts and comparisons drug information* (pp. 1398–1413). St. Louis, MO: Facts and Comparisons.

Oliver, J. E. (1993). Intergenerational transmission of child abuse: Rates, research, and clinical interpretations. *American Journal of Psychiatry, 150,* 1315–1324.

Ollendick, T. H., & King, N. J. (1998). Empirically supported treatments for children with phobic and anxiety disorders: Current status. *Journal of Clinical Child Psychology, 27*(2), 156–167.

Olsen, P. (1975). *Emotional flooding.* Baltimore, MD: Penguin Books.

Olson, H. C., & Burgess, D. M. (1997). Early intervention for children prenatally exposed to alcohol and other drugs. In M. J. Guralnick (Ed.), *The effectiveness of early intervention* (pp. 109–146). Baltimore: Brookes.

Olulade, O. A., Jamal, N. I., Koo, D. S., Perfetti, C. A., LaSasso, C., & Eden, G. F. (2015). Neuroanatomical evidence in support of the bilingual advantage theory. *Cerebral Cortex.* doi: 10.1093/cercor/bhv152

Olver, J. S., Pinney, M., Maruff, P., & Norman, T. R. (2015). Impairments of spatial working memory and attention following acute psychosocial stress. *Stress and Health, 31,* 115–123.

Oman, C. M. (1990). Motion sickness: A synthesis and evaluation of the sensory conflict theory. *Canadian Journal of Physiological Pharmacology, 68,* 294–303.

Onken, L. S., Blaine, J. D., & Battjes, R. J. (1997). Behavioral therapy research: A conceptualization of a process. In S. W. Henggeler & A. B. Santos (Eds.), *Innovative approaches for difficult-to-treat populations* (pp. 477–485). Washington, DC: American Psychiatric Press.

Open Science Collaboration. (2015). Estimating the reproducibility of psychological science. *Science, 349*(6251), aac4716. DOI 10.1126/science.aac4716

Ophir, E., Nass, C., & Wagner, A. D. (2009). Cognitive control in media multitaskers. *Proceedings of the National Academy of Sciences of the United States of America, 106*(37), 15583–15587.

Osborne, J. W. (2007). Linking stereotype threat and anxiety. *Educational Psychology, 27,* 135–154.

Osshera, L., Flegala, K. E., & Lustiga, C. (2012). Everyday memory errors in older adults. *Aging, Neuropsychology, and Cognition, 20*(2), 220–242. doi: 10.1080/13825585.2012.690365

Oster, J. R. (1987). The binge-purge syndrome: A common albeit unappreciated cause of acid-base and fluid-electrolyte disturbances. *Southern Medical Journal, 80,* 58–67.

Österman, K., Björkqvist, K., & Wahlbeck, K. (2014). Twenty-eight years after the complete ban on the physical punishment of children in Finland: Trends and psychosocial concomitants. *Aggressive Behavior, 40*(6), 568–581.

Oswald, I. (1959). Sudden bodily jerks on falling asleep. *Brain, 82,* 92–103.

Ottaway, N., Mahbod, P., Rivero, B., Norman, L. A., Gertler, A., D'Alessio, D. A., & Perez-Tilve, D. (2015). Diet-induced obese mice retain endogenous leptin action. *Cell Metabolism, 21*(6), 877–882.

Oudiette, D., Antony, J. W., Creery, J. D., & Paller, K. A. (2013). The role of memory reactivation during wakefulness and sleep in determining which memories endure. *Journal of Neuroscience, 33*(15), 6672. doi: 10.1523/JNEUROSCI.5497-12.2013

Overeem, S., Mignot, E., Gert van Dijk, J., & Lammers, G. J. (2001). Narcolepsy: Clinical features, new pathophysiological insights, and future perspectives. *Journal of Clinical Neurophysiology, 18*(2), 78–105.

Overmier, J. B., & Seligman, M. E. P. (1967). Effects of inescapable shock on subsequent escape and avoidance behavior. *Journal of Comparative Physiology and Psychology, 63,* 23–33.

Owen, A. M., Hampshire, A., Grahn, J. A., Stenton, R., Dajani, S., Burns, A. S., . . . Ballard, C. G. (2010). Putting brain training to the test. *Nature, 465*(7299), 775–778. doi: 10.1038/nature09042

Owen, M. T., Easterbrooks, M. A., Chase-Lansdale, L., & Goldberg, W. A. (1984). The relation between maternal employment status and the stability of attachments to mother and to father. *Child Development, 55,* 1894–1901.

Ozer, D. J., & Benet-Martinez, V. (2006). Personality and the prediction of consequential outcomes. *Annual Review of Psychology, 57,* 401–421. doi: 10.1146/annurev.psych.57.102904.190127

Paap, K. R. (2014). The role of componential analysis, categorical hypothesising, replicability and confirmation bias in testing for bilingual advantages in executive functioning. *Journal of Cognitive Psychology, 26*(3), 242–255. doi: 10.1080/20445911.2014.891597

Paap, K. R., & Greenberg, Z. I. (2013). There is no coherent evidence for a bilingual advantage in executive processing. *Cognitive Psychology, 66*, 232–258. doi: 10.1016/j.cogpsych.2012.12.002

Paap, K. R., Johnson, H. A., & Sawi, O. (2014). Are bilingual advantages dependent upon specific tasks or specific bilingual experiences? *Journal of Cognitive Psychology, 26*(6), 615–639. doi: 10.1080/20445911.2014.944914

Palacios-Ceña, D., Carrasco-Garrido, P., Hernandez-Barrera, V., Alonso-Blanco, C., Jiménez-Garcia, R., & Fernández-de-Las-Peñas, C. (2011). Sexual behaviors among older adults in Spain: Results form a population-based national sexual health survey. *Journal of Sexual Medicine, 9*(1), 121–129.

Palmatier, J. J., & Rovner, L. (2015). Credibility assessment: Preliminary process theory, the polygraph process, and construct validity. *International Journal of Psychophysiology, 95*(1), 3–13.

Palmer, S. E. (1992). Common region: A new principle of perceptual grouping. *Cognitive Psychology, 24*(3), 436–447.

Palva, J. M., Monto, S., Kulashekhar, S., & Palva, S. (2010). Neuronal synchrony reveals working memory networks and predicts individual memory capacity. *Proceedings of the National Academy of Sciences, USA, 107*(16), 7580–7585.

Pan, A. S. (2000). Body image, eating attitudes, and eating behaviors among Chinese, Chinese-American and non-Hispanic White women. *Dissertation Abstracts International, Section B: The Sciences and Engineering, 61*(1–B), 544.

Pan, H., Guo, J., & Su, Z. (2014). Advances in understanding the interrelations between leptin resistance and obesity. *Physiology & Behavior 130*, 157–169.

Pant, H., McCabe, B. J., Deskovitz, M. A., Weed, N. C., & Williams, J. E. (2014). Diagnostic reliability of MMPI-2 computer-based test interpretations. *Psychological Assessment, 26*(3), 916–924. doi: 10.1037/a0036469

Paparelli, A., Di Forti, M., Morrison, P. D., & Murray, R. M. (2011). Drug-induced psychosis: How to avoid star gazing in schizophrenia research by looking at more obvious sources of light. *Frontiers in Behavioral Neuroscience, 5*: 1. doi: 10.3389/fnbeh.2011.00001

Parent, A., Teilmann, G., Juul, A., Skakkebaek, N. E., Toppari, J., & Bourguignon, J. P. (2003). The timing of normal puberty and age limits of sexual precocity: Variations around the world, secular trends, and changes after migration. *Endocrine Reviews, 24*(5), 668–693.

Pargament, K. I. (1997). *The psychology of religion and coping: Theory, research, and practice.* New York: Guilford Press.

Park, J., Turnbull, A. P., & Turnbull, H. R. (2002). Impacts of poverty on quality of life in families of children with disabilities. *Exceptional Children, 68*, 151–170.

Parkes, C. M., Laungani, P., & Young, W. (1997). *Death and bereavement across cultures.* Routledge: New York.

Parkinson, W. L., & Weingarten, H. P. (1990). Dissociative analysis of ventromedial hypothalamic obesity syndrome. *American Journal of Physiology: Regulatory, Integrative, and Comparative Physiology, 259*, R829–R835.

Parsons, H. M. (1992). Hawthorne: An early OBM experiment. *Journal of Organizational Behavior Management, 12*(1), 27–43.

Partnership for Drug-Free Kids. (2014). The medicine abuse project: 2014 report. Retrieved from http://medicineabuseproject.org/assets/documents/MAP_2014_Report_final.pdf

Partonen, T., & Lonnqvist, J. (1998). Seasonal affective disorder. *Lancet, 352*(9137), 1369–1374.

Pashkow, F. J. (2011). Oxidative stress and inflammation in heart disease: Do antioxidants have a role in treatment and/or prevention? International Journal of Inflammation, 2011, Article ID 514623.

Patel, A., Yamashita, N., Ascaño, M., Bodmer, D., Boehm, E., Bodkin-Clarke, C., . . . Kuruvilla, R. (2015). RCAN1 links impaired neurotrophin trafficking to aberrant development of the sympathetic nervous system in Down syndrome. *Nature Communications, 6*, 10119.

Paul, B. M., ElvevÅg, B., Bokat, C. E., Weinberger, D. R., & Goldberg, T. E. (2005). Levels of processing effects on recognition memory in patients with schizophrenia. *Schizophrenia Research, 74*(1), 101–110.

Pavlov, I. P. (1906). The scientific investigation of the psychical faculties or processes in the higher animals. *Science, 24*, 613–619.

Pavlov, I. P. (1926). *Conditioned reflexes.* London: Oxford University Press.

Pavlov, I. P. (1927). *Conditioned Reflexes: An Investigation of the Physiological Activity of the Cerebral Cortex. Translated and Edited by G. V. Anrep.* London: Oxford University Press.

Peever, J., Luppi, P.-H., & Montplaisir, J. (2014). Breakdown in REM sleep circuitry underlies REM sleep behavior disorder. *Trends in Neurosciences, 37*(5), 279–288. doi: 10.1016/j.tins.2014.02.009

Peng, K., Ames, D. R., & Knowles, E. D. (2000). Culture and human inference: Perspectives from three traditions. In D. Matsumoto (Ed.) (2001). *The handbook of culture and psychology* (pp. 245–264). New York: Oxford University Press.

Peng, L., Verkhratsky, A., Gu, L., & Li, B. (2015). Targeting astrocytes in major depression. *Expert Review of Neurotherapeutics, 1–8.* doi: 10.1586/14737175.2015.1095094

Pennsylvania State University. (2014). Why plagiarism is wrong. Retrieved from http://tlt.psu.edu/plagiarism/student-tutorial/why-plagiarism-is-wrong/

Peplau, L. A., & Fingerhut, A. W. (2007). The close relationships of lesbians and gay men. *Annual Review of Psychology, 58*, 10.1–10.20.

Peplau, L. A., & Taylor, S. E. (1997). *Sociocultural perspectives in social psychology: Current readings.* Upper Saddle River, NJ: Prentice-Hall.

Pepperberg, I. M. (1998). Talking with Alex: Logic and speech in parrots. *Scientific American Presents: Exploring Intelligence, 9*(4), 60–65.

Pepperberg, I. M. (2007). Grey parrots do not always "parrot": The roles of imitation and phonological awareness in the creation of new labels from existing vocalizations. *Language Sciences, 29*(1), 1–13.

Perls, F. (1951). *Gestalt therapy.* New York: Julian Press.

Perls, F. (1969). *Gestalt therapy verbatim.* Moab, UT: Real People Press.

Perrin, S., & Spencer, C. (1980). The Asch effect—A child of its time. *Bulletin of the British Psychological Society, 33*, 405–406.

Perrin, S., & Spencer, C. P. (1981). Independence or conformity in the Asch experiment as a reflection of cultural and situational factors. *British Journal of Social Psychology, 20*(3), 205–209.

Perrine, D. M. (1997). *The chemistry of mind-altering drugs.* Washington, DC: American Chemical Society.

Perry, W. G., Jr. (1970). *Forms of intellectual and ethical development in the college years: A scheme.* New York: Holt, Rinehart, and Winston.

Peters, W. A. (1971). *A class divided.* Garden City, NY: Doubleday.

Peterson, C., & Park, N. (2010). What happened to self-actualization? *Perspectives on Psychological Science, 5*(3), 320–322.

Peterson, D. R. (1976). Need for the doctor of psychology degree in professional psychology. *American Psychologist, 31*, 792–798.

Peterson, D. R. (1982). Origins and development of the Doctor of Psychology concept. In G. R. Caddy, D. C. Rimm, N. Watson, & J. H. Johnson (Eds.), *Educating professional psychologists* (pp. 19–38). New Brunswick, NJ: Transaction Books.

Peterson, L. R., & Peterson, M. J. (1959). Short-term retention of individual items. *Journal of Experimental Psychology, 58*, 193–198.

Petersen, R. (2015). Can exercise prevent memory loss and improve cognitive function? *Mayo Clinic: Diseases and Conditions: Alzheimer's Disease.* Retrieved from http://www.mayoclinic.org/diseases-conditions/alzheimers-disease/expert-answers/alzheimers-disease/faq-20057881

Petit, D., Pennestri, M. H., Paquet, J., Desautels, A., Zadra, A., Vitaro, F., . . . Montplaisir, J. (2015). Childhood sleepwalking and sleep terrors: A longitudinal study of prevalence and familial aggregation. *JAMA Pediatrics, 169*(7), 653–658. doi: 10.1001/jamapediatrics.2015.127

Petitto, L. A., Holowka, S., Sergio, L. E., & Ostry, D. (2001). Language rhythms in baby hand movements. *Nature, 413*, 35.

Petitto, L. A., & Marentette, P. F. (1991). Babbling in the manual mode: Evidence for the ontogeny of language. *Science, 251*, 1493–1496.

Petri, H. (1996). *Motivation: Theory, research and application* (4th ed.). Belmont, CA: Wadsworth.

Petrides, G., Tobias, K. G., Kellner, C. H., & Rudorfer, M. V. (2011). Continuation and maintenance electroconvulsive therapy for mood disorders: A review of the literature. *Neuropsychobiology, 64*(3), 129–140. doi: 10.1159/000328943

Petrova, P. K., Cialdini, R. B., & Sills S., J. (2007). Compliance, consistency, and culture: Personal consistency and compliance across cultures. *Journal of Experimental Social Psychology 43*: 104–111.

Pettigrew, T. F., & Tropp, L. R. (2000). Does intergroup contact reduce prejudice? Recent meta-analytic findings. In S. Oskamp (Ed.), *Reducing prejudice and discrimination: Social psychological perspectives* (pp. 93–114). Mahwah, NJ: Erlbaum.

Petty, R., & Cacioppo, J. (1986). *Communication and persuasion: Central and peripheral routes to attitude change.* New York: Springer-Verlag.

Petty, R., & Cacioppo, J. (1996). *Attitudes and persuasion: Classic and contemporary approaches* (Reprint). Boulder, CO: Westview Press.

Petty, R. E. (1995). Attitude change. In A. Tesser (Ed.), *Advances in social psychology* (pp. 194–255). New York: McGraw-Hill.

Petty, R. E., & Briñol, P. (2015). Processes of social influence through attitude change. In E. Borgida & J. Bargh (Eds.), APA handbook of personality and social psychology (Vol.1), Attitudes and social cognition (pp. 509–545). Washington, DC: APA Books.

Petty, R. E., Wheeler, S. C., & Tormala, Z. L. (2003). Persuasion and attitude change. In T. Millon & M. J. Lerner (Eds.), *Handbook of psychology: Volume 5: Personality and social psychology* (pp. 353–382). Hoboken, NJ: John Wiley & Sons.

Pew Research Center. (2013). *The global divide on homosexuality.* Retrieved from http://www.pewglobal.org/files/2013/06/Pew-Global-Attitudes-Homosexuality-Report-FINAL-JUNE-4-2013.pdf

Pezdek, K., Finger, K., & Hodge, D. (1997). Planting false childhood memories: The role of event plausibility. *Psychological Science, 8*, 437–441

Pezdek, K., & Hodge, D. (1999). Planting false childhood memories in children: The role of event plausibility. *Child Development, 70*, 887–895.

Pfeiffer, W. M. (1982). Culture-bound syndromes. In I. Al-Issa (Ed.), *Culture and psychopathology* (pp. 201–218). Baltimore: University Park Press.

Phan, T., & Silove, D. (1999). An overview of indigenous descriptions of mental phenomena and the range of traditional healing practices amongst the Vietnamese. *Transcultural Psychiatry, 36*, 79–94.

Piaget, J. (1926). *The language and thought of the child*. New York: Harcourt Brace.

Piaget, J. (1952). *The origins of intelligence in children*. New York: W. W. Norton.

Piaget, J. (1962). *Play, dreams and imitation in childhood*. New York: W. W. Norton.

Piaget, J. (1983). Piaget's theory. In W. Kessen (Ed.), *Handbook of child psychology: Volume 1. Theoretical models of human development* (pp. 103–128). New York: Wiley.

Pilkington, J. (1998). "Don't try and make out that I'm nice": The different strategies women and men use when gossiping. In J. Coates (Ed.), *Language and gender: A reader* (pp. 254–269). Oxford, UK: Blackwell.

Pilon, M., Montplaisir, J., & Zadra, A. (2008). Precipitating factors of somnambulism: Impact of sleep deprivation and forced arousals. *Neurology, 70*: 2284–90.

Pinker, S. (1995). Language acquisition. In Gleitman and M. Liberman. (Eds.), *An invitation to cognitive science* (2nd ed., pp. 135–182). Cambridge, MA: MIT Press.

Pinker, S., & Bloom, P. (1990). Natural language and natural selection. *Behavioral and Brain Sciences, 13*(4), 707–784.

Pinsof, W. M., & Wynne, L. C. (1995). The efficacy of marital and family therapy: An empirical overview, conclusions, and recommendations. *Journal of Marital and Family Therapy, 21*, 585–613.

Pittenger, D. J. (2005). Cautionary comments regarding the Myers-Briggs Type Indicator. *Consulting Psychology Journal: Practice and Research, 57*(3), 210–221. doi: 10.1037/1065-9293.57.3.210

Plaks, J. E, Grant, H., & Dweck, C. S. (2005). Violations of implicit theories and the sense of prediction and control: Implications for motivated person perception. *Journal of Personality and Social Psychology, 88*, 245–262.

Plaut, D. C., & McClelland, J. L. (2010). Locating object knowledge in the brain: A critique of Bowers' (2009) attempt to revive the grandmother cell hypothesis. *Psychological Review, 117*, 284–288.

Pliatsikas, C., Moschopoulou, E., & Saddy, J. D. (2015). The effects of bilingualism on the white matter structure of the brain. *Proceedings of the National Academy of Sciences of the United States of America, 112*(5), 1334–1337. doi: 10.1073/pnas.1414183112

Plomin, R. (1994). The nature of nurture: The environment beyond the family. In R. Plomin (Ed.), *Genetics and experience: The interplay between nature and nurture* (pp. 82–107). Thousand Oaks, CA: Sage.

Plomin, R., & Deary, I. J. (2015). Genetics and intelligence differences: Five special findings. *Molecular Psychiatry, 20*, 98–108.

Plomin, R., & DeFries, J. C. (1998, May). Genetics of cognitive abilities and disabilities. *Scientific American*, 62–69.

Plomin, R., Owen, M. J., & McGuffin, P. (1994). The genetic basis of complex human behaviors. *Science, 264*(5166), 1733–1739.

Plomin, R., & Spinath, F. M. (2004). Intelligence: Genetics, genes, and genomics. *Journal of Personality and Social Psychology, 86*(1), 112–129.

Plomin, R. N. L., Pederson, G. E., McClearn, J. R., Nesselroade, C. S., & Bergman, H. F. (1988). EAS temperaments during the last half year of the life span: Twins reared apart and twins raised together. *Psychology of Aging, 4*, 43–50.

Plotkin, S., Fine, P., Eames, K., & Heymann, D. L. (2011). "Herd immunity": A rough guide. *Clinical Infectious Diseases, 52*(7), 911–916.

Plug, C., & Ross, H. E. (1994). The natural moon illusion: A multi-factor angular account. *Perception, 23*, 321–333.

Plum, F., & Posner, J. B. (1985). *The diagnosis of stupor and coma*. Philadelphia: F. A. Davis.

Poe, G. R., Walsh, C. M., & Bjorness, T. E. (2010). Cognitive neuroscience of sleep. In G. A. Kerkhof and H. P. A. van Dongen (Eds.), *Human Sleep and Cognition, 185*, 1–19. Oxford: Elsevier Science.

Polce-Lynch, M., Myers, B. J., Kilmartin, C. T., Forssmann-Falck, R., & Kliewer, W. (1998). Gender and age patterns in emotional expression, body image, and self-esteem: A qualitative analysis. *Sex Roles, 38*, 1025–1050.

Polderman, T. J. C., Benyamin, B., de Leeuw, C. A., Sullivan, P. F., van Bochoven, A., Visscher, P. M., & Posthuma, D. (2015). Meta-analysis of the heritability of human traits based on fifty years of twin studies. *Nature Genetics, 47*, 702–709.

Polewan, R. J., Vigorito, C. M., Nason, C. D., Block, R. A., & Moore, J. W. (2006). A cartesian reflex assessment of face processing. *Behavioral and Cognitive Neuroscience Reviews, 3*(5), 3–23.

Pollack, M. H., Simon, N. M., Fagiolini, A., Pitman, R., McNally, R. J., Nierenberg, A. A., . . . Otto, M. W. (2006). Persistent posttraumatic stress disorder following September 11 in patients with bipolar disorder. *Journal of Clinical Psychiatry, 67*(3), 394–399.

Pollitt, E., & Mathews, R. (1998). Breakfast and cognition: An integrative summary. *The American Journal of Clinical Nutrition, V67*: 804S–813S.

Pompili, M., Lester, D., Dominici, G., Longo, L., Marconi, G., Forte, A., . . . Girardi, P. (2013). Indications for electroconvulsive treatment in schizophrenia: A systematic review. *Schizophrenia Research, 146*(1–3), 1–9. doi: 10.1016/j.schres.2013.02.005

Pormerleau, C. S., & Pormerleau, O. F. (1994). Euphoriant effects of nicotine. *Tobacco Control, 3*, 374.

Posada, G., Lu, T., Trumbell, J., Kaloustian, G., Trudel, M., Plata, S. J., . . . Lay, K.-L. (2013). Is the secure base phenomenon evident here, there, and anywhere? A cross-cultural study of child behavior and experts' definitions. *Child Development, 84*, 1896–1905.

Posthuma, D., de Geus, E. J. C., & Deary, I. J. (2009). The genetics of intelligence. In T. E. Goldberg & D. R. Weinberger (Eds.), *The genetics of cognitive neuroscience*. Cambridge, MA: MIT Press.

Postman, L. (1975). Tests of the generality of the principle of encoding specificity. *Memory & Cognition, 3*, 663–672.

Poulin, M. J., Holman, E. A., & Buffone, A. (2012). The neurogenetics of nice: Receptor genes for oxytocin and vasopressin interact with threat to predict prosocial behavior. *Psychological Science, 23*(5), 446–452. doi: 10.1177/0956797611428471

Powers, M. H. (1984). A computer-assisted problem-solving method for beginning chemistry students. *The Journal of Computers in Mathematics and Science Teaching, 4*(1), 13–19.

Powell, R. A. (2010). Little Albert still missing. *American Psychologist, 65*(4), 299–300. doi: 10.1037/a0019288

Prakash, R. S., Voss, M. W., Erickson, K. I., & Kramer, A. F. (2015). Physical activity and cognitive vitality. *Annual Review of Psychology, 66*, 769–797. doi: 10.1146/annurev-psych-010814-015249

Pratkanis, A. R. (1992). The cargo-cult science of subliminal persuasion. *Skeptical Inquirer, 16*, 260–272.

Pratkanis, A. R., & Greenwald, A. G. (1988). Recent perspectives on unconscious processing: Still no marketing applications. *Psychology and Marketing, 5*, 337–353.

Pratt, J. A. (1991). Psychotropic drug tolerance and dependence: Common underlying mechanisms? In E. Pratt (Ed.), *The biological bases of drug tolerance and dependence* (pp. 2–28). London: Academic Press/Harcourt Brace Jovanovich.

Prause, N., & Graham, C. A. (2004). Asexuality: Classification and characterization. *Archives of Sexual Behavior, 36*(3), 341–356.

Preston, J. D., O'Neal, J. H., & Talaga, M. C. (2008). *Handbook of clinical psychopharmacology for therapists* (5th ed.). Oakland, CA: New Harbinger.

Priester, J. M., & Petty, R. E. (1995). Source attributions and persuasion: Perceived honesty as a determinant of message scrutiny. *Personality and Social Psychology Bulletin, 21*, 637–654.

Prigerson, H. G., Bierhals, A. J., Kasi, S. V., Reynolds, C. F., Shear, M. K., Day, N., . . . Jacobs, S. (1997). Traumatic grief as a risk factor for mental and physical morbidity. *American Journal of Psychiatry, 154I*, 616–623.

Pritchard, T. C. (2012). Gustatory system. In J. K. Mai & G. Paxinos (Eds.), *The human nervous system* (pp. 1187–1218). London, UK: Academic Press.

Prochaska, J. O., & Norcross, J. C. (2009). *Systems of psychotherapy: A transtheoretical analysis*. Belmont, CA: Brooks/Cole, Cengage Learning.

Prochaska, J. O., & Norcross, J. C. (2014). *Systems of psychotherapy: A transtheoretical analysis* (8th ed.). Stamford, CT: Cengage Learning.

Prot, S., Gentile, D. A., Anderson, C. A., Suzuki, K., Swing, E., Lim, K. M., . . . Lam, B. C. P. (2014). Long-term relations among prosocial-media use, empathy, and prosocial behavior. *Psychological Science, 25*(2), 358–368.

Przybylski, A. K., Deci, E. L., Rigby, C. S., & Ryan, R. M. (2014). Competence-impeding electronic games and players' aggressive feelings, thoughts, and behaviors. *Journal of Personality and Social Psychology, 106*(3), 441. doi: 10.1037/a0034820

Pullum, G. K. (1991). *The great Eskimo vocabulary hoax: And other irreverent essays on the study of language*. Chicago: University of Chicago Press.

Pumariega, A. J., & Gustavson, C. R. (1994). Eating attitudes in African-American women: The essence. *Eating Disorders: Journal of Treatment and Prevention, 2*, 5–16.

Purdy, D., Eitzen, D., & Hufnagel, R. (1982). Are athletes also students? The educational attainment of college athletes. *Social Problems, 29*, 439–448.

Puspitasari, A., Kanter, J. W., Murphy, J., Crowe, A., & Koerner, K. (2013). Developing an online, modular, active learning training program for behavioral activation. *Psychotherapy, 50*(2), 256–265. doi: 10.1037/a0030058

Putnam, S. P., & Stifter, C. A. (2002). Development of approach and inhibition in the first year: Parallel findings for motor behavior, temperament ratings and directional cardiac response. *Developmental Science, 5*, 441–451.

Puts, D. A., Jordan, C. L., & Breedlove, S. M. (2006). O brother, where art thou? The fraternal birth-order effect on male sexual orientation. *Proceedings of the National Academy of Sciences, USA, 103*(28), 10531–10532.

Pyc, M. A., Agarwal, P. K., & Roediger, H. L. (2014). Test-enhanced learning. In V. A. Benassi, C. E. Overson & C. M. Hakala (Eds.), *Applying the science of learning in education: Infusing psychological science into the curriculum*, pp. 78–90. Retrieved from the Society for the Teaching of Psychology web site: http://teachpsych.org/ebooks/asle2014/index.php.

Qin, J., Wang, H., Sheng, X., Liang, D., Tan, H., & Xia, J. (2015). Pregnancy-related complications and adverse pregnancy outcomes in multiple pregnancies resulting from assisted reproductive technology: A meta-analysis of cohort studies. *Fertility and Sterility, 103*, 1492–1508.

Quintero, J. E., Kuhlman, S. J., & McMahon, D. G. (2003). The biological clock nucleus: A multiphasic oscillator network regulated by light. *Journal of Neuroscience, 23*, 8070–8076.

Raaijmakers, J. G. W. (1993). The story of the two-store model of memory: Past criticisms, current status, and future directions. In D. E. Meyer & S. Kornblum (Eds.), *Attention and Performance. XIV (Silver Jubilee Volume)* (pp. 467–488). Cambridge, MA: MIT Press.

Raaijmakers, J. G. W., & Shiffrin, R. M. (1992). Models for recall and recognition. *Annual Review of Psychology, 43*, 205–234.

Raaijmakers, J. G. W., & Shiffrin, R. M. (2003). Models versus descriptions: Real differences and language differences. *Behavioral and Brain Sciences, 26*, 753.

Rabins, P., Appleby, B. S., Brandt, J., DeLong, M. R., Dunn, L. B., Gabriels, L., . . . & Matthews, D. J. (2009). Scientific and ethical issues related to deep brain stimulation for disorders of mood, behavior, and thought. *Archives of General Psychiatry, 66*(9), 931–937.

Rachman, S. (1990). The determinants and treatments of simple phobias. *Advances in Behavioral Research and Therapy, 12*(1), 1–30.

Rachman, S. J., & Hodgson, R. J. (1980). *Obsessions and compulsions.* Englewood Cliffs, NJ: Prentice Hall.

Racsmány, M., Conway, M. A., & Demeter, G. (2010). Consolidation of episodic memories during sleep: Long-term effects of retrieval practice. *Psychological Science, 21:* 80–85.

Raffin, E., Richard, N., Giraux, P., & Reilly, K. T. (2016). Primary motor cortex changes after amputation correlate with phantom limb pain and the ability to move the phantom limb. *Neuroimage, 130,* 134–144. doi: 10.1016/j.neuroimage.2016.01.063

Rahman, Q., & Yusuf, S. (2015). Lateralization for processing facial emotions in gay men, heterosexual men and heterosexual women. *Archives of Sexual Behavior, 44*(5), 1405–1413.

Rai, R., Mitchell, P., Kadar, T., & Mackenzie, L. (2014). Adolescent egocentrism and the illusion of transparency: Are adolescents as egocentric as we might think? *Psychological Studies, 67*(1), 58–66.

Raikkonen, K., Matthews, K. A., & Salomon, K. (2003). Hostility predicts metabolic syndrome risk factors in children and adolescents. *Health Psychology, 22,* 279–286.

Rainforth, M. V., Schneider, R. H., Nidich, S. I., Gaylord-King, C., Salerno, J. W., & Anderson, J. W. (2007). Stress reduction programs in patients with elevated blood pressure: A systematic review and meta-analysis. *Current Hypertension Reports, 9,* 520–528.

Rakoff-Nahoum, S. (2006). Why cancer and inflammation? Yale *Journal of Biology and Medicine, 79*(3–4), 123–130.

Ramachandran, V. S., & Blakeslee, S. (1998). *Phantoms in the brain.* New York: Quill William Morrow.

Ramdhonee, K., & Bhowon, U. (2012). Acculturation strategies, personality traits and acculturation stress: A study of first generation immigrants from transnational marital context. *Psychology & Developing Societies, 24*(2), 125–143.

Ramón y Cajal, S. (1995.) *Histology of the nervous system of man and vertebrates.* New York: Oxford University Press. English translation by N. Swanson and L. M. Swanson.

Ramos, M. R., Cassidy, C., Reicher, S., & Haslam, S. A. (2015). Well-being in cross-cultural transitions: Discrepancies between acculturation preferences and actual intergroup and intragroup contact. *Journal of Applied social Psychology, 45*(1), 23–34.

Rangmar, J., Hjern, A., Vinnerljung, B., Strömland, K., Aronson, M., & Fahlke, C. (2015). Psychosocial outcomes of fetal alcohol syndrome in adulthood. Pediatrics, 135, e52–e58.

Ranke, M. B., & Saenger, P. (2001, July 28). Turner's syndrome. *Lancet, 358*(9278), 309–314.

Rao, S. C., Rainer, G., & Miller, E. K. (1997). Integration of what and where in the primate prefrontal cortex. *Science, 276,* 821–824.

Rapoport, J. L., Addington, A. M., Frangou, S., & Psych, M. R. (2005). The neurodevelopmental model of schizophrenia: Update 2005. *Molecular Psychiatry, 10*(5), 434–449. doi: 10.1038/sj.mp.4001642

Rapoport, J. L., Giedd, J. N., & Gogtay, N. (2012). Neurodevelopmental model of schizophrenia: Update 2012. *Molecular Psychiatry, 17*(12), 1228–1238. doi: 10.1038/mp.2012.23

Raposa, E. B., Bower, J. E., Hammen, C. L., Najman, J. M., & Brennan, P. A. (2014). A developmental pathway from early life stress to inflammation the role of negative health behaviors. *Psychological Science, 25,* 1268–1274.

Rasenberger, J. (2006). Nightmare on Austin Street. *American Heritage Magazine, 57*(5). Retrieved July 8, 2010, from http://www.americanheritage.com/articles/magazine/ah/2006/5/2006_5_65.shtml

Ratey, J. J., & Hagerman, E. (2008). *Spark: The revolutionary new science of exercise and the brain.* New York: Little, Brown.

Ratiu, P., Talos, I. F., Haker, S., Lieberman, D., & Everett, P. (2004). The tale of Phineas Gage, digitally remastered. *Journal of Neurotrauma, 21*(5), 637–643. doi: 10.1089/089771504774129964

Rauch, S. L., Shin, L. M., & Wright, C. I. (2003). Neuroimaging studies of amygdala function in anxiety disorders. *Annals of the New York Academy of Sciences, 985,* 389–410.

Raynor, H. A., & Epstein, L. H. (2001). Dietary variety, energy regulation and obesity. *Psychological Bulletin, 127*(3), 325–341.

Reason, J. T., & Brand, J. J. (1975). *Motion sickness.* London: Academic Press.

Reece, M., Herbenick, D., Schick, V., Sanders, S. A., Dodge, B., & Fortenberry, J. D. (2010). Condom use rates in a national probability sample of males and females ages 14 to 94 in the united states. *Journal of Sexual Medicine, 7*(Suppl 5), 266–276.

Rechtschaffen, A., & Kales, A. (1968). *A manual of standardized terminology, techniques, and scoring system for sleep stages of human subjects.* U.S. Department of Health, Education, and Welfare Public Health Service - NIH/NIND.

Redick, T. S. (2015). Working memory training and interpreting interactions in intelligence interventions. *Intelligence, 50,* 14–20. doi: 10.1016/j.intell.2015.01.014

Reese, H. W. (2010). Regarding Little Albert. *American Psychologist, 65*(4), 300–301. doi: 10.1037/a0019332

Reichborn-Kjennerud, T. (2008). Genetics of personality disorders. *Psychiatric Clinics of North America, 31,* 421.

Reichborn-Kjennerud, T., Czajkowski, N., Neale, M. C., Orstavik, R. E., Torgersen, S., Tambs, K., . . . Kendler, K. S. (2007). Genetic and environmental influences on dimensional representations of DSM-IV cluster C personality disorders: A population-based multivariate twin study. *Psychological Medicine, 37*(5), 645–653. doi: 10.1017/s0033291706009548

Reicher, S. D., Haslam, S. A., & Smith, J. R. (2012). Working toward the experimenter: Reconceptualizing obedience within the Milgram paradigm as identification-based followership. *Perspectives on Psychological Science, 7*(4), 315–324. doi: 10.1177/1745691612448482

Reinders, A., Quak, J., Nijenhuis, E. R., Korf, J., Paans, A. M., Willemsen, A. T., & den Boer, J. A. (2001, June). *Identity state-dependent processing of neutral and traumatic scripts in dissociative identity disorder as assessed by PET.* Oral presentation at the 7th Annual Meeting of the Organisation for Human Brain Mapping, Brighton, UK. *NeuroImage 13*(Suppl.), S1093.

Reiner, W. G. (1999). Assignment of sex in neonates with ambiguous genitalia. *Current Opinions in Pediatrics, 11*(4), 363–365.

Reiner, W. G. (September 29, 2000). *The genesis of gender identity in the male: Prenatal androgen effects on gender identity and gender role.* Oral presentation at New York University Child Study Center, Grand Rounds Summary.

Reiner, W. G., & Gearhart, J. P. (2004). Discordant sexual identity in some genetic males with cloacal exstrophy assigned to female sex at birth. *The New England Journal of Medicine, 350*(4), 333–341. http://doi.org/10.1056/NEJMoa022236

Reisenzein, R. (1983). The Schachter theory of emotion: Two decades later. *Psychological Bulletin, 94,* 239–264.

Reisenzein, R. (1994). Pleasure-arousal theory and the intensity of emotions. *Journal of Personality and Social Psychology, 7*(6), 1313–1329.

Remini, L. (2015). *Troublemaker: Surviving hollywood and scientology.* New York: Ballantine Books.

Renchler, R. (1993). Poverty and learning. *ERIC Digest No. 83,* Eugene, OR: ERIC Clearinghouse on educational management. (ERIC Document Reproduction Service No. ED 357 433).

Renneboog, B. (2012). Andropause and testosterone deficiency: How to treat in 2012? *Revue Médicale de Bruxelles, 33*(4), 443–449.

Renner, M. J., & Mackin, R. S. (1998). A life stress instrument for classroom use. *Teaching of Psychology, 25,* 47.

Rescorla, R. A. (1968). Probability of shock in the presence and absence of CS in fear conditioning. *Journal of Comparative and Physiological Psychology, 66,* 1–5.

Rescorla, R. A. (1988). Pavlovian conditioning—It's not what you think. *American Psychologist, 43,* 151–160.

Resick, P. A., Monson, C. M., & Rizvi, S. (2008). Posttraumatic stress disorder. In D. H. Barlow (Ed.), *Clinical handbook of psychological disorders* (pp. 65–122). New York: Guilford Press.

Rethorst, C. C., Greer, T. L., Toups, M. S. P., Bernstein, I., Carmody, T. J., & Trivedi, M. H. (2015). IL-1β and BDNF are associated with improvement in hypersomnia but not insomnia following exercise in major depressive disorder. *Translational Psychiatry, 5*(8), e611. doi: 10.1038/tp.2015.104

Reynolds, C. F., Frank, E., Perel, J. M., Imber, S. D., Cornes, C., Miller, M. D., . . . Kuper, D. J. (1999). Nortriptyline and interpersonal psychotherapy as maintenance therapies for recurrent depression: A randomized controlled trial in patients older than 59 years. *Journal of the American Medical Association, 281* (1), 39–45.

Reynolds, J. A. (2002). *Succeeding in college: study skills and strategies, 2e.* Needham Heights: Allyn and Bacon.

Reynolds, R. M., Strachan, M., Frier, B. M., Fowkes, F. G., Mitchell, R., Seckl, J. R., . . . Prices, J. F. (2010). Morning cortisol levels and cognitive abilities in people with Type 2 diabetes. *American Diabetes Association: Diabetes Care, 33*(4), 714–720.

Rezvani, A. H., & Levin, E. D. (2001). Cognitive effects of nicotine. *Biological Psychiatry, 49,* 258–267.

Rhodes, M. G., & Castel, A. D. (2008). Memory predictions are influenced by perceptual information: Evidence for metacognitive illusions. *Journal of Experimental Psychology: General, 137*(4), 615–625. doi: 10.1037/a0013684

RIA Novosti. (2010, January 7). Some 80 people die from drug abuse in Russia every day—minister. Retrieved June 30, 2010, from http://en.rian.ru/russia/20100616/159443005.html

Rice, W. R., Friberg, U., & Gavrilets, S. (2012). Homosexuality as a consequence of epigenetically canalized sexual development. *The Quarterly Review of Biology, 87*(4), 344–368.

Richard, O. D., Stewart, M. M., McKay, P. F., & Sackett, T. W. (2015). The impact of store-unit-community racial diversity congruence on store-unit sales performance. *Journal of Management.* doi: 10.1177/0149206315579511

Richards, C. F., & Lowe, R. A. (2003). Researching racial and ethnic disparities in emergency medicine. *Academic Emergency Medicine, 10*(11), 1169–1175.

Richardson, J., & Morgan, R. (1997). *Reading to learn in the content areas.* Belmont, CA: Wadsworth.

Rideout, V. J., Foehr, U. G., & Roberts, D. F. (2010). *Generation M2: Media in the lives of 8- to 18-year-olds:* Menlo Park, CA: Henry J. Kaiser Family Foundation.

Ridley, M. (1999). *Genome: The autobiography of a species in 23 chapters*. London: Fourth Estate.

Ridley, M. (2002). Crop Circle Confession. *Scientific American*. Retrieved February 17, 2010, from http://www.sciam.com/article.cfm?chanID=sa006&articleID=00038B16-ED5F-1D29-97CA809EC588EEDF

Rieber, R. W., & Robinson, D. K. (2001). *Wilhelm Wundt in history: The making of a scientific psychology*. New York: Kluwer Academic.

Rigby, C. S., Schultz, P. P., & Ryan, R. M. (2014). Mindfulness, interest-taking, and self-regulation: A self-determination theory perspective on the role of awareness in optimal functioning. In A. Ie, C. T. Ngnoumen, & E. Langer (Eds.), *Handbook of mindfulness* (pp. 216–235). Cambridge, UK: Cambridge University Press.

Rijsdijk, F. V., Gottesman, I. I., McGuffin, P., & Cardno, A. G. (2011). Heritability estimates for psychotic symptom dimensions in twins with psychotic disorders. *American Journal of Medical Genetics Part B, Neuropsychiatric Genetics, 156B*(1), 89–98. doi: 10.1002/ajmg.b.31145

Ritchey, M., LaBar, K. S., & Cabeza, R. (2011). Level of processing modulates the neural correlates of emotional memory formation. *Journal of Cognitive Neuroscience, 4*, 757–775.

Ritts, V. (1999). Infusing culture into psychopathology: A supplement for psychology instructors. Retrieved from the Internet on June 19, 2004, at www.stlcc.cc.mo.us/mc/users/vritts/psypath.htm.

Rizzolatti, G., Fabbri-Destro, M., & Cattaneo, L. (2009). Mirror neurons and their clinical relevance. *Nature Clinical Practice Neurology, 5*(1), 24–34.

Ro, E., & Clark, L. A. (2009). Psychosocial functioning in the context of diagnosis: Assessment and theoretical issues. *Psychological Assessment, 21*(3), 313–324.

Roane, B. M., Seifer, R., Sharkey, K. M., Van Reen, E., Bond, T. L., Raffray, T., & Carskadon, M. A. (2015). What role does sleep play in weight gain in the first semester of university? *Behavioral Sleep Medicine, 13*(6), 491–505.

Roberto, C. A., & Kawachi, I. (2014). Use of psychology and behavioral economics to promote healthy eating. *American Journal of Preventive Medicine, 47*, 832–837.

Robins, L. N. (1996). *Deviant children grown up*. Baltimore: Williams & Wilkins.

Robinson, F. P. (1946). *Effective study*. New York: Harper & Bros.

Robinson, J. W., & Preston, J. D. (1976). Equal status contact and modification of racial prejudice: A reexamination of the contact hypothesis. *Social Forces, 54*, 911–924.

Robinson, P. (1993). *Freud and his critics*. Berkeley: University of California Press.

Roche, A. F. (1979). Secular trends in human growth, maturation, and development. *Monographs of the Society for Research in Child Development, 44*(3–4), 1–120.

Rodin, J. (1981). Current status of the internal-external hypothesis for obesity. *American Psychologist, 36*, 361–372.

Rodin, J. (1985). Insulin levels, hunger, and food intake: An example of feedback loops in body weight regulation. *Health Psychology, 4*, 1–24.

Rodin, J., & Langer, E. J. (1977). Long-term effects of a control-relevant intervention among the institutionalized aged. *Journal of Personality and Social Psychology, 35*, 275–282.

Roediger, H. L. (1990). Implicit memory: Retention without remembering. *American Psychologist, 45*, 1043–1056.

Roediger, H. L., III (2000). Why retrieval is the key process to understanding human memory. In E. Tulving (Ed.), *Memory, consciousness and the brain: The Tallinn Conference* (pp. 52–75). Philadelphia: Psychology Press.

Roediger, H. L., III, & Guynn, M. J. (1996). Retrieval processes. In E. L. Bjork & R. A. Bjork (Eds.), *Memory* (pp. 197–236). New York: Academic Press.

Roediger, H. L., & Karpicke, J. D. (2006). The power of testing memory: Basic research and implications for educational practice. *Perspectives on Psychological Science, 1*, 181–210.

Roediger, H. L., & McDermott, K. B. (1995). Creating false memories: Remembering words not presented in lists. *Journal of Experimental Psychology, 21*(4), 803–814.

Roethlisberger, F. J., & Dickson, W. J. (1939) *Management and the Worker*. Cambridge, MA: Harvard University Press.

Roffman, I., Savage-Rumbaugh, S., Rubert-Pugh, E., Ronen, A., & Nevo, E. (2012). Stone tool production and utilization by bonobo-chimpanzees (pan paniscus). *Proceedings of the National Academy of Sciences of the United States of America, 109*(36). doi: 10.1073/pnas.1212855109

Roffman, R. A., Stephens, R. S., Simpson, E. E., & Whitaker, D. L. (1988). Treatment of marijuana dependence: Preliminary results. *Journal of Psychoactive Drugs, 20*(1), 129–137.

Roffwarg, H. P., Muzio, J. N., & Dement, W. C. (1966). Ontogenetic development of the human sleep-dream cycle. *Science, 152*(3722), 604–619.

Rogers, C. R. (1951). *Client-centered therapy*. Boston: Houghton Mifflin Co.

Rogers, C. R. (1961). *On becoming a person: A therapist's view of psychotherapy*. Boston: Houghton Mifflin Co.

Rogers, R. W., & Mewborn, C. R. (1976). Fear appeals and attitude change: Effects of a threat's noxiousness, probability of occurrence, and the efficacy of the coping responses. *Journal of Personality and Social Psychology, 34*, 54–61.

Rogoff, B. (1994). Developing understanding of the idea of communities of learners. *Mind, Culture, and Activity, 1*(4), 209–229.

Roid, G. H. (2003). *Stanford-Binet intelligence scales* (5th ed.). Itasca, IL: Riverside.

Roos, P. E., & Cohen, L. H. (1987). Sex roles and social support as moderators of life stress adjustment. *Journal of Personality and Social Psychology, 3*, 576–585.

Ros, T., Theberge, J., Frewen, P. A., Kluetsch, R., Densmore, M., Calhoun, V. D., & Lanius, R. A. (2013). Mind over chatter: Plastic up-regulation of the fMRI salience network directly after EEG neurofeedback. *Neuroimage, 65*, 324–335. doi: 10.1016/j.neuroimage.2012.09.046

Rosch, E. (1973). On the internal structure of perceptual and semantic categories. In T. E. Moore (Ed.), *Cognitive development and the acquisition of language* (pp. 111–144). New York: Academic Press.

Rosch, E. (1977). Human categorization. In N. Warren (Ed.), *Advances in cross-cultural psychology, 1* (pp. 1–72). London: Academic Press.

Rosch, E., & Mervis, C. (1975). Family resemblances: Studies in the internal structures of categories. *Cognitive Psychology, 7*, 573–605.

Rosch-Heider, E. (1972). Universals in color naming and memory. *Journal of Experimental Psychology, 93*, 10–20.

Rosch-Heider, E., & Olivier, D. C. (1972). The structure of the color space in naming and memory for two languages. *Cognitive Psychology, 3*, 337–354.

Rosenbloom, T., Shahar, A., Perlman, A., Estreich, D., & Kirzner, E. (2007). Success on a practical driver's license test with and without the presence of another testee. *Accident Analysis & Prevention, 39*(6), p. 1296–1301.

Rosenfeld, J. P., Labkovsky, E., Winograd, M., Lui, M. A., Vandenboom, C., & Chedid, E. (2008). The Complex Trial Protocol (CTP): A new, countermeasure-resistant, accurate, P300-based method for detection of concealed information. *Psychophysiology, 45*(6), 906–919.

Rosenhan, D. L. (1973), On being sane in insane places, *Science, 179*, 250–258.

Rosenman, R. H., Brand, R. I., Jenkins, C. D., Friedman, M., Straus, R., & Wurm, M. (1975). Coronary heart disease in the Western Collaborative Group Study, final follow-up experience of 2 years. *Journal of the American Medical Association, 233*, 812–817.

Rosenthal, A. M. (1964). *Thirty-eight witnesses: The Kitty Genovese case*. New York: McGraw-Hill.

Rosenthal, R., & Jacobson, L. (1968). *Pygmalion in the classroom*. New York: Holt, Rinehart & Winston.

Rose, S., Kamin, L. J., & Lewontin, R. C. (1984). *Not in our genes: Biology, ideology and human nature*. Harmondsworth, UK: Penguin.

Ross, C. A., Ferrell, L., & Schroeder, E. (2014). Co-occurrence of dissociative identity disorder and borderline personality disorder. *Journal of Trauma & Dissociation, 15*(1), 79–90. doi: 10.1080/15299732.2013.834861

Ross, H. E., & Ross, G. M. (1976). Did Ptolemy understand the moon illusion? *Perception, 5*, 377–385.

Rossini, P. M., Altamura, C., Ferreri, F., Melgari, J. M., Tecchio, F., Tombini, M., . . . Vernieri, F. (2007). Neuroimaging experimental studies on brain plasticity in recovery from stroke. *Eura Medicophys, 43*(2), 241–254.

Rostron, B., Chang, C. M., van Bemmel, D. M., Xia, Y., & Blount, B. C. (2015). Nicotine and toxicant exposure among U.S. smokeless tobacco users: Results from 1999 to 2012 National Health and Nutrition Examination Survey data. *Cancer Epidemiology, Biomarkers & Prevention*. doi: 10.1158/1055-9965.EPI-15-0376

Rothbaum, B. O., Hodges, L. F., Kooper, R., Opdyke, D., Williford, J. S., & North, M. (1995). Effectiveness of computer-generated (virtual reality) graded exposure in the treatment of acrophobia. *American Journal of Psychiatry, 152*, 626–628.

Rothbaum, R., Weisz, J., Pott, M., Miyake, K., & Morelli, G. (2000). Attachment and culture: Security in Japan and the U.S. *American Psychologist, 55*, 1093–1104.

Rothenberg, A. (2001). Bipolar illness, creativity, and treatment. *Psychiatric Quarterly, 72*(2), 131–147.

Rothman, A. J., Gollwitzer, P. M., Grant, A. M., Neal, D. T., Sheeran, P., & Wood, W. (2015). Hale and hearty policies: How psychological science can create and maintain healthy habits. *Perspectives on Psychological Science, 10*, 701–705.

Rothstein, H. R., & Bushman, B. J. (2015). Methodological and reporting errors in meta-analytic reviews make other meta-analysts angry: A commentary on Ferguson (2015). *Perspectives on Psychological Science, 10*(5), 677–679. doi: 10.1177/1745691615592235

Rothstein-Fisch, C., & Trumbell, E. (2008). *Mangaging diverse classrooms: How to build on students' cultural strengths*. Alexandria, VA. Association for Supervision and Curriculum Development.

Rotter, J. B. (1966). Generalized expectancies for internal versus external control of reinforcements. *Psychological Monographs, 80* [Whole no. 609].

Rotter, J. B. (1978). Generalized expectancies for problem solving and psychotherapy. *Cognitive Therapy and Research, 2*, 1–10.

Rotter, J. B. (1981). The psychological situation in social learning theory. In D. Magnusson (Ed.), *Toward a psychology of situations: An interactional perspective*. Hillsdale, NJ: Lawrence Erlbaum.

Rotter, J. B. (1990). Internal versus external control of reinforcement: A case history of a variable. *American Psychologist, 45*, 489–493.

Rotton, J., & Frey, J. (1985). Air pollution, weather, and violent crime: Concomitant time-series analysis of archival data. *Journal of Personality and Social Psychology, 49*, 1207–1220.

Rotton, J., Frey, J., Barry, T., Milligan, M., & Fitzpatrick, M. (1979). The air pollution experience and physical aggression. *Journal of Applied Social Psychology, 9*, 397–412.

Rouru, J., Wesnes, K., Hänninen, J., Murphy, M., Riordan, H., & Rinne, J. (2013, March 16–23). Safety and efficacy of ORM-12741 on cognitive and behavioral symptoms in patients with Alzheimer's disease: A randomized, double-blind, placebo-controlled, parallel group, multicenter, proof-of-concept 12 week study. Paper presented at American Academy of Neurology 65th Annual Meeting, San Diego, CA.

Rouse, B. A. (1998). *Substance and mental health statistics source book*. Rockville, MD: Department of Health and Human Services, Substance Abuse and Mental Health Services Administration (SAMHSA).

Rovet, J. (1993). The psychoeducational characteristics of children with Turner's syndrome. *Journal of Learning Disabilities, 26*, 333–341.

Rowan, J. (2001). *Ordinary ecstacsy*. Hove, UK: Brunner-Routledge.

Rowe, D. C., Almeida, D. A., & Jacobson, K. C. (1999). School context and genetic influences on aggression in adolescence. *Psychological Science, 10*, 277–280.

Roysircar-Sodowsky, G. R., & Maestas, M. V. (2000). Acculturation, ethnic identity, and acculturative stress: Evidence and measurement. In R. H. Dana (Ed.), *Handbook of cross-cultural and multicultural assessment* (pp. 131–172). Mahwah, NJ: Lawrence Erlbaum.

Rozeske, R. R., Evans, A. K., Frank, M. G., Watkins, L. R., Lowry, C. A., & Maier, S. F. (2011). Uncontrollable, but not controllable, stress desensitizes 5-HT1A receptors in the dorsal raphe nucleus. *The Journal of Neuroscience, 31*(40), 14107–14115. doi: 10.1523/jneurosci.3095-11.2011

Rubio-Fernandez, P., & Glucksberg, S. (2012). Reasoning about other people's beliefs: Bilinguals have an advantage. *Journal of Experimental Psychology: Learning, Memory, and Cognition, 38*(1), 211–217. doi: 10.1037/a0025162

Ruble, D., Alvarez, J., Bachman, M., Cameron, J., Fuligni, A., Garcia Coll, C., & Rhee, E. (2004). The development of a sense of "we": The emergence and implications of children's collective identity. In M. Bennett & F. Sani (Eds.), *The development of the social self*. New York: Psychology Press.

Rudd, P., & Osterberg, L. G. (2002). Hypertension: Context, pathophysiology, and management. In E. J. Topol (Ed.), *Textbook of cardiovascular medicine* (pp. 91–122). Philadelphia: Lippincott Williams & Wilkins.

Rudmin, F. W. (2003). Critical history of the acculturation psychology of assimilation, separation, integration, and marginalization. *Review of General Psychology, 7*, 3–37.

Ruff, R. M., Iverson, G. L., Barth, J. T., Bush, S. S., & Broshek, D. K. (2009). Recommendations for diagnosing a mild traumatic brain injury: A National Academy of Neuropsychology education paper. *Archives of Clinical Neuropsychology, 24*(1), 3–10.

Ruhe, H. G., Mason, N. S., & Schene, A. H. (2007). Mood is indirectly related to serotonin, norepinephrine and dopamine levels in humans: A meta-analysis of monoamine depletion studies. *Molecular Psychiatry, 12*(4), 331–359.

Ruiz, S., Lee, S., Soekadar, S. R., Caria, A., Veit, R., Kircher, T., . . . Sitaram, R. (2013). Acquired self-control of insula cortex modulates emotion recognition and brain network connectivity in schizophrenia. *Human Brain Mapping, 34*(1), 200–212. doi: 10.1002/hbm.21427

Rumelhart, D. E., Hinton, G. E., & McClelland, J. L. (1986). A general framework for parallel distributed processing. In D. E. Rumelhart, J. L. McClelland, & the PDP Research Group (Eds.), *Parallel distributed processing: Explorations in the microstructure of cognition: Vol. 1. Foundations* (pp. 45–76). Cambridge, MA: MIT Press.

Rundus, D. (1971). An analysis of rehearsal processes in free recall. *Journal of Experimental Psychology, 89*, 63–77.

Running, C. A., Craig, B. A., & Mattes, R. D. (2015). Oleogustus: The unique taste of fat. *Chemical Senses, 40*(7), 507–516. doi: 10.1093/chemse/bjv036

Runyan, D. K., Shankar, V., Hassan, F., Hunter, W. M., Jain, D., Paula, C. S., . . . Bordin, I. A. (2010). International variations in harsh child discipline. *Pediatrics, 126*(3), e701–711.

Ruscio, A. M., Borkovec, T. D., & Ruscio, J. (2001). A taxometric investigation of the latent structure of worry. *Journal of Abnormal Psychology, 110*, 413–422.

Russell, D. E. (1986). *The secret trauma: Incest in the lives of girls and women*. New York: Basic Books.

Russo, S. J., & Nestler, E. J. (2013). The brain reward circuitry in mood disorders. *Nature Reviews Neuroscience, 14*, 609–625.

Rutherford, A. (2000). Mary Cover Jones (1896–1987). *The Feminist Psychologist, 27*(3), 25.

Ruzek, J. I., Eftekhari, A., Rosen, C. S., Crowley, J. J., Kuhn, E., Foa, E. B., . . . Karlin, B. E. (2014). Factors related to clinician attitudes toward prolonged exposure therapy for PTSD. *Journal of Traumatic Stress, 27*(4), 423–429. doi: 10.1002/jts.21945

Ryan, R. M., Chirkov, V. I., Little, T. D., Sheldon, K. M., Timoshina, E. L., & Deci, E. L. (1999). The American dream in Russia: Extrinsic aspirations and well-being in two cultures. *Personality and Social Psychology Bulletin, 25*, 1509–1524.

Ryan, R. M., & Deci, E. L. (2000). Intrinsic and extrinsic motivations: Classic definitions and new directions. *Contemporary Educational Psychology, 25*, 54–67.

Ryan, R. M., Legate, N., Niemiec, C. P., & Deci, E. L. (2012). Beyond illusions and defense: Exploring the possibilities and limits of human autonomy and responsibility through self-determination theory. In P. R. Shaver & M. Mikulincer (Eds.), *Meaning, mortality, and choice: The social psychology of existential concerns* (pp. 215–233). Washington, DC: American Psychological Association.

Rydell, R. J., & Boucher, K. L. (2010). Capitalizing on multiple social identities to prevent stereotype threat: The moderating role of self-esteem. *Personality and Social Psychology Bulletin, 36*(2), 239–250.

Rysavy, M. A., Li, L., Bell, E. F., Das, A., Hintz, S. R., Stoll, B. J., . . . Higgins, R. D. (2015). *The New England Journal of Medicine, 372*, 1801–1811.

Sabatini, E., Della Penna, S., Franciotti, R., Ferretti, A., Zoccolotti, P., Rossini, P. M., . . . Gainotti, G. (2009). Brain structures activated by overt and covert emotional visual stimuli. *Brain Research Bulletin, 79*(5), 258–264.

Sacchet, M. D., Livermore, E. E., Iglesias, J. E., Glover, G. H., & Gotlib, I. H. (2015). Subcortical volumes differentiate major depressive disorder, bipolar disorder, and remitted major depressive disorder. *Journal of Psychiatric Research, 68*, 91–98. doi: 10.1016/j.jpsychires.2015.06.002

Sackeim, H. A., Prudic, J., Fuller, R., Keilp, J., Lavori, P. W., & Olfson, M. (2007). The cognitive effects of electroconvulsive therapy in community settings. *Neuropsychopharmacology, 32*, 244–254.

Sackett, P. R., Borneman, M. J., & Connelly, B. S. (2008). High stakes testing in higher education and employment: Appraising the evidence for validity and fairness. *American Psychologist, 63*(4), 215–227. doi: 10.1037/0003-066X.63.4.215

Sacks, O. (1990). *The man who mistook his wife for a hat and other clinical tales*. New York: HarperPerennial.

Sadker, M., & Sadker, D. (1994). *Failing at fairness: How America's schools cheat girls*. New York: Scribner.

Sadock, B. J., Kaplan, H. I., & Sadock, V. A. (2007). *Kaplan & Sadock's synopsis of psychiatry: Behavioral sciences/clinical psychiatry* (10th ed.). Philadelphia: Lippincott Williams & Wilkins.

Safer, D. J. (2015). Recent trends in stimulant usage. *Journal of Attention Disorders*. Published online before print. doi: 10.1177/1087054715605915

Sagan, C. (1977). *The dragons of Eden: Speculations on the evolution of human intelligence*. New York: Random House.

Saha, S., Chant, D., Welham, J., & McGrath, J. (2005). A systematic review of the prevalence of schizophrenia. *PLoS Medicine, 2*(5), e141.

Sahin, M., & Sur, M. (2015). Genes, circuits, and precision therapies for autism and related neurodevelopmental disorders. *Science*. doi: 10.1126/science.aab3897

Salamone, J. D., & Correa, M. (2012). The mysterious motivational functions of mesolimbic dopamine. *Neuron, 76*(3), 470–485.

Salend, S. J. (1987). Contingency management systems. *Academic Therapy, 22*, 245–253.

Salgado, S., & Kaplitt, M. G. (2015). The nucleus accumbens: A comprehensive review. *Stereotactic and Functional Neurosurgery, 93*(2), 75–93.

Salovey, P., & Mayer, J. D. (1990). Emotional intelligence. *Imagination, cognition, and personality, 9*, 185–211.

Salthouse, T. A. (1984). The skill of typing. *Scientific American, 250*(2), 128–135.

Sam, D. L., & Berry, J. W. (2010). Acculturation when individuals and groups of different cultural backgrounds meet. *Perspectives on Psychological Science, 5*(4), 472.

Sanbonmatsu, D. M., Strayer, D. L., Medeiros-Ward, N., & Watson, J. M. (2013). Who multi-tasks and why? Multi-tasking ability, perceived multi-tasking ability, impulsivity, and sensation seeking. *PLoS ONE, 8*(1), e54402. doi:10.1371/journal.pone.0054402

Sanders, A. R., Martin, E. R., Beecham, G. W., Guo, S., Dawood, K., Rieger, G., . . . Bailey, J. M. (2015). Genome-wide scan demonstrates significant linkage for male sexual orientation. *Psychological Medicine, 45*(7), 1379–1388.

Sanders, L. D., Weber-Fox, C. M., & Neville, H. J. (2008). Varying degrees of plasticity in different subsystems within language. In J. R. Pomerantz & M. Crair (Eds.), *Topics in integrative neuroscience: From cells to cognition*. New York: Cambridge University Press.

Sanders, S., Hill, B., Yarber, W., Graham, C., Crosby, R., & Milhausen, R. (2010). Misclassification bias: Diversity in conceptualisations about having "had sex." *Sexual Health, 7*(1), 31–34.

Sands, L. P., & Meredith, W. (1992). Intellectual functioning in late midlife. *Journal of Gerontological and Psychological Science, 47*, 81–84.

Sanes, J. R., & Jessell, T. M. (2013a). Experience and the refinement of synaptic connections. In E. R. Kandel, J. H. Schwartz, T. M. Jessell, S. A. Siegelbaum, & A. J. Hudspeth (Eds.), *Principles of neural science* (5th ed., pp. 1259–1283). USA: McGraw-Hill.

Sanes, J. R., & Jessell, T. M. (2013b). Repairing the damaged brain. In E. R. Kandel, J. H. Schwartz, T. M. Jessell, S. A. Siegelbaum, & A. J. Hudspeth (Eds.), *Principles of neural science* (5th ed., pp. 1284–1305). USA: McGraw-Hill.

Santhakumar, V., Wallner, M, & Otis, T. S. (2007). Ethanol acts directly on extrasynaptic subtypes of GABAA receptors to increase tonic inhibition. *Alcohol, 41*(3), 211–221.

Sanz, C., Andrieu, S., Sinclair, A., Hanaire, H., & Vellas, B. (2009). Diabetes is associated with a slower rate of cognitive decline in Alzheimer disease. *Neurology, 73*, 1359–1366.

Saper, C. B., Chou, T. C., & Scammell, T. E. (2001). The sleep switch: Hypothalamic control of sleep and wakefulness. *Trends in Neurosciences, 24*, 726–731.

Sapir, E. S. (1921). *Language: An introduction to the study of speech*. New York: Harcourt, Brace.

Sapolsky, R. M. (2004). *Why zebras don't get ulcers* (3rd ed.). New York: Owl Books.

Sarada, P. A., & Ramkumar, B. (2014). Positive stress and its impact on performance. *Research Journal of Pharmaceutical, Biological, and Chemical Sciences, 6*(2), 1519–1522.

Sarbin, T. R., & Coe, W. C. (1972). *Hypnosis: A social psychological analysis of influence communication.* New York: Holt, Rinehart, & Winston.

Sartorius, A., Demirakca, T., Bohringer, A., Clemm von Hohenberg, C., Aksay, S. S., Bumb, J. M., . . . Ende, G. (2015). Electroconvulsive therapy increases temporal gray matter volume and cortical thickness. *European Neuropsychopharmacology, 26*(3), 506–517. doi: 10.1016/j.euroneuro.2015.12.036

Sartory, G., Cwik, J., Knuppertz, H., Schürholt, B., Lebens, M., Seitz, R. J., & Schulze, R. (2013). In search of the trauma memory: A meta-analysis of functional neuroimaging studies of symptom provocation in posttraumatic stress disorder (PTSD). *PLoS ONE, 8*(3), e58150. doi: 10.1371/journal.pone.0058150

Sastry, K. S., Karpova, Y., Prokopovich, S., Smith, A. J., Essau, B., Gersappe, A., . . . Kulik, G. (2007). Epinephrine protects cancer cells from apoptosis via activation of cAMP-dependent protein kinase and BAD phosphorylation. *Journal of Biological Chemistry, 282*(19), 14094–14100.

Satterly, D. (1987). Piaget and education. In R. L. Gregory (Ed.), *The Oxford companion to the mind* (pp. 110–143). Oxford: Oxford University Press.

Sattler, J. M. (1977). The effects of therapist–client racial similarity. In A. S. Gurman & A.M.Razin(Eds.),*Effective psychotherapy: A handbook of research* (pp.252–290). Elmsford, NY: Pergamon.

Savage-Rumbaugh, S., & Lewin, R. (1994). *Kanzi.* New York: Wiley.

Savage-Rumbaugh, S., Shanker, S., & Taylor, T. J. (1998). *Apes, language and the human mind.* Oxford, UK: Oxford University Press.

Savard, J., Ivers, H., Savard, M. H., & Morin, C. M. (2014). Is a video-based cognitive behavioral therapy for insomnia as efficacious as a professionally administered treatment in breast cancer? Results of a randomized controlled trial. *Sleep, 37*(8), 1305–1314. doi: 10.5665/sleep.3918

Savic, I., Berglund, H., & Lindstrom, P. (2005). Brain response to putative pheromones in homosexual men. *Proceedings of the National Academy of Sciences, USA, 102*(20), 7356–7361.

Savic, I., & Lindström, P. (2008). PET and MRI show differences in cerebral asymmetry and functional connectivity between homo- and heterosexual subjects. *Proceedings of the National Academy of Sciences, USA, 105*(27), 9403–9408.

Scarpa, A., Raine, A., Venables, P. H., & Mednick, S. A. (1995). The stability of inhibited/uninhibited temperament from ages 3 to 11 years in Mauritian children. *Journal of Abnormal Child Psychology, 23,* 607–618.

Schilbach, L., Hoffstaedter, F., Müller, V., Cieslik, E. C., Goya-Maldonado, R., Trost, S., . . . Eickhoff, S. B. (2016). Transdiagnostic commonalities and differences in resting state functional connectivity of the default mode network in schizophrenia and major depression. *NeuroImage: Clinical, 10,* 326–335. doi: 10.1016/j.nicl.2015.11.021

Schlumpf, Y. R., Reinders, A. A., Nijenhuis, E. R., Luechinger, R., van Osch, M. J., & Jancke, L. (2014). Dissociative part-dependent resting-state activity in dissociative identity disorder: A controlled fMRI perfusion study. *PLoS One, 9*(6), e98795. doi: 10.1371/journal.pone.0098795

Schvey, N. A., Sbrocco, T., Stephens, M., Bryant, E. J., Ress, R., Spieker, E. A., . . . Tanofsky-Kraff, M. (2015). Comparison of overweight and obese military-dependent and civilian adolescent girls with loss-of-control eating. *International Journal of Eating Disorders, 48*(6), 490–494. doi: 10.1002/eat.22424

Schachter, S., & Singer, J. E. (1962). Cognitive, social and physiological determinants of emotional states. *Psychological Review, 69,* 379–399.

Schacter, D. L., & Wagner, A. D. (2013). Learning and memory. In E. R. Kandel, J. H. Schwartz, T. M. Jessell, S. A. Siegelbaum, & A. J. Hudspeth (Eds.), *Principles of neural science* (5th ed., pp. 1441–1460). USA: McGraw-Hill.

Schafer, M., & Crichlow S. (1996). Antecedents of groupthink: A quantitative study. *Journal of Conflict Resolution, 40,* 415–435.

Schaie, K. W., & Willis, S. L. (2010). The Seattle longitudinal study of adult cognitive development. *Bulletin of the International Society for the Study of Behavioral Development, 37,* 24–29.

Schapiro, A. C., & McClelland, J. L. (2009). A connectionist model of a continuous developmental transition in the balance scale task. *Cognition, 110*(1), 395–411.

Scharnowski, F., Hutton, C., Josephs, O., Weiskopf, N., & Rees, G. (2012). Improving visual perception through neurofeedback. *The Journal of Neuroscience, 32*(49), 17830–17841. doi: 10.1523/jneurosci.6334-11.2012

Scheele, D., Striepens, N., Güntürkün, O., Deutschländer, S., Maier, W., Kendrick, K. M., & Hurlemann, K. (2012). Oxytocin modulates social distance between males and females. *The Journal of Neuroscience, 32*(46), 16074–16079. doi: 10.1523/jneurosci.2755-12.2012

Schiller, P. H., & Carvey, C. E. (2005). The Hermann grid illusion revisited. *Perception, 34*(11), 1375–1397.

Schizophrenia Working Group of the Psychiatric Genomics, C. (2014). Biological insights from 108 schizophrenia-associated genetic loci. *Nature, 511*(7510), 421–427. doi: 10.1038/nature13595

Schmitt, D. P. (2002). Personality, attachment and sexuality related to dating relationship outcomes: Contrasting three perspectives on personal attribute interaction. *British Journal of Social Psychology, 41*(4), 589–610.

Schmitt, D. P., Allik, J., McCrae, R. R., & Benet-Martínez, V. (2007). The geographic distribution of big five personality traits: Patterns and profiles of human self-description across 56 nations. *Journal of Cross-Cultural Psychology, 38*(2), 173–212. doi: 10.1177/0022022106297299

Schmitt, K. C., & Reith, M. E. A. (2010). Regulation of the dopamine transporter. *Annals of the New York Academy of Sciences, 1187:* 316.

Schmitz, C., Wagner, J., & Menke, E. (2001). The interconnection of childhood poverty and homelessness: Negative impact/points of access. *Families in Society, 82*(1), 69–77.

Schnabel, J. (1994). *Round in circles* (pp. 267–277). London: Hamish Hamilton.

Schneider, K. J., Bugental, J. F. T., & Fraser, J. F. (Eds.). (2001). *Handbook of humanistic psychology.* Thousand Oaks, CA: Sage.

Schneider, R., Grim, C., Rainforth, M., Kotchen, T., Nidich, S., Gaylord-King, C., . . . Alexander, C. (2012). Stress reduction in the secondary prevention of cardiovascular disease: Randomized controlled trial of transcendental meditation and health education in blacks. *Circulation: Cardiovascular Quality and Outcomes. 5:*750–758.

Schneider, R. H., Staggers, F., Alexander, C. N., Sheppard, W., Rainforth, M., Kondwani, K., Smith, S., & King, C. G. (1995). A randomized controlled trial of stress reduction for hypertension in older African Americans. *Hypertension, 26*(5), 820–827.

Schneider, W., Dumais, S., & Shriffrin, R. (1984). *Automatic and control processing and attention.* London: Academic Press.

Schneider, W. J., & McGrew, K. S. (2012). The Cattell-Horn-Carroll model of intelligence. In D. P. Flanagan & P. L. Harrison (Eds.), *Contemporary intellectual assessment: Theories, tests, and issues* (3rd ed., pp. 99–144). New York, NY: Guilford Press.

Schneider, W. J., & McGrew, K. S. (2013). The cattell-horn-carroll (chc) model of intelligence v2.2: A visual tour and summary, from http://www.iapsych.com/chcv2.pdf

Schneidman, E. (1983). *Death of man.* New York: Jason Aronson.

Schneidman, E. (1994). *Death: Current perspectives.* New York: McGraw-Hill.

Schöls, L., Haan, J., Riess, O., Amoiridis, G., & Przuntek, H. (1998). Sleep disturbance in spinocerebellar ataxias: Is the SCA3 mutation a cause of restless legs syndrome? *Neurology, 51,* 1603–1607

Schroeder, R. D., Higgins, G. E., & Mowen, T. J. (2014). Maternal attachment trajectories and criminal offending by race. *American Journal of Criminal Justice, 39,* 155–171.

Schroeder, S. R. (2000). Mental retardation and developmental disabilities influenced by environmental neurotoxic insults. *Environmental Health Perspectives, 108*(Suppl. 3), 395–399.

Schroth, M. L., & McCormack, W. A. (2000). Sensation seeking and need for achievement among study-abroad students. *The Journal of Social Psychology, 140,* 533–535.

Schultz, D. P., & Schultz, S. E. (2004). *A History of Modern Psychology,* pp. 239–242. Belmont, CA: Wadsworth.

Schutzwohl, A., Fuchs, A., McKibbin, W. F., & Shackelford, T. K. (2009). How willing are you to accept sexual requests from slightly unattractive to exceptionally attractive imagined requestors? *Human Nature, 20*(3), 282–293.

Schuwerk, T., Vuori, M., & Sodian, B. (2015). Implicit and explicit theory of mind reasoning in autism spectrum disorders: The impact of experience. *Autism, 19,* 459–468.

Schwanenflugel, P., & Rey, M. (1986). Interlingual semantic facilitation: Evidence from common representational system in the bilingual lexicon. *Journal of Memory and Language, 25,* 605–618.

Schwartz, C. E., Kunwar, P. S., Greve, D. N., Moran, L. R., Viner, J. C., Covino, J. M., . . . Wallace, S. R. (2010). Structural differences in adult orbital and ventromedial prefrontal cortex predicted by infant temperament at 4 months of age. *Archives of General Psychiatry, 67*(1), 78–84. doi: 10.1001/archgenpsychiatry.2009.171

Schwartz, J. H., Barres, B. A., & Goldman, J. E. (2013). The cells of the nervous system. In E. R. Kandel, J. H. Schwartz, T. M. Jessell, S. A. Siegelbaum, & A. J. Hudspeth (Eds.), *Principles of neural science* (5th ed., pp. 71–99). USA: McGraw-Hill.

Schwartz, J. H., & Javitch, J. A. (2013). Neurotransmitters. In E. R. Kandel, J. H. Schwartz, T. M. Jessell, S. A. Siegelbaum, & A. J. Hudspeth (Eds.), *Principles of neural science* (5th ed., pp. 289–306). USA: McGraw-Hill.

Schwartz, S. K. (2000). *Working your degree.* Retrieved March 6, 2010, from http://cnnfn.cnn.com/2000/12/08/career/q_degreepsychology/

Schweickert, R. (1993). A multinomial processing tree model for degradation and redintegration in immediate recall. *Memory and Cognition, 21,* 168–175.

Schwitzgebel, E. (1999). Representation and desire: A philosophical error with consequences for theory-of-mind research. *Philosophical Psychology, 12,* 157–180.

Scott, E., Zhang, Q.-g., Wang, R., Vadlamudi, R., & Brann, D. (2012). Estrogen neuroprotection and the critical period hypothesis. *Frontiers in Neuroendocrinology, 33*(1), 85–104. doi: 10.1016/j.yfrne.2011.10.001

Scott, S. K., Young, A. W., Calder, A. J., Hellawell, D. J., Aggleton, J. P., & Johnson, M. (1997). Impaired auditory recognition of fear and anger following bilateral amygdala lesions. *Nature, 385*(6613), 254–257.

Scott, W. D. (1908). *The theory and practice of advertising.* Boston, MA: Small, Maynard, & Company,

Seedat, S., Scott, K. M., Angermeyer, M. C., Berglund, P., Bromet, E. J., Brugha, T. S., . . . Kessler, R. C. (2009). Cross-national associations between gender and mental disorders in the World Health Organization world mental health surveys. *Archives of General Psychiatry, 66*(7), 785–795. doi: 10.1001/archgenpsychiatry.2009.36

Seehagen, S., Konrad, C., Herbert, J. S., & Schneider, S. (2015). Timely sleep facilitates declarative memory consolidation in infants. *Proceedings of the National Academy of Sciences of the United States of America, 112*(5), 1625–1629.

Segal, S. K., Cotman, C. W., & Cahill, L. F. (2012). Exercise-induced noradrenergic activation enhances memory consolidation in both normal aging and patients with amnestic mild cognitive impairment. *Journal of Alzheimer's Disease, 32*(4), 1011–1018. doi: 10.3233/JAD-2012-121078

Segall, M. H., Campbell, D. T., & Herskovits, M. J. (1966). *The influence of culture on perception.* Indianapolis, IN: Bobbs-Merrill.

Segerstrom, S. C., & Sephton, S. E. (2010). Optimistic expectancies and cell-mediated immunity: The role of positive affect. *Psychological Science, 21*(3), 448–455.

Segerstrom, S. C., Taylor, S. E., Kemeny, M. E., & Fahey, J. L. (1998). Optimism is associated with mood, coping, and immune change in response to stress. *Journal of Personality and Social Psychology, 74*(6), 1646–1655.

Sehon, S., & Stanley, D. (2010). Applying the simplicity principle to homeopathy: What remains? *Focus on Alternative and Complementary Therapies, 15*(1), 8–12.

Sekar, A., Bialas, A. R., de Rivera, H., Davis, A., Hammond, T. R., Kamitaki, N., . . . McCarroll, S. A. (2016). Schizophrenia risk from complex variation of complement component 4. *Nature*, advance online publication. doi: 10.1038/nature16549

Sekar, A., Bialas, A. R., de Rivera, H., Davis, A., Hammond, T. R., Kamitaki, N., . . . McCarroll, S. A. (2016). Schizophrenia risk from complex variation of complement component 4. *Nature, 530,* 177–183. doi: 10.1038/nature16549

Seligman, M. (1975). *Helplessness: Depression, development and death.* New York: W. H. Freeman.

Seligman, M. (1989). *Helplessness.* New York: W. H. Freeman.

Seligman, M. (1995). The effectiveness of psychotherapy: The *Consumer Reports* study. *American Psychologist, 50,* 965–975.

Seligman, M. (1998). *Learned optimism: How to change your mind and your life* (2nd ed.). New York: Pocket Books.

Seligman, M. (2002). *Authentic happiness.* New York: Free Press.

Seligman, M. E. P. (2005). Positive psychology, positive prevention, and positive therapy. In C. R. Snyder & S. J. Lopez (Eds.), *Handbook of positive psychology* (pp. 3–9). New York: Oxford University Press.

Seligman, M. E. P., & Csikszentmihalyi, M. (2000). Positive psychology: An introduction. *American Psychologist, 55*(1), 5–14. doi: 10.1037/0003-066x.55.1.5

Seligman, M., & Maier, S. F. (1967). Failure to escape traumatic shock. *Journal of Experimental Psychology, 74,* 1–9.

Selye, H. (1956). *The stress of life.* New York: McGraw-Hill.

Selye, H. (1976). *The stress of life* (Rev. ed.). New York: McGraw-Hill.

Selye, H. A. (1936). Syndrome produced by diverse nocuous agents. *Nature, 138,* 32.

Seo, D., Tsou, K. A., Ansell, E. B., Potenza, M. N., & Sinha, R. (2014). Cumulative adversity sensitizes neural response to acute stress: Association with health symptoms. *Neuropsychopharmacology, 39,* 670–680.

Shackelford, T. K., Buss, D. M., & Bennett, K. (2002). Forgiveness or breakup: Sex differences in responses to a partner's infidelity. *Cognition and Emotion, 16*(2), 299–307.

Shadish, R., Cook, T. D., & Campbell, D. T. (2002). *Experimental and quasi-experimental designs for generalized causal inferences.* New York: Houghton Mifflin.

Shaffer, J. J., Peterson, M. J., McMahon, M. A., Bizzell, J., Calhoun, V., van Erp, T. G. M., . . . Belger, A. (2015). Neural correlates of schizophrenia negative symptoms: Distinct subtypes impact dissociable brain circuits. *Molecular Neuropsychiatry, 1*(4), 191–200. doi: 10.1159/000440979

Shafiro, M. V., Himelein, M. J., & Best, D. L. (2003). Ukrainian and U.S. American females: Differences in individualism/collectivism and gender attitudes. *Journal of Cross-Cultural Psychology, 34*(3), 297–303.

Shafton, A. (1995). *Dream reader: Contemporary approaches to the understanding of dreams (SUNY series in dream studies)* (pp. 40–46). New York: State University of New York Press.

Shakespeare, W., & Hubler, E. (1987). *The tragedy of Hamlet, Prince of Denmark.* New York: Penguin Group.

Shang, J., Fu, Y., Ren, Z., Zhang, T., Du, M., Gong, Q., . . . Zhang, W. (2014). The common traits of the ACC and PFC in anxiety disorders in the DSM-5: Meta-analysis of voxel-based morphometry studies. *PLoS One, 9*(3), e93432. doi: 10.1371/journal.pone.0093432

Shapiro, A. K., & Shapiro, E. (1997). *The powerful placebo.* Baltimore: Johns Hopkins University Press.

Shapiro, F. (2001). *Eye movement desensitization and reprocessing: Basic principles, protocols, and procedures.* New York: Guilford Press.

Shapiro, F. (2012). *Getting past your past: Take control of your life with self-help techniques from EMDR therapy.* New York: Rodale.

Shapiro, K. L., Jacobs, W. J., & LoLordo, V. M. (1980). Stimulus relevance in Pavlovian conditioning in pigeons. *Animal Learning and Behavior, 8,* 586–594.

Sharif, Z., Bradford, D., Stroup, S., & Lieberman, J. (2007). Pharmacological treatment of schizophrenia. In P. E. Nathan & J. M. Gorman (Eds.), *A guide to treatments that work* (3rd ed., pp. 203–241). New York: Oxford University Press.

Sharot, T., Delgado, M. R., & Phelps, E. A. (2004). How emotion enhances the feeling of remembering, *Nature Neuroscience, 7*(12), 1376–1380.

Shaw, N. D., Butler, J. P., McKinney, S. M., Nelson, S. A., Ellenbogen, J. M., & Hall, J. E. (2012). Insights into puberty: the relationship between sleep stages and pulsatile LH secretion. *Journal of Clinical Endocrinology & Metabolism, 97*:11, E2055–E2062.

Shean, R. E., de Klerk, N. H., Armstrong, B. K., & Walker, N. R. (1994). Seven-year follow-up of a smoking-prevention program for children. *Australian Journal of Public Health, 18,* 205–208.

Sheldon, K. M. (2012). The self-determination theory perspective on positive mental health across cultures. *World Psychiatry, 11*(2), 101–102.

Sheldon, S. H. (2002). Sleep in infants and children. In T. L. Lee-Chiong, M. J. Sateia, & M. A. Carskadon (Eds.), *Sleep medicine* (pp. 99–103). Philadelphia: Hanley & Belfus.

Shelton, J. (2004). *Homeopathy: How it really works.* Amherst, NY: Prometheus Books.

Shepard, R. N., & Metzler, J. (1971). Mental rotation of three-dimensional objects. *Science, 171,* 701–703.

Shepherd, G. M. (2012). *Neurogastronomy: How the brain creates flavor and why it matters.* New York, NY: Columbia University Press.

Sherif, M. (1936). *The psychology of social norms.* New York: Harper & Row.

Sherif, M., Harvey, O. J., White, B. J., Hood, W. R., & Sherif, C. W. (1961). *Intergroup conflict and cooperation: The Robber's Cave experiment.* Norman: University of Oklahoma Book Exchange.

Sherlin, L. H., Arns, M., Lubar, J., Heinrich, H., Kerson, C., Strehl, U., & Sterman, M. B. (2011). Neurofeedback and basic learning theory: Implications for research and practice. *Journal of Neurotherapy: Investigations in Neuromodulation, Neurofeedback and Applied Neuroscience, 15*(4), 292–304.

Sherry, P., Gaa, A., Thurlow-Harrison, S., Graber, K., Clemmons, J., & Bobulinski, M. (2003). *Traffic accidents, job stress, and supervisor support in the trucking industry.* Paper presented at the International Institute for Intermodal Transportation, University of Denver, CO.

Shore, L. A. (1990). Skepticism in light of scientific literacy. *Skeptical Inquirer, 15*(1), 3–4.

Shorter, E. (1997). *A history of psychiatry: From the era of the asylum to the age of Prozac.* New York: John Wiley & Sons.

Showalter, E. (1997). *Hysteries: Hysterical epidemics and modern culture.* New York: Columbia University Press.

Shuglin, A. (1986). The background chemistry of MDMA. *Journal of Psychoactive Drugs, 18*(4), 291–304.

Shweder, R. A., Haidt, J., Horton, R., & Joseph, C. (2008). The cultural psychology of the emotions. In M. Lewis, J. M. Haviland-Jones & L. F. Barrett (Eds.), *Handbook of emotions* (3rd ed., pp. 409–427). New York: Guilford Press.

Siegel, J. M. (2001). The REM sleep-memory consolidation hypothesis. *Science, 294,* 1058–1063.

Siegel, J. M. (2011). Neural control of sleep in mammals. In M. H. Kryger, T. Roth & W. C. Dement (Eds.), *Principles and practice of sleep medicine.* St. Louis, MO: Elsevier Saunders.

Siegel, R. K., & West, L. J., Eds. (1975). *Hallucinations: Behavior, experience, and theory* (2nd ed.). New York: Wiley.

Siegel, S. (1969). Effects of CS habituation on eyelid conditioning. *Journal of Comparative and Physiological Psychology, 68*(2), 245–248.

Siegelbaum, S. A., Kandel, E. R., & Yuste, R. (2013). Synaptic integration in the central nervous system. In E. R. Kandel, J. H. Schwartz, T. M. Jessell, S. A. Siegelbaum, & A. J. Hudspeth (Eds.), *Principles of neural science* (5th ed., pp. 210–235). New York: McGraw-Hill.

Siegler, I. C., Costa, P. T., Brummett, B. H., Helms, M. J., Barefoot, J. C., Williams, R. B., Dahlstrom, G., Kaplan, B. H., Vitaliano, P. P., Nichaman, M. Z., Day, S., & Rimer, B. K. (2003). Patterns of change in hostility from college to midlife in the UNC alumni heart study predict high-risk status. *Psychosomatic Medicine, 65,* 738–745.

Siegler, R. S. (1996). *Emerging minds: The process of change in children's thinking.* New York: Oxford University Press.

Silva, K., Chein, J., & Steinberg, L. (2016). Adolescents in peer groups make more prudent decisions when a slightly older adult is present. *Psychological Science, 20,* doi: 10.1177/0956797615620379

Silva, M. N., Marques, M., & Teixeira, P. J. (2014). Testing theory in practice: The example of self-determination theory-based interventions. *The European Health Psychologist, 16,* 171–180.

Simeon, D., Guralnik, O., Hazlett, E. A., Spiegel-Cohen, J., Hollander, E., & Buchsbaum, M. S. (2000). Feeling unreal: A PET study of depersonalization disorder. *American Journal of Psychiatry, 157,* 1782–1788.

Simkin, D. R., & Black, N. B. (2014). Meditation and mindfulness in clinical practice. *Child and Adolescent Psychiatric Clinics of North America, 23,* 487–534.

Simner, J. (2013). Why are there different types of synesthete? *Frontiers in Psychology, 4,* 558. doi: 10.3389/fpsyg.2013.00558

Simner, J., Mulvenna, C., Sagiv, N., Tsakanikos, E., Witherby, S. A., Fraser, C., . . . Ward, J. (2006). Synaesthesia: The prevalence of atypical cross-modal experiences. *Perception, 35*(8), 1024–1033. doi: 10.1068/p5469

Simon, D. A., & Bjork, R. A. (2001). Metacognition in motor learning. *Journal of Experimental Psychology: Learning, memory, and cognition, 27*(4), 907–912.

Simon, S. L., Field, J., Miller, L. E., DiFrancesco, M., & Beebe, D. W. (2015). Sweet/dessert foods are more appealing to adolescents after sleep restriction. *PLoS ONE, 10*(2), e0115434. doi: 10.1371/journal.pone.0115434

Simpson, D. (2005). Phrenology and the neurosciences: Contributions of F. J. Gall and J. G. Spurzheim. *ANZ Journal of Surgery, 75*(6), 475–482.

Sin, N. L., Graham-Engeland, J. E., Ong, A. D., & Almeida, D. M. (2015). Affective reactivity to daily stressors is associated with elevated inflammation. *Health Psychology, 34*(12), 1154–1165.

Singer, M. T., & Lalich, J. (1995). *Cults in our midst.* San Francisco: Jossey-Bass.

Singh-Manoux, A., Richards, M., & Marmot, M. (2003). Leisure activities and cognitive function in middle age: Evidence from the Whitehall II study. *Journal of Epidemiology and Community Health, 57*, 907–913.

Skinner, B. F. (1938). *The behavior of organisms: An experimental analysis.* New York: Appleton-Century-Crofts.

Skinner, B. F. (1956). A case history in scientific method. *American Psychologist, 11*, 221–233.

Skinner, B. F. (1961). *Cumulative record: Definitive edition.* New York: Appelton-Century-Crofts.

Skinner, B. F. (1971). *Beyond freedom and dignity.* New York: Alfred A. Knopf.

Skinner, B. F. (1974). *About behaviorism.* New York: Alfred A. Knopf.

Skinner, B. F. (1989) The origins of cognitive thought. *Recent Issues in the Analysis of Behavior*, Princeton, NC: Merrill Publishing Company.

Skolnick, A. (1986). Early attachment and personal relationships across the life course. In P. B. Baltes, D. L. Featherman, & R. M. Lerner (Eds.), *Life-span development and behavior* (vol. 7). Hillsdale, NJ: Erlbaum.

Skorska, M. N., Geniole, S. N., Vrysen, B. M., McCormick, C. M., & Bogaert, A. F. (2015). Facial structure predicts sexual orientation in both men and women. *Archives of Sexual Behavior, 44*, 1377–1394.

Slater, A. (2000). Visual perception in the young infant: Early organisation and rapid learning. In D. Muir & A. Slater (Eds.), *Infant development: The essential readings.* Oxford, UK: Blackwell.

Slater M., Antley, A., Davison, A., Swapp, D., Guger, C., Barker, C., . . . Sanchez-Vives, M. V. (2006). A virtual reprise of the Stanley Milgram obedience experiments. *PLoS ONE 1*(1), e39. doi:10.1371/journal.pone.0000039

Sleddens, E. F., Gerards, S. M., Thijs, C., de Vries, N. K., & Kremers, S. P. (2011). General parenting, childhood overweight and obesity-inducing behaviors: A review. *International Journal of Pediatric Obesity, 6*, (2–2), e12–27.

Slipp, S. (1993). *The Freudian mystique: Freud, women and feminism.* New York: New York University Press.

Sloan, D. M., & Mizes, J. S. (1999). Foundations of behavior therapy in the contemporary healthcare context. *Clinical Psychology Review, 19*, 255–274.

Smith, A. R., Steinberg, L., Strang, N., & Chein, J. (2015). Age differences in the impact of peers on adolescents' and adults' neural response to reward. *Developmental Cognitive Neuroscience, 11*, 75–82.

Smith, M. A., Roediger, H. L., & Karpicke, J. D. (2013). Covert retrieval practice benefits retention as much as overt retrieval practice. *Journal of Experimental Psychology. Learning, Memory, and Cognition.* doi: 10.1037/a0033569

Smith, T. C., Ryan, M. A. K., Wingard, D. L., Sallis, J. F., & Kritz-Silverstein, D. (2008). New onset and persistent symptoms of post-traumatic stress disorder self-reported after deployment and combat exposures: Prospective population based U.S. military cohort study. *British Medical Journal, 336*(7640), 366–371.

Smolen, P., Baxter, D. A., Byrne, J. H., (2006). A model of the roles of essential kinases in the induction and expression of late long-term potentiation. *Biophysical Journal, 90*, 2760–2775.

Snarey, J. R. (1985). Cross-cultural universality of social-moral development: A critical review of Kohlbergian research. *Psychological Bulletin, 97*(2), 202–232.

Snitz, B. E., O'Meara, E. S., Carlson, M. C., Arnold, A. M., Ives, D. G., Rapp, S. R., . . . DeKosky, S. T. (2009). Ginkgo biloba for preventing cognitive decline in older adults. *The Journal of the American Medical Association, 302*(24), 2663–2670.

Snyder, C. R., & Lopez, S. J. (2005). The future of positive psychology. In C. R. Snyder & S. J. Lopez (Eds.), *Handbook of positive psychology* (pp. 751–767). New York: Oxford University Press.

Snyder, D. J., & Bartoshuk, L. M. (2009). Epidemiological studies of taste function: Discussion and perspectives. *Annals of the New York Academy of Sciences, 1170*, 574–580.

Snyder, H. R., Kaiser, R. H., Warren, S. L., & Heller, W. (2015). Obsessive-compulsive disorder is associated with broad impairments in executive function: A meta-analysis. *Clinical Psychological Science, 3*(2), 301–330. doi: 10.1177/2167702614534210

Snyder, M., Tanke, E. D., & Berscheid, E. (1977). Social perception and interpersonal behavior: On the self-fulfilling nature of social stereotypes. *Journal of Personality and Social Psychology, 35*, 656–666.

Snyder, T. D., & Dillow, S. A. (2010). Digest of education statistics 2009 (NCES Publication No. NCES 2010-013). Washington, DC: National Center for Education Statistics, Institute of Education Sciences, U.S. Department of Education.

Söderlund, J., Schröder, J., Nordin, C., Samuelsson, M., Walther-Jallow, L., Karlsson, H., . . . Engberg, G. (2009). Activation of brain interleukin-1® in schizophrenia. *Molecular Psychiatry, 14*(12), 1069.

Sodowsky, G. R., Lai, E. W., & Plake, B. S. (1991). Moderating effects of socio-cultural variables on acculturation attitudes of Hispanics and Asian Americans. *Journal and Counseling and Development, 70*, 194–204.

Soomro, G. M. (2001). Obsessive-compulsive disorder. *Clinical Evidence, 6*, 754–762.

Somerville, L. H., Jones, R. M., Ruberry, E. J., Dyke, J. P., Glover, G., & Casey, B. J. (2013). The medial prefrontal cortex and the emergence of self-conscious emotion in adolescence. *Psychological Science, 24*, 1554–1562.

Song, Y., Ma, J., Wang, H.-J., Wang, Z., Lau, P. W. C., & Agardh, A. (2015). Age at spermarche: 15-year trend and its association with body mass index in Chinese school-aged boys. *Pediatric Obesity.* doi: 10.1111/ijpo.12073

Sorkhabi, N. (2005). Applicability of Baumrind's parent typology to collective cultures: Analysis of cultural explanations of parent socialization effects. *International Journal of Behavioral Development, 29*(6), 552–563. doi: 10.1177/01650250500172640

Spalding, K. L., Bergmann, O., Alkass, K., Bernard, S., Salehpour, M., Huttner, H. B., . . . Frisen, J. (2013). Dynamics of hippocampal neurogenesis in adult humans. *Cell, 153*(6), 1219–1227. doi: 10.1016/j.cell.2013.05.002

Spangler, W. D. (1992). Validity of questionnaire and TAT measures of need for achievement: Two meta-analyses. *Psychological Bulletin, 112*, 140–154.

Sparing, R., Mottaghy, F., Ganis, G., Thompson, W. L., Toepper, R., Kosslyn, S. M., & Pascual-Leone, A. (2002). Visual cortex excitability increases during visual mental imagery—A TMS study in healthy human subjects. *Brain Research, 938*, 92–97.

Spearman, C. (1904). "General intelligence" objectively determined and measured. *American Journal of Psychology, 15*, 201–293.

Speca, M., Carlson, L. E, Goodey, E., & Angen, E. (2000). A randomized wait-list controlled clinical trial: The effects of a mindfulness meditation-based stress reduction program on mood and symptoms of stress in cancer outpatients. *Psychosomatic Medicine, 6*, 2613–2622.

Sperling, G. (1960). The information available in brief visual presentations. *Psychological Monographs, 74*(11), 1–29.

Speroff, L., Glass, R. H., & Kase, N. G. (1999). Recurrent early pregnancy loss. In *Clinical Gynecologic endocrinology and infertility* (pp. 1042–1055). Philadelphia: Lippincott Williams & Wilkins.

Sperry, R. W. (1968). Mental unity following surgical disconnection of the cerebral hemispheres. *The Harvey Lectures. Series, 62*, 293–323. New York: Academic Press.

Spiegel, D., Bloom, J. R., & Gottheil, E. (1989). Effects of psychosocial treatment on survival of patients with metastatic breast cancer. *Lancet, 2*, 888–891.

Springer, S. P., & Deutsch, G. (1998). *Left brain, right brain: Perspectives from cognitive neuroscience* (5th ed.). New York: Freeman.

Squire, L. R., & Alvarez, P. (1995). Retrograde amnesia and memory consolidation: A neurobiological perspective. *Current Opinion in Neurobiology, 5*(2), 169–177.

Squire, L. R., & Kandel, E. (1999). *Memory: From mind to molecule.* New York: Scientific American Library.

Squire, L. R., & Kandel, E. R. (2009). *Memory: From mind to molecules.* Greenwood Village, CO: Roberts and Company Publishers.

Squire, L. R., Knowlton, B., & Musen, G. (1993). The structure and organization of memory. *Annual Review of Psychology, 44*, 453–495.

Squire, L. R., Slater, P. C., & Chace, P. M. (1975). Retrograde amnesia: Temporal gradient in very long-term memory following electroconvulsive therapy. *Science, 187*, 77–79.

Stahl, S. M. (2013). *Stahl's essential psychopharmacology: Neuroscientific basis and practical applications* (4th ed.). New York: Cambridge University Press.

Standing, L., Conezio, J., & Haber, R. N. (1970). Perception and memory for pictures: Single-trial learning of 2500 visual stimuli. *Psychonomic Science, 19*, 73–74.

Stanovich, K. E., & West, R. F. (2000). Individual differences in reasoning: Implications for the rationality debate? *Behavioral and Brain Sciences, 23*(5), 645–665; discussion 665–726.

Steele, C. M. (1992). Race and the schooling of Black Americans. *The Atlantic Monthly, 269*(4), 68–78.

Steele, C. M. (1997). A threat in the air: How stereotypes shape intellectual identity and performance. *American Psychologist, 52*, 613–629.

Steele, C. M. (1999, August). Thin ice: "stereotype threat" and Black college students. *The Atlantic Monthly, 284*, 44–54.

Steele, C. M., & Aronson J. (1995). Stereotype threat and the intellectual test performance of African Americans. *Journal of Personality and Social Psychology, 69*, 797–811.

Steele, J., James, J. B., & Barnett, R. C. (2002). Learning in a man's world: Examining the perceptions of undergraduate women in male-dominated academic areas. *Psychology of Women Quarterly, 26*, 46–50.

Stefanovic-Stanojevic, T., Tosic-Radev, M., & Velikic, D. (2015). Maternal attachment and children's emotional and cognitive competencies. *Psihologijske Tema, 24*, 51–69.

Stein, H. T. (2001). Adlerian overview of birth order characteristics. Alfred Adler Institute of San Francisco. Retrieved June 16, 2004, at http://pws.cablespeed.com/~htstein/birthord.htm

Stein, S. (1984). *Girls and boys: The limits of non-sexist rearing.* London: Chatto & Windus.

Stein-Behrens, B., Mattson, M. P., Chang, I., Yeh, M., & Sapolsky, R. (1994). Stress exacerbates neuron loss and cytoskeletal pathology in the hippocampus. *Journal of Neuroscience, 14*, 5373–5380.

Steinberg, L., & Silverberg, S. B. (1987). Influences on marital satisfaction during the middle stages of the family life cycle. *Journal of Marriage and the Family, 49*, 751–760.

Steriade, M., & McCarley, R. W. (1990). *Brainstem control of wakefulness and sleep.* New York: Plenum.

Stern, W. (1912). *The psychological methods of testing intelligence* (G. M. Whipple, Trans.) (Educational Psychology Monograph No. 13). Baltimore, MD: Warwick & York, Inc.

Sternberg, R. J. (1986). A triangular theory of love. *Psychological Review, 93*, 119–135.

Sternberg, R. J. (1988a). *The triarchic mind: A new theory of human intelligence.* New York: Viking-Penguin.

Sternberg, R. J. (1988b). Triangulating love. In R. Sternberg & M. Barnes (Eds.), *The psychology of love* (pp. 119–138). New Haven, CT: Yale University Press.

Sternberg, R. J. (1996). *Successful intelligence: How practical and creative intelligence determine success in life.* New York: Simon & Schuster.

Sternberg, R. J. (1997a). Construct validation of a triangular love scale. *European Journal of Social Psychology, 27*, 313–335.

Sternberg, R. J. (1997b). The triarchic theory of intelligence. In P. Flannagan, J. L. Genshaft, & P. L. Harrison (Eds.), *Contemporary intellectual assessment: Theories, tests, and issues* (pp. 92–104). New York: Guilford Press.

Sternberg, R. J. (2005). The triarchic theory of successful intelligence. In *Contemporary Intellectual Assessment: Theories, Tests, and Issues.* New York: Guilford Press.

Sternberg, R. J. (2015). Successful intelligence: A model for testing intelligence beyond IQ tests. *European Journal of Education and Psychology, 8*(2), 76–84. doi: 10.1016/j.ejeps.2015.09.004

Sternberg, R. J., & Grigorenko, E. L. (2006). Cultural intelligence and successful intelligence. *Group Organization Management, 31*, 27–39.

Sternberg, R. J., & Kaufman, J. C. (1998). Human abilities. *Annual Review of Psychology, 49*, 479–502.

Sternberger, R. R., Turner, S. M., Beidel, D. C., & Calhoun, K. S. (1995). Social phobia: An analysis of possible developmental factors. *Journal of Abnormal Psychology, 194*, 526–531.

Stevenson, M. B., Roach, M. A., Leavitt, L. A., Miller, J. F., & Chapman, R. S. (1988). Early receptive and productive language skills in preterm and full-term 8-month-old infants. *Journal of Psycholinguistic Research, 17*(2), 169–183.

Stewart, S. (2012). Hurricane Sandy discussion number 25? (report). National Hurricane Center. Retrieved May 28, 2013, from http://www.nhc.noaa.gov/archive/2012/al18/al182012.discus.025.shtml?

Stickgold, R., Hobson, J. A., Fosse, R., & Fosse, M. (2001). Sleep, learning and dreams: Off-line memory reprocessing. *Science, 294*, 1052–1057.

Stickgold, R., & Ellenbogen, J. M. (2008). Quiet! Sleeping brain at work. *Scientific American Mind, 19*(4), 23–29.

Stiff, J. B., & Mongeau, P. A. (2002). *Persuasive communication* (2nd ed.). New York: Guilford Press.

Stigler, S. M. (1997). Regression towards the mean, historically considered. *Statistical Methods in Medical Research, 6*(2), 103–114.

Stipek, D. J., Gralinski, J. H., & Kopp, C. B. (1990). Self-concept development in the toddler years. *Developmental Psychology, 26*(6), 972–977.

Stockhorst, U., Gritzmann, E., Klopp, K., Schottenfeld-Naor, Y., Hübinger, A., Berresheim, H., . . . Gries, F. A. (1999). Classical conditioning of insulin effects in healthy humans. *Psychosomatic Medicine, 61*, 424–435.

Stoesz, B. M., Hare, J. F., & Snow, W. M. (2013). Neurophysiological mechanisms underlying affiliative social behavior: Insights from comparative research. *Neuroscience and Biobehavioral Reviews, 37*(2), 123–132. doi: 10.1016/j.neubiorev.2012.11.007

Stoodley, C. J., & Schmahmann, J. D. (2009). Functional topography in the human cerebellum: A meta-analysis of neuroimaging studies. *NeuroImage, 44*(2), 489–501. doi: 10.1016/j.neuroimage.2008.08.039

Stoodley, C. J., Valera, E. M., & Schmahmann, J. D. (2012). Functional topography of the cerebellum for motor and cognitive tasks: An fMRI study. *NeuroImage, 59*(2), 1560–1570. doi: 10.1016/j.neuroimage.2011.08.065

Stoeckel, L. E., Garrison, K. A., Ghosh, S., Wighton, P., Hanlon, C. A., Gilman, J. M., . . . Evins, A. E. (2014). Optimizing real time fMRI neurofeedback for therapeutic discovery and development. *Neuroimage: Clinical, 5*, 245–255. doi: 10.1016/j.nicl.2014.07.002

Storey, A. E., Walsh, C. J., Quinton, R. L., & Wynne-Edwards, K. E. (2000). Hormonal correlates of paternal responsiveness in new and expectant fathers. *Evolution and Human Behavior 21*, 79–95.

Stowell, J. R., Kiecolt-Glaser, J. K., & Glaser, R. (2001). Perceived stress and cellular immunity: When coping counts. *Journal of Behavioral Medicine, 24*(4), 323–339.

Stratton, K., Gable, A., & McCormick, M. C. (Eds.). (2001a). *Immunization safety review: Thimerosal-containing vaccines and neurodevelopmental disorders.* Washington, DC: National Academies Press.

Stratton, K., Wilson, C. B., & McCormick, M. C. (Eds.). (2001b). *Immunization safety review: Measles-mumps-rubella vaccine and autism.* Washington, DC: National Academies Press.

Straus, M. A. (2000). Corporal punishment of children and adult depression and suicidal ideation. *Beating the devil out of them: Corporal punishment in American families and its effects on children* (pp. 60–77). New York: Lexington Books.

Strauss, A. S. (2004). The meaning of death in Northern Cheyenne culture. In A. C. G. M. Robben (Ed.), *Death, mourning, and burial: A cross-cultural reader* (pp. 71–76). Malden, MA: Blackwell.

Strauss, C., Rosten, C., Hayward, M., Lea, L., Forrester, E., & Jones, A. M. (2015). Mindfulness-based exposure and response prevention for obsessive compulsive disorder: Study protocol for a pilot randomised controlled trial. *Trials, 16*, 167. doi: 10.1186/s13063-015-0664-7

Strawbridge, W. J., Cohen, R. D., Shema, S. J., & Kaplan, G. A. (1997). Frequent attendance at religious services and mortality over 28 years. *American Journal of Public Health, 87*, 957–961.

Strayer, D. L., & Drews, F. A. (2007). Cell-phone-induced driver distraction. *Current Directions in Psychological Science, 16*, 128–131.

Strayer, D. L., Drews, F. A., & Crouch, D. J. (2006). A comparison of the cell phone driver and the drunk driver. *Human Factors, 48*, 381–391.

Strayer, D. L., & Johnston, W. A. (2001). Driven to distraction: Dual-task studies of simulated driving and conversing on a cellular phone. *Psychological Science, 12*, 462–466.

Strayer, D. L., Turrill, J., Coleman, J. R., Ortiz, E. V., & Cooper, J. M. (2014). Measuring cognitive distraction in the automobile II: Assessing in-vehicle voice-based interactive technologies. AAA Foundation for Traffic Safety Fact Sheet. Retrieved from https://www.aaafoundation.org/sites/default/files/Cog%20Distraction%20Phase%202%20FINAL%20FTS%20FORMAT_0.pdf

Strehl, U., Birkle, S., Wörz, S., & Kotchoubey, B. (2014). Sustained reduction of seizures in patients with intractable epilepsy after self-regulation training of slow cortical potentials—10 years after. *Frontiers in Human Neuroscience, 8*(1), 604.

Strick, P. L., Dum, R. P., & Fiez, J. A. (2009). Cerebellum and nonmotor function. *Annual Review of Neuroscience, 32*, 413–434. doi: 10.1146/annurev.neuro.31.060407.125606

Stromeyer, C. F., III, & Psotka, J. (1971). The detailed texture of eidetic images. *Nature, 237*, 109–112.

Stroth, S., Hille, K., Spitzer, M., & Reinhardt, R. (2009). Aerobic endurance exercise benefits memory and affect in young adults. *Neuropsychological Rehabilitation, 19*(2), 223–243.

Strunk, D. R., Brotman, M. A., & DeRubeis, R. J. (2010). The process of change in cognitive therapy for depression: Predictors of early inter-session symptom gains. *Behaviour Research and Therapy, 48*(7), 599–606.

Stubbs, R. J., van Wyk, M. C., Johnstone, A. M., & Harbron, C. G. (1996). Breakfasts high in protein, fat or carbohydrate: Effect on within-day appetite and energy balance. *European Journal of Clinical Nutrition, 50*(7), 409–417.

Stuss, D. T., Binns, M. A., Murphy, K. J., & Alexander, M. P. (2002). Dissociations within the anterior attentional system: Effects of task complexity and irrelevant information on reaction time speed and accuracy. *Neuropsychology, 16*, 500–513.

Su, L., Cai, Y., Xu, Y., Dutt, A., Shi, S., & Bramon, E. (2014). Cerebral metabolism in major depressive disorder: A voxel-based meta-analysis of positron emission tomography studies. *BMC Psychiatry, 14*, 321. doi: 10.1186/s12888-014-0321-9

Sue, D. W. (2010). *Microaggressions and marginality: Manifestation, dynamics, and impact.* Hoboken, NJ: John Wiley & Sons.

Sue, D. W., & Sue, D. (2016). *Counseling the Culturally Diverse: Theory and Practice* (7th d.). Hoboken, NJ: John Wiley & Sons.

Sue, S. (1977). Community mental health services to minority groups: Some optimism, some pessimism. *American Psychologist, 32*, 616–624.

Sue, S. (1992). Ethnicity and mental health: Research and policy issues. *Journal of Social Issues, 48*(2), 187–205.

Sue, S., Zane, N., & Young, K. (1994). Research on psychotherapy in culturally diverse populations. In A. Bergin & S. Garfield (Eds.), *Handbook of psychotherapy and behavior change* (pp. 783–817). New York: Wiley.

Suleiman, J., & Watson, R. T. (2008). Social loafing in technology-supported teams. *Computer Supported Cooperative Work, 17*, 291–309.

Sullivan, D. R., Liu, X., Corwin, D. S., Verceles, A. C., McCurdy, M. T., Pate, D. A., . . . Netzer, G. (2012). Learned helplessness among families and surrogate decision-makers of patients admitted to medical, surgical, and trauma ICUs. *Chest, 142*(6), 1440–1446. doi: 10.1378/chest.12-0112

Sullivan, P. F. (2005). The genetics of schizophrenia. *PLoS Med, 2*(7), e212. doi: 05-PLME-RIT-0198R1

Sullivan, P. F., Neale, M. C., & Kendler, K. S. (2000). Genetic epidemiology of major depression: Review and meta-analysis, *American Journal of Psychiatry, 157*, 1552–1562.

Sulloway, F. J. (1996). *Born to rebel: Birth order, family dynamics, and creative lives.* New York: Pantheon.

Sulzer, J., Sitaram, R., Blefari, M. L., Kollias, S., Birbaumer, N., Stephan, K. E., . . . Gassert, R. (2013). Neurofeedback-mediated self-regulation of the dopaminergic midbrain. *Neuroimage, 75C*, 176–184. doi: 10.1016/j.neuroimage.2013.02.041

Suryani, L., & Jensen, S. (1993). *Trance and possession in Bali: A window on western multiple personality, possession disorder, and suicide.* New York: Oxford University Press.

Sutcliffe, N., Clarke, A. E., Levinton, C., Frost, C., Gordon, C., & Isenberg, D. A. (1999). Associates of health status in patients with systemic lupus erythematosus. *Journal of Rheumatology, 26*, 2352–2356.

Sutherland, P. (1992). *Cognitive development today: Piaget and his critics.* London: Paul Chapman.

Svebak, S., Romundstad, S., & Holmen, J. (2010). A 7-year prospective study of sense of humor and mortality in an adult county population: The HUNT-2 study. *The International Journal of Psychiatry in Medicine, 40*(2), 125–146.

Swaab, D. F., Bao, A.-M., Garcia-Falgueras, A., Hofman, M. A., & Ishunina, T. A. (2012). Sex differences in the forebrain. In J. K. Mai & G. Paxinos (Eds.), *The human nervous system* (pp. 739–758). London, UK: Academic Press

Swann, J. (1998). Talk control: An illustration from the classroom of problems in analyzing male dominance of conversation. In J. Coates (Ed.), *Language and gender: A reader* (pp. 185–196). Oxford, UK: Blackwell.

Swanson, H. (1994). Index of suspicion. Case 3. Diagnosis: Failure to thrive due to psychosocial dwarfism. *Pediatric Review*, 15(1), 39, 41.

Swayze, V. W., II. (1995). Frontal leukotomy and related psychosurgical procedures in the era before antipsychotics (1935–1954): A historical overview. *American Journal of Psychiatry*, 152(4), 505–515.

Swenson, D. D., & Marshall, B. (2005, May 14). Flash flood: Hurricane Katrina's inundation of New Orleans, August 29, 2005. *Times-Picayune*, p. 3.

Sykes-Muskett, B. J., Prestwich, A., Lawton, R. J., & Armitage, C. J. (2015). The utility of monetary contingency contracts for weight loss: A systematic review and meta-analysis. *Health Psychology Review*, 9(4), 434–451. doi: 10.1080/17437199.2015.1030685

Szalavitz, M. (2009). Popping smart pills: the case for cognitive enhancement. *Time* in partnership with CNN. Retrieved May 5, 2010, from http://www.time.com/time/health/article/0,8599,1869435,00.html

Szell, M., & Thurner, S. (2013). How women organize social networks different from men. *Scientific Reports*, 3, 1214. doi: 10.1038/srep01214

Tagliatela, J. P., Savage-Rumbaugh, E. S., & Baker, L. A. (2003). Vocal production by a language-competent bonobo (*Pan paniscus*). *International Journal of Comparative Psychology*, 24, 1–17.

Tajfel, H., & Turner, J. C. (1986). The social identity theory of intergroup behaviour. In S. Worchel & W. G. Austin (Eds.), *The psychology of intergroup relations* (Vol. 2, pp. 7–24) New York: Nelson Hall.

Takahashi, A., Lee, R. X., Iwasato, T., Itohara, S., Arima, H., Bettler, B., . . . Koide, T. (2015). Glutamate input in the dorsal raphe nucleus as a determinant of escalated aggression in male mice. *Journal of Neuroscience*, 35(16), 6452. doi: 10.1523/JNEUROSCI.2450-14.2015

Takeuchi, T., Ogilvie, R. D., Murphy, T. I., & Ferrelli, A. V. (2003). EEG activities during elicited sleep onset. REM and NREM periods reflect difference mechanisms of dream generation. *Clinical Neurophysiology*, 114(2), 210–220.

Talbott, G. D., & Crosby, L. R. (2001). Recovery contracts: Seven key elements. In R. H. Coombs (Ed.), *Addiction recovery tools* (pp. 127–144). Thousand Oaks, CA: Sage.

Tammen, S. A., Friso, S., & Choi, S. W. (2013). Epigenetics: The link between nature and nurture. *Molecular Aspects of Medicine*, 34(4), 753–764. doi: 10.1016/j.mam.2012.07.018

Tan, M. S., Yu, J. T., Tan, C. C., Wang, H. F., Meng, X. F., Wang, C., . . . Tan, L. (2015). Efficacy and adverse effects of ginkgo biloba for cognitive impairment and dementia: A systematic review and meta-analysis. *Journal of Alzheimer's Disease*, 43(2), 589–603.

Tannenbaum, M. B., Hepler, J., Zimmerman, R. S., Saul, L., Jacobs, S., Wilson, K., & Albarracín, D. (2015). Appealing to fear: A meta-analysis of fear appeal effectiveness and theories. *Psychological Bulletin*, 141(6), 1178–1204.

Tang, Y.-Y., Holzel, B. K., & Posner, M. I. (2015). The neuroscience of mindfulness meditation. *Nature Reviews Neuroscience*, 16, 213–225.

Tarescavage, A. M., Fischler, G. L., Cappo, B. M., Hill, D. O., Corey, D. M., & Ben-Porath, Y. S. (2015). Minnesota Multiphasic Personality Inventory-2—Restructured Form (MMPI-2-RF) predictors of police officer problem behavior and collateral self-report test scores. *Psychological Assessment*, 27(1), 125–137. doi: 10.1037/pas0000041

Tatke, S. (2012). Bystander effect typifies Indian psyche. The Times of India, July 15, 2012. Retrieved from http://timesofindia.indiatimes.com/city/mumbai/Bystander-effect-typifies-Indian-psyche/articleshow/14924402.cms

Taylor, B., Miller, E., Farrington, C. P., Petropoulos, M. C., Favot-Mayaud, I., Li, J., & Waight, P. A. (1999). Autism and measles, mumps, and rubella vaccine: No epidemiological evidence for a causal association. *Lancet*, 353, 2026–2029.

Taylor, C., Manganello, J. A., Lee, S. J., & Rice, J. C. (2010). Mothers' spanking of 3-year-old children and subsequent risk of children's aggressive behavior. *Pediatrics*, 125, 1057–1065.

Taylor, D. M., & Moghaddam, F. M. (1994). *Theories of intergroup relations: International social psychological perspectives* (2nd ed.). Westport, CT: Praeger.

Taylor, E. (2001). Positive psychology and humanistic psychology: A reply to Seligman. *Journal of Humanistic Psychology*, 41(1), 13–29. doi: 10.1177/0022167801411003

Taylor, S. E. (2006). Tend and befriend: Biobehavioral bases of affiliation under stress. *Current Directions in Psychological Science*, 15, 273–277.

Taylor, S. E., Klein, L. C., Lewis, B. P., Gruenewald, T. L., Gurung, R. A. R., & Updegraff, J. A. (2000). Biobehavioral responses to stress in females: Tend-and-befriend, not fight-or-flight. *Psychological Review*, 107(3), 411–429.

Teigen, K. (1994). Yerkes–Dodson: A law for all seasons. *Theory & Psychology*, 4, 525–547.

Temoshok, L., & Dreher, H. (1992). *The Type C connection: The behavioral links to cancer and your health*. New York: Random House.

Temple, J. R., & Choi, H. J. (2014). Longitudinal association between sexting and sexual behavior. *Pediatrics*, 134(5), e1287–e1292. doi: 10.1542/peds.2014-1974

Terracciano, A., Sutin, A. R., An, Y., O'Brien, R. J., Ferrucci, L., Zonderman, A. B., & Resnick, S. M. (2014). Personality and risk of Alzheimer's disease: New data and meta-analysis. *Alzheimer's & Dementia*, 10(2), 179–186. doi: 10.1016/j.jalz.2013.03.002

Terman, L. M. (1916). *The measurement of intelligence*. Boston: Houghton Mifflin.

Terman, L. M. (1925). *Mental and physical traits of a thousand gifted children (I)*. Stanford, CA: Stanford University Press.

Terman, L. M., & Oden, M. H. (1947). *The gifted child grows up: 25 years' follow-up of a superior group: Genetic studies of genius (Vol. 4)*. Stanford, CA: Stanford University Press.

Terman, L. M., & Oden, M. H. (1959). *The gifted group at mid-life, thirty-five years follow-up of the superior child: Genetic studies of genius (Vol. 3)*. Stanford, CA: Stanford University Press.

Tesler, N., Gerstenberg, M., Franscini, M., Jenni, O. G., Walitza, S., & Huber, R. (2016). Increased frontal sleep slow wave activity in adolescents with major depression. *Neuroimage: Clinical*, 10, 250–256. doi: 10.1016/j.nicl.2015.10.014

Tevis, M. (1994). "George I. Sanchez." In *Lives in education: A narrative of people and ideas*, 2nd ed., ed. L. Glenn Smith, Joan K. Smith, pp. 346–354. New York: St. Martin's Press.

Thall-Bastow, B. D. (2016). Teratology and drug use during pregnancy. *Medscape: News & Perspective: Drugs & Diseases: CME & Education*. Retrieved from http://emedicine.medscape.com/article/260725-overview#showall

Thase, M. E. (1999). When are psychotherapy and pharmacotherapy combinations the treatment of choice for major depressive disorders? *Psychiatric Quarterly*, 70(4), 333–346.

Thase, M. E., & Sachs, G. S. (2000). Bipolar depression: Pharmacotherapy and related therapeutic strategies. *Biological Psychiatry*, 48(6), 558–572.

The College Board. (2011). Time management tips for students. Retrieved May 31, 2013, from http://www.collegeboard.com/student/plan/college-success/116.html

Thibodeau, P. H., & Boroditsky, L. (2013). Natural language metaphors covertly influence reasoning. *PLoS One*, 8(1). doi: 10.1371/journal.pone.0052961

Thibodeau, P. H., & Boroditsky, L. (2015). Measuring effects of metaphor in a dynamic opinion landscape. *PLoS One*, 10(7), e0133939. doi: 10.1371/journal.pone.0133939

Thiedke, C. C. (2001). Sleep disorders and sleep problems in childhood. *American Family Physician*, 63, 277–284.

Thomas, A., & Chess, S. (1977). *Temperament and development*. New York: Brunner/Mazel.

Thomas, A. G., Dennis, A., Rawlings, N. B., Stagg, C. J., Matthews, L., Morris, M., . . . Johansen-Berg, H. (2015). Multi-modal characterization of rapid anterior hippocampal volume increase associated with aerobic exercise. *Neuroimage*. doi: 10.1016/j.neuroimage.2015.10.090

Thomas, E. F., McGarty, C., & Mavor, K. (2016). Group interaction as the crucible of social identity formation: A glimpse at the foundations of social identities for collective action. *Group Processes & Intergroup Relations*, 19(2), 137–151.

Thomas, M., Thorne, D., Sing, H., Redmond, D., Balkin, T., Wesensten, N., Russo, M., Welsh, A., Rowland, L., Johnson, D., Aladdin, R., Cephus, R., Hall, S., & Belenky, G. (1998). The relationship between driving accidents and microsleep during cumulative partial sleep deprivation. *Journal of Sleep Research*, 7(2), 275.

Thomas, R. K. (1994). Pavlov's rats "dripped saliva at the sound of a bell." *Psycoloquy*, 5(80). Retrieved May 9, 2008, from http://www.cogsci.ecs.soton.ac.uk/cgi/psyc/newpsy?5.80

Thompson, W. W., Price, C., Goodson, B., Shay, D. K., Benson, P., Hinrichsen, V. L., . . . DeStefano, F. (2007). Early thimerosal exposure and neuropsychological outcomes at 7 to 10 years. *The New England Journal of Medicine*, 357(13), 1281–1292.

Thoresen, C. E., & Harris, H. S. (2002). Spirituality and health: What's the evidence and what's needed? *Annals of Behavioral Medicine*, 24, 3–13.

Thorndike, E. L. (1911). *Animal intelligence: Experimental studies*. New York: MacMillan.

Thorndike, E. L. (1920). A constant error on psychological rating. *Journal of Applied Psychology*, 5, 25–29.

Thornton, A., & Hui-Sheng, L. (1994). Continuity and change. In A. Thornton & Hui-Sheng (Eds.), *Social change and the family in Taiwan* (pp. 396–410). Chicago: University of Chicago Press.

Thurstone, L. (1938). *Primary mental abilities*. Chicago: University of Chicago Press.

Tian, R., Hou, G., Li, D., & Yuan, T.-F. (2014). A possible change process of inflammatory cytokines in the prolonged chronic stress and its ultimate implications for health. The Scientific World Journal, 2014, Article ID 780616. doi: 10.1155/2014/780616

Tienari, P., Wynne, L. C., Sorri, A., Lahti, I., Läksy, K., Moring, J., . . . Wahlberg, K-E. (2004). Genotype-environment interaction in schizophrenia-spectrum disorder: Long-term follow-up study of Finnish adoptees. *The British Journal of Psychiatry*, 184, 216–222.

Tobach, E. (2001). Development of sex and gender. In J. Worell (Ed.), *Encyclopedia of women and gender* (pp. 315–332). San Diego, CA: Academic Press.

Toga, A. W., & Thompson, P. M. (2003). Mapping brain asymmetry. *Nature Reviews Neuroscience*, 4, 37–48.

Toker, S., Shirom, A., Melamed, S., & Armon, G. (2012). Work characteristics as predictors of diabetes incidence among apparently healthy employees. *Journal of Occupational Health Psychology*, 17(3), 259. doi: 10.1037/a0028401

Tolman, E. C., & Honzik, C. H. (1930). Introduction and removal of reward and maze learning in rats. *University of California Publications in Psychology*, 4, 257–275.

Tomassy, G. S., Berger, D. R., Chen, H.-H., Kasthuri, N., Hayworth, K. J., Vercelli, A., . . . Arlotta, P. (2014). Distinct profiles of myelin distribution along single axons of pyramidal neurons in the neocortex. *Science, 344*(6181), 319–324. doi: 10.1126/science.1249766

Tomasello, M., Carpenter, M., & Lizskowski, U. (2007). A new look at infant pointing. *Child Development, 78*, 705–722.

Tor, P. C., Bautovich, A. Wang, M. J., Martin, D., Harvey, S. B., & Loo, C. (2015). A systematic review and meta-analysis of brief versus ultrabrief right unilateral electroconvulsive therapy for depression. *The Journal of Clinical Psychiatry, 76*(9), e1092–1098. doi: 10.4088/JCP.14r09145

Torgersen, S., Czajkowski, N., Jacobson, K., Reichborn-Kjennerud, T., Roysamb, E., Neale, M. C., & Kendler, K. S. (2008). Dimensional representations of DSM-IV cluster B personality disorders in a population-based sample of Norwegian twins: A multivariate study. *Psychological Medicine, 38*(11), 1617–1625. doi: 10.1017/s0033291708002924

Torrance, E. P. (1993). The Beyonders in a thirty-year longitudinal study of creative achievement. *Roeper Review, 15*(3), 131–135.

Townsend, S., Kim, H. S., & Mesquita, B. (2014). Are you feeling what I'm feeling? Emotional similarity buffers stress. *Social Psychological and Personality Science, 5*(5), 526–533.

Trace, S. E., Baker, J. H., Penas-Lledo, E., & Bulik, C. M. (2013). The genetics of eating disorders. *Annual Review of Clinical Psychology, 9*, 589–620. doi: 10.1146/annurev-clinpsy-050212-185546

Traffanstedt, M. K., Mehta, S., & LoBello, S. G. (2016). Major depression with seasonal variation: Is it a valid construct? *Clinical Psychological Science.* doi: 10.1177/2167702615615867

Trappey, C. (1996). A meta-analysis of consumer choice and subliminal advertising. *Psychology and Marketing, 13*, 517–530.

Trauer, J. M., Qian, M. Y., Doyle, J. S., Rajaratnam, S. M. W., & Cunnington, D. (2015). Cognitive behavioral therapy for chronic insomnia: A systematic review and meta-analysis. *Annals of Internal Medicine, 163*(3), 191–204. doi: 10.7326/M14-2841

Treadway, M. T., Buckholtz, J. W., Martin, J. W., Jan, K., Asplund, C. L., Ginther, M. R., . . . Marois, R. (2014). Corticolimbic gating of emotion-driven punishment. *Nature Neuroscience, 17*, 1270–1275.

Treisman A. [M.] (2006). How the deployment of attention determines what we see. *Visual Cognition, 14*, 411–443.

Treisman, A. M., & Gelade, G. (1980). A feature integration theory of attention. *Cognitive Psychology, 12*, 97–136.

Treisman, M. (1977). Motion sickness: An evolutionary hypothesis. *Science, 197*, 493.

Tremblay, A., Doucet, E., & Imbeault, P. (1999). Physical activity and weight maintenance. *International Journal of Obesity, 23*(3), S50–S54.

Triandis, H. (1971). *Attitude and attitude change.* New York: Wiley.

Trivers, R. L. (1972). Parental investment and sexual selection. In B. Campbell (Ed.), *Sexual selection and the descent of man, 1871–1971* (pp. 136–179). Chicago: Aldine-Atherton.

Trocmé, N., MacLaurin, B., Fallon, B., Daciuk, J., Billingsley, D., Tourigny, M., . . . McKenzie, B. (2001). *Canadian incidence study of reported child abuse and neglect: Final report* (pp. 30–31). Ottawa, ON: Minister of Public Works and Government Services Canada.

Troncoso, X. G., Macknik, S. L., Otero-Millan, J., & Martinez-Conde, S. (2008). Microsaccades drive illusory motion in the enigma illusion. *Proceedings of the National Academy of Sciences, USA, 105*(41), 16033–16038.

Trumbull, E., & Rothstein-Fisch, C. (2011). The intersection of culture and achievement motivation. *eSchool Community Journal, 21*(2), 25–53.

Truong, K. D., Reifsnider, O. S., Mayorga, M. E., & Spitler, H. (2012). Estimated number of preterm births and low birth weight children born in the United State due to maternal binge drinking. *Maternal and Child Health Journal, 17*(4), 677–688.

Trut, L. M. (1999). Early canid domestication: The Farm-Fox experiment. *Science, 283*.

Trzaskowski, M., Harlaar, N., Arden, R., Krapohl, E., Rimfeld, K., McMillan, A., . . . Plomin, R. (2014). Genetic influence on family socioeconomic status and children's intelligence. *Intelligence, 42*(100), 83–88. doi: 10.1016/j.intell.2013.11.002

Tsai, G. E., Condle, D., Wu, M-T., & Chang, I-W. (1999). Functional magnetic resonance imaging of personality switches in a woman with dissociative identity disorder. *Harvard Review of Psychiatry, 7*, 119–122.

Tsai, J. L., Simeonova, D. I., & Watanabe, J. T. (2004). Somatic and social: Chinese Americans talk about emotion. *Personality and Social Psychology Bulletin, 30*(9), 1226–1238.

Tucker, E. W., & Potocky-Tripodi, M. (2006). Changing heterosexuals' attitudes toward homosexuals: A systematic review of the empirical literature. *Research on Social Work Practice, 16*(2), 176–190.

Tucker, M. A., Hirota, Y., Wamsley, E. J., Lau, H., Chaklader, A., & Fishbein, W. (2006). A daytime nap containing solely non-REM sleep enhances declarative but not procedural memory. *Neurobiology of Learning and Memory, 86*(2), 241–247.

Tugade, M. M., & Fredrickson, B. L. (2004). Resilient individuals use positive emotions to bounce back from negative emotional experiences. *Journal of Personality and Social Psychology, 86*(2), 320–333.

Tukuitonga, C. F., & Bindman, A. B. (2002). Ethnic and gender differences in the use of coronary artery revascularisation procedures in New Zealand. *New Zealand Medical Journal, 115*, 179–182.

Tulving, E., & Thomson, D. M. (1973). Encoding specificity and retrieval processes in episodic memory. *Psychological Review, 80*, 352–373.

Tupak, S. V., Dresler, T., Badewien, M., Hahn, T., Ernst, L. H., Herrmann, M. J., . . . Fallgatter, A. J. (2013). Inhibitory transcranial magnetic theta burst stimulation attenuates prefrontal cortex oxygenation. *Human Brain Mapping, 34*(1), 150–157. doi: 10.1002/hbm.21421

Turk, C. L., Heimberg, R. G., & Magee, L. (2008). Social anxiety disorder. In D. H. Barlow (Ed.), *Clinical handbook of psychological disorders* (pp. 123–163). New York: Guilford Press.

Turner, W. J. (1995). Homosexuality, Type 1: An Xq28 phenomenon. *Archives of Sexual Behavior, 24*(2), 109–134.

Tusel, D. J., Piotrowski, N. A., Sees, K., Reilly, P. M., Banys, P., Meek, P., & Hall, S. M. (1994). Contingency contracting for illicit drug use with opioid addicts in methadone treatment. In L. S., Harris (Ed.), *Problems of drug dependence: Proceedings of the 56th Annual Scientific Meeting.* (National Institute on Drug Abuse Research Monograph No. 153, pp. 155–160). Washington, DC: U.S. Goverment Printing Office.

Tversky, A., & Kahneman, D. (1973). Availability: A heuristic for judging frequency and probability. *Cognitive Psychology, 5*(2), 207–232.

Tversky, A., & Shafir, E. (1992). The disjunction effect in choice under uncertainty. *Psychological Science, 3*(5), 305–309.

UNAIDS. (2008). 2008 Report on the global AIDS epidemic. Retrieved June 8, 2010, from http://www.unaids.org/en/KnowledgeCentre/HIVData/GlobalReport/2008/2008_Global_report.asp

UNAIDS. (2009). AIDS epidemic update. Retrieved June 8, 2010, from http://data.unaids.org/pub/Report/2009/JC1700_Epi_Update_2009_en.pdf

UNAIDS. (2014). *Fact sheet: Global statistics.* Retrieved from http://www.unaids.org/sites/default/files/en/media/unaids/contentassets/documents/factsheet/2014/20140716_FactSheet_en.pdf

Underwood, M. K., Beron, K. J., & Rosen, L. H. (2009). Continuity and change in social and physical aggression from middle childhood through early adolescence. *Aggressive Behavior, 35*(5), 357–375.

Unger, R. (1979). Toward a redefinition of sex and gender. *American Psychologist, 34*, 1085–1094.

United Nations Office on Drugs and Crime (UNODC). (2014). World drug report. Retrieved from http://www.unodc.org/documents/wdr2014/World_Drug_Report_2014_web.pdf.

Unsworth, N., Fukuda, K., Awh, E., & Vogel, E. K. (2014). Working memory and fluid intelligence: Capacity, attention control, and secondary memory retrieval. *Cognitive Psychology, 71*, 1–26. doi: 10.1016/j.cogpsych.2014.01.003

Unsworth, N., Fukuda, K., Awh, E., & Vogel, E. K. (2015). Working memory delay activity predicts individual differences in cognitive abilities. *Journal of Cognitive Neuroscience, 27*(5), 853–865. doi: 10.1162/jocn_a_00765

Upthegrove, T., Roscigno, V., & Charles, C. (1999). Big money collegiate sports: Racial concentration, contradictory pressures, and academic performance. *Social Science Quarterly, 80*, 718–737.

U.S. Department of Health and Human Services. (2010). *How tobacco smoke causes disease: What it means to you.* Atlanta, GA: U.S. Department of Health and Human Services, Centers for Disease Control and Prevention, National Center for Chronic Disease Prevention and Health Promotion, Office on Smoking and Health.

U.S. Department of Health and Human Services. (2014). *The health consequences of smoking—50 years of progress: A report of the Surgeon General.* Atlanta, GA: U.S. Department of Health and Human Services, Centers for Disease Control and Prevention, National Center for Chronic Disease Prevention and Health Promotion, Office on Smoking and Health (accessed October 5, 2015) at http://www.surgeongeneral.gov/library/reports/50-years-of-progress/full-report.pdf.

Vail, E. (1976). Factors influencing lower class, black patients' remaining in treatment. *Clinical Psychology, 29*, 12–14.

Vaillant, G. E. (2002). Adaptive mental mechanisms: Their role in a positive psychology. *American Psychologist, 55*, 89–98.

Valerio, S., & Taube, J. S. (2016). Head direction cell activity is absent in mice without the horizontal semicircular canals. *The Journal of Neuroscience, 36*(3), 741–754. doi: 10.1523/JNEUROSCI.3790-14.2016

Val-Laillet, D., Aarts, E., Weber, B., Ferrari, M., Quaresima, V., Stoeckel, L. E., . . . Stice, E. (2015). Neuroimaging and neuromodulation approaches to study eating behavior and prevent and treat eating disorders and obesity. *Neuroimage: Clinical, 8*, 1–31. doi: 10.1016/j.nicl.2015.03.016

Valverde, R., Pozdnyakova, I., Kajander, T., Venkatraman, J., & Regan, L. (2007). Fragile X mental retardation syndrome: Structure of the KH1-KH2 domains of fragile X mental retardation protein. *Structure, 9*, 1090–1098.

Van de Castle, R. (1994). *Our dreaming mind.* New York: Ballantine Books.

Van de Garde-Perik, Markopoulos, P., de Ruyter, B., Eggen, B., IJsselsteijn, W. A., (2008). Investigating privacy attitudes and behavior in relation to personalization. *Social Science Computer Review, 26*(1), 20–44.

VanderLaan, D. P., Ren, Z., & Vasey, P. L. (2013). Male androphilia in the ancestral environment. *Human Nature, 24*, 275–301. doi: 10.1007/s12110-013-9182z.

van der Linden, S., Maibach, E., & Leiserowitz, A. (2015). Improving public engagement with climate change: Five "best practice" insights from psychological science. *Perspectives on Psychological Science, 10*, 758–763.

van der Merwe, A., & Garuccio, A. (Eds.). (1994). *Waves and particles in light and matter.* New York: Plenum Press.

van der Stelt, O., van der Molen, M., Boudewijn Gunning, W., & Kok, A. (2010). Neuro-electrical signs of selective attention to color in boys with attention-deficit hyperactivity disorder. *Cognitive Brain Research, 12*(2), 245–264.

Van Dongen, H. P. A., Maislin, G., Mullington, J. M., & Dinges, D. F. (2003). The cumulative cost of additional wakefulness: Dose-response effects on neurobehavioral functions and sleep physiology from chronic sleep restriction and total sleep deprivation. *Sleep, 26*, 117–126.

van Duijl, M., Nijenhuis, E., Komproe, I. H., Gernaat, H. B., & de Jong, J. T. (2010). Dissociative symptoms and reported trauma among patients with spirit possession and matched healthy controls in Uganda. *Culture, Medicine, and Psychiatry, 34*(2), 380–400. doi: 10.1007/s11013-010-9171-1

Van Horn, J. D., Irimia, A., Torgerson, C. M., Chambers, M. C., Kikinis, R., & Toga, A. W. (2012). Mapping connectivity damage in the case of Phineas Gage. *PLoS One, 7*(5), e37454. doi: 10.1371/journal.pone.0037454

Varela, J. A., Wang, J., Christianson, J. P., Maier, S. F., & Cooper, D. C. (2012). Control over stress, but not stress per se increases prefrontal cortical pyramidal neuron excitability. *The Journal of Neuroscience, 32*(37), 12848–12853. doi: 10.1523/jneurosci.2669-12.2012

Vartanian, L. R. (2000). Revisiting the imaginary audience and personal fable constructs of adolescent egocentricism: A conceptual review. *Adolescence, 35*(140), 639–661.

Vecsey, C. G., Baillie, G. S., Jaganath, D., Havekes, R., Daniels, A., Wimmer, M., ... Abel, T. (2009). Sleep deprivation impairs cAMP signaling in the hippocampus. *Nature, 461*(7267), 1122–1125.

Verkhratsky, A., Marutle, A., Rodriguez-Arellano, J. J., & Nordberg, A. (2014). Glial asthenia and functional paralysis: A new perspective on neurodegeneration and Alzheimer's disease. *Neuroscientist.* doi: 10.1177/1073858414547132

Vernon, R. J. W., Sutherland, C. A. M., Young, A. W., & Hartley, T. (2014). Modeling first impressions from highly variable facial images. *Proceedings of the National Academy of Science, 111*(32), E3353–E3361. doi: 10.1073/pnas.1409860111

Vernon, S. W., & Roberts, R. E. (1982). Use of RDC in a tri-ethnic community survey. *Archives of General Psychiatry, 39*, 47.

Villani, S. (2001). Impact of media on children and adolescents: A 10-year review of the research. *Journal of the American Academy on Child and Adolescent Psychiatry, 40*(4), 392–401.

Virkkunen, M., & Linnoila, M. (1996). Serotonin and glucose metabolism in impulsively violent alcoholic offenders. In D. M. Stoff, & R. B. Cairns (Eds.), *Aggression and violence* (pp. 87–100). Mahwah, NJ: Lawrence Erlbaum.

Visser, P. S., & Krosnick, J. A. (1998). Development of attitude strength over the life cycle: Surge and decline. *Journal of Personality and Social Psychology, 75*(6), 1389–1410.

Visser, P. S., & Mirabile, R. R. (2004). Attitudes in the social context: The impact of social network composition on individual-level attitude strength. *Journal of Personality and Social Psychology, 87*(6), 779–795.

Vitorovic, D., & Biller, J. (2013). Musical hallucinations and forgotten tunes—case report and brief literature review. *Frontiers in Neurology, 4*, 109. doi: 10.3389/fmeir/2013.00109

Vogel, G. W. (1975). A review of REM sleep deprivation. *Archives of General Psychiatry, 32*, 749–761.

Vogel, G. W. (1993). Selective deprivation, REM sleep. In M. A. Carskadon (Ed.), *The encyclopedia of sleep and dreaming.* New York: Macmillan.

Vogt, B. A., & Palomero-Gallagher, N. (2012). Cingulate cortex. In J. K. Mai & G. Paxinos (Eds.), *The human nervous system* (pp. 943–987). London, UK: Academic Press.

Vokey, J. R., & Read J. D. (1985). Subliminal messages: Between the devil and the media. *American Psychologist, 40*, 1231–1239.

Volkow, N. D., Wang, G.-J., Newcorn, J., Telang, F., Solanto, M. V., Fowler, J. S., ... & Swanson, J. M. (2007). Depressed dopamine activity in caudate and preliminary evidence of limbic involvement in adults with Attention-Deficit/Hyperactivity Disorder. *Archives of General Psychiatry, 64*(8), 932–940.

von Bastian, C. C., Souza, A. S., & Gade, M. (2016). No evidence for bilingual cognitive advantages: A test of four hypotheses. *Journal of Experimental Psychology: General, 145*(2), 246–258. doi: 10.1037/xge0000120

von Helmholtz, H. (1852). On the theory of compound colours. *Philosophical Magazine, 4*, 519–535.

von Helmholtz, H. L. F. (1863). *Die Lehre von den Tonempfindungen als physiologische Grundlage fur die Theorie der Musik* (1954, XX, trans. by Alexander J. Ellis). *On the sensations of tone as a physiological basis for the theory of music.* New York: Dover.

von Hofsten, O., von Hofsten, C., Sulutvedt, U., Laeng, B., Brennen, T., & Magnussen, S. (2014). Simulating newborn face perception. *Journal of Vision, 14*, 16.

von Stumm, S., & Plomin, R. (2015). Socioeconomic status and the growth of intelligence from infancy through adolescence. *Intelligence, 48*, 30–36. doi: 10.1016/j.intell.2014.10.002

Voogd, J., & Ruigrok, T. J. H. (2012). Cerebellum and precerebellar nuclei. In J. K. Mai & G. Paxinos (Eds.), *The human nervous system* (pp. 471–545). London, UK: Academic Press.

Voss, M. W., Erickson, K. I., Prakash, R. S., Chaddock, L., Malkowski, E., Alves, H., ... Kramer, A. F. (2010). Functional connectivity: A source of variance in the association between cardiorespiratory fitness and cognition? *Neuropsychologia, 48*(5), 1394–1406.

Voyer, D., & Rodgers, M. (2002). Reliability of laterality effects in a dichotic listening task with nonverbal material. *Brain & Cognition, 48*, 602–606.

Voyer, D., Voyer, S., & Bryden, M. (1995). Magnitude of sex differences in spatial abilities: A meta-analysis and consideration of critical variables. *Psychological Bulletin, 117*(2), 250–270.

Vrij, A. (2015). The protection of innocent suspects: A comment on Palmatier and Rovner (2015). *International Journal of Psychophysiology, 95*(1), 20–21.

Vygotsky, L. S. (1934/1962). *Thought and language.* Cambridge, MA: MIT Press.

Vygotsky, L. S. (1978). *Mind in society: The development of higher psychological processes.* Cambridge, MA: Harvard University Press.

Vygotsky, L. S. (1987). Thought and word. In R. W. Riebe & A. S. Carton (Eds.), *The collected works of L. S. Vygotsky: Vol. 1. Problems of general psychology* (pp. 243–288). New York: Plenum.

Wade, T. D., Gordon, S., Medland, S., Bulik, C. M., Heath, A. C., Montgomery, G. W., & Martin, N. G. (2013). Genetic variants associated with disordered eating. *The International Journal of Eating Disorders.* doi: 10.1002/eat.22133

Wahlsten, D. (1997). The malleability of intelligence is not constrained by heritability. In B. Devlin, S. E. Fienberg, & K. Roeder, *Intelligence, genes, and success: Scientists respond to the bell curve* (pp. 71–87). New York: Springer.

Wakefield, A. J., Murch, S. H., Anthony, A., Linnell, J., Casson, D. M., Malik, M., ... Walker-Smith, J. A. (1998). Ileal-lymphoid-nodular hyperplasia, non-specific colitis, and pervasive developmental disorder in children. *The Lancet, 351*, 9103.

Walker, L. J. (1991). Sex differences in moral reasoning. In W. M. Kurtines & J. L. Gewirtz (Eds.), *Handbook of moral behavior and development: Vol. 2. Research* (pp. 333–364). Hillsdale, NJ: Lawrence Erlbaum.

Walker, M. P. (2005). A refined model of sleep and the time course of memory formation. *Behavioral and Brain Sciences, 28*, 51–64.

Walker, P., Francis, B. J., & Walker, L. (2010). The brightness-weight illusion. *Experimental Psychology, 57*(6), 462–469. doi: 10.1027/1618-3169/a000057

Walter, C. (2008). Affairs of the lips. *Scientific American Mind, 19*(6), 24.

Wampold, B. E. (1997). Methodological problems in identifying efficacious psychotherapies. *Psychotherapy Research, 7*, 21–43.

Wang, T., Shi, F., Jin, Y., Yap, P. T., Wee, C. Y., Zhang, J., ... Shen, D. (2016). Multilevel deficiency of white matter connectivity networks in Alzheimer's disease: A diffusion MRI study with DTI and Hardi models. *Neural Plasticity, 2016*, 2947136. doi: 10.1155/2016/2947136

Wang, Z., David, P., Srivastava, J., Powers, S., Brady, C., D'Angelo, J., & Moreland, J. (2012). Behavioral performance and visual attention in communication multitasking: A comparison between instant messaging and online voice chat. *Computers in Human Behavior, 28*(3), 968.

Ward, A. S., Li, D. H., Luedtke, R. R., & Emmett-Oglesby, M. W. (1996). Variations in cocaine self-administration by inbred rat strains under a progressive-ratio schedule. *Psychopharmacology, 127*(3), 204–212.

Ward, B. W., Dahlhamer, J. M., Galinsky, A. M., & Joestl, S. S. (2014). Sexual orientation and health among U.S. adults: National Health Interview Survey, 2013. *National Health Statistics Reports, 77*, 1–12.

Ward, C., & Rana-Deuba, A. (1999). Acculturation and adaptation revisited. *Journal of Cross-Cultural Psychology, 30*, 422–442.

Ward, I. L. (1992). Sexual behavior: The product of parinatal hormonal and prepubertal social factors. In A. A. Gerall, H. Moltz, & I. L. Ward. (Eds.), *Handbook of behavioral neurobiology: Vol. 11. Sexual differentiation* (pp. 157–178). New York: Plenum Press.

Ward, J., Mattic, K. R. P., & Hall, W. (1999). *Methadone maintenance treatment and other opioid replacement therapies.* Sydney, Australia: Harwood Academic.

Ward, M. M., Lotstein, D. S., Bush, T. M., Lambert, R. E., van Vollenhoven, R., & Neuwelt, C. M. (1999). Psychosocial correlates of morbidity in women with systemic lupus erythematosus. *Journal of Rheumatology, 26*, 2153–2158.

Ward, R. D., Gallistel, C. R., Jensen, G., Richards, V. L., Fairhurst, S., & Balsam, P. D. (2012). Conditioned stimulus informativeness governs conditioned stimulus-unconditioned stimulus associability. *Journal of Experimental Psychology: Animal Behavior Processes, 38*: 217–232.

Ware, M. A., Wang, T., Shapiro, S., & Collet, J.-P. (2015). Cannabis for the management of pain: Assessment of safety study (COMPASS). *The Journal of Pain.* doi: 10.1016/j.jpain.2015.07.014

Wartner, U. G., Grossmann, K., Fremmer-Bombik, E., & Suess, G. (1994). Attachment patterns at age six in south Germany: Predictability from infancy and implications for preschool behavior. *Child Development, 65*, 1014–1027.

Washburn, M. F. (1908). *The animal mind: A text-book of comparative psychology.* New York: Macmillan.

Wasserman, E. A., & Miller, R. R. (1997). What's elementary about associative learning? *Annual Review of Psychology, 48*, 573–607.

Waterhouse, L. (2006a). Inadequate evidence for multiple intelligences, Mozart effect, and emotional intelligence theories. *Educational Psychologist, 41*(4), 247–255.

Waterhouse, L. (2006b). Multiple intelligences, the Mozart effect, and emotional intelligence: A critical review. *Educational Psychologist, 41*, 207–225.

Waterman, A. S. (2013). The humanistic psychology–positive psychology divide: Contrasts in philosophical foundations. *American Psychologist, 68*(3), 124–133. doi: 10.1037/a0032168

Watkins, C. E., Campbell, V. L., Nieberding, R., & Hallmark, R. (1995). Contemporary practice of psychological assessment by clinical psychologists. *Professional Psychology: Research and Practice, 26*, 54–60.

Watkins, C. E., Jr., & Savickas, M. L. (1990). Psychodynamic career counseling. In W. B. Walsh & S. H. Osipow (Eds.), *Career counseling: Contemporary topics in vocational psychology* (pp. 79–116). Hillsdale, NJ: Lawrence Erlbaum.

Watson, D. L., Hagihara, D. K., & Tenney, A. L. (1999). Skill-building exercises and generalizing psychological concepts to daily life. *Teaching of Psychology, 26*, 193–195.

Watson, J. B. (1913). Psychology as the behaviorist views it. *Psychological Review, 20*, 158–177.

Watson, J. B. (1924). *Behaviorism.* New York: W. W. Norton.

Watson, J. B., & Rayner, R. (1920). Conditioned emotional responses. *Journal of Experimental Psychology, 3*, 1–14.

Watson, J. C., Steckley, P. L., & McMullen, E. J. (2014). The role of empathy in promoting change. *Psychotherapy Research, 24*(3), 286–298. doi: 10.1080/10503307.2013.802823

Watson, J. M., & Strayer, D. L. (2010). Supertaskers: Profiles in extraordinary multitasking ability. *Psychonomic Bulletin & Review, 17*(4), 479–485.

Watt, H. M. G. (2000). Measuring attitudinal change in mathematics and English over the 1st year of junior high school: A multi-dimensional analysis. *Journal of Experimental Education, 68*, 331–361.

Waytz, A., Young, L. L., & Ginges, J. (2014). Motive attribution asymmetry for love vs. hate drives intractable conflict. *Proceedings of the National Academy of Sciences, 111*(44), 15387.

Weaver, F. M., Follett, K., Stern, M., Hur, K., Harris, C., Marks, W. J., Jr., . . . & Huang, G. D. (2009). Bilateral deep brain stimulation vs. best medical therapy for patients with advanced Parkinson disease: A randomized controlled trial. *Journal of the American Medical Association, 301*(1), 63–73.

Webb, W. B. (1992). *Sleep: The gentle tyrant* (2nd ed.). Bolton, MA: Ander.

Weber, F., Chung, S., Beier, K. T., Xu, M., Luo, L., & Dan, Y. (2015). Control of REM sleep by ventral medulla GABAergic neurons. *Nature, 526*(7573), 435–438. doi: 10.1038/nature14979

Wechsler, D. (1975). *The collected papers of David Wechsler.* New York: Academic Press.

Wechsler, D. (2008). *Wechsler adult intelligence scale* (4th ed.). Bloomington, MN: Pearson.

Wechsler, D. (2012). *Wechsler preschool and primary scale of intelligence* (4th ed.). Bloomington, MN: Pearson.

Wechsler, D. (2014). *Wechsler intelligence scale for children* (5th ed.) Bloomington, MN: Pearson.

Wedding, D. (2004). Cross-cultural counseling and psychotherapy. In R. J. Corsini & D. Wedding (Eds.), *Current psychotherapies* (7th ed., p. 485). Itasca, IL: Peacock.

Weinberger, D. R. (1987). Implications of normal brain development for the pathogenesis of schizophrenia. *Archives of General Psychiatry, 44*, 660–668.

Weiner, B. (1985). An attributional theory of achievement motivation. *Psychological Review, 92*, 548–573.

Weiner, I. B. (1997). Current status of the Rorschach Inkblot Method. *Journal of Personality Assessment, 68*, 5–19.

Weiner, I. B. (2013). Applying Rorschach assessment. In G. P. Koocher, J. C. Norcross & B. A. Greene (Eds.), *Psychologists' desk reference* (pp. 148–152). New York, NY: Oxford University Press

Weiner, R. D. (2000). Retrograde amnesia with electroconvulsive therapy: Characteristics and implications. *Archives of General Psychiatry, 57*, 591–592.

Weis, S., Klaver, P., Reul, J., Elger, C. E., & Fernandez, G. (2004). Temporal and cerebellar brain regions that support both declarative memory formation and retrieval. *Cerebral Cortex, 14*, 256–267.

Weisman, A. (1972). *On dying and denying.* New York: Behavioral Publications.

Weiss, J. M. (1972). Psychological factors in stress and disease. *Scientific American, 26*, 104–113.

Weisse, C. S. (1992). Depression and immunocompetence: A review of the literature. *Psychological Bulletin, 111*, 475–489.

Weissman, M. M., & Klerman, G. L. (1977). Sex differences and the epidemiology of depression. *Archives of General Psychiatry, 34*, 98–111.

Wellings, K., Nanchahal, K., Macdowall, W., McManus, S., Erens, B., Mercer, C. H., . . . Field, J. (2001). Sexual behaviour in Britain: Early heterosexual experience. *Lancet, 358*(9296), 1843–1850.

Welch, E., Ghaderi, A., & Swenne, I. (2015). A comparison of clinical characteristics between adolescent males and females with eating disorders. *BMC Psychiatry, 15*, 45. doi: 10.1186/s12888-015-0419-8

Wenneberg, S. R., Schneider, R. H., Walton, K. G., Maclean, C. R., Levitsky, D. K., Mandarino, J. V., Waziri, R., & Wallace, R. K. (1997). Anger expression correlates with platelet aggregation. *Behavioral Medicine, 22*(4), 174–177.

Werker, J. F., & Lalonde, C. E. (1988). Cross-language speech perceptions: Initial capabilities and developmental change. *Developmental Psychology, 24*, 672–683.

Wertheimer, M. (1982). *Productive thinking.* Chicago: University of Chicago Press.

Westen, D. (2005). Cognitive neuroscience and psychotherapy: Implications for psychotherapy's second century. In G. Gabbard, J. Beck, & J. Holmes (Eds.), *Oxford textbook of psychotherapy.* Oxford, UK: Oxford University Press.

Wetherell, J. L. (2002). Behavior therapy for anxious older adults. *Behavior Therapist, 25*, 16–17.

Wever, E. G. (1949). *Theory of hearing.* New York: John Wiley & Sons.

Wever, E. G., & Bray, C. W. (1930). The nature of acoustic response: The relation between sound frequency and frequency of impulses in the auditory nerve. *Journal of Experimental Psychology, 13*(5), 373–387.

Weyant, J. M. (1996). Application of compliance techniques to direct-mail requests for charitable donations. *Psychology and Marketing, 13*, 157–170.

White, G. L. (1980). Physical attractiveness and courtship progress. *Journal of Personality and Social Psychology, 39*, 660–668.

White, J. N., Hutchens, T., & Lubar, J. (2005). Quantitative EEG assessment during neuropsychological task performance in adults with attention deficit hyperactivity disorder. *Journal of Adult Development, 12*(2), 113–121.

White, S. (2000). *The transgender debate (the crisis surrounding gender identity).* Reading, UK: Garnet.

Whiting, D. M., Tomycz, N. D., Bailes, J., de Jonge, L., Lecoultre, V., Wilent, B., . . . Oh, M. Y. (2013). Lateral hypothalamic area deep brain stimulation for refractory obesity: A pilot study with preliminary data on safety, body weight, and energy metabolism. *Journal of Neurosurgery, 119*(1), 56–63. doi: 10.3171/2013.2.jns12903

Whorf, B. L. (1956). *Language, thought and reality.* New York: Wiley.

Wicker, A. W. (1971). An examination of the "other variables" explanation of attitude–behavior inconsistency. *Journal of Personality and Social Psychology, 19*, 18–30.

Wierenga, C. E., Stricker, N. H., McCauley, A., Simmons, A., Jak, A. J., Chang, Y. L., . . . & Bondi, M. W. (2010). Increased functional brain response during word retrieval in cognitively intact older adults at genetic risk for Alzheimer's disease. *Neuroimage, 15*, 15.

Wiesemann, C., Ude-Koeller, S., Sinnecker, G. H., & Thyen, U. (2010). Ethical principles and recommendations for the medical management of differences of sex development (DSD)/intersex in children and adolescents. *Euopean Journal of Pediatrics, 169*, 671–679.

Wiggert, N., Wilhelm, F. H., Derntl, B., & Blechert, J. (2015). Gender differences in experiential and facial reactivity to approval and disapproval during emotional social interactions. *Frontiers in Psychology, 6*, 1372.

Wiley, J., & Jarosz, A. F. (2012). Working memory capacity, attentional focus, and problem solving. *Current Directions in Psychological Science, 21*(4), 258.

Wilhelm, I., Kurth, S., Ringli, M., Mouthon, A. L., Buchmann, A., Geiger, A., . . . Huber, R. (2014). Sleep slow-wave activity reveals developmental changes in experience-dependent plasticity. *Journal of Neuroscience, 34*(37), 12568–12575. doi: 10.1523/JNEUROSCI.0962-14.2014

Wilhelm, I., Rose, M., Imhof, K. I., Rasch, B., Buechel, C., & Born, J. (2013). The sleeping child outplays the adult's capacity to convert implicit into explicit knowledge. *Nature Neuroscience.* doi: 10.1038/nn.3343

Wilkinson, D., Schaefer, G. O., Tremellen, K., & Savulescu, J. (2015). Double trouble: Should double embryo transfer be banned? *Theoretical Medicine and Bioethics, 36*, 121–139.

Williams, J. A., Pascual-Leone, A., & Fregni, F. (2010). Interhemispheric modulation induced by cortical stimulation and motor training. *Physical Therapy, 90*(3), 398–410.

Williams, J. F., & Smith, V. C. (2015). Fetal alcohol spectrum disorders. *Pediatrics, 136*(5), e1395–e1406.

Williams, M. A., & Sachdev, P. S. (2010). Magnetoencephalography in neuropsychiatry: Ready for application? *Current Opinion in Psychiatry, 4*, 4.

Williams, M. E. (1995). *The American Geriatrics Society's complete guide to aging and mental health.* New York: Random House.

Williams, R. B. (1999). A 69-year-old man with anger and angina. *Journal of the American Medical Association, 282*, 763–770.

Williams, R. B. (2001). Hostility: Effects on health and the potential for successful behavioral approaches to prevention and treatment. In A. Baum, T. A. Revenson, & J. E. Singer (Eds.), *Handbook of Health Psychology.* Mahwah, NJ: Erlbaum, 661–668.

Williams, R. B., Haney, T. L., Lee, K. L., Kong, Y. H., Blumenthal, J. A., & Whalen, R. E. (1980). Type A behavior, hostility, and coronary atherosclerosis. *Psychosomatic Medicine, 42*(6), 539–549.

Willoughby, T., Good, M., Adachi, P. J. C., Hamza, C., & Tavernier, R. (2013). Examining the link between adolescent brain development and risk taking from a social-developmental perspective. *Brain and Cognition, 83*, 315–323.

Wimber, M., Alink, A., Charest, I., Kriegeskorte, N., & Anderson, M. C. (2015). Retrieval induces adaptive forgetting of competing memories via cortical pattern suppression. *Nature Neuroscience, 18*, 582–589.

Winningham, R. G., Hyman, I. E., Jr., & Dinnel, D. L. (2000). Flashbulb memories? The effects of when the initial memory report was obtained. *Memory, 8*, 209–216.

Winslow, J. T., Hastings, N., Carter, C. S., Harbaugh, C. R., & Insel, T. R. (1993). A role for central vasopressin in pair bonding in monogamous prairie voles. *Nature, 365*(6446), 545–548. doi: 10.1038/365545a0

Winton, W. M. (1987). Do introductory textbooks present the Yerkes-Dodson law correctly? *American Psychologist*, 42(2), 202–203.

Wiseman, R. (2007). *Quirkology: How we discover the big truths in small things* (pp. 7–8, 28–29). New York: Basic Books.

Wisniewski, A. B., Migeon, C. J., Meyer-Bahlburg, H. F. L., Gearhart, J. P., Berkovitz, G. D., Brown, T. R., & Money, J. (2000). Complete androgen insensitivity syndrome: Long-term medical, surgical and psychosexual outcome. *The Journal of Clinical Endocrinology and Metabolism*, 85, 2664–2669.

Witelson, S. F. (1991). Neural sexual mosaicism: Sexual differentiation of the human temporo-pariatal region for functional asymmetry. *Psychoneuroendocrinology*, 16, 131–153.

Witt, W. P., Litzelman, K., Cheng, E. R., Wakeel, F., & Barker, E. S. (2014). Measuring stress before and during pregnancy: A review of population-based studies of obstetric outcomes. *Maternal and Child Health Journal*, 18, 52–63.

Wohn, D. Y. (2011). Gender and race representation in casual games. *Sex Roles*, 65, 198–207.

Wolberg, L. R. (1977). *The technique of psychotherapy*. New York: Grune & Stratton.

Wolfe-Christensen, C., Fedele, D. A., Kirk, K., Philips, T. M., Mazur, T., Mullins, L. L., . . . & Wisniewski, A.B. (2012). Degree of external genital malformation at birth in children with a disorder of sex development and subsequent caregiver distress. *Journal of Urology*, 188, 1596–1600.

Wood, J. M., Lilienfeld, S. O., Nezworski, M. T., Garb, H. N., Allen, K. H., & Wildermuth, J. L. (2010). Validity of Rorschach inkblot scores for discriminating psychopaths from non-psychopaths in forensic populations: A meta-analysis. *Psychological Assessment*, 22(2), 336–349. doi: 10.1037/a0018998

Wood, J. M., Nezworski, M. T., & Stejskal, W. J. (1996). The comprehensive system for the Rorschach: A critical examination. *Psychological Science*, 7(1), 3–10, 14–17.

Woodhouse, A. (2005). Phantom limb sensation. *Clinical and Experimental Pharmacology and Physiology*, 32(1–2), 132–134.

World Health Organization. (2010). Guidelines on HIV and infant feeding 2010: Principles and recommendations for infant feeding in the context of HIV and a summary of evidence. Retrieved from http://www.who.int/maternal_child_adolescent/documents/9789241599535/en/

World Health Organization. (2012). HIV/AIDS. Retrieved from http://www.who.int/mediacentre/factsheets/fs360/en/

Wu, C-C., Lee, G. C., & Lai, H-K. (2004). Using concept maps to aid analysis of concept presentation in high school computer textbooks. *Journal of Education and Information Technologies*, 9(2), 10.1023/B:EAIT.0000027930.09631.a5

Wyman, P. A., Moynihan, J., Eberly, S., Cox, C., Cross, W., Jin, X., & Caserta, M. T. (2007). Association of family stress with natural killer cell activity and the frequency of illnesses in children. *Archives of Pediatric and Adolescent Medicine*, 161, 228–234.

Wynne, C. (1999). Do animals think? The case against the animal mind. *Psychology Today*, 32(6), 50–53.

Xie, L., Kang, H., Xu, Q., Chen, M. J., Liao, Y., Thiyagarajan, M., . . . Nedergaard, M. (2013). Sleep drives metabolite clearance from the adult brain. *Science*, 342(6156), 373–377.

Yaffe, K., Vittinghoff, E., Lindquist, K., Barnes, D., Covinsky K. E., Neylan, T., . . . Marmar, C. (2010). Posttraumatic stress disorder and risk of dementia among U.S. veterans. *Archives of General Psychiatry*, 67(6), 608–613.

Yalom, I. (1995). *The theory and practice of group psychotherapy* (4th ed.). New York: Basic Books.

Yamaguchi, S., Isejima, H., Matsuo, T., Okura, R., Yagita, K., Kobayashi, M., & Okamura, H. (2003). Synchronization of cellular clocks in the suprachiasmatic nucleus. *Science*, 302, 1408–1412.

Yamamuro, K., Kimoto, S., Rosen, K. M., Kishimoto, T., & Makinodan, M. (2015). Potential primary roles of glial cells in the mechanisms of psychiatric disorders. *Frontiers in Cellular Neuroscience*, 9, 154. doi: 10.3389/fncel.2015.00154

Yang, Y., Raine, A., & Colletti, P. (2010). Morphological alterations in the prefrontal cortex and the amygdala in unsuccessful psychopaths. *Journal of Abnormal Psychology*, 119, 546–554.

Yarkoni, T. (2015). Neurobiological substrates of personality: A critical overview. In M. Mikulincer & P. R. Shaver (Eds.), APA handbook of personality and social psychology: Vol. 4. Personality processes and individual differences (pp. 61–83). Washington, DC: American Psychological Association.

Yavuz, E., Maul, P., & Nowotny, T. (2015). Spiking neural network model of reinforcement learning in the honeybee implemented on the GPU. *BMC Neuroscience*, 16(1), 181.

Yeager, D. S., Johnson, R., Spitzer, B. J., Trzesniewski, K., Powers, J., & Dweck, C. S. (2014). The far-reaching effects of believing people can change: Implicit theories of personality shape stress, health, and achievement during adolescence. *Journal of Personality and Social Psychology*, 106, 867–884.

Yerkes, R. M. (Ed.). (1921). Psychological examining in the United States Army. *Memoirs of the National Academy of Sciences*, 15, 1–890.

Yerkes, R. M., & Dodson, J. D. (1908). The relation of strength of stimulus to rapidity of habit formation. *Journal of Comparative Neurology and Psychology*, 18, 459–482.

Ying, Y. W. (1990). Explanatory models of major depression and implications for help-seeking among immigrant Chinese-American women. *Culture, Medicine, and Psychiatry*, 14, 393–408.

Yip, Y. L. (2002, Autumn). Pivot–Qi. *The Journal of Traditional Eastern Health and Fitness*, 12(3).

Yopyk, D., & Prentice, D. A. (2005). Am I an athlete or a student? Identify salience and stereotype threat in student-athletes. *Basic and Applied Social Psychology*, 27 (4), 29–336.

Young, J. E., Rygh, J. L., Weinberger, A. D., & Beck, A. T. (2008). Cognitive therapy for depression. In D. H. Barlow (Ed.), *Clinical handbook of psychological disorders* (pp. 250–305). New York: Guilford Press.

Young, S. N. (Ed.). (1996). Melatonin, sleep, aging, and the health protection branch. *Journal of Psychiatry Neuroscience*, 21(3), 161–164.

Yule, G. (1996). *Pragmatics*. Oxford: Oxford University Press.

Zadra, A., Desautels, A., Petit, D., & Montplaisir, J. (2013). Somnambulism: Clinical aspects and pathophysiological hypotheses. *The Lancet Neurology*, 12(3), 285.

Zadra, A., Pilon, M., & Montplaisir, J. (2008). Polysomnographic diagnosis of sleepwalking: Effects of sleep deprivation. *Annals of Neurology*, 63(4), 513–519.

Zajonc, R. B. (1965). Social facilitation. *Science*, 149, 269–274.

Zajonc, R. B. (1968). Attitudinal effects of mere exposure. *Journal of Personality and Social Psychology Monographs*, 9(2), 1–27.

Zajonc, R. B. (1980). Feeling and thinking: Preferences need no inferences. *American Psychologist*, 35, 151–175.

Zajonc, R. B. (1984). On the primacy of affect. *American Psychologist*, 39, 117–123.

Zajonc, R. B. (1998). Emotions. In D. T. Gilbert & S. T. Fiske (Eds.), *Handbook of social psychology* (4th ed., Vol. 1, pp. 591–632). New York: McGraw-Hill.

Zajonc, R. B., Heingartner, A., & Herman, E. M. (1970). Social enhancement and impairment of performance in the cockroach. *Journal of Social Psychology*, 13(2), 83–92.

Zarate, C. A., Jr., Brutsche, N. E., Ibrahim, L., Franco-Chaves, J., DiazGranados, N., Cravchik, A., . . . Luckenbaugh, D. A. (2012). Replication of ketamine's antidepressant efficacy in bipolar depression: A randomized controlled add-on trial. *Biological Psychiatry*, 71(11), 939–946. doi: 10.1016/j.biopsych.2011.12.010

Zarate, C. A., Jr., Singh, J. B., Carlson, P. J., Brutsche, N. E., Ameli, R., Luckenbaugh, D. A., . . . Manji, H. K. (2006). A randomized trial of an N-methyl-D-aspartate antagonist in treatment-resistant major depression. *Archives of General Psychiatry*, 63(8), 856–864. doi: 10.1001/archpsyc.63.8.856

Zedler, B. (1995). "Mary Whiton Calkins." In M. E. Waithe (Ed.), *A history of women philosophers: Vol. 4* (pp. 103–123). Netherlands: Kluwer Academic Publishers.

Zeidner, M., & Matthews, G. (2005). Evaluative anxiety. In A. Elliott & C. Dweck (Eds.), *Handbook of competence and motivation* (pp. 141–146). New York: Guilford Press.

Zeki, S. (2001). Localization and globalization in conscious vision. *Annual Review of Neuroscience*, 24, 57–86.

Zentall, T. R. (2000). Animal intelligence. In R. J. Sternberg (Ed.), *Handbook of intelligence*. Cambridge, MA: Cambridge University Press.

Zentner, M., & Mitura, K. (2012). Stepping out of the caveman's shadow: Nations' gender gap predicts degree of sex differentiation in mate preferences. *Psychological Science*, 23(10), 1176–1185. doi: 10.1177/0956797612441004

Zhan, Y., Paolicelli, R. C., Sforazzini, F., Weinhard, L., Bolasco, G., Pagani, F., . . . & Gross, C. T. (2014). Deficient neuron-microglia signaling results in impaired functional brain connectivity and social behavior. *Nature Neuroscience*, 17, 400–406. doi: 10.1038/nn.3641

Zhang, A., Ferretti, V., Güntan, I., Moro, A., Steinberg, E. A., Ye, Z., . . . Franks, N. P. (2015). Neuronal ensembles sufficient for recovery sleep and the sedative actions of α2 adrenergic agonists. *Nature Neuroscience*, 18, 553–561. doi: 10.1038/nn.3957

Zhao, Y., Montoro, R., Igartua, K., & Thombs, B. D. (2010). Suicidal ideation and attempt among adolescents reporting "unsure" sexual identity or heterosexual identity plus same-sex attraction or behavior: Forgotten groups? *Journal of the American Academy of Child & Adolescent Psychiatry*, 49(2), 104–113.

Zhou, J. N., Hofman, M. A., Gooren, L. J. G., & Swaab, D. F. (1995). A sex difference in the human brain and its relation to transsexuality. *Nature*, 378, 68–70.

Zilles, K. (1990). Cortex. In G. Paxinos (Ed.), *The human nervous system* (pp. 757–802). San Diego, CA: Academic.

Zilles, K., & Amunts, K. (2012). Architecture of the cerebral cortex. In J. K. Mai & G. Paxinos (Eds.), *The human nervous system* (pp. 836–895). London, UK: Academic Press.

Zillmann, D., Baron, R., & Tamborini, R. (1981). Social costs of smoking: Effects of tobacco smoke on hostile behavior. *Psychology Journal of Applied Social*, 11, 548–561.

Zimbardo, P. G. (1970). The human choice: Individuation, reason, and order versus deindividuation, impulse, and chaos. In N. J. Arnold & D. Levine (Eds.), *Nebraska Symposium on Motivation, 1969*. Lincoln: University of Nebraska Press.

Zimbardo, P. G. (1971). The pathology of imprisonment. *Society*, 9(4–8), 4.

Zimbardo, P. G., & Hartley, C. F. (1985). Cults go to high school: A theoretical and empirical analysis of the initial stage in the recruitment process. *Cultic Studies Journal*, 2, 91–148.

Zimbardo, P., Maslach, C., & Haney, C. (2000). Reflections on the Stanford Prison Experiment: Genesis, transformations, consequences. In T. Blass (Ed.), *Obedience to authority: Current perspectives on the Milgram paradigm* (pp. 193–237). London: Lawrence Erlbaum.

Zisapel, N. (2001). Circadian rhythm sleep disorders: Pathophysiology and potential approaches to management. *CNS Drugs*, 15(4), 311–328.

Zlatin, D. M. (1995). Life themes: A method to understand terminal illness. *Omega: Journal of Death and Dying, 31*(3), 189–206. doi: 10.2190/E4BA-ML04-E2BK-7YJE

Zolotor, A. J., & Puzia, M. E. (2010). Bans against corporal punishment: A systematic review of the laws, changes in attitudes and behaviours. *Child Abuse Review, 19*(4), 229–247.

Zolotor, A. J., Theodore, A. D., Chang, J. J., & Laskey, A. L. (2011). Corporal punishment and physical abuse: Population-based trends for three- to 11-year-old children in the United States. *Child Abuse Review, 20*(1), 57–66.

Zorilla, E. P., Luborsky, L., McKay, J. R., Rosenthal, R., Houldin, A., Tax, A., . . . & Schmidt, K. (2001). The relationship of depression and stressors to immunological assays: A meta-analytic review. *Brain, Behavior, and Immunity, 15*, 199–226.

Zosuls, K. M., Miller, C. F., Ruble, D. N., Martin, C. L., & Fabes, R. A. (2011). Gender development research in Sex Roles: Historical trends and future directions. *Sex Roles, 64*(11–12), 826–842. http://doi.org/10.1007/s11199-010-9902-3

Zucchi, F. C. R., Kirkland, S. W., Jadavji, N. M., van Waes, L. T., Klein, A., Supina, R. D., & Metz, G. A. (2009). Predictable stress versus unpredictable stress: A comparison in a rodent model of stroke. *Behavioural Brain Research, 205*(1), 67–75.

Zuckerman, M. (1979). *Sensation seeking: Beyond the optimal level of arousal.* Hillsdale, NJ: Lawrence Erlbaum.

Zuckerman, M. (1994). *Behavioral expression and biosocial bases of sensation seeking.* New York: Cambridge University Press.

Zuckerman, M. (2002). Zuckerman-Kuhlman Personality Questionnaire (ZKPQ): An alternative five-factorial model. In B. De Raad & M. Perugini (Eds.), *Big Five assessment* (pp. 377–396). Seattle, WA: Hogrefe & Huber.

Zuo, L., & Cramond, B. (2001). An examination of Terman's gifted children from the theory of identity. *Gifted Child Quarterly, 45*(4), 251–259.

Zuvekas, S. H., & Vitiello, B. (2012). Stimulant medication use in children: A 12-year perspective. *American Journal of Psychiatry, 193*:160–166.

Zvolensky, M. J., Schmidt, M. B., & Stewart, S. H. (2003). Panic disorder and smoking. *Clinical Psychology: Science and Practice, 10*, 29–51.

# Credits

## Photo Credits

329 Zurijeta/Shutterstock; Page 332 Radius Images/Alamy Stock Photo; Page 334 Nina Leen/The LIFE Picture Collection/Getty Images; Page 339 shock/Fotolia; Page 341 Ansgar Photography/Getty Images; Page 343 Piti Tan/Shutterstock; Page 344 Olivier Voisin/Photo Researchers, Inc.; Page 347 Amble Design/Shutterstock; Page 349 Yadid Levy/Alamy Stock Photo.

**Chapter 9**   Page 355 Rocketclips/Fotolia; Page 358 Norbert Schaefer/Getty Images; Page 358 Greg Epperson/Shutterstock; Page 359 JEP Celebrity Photos/Alamy Stock Photo; Page 360 David Roth/Stone/Getty Images; Page 361 benng/Shutterstock; Page 364 Pictorial Press Ltd/Alamy Stock Photo; Page 365 imtmphoto/Shutterstock; Page 365 Lee Lorenz/The New Yorker Collection/The Cartoon Bank; Page 369 Olivier Voisin/Science Source; Page 371 Camera Press Ltd/Alamy Stock Photo; Page 371 Ryan McVay/Lifesize/Getty Images; Page 372 Juice Images/Alamy Stock Photo; Page 376 Barbara Penoyar/Photodisc/Getty Images; Page 376 J. Christopher Briscoe/Science Source; Page 376 vladimirfloyd/Fotolia; Page 376 Guido Alberto Rossi/AGE Fotostock; Page 376 Photo Researchers, Inc./Science Source; Page 376 Cheryl Casey/Shutterstock; Page 377 imtmphoto/Alamy Stock Photo; Page 381 Jack Hollingsworth/Getty Images; Page 386 Ian Dagnall/Alamy Stock Photo.

**Chapter 10**   Page 391 Tom Wang/Shutterstock; Page 393 ZUMA Press, Inc./Alamy Stock Photo; Page 396 National Archives and Records Administration; Page 399 BJI/Blue Jean Images/Getty Images; Page 399 Jeffrey Blackler/Alamy Stock Photo; Page 400 Beyond Fotomedia GmbH/Alamy Stock Photo; Page 401 MARKA/Alamy Stock Photo; Page 402 Donald Reilly/The New Yorker Collection/The Cartoon Bank; Page 402 Pixtal/SuperStock; Page 405 Bettmann/Getty Images; Page 407 Wallace Kirkland/Getty Images; Page 410 David McNew/Getty Images; Page 414 Sean Sprague/Alamy Stock Photo; Page 415 Rachel Epstein/Photo Edit; Page 415 Bill Aron/PhotoEdit.

**Chapter 11**   Page 421 Kenneth Man/Fotolia; Page 422 Lisa F. Young/Alamy Stock Photo; Page 426 Myrleen Pearson/PhotoEdit; Page 427 Stockbroker/Alamy; Page 428 Profimedia International s.r.o./Alamy Stock Photo; Page 429 Kablonk/SuperStock; Page 440 Mischa Richter/The New Yorker Collection/The Cartoon Bank; Page 442 Donald Reilly/The New Yorker Collection/The Cartoon Bank; Page 443 Jaren Jai Wicklund/Shutterstock; Page 443 Nathan Benn/Getty Images; Page 444 Gary Conner/PhotoEdit; Page 449 Adrian Weinbrecht/Getty Images; Page 451 David Pollack/Getty Images; Page 452 Judy Bellah/Alamy Stock Photo; Page 454 Tyler Olson/Shutterstock.

**Chapter 12**   Page 459 Scanrail/123RF; Page 460 Alex Gregory/The New Yorker Collection/The Cartoon Bank; Page 462 Bloomberg/Getty Images; Page 464 Tom Merton/Alamy Stock Photo; Page 467 The University of Akron/Archives of the History of American Psychology; Page 473 neal and molly jansen/Alamy Stock Photo; Page 475 Fuse/Getty Images; Page 477 Xinhua/Alamy Stock Photo; Page 483 Dmitriy Shironosov/123RF; Page 483 David Grossman/Alamy Stock Photo; Page 484 Allan Tannenbaum/Polaris/Newscom; Page 486 highwaystarz/Fotolia; Page 486 Bill Aron/PhotoEdit; Page 492 Philip G. Zimbardo, Inc.; Page 492 AP Images.

**Chapter 13**   Page 505 Kabakova Tatyana/Fotolia; Page 506 Bjanka Kadic/Alamy Stock Photo; Page 510 shalunts/Shutterstock; Page 512 Clearviewimages RF/Alamy; Page 516 Andresr/Shutterstock; Page 518 Peter Steiner/The New Yorker Collection/The Cartoon Bank; Page 520 Radius Images/Alamy Stock Photo; Page 523 Corbis Premium RF/Alamy; Page 523 Gravicapa/Shutterstock; Page 526 AP Photos; Page 536 Bill Aron/PhotoEdit; Page 536 Noland White, Ph.D.

**Chapter 14**   Page 543 nito500/123RF; Page 544 New York Public Library/Science Source; Page 545 ZoomTeam/Fotolia; Page 545 ZoomTeam/Fotolia; Page 548 David R. Frazier Photolibrary, Inc./Alamy; Page 550 Rafael Ramirez Lee/Shutterstock; Page 553 iStockphoto/Getty Images; Page 555 Cartoonresource/Shutterstock; Page 556 Mike Fryer/MAG/Alamy Stock Photo; Page 557 Bernd Vogel/Getty Images; Page 560 Elaine Thompson/AP Images; Page 568 Karl Prouse/Catwalking/Getty Images; Page 571 Alex Segre/Alamy Stock Photo; Page 573 Joerg Carstensen Deutsche Presse-Agentur/Newscom; Page 574 Archive Pics/Alamy Stock Photo; Page 575 Marek Kubicki, MD, PhD/Psychiatry Neuroimaging Laboratory, Department of Psychiatry, Brigham and Women's Hospital, Harvard Medical School.

**Chapter 15**   Page 587 Belight/Shutterstock; Page 588 Charles Ciccione/Photo Researchers, Inc.; Page 590 Arnie Levin/The New Yorker Collection/The Cartoon Bank; Page 592 Marcin Balcerzak/Shutterstock; Page 593 Zigy Kaluzny/Stone/Getty Images; Page 594 TongRo Images/Alamy Stock Photo; Page 600 MBI/Alamy Stock Photo; Page 602 Helder Almeida/Fotolia; Page 605 Jodi Jacobson/E+/Getty Images; Page 606 Wavebreakmedia/Shutterstock; Page 608 Mike Twohy/The New Yorker Collection/The Cartoon Bank; Page 612 Rob Marmion/Shutterstock; Page 620 Marty Slagter/The Ann Arbor News/AP Images; Page 621 Bettmann/Getty Images; Page 622 Phanie/Alamy Stock Photo; Page 623 Phanie/Alamy Stock Photo; Page 624 Z2A1/Alamy Stock Photo.

**Appendix**   Page B-4 Photographee.eu/Fotolia; Page B-5 Picture Partners/Alamy Stock Photo; Page B-7 Christopher Futcher/Getty Image; Page B-8 Paul Conklin/PhotoEdit, Inc; Page B-10 Restyler/Shutterstock; Page B-13 Joel Page/AP Images.

## Text Credits

**Chapter 1**   Page 7 American Psychological Association; Page 16 Figure 1.3a Michalski, D., Kohout, J., Wicherski, M., & Hart, B. (2011). 2009 Doctorate Employment Survey (Table 3). Washington, DC: American Psychological Association. Retrieved from https://www.apa.org/workforce/publications/09-doc-empl/report.pdf.; Page 16 Figure 1.3b American Psychological Association. (2014). How many psychology doctorates are awarded by U.S. institutions? News from APA's Center for Workforce Studies. Monitor on Psychology, 45(7), 13.; Page 34 Jameson, M., Diehl, R., & Danso, H. (2007). Stereotype threat impacts college athletes' academic performance. *Current Research in Social Psychology*, 12(5), 68–79.

**Chapter 3**   Page 99 Figure **3.3** St. Luke's Cataract & Laser Institute; Page 128 Figure 3.25 Created by and courtesy of Jorge Otero-Millan, Martinez-Conde Laboratory, Barrow Neurological Institute.

**Chapter 4**   Page 143 Figure 4.1 H. P. Roffwarg; J. N. Muzio; W. C. Dement, "Ontogenetic Development of the Human Sleep-Dream Cycle" *Science,* (1966), 152, pp. 604–619. American Association for the Advancement of Science (AAAS).

**Chapter 5**   Page 181 Figure 5.2 Hovland, C. I. (1937). The generalization of conditioned responses. I. The sensory generalization of conditioned responses with varying frequencies of tone. *Journal of General Psychology*, 17, 125–48; Page 182 Figure 5.3 Pearson Education; Page 209 Figure 5.10 Tolman, E. C., & Honzik, C. H. (1930).

Introduction and removal of reward and maze learning in rats. *University of California Publications in Psychology,* 4, 257–275; Page 216 Applying Psychology to Everyday Life: Can You Really Toilet Train Your Cat?/Karawynn Long.

**Chapter 6** Page 244 Loftus, E. (1975). Leading questions and the eyewitness report. *Cognitive Psychology,* 7, 560–572.

**Chapter 7** Page 269 Figure 7.1 Kosslyn, S. M., Ball, T. M., & Reiser, B. J. (1978). Visual images preserve metric spatial information: Evidence from studies of image scanning. *Journal of Experimental Psychology: Human Perception and Performance,* 4, 47–60; Page 279 Table 7.2 Gardner, H. (1998). Are there additional intelligences? The case for naturalist, spiritual, and existential intelligences. In J. Kane (Ed.), *Education, information, and transformation* (pp. 111–131). Upper Saddle River, NJ: Merrill-Prentice Hall. Gardner, H. (1999b, February). Who owns intelligence? *Atlantic Monthly,* 67–76; Page 283 Table 7.3 Wechsler, D. (2008). WAIS-IV (Weschsler Adult Intelligence Scale—4th ed.) Administration and scoring manual. San Antonio, TX: Pearson.

**Chapter 8** Page 320 Table 8.2 March of Dimes Foundation (2009); Organization of Teratology Information Specialists (2011); Shepard, T. H. (2001); Page 334 Harlow, H. F. (1958). The nature of love. *American Psychologist,* 13, 573–685; Page 335–336 Table 8.4 Erikson, E. H. (1950). *Childhood and society.* New York: Norton; Page 340 Table 8.5 Based on Kohlberg, L. (1969). Stage and sequence: the cognitive-developmental approach to socialization. In D. A. Goslin (Ed.), *Handbook of socialization: Theory in research* (pp. 347–480). Boston: Houghton-Mifflin./Ciccarelli, Saundra; Page 349 Twentieth Century Fox.

**Chapter 9** Page 362 Table 9.1 Reproduced with permission. Originally published in *Big Five Assessment* by Boele De Raad and Marco Perugini, ISBN 0-88937-242-X, ©2002 Hogrefe & Huber Publishers www.hogrefe.com. Permission is granted for this edition only; Page 364 Figure 9.3 Maslow, Abraham H., Frager, Robert D., Fadiman, James, *Motivation and Personality,* 3rd Ed., ©1987. Reprinted and electronically reproduced by permission of Pearson Education, Inc., New York, NY; Page 375 Figure 9.6 from Marin/Hock, 1e The "Low Road" and "High Road". Based on Pearson-created figure from the Krause/Corts, *Psychology* text (Figure 11.12, p. 428).

**Chapter 10** Page 408 Palacios-Ceña, D., Carrasco-Garrido, P., Hernandez-Barrera, V., Alonso-Blanco, C., Jiménez-Garcia, R., & Fernández-de-Las-Peñas, C. (2011). Sexual behaviors among older adults in Spain: Results from a population-based national sexual health survey. *Journal of Sexual Medicine,* 9(1), 121–129; Page 413 Temple, J. R., & Choi, H. J. (2014). Longitudinal association between sexting and sexual behavior. *Pediatrics,* 134(5), e1287–e1292. doi: 10.1542/peds.2014-1974.

**Chapter 11** Page 425 Table 11.1 Adapted and abridged from Holmes & Rahe (1967); Page 426 Lazarus, R. S., & Folkman, S. (1984). *Stress, appraisal and coping.* New York: Springer; Page 447 Hall, H. (2014). An intro to homeopathy. *Skeptical Inquirer,* 38(5). Retrieved from http://www.csicop.org/si/show/an_introduction_to _homeopathy/Center for Inquiry; Page 448 Pearson Education.

**Chapter 12** Page 461 Figure 12.1 Asch, S. E. (1956). Studies of independence and conformity: A minority of one against a unanimous majority. *Psychological Monographs,* 70 (Whole no. 416); Page 463 Table 12.1 Adaptation of Table 10.1, "Symptoms of Groupthink" from *GROUPTHINK: Psychological Studies of Policy Decisions and Fiascoes* 2nd edition by Janis. Copyright (c) 1982 by Wadsworth, a part of Cengage Learning, Inc. Reproduced by permission. www.cengage.com/permissions; Page 467 Figure 12.2 Milgram (1964a, 1974). Milgram, S. (1964a). Behavioral study of obedience. *Journal of Abnormal and Social Psychology,* 67, 371–378; Milgram, S. (1974). *Obedience to authority: An experimental view.* New York: Harper & Row./Pearson Education; Page 476 Figure 12.4 Festinger, L., & Carlsmith, J. (1959). $1/$20 experiment: Cognitive consequences of forced compliance. *Journal of Abnormal and Social Psychology,* 58(2), 203–210; Page 496 Figure 12.5 Latané, B., & Darley, J. M. (1969). Bystander "apathy." *American Scientist,* 57(2), 244–268.

**Chapter 13** Page 523 Figure 13.4 Based on Cattell, R.B. (1973). Personality and mood by questionnaire. San Francisco: Jossey-Bass./Jossey-Bass; Page 523 Table 13.2 McCrae, R. R., & Costa, P. T. (1990). *Personality in adulthood.* New York: Guilford Press; Page 527 Figure 13.5 Kandler, C., Riemann, R., Spinath, F. M., & Angleitner, A. (2010). Sources of variance in personality facets: A multiple-rater twin study of self–peer, peer–peer, and self–self (dis)agreement. *Journal of Personality,* 78(5), 1565–1594. doi:10.1111/j.1467-6494.2010.00661.x.

**Chapter 14** Page 550 Figure 14.1 Insel, T. R., & Cuthbert, B. N. (2015). Medicine. Brain disorders? Precisely. *Science,* 348(6234): 499–500. American Association for the Advancement of Science. (AAAS); Page 551 Table 14.1 Adapted from National Institute of Mental Health (2016). Table uses terminology from both the DSM-IV and DSM-5 (American Psychiatric Association, 2000, 2013); Page 570 http://media.pearsoncmg.com/ph/streaming/ssa/mypsychlab/ Ciccarelli_4e/videos/Video_Index/E14_S05_ALT.html.

**Chapter 15** Page 593 Miller, W. R., & Rollnick, S. (2002). *Motivational interviewing: Preparing people for change* (2nd ed.). New York: Guilford Press; Page 612 Sue, D. W., & Sue, D. (2016). *Counseling the Culturally Diverse: Theory and Practice* (7th ed.). Hoboken, NJ: John Wiley & Sons.

**Appendix** Page A-3 Pearson Education.

# Name Index

Swann, J,402
Swanson, H,146
Swayze, V. W, II,621
Sweetnam, H., 250
Swendsen, J., 565
Swenne, I., 569
Swenson, D. D,424
Swets, J. A., 96
Swindells, S., 416
Swing, E., 215
Swing, E. L., 493–494
Syed, M., 342
Sykes, C. M., 437
Sykes-Muskett, B. J,600
Symes, B., 443
Symmons, D. P., 212
Szabo, A., 306
Szalavitz, M,140
Szell, M,489

**T**

Taconnat, L., 344
Taglialatela, J. P,302
Taha, T. E., 416
Tajfel, H,483, 485
Tajima, S., 215
Takahashi, A,491
Takahashi, R., 442
Takano, T., 144
Takeuchi, T,147
Talaga, M. C., 54, 615–618
Talbott, G. D,600
Talos, I. F., 24, 79, 85
Tamborini, R., 491
Tambs, K., 578
Tammen, S. A,59
Tan, H., 318
Tan, M. S,250
Tan, S., 59, 415
Tan, S. A., 450
Tang, T. Z., 603
Tang, Y.-Y,454
Tannenbaum, B., 59
Tannenbaum, M. B,474
Tannock, R., 233
Tanzi, R. E., 259
Tapia, G., 344
Tarescavage, A. M,533
Tatarko, A., 366
Tatke, S,13
Taub, E., 118
Taube, J. S., 119
Tavernier, R., 362
Tax, A., 436
Taylor, B,331
Taylor, C,198
Taylor, C. B., 554
Taylor, D. M., 484
Taylor, E., 520
Taylor, J., 611
Taylor, S. E,13
Taylor, S. E., 451
Teasdale, J. D., 516, 565
Tecchio, F., 58
Teigen, K., 361
Teitelbaum, P., 369
Teitelbaum, S., 393
Telang, F., 87
Tellegen, A., 528, 533
Temoshok, L., 441
Temple, J. R, 413
Tenney, A. L., 225
Tennstedt, S. L., 71, 344
Tenorio, G., 250, 251, 261
Tereno, S., 333
Terman, L. M., 282, 290, 291, 292
Terracciano, A., 524, 525
Tesler, N., 59
Tevis, M., 7
Thase, M. E., 424, 608, 617
Theberge, J., 205
Thelen, M. H., 561
Theodore, A. D., 207
Theriault, G., 369, 526

Therrien, Z., 608
These, M., 608
Thibodeau, P. H., & Boroditsky, L., 301
Thiedke, C. C., 146
Thierry, H., 364
Thiyagarajan, M., 144
Thomae, H., 440
Thomas, A., 331–332
Thomas, A. G., 306
Thomas, M., 143
Thomas, R. K., 181
Thomas, S. B., 611
Thomas, S. L., 493
Thombs, B. D., 410
Thompson, P. M., 82, 566, 576
Thompson, W. L., 269
Thompson, W. W., 331, 337
Thomson, D. M., 240
Thomson, M. A., 331
Thorand, B., 435
Thoresen, C. E., 453
Thorndike, E. L., 188, 534
Thorne, D., 143
Thornton, A., 490
Thorsen, C., 330
Thurner, S,489
Thurstone, L., 278
Thyen, U., 394
Tian, R., 435, 436
Tian, X., 165, 298, 319
Tienari, P., 574
Timbo, B. B., 162
Timoshina, E. L., 366
Timulak, L., 595
Tisdale, J., 58
Tobach, E., 395
Tobin S. N. S., 347
Todd, C. S., 417
Toga, A. W., 24, 79, 82, 85, 86
Tojo, L. M., 169
Toker, S., 436
Tolman, E. C., 208, 209
Toma, R. A., 215
Tomasello, M., 299
Tomassy, G. S., 48
Tombini, M., 58
Tomes, N., 547
Tomycz, N. D., 622
Toner, K., 520, 595
Tononi, G., 144
Tooby, J., 491
Tor, P. C., 620
Torén, K., 306
Torgersen, S., 578
Torgerson, C. M., 24, 79, 85, 86
Tormos, J. M. P., 622
Torrance, E. P., 292
Torrens, M., 164
Toups, M. S. P., 150
Tourigny, M., 197, 198
Townsend, S., 451
Towsley, S., 331
Trabulsi, J. C., 112
Trace, S. E., 568
Tracy, D. K., 169
Traffanstedt, M. K., 564
Tranel, D., 77, 79, 374
Trapnell, P. D., 464
Trappey, C., 95
Trauer, J. M., 603
Treadway, M. T., 375
Treccani, R., 304
Treisman, A. M., 119, 230
Tremblay, A., 369, 526
Tremellen, K., 318
Triandis, H., 471
Trifilieff, P., 256
Trivedi, M. H., 150
Trivers, R. L., 408
Trocmé, N., 197, 198
Troncoso, X. G., 127, 128
Tropp, L. R,487
Trost, M. R., 465
Trudel, M., 333
Trumbell, E., 367

Trumbell, J., 333
Trumbull, E., 367
Truong, K. D., 166
Trut, L. M., 526
Trzaskowski, M., 295
Trzesniewski, K., 360
Tsai, G. E., 562
Tsai, J. L., 378
Tsai, N., 306
Tucker, D., 441
Tucker, E. W., 410
Tucker, M. A., 148
Tucker, P., 141
Tugade, M. M., 451
Tukuitonga, C. F., 497
Tulving, E,235
Tulving, E., 225, 234, 240
Tupak, S. V., 68
Turk, C. L., 603, 606, 610
Turner, J. C,483, 485
Turner, R. B., 435
Turner, S., 610
Turner, W. J., 412
Tusel, D. J., 162
Tversky, A., 272, 429
Tyrrell, D. A., 435
Tyson, J. E., 321

**U**

Uckert, K., 362
Ude-Koeller, S., 394
Underwood, M. K., 346
Unger, R., 395
Unsworth, N., 281
Unverzagt, F. W., 71, 344
Updegraff, J. A., 451
Upthegrove, T., 34
Urbanowski, F., 375
Urbina, S., 534–535

**V**

Vago, R., 454
Vail, A., 611
Vaillant, G. E., 451
Val-Laillet, D., 622
Valasek, C., 68
Valasek, C. A., 68
Valentine, A., 331
Valera, E. M., 77, 87
Valerio, S., 119
Valverde, R., 289
van Bemmel, D. M., 165
van Bochoven, A., 313
van Dam, R. M., 165, 298, 319
Van de Castle, R., 157
Van de Garde-Perik,473
Van de Vijver, F. J. R., 286
van den Munckhof, P., 622
van der Heijden, K. B., 88
van der Linden, S., 4
van der Merwe, A., 97
van der Molen, M., 87
van der Stelt, O., 87
Van Dongen, H. P. A., 145
van Duijl, M., 561
Van Goozen, S. H., 578
Van Hemert, D. A., 286
Van Horn, J. D., 24, 79, 85, 86
Van Reen, E., 153, 372
Van Straten, A., 600, 601
van Vollenhoven, R., 451
van Waes, L. T., 427
van Wyk, M. C., PIA-14
Vandell, D., 333
Vandenboom, C., 70
Vandenbulcke, M., 620
VanderLaan, D. P., 396
Vanneste, S., 344
Varela, J. A., 212
Vartanian, L. R., 339
Vasey, P. L., 396
Vasquez, M. J. T., 608
Vecchio, F., 95

Vecsey, C. G., PIA-14
Veit, R., 71, 205
Vellas, B., 436
Venables, P., 578
Venkatraman, J., 289
Vercelli, A., 48
Verfaellie, M., 70
Verhaeghen, P., 306
Verissimo, L., 34
Verissimo, M., 333
Verkhratsky, A., 47
Vernieri, F., 58
Vernon, P. A., 528, 547
Vernon, R. J. W., 477, 611
Vernon, S. W., 611
Verschuere, B., 374
Verstappen, S. M., 212
Vervliet, B., 601
Viberg, H., 289
Vichayapai, M., 19
Vidal, J. P., 622
Vigorito, C. M., 181
Vilain, E., 411
Villani, S., 493
Villarreal, R., 517
Vincent, J., 465
Vinnerljung, B., 320
Vinogradov, S., 305–306
Virkkunen, M., 491
Visscher, P. M., 313
Visser, P. S., 474
Vitiello, B., 140
Vitorovic, D., 164
Vittinghoff, E., 557
Vizcarra, B., 207
Vogel, E. K., 281
Vogel, G., 319
Vogel, G. W., 148, 319
Vogt, B. A., 77
Vohr, B. R., 321
Vohs, K. D., 153
Voirin, N., 170
Volkow, N. D., 87
Vollenweider, F. X., 169
von Bastian, C. C., 304
von Eisenhart Rothe, A., 435
von Helmholtz, H., 5, 103, 109
von Hipple, W., 478
von Hofsten, C., 325
von Hofsten, O., 325
von Stumm, S., 295
Voogd, J., 75
Voss, M. W., 306, 402
Voyer, D., 375, 402
Voyer, S., 402
Vrij, A., 374
Vu, M. A., 344
Vul, E., 253
Vygotsky, L. S., 13, 300, 330
Vyssotski, A. L., 142

**W**

Wade, E., 241
Wade, T. D., 568
Wager, T. D., 376, 432
Wagner, A. D., 235, 251, PIA-6
Wahlberg, K-E., 574
Wahlsten, D., 313
Wake, W. K., 313
Wakeel, F., 424
Wakefield, A. J., 331
Wald, G., 103
Wales, J., 569
Walitza, S., 59
Walk, R. D., 325
Walker, B., 435
Walker, B. N., 443
Walker, B. R., 436
Walker, L., 130
Walker, L. J., 340
Walker, M. C., 172
Walker, M. P., 148
Walker, P., 130
Walker, R., 113

# Subject Index

Drive, 357
Drive-reduction theory, 357–358
Drugs. *See also* Psychoactive drugs
    reuptake and, 53–54
Drug tolerance, 161
DSM. *See under* Diagnostic and Statistical Manual of
    Mental Disorders (DSM)
DTI. *See* Diffusion tensor imaging (DTI)
Dweck, Carol, 359–360

**E**

Easy temperament, 331
Eat-drink-and-rest system, 62
Eating disorders, 372, 567–558
    anorexia nervosa, 371, 567, 622
    binge-eating disorder, 371, 568
    bulimia nervosa, 368, 567–568
    causes of, 568–569
    culture and, 568
    treatmrnt of, 569–570
Eating habits, 371
Ebbinghaus, Hermann, 252
EBT. *See* Evidence-based treatment (EBT)
Echoic sensory memory, 229–230
Eclectic perspective, 15
Eclectic techniques, 588
Ecological validity, 284
ECT. *See* Electroconvulsive therapy (ECT)
Education, overcoming prejudice and, 486–487
Educational psychology, 7, B-7
EEG. *See* Electroencephalogram (EEG)
*Effective Study* (Robinson), PIA-8
Efferent (motor) neurons, 57
Ego, 508, 510–511
Egocentrism, 327–328
Ego integrity, 346
Eidetic imagery, 229
Einstein, Albert, 97, 520
Elaboration likelihood model, 475
Elderly, hassles and, 427
Electra complex, 510
Electrical stimulation of the brain (ESB), 67
Electroconvulsive therapy (ECT), 68, 257, 619–620
    retrograde amnesia and, 257
Electroencephalogram (EEG), 70, 145, 147, 205
Electroencephalograph, 70, 205, 375
Electrostatic pressure, 48
Elliot, Jane, 484–485
Ellis, Albert, 603
Embryo, 320, 393–394
Embryonic period, 320
EMDR. *See* Eye-movement desensitization and
    reprocessing (EMDR)
Emerging adulthood, 342
Emotion, 373–387
    behavior of, 376–377
    Cannon-Bard theory of, 379–380, 384
    cognitive arousal theory (Schachter/Singer),
        381, 384
    cognitive-mediational theory, 382–384, 384
    common sense theory of, 378, 379, 384
    comparison of theories of, 384
    defined, 373
    display rules, 377
    elements of, 373–378
    emotional expression, 376–377
    facial expressions, 376–377
    facial feedback hypothesis, 380–381
    facial feedback theory, 380–381, 384
    James-Lange theory of, 379, 384
    labeling, 378
    physiology of, 374–376
    range of, 563
    theories of, 378–384
Emotional expression, 376–377

Emotional intelligence, 292–293
Emotion-focused coping, 449–450
Empathy, 292–293, 527, 593
Encoding, 224
    automatic, 244–245
Encoding failure, 253, 254
Encoding specificity, 240
Endocrine glands, 63–66
Endogenous morphine, 53
Endorphins, 52, 53, 117
End-stopped neurons, 132
*The Enigma* (Levant), 128
Environment
    gender and, 398
    sexual orientation and, 410–412
Environmental psychology, B-9
Environmental stressors, 423–427
    catastrophes, 423–424
    College Undergraduate Stress Scale (CUSS),
        425–426
    hassles, 426–427
    major life changes, 424–426
    psychological, 427–430
    Social Readjustment Rating Scale (SRRS), 424,
        425, 426
Enzymatic degradation, 54
Epilepsy, 82
Epi-marks, 411
Epinephrine, 66, 382
Episodic memory, 236
Equal status contact, 486–487
Erectile disorder, 570, 571
Ergot, 169
Erikson, Erik, 8, 334–335, 340–341, 344, 345–346,
    365, 512
Erikson's psychosocial stages of development, 335
Erogenous zones, 509–510
ERPs. *See* Event-related potentials (ERPs)
ESB. *See* Electrical stimulation of the brain (ESB)
Escape, 429
Esteem needs, 364
Estrogens, 394
Ethics
    Milgram's shock experiment and, 468
    of psychological research, 35–37
Ethnicity
    helping behavior and, 497
    psychotherapy and, 611
    social networking and, 488
*Ethnicity and Health in America Series*, 7
Etiology, 544
Eustress, 422–423
Event-related potentials (ERPs), 70, 95
Evidence, evaluating, 39
Evidence-based treatment (EBT), 610
Evolutionary perspective, 14–15
Evolutionary psychologists, 14
Evolutionary psychology, 7, 14
Evolutionary purpose of homosexuality, 408–409
Exams, studying for, PIA-11–PIA-14
    applied questions, PIA-12
    concept maps, PIA-13
    conceptual questions, PIA-12
    cramming, PIA-11–PIA-14
    factual questions, PIA-12
    memorizing facts, PIA-12
    old tests, review of, PIA-13
    physical needs, taking care of, PIA-14
    resources, making use of, PIA-13
    SQ3R (reading method), PIA-13
    test time, using wisely, PIA-14
Excitatory synapses, 51
Excitement phase, 404, 405
Exercise
    cognitive health and, 305–306
    immune system and, 443

insomnia and, 150
    memory and, 260–261
Exhaustion stage, 432, 433
Exorcism, 544
Expectancies, 516–517
Experimental group, 30
Experimental psychology, B-6
Experimenter effect, 31–32
Experiments, 28–32
Expertise, 39
Explanation, 19, 20, 21
Explanatory style, 442–443
Explicit memory, 235–236, 259
Exposure therapy, 598
    virtual reality and, 623
*The Expression of the Emotions in Man and Animals*
    (Darwin), 380
External frustration, 428
Extinction, 181–182, 200, 600
Extrapyramidal symptoms, 615
Extraversion, 523, 524, 527, 533, 538
Extraverts, 524
Extrinsic motivation, 356
Eye
    function of, 101–102
    light and, 97–101
    REM sleep (*See under* REM (rapid eye
        movement))
    structure of, 98–101
Eye-movement desensitization and reprocessing
    (EMDR), 598
Eyewitness recognition, 243, 244
Eysenck, Hans, 607, 608
Eysenck Personality Questionnaire, 532, 534

**F**

Facebook, 488–489
Facial expressions, emotion and, 374, 375, 376–377
Facial feedback hypothesis, 380–381
Facial feedback theory, 380, 384
Factor analysis, 522
Factual questions, PIA-12
False-memory syndrome, 246–247
False positives, 243
Family counseling/family therapy, 605–606
Family studies on schizophrenia, 574
Farsightedness, 99
FAS. *See* Fetal alcohol syndrome (FAS)
FASD. *See* Fetal alcohol spectrum disorders (FASD)
Fear, 377, 378
    biological preparedness for, 186
Fear hierarchy, 598
Feature detectors, 126
Fechner, Gustav, 5, 95
Female gender stereotypes, 400
Female orgasmic disorder, 570
Female primary sex characteristics, 392
Female secondary sex characteristics, 392–393
Female sexual interest/arousal disorder, 570
Female sexual-response cycle, 404–405
Feminine cultures, 529
Fertilization, 318–319
Festinger, Leo, 476
Fetal alcohol spectrum disorders (FASD), 320
Fetal alcohol syndrome (FAS), 289, 320
Fetal development, hormonal exposure during, 397
Fetal period, 320
Fetus, 320
Fever, stress and, 437
Fight-or-flight system, 60–61, 211, 379, 432
Figure-ground relationships, 121
*Finding Meaning in Dreams* (Domhoff), 156
Five-factor model, 523–524
Fixation, 509, 510
Fixed interval schedule of reinforcement, 194–195

Russia, AIDS epidemic in, 417
Rutherford, Ernest, 109
Ryan, Richard, 365

**S**

Sacks, Oliver, 79
SAD. *See* Seasonal affective disorder (SAD)
Safety needs, 364
Salovey, Peter, 292
Sample, A3
    representative, 24
Sanchez, George (Jorge), 7
Sapir, Edward, 301
Sapir-Whorf hypothesis, 301
SARIs. *See* Serotonin antagonist/reuptake
    inhibitors (SARIs)
Saturation, 98
Scaffolding, 330
Scapegoating/scapegoats, 429, 483–484
Scatterplots, 28
Schachter, Stanley, 381, 382
Schachter-Singer cognitive arousal theory of
    emotion, 381, 383
Schedules of reinforcement, 192–196
Schema, 271, 298, 478
Schemes, 326
    gender schema theory and, 400
Schizophrenia, 572–576
    brain imaging and, 70
    catatonic, 573
    categorization of, 551
    causes of, 573–575
    cognitive exercises and, 305–306
    defined, 572
    delusions, 572
    development of, 14
    drug treatment of, 616–617
    electroconvulsive therapy for, 619–620
    genetics and, 14, 574–575
    glial cells and, 47
    hallucinations, 573
    negative symptoms, 573
    occurrence of, 545
    positive symptoms, 573
    psychotherapy for, 602
    stress-vulnerability model, 575
    symptoms, 572–573
School psychology, B8
School shootings, 493
Schwann cells, 47
Science, sex differences in, 402
Scientific method, 4, 20–32
    correlations, 26–27
    descriptive methods, 23–26
    experiment, 28–32
    five steps of, 20–22
Scott, Walter D., B11
Scripts, 271
Scrotum, 392
SD. *See* Standard deviation (SD)
SDT. *See* Self-determination theory (SDT)
Sears, Robert, 291
Seasonal affective disorder (SAD), 564
Secondary appraisal, 438
Secondary drives, 357
Secondary reinforcer, 190
Secondary sex characteristics, 392–393
Secular trend, 392
Secure attachment, 332
Seeing. *See also* Sight
    science of, 97–105
Segall, Marshall, 127
Selection, for experiment, 28
Selective attention, 230–231
Selective norepinephrine reuptake inhibitors (NRIs), 618

Selective serotonin reuptake inhibitors (SSRIs), 54,
    569, 618
Selective thinking, 601
Self, 519
    ideal and real, in Roger's theory, 519
    intelligence and sense of, 290
Self-actualization, 12, 363–365
Self-actualizing tendency, 518
Self-concept, 334, 519
Self-consciousness, adolescence and, 339–340
Self-determination theory (SDT), 365–366
Self-efficacy, 515–516
Self-esteem, 360, 516
Self-fulfilling prophecy, 486
Self-help groups, 606
Self-perception theory, 477
Self-theory of motivation, 359–360
Seligman, Martin, 208, 210–212, 443
Selye, Hans, 422–424
Semantic memory, 235
    brain and, 255, 256
Semantic network model, 237
Semantics, 299
Semicircular canals, 119
Semipermeable membrane, 48
Senile dementia, 257
Sensate focus, 571
Sensation
    absolute threshold, 95
    chemical senses, 111–115
    defined, 94
    difference threshold, 94–95
    habituation, 96
    hearing, 107–110
    just noticeable differences (jnd), 94–95
    olfaction, 114–115
    sensory adaptation, 96
    sight, 97–105
    signal detection theory, 96
    somesthetic senses, 116–118
    subliminal perception, 95
    synesthesia, 94
    taste, 111–114
    transduction, 94
Sensation seeker, 361
Sensing/intuition (S/N), 534
Sensorimotor stage of cognitive development,
    326–327
Sensory adaptation, 96
Sensory conflict theory, 119
Sensory development, infancy and childhood
    development, 323–326
Sensory memory, 227–230
    echoic, 229–230
    iconic, 228–229
Sensory pathway, 59
Sensory receptors, 94
Sensory thresholds, 94–96
Separation, 444–445
Separation anxiety, 332
September 11, 2001 attacks, 245, 423, 452, 484
Serial position effect, 241
Serotonin antagonist/reuptake inhibitors
    (SARIs), 618
Serotonin (5-HT), 52, 54, 306
    aggression and, 491
    drugs and, 54
    MDMA and, 169
    mood disorders and, 565–566
    sleep and, 141–142
Serotonin-norepinephrine reuptake inhibitors
    (SNRIs), 618
Serotonin partial agonist/reuptake inhibitors
    (SPARIs), 618
Sertraline (Zoloft), 618
Sex chromosomes, 314

Sex differences, in science and math, 402
Sexism, 400
Sex-linked inheritance, 105
Sexting, 413–414
Sexual behavior, 404–412
    types of, 406–409
Sexual behavior surveys
    explaining findings, 408–409
    Janus, 407
    Kinsey, 406–407
    National Survey of Sexual Health and Behavior
        (NSSHB), 407–408
Sexual characteristics
    development of, 393–394
    primary, 392
    secondary, 392–393
Sexual content, in dreams, 156
Sexual desire/arousal disorders, 570
Sexual dysfunction/problems, 570–571
    causes and influences, 571
    prevalence of, 570
    treatment, 571
Sexuality
    female primary sex characteristics, 392
    female secondary sex characteristics, 392
    male primary sex characteristics, 392
    male secondary sex characteristics, 393
    physical side of, 392–394
    primary sex characteristics, 392–393
    psychological side of, 395–402
    secondary sex characteristics, 392–393
    sexual behavior, 404–412
    sexual dysfunction, 570–571
    sexually transmitted infections (STIs), 414–416
    sexual orientation, 409–412
    sexual response, 404–406
    types of sexual behavior, 406–409
Sexually transmitted infections (STIs), 414–416
    AIDS (acquired immune deficiency syndrome),
        414, 415–416
    chlamydia, 414, 415
    genital herpes, 414
    genital warts, 414
    gonorrhea, 414
    syphilis, 414
Sexual orientation, 14, 409–412
    bisexual, 410, 411
    categories, 409–410
    defined, 409
    development of, 410–412
    heterosexual, 409, 410
    homosexual, 408, 409, 410
Sexual response, 404–406
    excitement, 404
    observational study of, 405–406
    orgasm, 404
    plateau, 404
    resolution, 404–405
s factor (specific intelligence), 278
Shadow, 511
Shape constancy, 121
Shaping, 201–202, 217–218
Sheep brain, 78
Sherif, Muzafer, 460
Sherlin, Leslie, 147
Shock experiment, Milgram's, 466–468
Short-term memory (STM), 227, 230–233
    brain and, 256
    capacity, 231–232
    chunking, 232
    defined, 230
    encoding, 231
    interference in, 232–233
    maintenance rehearsal, 232
    selective attention, 230–231
    working memory, 231